GLORIOUS FRENCH FOOD

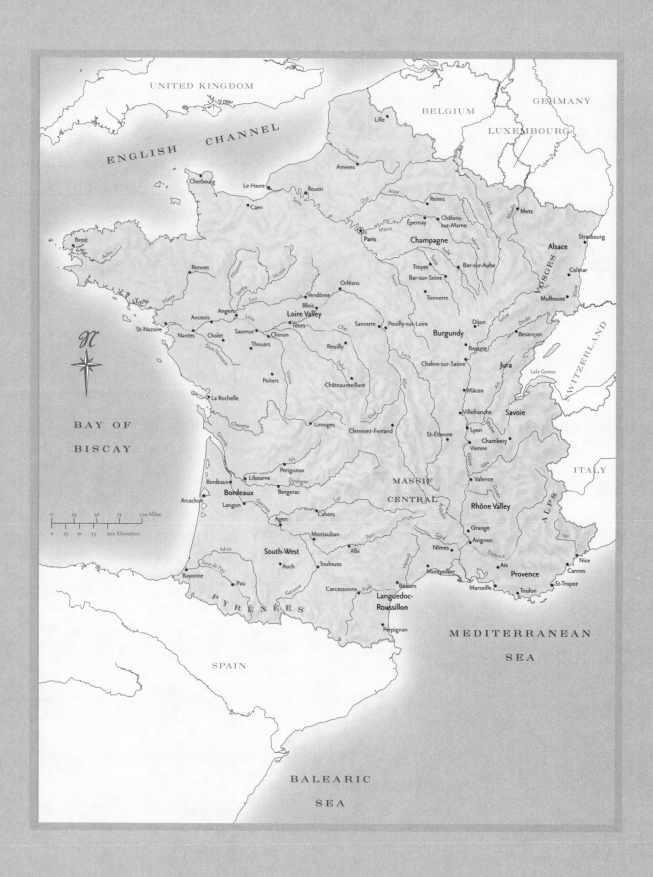

UNITED KINGDOM

ENGLISH CHANNEL

BELGIUM

LUXEMBOURG

GERMANY

Lille

Cherbourg

Le Havre

Rouen

Amiens

Somme

Caen

Seine

Oise

Aisne

Reims

Marne

Châlons-sur-Marne

Épernay

Moselle

Metz

Brest

Aulne

Paris

Champagne

Marne

Strasbourg

Alsace

Colmar

Rhine

Rennes

Mayenne

Huisne

Sarthe

Vendôme

Blois

Orléans

Yonne

Troyes

Seine

Aube

Bar-sur-Aube

Bar-sur-Seine

Mulhouse

VOSGES

Vilaine

Angers

Loir

Loire Valley

Tours

Sancerre

Pouilly-sur-Loire

Tonnerre

Doubs

Dijon

Saône

Besançon

Ancenis

St-Nazaire

Nantes

Cholet

Saumur

Chinon

Cher

Reuilly

Burgundy

Beaune

Jura

Sèvre Nantaise

Thouars

Indre

Châteaumeillant

Chalon-sur-Saône

Lake Geneva

SWITZERLAND

Poitiers

Vienne

Loire

Mâcon

Ain

Villefranche

Savoie

La Rochelle

Allier

Saône

Lyon

Rhône

Chambery

BAY OF

BISCAY

Limoges

Clermont-Ferrand

St-Étienne

Vienne

Isère

Charente

Sioule

Isle

Perigueux

Dordogne

Libourne

MASSIF

CENTRAL

Valence

Drôme

ITALY

Garonne

Bordeaux

Bergerac

Rhône Valley

ALPS

Langon

Lot

Ardèche

Orange

Arcachon

Agen

Cahors

Avignon

Aix

Var

Nice

Montauban

Tarn

Albi

Gard

Nîmes

Durance

Provence

Cannes

South-West

Adour

Auch

Toulouse

Hérault

Montpellier

St-Tropez

Bayonne

Gave de Pau

Pau

Garonne

Carcassonne

Aude

Béziers

Marseille

Toulon

PYRÉNÉES

Languedoc-Roussillon

MEDITERRANEAN

SEA

Perpignan

SPAIN

0   25   50   75   100 Miles

0   25   50   75   100 Kilometers

BALEARIC

SEA

CONTENTS

OYSTERS | Huîtres 250

Sauce Mignonnette 250

Sauce Hollandaise 256

Gratinéed Oysters with Curried Hollandaise Sauce | Huîtres Gratinées au Curry 258

Gratinéed Oysters with Bacon, Tomatoes, and Tarragon | Huîtres Gratinées au Lard Maigre aux Tomates et à l'Estragon 259

Oyster Stew with Spinach and Chives | Huîtres en Ragoût aux Épinards et à la Ciboulette 261

New York Strip Steak with Red Wine and Oysters | Contre-filet à la Sauce Vin Rouge et aux Huîtres 264

STEAMED MUSSELS WITH WHITE WINE, SHALLOTS, AND PARSLEY
| Moules à la Marinière 265

Steamed Mussels with White Wine, Shallots, and Parsley | Moules à la Marinière 268

Steamed Mussels with Cream, Saffron, and Mint | Moules à la Crème au Safran et à la Menthe 269

Broiled Mussels with Onions and Mussel-flavored White Wine Sauce
| Moules Gratinées aux Oignons et à la Sauce Vin Blanc 270

Miniature Servings of Mussels with Sea Urchin Sauce | Cassolettes de Moules à la Sauce d'Oursins 271

Mussel Soup with Garlic Purée and Saffron | Soupe aux Moules à la Purée d'Ail et au Safran 274

Hot Broiled Mussels with Garlic and Parsley Butter | Moules Gratinées au Beurre d'Escargots 274

SEA SCALLOPS POACHED IN VEGETABLE BROTH | Coquilles Saint-Jacques à la Nage 277

Beurre Blanc 281

Court Bouillon for Cooking à la Nage | Court-bouillon pour Cuisson à la Nage 283

Sea Scallops with Vegetable Broth and Julienned Vegetable | Coquilles Saint-Jacques à la Nage 284

Sea Scallops with Vegetable Broth Finished with Flavored Butters | Coquilles Saint-Jacques à la Nage au Beurre Composés 284

Sea Scallops à la Nage Finished with the Scallops' Roe | Coquilles Saint-Jacques à la Nage et au Beurre de Corail 286

Bay Scallops and Shrimp or Crayfish à la Nage | Pétoncles et Crevettes ou Écrevisses à la Nage 288

Blue Trout | Truite au Bleu 289

Medallions of Salmon à la Nage | Médaillons de Saumon à la Nage 290

SOLE WITH HOT BUTTER AND LEMON | Sole Meunière 292

Skate with Capers and Lemon | Raie à la Grenobloise 298

Salmon Fillets with Powdered Cèpes and Balsamic Vinegar | Filets de Saumon à la Poudre
de Cèpes et au Vinaigre Balsamique 299

Trout with Paprika and Almonds | Truite Amandine au Paprika 300

Sautéed Striped Bass Fillets with Vegetable "Marmalade" | Sauté de Filets de Bar à la Marmelade de Legumes 301

Fillets of Sole with a Light Bread-Crumb Coating | Filets de Sole à l'Anglaise 304

PREFACE

FRIENDS AND COLLEAGUES SEEM PERPLEXED WHEN I TELL THEM I'VE written a book about French cooking. They're gentle and discreet, and instead of just coming out with, "Why yet another book about French food?" they ask how my book differs from other books about French cooking and why I would put so much energy into such a thing. The more chauvinistic among them imply that I'm wasting my time, since cooking in America is now better and more inventive than cooking in France and French cuisine is too rich, complicated, expensive, and pretentious. These are the same people who tell me that California wines are the best in the world and who react to any contrary statement with annoyance.

I write about French food not because I think it's intrinsically better than food anywhere else in the world, but for reasons that have to do with more than just how food tastes. We all have the French to thank for encouraging a culture that takes a more than hedonistic interest in eating and drinking. In our current era of star chefs and TV cooking personalities, it's hard to remember America's attitude toward food in the 1960s and 1970s, when I was in my late teens and early twenties. When at that age I developed a fascination with fine food and wine, I was eyed with suspicion. Being a gourmet meant being at best an eccentric and at worst a hedonist intent only on sensual gratification. Mentioning the vintage of a bottle of wine was considered pure snobbery. Pursuing a career as a cook was considered far beneath the potential of anyone with even the lowest IQ. The idea of cuisine as an art form, or even a worthwhile craft, was laughable.

But the first day I set foot in France, on a Sunday afternoon in Strasbourg (I had hitchhiked from Munich), I knew I had found home. Food and drink seemed to be *all* that people were interested in, people who spent hours in restaurants and cafés, and who were always ready to strike up a conversation about their favorite dishes and wines. And these conversations weren't limited to any one social class; I could talk about food with truck drivers, bankers, shoe salesmen, and families on a Sunday outing who would pick me up when I hitchhiked.

A couple of years later, after I had settled in Paris to apprentice in restaurants, the French fascination with food and wine followed me wherever I went. The barber, straight razor in hand, would offer me tips for making his favorite crêpes; the woman at the dry cleaner would banter about the best bakeries in the neighborhood; the guy who pumped the kerosene mixture into my ancient moped would talk wine. Best of all, parents of friends were eager to have me taste their best bottles.

Late one summer night I was arrested. Some friends of mine from a Parisian mime school had learned about a network of tunnels, deep underground, where we could wander undetected anywhere in Paris. Well, we got lost. Worse, someone had reported us climbing down a manhole in the middle of the night and the police arrived just when we happened to be directly under the German embassy. Since the Red Brigade had just killed an important minister, this was no laughing matter. We were marched out at gunpoint to a waiting paddy wagon (known in Parisian slang as a *panier à salade,* a salad shaker) and taken to police headquarters for interrogation. My tiny hotel room was sacked for weapons, and this event improved my status immensely in the eyes of *la propriétaire,* whose hatred of the police was hardly surprising, since her rooms were for the most part rented by the hour to local prostitutes. Finally we were released. But I was detained somewhat longer than my friends because I had declared my métier as that of *cuisinier,* and so my interrogation involved discussion of favorite dishes and, as I remember, an exchange of tips about where to get the best *andouillettes* (tripe sausages). I was asked where I cooked and what my specialties were, and I was treated with sudden respect by my *interrogateurs,* who fortunately never asked to see my working papers.

My interest in French cooking is about far more than a love of food and drink. It is linked to an affection for an independent (and often irascible) people, their culture, their language, and their past. The history of French cooking reveals itself in dishes that are still served in various guises in restaurants and in some homes, in much the same way as the history of other arts is present in the gallery or concert hall. A particular dish or meal can evoke the past and, in some of us, a poignant, bittersweet nostalgia. French food also has a special place in my heart, or perhaps more accurately my liver, because it is enjoyed with wine. There have been periods in my life, best forgotten, in which I've experimented with not drinking wine and during which I lost all pleasure in eating, experiencing only a vague satisfaction in fulfilling a biological need. Of course, wine does all sorts of good things. It helps us digest our food by relaxing the stomach. It cleans out our blood vessels, and I at least am convinced that it helps us metabolize fats and in general makes us more fit and healthy. But it is in the realm of the psyche that wine brings real pleasure. Every bottle of wine is different; if it's a good wine, every glass is different; and if it's a great wine, every sip is different. This keeps the relationship between the flavors of the food and the aroma of the wine in constant flux, and while for many the process goes on unconsciously, it prolongs the pleasure of a particular dish and of a whole meal because each bite is experienced differently from the one before. But beyond wine's health benefits and its contribution to our gustatory titillation, its aroma and flavor are inextricably caught up with memory. I never stick my nose in a glass of Chianti without reliving for a short moment a wonderful month spent in Tuscany or sip a glass of Sancerre without tasting the fresh goat cheese nibbled (with Sancerre, of course) on a hill overlooking the vineyards of the Loire valley.

Because many of us have been exposed to French cooking in only a limited number of restaurants, we miss out on many of the traditions that make French food French. Though this is beginning to change, the food we encounter in the more expensive of these restaurants is representative of only one tradition, what the French call *la grande cuisine* or *la cuisine classique*. *La grande cuisine* was developed in the courts of royalty and in noble homes until the French revolution, when the royal chefs were put out of work (at least they still had their heads) and opened restaurants. Today, despite much talk about the death of *la cuisine classique,* its traditions are alive and well, although in a somewhat different guise, in restaurants in France, in the United States, and in countries all over the world. But other, less familiar cooking traditions have evolved, or at least persisted, simultaneously with those found in fine French restaurants. What the French call *la cuisine bourgeoise,* the cooking of well-run households, far more common in homes before the Second World War, is now most likely to be found in a good bistro. Cookbooks describing *la cuisine bourgeoise* date back to the seventeenth century and culminate in the wonderful cookbook *La Cuisine de Madame Saint-Ange,* published in the 1920s. Madame Saint-Ange describes many of the same techniques that Auguste Escoffier outlined twenty years earlier in *Le Guide Culinaire,* a book written for professionals, but explains them in better detail and with far less superfluity, as though the bourgeois cook and diner wanted to get to the heart and soul of the matter without needless chichi. There is also *la cuisine du terroir,* hearty regional cooking made with local products and reflective of centuries of eating habits in various parts of France. In France, and to some degree in other places, the distinctions between classic cuisine, *nouvelle cuisine, cuisine bourgeoise,* and regional cooking are beginning to break down as chefs trained in the techniques of classic cooking apply their savoir faire and finesse to dishes once served only at home or in the least expensive restaurants. While in the 1970s, *nouvelle cuisine* chefs were eager to invent dishes, often by using baroque juxtapositions of ingredients, contemporary cooks are turning to French regional and bourgeois cooking and are bringing back cooking rooted in solid tradition and common sense.

I call this book *Glorious French Food: A Fresh Approach to the Classics,* a confusing title for French readers for whom *la cuisine classique* has a very specific meaning, while for Americans the term means simply familiar or traditional French cooking. Because I want the reader to have at least heard of most of the dishes or to have tasted them in restaurants or perhaps even made them at home, I've taken a very un-French approach and combined every style of French cooking, drawing from refined and extravagant lunches, meals in truck stops and in people's homes (both poor and not so poor), and my houseful of old cookbooks.

As Americans we have certain advantages and disadvantages. Most of us weren't raised with a solid cooking tradition that we can use as a point of reference in our own cooking. As time moves on, fewer of us have grandmothers who can teach us traditional recipes and "little secrets." On the other hand, as Americans we're open to new combinations and approaches because we're not trying to duplicate something we've never even tasted. When I was studying cooking at Le Cordon Bleu in Paris, a student raised his hand and had the audacity to ask if we could substitute raspberries for strawberries in a particular dessert. The answer was a simple no. When the student pressed further, the chef retorted, "Every dish was already invented by the end of the nineteenth century. There's no room for anything new." My own encounter with the rigidity of French tradition occurred in a Parisian restaurant where I, the chef, was often coming up with logically conceived combinations of ingredients dictated by what I found at the market. One evening I served some lovely little string beans with a red wine beef stew. The customer complained that such a combination was not classic. For me the contrast of the bright fresh beans with the deep color and flavor of the stew was delightful; for my customer it bordered on the bizarre.

But back to the book. I've organized it in a somewhat unorthodox way and have drawn on my own experience, experiments, whims, and reading to give logic and context to the recipes. Despite parallel traditions and a cuisine that has evolved over the centuries in many economic milieus, there is an interrelatedness in French cooking that makes it possible for the thoughtful or creative cook to prepare a wide variety of French dishes starting with only a few recipes. If the cook understands what's going on in a dish and how it relates to other similar (or not-so-similar) dishes, he or she can cook from principles rather than from recipes. Cooking from recipes is much like painting by numbers: You may produce a few dishes or come up with a decent canvas, but you won't learn how to cook or paint. So each of the fifty chapters is about a dish, one that I hope you have heard of and that will entice you; but this is a ruse designed to lead you into a series of cooking lessons that use the dish as a point of reference. A cassoulet made from scratch (really from scratch—you make your own sausages and confit, stew lamb, soak and simmer dried beans) is something most of us aren't likely to undertake very often. I've made a lot of them because I've had to teach them, not because I wanted to spend too many weekends simmering things in duck fat. But if you understand what a cassoulet really is, that it's the culmination of many techniques, traditions, and ways of using ingredients that have long been available in a particular region, you have access to something far more valuable than a recipe for cassoulet. Instead you have its logic and context and you understand the techniques needed to prepare it, and so you are able to invent your own variations or to simplify the recipe to suit your schedule or energy level. The curtain is pulled back and the daunting and mysterious cassoulet is suddenly revealing it for what it is, a casserole of baked beans. Very special baked beans, of course.

Paradoxically, French cooking can no longer be left to the French. Modern society has changed the way we eat, cook, and learn to cook. The great dishes of French cooking, ranging from rustic peasant dishes to refined derivatives of a cuisine once served to kings and queens, are no longer maintained in a day-to-day unself-conscious way in farmhouses, wealthy homes, or Paris apartments. It is now left to restaurant chefs and us home cooks to preserve and, at times, to reinterpret these traditions. And while restaurants thrive, their dishes will always be those of the restaurant and no matter how well prepared will lack the soul of food cooked at home. Though I don't expect to change America's eating habits overnight, I hope to give, to those who enjoy cooking, access to traditions and techniques and to the intuition and spontaneity that inhabit the heart and stomach of any good cook. Though I've made no attempt to simplify the traditional French dish (unless simplification improves it), many of the dishes in this book are almost absurdly straightforward. Also, a relatively large number are made with leftovers, so if you've spent more time than usual in the kitchen preparing a Sunday dinner or getting ready for a dinner party, you can use the remnants to make an array of salads, gratins, or even pasta dishes in very little time, with recipes in this book a guidelines rather than as dictates.

It has long been my dream to write a cookbook with no recipes at all. This would save me a lot of time, energy, and money, since there would be no recipes to test. It would relieve a lot of frustration, too, because as soon as I write down a recipe I think of dozens of different things I'd like to try or say. But since I've written a book with lots of recipes, I suggest that you read around in them so you'll understand how they work and then just use the recipe itself when you're making your shopping list, for helpful tips, or if you get stuck somewhere. It still makes me happiest when someone comes up to me and says, "Well, I didn't follow your recipe exactly. . . ." That makes me feel I've accomplished my goal of genuinely giving people a metaphorical hand in the kitchen.

ACKNOWLEDGMENTS

I WISH I COULD PERSONALLY THANK THE MYRIAD OF COOKS, CHEFS, WRITERS, gourmets, and lovers of good food who've helped me over the course of the last 25 years to have a rich experience with French cooking. More specifically, it has been the great cooks—Paul Bocuse, Claude Peyrot, George Blanc, Thomas Keller, the late Richard Olney, and many others—who have expressed their own vision of French food in an inimitable way.

I'd like to thank those at Wiley who transformed an enormous manuscript into something manageable, especially Pam Chirls, my editor. Others at Wiley who've helped with publication and promotion are, Fred Bernardi, Diana Cisek, Kate Fisher, Adrianne Maher, Valerie Peterson, Michele Sewell, and Aditi Shah.

I'd also like to thank my friend and former editor, Maria Guarnaschelli, for helping me generate the original idea for this book.

A number of people have helped me test and edit recipes. Geraldine Cresci (to whom this book is dedicated) has helped me on this book and many others. Allison Fishman, Stefanie Shapiro, and Susan Ryan Ackell also devoted their time and attention to the recipes and the manuscript. I'd like to thank Erica Marcus for editing the manuscript to make sure I was making sense.

Thanks to food stylist Ann Disrude for her amazing eye and for making food look great and to Betty Alfenito for letting us use her amazing collection of props. Thanks also Maggie Ruggiero, for assisting Ann during the styling.

Many thanks to my tenacious agents Elise and Arnold Goodman for their help and encouragement over what is now becoming a rather large number of years. Thank you to my friends, Paul Geltner and Debré DeMers (Debré helped style the photographs), for being my friends and for encouraging me when I'm racked with self doubt. Special thanks to my partner Zelik for putting up with various culinary experiments (sauerkraut in the bathroom, ham curing in the bedroom) and for just being there.

READ THIS FIRST

BECAUSE MANY OF THE TECHNIQUES AND INGREDIENTS USED IN FRENCH cooking appear repeatedly throughout the book, I suggest you read through this section first so that the recipes and discussions will make more sense. Because some of this information is very basic, experienced cooks should be able to scan it fairly quickly.

Ingredients

BACON: My favorite bacon is Schaller & Weber (see Sources), a brand of "double-smoked" bacon that comes in a slab with the rind already removed. Not only is this bacon lean and flavorful, but its being in a single slab allows you to slice it to whatever thickness you want. Once you open the package, wrap the bacon in a clean kitchen towel and put it in the refrigerator, where it will keep for several weeks. (You can keep it even longer, but it gets hard.) Most slab bacon, however, is sold with the rind attached. To remove it, slide a long, thin knife between the fat and the rind before slicing the bacon. Leave the rind attached to that part of the slab you're not slicing and then fold the flap over the rest of the bacon to keep the bacon moist. Presliced bacon is easier to find than slab bacon, and there are several good brands. Use thick-sliced bacon for cooking; it makes more substantial *lardons* and has more texture. Inspect it carefully and select the brand with the most lean. Be sure the package says "naturally smoked" and not "smoke-flavored." "Smoke-flavored" bacon has an unpleasant soapy taste.

BREAD CRUMBS: When most of us think of bread crumbs we think of the store-bought variety or our own version, made with stale or lightly toasted bread. But French cooks use stale, crunchy bread crumbs only as a layer for a gratin or in some dish—cassoulet comes to mind—in which the bread crumbs provide a needed contrast in texture. For breading sautéed or fried foods, the French use fresh bread crumbs—which they call *chapelure*—because they absorb less fat and form a more delicate coating. Making your own fresh bread crumbs is easy. Cut the crusts off slices of dense-crumbed white bread—I use Pepperidge Farm sandwich bread—and pulse the slices in a food processor for about 30 seconds. For very fine bread crumbs, which will absorb the least fat and make the most delicate layer of breading, work the crumbs through a large strainer (or better yet, a drum sieve: see page 15) with your fingers.

BOUQUET GARNI: Few cooking terms cause more needless confusion than "bouquet garni." French cookbooks are casual in calling for a bouquet garni in just about any long-simmered dish, be it soup, stew, or sauce, but rarely go into any detail about how to make one. American cooks, probably as a result of having had to rely on chopped or ground dried herbs, go through the laborious process of making little packets of herbs tied up in cheesecloth. Much of the time there's no need for a bouquet garni. If, for example, you're making a soup that doesn't require skimming or that's going to be strained, just throw the herbs into the pot. But in many dishes, stew, for instance, loose herbs can be hard to strain out, and even when finely chopped they leave a distracting feel in the mouth. In other preparations, such as broth, loose herbs may float to the top and interfere with the skimming off of fat and froth.

While making a bouquet garni by tying up herbs in cheesecloth is still necessary when the herbs have been dried and chopped, when using sprigs of fresh herbs, just tie the sprigs together in a bundle with a couple of loops of string. The standard ingredients for a bouquet garni are imported bay leaves (don't use California bay leaves, they're too pungent), thyme, and parsley. You can vary the herbs depending on your whim and what you have around. I often include fresh tarragon in a bouquet garni to be used in chicken broth and, following Provençal tradition, an orange rind and a sprig of marjoram in a beef daube.

Most bouquets garnis are too small. I've seen students add a single bouquet garni the thickness of a thumb to a 25-quart [25 l] stockpot. The size of the bouquet garni should be proportional to the amount of liquid in which it's being simmered and to the robustness of the liquid and the final dish. Here are some approximate sizes for a standard bouquet garni made with both fresh and dried herbs:

Small (1 to 2 quarts [liters] of liquid)	**Medium** (2 to 4 quarts [liters] of liquid)	**Large** (per gallon [4 liters] of liquid)
1 small bunch parsley (bunched stems about the thickness of a middle finger)	1 bunch parsley (bunched stems about the thicknessof a large thumb)	1 large bunch parsley
½ imported bay leaf	1 imported bay leaf	2 imported bay leaves
3 sprigs thyme, or ½ teaspoon dried thyme leaves (never powdered thyme)	5 sprigs thyme, or 1 teaspoon dried thyme	7 sprigs fresh thyme or 1 teaspoon dried thyme

BROTHS, STOCKS, BOUILLON, CONSOMMÉ, CONCENTRATED BROTHS, GLACE DE VIANDE, DEMI-GLACE, JUS, GRAVY: The question most often asked in my cooking classes is, "Is it all right to use canned broth?" If you're using broth for a simple soup in which the broth acts as a backdrop for flavor instead of as the principal source of flavor, go ahead and use canned broth. If you're boiling down broth for a gelatinous sauce base (such as *glace de viande*; see page 221), you must make your own broth because the salt in canned broth becomes too concentrated and because canned broth contains very little natural gelatin (notice how canned broth never sets in the fridge, while homemade does). If you're braising meats, say for a pot roast or stew, you can use half canned broth and half some other liquid such as wine, water, or homemade broth, so that when you simmer down the braising liquid it isn't too salty. If you're using canned broth for a soup, liven it up by simmering 2 quarts [2 l] of low-sodium beef or chicken broth with half a stalk of celery, a finely chopped medium-size carrot, a chopped onion, a crushed garlic clove, and a small bouquet garni, or any combination of the above, for 20 minutes and strain. Skip the onion or any of the other vegetables if you're using the broth in a soup that contains that vegetable.

The second most often asked question is, "What is the difference between stock and broth?" Well, there is none. "Stock" is the word used in restaurants and implies that it's going to be used for something else, such as sauce or soup, rather than as an end in itself.

Bouillon is just the French name for broth. A consommé is a double-strength (or triple-strength) broth that's made by cooking meat in broth instead of water. When care is taken in its preparation, a consommé should be perfectly clear with no trace of fat on its surface, but most recipes call for clarifying consommé with egg whites (see also Chapter 16).

In addition to needing broth for stews, soups, and braised or poached meats, you also need it to make concentrated sauce bases such as *glace de viande* (meat glaze) or demi-glace ("half" meat glaze). *Glace de viande* is a simple reduction of full-flavored gelatinous broth to about one-tenth its original volume. Demi-glace, rarely called for in modern recipes, involves less reduction after first thickening the broth with roux.

In recent years, packaged concentrated broths and glazes have become available in gourmet stores and even in supermarkets. There are several brands of concentrated broths. My favorite is manufactured by More Than Gourmet (see Sources), whose original product, Demi-Glace Gold, contains flour, but in such small amounts that it's hardly detectable. Demi-Glace Gold, which is claimed to be ten times as concentrated as demi-glace, is very much like *glace de viande* and can be used in its place in recipes or when improvising brown sauces (see below). More Than Gourmet also markets a *glace de viande,* very close to one you would make yourself, as well as a duck glaze, *glace de canard.* In addition to their use in sauces, when thinned these concentrates provide an excellent broth, the concentration of which is easy to control by adding more or less water. In many recipes, especially those for stews where additional flavorful liquid is needed to supply enough sauce, I call for a cup [250 ml] of broth or even a cup [250 ml] of concentrated broth. The difference between broth and concentrated broth is somewhat arbitrary, but I usually think of concentrated broth as broth that has been reduced to one-fourth its original volume. If you want to use Demi-Glace Gold or *glace de viande* to make concentrated broth, dissolve 4 tablespoons (60ml) in 1 cup [250 ml] of hot water.

When reduced down by three-quarters, 30 fluid ounces (900 ml) good-quality home-made broth yields 7 fluid ounces (200 ml)—about a cup—concentrated broth. When reduced to one-tenth its original volume, 30 fluid ounces yield 3 fluid ounces (about 6 tablespoons/90 ml) *glace de viande.* Commercial demi-glace or *glace de viande* (specifically the More Than Gourmet brand) is roughly the equivalent to homemade *glace de viande.* To make concentrated broth with commercial demi-glace or *glace de viande,* combine 4 to 6 tablespoons *glace de viande* or demi-glace with 8 tablespoons water.

A *jus* is the liquid released by a roast (see Chapter 26); it is usually passed at the table as a pure natural sauce to accompany slices of meat. A *jus* has a full, meaty aroma and intense flavor that for centuries cooks have tried to duplicate without having to make a whole roast to get a cup [250 ml] or so of *jus.* Many cooks incorrectly assume that a concentrated broth, one that has been slowly simmered to a fraction of its original volume, will have the same vibrant, authentic flavor as a natural *jus.* Well-made concentrated broth does have body and a lightly syrupy consistency (because of the natural gelatin it contains), but the fresh, aromatic flavor of meat will have dissipated after long cooking. Concentrated broths taste flat, but since they're usually flavored with other ingredients, as in a sauce, this isn't important; they provide a backdrop for the sauce's flavor and contribute to its saucelike consistency. To make a light sauce that tastes a lot like a natural *jus,* brown pieces of meat and bones with a little onion, carrot, and celery (mirepoix) until the juices caramelize on the bottom of the pan; deglaze the pan with a little broth or white wine; caramelize the juices a second time; and deglaze again with just a little broth. Simmer the mixture for only 5 minutes or so, so the fresh direct flavor of the *jus* doesn't have time to cook off. (See also "Caramelization," page 16.)

BROWN SAUCES: Made from foods, usually meats, that have been browned before being simmered in liquid, brown sauces are based on broth, which in traditional farmhouse cooking is taken from the ever-present pot-au-feu and nowadays more likely is taken out of a can or made with a bouillon cube. In classic French restaurants up until a generation ago, brown sauces were based on demi-glace, which is reduced and concentrated *sauce espagnole,* a rich veal or beef bone broth with tomatoes added and lightly thickened with brown roux. In modern French restaurants, most brown sauces are based on *glace de viande,* a very concentrated veal broth (more often than not made with bones) that contains no flour.

While it is possible to make demi-glace or *glace de viande* at home, very few of us are willing to spend the time, on a regular basis, to ensure us a steady supply. Because reliable brands of commercially made demi-glace and *glace de viande* are now available (see above, page 221, and Sources) it's now possible to make brown sauces at home that rival those made in the best restaurants. It is also possible when making your own brown sauce to simply reduce homemade veal or chicken broth (canned is too salty) in a deglazed roasting or sauté pan, concentrating the flavor of the broth at the last minute. Cooking down a well-made broth also concentrates its gelatin, which gives body to the sauce. (See page 484 for more about brown sauces.)

Though classic brown sauces are intimidating to beginning cooks, a little analysis reveals that most of them are made in a somewhat formulaic way. Once you've mastered a few, you can make others, as well as improvising your own sauces, by plugging in different ingredients. Often, a brown sauce is made by gently cooking aromatic ingredients such as mirepoix (onions, carrots, and celery), onions (alone), shallots, garlic, or prosciutto in a small amount of fat. A liquid is then added, often red or white wine or a fortified wine such as port or Madeira. In a classic poivrade sauce, vinegar is used at this stage. Usually the sauce is reduced and demi-glace (in traditional sauces) or *glace de viande* (in modern sauces) added to give the sauce body and a meaty flavor. Some sauces are then strained to take out the aromatic ingredients that have surrendered their flavor to the surrounding liquid. Cream is sometimes added at this point and lightly reduced to thicken the sauce, unify its flavors, and give it body. Other, more delicate flavorings, such as finely chopped fines herbes (chervil, parsley, chives, and tarragon) alone or in combination; mustard (not so delicate, but it will separate if added earlier); chopped or sliced mushrooms; truffles; or delicate spirits such as Cognac are then often added. Last, the sauce is finished with a swirl of butter to give it a satiny texture and, like cream, to unify the flavors. In more homespun red wine sauces, a paste of flour and butter (*beurre manié*) may be whisked in as a thickener. Traditional sauces, based on demi-glace, contain relatively little cream and butter compared to sauces made with *glace de viande,* because the flour added to the demi-glace acts as a thickener. Here are some ideas for improvising your own brown sauces:

Aromatic ingredients, chopped fine and gently sweated in a small amount of fat before liquid is added

MIREPOIX
onions, carrots, celery (see meurette sauce, page 115)

ONIONS

SHALLOTS
(see Bordelaise Sauce, page 483)

GARLIC
(see Lamb Chops with Garlic and Marjoram, page 503)

MUSHROOMS
(see *Poulet Sauté Chasseur*, page 370)

CUBES OF PROSCIUTTO, PANCETTA
the closest equivalent to French unsmoked bacon, or meat trimmings (see meurette sauce, page 115)

Flavorful liquids added to the aromatic ingredients already in the pan and cooked down to varying degrees

WINES
red or white, Madeira, port, marsala, Sauternes (see Tournedos Rossini, page 494)

VINEGAR
(see Sauce Poivrade, page 406)

GASTRIQUE MIXTURE
made by adding vinegar to caramel (see page 390 for more about this method)

MUSHROOM COOKING LIQUID
(see recipe, page 8)

CURRANT JELLY
(see Sauce Poivrade, page 406)

FRUIT JUICES
such as orange juice for duck à l'orange

Meat base to give body to the sauce

DEMI-GLACE
commercial or homemade

GLACE DE VIANDE
(homemade, see recipe, page 221; or commercial)

GOOD-QUALITY VEAL, BEEF, OR CHICKEN BROTH
the more concentrated the better, so you're not reducing at the last minute

Enricheners/thickeners

HEAVY CREAM

BUTTER

HERB BUTTER
(see recipes, page 490)

CRUSTACEAN BUTTER
(see recipe, page 335, and Lobster Newburg, page 337)

BUTTER FLAVORED WITH AROMATIC INGREDIENTS
such as reduced tomato purée, chopped truffles, or cèpes (porcini)

BEURRE MANIÉ
(butter-and-flour paste, see page 116; see also recipe, page 115)

Final aromatic ingredients and flavorings

COGNAC
(or other spirits such as dry fruit brandies; see below, page 10, for more about using spirits in cooking)

DELICATE HERBS
tarragon, chervil, parsley, chives

CHOPPED OR SLICED MUSHROOMS

CHOPPED, JULIENNED, OR SLICED TRUFFLES

MUSTARD
(see Veal Kidneys with Mushrooms, Mustard, and Port, page 541)

DICED CARAMELIZED ROOT VEGETABLES
such as carrots, celeriac, and onions

DICED CARAMELIZED MEATS
such as prosciutto (see Roast Top Round of Veal with Diced Aromatic Vegetables, page 52)

FRUITS

LEFT
GREEN SALAD
52

BELOW
BABY ARTICHOKES WITH
TOASTED WALNUTS
40

BELOW
NICE-STYLE ONION, OLIVE,
AND ANCHOVY TART
169

ABOVE
GRATINÉED OYSTERS WITH
CURRIED HOLLANDAISE SAUCE
256

BELOW
CRAYFISH, ASPARAGUS,
FAVA BEAN, ARTICHOKE BOTTOMS,
AND MOREL SALAD
63

LEFT
RIB STEAK WITH
RED WINE SAUCE AND
BEEF MARROW
483

RIGHT
POACHED SEA SCALLOPS WITH
VEGETABLE BROTH FINISHED WITH
FLAVORED BUTTERS
285

BELOW
SEAFOOD CASSOULET
WITH LOBSTER AND MUSSELS
475

ABOVE
SALAD DRESSING
79

BELOW
CHICKEN WITH RED WINE SAUCE AND
WILD MUSHROOMS
366

BELOW
ROAST VEGETABLES
563

ABOVE
ROAST CHICKEN
352

LEFT
RAGOUT OF SPRING
VEGETABLES
586

RIGHT
THE FAMOUS MONT ST. MICHEL
OMELET
124

RIGHT
PASTA GRATIN
574

BELOW
TRADITIONAL RACLETTE
144

BELOW
BEEF STEW WITH PEARL ONIONS,
MUSHROOMS, AND BACON
438

BUTTER: Waverley Root, in his marvelous work *The Food of France*, divides France into four regions based on the principal cooking fat used in each. In the southwest it's goose fat; in the southeast, olive oil; in the northeast, lard; and in the northwest, butter. While the distinctions among the cooking styles of France's many regions have blurred a great deal since the Second World War, these divisions are still applicable to traditional regional cooking. For most of us, French cooking is almost synonymous with cooking with butter. This is because classic French cooking—the cooking that evolved in the French court and later in fine restaurants—has been based on butter since the seventeenth century. (In medieval cooking, lard was more common.)

Butter is used in French cooking in many ways: for sautéing all manner of foods; for thickening sauces (see beurre blanc, page 281, and *monter au beurre*, page 20); for giving them a silky texture and unifying flavors; for pouring over cooked fish or poultry (see the recipe for *sole meunière*, page 294); as a sauce unto itself; and for baking into pastries.

Butter is used to sauté foods because of its delicious flavor, but since it burns at a relatively low temperature, it is often clarified—its water and milk solids removed—so that it can be heated to a high temperature. If you're sautéing foods over medium heat, regular whole butter works fine and in fact is tastier than clarified butter because the milk solids in the butter cling to the food and caramelize. When foods like chicken are cut into pieces and cooked in butter entirely in a sauté pan, they are flavored with butter but end up containing very little fat because it's largely the caramelized milk solids—which are proteins—that impart the buttery flavor, not the fat, which is poured off. But if you need to sauté on high heat, for example when sautéing something thin, like a veal cutlet, which must be browned quickly so it doesn't overcook, the milk solids in whole butter will burn. Don't brown foods over high heat in a mixture of butter and oil, as suggested in many recipes, because the oil will not keep the milk solids from burning. And last, don't try to clarify salted butter; it froths up and is almost impossible to work with. (See page 296 for information about clarified butter.)

There are two methods for taking the milk solids out of butter to clarify it. If you're clarifying more than a couple of pounds, do what they do in restaurants: Melt the butter in a pot on the stove, let it sit, and skim off the froth with a ladle. (Ideally, the pot should be tall and narrow to make skimming easier.) Discard the froth and ladle out the pure golden clarified butter. Don't reach too far down in the pot with the ladle or you'll bring up water and milk solids that have settled to the bottom. It's worth making more than you need, since clarified butter keeps for months in the fridge and forever in the freezer. But if you're clarifying only 1 or 2 pounds [450 or 900 g] of butter, cook the butter over medium heat in a heavy-bottomed saucepan. The butter will froth and bubble as the water in it (butter contains about 30 percent water) boils away. After about 5 minutes, keep a close eye on the butter. Tilt the pan and look at the bottom, where some of the milk solids will cling. When the milk solids coagulate, first into white specks, and then into lightly brown ones, remove the butter from the heat and set the bottom of the saucepan in a bowl of cold water for a few seconds to stop the cooking. Pour the butter into another container, leaving the golden-brown milk solids clinging to the saucepan. Or if you really want to be fastidious, strain the butter through a fine-mesh strainer, a triple layer of cheesecloth, or a coffee filter. This second method produces a tastier version of clarified butter than the first method because the milk solids have caramelized, producing what French cooks called *beurre noisette* and Indian cooks call *ghee*. Beurre noisette is used in the same way as clarified butter but can also be used in butter sauces (such as hollandaise) or in pastries to give a more pronounced butter flavor.

CAUL FAT: In French called *crépine,* caul fat is a thin, veil-like sheet of fat that lines the inside of a pig's abdominal wall. Pork caul fat is useful for making sausages because it renders away as the sausages cook. It can also be used to line terrines for making pâtés instead of the usual sheets of fatback (see Chapter 5), which can be harder to slice and work with. Caul fat is also used to wrap fragile foods such as braised oxtails to keep them from falling apart as they're being reheated. A butcher should be able to order caul fat for you—it's rarely in stock—and you may have to take more than you need. Because it freezes well and is inexpensive, I never hesitate. If you get a large batch, divide it into easier-to-manage portions and wrap them individually before freezing them.

FEET: French recipes for stews and braised dishes often call for pigs' or calves' feet to supply additional natural gelatin. Unless you live in the right ethnic neighborhood, you may have to order your feet in advance. They're not expensive and they can be kept frozen almost indefinitely. When ordering feet, have the butcher saw them lengthwise in half. If you're ordering calves' feet, have them cut in half crosswise, too, so the pieces—you'll now have 4 from each foot—aren't too large for the pot. Before using pigs' or calves' feet, you must boil them, starting with just enough cold water to cover, for 5 minutes to rid them of the scum they throw off. After the boiling, drain them in a colander and rinse thoroughly with cold water.

FENNEL: In some recipes I call for one or more of the three parts of the fennel plant: the bulb; the tough, fibrous stalks; and the fronds. When I don't specify the part, I'm referring to the bulb.

MUSHROOM COOKING LIQUID: Because mushrooms have an almost meaty flavor that's both subtle and robust, mushroom cooking liquid is often called for in French cooking for making sauces. I sometimes use it as a substitute for meat broth or concentrated broth when I'm cooking for vegetarians. You can make mushroom cooking liquid as strong or light as you like by steaming mushrooms with more or less liquid. I use the cooked mushrooms to make the crudité salad on page 40. Here's a recipe for 1 cup (250 ml) of liquid.

1 pound [450 g] cultivated mushrooms, preferably cremini

1 cup [250 ml] water

PUT the mushrooms and water in a pot with a lid. Cover the pot, bring to a boil, and then turn down the heat to maintain at a gentle simmer. Simmer gently for 15 minutes. Most of the mushrooms won't be submerged in liquid, but don't worry; you're actually steaming, not poaching, them.

PARMESAN CHEESE: Despite having more than four hundred cheeses of their own, French cooks often use Parmesan because of its forthright flavor and because it is dry and won't become stringy when cooked. Unfortunately, most of what's called Parmesan cheese in the United States is not authentic and in fact barely resembles the original. Authentic Parmesan cheese, Parmigiano-Reggiano, is produced only in three Italian provinces, Parma, Mantova, and Bologna. Parmigiano is aged from 18 months to 5 years, becoming dryer and more aromatic as it gets older. *Grana padana,* sometimes called simply grana, a less expensive but very similar cheese from north of the Po River, makes a suitable substitute. Grana is usually aged 1 to 2 years. Always grate Parmesan cheese shortly before you use it; it loses its aroma when grated in advance.

PORK: FRENCH PRODUCTS AND THEIR AMERICAN AND ITALIAN EQUIVALENTS: French pork products are rarely imported into the United States and often don't have exact American equivalents. Italian ingredients and Italian-style products made in the United States and Canada often make closer substitutes than traditional American ingredients such as salt pork. French terminology is also confusing because the same words in English may mean something different. For example, in English, "lard" refers to unsalted fresh pork fat that has been rendered. In French, rendered pork fat is called *saindoux,* while unsalted pork fat, which we call fatback, is called *lard gras* or simply *lard.* The French equivalent to American bacon (smoked pork belly) is called *lard maigre* or *lard fumé,* while fresh unsmoked bacon is called *poitrine fraîche.* The French also have salt pork, called *lard salé,* which is leaner than our salt pork (which has no lean at all), and *demi-sel,* which is pork, usually pork breast (unsmoked bacon), that's been partially cured with salt (see recipe, page 528). *Jambon de Paris* is much like our cooked ham and Italy's *prosciutto cotto* (*cotto* means cooked), which have been rubbed with salt and saltpeter (see recipe, page 106) or soaked in a salt, sugar, and saltpeter brine. There are dozens of other regional pork products, made from different parts of the animal and involving various degrees of salting, brining, or smoking. *Ventrêche,* from the southwest, is lean pork breast (brisket) that has been cured with salt but not always smoked, and is roughly the equivalent, when unsmoked, of the Italian pancetta. The French also have a variety of hams, both raw cured (*jambon cru,* the equivalent of Italy's *prosciutto crudo*) and cooked (*jambon cuit,* the equivalent of Italy's *prosciutto cotto*). The best known French raw cured ham is *jambon de Bayonne,* from the southwest. *Jambon de Bayonne* is served raw and thinly sliced, in the same way as Italian prosciutto.

The obvious substitute for *saindoux* would be lard, but because I find that American lard has a soapy taste and smell, I prefer to render the fat from pancetta or the outside of a prosciutto, the closest equivalents I can find to *poitrine fraîche.* French recipes calling for *lard maigre* or *lard fumé* (both smoked) aren't a problem, because they are exact equivalents to American bacon. Because I can't find *jambon de Bayonne* in the United States, for cooking I use the less expensive end piece of Italian *prosciutto di Parma,* which isn't as assertive but, once cooked, is pretty close.

French	American	Italian
saindoux	lard (rendered pork fat)	strutto
lard gras	fatback	lardo
lard maigre or lard fumé	bacon (smoked)	
ventrêche	bacon (smoked or not)	pancetta
poitrine fraîche	bacon (unsmoked)	
demi-sel	brined pork breast	
jambon cru	cured, uncooked ham	prosciutto crudo
jambon cuit	cooked ham	prosciutto cotto

ROOT VEGETABLES: BUYING TURNIPS AND CELERIAC (CELERY ROOT): Some vegetables are easy to avoid when they get too old, because they wilt, develop soft spots, or smell funny. But turnips and celeriac may look fine, but still be old and stale. Buy those that feel heavy. If they are light, they are spongy in the middle and will probably be bitter. Another thing to look out for: Don't mistake tiny leaves coming out of the top for the cut-off greens. Tiny leaves mean that the turnip or celeriac has been sitting around for a good while and is sprouting.

WHITE SAUCES: Traditional white sauces are based on either béchamel sauce or velouté sauce. A béchamel is essentially milk that's been thickened with roux (see page 577 for more about béchamel) and a velouté is white broth—made from veal, chicken, or fish—that's been thickened with roux. All of the classic French white sauces are made by adding various ingredients to one or the other of these two "mother" sauces. Modern white sauces, made without flour, are based on white veal stock that is reduced and given body with cream (which is usually reduced) and/or egg yolks (cooked gently, like a crème anglaise; see page 641) or butter.

WINES AND SPIRITS FOR COOKING: French recipes have an annoying way of being cavalier about using expensive wines. Some insist that you pour a bottle of Burgundy over an old rooster to make an authentic *coq au vin*, others call for a wine that's at least 10 years old; and some have you simmering a bunch of little fish in a good bottle of Champagne. Better to crack open the Champagne and, while sipping, use something else for the fish. I do admit to having once made a red wine sauce—a beurre rouge, I think—with a bottle of Échézeaux and, yes, I could taste a difference—a very slight difference. But the sauce wasn't any better than when made with my usual cooking zinfandel.

The things that make expensive wines expensive—subtle nuances of perfume and flavor—are for the most part lost when the wine is exposed to heat. And qualities that make wine connoisseurs scoff, such as low acidity, too high an alcohol content, fatness, or clumsiness, are often the qualities that make wine good in a sauce or a stew. Red wines for cooking should be full-bodied and deeply colored, with low acidity and little or no tannin. Alcohol content makes no difference, since the alcohol cooks off anyway. Lighter-colored wines (such as Burgundy, in fact) give sauce an insipid, unappetizing milk of magnesia–like color, and red wines with high acidity (essential in the glass but not in the pot) make overly tart sauces because the acid is concentrated during reduction. Tannin (the stuff that makes your mouth pucker when you take a sip) in a red wine can cause the wine to separate when it's cooked with proteins such as those from fish, meat, or bones; the liquid ends up almost colorless and the pigment from the wine clings to the fish, meat, or bones. My favorite cooking red wines are California zinfandels (they're soft and full-bodied and not too expensive), Côtes-du-Rhône from a good maker (but these are starting to get too dear), Rioja (again, getting expensive), and cabernets, malbecs, and merlots from Chile or Argentina.

White wines are another story. In most sauces or soups based on white wine, the wine provides a welcome tart acidity. So whereas I'm likely to choose one of the "New World" red wines (wines from places other than Europe), which tend to have less acid, I almost always use more highly acidic European white wines. Muscadet used to be my old standby, and in fact it's the traditional wine used for making beurre blanc. But it has gotten too pricey, so I often use a nondescript French sauvignon blanc (usually just labeled "sauvignon"), a pinot grigio from the Veneto (buy a cheap one, they can be expensive), or a Sylvaner or pinot blanc from Alsace. There are occasional dishes, such as sorbets, granités, and sabayon sauces, in which the wine is exposed only to gentle heat or to no heat at all. In these situations it's sometimes worth using a somewhat special wine with a distinct character. If you can stand the extravagance, a *sauce sabayon* (made by whisking together sugar, egg yolks, and white wine over medium heat until the mixture stiffens into a frothy sauce) is marvelous made with Champagne, French Chablis, Gewürztraminer, or a decent Riesling.

Most of the fortified wines used in cooking have a nutty sweetness that adds a delightful complexity to sauces and stewing liquids. Madeira is a particularly useful wine to have around, but keep in mind that it comes in different degrees of sweetness. Until recently, Madeira was named according to the original grape varieties used to make it. Since many of these vines were wiped out by disease in the nineteenth century, the names ended up referring to degrees of sweetness rather than actual grape varieties. Since 1993, the laws governing Madeira have changed; they now require that any Madeira labeled after a grape must actually contain at least 85 percent of that grape. Today, much Madeira is simply labeled "dry," "semidry," "semisweet," or "sweet" instead of after the traditional grape names: sercial, which is dry; verdelho, which is dry to semidry; bual, which is sweeter still; and malmsey, which is the sweetest of all and should be used in very small amounts for cooking. A Madeira labeled "semidry," "Verdelho," or "Rainwater" (a brand name, which implies a blend) is best for cooking.

Ruby port is the least expensive of ports and because of this is the most practical for cooking, but a good tawny port will have more nuttiness and complexity, and if not too expensive is worth paying a bit more for.

Spirits are often called for in French cooking and are often misused or poorly chosen in a misguided effort to save money—it's better to use less of something good than a lot of something cheap. Cheap brandy is often substituted in recipes calling for Cognac or Armagnac. There's nothing wrong with substituting a well-made brandy from another place; there are some very good ones from California and Spain. But using a generic brandy (they're usually called something like "old Napoleon brandy") at best will do nothing for the dish and at worst will give it an unpleasant medicinal taste. On the other hand, using the best Cognac is a waste because its delicate perfumes are lost when it is exposed to heat. I opt for inexpensive but authentic Cognac, which doesn't have a lot of complexity but is full of honest fruit flavor. Just remember that it must say "Cognac" on the label.

Other fruit brandies, such as kirsch (cherries), framboise (raspberries), mirabelle (yellow plums), and Poire William (pears), are sometimes called for in recipes, especially desserts. They vary in quality; the best capture the delicate essence of fruit, others the essence of kerosene. French and Swiss brands of these clear fruit brandies are reliable, and expensive. Don't confuse these clear and sugarless brandies, called eaux-de-vie, with fruit-*flavored* brandies made by adding a very sweet fruit syrup to grape brandy, with a result more like cough medicine than anything you'd want to put into a sauce. Marc, a brandy made from the stems and grape pits left over from pressing the juice for wine making, has a distinctive earthy flavor that's delicious in game sauces and with chocolate. Again, marc can be marvelously complex and nuanced or it can smell like medicine. Grappa, originally the Italian equivalent of marc, is now often made with wine instead of grape pressings and much of the time is really an eau-de-vie with the distinctive varietal character of specific grapes, such as muscat. You can use these grappas as you would a clear fruit brandy—as a finish for a meat sauce or dessert sauce. But beware, they can be very expensive.

Equipment

BAKING DISHES: Many recipes call for baking in one sort of container or another. Fortunately, you don't need a collection of all types of containers in various sizes, since you can often substitute one for the other. Here are some of those most often called for in this book:

Charlotte Molds: Usually metal, shaped like a fez with heart-shaped handles on either side, charlotte molds are used for baking apple charlottes (see recipe, page 614) and for serving various mousses and Bavarian creams. In older recipes, the inside walls of the charlotte mold are lined with ladyfingers before mousse mixture is poured in and allowed to set. Charlotte molds are available in 3-cup [750-ml], 4-cup [1-l], and 2-quart [2-l] sizes.

Dariole Molds: These metal molds are straight-sided little cups with slightly sloping sides. Most hold 2 to 3 fluid ounces [60 to 90 ml]. They are used for baking both sweet and savory custards and mousses, and for babas (see variations, page 655). If you're shopping for dariole molds, buy nonstick ones.

Gratin Dishes: A gratin is really just the French equivalent of a casserole, but when baking a gratin the emphasis should be on the crust that forms on the top. (In some gratins, such as cassoulet, the crust is folded into the mixture to allow a second or even third crust to form.) For most gratins the dish should be large enough to hold the mixture so that it is ½ inch to 2 inches [1.5 to 5 cm] deep. Gratin dishes come in different sizes and shapes (although they're usually oval) and are made out of materials such as porcelain, enameled cast iron, or copper, all of which are interchangeable. For the recipes in this book I used two oval copper gratin dishes, one 9 inches wide by 13 inches long [23 by 33 cm] and the other 10 by 17 inches [25.5 by 43 cm]. For smaller gratins (and for creme brûlée) I use an assortment of oval and round porcelain gratin dishes. If I were buying gratin dishes for the first time, my first choices would be the 9-by-13-inch [23-by-33-cm] oval and a 10-by-17-inch [25.5-by-43-cm] oval for large gratins, and four or more 8-by-5-inch [20.5-by-12.5-cm] oval gratin dishes for smaller servings. Round porcelain quiche dishes (about 5 inches [12.5 cm] across) also work for gratins, creme brûlée, and individual servings of quiche or dessert tarts.

Pot-de-créme Molds: Some kinds of these pot-shaped porcelain molds have a handle, others do not, but all have lids. They are perfect for rich custards. I've seen them in 2-ounce [60-ml], 3-ounce [90-ml], and 4-ounce [125-ml] sizes.

Pyrex Custard Cups: These familiar glass cups with slanted sides come in 6-ounce [175-ml] and 10-ounce [300-ml] sizes and make an inexpensive if less elegant substitute for porcelain ramekins and small baking dishes. The 6-ounce [175-ml] size, perfect for individual custards, measures 3¾ inches [9.5 cm] across the top and is 2 inches [5 cm] high.

Ramekins: Small porcelain ramekins are useful for a myriad of dishes, including individual soufflés or cakes, mousses (both sweet and savory), and dishes served *en gelée.* Ramekins come in sizes ranging from 2 to 10 ounces [60 to 300 ml]; I find the 5-ounce [155-ml] size and the 10-ounce [300-ml] size (which is really more like a small soufflé dish) the most useful.

BLENDERS AND FOOD PROCESSORS: When hot liquids are puréed in a blender, the air in the blender quickly expands and may cause the top to fly off and the hot liquid to spatter. To avoid this, don't fill the blender more than two-thirds full. Wrap a towel around the top of the blender and hold the top firmly, through the towel, so it can't fly off. Begin blending using very short pulses with the blender on the lowest speed, and gradually increase their duration and, if necessary, the speed of the blender. While a food processor is excellent for puréeing stiff or dry mixtures, a blender is best for puréeing liquids, which would leak out of the bottom of a food processor. Immersion blenders, which can be placed right in a saucepan, are easiest and safest for hot soups and sauces.

MANDOLINES AND VEGETABLE SLICERS: Slicing vegetables by hand with a knife can be tricky, especially if you want paper-thin slices and you're slicing something round or cylindrical that has no flat surface to stabilize it on the cutting board. There's no shame in using a gadget to do this. In restaurants in France, a metal plane-like device, called a mandoline, with an adjustable blade is used almost constantly for jobs of this kind. A French mandoline is handy in any home kitchen, but expensive. In the last several years, inexpensive plastic mandolines with razor-sharp blades have become available in kitchen supply stores for about one-fifth the price of the classic metal model. There are two kinds. One has two or three inserts, each allowing you to slice at a different thickness. Another kind, the kind I prefer, is called a Benriner cutter and has little screws on the back that allow you to adjust the blade to produce slices the exact thickness you want. This kind of cutter is perfect for slicing fennel, root vegetables, radishes, and truffles into very thin slices. There is also a special wide model, slightly harder to find, that better accommodates larger vegetables like celeriac and cabbage (see Sources). If you're slicing truffles, you can use a truffle slicer, but since the Benriner cutter works just as well, I recommend spending your money on the Benriner instead. If you're slicing truffles at the table, however, as when slicing white truffles over pasta or other goodies, a truffle slicer is more compact and prettier. If you trust your guests or love them dearly, you can pass the truffle and slicer at the table so they can help themselves.

MICROWAVE OVENS: Students are sometimes horrified when I suggest using the microwave, but I use it for heating plates that don't have any metal on them, for reheating leftovers, and for cooking small numbers of potatoes, beets, or squash. Keep in mind that a microwave, unlike a regular oven, takes more time to cook the more you put in it; thus it is impractical for large amounts. When using the microwave, reposition whatever it is you're cooking or reheating every few minutes so you redistribute the heat. Heat leftovers covered loosely with plastic wrap (or cover with a microwavable plate or bowl) and let them sit for a couple of minutes between zaps so the heat has a chance to even itself out.

PARCHMENT PAPER: One mention of the words "parchment paper" used to send would-be cooks running, but now that parchment paper is sold in most supermarkets it no longer requires a special trip or a mail order. Parchment paper is sold in rolls (which are what you'll most likely find at the supermarket) and sheets. You can use it in the same way you would use wax paper, but you can also use it in the oven, whereas the wax on wax paper would melt and cling to your food. Parchment paper is especially useful for baking, making it easier to work with pastries that would otherwise stick to the baking sheet.

PASTRY BAGS: Pastry bags intimidate beginning cooks, probably because most of us have seen cooking shows where some pastry chef demonstrated his or her virtuosity so convincingly that the feat looked impossible to duplicate without having spent years in Europe under the tutelage of a master. While it's true that using a pastry bag to make perfect little curlicues on a cake takes practice, there are lots of tricks that you can master the first time and that are immediately much easier than trying to do the same thing with a spoon.

Most pastry bags are cone-shaped pieces of cloth, lined with plastic, although I have recently seen disposable versions, which are like plastic bags. In fact, you can improvise your own pastry bag by cutting a corner out of a small Ziploc bag. But the real thing is inexpensive and easy to find, so unless you're in your mountain cabin and feel suddenly compelled to make an elaborate dessert, you're better off just going out and buying a pastry bag. A variety of metal and plastic tips for the bags are available; some are plain round, others fluted, and some flattened and fluted. The tips are sold in different sizes, so it's probably worth picking up an assortment while you're at it. Most pastry bags just have a hole at the small end for inserting the tip; you may need to enlarge the hole with scissors if the tip won't fit in it. Recently I've seen plastic rings, called couplers, that fit on the end of the pastry bag and allow you to change tips without emptying the bag.

To fill a pastry bag, fold down the top of the bag, as though folding back a shirtsleeve, so that you get a cuff 3 to 4 inches [7.5 to 10 cm] wide around the top rim of the bag. At the tip end, push about 3 inches of the bag into the top of the tip so that when you load the bag with mixture the mixture doesn't just flow out the tip. Assuming you're right-handed, hold the bag in your left hand by reaching your fingers under the cuff and holding the top of the bag open.

Use a rubber spatula, large spoon, or ladle (depending on the consistency of the mixture) to fill the bag about two-thirds full. Unfold the cuff, pulling it up with your right hand, and pinch the top end of the bag together like an accordion. Clamp the loose top of the bag between the base of the thumb and forefinger of your right hand. Rotate the bag so the top twists and forms a seal, keeping the mixture from shooting out the top when you squeeze. When you're ready to use the bag, hold the bag with the tip facing upward and pull against the tip so the part of the bag you crammed into the tip comes out, releasing the mixture into the tip. Squeeze the bag, with the tip still facing upward, until the mixture just starts to come out. Then turn the bag over so that the tip faces downward. When using the pastry bag, keep it taut by twisting the top as the mixture comes out of the tip. If the bag gets limp, it will be almost impossible to control. Hold the bag in your right hand—again, keep the top pinched between your thumb and forefinger—and guide the tip with your left hand.

ROASTING PANS: Until recently, I only had one roasting pan, too big for everything except a turkey; it forced me to improvise and use a heavy iron skillet or an oval enameled gratin dish. Buy or improvise a roasting pan that matches as closely as possible the size and shape of whatever it is you're roasting. If the roasting pan is too big, the juices from the roast spread out over the surface of the pan, get too hot, and burn. Ideally, a roasting pan should be heavy, so the heat is evenly distributed and so it won't get too hot in the areas not being touched by the roast, a condition that, again, causes the juices to burn. Another factor is the color of the roasting pan. A dark pan, like my improvised iron skillet, makes it difficult to see whether or not the juices are burning. If you have a choice, opt for a pan with a shiny, silvery inside surface. Though I have many uses for nonstick pans, I don't like nonstick roasting pans because the juices don't cling to their surface, and thus it is difficult if not impossible to separate juices and fat. My roasting plans are made of aluminum (plain, not anodyzed) and copper lined with stainless steel.

ROLLING PINS: There are three kinds. The American kind has a handle on either end; the Italian kind is a plain wooden rod that tapers at each end; and the French kind is a single wooden baton about 2½ inches [6.5 cm] thick. The French and American kinds work equally well for pastry, but I prefer my French pin because I can use it, holding it on end, to break up mixtures of simmering crustacean shells, tomatoes, fish heads, and so on.

STRAINERS AND FOOD MILLS: Most of us are familiar with a basic strainer used to strain mixtures such as soups or to sift flour. Less familiar is a fine-mesh strainer, useful for straining minute particles out of broths and sauces. Fine-mesh strainers come in two types. The less expensive looks like a regular strainer except for its fine mesh. The other, sometimes called a *chinois*, has a relatively large cone-shaped screen. Be careful when using fine strainers not to tear the mesh by working the mixture with a spoon. French professionals move a small ladle, bowl downward in the strainer, up and down to work mixtures through. To avoid clouding broth, pour it gently into the strainer and then tap the side of the strainer with a wooden spoon to get the mixture to go through without working it.

While I'm not big on exotic or contrived kitchen equipment, there are a couple of useful things that even the best-stocked kitchen stores often don't sell. One is a drum sieve, essential for making silken purées of such things as mashed potatoes. A drum sieve is a round metal or wooden frame with a screen, available in coarser or finer mesh, stretched over it. Metal drum sieves, which are more expensive, have an additional ring that tightens and loosens, allowing you to change the screen when it wears out or when you need a different mesh. Wooden drum sieves, while about one-fourth the price of the metal ones, are useless once the nylon screen wears out. To use a drum sieve, simply place it, screen-side up, on a large sheet pan or over a large mixing bowl and work whatever it is you're purée-ing through the screen. I use a flat wooden spatula or the bottom of a small mixing bowl to work the ingredient to be puréed over the surface of the screen.

A china cap comes in handy when straining rough-and-tumble mixtures such as fish bones or crustacean shells that could easily poke through a regular strainer. A china cap is a cone-shaped strainer that instead of having a mesh screen has a sturdy sheet of perforated metal that allows you to apply a lot of pressure to mixtures to work them through. I often use a French rolling pin (see above, page 15) to work broths and stocks through.

Food mills, rarely seen anymore except in grandmothers' kitchens, are far more useful than we give them credit for; they strain and purée at the same time. There are two basic types. The simplest is a straight-sided bowl, perforated on the bottom, with a propeller-like paddle and crank stuck in it. You put the mixture to be strained and puréed (a combination perfect for tomatoes) in the bowl and turn the crank. A slightly more elaborate version has removable perforated grids that allow you to change the consistency and fineness of your purées. When buying a food mill, buy the largest size you think you'll ever need—the larger the more efficient.

TWO-PRONGED FORKS: Most people use tongs or a spatula to turn foods over on the grill or in a sauté pan. In restaurants, cooks are more likely to use a fork with two long, thin tines to quickly turn steaks, chops, or poultry, but a two-pronged fork is most valuable to help you loosen fish, especially whole fish, that sticks to the grill. When lifting fish off the grill to turn it over or serve it, slide the two-pronged fork between the grill bars under the fish. Gently lift up under the fish, detaching it from the grill. Then slide a spatula under the fish while holding the fish up with the fork.

WINDSOR PANS: These saucepans have sloping sides and are perfect for making sauces such as hollandaise that contain egg yolks because you can reach with the whisk into the corners, where the yolk would otherwise curdle.

Techniques

CARAMELIZATION: Antonin Carême, the most famous cook and food writer of the early nineteenth century, was obsessed with finding out what made certain sauces more flavorful than others. Why, for example, are the pure juices from a simple roast chicken so much tastier than concentrated chicken broth, even broth made from whole chickens instead of bones? Carême attributed the source of meaty flavor to a substance he called *osmazone*. As it turns out, there's no such thing, but there are compounds, including peptides, that contribute savor to meat dishes. Peptides are formed by the partial breakdown of certain proteins during cooking. When proteins are broken down completely, with acids or during digestion, they separate into their basic components, amino acids, which are essential to animal life. But it's the interim compounds, the peptides and others, that are responsible for the flavor of a well-made *jus*.

Whatever we call them, peptides or *osmazone,* how do we get the most out of meats and bones? The secret is caramelization. When proteins are broken down in the presence of air, flavorful compounds are formed that are different from those extracted, for example, during the simple simmering of broth or poached foods. Try making chicken *jus* out of chicken broth by boiling a cup [250 ml] of the broth down in a frying pan until it completely evaporates and browns on the bottom of the pan. Just before the broth is about to burn, add another cup [250 ml] of broth. Repeat the process several times and you'll end up with a delicious concentrated broth that's a lot better than if you had simply reduced the broth without letting it caramelize. Admittedly, the broth won't taste as good as a real *jus,* but you get the idea. Variations on this broth technique have been used in kitchens for centuries. Nowadays, when meats are braised or when meat is used to prepare broth, the meat is often browned, usually with aromatic vegetables such as onions and carrots, and then moistened with water or broth. In the best eighteenth-century cooking, a small amount of liquid was added to the meats and aromatic vegetables after the meats had been browned, and the pot was put on the stove until the liquid completely evaporated and caramelized on the bottom of the pan. This process causes the meats to release their juices, which then caramelize and break down into a variety of flavorful peptides on the bottom of the pan. More liquid is added for the final deglazing and the result is simmered for only a few minutes. Caramelized juices that are simmered in liquid for too long lose much of their flavor.

CHIFFONADE: CUTTING LEAFY VEGETABLES INTO FINE STRIPS: When leafy vegetables are cut into thin shreds, they are called chiffonade—the leafy equivalent to julienne. To cut leafy vegetables such as sorrel, spinach, or chard into chiffonade, roll up 2 to 3 leaves at a time and slice the roll.

CUTTING UP CHICKEN: Throughout this book there are many recipes that call for quartered chicken or chicken legs or sometimes chicken thighs and drumsticks. This can all be confusing, especially since cooks in restaurants cut their chicken differently than most butchers do.

When you buy a quartered chicken from the butcher or at the supermarket, you're getting a whole chicken that's been cut into 4 pieces, not including the head, feet, and neck. This leaves you with 2 whole legs, which include the thighs and drumsticks, and 2 breasts, with the ribs and wings attached. Since the ribs make it harder to brown the chicken breasts and have very little meat on them, I use a heavy knife or scissors to cut off the ribs below the meaty part of the breast. I save the ribs for broth. I cut the wings off where they join the breast, or at the first joint so that only a section of wing stays attached to the breast. The legs will come with a section of the back attached, and this makes them harder to eat. I bone out the piece of back and, again, save it for broth. But because of the way chickens are butchered, I prefer to buy whole chickens and cut them up myself.

Depending on your guests' appetites, a chicken cut into 2 breasts and 2 legs (thighs plus drumsticks) should make 4 main-course servings. If you've got big eaters and you're not serving a first course, you may want to buy 1 chicken for every 2 people. When you "quarter" a chicken, you'll actually end up with 7 pieces: 2 breasts, 2 legs (each of which includes a drumstick and a thigh), 2 wings, and the back; but only the legs and breasts are substantial enough to make a full serving. If you want more than 4 meaty pieces per chicken, as when making a chicken sauté or fricassee, separate the drumsticks and thighs so that each leg provides 2 pieces, and cut each single breast crosswise in half this way; you get 4 pieces of breast, 2 drumsticks, and 2 thighs, and you'll be able to serve everyone a piece of dark meat (thigh or drumstick) and a piece of white meat (breast).

If you're making broth cut the back, which has very little meat on it, into 3 pieces with a cleaver or heavy chef's knife. If you're serving the wings, fold the tip of the wing under the first joint so each wing forms a triangle, making them easier to fit in the pan. The wings can also be halved through the middle joint if you left the first joints attached to the breasts. Here's how to "quarter" a chicken:

1. Trim off the tail (better known as the pope's or parson's nose or puppick) at the back end of the chicken, below where the drumsticks come to points, and discard it. Pull out any large clumps of fat from the cavity and discard them, unless you like rendering them for cooking fat.

2. Pull out each wing and separate it from the rest of the chicken by cutting through the joint where the wing joins the body or at the second joint.

3. Turn the chicken on its side and pull one of the thighs forward so that the breast meat is completely covered with skin. (Otherwise, when you cut off the thigh you'll cut off too much skin and leave part of the breast meat exposed.) Cut through the skin, between the thigh and breast, along the side of the chicken all the way to the back, following the natural line of fat that runs along the edge of the thigh. Hold your thumb under the joint where the thigh connects to the rest of the chicken and snap open the thigh. You'll feel the joint snap out. Slide the knife along the back, keeping the knife against the bone, pulling on the thigh with the other hand as you go. Be sure to cut under the small morsel of meat (the oyster) embedded in the back so that you leave it attached to the thigh. Continue sliding the knife along the backbone while pulling on the thigh until the thigh comes away. Turn the chicken onto its other side and repeat with the other thigh.

4. Holding the chicken on the cutting board with the tip of the breast pointing up, make a series of rapid chops with a chef's knife to cut through the rib cage, almost all the way down to the cutting board. Keep the knife toward the back so you don't cut through any of the breast meat. Continue until you've cut through all the ribs. Snap the back away from the double breast and cut through the joints that attach the double breast to the back. Pull the back away from the double breast. Split the double breast lengthwise by placing it skin-side down on a cutting board and cutting straight down through the center of the breastbone. Pull the knife toward you, separating the back half of the breast. Turn the breast around and cut in the other direction, separating the halves.

5. If you're serving whole thighs, cut off the ends of the thigh bones by giving them a quick whack with a chef's knife. Use the section of the blade nearest the handle—where the metal is thickest—so you don't damage the edge.

DEGLAZING: Any book about French cooking at some point mentions deglazing, which, for some, is immediately intimidating. Fortunately there's nothing to it. Deglazing simply means adding liquid to the caramelized juices in a sauté pan or roasting pan after pouring or spooning out the fat (see "Degreasing," below). The dissolved juices are then served as a *jus* or thickened and served as gravy (for roasts), or used as the basis for a pan sauce (for sautéed meats and occasionally seafood).

DEGREASING: In French cooking, you'll often end up with liquids, such as braising liquids, roasting juices, and broths, that have fat floating on top. In professional kitchens, the fat is skimmed off liquids with a small ladle as the liquid simmers. This method requires a bit of technique so you don't end up scooping up too much of the flavorful liquid while trying to skim off the fat. To skim fat with a ladle, simmer the liquid on the stove with the saucepan moved to one side of the heat source so that the liquid simmers only on one side. This pushes the fat to the opposite side and makes it easier to lift off with the ladle. I use a 1-ounce or 2-ounce [30- or 60-ml] ladle for small pots, a 6-ounce or 8-ounce ladle for stockpots. Hold the ladle so that the top of its bowl is almost level with the liquid and, while tilting it just slightly toward the edge of the saucepan, make a circular motion with the ladle, skimming off the fat where it accumulates against the edge. As braising liquids and broths simmer, they typically throw off more fat and sometimes froth, so it's best to wait 5 or 10 minutes—or even longer in making slowly reduced liquids such as *glace de viande*—between skimmings.

If skimming the fat off hot liquids with a ladle sounds too tricky, you can use a degreasing cup. A degreasing cup is a clear plastic or glass cup with a spout that comes out of the bottom, so that when you pour out liquid it comes from the bottom of the cup instead of the top. In this way you can pour liquid into a clean saucepan and leave the fat, which floats to the top, behind in the cup. You still may need to skim the liquid as it reduces, since simmering broth continues to release fat and protein. Degreasing cups come in various sizes.

You can also refrigerate liquids until the fat congeals; you can then easily remove the fat with a spoon. If, after removing the congealed fat, you find that the liquid is cloudy, make it clearer by bringing it to a gentle simmer, which will cause it to release more fat and insoluble proteins, and then skimming it with a ladle as described above.

In some instances, as in roasting, you may end up with liquid fat floating over a small amount of concentrated drippings. Because there's so little liquid, it's almost impossible to remove fat without taking the savory juices with it. To avoid this, place the roasting pan on the stove and boil down the juices until they caramelize and stick to the bottom of the roasting pan. (This is why it isn't good to use nonstick roasting pans.) Reposition the pan every few minutes so that the juices brown evenly. Pour off the liquid fat which will now be floating over the caramelized juices, leaving the juices in the pan where they can be dissolved by deglazing with broth, wine, or water.

JULIENNE: A vegetable is said to be cut in julienne when it is cut into small sticks about 3 inches [7.5 cm] long and ¹⁄₁₆ inch to ⅛ inch [about 3 mm] on each side. Vegetable slicers (see "Mandolines and Vegetable Slicers," page 13) have julienne attachments, but they never seem to cut things the right size, and if the vegetable is hard, like celeriac or carrots, too much force is required to work it through the blades. When julienning, it's best to begin by slicing the vegetable with a vegetable slicer. You can of course use a knife, but it's hard to keep everything even. Then stack the slices 3 to 5 slices deep and thinly slice the stack with a knife. All vegetable slicers and mandolines come with a guard to keep you from slicing your hand instead of the vegetable. Even though the guards are often awkward, especially as you get near the end of the vegetable, resist the temptation to dispense with something to protect your hand.

Leeks must be julienned by hand. Cut the root end off the leek and cut off the greens. Wash the whites thoroughly, and take 2 or 3 stalks at a time and fold them end to end to make them easier to slice. Slice the stalks lengthwise into fine strips.

KNOWING WHEN FISH IS DONE: Fish is usually done after about 9 minutes of cooking per inch [2.5 cm] of thickness at the thickest part, but any number of factors—a slow oven, fish that is very thick or thin, and whole fish versus steaks or fillets—can make the actual cooking time longer or shorter than you expect. The easiest method for determining doneness is to just stick a knife in the fish and look at the flesh. If it's shiny and translucent, it's still slightly undercooked. On the other hand, if the fish is flaking, it's at least starting to overcook. The ideal appearance is just slightly translucent in the very center. With a little experience, you can judge the doneness of steaks and fillets by poking them with your forefinger in the same way you would meat (see Chapter 35). Fish that is cooked through will feel firm to the touch rather than fleshy. If you remove the fish from the heat as soon as it begins to feel firm, it will be the equivalent of medium, which is usually perfect for fish. Some fish, specifically fresh tuna, is often served rare, and salmon is best left a tad shiny and translucent in the middle. If you're cooking whole fish, slide a small knife along one side of the back fin down to the backbone and peek under the flesh. If the flesh pulls away from the bone easily, the fish is done. If it looks translucent and clings to the bone, cook it longer. If you're cooking very large whole fish, or don't want to deal with the knife method, slide a meat thermometer into the back of the fish down to the backbone; the temperature should read 135°F [55°C].

MONTER AU BEURRE: Literally "to work up with butter," the expression *monter au beurre* refers to whisking whole butter into small amounts of concentrated liquids to create a sauce. Beurre blanc (see page 281) is the best example of this technique, but you can finish virtually any flavorful liquid with butter to convert it into a sauce. When finishing a sauce with butter, keep in mind that butter is a fragile emulsion that if mishandled will separate into fat, water, and proteins. To prevent the emulsion from breaking apart, use whole unsalted butter and make sure it is cold. Whisk the butter in, a tablespoon or so at a time, while moving the pan back and forth over high heat. If you're making a lot of sauce, add more of it at once. Keep whisking until the butter is incorporated and the sauce has the texture and flavor you like. Don't let the sauce boil for more than 1 or 2 seconds or the butter will separate. Serve the sauce within 30 minutes of finishing it with butter; ideally, you should serve it sooner. (See also "Brown Sauces," page 5.)

PEELING AND SEEDING BELL PEPPERS: To peel a bell pepper, cook it until it is totally black by setting it directly on the flame of a gas stove or on a grill and turning it every couple of minutes with tongs. If you have an electric stove, bend down the ends of a metal coat hanger and set the hanger on the electric coils. Turn the heat to high and set the pepper on the hanger so that it stays about ⅛ inch [3 mm] above the coils. After charring the pepper, put it in a plastic bag or in a bowl covered with plastic wrap for 10 minutes so the steam it releases loosens the skin. Remove the charred skin by pulling it away with your fingers and then scraping off stubborn patches with a paring knife. Rinse the pepper quickly under cold water, cut out the stem, and make a slit through one side of the pepper. Open the pepper and cut away any pieces of white pulp. Rinse out the seeds under cold running water.

PEELING AND SEEDING TOMATOES: Bring about 2 quarts [liters] of water, enough to cover 1 or 2 of the tomatoes, to a boil in a small saucepan. Submerge the tomatoes 1 or 2 at a time in the boiling water and boil for 30 seconds. Drain them in a colander and rinse immediately with cold water. If you're peeling a lot of tomatoes, use more water, cook about 10 tomatoes at once, take them out with a skimmer (again, rinse immediately), and wait for the water to return to a boil before adding more tomatoes.

While seeding is usually not necessary, there are times when you will want your tomatoes seeded: for example, when making sauces that aren't being strained, or when using them in salads, where the seeds and the liquid that surrounds them can dilute the vinaigrette. There are two ways to go about it. The easiest way, best for sauces and baked tomatoes, is to cut the tomato crosswise in half and just squeeze the seeds out of each half. If you're using tomato wedges in a salad, cut the tomato in half vertically and then cut each half into the number of wedges you want. Push the seeds out of each wedge with a finger.

PEELING WINTER SQUASH: I'm always amused by recipes that call for peeling winter squash, especially acorn squash or other squashes with an irregular peel that make peeling impossible. If you have a recipe that calls for squash, cook the squash first in the microwave, just long enough to allow you to pull off the peel, usually about 10 minutes, or in the oven for about 50 minutes.

SHAPING ROOT VEGETABLES: In old-fashioned presentations, carrots, turnips, celeriac, and other root vegetables were cut into little balls with a melon baller or "turned" into elongated shapes. You still might encounter these if you go out to eat in an old-fashioned restaurant in Paris or New York, but nowadays chefs prefer to leave vegetables as unaltered and as natural as possible—this also saves a lot of work. If you find baby turnips and carrots, the turnips don't need peeling and the carrots just need to be lightly peeled or scraped and left whole with a tiny bit of the green attached. (Michel Guérard started this trend of leaving the greens attached in the early 1970s.) If you're confronted with larger carrots (or parsnips), peel them, cut them into 2-inch-long [5-cm] sections (or any size you like), and then cut the sections lengthwise into wedge-shaped lengths. The number of wedges you get out of each carrot section will depend on the size of the carrot. If the carrots are thin, you may want only to cut the sections lengthwise in half; if the carrots are very thick, you may want to cut the sections into as many as 5 wedges. Slide a paring knife along each side of the carrot sections between the yellowish core and the surrounding orange. Snap out the cores and discard. I rarely take it further than this, but if you like, turn the vegetables (see below) to give them a slightly elliptical shape. To deal with large turnips, cut them vertically into wedges (you can turn the wedges, if you like) or cut them into sticks—the French call these *bâtonnets*—by squaring off the edges and cutting the resulting cube into thick slices and then slicing each slice. This is also the way to make perfect dice.

If you do want to turn vegetables, you need to round off the sharp edges with a small knife. Turned vegetables look a little like elongated footballs or garlic cloves, thick in the middle and gently tapering at each end. Turning vegetables takes a little practice, and even once mastered, the technique takes time. I'll occasionally turn carrots, sectioned in the way explained above, and turnips or celeriac, which I first cut into thick *bâtonnets*. There are special little claw-shaped knives made for turning, but most people get by with a paring knife. The trick to turning is to move the vegetable against the blade of the knife in a continuous uninterrupted arc. Since I'm right-handed, I hold the knife in my right hand and the vegetable in my left and rotate the vegetable against the blade as though peeling, cutting deeper nearer the ends and allowing the knife to form arcs on the sides of the vegetables.

SLICING AND DICING: Cutting carrots into perfect dice is annoying, since carrots are cylindrical, which makes it necessary to cut each carrot into sections and then to square off the sides and waste the outer, reddest and sweetest, part. Except for very formal dishes in which you want the eye-catching geometry of perfect cubes, it makes more sense to slice the carrots instead. If you need perfect round slices, just slice the carrots as they are and put up with their tendency to roll all over the cutting board and onto the kitchen floor (angling the knife slightly toward the cutting board while slicing helps prevent this). An easier method, called slicing *en paysanne,* is to slice the carrots lengthwise into 3 or more wedge-shaped lengths (the number will depend on the size of the carrot and how big you want the slices) and then slice the lengths into tiny triangles. The triangles stay put and look attractive in informal soups and stews. This same method can be used for parsnips, zucchini, summer squash, or any cylindrical vegetable.

To make perfectly even fine dice called *brunoise,* cut the vegetables into julienne (see page 19) and while holding together the julienne strips slice them, producing minuscule cubes. To make macédoine, cut the vegetables into ³⁄₁₆-inch-wide [about .5 cm] sticks (*bâtonnets*) and slice these in the same way.

STEMMING, CLEANING, AND PREPARING SPINACH, SWISS CHARD, AND SORREL: Unless you're using it in a salad, look for the kind of spinach with large crinkly leaves—removing the stems will take much less time. I sometimes buy spinach in bags, but if you do this, look through the bag to make sure the spinach isn't spoiling (it will look slimy where the leaves touch the bag). When you get home, remove the stems and wash the spinach one more time.

To de-stem spinach and sorrel, peel the stem away from the back of the leaf so you don't remove the stem just where it joins the leaf but also where it runs up the leaf. To de-stem Swiss chard, cut the stems away from the leafy part with a knife. Next, put the leaves in a large bowl of cold water, lift them out with your splayed fingers, and feel the bottom of the bowl. If you feel sand or grit, rinse out the bowl and repeat until there's no grit. Spin the leaves dry in a salad spinner.

To cook spinach or chard in advance, or for immediate creaming or buttering, plunge the cleaned leaves into a 4 quarts [liters] of boiling salted water (for 1 or 2 bunches of leaves). The salt helps the spinach stay green; very little ends up in the finished dish. Stir for about 30 seconds, until the spinach "melts." Drain immediately in a colander and press on the spinach with the back of a spoon to force out water. If you're using the spinach later, rinse it immediately with cold water and, once it is cool, squeeze out the water by forming the spinach into balls in the palm of your hand. If you're serving the spinach right away, put it in a pot with some reduced cream (for more details, see page 118) or beurre noisette (see page 545).

Pronunciation Guide

SINCE MANY FRENCH SOUNDS HAVE NO ENGLISH EQUIVALENT, THIS CHART IS an approximation. Keep in mind a few rules. Unless otherwise directed, always accent the last syllable. Most of the words I list here are singular, so pronouncing the plural isn't an issue, but most French plurals end in *s*, which should be pronounced only if the next word in the sentence starts with a vowel. An *s* that is followed by a vowel should be pronounced like a *z*; a double *s* is pronounced with a hard *s* sound, as in "hiss." Here I've done my best to describe the sound of French words without using symbols. Keep in mind that when shown alone, vowels are pronounced with their long sound. For example, *a* is pronounced like the *a* in "paint"; *e* is pronounced like the *e* in "e-mail." The French *on* sound is impossible to replicate in English. I've written it "ohn (*n* silent)," meaning you should start to pronounce the English "on" but don't stop short of touching your tongue to the roof of your mouth to make the final *n* sound. Letters written as consonants (eg., *s*, *n*) are pronounced as though you are saying the word for the letter.

à/ah

abricotage/ah-bree-koh-tahje

agile/ah-jeel

agneau/ah-nyoh

aigre-doux/a-gr-du

aiguille/a-gwee

ail/eye

aile/el

aillade/eye-ahd

aïoli/eye-oh-lee

algérienne/ahl-jay-ree-en

aligot/al-e-go

aloyau/ah-loh-yo

alsacienne/ahl-zah-see-en

amandes/ah-mahnd

amandine/ah-mahn-dean

améliorée/ah-may-lee-or-ay

américaine/ah-may-ree-ken

amuse/ah-muuz

ananas/ah-nah-nah

anchoïde/ah-nshwahd

ancienne/ah-nsee-en

andalouse/ahn-dah-looze

andouille/ah-ndooya

anglaise/ahn-glez

anguille/ahng-gee (second g hard)

Anna/ah-nah

arachide/ah-rah-sheed

Aragon/ahr-ah-gon (n not pronounced)

archiduc/arsh-ee-duke

argent/ahr-jaunt (t not pronounced)

armoricaine/ahr-moh-ree-ken

aromatique/ahr-oh-mah-teek

artichauts/ahr-tee-show

asperges/ah-spairje

assiette/ah-see-et

attendre/ah-tahndr

attendu/ah-tah-ndo

au/o

aubergine/oh-bear-jeen

Auge/oje

Augustin/oh-guus-tan (don't pronounce n)

aux/o (ohz if in front of a vowel)

avec/ah-vek

azure/ah-zuur

bagatelle/bah-gah-tell

bagna/bahn-yah

bagration/bah-grah-see-ohn (n not pronounced)

baie/bay

bain-marie/ba-mah-ree (first a as in "ran")

ballon/bah-lohn (n not pronounced)

balsamique/ball-sah-meek

bar/bahr

bard/bahr

baron/bar-ohn (n not pronounced)

basilic/bah-zee-leek

basquaise/bahss-kez (first s hard; second s is soft like z)

bassin/bah-ssan (n not pronounced)

bâtonnets/bah-toe-nay

bavette/bah-vet

bayonnaise/bah-yoh-nez

Bayonne/bah-yohn

béarnaise/bay-air-nez

béatitude/bay-ah-tee-tude

béchamel/bay-shah-mell

beignet/bay-nyay

Bercy/bair-see

betterave/bet-rahve

beurre/beur

bien/be-yen (n not pronounced)

bifteck/bif-tek

bigarade/be-gahr-ahd

biscuit/bees-kwee

bisque/beesk

blanc/blahnk (k not pronounced, just approached)

blancmange/blahnk-mahnj (k not pronounced)

blanquette/blahn-ket

blette/blet

blettes/blet

bleu/blu (u as in "put")

blinis/blee-nee

bloc/block

blond/blohng (ng not pronounced)

blonde/blohnd

boeuf/boof (oo sound as in "foot")

bonne/bohn

Bordaberry/bohr-dah-bair-e

Bordaloue/boar-dah-loo

bordelaise/bohr-duh-lez

bouche/boush

boudin/boo-da (a as in "Dan")

bouillabaisse/booya-bess

bouillie/boo-e-yee

bouillon/booy-on (don't pronounce the last n, move your mouth toward it)

bourgoule/boor-gool

bourguignonne/boor-gee-nyohn (hard g)

bourride/boor-eed

bouzigue/boo-zeeg (hard g)

braise/brez

braisé[e]/bre-zay

braiser/bray-zay

brandade/brah-ndahd

Bresse/bress

bretonne/bru-tohn (u as in "put")

bretons/bru-ton (u pronounced like oo in "foot"; don't pronounce the n, move your mouth toward it)

bretzel/(pronounced like "pretzel")

Brillat-Savarin/bree-yah-saw-ver-an (last n not pronounced)

brioche/bree-ohsh (o pronounced like "oh")

brioché/bree-oh-shay

brouillés/broo-e-yay

brûlée/brew-lay

brun/bra (a pronounced like ua in "quack")

brunoise/broo-nwahz

bûcheron/boo-sher-on (last n not pronounced)

ça/saw

cabillaud/kah-b-yoh

Caen/kahn (n not pronounced)

caennaise/kah-nez

cameline/kah-muh-lean (u as in put)

campagne/kahn-pah-nyuh

canaille/kah-neye

canaleur/kah-nah-lir (lir as in "sir")

canard/kah-nahr

caneton/kah-nton (n not pronounced)

canut/kah-new

caouda/kah-ooda

caramel/cah-rah-mel

carbonnade/kahr-bow-nod

carottes/kar-oat (ar pronounced like letter r)

carré/kah-ray

cassole/kah-ssol

cassolette/kah-soh-let

cassoulet/kah-soo-lay

caudière/koh-d'yair

céleri-branch/say-lu-ree-brahnsh (u pronounced as in "put"; last n not pronounced)

céleri-rave/say-lur-ree-rahv

célestine/say-les-teen

cendre/sah-ndrah

Cendrillon/sah-ndree-ohn (last n not pronounced)

cent/sawn (n not pronounced)

central/sahn-trahl (n not pronounced)

cèpes/sep

cerises/suh-reez

certain age/sair-ten-ahj

cervelas/sair/vel-ah

cervelle/sair-vell

chaînette/shen-ett

champignons/shah-npee-yong (g not pronounced)

Chandeleur/shan-d'lur

Chantilly/shah-ntee-yee

chapelure/shah-pluur

charcutier/shar-cuu-tyay

Charentes/shar-ahnt

charlotte/shar-loat

charolais/shar-o-lay

charolaise/shar-o-lez

chartreuse/shar-truz (u as in "put")

chasseur/shaw-sir

chaud-froid/show-fwah

chaudrée/show-dray

chèure/shevr

chez/shay

chichi/she-she

chiffonnade/shee-foh-nahd

chinoise/sheen-wahs

chocolat/shoh-koh-lah

Choron/show-rohn (n not pronounced)

chou/shoe

choucroute/shoe-kroot

choufleur/shoe-flur

choux/shoo

ciboulette/see-boo-let

citron/see-tron (n not pronounced)

civet/see-vay

clafoutis/klah-foo-tee

claire/clair

classique/klah-seek

clémentine/clay-mahn-teen

cocotte/koh-kott

coeurs/kuhr

coing/kwan (n not pronounced)

comme/kohm

composé/koh-mpoh-zay

concassé/koh-nkah-say

concassée/kohn-kah-say

concombres/kohn-kohn-bruh

confit/koh-nfee

confiture/koh-nfee-teewr

congre/kohngr

conserve/koh-nsairv

consommé/koh-nso-may

contre-filet/koh-ntra-fee-lay

coq/coke

coquetier/koh-k'tyay

coquilles/ko-key

corail/kor-eye

corniotte/kor-nee-yoat

côte/koht

côtelette/koat-let

côtes/koht

cotignac/koh-tee-nyahk

cotriade/koh-tree-ahd

coulis/koo-lee

coupés/kou-pay

courge/koorj

courgette/koor-jet

court-bouillon/koor-booy-on (don't pronounce the last n, move your mouth toward it)

cousinat/coo-zee-nah

crabe/kwrab

crème/kwrem

crèmé/kwrem-a

crêpes/kwrep

cressonière/kre-soh-nyair

creuses/kruz (u as in "put")

crevette/kruh-vet

crevettes/kruh-vet

croque/kwroak

croûte/kroot

croûton/kroo-tohn (n not pronounced)

cru/kwrew

crudité/kwrew-dee-tay

cuiller/kwee-yair

cuillière/kwee-yair

cuisinier/kwee-z-nyay

cuisses/kwees (hard s)

cuisson/kwee-sohn (n not pronounced)

cuit/kwee

cul/kewe

culinaire/coo-lee-nair

cultivateur/kul-tee-vah-tir (ir as in "sir")

curry/kuu-ree

d'hôtel/doh-tel

dacquoise/dahk-wahz

Danicheff/dah-nee-shef

dariole/dah-ree-ol

darne/dahrn

daube/dohb

daubière/doh-be-yair

dauphine/doh-feen

dauphinois/doh-feen-wah

daurade/doh-rod

de/du (u barely pronounced; pronounced as in "put")

demi-deuil/d'me-doiya (oi sound between o and "oink")

demi-glace/duh-mee-glahss

désossé/day-zoh-say

Diane/dee-ahn

dieppoise/dee-ep-wahz

digestif/dee-jes-teef

dijonnaise/dee-joh-nez

doit/dwah

doré/door-ay

du/dew

duchesse/du-shess

dugléré/duu-glay-ray

duxelles/doox-el

échalote/ay-shah-lot

Echiré/a-sheer-ay

écorce/a-korss

écrevisse/ay-kruh-veess

en/on (o sound similar to "on", but n not pronounced)

entier/on-tee-yay (n not pronounced)

entrecôte/on-tra-coat (n not pronounced)

entrée/on-tray (n not pronounced)

épaule/a-pole

épices/a-peese (hard s)

épinard/a-pee-nahr

épinards/a-pee-nahr

escabeche/s-kah-besh

escalope/s-kah-lop

escargot/s-car-go

Escoffier/s-koh-fee-yay

Espagne/s-pah-nya

espagnole/s-pah-nyole

espelette/s-pu-let (u as in "put")

estragon/s-tra-gohn (n not pronounced)

et/a

étouffer/a-two-fay

étuvage/a-two-vahj

étuvé/a-two-vay

étuver/a-two-vay

évasé/a-vaw-zay

facile/fah-seel

faire/fair

fallue/fal-oo

far/fahr

farci/fahr-see

farine/fah-reen

favorite/fah-voh-reet

femme/fahm

fenouil/fen-ooye (last e barely pronounced)

fermier/fair-mee-yay

fête/fett

feuilletée/foi-e-tay (oi pronounced as in "oink")

fèves/fev

ficelle/fee-sel

figue/feeg (hard g)

filets/fee-lay

financier/fee-nah-nsee-ay

fines/feen

flageolets/flahj-oh-lay

flan/flahn (n not pronounced)

flétan/flay-tahn (n not pronounced)

fleur/flir (ir as in "sir")

flimiche/flee-meesh

flottante/flow-taunt ("aunt" with broad a)

flottantes/flow-tahnt

foies/fwah

fonçage/foh-nsahje

fonds/fohn (n not pronounced)

fondue/phone-due

fou/foo

fougasse/fou-gahss (hard s)

four/foor

frâiche/freysh

frais/fray

fraisage/fray-zahj

fraise/frez

fraiser/frez-a

framboises/frah-mbwaz

française/frahn-sez

françois/frah-nswa

fricandeau/free-kahn-doh

fricassée/free-cah-say

frisée/free-zay

frit/free

froid/fwrahd

fromage/fro-mahje

fruits/fwree

fumet/foo-may

gâche/gawsh

galettes/gah-let

ganache/ga-nahsh

garage/gah-rahje

garbure/gahr-buur

garenne/gahr-n

garnie/gar-knee

garniture/gar-knee-tur

gastrique/gahs-tweek

gastronomique/gahs-troh-noh-meek

gâteau/gah-toe

gâteaux/gah-toe

gelée/jel-ay

genevoise/je-nuh-vwahz

Georges/jorje

georgette/jorj-ett

germiny/jur-meeny (u as in "put")

gibelotte/gee-b'loat

gigot/gee-go (first g soft)

gingembre/jan-jahn-bruh

girelle/jee-rel

glaçage/glahce-ahje

glace/glahss

glacé/glah-say

godiveau/go-dee-voh

gorge/gorj

gougères/goo-jerr

gourmandise/gour-mah-ndeez

gousse/goose

grand/gwrahn (n not pronounced)

grande/grah-nd

gras/gwrah

gratin/grah-ta (last a pronounced as in "and")

gratinée/grah-tee-nay

gravette/grah-vet

grecque/grek

grenobloise/gruh-no-blwahz (u as in "put")

gribiche/gree-beesh

grillé/gree-ya (a pronounced as in "paint")

grondin/grow-ndan (last n not pronounced)

gros/groh

groseilles/grow-zay

guérande/gay-rahnd (last n not pronounced)

gueules/gull

guide/geed (hard g)

gwen aman/gwe-nahmahn

hachis/ah-shee

hallé/ah-lay

haricots/ah-ree-koh

haute/oat

herbe/airb

heures/urr (like "purr")

hochepot/ohsh-poe

hollandaise/oh-lah-ndezs

homard/o-mahr

huile/wheel

huîtres/wee-tra (a barely pronounced)

hure/oor

île/eel

îles/eel

impératrice/an-pay-rah-treece (first a pronounced as in "ran")

impériale/an-pay-ree-all (n not pronounced; first a as in ran)

improvisé/an-pro-vee-zay (don't pronounce the n)

indienne/a-ndee-n (a pronounced as in "ran")

inmangeable/an-mah-njable (first a pronounced as in "ran")

Irma/ear-mah

Isigny/e-z-nyee

italienne/e-tal-yen

jamais/jah-may

jambon/jah-mbohn (n not pronounced)

jamboneaux/jah-mboh-no

japonaise/jah-poh-nez

jarret/jahr-ay

Jean/john (n not pronounced)

julienne/joul-e-n

jus/joo

kirsch/keersh

kugelhopf/kooglof

la/lah

Laguiole/lah-yol

laiteuse/let-uz (u as in put)

landaise/lah-ndez

Landes/lahnd

langoustine/lah-ngoo-steen

lapereau/lah-proh

Laperouse/lah-pair-rooz

lapin/lah-pan (n not pronounced)

lard/lahr

lardoir/lahr-dwah

lardon/lahr-dohn (n not pronounced)

lavandade/lah-vah-ndahd

le/luh

lèchefrite/lesh-freet

légume/lay-goom (hard g)

les/lay (when followed by a consonant), layz (when followed by a vowel)

les Halles/lay-all

leur/ler (er pronounced as in "her")

lié/lee-a

lièvre/lee-evr (last e as in "edge")

limonadier/lee-moh-nahd-ee-a

limousin/lee-mou-zan (a as in "ran")

limousine/lee-mou-zeen

linzer/lean-zer (second e as in "her")

lorraine/lore-n

lotte/lot

loup/loo

luxe/loox

lyonnaise/lee-oh-nez

macaron/mah-kah-rohn (n not pronounced)

macaroni/mah-kah-row-knee

macédoine/mah-say-dwan (last a as in "ran")

madeleines/mahd-len (mahd as in "modern")

madère/mah-dair

magret/mah-gray

maigre/meggr (egg pronounced like "egg")

mais/may

maïs/mah-eess

maître/metr (e as in "edge")

maïze/mah-eez

maladie/mah-lah-dee

maltaise/mahl-tez

mandarin/mahn-dah-ran (n not pronounced)

manié/mah-nyay

maquereaux/mah-kroh

marc/mahr

marchand/mar-shahn (n not pronounced)

marché/mahr-shay

marennes/mah-ren

mareyeur/mahr-e-yir (as in "sir")

Marguéry/marg-air-ee (g hard)

marinés/mah-ree-nay

marinière/mah-ree-nyair

marjolaine/mar-jo-len

marmelade/mahr-muh-lahd (u as in "put")

marmite/mahr-meet

marnier/mahr-nyay

marron/mah-rohn (n not pronounced)

marseillaise/mahr-say-yez (e as in edge)

massif/mah-seef

matelote/mah-tloat

matignon/mah-tee-nyon (last n not pronounced)

mayonnaise/mah-o-nayz

médaillon/may-dah-yohn (last n not pronounced)

meilleur/may-yuhr

méjanel/may-jaw-nell

ménagère/may-nah-jair

mer/mair

Mercédès/mair-say-dees

mère/mair

meringue/mair-ang (ang as in "anger")

meringué/mair-ang-gay

merlan/mair-lahn (n not pronounced)

merveilles/mair-vay

mesclun/mu-sclan (u as in "put"; a as in "ran"; n not pronounced)

meunière/muh-nyair (u as in "put")

meurette/mur-ett (u as in "murder")

mie/me

mignon/me-nyon (last n not pronounced)

mignonnette/me-nyoh-net

mijoter/me-jo-tay

milanaise/me-lah-nez

milhas/me-lah

minceur/ma-nsir (a as in "ran")

mirabelle/meer-ah-bell

mirepoix/meer-pwah

mirliton/meer-lee-tohn (n not pronounced)

miroton/mee-roh-tohn (n silent)

mise en place/meez-on-plahss (n not pronounced)

mode/mode

moelleux/mwall-u (u as in "put")

monde/mohnd

monsieurs/muh-ssyuh

monter/moh-ntay

montpelier/moh-npel-e-a

morilles/mor-e

Mornay/mor-nay

mortier/mor-tee-yay

morue/mor-oo

morvandelle/more-vahn-del

moscovite/moe-sko-veet

mouclade/moo-clod

mougins/moo-jan (a as in "ran"; n not pronounced)

moule/mool

moulin/moo-lan (a as in "ran"; n not pronounced)

mourtayrol/moor-tah-rol

mousse/mousse

mousseline/moos'l-een

moutarde/moo-tard

mouton/mou-tohn (n silent)

n'importe quoi/nan-pohr-tuh-kwah (a as in "ran")

nage/nahje

nantais/nah-ntayz

nantua/nahn-twah

navarin/nah-vah-ran (last n not pronounced)

navet/nah-vay

navette/nah-vet

neige/nej (e sound as in "edge"; j soft)

niçoise/nee-swahz

ninon/knee-nohn (last n not pronounced)

noël/no-el

noir/nwar

noisettes/nwah-zet

noix/nwah

normande/nor-mahnd

norvégienne/nohr-vay-jee-en

nougatine/new-ga-teen

nouille/noo-ya

nouvelle/new-vel

nuage/new-ahje

oeuf/u (like the u in "put")

oignon/u-nyon (u as in "put"; last n not pronounced)

oignons/oi-nyon (n silent)

olive/oh-leave

omelette/ohm-let

onglet/ohn-glay (n not pronounced)

opéra/oh-pay-rah

orange/oh-rahnje (n not pronounced)

orangerie/oh/rah-njair-e

ordinaire/or-dee-nair

oseille/oh-zay

ou/oo (as in "roof")

oursin/oor-san (a as in "ran")

oursinade/oor-see-nahd

pain/pa (a as in "ran")

palmier/pahl-me-a

paloise/pawl-wahz

pamplemousse/pahm-pl-mousse

panaché/pah-nah-shay

panade/pah-nod

panais/pah-nay

paner/pah-nay

panier/pah-n'yay

panisse/pah-niece

panne/pahn

pantin/pah-nta (last a as in "tan")

papillote/pah-pee-yote

paprika/pah-pree-kah

Pâques/pahk

parfait/pahr-fay

parisienne/pah-ree-zee-en

parmentier/pahr-mah-ntee-yay

pastis/pahss-teesse

pâte/paht

pâté/pah-tay

pâtissière/pah-tee-see-air

paysanne/pay-ee-zahn

peau/poh

pithiviers/pee-tee-vee-yay (with the a pronounced as in "paint")

pépin/pay-pan (n not pronounced)

perce-pierre/pairss-pee-air

Périgord/pay-ree-gore

périgoourdine/pay-ree-goor-deen

Pernod/pair-noh

pérougienne/pay-rouge-e-n

persillade/pair-see-yahd

persil/pair-see

persillé/pair-see-yay

petit/pu-tee (u as in "put")

petite/pu-teet

pétoncle/pay-tohnk-lu (u as in "put")

picquer/pee-kay

pièce/pee-yes

pigeon/pee-jo (o sound between "Joe" and "John")

pignola/pee-nyo-lah

pignon/pee-nyon (n not pronounced)

pincer/pan-say (n not pronounced)

pipérade/pee-pay-rod

pissala/pee-ssah-lah

pissaladière/pee-ssah-lah-dyair

pistaches/pee-stahsh

pistou/pee-stew

plant/plahn (n not pronounced)

plat/plah

plate/plaht

plus/plu (meaning "none" or "no more"), plouss (meaning "in addition to")

poêlage/pwahl-ahj

poêle/pwall

poilane/pwah-lahn

point/pwa (a as in "ran")

poireaux/pwah-roh

poires/pwar

pois/pwah

poisson/pwah-sohn (n not pronounced)

poitrine/pwah-tween

poivrade/pwah-vrahd

poivre/pwah-vr

pommade/poe-mahd

pommes/pohm

porc/por

porto/por-toe

portugaise/por-to-gez (hard g; e as in "edge")

pot/poh

pot-au-feu/poh-toe-fu (u as in "put")

potage/poh-tahje

potée/poe-tay

pots/poh

poudre/poo-dr

poularde/poo-lahrd

poule/pool

poulet/poo-lay

poulette/pool-ett

poulpe/poolp

pounti/poo-ntee

pour/poor (oo as in "pool")

presse/pwress

printanier/pra-ntah-nyay (first n not
   pronounced)

propriétaire/pro-pree-a-tair

provençal/pro-vah-nsahl

pruneau/pru-no

pruneaux/pru-no

purée/puu-ray

quarante/kahr-aunt ("aunt" with a
   broad a)

quatre/catr

quatre-quarts/cat-cahr

quenelle/ku-nell (u as in "put," barely
   pronounced)

quetsche/kwetsh

queue/ku (u as in "put")

quiche/keesh (sh as in "she")

râble/rah-bl

racler/rah-klay

raclette/rah-klet

ragoût/rah-goo

raie/ray

raisiné/ray-zee-nay

raïto/rah-e-toe

ramequin/ram-kan (n not pronounced)

râpé/rah-pay

râpées/rah-pay

rascasse/rahs-kahss

ratafia/rah-tah-fee-ah

ratatouille/rah-tah-too-yuh

ratte/raht

régionaux/ray-jee-oh-noh

reine/ren (en as in "yen")

rémoulade/ray-moo-lahd (u as in "put")

renversée/rah-nver-say

reste/wrest

Ricard/ree-kahr

rigodon/ree-go-dohn (n not pronounced)

rillettes/ree-yet

ris/ree

riz/ree

Rochebonne/rosh-bon

rognon/roh-nyohn (last n not
   pronounced)

rondeau/row-ndoe

roquefort/rok-for

rosette/rose-ett

Rossini/row-see-knee

rôti/roh-tee

rouge/rouge

rouget/roo-jay

rouille/roo-ya (last a barely pronounced)

rousse/rooss

royale/ro-yahl

romsteck/room-stek

sa/saw

sable/sah-bl

sablé/saw-blay

sablés/saw-blay

safran/sah-fron (n not pronounced)

saignant/sen-yahn (last n not
   pronounced)

saindoux/san-do (a as in "ran"; n not
   pronounced)

saint/san (n not pronounced; a as
   in "ran")

Saint-Ange/san-tahnj (first a as in "ran")

Saint-Jacques/san-jawk (first a
   pronounced as in "ran"; n silent)

Sainte-Ménehould/sant-may-new

Saint-Pierre/sa-pee-air (first a as in "ran")

salade/sa-lahd

salmis/sal-me

salon/sah-lohn (n not pronounced)

salpicon/sahl-pee-kohn (n not
   pronounced)

sandre/sah-ndr

sang/sahn (n not pronounced)

sans/sawn (n not pronounced)

sarladaise/sahr-lah-dez

sarrasin/sah-rah-zan (a as in "ran"; n not
   pronounced)

sauce/sohss

saucisse/so-cease

saucisson/sew-see-sohn (n not
   pronounced)

saumon/so-mohn (n not pronounced)

saupiquet/so-pee-k

sauté/soh-tay

savarin/saw-ver-a (a pronounced as in
   "and")

savoyarde/sah-vwah-yahrd

Schifeta/she-fah-lah

sec/sek

sèche/sesh

sèches/sesh

sel/sell

selle/sell

sept/set

sètoise/set-wahz

simple/sa-mple (a as in "ran")

singer/san-jay (n not pronounced)

socca/so-kah

sole/sole

soubise/sue-beez

soufflé/soo-flay

soupe/soup

sous/soo

spéciale/spay-see-all

suavité/swah-vee-tay

succès/sook-say

sucre/sookr

sucré/soo-kray

suédoise/suede-wahz

suissesse/swee-ssess

suprême/sue-prem

sur/soor

surprise/sur-preeze (u pronounced like
    the letter u)

suzette/soo-zett

table/tah-bl

Taillevent/tie-vahn (n not pronounced)

tapénade/tah-pay-nahd

tarte/tart

Tatin/tah-tan (n not pronounced)

tendron/tahn-drohn (n not pronounced)

terre/tair

terrine/tu-reen (u as in "put")

terrinée/tuh-ree-nay

terroir/tair-wahr

thé/tay

thon/tohn (n silent)

tian/tee-ahn (n silent)

tomate/toe-maht

tome/tome

torchon/tor-shohn (n not pronounced)

tour/toor

tourangelle/toor-ahn-jel

tournedo/toor-nuh-doh

tourte/toort

tourteaux/tour-toh

tripes/twreep

tronçon/trohn-sohn (neither n
    pronounced)

truffes/twroof

truite/twreet

ttoro/toro

tyrolienne/tee-roll-e-n

un/an (n not pronounced)

vallée/vahl-a

ASSORTED
VEGETABLE SALADS

CRUDITÉS

HOW TO	HOW TO	HOW TO	HOW TO
PEEL, SLICE, AND CHOP A VARIETY OF VEGETABLES	USE SALT TO GET EXCESS LIQUID OUT OF VEGETABLES	MAKE MAYONNAISE	MAKE CRÈME FRAÎCHE

WHEN LIVING IN PARIS IN THE 1970S, I'D TAKE PILGRIMAGES TO THE countryside and spend a week's wages from my low-paying restaurant job on lunch in some famous and extravagant restaurant. These trips would often take a couple of days each way. I had to pinch pennies, and I was careful not to spend my lunch money just getting to the restaurant. Most of the time I'd hitchhike, which in the early days of my limited French might mean hours of silence in the cab of some unfortunate trucker who was dying for a little conversation. I'd stay at fleabag hotels and at youth hostels (at least French youth hostels would have a bar) and eat in the least expensive restaurants I could find along the way. While often far from great, these little local places sometimes provided me with a deeper sense of the roots of French cooking than I'd find at the luxury spot where I was heading. The menus usually included regional specialties, and when my French got better I'd get to chat with French families and traveling salesmen, since customers often shared tables. I enjoyed the hustle and bustle after a day spent mostly alone with my thumb out. But what I remember most about these simple meals is the abundant platter of assorted vegetable salads—*l'assiette de crudités*—offered as a way to start dinner. Usually the waiter or waitress would set the platter next to my table and let me serve myself as much as I wanted. I'd linger as long as I could, munching vegetables and sipping a cool local wine.

When I returned to the United States, I was surprised to see crudités on a list of hors d'oeuvres at a dinner at someone's wedding, but when they never appeared and I asked a friend where they were, she pointed to a little glass of limp carrot sticks that had been set at the center of the table. Nowhere were the mounds of colorful salads I remembered.

The word "crudités" comes from *cru,* meaning raw. While in fact cooked things such as beets and hard-boiled eggs often find their way onto a crudité platter, most crudités are simple salads made of raw vegetables that have been seasoned with vinaigrette, homemade mayonnaise, or mustardy cream sauce. You can make a crudité selection as simple or as complicated as you like by providing just one or two salads at a family dinner, or you can pull out all the stops and serve as many as seven. While most crudité salads have their traditional sauces, it's more important to use contrasting ingredients so the salads don't end up tasting all the same, and at the same time use ingredients that underline the vegetable's character without disguising it. I keep on hand a selection of vinegars that includes my own homemade vinegar (see page 50) made from unfinished bottles of red wine (an admittedly rare occurrence), a champagne vinegar, several kinds of balsamic vinegar (from an inexpensive supermarket brand to rare *aceto balsamico tradizionale* that I measure out with an eyedropper), and various herb vinegars made by stuffing bundles of thyme, marjoram, and tarragon into separate bottles of my own vinegar or champagne vinegar and letting them sit for a couple of weeks. I have a similar variety of oils, including an inexpensive extra-virgin olive oil I buy in large cans and a golden (and frightfully expensive) bottle of unfiltered Provençal olive oil. Nut oils, which provide a welcome contrast in crudités, must be used quickly because they're very perishable. While I never seem to have them all on hand at once, I buy a special brand of hazelnut oil, walnut oil, and a gorgeous green pistachio oil made from roasted nuts (see Sources). The roasting not only intensifies the flavor of the nuts but makes the oils much less perishable. I also keep a bottle of canola oil on hand for those rare occasions when I want an oil with virtually no taste.

CELERIAC RÉMOULADE

CÉLERI-RAVE RÉMOULADE

MAKES 6 FIRST-COURSE SERVINGS

WHEN SERVED ALONE, OR PROPORTIONATELY MORE

WHEN SERVED WITH OTHER SALADS

Americans don't eat much celeriac (also called celery root), no doubt in part because of its intimidating appearance. Celeriac shows up in markets, usually without its greens, as a knobby and hairy-looking vaguely spherical root that is rather large, between a rutabaga and a turnip in size. Most of us don't know how to peel such a thing, much less how to prepare and eat it. As you may have guessed, celeriac is closely related to our everyday celery, which the French call céleri-branche. But you won't get a decent celeriac by just yanking a bunch of celery out of the ground, because celeriac is grown specifically for the root. While celeriac does smell like celery, it has an alluring complexity and earthy subtlety of taste that celery stalks lack. Celeriac is good cut up and glazed in the same way as turnips (see page 560), but it is at its very best as a flavoring for mashed potatoes (add about a third as much celeriac as you have potatoes to the potatoes before puréeing) and in Celeriac Rémoulade.

To make Celeriac Rémoulade you only need to peel the root with a paring knife—vegetable peelers don't cut deep enough—and then slice it into julienne. If you have a mandoline or plastic vegetable slicer (see page 13), slicing it isn't as difficult as it sounds. You then toss the julienne in homemade mayonnaise, well seasoned with mustard. The first time I made Celeriac Rémoulade I made the easily committed mistake of using rémoulade sauce (a mayonnaise that includes capers, gherkins, anchovies, and herbs) instead of the mustardy mayonnaise that in French classic cooking is called sauce dijonaise. (Why this discrepancy, I have no idea. My Larousse Gastronomique claims that the French word rémoulade comes from the Latin armorcia, meaning horseradish. But the earliest reference I can find to rémoulade sauce is in Antonin Carême's 1830s work L'Art de la Cuisine Française, which gives seven versions, none with horseradish. Escoffier mentions only one version.)

- 1 very large celeriac (1½ to 2 pounds [675 g to 900 g] without greens), peeled
- 1 tablespoon lemon juice
- ¾ cup [175 ml] Basic Mayonnaise (page 34)
- 1 tablespoon Dijon mustard (in addition to the mustard in the Basic Mayonnaise recipe), or more to taste
- salt
- pepper
- 1 tablespoon finely chopped parsley

CUT the celeriac in half through the top. Place each half on a vegetable slicer, with the flat side of the half facing the blade, and slice it into ⅛-inch [3 mm] slices. Stack the slices two or three together and cut them into ⅛-inch-wide [3 mm] julienne with a chef's knife. Toss the julienned celeriac with the lemon juice. Combine the Basic Mayonnaise with the mustard and season to taste with salt and pepper and, if you like, more mustard. Stir this sauce and the parsley into the celeriac. Taste the Celeriac Rémoulade and add more salt and pepper if needed.

BASIC MAYONNAISE

The idea of homemade mayonnaise makes a lot of us nervous, probably because we've read so many recipes that describe tediously adding oil drop by drop, insist the eggs and oil be at exactly a certain temperature, and warn us of dire consequences if any steps are missed or any rules broken. If you have a blender, a batch of Basic Mayonnaise will take you about a minute, and even if you don't have a blender, you can make a cup or two in about five minutes. One caveat: If you're making a mayonnaise, such as aïoli, with extra-virgin olive oil, you'll have to make it by hand, using a wooden spoon, because hard beating in an electric mixer or even with a hand whisk turns the oil bitter. (See Aïoli, page 491.)

All of this of course brings us to the question, always asked in my cooking classes, of whether it is safe to eat raw egg yolks. It depends. The latest statistics say that one in twenty thousand egg yolks may be contaminated. So if you're using 2 yolks for four servings of mayonnaise, the chances of making your guests sick is very small, but if you're cooking for a thousand, the chances increase because you're using more yolks and it only takes one bad one to make everyone sick. For the most part, I live dangerously and eat and serve mayonnaise made with raw yolks. But if I'm cooking for a large crowd, I cook the yolks, but not to the point where they curdle, by combining them with ½ tablespoon of water per egg yolk and whisking them in a bowl over a pot of boiling water until they become airy and start to thicken, at about 180°F [82°C], which is more than hot enough to kill salmonella bacteria. I then whisk the oil into the hot yolks, off the heat.

MAKES 1½ CUPS [375 ML]

2 egg yolks

2 teaspoons Dijon mustard

1 tablespoon lemon juice, or 2 teaspoons white wine vinegar, or more to taste

1⅓ cup [325 ml] canola or safflower oil

salt

pepper

COMBINE the egg yolks, Dijon mustard, and lemon juice in a blender or food processor. If you're using a blender, turn it on low. If you're using a food processor, just turn it on. Pour the canola or safflower oil in a thin steady stream through the hole in the blender or food processor lid. When you've added all the oil, the mayonnaise should be very thick. Season the mayonnaise to taste with salt and pepper and, if needed, more lemon juice. If while you're adding the oil the mayonnaise becomes so stiff that it won't move around in the blender or food processor, add a tablespoon or so of water, a bit at a time, to keep the mayonnaise at the consistency you like.

GRATED
CARROTS

CAROTTES RÂPÉES

Before I ever tasted my first plate of crudités, I had encountered grated carrots, tossed in salads with raw sunflower seeds and lots of alfalfa sprouts, in American health food restaurants. Frankly, the carrots always seemed to me more appropriate as rabbit food than as part of a salad. As I later found out, there's more to grating a carrot than most people think. If the carrots are grated too coarsely, they'll take forever to chew, for man or rabbit, and if the carrots are grated too finely, they'll turn into mush. The solution lies in your choice of graters. I use a box grater, one of those old-fashioned stand-up models with four sides, with a different-gauge grater on each side. But, to further complicate matters, not all such graters are made alike. The finest side on some brands is covered with tiny little holes that have been punched out from the inside. Don't try grating carrots with one of these or you'll end up with carrot sludge. Look for a grater with tiny scooplike teeth (the same shape as the coarse teeth on the other side of the grater) that protrude; these are perfect for grated carrots. If this is all just too much, grate the carrots in a food processor with the finest grating attachment, placing the carrots, cut in sections, on their sides against the blade.

As part of a serving of crudités, grated carrots aren't combined with other vegetables or greens, but are kept separate in their own little mound on the plate or in a bowl so that their clean, sweet flavor isn't obscured by other ingredients. Seasonings for grated carrots are kept simple. In most French versions, the carrots are tossed with a little flavorless vegetable oil, lemon juice, salt and pepper, and freshly chopped parsley. The French usually use a tasteless version of peanut oil, *huile d'arachide*, but because American peanut oil has too strong a flavor, we're better off using canola oil, safflower oil, or "pure" olive oil. If you're serving grated carrots by themselves or with only one or two other salads, experiment with any oil you like; just make sure it's different from what you use in the other salads.

8 large or 16 medium-size carrots, peeled and cut into 3-inch [7.5 cm] lengths

1½ tablespoons lemon juice

3 tablespoons canola oil, "pure" olive oil, or olive oil

3 tablespoons finely chopped parsley, chopped at the last minute

salt

freshly ground white pepper

½ teaspoon sugar (optional)

GRATE the carrots by pushing them lengthwise along the grater teeth. Grate one side of the carrot section until you get down to the woody core. Rotate the carrot a half turn, again grate down to the core, give a quarter turn, and repeat until you've grated all four sides and are left with the core. Discard the cores. If you're grating the carrots with a food processor, use the finest attachment and don't worry about the cores.

TOSS the grated carrots with the lemon juice, oil, parsley, salt, and pepper. Taste the carrots and toss them with the sugar if you think they need to be sweeter.

Variations: If I'm serving Grated Carrots with a number of other salads as part of a selection of crudités, I leave it as is, but if I'm serving it alone as a first-course salad or as a side dish at a summer barbecue, I often liven it up with other ingredients: little cubes of celery, which add crunch; toasted pine nuts, for crunch and a nutty accent; golden raisins (sometimes combined with pine nuts), which add sweetness and complexity; a little saffron (soaked for 30 minutes in a teaspoon of water), which is good with the raisins; curry powder (cooked for a few seconds in oil, stirred in to taste); diced or shredded hot chiles, fresh or dried (if dried, toasted and softened in water), or cilantro (combined with the chiles).

Extra-virgin olive oil is oil that's gently squeezed out of the olives after they are crushed, along with their pits, into a paste. The paste is layered between rounds of wicker (or, nowadays, plastic) and allowed to exude oil, the weight of the paste providing sufficient pressure to release the oil. When, on a recent trip to Tunisia, I saw olive oil being made in this way, the oil that was released without pressure was called first-pressed olive oil or *première pression à cru*. The paste was then put under a press, yielding a less golden oil, the second pressing. Both of these oils are still considered extra-virgin olive oils because the oil is never exposed to heat or chemicals. To qualify as extra-virgin olive oil, the oil must contain no more than 1 percent of oleic acid, an acid that results from rancidity. To avoid rancidity, the olives must be pressed within days—ideally, within hours—of being harvested. Virgin olive oil is allowed to contain more oleic acid than extra-virgin olive oil. "Pure" olive oil is made from oil that has a higher-than-acceptable amount of oleic acid and hence must be "purified" by treating it with chemicals. "Pure" olive oil, while far less expensive, never approaches the flavor of extra-virgin olive oil. It is, however, useful for frying and sautéing, processes whose high heat destroys the flavor of extra-virgin olive oil. I use "pure" olive oil where others might use vegetable oils, because, while its flavor is hard to detect, it's at least innocuous.

I'm often asked what my favorite olive oil is. Like wine, extra-virgin olive oil is interesting because every kind is different. It even changes with each vintage. I use so much olive oil that I buy 3-liter cans of an inexpensive brand such as Colavita or Bertolli extra-virgin for daily use in salads and sauces. A can lasts me about three months; it is finished well ahead of when the oil would turn rancid. Adjust the amount of extra-virgin olive oil you buy at one time so that you take home three months' worth, since the more you buy at once, the less expensive it is. In addition to the everyday olive oil, other, more expensive kinds of olive oil come and go in my kitchen; these are usually gifts from friends returning from Europe or the result of occasional splurges at a fancy food shop.

NUT OILS

Nut oils are wonderful in all sorts of sauces, especially cold sauces and sauces for salads. There is, however, an enormous range in quality from one brand to another. I use oils made by Le Blanc (see Sources), which are made from roasted nuts. The roasting intensifies the nuts' flavor and makes the oil much less perishable. My favorite oils are walnut, hazelnut, and pistachio. Le Blanc also makes an almond oil, which I have never used.

RED CABBAGE SALAD WITH PISTACHIOS

SALADE DE CHOU ROUGE AUX PISTACHES

MAKES 6 SIDE-DISH OR FIRST-COURSE SERVINGS IF SERVED ALONE, OR PROPORTIONATELY MORE IF OTHER SALADS ARE BEING SERVED AT THE SAME TIME

I always feel a trifle guilty when I throw out those little cups of coleslaw that come with the take-out pastrami sandwiches that have become an all-too-important part of my everyday lunch diet. But I've never been fond of coleslaw, the closest American equivalent to red cabbage salad, partly because I'm not a fan of bottled mayonnaise and partly because the cabbage is either too tough and chewy, or limp and mushy. This salad solves both problems. The mayonnaise is replaced with vinegar and oil, and the shredded cabbage is rubbed with salt, which softens it while still leaving some texture. Pistachios or pecans provide a delightful contrasting crunch. Since the flavor of nuts goes well with cabbage, I usually use walnut, hazelnut, or pistachio oil from my favorite producer, Le Blanc (see Sources), who roasts the nuts, enhancing their flavor and shelf life, before pressing out the oil. (For more about nut oils, see above.) Extra-virgin olive oil will do in a pinch, but if you're making an assortment of crudités, don't use it on everything or the salads will taste too much alike. Sherry vinegar is my favorite vinegar for this salad because its own nutty flavor underlines the character of the oil. While I usually serve this salad as part of a crudité plate, it also makes an excellent side dish for grilled foods, sandwiches, or anything that might normally be served with coleslaw.

1   small red cabbage (1½ pounds [675 g]), loose or wilted outer leaves pulled off and discarded

1   tablespoon coarse salt

⅓   cup [75 ml] sherry vinegar or other flavorful wine vinegar, such as balsamic

½   cup [125 ml] walnut, hazelnut, or pistachio oil made from roasted nuts, or extra-virgin olive oil

1   cup husked pistachios [125 g], whole pecans, or walnut halves, toasted for 10 to 15 minutes in a 350°F [175°C/gas mark 4] oven until fragrant, then allowed to cool; walnut halves chopped coarse

freshly ground pepper

CUT the cabbage in four pieces through the bottom core. Slice the wedge of white core out of each quarter. Shred each quarter as finely as you can. This is easiest if you have a plastic vegetable slicer or a mandoline (see page 13), but if you don't have one, place each quarter on a cutting board and slice it as fine as you can with a very sharp chef's knife.

PUT the cabbage in a mixing bowl with the salt, and rub it between your fingers for about 2 minutes until the salt dissolves and you can't feel any more salt. Transfer the cabbage to a colander, set the colander over the mixing bowl, and let drain for about 30 minutes. Squeeze the cabbage in your hands, in little balls, to extract as much liquid and salt as you can—you'll be amazed how much liquid comes out—and put the squeezed cabbage in a clean mixing or salad bowl (if you're serving or passing it at the table). Use a fork to toss the cabbage with the vinegar and oil. Stir in the nuts just before serving so they don't get soggy. Season to taste with pepper.

COLD CUCUMBERS WITH CRÈME FRAÎCHE

SALADE DE CONCUMBRES À LA CRÈME

This is one of those simple salads that you can serve on a crudité plate with other salads, but it's so satisfying in itself that in France you'll often see it offered as a first course in neighborhood restaurants. The French have delicious crème fraîche (see page 39), which they use generously, but if the fat makes you nervous, use yogurt instead. My own taste veers to crème fraîche in the winter and yogurt in the summer. If you do want to use crème fraîche, you can buy it, but it's so expensive that it makes sense to prepare your own (see page 39). The French like to flavor this salad with little slivers of mint leaves, but I improvise freely and use other herbs, such as tarragon or a mixture of chervil and chives. I sometimes make a decidedly un-French version by using cilantro and spicing the whole thing up with finely chopped jalapeños, or better yet, chipotles, which are jalapeños that have been smoked and are sold in cans or dried. (The canned ones are usually packed in adobo sauce, which I rinse off.) My favorite cucumber salads from other places include raita from India (use tangy plain yogurt). I also like an Iranian version with raisins and walnuts.

To make a successful cucumber salad, you need to get rid of the excess water in both the cucumber and the yogurt. Otherwise, when you season the salad with salt, the salt will draw the water into the sauce. To get the excess water out of cucumber, toss the slices with salt, as in this recipe. To get the excess water out of yogurt, let it drain in a cloth-lined strainer or coffee filter for a couple of hours or overnight. If you live near a Middle Eastern market, you may be able to find leban yogurt, which has the consistency of cream cheese and doesn't need to be drained—in fact, you may need to thin it a little with milk or water.

5 regular cucumbers, or 3 long hothouse cucumbers

1 tablespoon coarse salt

¾ cup [175 ml] Crème Fraîche (below), or 2 cups [500 ml] plain whole-milk yogurt, drained from 3 hours to overnight in a cloth-lined strainer or coffee filter set over a bowl in the refrigerator

1 bunch fresh mint

pepper

PEEL the cucumbers. If you want a little added crunch and color, don't remove all the peel but cut it off in strips so the cucumber ends up striped. If you are leaving some peel, wash the cucumbers thoroughly. And if you're using regular cucumbers, which are usually coated with mineral oil to help preserve them, use plenty of detergent and water and rinse them thoroughly.

CUT the cucumbers in half lengthwise and scrape out the seeds with a spoon. Slice the halves into crescents, about ⅛ inch [3 mm] thick. Toss the slices with the salt in a mixing bowl and rub them between your fingers for about 2 minutes, until the salt dissolves and you can't feel it anymore. Transfer the slices to a colander and set the colander over the mixing bowl. Let drain for 30 minutes. Squeeze the slices in small bunches in your first to get rid of as much of their liquid as you can. Stir the slices with the crème fraîche. Coarsely chop or tear the mint and stir it into the cucumbers. Season to taste with pepper.

CRÈME FRAÎCHE

In most recipes, heavy cream can be substituted for crème fraîche, but in dishes that require that the cream be thick, or when the tanginess of crème fraîche is important, you'll have to either go out and buy a small and very expensive little container or make it yourself.

Translated literally, *crème fraîche* just means fresh cream, but crème fraîche is actually more like what we call sour cream than it is like heavy whipping cream. The tang makes a delightful counterbalance to the sugar in sweet dishes. On a traditional French dairy farm, crème fraîche is made by letting fresh cream sit until the natural beneficial bacteria in the cream ferment the milk sugar (lactose), converting it to lactic acid, which causes the cream to thicken. Nowadays, most crème fraîche is made by inoculating pasteurized cream, in which the naturally occurring bacteria have been killed, with cloned bacteria, all genetically identical, grown in a laboratory. You can produce the same effect at home by combining heavy cream with a small amount of buttermilk, which contains the active culture. Use 2 cups [500 ml] of cream to ¼ cup [60 ml] of buttermilk and let the mixture sit, covered, in a warm place for 24 hours.

Crème fraîche keeps longer than heavy cream because it has already been allowed to sour, but with good rather than harmful bacteria. Don't try to substitute sour cream for crème fraîche in sauces that are served hot, because sour cream has a lower butterfat content and will curdle when heated. Crème fraîche will keep for several weeks in the refrigerator.

MUSHROOMS MARINATED WITH OLIVE OIL, VINEGAR, AND TARRAGON

CHAMPIGNONS MARINÉS À L'ESTRAGON

MAKES 6 SIDE-DISH OR FIRST-COURSE SERVINGS IF
SERVED ALONE, OR PROPORTIONATELY MORE IF OTHER
SALADS ARE BEING SERVED AT THE SAME TIME

I've never been a big fan of raw mushrooms. When encountered in health food restaurant salads, they always seem spongy and tasteless. But when mushrooms are marinated with a little good olive oil and vinegar, their flavor blossoms. And they are magical with fresh tarragon. If you can't find fresh tarragon, use parsley instead. I prefer cremini to regular white cultivated mushrooms because cremini contain less water, have more flavor, and are often the same price or just slightly more expensive.

    1   pound [450 g] cultivated mushrooms, preferably cremini

    ½   cup [125 ml] extra-virgin olive oil, or more as needed

    ¼   cup [60 ml] sherry vinegar or balsamic vinegar, or
        more to taste

    2   tablespoons fresh tarragon leaves

        salt

        pepper

IF the ends of the mushroom stems are dark, dried out, or dirty, slice off and discard about ¼ inch [.5 cm] of each stem. Put the mushrooms in a colander and rinse them under cold running water while rubbing them together between your hands. Don't soak them. Allow them to drain, and pat dry. Slice the mushrooms as thin as you can—you may even want to use a vegetable slicer set to the thinnest setting. Toss the mushrooms with the oil and vinegar in a large mixing bowl. Coarsely chop the tarragon leaves and toss them with the mushrooms. Season to taste with salt and pepper, cover the bowl with plastic wrap, and refrigerate for between 4 and 24 hours before serving. As the mushrooms sit, they'll get darker but also more flavorful. Just before serving the mushrooms, taste them again because they may need more oil, vinegar, salt, or pepper; season them accordingly.

BABY ARTICHOKES WITH TOASTED WALNUTS

SALADE D'ARTICHAUTS AUX NOIX

MAKES 6 SIDE-DISH OR FIRST-COURSE SERVINGS IF
SERVED ALONE, OR PROPORTIONATELY MORE IF OTHER
SALADS ARE BEING SERVED AT THE SAME TIME

Reading the details of a great meal is for me every bit as exciting as the spicy climax of a juicy spy novel. M.F.K. Fisher, Henry James, Honoré de Balzac, or Émile Zola, who uses fifty pages to build up to a goose dinner in L'Assommoir, can have me sitting on the edge of my seat, eagerly anticipating what's to be served next. In a similar vein, I'll remember the wines had at a lunch in some obscure restaurant twenty years ago, even if I forget who was there. So it is that I remember, from an article by Elizabeth David about French restaurants in the 1960s, the description of a perfect and simple meal served at Chez Madame Brazier in Lyons. That was where I got the idea for this dish.

The Italians, and to a lesser degree the French, are fond of serving baby artichokes, thinly sliced and raw, dressed with lemon juice and extra-virgin olive oil. This is, in fact, a marvelous way of serving them (see page 69). But that is not what we're doing here.

Baby artichokes, at most 1½ inches [4 cm] thick at the thickest part, can sometimes be hard to find; when they are available they're sold by the pound and are often a good value. You need to trim off the tops and outer leaves before you cook them, but once they're cooked they can be eaten whole, and there's no need to remove the choke as there is when serving or eating large artichokes. Serve 3 or 4 of these artichokes as part of a crudité plate or serve 6 as a light first course.

30 baby artichokes (about 3 pounds) [1.34 g], all the same size (so they cook evenly)

juice of 1 lemon

1 tablespoon sherry vinegar or good-quality white wine vinegar, or more to taste

3 tablespoons walnut or hazelnut oil made from roasted nuts (see Sources) or extra-virgin olive oil, or more to taste

salt

pepper

¾ cup [100 g] walnut halves, toasted for 10 to 15 minutes in a 350°F [175°C/gas mark 4] oven

PULL any loose leaves away from the bottom of each artichoke. Cut off the bottom stem where it joins the base. Rotate the artichoke against the blade of a very sharp paring knife until you see the pale green, almost white, flesh. Rotate the bottom of the artichoke against the knife to remove patches of dark green. Cut off and discard the top half of the artichoke. Toss the artichokes in the lemon juice as you trim them to keep them from turning dark.

PUT the artichokes in a nonaluminum pot with plenty of water to cover and bring to a gentle simmer. Simmer for 10 to 15 minutes, until a knife poked into one of the artichokes goes through with just slight resistance. Drain the artichokes and immediately toss them with the vinegar and oil and salt and pepper. Just before serving, toss in the nuts; don't do this ahead of time or the nuts will lose their crunch. This salad, apart from adding the nuts, can be made two days in advance.

SHAVED FENNEL SALAD
SALADE DE FENOUIL CRU

MAKES 6 COURSES WHEN SERVED WITH OTHER SALADS

AS PART OF A COLLECTION OF CRUDITÉS, OR

2 GENEROUS FIRST COURSES WHEN SERVED ALONE

The French have never been particularly fond of fennel. They probably know it best as a component, if not an actual ingredient, in the famous Mediterranean sea bass grilled over dried fennel stalks, served in restaurants all over Provence (see Chapter 24). Occasionally, chopped fennel fronds are smeared on the inside of a fish. Fennel's flavor, if not the vegetable itself, is often added, in the form of a fennel-flavored pastis such as Ricard, to fish soups, including bouillabaisse.

In all honesty, this salad is more Italian than French. I first encountered it in New York in an Italian restaurant where it was served as a first course, topped with thin curls of Parmigiano-Reggiano. It's become one of my favorite salads, served either as a first course, with the cheese, or as part of a collection of crudité salads, without the cheese. Assuming you have a vegetable slicer, this is one of the quickest things you can make. (The mystery is why it continues to be expensive in big-city restaurants.) If you don't have a slicer, slice the fennel as thin as you can with a knife.

1 large fennel bulb, or 2 medium-size bulbs

2 tablespoons lemon juice

¼ cup [60 ml] extra-virgin olive oil

salt

pepper

CUT the stalks off the fennel where they join the bulb. Pull off and reserve a small handful of the frizzy fronds. Discard the stalks or use them in broths or braised dishes, to which they add a lovely subtle freshness. Pull off and discard any dark or dried-out layers from the bulb and use a vegetable peeler to peel away the outermost stringy membrane as you would peel a stalk of celery. Use a vegetable peeler or paring knife to cut out the cone-shaped core at the base of the bulb.

SLICE the fennel bulb, vertically, as thin as you can with a vegetable slicer or chef's knife. Coarsely chop the reserved fronds. Toss the fennel slices and the reserved fronds with the lemon juice, olive oil, and salt and pepper.

TOMATO SALAD

SALADE DE TOMATES

MAKES 6 SIDE-DISH OR FIRST-COURSE

SERVINGS IF SERVED ALONE, OR PROPORTIONATELY

MORE IF OTHER SALADS ARE BEING SERVED

AT THE SAME TIME

I serve this salad during only a few months out of the year—from August to October—a time when I'm likely to eat, in one form or another, a couple of pounds of tomatoes a day. The rest of the year I don't bother with tomatoes except for making sauces and stews, in which case I use tomatoes out of a can. You can serve this salad as part of a crudité plate, but when tomatoes are at their best, most meals turn into tomato festivals of sorts, making other vegetables almost superfluous. Sometimes I just serve tomato slices on a big plate and dribble them with my best olive oil, but most of the time I peel the tomatoes, cut them into wedges, seed the wedges, and toss them with olive oil and my homemade vinegar (see page 50 for more information about homemade vinegar). Some people think peeling the tomatoes is a needless affectation, but I find

it enhances the salad. Seeding is another fastidious step that amazes guests, but I consider it essential to keep the liquid that clings to the seeds from diluting the vinaigrette. Generally I add a handful of basil leaves—I don't bother chopping—and that's it. Sometimes other favorite herbs such as tarragon and marjoram, but not both at once, replace the basil. At the end of the tomato season, when the weather turns crisp, I sometimes replace the olive oil with heavy cream; the acidity of the vinegar thickens it enough to allow it to coat the tomatoes. Or I may even add a few thick slices of bacon, cut into cubes, rendered, only some of the fat discarded, and cream added to the pan; this is a mixture that, again, replaces the olive oil. (Guests are often reminded of a BLT.) When I can find them, I combine different heirloom tomatoes—yellow, orange, even striped, or just those that have different nuances of red—in the same bowl.

6 large ripe tomatoes (about 12 ounces [350 g] [2 kilos] each or 4½ pounds total weight), or the equivalent in smaller tomatoes

½ cup [125 ml] extra-virgin olive oil

2 tablespoons sherry vinegar or other good-quality wine vinegar, or more to taste

1 handful fresh basil leaves, or 1 tablespoon chopped fresh marjoram, or 2 tablespoons fresh tarragon leaves, chopped at the last minute (all optional)

salt

pepper

PLUNGE the tomatoes, 2 at a time, into about 4 quarts [4 l] of boiling water, and leave them in the water for about 15 seconds. (If your tomatoes aren't at season's height, you may need to leave them in for 30 seconds or even longer to loosen the peel.) Take the tomatoes out with a slotted spoon and immediately rinse with cold water or plunge into a bowl of ice water so the tomato flesh doesn't start to cook and get mushy. Repeat with the rest of the tomatoes. Cut out the stem end of each scalded tomato by twisting a paring knife around underneath the stem. Pinch the skin between your forefinger and the side of the paring knife and peel it away in big strips.

CUT the tomatoes vertically into about 8 wedges each, depending on the size of the tomatoes and how big you want the wedges, and push the seeds out of the wedges with your forefinger.

TOSS the salad, just before serving, with the olive oil, vinegar, basil, and salt and pepper. (If you toss it ahead of time, the salt will draw the water out of the tomatoes and dilute the oil and vinegar, and the basil will wilt.)

Potato Salad

SALADE DE POMMES DE TERRE

I'VE ALWAYS BEEN A BIG FAN OF ALMOST ANY potato salad, from the kind that shows up at church picnics to fancy truffled versions sampled in Paris. There's something satisfying about the fragile yet substantial texture of cooked potatoes in a tangy sauce—mayonnaise, vinaigrette, or cream—brought into focus with a few chopped herbs or, in the church-picnic version, a little sliced celery.

Variations are limitless because you can alter the texture of the salad by what kind of potatoes you use (see page 44), how you cut them, how thickly you slice them, and so on. Potatoes lend themselves to combining with seafood, so that virtually any sauce you would make for fish or shellfish can be used in the salad (cream is especially good here) and the fish or shellfish itself combined in the salad. This is one good method of extending the flavor of expensive ingredients such as lobster. Make a sauce similar to the sauce for the lobster newburg on page 337, leaving out the lobster butter, and use it, cold, as a sauce for the salad. Garnish the salad with pieces of lobster and serve as an elegant first course.

If you're serving potato salad as part of a crudité platter, you can get by with serving very little. Below is the classic version made by layering still-warm potatoes with olive oil, vinegar, white wine, shallots, and parsley; but see the bottom of the recipe for some variations.

CLASSIC PARISIAN-STYLE POTATO SALAD

SALADE DE POMMES DE TERRE À LA PARISIENNE

MAKES 6 SIDE-DISH OR FIRST-COURSE SERVINGS IF SERVED ALONE, OR PROPORTIONATELY MORE IF OTHER SALADS ARE BEING SERVED AT THE SAME TIME

2 pounds [900 g] red or white waxy potatoes (large ones, for easier peeling), or fingerlings

2 tablespoons dry white wine

4 tablespoons good-quality white wine vinegar

½ cup [125 ml] extra-virgin olive oil

3 shallots, chopped fine

3 tablespoons coarsely chopped parsley, preferably flat-leaf (chopped at the last minute; see page 110 for more information about parsley)

salt

pepper

PUT the potatoes, unpeeled, in a 4-quart [4 l] pot with enough cold water to cover. The potatoes are started in cold water so that the heat penetrates evenly; if they are started in hot water, the outside cooks faster than the inside. Bring to a boil, lower to a simmer. Simmer gently until the potatoes can easily be penetrated with a paring knife or skewer but still offer a little resistance. Don't cook the potatoes until they crack, or they will be overcooked. Drain the potatoes in a colander and let cool for about 10 minutes to make them easier to handle. But don't let them cool for too long, or they'll be harder to peel.

WHISK together the wine, vinegar, olive oil, and shallots in a small bowl. Peel the potatoes by holding one at a time in a towel with one hand and pulling off the peel in long strips with a paring knife. Slice the potatoes into ¼-inch-thick [.5 cm] rounds and layer the slices in a square or oval glass, earthenware, or porcelain gratin or baking dish large enough to hold them in about four layers. Sprinkle each layer with one-fourth of the oil mixture, quickly stirring the mixture each time so the ingredients stay evenly distributed. Sprinkle each layer with parsley, salt, and pepper. Serve at room temperature or slightly cooler, but not directly out of the refrigerator. When serving the salad, be sure to reach all the way to the bottom of the dish—the dressing tends to settle to the bottom.

Variations: Joel Robuchon in his book *Le Meilleur & le Plus Simple de la Pomme de Terre*—or, roughly translated, "The Best and Simplest Potato Recipes"—gives thirteen potato salad recipes, including a version from Normandy made with apples, apple cider, sorrel, and a mayonnaise containing plenty of mustard and crème fraîche; a *salade cressonnière* made by layering hard-boiled eggs in with the potatoes and plenty of chervil, tarragon, and chives, and a little bundle of watercress, placed in the middle; a *salade de pommes céleri* that's a lot like the American version except that celeriac is used instead of branch celery,

a little wine sneaks in, and crème fraîche flavored with horseradish and lots of mustard replaces the mayonnaise . . . and the list goes on.

Vinaigrette is a lighter alternative to the mayonnaise we're more used to. You can make a classic vinaigrette by combining mustard with vinegar and whisking in oil (see page 48), or a deconstructed version by just sprinkling the layers of potato slices with oil, vinegar, herbs, salt and pepper, and (in the classic Parisian version given above), white wine. Experiment with different vinegars and oils. Cream flavored with mustard, salt, and pepper also makes a great sauce for a potato salad. Crème fraîche (see page 39) is naturally thick and will cling to the potatoes, but heavy cream will thicken when combined with lime juice or vinegar, whose acidity provides a welcome note. Figure about 3 tablespoons of lime juice to 1 cup of heavy cream; add mustard to taste.

It's hard to imagine any single herb that, when used alone, wouldn't enhance the sauce for a potato salad, but things get more complicated when herbs are used in combination with other herbs or with ingredients, other than the potatoes, that are more assertively flavored. While tarragon makes up a quarter of the classic mixture *fines herbes*, which also includes chervil, parsley, and chives, it has such a distinctive flavor that I rarely bother to add the other herbs, since it takes over anyway. Basil is great in a summer potato salad. The leaves can be torn at

WHICH POTATOES TO USE?

I recently sent a friend to the store to buy some waxy potatoes. She returned, confused, with a bagful of russets. First, let it be said that any potato can be used in any potato dish with results far from catastrophic. But some potatoes are better in certain recipes. Waxy potatoes, the red or white kind with a relatively smooth, shiny, and almost translucent skin, are best in dishes in which you don't want the potato to fall apart. Choose them for salads and gratins (see Chapter 41). On the other hand, avoid waxy potatoes in making soups or mashed potatoes, or in any situation in which the potatoes are being puréed, since they may become glutinous and produce a slightly sticky feeling in the mouth. Yukon Golds and Yellow Finns are best for mashed potatoes; they produce a silken texture. Russets are best for baking.

the last minute into little pieces and strewn over the potato layers, or chopped and added to the sauce, or ground into a pesto, which along with a sprinkling of vinegar becomes the sauce; or the pesto can be stirred into a cream sauce or mayonnaise. Sorrel or mint can be chopped or cut into chiffonade (see page 17) at the very last minute (or it will turn dark) and sprinkled over the potatoes. Sorrel can also be stewed and puréed, combined with cream, and used as the sauce. More assertive herbs, such as thyme, rosemary, marjoram, hyssop, lavender flowers, savory, and oregano, can be sprinkled over the potato layers in various combinations and proportions that you invent yourself, or you can buy them already mixed, in herbes de Provence (see Sources). If you make your own mixture, be especially careful of rosemary and lavender, which tend to take over.

The French are relatively naïve about spices and are likely to reach for the jar of curry powder, whereas Indian cooks carefully make their own combinations of roasted spices for specific dishes. The Indian equivalent of the potato salad, *aloo chaat,* is flavored with a mixture of cumin, various ground peppers, asafetida, mango powder, and a tangy seasoning called black salt—but this takes us to another realm. Because the spices in curry powder haven't been roasted, when using curry powder, wake up its flavor by cooking it for about 30 seconds— until you smell its fragrance—in a little oil and then whisking this mixture into the sauce to taste. Saffron threads, soaked for 30 minutes in a tiny bit of water, threads and soaking liquid added to the sauce, are delicious when combined with aïoli (see page 491), and they also give the salad a great color.

You'll probably find yourself inventing your own flavorings based on what else you're putting in the salad and what you have around. I'm not crazy about whole pieces of tomato in a potato salad, but sometimes I add a reduced tomato purée (or even ketchup, recently encountered in a couple of fashionable Paris restaurants), along with a little tarragon, to a mustardy cream sauce. Dried mushrooms, especially cèpes (porcini) and morels, soaked in the smallest amount of water needed to get them to soften, chopped, and whisked into a mayonnaise, will turn a potato salad into something luxurious. Some fresh mushrooms, such as cèpes or chanterelles, are best sautèed (with garlic and parsley or other herbs), while others, such as morels, can be stewed in a little cream or broth and the stewing liquid, lightly reduced, added to the basic mayonnaise or cream sauce (omit the mustard). Tiny dice of prosciutto, stewed with

the mushrooms, add complexity. Sliced truffles can be sliced and tossed or layered with the potatoes, but it is more practical to stir a little truffle oil or juice into the sauce. Grated fresh horseradish is great in a cream sauce and even better when juxtaposed with something sweet, such as apple. Sliced apples can be added between the layers of potatoes to provide sweetness and textural contrast, or apple juice can be reduced and stirred into the sauce. Chiles take us out of the realm of French cooking (and they ruin wine), but, while we're at it, dried chiles (anchos, pasillas, and so on) chopped and simmered with a little cream, and the sauce then flavored with cilantro, are spectacular in a potato salad. Chipotles (smoked jalapeños) add an intriguing smoky note. Speaking of smoke, bacon, cut into cubes, rendered, cream added, reduced slightly, and used as the sauce, is marvelous, as are thin strips of smoked salmon.

Some flavorings will be dictated by ingredients you've added to the salad. Mollusks, such as clams, mussels, or cockles, can be steamed with a little white wine, shallot, and parsley and the steaming liquid reduced and added to a cream sauce or mayonnaise. Crustacean shells can be stewed in cream (as in lobster newburg, page 33), and the strained and reduced stewing liquid added to the salad sauce.

You can make your potato salad completely original by layering or gently tossing other ingredients—perhaps leftovers from the night before or something inspiring seen at the market—with the potatoes. Leftover meats, especially braised meats from stews or pot-au-feu, can be sliced thin and layered with the potatoes. Extra mustard in the sauce is welcome when you've included stewed meats. Leftover steak, sliced into thin strips, can also be layered or tossed with the potatoes. Slices or strips of cooked or smoked fish can be layered in sheets between the potatoes or tossed with them; horseradish in a cream sauce is good here. Strips of leftover undercooked tuna or other fresh fish, or chunks of canned tuna, grilled sardines, or anchovies (desalted or fresh marinated, see page 168) make delicious additions. Clams, mussels, or cockles; shrimp or crayfish tails; and lobster cut into medallions can all be used.

Cubes of vegetables such as celery (or celeriac, cut in very small cubes), cooked artichoke bottoms, cooked beets cut in rounds, thinly sliced fennel or onions (the onion slices rubbed with salt to soften them), capers, cornichons or other pickles, and chopped garlic (used instead of the shallots in the classic salad above), will vary the texture, and some of them will add a welcome tang.

GREEN SALADS

SALADES VERTES

HOW TO	HOW TO	HOW TO	HOW TO	HOW TO
CUT, WASH, AND DRY LETTUCE	MAKE A VINAIGRETTE	MAKE IMPROVISED SALADS	MAKE A "WILTED" SALAD	MAKE YOUR OWN VINEGAR

DURING MY YEARS OF TEACHING PROFESSIONAL COOKING CLASSES, A simple green salad was the hardest dish to teach students to prepare well. Students typically thought of it as an appendage to a meal, just a way of making sure everyone got a daily dose of raw greens. The gravest sins weren't to do with making the vinaigrette. That was easy to teach, and since we used good vinegar and olive oil, most everyone could handle it. But no one knew how to handle the greens. Despite my directions, the students invariably set out in their own way, some ferociously ripping up the lettuce, others choosing a weapon, usually a chef's knife, and hacking the lettuce into minuscule pieces. When it came to washing and drying the lettuce, the situation would go from bad to worse. Some plunged the lettuce in and out of water before spinning it at 1,000 rpm in a salad spinner and cramming it into a too-small bowl. And then there were those who were fond of the one-leaf-at-a-time approach and would stand dreamily by the sink, holding a lettuce leaf under the running water for a good 30 seconds before moving on to the next leaf. They would use half the evening and as much water as a long shower, and the leaves would droop like wet rags.

Making a green salad needn't be hard, but you must treat the greens lovingly. First, gently coax the leaves, one by one, away from the lettuce bunch. Don't bend or break the leaves or you'll leave little cracks that will make the leaf limp and soggy as soon as you add the vinaigrette. If the outer lettuce leaves are tough or wilted, throw them out and work your way down to the tender leaves nearer the center of the lettuce. Snap the leaves away from the lettuce where they join the core. Don't cut or tear the leaves into too-small pieces; if the leaves are unwieldy, carefully tear, snap, or cut them into smaller pieces, following their natural shape. Large romaine leaves, for example, can be split lengthwise down the middle so the halves still retain the shape of the leaf. Don't serve lettuce leaves so large they hang over the edge of the plate, but don't worry if your guests need to use a knife to eat their salad, something that was once considered bad manners.

WASHING GREENS

Once you get the leaves off the head, you have to wash them. Put the lettuce leaves in a large bowl and fill the bowl with cold water by running the water down the side of the bowl, being careful not to let the water hit the lettuce and bruise it. Let the lettuce sit in the bowl for 5 or 10 minutes; don't swirl it around, just let it sit. Then gently lift it with your fingers and transfer it to a second bowl. Pour the water out of the first bowl and feel for sand or grit in the bottom of the bowl. Sometimes there is none, in which case you're ready to move on to drying. More often you'll need to repeat the washing once, or even twice.

While purists still insist that lettuce be gently patted dry between kitchen towels, the salad spinner is so quick and easy that it's hard to resist. But most people spin the lettuce too fast and too hard, so it ends up crushed against the spinner's inside walls. The trick is to spin gently, remove the lid, gently toss the leaves to redistribute them, spin again, and repeat until the leaves are dry. If you can't tell whether you're done, pour the water out of the spinner, spin the leaves, and see if any more water shows up in the bottom of the bowl.

TOSSING

Another salad error, common in restaurants, is to serve an individual portion of salad in a bowl, with no plate and no spoons for tossing, the implication being that it's supposed to be eaten directly out of the bowl. But the purpose of transferring the salad from bowl to plate is to allow any excess vinaigrette to stay behind in the bowl, not form a puddle on the plate. A small amount of salad, placed on the plate, is also easier to eat. More grievous still is putting the salad on the plate and then pouring the vinaigrette over it, so that some of the leaves never get coated and others are drenched. Instead, you should toss the entire salad just before serving. Don't do it earlier or the lettuce will wilt. Anyway, it's nice to toss the salad in front of guests. Toss it in a large enough bowl—the lettuce shouldn't come more than two-thirds up the sides—so you don't end up with lettuce all over the table. Toss gently with two spoons, preferably spoons that are longer than the bowl is wide so that the handles can't slip into the bowl and end up covered with vinaigrette. With the spoons, gently lift the lettuce leaves out of the bowl and onto plates.

Most of us are in the habit of serving salad at the beginning of a meal. A first-course salad has the advantage of not filling you up and will taste best when your hunger is at its peak. Guests are likely to pay more attention to it and notice your efforts, which can be appreciable if your lettuce was sandy and you spent some time arranging the leaves in the bowl. In France, a simple green salad (other salads follow different rules) is usually served after the main course and before the cheese. The magic to this system is that eating a small salad will actually make you feel less full so you'll be in better shape for cheese or dessert or fruit. The problem, however, is that after a main course a lot of guests *think* they don't want a green salad because they're feeling full. Don't ever ask, just serve it. Sometimes I serve a green salad at the same time as steaks or other rich foods, to lighten their effect.

Few sauces cause as much anxiety as vinaigrette. In its simplest and most classic form, a vinaigrette is simply an emulsion of oil and vinegar held together with a little mustard. The mustard and vinegar are combined, usually with a little salt and pepper, and the oil is slowly whisked in as though you were making a mayonnaise. This is all very nice if you include mustard in your vinaigrette; I leave it out when using good olive oil, which is almost always. Making a vinaigrette is also fine if you're using it as a sauce for something other than a salad and you don't want it to separate, or if you're adding garlic, herbs, orange zests, or other special flavorings that you want to infuse in the sauce. Otherwise, it's completely unnecessary to make a vinaigrette for a salad because the vinegar and oil, when added to the salad separately, end up coating the leaves more or less evenly anyway. I just dribble a little vinegar over the salad, keeping in mind the usual proportions of 1 part vinegar to 4 parts oil, pour some olive oil over it, sprinkle with salt, grind some pepper on top, and toss. I pick a leaf out and taste it, and if necessary I add a little more oil or vinegar, or seasoning. If this makes you nervous, just measure out the liquids ahead of time and put them in a little pitcher. There's no need to whisk them into an emulsion, and for some mysterious reason, beating extra-virgin olive oil turns it bitter anyway. If you're unsure of how much vinaigrette to use, start with just a little—you should have just enough to barely coat and season the leaves.

You can vary the character of a classic vinaigrette in more or less simple ways. The most obvious is to use different kinds of flavored oil and vinegar and different kinds of mustard. (For more about vinegar, see page 50; and for more about oil, see page 36.) Other additions might include chopped or ground herbs. Aromatic fresh herbs such as basil or mint or tarragon can be chopped fine and tossed in the salad with the other vinaigrette ingredients, or, for a more subtle effect, can be ground to a paste in a mortar with a little salt (which helps with the grinding) or sugar (in the case of mint). Stronger-flavored herbs such as thyme, rosemary, and sage can also be chopped fine and tossed in the salad, but the effect will be more subtle if you infuse these herbs in the oil for a week or two. While some herbs, especially tarragon, infuse better in vinegar, the flavor of most other herbs is left more intact when the herb is infused in olive oil. Shallots and garlic, finely minced and crushed to a paste with the side of a chef's knife or in a mortar, can be infused for a few minutes in the vinegar before being tossed in a salad. Finely chopped orange or lemon zests are delicious in a vinaigrette containing a tiny hint of sugar, especially when tossed with bitter greens such as endive. Mustard can simply be left out when you are making a green salad containing only greens, but for salads containing meats or strongly flavored vegetables such as beets or leeks, the mustard is almost essential. Instead of mustard, you can use cooked vegetable purées made from tomatoes, roasted garlic or onion, or sautéed mushrooms, wild or otherwise; these add flavor and hold the vinegar and oil together in a more or less tenuous emulsion. (For more salad dressing ideas, see Chapter 1, "Assorted Vegetable Salads.")

CHOOSING THE BEST GREENS FOR MAKING A GREEN SALAD

Now to the most important question of all: Which are the best greens and what are the best mixtures? This is largely a matter of taste and season. I have certain fallback greens and combinations. My summer salads almost always consist of a mixture of equal parts arugula (rocket) and basil. If I get to a greenmarket or some interesting things pop up in the garden, I'm likely to add nasturtium flowers or leaves (both have a spicy cinnamon-like flavor and the flowers add a brilliant orange), purslane, a little red oak leaf lettuce, or some baby watercress. (In the spring, choices may include a few wild dandelion leaves or wisteria flowers.) These summer salads are actually mesclun salads (the French word *mesclun* comes from the Latin *miscellanea*). They were long popular in Provence before they caught on in the 1970s in the rest of France, where they appeared as first courses in virtually every restaurant with even the slightest nouvelle cuisine pretension. *Salade mesclun* has taken hold in America, and mixtures containing seemingly dozens of greens are sold, already washed, at the corner supermarket. Restaurant salads now all taste the same because they all use the same mixtures sold by various mesclun farmers. To make matters worse, whoever composes these mixtures seems more concerned with including as many different greens as possible than with worrying about what these greens actually taste like. The greens in some mixtures are so tough and bitter that most of us would be better off pulling up a few weeds in the garden. A more reliable system is to compose your own summer green salads using arugula and basil as a base and then adding greens and flowers that are available and that taste good and look pretty.

When the cold weather sets in and basil and arugula go out of season, you can no longer rely on a single basic mixture on which to build. One option is a watercress salad, the easiest of all salads to make. You just cut off the tough stems on the bottom half of the bunch all at once, give the leaves with the small edible stems attached a single washing (store-bought watercress never seems to contain sand or grit), dry, and toss with vinaigrette. Balsamic vinegar (a medium-priced brand bought at a gourmet store or a supermarket brand boiled down by half, see page 50) is good here because its sweetness balances the spicy bitterness of the watercress. Another of my standards is a chicory salad, made with the pale yellow center of curly endive or chicory (nowadays usually called by its French name *frisée*, which means curly), radicchio or treviso (they're both scarlet and a little bitter, but treviso, harder to find and more expensive, is spiky, while radicchio comes in fist-size balls), and usually a little Belgian endive or escarole. If I'm serving this salad after the main course, I dress it with sherry vinegar (see page 51) and walnut, pistachio, or hazelnut oil made from roasted nuts. I also use this salad, or sometimes just the frisée, as the base for a salad with bacon (see page 52) that I serve as a first course.

Romaine lettuce is also a cool-weather favorite, but most of the time it is so overgrown that I peel off and waste most of the leaves, which are hard and tough to chew, and work down to the delicate and crispy yellow core. (Having a compost heap makes me feel a little less guilty about this.) You may also see hearts of romaine for sale in little plastic bags. These are usually fine, but keep in mind that they may not be at the peak of freshness, since some stores peel away leaves as the lettuce wilts. However you go about it, a Caesar salad made from these delicate yellow leaves is a glorious thing. While there are those who will claim there's nothing French about a Caesar salad, the concept of tossing leaves with egg, croutons, and anchovies in a salad is an idea very close to the French way of doing things. (I use soft-boiled egg instead of raw, not because of salmonella phobia, but because I think it tastes better.) Other favorite salad greens: Bibb lettuce, which is tiny and crisp (serve it alone or with Boston lettuce, or add it when you want to soften the flavor of aggressive or bitter greens such as treviso); Boston lettuce, for its delicate flavor and texture; escarole, which is very bitter, but great with orange-flavored vinaigrette, with beets, or with bacon; mâche (also called lamb's lettuce), which is delicate and lovely (I serve it with a delicate vinaigrette and no other greens); and oak leaf lettuces, which are pretty and delicate and available in small bunches.

VINEGAR

Vinegar can be made out of virtually anything that contains alcohol or sugar. Liquids that contain sugar and no alcohol must go through some fermentation, which turns the sugar into alcohol, before the final stage, the conversion of alcohol into acetic acid, can occur. Yeast ferments sugar into alcohol and harmless bacteria ferment alcohol into vinegar.

Vinegar used in cooking should always be vinegar made from fermented fruit or grain, not "distilled white vinegar," which is made from wood. In French cooking this usually means wine vinegar, although I have encountered a few recipes from Normandy that call for cider vinegar. Wine vinegar varies enormously in quality and style and there are, frankly, very few brands I'd willingly use on my salads. I'm often asked whether I prefer white-wine or red-wine vinegar. My favorite wine vinegars are balsamic vinegar, sherry vinegar, and my own homemade red-wine vinegar. If none of these is available, I use champagne vinegar. If that's not available, I use the most expensive red-wine vinegar I can find, which is never really too much.

Balsamic vinegar ranges from a sweetened indifferent wine vinegar with a vague taste of caramel, which sells for the same price as any other inexpensive wine vinegar, to *aceto balsamico tradizionale,* which sells for about $1,000 a liter. (I did the math—this works out to about 10 cents per drop.) *Aceto balsamico tradizionale*, which I usually refer to simply as authentic balsamic vinegar (see Sources), is made by aging grape juice, not wine, in a series of barrels made from various woods such as juniper, oak, ash, and mulberry. It must be at least ten years old but is often much older. Fortunately there are affordable yet high-quality versions between these two poles. Inexpensive and medium-priced versions can be used to deglaze pans and dress salads, while the authentic vinegar should be saved for applying to finished dishes—meats, fish, even fruit—with an eyedropper. I sometimes boil down supermarket vinegar by half to intensify the flavor and take away some of the harshness. There are many fine balsamic-style vinegars that approach the quality of *aceto balsamico tradizionale*. Some are made in the same way but, because they are made in regions not allowed to use the official name, are good values. Others, made by combining concentrated grape must (unfermented grape juice) with good-quality vinegar, while nowhere near the quality of the real thing, are still very fine vinegars.

Sherry vinegar was almost universally excellent twenty years ago, when it first became popular. Unfortunately, the quality of the less expensive brands has slipped over the years, the original nutty complexity having given way to harsh acidity. I look for brands that claim to be aged 25 years, although I suspect they're made from a *solera* sherry, which may contain only a minute amount of 25-year-old sherry. As always when I'm in doubt, I look for the most expensive. (See Sources for where to buy vinegar.)

For the best affordable vinegar, make your own. Buy a small oak barrel (see Sources, vinegar-making supplies), larger than you think you'll need. (Mine holds 2 gallons [8 l].) The extra volume is important, since wine needs lots of air to turn into vinegar; a completely full barrel will barely ferment. Combine about ½ cup [125 ml] of vinegar mother (a vinegar containing the active bacteria, see Sources) or a friend's homemade vinegar with ½ cup [125 ml] of red wine in the barrel and put the barrel in a warm place. Stuff a piece of cheesecloth in the hole at the top of the barrel to keep out dust and fruit flies but allow air in. Wait a week, pour in 1 cup of red wine, and wait another week. Add 2 cups [500 ml] of red wine, wait another week, and continue doubling the amount of wine you add each time until the barrel's about two-thirds full. Give the vinegar about 3 months to ferment fully. When it reaches that point, you can draw off a quart or so and replace it with wine. By the time you need more vinegar—in a month or so—the wine you added will be vinegar. Don't add fortified wines such as port to your barrel because the extra alcohol can kill the bacteria. Another tip: Keep the vinegar warm, preferably about 85°F [30°C]. I didn't realize this was important until I discovered that my vinegar went great guns in summer and ground to a halt in the fall. Since then, I keep the barrel on top of the hot-water heater.

SIMPLE GREEN SALAD

SALADE VERTE

MAKES 4 FIRST-COURSE SERVINGS

4 large handfuls salad greens, washed and dried

4 tablespoons extra-virgin olive oil or other flavorful oil

1 tablespoon good-quality wine vinegar (see page 50)

   salt and pepper to taste

COMBINE all the ingredients in a large salad bowl and toss gently until all the leaves are coated with oil and vinegar. Taste a leaf and add more of any of the ingredients accordingly.

Garnished Green Salads

A GARNISHED GREEN SALAD IS A GREEN SALAD with something more substantial than greens tossed in it. Simple additions, such as shallots or garlic or a few chopped nuts, aren't important enough to change a green salad into a garnished salad, but once you start adding meat or seafood, eggs, or vegetables, the salad's role in the meal is changed. No longer is the salad an accompaniment to a main course or as a re-freshing digestif, served at the end, but it becomes a substantial first course or even main course. I distin-guish somewhat arbitrarily between garnished green salads and composed salads (see Chapter 3), which contain few if any salad greens.

Once you start adding ingredients to a basic green salad, the possible combinations become endless. The French have their well-known classics like *salade niçoise* and *salade aux lardons*. While I'm not trying to diminish their marvelousness, the real fun begins when you invent your own salad combinations. But first, here are a couple of classics.

GREEN SALAD WITH BACON

SALADE AUX LARDONS

MAKES 4 FIRST-COURSE OR

LIGHT MAIN-COURSE SERVINGS

I don't remember when it started, but it seems as if every Parisian corner bistro now offers this salad as a first course. If followed with a bite of cheese or fruit, it's often even enough for a whole lunch. Fortunately I, and apparently a lot of other people, never tire of it. And while each place gives this salad its own twist, it's basically a bowl of frisée tossed with little strips of cooked bacon and a vinaigrette made with the hot bacon fat and usually some additional oil. It's important to use frisée instead of lettuces with smooth leaves because the smooth leaves get coated with the fat and feel greasy in the mouth, while the irregular surface of the frisée somehow prevents this. Little croûtons are often added for crunch and substance (they too are sometimes crisped up in the bacon fat), and I've encoun-tered some versions that include Roquefort cheese tossed in little slivers—the closest the French will ever get to American blue cheese dressing.

When shopping for frisée, look for heads with a large proportion of yellow, rather than green, leaves—the green outer leaves tend to be too tough. I've noticed two varieties of curly endive in the market: the classic frisée that's used in France, and a more delicate variety, which I prefer, with a greater proportion of yellow, sometimes sold under the Italian name for frisée, *riccia*.

1 large bunch or 2 small heads frisée (curly endive) or other leafy salad green

1½ cups bread cubes, made by cutting two ¾-inch-thick [2 cm] slices from a large country loaf, then cutting the slices into ¾-inch [2 cm] cubes

½ pound [225 g] slab bacon without rind or 10 ounces [280 g] with rind, or ½ pound [225 g] thick-sliced bacon

2 tablespoons Dijon mustard

3 tablespoons sherry vinegar or other good-quality wine
vinegar

½ cup [125 ml] extra-virgin olive oil

freshly ground pepper

PEEL away and discard any tough, dark-green outer leaves from the frisée. Detach the delicate yellow leaves where they attach at the bottom of the head and gently snap them into manageable pieces, but don't make them too small or the salad will absorb too much fat and be heavy. Wash and dry the leaves and refrigerate them until you're ready to serve the salad.

PREHEAT oven to 350°F [175°C/gas mark 2]. Spread the bread cubes on a sheet pan and bake them for about 15 minutes, until they are lightly browned and crispy. Reserve.

IF the bacon still has its rind, cut it off. Slice the bacon into ¼-inch [.5 cm] thick slices, and slice the slices crosswise into 1-inch [2.5 cm] *lardons*. Cook the *lardons* over low-to-medium heat in a heavy-bottomed pan until they just start to turn crispy. Take them out of the pan with a slotted spoon and reserve.

COMBINE the mustard and vinegar and stir the mixture, and the olive oil, into the hot bacon fat. Immediately toss together the frisée, bacon, and bread cubes and the contents of the pan in a large bowl. Season with pepper and toss. Serve immediately.

Variations: This *salade aux lardons* is only one example of what is often called a wilted salad. The name doesn't really mean that the greens are wilted—although they do end up softened a bit—but rather that a hot vinaigrette and hot ingredients are added to the salad just before serving instead of a cold vinaigrette and cold ingredients. This is such a versatile idea that virtually any hot ingredient can be sliced or cut into manageable pieces and tossed with various salad greens. When the hot ingredient is sautéed, the sauté pan is usually deglazed with vinegar and, depending on the type and amount of fat in the pan, additional oil may be added to make a hot vinaigrette. If the ingredient is roasted, the juices from the roasting pan should be poured over the salad along with a vinaigrette that is prepared separately.

The meat of various birds is especially good in salads. Confit of duck can be shredded and gently cooked just like the bacon in the *lardon* salad (see the green salad with duck confit and wild mushrooms, page 384), and the meat of any roast bird—chicken, game, or, best of all, squab—can be sliced or pulled away in strips and tossed in a salad, the hot roasting juices poured over it along with the vinaigrette, and the chopped cooked giblets tossed in or crushed into a paste in the vinaigrette. Seafood is also good, especially grilled or sautéed oily fish, such as fresh sardines or mackerel, but don't deglaze the pan or your sauce will taste fishy.

NIÇOISE SALAD

SALADE NIÇOISE

MAKES 4 FIRST-COURSE SERVINGS OR

LIGHT MAIN-COURSE LUNCH SERVINGS

There seem to be dozens of recipes for *salade niçoise*, and of course everybody claims his or her own to be the only one that could possibly be authentic, all others being pale and affected imitations. I've never been terribly concerned about authenticity and the need to adhere strictly to a given recipe because I quickly grow bored and like changing things. This has gotten me into trouble at a number of restaurant jobs.

My own notions of a *salade niçoise* aren't even inspired by salads tasted in Nice, but rather by the typical *salade niçoise* served in virtually every Parisian café. There's nothing particularly fabulous about the *salade niçoise* I recall; in fact, most café versions seem rather hurriedly put together. It is more like the memory of a reliable friend available *à toute heure*.

While the original *salade niçoise* apparently never contained lettuce or the now ubiquitous canned tuna, the Parisian version is presented in a lettuce-lined bowl and topped with chunks of tuna, boiled potatoes and green beans (both apparently heretical in Nice), hard-boiled eggs, anchovies, tiny black niçoise olives (warn your guests about the pits), and slices of raw bell peppers. My only objection is to the raw bell peppers, which I find aggressive; I prefer mine charred and peeled or left out altogether. I like to assemble all the ingredients for a *salade niçoise* in a big salad bowl and toss everything together at the table. With this method, however, it is hard to make sure that everyone gets a fair share of all the ingredients. An alternative is to toss each of the ingredients separately in the kitchen and assemble the salads on individual plates.

4 large handfuls assorted lettuces such as Boston, Bibb, arugula, and frisée, or 10 ounces [280 g] assorted greens, such as mesclun mix, that have already been washed

1 clove garlic, minced, crushed to a paste with the side of a chef's knife

2 tablespoons good-quality wine vinegar

pinch of salt

⅔ cup [150 ml] extra-virgin olive oil

1 waxy potato (8 ounces [225 g]), gently simmered in its skin until easily penetrated with a paring knife, about 20 minutes

½ pound [225 g] string beans, preferably haricots verts, ends broken off

3 large eggs

1 red or yellow bell pepper, charred, peeled, and seeded (see page 20) (optional)

2 medium-size tomatoes

1 jar (2 ounces [50 g]) anchovy fillets, or 16 anchovy fillets taken from salted anchovies (see page 168)

1 can (6 ounces [170 g]) Italian tuna packed in olive oil, drained

½ cup [65 g] niçoise olives or other brine-cured black olives (not canned olives), drained

WASH and dry the lettuces, gently tear them into manageable pieces if the leaves are large—don't overdo it—and refrigerate. In a small mixing bowl, stir together the garlic, vinegar, and salt and mix in the olive oil without beating, to form a vinaigrette. Drain the potato and peel off the skin in strips while the potato is still warm. Slice the potato thick and stir the slices very gently, in a small mixing bowl,

with 3 tablespoons of the vinaigrette. (Stir the vinaigrette each time you use it so the vinegar and oil are evenly distributed.)

BOIL the green beans for 5 to 8 minutes in a large pot of boiling salted water until you feel only the slightest crunch when you bite into one. Drain them in a colander and immediately rinse with cold water. Pat dry or spin dry in a salad spinner. If you're serving the salad right away, toss the beans with 3 tablespoons of the garlic vinaigrette. If not, toss them with the vinaigrette just before serving. Tossing too early will turn the beans gray.

PUT the eggs in a saucepan with enough cold water to cover by an inch [2.5 cm] and simmer gently for 7 minutes. This will leave the yolk bright yellow and moist. Drain in a colander and immediately rinse with cold water to cool. Peel and reserve.

CUT the cooked pepper lengthwise into ¼-inch [.5 cm] strips and reserve. If you like, peel the tomatoes (if I have perfect summer tomatoes I don't bother) by plunging them in boiling water for about 30 seconds, immediately rinsing with cold water, and pulling the peel away in strips with a paring knife. Cut out the stem end, and cut each tomato into 8 wedges. Push the seeds out of each wedge with your fingertip.

DRAIN the anchovy fillets and cut them in half crosswise. Break the tuna up into chunks but don't shred it.

ARRANGE the lettuces around the inside of a large salad bowl or on individual plates. If you're placing the individual salads on plates, first toss each of the ingredients (except the eggs, which would fall apart, and the potatoes and beans, which have already been marinated), including the lettuces, in the remaining vinaigrette. Cut each of the eggs into 4 wedges. Arrange all the ingredients decoratively on top of the lettuces in the bowl or on each plate. If you're serving at the table out of one big bowl, just before serving pour the sauce over the salad and gently toss. Transfer to plates at the table.

Variations: Again we've entered the realm of the limitless, but the most obvious *salade miçoise* derivative is made by replacing the canned tuna with strips of fresh tuna that have been grilled or sautéed and left rare in the middle. You can replace the tuna with almost any other seafood, including chunks or strips of fish either left over or tossed into the salad sizzling hot from the grill or sauté pan. Smoked salmon or other fish and cooked shellfish will also work. Grilled shrimp, fried squid, and leftover lobster are marvelous, and sophisticated vinaigrettes can be made from the shells and coral of crustaceans (see page 66). One of my favorite tossed seafood salads involves grilled sardines, filleted while still hot, tossed with wild dandelions and a mustardy vinaigrette. If you or your guests don't like anchovies, slip them in by pounding or chopping them to a paste and stirring them into the vinaigrette—their flavor will still be present, but more subtly.

The niçoise *pan bagnat* originated as a salad by adding cubes of stale bread to a *salade niçoise*, somewhat like the now fashionable Tuscan *panzanella*, but has since evolved into a kind of *salade niçoise* sandwich, with the salad placed between two halves of a thin round loaf that's been rubbed with olive oil and garlic. I make *fougasse*, but without the slits (see page 272), cut it in half crosswise, and sandwich in goodies such as tomatoes, anchovies, capers, or pitted olives.

SQUAB AND FLOWER SALAD

SALADE DE FLEURS

AU PIGEONNEAU

MAKES 4 FIRST-COURSE OR LIGHT MAIN-COURSE SERVINGS

One way to give a full flavor to a salad is to cook meats and toss their cooking juices, from the roasting pan or deglazed sauté pan, with the salad greens (or, as here, flowers) or add them to the vinaigrette. If you're lucky enough to have an assortment of flowers, this salad makes a dramatic first course or light main course. Squab (fledgling pigeon) makes a perfect garniture because it's full-flavored and will hold up to the flowers. I make a jus with the squab bones and add the

jus and the chopped giblets to the vinaigrette, but you can make this kind of salad with slices of cold meats—paper-thin slices of prosciutto are great—and a simple mixture of the best extra-virgin olive oil and wine vinegar, and forget about the jus. I never present this salad, already tossed, on plates but bring it to the table in a big bowl and toss and serve in front of the guests. Squabs are certainly not everyday fare, so if the idea of cooking them is a little scary, try this recipe with a baby chicken (sometimes called a poulette) or a Cornish game hen.

2 handfuls small-leafed greens such as arugula, mâche, basil, oak leaf lettuce, nasturtium leaves (unless you're using nasturtium flowers), or Bibb lettuce

2 handfuls assorted flowers or flower petals (nasturtium flowers are best; see page 56)

2 squabs, with giblets

2 tablespoons pure olive oil

1 shallot or small onion, minced

1 clove garlic, chopped

1 sprig fresh thyme or dried thyme, or ½ teaspoon dried thyme leaves

1 cup chicken broth

½ cup [125 ml] good-quality wine vinegar, sherry vinegar, or balsamic vinegar

salt

pepper

6 tablespoons extra-virgin olive oil

GENTLY wash and dry the greens. Pick through the flowers, checking for bugs and soil. Make sure the flowers were grown to be served as food, so you don't have to wash them (they're too fragile). Handle them gently and store them in a plastic bag in the refrigerator until you're ready to serve the salad.

CUT the legs and breasts off the squabs, being careful to leave the breasts covered with skin. Set the legs aside and reserve the breasts on a plate in the refrigerator. Remove the liver, heart, and lungs (if the lungs are included with the giblets), chop them fine with a chef's knife, and refrigerate. Heat 1 tablespoon of the pure olive oil in a small sauté pan and stir in the shallot and garlic. Chop up the squab legs, necks, and carcasses with a heavy chef's knife or cleaver and add them and the thyme to the pan. Continue browning over medium heat, stirring every few minutes until the bones in the squab pieces are well caramelized, about 15 minutes.

POUR the chicken broth into the sauté pan and boil it down over high heat until it evaporates completely. Continue cooking until the juices caramelize, but be very careful that they don't burn. Pour in the vinegar and stir the bones over medium heat with the vinegar for about 2 minutes, so that all the caramelized juices dissolve into the vinegar.

Strain into a small saucepan, discard the bones, and reserve the *jus.*

SEASON the breasts with salt and pepper and sauté them on high heat, about 1½ minutes on each side, in the remaining tablespoon of plain olive oil.

WHISK the chopped giblets into the reserved *jus* and gently heat to the barest simmer. Immediately remove from the heat, season to taste with salt and pepper, and pour the extra-virgin olive oil into the saucepan.

THINLY slice the breasts and arrange them on top of the flowers in a large salad bowl. Pour the hot *jus* over them, toss, and serve immediately.

FLOWERS

One summer in the mid-1970s I had lunch with my mentor Richard Olney, who lived on an idyllic little hill in a village in Provence. It was at his table that I first ate flowers—glorious nasturtium flowers tossed atop a *salade mesclun* that was at once elaborate, because it contained so many varieties of green things, and simple, in its light and festive effect. Several years later I had a restaurant where I was forever making flower salads for startled but delighted guests. We had a flower garden and I'd go out and pick whatever blossoms looked pretty and tasted good. I'd flick off any obvious insects and toss them—the flowers, not the insects—into the salads. It was during this period that I was asked to give a cooking demonstration for the YWCA. When I showed up with my shopping bags of foods and flowers from the restaurant garden, one of the women at the gathering said how kind it was of me to bring the flowers, too. Her smile quickly waned when I told her they were going into the salad. Now that I look back, I realize that things had gotten out of hand—not all flowers taste good and frankly it's a wonder I didn't poison anyone—but some flowers are so delicately flavored and textured that they provide the perfect accent to delicate meats, herbs, and vegetables.

When buying flowers, buy them at a food store, not a flower store. Flowers grown for decoration often contain dangerously high amounts of pesticides. If you grow your own flowers, use only organic fertilizers and pesticides designed for growing foods. Eat only the petals, not the stamens and pistils, which you should cut off. Gently rinse and pat your flowers dry before you use them, which should be as soon as possible, since the petals wilt very quickly. You should also be aware that some people are allergic to certain flowers.

COMPOSED SALADS

SALADES COMPOSÉES

HOW TO COMBINE	MORE IDEAS	THE DIFFERENCE	HOW TO	HOW TO
VEGETABLES, MEAT, OR SEAFOOD INTO INVENTIVE SALADS	ABOUT SALAD SAUCES	BETWEEN TRUFFLE OIL AND "TRUFFLE JUICE" AND HOW TO MAKE YOUR OWN TRUFFLE OIL	PEEL ASPARAGUS	TRIM ARTICHOKES

A SALADE COMPOSÉE IS A SALAD IN WHICH VARIOUS COLD INGREDIENTS are cut, usually into cubes, and tossed together in some kind of cold sauce. What the French call *salades simples* contain only one central ingredient, such as carrots, cucumbers, mushrooms, or string beans, and are often served together as an assortment for a crudité platter. Green salads, of course, may have any number of ingredients tossed with the lettuce, but it's the greens in the salad that set the tone. A composed salad may contain greens but they're often just decorative and are rarely the main element. Usually a composed salad consists of vegetables and sometimes meats or seafood tossed together in a mayonnaise, vinaigrette, or occasionally a cold cream sauce. Many of my own composed salads are based on leftovers. If I'm cooking to impress, I'll run out in search of ingredients to combine with my leftovers, but otherwise and when feeling lazy, I'll just toss leftover vegetables, or strips of leftover meat or fish, with a little olive oil, vinegar, salt and pepper, and a few herbs from the garden. In old French cookbooks, salads made by combining ingredients carefully cut into cubes (macédoine, see page 22) are sometimes called salades macédoines or salpicons, but I like to leave the natural shape of the salad ingredients as intact as possible. When combining ingredients in a composed salad it's hard to go terribly wrong, and in fact combinations that at first sound odd often reveal themselves to be surprisingly good (although I've yet to try a pineapple and truffle salad mentioned in Proust). It's helpful, though, to keep in mind certain principles. Much of the time you should be able to taste all the ingredients in a composed salad without one or two taking over the flavor of the whole thing. On the other hand, especially if you're showing off special ingredients like cooked lobster or crayfish, there shouldn't be too many competing elements. As when inviting guests to a dinner party, you want a happy blend of talkers and listeners. One flavor should predominate but not dominate. (If, for example, I'm making a salad containing lobster, I'll probably work some of the lobster coral into the sauce so the salad all tastes of lobster but not so strongly that I can't taste other ingredients through the sauce.) Texture is also important. Salads containing relatively soft ingredients such as cooked beets or potatoes usually benefit from other ingredients of contrasting texture. This contrast can be subtle—cooked artichoke bottoms aren't terribly firm, but they still have more texture than potatoes—or the contrast can be made dramatic by adding something distinctly crunchy like roasted walnuts or pecans. The richness of ingredients should also contrast. A salad of peas, green beans, and asparagus can function as a backdrop of richer ingredients such as strips of prosciutto or even cubes of foie gras. Starchy ingredients such as rice, potatoes, and pasta benefit from lightly crunchy greens. Cubes of cheese are surprisingly good with sweet and crunchy pieces of apple.

APPLE, CELERIAC, AND WALNUT SALAD

SALADE WALDORF

MAKES 6 FIRST-COURSE SERVINGS

While a Waldorf salad is decidedly American, it is still a useful model for what the French used to call "Salades Américaines", made by combining various ingredients, often diced, in some kind of cold sauce. The salade américaine has since become more French than American.

- 1 cup (¼ pound [125 g]) walnut halves, very coarsely chopped
- 1½ pounds [675 g] crisp, tart apples (3 to 5 apples, depending on their size)
- 2 tablespoons lemon juice
- 1 medium-size celeriac (about 8 ounces [225 g])
- ½ cup [125 ml] Basic Mayonnaise (page 34)
- 2 tablespoons heavy cream (optional)

  salt

TOAST the walnuts for 10 to 15 minutes in a 350°F [175°C/gas mark 4] oven, until they smell nutty and turn slightly darker. Let cool.

PEEL the apples and cut them in half vertically. Cut out the cores with a paring knife or melon baller and cut the apple halves into ¼-inch [.5 cm] cubes. Don't worry if some of the cubes are irregular; this is inevitable unless you're going to be rigidly formal and square off the ends and sides of the halves, in which case you'll need 2 or 3 extra apples. In a mixing bowl, toss the apple cubes with the lemon juice.

PEEL the celeriac with a pairing knife and cut it into cubes slightly smaller than the apple cubes. (The cubes are made smaller because celeriac has a firmer texture than the apples.) Toss the celeriac cubes with the apple cubes, along with the walnuts and mayonnaise. If the salad seems too thick, stir in the heavy cream or a little water to thin it. Season to taste with salt.

SERVE slightly chilled in mounds or individual plates. For a more formal presentation, pack the salad into six 5-ounce [150 ml] (3½-inch [9 cm] diameter) ramekins lined with plastic wrap, place a plate on top of each ramekin, flip over the plate and ramekin together, lift off the ramekin, and peel off the plastic wrap.

Variations: The easiest and most obvious variations involve the mayonnaise. You can underline the walnut theme of the salad by finishing the mayonnaise with a few tablespoons of full-flavored roasted nut oil, such as walnut, hazelnut, or pistachio oil (see page 37). Or you can accentuate the flavor of the apples by stirring some reduced apple juice or apple cider into the mayonnaise, instead of adding the heavy cream. This will also give the salad a welcome hint of sweetness that you may want to balance with a little extra lemon juice. If you don't want to use mayonnaise, make a simple *citronette* (a vinaigrette in which the vinegar is replaced with lemon juice) by combining lemon juice with oil, ideally one of the nut oils mentioned above either used alone or attenuated with a little flavorless oil such as canola. I sometimes make this salad more substantial by adding about a cup [225 g] of Gruyère cubes cut the same size as the celeriac. This sounds bizarre but is surprisingly good. Tiny cubes or thin strips of prosciutto also give a "Waldorf" salad a savory accent.

Classic French Salades Composées

ESCOFFIER, IN *Le Guide Culinaire*, FIRST published in 1903, lists 69 *salades composées*, most with romantic names like *Opéra* (chicken, celery, truffles, asparagus), *Rachel* (celery, truffles, artichoke bottoms, potatoes, and asparagus), and *Victoria* (lobster, truffles, cucumbers, and asparagus). Except for the preponderance of truffles, all of Escoffier's classic salads can easily be tossed together at home, but nowadays one rarely bothers duplicating a nineteenth-century salad when it makes much more sense to improvise, based on what's around and what's in season. These old recipes can, however, be a source of ideas. Here are a few classics. Don't worry about the truffles—just leave them out or add a little truffle oil or truffle juice (see page 62) to your sauce. Sliced mushrooms, while no substitute, are also good in salads that call for truffles.

AMÉRICAINE: Slices of seeded tomatoes, sliced rounds of cooked potatoes, julienned celery, thinly sliced onions, and hard-boiled eggs. Toss with vinaigrette just before serving.

ANDALOUSE: Seeded tomato wedges, julienne of roasted and peeled red bell peppers, rice, and chopped onions, garlic, and parsley. Toss with vinaigrette just before serving.

ARCHIDUC: Cooked beets cut into julienne, julienned endive, julienned cooked potatoes, and julienned truffles, everything tossed with vinaigrette.

AUGUSTIN: String beans (haricots verts) cut into 1-inch [2.5 cm] lengths, peeled and seeded tomato wedges, wedges of hard-boiled eggs, and cooked baby peas, everything tossed with mayonnaise that has been flavored with Worcestershire sauce.

BAGATELLE: Julienne of carrots and mushrooms and whole asparagus tips, tossed with vinaigrette.

BAGRATION: Julienned celery, julienne of chicken breasts, artichoke bottoms (sliced thin or julienned, see page 68), cooked macaroni, tomato wedges, and hard-boiled eggs. Toss with mayonnaise.

BEAUCAIRE: Julienne of celery, celeriac, endive, cooked ham, and apples. Toss with chopped parsley, chervil, and tarragon and rounds of cooked potatoes and beets.

CANAILLE: Tomato wedges, asparagus tips, thinly sliced onions, banana slices, cooked rice, and celery julienne. Toss with sour cream.

CENDRILLON: Julienned celeriac, julienned truffles and artichoke bottoms, apple and potato slices, and asparagus tips. Toss with vinaigrette.

DANICHEFF: Asparagus tips, celeriac julienne, sliced potatoes, julienned artichoke bottoms and very thinly sliced raw baby artichokes, and wedges of hard-boiled egg, everything tossed with vinaigrette.

ESPAGNOLE: String beans cut into 1-inch [2.5 cm] lengths, tomato wedges, strips of grilled and peeled bell peppers, and thinly sliced onions and mushrooms. Toss with vinaigrette.

GRANDE DUCHESSE: String beans cut into 1-inch [2.5 cm] lengths, cooked potatoes cut into French-fry shapes, and julienned celery. Toss with a lightened mayonnaise.

IMPÉRIALE: String beans cut into 1-inch [2.5 cm] lengths and julienned carrots, apples, and truffles. Toss with vinaigrette flavored with fines herbes (tarragon, chervil, chives, parsley).

INDIENNE: Cooked rice, asparagus tips, strips of grilled and peeled bell peppers, and diced apples. Toss with crème fraîche or heavy cream and vinegar flavored with curry powder that has been heated for a minute in oil to release its flavor.

IRMA: Thinly sliced seeded cucumbers, asparagus tips, string beans cut into 1-inch [2.5 cm] lengths, and small florets of cauliflower. Toss with a tarragon-flavored mayonnaise.

LAPEROUSE: Peeled and seeded tomato wedges, diced ham, string beans cut into 1-inch [2.5 cm] lengths, sliced artichoke bottoms, and thinly sliced onions. Toss with sour cream.

LEGUMES: Thick julienne of cooked potatoes, string beans cut into 1-inch [2.5 cm] lengths, baby peas, and tiny cauliflower florets. Toss with vinaigrette flavored with fines herbes.

MERCÉDÈS: Julienne of celery and beets, sliced tomatoes, and sliced hard-boiled eggs, everything tossed with vinaigrette.

RUSSE: Carrots and turnips cut into dice, string beans cut into 1-inch [2.5 cm] lengths, baby peas, diced truffles, sliced mushrooms, capers, and diced ham, lobster, and cornichons. Toss with mayonnaise.

SAINT-JEAN: Asparagus tips, string beans cut into 1-inch [2.5 cm] lengths, baby peas, raw artichoke bottoms (sliced thin, see 68), and sliced seeded cucumbers. Toss with mayonnaise containing a lot of vinegar.

YAM-YAM: String beans cut into 1-inch [2.5 cm] lengths, sliced seeded cucumbers, celeriac julienne, and Bibb lettuce, cut in quarters, everything tossed with vinaigrette.

STRING BEANS, GREEN BEANS, AND HARICOTS VERTS

We don't actually have "string" beans anymore because the thick string of fiber running up their sides was bred out near the beginning of the twentieth century, but the name persists. The terms "green bean" and "string bean" can be used interchangeably. *Haricots verts* is the French term for green beans, but because French string beans are much thinner than the usual American varieties, the term is often used in this country to mean the much thinner (and more expensive) French variety. Unless they're outrageously priced, I opt for haricots verts because of their bright green color and delicate taste, and because they're never mealy. If you're stuck with thick green beans, you can "French" them by slicing them in half lengthwise. If they're very thick, slice each half in half.

TRUFFLE OIL AND TRUFFLE JUICE

French chefs in the late nineteenth and early twentieth centuries were forever combining their favorite salad ingredients—vegetables, seafood, and meat—with sliced, shaved, or julienned black, and occasionally white, truffles. Sadly, truffles are just one of those things that most of us have to do without. Even those among us who may buy a truffle or two as a holiday splurge can't count on them as an everyday staple the way Escoffier and his clientele did at the turn of the last century. Truffle oil and truffle juice can help us all through this unfortunate circumstance. Neither of these is cheap, but both provide the flavor if not the texture and black color of the real thing. The situation is complicated by the big differences among brands. Some of the oils and juices are so intensely flavored that a couple of teaspoons in half a cup of sauce will more than do the trick; with others, half the bottle is required. I'd recommend specific brands, but even bottles from the same manufacturer seem to differ. You can buy small bottles of truffle oil and truffle juice and try them out, but even this is an expensive and potentially discouraging undertaking.

You can save money and come up with something better by making your own truffle oil. If you want to make white truffle oil, buy a white truffle from a reliable supplier (see Sources) sometime in late October or early November. It will cost about as much as a modest dinner for two. Push the truffle through the mouth of a quart or liter bottle of good extra-virgin olive oil. Screw the bottle top on tightly and store the oil for a week before you use it. If you want to make black truffle oil, do the same thing, using either extra-virgin olive oil or a relatively tasteless vegetable oil such as "pure" olive oil or canola oil, but wait until December or January to buy the truffles. The prices usually drop a little in January, since most of us want our truffles for the holidays. The oil should last, kept in a cool place or in the fridge, for most of the next year.

Truffle juice is something else again. It isn't really juice but what the French call *cuisson,* meaning cooking liquid; it is the juice released by the truffles that are cooked for bottling and canning. This liquid can be full of flavor but it can also be insipid or overly salty, and unless you happen to can your own truffles is not something you can reasonably make yourself.

Truffle oil and truffle juice are used in somewhat different ways because the oil is soluble in fat—including oil, butter, cream, egg, and poultry fat—and the juice is soluble in water and other liquids. If you're using either one in vinaigrette or in an emulsified sauce such as mayonnaise, hollandaise, or beurre blanc (which contain both fat and water), you can use the oil, the juice, or both. In some sauces—hollandaise, for instance—you may not want the flavor of the olive oil used to make commercial truffle oil. You're better off using truffle juice or your own homemade oil made with flavorless oil. (See Chapter 43 for more information about truffles.)

Seafood Salads

FRENCH COOKBOOKS ABOUND WITH SEA-
food salads. Escoffier's are elegant and hopelessly
extravagant: *salade favorite* is made by tossing equal
parts of crayfish tails, white truffle slices, and white
asparagus tips with lemon juice and olive oil (it's not
hard to figure out how it got its name); *salade hollandaise* contains cubes of smoked salmon, cubes of
potato, minced onion, and caviar; *salade japonaise*
combines diced herring fillets, poached oysters,
sliced potatoes, and truffle slices; *salade mignon* calls
for tossing together shrimp tails, cubes of cooked
artichoke bottoms, and truffle slices in a mayonnaise–crème fraîche combination (sounds like a
winner). The list goes on.

In the 1960s and 1970s, when the innovations
(and, often, pretenses) of *la nouvelle cuisine* supplanted many of the old classic dishes, there was
surprisingly little difference in the old and the new.
Most of the differences had to do with how the salads were presented. In a classic French restaurant, a
seafood salad would be brought to the table in a
salad bowl, tossed at table side, and served in front
of the diners. In nouvelle cuisine restaurants, the
salads were arranged on the plates in the kitchen,
and this allowed the chefs to create their own elaborate arrangements on the plates. The portions also
got smaller and the old fanciful classic names were
replaced with more or less elaborate descriptive
titles. But not much actually changed.

George Blanc, one of France's greatest living
chefs, serves a salad called *salpicon de homard à la
brunoise de légumes,* which consists of pieces of lobster,
truffles, and carrots cut into tiny cubes, and julienned
leeks, tossed with a mayonnaise that is lightened with
a little court bouillon and truffle juice. He occasionally varies the vegetables and, depending on the season, includes peas, tiny cubes of haricots verts, fava
beans, or tomatoes. Another of Monsieur Blanc's salads consists of tossing together crayfish tails and asparagus tips in a mayonnaise containing mustard and
crème fraîche, and again lightened with court bouillon. He may add one or more of the fines herbes
(parsley, chervil, chives, and tarragon) to the mayon-

naise, or tomatoes, if in season—again, all very classic. Other chefs apply similar treatments to other
shellfish, such as scallops or langoustines, and use
peas, string beans, snow peas, fava beans, or asparagus
tips to lighten the dish and to add color and crunch.

CRAYFISH, ASPARAGUS, FAVA BEAN, ARTICHOKE BOTTOMS, AND MOREL SALAD

SALADE AUX QUEUES D'ÉCREVISSES, ASPERGES, FÈVES, FONDS D'ARTICHAUTS, ET MORILLES

MAKES 6 FIRST-COURSE SERVINGS

Don't be intimidated by all these ingredients. This is a magnificent salad, based on
classic techniques and traditions, but unless you
live near a very fancy market you probably
won't be able to find everything and you'll end up making
substitutions. In truth, you could replace everything and
just follow the principle of delicately binding together
shellfish and seasonal vegetables in a light and flavorful
homemade mayonnaise. You'd be far better off using
what's fresh and in season instead of blindly tracking
down everything listed here. Assuming you do find all the
ingredients, or similar ones, you can simplify this recipe
by just buying crayfish tails (which come already cooked)
instead of live crayfish, leaving out the ingredients listed
below for cooking the crayfish, and tossing together the
ingredients with the homemade mayonnaise, flavored
according to your own whims (see "Seafood Salad Variations," below, for a few ideas). But what I describe here is

a bit more conscientious because it involves extracting the flavor from whole crayfish and then using this to flavor the sauce. If you are buying crayfish, make sure they're all alive by picking them out yourself or by watching very carefully to make sure they all put up a good fight as the guy at the fish store tries to get them into a bag.

FOR COOKING THE CRAYFISH AND EXTRACTING
THE FLAVOR FROM THE SHELLS:

36 live crayfish

1 tablespoon olive oil

2 shallots, or 1 small onion, chopped

1 medium-size carrot, chopped

4 medium-size tomatoes, chopped coarse, or 1 can (15 ounces [400-450 g]) tomatoes, drained, chopped coarse

½ cup [125 ml] heavy cream

FOR THE VEGETABLES AND SAUCE:

18 thick stalks asparagus, or 36 thin stalks, peeled (see page 67)

salt

½ pound [225 g] fresh morels, or 1 ounce [30 g] dried

1 pound [450 g] fava beans (weighed in the pod), shucked and peeled (see page 65)

3 large, 6 medium-size, or 12 baby artichokes, trimmed and cooked (see page 68)

1 tablespoon extra-virgin olive oil (for the morels)

pepper

½ cup [125 ml] Basic Mayonnaise (page 34)

2 tablespoons sherry vinegar or other good quality wine vinegar (except balsamic, which discolors the salad), or more to taste

1 tablespoon finely chopped parsley, chervil, or chives, or a combination

1 small bunch chervil (optional)

TO COOK THE CRAYFISH AND EXTRACT
THE FLAVOR FROM THE SHELLS

DUMP the crayfish onto a sheet pan and transfer them, a few at a time, to a colander to make sure they're all alive. Rinse them under cold water. Heat the olive oil over medium heat in a heavy-bottomed pot—one that has a lid—and stir in the shallots and carrots. Stir these for a couple of minutes until they smell fragrant, but don't let them brown. Toss in the crayfish. Immediately put on the lid and cook the crayfish, covered, for about 5 minutes until, when you lift the lid, the crayfish have all turned red. Turn off the heat and let cool. When you take out the crayfish to remove their meat, leave the shallots and the carrots in the pot. You'll need them later.

TWIST the tails and claws away from the main part (the thorax) of the crayfish, keeping each of the parts in a separate pile. To devein the crayfish tails, pull off the tiny flipper at the end of the tail—most of the time, the "vein" (actually the intestine) will come away with it. Set aside any tails whose vein didn't come out. Peel the crayfish tails, including those you set aside, by pinching them gently on the sides—you'll feel a little crack—and then pulling away the shells. Devein the tails that still have their intestine by pushing against the back of the tail with your thumb to tear back, but not off, the small piece of meat covering the vein. Just pull the vein out with your fingers.

CRUSH the crayfish claws with the end of a European-style rolling pin (the kind without handles), with the end of cleaver, or by leaning on them with a heavy-bottomed pot. Don't put the claw shells in a food processor or they'll damage the blade. Break up the remaining shells by grinding them for about a minute in a food processor (don't overwork them or the sauce will be muddy) or, again, with the end of a rolling pin or with a cleaver. Put the broken-up shells and claws in the pan with the shallots, pour in the tomatoes and cream, and simmer gently, stirring every few minutes, for 30 minutes. Strain the sauce through a coarse-mesh strainer, pushing hard with the back of a ladle to extract the maximum amount of liquid. Then strain it through a fine-mesh strainer. (The coarse strainer is used first to get rid of the shells, which could damage a fine strainer.) You should end up with about ¾ cup [175 ml] of liquid. If you have more, simmer it down to ¾ cup [175 ml]. Refrigerate this liquid while preparing the other ingredients.

CUT the tips off the asparagus and cut the stalks, on a diagonal, into 1-inch lengths. Plunge the pieces into a pot of boiling salted water and boil until tender, 2 to 5 minutes, depending on the thickness. Drain in a colander and rinse with cold water.

IF you're using dried morels, toss them with about ¼ cup [60 ml] of cold water. Let them steep, moving them around every 15 minutes or so to make sure they absorb the water evenly, for about 30 minutes, until they have softened. If you're using fresh morels, check the outsides and insides for dirt. If they seem dirty, rinse them quickly, in a colander. Otherwise, don't bother.

PLUNGE the fava beans into a small pot of boiling salted water and boil for 1 to 4 minutes, depending on their size and freshness. Drain in a colander and rinse with cold water.

CUT the artichoke bottoms into wedges, as though cutting a cake: about 6 wedges for large artichokes and 4 for medium-size. If you're using baby artichokes, cut them in half vertically.

IF you're using dried morels, squeeze out their soaking liquid and reserve it. Cook the morels, either dried or fresh, in the extra-virgin olive oil in a sauté pan over medium heat until they smell fragrant, about 10 minutes. Season with salt and pepper and let cool.

COMBINE the mayonnaise, the reserved crayfish liquid, the vinegar (adding it a bit at a time, tasting as you go), the chopped herbs, and any reserved soaking liquid from the morels (decanting it slowly into the sauce so any grit is left behind), and season to taste with salt and pepper. If necessary, thin the sauce with a little water so that it has a consistency just slightly thicker than heavy cream. At this point, you can toss everything (except the chervil) together. But if you want to make sure that everyone gets the same amount of each component, separately toss everything with sauce in little bowls and then construct each salad, in a small mound, on an individual plate. Decorate each mound with a few sprigs of chervil.

PEELING FAVA BEANS

Until recently, fava beans were almost impossible to find in American markets. When I used to buy them, at an Italian market in New York, I could pick through them at my leisure—it's important to feel each pod to make sure that there are plenty of beans in it. But now I'm rarely alone. When quickly blanched, fava beans are bright green and tender and have a flavor that's vaguely cauliflower-like, but more delicate. The downside is that fava beans have to be "peeled" twice: first shucked by running your thumb along the seam of the felt-lined pod and then peeled individually with a thumbnail or paring knife. If you're peeling a lot of fava beans, it's worthwhile to plunge the shucked but unpeeled beans into a pot of boiling water for a minute and then quickly rinse with cold water to loosen the skin. But when doing only a few, I rarely bother.

SEAFOOD SALAD VARIATIONS

CRUSTACEANS: The sauce used for the crayfish salad on page 63 is flavored with a rich extract made by simmering the crayfish shells with aromatic vegetables, herbs, and heavy cream—the classic technique used for making crustacean sauces and bisques (see Chapter 25). If you're feeling conscientious, you can make the same kind of extract when preparing any salad containing crustaceans such as lobster or shrimp. If you can't find shrimp with heads on, just use the shells to flavor the sauce. When I'm in a rush, I toss the shells and/or heads in a saucepan with a couple of hacked-up tomatoes (no need for finesse, they're getting strained out), a sprig of thyme or tarragon, and a little chopped shallot or onion. I then simmer for about ½ hour with barely enough heavy cream to cover, leaving the saucepan uncovered so that the cream will not separate. I break the shells up, while they're simmering, with the end of a European-style rolling pin or a cleaver held on end. Then I strain the sauce, first through a coarse strainer, to get rid of the shells, and then through a fine one. You can use this rich extract as the base for a salad sauce, by working it into a mayonnaise as we did above, or by thinning it with broth, vinegar, or another flavorful liquid, such as truffle oil. It must be thinned or it will be too stiff once it gets cold. Vinegar is usually an ideal liquid for thinning, since seafood salads need a little tangy acidity anyway. Other liquids, such as broth, truffle juice (see page 62), or raw tomato coulis (strained raw tomato purée; see page 374), can also be used, to provide flavor and color at the same time. In addition to the vegetables included in the crayfish salad above, any of the following can be tossed with crustaceans: seeded, sliced cucumbers; celeriac, diced or cut into julienne; baby peas; haricots verts; raw, thinly sliced regular mushrooms; diced tomatoes; salsify, peeled, blanched, and diced; diced potatoes; fresh beans; dried beans, which can be simmered in a broth made from the crustacean shells; grilled or roasted and peeled red bell peppers; avocados; and diced and blanched turnips.

MOLLUSKS: Escoffier was fond of including cold cooked oysters in salads, but despite being a dedicated oyster addict, I don't find this appealing. So by mollusks I mean mussels, clams, and cockles, all three of which release full-flavored briny liquid when steamed. When using mollusks in a salad, steam them open in the usual way, with a little white wine, and shallots or garlic (see Chapter 20). Reduce the briny steaming liquid and incorporate it into a mayonnaise, or combine it with heavy cream or crème fraîche, or whisk it into a mustardy vinaigrette. Toss the cooked mollusks with the sauce and cubes of vegetables and/or cooked pasta. When you have important guests or just feel like hanging out in the kitchen, try adding tomato coulis (see page 581) to give the sauce a delightful sweetness and color, and add delicate herbs such as chives, tarragon, parsley, or chervil. On hot summer days, when you may want to keep things simpler and lighter (and less traditionally French), toss the cooked mollusks with the cold reduced steaming liquid, olive oil, plenty of lime juice, and maybe some tomato cubes, chopped cilantro, and finely chopped chiles for a salad that's refreshing, spicy, and ceviche-like.

SQUID, OCTOPUS, AND CUTTLEFISH: All of these lovely tentacled creatures have such a full flavor that I never bother making a salad sauce out of their cooking liquid; the result is just too strong. I just braise them (see the octopus daube on page 245) or sauté them and serve them cold, tossed with lemon juice and olive oil, tomatoes when in season, basil leaves if they're around, parsley if they're not, and, if I have the energy, pitted black olives. (Never use canned pitted olives, buy loose olives in brine. In a fancy store you might find them already pitted; otherwise, pit them yourself.) Cubes of bread—sautéed in olive oil, added for crunch—and, occasionally, anchovy fillets also work their way in.

FISH: Pieces of fish in a salad can be tricky because most fish is fragile and may fall apart once cooked and tossed. I don't use fish broth or the cooking liquid from fish in a salad because it just makes everything taste fishy. When I do use fish in a salad, it's usually grilled and tossed with salad greens (see page 63). If you do want to use fish in *salade composée*, choose a firm variety such as barely cooked tuna that won't fall apart when tossed.

SMOKED FISH: Because of its firm texture and full flavor, smoked fish makes an excellent salad ingredient. Thin strips of smoked salmon, or pieces of smoked trout, eel, or sable, give a savory accent to mixtures of vegetables or starchy ingredients with understated flavor, such as potatoes and pasta.

Cubes of smoked fish also balance the flavor of spicy mixtures containing chiles and cilantro. (Strips or cubes of smoked fish are great in a spicy gazpacho, ceviche, or guacamole.) Slices of smoked fish can also take a starring role and be spread, in thin slices, on large plates. Delicate sauces, such as vinaigrette or mayonnaise flavored with nut oil and truffle juice or wild-mushroom soaking liquid, can be served on the side. Smoked salmon requires no sauce, but crème fraîche isn't bad, especially if you're serving it with blinis (see Chapter 47), but this takes us into another realm. Or the sauce can be brushed over thin slices of the fish.

PEELING ASPARAGUS

The French peel a lot of things that Americans don't. Most of us never peel a tomato unless forced to by a finicky recipe (like one of mine). Peeling a mushroom would be unthinkable here, and even in France this habit is dying out. So peeling asparagus sounds like just another silly affectation. In fact, peeling is very practical because it allows you to boil or steam the asparagus and have it come out with both tip and stalk done at the same time. This brings up the thick-versus-thin controversy. I, for one, try to avoid asparagus any thinner than a thumb, because I like thick asparagus's flavor and meaty texture. And because fewer thick meaty stalks are needed for a serving, peeling is less of a project.

To peel asparagus, first cut off and discard 1 or 2 inches [2.5 to 5 cm] of the woody part on the bottom end. Lay the asparagus flat on a cutting board and peel the stalk, up to the base of the tip, with a vegetable peeler. Move the peeler rapidly back and forth with one hand while you give the stalk a small roll with the other hand. Rinse under running cold water and pull away any strips of peel left attached to the stalks.

TRIMMING AND COOKING ARTICHOKES

In most French homes and simple restaurants, artichokes are served whole with a sauce, usually vinaigrette if the vegetable is being served cold, and melted butter or hollandaise if it's being served hot. (I also like aïoli for both hot and cold.) In fancy French restaurants, artichokes are usually trimmed of their leaves and chokes and only the meaty leafless bottoms used. In old-fashioned classic cooking, the bottoms made convenient holders for complicated mixtures of vegetables or vegetable purées and were typically arranged around some extravagant roast. The bottoms were, and still are, also sliced or diced and incorporated into salads or light vegetable stews.

To trim the leaves off a large or medium-size artichoke, cut the thick stem off the bottom, level with the base of the artichoke, so that the artichoke bottom—if you're serving it whole—will stay flat on the plate. If you're cutting the artichoke bottom into pieces, reserve the stem—you can use it too. If you're right-handed, hold the artichoke in your left hand. With a very sharp paring knife in your right hand, rotate the artichoke against the blade of the knife while holding the knife perpendicular to the base of the artichoke. Continue rotating until you see the white flesh of the artichoke bottom appear where the leaves have fallen off. When you've exposed the artichoke bottom on all sides, switch the angle of the knife and, again, while rotating the artichoke, trim off any patches of green on the bottom. Cut off and discard the top two-thirds of the artichoke. Trim off any remaining dark green spots or leaves on the upper side of the artichoke bottom. Rub the artichoke bottoms with half a lemon to help keep them from turning dark. You can cut the choke out of the bottom before cooking, but this is annoying; it's much easier to scoop out the choke after cooking. To use the artichoke stems, cut off and discard the dark bottom ends. Peel the stems deeply with a paring knife, rub them with lemon, and simmer them along with the artichoke bottoms.

Cook the artichoke bottoms the same way you cook whole artichokes, by tossing them into a pot of boiling water with a little olive oil added to protect the artichokes from air. Be sure to use a nonaluminum pot, since aluminum will turn the artichokes dark. Simmer about 20 minutes, then test for doneness by poking one of the artichoke bottoms with a paring knife; it should offer only slight resistance. Drain the artichoke bottoms, let cool, and scoop out the chokes with a spoon, being careful not to cut too deeply and waste any of the flesh. Toss the artichoke bottoms with just enough lemon juice to coat them, to keep them from turning dark. If you do this the day before using the artichoke bottoms and leave them covered in the refrigerator, the lemon juice will bleach them to an appealing pale green.

Baby artichokes are easier to deal with than mature ones because you don't have to take out the choke, which is underdeveloped and harmless. Just cut off the stem and the top half of the baby artichoke. Trim around the bottom half until you've removed most of the green. Simmer the artichokes in the same way as artichoke bottoms, 10 to 15 minutes, depending on their size. Drain, let cool, and toss with lemon juice.

Baby artichokes are sometimes left raw and sliced thinly. To use raw baby artichokes, trim them in the same way as for cooking and then slice them, at the very last minute since they turn dark very quickly, with a mandoline or plastic vegetable slicer (see page 13). Immediately toss them with lemon juice or vinegar and olive oil.

Whole cooked baby artichokes or artichoke bottoms are delicious in salads, but if you're not up to trimming and cooking them yourself, use frozen baby artichokes, which you'll have to cook, or rinsed and drained bottled artichokes instead.

Meat and Poultry Salads

OLD-FASHIONED FRENCH COOKBOOKS always include a cold beef salad or two made from leftover beef, since farmhouse cooks were forever making pot-au-feu and other slow-simmering concoctions, and the idea of a cool salad made with the cold meat instead of a repeat of the night before no doubt led to the invention of many a variation. When I owned a restaurant, I stretched my imagination to serve the staff the beef and veal left over from making the broths, and I incorporated these meats in various salads. One of my absolute favorite beef salads is made with beets. Beets have a special affinity for cold beef, maybe because both do so well coated with mustardy vinaigrette. Cold meats can be gently tossed or brushed with virtually any flavored mayonnaise, and vegetables can be added to provide color and contrasting texture.

COLD BEEF AND BEET SALAD
SALADE DE BOEUF ET DE BETTERAVES

MAKES 4 MAIN-COURSE OR 6 FIRST-COURSE SERVINGS

4   beets (about 1¼ pounds [550 g] without greens), or the equivalent in smaller beets

4   to 6 slices (¼ inch thick) leftover pot-au-feu beef, pot roast, roast, or steak, or more slices of stew meat (¾ pound to 1 pound [335 g to 450 g] total)

3   tablespoons Dijon mustard

2   large shallots, chopped fine

2   tablespoons good-quality wine vinegar

6   tablespoons extra-virgin olive oil or vegetable oil

    leaves from 1 small bunch parsley, preferably flat-leaf, chopped coarse at the last minute

    salt

    pepper

THE tastiest way to cook beets is to roast them unpeeled. Rub them with oil or wrap them in aluminum foil and put them on a sheet pan in a 375°F [190°C/gas mark 5] oven for 1 to 1½ hours, until a skewer goes in easily. On hot summer days, when I hate to turn on the oven, I boil them for the same length of time or cook them in the microwave for about 20 minutes, turning them over and around every 5 minutes. When they're done, drain them or take them out of the oven or microwave, let them cool for about 20 minutes, and pull off the skins with your thumb and a paring knife. Slice into ¼-inch-thick [.5 cm] rounds and then cut each of the rounds into French-fry shapes, which the French call *bâtonnets*.

IF the slices of meat are large, cut them into a more manageable size—the more tender the meat, the larger the pieces can be. You might want to cut them into French-fry shapes, just like the beets. Toss them gently in a mixing bowl with the beets, mustard, shallots, vinegar and oil, and parsley. Serve lightly chilled. Season with salt and pepper.

Variations: Sliced or coarsely chopped pickles, especially cornichons, and capers are great when tossed into this salad. Different herbs, especially marjoram, can be used in addition to or instead of the parsley. Red onions, thinly sliced on a plastic vegetable slicer or a mandoline, can also go in the layers in place of the chopped shallots in the sauce. (When I use onion slices I rub them with salt, drain them for 30 minutes to 1 hour, and squeeze out their excess liquid. This softens them and makes them less aggressive.) Tomatoes can be used instead of the beets, in which case I leave out the mustard and substitute lots of basil for the parsley. During cooler months, I combine mustard with heavy cream or crème fraîche and grate in some fresh horseradish and sometimes add little cubes of celeriac or thinly sliced branch celery for a subtle dissonance that goes well with the horseradish. The sweetness of apples also goes well with horseradish, and their cool crispness is a delight next to the soft, rich texture of the meat. If you're stuck with stew meat, which is difficult to slice into attractive layers, or have at hand very tender leftover roast beef, you can turn this salad and all its variations into a salpicon by cutting everything into ¼-inch [.5 cm] cubes and tossing together with whatever sauce you come up with.

CHICKEN SALAD

SALADE DE POULET

MAKES 4 LIGHT MAIN-COURSE SERVINGS

Most of us are familiar with chicken salad in one of two guises: the original deli version, made much like American potato salad—with mayonnaise and celery—and the new yuppie version, the chicken Caesar. I'm not crazy about either version, because the original always tastes like bottled mayonnaise and the new version is so often made with the outer tough leaves of the romaine, never contains enough anchovies, and in restaurants at least is too expensive. I talk about a few potential variations on the chicken Caesar (see chapter 2 for ideas about garnished green salads), but the deli version, much like potato salad, can be improvised upon almost endlessly.

The bottled-mayonnaise problem is easily solved. Make your own, or make a different sauce entirely. My own simplest chicken salad is made by pulling strips of meat away from last night's roast chicken and tossing them with extra-virgin olive oil, vinegar, chopped herbs—usually parsley, but tarragon is always a delight—a little chopped or sliced onion, and something crunchy like celery. To make this salad for one or two, the chicken leftovers are enough, but for 4 servings, you'll need a whole chicken. If you're roasting a chicken and know it will all get eaten, roast an extra one and serve this salad the next day, or use a preroasted chicken from the supermarket.

1 large red onion, sliced as thin as possible

1 tablespoon coarse salt (for softening the onion)

1 cold roasted, grilled, or poached chicken

½ cup [60 g] coarsely chopped walnut halves or whole pecan halves, toasted for 10 to 15 minutes in a 350°F [175°C/gas mark 4] oven

2 stalks celery, sliced about ¼ inch [.5 cm] thick

8 anchovy fillets (optional)

2 tablespoons chopped parsley or tarragon (chopped at the last minute; sprinkle tarragon with a few drops of olive oil to keep it from turning black)

½ cup [30 g] short tubular pasta such as macaroni or penne or orechiette, boiled according to package instructions and drained

3 tablespoons good-quality wine vinegar, such as sherry vinegar

6 tablespoons extra-virgin olive oil

salt

pepper

TOSS the onion with the coarse salt and rub the slices between your fingers for about 1 minute, until you don't feel any more salt. Drain the onion in a colander for 30 minutes to 1 hour.

PULL the chicken meat away from the carcass in strips. If the chicken was roasted or grilled, leave the skin on the meat. Otherwise, remove the skin and discard it.

SQUEEZE the onion slices tightly in your hands to extract as much liquid as possible. Toss the onion in a salad bowl with the chicken and the rest of the ingredients. You can also arrange the ingredients in the bowl in a decorative way and toss at the table. (If you're setting up the salad ahead of time, don't add the oil, walnuts, and vinegar until just before serving.)

Meat and Poultry Salad Variations:

Almost any cooked vegetable, and some raw ones, will provide a nice contrast to the richness of the meat. Green vegetables include string beans, asparagus (just the tips or the whole peeled stalk cut into sections or cubes), cucumber (seeded, sliced or julienned), artichokes (baby or large artichoke bottoms—see page 68—or bottled artichoke hearts, halved or cubed), avocados, celery (sliced or julienned), chiles (for spice), fennel (sliced thin with a vegetable peeler or cooked and cut into cubes or strips), fresh fava beans (shucked, blanched, and peeled—see page 65), peas (quickly blanched and refreshed if fresh; thawed, but not cooked, if frozen), zucchini (grilled—it doesn't have enough taste otherwise). Other vegetables could include bell peppers (grilled or roasted, peeled, cut into strips), carrots (julienned or diced, sweated gently in a little olive oil or left raw), celeriac (cut into small cubes or julienne), beets (roasted, then sliced, cubed, or julienned), garlic, mush-

rooms, salsify (peeled, rubbed with lemon, cut into sections, simmered until it has the texture of a cooked artichoke), and tomatoes (cut into wedges, seeded). And, of course, there are truffles. Few if any of us are going to toss them into a salad, but their flavor can be added in the form of oil or juice (see page 62).

Starchy Ingredients

ANY COMPOSED SALAD CAN BE STRETCHED with a starchy ingredient such as pasta or rice. The French have never been very fond of pasta salads, although *La Cuisine de Madame Saint-Ange,* the French equivalent to *Joy of Cooking,* offers a *salade de spaghetti* that includes cold chicken, ham, celery, artichoke hearts, a truffle, hard-boiled eggs, and parsley. I find the idea of cold long pasta a little creepy and prefer to use easier-to-manage short pasta, such as macaroni, penne, or orechiette. I also find that most pasta salads contain too much pasta and not enough bright, tasty ingredients to provide contrasting flavors, textures, and colors. I prefer to add relatively small amounts of cooked pasta to seafood or meat salads.

On the other hand, the French are very fond of rice salads, which appear in charcuteries throughout France as quick take-out side dishes. Most of the time these are very simple and inexpensive affairs: just cooked rice tossed with oil and little cubes of vegetables. I myself never set out to make a rice salad, but I do use leftover long-grain rice. I use basmati rice, which has not only a better flavor but also a firmer texture that prevents it from falling apart or getting gummy when it's tossed with other ingredients. Meats, poultry, vegetables, and seafood can all be tossed with rice in varying proportions—from a rice salad with a few little cubes of other ingredients tossed in to a meat or vegetable salad made fuller with a little rice.

ASSORTED COOKED VEGETABLES, HARD-BOILED EGGS, AND SALT COD WITH GARLIC MAYONNAISE

GRAND AÏOLI

HOW TO	HOW TO	HOT TO	HOW TO
COOK LEEKS AND CARDOONS	MAKE MAYONNAISE AND IMPROVISE YOUR OWN VARIATIONS	PREPARE SALT COD	MAKE A VARIETY OF SAUCES FOR VEGETABLES

MOST VEGETABLES ARE ADAPTABLE TO A VARIETY OF COOKING METHODS and take well to steaming, grilling, sautéing, or boiling. However you cook them, vegetables are inevitably enhanced by sauces such as compound butters, flavored mayonnaises (see Chapter 35), emulsified egg and butter sauces such as hollandaise or béarnaise sauce, or butter sauces such as beurre blanc and its derivatives (see page 281). But of all the sauces served with vegetables, garlic mayonnaise, *sauce aïoli,* is the most famous and is the focal point of the

Provençal *grand aïoli,* a traditional festival at which heaping platters of hot vegetables and other goodies such as poached salt cod and hard-boiled eggs are passed along with a big bowl or mortar full of aïoli for dolloping in obscene quantities on all of the above.

When I was living in San Francisco in the late 1970s, aïoli saved me. I had gone for several months without finding a job and as my diet approached the starvation level, I became an expert at making homemade pasta, sautéing chicken livers, and cooking squid. But my real coup was the Napa Valley extra-virgin olive oil sold at the local health food store for a dollar a quart if you brought your own jar. So I'd get my olive oil and a bagful of whatever vegetables were cheap and go home and have my own *grand aïoli,* minus the salt cod, which hadn't yet become fashionable and which I wouldn't have been able to afford anyway. You can really make a *grand aïoli* with anything you want, but I must warn you that you and your guests will find themselves able to eat massive quantities of the aïoli itself— so make a lot and for heaven's sake don't think about the calories. Because this dish is fun for a crowd, I like to make it for summer evenings. I often serve barbecued chicken or fish instead of the traditional poached salt cod. If you can't find all the vegetables listed below, just serve more of the others.

MEDITERRANEAN SAUCES

Southern French and other Mediterranean sauces are distinct from classic French sauces with their roux, concentrated stocks, and buttery emulsions. Most traditional Mediterranean sauces are pastes made by working various ingredients in a large mortar and pestle into what the French call a *pommade* and then spreading the sauces on cooked meats, seafood, or vegetables or whisking them into hot liquids such as fish soups, in the way aïoli is whisked into a bourride (see page 237) and *rouille* is whisked into a bouillabaisse (see page 236). In older recipes these sauces are held together by and get much of their substance from bread (often soaked in fish broth or milk) and are flavored with indigenous ingredients such as anchovies (often fermented—see page 168—or at least salted, used to make the sauce or condiment *anchoïade*), sea urchin roe (for *oursinade,* a magnificent thing), and olives, capers, and olive oil (for tapenade—see page 83). When New World ingredients were introduced into European cooking, cooked potatoes began to replace the bread, chiles were rapidly adopted for their flavor and color, and later, tomatoes were used. Egg yolks, probably through the influence of classic French cooking, are now often added, converting the original *pommades* into rustic forms of mayonnaise, giving them a smoother texture but also making them more vulnerable to heat—a *rouille* or virtually any sauce made with egg yolks can't be allowed to boil or the egg yolks will curdle (sauces containing a lot of flour are the exception).

ASSORTED COOKED VEGETABLES, HARD-BOILED EGGS, AND SALT COD WITH GARLIC MAYONNAISE

GRAND AÏOLI

MAKES 8 MAIN-COURSE SERVINGS

8 medium-size beets

8 medium-size white or red waxy potatoes, or 16 new or fingerling potatoes

8 eggs

salt

1 head cauliflower or broccoli

1 pound [450 g] string beans, preferably haricots verts, ends broken off

24 baby artichokes

2 tablespoons olive oil

8 medium-size carrots, peeled

pepper

2 pounds [900 g] salt cod, soaked for 24 to 36 hours, any bones or skin removed (see page 75); or freshly grilled fish, chicken, or meat; or cold chicken, fish, or meat

1 medium-size bouquet garni

4 cups (2 recipes) Garlic Mayonnaise (aïoli) (page 491)

BOIL the beets until they're easily penetrated with a skewer or knife, about 45 minutes. Drain, allow to cool slightly, and peel by pinching the peel between your thumb and the side of a paring knife and pulling it away in strips. Cut off stubborn patches with a knife. Cut into wedges or slice into rounds about ¼ inch [.5 cm] thick.

PUT the potatoes into a pot with enough cold water to cover and bring slowly to a simmer. Simmer until they're easily penetrated with a knife or skewer. If you're using new potatoes, you can leave the peel on. Otherwise, pull the peel away in strips.

PUT the eggs into a pot with enough cold water to cover, bring to a boil over high heat, and turn down the heat to maintain a gentle simmer. Simmer the eggs for 10 minutes from the time they reached the boil. Drain the eggs, cover them with cold water, and let cool for 5 minutes. Peel.

BRING a pot of water to a rapid boil and toss in a small handful of salt. Cut the cauliflower or broccoli into florets by first peeling away the green leaves at the base and then cutting around the core with a small knife. Boil the florets for about 3 minutes for broccoli or 5 minutes for cauliflower. Drain in a colander and rinse with cold water.

BRING another pot of water to a rapid boil, toss in salt, and boil the string beans until they just loose their crunch. Drain in a colander and rinse with cold water.

CUT the top one-third off the artichokes and rotate the artichokes against the blade of a sharp paring knife until you've trimmed any patches of dark green away from the hearts. Trim any dark patches off the ends of the stems. Peel the stems with a vegetable peeler. Put the artichokes in a nonaluminum pot with enough water to cover, a small handful of salt, and a tablespoon of olive oil (to keep them from turning dark). Bring to a gentle simmer and simmer for about 20 minutes, until the artichokes offer only slight resistance when poked with a skewer or paring knife. Drain in a colander and toss with the remaining olive oil.

ARRANGE the carrots in a skillet or straight-sided sauté pan just large enough to hold them in a single layer; cut them into 1-inch [2.5-cm] sections if they won't fit. Add enough water to come about one-third of the way up the sides of the carrots. Sprinkle with salt. Cover the carrots lightly with a round of parchment paper or aluminum foil, or partially cover the pan with its lid. Simmer about 20 minutes, until the carrots are cooked through and the water has evaporated. Be careful not to burn the carrots. Season with pepper.

IF you're serving salt cod, cut it into 8 equal pieces and put it into a pan just large enough to hold it. Add enough water to cover. Nestle the bouquet garni in and bring the water to a gentle simmer over medium heat. Simmer the cod for about 10 minutes per inch of thickness. Remove the cod pieces gently with a long spatula.

PASS the warm or cool vegetables, the seafood or meat, and bowls of the aïoli at the table. Encourage your guests to take a little (or a lot) of everything and a big dollop of aïoli. Serve lots of wine. In the summer, I serve a cool rosé and eat outside.

SALT COD

Cod swim in the north Atlantic, from Norway to Iceland to Newfoundland. I refer here to authentic Atlantic cod, *Gadus morhua*, and not to any of a number of southern and even freshwater relatives. According to Mark Kurlansky, in his revealing historical book *Cod*, it was the Basques who first salted cod in large quantities and marketed it in Europe. They weren't, however, fishing for cod in local waters or even in the European side of the north Atlantic, but off the coast of Newfoundland, where cod were especially abundant. And this was before Columbus "discovered" America.

Guillaume Taillevent, in his late-fourteenth-century classic *Le Viandier*, calls for cod, both salted and fresh, in various recipes.

Before refrigerators, trucks, and railroads, the only people who got to eat fresh fish were those who lived near the sea or who were rich enough to have fish brought to them, packed in expensive ice, pulled by a horse or tugged along in a canal. This lack of fresh fish required a far greater sacrifice than it would today, because until the twentieth century Catholics were forbidden to eat meat during Lent—a 40-day fast. So salt cod, which keeps well even without refrigeration, was popular in inland regions. And because of its special flavor, it was popular even in places where fresh fish was a year-round staple.

When shopping for salt cod, buy the thickest piece you can find—these pieces are sometimes called loins—sealed, vacuum-packed in plastic, preferably with the skin and bones already removed. If you can find only thin pieces, or chunks with the skin and bones still attached, these will still do fine; you just may have to soak them a while longer and cut away the skin and bones after soaking. Most salt cod available in the United States comes from Canada or Norway. Norwegian cod is cured twice as long as Canadian cod and, I think, has a better flavor.

When using cod, first soak it in cold water in the refrigerator for 36 to 48 hours, changing the water every 8 hours. The only way to tell if you've soaked it long enough is to cut off a piece, taste it, and see if it seems too salty. When it's done soaking it will have plumped up from the water it has absorbed. (If you want to mail-order salt cod, see Sources.)

Dishes based on salt cod can be found all over France. In the Périgord region cooked salt cod is mashed with potatoes, garlic, eggs, and walnut oil and baked into a kind of savory cake. In a Basque dish, *morue basquaise,* salt cod is simmered with onions, peppers, garlic, tomatoes, and herbs, and the cod is flaked and everything combined into a kind of coarse stew. In Provence, meaty chunks of salt cod are served *en raïto.* A *raïto* is a sauce made with red wine, tomatoes, aromatic vegetables, a big bouquet garni, and a few crushed walnuts. The sauce is thickened with roux, strained, and finished with chopped olives and capers. In Brittany, puréed beans replace the potatoes in a kind of *brandade* made with tuna preserved in brine instead of salt cod. The mixture is sprinkled with cheese and breadcrumbs and served as a *gratin.*

A long-popular treatment for salt cod involves mashing or flaking the fish—first soaked to rid it of its salt—and then working it into a paste with garlic, potatoes, and olive oil. *Brandade de morue,* from Provence or the Languedoc, is the best known of these potato/cod mixtures. (A number of food historians say brandade was invented in Nîmes, a city in the Rhone valley famous for its Roman ruins.)

PROVENÇAL POTATO AND SALT COD SPREAD

BRANDADE DE MORUE

MAKES ABOUT 60 HORS D'OEUVRES OR
8 FIRST-COURSE SERVINGS

I serve *brandade de morue* as a dip at cocktail parties or as a first course. In either situation, I serve toasted thin slices of baguette.

- 1 pound [450 g] center-cut fillet of salt cod, or a somewhat larger piece if skin and bones are still attached

- 1¼ pound [560 g] medium-starchy potatoes, such as Yukon Gold or Yellow Finn or russet, peeled

- 3 peeled garlic cloves (for the potatoes), plus 1 head of garlic cut crosswise in half

- 1 medium-size bouquet garni

- ½ cup [125 mL] milk or heavy cream

- ½ cup [125 mL] extra-virgin olive oil

  salt, if needed

  pepper

- 2 baguettes, cut into thin slices, slices toasted on one side only on a sheet pan under the broiler (to accompany the brandade)

SOAK the salt cod in cold water for 24 to 36 hours, changing the water and turning the cod over every 8 hours, until the cod no longer tastes salty when you nibble on a piece.

CUT the potatoes into about four pieces each, and put them in a pot with the garlic cloves and enough water to come about halfway up their sides. Cover the pot and simmer the potatoes until the potatoes and garlic are tender, about 25 minutes.

SIMMER the bouquet garni and the halves of whole garlic in enough water to cover the cod in a covered pot or pan, just large enough to hold the cod, for 20 minutes, to infuse the flavor of the garlic and herbs. Add the cod and simmer it until it is flaky, about 20 minutes. Drain the cod and garlic and discard the poaching liquid and bouquet garni.

DRAIN the potatoes and garlic, reserving the liquid, and work them through a food mill, drum sieve, or ricer. Use a wooden spoon to combine them with the cod and the milk in a mixing bowl for a rustic version, or use a food processor for 2 to 3 minutes (until smooth) for a finer consistency. Work in the olive oil. If the mixture seems too stiff—it should have the consistency of mashed potatoes—work in a little of the reserved potato-cooking liquid. Peel the reserved garlic halves, purée, and add to taste. Season to taste with salt and pepper. Serve with the toasted slices of baguette.

Vinaigrette and Other Sauces for Vegetables

MUCH OF THE GENIUS BEHIND FRENCH cooking rests in its sauces, which have the magical ability to transform the simplest foods into something far more tempting than they would be otherwise. Most of us restrict our use of vinaigrette to tossing with a green salad, but vinaigrette is also delicious with asparagus, artichokes, and best of all, leeks. While vinaigrette is best served with cold vegetables, hollandaise and its derivatives are best dolloped on vegetables that are hot. The most famous is *sauce mal-*

taise—hollandaise made with orange juice—on top of asparagus, but hollandaise and its relative sauce, *mousseline,* which is made by folding whipped cream with hollandaise, can go with artichokes, steamed green vegetables such as broccoli, and even root vegetables such as beets. *Bagna caouda* is made by dipping assorted vegetables into a hot sauce made with olive oil, garlic, anchovy paste, and, in my own version, a little heavy cream and truffle oil.

LEEKS WITH VINAIGRETTE

POIREAUX EN VINAIGRETTE

MAKES 4 FIRST-COURSE SERVINGS

At one time leeks were called the poor man's asparagus. This may still be true in France, where asparagus have a short season and come to market fat and white and tied up with purple ribbon, and sell for a small fortune. But in America the reverse seems to be true. Asparagus have lost their cachet and can be found not just in spring but year-round, even at Christmastime dinners, while leeks, which like shallots still have gourmet-cook connotations, remain pricey. And unless my asparagus are big and thick and in season, I'd rather eat leeks anyway.

In the winter I serve leeks in a rich creamy gratin (see page 575), but the rest of the year I prefer them as a first course, doused with a mustardy vinaigrette, the way they're served in half of Paris's corner bistros—at least those without pretensions of being anything else. Few dishes are easier to make. The leeks are trimmed and boiled in lots of salted water, rinsed and patted dry, and served with the vinaigrette. This is one of the few occasions when I actually set out to make a vinaigrette instead of just tossing the item in question with vinegar and oil, as I do the green salads in Chapter 2. I do this because I want the oil and vinegar to be well integrated with the mustard into a sauce that won't separate on the plate. And because the sauce contains mustard, the French use *huile d'arachide*, a version of peanut oil that has virtually no taste and really just functions as a medium for the mustard and vinegar. There are of course those of us who use olive oil for just about everything, but because of the mustard, which clashes with the flavor of olives, I stick to French tradition and use the closest thing I can find to *huile d'arachide*, "pure" olive oil (see page 36), canola oil, or safflower oil. I don't use American peanut oil because of its peanut taste. You can prepare the leeks earlier the same day and keep them in the refrigerator. But take them out at least an hour before serving—they should be cool but not cold.

salt

6 medium-size leeks, or 12 small leeks

1 medium-size shallot, chopped fine

½ cup (1 recipe) Mustard Vinaigrette (page 79)

1 tablespoon finely chopped parsley (chopped at the last minute; see page 110 for more information about parsley)

BRING about 4 quarts [4 l] of water with a small handful of salt to a rapid boil.

CUT the hairy roots off the ends of the leeks, but be careful not to cut too far into the white of the leek or it will fall apart. Cut off all but 1 inch of the green. (You can use the greens for broths.) Cut the leeks in half lengthwise.

RINSE the leek halves by holding them at a slant under cold running water with the root end facing up. If the root end is held lower and the end where you cut off the greens held higher, sand will be forced down into the leek and you'll never get it out. Fold back each layer of leek and rub it between your thumb and forefinger under the running water to dislodge any sand or grit. Tie the leeks up into 2 bundles with string to keep them from falling apart while they're cooking.

PUT the leeks in the boiling water and boil for about 15 minutes, until they're tender but not mushy. To test for doneness, fish out a bunch with a slotted spoon, pull out one of the leeks, cut off a small piece, and bite into it. Drain the leeks in a colander and rinse them under cold running water. Take the leek halves, one at a time, and press them between your two flattened hands to force out water.

STIR the shallot into the mustard vinaigrette.

PUT the leeks into a mixing bowl and pour most of the mustard vinaigrette over them. Gently stir the leeks around in the vinaigrette with your hands. Arrange the leeks in neat rows on plates and spoon another tablespoon of mustard vinaigrette on top. Sprinkle each serving with parsley.

Variations: Apart from varying the sauce, there's very little you can do to change a plate of leeks in vinaigrette. Michel Trama, at his restaurant in Puymirol, a village in western France, packs the cooked leeks into a terrine, chills it thoroughly, removes the molded mass of leeks and slices it, and then garnishes it with slices of black truffles, a few specks of *fleur de sel* (see page 598), and a mustardless vinaigrette made with sherry vinegar, truffle juice, and puréed fresh truffles, the puréed truffles replacing the mustard as the emulsifier. I like to serve leeks *en geleé* by braising them in just enough concentrated chicken or veal broth to cover and, unless the broth's sparklingly clear already, clarifying the broth as though making consommé (see Chapter 16). I add chopped chives (or chopped wild mushrooms or truffles) to the *geleé* before it sets and serve the leeks at the table, molded in a terrine with the *gelée*. If Michel Trama's truffle vinaigrette isn't in the budget, try dried morels, soaked in a little Madeira that has been simmered to cook off the alcohol—some of the morels puréed and used instead of mustard in the vinaigrette, others used as a garniture atop the leeks. Dried cèpes (porcini), soaked in a little of the vinegar destined for the vinaigrette and then pureed into the vinaigrette, add a marvelous flavor and replace the mustard. If you're making any vinaigrette in which a vegetable purée, such as tomato, mushroom, roasted garlic, roasted onion, or cooked green vegetable, is used instead of mustard as the emulsifier, you can use extra-virgin olive oil instead of a tasteless vegetable oil. (See page 374 for vegetable purée recipes.) Again, truffle oil could come into play.

Combine 2 tablespoons Dijon mustard with 1 tablespoon good-quality wine vinegar and slowly whisk in 4 tablespoons canola oil or safflower oil. Grind in some fresh pepper.

ASPARAGUS WITH MALTAISE SAUCE

ASPERGES À LA SAUCE MALTAISE

MAKES 6 FIRST-COURSE SERVINGS

Asparagus with *sauce maltaise*, a hollandaise made with the juice of blood oranges, is an example of one of those combinations, discovered a century or more ago, that are so perfect they need never be changed.

The French revere asparagus far more than we Americans do, and when the short season arrives in the spring, they pay dearly for those glorious fat white spikes, whose flavor and meaty texture put our poor omnipresent stalks to shame. When I worked at Paris's then-three-star Vivarois, they let me prepare the *sauce maltaise*, but I was far too inept to be trusted with the asparagus, which were carefully peeled with a knife. (American asparagus stalks have a thinner skin and can be peeled with a vegetable peeler; see page 67.) The asparagus were cooked in boiling salted water minutes before the restaurant opened and kept in a warming oven until needed. While this works in a classic French restaurant where everyone arrives at once, don't try holding cooked asparagus for more than an hour. In fact, it's best to cook asparagus at the last minute.

The Maltaise sauce is nothing more than a hollandaise in which reduced orange juice infused with some of the zests replaces or augments the lemon juice. I like the acidity the lemon provides. You don't have to use blood oranges for the juice, although the colorful effect is more dramatic. I never serve asparagus as a side dish. In the spring, when I can find them at the farmers' market, I search out the thickest, meatiest stalks I can find and serve them as a first course, with the luxurious buttery sauce passed at the table. The asparagus can be peeled earlier the same day and kept in the refrigerator covered with a damp towel.

30 fat asparagus stalks, or 2 bunches (1 pound each) smaller stalks

    salt

2 blood oranges or regular juicing oranges

1½ cups (1 recipe) hollandaise sauce (see page 257)

    freshly ground white pepper

CUT about 1 inch [1.5 cm]—the woody part—away from the base of each of the asparagus stalks. Peel the stalks. Bring about 4 quarts [4 l] of water with a small handful of salt to a rapid boil.

WHILE the water's coming to the boil, cut about three 2-inch-long [5 cm] strips of zest off the side of one of the oranges, using a knife or a zester. If you've used a knife, cut the zest into fine julienne. Squeeze the juice out of the oranges and strain it into a saucepan. Boil it down to about ¼ cup [60 ml]. Add the orange zests and simmer for 2 minutes more.

PREPARE the hollandaise sauce and stir in the orange-juice mixture. Season to taste with salt and pepper. Keep warm but not hot, or the sauce will curdle.

BOIL the asparagus, uncovered, until a stalk retains only the barest hint of crunch when tested—5 to 10 minutes, depending on its thickness. Drain the asparagus in a colander and, without rinsing, transfer to heated plates. Pass the sauce in a sauce boat at the table.

Variations: Asparagus can be steamed, grilled (brush it with a little bunch of thyme dipped in olive oil), or roasted (coat it with olive oil or butter), but the most dramatic variations have to do with the sauce. I sometimes make a *sauce mousseline,* by folding whipped cream into a hollandaise sauce. The effect is light, frothy, and luxurious.

While all hollandaise sauce relatives make perfect accompaniments to virtually any category of food—vegetable, seafood, or meat—they also terrify people because they're based on butter and egg yolks. (I know this is so because I watch students gaping in horror when I demonstrate them during my cooking classes.) A number of chefs have tried to get around this problem by lightening hollandaise-type sauces in various ways. One method, popularized by Michel Guérard in the 1970s, is to simply add less butter to the frothy *sabayon* created in the first step of making a hollandaise, resulting in a sauce that contains a higher proportion of air. I use this same technique, but replace whole or clarified butter with *beurre noisette* (see page 545), which has a more intense butter flavor and allows you to get by using less. Other chefs, especially those in the south of France, replace the butter in traditional hollandaise-type sauces with olive oil (similar, in fact, to a classic *sauce tyrolienne,* but with less oil so the sauce stays airier and lighter) or, in the southwest, with goose or duck fat. *Foie gras* fat—the yellow fat on top of a terrine of *foie gras,* see page 97—is a spectacular finish to any emulsified egg yolk sauce. The trick with any of these approaches is to use a particular fat as a flavoring but to use less of it, so the sauce is lighter but still has plenty of flavor.

ANCHOVY AND GARLIC SAUCE WITH MIXED VEGETABLES

BAGNA CAOUDA

MAKES ENOUGH FOR 6 FIRST-COURSE SERVINGS

I'm using the spelling—*bagna caouda*—that Jacques Médecin uses in his book La Cuisine Niçoise, but more often than not this warm anchovy-and-garlic sauce is called by its Piemontese name, *bagna cauda.* However you spell it, it doesn't take much to figure out that it means, literally, hot bath. Most recipes call for heating puréed anchovy fillets and garlic in a mixture of butter and olive oil and dipping various raw vegetables—cardoons are a favorite—in the warm sauce as an hors d'oeuvre. Italian recipes, again from the Piedmont, occasionally call for a sliced or chopped white truffle, a natural companion to garlic and anchovies but not always available or affordable. Because traditional recipes for *bagna caouda* garlic-anchovy sauce call for first cooking the garlic in butter or oil and then adding more butter or oil, the sauce inevitably separates. Some recipes solve this problem by including an egg yolk in the sauce, thereby turning it into a mayonnaise. But because egg yolks curdle if they get too hot, I prefer to emulsify the ingredients so that they produce a creamy sauce, by first reducing some heavy cream, whisking in butter, whisking in olive oil (which is then held in an emulsion by the cream) or even truffle oil, and then finishing the sauce with a garlic and anchovy paste.

Sauces similar to aïoli and the sauce used for *bagna caouda* are the Catalan allioli (made by slowly working oil into puréed garlic, without egg yolks) or a *sauce aillade* from Toulouse (made by working oil into a paste of garlic and walnuts), cousins of the southern French aïoli. An aïoli, however, contains egg yolks and is hence a mayonnaise, while authentic alliou, *sauce aillade,* and *bagna caouda* do not. (I have read about a Provençal aïloh sans oeufs—

an eggless aïoli—but I've never encountered one.) Most versions of *bagna caouda* I find in restaurants are actually mayonnaises, and while they're not bad, they're little more than aïoli containing anchovy purée, a mixture sometimes called an *anchoïade.*

Regulating the temperature for the sauce for a *bagna caouda* can sometimes be a problem. If the sauce gets too hot, the fragile emulsion will break and the oil will lose its savor, and you'll start frying the vegetables, which isn't the point at all. I sometimes use a fondue dish with a flame tamer between the flame and the dish and turn off the flame when the sauce starts to get hot. Or I serve the sauce in a porcelain dish and put it in the microwave for a just few seconds if it cools off too much before everyone has finished. If all this toying around with the temperature of the sauce is just too much, serve the sauce at room temperature; the dish then becomes a traditional *bagna fredda.*

Serve plenty of crusty French bread with *bagna caouda.* The bread isn't for dipping but for holding under the vegetables as you move them, dripping with sauce, from pot to mouth.

While *bagna caouda* is traditionally used as a warm dip, I sometimes use it as a warm salad sauce, and instead of leaving the vegetables in large pieces, I slice them thin, pass them at the table, and let guests dollop the hot sauce over them. Ultimate luxury: Instead of adding grated raw white truffles to the sauce as the Italians do, slice the truffles over the servings of vegetables after having dolloped the sauce.

FOR THE SAUCE:

- 12 anchovy fillets (packed in olive oil), drained, chopped fine
- 2 large cloves garlic, chopped fine
- ⅔ cup [150 ml] heavy cream
- 6 tablespoons butter, in 6 pieces, cold
- 1 cup [250 ml] extra-virgin olive oil
- 1 tablespoon truffle oil (optional)

THE VEGETABLES (AS MANY OR AS FEW AS YOU LIKE):

baby artichokes

broccoli

cardoons

cauliflower

celery

fennel

lettuce leaves from crisp varieties, such as romaine

mushrooms

radishes

scallions, root end cut off

TO PREPARE THE SAUCE

CRUSH the anchovies and garlic to a paste by working them over, back and forth, with the side of a chef's knife.

BOIL the cream for about 2 minutes in a saucepan to reduce it slightly. Turn down the heat and whisk in the butter, keeping the sauce hot but not boiling. When all the butter is in, whisk in the olive oil, pouring in a thin but even stream. Whisk in the anchovy paste mixture. Add truffle oil, if using. Keep the sauce over very low heat while serving.

TO PREPARE THE VEGETABLES

BABY ARTICHOKES: Unlike the baby artichokes available in Provence, American baby artichokes need to be trimmed and precooked (see page 68), in which case they can be dipped whole in the sauce, or they can just be trimmed and sliced raw, paper thin, at the last minute with a vegetable slicer and tossed in lemon juice (to prevent blackening), so guests can put the slices on their plates and dollop the sauce on them instead of dipping.

BROCCOLI OR CAULIFLOWER: If you're using cauliflower, pull off any leaves attached at the base and cut around the core, detaching the florets. You can make the broccoli or cauliflower florets any size you want by cutting through their base in one or more places, but I like them about 1 inch [2.5 cm] wide at the floret end.

CARDOONS: In America it's hard to find the baby cardoons sold in Italy and the south of France. Cardoons show up here in the fall, looking like giant, rather scraggly celery. They're related to artichokes (both are in the thistle family), and because they turn dark in the same way when exposed to air, they should be cooked with a little lemon juice and oil. To prepare them, pull away and discard the outermost ribs or any pieces that are limp or dark—be careful when handling cardoons, because they prick. When you've removed the outermost ribs, pull away the inner ribs as though taking apart a bunch of celery and peel them on the outside with a vegetable peeler to eliminate the tough outer fibers. Cut the ribs into 2-inch [5-cm] sections and simmer them in water with a little lemon juice and olive oil in a nonaluminum pan as you would artichokes, for about 20 minutes, until they've lost most but not all of their texture. Drain them and pass them at the table while they're still warm.

CELERY: Just dip celery stalks in the *bagna caouda*.

FENNEL: You can use fennel in a *bagna caouda* in two ways. Regardless of which method you use, cut the stalks and fronds off the bulb and peel the stringy fibers away from the outside of the bulb with a vegetable peeler. You can cut the bulb into thin wedges by first cutting it in half vertically, through the core at the bottom, and then cutting each half into thin wedges, being sure to leave part of the core attached to each wedge so the wedges don't fall apart. These wedges can then be dipped in the *bagna caouda*. My own favorite approach is to shave the fennel paper thin with a vegetable slicer and then dollop the sauce on the slices to produce a kind of instant savory salad.

LETTUCE: The lettuce leaves can be put on each person's plate so that they catch the dipping sauce.

MUSHROOMS: Depending on their size, leave the mushrooms whole or cut them vertically in quarters.

RADISHES: Leave whole, except for an inch of green that guests can use as a handle. If the radishes are very large, slice them thinly—a plastic vegetable slicer works well for this—and have guests spoon the sauce over the slices on their plates instead of trying to dip.

SCALLIONS: Leave whole for dipping.

PASS the sauce and vegetables with plenty of crusty bread and cool wine.

HOW THE FRENCH COOK VEGETABLES

The French cook green vegetables by plunging them in boiling salted water (*à l'anglaise*, English style) and draining them as soon as they're done; by cooking them slowly covered with butter until soft and sullen gray (*à la française*, French style); by steaming; or by simmering, partially covered, with a little olive oil and lemon juice, a method used for vegetables, such as artichokes, cardoons, or salsify, that turn black when exposed to air. Traditional recipes also include flour with the lemon and olive oil, turning the cooking liquid into what is referred to as a *blanc*.

Root vegetables require different methods and, unless cooked with the peel on, should not be boiled *à l'anglaise*, which would leach out their natural sugars and flavor. Root vegetables such as turnips, carrots, celeriac, potatoes, and parsnips can be peeled, tossed with a little melted butter, and roasted. Roasting evaporates the water contained in the vegetable and concentrates its flavor. Root vegetables, though not potatoes, can be glazed in a small amount of liquid, which, like roasting, concentrates their flavor. (For more about glazing vegetables, see Chapter 40.)

The anchovies in a *bagna caouda* were once (and perhaps somewhere still are) replaced by a paste, called *pissala*, made by layering gutted and beheaded baby anchovies and sardines with salt, cloves, bay leaves, thyme, and lots of pepper and stirring the mixture every day for a month before working it through a drum sieve to eliminate bones. (The resulting mixture sounding suspiciously similar to the garum, a condiment popular in ancient Rome.) The Niçoise-style pizza called *pissaladière* (see Chapter 12) gets its name from *pissala* because in original versions the dough was spread with *pissala* before the onions were added. I'm not giving a recipe for *pissala* because it requires baby anchovies and sardines of impeccable freshness, which can be hard to find even in France. But a recipe can be found in Jacques Médicin's book, which has been translated into English, *Cuisine Niçoise*.

OLIVE AND CAPER SPREAD

TAPÉNADE

MAKES 2 CUPS [500 ML], ENOUGH FOR
HORS D'OEUVRES FOR 8 (OR MORE IF YOU'RE ALSO
SERVING OTHER HORS D'OEUVRES)

Tapenade (from the Provençal word *tapeno*, meaning caper) is one of the most versatile and delicious of southern French condiments, and apart from the necessity of pitting a bunch of olives, it is also one of the easiest. I suppose to be authentic it should be made with niçoise olives, but because niçoise olives are so small that pitting them takes forever, I use larger black olives from other parts of France, such as Nyons olives from the Drôme and the Vaucluse, or Gaeta olives from Italy, Kalamata olives from Greece, or oil-cured wrinkly olives from Morocco. Tapenade can be used as a salad sauce (see Provençal Tapenade salad, page 84), but I like to serve it with apéritifs, on toasted thin slices of baguette or on crackers. While some cooks add dried figs to their tapenade, I used dried currants. Either way, the sweetness gently balances the saltiness of all the other ingredients.

1 pound [450 g] imported large black olives (not canned olives)

3 heaping tablespoons small nonpareil capers, rinsed

12 anchovy fillets packed in oil, soaked in cold water for 5 minutes, patted dry

¼ cup [35 g] dried currants or raisins, soaked in ½ cup [125 ml] cold water for 15 minutes, drained

3 cloves garlic, chopped fine, crushed to a paste with the side of a chef's knife

¼ cup [60 ml] extra-virgin olive oil, or more as needed to give the tapenade the texture you like

PIT the olives by squeezing them on each end between your thumb and forefinger to get the pit to slide out. If this doesn't work, cut them along one side with a small knife and pull out the pit.

CHOP the olives, capers, anchovies, and currants into a coarse paste with the texture of hamburger relish; you can either use a chef's knife or pulse the mixture in a food processor, scraping down the sides several times with a rubber spatula. Don't work the mixture to a smooth paste, as is often done in restaurants, or the flavors will meld and the tapenade won't be as interesting. Stir in the garlic and olive oil. Serve on baguette toasts or crackers.

PROVENÇAL TAPENADE SALAD

SALADE PROVENÇALE

MAKES 8 FIRST-COURSE SERVINGS

This simple salad, from Austin de Croze's classic *Les Plats Régionaux de France*, published in the 1920s, is an example of how tapenade can be used as a salad sauce.

- 8 medium-size new potatoes (about 2 pounds total)
- ½ cup [125 ml] extra-virgin olive oil
- 6 medium-size tomatoes, stemmed and peeled (see page 42)
- 1 cup [250 ml] (½ recipe) Olive and Caper Spread (tapenade) (page 83)
- 2 tablespoons chopped parsley (chopped at the last minute)

PUT the potatoes in a pot with enough water to cover and bring to a gentle simmer over medium heat. When the potatoes are cooked through, so that they offer only slight resistance when you poke them with a paring knife, drain them and, while they're still hot, pull away the peels in strips with a paring knife while holding the potato in a towel. Cut the potatoes in half lengthwise and gently toss with the olive oil; it's best to use your hands for this so you don't break up the potatoes.

CUT the tomatoes into wedges so you get about 8 wedges out of each tomato. Push the seeds out of each wedge by sliding the tip of your forefinger along the side of the wedge.

COMBINE the potatoes, tomatoes, and tapenade and sprinkle with parsley. Toss gently, again using your hands, to combine the ingredients. Serve immediately. Ideally, the potatoes will still be slightly warm.

COUNTRY-STYLE PORK PÂTÉ

TERRINE DE CAMPAGNE

ONE OF MY FIRST EXPERIENCES WITH FRENCH FOOD WAS A SLICE OF pâté my parents brought home from a dinner party. Always ready to try anything that smacked of elegance or extravagance and having had several positive experiences with dinner party leftovers, I eagerly took a bite, awaiting new heights of flavor. But, alas, the pâté, which looked so glorious in its golden crust, tasted like meat loaf. And while I've always enjoyed meat loaf, I was left wondering what all the fuss was about. Later in life, when slices of pâté appeared, along with the obligatory wedges of Brie, at every cocktail party, I began to appreciate pâté as a filling snack, but little else. Revelation didn't come until I worked in a restaurant in Paris where we made thrush pâté. Large wicker baskets of thrushes would arrive in the early morning, and it was my job to pluck them and scrape the meat from their little bones. A day's work would yield about a quart of meat, which was turned into a pâté. The pâté still stands out as one of the most delicious things I've ever tasted. Fortunately for thrushes, such extravagant use of innocent little birds is no longer permitted; fortunately for lovers of good food, there are other ways to make great pâté.

Even though the two terms are often used interchangeably, there's a difference between a pâté and a terrine. Technically, a pâté has a crust and a terrine—named after the container, often made of glazed earthenware, in which it is baked—doesn't. (In the recipes that follow, the terms "terrine" and "terrine mold" are used interchangeably to refer to the container.) Because nowadays the word "pâté" is often used loosely to mean either one, the French now call an authentic pâté (one with a crust) a *pâté en croûte*. While a *pâté en croûte* may look more dramatic, I prefer crustless pâtés, called terrines, because the meats in either a *pâté en croûte* or a terrine release liquid as they cook, and as a result the pastry crust of a *pâté en croûte* becomes dense and soggy, whereas any liquid released in a terrine is trapped inside with the meat.

The simplest terrines are, in fact, made in the same way as meat loaf, except that ground pork replaces ground beef and a fair amount of pork fat (at least one-third of the total) is included in the mixture to keep it moist and to help hold it together. Seasonings, usually spices (*quatre-épices*, a mixture of white pepper, cloves, powdered ginger, and nutmeg; see page 386), garlic, cooked shallots or onions, and herbs (usually thyme), salt, and pepper are worked into the mixture. The mixture is packed into a terrine mold lined with sheets of fatback (unsmoked unsalted fatty bacon, see page 10), caul fat (see page 8), or occasionally bacon, and baked, in a pan of hot water called a bain-marie. When the terrine comes out of the oven, a cutting board or other flat-bottomed object is placed on top and the terrine weighted while it cools to hold it together and keep it from crumbling when sliced. Because such a version takes so little effort, the first recipe in this chapter is for the simplest country pâté.

If you want to take your terrines out of the realm of the ordinary and make something better than you could ever buy, you must make certain refinements. The secret to the best terrines is a continuous variation in texture and flavor as you savor a bite. Because this effect is impossible to achieve by just grinding everything together, you have to divide up the ingredients for the terrine and then flavor and chop them in different ways. First, you need a smooth and flavorful forcemeat—essentially a meat purée—to hold the terrine together and to provide a melting background texture. I usually base this mixture on pork, pork fat (fatback), chicken livers, seasonings, and bread crumbs soaked in reduced broth or, in a pinch, in milk. French *charcutiers* use pork liver, but pork livers are a nuisance to track down. The bread crumbs lighten the forcemeat; the reduced broth contributes depth of flavor, and the gelatin it contains helps hold the terrine together. You can make this smooth forcemeat by puréeing the ingredients (except the soaked bread crumbs) in a food processor. Second, I make a coarse mixture of chopped raw meat such as pork and veal, trimmings from whatever animal is being featured (such as chopped duck legs for a duck terrine), and often prosciutto. I chop these ingredients to the consistency of hamburger relish, either by hand with a very sharp chef's knife or by getting them very cold in the freezer and then pulsing them, a bit at a time, in a food processor. I don't use a meat grinder because it pulls and tears the flesh, turning the meat into a paste instead of leaving it in small discrete pieces. If I'm going all-out, I may season or marinate each of the different meats differently—one may get soaked in a little Madeira, another in port, another tossed with chopped fresh marjoram and chopped garlic. Third, there is what the French call the *garniture*: cubes, strips, or chunks of lean meat, fatback, pistachios, truffles, or foie gras, cut by hand and layered into the terrine, again to provide flavor and texture but also to give each slice a colorful checkerboard pattern.

COUNTRY-STYLE PORK PÂTÉ

TERRINE DE CAMPAGNE

MAKES ABOUT 10 FIRST-COURSE SERVINGS

(A 1-QUART [1 L] TERRINE)

This is the simplest possible terrine because you (or your butcher) just grind all the ingredients for the filling together in a meat grinder or in a food processor, push the mixture down into the terrine, and bake it. Ideally, the terrine should be porcelain or enameled iron (see Sources), but a metal loaf pan will work in a pinch. The only possible problem is tracking down the right kind of fat for the filling and to use for lining the terrine. In French charcuteries, terrines are lined with thin sheets of fatback, which is unsmoked, unsalted bacon with no streaks of lean. Making terrines at home is unusual in France, since everyone has access to a wide assortment of terrines and pâtés at the charcuterie. But when terrines are made in French home kitchens, caul fat (the netlike lining of the pig's abdomen; see page 8) is used in place of fatback. In America, especially if you don't have a butcher used to eccentric requests, asking for either of these will get you a funny look. Ask first for fatback (not salt pork) and then ask the butcher, in the most charming way, to slice it into thin sheets on his electric meat slicer. If you can't get the butcher to slice the fatback, you can slice it yourself. Don't try to cut it crosswise in sheets, since that is very difficult to do by hand, but cut off the rind and slice the fat into long slices as you would with slab bacon, making the slices as thin as you can. The fatback will be easier to slice if you put it in the freezer for 20 minutes beforehand. If you can't find fatback, ask for caul fat. The butcher may have to order it and will probably have to order more than you or he will need. But caul fat is cheap and keeps well in the freezer, so, as long as your freezer has room, be willing to take more than the recipe calls for. If you can't find caul fat or fatback, use strips of bacon to line the terrine, but not in the filling. They will give your terrine a smoky taste, which isn't really bad but which does reinforce the meat loaf associations.

Terrines will keep (and improve) for at least 3 weeks in the refrigerator, as long as you don't peel the foil off when they come out of the oven.

- 1 pound [450 g] pork shoulder meat or pork butt, or 1½ pounds [675 g] bone-in pork shoulder chops

- ¾ pound [350 g] fatback (not including the rind), slightly more if the rind is attached, or ½ pound [225 g] caul fat, or ¾ pound [350 g] thin-sliced bacon

- ¼ pound [115 g] chicken livers, cleaned and rinsed

- 2 large eggs

- 2 cloves garlic, chopped fine, crushed to a paste with the side of a chef's knife

- 1 tablespoon finely chopped fresh thyme, or 2 teaspoons dried thyme, finely crumbled

- 2 teaspoons fine salt

- 2 teaspoons freshly ground black pepper

- ½ teaspoon ground cloves

- ½ teaspoon ground ginger

- ¼ teaspoon ground nutmeg

- 1 tablespoon olive oil

- ½ pound [225 g] fatback (not including the rind), slightly more if the rind is attached, sliced into thin sheets, or ½ pound [225 g] caul fat, or ½ pound [225 g] thinly sliced bacon, for lining the terrine

CUT the pork shoulder into 1-inch [2.5 cm] cubes and chill it in the freezer until it's almost frozen. If you're using pork shoulder chops, which are easier to find, cut the meat away from the bone, cut it into cubes, and chill it in the same way. Chop the pork shoulder in a food processor using the pulse mechanism until it has the consistency of hamburger relish. Cut the rind off the fatback. (You can freeze the rind and use it in stews and braised dishes.) Cut the fat into 1-inch [2.5 cm] cubes and purée them in the food processor, with the chicken livers, until smooth. Use a wooden spoon to combine the chopped pork, the chicken liver mixture, and the eggs, garlic, thyme, salt, and spices in a mixing bowl until all the ingredients are evenly distributed. Form a walnut-size piece of the filling into a small patty and sauté it, like a hamburger, in the olive oil. Taste it and adjust the seasoning, adding more salt or pepper or herbs or spices as needed.

LINE the terrine with a single layer of fatback sheets, caul fat, or bacon, leaving enough hanging over the two long sides to fold over and cover the top of the terrine once it is filled. The fatback should overlap on top by about ½ inch [1.5 cm]. (The 1-quart terrine I use for this recipe is porcelain and measures 10 by 3½ by 3½ inches [25.5 by 8.5 by 9 cm].) Add the filling.

PUSH down on the filling and rap the terrine firmly, but not too hard, on a cutting board (not on a tile counter) to settle the filling and eliminate any air pockets. Fold the sheets of fat over the top of the terrine, completely covering the filling. Make a triple-layer sheet of aluminum foil large enough to fit over the top of the terrine with a couple of extra inches on each side. Press the foil down on top of the terrine and seal it firmly around the sides.

HEAT the oven to 350°F [175°C/gas mark 4] and place the terrine in a baking pan or shallow pot large enough to hold the water that will surround the terrine. The water bath keeps the terrine from overheating and helps it cook evenly. Place the baking pan with the terrine in the oven and pour hot tap water into the pan until the water comes two-thirds of the way up the sides of the terrine. I use a teakettle to pour in the water. Bake the terrine until an instant-read thermometer stuck into the center of the foil reads 145°F [62°C], about 1½ hours, depending on the shape of your terrine. The juices that run out of the hole should be clear, not pink.

PUT the terrine on a sheet pan to catch any fat that may drip down its sides, and place a small cutting board on top of the terrine and put a can or heavy saucepan on top. If, however, the top of the filling doesn't protrude above the rim of the terrine, the cutting board will be ineffective. Instead, you can use several layers of cardboard, cut to the inside size of the terrine and stacked together and wrapped in aluminum foil, before putting on the weight. Let the terrine cool for a couple of hours at room temperature and then place it in the refrigerator, with the weight still on, for at least 12 hours, after which you can remove the weight, or up to 3 weeks well wrapped. (Once you unwrap the terrine, you should serve it within several days.)

IF you've lined the terrine mold with caul fat, unmold the whole terrine and peel and cut away the caul fat before slicing the terrine into ¼-inch to ½-inch [.5 cm to 1.5 cm] slices. If you've lined the mold with fatback, you can slice the terrine in it and let guests peel away the fat that surrounds each slice. (The fat isn't eaten.) Pass a bowl of cornichons and some mustard.

DUCK TERRINE

TERRINE DE CANARD

MAKES ABOUT 20 FIRST-COURSE SERVINGS

(A 2-LITER TERRINE)

In this duck terrine, a fine forcemeat—a purée of meat, fat, and chicken livers—provides a smooth texture and deep meaty flavor, keeps the terrine moist, and acts as a binder to hold it together. Coarsely chopped duck meat and prosciutto contribute texture and bright bits of flavor. Strips of duck breast, fatback, and bright green pistachios vary the flavor and provide color and contrasting textures. A concentrated broth made from the duck trimmings is combined with bread crumbs and worked into the fine forcemeat to lighten the terrine and contribute more flavor. If you want to skip this step, which admittedly makes for more work, moisten the bread crumbs with milk or good chicken broth instead.

FOR THE DUCK BROTH (OPTIONAL):

    carcass of a 5-lb duck used in the main recipe, with breasts and whole legs removed

2 tablespoons olive oil

1 small onion, peeled and halved

1 small bouquet garni

1 quart [1 l] chicken broth or water (or ⅔ cup [150 ml] milk or ⅔ cup [150 ml] concentrated chicken broth)

FOR THE GARNITURE:

6 ounces [170 g] fatback, not including rind, or slightly more (about 9 ounces [255 g]) if the rind is attached

1 small clove garlic, finely chopped, crushed to a paste with the side of a chef's knife

2 tablespoons Cognac

2 duck breasts, about 8 ounces each

¼ cup semidry Madeira or port (optional)

FOR THE FINE FORCEMEAT:

¼ pound [115 g] chicken livers (2 whole livers)

1 duck liver

6 ounces [170 g] pork shoulder meat, or one ¾-pound [350 g] pork shoulder chop, boned; meat cut into 1-inch [2.5 cm] cubes

6 ounces [170 g] fatback, not including rind, cut into ½-inch [1.5 cm] cubes

2 large eggs

2 large cloves garlic, finely chopped, crushed to a paste with the side of a chef's knife

1 teaspoon finely chopped fresh thyme, or ½ teaspoon dried

2 teaspoons freshly ground black pepper

½ teaspoon ground cloves

½ teaspoon ground ginger

¼ teaspoon ground nutmeg

the reduced duck broth (see below), if you're making the broth, or ⅔ cup [150 ml] milk or good chicken broth

4 slices dense-crumb white bread such as Pepperidge Farm, crusts removed

FOR THE COARSE FORCEMEAT:

2 duck legs

6 ounces [170 g] prosciutto

½ cup shelled pistachios (2 ounces [150 g] by weight)

1 teaspoon finely chopped fresh marjoram (optional)

FOR TESTING THE TERRINE MIXTURE:

1 tablespoon olive oil

FOR ASSEMBLING THE TERRINE:

¾ pound [350 g] fatback without the rind, sliced into thin sheets, or ½ pound [225 g] caul fat, or ¾ pound [350 g] thin-sliced bacon

TO PREPARE THE OPTIONAL DUCK BROTH

CHOP the duck carcass into about 10 pieces with a cleaver or heavy chef's knife. Brown the pieces in the olive oil with the onion over medium-to-high heat in a medium-sized heavy-bottomed pot, stirring every few minutes, for about 15 minutes. Add the bouquet garni and the chicken broth or water, just enough to cover by about 1 inch [2.5 cm]. (If you're using broth and don't have enough, add just enough water to cover.) Simmer gently for two hours, skimming off fat and froth. Strain the broth into a clean saucepan and simmer it down over medium heat, again skimming off fat, until you're left with only about ⅔ cup [150 ml] of concentrated syrupy duck broth. You can prepare the duck broth up to several days ahead and refrigerate it, or even months ahead, if you freeze it. Unless you've made the broth ahead of time, work on the terrine while the broth is simmering.

TO PREPARE THE GARNITURE

CUT the fatback crosswise into strips about ¼ inch [.5 cm] thick. Toss the strips with the garlic and Cognac and marinate in the refrigerator for 2 hours or overnight. Cut the skin off the duck breasts—this is easiest if you peel back the meat and use a sharp paring knife to cut through the delicate membrane that connects the skin to the meat. Cut the breasts lengthwise into strips ¼ inch [.5 cm] thick. Marinate the duck strips in semidry Madeira or port in the refrigerator for 2 hours or overnight. The marinating is optional, but it adds a wonderful flavor.

TO PREPARE THE FINE FORCEMEAT

COMBINE the chicken livers, duck liver, pork shoulder, fatback, eggs, garlic, thyme, and spices in a food processor and purée until smooth, about 3 minutes, scraping down the inside of the processor every minute. Transfer the forcemeat to a mixing bowl. If the concentrated duck broth has set in the refrigerator, melt it on the stove. Use your fingers to work the broth or the milk into the bread, but don't overdo it or you'll make the mixture heavy. Work the soaked bread into the rest of the forcemeat. Refrigerate until you're ready to assemble the terrine.

TO PREPARE THE COARSE FORCEMEAT

PEEL the skin off the duck legs and discard it (or save it and render it for cooking). Cut the meat away from the bone and cut away any obvious strips of sinew. Coarsely chop the duck meat and the prosciutto, either by hand with a sharp chef's knife or by chilling almost until frozen in the freezer and then quick pulsing in a food processor, until the pieces are about the size of baby peas. If the pistachios still have their thin hulls, plunge them in boiling water for about 30 seconds and rub them quickly in a kitchen towel to remove the hulls. If the pistachios are large, chop them coarse. If you're using the marjoram, use your fingers to combine it with the duck, prosciutto, and pistachios in a small mixing bowl. Reserve the mixture until you're ready to assemble the terrine. If you're not using the marjoram, just stir the chopped duck, prosciutto, and pistachios into the fine forcemeat.

TO TEST THE FILLING

STIR the coarse forcemeat into the fine forcemeat. Stir any cognac, Madeira, or port used for marinating the garniture into the forcemeat. Form a walnut-size piece of the filling into a small patty and cook it, like a hamburger, in the olive oil. Taste it and adjust the seasoning, adding more salt or pepper or herbs or spices as needed.

TO ASSEMBLE THE TERRINE

LINE a 2-liter rectangular terrine with a single layer of fatback sheets, caul fat, or bacon, leaving enough hanging over both long sides to fold over and cover the top of the terrine once it is filled. (The 2-liter rectangular terrine I use for this recipe measures 11½ by 4 by 4 inches [29 by 10 by 10 cm].) Using an offset spatula or a large spoon, spread the bottom of the terrine with one-fourth of the forcemeat and arrange one-third of the fatback strips and one-third of the duck strips lengthwise in the terrine. Spread over these another fourth of the forcemeat, layer in another third of the fatback and duck strips, and repeat, so that you have 3 layers of garniture and 4 of forcemeat, ending with forcemeat. Push down on the filling and rap the terrine firmly, but not too hard, on

a cutting board (not on a tile counter) to settle the filling and eliminate any air pockets. Fold the sheets of fat over the top of the terrine, completely covering the top of the filling. Make a triple-layer sheet of aluminum foil large enough to fit over the top of the terrine with a couple of extra inches on each side. Press the foil down on top of the terrine and seal it firmly around the sides.

TO BAKE AND WEIGHT THE TERRINE

HEAT the oven to 350°F [175°C/gas mark 4] and place the terrine in a baking pan or shallow pot large enough to hold the water that will surround the terrine. The water bath keeps the terrine from overheating and helps it cook evenly. Place the baking pan with the terrine in the oven and pour hot tap water into the pan until the water comes two-thirds of the way up the sides of the terrine. I use a teakettle to pour in the water. Bake the terrine until an instant-read thermometer stuck into the center through the foil reads 140°F [60°C], about 1½ hours. The juices that run out of the hole should be clear, not pink.

PUT the terrine on a sheet pan, to catch any fat that may drip down its sides, and place a small cutting board on top of the terrine. Put a can or heavy saucepan on top. If, however, the top of the filling doesn't protrude above the rim of the terrine mold, the cutting board will be ineffective. Instead, you can use several layers of cardboard, cut to the inside size of the terrine, stacked together, and wrapped in aluminum foil, before putting on the weight. Let the terrine cool for about 2 hours at room temperature and then place it in the refrigerator, with the weight still on it, for at least 12 hours, after which you can remove the weight, or for up to a month, sealed (provided that the seal is never broken).

IF you've lined the terrine with caul fat, unmold the whole terrine and peel and cut away the caul fat before slicing the terrine into ¼-inch to ½-inch [.5 cm to 1.5 cm] pieces. If you've lined the terrine mold with fatback, you can slice the terrine in it and let guests peel away the fat that surrounds each slice. (The fat isn't eaten.) Pass a bowl of cornichons and some mustard.

Variations: You can use this terrine as a model for making terrines from the meat of other animals, such as game, squabs, or rabbits, using irregular pieces trimmed off the rib cages and legs as part of the forcemeat (either puréed with fatback as part of the fine forcemeat or chopped coarsely for the coarse forcemeat) and more regular and presentable pieces, usually the breast meat, as part of the garniture. The garniture, those solid pieces of meat or other ingredients that appear in cross-section when the terrine is sliced, can be varied almost endlessly. Cubes, chunks, or slices of foie gras are common but make any terrine expensive. Truffles are often included, but if they are not used abundantly, you can't taste them, and if they are, the price of the terrine, well, goes through the roof. I sometimes include dried morels, soaked in a little Madeira and chopped coarse, in the coarse forcemeat. Pistachios are very common because their bright green color is attractive and they provide a delightful crunch that contrasts with the texture of the forcemeat. Some more fanciful recipes call for other nuts, including hazelnuts, but these don't provide the color and they're so hard that they can cause the terrine to tear when you slice it. Ham is used in various ways. Cured hams such as Italian prosciutto and American Smithfield hams, including their fat (but not their rind), give depth and subtlety of flavor when puréed into a fine forcemeat or chopped and used in a coarse forcemeat. (Since prosciutto and Smithfield ham are very salty, don't add salt to your mixture until you have tested it by cooking a small piece.) These hams can also be cut into ¼-inch [.5 cm] cubes and stirred in with the forcemeat so they make a decorative pattern when you slice the terrine. (See Chapter 6 for more about ham.)

GALANTINES AND BALLOTTINES

A galantine is an elaborate pâté that, instead of being baked in a mold, is wrapped in the skin of whatever bird—usually a duck—is being featured. When we made them at a restaurant where I once worked in Paris, a duck was first boned by making a slit the length of its back, carefully removing the skin so it ended up as a neat rectangle, and then boning the breasts and whole legs. The skin was spread with a layer of fine forcemeat, and strips of duck breast and fatback, pistachios, and thickly julienned truffles were arranged in neat rows on top of the forcemeat. A whole foie gras goose liver was rolled into a cylinder and placed, lengthwise, in the middle of the whole concoction, and everything tied up into what looked like a giant sausage. Meanwhile, a gelatinous broth was prepared with meat and calves' feet, which release a lot of gelatin. The galantine was wrapped tightly in a sheet of muslin and poached, bobbing up like something out of Loch Ness, and cooled in the broth. When the broth chilled and jelled, we'd fish out the galantine, unwrap it, and serve it in round slices with a little of the chopped *gelée* on the side. The effect was lovely to look at, but it didn't taste any better than a terrine made with the same luxurious ingredients.

A ballottine differs from a galantine in ways that depend on whom you read. At the restaurant, we would occasionally roast the galantine rather than poach it, and then serve it hot—the thing was so rich I couldn't imagine eating a big hot chunk of it—and because it was roasted and hot instead of poached and cold, we'd call it a ballottine. Older editions of *Larousse Gastronomique* insist that an authentic ballottine must be made with a "butchery" animal like a lamb, not with birds, while the latest edition explains that ballottines are individual small birds cooked like galantines.

CHICKEN LIVER TERRINE OR MOUSSE

TERRINE OU MOUSSE DE FOIES DE VOLAILLE

MAKES 6 FIRST-COURSE SERVINGS OF TERRINE
(2 CUPS [450 ML] OF TERRINE) OR 12 HORS D'OEUVRES
OR 8 FIRST-COURSE SERVINGS OF MOUSSE OR
15 HORS D'OEUVRES (4 CUPS [850 G] OF MOUSSE)

A chicken liver terrine or mousse, unlike most terrines and pâtés, is made by combining raw meats in various ways before baking, a chicken liver terrine is made by puréeing with, butter, chicken livers that have been sautéed in hot oil. To turn the mixture into a mousse, which has a lighter texture than a terrine, you fold it with whipped cream before you chill it. I give the terrine or mousse extra flavor by deglazing the sauté pan with finely chopped shallots and garlic, herbs, and port or Madeira, and incorporating this little sauce into the liver mixture. You can make chicken liver mousse a day or two ahead of time, but unlike terrines that are tightly sealed and will keep for a long time in the refrigerator, chicken liver mousse is somewhat perishable and should be served within a day or two of when you make it.

In this recipe, I offer two versions. The first, which is basically a purée of livers and butter, has the relatively dense consistency of a traditional terrine. The second version, made out of the first, has the consistency of mousse because it is lightened with whipped cream.

FOR EACH VERSION:

12 ounces chicken livers (¾ pound [350 g]), cleaned of blood vessels and fat

2 tablespoons "pure" olive oil

salt

pepper

2 medium-size shallots, chopped fine

1 small clove garlic, chopped fine

½ teaspoon finely chopped fresh thyme or marjoram, or ¼ teaspoon dried

¼ cup [60 ml] port or semidry Madeira (see page 10), or cream sherry

2 tablespoons Cognac, optional

½ pound [225 g] butter, plus ¼ pound [115 g] butter (optional), melted

FOR THE MOUSSE VERSION:

1 cup [250 ml] heavy cream, well chilled

TO MAKE THE TERRINE

RINSE and drain the livers and pat them dry. In a sauté pan or skillet just large enough to hold the livers in a single layer, heat the olive oil over high heat until it begins to smoke. The pan must be very hot or the livers will release liquid, won't brown, and will end up simmering in their own juices. Season the livers with salt and pepper and lower them, one by one, into the hot skillet—stand back, because chicken livers tend to spatter. Brown the livers for about 3 minutes on each side, until they just begin to feel firm to the touch. Use a slotted spoon to scoop them out of the pan and into a bowl.

POUR the oil out of the pan and discard it. While the pan is still hot, use a wooden spoon to stir in the shallots, garlic, and thyme. Stir the mixture around in the pan for about 1 minute until it releases its fragrance, and pour in the port. Boil the port down to about half, add the Cognac, boil for about 10 seconds, and pour the mixture over the livers. Let the livers cool for 10 minutes.

CUT the butter into about 6 chunks and put these into the bowl with the livers. Let sit for about 15 minutes, allowing the livers to cool further and the butter to soften slightly. Don't, however, let the butter melt. Purée the mixture in a food processor until smooth and then work it through a drum sieve or coarse-mesh strainer with the back of a large spoon. Season the mixture to taste with salt and pepper.

THERE are several ways to serve this. You can pack the mixture into a bowl, chill it, and pass it at the table for guests to help themselves, or you can use two wet spoons to shape the mixture into egg shapes (quenelles) and put two on each plate. You can also pack the mixture into a terrine lined with blanched leek greens, spinach, or cabbage, chill it, unmold it, and slice it as you would any terrine. Or you can pack it into individual 3-ounce or 4-ounce [90 to 125 ml] ramekins, spoon a little more than a tablespoon of melted butter over each one, and chill until the butter sets and forms a seal. Whichever method you use, pass around quartered slices of toasted white bread or pieces of crusty baguette.

TO MAKE THE MOUSSE

PREPARE the mixture above, but as soon as you work it through a strainer, beat the chilled cream to medium peaks and quickly whisk one-fourth of the cream into the liver mixture, which should be at about room temperature, not hot. Fold the liver mixture with the rest of the cream and season again to taste with salt and pepper. Cover the mousse with plastic wrap, pressing the wrap against the surface of the mousse to keep it from coming into contact with air. Chill the mousse for 3 hours or overnight. You can serve chicken liver mousse in individual ramekins, like the stiffer mixture described above. But don't spoon melted butter over them; just cover them with plastic wrap until you're ready to serve. I usually spoon the mousse out in egg shapes, as described above, and arrange two each on individual chilled plates. Chicken liver mousse is too soft to slice like a terrine.

Hot Pâtés

THE LINES THAT DISTINGUISH HOT PÂTÉS, *tourtes*, and foods cooked *en brioche* are sometimes so indistinct that these terms end up being used almost interchangeably. A *pâté pantin* is a rectangular pâté wrapped either in *pâté à pâté* (a kind of heavy pie dough made with lard) or *pâté feuilletée* (puff pastry). Fillings can range from a mixture of pork, veal, fatback, and cured ham—the same ingredients used in a well-made cold terrine—to luxurious combinations containing truffles and foie gras. A *tourte* can be made in the same way, but the implication is that a *tourte* is round and flat rather than rectangular. (Unlike a tart, a *tourte* has pastry on the top as well as the bottom, making it roughly equivalent to a pie). Something cooked *en brioche* is exactly as it sounds—the most famous version is the classic Lyonnaise *saucisse en brioche*, a sausage baked in brioche dough. But in Lyons you may also encounter *foie gras en brioche*, made famous by Ferdinand Point at his restaurant La Pyramide.

While I've never been crazy about cold *pâté en croûte*, a well-made hot pâté is a different thing altogether. The perfumes of the various elements fill the kitchen and dining room, and the pastry, when well made, provides a flaky counterpoint to the rich filling. But cooks who take shortcuts often go wrong. Because any meat filling releases moisture as it cooks, the bottom crust can become soggy. I have two solutions to this problem. One is to wrap the filling in several layers of crêpes, so the crêpes absorb liquid released by the filling and the outside pastry stays crisp. (Yes, the crêpes get soggy, but a soggy crêpe is a surprisingly good thing and a lot better than a soggy crust.) The second solution is to surround the filling with finely chopped mushrooms, cooked until perfectly dry; the preparation, called a duxelles (see page 96), absorbs liquid. Once in a while, if I'm being really careful, I use both crêpes and duxelles.

While cold pâtés must have a firm enough texture so they don't fall apart when sliced, and at times require a denser-than-desirable forcemeat, hot pâtés need just enough structure so they don't fall apart on the plate. This means that you can incorporate meaty chunks or slices of veal, ham, game, poultry, rabbit, or other meats, using a small amount of forcemeat, if any at all, to reinforce and balance their flavors instead of simply for the purpose of holding the whole thing together.

HOT RECTANGULAR PÂTÉ IN A CRUST

PÂTÉ PANTIN

MAKES 8 FIRST-COURSE SERVINGS

My Larousse defines a pantin first as a cardboard puppet, manipulated with strings, and second as a person who is forever changing his or her opinion. How a pâté inherited the name, I have no idea, but suspect it refers to the makeshift quality of many a pâté pantin, which can be quickly thrown together by wrapping various leftovers in puff pastry, brioche, or pie dough and sliding the concoction into the oven.

You can approach a pâté pantin as you do most any terrine, but because a pâté pantin doesn't have to hold together in the same way, you can leave more of the ingredients in chunks, strips, or slices and cut down on the amount of forcemeat (and hence, fat). Recipes for pâté pantin vary widely. Here is my own version, made with veal and pork and no forcemeat at all. Instead of forcemeat, I use a cooked mixture of chopped mushrooms called a duxelles (see page 96), which makes the pâté much lighter and absorbs juices released by the meats. I marinate the veal and pork separately to underline the individual character of each. You can use this recipe as a model and substitute other meats for the solid ingredients and a classic fine or coarse forcement (like those used in the pâtés on pages 87 and 88) for part or all of the

duxelles. You can make your own puff pastry, but it's tricky to make and easy to buy (see Sources); just make sure you buy a brand that's made with all butter and contains no margarine or shortening (usually disguised on the ingredients label as hydrogenated vegetable or cottonseed oil). Traditionally, pâté pantin is served as a first course, but it also makes a good luncheon main course when served with a green salad.

½ pound [225 g] pork tenderloin

½ pound [225 g] top round or boneless loin of veal

  salt

  pepper

1 clove garlic, finely chopped, crushed to a paste with the side of a chef's knife

1 bunch parsley, preferably flat-leaf, chopped just before using

¼ cup [60 ml] port, semidry Madeira, or sweet sherry

¼ cup [60 ml] dry white wine

1 teaspoon finely chopped fresh thyme or marjoram, or ½ teaspoon dried

1 pound [450 g] mushrooms, quickly rinsed, drained

2 large shallots, or 1 small onion, chopped fine

1 tablespoon butter

4 tablespoons heavy cream

1 pound [450 g] puff pastry, or one 14-ounce [about 400 g] package, allowed to thaw in a cool place or in the refrigerator

1 egg, lightly beaten with 1 teaspoon salt

USE a boning knife or paring knife to trim any strips of membrane off the pork tenderloins. Cut the tenderloins lengthwise into strips about ¼ inch [.5 cm] wide. Cut the strips into ¼-inch [.5 cm] cubes. Cut the veal into ¼-inch [.5 cm] cubes. Toss the pork cubes, in a mixing bowl, with salt, pepper, the garlic, 1 heaping tablespoon of the parsley, and the port. Cover the bowl and marinate in the refrigerator for 2 to 6 hours. In another mixing bowl, toss the veal cubes with the white wine, salt, pepper, and thyme, and marinate, in the same way as the pork.

USE the mushrooms, shallots, butter, heavy cream, and the remaining parsley to make a duxelles (see page 96).

WHEN the pastry has thawed but is still cold, roll it out into a 13-by-10-inch [33 by 25.5 cm] rectangle, between ⅛ and ¼ inch [about .5 cm] thick, and cut the rectangle in half lengthwise to make 2 rectangles each measuring 13 by 5 inches [33 by 12.5 cm]. If the pastry becomes difficult to roll out, starts to melt, or contracts slightly after each roll, let it rest in the refrigerator for 30 minutes and try again. If you force it, it will contract in the oven and be tough. Place one of the rectangles on a sheet pan sprinkled with cold water, to keep the bottom of the pastry from burning, and spread over it one-half of the duxelles, leaving a 1-inch [2.5 cm] border all around the pastry with no duxelles on it. Drain the pork and veal cubes, pat them dry, and combine them with the remaining duxelles to make the pâté. Arrange the pâté on top of the duxelles on the rectangle of puff pastry that is on the sheet pan. Fold the borders of the pastry up along the sides of the pâté and brush the outsides of the pastry—which are now the sides of the pâté—with some of the beaten egg. Place the second rectangle of pastry over this whole construction by rolling up the pastry on a rolling pin and then unrolling it over the pâté. Tuck the sides of this top layer around the pâté, pressing to seal it against the egg-brushed sides. Brush the tops and sides of the pâté with the remaining egg. Refrigerate the pâté for 30 minutes to an hour.

PREHEAT the oven to 425°F [220°C/gas mark 7]. Make a series of diagonal slashes, about 1 inch [2.5 cm] apart, along the top of the pâté, being careful to cut only about ¹⁄₃₂ inch [1 mm] into the pastry, not all the way through to the stuffing. Repeat, going in the other direction, to create a crisscross pattern, a decorative effect that also allows the pastry to expand without cracking. Bake the pâté for 30 minutes. If, after 20 minutes, the pâté starts to get too dark, turn the oven down to 300°F [150°C/gas mark 2]. When the inside of the pâté measures 140°F [60°C]

with an instant-read thermometer and the pastry is well browned, remove the pâté from the oven and cover it loosely with aluminum foil. Keep it warm for at least 10 minutes and up to 30 minutes before serving. Slice the pâté at the table with a sharp serrated bread knife.

Variations: I once made a version of this pâté with squabs, using morels for the duxelles and lightly browning the squab breasts before layering them in the pâté with thin slices of foie gras. I then made a concentrated sauce with the squab carcasses, finished it with butter and the puréed squab livers, and just before serving poured it, using a small funnel, into holes on top of the pâté. Variations on this theme are obvious. Any flavorful winged or four-legged creature will work. But keep in mind that red meats, such as duck breast or saddle of hare, should be lightly browned before being arranged in the pâté, and the pâté should be cooked at a higher temperature for less time than for one containing white meats, such as veal, pork, rabbit, or chicken, so that the duxelles cooks through without overcooking the red meat garniture to a dull brown. Any sauce you would use for the meat in the pâté can be poured through one or more holes made in the top of the pâté before baking.

Many stuffings are too heavy, too rich, or too starchy, but a duxelles—chopped mushrooms cooked down to concentrate their flavor—is intensely flavored and light. It makes a versatile stuffing for small birds and a substitute for rich forcemeats in hot pâtés. Usually, a duxelles is made with ordinary mushrooms, or sometimes just their stems, frozen until a pound or more accumulate. But wild mushrooms, especially morels and cèpes (porcini), give the duxelles a deep luxurious flavor that complements other deep-flavored foods like game, foie gras, and truffles. I often add a few dried morels or cèpes, soaked in a little water and chopped fine, to a duxelles made with cultivated mushrooms.

Making duxelles is easy. Chop the mushrooms to the texture of hamburger relish, by hand or in a food processor (use the pulse mechanism and don't overdo it). Cook some chopped shallot and/or garlic in a little butter in a sauté pan and add the mushrooms. Cook the mushrooms over high heat until the water they release completely evaporates, about 10 minutes. At this point you can add a little cream to help hold the mixture together and give a certain suaveness to the flavor, but you don't have to. Let cool to room temperature and refrigerate, covered, for at least 1 hour. Stir in chopped parsley.

Foie Gras

FOIE GRAS—LITERALLY, "FAT LIVER"—IS THE liver of a duck or goose that has been allowed to eat voraciously or has been force-fed by means of sliding a long funnel down its neck and pouring in grain, usually corn. Pictures of elderly women performing this seemingly cruel procedure, called gavage, often adorn the walls of restaurants and of charming little inns in the region in France best known for its foie gras, the Dordogne. It does indeed seem cruel, but I've seen gavage being performed and it's clearly something that geese, which were what I saw, and presumably ducks, can't get enough of, the sight of the funnel almost prompting a stampede in its direction. In any case, the liver grows from a couple of ounces to about a pound and a half and turns from a dark livery reddish brown to pale yellowish pink, the change in color due to the fact that the liver is now largely fat, and very tasty fat. The most classic way to prepare and eat foie gras is to carefully pull the veins out of the livers, season the livers and sometimes marinate them with a little Madeira, and press them into a terrine, which is then sealed with a lid or with several layers of aluminum foil and baked, in a bain-marie. The foie gras terrine is served cold, in slices, with squares of sandwich bread (what the French call *pain de mie*) toasts. The whole raw livers can also be sliced and sautéed, poached whole (when wrapped in a kitchen towel these are referred to as foie gras *en torchon*), or roasted whole and served hot. Foie gras is sold in several forms: the whole livers (with which you can make your own terrine), already cooked in a terrine, and as mousse. Terrines made from the whole livers are the most expensive because water is released during cooking, causing the liver to lose weight, increasing its proportion of fat and intensifying its flavor. Terrines made from the whole livers are often labeled "*entier*" or "*bloc*" to distinguish them from mousse. Foie gras mousse is considerably less expensive and is made from the trimmings of the liver and sometimes unfattened liver, puréed and strained for a smooth, spreadable texture. If you're using foie gras as flavoring for a sauce or to purée in a foie gras butter, you can get by with mousse. To appreciate foie gras with the deepest flavor and its firm yet buttery texture intact, buy *entier* or *bloc* already cooked into a terrine. Unlike most cooks, who slice whole raw livers for sautéing and serving hot, I prefer to use terrine for such dishes because it holds its shape better, releases less water, and has a denser texture and a more intense flavor.

One advantage to making your own terrine of foie gras with whole livers is that you can choose the livers yourself, making sure you get the best quality. (Look for even, pale yellowish pink color; large size; and a surface with no bruises or stains.) A second advantage is that you'll learn to work with whole livers and can cook them in other ways (see page 100).

FOIE GRAS TERRINE

TERRINE DE FOIE GRAS

MAKES 15 TO 20 SINGLE-SLICE SERVINGS

(A 2-LITER TERRINE)

Even though I spend a disproportionate amount of my income on food, the cost of certain foods intimidates even me. And because a terrine of foie gras is one of them, I make it for grand occasions like Christmas or New Year's Eve when I can justify indulging in my favorite luxury foods. Before setting out, you should give some thought to how large a terrine you want to make so that you don't end up with more than you need or can afford. Of my two terrine molds, I prefer to use the 2-liter one (capacity slightly more than 2 quarts) for this dish, since it's just the right size for cooking two 2-pound [900 g] livers and producing enough for 15 to 20 servings. (It measures 11½ by 4

by 4 inches.) My terrine molds, made of porcelain and enameled iron, don't need to be lined with fat for a terrine of foie gras, since foie gras doesn't stick to these materials in the same way other pâté mixtures do. If you're using a metal terrine, such as a loaf pan, you'll need to line it. You can use thin sheets of fatback or caul fat in the way described on page 88 or brush the terrine with some softened butter and line each side with a rectangle of parchment paper. All of this is to avoid imparting a metallic taste to the foie gras. Terrine of foie gras will keep for 3 weeks in the refrigerator if you don't cut into it, but once you do you should eat it within several days.

- 2 foie gras duck livers (about 1 ½ pounds [675 g] each)
- ¼ cup [60 ml] port (an old tawny is ideal), Sauternes, or semidry Madeira
- 2 teaspoons fine salt
- 1 teaspoon freshly ground white pepper
- 1 teaspoon softened butter (if using parchment paper), or ½ pound [225 g] fatback cut into thin sheets, or ½ pound [225 g] caul fat (for lining the terrine mold or loaf pan if it does not have a nonstick surface)

WHEN you get the livers home, soak them in cold tap water for 2 hours in the refrigerator to remove traces of blood and make it easier to peel off the thin translucent membrane that covers each liver. Pat the livers dry with a clean kitchen towel and gently peel away the membrane by pinching it on one end between your thumb and the side of a small paring knife. Don't worry if you can't get all the membrane off. Gently fold back the smaller of the two lobes and pull out the veins that connect the lobes. If the livers start to crack as you're removing veins, let them warm slightly. You may have to use a small paring knife to cut along one side of the veins to make them easier to remove. Cut away and discard any patches of green, which are caused by the gall bladder and may be bitter. Reserve the veins and any pieces of the liver that cling to them. (Later, work these through a drum sieve or fine-mesh strainer; this will give you a small amount of foie gras purée that you can add to the terrine or freeze and save for finishing sauces.)

SPRINKLE one-half the port and one-half the salt and pepper on the bottom of a large stainless steel or glass mixing bowl large enough to hold the livers, when they are pressed down, in a single layer. Press the livers down into the bowl and sprinkle the remaining port, salt, and pepper over them. Cover with plastic wrap and refrigerate for 12 to 24 hours, turning the livers several times while they're marinating.

IF you're using a metal terrine or loaf pan that does not have a nonstick surface, brush it with butter and line each side with a piece of parchment paper, or line it with sheets of fatback (without overlapping) or caul fat, leaving enough hanging over the sides to cover the top of the terrine.

PRESS the foie gras firmly into the terrine. Pour over it the marinade left in the bowl and let the marinade settle down into the terrine. Press a rectangle of parchment paper just large enough to cover the foie gras on top to prevent the aluminum foil from touching the foie gras, since it can leave tiny specks if it does. Fold a three-layer rectangle of aluminum foil about 2 inches [5 cm] larger on all sides than the top of the terrine. Press the foil down firmly on the top of the terrine and fold it over the sides, being especially careful to fold over the corners so the terrine is well sealed. Let the terrine come to room temperature (about 3 hours) before baking. This helps it bake evenly.

PREHEAT the oven to the very lowest temperature, about 200°F [95°C]. Place the terrine in a container such as a baking dish with high sides or a pot, to serve as a bain-marie. Bring water to a boil, ideally in a teakettle. Set the bain-marie in the oven and pour in enough boiling water to come halfway up the sides of the terrine. Bake for about 3 hours. After 2 hours of cooking, start checking the terrine by poking an instant-read thermometer through the foil. The terrine is ready when the thermometer reads 137°F [58°C] (see "Internal Temperature for Foie Gras Terrine," page 99). Take the whole bain-marie out of the oven and gently lift out the terrine. Put the terrine on a sheet pan to catch any fat that may drip down its sides (and which you should save) and place a heavy rectangular object on the terrine so that it presses down on the foie gras and doesn't just rest on the edges of the terrine mold (I use my 1-quart terrine for this). If you don't have something the right size, cut a piece of stiff cardboard to fit inside the mold on top of the foie gras, wrap it in aluminum foil, and put small cans on top to act as weights. Let the terrine cool for a couple of hours at room temperature and then place it in the refrigerator, with the weight still on, for at least 24 hours, after which you can remove the weight, or up to 2 weeks.

WHEN serving the terrine, gently pull away the foil. You'll see that the foie gras is covered with a layer of yellow fat. You can slice the terrine, leaving the fat attached to each slice, but since a lot of people don't eat it, I scrape it off and save it in the freezer for brushing on croûtons as a little snack, for cooking omelets, or for finishing emulsified sauces such as hollandaise. Traditionally, *terrine de foie gras* is served with white-bread toast, but since good dense-crumbed white bread can be hard to find, I sometimes serve it with crusty French bread instead. Once you've cut into the terrine, eat it within 2 or 3 days.

INTERNAL TEMPERATURE FOR FOIE GRAS TERRINE

Cooks in the United States are often in disagreement with the Food and Drug Administration (FDA) about what internal temperature foie gras should have reached in a terrine. I cook mine to 137°F [58°C], which as the terrine stands after cooking actually increases to over 140°F [60°C], a high enough temperature to kill most pathogens. Cooks in France sometimes cook foie gras to only 120°F [48°C] or even less, with delicious results, but after a miserable case of food poisoning spent in a rather speedy Paris hotel, I stick to 137°F [58°C]. The FDA requires that foie gras that is sold commercially be cooked to 160°F [71°C], a temperature that makes it too dry for my taste. Canned foie gras must be cooked to 212°F [100°C]. That's one reason I never bother with it.

SALT-CURED WHOLE FOIE GRAS

FOIE GRAS SALÉ

MAKES ENOUGH FOR 6 GENEROUS FIRST-COURSE SERVINGS, OR MORE IF TOSSED IN A SALAD

I first discovered a version of this dish in Alice Waters's charming *Chez Panisse Café Cookbook*, which includes a recipe for an arugula salad with cured foie gras shaved over it. The curing technique produces delicious foie gras with a somewhat lighter consistency than foie gras that's been cooked in a terrine. While Alice serves her cured liver in a salad, I like to slice it and smear it on crunchy slices of toasted French bread as I would Terrine of Foie Gras.

1 duck foie gras (1½ pounds [675 g])

6 to 8 pounds [2.7 to 3.6 kg] coarse salt (depending on the shape of your dish)

LET the foie gras come to room temperature and remove the membrane and veins as described on page 97. Don't worry if you can't get the membrane off—it's very thin and can be difficult to remove—or if you break the liver into a couple of pieces while deveining it. Wrap the foie gras in a sheet of muslin or a quadruple layer of well-rinsed and still-wet cheesecloth. Twist the ends of the cloth in opposing directions so that the cloth clings tightly to the foie gras and roll the liver as necessary to form it into an even sausage shape. Tie the cloth with string at each end.

POUR a 1½-inch-thick [4 cm] layer of coarse salt into an oval porcelain, glass, or ceramic terrine. You can also use a large soufflé dish or glass mixing bowl; you'll just need more salt. Set the foie gras on the salt in the middle of the dish, making sure there's at least 1 inch of space between the foie gras and the sides of the dish. Surround the foie gras with a 1-inch layer of salt. Set a small, heavy saucepan or a few full cans on top of dish and refrigerate it for 4 days. When you unpack the foie gras, unwrap it and slice it. Or if you're using it in a salad, shave it into thin slivers with a vegetable peeler. Because the outside ⅛ inch [3 mm] or so of the foie gras is very salty, I shave it off with a knife and render it for making omelets or for sautéing vegetables such as potatoes or mushrooms.

COOKING WHOLE RAW FOIE GRAS

Hot foie gras is all the rage in fancy restaurants, and while I have nothing against it, its texture never satisfies me in the same way as that of cold foie gras baked in a terrine. If you like hot foie gras, just slice the whole liver crosswise, angling the slices according to how wide you want them to be (not any thinner than ½ inch or they'll melt into nothing). Pick out any obvious pieces of vein. Preheat a sauté pan until it is very hot, and sauté the slices, without any added fat, for about 1 minute on each side. When cooked properly, the slices should be well caramelized on the outside but melting on the inside. I like to serve slices of sautéed foie gras with sautéed wild mushrooms (thick, meaty ones like cèpes or portobellos, chanterelles, morels, or the mushrooms with truffles on page 604), on top of other meats, or even atop a crispy fried croûton to provide a contrast to the slightly cloying texture of the hot foie gras.

There are things you can do with whole foie gras livers other than packing them into a terrine. You can make *foie gras en torchon* by wrapping the liver tightly in a muslin cloth and poaching it in gelatinous broth—one that jells in the refrigerator, as do most homemade broths—maintained at a constant 140°F [60°C], and either serving it hot in slices or letting it cool in the broth, refrigerating it before unwrapping it, and then serving it cold in slices, much like a terrine. Or you can roast the whole liver in a 425°F [220°C/gas mark 7] oven for about 20 minutes, while basting it with its own fat, until it is well caramelized on the outside but only 137°F [58°C] on the inside. The best-known version of roasted foie gras is *à la bordelaise*, in which the liver is surrounded with peeled grapes during its last 5 minutes of cooking. I admit to having made it with unpeeled grapes with perfect success. I imagine this method would be good with other fruits, such as peaches or apples, but I've yet to try it.

Whole raw foie gras livers can also be cured in salt in the same way as other meats (see recipe, page 99) or fish used for gravlax. In this way, the liver is actually never cooked but can be sliced and served on pieces of toast or tossed in salads.

HAM AND PARSLEY TERRINE

JAMBON PERSILLÉ

WHAT A PARADOX THAT PIGS, LOVABLE AND GENEROUS CREATURES WHO, useful in life, help us find truffles and, noble in death, end up on our tables, have become synonymous with gluttony, slobbishness, and avarice. Pigs are neither gluttons nor slobs (they prefer water to mud), and they are no greedier than any other creature and far less greedy than man. What's more, the pig is the most versatile of beasts. Every part is used: the head to make headcheese, the blood to make sausages (*boudins noirs*), the feet to be grilled or to make *gelée,* the loins to make lovely roasts and chops, and the hind legs to make one of the greatest of all foods, ham.

Ham confuses us because it comes in so many forms, from banal sandwich meat to the finest *jamón de jabugo,* a Spanish Serrano ham made from black-hooved pigs fed with acorns. This almost endless variety of hams can be broken down into three categories: fresh ham, which is just the whole pig's leg with nothing done to it (in fact, it's often sold as "pork leg"); cooked hams, of which there are many subdivisions based largely on the time spent curing in brine, rubbed with salt, and/or smoking; and raw fully cured hams such as prosciutto, Smithfield hams, and Serrano hams, which are never exposed to heat. If you order a ham sandwich in a typical French café, you'll have two choices: *jambon cuit* (cooked) or *jambon cru* (raw, cured). I always opt for the more expensive *jambon cru,* the French equivalent of prosciutto. Whichever you choose, your sandwich will be made with a crusty baguette halved down the middle and smeared with good Norman butter.

FRESH (RAW) HAM

A fresh ham is just a whole pig leg, sold bone in or bone out. It can weigh from 15 to more than 30 pounds [from 7 to 14 kg]. Sometimes fresh hams are sawed crosswise in half into a sirloin end and a shank end so you don't have to buy as much. They are even broken down further into pork roasts, or are sliced into steaks. When cooked, fresh ham is much like any other pork roast, pink and juicy—and especially dramatic to serve at the table. The labels on fresh ham read "fresh ham" or, more recently, "leg of pork." I roast fresh ham at 350°F [175°C/gas mark 4] to an internal temperature of 140°F [60°C]. (I actually take the leg out at 135°F [57°C] and let it come to 140°F [60°C] as it's resting.) The United States Department of Agriculture (USDA) recommends higher temperatures, the result being dried-out meat. A 20-pound [9 kg] fresh ham, allowed to come to room temperature for several hours before it goes into the oven, takes about 3½ hours to bake and another ½ hour to rest. Half a ham, such as a 10-pound [4.5 kg] shank end, takes about 2 hours to bake and another ½ hour to rest.

SMOKED OR UNSMOKED

Both cooked and fully cured hams are sometimes smoked. I prefer cooked hams to be smoked, because the smoking bolsters their flavor. However, I prefer fully cured hams unsmoked, because the smoking obscures their delicate flavor. When buying smoked ham, make sure the label says "naturally smoked" or "hickory smoked" and not "smoke flavored." Smoked-cured hams such as German Westphalian and Black Forest hams, and some hams from Virginia, Kentucky, or Vermont (where sugar enters the cure), while tasty, don't have the delicacy or finesse of unsmoked ones, such as *prosciutto di Parma, jambon de Bayonne* (France's best-known cured ham), and Serrano hams.

ROAST FRESH HAM (SHANK END)

JAMBON RÔTI

MAKES 12 SERVINGS

1 bone-in fresh uncooked ham shank (the shank end of a whole ham) with rind on (about 10 pounds [4.5 kg])

4 cups [950 g] kosher salt, or 2 cups [550 g] regular fine salt

3 cups [600 g] granulated sugar

1 bulb fennel, preferably with stalks and fronds, bulb sliced thin, stalks and fronds chopped

1 head garlic, cut in half crosswise

MAKE a series of lengthwise and crosswise incisions in the ham, about 1 inch [2.5 cm] apart, deep enough to cut through the rind but not deep enough to expose the meat.

FIND a nonaluminum container that holds your ham as snugly as possible and that, ideally, will fit in the refrigerator. Combine the salt, sugar, fennel, and garlic in the container with 2 quarts [2 l] of hot tap water. Stir the mixture to dissolve the salt and sugar. If the container fits in the refrigerator, add 4 cups [1 l] of cold water and refrigerate until cool. If the container doesn't fit, add only 2 cups [500 ml] of cold water, let the mixture cool, and then add 2 quarts [2 l] of ice cubes. Submerge the ham in the brine and put a plate on it to keep it from bobbing up. Refrigerate it or keep it in a cool place for 24 hours.

PREHEAT the oven to 350°F [175°C/gas mark 4]. Pat the ham dry and place it, flat side down, in a roasting pan or skillet just large enough to hold it, or in a skillet, and slide it into the oven. Bake until an instant-read thermometer stuck through the side of the shank, almost to the bone but not touching the bone, reads 135°F [57°C]. Turn off the oven, crack open the door, and let the ham rest for 30 minutes. Recheck the temperature to make sure that it has risen to between 140° and 145°F [60° and 63°C].

TRANSFER the ham to a cutting board (one with a moat is best) and pour the juices from the roasting pan into a glass measuring cup or a degreasing cup. Let the juices set for 10 minutes so that the fat floats to the top, and either skim the fat from the measuring cup with a small ladle and pour the *jus* into a sauceboat, or pour the *jus* into the sauceboat from the degreasing cup. Carve the ham at the table, first removing a sheet of rind and then slicing lengthwise and parallel to the bone. Pass the *jus* at the table.

COOKED AND PARTIALLY COOKED HAMS

Most hams we encounter in supermarkets have been treated in some way and at least partially cooked. Hams are often cut in half into a butt and a shank. I'm wary of this practice, because butchers sometimes cut out the best slices from the middle of the ham to sell as steaks, and leave the two big ends without the best slices. My first choice is to roast a whole ham, which will make enough for a big dinner party and still provide plenty of leftovers. My second choice is a bone-in butt end.

Most cooked and partially cooked hams have been lightly cured, usually in brine but sometimes with dry salt, before being cooked. Less expensive hams are injected with brine or water, the best-quality hams being those with the least water. The USDA has a labeling system that tells you indirectly the amount of water in (and hence the quality of) the ham. Ham that's labeled simply "ham" contains no water and must be at least 20.5 percent protein, while "ham with natural juices" contains brine or water and must be at least 18.5 percent protein. "Ham—added water" contains more water and 17 percent protein. Last in line is "ham and water product," with the percentage of "added ingredients" specified on the label. Even though these hams are at least partly cooked, you're supposed to cook them again, to a temperature of 160°F [71°C]. Among the most popular of cooked hams are "spiral cut" hams, which have already been sliced so that you just lift the slices away instead of actually carving the ham. When buying a cooked or partially cooked ham, I buy bone-in hams because they have more flavor. In any case, carve the ham by just slicing the meat off the bone.

Cooked ham is easily recognized because it's pink and opaque (versus fully cured uncooked hams, which are dark red-purple and translucent) and in France is called *jambon cuit* (literally, cooked ham) or *jambon de Paris* or sometimes *jambon d'York*. In Italian markets, cooked ham is sold as *prosciutto cotto*, as opposed to *prosciutto crudo*, what we call simply prosciutto. All these hams, except *proscutto crudo*, are fully cooked.

SHOULDER HAMS

Shoulder ham is pork shoulder cured like ham. It is sometimes called picnic ham (in French, *jambonneau*, which refers to a shoulder ham or a "ham" taken from the lower part of either the forelegs or hind legs). These "hams" are not only less tasty and tender than regular hams, but they're a bit of an oxymoron, since ham by definition is the leg. In America, they are sold both raw and already cooked.

CURED HAMS (COUNTRY HAMS)

I've saved the best for last, because ham, however good it may be, doesn't reach celestial heights when it is cooked. Cured hams, called country hams in the United States, are wet-cured by soaking in brine, dry-cured by rubbing with salt, or cured first with dry salt and later in the process with brine. The best hams are dry-cured and are allowed to dry in the open air. *Prosciutto di Parma* must be made in the region of Parma, be dry-cured with salt and no chemicals, such as nitrites, and be hung in the open air to age for at least 300 days. *Prosciutto di San Daniele* and Serrano hams are cured in a similar way and have a delicate character of their own. The USDA requires prosciutto that's imported into the United States to be aged for 400 days. The best ham I've ever tasted is Serrano ham from Spain, which happily is now being imported into the United States, though at rather daunting prices. Authentic dry-cured French hams such as *jambon de Bayonne* and hams from the Morvan (a region near Burgundy) are not yet sold in the United States.

Before *prosciutto di Parma* was allowed back into the United States after a 20-year ban, I ate a lot of Smithfield ham, the best known of American country hams, which is dry-cured and well aged. I had been eating it raw for years before I discovered that most people cook it. It's delicious when sliced thin and served with figs or melon in the same way as *prosciutto di Parma*. Because Smithfield ham is very salty, it must be sliced very thin when eaten raw or must be thoroughly soaked before it is cooked. Most recipes suggest soaking for only 1 day, but I soak mine for 3 days and then poach it rather than roast it to further draw out the salt.

HAM AND PARSLEY TERRINE

JAMBON PERSILLÉ

MAKES 12 FIRST-COURSE SERVINGS

(A 1½-LITER OR 6-CUP TERRINE)

While no two versions are exactly the same, jambon persillé is cooked ham that's been layered in a terrine with chopped parsley and the gelatinous poaching liquid used for cooking the ham. Depending on whose recipe you follow, the terrine may consist of pieces of ham suspended in gelée or contain very little gelée at all, just enough to hold the terrine together.

An exact recipe for jambon persillé is hard to give because ham is one of the few things that aren't made the same way in different parts of the country. How you make jambon persillé depends on the ham or ham shoulder you start out with and how ambitious you're feeling. The traditional method consists of soaking a fully cured raw ham for several days to rid it of excess salt and then braising it for several hours in a wine-and-carrot-flavored court bouillon (vegetable stock) to soften it. The ham would probably be a jambon de Morvan in Burgundy, where jambon persillé originates, but prosciutto di Parma, or a less expensive domestic prosciutto, or Smithfield ham would make a good substitute. Split calves' or pigs' feet are simmered in the court bouillon with the ham to provide gelatin, which holds the finished jambon persillé together. The ham is cut into cubes or shredded and combined with freshly chopped parsley and the braising liquid in a terrine and allowed to set.

My own approach is somewhat different and takes a few days of forethought. I salt a fresh, raw ham and convert it into demi-sel (see page 528), a trick that enhances its flavor, and then make stock with pigs' or calves' feet (see page 424), reduce it, and and use it along with vegetables, herbs, and white wine to poach the ham instead of simmering the feet along with the ham in the way most recipes suggest. There are two reasons for making a separate jelly stock. First, this allows you to cook the stock for 10 hours instead of only 6 or so, to extract the maximum of natural gelatin. Second, jambon persillé needs a very gelatinous stock to hold it together, and making the stock in advance allows you to reduce it before you poach the ham.

While my own preference is for homemade demi-sel, you can make a jambon persillé out of just about any form of ham. If you have some decent cooked ham, you don't need to cook it more. Just slice it, cut it into cubes, and layer it in the terrine with melted fonds gelée, clear stock with some extra gelatin added to hold it together. If you have a fully cured ham, soak a piece of it for 3 days in cold water, changing the water a couple of times a day, and then cook the piece as I describe in the recipe.

- 6 quarts when melted (1 recipe) fonds gelée (page 424) (optional)

- 4 pounds [1.8 kg] boneless raw uncured fresh ham or shoulder (5 pounds [2.3 kg] if the bone is in), partially salted (see directions on page 106) or left raw and uncured

- 4 medium-size carrots, peeled, cut into 1-inch [2.5 cm] sections

- 2 large red onions, peeled, cut in half through the root end

- 3 cups [750 ml] dry white wine

- 1 medium-size bouquet garni

- 1 large bunch flat-leaf parsley, large stems cut off and used in the bouquet garni

BRING the gelée to a gentle simmer on the stove and simmer about 2 hours to reduce it to 10 cups [2.5 l]. Skim.

PUT the ham in a pot just large enough to hold it. Pour enough of the fonds gelée over the ham to cover it. If you don't have enough fonds, turn the ham over after 2½ hours. Add the carrots, onions, wine, and bouquet garni, and bring to a simmer over high heat. Turn down to between low and medium heat to maintain a gentle simmer for 5 to 6 hours, until a knife slides easily in and out of the meat. Add water or more broth from time to time to make up for evaporation.

TRANSFER the ham to a cutting board and strain the poaching liquid into a clean container. Chop the parsley very fine. Ladle ½ cup [125 ml] of poaching liquid into the bottom of a 1½-liter (6-cup) terrine and sprinkle over it about 1 tablespoon of the chopped parsley. Pull the ham into shreds and put a layer on top of the parsley and poaching liquid. Pour just enough poaching liquid over the meat to barely cover it, sprinkle more parsley, and add another layer of meat. Keep layering the terrine in this way, finishing it with a layer of broth and parsley. Refrigerate overnight.

WHEN you're ready to serve, just cut slices right out of the terrine. Or, for a more dramatic effect, you can unmold the whole thing: put a platter upside down over the terrine, invert both together, and lift off the terrine. If you like, serve with mustard or cornichons.

Variations: Virtually any meat and some seafood can be poached or braised and layered in a terrine with the reduced braising or poaching liquid, allowed to chill, and served in slices. The Individual Octopus Terrines on page 247, the Sweetbread Terrine on page 417 (in which concentrated broth is finished with cream), and the Cold Beef Terrine on page 427 are a few examples. Traditional jambon persillé is a rough-hewn country terrine, designed to be eaten in generous slices with a robust country wine. While I have nothing against rustic dishes, there are times, such as when old or fragile wines are being served or when a dinner has been conceived to contain more than the usual number of courses, that a traditional country dish benefits from reinterpretation with an eye toward lightness and subtlety of flavor. When I had my restaurant, my wine-importer friend Neal Rosenthal and I decided to host a dinner featuring his favorite Burgundies. I had the task of featuring dishes from Burgundy (such as jambon persillé), but the dishes couldn't be so full-flavored as to overpower Neal's Volnays and Pommards. So I came up with a lightened version of jambon persillé: individual servings of prosciutto shreds, artichokes, and parsley, set in a natural gelée.

When meat is fully cured, it won't go bad if it is left exposed to air and in a relatively cool place. To cure meat to this degree takes prolonged contact with salt, brine, and/or sugar, all of which resist bacteria. Since most bacteria need water to live, drying also helps preserve meat, which is why salted or brined hams are hung up to a year or even longer. Smoking can also help cure a ham, because smoke contains compounds that kill bacteria.

Sometimes curing techniques are used to enhance the flavor of hams and other meats, but not used long enough actually to preserve the meat. It's important to know the difference between fully cured and partially cured hams so you aren't left thinking that your partially cured ham will last indefinitely. A raw fresh ham always benefits from contact with salt and sugar, both of which enhance its flavor and texture. You can simply soak the ham in brine for several days in a cool place before you roast it in the same way you would other cuts of pork, using 3 gallons [12 l] of water, 12 cups [2.9 kg] of kosher salt (or 6 cups [1.5 kg] of regular fine salt), and 12 cups [2.5 kg] of granulated sugar for a half ham or proportionately more brine as needed to cover your ham in a nonaluminum pot. I like to add garlic and fennel to the brine for extra flavor.

Curing a ham so that you can preserve it and store it is a more elaborate process. It takes up to a year and requires a cool airy place to hang the ham—a beam in the cellar, for example. Because of this, I start the project in the fall or early winter. I follow a technique described in Paul Bocuse's *La Cuisine du Marché*. The spices are crushed by rocking over them with a heavy saucepan.

MAKES 1 CURED HAM

1 raw ham (about 15 pounds [6.8 kg])

7 cups [1.25 g] sea salt, or more as needed

1½ cups [200 g] granulated sugar, or more as needed

¼ cup [65 g] saltpeter (optional)

6 bay leaves

10 fresh thyme sprigs, or 1 pinch dried thyme

25 juniper berries, crushed

20 black peppercorns, crushed

30 coriander seeds, crushed

CUT out the hip bone and any backbone left at the top of the ham, following the contours of the bone with the knife. This should expose a shiny round joint, which can be left where it is. Combine

1 cup of the sea salt, ½ cup of the granulated sugar, and the optional saltpeter to keep the flesh pink. Set the ham on a clean table, flesh-side up, skin-side down, and with very clean hands massage the ham with the salt mixture, rubbing it back and forth to get it to penetrate the meat. Be especially attentive to the end of the ham where you cut out the bones. Turn the ham over and rub the skin side in the same way until you've used up all the mixture.

PUT the ham, skin-side down, in a clean container with a lid. For this I use a food-grade plastic storage container. Cover the top flesh side of the ham with 2 cups [480 g] of the sea salt. Put an immaculate kitchen towel gently over the ham and put the lid on the container. Leave the container in a cool place for 2 days, turn the ham over, and repeat with 2 more cups [480 g] of sea salt on the other side. Leave for 2 days more.

AT this point it's best to work with surgical gloves on to protect the ham from bacteria. Place the ham on a very clean platter or surface. Brush any salt mixture off the ham into a large pot and pour 2 quarts [2 l] of water into the container used for salting the ham. Swirl the water around to partially dissolve the mixture, then pour the contents of the container into the pot. Add 1 cup [200 g] of sugar, the bay leaves, the thyme sprigs, and the crushed juniper berries, black peppercorns, and coriander seeds and bring the water to a simmer. Stir in the remaining 4 cups [1 kg] of salt and 6 more quarts [6 l] of water. Bring back to a simmer, simmer for 5 minutes—until the salt and sugar dissolve—and let cool. Thoroughly wash the container used for salting the ham. Put the ham back in the container and pour the cool brine over it. The brine—you'll have about 10 quarts [10 l]—should completely cover the ham. If it doesn't, place a towel over the ham with the ends submerged in the brine—this will keep the top of the ham covered with brine. If the brine doesn't cover at least two-thirds of the ham, look for another container that better fits the ham or make more brine, keeping the same proportions. Turn the ham over every 2 days, again using surgical gloves so you don't contaminate it. After 20 days in brine, the ham is ready to be hung in a cool, dry place. If you're going to serve the ham cooked, you only need to hang it for 20 days and then soak it for 3 days, changing the water each day, to rid it of excess salt. (I know it sounds peculiar that you spend all this time getting the ham to absorb salt and then you desalt it, but the flavor is much improved.) If you want to serve the ham raw, in thin slices, you must hang it for at least 6 months; it will continue to improve for up to 15 months. To hang the ham, thread a length of heavy string through a trussing needle and thread it through the foot end of the ham, about 2 inches [5 cm] in from the edge of the rind. Hang the ham from a hook or nail in a cool place.

INDIVIDUAL PROSCIUTTO, ARTICHOKE, AND PARSLEY TERRINES

JAMBON CRU ET COEURS D'ARTICHAUTS EN GELÉE AU PERSIL

MAKES 8 FIRST-COURSE SERVINGS

6 cups [1.5 l] clear homemade Brown Chicken Broth (page 209) or beef bone broth (page 219) without salt, pot-au-feu broth (page 456), or oxtail soup broth (page 200), or a combination

salt

4 large artichokes

½ lemon

1 tablespoon olive oil

½ pound [225 g] raw fully cured ham such as prosciutto di Parma, prosciutto di San Daniele, Smithfield ham, or Serrano ham, thinly sliced

1 package gelatin (if needed to make the broth jell)

1 large bunch flat-leaf parsley, large stems cut off

BRING the broth to a gentle simmer in a saucepan over low-to-medium heat. Keep the saucepan to one side of the heat to make skimming easier. Reduce the broth to 3 cups [750 ml] while skimming off fat and froth with a small ladle. Let the broth cool slightly and season to taste with salt, leaving the broth a little undersalted because the ham will be salty. Strain the broth through a fine-mesh strainer or a strainer lined with a triple layer of cheesecloth and let cool. Chill it in the refrigerator until set.

WHILE the broth is reducing, trim the leaves off the artichokes (see page 68) and rub the artichoke bottoms with the lemon half. Put the artichoke bottoms in a nonaluminum pot with the olive oil, the juice from the lemon half, and enough water to cover by 3 inches [7.5 cm]. Don't put the lemon itself in the water or it will give the artichokes a bitter lemon flavor. Simmer gently until the artichoke bottoms are easily penetrated with a knife but still offer some resistance, about 20 minutes. Drain in a colander, let cool for 5 minutes, and scoop the choke out of each artichoke with a spoon.

TRIM the fat off the ham slices (save it and render it for cooking) and roll up the slices. Slice each roll crosswise so you end up with ¹⁄₁₆-inch-wide [2 mm] strips.

CHECK to make sure the broth has set—you're chilling it to verify that it contains enough natural

SLICING A TERRINE

Keep in mind that full-size terrines in which solids are suspended in gelled broth can be hard to slice without causing the slices to fall apart. To avoid this, unmold the terrine, freeze, slice it with a serrated bread knife, and allow the individual slices to thaw in the refrigerator or at room temperature.

gelatin to hold it together. If the broth is cold but still liquid, bring it to a bare simmer. Soften the gelatin with 3 tablespoons of water and stir it into the broth. Chill the broth again, only enough to cool it without allowing it to set. Chill eight 5-ounce [150 ml] ramekins. When the broth is ready, wash and dry the parsley, chop it fine, and stir it into the broth. Spoon 2 tablespoons of the parsley broth into each of the molds and refrigerate until set.

CUT the artichoke bottoms into more-or-less regular ½-inch [1.5 cm] cubes and toss them with the shredded prosciutto. Arrange the prosciutto and artichokes in the ramekin molds. Ladle in enough parsley broth to cover the ham and artichokes, and chill the molds until set. Chill for at least 4 hours, or overnight.

ABOUT 10 minutes before you're ready to serve, chill 8 plates. Dip each mold for about 10 seconds in a bowl of hot tap water. Turn the plate over the mold, invert, and give a shake. If the terrines don't just pop out, run a knife around the inside of the mold. Serve immediately.

Variations: Any of the ingredients can be changed. The broth can be made from any creature you like and the ham replaced with thinly sliced meats, such as squab, quail, or duck, or, in seafood versions, with smoked salmon. To use squab, quail, or duck, remove the breasts, pull off the skin, rub them thoroughly with salt and pepper, and store overnight in the refrigerator. The next day, rinse off the breasts, pat dry, rub again with salt and pepper, and store overnight again. Rinse off the salt and pepper and pat dry. Salting twice like this gives the meat a light cure. Sauté in olive oil or clarified butter until the meat is cooked between rare and medium rare. Let cool and slice into thin strips like the ham. I also like to use cubes of foie gras—the combination of foie gras and artichokes is classically Lyonnaise—and substitute chervil or tarragon for the parsley. Truffles, of course, would do no harm.

The delicate leanness of these individual terrines can be beautifully accented with a cold sauce that is more or less rich—light tomato cream sauce, creamed sorrel purée, or crayfish or lobster sauce (see Chapter 25) for seafood terrines, dollops of caviar or sea urchin roe, or cold oysters.

GRILLED HAM AND CHEESE SANDWICHES

CROQUE-MONSIEURS

MAKES 4 SANDWICHES

A croque-monsieur is a French-style ham and cheese sandwich, sold in every café and sometimes even on the street. When I first went to France, croque-monsieurs were dipped in béchamel sauce before being cooked on a griddle, but lately the béchamel seems to have disappeared. In the 1970s a law was passed controlling the price of croque-monsieurs and croissants—France's equivalent of the Federal Reserve controlling interest rates. The result, in those inflationary days, was that croque-monsieurs just kept getting more shoddy until they were hardly worth eating. But there were certain cafés where it was possible to get a well-made, more expensive (and illicit) croque-monsieur—nothing like the thrill of eating a black market sandwich.

Ham and cheese sandwiches remain a staple of my own day-to-day existence and sustain me on many an afternoon when I'm too lazy to cook something serious. When I have the ingredients, I make my ultimate version with thinly sliced Smithfield ham and aged Gouda cheese. Aged Gouda, which is appreciated in France, has the texture of authentic Parmigiano-Reggiano but melts better and has an irresistible nutty complexity that's perfect with ham. If I've got it, I eat these sandwiches with a glass of chilled old amontillado, which also has a nutlike flavor that stands up to the ham and cheese.

When you make a ham and cheese sandwich you have the choice of making it open-faced or closed-faced. My favorites are closed, like an authentic croque-monsieur, but these are richer because they have to be cooked in butter, whereas open-faced versions can be cooked under the broiler with no additional fat. If you don't have raw cured ham such as American country ham or prosciutto, use a good-quality cooked ham.

4 large slices of crusty French bread taken from near the center of a round loaf (for open-faced sandwiches), or 8 slices dense-crumbed white bread such as Pepperidge Farm (for closed-faced)

12 ounces [340 g] prosciutto, country ham, or good-quality cooked ham, sliced thin but not paper thin

12 ounces [340 g] aged Gouda, Gruyère, English or American Cheddar, or other full-flavored hard cheese, sliced thin

4 tablespoons [60 g] butter (for closed-faced sandwiches)

IF you're making open-faced sandwiches, heat the broiler and toast the bread on one side only. Spread a layer of ham on the untoasted side of each slice and top with the cheese slices. Slide the sandwiches under the broiler and broil until the cheese has bubbled up and is melted all the way through.

IF you're making closed-faced sandwiches, put the ham and cheese slices in between 2 slices of bread for each sandwich. Melt half the butter in a heavy-bottomed skillet (or two, if one isn't big enough) and put in the sandwiches. Move them around for a few seconds so they absorb the butter evenly, cover the pan only partially so that trapped steam won't make the sandwiches soggy, and turn the heat to low so the cheese melts without the bread burning. When the bottoms of the sandwiches are browned and the cheese is melting and oozing out the sides, take the sandwiches out of the pan, put in the rest of the butter, and put the sandwiches back in the pan, uncooked side down. Cook, uncovered, until the second side is well browned, about 5 minutes. Don't worry if the cheese oozes out and browns in the skillet—that's the best part.

FRENCH REGIONAL HAM DISHES

A *rigodon* is a kind of crustless quiche made in Burgundy by cooking cubes of ham in a flan mixture (beaten eggs and milk) with a little flour in it to give it some texture. A *jambon de Pâques* (Easter ham) is a

PARSLEY

Parsley has such a presence in my kitchen that I think of it almost as I do salt or pepper. I add it, finely chopped, at the last minute to sauces and stews, to which it lends a fragile, elegant freshness. In restaurant kitchens, parsley may be chopped so far in advance, often by apprentices well drilled in the necessity of preparedness or *mise en place*, that it loses its aroma and ends up smelling like lawnmower clippings. If it is chopped while wet, it clumps and becomes impossible to sprinkle, so it is then wrung out in a towel and all the flavor is squeezed out.

Parsley must be perfectly dry before you chop it. Wash parsley by passing the leaf-end of the bunch under cold running water. Don't take the bunch apart or it'll be harder to cut off the stems. Give the parsley a good shake and cut off the thickest stems at the base of the leaves. Don't bother with the smaller stems within the leaves and certainly don't make yourself crazy by taking the leaves off the bunch one by one. Spin the parsley dry in a salad spinner and then pat it in a kitchen towel so it's perfectly dry. Chop it with a very sharp knife to avoid crushing it. Ideally, parsley should be chopped at the last minute. My solution to this last-minute part is to coarsely chop the parsley ahead of time and then give it a second, fine chopping, which releases its flavor, just before I use it.

jambon persillé with hard-boiled eggs layered with the ham. A *pounti*, from the Auvergne, is a kind of meat loaf made with chopped ham and Swiss chard held together with eggs, milk, and flour. A *saupiquet* was originally a spicy sauce—Taillevent writes about it in the fourteenth century—made with bread soaked in broth (the most common thickener before the invention of roux), onions cooked in lard, plenty of cinnamon and ginger, red wine, and vinegar. The word *saupiquet* now refers to ham steaks in a sauce, not just the sauce, and today's regional French recipes for it have little to do with Taillevent's version except that the sauce contains vinegar and is made spicy with pepper. A typical Burgundian *saupiquet* is made with white wine, broth, juniper berries, shallots, crushed black pepper, and vinegar held together with roux and heavy cream.

French classic cooks, versed in the elaborate cuisine of Escoffier, eschewed pork because they considered it low-class. The exception was ham. Escoffier's *Le Guide Culinaire*, which extolls the virtues of Prague ham, is filled with the usual contrivances, including braising in sherry (which I must say sounds pretty good), various mousses, cold and hot mousselines, and soufflés.

HAM STEAKS WITH JUNIPER CREAM SAUCE

LE SAUPIQUET

MAKES 6 MAIN-COURSE SERVINGS

2 tablespoons flour

4 tablespoons [60 g] butter

1 cup [250 ml] dry white wine

½ cup [125 ml] concentrated broth (see page 4)(optional)

4 shallots, chopped fine

12 juniper berries, crushed

10 peppercorns, crushed

¼ cup [60 ml] good-quality red wine vinegar or sherry vinegar

½ cup [125 ml] heavy cream

2 tablespoons parsley, chopped fine

   salt

6 thick ham steaks (6 to 8 ounces [170 to 225 g] each) from cooked ham, preferably smoked (the ham steaks sold at the supermarket usually work fine)

MAKE a roux by combining the flour with 2 tablespoons of the butter in a small saucepan and cook over medium heat, while stirring with a wooden spoon until the flour smells toasty, about 5 minutes. Whisk in half the wine and continue whisking until it comes to a simmer and the sauce gets thick. (The wine is added in increments so that you can smooth out the sauce; if you add it too quickly, the flour will remain lumpy.) Whisk in the rest of the wine and the optional broth. Simmer the sauce on low heat for 30 minutes—slightly longer if you're using the broth—until the sauce has the consistency you like, but isn't too thick. I like most sauces slightly thicker than heavy cream. With a ladle, skim off any scum that floats to the top. Add the shallots, crushed juniper berries and peppercorns, vinegar, and cream to the sauce and simmer for 5 minutes more or, again, until the sauce has the consistency you like. Strain the sauce into another saucepan, add the parsley, and season to taste with salt.

COOK the ham steaks in a skillet in the remaining butter for about 5 minutes on each side to heat them through. Pat the cooked butter off both sides with a kitchen towel so it doesn't cause the sauce to run off the ham steaks. Arrange the ham steaks on hot plates and ladle the sauce over them.

POACHED EGGS WITH RED WINE SAUCE

OEUFS EN MEURETTE

HOW TO	HOW TO	HOW TO	HOW TO	HOW TO
POACH AN EGG	MAKE A RED WINE SAUCE WITHOUT STOCK	BAKE EGGS	MAKE A QUICK FRESH TOMATO SAUCE	MAKE FRENCH-STYLE Croûtons

I ALWAYS GET PECULIAR LOOKS WHEN I SERVE THIS TRADITIONAL Burgundian dish at a weekend brunch. Eggs with red wine sauce? A single bite convinces guests of the genius of the combination and leaves them wondering why they've never before encountered *les oeufs en meurette*. My own introduction to the dish, 20 years ago, was less than encouraging. I was hitchhiking around France, consulting Waverley Root's marvelous book *The Food of France*, and doing my best to sample regional specialties, but without the funds to indulge myself in the best places. And being in Burgundy, I naively expected that my proximity to noble vines would guarantee marvelous food even on my bare-bones budget. The result was a somewhat warped and disillusioning view of France's country cooking, but probably a more accurate reflection of everyday eating habits than I would have encountered in the top Michelin-starred restaurants. In any case, my plate of *oeufs en meurette*, at a simple bistro within walking distance of the vineyards of Gevrey-Chambertin, was a disastrous mess of two overcooked eggs sitting on a couple of slices of soggy toast and masked with a sauce that looked like a bottle of *gros rouge*—the kind of red wine sold by the liter in plastic bottles—thickened with a handful of raw flour.

Such catastrophes should not cause us to give up too easily. In fact, careful deconstruction of bad meals often helps us to be better cooks. As far as *oeufs en meurette* is concerned, one must first learn to poach an egg. I've tried various methods. Swirling the water around and carefully cracking the egg into the vortex is tedious because you can cook only one egg at a time, and ineffective because the filaments of coagulated egg white that are normally trimmed off adhere to the top of the egg. Adding vinegar to the poaching water supposedly helps the white coagulate, but in fact it just gives the kitchen a funny smell. And poaching the eggs in little cups is simply more nuisance than it's worth. I now just crack the eggs into a frying pan filled with simmering well-salted water. The salt helps the egg float and prevents it from sticking to the bottom of the pan (the sticking makes it more likely that the yolk will rupture when you take out the egg). I break the egg as close to the surface of the gently simmering water as possible so the white holds together as it slips into the water. I also use the freshest eggs I can find, because the white of fresh eggs is firmer and holds more neatly around the yolk. Fresh eggs aren't easy to identify while they're still in the shell, but if you shake a distinctly older egg you'll feel it sloshing around in the shell, because over a period of weeks some of its liquid will have evaporated through the shell and been replaced with air. If you crack a very fresh egg onto a plate, you'll notice that most of the white holds around the yolk with very little liquid running to the edges of the plate. The white of a stale egg won't hold its shape and the lonely yolk will end up sitting in a puddle of watery white.

But back to my sad little lunch. The second problem with the eggs *en meurette* was the toast. If the round slices of bread called *croûtons* are merely toasted, they immediately absorb sauce (and, once you start eating, the runny egg yolk) and turn soggy. To avoid this, the *croûtons* must be cooked in butter, which waterproofs them so they stay crunchy even when surrounded by liquid. While cooking the *croûtons* in butter will make our dish a little richer, the flavors of butter and egg yolk are so well suited to each other that no one seems to mind. If you want to make the *croûtons* less rich, cook them in butter and then carefully slice them in half through the side with a sharp serrated knife, the original method used to make melba toast. Serve each egg on a *croûton* half (buttered-side up), instead of a whole *croûton*.

Now, on to the sauce. Red wine sauces are tricky for a couple of reasons. When red wine is simmered down to concentrate its flavor and color, the tannins (the compounds that make wine feel rough-textured in the mouth) are also concentrated and the acidity is increased; this can result in a sour sauce that makes your mouth pucker. In restaurants, red wine sauces are usually constructed by combining reduced red wine with meat glaze (*glace de viande*, see page 221) and butter, both which soften the acids and tannin in the wine. A better method is to simmer meat with a full-bodied, low-tannin red wine so that the proteins in the meat actually combine with the wine's tannins as the wine reduces and make the sauce less harsh. (See page 10 for more information about the best wines for cooking.)

My own trick is to ask for a prosciutto end, which is a lot cheaper than a chunk of prosciutto, and cut it into small cubes before gently caramelizing it with aromatic vegetables. I then add about one-third of the wine to be used for the sauce and cook it down until it caramelizes on the bottom of the pan. This gives the sauce color and body while partially neutralizing the tannins and acids. Then I add the rest of the wine and, if I have it, a chunk of homemade or store-bought *glace de viande* or demi-glace (see Sources). (These concentrated veal broths, or glazes, aren't essential; in fact, one of the great things about a *sauce meurette* is that it can be made without broth.) I then simmer the sauce with a bouquet garni until it has the necessary flavor and color.

As the sauce simmers and reduces, you must choose how to thicken it. The traditional method for thickening a *sauce meurette* is to whisk in a little beurre manié (literally, kneaded butter), a paste made by working together softened butter and flour, and quickly bringing the sauce to a simmer before immediately serving. (Unlike roux-thickened sauces, which are simmered for at least 30 minutes to eliminate their flour taste, beurre manié-thickened sauces are served before the starchy taste has a chance to develop.) Such a sauce will be perfectly delicious and not as rich as a flourless sauce, such as those popularized in the 1970s during the rage for nouvelle cuisine, in which the red wine is reduced even further and a rather large amount of plain butter is added to finish the sauce. This second method produces a sauce with a deeper, more forthright flavor and a luxurious satiny texture, but with about triple the calories. You also end up with less sauce. Last, either sauce needs seasoning, although because of the prosciutto it may not need salt. I add finely chopped parsley to liven up its color and give it a fresh herbal flavor, a few drops of Cognac for complexity, and in what seems like a contradiction, since we've tried to avoid concentrating the wine's acidity, a few drops of good wine vinegar. The acidity in vinegar seems to affect a different part of the mouth and wakes up the flavor of red-wine and brown sauces without making them sour.

POACHED EGGS WITH RED WINE SAUCE

OEUFS EN MEURETTE

MAKES 6 BRUNCH OR BREAKFAST SERVINGS,

OR 12 FIRST-COURSE SERVINGS AT A LARGER MEAL

FOR THE EGGS AND SAUCE BASE:

- 12 eggs, as fresh as possible

    salt

- ⅓ pound [150 g] prosciutto end, pancetta, or veal or pork trimmings, cut roughly into ¼-inch [.5 cm] cubes

- 1 medium carrot, peeled, cut lengthwise into 3 or 4 strips, and sliced thin

- 1 medium onion, chopped coarse

- ½ stalk celery, sliced thin (optional)

- 1 tablespoon butter

- 3 cups [750-ml bottle] full-bodied red wine

- 1 small bouquet garni

FOR THE CROÛTONS:

- 12 thin slices dense-crumbed white bread (such as thin-sliced white bread)

- 4 tablespoons butter

IF YOU'RE THICKENING THE SAUCE WITH BEURRE MANIÉ:

- 1½ tablespoons butter, softened

- 1½ tablespoons all-purpose flour

IF YOU'RE THICKENING THE SAUCE WITH BUTTER ALONE:

- ¼ pound [115 g] cold butter, cut into 6 slices

FOR FINISHING THE SAUCE:

- 2 tablespoons finely chopped parsley (chopped at the last minute)

- 2 teaspoons Cognac (optional)

- 1 teaspoon good wine vinegar

    salt

    pepper

TO PREPARE THE EGGS AND THE SAUCE BASE

POACH the eggs by cracking them just above the surface of a frying pan filled with well-salted, gently simmering water. You may have to turn up the heat as you add eggs and they cool the water, but don't let the water actually boil. Poach the eggs 4 at a time for about 4 minutes each, take them out of the water with a slotted spoon, and quickly cut off and push away any shaggy amorphous white surrounding each egg. Gently slip the eggs into a bowl of ice water and refrigerate until needed.

COMBINE the prosciutto, carrot, onion, celery, and 1 tablespoon of butter in a heavy-bottomed 2-to-4-quart [2 to 4 l] saucepan and stir over medium heat until the mixture smells fragrant and turns a deep golden brown, about 10 minutes. Pour in 1 cup of wine, turn the heat to high, and boil down the wine until it completely evaporates and the bottom of the pan is coated with a brown glaze. (When the wine is just about gone, turn the heat to low so you don't risk burning the glaze.) Pour in the rest of the wine, add the bouquet garni, and simmer gently over low to medium heat, skimming off froth and fat, until there's only about 1 cup of wine left, about 30 minutes.

TO PREPARE THE CROÛTONS

WHILE the sauce is cooking, prepare the *croûtons*. Cut the bread slices into rounds 3 to 4 inches [6 to 10 cm] in diameter with a fluted cookie cutter or by placing a glass or small bowl over each slice and cutting around it with a knife. Melt 2 tablespoons of the butter in a wide skillet and cook half the rounds, over low to medium heat, on both sides until they are crispy and golden brown. Repeat with the remaining 2 tablespoons of butter and the remaining rounds. (You can also use two skillets and cook all the rounds at once.) Reserve the *croûtons* on paper towels.

TO THICKEN THE SAUCE

STRAIN the sauce into a clean saucepan, pushing firmly against the meat mixture to extract as much liquid as possible.

IF you're using beurre manié to thicken the sauce, work together the softened butter and flour on a plate, with the back of a fork, until smooth. Reserve this mixture until just before serving.

IF you're using just butter to thicken the sauce, simmer the sauce base down by half, so you end up with about ½ cup [125 ml]. (The butter will be added later.)

TO FINISH

BRING about 2 quarts [2 l] of water to a boil. Remove any ice cubes from the bowl with the eggs and gently pour off the water, holding the eggs back with one hand. Warm the plates and the *croûtons*. Bring the sauce base to a simmer and whisk in the beurre manié or the slices of cold butter. Bring to a quick simmer and whisk in the parsley, Cognac, and vinegar, and season to taste with salt and pepper. Pour the boiling water over the eggs and let sit for 1 minute. Take the eggs out, one by one, with a slotted spoon, gently press the bottom of the spoon on a folded kitchen towel, and then place the eggs on the *croutons* set on the warmed plates: 1 per person as a first course, 2 per person as a main course. Ladle or spoon the sauce over each egg. Serve immediately.

Variations: Some recipes for *oeufs en meurette* call for mushrooms while others call for the entire Burgundian garniture of mushrooms, pearl onions, and bacon *lardons*—not a bad idea, but one that makes a basically simple dish into a rather difficult one. Mushrooms alone, however, are easy enough to handle, and they add

dimension to the sauce and another element to the finished dish. I look for the smallest mushrooms, break off their stems, and cook the stems with the aromatic ingredients before I add the wine, and simmer the caps—either whole or cut vertically in quarters—in a little of the wine, and return the resulting winy mushroom-juice mixture to the sauce during reduction. A few dried cèpe (porcini) slices, cooked with the aromatic vegetables at the beginning, add an almost magical earthy note, the origin of which few people will suspect (it will be attributed to your culinary genius).

Of all poached-egg dishes, eggs Benedict is the most famous, and perhaps deservedly so; the combination of melting egg yolk and the rich, mildly acidic hollandaise, while seemingly redundant, is hard to match. I make eggs Benedict with béarnaise sauce (see page 488) instead of hollandaise and substitute a thin slice of prosciutto for the usual Canadian bacon. I also like to prepare *croûtons*, like those described in this recipe, instead of English muffins, which always seem too thick and doughy. Anyone who goes out to brunch with any regularity will have already encountered a collection of eggs Benedict variations, some delicious, some ill conceived. The better-known variations include replacing the Canadian bacon with spinach (Florentine), chopped mushrooms (duxelles; see page 96), or asparagus. Classic French versions are extravagant and baroque—slices of foie gras, crayfish tails, truffles, rich sauces all have their encounters with poached eggs. Often the *croûton* is replaced with a tartlet filled with some elaborate concoction of lobster or game, finely diced and held together with an elaborate (often truffled) sauce. Vegetable purées are sometimes used to fill the tartlets before the poached eggs are set on top, and the purées are sometimes added to the velouté or béchamel used to coat the eggs.

In Burgundy they sometimes serve poached brains (see page 544 for how to cook brains) on *croûtons* and coat them with *sauce meurette*, just like poached eggs.

BEURRE MANIÉ

Beurre manié is a paste made by working together flour and butter with the back of a fork and is whisked into sauces and stews as a thickener. Unlike roux, which should be cooked with liquid for at least 30 minutes before it is served (to get rid of the flour taste), beurre manié should be whisked in at the last minute. Use one to two tablespoons of beurre manié to thicken a cup of liquid.

Poaching eggs a couple at a time is fine for an intimate little breakfast. But the logistics of poaching a large number of eggs, keeping some warm while not allowing others to overcook, can be daunting. One way around this is to poach the eggs up to several hours ahead of time (or even the night before), keep them in a bowl of ice water, and reheat them all at once. Just set a bowl of ice water next to you as you poach, trim the eggs with a paring knife as you go, and gently put them in the bowl. Go ahead and pile the eggs on top of each other, you don't need to arrange them in a single layer. Put the bowl in the fridge until you need the eggs. When you're ready to reheat them, pick out the ice cubes and gently drain away the cold water by tilting the bowl and holding the eggs back with your hand. Pour boiling water over the eggs (pour it down the side of the bowl so you don't break a yolk), let them sit for 1 minute, and then quickly take them out with a slotted spoon, setting the spoon over a towel for a second to absorb water, and serve.

Eggs Baked in Ramekins

OEUFS EN COCOTTE

I'VE NEVER UNDERSTOOD WHY BAKED EGGS haven't caught on in the United States. They're easy to prepare, infinitely adaptable to whims and leftovers, and delicious. In their simplest form, small *cocottes,* or ramekins, are buttered, an egg cracked inside, and the eggs cooked in a covered sauté pan for about 8 minutes on top of the stove or in the oven until the white sets but the yolk stays runny—a kind of poached egg in a mold. For my own slightly richer version, I dribble some heavy cream over the egg; the cream mingles with the white, keeping it custardlike as it cooks. Then I grate some Parmegiano-

Reggiano over it before cooking. Classic recipes abound with the usual rococo variations—purées and forcemeats are placed under the eggs and rich and complicated sauces on top. My own versions follow the same principles but contain far more humble ingredients, often leftovers from the previous night's dinner. I put cooked and diced vegetables—asparagus, string beans, mushrooms, tomato sauce—or diced cooked seafood—shrimp, lobster—or diced pieces of leftover stew with their stewing liquid—in the bottom of the ramekin, crack in the egg, dribble with cream, and sprinkle with Parmigiano-Reggiano. If I'm having brunch guests, I make a couple of different kinds and serve each guest a set of 2. (My ramekins hold 6 fluid ounces [175 ml] and measure about 3½ inches [8.5 cm] in diameter; you can also use 6-ounce [175 ml] Pyrex custard cups.) The variations that follow the recipe are among my favorites.

BAKED EGGS WITH CREAMED SPINACH

OEUFS EN COCOTTE AUX ÉPINARDS À LA CRÈME

MAKES 6 RAMEKINS (6 SMALL FIRST-COURSE
SERVINGS, OR PART OF 6 MAIN-COURSE SERVINGS
WHEN SERVED WITH OTHER VERSIONS)

    salt

1   pound [450 g] spinach, or one 10-ounce [280 g] bag spinach leaves, or ¾ cup [40 g] (12 tablespoons) cooked leftover spinach (2 tablespoons per serving)

⅔   cup [150 ml] heavy cream

    salt

    pepper

1   tablespoon butter, softened

6   large eggs

½   cup (about 2 ounces [60 g]) freshly grated Parmigiano-Reggiano or grana padana

6   slices white bread, crusts removed, toasted, each slice cut diagonally into 4 triangles

IF you're cooking spinach, bring about 3 quarts [3 l] of water with a small handful of salt to a rapid boil.

TAKE the stems off the spinach leaves by pinching the leaf at the base between thumb and forefinger and pulling back the stem with the other hand so that you remove the stem where it runs up the center of the leaf instead of just breaking it off at the base. Wash the leaves thoroughly, plunge them in the boiling water, and simmer them until they "melt," about 30 seconds. Immediately drain in a colander and rinse with cold water. Gently squeeze the leaves in small bunches to get rid of excess water. Slice the small bunches into 2 or 3 pieces each, so the spinach ends up coarsely chopped.

BRING ¼ cup [60 ml] of the cream to a simmer in a sauté pan, season it with salt and pepper, and cook it down until it's so thick it looks almost like a paste. Stir the fresh-cooked or leftover spinach into the cream for about 30 seconds and turn off the heat.

USE a brush or your finger to smear the insides of 6 ramekins or custard cups with softened butter. Distribute the creamed spinach among the ramekins and crack an egg into each ramekin. Spoon the rest of the cream, about 1 tablespoon per ramekin, over the eggs. Sprinkle with salt and pepper and the grated Parmigiano-Reggiano.

LINE the bottom of a lidded sauté pan with a kitchen towel (to keep the ramekins from rattling around), arrange the ramekins in the pan, and pour in enough water to come about one-third of the way up the sides of the ramekins. Put the pan over high heat, and as soon as the water comes to the simmer, turn the heat down to low and cover the pan. Cook until the egg whites set but the yolks are still runny, 10 to 12 minutes. Because of the cream, the eggs may look runny on top, so judge doneness by quickly touching the egg white with your finger, not by how the *cocottes* look on top. Serve on little folded napkins set on small plates, with the toasts passed at the table or arranged around the rim of each plate.

Variations: You can replace all or half of the spinach with sorrel. Stem and wash the sorrel the same way as spinach, but instead of boiling it, put the sorrel leaves directly into the reduced cream and cook the mixture over medium heat until the liquid released by the sorrel evaporates, about 2 minutes.

In the summer I bake my eggs with a chunky tomato sauce (*tomates concassées*). I simmer 2 big, ripe, peeled and seeded and chopped tomatoes until the mixture stiffens, about 10 minutes, and then I add about ¼ cup [60 ml] of heavy cream and simmer again for about 5 minutes until the mixture takes on a saucelike consistency. I put the sauce on the bottom of the 6 ramekins or custard cups, crack the eggs over the sauce, spoon about 1 tablespoon of heavy cream over each egg, sprinkle with Parmigiano-Reggiano, and bake as described in the main recipe.

A third version, and another of my favorites, is eggs baked with duxelles. I make the duxelles by finely chopping ½ pound of mushrooms and cooking them in a sauté pan in which I've cooked a shallot or two in butter until all their liquid is released and evaporates in the pan. I add a little cream to the duxelles, sprinkle cream over the eggs when they are in the ramekins, sprinkle with cheese, and bake in the same way as described above.

Since eggs and seafood make a great combination, I occasionally bake eggs over 1 cup of coarsely chopped cooked shrimp or crabmeat, finishing with cream but leaving out the cheese.

French-style "Fried" Eggs

OEUFS SUR LE PLAT

MOST WAYS THE FRENCH COOK EGGS CAN'T be translated exactly into English. What they call a fried egg (an *oeuf frit*) is a deep-fried egg, plunged in hot oil; the white is spooned up around the yolk as the oil bubbles furiously, enclosing the still-runny yolk in a brown crispy crust. I prefer the American method of "frying," more accurately called panfrying. In panfrying we cook the eggs in a small amount of butter or oil, a technique the French call cooking *à la poêle* (loosely translated as "cooking in a frying pan") or cooking "*à l'américaine.*" Apparently the bare-bones simplicity of cooking an egg in a little butter in a frying pan doesn't appeal to the French, who have developed their own method, endlessly variable, called *sur le plat*. An *oeuf sur le plat* is an egg (or often two) cracked into a buttered round dish—I use individual round porcelain dishes like those used for making crème brulée—and then baked in a preheated oven until the white sets and the yolk stays runny, just like an American fried egg. But unlike American fried eggs, French recipes include an infinity of variations, accomplished by putting various garnitures in the dishes before cracking the eggs over them, and assorted sauces over the eggs once they're in the dishes. In many ways an egg *sur le plat* is like an *oeuf en cocotte*—many of the same variations can come into play—except that an *oeuf sur le plat* spreads out over the dish (like an American fried egg) instead of being held, custardlike, in a ramekin.

Here's my own favorite and simple version:

BAKED EGGS WITH CREAM AND PARMIGIANO-REGGIANO

OEUFS SUR LA PLAT

À LA CRÈME ET AU FROMAGE

MAKES 4 BREAKFAST OR BRUNCH SERVINGS

2 teaspoons butter, softened

8 large eggs

½ cup [12.5 ml] heavy cream

salt

pepper

½ cup [60 g] freshly grated Parmigiano-Reggiano or grana padana

4 slices white bread, crusts removed, toasted, each slice cut diagonally into 4 triangles

PREHEAT the oven to 375°F [190°C/gas mark 5].

BRUSH or rub the insides of 4 round low-sided casserole dishes—sometimes called egg dishes, quiche dishes, or gratin dishes—with butter and crack 2 eggs into each dish. My dishes are about 5 inches [13 cm] in diameter, but an inch or so more or less won't matter.

DRIBBLE the cream over the egg yolks; it will slide down and mingle with the whites. Season the eggs with salt and pepper and sprinkle the cheese over them. Place the egg dishes on sheet pans and slide them into the oven. Bake the eggs until the whites have set—quickly poke one with your finger to see if it's firm—but the yolks stay runny, about 10 minutes. Serve immediately, with the toast points passed at the table.

Variations: Any of the variations that work for *oeufs en cocotte* will also work for *oeufs sur le plat*, but it's best to keep things simple. Sometimes I put a little slice of toasted bread under the eggs and use more cream so it gets absorbed into the bread and makes the whole thing irresistibly rich. Sometimes I rub the bread with a little garlic or, if I'm being sneaky, some of the yellow foie gras fat that forms on top of a Foie Gras Terrine (see page 97). Duxelles, chopped and cooked mushrooms, are fantastic, but since *oeufs sur le plat* are more visible than *oeufs en cocotte,* I sometimes sauté whole or thick-sliced mushrooms and spoon them over the eggs just before serving. Morels and cèpes are great for this—when sautéed in goose or foie gras fat, divine. Shaved white truffles or grated black truffles on top of each serving are great.

OMELETS

OMELETTES

FOUR WAYS	HOW TO	TIPS FOR	HOW TO
TO MAKE AN OMELET	MAKE THE WORLD-FAMOUS OMELETTE DE LA MÈRE POULARD	IMPROVISING OMELETS FOR ELEGANT FIRST OR MAIN COURSES	MAKE LUXURIOUS FRENCH-STYLE SCRAMBLED EGGS

I SPENT YEARS TRYING TO MAKE A DECENT OMELET. MY FIRST ATTEMPT, made as a teenager after watching Julia Child on TV, was green (I used a rusty iron skillet) and leaden, and it left the kitchen smelling like something had died. When my mother bought a nonstick pan, I started to get the knack, and when I was in my twenties and working my first restaurant job as a short-order cook, I learned, during the do-or-die frenzy of Sunday brunch, to make five omelets at a time.

If you've never made an omelet, it may cost you a dozen eggs to get the knack, but once you do you will have found a quick and easy way to make a little breakfast or a midnight snack. There are two ways to make a classic French omelet and a couple of other methods for making a not-so-classic omelet, but here's the most common approach:

OMELETS

OMELETTES

MAKES 1 OMELET

3 large eggs

2 tablespoons heavy cream (optional)

  salt

  freshly ground pepper

1 tablespoon butter

USE a fork to beat the eggs with the cream. The cream gives the omelet a melting, custardlike consistency and makes it harder to overcook and toughen the eggs. Then add the salt and pepper. The egg should be well broken up but they don't have to look perfectly homogenous. When making more than 1 omelet, keep the others warm on plates in a low oven.

TRADITIONAL METHOD

HEAT the butter, over high heat, in an 8-inch [20.5 cm] nonstick or well-seasoned cast-iron omelet pan (the bottom will be 7 to 8 inches [18 to 20.5 cm] across). The pan should have curved sides that slope outward to make it easy to get the eggs to fold back in on themselves. Heat until the butter froths and the froth begins to subside, just before the butter burns. Immediately pour in the beaten eggs and quickly work the eggs around in the pan with the back of a fork until they're almost completely scrambled and their surface is runny but not raw. Tilt the pan away from you and use a fork to gently fold the side of the omelet nearest you over the rest of the eggs. Hold the pan level with your left hand and with your right fist give a couple of quick whacks to the handle near where it joins the pan. This causes the side of the omelet opposite the handle to come up above the edge of the pan. Use a fork to fold this flap of omelet back, toward the center of the pan. Lift the pan and turn the omelet out onto a heated plate so that the folds are now facing down on the plate. If the omelet

doesn't have a perfect tapering shape, push it together on the plate with your fingers.

ROLLED METHOD

THIS method sounds harder than the traditional method, but I actually have found it easier to master. Use a fork to beat the eggs with the cream and seasonings, just enough to break up the eggs—they don't need to be perfectly homogeneous.

HEAT the butter, over high heat, in an 8-inch [20.5 cm] nonstick or well-seasoned cast-iron omelet pan, one with curved sides that slope outward to make it easy to get the eggs to fold back in on themselves. Heat until the butter froths and the froth begins to subside, just before the butter burns. Immediately pour in the beaten eggs, but instead of scrambling them—the most classic method—give them 5 to 10 seconds to set (the exact time will depend on your stove). Then quickly jerk the pan toward you, causing the portion of the omelet away from you to fold partly over the rest and leave about one-third of the pan—the side toward the handle—exposed. Tilt the omelet slightly back toward you, so the loose egg covers the part of the pan left exposed after jerking, and allow it to set again, for 5 to 10 seconds, and repeat the jerking motion. Continue in this way—you'll probably need to jerk the omelet 4 or 5 times, until the omelet completely rolls up on itself and all the runny egg has set. Ideally, the omelet should be firm on the outside, but like loose scrambled eggs on the inside. Turn the omelet out onto a heated plate.

OMELET FLAVORINGS AND FILLINGS

There are three ways to add filling or flavorful ingredients to an omelet. You can whisk them into the eggs before cooking; you can sprinkle them in while the eggs are in the pan, just before folding or rolling the omelet; or you can make a lengthwise slit along the top of the cooked omelet and arrange ingredients (and/or a sauce) on top. Small amounts of flavorful ingredients such as herbs, very dry cheeses such as Parmigiano-Reggiano, mustard, chopped truffles, and spices are best just beaten into the eggs before cooking. More substantial ingredients that might cause the omelet to stick (such as softer cheeses) or break apart (substantial amounts of cooked vegetables such as mushrooms) are better sprinkled in the omelet as you're folding or rolling it up. Elegant-looking or expensive ingredients that you want to highlight (lobster) or that would cook if you put them in with the eggs (caviar) should be nestled into a slit made lengthwise along the top of the finished omelet. Here are few of my favorite combinations:

OMELET WITH CHOPPED PARSLEY, CHERVIL, TARRAGON, AND CHIVES (Omelette aux Fines Herbes): A classic fines herbes mixture contains equal parts of each of these herbs. I cut the amount of tarragon in half because it's stronger and takes over the flavor of the other herbs. If you don't have all four herbs, just substitute more of the others. Chop the herbs at the last minute and count about 1 tablespoon total chopped herbs per omelet. Beat the herbs right into the eggs (and cream, if you're using it) before making the omelet.

MUSTARD AND PARMIGIANO-REGGIANO CHEESE OMELET (Omelette à la Moutarde et Parmigiano-Reggiano): I discovered this combination one night after creeping around the house trying to figure out how to eat from a virtually empty fridge. The effect is fabulous and if you're careful not to use too much mustard or cheese, the omelet is just marvelously savory and the source of the flavor hard to identify, keeping guests guessing. I use about 1 teaspoon of Dijon mustard and 1 tablespoon of freshly grated Parmigiano-Reggiano per omelet. Because you're using so little cheese and the cheese is hard, and therefore won't cause sticking, just beat these ingredients in with the eggs.

GRUYÈRE CHEESE OMELET (Omelette au Gruyère): This is my standard cheese omelet. Sprinkle about ⅓ cup [35 g] grated Gruyère over the omelet just before folding it or, if you're making a rolled omelet, after the first couple of jerks.

MUSHROOM OMELET (Omelette aux Champignons): The way I approach this omelet depends on whim,

degree of laziness, and what kind of mushrooms I have. If I have ordinary cultivated mushrooms, I slice them, sauté them in butter until they are completely dry and well browned, and add a sprinkling of shallot or garlic and chopped parsley near the end of sautéing. I make a slit along the top of the finished omelet and spoon the mushrooms over it. I also sometimes chop the mushrooms, make a duxelles (see page 96), and fold or roll the duxelles up into the omelet. If I have wild mushrooms, I sauté them in the same way as cultivated mushrooms but I either leave them whole (morels, chanterelles) or in thick dramatic slices (cèpes) and then arrange them on top of the omelets. Use as many mushrooms as you like—I've made omelettes aux cèpes with so many mushrooms that you couldn't even see the eggs underneath. Nobody complained.

TRUFFLE OMELET (Omelette aux Truffes): There's more than one way to make a truffle omelet. You can beat chopped truffles into the eggs and cook the omelet as you would an omelette aux fines herbes; you can make a sauce périgourdine by boiling down some semidry Madeira, adding glace de viande or demi-glace, whisking in a little butter, adding sliced truffles, and spooning the sauce over the omelet, which can but doesn't have to contain truffles; or, most subtle of all, you can store your truffles overnight in a jar with the uncracked eggs for your omelets so that the fleeting and ephemeral truffle scent passes mysteriously through the shells and scents the eggs on the inside. Or you can go all out and use all three methods.

LOBSTER OMELET (Omelette à l'Homard): Omelets are useful for turning small amounts of something luxurious into something more substantial. If, for example, you have a leftover lobster, you can make miniature 1-egg omelets (I use a 6-inch [15 cm] nonstick sauté pan with sloping sides) and then serve three slices of lobster on top of each one. If you don't have any leftover sauce, peel, seed, and chop a couple of tomatoes, simmer them with a little cream, add a little chopped tarragon or parsley, and you'll have a halfway decent sauce to spoon over the omelets, creating an elegant first course.

THE FAMOUS MONT-SAINT-MICHEL OMELET

OMELETTE DE LA MÈRÈ POULARD

MAKES 1 LARGE OMELET (2 MAIN-COURSE SERVINGS)

France is filled with pilgrimage sites, from places whose claim to fame is a bone from some obscure saint to Gothic cathedrals so grand that it's easy to imagine the devout of the Middle Ages staring in awe at the rose windows. Mont-Saint-Michel is in the latter category. It is a fortified rock, and depending on the tides, at times it is an island and at times not. At the summit is an ancient abbey, now visited by tourists instead of pilgrims. But lower down is a restaurant that once became the goal of my own pilgrimage, Le Restaurant de la Mère Poulard. La Mère Poulard and her descendants have long been famous for the almost mythical omelets of Mont-Saint-Michel. So one March weekend, determined to discover the secret, I set out to this demi-isle, just off the coast between Normandy and Brittany. Mont-Saint-Michel was beautiful, but the restaurant was clearly a tourist trap. The price of a plain omelet was about the same as for a T-bone for two in a top New York steak house. But I ventured in anyway and ordered the omelet, which arrived on an enormous platter, surrounded with what looked like some kind of sauce. When I asked the waiter whether this liquid was indeed a sauce he stiffened and, almost trembling with indignation, informed me, "Monsieur, c'est du beurre!"—roughly translatable as "It's butter, you idiot." Well, he was right and the omelet was a triumph. Later in the evening I was invited into the kitchen to watch the omelets being prepared. I've since figured out how to reproduce them at home.

Contrary to most recipes I've read for the famous omelets, the eggs are not separated (as though making a soufflé omelet) but are whisked up, by hand, until frothy in a copper bowl. (Fortunately you can also whisk them up in a noncopper bowl or in an electric mixer.) For this to work, the eggs must be slightly warm and you shouldn't try whisking more than 4 or 5 eggs at once. In Mont-Saint-Michel, a fist-size chunk of butter is heated over a small fire in the hearth, until frothy, in a big copper omelet pan with a 5-foot [1.5 m] handle. The eggs are poured in, allowed to set for a minute or so, and another fist-size chunk of butter is set in the middle. The omelet sits there for another minute, is gently folded over in half, and is slid onto a platter. Here's how I do it at home. If you don't have a 12-inch [30 cm] skillet, you can make single omelets (see variations), using the same amount of butter for a single omelet as you do the two-serving omelet given below.

5 large, best-quality, very fresh eggs

6 tablespoons best-quality American butter, or, better, ⅓ of a 250-gram packet of French butter (beurre d'Isigny, beurre de Charentes, or beurre d'Echiré if you're getting really picky)

salt

pepper

PREHEAT the oven to 350°F [175°C/gas mark 4].

WARM the eggs to body temperature by putting them (uncracked) in a bowl, covering them with warm water, and letting them sit for 10 minutes. Cut half of the butter into four equal slices. Crack the eggs into a large stainless steel or copper bowl or the bowl of an electric mixer. Beat by hand for 10 minutes or in an electric mixer for 5 minutes, until the eggs triple in volume, and hold medium peaks.

HEAT the butter you didn't slice until it froths, over medium heat, in a 12-inch [30 cm] nonstick or well-seasoned omelet pan that will fit in the oven and that has a handle that won't melt. Pour in the eggs and cook the omelet for a total of 2 minutes on the stove, repositioning it every 30 seconds so that it browns evenly, over low to medium heat. Set the butter slices gently on top of the omelet in the pan. Reposition the pan on the flame until air pockets form in the eggs, another minute or so. Sprinkle salt and pepper over the omelet and slide the pan into the oven. Bake for 1 to 2 minutes—leave the omelet runny because it will continue to cook after you fold it.

SLIDE a rubber spatula under the side of the omelet nearest the handle, and while lifting the pan up with your left hand, gently fold the omelet in half and slide it onto a warm platter. Serve immediately, cutting the omelet in half at the table and using a large spoon and spatula to serve it onto hot plates.

Variations: In Mont-Saint-Michel, the famous omelet is served with every imaginable flavor, both sweet and savory. I like the plain omelets best because they show off the flavor of the eggs and butter, but a sprinkling of Grand Marnier, a little cocoa powder and sugar, or fruit preserves turn the omelet into a lovely dessert. If you're making an omelet for 1 serving, use 3 eggs and a 9-inch or 10-inch [23 or 25.5 cm] nonstick pan. If you're making 2 omelets, beat the eggs in 2 batches, beating the second batch as soon as you pour the first batch into the pan. Instead of sliding the omelets into a 350°F [175°C/gas mark 4] oven, keep the first omelet warm in a 250°F [120°C/gas mark ½] oven while you're making the second one.

Flat Omelets

A FLAT OMELET IS SIMPLY AN OMELET THAT isn't folded or rolled over itself. This makes it easier to prepare because there's no folding of the omelet or shaking of the pan, either of which can be intimidating to neophyte cooks. Most French recipes recommend flipping the omelet as soon as it starts to set on the bottom—a technique that usually ends in disaster. My own foolproof solution is to cook the omelet for a few seconds on top of the stove and then slide it under the broiler to get the top to barely set so the omelet is still slightly runny (what the French call *baveuse*).

FLAT OMELET WITH ONIONS AND WINE VINEGAR

OMELETTE LYONNAISE

MAKES 4 LIGHT LUNCH OR FIRST-COURSE SERVINGS

An omelette lyonnaise is made with lots of onions and is finished with a sprinkling of wine vinegar, a typically Lyonnaise trick that balances the onions' sweetness.

Since cooking the onions takes about 45 minutes, I like to make this omelet for 4 people, in my 12-inch [30 cm] nonstick pan. I often serve it for lunch with plenty of red wine, most often Beaujolais. If you don't have a 12-inch [30 cm] pan, make individual omelets—use 2 or 3 eggs each—in a 9-inch or 10-inch [23 or 25.5 cm] pan. For late risers, the onions can be cooked the night before.

3   large red onions (about 3 pounds total), peeled

3   tablespoons butter

10 large eggs

¼   cup [60 ml] heavy cream (optional)

    salt

    pepper

    good red-wine vinegar or balsamic vinegar

SLICE the onions as thin as you can. I use a plastic vegetable slicer (see page 13) and slice the onions into whole rounds. If you're using a chef's knife, cut the onions in half through the root end before slicing, since half-onions are easier to slice than whole ones.

MELT the butter in a heavy-bottomed pot and add the onions, which will seem like far too many. Cook the onions over medium heat, stirring every few minutes, for about 15 minutes, until they shrink and release liquid. Turn the heat to high to evaporate the liquid. Stir every minute to prevent sticking and watch the onions carefully so they don't burn. When all the liquid has evaporated, turn the heat to low and stir the onions every couple of minutes until they are evenly caramelized, about 15 minutes more.

TRANSFER the onions to a 12-inch [30 cm] nonstick sauté pan or well-seasoned iron skillet and spread them out with a wooden spoon.

PREHEAT the broiler for at least 5 minutes.

BEAT the eggs in a mixing bowl with the cream, salt, and pepper and pour them into the pan with the onions. Cook over medium heat for about 4 minutes, repositioning the pan over the flame so the bottom cooks evenly and gently pushing the eggs down into the onions with a wooden spoon. Slide the pan under the broiler, again repositioning it so the top cooks evenly, for 1 or 2 minutes, until the omelet is barely set and still slightly runny. Slide the omelet out of the pan onto a hot platter and sprinkle it with a few drops of vinegar. Serve at the table in wedges. Pass the vinegar bottle for those who want more.

Variations: Many areas in France have, in addition to the old standbys such as *omelette aux fines herbes,* their own regional omelets. The Basque country is known for its *pipérade,* which I prepare with poblano chiles (heretical) because I'm not terribly fond of sweet peppers, or I replace the traditional *piments d'espelette,* which are nearly impossible to find here, with Italian dried *peperoncini.* In nearby Béarn they make an *omelette bayonnaise* with cubes of ham and cèpes, and a similar *omelette bordaberry,* which contains crème fraîche. The Auvergne has its *omelette bravaude,* made by gently cooking small cubes of potatoes in bacon fat (I add cubes of bacon, too), pouring over them eggs mixed with cream, sprinkling the whole thing with grated cheese, and then lightly broiling. Norman cooks make omelets with cockles or shrimp. (When using cockles, I make a little cream sauce from the cockle-steaming liquid or the shrimp shells and spoon it over the finished omelets, along with the cockles in their shells.) An *omelette landaise,* named after the Landes region in Gascony, contains ham and bread cubes gently browned in goose fat or foie gras fat. An *omelette limousine,* named after the Limousin region, is a lot like an *omelette bravaude* with the cubes of potatoes replaced with mushrooms. One of my old cookbooks describes an omelet from the Languedoc made with lightly toasted pine nuts, half of which are ground and added to the eggs, the other half added whole. An *omelette savoyarde,* named after the mountainous Savoy region known for its cheeses, is made with plenty of grated cheese and thinly sliced potatoes gently sautéed in butter in a separate pan. Provençal cooks make any number of flat omelets they call *crespèus* by cooking various vegetables, such as chard, tomatoes, zucchini, mushrooms, and artichokes, pouring the eggs over them, allowing the eggs to set on the bottom, and then finishing the omelet under the broiler or by continually lifting the edges of the omelet so that any uncooked egg flows underneath and cooks. In Florence I once tasted a frittata no thicker than a crepe that had thin slices of porcini embedded in it. Try making up your own different-flavored flat omelets, stacking them in a loaf pan or cake pan with various sauces, and then serving the whole assembly in slices.

Scrambled Eggs

OEUFS BROUILLÉS

THE FRENCH HAVE A COMPLETELY DIFFER-ent attitude about scrambled eggs and omelets than Americans do. We tend to think of omelets as something special and more likely to be eaten at a restaurant, and of scrambled eggs as a quick home breakfast. In France, where scrambled eggs are rarely made at home but are likely to be encountered in the most elegant restaurants, the reverse is true. This is because the French scramble their eggs differently than we do. We just stir our eggs in a frying pan or skillet over fairly high heat until they curdle. In France, this won't do at all. There, the eggs must first be thoroughly beaten and then strained so they're perfectly smooth. They are then combined with prodigious amounts of cream and/or butter and cooked in a double boiler until smooth and custardlike. Luxurious ingredients such as morels, cubes of foie gras, and truffles are often added to the eggs as they're being stirred, and it's not uncommon to find scrambled eggs topped with beluga caviar. Scrambled eggs are usually served in little ramekins, but in fancier places, the top of the egg is carefully cut off with a knife or eggshell cutter, the egg poured out, the shell carefully washed, and the scrambled eggs put back in the shell, which is set in an egg cup. This may seem like a complicated and extravagant way to go about things, but if you serve the eggs as an elegant little first course instead of for breakfast, the work, expense, and calories are easier to justify. You can also get by with serving far less.

SCRAMBLED EGGS WITH MORELS

OEUFS BROUILLÉS AUX MORILLES

MAKES 4 FIRST-COURSE SERVINGS OR
6 SIT-DOWN HORS D'OEUVRES

You don't have to limit this dish to those times when you have morels. It also works marvelously well with other wild mushrooms, especially cèpes, chanterelles, or hedgehogs, gently sautéed in butter and stirred in with the eggs. Scrambled eggs are also the perfect medium for truffles. Store the uncracked eggs overnight in a tightly sealed jar with the truffles and then beat chopped truffles into the eggs before cooking.

½ ounce [15 g] dried morels, or ⅓ pound [150 g] fresh

6 tablespoons butter (or 4 tablespoons, if using dried morels)

salt

pepper

4 large eggs

¼ cup [60 ml] heavy cream

IF you're using dried morels, put them in a bowl with ½ cup [125 ml] water and let soak for 30 minutes, repositioning them with your finger every few minutes so that they soak the water up evenly, until soft. Squeeze them firmly over the bowl to extract any liquid and eliminate sand. Save the soaking liquid in a small bowl.

IF you're using fresh morels, quickly swirl them around in a bowl of cold water, lift them out with your fingers, and drain them on paper towels.

IF the morels, either dried or fresh, are large, cut them lengthwise in half or in quarters.

IF you're using fresh morels, sauté them over medium heat in 2 tablespoons of the butter until they are soft and fragrant and any water they release evaporates, about 10 minutes. Sprinkle with salt and pepper and reserve.

IF you're using dried morels, put them in a small saucepan and slowly pour their reserved soaking liquid over them, leaving any sand behind in the bowl. Cover the saucepan and cook over low heat for about 10 minutes. Watch the morels carefully to make sure the liquid doesn't run dry.

IF you want to serve the eggs in their shells, cut the narrower end off each egg, about ¼ inch down from the top. If you have an egg cutter, just fit it over the egg and squeeze the handles. If you don't, gently saw through the shell with a fine-serrated knife. Rinse out the lower shells and reserve. Discard the tops.

BEAT the eggs and work them through a strainer into the top of a double boiler or heavy-bottomed saucepan and stir in the cream, 4 tablespoons butter, salt, and pepper. Bring the water in the double boiler to a barely perceptible simmer, making sure the insert isn't touching the water. If you're using a saucepan, put it on a flame-tamer over very low heat. Stir the eggs with a wooden spoon, being careful to reach into the corners of the saucepan so the eggs don't curdle. Be patient; it will take about 10 minutes for the eggs to start to thicken. As soon as they do, add the morels, and continue stirring off the heat. The eggs should have a semiliquid consistency, but if you like them slightly thicker, just cook them a few seconds longer. Season to taste with salt and pepper.

SERVE in individual 4-ounce or 5-ounce [125 ml or 155 ml] ramekins or the cleaned-out eggshells set in egg cups. The eggs are easiest to eat with demitasse spoons or small teaspoons.

GEORGE BLANC'S EGG CUP HORS D'OEUVRE

L'AMUSE-BOUCHE COQUETIER DE GEORGES BLANC

MAKES 6 SIT-DOWN HORS D'OEUVRES, OR 8 IF YOU'RE USING A TOPPING

When I first went to France on my quest to learn cooking, I went to see Richard Olney, who at the time no longer taught his famous Avignon cooking classes. I asked him which would be the best restaurants in France in which to work for an apprenticeship. He named only two: Vivarois in Paris and Chez la Mère Blanc (now Georges Blanc) in Vonnas, a tiny village in the mountains east of Burgundy.

Every fancy restaurant in France puts amazing effort into the tiny hors d'oeuvres that are served, usually with an aperitif, before the meal is even ordered. Nowadays it's fashionable to call them amuse-gueules or amuse-bouches—barely translatable, but gueule is slang for "face" and bouche means "mouth." Competition is intense. Of all the amuse-gueules I sampled, this one is the best, and fairly generous, too. When I first tasted it, before I landed a job in the kitchen of Chez la Mère Blanc, I was confused by a layer of what seemed like scrambled eggs. As it turns out, the layer is made of puréed hard-boiled eggs combined with mayonnaise—a little, in fact, like my mother's deviled-egg sandwich filling. In any case, this makes a lovely little starter to a fancy dinner. It's best in 2- to 3-ounce [60 to 90 ml] egg cups, but if you don't have any, small ramekins or liqueur glasses will do. Because this recipe is very rich, it makes only about 2 ounces [70 g] per serving, so select your serving dishes accordingly. I try to coordinate preparation so that I make this hors d'oeuvre within a day or two of making Chicken Liver Mousse.

FOR THE FIRST LAYER:

½ cup [110 g] Chicken Liver Mousse (page 92)

FOR THE SECOND LAYER:

1 tablespoon extra-virgin olive oil

1 medium shallot, chopped fine

2 ripe medium-size tomatoes, peeled, seeded, chopped
fine

2 tablespoons heavy cream (optional)

½ teaspoon good wine vinegar

salt

pepper

FOR THE THIRD LAYER:

2 hard-boiled eggs

¼ cup [60 ml] Basic Mayonnaise (page 34)

salt

pepper

OPTIONAL TOPPINGS:

1 ounce [30 g] caviar or other fish roe

chervil sprigs

flat-leaf parsley, tiny leaves only

3 ounces [90 ml] clear concentrated broth or consommé
(pages 4 and 212), chilled

TO PREPARE MIXTURE
THE FIRST LAYER

RESERVE the chicken liver mousse in the refrigerator, covered with plastic wrap, until you're ready to assemble the hors d'oeuvres.

TO PREPARE MIXTURE
THE SECOND LAYER

HEAT the olive oil over medium heat in a saucepan and stir in the shallot. Cook the shallot for about 10 minutes, until it turns translucent, lowering the heat if it starts to brown. Add the tomatoes and turn up the heat to cook the tomatoes until they form a stiff mixture. Add the cream and the vinegar, cook for about a minute more, and season to taste with salt and pepper. Reserve, covered, in the refrigerator.

TO PREPARE MIXTURE
THE THIRD LAYER

COMBINE the hard-boiled eggs with the mayonnaise and mash together to the consistency of finely chopped eggs with the back of a fork or in a mini-processor. Season to taste with salt and pepper.

TO ASSEMBLE
THE HORS D'OEUVRES

DIVIDE the chilled chicken liver mousse among the 6 or 8 egg cups, smoothing it as best you can with the back of a spoon so that it makes an even layer. Spread a layer of the tomatoes over it and give the egg cups a tap to settle the mixture down. Cover with a layer of the egg mixture and again tap the egg cups. If you're using the chilled concentrated broth or consommé, chop it and spoon it on top of the egg cups and put them back in the refrigerator long enough for the broth to set.

COVER the top of the egg cups with one of the other optional toppings, or just serve the egg cups as they are.

CHEESE SOUFFLÉ

SOUFFLÉ AU FROMAGE

HOW TO	HOW TO	HOW TO
BEST BEAT EGG WHITES	JUDGE WHEN A SOUFFLÉ IS DONE	MAKE SOUFFLÉS AHEAD OF TIME

MANY OF US HAVE TASTED DESSERT SOUFFLÉS, USUALLY CHOCOLATE OR Grand Marnier, in restaurants, but cheese soufflés rarely show up on restaurant menus because they're served as a first course and have to be assembled and baked while the customer sits, taking up valuable real estate. Dessert soufflés, on the other hand, are ordered ahead of time, during the meal, and can be prepared while the customer finishes the main course. So the only place you're likely to eat cheese soufflé is at home, either your own or someone else's, a fact that adds to the dramatic effect, since you can be sure your guests didn't eat one the night before at some restaurant. A big soufflé never fails to impress.

Cheese soufflés, at least in the form we know them today, are relatively recent inventions. The earliest mention of any soufflé at all was made in the early part of the eighteenth century by Vincent de la Chapelle; that dish resembles modern versions only in that it is lightened with beaten egg whites. Later in the eighteenth century, the word occurs again, but not in the way we use it today. (*Soufflé*, the past participle of *souffler*, is translated as "breathed" or, more loosely, as "puffed.") Menon, one of the most popular writers of the late eighteenth century, uses it to describe a kind of beignet made with cream-puff pastry, *pâte à choux*. By the early nineteenth century, modern soufflés, made with beaten egg whites, appear consistently in cookbooks and are usually rather elegant affairs made with game and exotic seafood, but cheese soufflés, which seem to have been the country cousins of their classic counterparts, don't show up in cookbooks with any regularity until the end of the nineteenth century.

Regardless of their history, soufflés terrify novice and even experienced cooks. I don't know why this is, exactly. I make them often, usually on those days when there's nothing but cheese and eggs in the fridge and it's too late to go out and shop. With a tangy little salad and a glass of white wine, a cheese soufflé makes a perfect, luxurious little meal.

Despite all the anxiety about making soufflés, very little can go wrong. The worst thing you can do is overcook it, which will cause it to fall as soon as it comes out of the oven and will make it dry, or overbeat the egg whites, which will result in a soufflé that won't rise as dramatically but will still rise and taste great. One thing you must do is use good cheese. If the cheese doesn't have enough flavor, neither will the soufflé. The classic cheeses for a soufflé are Gruyère and authentic Parmigiano-Reggiano. Any number of substitutes work wonderfully. These include good Cheddar (I've made lovely soufflés with the sharpest Cheddar from the supermarket), blue cheese (good blue cheese such as Stilton, Roquefort, Gorgonzola), and goat cheese (see recipe, page 135). For the most dramatic soufflés, you'll need to make a "collar," a double-folded sheet of aluminum foil that wraps around the soufflé dish. It allows you to overfill the dish and prevents the soufflé mixture from pouring over the sides of the dish as it expands, but before it has set. The dish and the collar must be well coated with butter and finely grated Parmigiano-Reggiano (or flour) to prevent the mixture from sticking to the dish, since that would keep the mixture from rising as it expands.

A cheese soufflé is made by folding beaten egg whites into a béchamel sauce to which cheese has been added (turning the béchamel into a Mornay sauce), along with some but not all of the egg yolks. In most recipes, additional cheese is sprinkled over the mixture as the egg whites are being folded with the sauce base; the purpose is to avoid adding too much cheese to the sauce base and thus making it and the finished soufflé too heavy. The egg whites should be beaten with a balloon whisk, or in an electric mixer, to stiff peaks, but they mustn't be overbeaten or they'll break apart and the soufflé won't rise as well. An electric mixer can wreak havoc if left on for a few minutes too long. Using a blender—which I did on my first attempt—is folly. I beat my egg whites in a big copper bowl that I polish thoroughly beforehand with copper cleaner or in the traditional (and less expensive) French way, with about ½ cup [125 ml] of vinegar and a small handful of salt. In either case I then thoroughly rinse the bowl in hot water and wipe it perfectly dry with paper towels or a clean kitchen towel. Traces of fat or water in the bowl will keep the egg whites from fluffing up. Needless to say, the beating requires physical effort and becomes exhausting if you use only one arm (it's worth acquiring a little ambidexterity so you can switch arms). Most cooks don't share my aversion for electric things and use a mixer. A sturdy stand-up mixer with a "planetary" motion best simulates hand beating, but you can get by using a handheld mixer, moving it around in the whites so they beat evenly. Unless you have a copper bowl for your mixer, you'll need to add a small pinch of cream of tartar to the whites before beating to stabilize them and keep them from breaking apart. You don't need the cream of tartar when using a copper bowl since traces of copper react with the whites and perform the same function. A pinch of salt is also added to the whites regardless of how they're beaten.

A soufflé should be baked on the bottom rack of the oven so that the heat rises from below. Some recipes even suggest setting the soufflé directly on the floor of the oven. If the oven is too hot, or the heat is coming from the top, the soufflé will brown too quickly, and the hard crust that forms will keep the soufflé from rising as dramatically as it might have. If, on the other hand, the oven isn't hot enough, the soufflé will dry out in the center before it browns on the outside. The temperature of the oven should also be adjusted according to the size of the soufflé; smaller soufflés should be baked in a hotter oven. Whatever temperature I'm using, I preheat the oven and then turn it up 25°F [14°C] more once I put the soufflé in. This causes the heat source at the bottom of the oven to ignite and gives the soufflé an extra little push. When making a large soufflé, preheat the oven to 350°F [175°C/gas mark 4] and turn it up to 375°F [190°C/gas mark 5] as soon as you put in the soufflé. When making individual soufflés, start the oven at 375°F [190°C/gas mark 5] and turn it up to 425°F [220°C/gas mark 7]. If you have a convection oven—one that blows the hot air around—turn off the convection fan when making soufflés.

CHEESE SOUFFLÉ

SOUFFLÉ AU FROMAGE

MAKES 4 INDIVIDUAL FIRST-COURSE SERVINGS

OR 2 MAIN-COURSE SERVINGS

FOR LINING THE DISHES AND COLLARS:

1 tablespoon softened butter

4 tablespoons [25 g] finely grated Parmigiano-Reggiano or grana padana

FOR THE MORNAY SAUCE BASE:

4 tablespoons [55 g] butter

4 tablespoons plus 1 teaspoon all-purpose flour

1½ cups [375 ml] whole milk

¾ cup (2 to 3 ounces/75 g) finely grated Parmigiano-Reggiano or grana padana

salt

pepper

very small pinch of nutmeg

5 large egg yolks

FOR THE FINAL FOLDING:

8 egg whites

pinch of salt

cream of tartar (if you're not using a copper bowl), a small pinch

¾ cup (2 to 3 ounces/80 g) Gruyère or other hard, flavorful cheese such as Cheddar, grated fine

TO MAKE THE COLLAR AND LINE THE DISH

BAKE the soufflé in a 6-cup or 8-cup [1.5 or 2 l] soufflé dish or in four individual 10-ounce [310 ml] soufflé dishes. Pull out a sheet of aluminum foil slightly more than 3 times longer than the diameter of the soufflé dish and fold it lengthwise over itself with the shiny side, which is less likely to stick, on the outside. The foil strip should be wide enough to cover the entire outside of the soufflé dish and rise at least 3 inches [7.5 cm] above the rim. Rub the shiny side of the foil and the inside of the soufflé dish with softened butter. Wrap the foil around the soufflé dish and attach it to itself with a paper clip or by just pinching it together at the top so it stays in place.

PUT the Parmigiano-Reggiano in the dish and turn the dish around and about until the dish and foil are all covered with a layer of cheese. Don't touch the inside after this point. Put the dish in the refrigerator.

TO MAKE THE MORNAY SAUCE BASE

MELT the butter in a small heavy-bottomed saucepan and stir in the flour with a whisk until smooth. Gradually pour in the milk while whisking and bring to a simmer over high heat, while continuing to whisk. Boil for about 30 seconds, whisking until the mixture is smooth. Remove from the heat, stir in the Parmigiano-Reggiano, and season to taste with salt, pepper, and nutmeg. Whisk in the egg yolks, one by one. Reserve up to 2 days, covered.

TO BEAT AND FOLD IN THE EGG WHITES AND BAKE THE SOUFFLÉ

PREHEAT the oven to 350°F [175°C/gas mark 4] if you're using a 6-cup or 8-cup soufflé dish, or to 375°F [190°C/gas mark 5], if you're using individual soufflé dishes.

PUT the egg whites into a bowl with the salt and, unless you're using a copper bowl, the cream of tartar. Beat the whites to stiff peaks (they'll stick straight out when you hold the whisk or beater sideways), starting slowly and gradually increasing speed, about 4 minutes with an electric mixer started on slow and ending on high, or 6 to 8 minutes by hand. Whisk about one-fourth of the beaten whites into the sauce base to lighten it and make it easier to fold. Pour the sauce base down the side of the bowl containing the remaining whites and fold together the sauce base and whites with a rubber spatula while sprinkling the grated Gruyère over the mixture. Pressing the spatula against the sides of the bowl, reach down to the bottom of the bowl where most of the heavier sauce base will have settled and lift up the base, gently folding it over the whites. Continue cutting into the whites, but not pushing against them, to combine the mixture. Don't overdo it; a few uncombined pieces of white are less of a problem than overworking the mixture.

GENTLY pour the mixture into the soufflé dish(es), place the dish(es) on a sheet pan, and slide the sheet pan into the oven. Turn up the oven to 375°F or higher [to 190°C/gas mark 5 or 200°C/gas mark 6]. Bake a large soufflé for 40 to 50 minutes or individual soufflés for 15 to 20 minutes. When done a soufflé should have risen by about half its original height. To determine when the inside is done (it should be somewhat on the runny side) open the oven as little as possible and move the sheet pan back and forth while closely watching the movement of the soufflé. If it's underdone and still liquid on the inside, you'll notice the top rocking slightly. As the inside begins to set, the top of the soufflé won't rock. If you rush the soufflé to the table and cut into it and see that it's undercooked, don't panic. Be as nonchalant as possible and just put the soufflé back in the oven and cook it a few more minutes. An underdone soufflé won't fall much once out of the oven; an overdone one will.

TO SERVE THE SOUFFLÉ

TAKE the sheet pan with the soufflé out of the oven, immediately pull away the collar, and bring the soufflé to the table. If you're serving individual soufflés, put each soufflé on a plate and set it before a guest. If you're serving one big soufflé, serve it at the table on heated plates. Make sure everyone gets some savory crust. The creamy center should function as a sauce for the rest.

Variations: You can make a Roquefort soufflé just like the cheese soufflé above by working 6 ounces [170 g] of Roquefort with the egg yolks and adding the mixture to the sauce base instead of the Parmigiano-Reggiano, leaving out the Gruyère that's added during the folding. Don't make blue-cheese soufflés with cheap blue cheese (such as Danish blue), which will give them a coarse and aggressive flavor.

French classic cookbooks contain dozens of savory soufflé recipes. (For more about dessert soufflés, see chapter 45.) Most of the savory soufflés are made by adding various ingredients, such as spinach, mushrooms, or cooked and puréed chicken or other meats or fish, to the same béchamel base used for a cheese soufflé; in older versions, a more savory béchamel based on aromatic vegetables and sometimes ham is used (see recipe for béchamel, page 577). Early nineteenth-century recipes for game and meat soufflés call for a concentrated velouté made from the bones or trimmings of whatever food is being souffléd instead of béchamel. Another approach, used for game and some seafood soufflés, involves making a mousseline by working heavy cream into the raw puréed flesh of poultry, game, or seafood, folding the mousseline with beaten egg whites, and baking the mixture until it expands. Some seafood soufflés aren't really soufflés in the usual sense but are elaborate gratins made by braising fish fillets (see chapter 23), quickly beating egg yolks with the braising liquid, converting it into a *sauce vin blanc* (or *Marguery*, see pages 257 and 310), coating the fish with the sauce, and immediately putting it back in the oven or under the broiler for a quick *glaçage* (glazing). Other seafood variations involve puréeing some of the cooked fish, combining it with a béchamel, folding with beaten whites, using this soufflé mixture to cover the fish in a gratin dish—in which it is immediately baked—and serving it with or without a *sauce vin blanc* that can be made by emulsifying egg yolks with the braising liquid as though making a hollandaise sauce.

Frankly, the more elaborate the procedure, the less likely the result will equal, much less exceed, the sum of the parts. A perfectly cooked vegetable or piece of fish with a simple sauce will almost always be more satisfying than the result of elaborate machinations. Unless I'm making *soufflés à la Suissesse* (see recipe, page 136), which better lend themselves to elaboration, I rarely make a soufflé with anything other than cheese. Eggs and cheese have an affinity, each seeming to heighten the goodness of the other, while the flavor of other ingredients—vegetables, fish, or meats—is muted and their texture lost in the soufflé treatment.

INDIVIDUAL GOAT CHEESE SOUFFLÉS

SOUFFLÉS AU FROMAGE DE CHÈVRE

MAKES 4 FIRST-COURSE SERVINGS

For four years I owned a small French restaurant in Manhattan where I was more concerned with duplicating experiences I had had in restaurants in France than I was in making money. Hence the restaurant's eventual demise—too many truffles, too many laborious dishes, and too much Champagne broken out if business was slow or a member of the kitchen staff was feeling a little low. The least practical dish, but a very popular one, was an individual goat cheese soufflé served as a first course. Not only did this keep the customers at the table an extra 20 minutes, but because I insisted the egg whites be beaten by hand (and because of our limited staff, this meant by me), I would be standing next to the stove beating egg whites in a copper bowl, sautéing chicken and steaks, whisking up sauces, and keeping track of those soufflés that were already in the oven.

These soufflés are very easy to prepare and you don't need to make a béchamel. I've never known anyone not to give them a rave review. It's important to use goat cheese that's not too hard, not too soft, and with plenty of flavor. I use bûcheron (loosely translated as "lumberjack"), which is shaped like a log, 1 foot [30 cm] long and 5 inches [12 cm] in diameter. It's often sold in cheese stores or fancy supermarkets sliced into chunks about 2 inches [5 cm] thick. If you can't find bûcheron, ask for a medium-textured full-flavored cheese, but don't pay a mint—goat cheese can be very expensive. I use individual 10-ounce [310 ml] porcelain soufflé dishes, 4 inches in diameter and 1¾ inches [5 cm] high. Charlotte molds, which are metal and have little heart-shaped handles, will also work. I don't use a collar for these soufflés, but if your soufflé dishes are small, you may want to make aluminium foil collars as described on page 133.

FOR LINING THE SOUFFLÉ DISHES:

- 1 tablespoon softened butter
- ⅓ cup finely grated Parmigiano-Reggiano or grana padana

FOR THE GOAT CHEESE BASE:

- 12 ounces [340 g] full-flavored, medium-textured goat cheese
- 6 egg yolks

FOR THE FINAL FOLDING:

- 10 egg whites
- pinch of salt
- small pinch of cream of tartar (if you're not using a copper bowl)

PLACE the dishes on their sides and brush the insides of the dishes with the softened butter. Put the Parmigiano-Reggiano in the dishes and turn the dishes around until the dishes and foil are all covered with a layer of cheese. Don't touch the inside after this point. Put the dishes in the refrigerator.

TO MAKE THE GOAT CHEESE BASE

TRIM any moldy rind off the goat cheese and discard. Using the back of a fork, or a Kitchen Aid with a paddle attachment, mash the cheese with the egg yolks until the mixture is fairly smooth—don't worry about a few little lumps of cheese. Reserve.

TO BEAT AND FOLD IN THE EGG WHITES AND BAKE THE SOUFFLÉ

PREHEAT the oven to 375°F [190°C/gas mark 5].

PUT the egg whites in a bowl with the salt and, unless you're using a copper bowl, the cream of tartar. Start beating slowly (slow speed on the mixer) and gradually increase speed. Beat the whites to stiff peaks, about 4 minutes with an electric mixer, 6 to 8 minutes by hand. Whisk about one-fourth of the egg whites into the goat cheese mixture to lighten it and make it easier to fold. Scoop the egg whites into the goat cheese mixture and fold the mixture together with a rubber spatula. Sliding the spatula firmly against the sides of the bowl, reach down to the bottom of the bowl, where most of the heavier sauce base will have settled, and lift up the base, gently folding it over the whites. Continue in this way, cutting into the whites, but not pushing against them, as needed to combine the mixture. Don't overdo it; a few uncombined pieces of white are less of a problem than overworking the mixture and making it heavy.

GENTLY pour the mixture into the soufflé dishes and place the dishes on a sheet pan. Slide the sheet pan into the oven. Turn up the oven to 425°F [200°C/gas mark 6]. Bake the soufflés for 15 to 20 minutes until they rise by 1 to 2 inches [5 to 7.5 cm]. Make sure your guests are all at the table. (*Un soufflé peut être attendu, mais il ne doit jamais attendre*—"A soufflé may be awaited but musn't ever wait"—is an often-quoted axiom.) Move the sheet pan back and forth while closely watching the movement of the soufflé. If you notice the top rocking slightly back and forth, the soufflés aren't done. As soon as the soufflés appear firm, place the soufflés on plates, and bring them to the table. Provide your guests with dinner forks or large spoons.

tion of soufflés à la Suissesse in Escoffier's *Le Guide Culinaire*. Escoffier's version is the simplest (for once) and consists of baking small Parmigiano-Reggiano cheese soufflés with less egg white than usual, unmolding them, and rebaking them with cream and cheese sprinkled over—a sort of cheese soufflé gratin. Richard Olney invents a variation (with shredded zucchini) that he calls a pudding and goes on to suggest using mushrooms and a savarin mold (a doughnut-shaped pan) instead of individual soufflé dishes, and, almost as an aside, mentions how marvelous the whole thing would be with a little creamed sorrel. The soufflés d'Aragon I taught in New York were closer to Escoffier's version—Parmigiano-Reggiano was the only flavoring in the soufflé itself—but they were finished with a creamy tomato sauce containing fresh tarragon. My own experiments have included mushrooms or sorrel in the soufflé base, and simple or complicated sauces, poured over the soufflés before (and occasionally after) the second baking. Every variation seems to please. Best of all, the soufflés can be baked earlier the same day and unmolded, and the soufflés given their final second baking, just before serving. The soufflés are practically foolproof because even if you overcook them, the sauce is absorbed into the soufflé and keeps it moist.

TWICE-BAKED CHEESE SOUFFLÉS WITH TOMATO SAUCE

SOUFFLÉS À LA SUISSESSE

MAKES 6 FIRST-COURSE SERVINGS

I was first alerted to these soufflés in Richard Olney's masterpiece, Simple French Food, and I encountered them again under a different name, soufflés d'Aragon, when teaching at Peter Kump's Cooking School in New York. I've been hard put to discover the origin of either name, finding only one men-

FOR COATING THE DISHES:

1 tablespoon softened butter

4 tablespoons [25 g] finely grated Parmigiano-Reggiano or grana padana

FOR THE SOUFFLÉ BASE AND FINAL FOLDING:

4½ tablespoons [35 g] flour

3 tablespoons butter

1½ cups [375 ml] milk

1 cup (about 3 ounces/100 g) finely grated Parmigiano-Reggiano or grana padana

salt

pepper

very small pinch of nutmeg

4 large eggs, separated

cream of tartar (if you're not using a copper bowl), a small pinch

FOR FINISHING THE SOUFFLÉS:

1   cup [250 ml] heavy cream

3   medium-size tomatoes, peeled, seeded and chopped

1   tablespoon coarsely chopped fresh tarragon

    salt

    pepper

½   cup [50 g] finely grated Parmigiano-Reggiano or grana padana cheese

TO PREPARE THE MOLDS

BRUSH the insides of six 5-ounce or 6-ounce [155 or 175 ml] ramekins or porcelain or Pyrex custard cups with 2 teaspoons of the softened butter and coat them with the grated cheese by putting all the cheese in one ramekin, rotating the ramekin until the sides are coated, pouring the cheese into the next ramekin, and so on, until all the ramekins are coated. Reserve the remaining softened butter.

TO PREPARE THE SOUFFLÉ BASE

PREHEAT the oven to 400°F [200°C/gas mark 6].

MAKE a béchamel by whisking the flour and butter together in a heavy-bottomed saucepan, over medium heat, until the mixture—the roux—is smooth and smells toasty, about 2 minutes. Whisk in the milk and bring to a boil, over high heat, while whisking. When the béchamel is smooth, remove it from the heat, stir in the cheese, and season the mixture with salt, pepper, and nutmeg. Stir in the egg yolks one by one. Reserve.

TO BEAT AND FOLD IN THE EGG WHITES AND FINISH THE SOUFFLÉ MIXTURE

PUT the egg whites in a bowl with a pinch of salt and, unless you're using a copper bowl, the cream of tartar. Start beating slowly (slow speed on the mixer) and gradually increase speed. Beat the whites to stiff peaks, about 4 minutes with an electric mixer, or 6 to 8 minutes by hand. Whisk about one-fourth of the egg whites into the sauce base to lighten it. Pour the sauce base down the side of the bowl containing the remaining whites and finish folding with a rubber spatula.

TO FILL THE RAMEKINS AND BAKE THE SOUFFLÉS

FILL the ramekins to the top (or until you've used all the mixture) with the soufflé mixture and run your thumb around the top edge of each of the molds, forming a small moat, about ½ inch [1.5 cm] wide, around the sides. This prevents the top of the soufflé mixture from attaching to the rim of the ramekins, which could cause the soufflés to rise unevenly.

ARRANGE the dishes in a baking dish with sides at least as high as the ramekins and ideally just large enough to hold them. Pour enough hot water—the hottest water from the tap is fine—into the dish to come two-thirds of the way up the sides of the ramekins to make a water bath, or bain-marie. Slide the baking dish into the oven.

BAKE until the soufflés rise 1 or 2 inches, about 20 to 30 minutes. Take the bain-marie out of the oven and take the ramekins out of the bain-marie. Let cool for 10 minutes. At this point, the soufflés will fall somewhat, but don't worry; they're going to puff up again during the second baking. Run a knife around the sides of the soufflés—flush against the mold—and carefully turn the soufflés out of the ramekins onto a gratin dish or baking dish just large enough to hold the soufflés in a single layer (it can be the same dish used for the bain-marie) that's been rubbed with the remaining teaspoon of softened butter. If you're not serving the soufflés right away, you can cover the dish with plastic wrap and refrigerate it for up to 24 hours.

TO PREPARE THE TOMATO CREAM SAUCE AND FINISH THE SOUFFLÉS

COMBINE the cream, tomatoes, and tarragon in a small saucepan and bring to a simmer. Season to taste with salt and pepper. (Like the soufflés, the sauce can be made up to 24 hours ahead of time and kept in the refrigerator.)

DRIBBLE the sauce over the soufflés—most of it will run down the sides—and sprinkle the soufflés with cheese. Turn the oven up to 450°F [230°C]. Slide the dish into the oven and bake for about 20 minutes, until the soufflés have risen again and turned golden brown on top, and the sauce in the bottom is bubbling. Use a spatula to transfer the soufflés to heated plates and spoon over any sauce left in the bottom of the baking dish.

Variations: You can add just about anything you like to the béchamel sauce base. To follow Richard Olney's advice, ½ cup [35 g] or so of duxelles (see page 96), especially if made with wild mushrooms, gives distinction and depth of flavor to the soufflés themselves. Mushrooms (especially morels) are great added to the sauce; gently simmering them in cream before pouring them over the soufflés gives their flavor a chance to infuse. Cubed cooked artichokes, coarsely chopped spinach or blanched chard, or other vegetables can be folded into the soufflé base to provide color and texture. Cubes of meat, such as leftover chicken or turkey, sweetbreads, or foie gras, or seafood, such as lobster or crabmeat, can also be added to the filling. (I use no cheese when including seafood in the base mixture.) In general, making *soufflés à la Suissesse* is a good way to convert small amounts of leftovers into something new and rather elegant. Leftover seafood stews or soups can be converted into soufflés by using the liquid in place of the milk when preparing the soufflé béchamel (in which case the base becomes a velouté, not a béchamel), and the solid pieces of seafood can be folded into the soufflé mixture or used as a final garniture, with pretty pieces of lobster or crayfish saved for topping the soufflés just before serving. If there's extra liquid from a seafood soup or seafood stew, it can replace or be combined with the cream used as the sauce in the final baking.

TWICE-BAKED MUSHROOM SOUFFLÉS WITH MOREL SAUCE

SOUFFLÉS À LA SUISSESSE AUX CHAMPIGNONS, SAUCE MORILLES

MAKES 8 FIRST-COURSE SERVINGS

These soufflés are almost identical to the soufflés à la Suissesse given above, except that 1 cup [70 g] of duxelles (finely chopped mushrooms cooked down until dry) is added to the béchamel base, the amount of cheese is reduced in the base and left out of the finishing sauce, and creamed morels, instead of the tomato sauce, are spooned over the soufflés just before serving.

FOR COATING THE DISHES:

1½ tablespoons softened butter

4 tablespoons [25 g] finely grated Parmigiano-Reggiano or grana padana

FOR THE DUXELLES:

1 large shallot or small onion, chopped fine

1 tablespoon butter

12 ounces [350 g] mushrooms or mushroom stems, chopped fine (but not puréed) by hand or in a food processor

FOR THE BÉCHAMEL BASE AND FINISHED SOUFFLÉ MIXTURE:

3 tablespoons butter

4½ tablespoons flour

1¼ cups [300 ml] milk

½ cup (about 1½ ounces/50 g) finely grated Parmigiano-Reggiano

salt

pepper

very small pinch of nutmeg

5 large eggs, separated

small pinch of cream of tartar (if you're not using a copper bowl)

FOR MAKING THE SAUCE AND FINISHING THE SOUFFLÉS:

1 ounce [30 g] dried morels, soaked for 30 minutes in ½ cup [125 ml] semidry Madeira or sherry

1 cup [250 ml] heavy cream

salt

pepper

TO PREPARE THE MOLDS

USE a brush or your finger to butter the insides of eight 5-ounce or 6-ounce [155 or 175 ml] ramekins or porcelain or Pyrex custard cups with 1 tablespoon of the softened butter and coat them with the grated cheese. Reserve the remaining softened butter.

TO PREPARE THE DUXELLES

COOK the shallot in the butter in a wide sauté pan for about 5 minutes over medium heat, until it smells fragrant, and add the chopped mushrooms. (The wider the pan, the more quickly the moisture will cook out of the mushrooms.) Turn the heat to high and cook the mushrooms until they release liquid into the pan and the liquid completely evaporates.

TO PREPARE THE SOUFFLÉ BASE

PREHEAT the oven to 400°F [200°C/gas mark 6].

MAKE a béchamel by cooking the flour and butter together in a heavy-bottomed saucepan, over medium heat, for about 2 minutes. Whisk in the milk and bring to the boil, over high heat, while whisking. When the béchamel is smooth, remove it

from the heat, stir in the duxelles and the cheese, and season the mixture with salt, pepper, and nutmeg. Stir in the egg yolks one by one.

TO BEAT AND FOLD IN THE EGG WHITES AND FINISH THE SOUFFLÉ MIXTURE

COMBINE the egg whites with a pinch of salt and, unless you're using a copper bowl, the cream of tartar. Beat to stiff peaks, starting slowly and gradually increasing speed. Whisk about one-fourth of the beaten whites into the sauce base to lighten it. Pour the sauce base down the side of the bowl containing the remaining whites and fold together with a rubber spatula.

TO FILL THE RAMEKINS AND BAKE THE SOUFFLÉS

FILL the ramekins with the soufflé mixture and run your thumb around the top edges of each of the molds, forming a small moat, about ½ inch [1.5 cm] wide, around the sides.

ARRANGE the dishes in a baking dish with sides at least as high as the ramekins and ideally just large enough to hold them. Make a water bath, or bain-marie, by pouring enough of the hottest tap water into the dish to come two-thirds of the way up the sides of the ramekins. Slide the baking dish into the oven.

BAKE until the soufflés rise 1 or 2 inches [2.5 cm], about 30 minutes. Take the bain-marie out of the oven and take the ramekins out of the bain-marie. Let cool for 10 minutes. At this point, the soufflés will fall somewhat, but don't worry because they're going to puff up again during the second baking. Run a knife around the soufflés, flush against the inside of the molds, and carefully turn the soufflés out of the ramekins into a gratin dish or baking dish just large enough to hold the soufflés, and buttered with the remaining softened butter. If you're not serving them right away, cover the dish with plastic wrap and refrigerate for up to 24 hours.

TO MAKE THE SAUCE
AND FINISH THE SOUFFLÉS

SQUEEZE the excess Madeira out of the morels, reserving it in a small bowl. Pour the soaking liquid into a small saucepan, being careful to leave any grit behind. Add the morels and the cream and combine. Bring to a simmer and season to taste with salt and pepper. Reserve.

POUR the morel cream sauce over the soufflés and bake for about 20 minutes, until the soufflés have risen again and turned golden brown on top, and the surrounding sauce is bubbling.

USE a spatula to transfer the soufflés to heated plates and spoon over them the morels and their sauce as well as any sauce left in the bottom of the baking dish.

CHEESE FONDUE

FONDUE DE FROMAGE

WAYS TO	HOW TO	HOW TO	HOW TO
USE MELTED CHEESE	COMBINE CHEESE WITH POTATOES	MAKE YOUR OWN FRESH CHEESE	USE FRESH CHEESE IN DESSERTS AND SAVORY DISHES

I HAVE TO ADMIT THAT MY FIRST FONDUE AND VIRTUALLY EVERY ONE I've had since have been enjoyed, not in a romantic chalet, but at my aunt Jane's house in Los Angeles, usually on a bright, sunny day. Long before cheese fondue became popular in the United States, Jane would return from lengthy trips to Europe with her husband, Frank, and would reproduce for their homebound friends and family their experiences in Greek tavernas, Italian trattorias, and Parisian bistros. Of all Jane's specialties, cheese fondue has become a tradition so entrenched that we have it whenever I visit her lovely home perched on a hill. Cheese fondue takes only about 10 minutes to make. It is always served with a glass or two of kirsch and an abundance of cool white wine.

If you read a lot of cookbooks you'll find an amazing array of fondue recipes, some containing cream; others roux, or egg yolks, or various cheeses. But my favorite recipe, derived from one in *Joy of Cooking,* is simple and straightforward. Dry white wine is brought to a boil with a garlic clove, the garlic is fished out, and a little cornstarch, dissolved in some kirsch or water, is added to keep the cheese from separating. Grated cheese is stirred around in the wine until it melts, and the whole thing is seasoned with salt, pepper, and nutmeg. We then pour it into our 1960s-era fondue pot set over a can of Sterno and happily sit around dripping in our chunks of bread, sipping wine and kirsch. Don't skimp on the quality of the cheese or the kirsch (see below for more about kirsch). Emmenthaler from Switzerland or France and authentic Swiss Gruyère, or its close (and even tastier) relative, Fribourg, are the cheeses most often used. Obviously you can experiment with any firm cheese, but Gruyère and Emmenthaler are so good and easy to find, I've never bothered.

KIRSCH

If you take a bushel of cherries, allow them to ferment, and then distill them, you get kirsch. Unlike other brandies such as Cognac or Armagnac, which are made from grapes and aged in wooden casks, kirsch is never aged and so is crystal clear. Since nothing is added to it, kirsch is perfectly dry, and for neophytes its 45 percent (90 proof) alcohol content makes it a bit on the fiery side.

The best kirsch comes from Switzerland, the second-best comes from France, and the lowest quality (except that from a few boutique distilleries in Oregon and California) is made in the United States. Lesser-quality kirsch tastes more like almonds than fruit and isn't worth the bother. My favorite brand, from Switzerland, is called ETTER, but I've never found kirsch from Switzerland that wasn't excellent. You can also play around with using other fruit brandies (see page 11) in a cheese fondue, but kirsch is my favorite.

CHEESE FONDUE

FONDUE DE FROMAGE

MAKES ENOUGH FOR

4 MAIN-COURSE SERVINGS

1 clove garlic, peeled

2 cups [500 ml] dry white wine

2 teaspoons cornstarch

2 tablespoons kirsch (optional) or water

½ pound [225 g] authentic Swiss Emmentaler, grated coarse

½ pound [225 g] authentic Swiss Gruyère, grated coarse

salt

pepper

tiny pinch of nutmeg

2 crusty baguettes, cut lengthwise in half or in quarters and then into bite-size pieces (for dipping)

CUT the garlic clove in half and put it in a saucepan with the wine. Bring the wine to a boil and boil it for about 3 minutes to cook off the alcohol. If you have a gas stove, you may want to tilt the pan to ignite the wine so it doesn't ignite accidently while you're leaning over the saucepan. Take out the garlic.

STIR together the cornstarch and the kirsch or water until the mixture is smooth—professional cooks sometimes call this mixture a "slurry"—and whisk it into the wine. Add the cheese and stir with a wooden spoon over low to medium heat until the cheese dissolves, about 5 minutes. At this point the fondue may seem too thin, but it will thicken as it sits over the Sterno flame. Season it to taste with salt, pepper, and nutmeg. Be careful when using nutmeg—it's very strong.

POUR the fondue into the fondue pot and set the pot over the Sterno can with the metal cover over most of the flame. You want to keep the heat as low as possible so you don't scorch the fondue. Gather round and pass the bread. Use long fondue forks or regular kitchen forks to dip your pieces of bread.

Raclette

"RACLETTE" REFERS TO BOTH A CHEESE AND a dish. Since the word derives from *racler,* meaning to scrape—what you do when serving the dish—it seems that the name of the dish must have preceded that of the cheese. To serve raclette the traditional way, take a large wedge of raclette cheese or some other variety (see variations to Untraditional Raclette, page 145) and set it close to a hot wood fire in a hearth. (I set mine on a small stack of bricks, the top one wrapped in aluminum foil.) As the surface of the cheese facing the flames begins to melt, scrape against the surface with a spatula or the back of a knife while holding a heated plate under the cheese. Served the melted cheese over boiled or steamed new potatoes in their skins and pass French sour gherkins—cornichons—as an accompaniment. If you don't have a fireplace or don't feel like building a big, hot fire in order to cook dinner, you can use an electric raclette maker (see Sources) or you can melt the cheese in the oven. Madeleine Kamman, in her delightful book *Madeleine Kamman's Savoie,* describes a version in which the potatoes are diced and cooked in butter, cream is poured over the potatoes in a gratin dish, and the slices of raclette are placed on top. The whole thing is then baked in the oven until the cheese melts. It's a marvelous interpretation, but the ritual of sitting around, taking turns scraping, is lost.

TRADITIONAL RACLETTE

RACLETTE TRADITIONELLE

MAKES 6 TO 8 MAIN-COURSE SERVINGS

- 1 wedge (1½ to 2 pounds [675 to 900 g]) raclette or other firm cheese such as Swiss Gruyère, Fribourg, Comté, or Cantal
- 3 pounds [1.25 kg] small red or white new potatoes or fingerling potatoes (if necessary, cut into uniform sizes)
- 1 white or black truffle (optional)

  salt

  pepper
- 1 jar (12 ounces [350 g]) cornichons
- 2 baguettes, cut into 5-inch-thick [1.5 cm] slices

BUILD a roaring fire in the fireplace or heat up the raclette maker.

CUT the rind off the raclette.

PUT the potatoes in a pot with enough cold water to cover by a couple of inches, bring to boil over high heat, and immediately turn down the heat to maintain a gentle simmer. When the potatoes are easily penetrated with a knife—anywhere from 15 to 25 minutes, depending on how big they are—drain them in a colander, pull off their peels, and keep them warm, either near the fire or in a 200°F [95°C] oven. Set the plates in the oven or near the fire to warm them.

SET the raclette on a heat-proof plate, with the inner part of cheese (not where the rind was) facing the fire. Set the plate on a couple of bricks or on an inverted small pot, with the plate extending over the edge, so that as the cheese is scraped off it can be slid down over a plate set beneath the first one (or the one on top).

PUT 1 or 2 new potatoes on each plate and, one at a time, set the plates under the plate that holds the cheese. With a spatula or the back of a knife, scrape the cheese over the potatoes. Shave the truffle, if using, over each serving; add salt and pepper to

taste. Pass the cornichons and bread. Keep repeating, giving everyone more potatoes and scraping more cheese over their plates.

UNTRADITIONAL RACLETTE

RACLETTE IMPROVISÉE

MAKES 6 TO 8 MAIN-COURSE SERVINGS

While the results of this raclette are almost identical to the traditional version made in front of a roaring fire, the appearance is more reminiscent of a gratin. The advantage to this version is that you need neither a fire nor a raclette maker—only a hot oven.

- 1 wedge (1½ to 2 pounds [675 to 900 g]) raclette or other firm cheese such as Swiss Gruyère, Fribourg, Comté, or Cantal
- 3 pounds [1.5 kg] small red or white new potatoes or fingerling potatoes (if necessary, cut into uniform sizes)

  salt

  pepper
- 1 jar (12 ounces [350 g]) cornichons
- 2 baguettes, cut into ½-inch-thick [1.5 cm] slices

CUT the rind off the raclette and cut it into ¼-inch-thick [.5 cm] slices.

PUT the potatoes in a pot with enough cold water to cover by a couple of inches, bring to a boil over high heat, and immediately turn down the heat to maintain a gentle simmer. When the potatoes can be penetrated with a knife but still offer a slight resistance—anywhere from 15 to 20 minutes, depending on how big they are—drain them in a colander, pull away their peels, and arrange them in a gratin dish or baking dish just large enough to hold them in a single layer. If you don't have a large enough dish, use two.

PREHEAT the oven to 400°F [200°C/gas mark 6].

ARRANGE the cheese slices over the potatoes and slide the gratin dish into the oven. Bake until the cheese has completely melted and covers the potatoes, 10 to 15 minutes. Be careful not to overcook the cheese or it will turn oily. Season with salt and pepper to taste.

SPOON the potatoes and cheese onto heated plates at the table and pass the cornichons and bread.

Variations: Austin de Croze, in his 1920s treatise *Les Plats Régionaux de France*, describes a dish, called a *truffado*, made in the Auvergne. Potatoes are sliced, sautéed in bacon fat, and finished with chopped garlic and the cooked bacon. (For more about sautéed potatoes—*pommes sautées à cru*—see page 602.) Just before serving, a fresh Cantal is diced and tossed with the hot potatoes for a minute or two before being served on hot plates. Since fresh Cantal isn't available in the United States, use a fresh Laguiole if you can find one or a good-quality ricotta, drained overnight in a muslin-lined strainer.

PURÉED POTATOES WITH CHEESE

ALIGOT

MAKES 6 SIDE-DISH SERVINGS

One of my favorite restaurants in Paris, L'Ambassade de l'Auvergne, prides itself on its rustic regional specialties: its tripe sausages, or andouillettes, and its aligot, a very stringy cheese-and-potato mixture that's slapped on the plates with great fanfare. A waiter at the restaurant told me that they make their aligot with fresh Laguiole, which comes from the same village where the famous Laguiole knives (the ones with the little honeybee on them) are made. When I make aligot in the United States, if I can't find fresh Laguiole, I use regular aged Cantal, which is easy to find at any decent cheese shop. If you've got a choice, ask for a relatively young Cantal fermier (from the farm) instead of an industrially produced version. If you can't find Cantal, use Swiss Gruyère. Your aligot won't be as dramatically stringy but it will still taste great.

2 pounds [900 g] medium-starchy potatoes such Yukon Golds or Yellow Finns, or russets

1 cup [250 ml] milk

1 pound [450 g] fresh Laguiole, or ¾ pound [340 g] Cantal (preferably fresh) or Gruyère, diced if using fresh cheese, grated coarse if using aged cheese (Cantal or Gruyère)

6 tablespoons [85 g] butter

salt

pepper

PEEL the potatoes, cut them in quarters, and put them in a pot with just enough water to come halfway up their sides. Bring to a simmer, cover the pot, and simmer over low to medium heat until the potatoes are easily penetrated with a knife, about 20 minutes. Drain the potatoes in a colander set over a bowl (to save the cooking liquid) and work the potatoes through a drum sieve or ricer. (For more about making "mashed" potatoes, see page 602.)

BRING the milk to a simmer. Put the drained potatoes in a pot and pour the milk over them. Stir in the cheese and butter with a heavy wooden spoon and stir the mixture vigorously until it becomes very stringy and elastic. If it becomes too stiff, thin it with some of the cooking liquid from the potatoes. Season to taste with salt and pepper. When serving *aligot*, you'll need to slap it on the plate quickly or it won't come away from the spoon.

CHEESE PUFFS

GOUGÈRES

MAKES ABOUT 50 SMALL GOUGÈRES,

HORS D'OEUVRES FOR 8 TO 10

As is true with so many French dishes, there is considerable argument about where gougères were first invented. They are usually thought of as Burgundian, and they do make a lovely hors d'oeuvre to accompany wine. But as Anne Willan points out in her book French Regional Cooking, the town of Sens, which is south of Paris on the way to Burgundy, claims gougères as its own. My Larousse Dictionnaire des Fromages says that gougères originated in Paris, where they were popular in the eighteenth century and were called ramequins. Wherever they came from, gougères are made by adding grated Gruyère cheese to cream puff pastry, pâte à choux (see page 148), not to be confused with flaky puff pastry, which is pâte feuilletée.

When you work grated cheese into pâte à choux, you'll have the stiff batter you need for making gougères. In virtually every recipe I read, gougères are made with Gruyère cheese. But whenever I've tried making them with Gruyère they come out heavy. Some recipes suggest stuffing them with Mornay sauce, béchamel finished with cheese, but this makes them even heavier and very rich. Instead of Gruyère, I use the oldest and hardest Parmigiano-Reggiano that I can find. Because it's so dry and full-flavored, I can use less of it, and the gougères come out lighter.

¼   pound [115 g] butter, plus 1 teaspoon softened butter for the sheet pan

1   cup [125 g] all-purpose flour

4   eggs for the batter, plus 1 large beaten egg for the egg wash, or more as needed

2   teaspoons Dijon mustard

2   teaspoons salt

1   cup [100 g] finely grated hard well-aged Parmigiano Reggiano, Grana Padano, or other very hard cheese such as aged Gouda

PREHEAT the oven to 425°F [220°C/gas mark 7].

RUB a sheet pan with the softened butter and put the pan in the refrigerator to chill, so that the dollops of batter will adhere.

COMBINE the ¼ pound [115 g] of butter with a cup of water in a saucepan and bring to a simmer over medium heat. When the liquid is simmering and all the butter has melted, pour in the flour all at once and work it vigorously with a large wooden spoon, still over medium heat, until the batter holds together in one piece and pulls away from the sides of the pan, about 1 minute. Transfer the flour mixture—the *panade*—into a mixing bowl and work in the 4 eggs, one at a time, adding another one only after the one before it is completely incorporated. Add the last egg, one-half at a time, white first. (Because the sizes of eggs and protein content of flour varies, it's useful to be able to recognize when you've added enough egg to the basic *panade*. Use the wooden spoon held sideways to make a ½-inch-wide [1.5 cm] groove in the top of the batter. The groove should slowly close in on itself. If you dip the spoon in the batter and lift it so it's pointing up, the very top of the batter should curve down rather than stick straight up.) Work in more egg if needed, the mustard, 1 teaspoon of the salt, and the grated cheese.

REMOVE the sheet pan from the refrigerator. Fit a pastry bag with a ½-inch [1.5 cm] tip and push part of the bag down into the tip so that none of the batter will ooze out of the tip until you're ready to start piping. Make a 3-inch [7.5 cm] cuff with the top of the bag by folding down the sides. Hold the bag open with your left hand by slipping your fingers under the cuff. Fill the bag about ⅔ full with your right hand, using a spatula. Unfold the cuff and twist the top of the bag in a coil to seal it. Keep twisting until the bag no longer sags. Pull the tip away from the bag—unclogging it—and, while guiding the tip with your left hand and gently squeezing the bag with your right, pipe out mounds about 1½ inches [4 cm] in diameter (they'll have the shape of Hershey's Kisses) and about 1½ inches

[4 cm] apart on the sheet pan, so that when they puff they won't stick together. (See page 14 for more information on how to use a pastry bag.)

BEAT the egg for the egg wash with the remaining 1 teaspoon of salt until it darkens and becomes runny, about 30 seconds. With a small pastry brush or the back of a fork, pat the top of each of the puffs with a very thin layer of beaten egg. This also evens off the top of the puffs.

SLIDE the sheet pan into the oven and bake for 25 minutes. Take a quick peek after 15 minutes to make sure that the puffs are browning evenly, but don't let the oven temperature fall or the *gougères* will deflate. If those on one end of the sheet pan are browning faster than those on the other end, turn the sheet pan around. Bake for 10 minutes more, or until the *gougères* are well puffed and golden brown. If the *gougères* are well puffed and browned before 25 minutes have passed, don't take them out of the oven, which will cause them to deflate. Instead, turn the oven down to 300°F [150°C/gas mark 2].

MAKING YOUR OWN FRESH CHEESE (FROMAGE FRAIS OR FROMAGE BLANC)

Fromage frais, sometimes called *fromage blanc,* is a light cheese similar to yogurt but with more texture and little tang. It has a depth of flavor that yogurt lacks. *Fromage frais* is a universal snack or breakfast food in France, but oddly it is only rarely encountered in the United States. It can be served in much the same way as yogurt, with fresh fruit or fruit preserves, or as a savory side dish, first course, or snack, flavored with fresh herbs. *Fromage frais* can occasionally be found in fancy gourmet stores, but it's easy to make at home.

Before you set out to make your own fresh cheese, it helps to understand a little of the science of it. The simplest cheese, made since antiquity, is produced when unpasteurized raw milk is simply allowed to sit in a reasonably warm place. The beneficial bacteria that occur naturally in the milk convert the lactose, a sugar contained in the milk, into lactic acid. As the amount of lactic acid increases, it causes the milk to curdle and separate into curds and whey. When you strain out the liquid whey, you're left with a simple curd that gets progressively more firm as you let it drain, and eventually takes on the consistency of cream cheese.

But cheese made by allowing raw milk to curdle has certain disadvantages. First, in most parts of the country it's illegal to sell raw milk. Second, raw milk is susceptible to the growth of various bacteria, both in the milk and in the air. While rarely pathogens, these bacteria can cause the milk and resulting curd to develop an unpleasant flavor. Third, and most important, milk that curdles completely as a result of a high concentration of lactic acid is very sour and has none of the delicate sweetness of *fromage frais.* The first and second problems can be avoided by culturing pasteurized milk with organic whole-milk yogurt, buttermilk, sour cream, or laboratory culture (see Sources), which have all the necessary lactic acid–producing bacteria. If you leave your cultured yogurt or buttermilk-milk mixture in a warm place, it will turn into yogurt (if you used yogurt) or a light sour cream (if you used buttermilk or sour cream). If you then drain it in cheesecloth (see page 149) or muslin, it will gradually thicken into a kind of cheese with the consistency of cream cheese but with much more tang. To address the third problem, if you want to make fresh cheese, not yogurt or sour cream, you must get the milk to curdle before the bacteria you've added have had a chance to convert too much of the lactose into lactic acid. Most cheese makers do this with rennet, taken from the lining of a calf's stomach, which contains a powerful enzyme, rennin, that causes milk to curdle very quickly. The exact time needed for curdling—technically called clabbering—depends on the temperature and acidity of the milk, the amount of rennet you add, and how long you culture the milk before adding the rennet.

You can control the sweetness and tanginess of your cheese by adding rennet at different times or in different amounts after culturing. The sooner you use rennet, or the more you use, the sweeter will be the cheese.

Pâte à choux, which is roughly translated as "cabbage dough"—no doubt a reference to the way a small mound of it looks when baked—is made by adding eggs to a stiff mixture of flour and liquid, called a *panade*. *Panades* have long been used to hold together old-fashioned stuffings, quenelles, and forcemeats. When destined for dessert, *pâte à choux* is piped into various shapes onto a sheet pan with a pastry bag (or, with more difficulty, spooned out) and baked. Once the dollops of *choux* pastry puff up, you can cut them crosswise in half and fill them with *crème Chantilly* (sweetened whipped cream flavored with vanilla) to make cream puffs. Or you can bore a little hole on the bottom of each puff with a fluted pastry bag tip and pipe in ice cream to create profiteroles, which make a delicious dessert, especially when topped with chocolate sauce. You can also pipe the *pâte à choux* into the shape for éclairs—essentially, elongated cream puffs—bake them, and fill them with pastry cream. Eclairs are usually topped with fondant, sugar that's cooked to the soft-ball stage and worked on a pastry marble. But I prefer a stiff dark chocolate sauce (see "Ganache," page 668), which is less sweet.

HOMEMADE FRESH CHEESE

FROMAGE FRAIS

MAKES ABOUT 3 CUPS

If you make a batch of cheese and get excited about the process, you may want to order special starters (see Sources). These starters contain various bacteria in carefully controlled amounts, allowing you to come up with different effects. If you're a vegetarian, you can also use vegetable "rennet" that contains no animal products. Some starters, especially designed for making *fromage frais*, contain combinations of active bacteria and rennet.

The two terms, *fromage frais* and *fromage blanc*—literally, fresh cheese and white cheese—are often used interchangeably, but strictly speaking there's a difference. Both types of cheese must be unripened, not aged like a Camembert or Roquefort. But *fromage frais* must contain some kind of bacterial culture, and in France this culture must be viable (still living) when the cheese is sold. *Fromage blanc* is sometimes defined as *fromage frais* that's made entirely with a bacterial culture and contains no rennet, and hence will be tangier; but I've seen plenty of recipes for *fromage blanc* made with rennet. What's more important than knowing the exact definition of each is to buy or make cheese to your own taste. Both *fromage frais* and *fromage blanc* can be more or less dense, from the consistency of runny yogurt to almost the consistency of cream cheese. To make your own cheese stiffer, just allow it to drain longer in muslin or cheesecloth, up to several days, covered, in the refrigerator.

1 gallon [4 l] whole pasteurized milk
and
1 cup [250 ml] organic plain whole milk yogurt, or
½ cup [125 ml] cultured buttermilk

or

1 packet fromage blanc starter (see cheesemaking supplies under Sources) (instead of the yogurt or buttermilk and rennet)

½ rennet tablet (animal or vegetable)

5 cup [125 ml] water

BRING the milk to a simmer in a very clean stainless steel pot, cover with the lid, and let cool to about 80°F [26°C]. Use a thermometer—or wing it by holding your hand on the side of the pot, which should feel just slightly cool—and stir in the yogurt or buttermilk or the packet of *fromage blanc* starter. Cover the pot again and let sit at room temperature (at least 72°F) for 8 hours.

IF you've used the *fromage blanc* starter, just let the milk sit for 2 to 4 hours more, until it stands up in peaks when you pull some out with a ladle. If you've inoculated the milk with only yogurt or buttermilk, dissolve the ½ rennet tablet in the ½ cup [125 ml] of water and stir the rennet solution into the milk mixture. Start checking the mixture after 4 hours more. It will be ready in 4 to 8 hours when, again, it stands up in peaks when you pull some out with a ladle.

THE exact time needed for the milk to curdle depends on the yogurt or buttermilk you've used and the temperature of your work area. But for a batch of homemade cheese, the only important thing is to know when the cheese has "clabbered" so you can then drain it. To determine when the cheese has clabbered to the right degree, I use the method described in Max Alth's *Making Your Own Cheese & Yogurt,* a book well worth having if you want to carry your cheesemaking experimentation further than I describe here. Alth suggests that you take a teaspoon and spoon out a bit of the curd. When the curd is too thin, it will be runny in the spoon. As it continues to clabber it will stiffen until, when tested, it forms a mound with sharp edges— the exact consistency of a crème caramel. This is the point at which you want to drain it. If you leave it to clabber longer than this, the curd will begin to thin and you'll have missed the best moment.

TO drain the curd, line a strainer with authentic cheesecloth, actually called butter muslin (see below), or a sheet of immaculately clean muslin. Leave enough extra cloth hanging over the sides of the strainer to cover the curd. Fold the cloth over the top of the curd and let the cheese drain in the refrigertor until it has the consistency you like (2 to 24 hours). You should end up with a rough equivalent to French *fromage frais,* a light cheese with a consistency between yogurt and cream cheese.

KEEP the cheese covered in a bowl in the refrigerator, and serve it with fresh fruit or fruit preserves.

CHEESECLOTH

The cheesecloth sold at the supermarket will not, despite its name, work for making cheese. The thread is so coarse that the curd runs through it. I use muslin or a piece of tightly woven cotton fabric. An old pillowcase, washed and thoroughly rinsed in hot water, is my favorite device. If you want authentic cheesecloth, called "butter muslin," the kind actually used to make cheese, see Sources under cheesemaking supplies.

HEART-SHAPED SWEET CHEESE DESSERTS

COEURS À LA CRÈME

MAKES 6 DESSERT SERVINGS

You can make these very tasty and romantic little desserts, which are perfect for Valentine's Day, by just combining fresh cheese or cream cheese with vanilla, sugar, and whipped cream and allowing the mixture to drain and stiffen. The result is a little like traditional Jewish cheesecake filling, but much lighter. The problem is getting the delicious cheese mixture into a heart shape. The standard solution is to drain the cheese in individual heart-shaped cheesecloth-lined porcelain molds with holes in them (see Sources). But unless you make *coeurs à la crème* often, you may not want to go out and buy a set of molds, since they're somewhat expensive. My molds have long since broken, so I dispense with the heart shape and mold the cheese in cheesecloth-lined muffin tins and then allow the rounds to drain overnight in the refrigerator.

You may find that this recipe makes varying amounts depending what kind of cheese you use. If using cream cheese, count on only 4 servings.

2   cups [450 g] fromage blanc (of a consistency slightly thicker than yogurt), or 1½ cups [360 g] fresh ricotta, or 1 package (8 ounces [225 g]) cream cheese (preferably containing no gum arabic)

⅓   cup [40 g] confectioners' sugar

1   teaspoon vanilla extract

1   cup [250 ml] heavy cream

1   package (14 ounces [400 g]) frozen raspberries, thawed, worked through a strainer or food mill (for the sauce)

IF you're using *fromage blanc* or ricotta, drain it overnight in the refrigerator in a strainer lined with a clean and well-rinsed kitchen towel. Cover the cheese with plastic wrap while it is draining.

WORK the drained cheese or cream cheese with the sugar and the vanilla extract in a mixing bowl with a heavy wooden spoon or in a mixer, turned on low, with the paddle blade. Work the mixture just long enough to make it smooth and malleable.

PUT the heavy cream in a mixing bowl and chill in the freezer for 5 minutes. Beat the cream until it starts to stiffen. Combine the whipped cream with the cheese by first vigorously working one-fourth of the whipped cream into the cheese and then folding in the rest of the cream with a rubber spatula. Fold the mixture just long enough to incorporate the cream.

LINE 6 *coeur à la crème* molds with a double layer of cheesecloth, press the cheese mixture into the molds, cover with plastic wrap, and let drain overnight on a sheet pan. If you don't have *coeur à la crème* molds, line 6 of the cups in a muffin tin with a double layer of cheesecloth, leaving enough cheesecloth hanging over the sides of each cup to cover the cheese mixture. Divide the mixture evenly among the muffin cups and pull the cheesecloth over the top of each. Gently transfer the wrapped cheese to a cake rack. Allow to drain overnight in the refrigerator.

IF you've used molds, turn the *coeurs à la crème* out onto chilled plates, peel off the cheesecloth, and serve. If you've used a muffin tin, gently take out the individual rounds of cheese, unwrap them, and place them on chilled plates.

PASS the sauce at the table.

HERB·FLAVORED FRESH CHEESE

CERVELLE DE CANUT

MAKES 4 FIRST-COURSE
OR HORS D'OEUVRE SERVINGS

This Lyonnaise dish is named after silk workers—canuts—who worked in Lyons's silk factories before the Second World War. A cervelle is a brain, and the culinary term cervelle refers to animal brains used as food. Fromage frais, the base for cervelle de canut, has a texture vaguely reminiscent of calves' brains, and this may explain the use of cervelle in the name of the dish.

In any case, cervelle de canut is a close relative to our American sour-cream-and-onion dip, the only significant difference being that in the French version fresh cheese is used and fresh herbs, usually chives and parsley, replace the dried onion-soup mix. My favorite way to serve cervelle de canut is as a light and inexpensive hors d'oeuvre or first course, spread on slices of toasted French bread, but this requires a relatively thick cheese and isn't really authentic. Authentic cervelle de canut has the consistency of runny yogurt and is usually just eaten with a spoon as a first course, in place of butter as an accompaniment to boiled or mashed potatoes, or as a cheese course. You can also experiment with adding different herbs—tarragon and marjoram, but not together, are two of my favorites.

- 2 cups [450 g] loose fromage frais, either store-bought or homemade (see page 148)

- 1 medium-size bunch fresh chives, chopped fine at the last minute

- 1 medium-size bunch parsley, chopped fine at the last minute

  salt

  pepper

WORK the fromage frais with the herbs and season to taste with salt and pepper. If you want a thicker version, more like a spread, drain the fromage frais in cheesecloth overnight in the refrigerator to thicken it, and serve with thin, toasted slices of French country bread or a baguette, or with crackers.

FRENCH·STYLE SWEET CHEESE TART

TARTE AU FROMAGE BLANC

MAKES ONE 10-INCH [25.5 CM] TART, ENOUGH
FOR 6 FIRST-COURSE SERVINGS OR
LIGHT LUNCH OR AFTERNOON SNACK SERVINGS

The French have cheese tarts, both savory and sweet, that are typically served as first courses or desserts. Either version may be offered as an afternoon snack in a salon de thé.

Sweet versions are similar to rich, creamy Jewish cheesecake (rather than to the more cakelike Italian cheesecake), except that fromage frais is used instead of cream cheese. Because of the cheese, the French version, tarte au fromage blanc, is lighter. And since it's baked in a traditional tart pan, it's also thinner. Both French and Jewish versions are essentially flans—the cheese is combined with whole eggs and gently baked until it sets, just like a custard. But the French version is made by lining the tart pan with regular pie dough (pâte brisée) instead of graham cracker crust mixture. If you can't find fromage blanc or haven't made your own, you can make this tart by puréeing organic yogurt and cottage cheese for a mixture that approximates the texture of authentic fromage blanc.

1 recipe Basic Tart Dough (page 155)

4 cups [450 g] firm *fromage blanc*, store-bought or homemade (page 148), or 2 cups [450 g] plain organic yogurt and 2 cups [450 g] small-curd cottage cheese

½ cup [125 ml] heavy cream

4 large eggs, beaten

½ cup [100 g] granulated sugar

1 teaspoon vanilla extract or grated lemon zest

ROLL out the pie dough. Use it to line a tart pan and bake it *à blanc*, as described on page 157.

IF you're using *fromage blanc*, work it with the cream until it's smooth. If you're using yogurt and cottage cheese, purée them together in a blender or food processor and drain them in the refrigerator for 4 hours or overnight in a strainer lined with muslin or authentic cheesecloth (see page 149) before combining with the cream.

PREHEAT the oven to 325°F [165°C/gas mark 3].

COMBINE the eggs, sugar, and vanilla or lemon in a small mixing bowl and whisk gently until the sugar dissolves. Work this mixture into the cheese mixture until smooth. If you're using yogurt and cottage cheese, work it through a strainer. Create a collar for the edge of the tart shell using a strip of aluminum foil and put it on the tart prior to cooking to keep the rim of the tart from becoming too brown. Spread the mixture in the baked tart shell and bake about 1 hour, until it is set—it doesn't jiggle in the middle when you move the tart back and forth. Serve warm or at room temperature.

Variations: Some recipes suggest serving a red-berry coulis (a purée that's been strained to eliminate seeds) with this tart. Whole berries in season, peaches, and kiwis also work well. If you want to make a savory cheese tart, leave out the sugar and vanilla and add herbs such as chopped chives and/or tarragon and salt and pepper to taste.

TRADITIONAL BACON AND CHEESE QUICHE

QUICHE LORRAINE

HOW TO	WHAT ARE	HOW TO	HOW TO	HOW TO
MAKE A BASIC DOUGH FOR PIES, TARTS, AND BRIOCHE	CUSTARDS AND HOW TO MAKE THEM	IMPROVISE YOUR OWN CUSTARDS AND QUICHES	TURN PURÉES INTO CUSTARDS AND QUICHES	USE LEFTOVERS

THE FIRST TIME I SAMPLED A QUICHE, SOMETIME IN THE LATE 1960s, I was convinced it was the most sophisticated and delicious thing I'd ever tasted. But since then, the poor quiche has had a hard time of it. Not long after my initial sampling, every little corner restaurant and fern bar was offering quiche. As the 1970s became the 1980s, the mixtures contained in the quiches became progressively more bizarre and unpleasant (broccoli springs to mind), the original and best, quiche lorraine, being all but forgotten. The quiche encountered its final humiliation after the publication of Bruce Feirstein's *Real Men Don't Eat Quiche*. A rugged and honest country dish had become a symbol of effete snobbery.

According to Anne Willan, in her informative book *French Regional Cooking*, quiche lorraine—in France also called *quiche au lard*—got its name from the German word *Kuchen*, which means cake or pastry. In nineteenth-century French cookbooks, quiche-like variations show up; they are mostly called *gâteaux au lard,* but rarely called *quiche.* According to *Larousse Gastronomique,* quiche was originally made with bread dough. Although that's a good idea (see Leek and Brioche Tart, page 162), I haven't been able to find any such recipes in even my oldest and dustiest cookbooks.

Essentially a quiche is a savory custard baked in a piecrust. A quiche lorraine is a tart made with a basic pie dough (*pâte brisée*) sprinkled with cooked bacon. A custard mixture (which is simply a liquid combined with eggs and gently baked until it sets) containing milk and/or cream is poured into a prebaked pastry shell and the tart is baked. Some recipes for quiche lorraine include onions, slowly sweated and caramelized, as though you were making French onion soup. Others, more common, contain cheese. In Alsace, onions cooked in goose fat are added along with the bacon and the result is called a *Zewelwai.* Of course, everyone who makes quiche lorraine claims that his or hers is the one true version, and that anything different is the most ignoble heresy. My own favorite version contains both the onions and the cheese, but more often than not I leave out the onions because they take a long time to sweat and caramelize. I like quiche made with milk instead of cream so I can eat more of it without feeling full, but if it's the main dish, I may use a combination of milk and cream. (It makes a decent lunch with a little green salad.)

What stops most people from making quiche (and a lot of other things) is the pastry dough. Some people go out and buy frozen ready-made pie shells, and that's fine as long as the dough is made with butter. Pastry dough made with margarine or shortening (usually disguised on the label as hydrogenated something-or-other) is at best flavorless and often distinctly unpleasant.

TART PANS

What are the best pans for tarts? My favorite tart pans are metal with fluted rims and a removable metal bottom. The advantage to these is that you can set the finished tart on an inverted bowl smaller than the bottom of the tart and just let the rim fall off the tart. You can then present the tart on a tray, leaving the metal bottom in place, so there's no cumbersome transferring from pan to serving plate. You can also use a Pyrex pie dish—just press the dough into it to line it—and serve wedges directly out of the dish. For a rustic touch, bake a quiche or tart in a porcelain quiche dish with a fluted rim and, again, serve the quiche directly out of the dish without unmolding it.

BASIC PIE AND TART DOUGH

PÂTE BRISÉE

MAKES ENOUGH PASTRY FOR ONE

10-INCH [25.5 CM] TART

1 stick (¼ pound/115 g) plus 1 tablespoon butter

1¾ cups [220 g] all-purpose bleached flour

1 large egg, plus 1 egg yolk right out of the refrigerator, beaten with ¼ teaspoon salt and 1 tablespoon water

1–2 tablespoons water, added ½ tablespoon at a time

It's no wonder piecrust makes people nervous—there is so much controversy about the right way to make it. For several reasons, the French have it easier than we Americans. First, they weigh ingredients, and doing so produces more consistent results than using cups and spoons for volume measurements. Second, their flour contains less protein than ours (and hence less of the gluten that makes tart dough tough) and their butter contains less water (water activates the gluten in the flour). Third, they're not concerned with making the dough "flaky," but rather want it to crumble in the mouth like sand. If they want flaky dough, they use the flakiest dough of them all, puff pastry (pâte feuilletée). Fourth, they use the metric system, which makes it easy to remember proportions and quickly understand the relationships between ingredients when comparing different recipes.

You can make tart dough by hand or in a food processor. Whichever method you use, you must chop the butter into the flour until it ends up distributed evenly, in little chunks the size of peas. The butter must stay cold during this chopping phase so it doesn't melt. Once the butter and flour are combined, cold liquid, usually water or eggs, is quickly stirred or chopped into the mixture. At this point the dough should look like a heap of gravel. Next, the mixture is quickly forced together into a smooth dough by smearing it with the heel of your hand (the French call this phase the *fraisage*) or by processing in a food processor. The dough may require additional water to come together depending on the dryness of your flour or humidity in the air. The dough is chilled to let any activated gluten relax. After chilling, the dough is ready to roll.

HAND METHOD: Once again, French and American cooks go about things differently. I can't say that one method is better than the other except that the American method involves dirtying an extra bowl, and so I use the French method. Both methods start out by chopping the butter into the flour. In America this is done in a bowl, ideally with a pastry blender, a gadget consisting of a handle to which a half dozen arcing wires are attached at either end—something you're likely to have seen only at the back of one of your grandmother's kitchen drawers. First the butter is cut into chunks with a knife; then it is worked into smaller pieces with the flour using the pastry blender. Liquid is added, then chopped into the flour with the pastry blender, and the nascent dough is dumped onto the work surface where it is worked until smooth. In France the butter is chopped into the flour right on the work surface with a flat metal or plastic pastry scraper sometimes called a bench scraper and then quickly worked into the flour with the tips of the fingers. A well is made in the flour mixture, the liquid ingredients are added to the well, and the mixture is quickly combined with the tips of the fingers. If the dough is still crumbly, add water (a half tablespoon at a time) and *fraisage* again. Repeat until the dough comes together. A rest in the fridge follows.

FOOD PROCESSOR METHOD: The cubes of cold butter are pulsed with the flour in the processor until the butter chunks are the size of peas. The liquid is added and the mixture is pulsed again until the dough forms a ball. The ball is then flattened into a disk and chilled.

PUT the butter and flour in the freezer for about 20 minutes so that they're very cold but not frozen. Use a chef's knife to cut the stick of butter in half lengthwise, turn the butter on its next slice and cut it again

TRADITIONAL BACON AND CHEESE QUICHE 155

in half lengthwise so you end up with 4 sticks the length of the stick of butter. Keeping the sticks together, slice them crosswise into eighths so that you end up with 32 little cubes. Toss the butter with the flour in a mixing bowl and put the bowl in the freezer for 20 minutes.

IF you're working by hand, dump the flour and the butter cubes onto the work surface and chop them together with a pastry scraper or the side of a metal spatula until the butter is in pieces the size of baby peas. Work the mixture further by lifting it a bit at a time with the tips of your fingers and quickly crushing the butter into the flour so that the "peas" end up flattened. Work quickly—don't do this for more than a minute. You don't want the warmth from your hands to melt the butter. Make a mound with the flour mixture and use your hand to make a well in the middle. Pour the egg mixture into the well and place all the fingertips of one hand into the liquid. Move your fingers around in the egg in a circular motion, gradually eroding the inside walls of the flour. Continue in this way until the egg mixture is incorporated into the flour and you end up with a rough heap. For the *fraisage,* start at the back of the pile and work the dough by crushing about one-sixth of it with the heel of your hand and smearing it backwards, away from the rest of the pile. Continue in this way until you've crushed all the dough. If the dough is still crumbly, add water (½ tablespoon at a time), squeeze it together into another pile, and repeat. It's sometimes necessary to *fraise* it three times to get it to come together. (If the butter starts to melt, put the dough, in a bowl, back in the freezer for 15 minutes before you continue.) When the dough is ready, press it into a flat disk about 1 inch [2.5 cm] thick. This will make it easier to roll out into the shape of the tart pan. Wrap the dough in plastic wrap and refrigerate it for 2 hours or overnight.

WHEN using a food processor, most of the work is done for you. Once you have added the amount of water to make the dough come together in a ball around the blade, stop immediately or you will make a highly elastic dough that will shrink when baked. Pulse the flour mixture, 2 to 3 seconds per pulse, about eight times, until the mixture has the consistency of fine gravel and there is no loose flour in the bottom of the bowl. Add the egg mixture and pulse two to three times more. Add the water a half tablespoon at a time, pulsing to combine after each addition. When the dough comes together into a ball, stop the food processor and form the dough into a disk about 1 inch (2.5 cm) thick, wrap it in plastic wrap, and put it in the refrigerator for 30 minutes to 12 hours.

ROLLING OUT TART DOUGH: Once the dough is chilled and rested, roll it out and put it in the tart pan. (See page 154 for more about tart pans.) Unwrap the dough before placing it on a lightly floured work surface. Most cooks put too much flour on the work surface, sprinkling flour directly over the surface and again on top of the dough. This can make the dough dry. French recipes say to *faire un nuage* (make a cloud) with the flour by taking a large pinch of it and tossing it with a quick snap of the wrist, releasing the flour about 6 inches [15 cm] from the work surface so that it settles in a thin, even coating. This takes a little practice—and while learning you'll mess up the kitchen. If you can't get the knack, slowly sprinkle the flour from about 2 feet [61 cm] above the work surface. When the dough comes out of the fridge it's usually too hard to roll out—give it a couple of good whacks with the rolling pin to soften it slightly. Place it on your lightly floured work surface and move it once in a circle so that it gets floured underneath. Flour it on top—again, lightly. Rub the rolling pin with flour to further prevent sticking and roll the dough out slightly, starting one-third of the way into the disk and rolling out the back two-thirds away from you. Don't try to roll out too much at one time—this can cause the dough to stick and tear, and don't roll all the way over the edge away from you—this will make the dough too thin at the edges. Between each roll or two, dust with flour and rotate the angle of the dough—*not* the pin—on the floured work surface so that the bottom of the dough keeps getting floured. At the same time, rotate the disk about a quarter turn, and roll out—again just the back two-thirds, not rolling over the end. Keep moving, rotating, dusting, and rolling until the dough forms a circle about 3 inches wider than your tart pan so that you'll have extra dough to line the sides of the pan and to form a border. (The circle of dough should be 13 inches/33 cm in diameter for a 10-inch/25.5 cm tart pan.) The dough should be between ⅛ inch and ¼ inch [about .5 cm] thick.

LINING THE TART PAN: Once you've rolled out the dough, you've got to get it into the pan. Brush any excess flour off the dough—there are special brushes for this but I just give it a quick swat with a towel. Most of the time you can simply roll the dough up on the rolling pin—again brushing off excess flour—and then unroll it over the pan. But if it's a hot day or the dough is cracking and being uncooperative, rolling it up on the pin may cause the dough to stick to the pin or to fall apart. In this situation, fold the dough in quarters, place the center corner in the middle of the tart pan, and unfold the dough in the pan.

Once you've transferred the dough, you need to fit it snugly into the tart pan and make a border. Lift the dough hanging over the side of the pan straight up and press it into the corners of the pan with your fingers. Don't stretch the dough, just feed as much as you need from the top as you're forming the corners. Rotate the tart pan and continue until you've formed an edge all around the pan. At this point, use your fingers to push the dough in slightly from the outer edge so that you have about ⅓ inch [about 8 mm] extra dough all around the tart to reinforce the sides and make them slightly thicker than the rest of the dough. Pinch the overhanging dough about ¼ inch away from the edge of the tart pan and push inward toward the center of the pan so that you create a little extra lip of dough along the inside rim of the pan. Push down on the top of the rim, using the edge to cut through the dough and leaving the excess dough on the outside of the tart and a little extra dough along the inside of the rim. Rotate the tart pan, pinching and cutting, until you've pinched all around the outside edge. Roll the rolling pin over the pan, cutting off any dough still clinging around the outside. With your thumb and forefinger, gently pinch and press straight down on the extra dough along the inside of the tart rim, making the sides slightly thicker and forming a smooth border that comes up a little less than ¼ inch above the rim of the tart pan. Refrigerate the lined tart pan for 1 hour.

PREBAKING THE TART SHELL (or Baking à Blanc): When you're baking wet ingredients in a tart, you've got to cook the dough ahead of time or it won't ever get hot enough and it will be pasty and soggy. (Remember, liquids can't get hotter than 212°F/100°C.) To bake the tart shell—what professionals call "cooking blind" and the French call cooking *à blanc*—preheat the oven to 425°F [220°C/gas mark 6]. Poke the tart shell in several places with a fork to help it cook through, and cover the shell with a sheet of parchment paper. Leave plenty of extra paper hanging over the sides so you'll be able to lift the paper out when the shell is hot. Don't use wax paper, because the wax melts, and don't use aluminum foil, because it leaves little metal specks on the dough. Fill the lined tart shell with something you don't care too much about—rice or dried beans—which I reuse, to keep the dough from rising. Bake the shell for about 20 minutes, until you notice that the edge of the dough is completely matte instead of shiny and is colored a very pale blond. Gently lift off the parchment, doing your best to not spill the rice or beans. Allow the shell to cool slightly and make an egg wash by beating a large egg with ¼ teaspoon of salt (not the egg and salt called for in the dough recipe.) Brush the shell with the egg mixture to create a seal that will prevent it from getting soggy when you cook it with the filling. Bake the empty shell for about 20 minutes more until the inside loses its shiny dull-gray look and turns matte and pale blond and the sides, which continue to cook, turn light brown. Turn the oven down to the temperature you need for baking the filled shell, or turn it off if you plan to finish the baking later in the day. Let the tart shell cool for at least 5 minutes before you use it. (You can make the shell earlier in the day, but the fresher the better.)

BACON·CUSTARD TART

QUICHE LORRAINE

MAKES 6 FIRST-COURSE OR LIGHT MAIN-COURSE
SERVINGS (ONE 10-INCH TART)

1 recipe Basic Pie and Tart Dough (page 155)

¾ pound [225 g] slab or thickly sliced bacon (see page 2)

3 large eggs

¼ teaspoon salt

¼ teaspoon pepper

2¼ cups [550 ml] milk, or 1 cup [250 ml] heavy cream combined with 1¼ cups [300 ml] milk

ROLL out the dough and prebake the tart shell as described on pages 156–157.

PREHEAT the oven to 325°F [165°C/gas mark 3]. (Or turn it down to 325°F [165°C/gas mark 3] if you've just baked the shell.)

IF you're using slab bacon, slice it into ¼-inch-thick [.5 cm] strips. Slice the strips crosswise into strips—*lardons*—¼ inch [.5 cm] on each side. Cook the *lardons* in a small heavy-bottomed pan over medium heat until they just begin to turn crispy, about 10 minutes, stirring every minute or two. Drain the *lardons* and sprinkle them in the tart shell.

BEAT the eggs with the salt and pepper and lightly beat in the milk. Strain. Set the tart pan on a sheet pan, pour the milk mixture into the shell, and gently slide the quiche into the oven.

TO tell when the quiche is done, gently move the sheet pan and see if the surface of the quiche ripples. As soon as it no longer ripples, the quiche is done, usually in 55 minutes to 1 hour. Let it cool for 15 minutes before serving.

Variations: Traditional variations from Lorraine include cheese and onions. For the cheese variation, sprinkle 1 cup of finely grated Gruyère or other flavorful firm cheese over the shell along with the bacon and cut the milk down to 2 cups [500 ml]. For the onion variation cut 2 large red onions into very thin slices— I use a vegetable slicer—and cook them gently in a heavy-bottomed pan on the stove for about 30 minutes, until they're soft and caramelized. Sprinkle them in the shell along with the bacon and, if you're using it, the cheese. Again, cut the milk (or milk and cream) down to 2 cups [500 ml] if you're using cheese as well as onions. Another version, called a *tarte tourangelle,* from the Loire valley is made by lining the bottom of the prebaked tart shell with rillettes (see page 384) instead of bacon, pouring the custard mixture over it, and baking.

You can make up your own quiche variations by sprinkling the prebaked shell with different ingredients or flavoring the custard mixture itself. When you experiment with adding ingredients to the prebaked shell, keep in mind that a quiche cooks slowly and some ingredients, especially green vegetables, turn a sullen gray when they're cooked too long. Remember also that most foods release liquid when they cook, so you have to precook them. If baked raw in the quiche, most foods will end up sitting in a pool of their own juices instead of setting in the custard. Mushrooms and sorrel (which turns a sullen gray no matter what you do to it) are the only vegetables, other than onions or leeks, that I use in quiche, because their flavor and texture aren't compromised by the long cooking. Dried wild mushrooms such as cèpes or morels, soaked in a little Madeira and sautéed before being used to fill the shell, make a magnificent quiche. (See the recipe that follows.) You can also sauté fresh cultivated mushrooms (sprinkled with a little thyme), but fresh wild mushrooms are so special, I don't like to bury them in a custard. Always sauté wild or cultivated mushrooms until any liquid they release completely evaporates before incorporating them into a quiche or custard.

I've always been fascinated by seafood quiche because I can incorporate the flavor of the seafood into the custard itself. I may, for example, steam open mussels or clams with white wine (as in the *moules à la marinière* recipe on page 268) and stir the briny liquid they release into the milk and egg mixture before baking. If I'm using crustaceans, I may simmer the broken-up shells with cream (as in the recipe on page 337) to extract their flavor and color, and then add this mixture to the custard. The one problem with a seafood quiche is that the long cooking time will leave fish falling apart and shellfish tough. Because of this, I use only shellfish, and I cut the flesh into small dice so that no one will detect any dryness or toughness. Don't include cheese in a seafood quiche.

Occasionally, quiche-like tarts are made by spreading a sheet or round of puff pastry or brioche (see page 161) with cooked ingredients and then simply baking the tart, much like a gratin, but without the egg contained in quiches or in custards. One of my favorite of these is the Leek and Brioche Tart on page 162, made by gently cooking sliced leeks or onions in butter until they soften, adding a small amount of cream, spreading the mixture over a round of brioche, and baking the tart until the surface turns golden brown. This method also works with a rectangle or round of puff pastry that is very thin—no thicker than ⅛ inch.

DRIED CÈPE QUICHE

QUICHE AUX CÈPES SÈCHES

MAKES 6 FIRST-COURSE OR LIGHT MAIN-COURSE SERVINGS (ONE 10-INCH TART)

1 recipe Basic Pie and Tart Dough (page 155)

1¼ cups (about 1 ounce/30 g) dried cèpes (porcini; Italian brands are usually the best)

½ cup [125 ml] semidry Madeira

¼ pound [115 g] pancetta or prosciutto (in one slice, prosciutto preferably from the end piece, see page 9; optional)

1 tablespoon butter (if you're using prosciutto)

2 tablespoons olive oil

1 large clove garlic, chopped fine

1 large shallot, chopped fine

  salt

  pepper

3 large eggs

2 cups [500 ml] milk, or more as needed

ROLL out the dough and prebake the tart shell as described on pages 156–157.

RINSE the cèpes quickly under cold running water. Toss them with the Madeira in a small mixing bowl and let them soak for 30 minutes; 15 minutes into the soaking, turn them in the Madeira so that they all soak evenly.

PREHEAT the oven to 325°F [165°C/gas mark 3].

CUT the pancetta or prosciutto into ¼-inch [.5 cm] dice and cook the dice in a sauté pan over low to medium heat until the aroma is released. If you're using prosciutto, which doesn't render enough fat for its own cooking, cook the dice in butter.

SQUEEZE the cèpes, reserving the juice in a small bowl. If you notice any hard parts on the cèpes, cut them off with a knife and discard them or save them to add to broths.

TAKE the pancetta out of the pan with a slotted spoon and sprinkle it over the prebaked shell. If the fat in the pan is burned, discard it. Add the olive oil to the pan and sauté the mushrooms over medium heat until they smell fragrant, about 5 minutes; 2 minutes into the sautéing, sprinkle the garlic and shallot over them. Season the mushroom mixture with salt and pepper and arrange it in the bottom of the pastry shell.

BEAT the eggs with ½ teaspoon salt and ¼ teaspoon pepper. Pour the soaking liquid from the cèpes into a measuring cup, leaving any grit behind in the bowl, and add enough milk to total 2¼ cups [550 ml]. Combine with the beaten eggs and strain. Set the tart pan on a sheet pan, pour the milk and egg mixture into the shell, and gently slide the quiche into the oven.

TO tell when the quiche is done, gently move the sheet pan and see if the surface of the quiche ripples. As soon as it no longer ripples, the quiche is done, usually in 55 minutes to 1 hour. Let cool for 15 minutes before serving.

Variation: *Larousse Gastronomique*, a limitless source of cooking lore, gives a recipe for *flan à la bordelaise* made by covering the bottom of a prebaked pastry shell with diced beef marrow and Bayonne ham (a prosciutto-like cured ham from the French southwest), covering it with layers of sautéd fresh cèpes, pouring bordelaise sauce (see page 483) over it, sprinkling with bread crumbs, and baking. Technically this tart isn't a flan—flans are custards and contain eggs—but for anything so delicious we have to allow a little poetic license.

SHRIMP AND SORREL QUICHE

QUICHE AUX CREVETTES ET À L'OSEILLE

MAKES 6 FIRST-COURSE OR LIGHT MAIN-COURSE SERVINGS (ONE 10-INCH TART)

Y̵ou can make this quiche the hard way or the easy way. The "hard way" isn't really hard but it does mean tracking down shrimp with heads (or saving up shrimp shells in the freezer). If you order the shrimp beforehand or live near an Asian market, this shouldn't be a problem and the quiche will taste more like shrimp than shrimp themselves. If you can't find sorrel, which gives the quiche a delightful tang, just leave it out or substitute spinach. The tastiest shrimp are white or pink gulf shrimp from the Gulf of Mexico or, despite being called "gulf" shrimp, the Atlantic coast of Florida. Since you're going to be dicing the shrimp, any size will do; larger shrimp always cost more, but have the advantage of leaving you with fewer to peel. Use the same techniques for making lobster or crayfish quiche by simmering the chopped cooked shells with cream and adding the strained cream to the custard mixture. (See chapter 25 for more about cooking crustaceans.)

1 recipe Basic Pie and Tart Dough (page 155)

1⅔ pounds [750 g] raw shrimp with heads, or 1 pound raw headless shrimp, or ¾ pound [340 g] peeled raw shrimp tails

10 ounces [280 g] frozen shrimp shells (which you can use instead of shrimp heads; optional)

1 medium onion, chopped fine (if you're using shrimp heads)

2 tablespoons butter (if you're using shrimp heads), plus 2 tablespoons for sautéing the shrimp

3 sprigs fresh thyme, or ½ teaspoon dried thyme

2 medium-size tomatoes, chopped coarse if you're using shrimp heads or frozen shells)

2 cups [500 ml] heavy cream (if you're using shrimp heads)

salt

pepper

3 large eggs

½ to 1 cup [125 to 250 ml] milk if you're using shrimp heads, 2¼ cups [550 ml] if you're not

¾ pound [340 g] fresh sorrel, or 1 bunch (10 ounces [280 g]) spinach, stems removed, leaves washed

ROLL out the dough and prebake the tart shell as described on pages 156–157.

IF you're using the heads, snap them off the shrimp and shell the shrimp tails. Pulse the heads and shells in a food processor about 5 times, 5 seconds each time, to break them up without puréeing them. (If you don't have a food processor, see paragraph below.)

IF you're using the heads or frozen shrimp shells, cook the onion in 2 tablespoons of butter in a heavy-bottomed saucepan large enough to hold the heads or shells, about 10 minutes, until translucent. Add the heads or shells, the thyme, tomatoes, cream, and ½ cup [125 ml] water. Simmer the mixture gently, stirring every few minutes, for about ½ hour. If you didn't break up the heads in the food processor, crush them in the pan while they're cooking; use the end of a European-style rolling pin (the kind without handles) or the front end of a cleaver held upright. Strain the shrimp mixture through a regular strainer, pushing down hard with a ladle to extract as much liquid as possible. Strain the mixture again through a fine-mesh strainer and reserve.

IF you're using headless shrimp, just shell and devein them.

SAUTÉ the shrimp tails in 2 tablespoons of butter for about 5 minutes, until they turn pink. Season with salt and pepper and reserve.

BEAT the eggs with ½ teaspoon salt and ¼ teaspoon pepper. If you use shrimp heads or frozen shells, put the cooking liquid in a mixing cup and add enough milk to total 2¼ cups [550 ml] of liquid. Whisk this mixture into the eggs. If you haven't used heads or shells, whisk 2¼ cups [550 ml] milk into the eggs.

IF you're using sorrel, heat it over high heat in a saucepan with 1 tablespoon of water, while stirring. When the sorrel has "melted" and any liquid in the pan has evaporated, after about 5 minutes, remove from the heat. Chop the sorrel coarse and spread it over the bottom of the prebaked tart shell. Slice the shrimp crosswise so you end up with pieces between ¼ inch and ½ inch [.5 and 1.5 cm] on each side, and sprinkle the pieces over the sorrel.

SET the tart pan on a sheet pan, and pour the egg and cooking liquid or milk mixture into the shell. Gently slide the quiche into the oven.

TO tell when the quiche is done, gently move the sheet pan and see if the surface of the quiche ripples. As soon as it no longer ripples, the quiche is done, usually in 55 minutes to 1 hour. Let cool for 15 minutes before serving.

OTHER SAVORY TARTS

For savory tarts, tart shells made with regular pie and tart dough (*pâte brisée*) are almost always filled with some kind of custard mixture. These tarts are cousins to traditional quiche. Other doughs, such as brioche or puff pastry (*pâte feuilletée*), can be used to provide a breadlike or crispy base for relatively thin layers of savory mixtures. In the case of brioche, the mixture seeps down into the bread, making a kind of savory coffee cake. The same mixture spread over a sheet of puff pastry makes a thin and buttery crispy tart that you can pick up like a piece of thin pizza. You can make up mixtures for savory tarts almost as though you were making a pizza, but use them in smaller amounts, so that the delicate texture of the pastry isn't lost. I like to top brioche or puff pastry with creamy mixtures rather than a pizza-like tomato sauce because the creaminess merges so beautifully with the buttery tart base.

BRIOCHE DOUGH

MAKES 1 POUND

Brioche dough is made in the same way as bread dough except that eggs are used instead of water and butter is incorporated into the dough before baking. This recipe is adapted from a specially successful brioche in Julia Child's Baking with Julia.

FOR THE SPONGE STARTER:

⅓ cup [75 ml] warm milk (it should barely feel warm when you touch it with the back of a finger)

1 packet (2¼ teaspoons) active dried yeast

1 large egg

2 cups [250 g] unbleached all-purpose flour

FOR THE DOUGH:

⅓ cup [75 ml] sugar

1 teaspoon kosher salt

4 large eggs, lightly beaten

1½ to 2 cups [175 to 250 g] unbleached all-purpose flour

1½ sticks (12 tablespoons) unsalted butter, cut into ½-inch cubes, warmed to room temperature

1 tablespoon unsalted butter for greasing the bowl

TO MAKE THE SPONGE

COMBINE the milk, yeast, egg, and 1 cup [150 g] of flour in a mixing bowl or the bowl of a heavy-duty electric mixer. Use a wooden spoon or the paddle blade to combine these ingredients just lightly—there's no need for actual kneading at this point—and then sprinkle the remaining cup of flour over the surface of the mixture. This prevents a crust from forming. Let rest for 1 hour in a warm place. The flour on top will appear cracked when the sponge is ready.

TO MAKE THE DOUGH

ADD sugar, salt, eggs, and 1 cup [150 g] of flour to the sponge. Replace the paddle blade with the dough hook and work the mixture on slow speed until it just starts to pull together, about 2 minutes. If you're working by hand, work the mixture also for about 2 minutes. Add another ½ cup [60 g] of flour and work the mixture on medium speed or by hand for 15 minutes. If using an electric mixer, periodically scrape down the sides of the bowl so everything gets incorporated. If, after 10 minutes, the dough seems loose, work in 1 to 3 tablespoons flour until the dough holds together in a single mass. At this point it may cling to the sides of the bowl (or to your fingers), but it shouldn't be so sticky that some of it remains attached.

IF it lets you, turn the mixer down to between low and medium; if not, turn it to medium. Add ⅓ of the softened butter and continue to work the dough for 5 minutes. Repeat with half the remaining butter, for 5 minutes more, and add the rest of the butter. When the last of the butter is incorporated, work the mixture for 1 minute on high and 5 minutes more on medium, scraping down the sides of the bowl and the hook so everything gets evenly mixed in. If the dough seems loose after 2 minutes, add up to 2 tablespoons more flour. Don't be tempted to add more. The looseness just means that the butter has melted or softened, giving the impression that the brioche is too wet. If you're working by hand, knead the brioche with the heel of your hand on the work surface, working in the butter and, if necessary, flour, as described above.

TRANSFER the dough to a bowl and cover with plastic wrap, with the plastic actually touching the dough's surface so a crust doesn't form. Don't cover the dough in such a way that it can't expand as it ferments. Let rise in a warm place for 4 hours or until doubled in volume. Press down the dough so it compacts to its original volume and, with the dough still covered with plastic wrap, refrigerate it for 6 hours or overnight. The dough may rise but not as much as it did in a warm place. After the cold rise, the deflated dough can be wrapped and frozen for up to 1 month and thawed overnight in the refrigerator.

LEEK AND BRIOCHE TART

TARTE AUX POIREAUX, PAIN BRIOCHÉ

MAKES 8 FIRST-COURSE SERVINGS OR 6 LIGHT MAIN-COURSE SERVINGS

Leeks, like so many things, are magnificent with cream. The mixture for this tart—actually more a spread than a filling—includes a little prosciutto and is spooned over a round of brioche as it's baking. The liquid gets absorbed by the brioche, making it moist and creamy, while the leeks and prosciutto form a delicate topping. Bacon or pancetta can be used in place of the prosciutto.

1 recipe (1 pound) Brioche Dough (page 161)
  butter for sheet pan
4 medium-size leeks
1 tablespoon butter
½ teaspoon sugar
1 thin slice prosciutto, chopped fine (about 1 heaping tablespoon when chopped; optional)

¾ cup [175 ml] heavy cream

salt

pepper

1 egg yolk

ROLL the brioche dough into a circle about 14 inches [35 cm] in diameter and transfer it to a buttered sheet pan. If your sheet pan isn't wide enough, roll the brioche into an oval or rectangle or use a 14-inch [35 cm] pizza pan. Cover the dough with a moist towel and set it in a warm place to rise until it has doubled in thickness, 30 minutes to 1 hour.

TRIM the greens off the leeks, cut the leeks in half lengthwise, wash them, and slice them as thin as you can.

PREHEAT the oven to 400°F [200°C/gas mark 6].

SWEAT the leeks in butter in a heavy-bottomed saucepan or small pot, stirring every few minutes with a wooden spoon until they smell fragrant and soften but don't brown, about 15 minutes. Sprinkle the sugar and prosciutto over the leeks, sweat for 1 minute more, and pour over the cream. Stir with a wooden spoon and simmer over high heat for 1 minute to thicken the mixture slightly. Season the mixture to taste with salt and pepper, remove from the heat, and let cool to room temperature.

BEAT the egg yolk with a large pinch of salt, which thins it and makes it easier to spread, and brush it over the entire surface of the brioche. Slide the brioche into the oven and bake for about 20 minutes. Use a large spoon to spread one-half the leek mixture in a circle in the middle of the brioche, leaving a 2-inch [5 cm] border and pressing down slightly with the back of the spoon so the mixture doesn't run off the sides of the brioche. Bake for 5 minutes more and repeat with the rest of the mixture. Bake for 5 to 10 minutes more, until the rim of the brioche is golden brown. If the brioche starts to puff up too much in one place, poke it with a fork. Serve warm in wedges.

Variations: If you make the base with *pâte feuilletée* instead of brioche, you'll end up with a crispy puff pastry leek tart, a *tarte feuilletée aux poireaux*. (Made with *pâte brisée*—regular pie dough—the tart becomes a *flimiche aux poireaux*.)

To make a *tarte feuilletée aux poireaux*, preheat the oven to 375°F [190°C/gas mark 5]. Roll out a 1-pound or 14-ounce [about 400 g] package of puff pastry (made with butter) into a 12-by-18-inch [30.5 by 46 cm] rectangle about ⅛ inch [3 mm] thick. You can also roll it out into a round, but since the dough comes already shaped like a rectangle, it's easier to keep it the same shape, and most sheet pans measure 12 by 18 inches. Roll the dough up on the rolling pin and roll it out on a sheet pan sprinkled with a couple of teaspoons of cold water to prevent the bottom of the tart from burning. With a sharp knife, trim about ¼ inch [.5 cm] of dough from all four sides of the rectangle, using a rapid movement to keep from crimping the dough. (The cutting removes any folded edges that would keep dough from rising.) Brush the dough with beaten egg yolk and salt mixture, just as you would the brioche tart. With a fork, poke holes in the pastry except for a 1-inch [2.5 cm] border around all sides of the tart (this keeps it from puffing too much) and refrigerate for 30 minutes.

Prepare the leek mixture as described above, until it thickens and you're left with about 1½ cups [350 g] of mixture. Chill this mixture.

Spread the leek mixture over the rolled-out dough, leaving a 1-inch [2.5 cm] border, and slide the tart into the oven. Bake for about 45 minutes. Check the tart every 5 minutes; if you see it starting to puff, poke any blisters with the tip of a knife or skewer to deflate them. If the tart puffs and pushes some of the leek mixture to one side, spread the mixture evenly with the back of a spoon. Cut the tart into 8 first-course servings.

Savory Custards: Quiches without the Pastry

A QUICHE IS A CUSTARD BAKED IN A PASTRY shell. Any filling you'd use to make a quiche can instead be baked in individual molds—ramekins or dariole molds, which look like miniature fezzes—and served as a savory custard. A custard can be made out of vegetable purées or leftover soups or sauces by beating a flavorful liquid or semiliquid mixture with eggs and a little bit of milk or cream and then baking. But when making a savory custard, keep in mind that a perfectly smooth texture can easily become monotonous if you don't contrast it with something crunchy or firm—not a problem in a quiche because of its crunchy crust, but otherwise something to think about. A simple smooth custard provides a delightful counterpoint to a chunk of firm grilled or roasted meat, but not to softer foods, such as delicate fish like flounder. If you're serving a custard as a first course, include something in the sauce or custard itself to provide texture and contrast. I like to use small pieces of sautéed mushrooms, cubes of artichoke hearts, chopped truffles, or sautéed cubes of zucchini. If I'm serving shellfish custard as a first course, I include cubes of the shellfish in the custard itself and the whole shellfish (baby shrimp, crayfish, mussels, oysters) or pieces of the shellfish (lobster, large shrimp) in the sauce or as a garniture.

INDIVIDUAL ARTICHOKE FLANS

FLANS AUX ARTICHAUTS

MAKES 6 FIRST-COURSE OR SIDE-DISH SERVINGS

This is an example of how you can take a soup and turn it into a flan by beating it with a little egg and baking it in individual molds. You only need to avoid soups that contain a lot of starch, such as potatoes or flour, because they make the custard too dense. This recipe is virtually identical to the *purée georgette* on page 184, except that the bread crumbs have been left out and eggs have been added to turn the soup into a flan. I serve these flans as an accompaniment to red meats. They are also good topped with meurette sauce (see page 115), or bordelaise sauce (see page 483) and sautéed wild mushrooms, or—ultimate extravagance—the sautéed wild mushrooms with truffles on page 604, and served as a first course.

- 6 medium-sized or 4 large artichokes (about 2½ pounds/1.1 kg total weight)
- 2 tablespoons olive oil
  juice of 1 lemon
- 1¼ cups [125 ml] heavy cream
  salt
  pepper
- 5 large egg yolks, beaten
- 1 tablespoon butter (for buttering the molds), at room temperature

CUT the top one-third off each artichoke and discard. Cut off the stems and reserve. Trim off and discard the outermost leaves by rotating the artichoke against a sharp paring knife or by just pulling away the leaves. Cut the artichokes vertically in quarters, peel the tough outermost fibers away from the stems with a paring knife, and simmer the artichokes and stems in a nonaluminum pot with plenty of water to cover, and 1 tablespoon of the olive oil. Put a plate directly on the artichokes to keep them from bobbing up.

WHEN the artichokes and stems are easily penetrated with a knife, after about 25 minutes, remove from cooking liquid and toss with the lemon juice and the remaining olive oil. Reserve the cooking liquid.

PURÉE the artichokes and stems in a blender with the olive oil in which they were tossed, along with 2 cups of the cool cooking liquid, for about 1 minute. Start on slow speed and gradually increase the speed to high. Work the purée through a food mill or, using the bottom of a ladle, through a coarse-mesh strainer. Strain a second time, ideally through a fine-mesh strainer. Combine the purée with the heavy cream and season to taste with salt and pepper—overseason slightly to make up for the eggs that will be added. Then whisk in the beaten egg yolks.

PREHEAT the oven to 275°F [165°C/gas mark 3].

BRUSH the inside of six 3 or 4-ounce ramekins or dariole molds with butter and ladle in the artichoke mixture. Put the ramekins in a baking dish with high sides and pour in enough hot tap water to come halfway up their sides. Loosely cover the whole baking dish with aluminum foil. Slide the baking dish into the oven and bake until the flans have set, about 45 minutes. Check if the flans are done by jiggling several back and forth, one at a time, and see if ripples form on top. If ripples form, cook the flans 10 more minutes and check again. When the flans are done, take the water bath out of the oven, remove the flans, and let them rest for 5 minutes. Unmold each flan by running a knife around the inside of the mold and then turning the flan over onto a towel held against the top of the mold, to catch any liquid released during baking. After holding each flan upside down against the towel for a few seconds, turn the flan back over so it settles back into its mold. Invert each flan on a small warm plate by placing the plate over the flan, turning over the plate and mold together, and lifting off the mold. Ladle any garniture or sauce (see headnote) over and around the flan.

CHICKEN LIVER FLANS WITH TOMATO-MARJORAM SAUCE

FLANS DE FOIE DE VOLAILLE, SAUCE TOMATE À LA MARJOLAINE

MAKES 8 FIRST-COURSE SERVINGS

In the Bresse region of eastern France, long famous for its chickens (poulardes de Bresse), they make a chicken liver flan and top it with a crayfish sauce (sauce nantua) similar to the sauce à la américaine on page 340. Combinations of seafood and poultry or veal were popular during the seventeenth and eighteenth centuries, but few of these dishes remain on modern menus, chicken liver flan with crayfish sauce being an exception. Modern chefs occasionally substitute foie gras, but the texture of foie gras is so special it seems a waste to purée it into a flan. Lucien Tendret, who in the late nineteenth century wrote La Table au Pays de Brillat-Savarin and who was one of the first to write about regional cooking, includes beef marrow in his version. But beef marrow is a nuisance to get out of the bones, so I make the flan in the more usual way: with cream, milk, and the puréed livers. Tendret serves his flan with the traditional crayfish sauce and describes the combination as one of the béatitudes de la gourmandise. He also insists on foies blonds, which are livers that are golden in color instead of the usual pink. I encounter them in chickens in France, but never in the United States. Frankly, I have never been able to detect any difference in flavor. When I worked at Claude Peyrot's restaurant Vivarois, we made a foie gras flan and topped it with oysters and oyster sauce—peculiar sounding maybe, but delicious to bite into. I make these flans with chicken livers from the best free-range organic chickens I can find—I save the livers up in the freezer—and serve it with a simple, slightly acidic tomato sauce to cut the richness.

FOR THE FLANS:

4   firm chicken livers from free-range organic chickens (enough to make ½ cup puréed liver)

½   small garlic clove, chopped fine, crushed to a paste with the side of a chef's knife

1½   cups heavy cream, warmed

5   egg yolks

½   teaspoon salt

¼   teaspoon freshly ground pepper, preferably white

3   tablespoons butter (for the molds), at room temperature

FOR THE SAUCE:

2   shallots, chopped fine

1   tablespoon butter or olive oil

4   medium-size tomatoes, chopped

2   teaspoons fresh marjoram leaves, or 1 teaspoon fresh thyme leaves, or ½ teaspoon dried thyme

¼   cup [60 ml] heavy cream

    salt

    pepper

PREHEAT the oven to 275°F [165°C/gas mark 3].

TO MAKE THE FLANS

COMBINE the livers, garlic, cream, the egg yolks, salt, and pepper in a blender and purée for about 1 minute. Strain the mixture through a fine-mesh strainer.

BRUSH the inside of eight 3 or 4-ounce [125 ml] ramekins or dariole molds with butter and ladle in the liver mixture so that each ramekin is about three-quarters full. Put the ramekins in a baking dish with high sides and pour enough hot tap water into the baking dish to come halfway up the sides of the ramekins. Slide the baking dish into the oven and bake until the flans have set, about 45 minutes. Check if the flans are done by jiggling one back and forth to see if ripples form on top. If ripples form, cook the flans 10 more minutes and check again.

TO MAKE THE SAUCE WHILE THE FLANS BAKE

COOK the shallots in the butter or olive oil in a heavy-bottomed saucepan for about 10 minutes until they smell fragrant. Don't let them brown. Stir in the tomatoes, cover the pan, and cook over medium heat for about 5 minutes, until the tomatoes release their liquid. Take off the lid, add the marjoram, and simmer for about 15 minutes more, until the tomatoes are completely soft and any liquid on the bottom of the pan has evaporated. Stir occasionally with a wooden spoon, scraping the bottom of the saucepan, to keep the tomatoes from sticking. Work the tomatoes through a food mill or use the bottom of a ladle to push them through a fine-mesh strainer into a clean saucepan. Add the cream. Simmer the sauce until it is just thick enough to coat the flans. Season to taste with salt and pepper.

TO FINISH AND SERVE THE FLANS

UNMOLD each of the flans by running a knife around the inside of the mold and then turning the flan over onto a towel held against the top of the mold. The towel catches any liquid released during baking so it won't run out onto the plate. After holding each flan upside down against the towel for a few seconds, turn the flan back over so it settles back into its mold. Invert the flans on small warm plates by placing the plate over the flan, turning over plate and mold together, and then lifting off the mold. Ladle the sauce over and around the flan.

Variations: If you want to try the oyster sauce, shuck a dozen oysters (for 4 servings), reserving all their liquor, and put both liquor and oysters in a saucepan. Heat over medium heat until the liquid approaches but doesn't reach a simmer and the oysters barely start to curl abound the edges. Use a slotted spoon to transfer the oysters to a small bowl. Add ¼ cup [60 ml] of dry white wine and one shallot, chopped fine, to the liquid left in the saucepan and boil the liquid down on high heat until you only have about ¼ cup [60 ml] left. Over medium heat, whisk in ¼ pound [115 g] of butter cut into 4 pieces. When all the butter has emulsified, strain the sauce through a fine-mesh strainer into a clean saucepan, put the oysters in the sauce, and season to taste with salt and pepper. Spoon some sauce and 3 oysters over each of the 4 flans.

ABOVE
ALSATIAN-STYLE
SAUERKRAUT WITH ASSORTED
SAUSAGES AND MEATS
527

BELOW
BRAISED VEAL SHANKS
(OSSO BUCCO) WITH VEGETABLE
"CONFITURE"
434

ABOVE
POT-AU-FEU BROTH WITH CRUSTY
CHEESE CROUTONS
455

LEFT
LEEK AND BRIOCHE TARTE
162

BELOW
CHICKEN WITH CRAYFISH
341

BELOW
COLD BEEF AND BEET SALAD
69

LEFT
SHREDDED
RED CABBAGE SALAD
WITH PISTACHIOS
37

BELOW
FRICASSEE OF YOUNG RABBIT WITH
PEARL ONIONS, BACON, AND MUSHROOMS
397

BELOW
POT-AU-FEU WITH CONDIMENTS
456

ABOVE
PORK TENDERLOIN WITH PRUNES
498

ABOVE
CRÊPES WITH ORANGE BUTTER SAUCE
649

LEFT
PEAR CLAFOUTIS
652

BELOW
ROAST PEARS WITH BUTTER
AND SUGAR
678

ABOVE
CHOCOLATE MOUSSE
623

BELOW
THIN APPLE TART
MADE WITH PUFF PASTRY
613

BELOW & RIGHT
CLASSIC MADELEINES
656

NIÇOISE ONION, OLIVE, AND ANCHOVY TART

PISSALADIÈRE

TWO WAYS	HOW TO	HOW TO	HOW TO
TO MAKE PIZZA DOUGH	USE A NATURAL BREAD STARTER	REPACK SALTED ANCHOVIES	MAKE TRADITIONAL FRENCH FLATBREADS AND "PANCAKES"

IF YOU EVER FIND YOURSELF TRAIPSING AROUND NICE, OR ANY LITTLE town within a short drive of the French Riviera, you'll see large square *pissaladières* in the windows of pastry shops. Sadly, most of them are rather drab looking—like pizzas that didn't quite make it.

But the comparison to pizza is unfair because a well-made *pissaladière* has a savory identity all its own. Even the origin of the words is different. In *La Cuisine Niçoise,* Jacques Médecin states that the word *pissaladière* comes from *pissala,* a kind of anchovy paste (see page 83) that, at least in traditional versions, is spread over the dough before baking.

So the decision to make *pissaladière* versus pizza or focaccia rests on your liking for onions, olives, and anchovies, the ingredients that give a *pissaladière* its own special identity.

I happen to be addicted to all of the above, and while I love pizza and focaccia, neither one satisfies these particular cravings like a slice or two of *pissaladière*, whose saltiness also makes it the perfect accompaniment to apéritifs or cocktails. (I serve it in little wedges or rectangles.) *Pissaladière* doesn't need to be hard to make, but since I'm always trying to improve things, often by reverting to laborious methods from earlier times, I make a version that does take a lot of time. Making *pissaladière* the hard way or the easy way depends on what you use for the dough. You can take the easy route and make a simple bread dough with yeast, flour, and water or a regular unsweetened pie dough (see Basic Pie and Tart Dough, page 155), or you can complicate your life but come up with something better than any *pissaladière* you'd encounter in Nice and make your dough with a natural sourdough starter instead of just packaged yeast. The topping of onions, olives, anchovies, and herbs stays the same, regardless of the dough. I use red onions instead of the traditional yellow onions (anyone from Nice would sneer) because I like their sweetness, a welcome counterpoint to the saltiness of the other ingredients.

SALTED ANCHOVIES

Because for years cooking-obsessed friends had been telling me that salted anchovies were far better than those that come packed in oil in little jars or cans, I went to my favorite fancy food shop several times to buy anchovies packed in salt. But the anchovies were always too strong and fishy. Finally I made the essential discovery that if you want anchovies packed in salt you must buy a whole unopened can (see Sources), desalt them, and repack them in extra-virgin olive oil.

If you're desalting anchovies for the first time, you'll probably want to buy the smallest amount you can, which is 600 grams, about 1¼ pounds. Cut the top off the pretty blue can and soak the whole can in a big bowl of cold water for about 10 minutes to loosen the salt. Rinse under cold running water to dissolve more salt and then turn the can over and shake it to get the anchovies to come out in one big clump. Soak the clump in a bowl of fresh water for about 10 minutes, then gently pull away the anchovies—don't force them or they'll tear—one by one. Soak the anchovies in another bowl of fresh water for about 20 minutes.

Snap the head off each anchovy by pushing it back, and separate the fillets from the backbone by running a finger along the backbone, gently pulling away the two fillets. Pat the fillets dry on a clean kitchen towel and pack them in small jars with tight-fitting lids. I use French canning jars with clamp-on lids and rubber seals. Pour in enough extra-virgin olive oil to cover, and use as needed. The anchovies will keep for at least 5 or 6 weeks in the refrigerator.

NICE-STYLE ONION, OLIVE, AND ANCHOVY TART

PISSALADIÈRE

MAKES 8 LIGHT FIRST-COURSE SERVINGS
OR 16 HORS D'OEUVRES (1 RECTANGULAR TART,
ABOUT 11 BY 17 INCHES [28 BY 43 CM])

FOR REGULAR BREAD DOUGH:

1 packet (about 2 teaspoons) active dry yeast

1¾ cups [400 ml] barely warm water

4 to 4½ cups [500 to 560 g] all-purpose flour

1 teaspoon salt

¼ cup [60 ml] extra-virgin olive oil, plus 1 tablespoon for the bowl

olive oil for the sheet pan

FOR THE TOPPING:

¼ cup [60 ml] extra-virgin olive oil

4 pounds [1.8 kg] red onions (or, to be traditional, yellow onions), sliced about ⅛ inch [3 mm] thick (traditionally, the onions would be sliced thicker)

2 teaspoons total of fresh herbs, such as whole thyme leaves, winter or summer savory leaves, or marjoram leaves, or chopped oregano leaves, or 1 teaspoon total of the same herbs dried, and/or ½ teaspoon fresh or dried rosemary leaves

20 salted anchovy fillets (see page 168) or anchovy fillets packed in olive oil in jars

salt

pepper

½ cup [65 g] black olives, preferably small Niçoise olives, pitted

TO MAKE THE DOUGH

COMBINE the yeast with ¼ cup of the barely warm water (hot water will kill the yeast). Let sit for 5 minutes. Toss 4 cups [500 g] of flour with the salt in a mixing bowl or the bowl of an electric mixer that has

a hook and paddle attachments. This will prevent a large amount of salt from touching the yeast and killing it. Stir in the yeast mixture, the remaining 1½ cups [375 ml] of water, and ¼ cup [60 ml] of extra-virgin olive oil and work the mixture slightly with a wooden spoon or your fingers until it comes together in a shaggy mass. (If you're using an electric mixer, start mixing with the paddle blade and as the dough thickens and the motor begins to strain, switch to the dough hook.) Let the mixture rest for 10 minutes. If you're working by hand, dump the dough out onto a work surface and knead it for 3 minutes. (In the mixer, work it for 3 minutes with the dough hook.) The dough should seem wetter and stickier than most bread dough. But if it's impossible to work with, work in another ¼ to ½ cup [30 to 60 g] of flour. Put 1 tablespoon of extra-virgin olive oil in a mixing bowl, put the dough in the bowl, turn the dough around to coat it all over with oil, and cover it with plastic wrap or a damp towel. Let the dough rise at room temperature until doubled, 1 to 3 hours depending on the temperature.

RUB a 12-by-18-inch [30.5 by 45.5 cm] sheet pan (what professionals call a half sheet pan) with olive oil. Push down on the dough in the bowl with your fist and turn it out onto the sheet pan. The dough will be too loose to roll. Press it into the sheet pan with the tips of your fingers until it completely covers the sheet pan. Cover the dough with plastic wrap and let it rise again until doubled, about 1 hour.

TO MAKE THE TOPPING

WHILE the dough is rising, heat the olive oil over medium heat in a wide, heavy-bottomed pot or pan large enough to hold the sliced onions. Put in the onions and stir them with a wooden spoon. Cook them gently, stirring every few minutes, until they release liquid. At this point, usually after about 10 minutes, you can turn the heat up to high to evaporate the liquid, but be careful not to let the onions burn. When all the liquid has evaporated and the onions are completely soft, after about 25 minutes more, remove from the heat. Stir in the herbs. Chop 8 of the anchovies into a paste, stir the paste into the onions, and season to taste with salt and pepper.

PREHEAT the oven to 425°F [220°C/gas mark 7]. If you have a pizza stone, slide it onto the lowest shelf in the oven.

SCATTER the onion mixture evenly over the dough, leaving about ½ inch [1.5 cm] of dough exposed along the edges. Arrange the anchovies on top of the onion mixture in a formal crisscross pattern or strew them nonchalantly. Arrange or sprinkle the olives on top and slide the sheet pan onto the pizza stone or directly onto the bottom shelf of the oven. Bake until the crust is golden brown around the edges, 25 to 30 minutes.

USING A SOURDOUGH CRUST MADE WITH A NATURAL STARTER

For years I struggled to make good bread, but now there are so many artisanal bakeries around that it's gotten hard to bake better bread than you can buy. But if you want a *pissaladière* with a *levain*—sourdough—crust that is savory and crispy, you have to make your own dough, unless, that is, you know a friendly baker who will sell you some dough.

The simplest bread dough, like the regular bread dough above, is made by combining packaged yeast, which is very aggressive and quick-acting, with wet flour. So-called natural starters are made by encouraging airborne yeasts or the yeasts in organic flour to take hold in various mixtures, such as potato cooking liquid, or by inoculating the dough with the natural yeasts that cling to the outside of certain ripe fruits, such as grapes or figs. Because these natural yeasts are less aggressive and more genetically diverse than packaged yeasts, they give the dough a more complex flavor, partly because they allow for the competition of naturally occurring benevolent bacteria. When the bacteria are given enough time to develop in the dough, they excrete lactic acid, which gives sourdough bread its distinctive tang, helps the bread develop a crunchy crust, and preserves the bread so it's slower to turn stale.

There are two problems with natural starters. They take longer and they're unpredictable. And while every natural starter I've ever made resulted in delicious bread, no loaf has ever turned out the same as another, which in fact is what makes the process so much fun. Sometimes, however, bread made with a natural starter refuses to rise enough. When this happens, I cheat, adding a small amount of commercial yeast to make the cooked dough lighter.

If you want to know more about artisanal baking and natural starters, the best information I've found is in *Chez Panisse Cooking,* by Paul Bertolli with Alice Waters. Here's a synopsis of Paul Bertolli's Sourdough Bread, adapted for making *pissaladière.* Once you have the starter, which takes almost a week to make, you can keep it alive by refrigerating it and adding flour and water to it every 4 days. When you're ready to make *pissaladière*, pizza, *fougasse* (see page 172), or just plain bread, take the starter out of the refrigerator and feed it for 2 days before you use it. It's important that the flour you use for the dough be organic and unbleached so it contains natural yeasts.

FOR THE SOURDOUGH STARTER:

- ½ medium-size russet potato, peeled and sliced
- 1 cup [125 g] organic unbleached all-purpose flour (available at health food stores), or more as needed to keep the starter active

PUT the potato slices in a pot with 2 cups of water and bring to a simmer with the lid ajar. Simmer until the potato is completely soft, about 15 minutes. Using a fork, mash the potato in the pot along with its cooking liquid. Let the mixture cool to room temperature. Transfer the mixture to a mixing bowl, stir in ¼ cup [30 g] of the flour, and add ¼ cup [60 ml] water. The mixture should have the consistency of pancake batter. If it's too stiff, add a small amount of water.

COVER the starter with plastic wrap and let it sit at room temperature—about 70°F [21°C]—for 24 hours. Add another ¼ cup [40 g] of flour and ¼ cup

[60 ml] of water, stir with a fork, cover the starter with plastic wrap, and let it sit for 24 hours more. By this time the batter will start to come alive and look like a science experiment gone terribly awry, but don't panic. Stir in another ¼ cup [40 g] of flour and ¼ cup [60 ml] of water to feed the natural yeasts, cover again, and wait for 24 more hours. Stir in the last ¼ cup of flour and another ¼ cup [60 ml] of water. At this point you can use the starter, but if you're not quite ready to make bread, you can keep the starter alive indefinitely by giving it its daily ration of ¼ cup [40 g] of flour and ¼ cup [60 ml] of water. Before long you'll have far more starter than you need. You can share it with friends, you can refrigerate it and feed it only every 4 days, or you can freeze it and then defrost it in the refrigerator and feed it at room temperature for a couple of days to bring it back to life. If the feeding gets completely out of hand you can discard some of the starter as you add fresh flour.

IN the recipe given here, a small amount of packaged yeast is added to help the dough to rise.

SOURDOUGH MADE WITH A HOMEMADE STARTER

- 1 cup [180 g] of the sourdough starter, ideally 1 hour after its last feeding (see above)

- 1 teaspoon active dry yeast combined with ¼ cup [60 ml] barely warm water and allowed to sit for 5 minutes

- 4 to 4½ cups [500 to 560 g] organic unbleached flour or all-purpose flour, or more as needed

- 1 teaspoon salt

- ¼ cup [60 ml] extra-virgin olive oil, plus 1 tablespoon for the bowl

  olive oil for the sheet pan

IN a mixing bowl or electric mixer bowl, combine the starter with the yeast mixture and 4 cups [500 g] of flour that has been tossed with the salt. Stir in ¾ cup [175 ml] of water and ¼ cup [60 ml] of olive oil, and work the mixture slightly with a wooden spoon or your fingers until the dough comes together in a shaggy mass. (If you're using the electric mixer, use the paddle attachment.) Let the mixture rest for 10 minutes, pour it out onto a work surface, and knead it by hand for 3 minutes. (Or replace the paddle attachment with the dough hook and work the dough for about 5 minutes.) The dough should seem wetter and stickier than most bread dough. But if it's impossible to work with, work in another ¼ cup to ½ cup [40 to 60 g] of flour. Put 1 tablespoon of extra-virgin olive oil in a mixing bowl, put the dough in the bowl, turn the dough around to coat it all over with oil, and cover it with plastic wrap or a damp towel. Let the dough rise at room temperature until doubled, 1 to 3 hours depending on the temperature.

RUB a 12-by-18-inch [30.5 by 45.5 cm] sheet pan with olive oil. Push down on the dough in the bowl with your fist and turn it out onto the sheet pan. The dough will be too loose to roll. Press it into the sheet pan with the tips of your fingers until it completely covers the sheet pan. Cover the dough with plastic wrap and let it rise again until doubled, about 1 hour.

PROVENÇAL FLATBREAD

FOUGASSE PROVENÇAL

MAKES 2 FLAT SNOWSHOE-SHAPED CRUSTY LOAVES, EACH
ABOUT 12 INCHES LONG, 10 INCHES WIDE AT ONE END,
AND NARROWING TO A ROUNDED POINT AT THE OTHER

We've all encountered foccacia, a kind of flatbread flavored with herbs and olive oil, often put on the table in restaurants at the beginning of the meal. The fougass sold in Provence is similar, except that it has distinctive slits cut into its surface and has a characteristic paddle or snowshoe shape. Historians are forever reminding us of how various peoples influenced the cooking of France's Mediterranean region. The Ligurians were among the first inhabitants, and then there were the Romans, the Visigoths, and the Saracens, to say nothing of the fact that Nice was a part of Italy until the nineteenth century. The first time I saw fougasse, it reminded me of the flatbread I encountered twenty years ago in Afghanistan.

Fougasse, like foccacia, is infinitely adaptable to whim and last-minute inspiration. You can incorporate olives, nuts, pieces of bacon, anchovies, or various herbs, so that your fougasse is a little different every time you make it.

1 recipe bread dough made with yeast (page 169) or sourdough bread dough (page 171)

1 cup [135 g] black olives, pitted, chopped coarse if large, patted dry if wet

4 teaspoons total of fresh herbs, such as whole thyme leaves, winter or summer savory leaves, or marjoram leaves, or chopped oregano leaves, or 2 teaspoons of the same herbs dried, and/or 1 teaspoon fresh or dried rosemary leaves

olive oil for the sheet pan and for sprinkling over the loaves

coarse sea salt for sprinkling over the loaves

AFTER you've punched down the dough after its first rising as described on page 169 (or page 171 if you're using a natural starter), knead in the olives and herbs until they're evenly distributed throughout the dough. Cut the dough into 2 equal-size pieces and press each batch down, with the tips of your fingers, into tapering oval shapes about ½ inch [1.5 cm] thick, 6 inches [15 cm] at the widest point, and 10 inches [25.5 cm] long, on olive-oiled sheet pans.

MAKE a series of 2-inch-long [5 cm] slits all the way through the dough, parallel with the sides of the ovals, 6 to 8 slits per oval. With your fingers, separate the sides of each slit so you can see the sheet pan underneath. This is to keep the slits from closing during baking. Cover the dough with plastic wrap or a damp towel and let it rise at room temperature until doubled in height, 1 to 2 hours.

PREHEAT the oven to 425°F [220°C/gas mark 7]. If you have a pizza stone, place it on the lowest rack in the oven.

SPRINKLE the *fougasses* with sea salt and dribble a few tablespoons of olive oil over them. Slide the sheet pans into the oven—if you have a pizza stone, place one of the pans on the stone and the other pan on the rack above it. Bake until golden brown, about 25 minutes. If the two *fougasses* aren't browning evenly, switch the pans after 15 minutes. If possible, serve while still warm.

Variations: Most parts of France have their own regional breads, and often these differ from those of their neighbors only by being worked into a different shape or by the addition of flavorings such as anise seeds, nuts, cheese, or dried fruit. In Normandy they make a bread—*la gâche*—similar to a Provençal *fougasse* except that olives or anchovies never get near it and it is made with eggs, butter, milk, and occasionally raisins. In the Auvergne, a *brioche de Gannat* is made much like regular brioche (a basic bread dough with butter and eggs), but with grated Cantal cheese worked into the dough.

Cornmeal, Buckwheat Flour, Chestnut Flour, and Chickpea Flour

BECAUSE WHEAT AND BREAD ARE NOW UNIversally available throughout France, it's hard to imagine that they were once luxuries and that until the middle of the twentieth century there were regions in France whose inhabitants had never tasted wheat bread. In poorer regions, cooks did their best to make edible foods out of starchy products like buckwheat, chestnuts, chickpeas, and later, after the discovery of the New World, corn and potatoes. But wheat has one characteristic that distinguishes it from these other cereals and starches. It contains gluten, a collection of proteins that give bread dough the elasticity that in turn traps the carbon dioxide produced by yeasts so the dough rises. In short, wheat breads rise while "breads" made from other starches do not. In areas where wheat was nonexistent or in short supply, these other starches were ground into flours and used to make polenta-like porridges, to be eaten like gruel or allowed to solidify and then grilled or sautéed, much as polenta is today. (Italian polenta was made with chestnuts before corn was brought back from America.) These porridges were also thinned with liquid and cooked into pancakes, like the Niçoise chickpea pancakes called *socca* and the crêpe-like *galettes* from Brittany, made with buckwheat flour. In some regions, these alternative flours were sweetened and leavened with beaten eggs—whole eggs to make cakes, separated eggs to make "soufflés." Breads were and still are made by combining these other flours with wheat flour, no doubt originally to get by with using less wheat flour, but now simply because many of these breads have a marvelous flavor and texture.

CORNMEAL (Farine de Maïs): Until *la nouvelle cuisine* lent corn an exotic gastronomic cachet, any French person would have recoiled in horror at the mention of corn on the cob—a treat normally saved for the pigs. But despite this rare lapse in culinary judgment, the French have been eating corn in various forms for years as a way of staving off hunger when wheat was too expensive or hard to find, especially during war years. Many of these corn dishes are so old that their origins have been forgotten, but they must have come into being since the discovery of the New World, since corn, according to almost all authorities, didn't exist in Europe before that time.

One of my favorite books about French regional cooking, *La Bonne Cuisine du Périgord*, written by La Mazille in 1929, describes a number of dishes made with combinations of cornmeal and wheat flour and sometimes with cornmeal alone. Included are various crêpes, soufflés, breads (one called *fougeasse*), fritters (called *miques* in the Périgord, *milhas* in Agen), savory porridges reminiscent of polenta (*bouillie de maïs*, called *rimotes* or *las pous* in the Périgord, *gaude* in the Franche-Comté, *broye* or *millas* in the Pyrenees), and cakes, similar to American corn bread, made with combinations of cornmeal and wheat flour and sometimes with cornmeal alone. The recipes were written before country people had stoves and ovens, so the directions describe cooking in an open hearth and call for pieces of equipment such as a *trépied* (a three-legged stand for holding the pan) and pans with 6-foot-long [1.83 m] handles so the cook didn't have to stand too near the heat. Here is a recipe for *périgourdin* corn crêpes called *tourteaux*. They're delicious served still warm with powdered sugar or jam—for breakfast, as a snack, or for dessert. They're at their best served with savory meat stews and braised dishes, the same way as polenta.

PÉRIGORD·STYLE CORN PANCAKES

TOURTEAUX

MAKES ABOUT 12 SMALL (4-INCH [10 CM]) PANCAKES

1 cup [140 g] yellow cornmeal

1 cup [125 g] white all-purpose flour

1 teaspoon salt

4 tablespoons melted butter or walnut oil, plus butter for the pan

1 tablespoon kirsch (optional)

2 tablespoons anise seeds, chopped coarse with a chef's knife

6 tablespoons milk

5 large eggs, beaten

powdered sugar or an assortment of fruit preserves (optional)

COMBINE the cornmeal and flour with the salt in a mixing bowl and dribble 4 tablespoons butter or walnut oil and the kirsch over the mixture. Add the anise seeds, milk, and the eggs and work the mixture with a large wooden spoon until it has the consistency of pancake batter.

HEAT 1 or 2 teaspoons of butter in a nonstick sauté pan or well-seasoned iron skillet. When the butter froths and the froth starts to subside, ladle between ⅓ and ⅔ cup [75 and 150 ml] of batter into the pan so that the batter has the thickness of a pancake. Cook over medium heat until golden brown on the bottom, 3 to 4 minutes. Turn the pancake over with a spatula or, if you're feeling confident, flip it. Cook for 2 minutes more. Slide onto a hot plate. Repeat until you've used all the batter. Serve the *tourteaux* in wedges with powdered sugar or fruit preserves, or without them as a savory accompaniment to stews and pot roasts.

CHICKPEA FLOUR (Farine de Pois Chiches): My first encounter with chickpeas was as a struggling college student in California, where we called chickpeas gar-

banzo beans. A wealthy friend of my roommate let us stay in his home in the Berkeley hills while he was on a prolonged vacation in Europe. As soon as we settled in, we searched the expansive kitchen for food, but the cupboards were bare except for a tall jar of chickpeas, set on the kitchen counter for decoration. Desperately, I poured them in a pot and simmered them in water. Hours later they finally softened and resulted in the most boring dinner of my life. Fortunately for them, Provençal cooks had the cleverness to grind chickpeas into flour and cook them into pancakes called *socca* and a polenta-like dish called *panisses*. *Socca* are an important Niçoise street food, and competition between *pissaladière* and *socca* vendors is fierce. *Panisses* are made with a stiffer chickpea flour batter, similar to *socca* batter, but are sautéed or deep-fried rather than baked and are served as a savory accompaniment to *boeuf en daube* or other stews. *Panisses* are also served as a sweet snack, dredged in sugar or accompanied by fruit preserves.

NIÇOISE CHICKPEA "POLENTA"

PANISSES

MAKES ENOUGH FOR SNACKS FOR 8 OR A STARCHY ACCOMPANIMENT TO 8 SERVINGS OF STEW

1 cup [120 g] chickpea flour (see Sources)

1½ cups [375 ml] water

4 tablespoons extra-virgin olive oil

½ teaspoon salt

pepper

1 tablespoon extra-virgin olive oil or butter for sautéing

STIR the chickpea flour, water, 4 tablespoons of the olive oil, and the salt and pepper together until smooth. Strain to get rid of lumps.

COOK the mixture in a saucepan on the stove about 4 to 5 minutes, or until a film develops on the bottom and the mixture thickens. Coat an 8-by-8-inch [20.5 cm by 20.5 cm] baking dish that has sides at least 1 inch [2.5 cm] high with 1 tablespoon of the olive oil. Pour the *panisse* mixture into the baking dish and cover it with a sheet of wax paper. Press down on the paper, pushing the batter toward the sides of the dish to form an even layer. Refrigerate for 1 hour. Turn the dish over, unmold the now firm mixture, and slice it into rectangles about ½ inch [1.5 cm] thick, 1 inch wide, and 2 inches [5 cm] long. Sauté the slices in the remaining butter or olive oil and serve them as an accompaniment to meat stews, or sprinkle them with sugar and serve them with fruit preserves.

NIÇOISE CHICKPEA
PANCAKES
SOCCA

MAKES TWO 12-INCH SOCCA, 4 TO 6 SERVINGS
AS AN ACCOMPANIMENT TO A MAIN COURSE

The first time I tasted socca, as a mid-morning snack, I wasn't terribly impressed, my palate jaded as it is by buttery goodies like croissants, Danish pastry, and, well, doughnuts. It wasn't until I tasted socca in Nice and read Robert Carrier's book Feasts of Provence, in which he suggests serving socca as a starchy accompaniment to seafood stews, that I realized they were worth the effort. I serve these chickpea pancakes in much the same way as polenta, with meat, seafood, and chicken stews.

Purists insist that authentic socca can be baked only in a hot wood-fired oven. No doubt they're better that way, since the gentle flavor of wood smoke improves most savory foods. But most of us are going to have to bake them in our home gas or electric ovens. In Nice, socca are made on and served from giant round metal plates that look a bit like paella pans without handles. But you're better off making socca in regular crêpe pans or ovenproof nonstick sauté pans. To simulate the effect of an intensely hot oven, the socca should be partially baked, with the heat coming from underneath, and partially broiled, with the heat coming from above.

    4   cups [1 l] cold water
    2½ cups [300 g] chickpea flour (see Sources)
    ½   cup [250 ml] extra-virgin olive oil
    ½   teaspoon salt
        olive oil for brushing the pan
        freshly ground pepper (if serving with meats) or powdered sugar (if serving as a sweet snack)

GENTLY whisk the water into the chickpea flour; start by adding just enough water to allow you to work the batter until it is smooth and then add the rest of the water. Let the batter rest at room temperature for 4 hours. Stir in the extra-virgin olive oil and salt.

PREHEAT the oven to 500°F [260°C/gas mark 10]. Brush a 12-inch [30.5 cm] well-seasoned or nonstick skillet—one that has a metal handle—with olive oil and place it over medium-to-high heat. When the pan is hot, ladle in half the batter. Rotate the pan, as though making a crêpe, until it is evenly coated with batter and slide it onto a middle rack in the oven. Bake for 5 minutes and then switch the oven to broil. If your broiler is beneath the oven, place the pan as far below the heat source as possible. If your broiler is on the top of the oven, place the pan about 8 inches [20.5 cm] below it. Broil the *socca* until it is lightly browned on top, about 3 to 5 minutes. Repeat with the remaining batter. Grind fresh pepper over the *socca* and serve them in wedges with stews or roasts, or sprinkle sugar over them and serve them as a sweet snack.

BUCKWHEAT FLOUR (Farine de Sarrasin): Why buckwheat flour is called *farine de sarrasin*—Saracen's flour—I'm not sure. According to Alan Davidson, in his magnificent tome *The Oxford Companion to Food*, buckwheat, not actually a wheat but a plant related to sorrel and rhubarb, is of East Asian origin and over the centuries has crept westward through Russia and Germany, and eventually on to France and Spain. Curiously, the only region in France where it is still used with any regularity is in Brittany, the farthest from Eastern Asia. The Breton people are of Celtic origin. The Celts did at one time wander as far as Asia Minor, the stomping grounds of the Saracens. So even though the Saracens didn't invade Brittany as they did Provence or Sicily, one wonders. Perhaps buckwheat flour stayed on in Brittany because it could be grown in Brittany's stormy climate and difficult soil where other grains wouldn't.

In any case, Breton cooks make buckwheat crêpes, stuff them with savory fillings, and call them *galettes,* reserving the word *crêpe* for dessert crêpes made with white flour. The buckwheat gives the *galettes* a slightly dissonant complexity that helps them match the stronger flavors of ham, eggs, sausages, or even seafood, and a good tumblerful of hard cider. The buckwheat *galettes* can be made a day or two ahead and then filled and cooked at the last minute.

BUCKWHEAT PANCAKES FILLED WITH BRETON CHEESE AND HAM

GALETTES BRETONNES AU FROMAGE ET AU JAMBON

MAKES 6 LIGHT MAIN-COURSE SERVINGS

1 cup [120 g] buckwheat flour (see Sources)

2 large eggs

½ teaspoon salt

¾ to 1 cup water [180 ml to 240 ml], or more as needed

1 tablespoon softened butter, plus 1 to 2 tablespoons cold butter

6 thin slices cooked ham, cut into strips about ¼ inch [.5 cm] wide and 2 inches [5 cm] long

1½ cups [225 g] coarse-grated Gruyère or other full-flavored cheese

PUT the buckwheat flour in a bowl with the eggs, the salt, and ½ cup [125 ml] of the water and work the mixture with a whisk until smooth. Stir in another ¼ cup to ½ cup [60 ml to 125 ml] of water or more as needed until the batter has a consistency between crêpe batter (which is slightly thicker than heavy cream) and pancake batter.

HEAT a 10-inch or 12-inch [25.5 to 30.5 cm] well-seasoned or nonstick sauté pan or skillet over medium to high heat. Brush the pan lightly with the softened butter and ladle in just enough of the buckwheat batter to cover the surface of the pan in a thin layer, about ⅛ inch [3 mm] thick. Lift the pan and rotate it as you're adding the batter so the batter completely and evenly covers the bottom of the pan. Cook over medium heat until the *galette* is golden brown on the bottom, about 3 minutes. Turn the *galette* over with a long spatula and cook it for about 2 minutes on the second side. When you've used all the batter, you should have a dozen buckwheat crêpes with a few left over. (I smear the extras with butter and eat them immediately.)

PLACE a *galette* on a large work surface with the prettiest side down and sprinkle the ham and cheese over the half that is closest to you. Fold the top of the *galette* over the filling, and then fold the resulting half circle in half, so that you end up with a triangular wedge. Repeat with the remaining crêpes.

HEAT 1 tablespoon of butter in a skillet large enough to hold all the crêpes in a single layer. (Or use two skillets, or make the *galettes* in two batches, keeping the first batch hot in a 200°F [93°C] oven while the second cooks.) Cook the *galettes* over low to medium heat for about 4 minutes on each side, long enough to melt the cheese on the inside. Serve immediately on hot plates.

COLD LEEK AND POTATO SOUP

VICHYSSOISE

HOW TO	HOW TO USE	A BIT
MAKE A VERSATILE SOUP BASE YOU CAN USE FOR ALMOST ANY VEGETABLE SOUP	EGG YOLKS TO FINISH SOUPS	ABOUT SORREL

THEY SAY THAT VICHYSSOISE WAS INVENTED IN THE UNITED STATES BY a French chef homesick for his birthplace, Vichy. This may very well be true, but leek and potato soups in various forms have been popular in France for close to two centuries. The fact that vichyssoise isn't listed in my edition of *Larousse Gastronomique* makes me suspect that the name, at least, came from somewhere other than France.

Vichyssoise is virtually identical to *potage Parmentier*, which has been around since the first half of the nineteenth century (the only difference is that vichyssoise is served cold) and is closely related to *soupe à la bonne femme*, a leek and potato soup in which the ingredients aren't puréed. There's nothing Vichy-esque about vichyssoise, but as far as I can tell there isn't much Vichy-esque about anything except Vichy water, a very minerally mineral water renowned for its ability to cure hangovers, and *carottes vichy*, which are carrots simmered in Vichy water. Perhaps our chef just gave an old soup a new name.

ESCOFFIER'S SYSTEM OF CLASSIC VEGETABLE SOUPS

In Escoffier's time there was little room for improvisation. Foods were prepared in one way and in one way only. All of France's great classic dishes were rigorously categorized. In categorizing soups, Escoffier first calls some *potages* and others *soupes*. Before and into the eighteenth century, *potages* contained large amounts of meat and were almost whole meals, much like a pot-au-feu (see page 456) or *potée* (see page 464). During the eighteenth and nineteenth centuries, *potages* were refined and simplified and were served, as they are today, at the beginning of a meal. *Potages* are often puréed and served with specific garnitures, such as tiny croutons or carefully cubed vegetables. Vegetable *potages* are categorized in terms of how the *potage* is thickened, what liquid it is based on, and what kind of fat is used to finish it. A vegetable *potage* is said to be a *purée* when it has been thickened with a starchy vegetable such as beans or potatoes or occasionally rice or bread crumbs. Vichyssoise is the perfect example of a *purée* soup because the puréed potatoes thicken it—no other thickener is needed. A *potage* that's thickened with roux, moistened with milk, and finished with cream is called a *crème*. One that's also thickened with roux, moistened with broth, and finished with butter, some cream, and sometimes egg yolks is called a *velouté*.

A *soupe* is of course a soup, but one that is more rough-hewn and hearty than a *potage*—more like what a *potage* was 200 years ago—and often a regional specialty. *Soupes* are generally served with bread, usually a bit stale. The bread is either placed in the bowl with the soup ladled over it or actually cooked in the soup; the latter soups, often stiff since they contain so much bread, are called *panades*. A good example of a traditional *soupe* is the *soupe à l'oignon* on page 189 or the *garbure* on page 465.

COLD LEEK AND POTATO SOUP

VICHYSSOISE

MAKES 6 SERVINGS

4   medium-size leeks

1   pound 2 ounces [500 g] medium-starchy potatoes
    such as Yukon Gold or Yellow Finn, or russet potatoes

4½ cups [1.1 l] water, milk, or chicken broth

½ to 1 cup [125 ml to 250 ml] heavy cream

    salt

    pepper

2   teaspoons finely chopped chives

CUT off all but a couple of inches [about 5 cm] of greens from the leeks. Cut the hairy root off each leek and whittle away the outermost green layers on the green end of the leek, exposing the white in the center. Cut the leeks in half lengthwise and rinse them under running water, flipping through the membranes as you go, rinsing out particles of dirt or sand. Slice thin.

PEEL the potatoes and cut them into thin slices. If you're not using them right away, put them in a bowl of water to keep them from turning dark.

COMBINE the leeks and potatoes with the liquid of your choice in a heavy-bottomed pot and simmer gently, covered, until you can easily crush the potatoes against the inside of the pot with the back of a fork and the leeks, when you taste a piece, have no hint of chewiness, about 25 minutes.

PURÉE the soup by working it through a food mill or through a large strainer with the back of a ladle. You can purée the soup before you strain it, in a blender (make sure you allow it to cool before doing so), but don't purée it for more than a few seconds or you'll overwork the potatoes and the soup will take on a slightly sticky consistency. Stir in the cream—if you're worried about fat, the smaller amount will do—and bring the soup back to a simmer.

CHILL the soup by putting the pot in a bowl of ice water. Stir the soup every few minutes to help it chill faster and to keep a skin from forming on its surface. If you're not in a rush, let it cool for about 1 hour at room temperature, cover it with plastic wrap, and refrigerate it for at least 6 hours. Season to taste with salt and pepper before serving. Put a pinch of chopped chives in the center of each serving.

OTHER VEGETABLE SOUPS THAT USE LEEK AND POTATO SOUP AS A BASE

First, keep in mind that a leek and potato soup doesn't have to be puréed. *Soupe à la bonne femme,* mentioned earlier, is served with the sliced leeks and the potatoes, diced and left chunky, in the soup. A chunk of butter is added to each bowl as the soup is served hot. The cream is left out. Some recipes call for gently cooking—sweating—the leeks in butter before any liquid is added, the idea being that this brings out their flavor; but I can't taste any difference, so I don't bother.

Many of France's soups seem to have been invented to stave off hunger as pleasantly as possible, and many of the techniques and ingredients are meant to make the soups nutritious. But nutrition in times past didn't mean what it does today. Nowadays something "nutritious" is typically low in fat, is often meatless, and may contain plenty of grains and raw vegetables. But throughout most of history, when people tried to take in as much energy-providing food as possible to stay alive, "nutritious" meant high-calorie. So if you could afford to add some egg yolks, a little cream, or butter to your food, so much the better. Home recipes for soup often contain some form of starch, such as beans, noodles, or bread. Bread crumbs may be used as a thickener; a stale piece of bread may be put in the bowl and the soup poured over it; or little pieces of toasted bread—croutons—may be sprinkled over each serving. Flour may be cooked into a roux with onions, leeks, or other vegetables before liquid is added. Fats are added at various stages. Butter or lard is sometimes used to sweat vegetables or meats, and butter is often dolloped on each serving of soup in the bowl. Vegetables may be simmered in milk; cream, sometimes combined with egg yolks, is often added at the end.

One way to improvise a vegetable soup is to make a leek and potato soup by simmering the chopped potatoes and the sliced leeks in milk, water, or broth—or a combination—until both the leeks and the potatoes are done. You can leave the soup as it is or purée it, and then pour in a little cream (or a lot) or stir in a few pats of butter, season, and you're done. If I'm making a base for a soup that features a single vegetable—say asparagus, carrots, or spinach—I add the vegetable to the leek and potato soup base just in time for the vegetable to cook. Diced or sliced carrots, for example, get simmered along with everything else, sliced asparagus stalks get added about 15 minutes before I predict the potatoes and leeks will be done, and spinach gets tossed in when the potatoes and leeks are completely done. I then purée or not—though I always purée asparagus soup. You can also make a vichyssoise as described above and then add shredded or diced vegetables so the soup consists of a purée base (the vichyssoise) but contains other solid vegetables that remain colorful and distinct.

Here are some examples. Each makes 8 servings or a little more because of the additional vegetable. In each of these recipes, I describe puréeing the soup, but you can also leave the vegetables whole—you may just want to be a little more attentive to how you cut them, so they look nice. When I purée the soup, I may serve it hot or cold. If I don't purée it, I serve it only hot.

ASPARAGUS: Start cooking the vichyssoise described on page 179. Take 1 large bunch (about 1½ pounds [675 g]) of asparagus and cut off and discard 2 inches [5 cm] from the base. Cut off and reserve the tips. Cut the stalks into 1-inch [2.5-cm] segments and toss them into the soup about 5 minutes after you've brought the leeks and potatoes to a boil. Boil the asparagus tips separately for 3 minutes in salted water. Drain in a colander, rinse with cold water, and reserve.

When the leeks, potatoes, and asparagus stalks are completely soft, in about 20 minutes, purée the soup in a blender and work it through a food mill or a medium-mesh strainer with the back of a ladle.

Add the heavy cream and bring the soup back to a simmer. Thin the soup if necessary with additional broth, milk, or water. Season with salt and pepper. Decorate the individual servings with the reserved asparagus tips.

BEETS: Take 2 pounds [1 kg] of beets, rub them with oil or wrap them in aluminum foil to keep them from drying out, and roast them in a 400°F [230°C/gas mark 8] oven for about 1½ hours, until a skewer slides easily in and out. (Or you can boil them for the same amount of time.) Make the vichyssoise described on page 179. Peel and slice the beets and add them to the soup when the potatoes have softened. Simmer for 2 minutes and then purée the soup in a blender and strain it through a food mill or strainer. Stir in the cream, bring the soup back to a simmer, and thin it with extra liquid if it seems too thick. Season to taste with salt and pepper. If you like, top each bowl with a dollop of sour cream, crème fraîche (see page 39), or lightly beaten heavy cream, or pass one of these toppings at the table. The chives called for in the vichyssoise recipe can be replaced with coarsely chopped dill for this version.

BROCCOLI: Start cooking the vichyssoise described on page 179. Remove the stems from 2 bunches of broccoli and set aside 8 small florets for decorating the soup. Cook the 8 florets for 4 minutes in boiling salted water, drain, rinse with cold water, and reserve. Chop and simmer the stems in the soup. When the potatoes start to soften, stir in the uncooked florets and simmer until the broccoli and potatoes have softened completely, about 7 minutes. Purée in a blender and work the soup through a food mill, or work it through a strainer with the back of a ladle. Thin the soup if necessary with additional liquid. Finish the soup with the cream, bring the soup back to a simmer, and season with salt and pepper. Decorate each bowl of soup with a reserved floret.

KEEPING GREEN SOUPS GREEN

If not served immediately, soups made with green vegetables turn a sad-looking gray. The obvious solution is of course to serve the soup right away. A second solution, best for quick-cooking vegetables like spinach, peas, and sorrel, is to cook the vichyssoise base and just before serving add the vegetable and finish the soup. You can also prepare the soup completely in advance, immediately put the pot in large bowl of ice water, and chill the soup as quickly as you can. Reheat the soup just before serving.

CARROT: Make the vichyssoise described on page 179 but cook 5 medium-size carrots, peeled and sliced, along with the potato. Simmer the soup until you can easily crush both the potatoes and the carrots against the inside of the pot. When the potatoes are soft, purée in a blender and work the soup through a food mill, or work it through a strainer with the back of a ladle. Finish the soup with the cream, bring it back to a simmer, and thin if necessary with additional liquid. Season to taste with salt and pepper.

CELERY: Make the vichyssoise described on page 179. When it's been simmering for about 5 minutes, add 8 celery ribs sliced fine. Purée the soup in a blender and work it through a food mill with the finest attachment, or work it through a strainer with the back of a ladle. Stir in the heavy cream, bring the soup back to a simmer, thin it if necessary with more broth or milk, and season to taste with salt and pepper.

FENNEL: Take 2 medium-size fennel bulbs, coarsely chop 1 tablespoon of the green leafy fronds and reserve them, remove and discard the stalks, and chop the bulbs coarse. Make the vichyssoise described on page 179 and simmer the chopped fennel bulbs along with the leeks and potatoes. Simmer until the vegetables are all completely cooked. Purée in a blender and strain through a medium-

mesh strainer or food mill. If the soup is too thick, thin it with additional liquid. Finish the soup with the cream, bring the soup back to a simmer, and season with salt and pepper. Decorate each bowl with a pinch of the chopped fronds.

MUSHROOM: Make the vichyssoise described on page 179 and simmer 1¼ pounds [565 g] (or two 10-ounce packages) of mushrooms, chopped coarsely, along with the leeks and potatoes until the potatoes are easily crushed against the inside of the pot. Purée the soup in a blender. If you want a fine consistency, strain it through a food mill or a strainer with the back of a ladle. Stir the cream into the soup and bring the soup back to a simmer. Thin if necessary with additional liquid and season to taste with salt and pepper.

FRESH OR FROZEN PEA: Make the vichyssoise described on page 179. When the potatoes have softened completely, stir in 3 cups [435 g] shucked peas (you'll need from 2 to 3 pounds [900 g to 1.3 kg] in the pod) or two 10-ounce [283 g] packages frozen peas (you don't even have to thaw them) and turn the heat to high. If you're using fresh baby peas or frozen peas, remove from the heat as soon as the soup returns to a boil. If you're using large, tough fresh-shucked peas, allow them to simmer in the liquid for 10 minutes. Purée in a blender. If you want the soup to be perfectly smooth, work it through a food mill, or work it through a strainer with the back of a ladle. Stir in the heavy cream and thin if necessary with additional milk, broth, or water. Season to taste with salt and pepper. If you're not serving the soup right away, chill it immediately so it doesn't change color.

SORREL: Make the vichyssoise described on page 179. When the potatoes are completely cooked, stir 1 pound [450 g] of sorrel, stems removed, into the soup and simmer for 5 minutes. Purée in a blender and strain through a food mill or medium-mesh strainer. If you want the soup to be very smooth, strain it again through a fine-mesh strainer. Finish the soup with the cream, and season to taste with salt and pepper. Thin if necessary with extra broth or milk. (See also the recipe for *potage germiny* on page 185.)

SPINACH: Make the vichyssoise described on page 179. When the potatoes have softened, stir in the leaves from two 10-ounce [283 g] bunches of spinach and simmer for about 1 minute, until the leaves "melt" in the soup. Purée in a blender and strain through a food mill or medium-mesh strainer. Add the cream and bring to a simmer. Season to taste with salt and pepper.

WATERCRESS: Prepare the vichyssoise described on page 179. Take 3 bunches of watercress and cut off and discard the bottom one-third. Boil the watercress for 1 minute in salted water, drain, and rinse with cold water to get rid of any bitterness. When the potatoes are cooked, add the watercress. Purée the soup in a blender and strain through a food mill or medium-mesh strainer. Add the cream, bring the soup back to a simmer, and thin if necessary with additional milk or broth. Season to taste with salt and pepper.

HOW TO KEEP CREAM SOUPS FROM SOURING

When you add heavy cream to the puréed base for a cream soup, be sure to bring the soup back to a simmer after adding the cream. Otherwise the cream may not be brought to a high enough temperature to kill bacteria. If you're planning to serve the soup hot but not to serve it right away, you can keep it at about 140°F [60°C], but this will cause a soup containing green vegetables to turn gray and may affect the soup's flavor. It's better to chill the soup and then reheat it just before serving. If you're making a small batch of cream soup, as with the recipes given here, take it off the heat and let it cool for about 1 hour, stirring it every 10 minutes to prevent a crust from forming. Cover it with plastic wrap and put it in the refrigerator, where it will keep for at least 3 or 4 days. If you're making soup for a crowd, follow the directions on page 218 for storing stocks and broths.

Cream Soups
without Potato

VICHYSSOISE WORKS AS A PERFECT BACKDROP for other vegetable purées. The potato is a flavorful natural thickener that makes a good replacement for the flour-and-butter roux so often called for in classic recipes. However, some vegetables, such as chestnuts, corn, parsnips, and squash, are starchy enough that the potato isn't needed and might even make the soup too thick. Other vegetables, such as artichokes, salsify, fava beans, and cardoons, have such subtle flavor that you wouldn't be able to taste them through the potatoes. Classic recipes thicken artichoke soups with a purée of bread cubes that have first been cooked in butter. Other soups, such as those based on tomato or tomatillo, just don't need starch and have enough body of their own.

TOMATO SOUP

MAKES 6 SERVINGS

Needless to say I'm an admirer of the great classics of French cooking, and I have nothing against going to great lengths if there's a payoff in flavor. But I get annoyed when I see a recipe that's needlessly complicated and needlessly rich, and that has too many ingredients. Nowhere is this more true than with the classic French recipes for tomato soup. One tomato soup classic, purée portugaise, has you sweat diced onions, carrots, and unsmoked bacon with thyme and a bay leaf. The tomatoes are added along with garlic, a rather large amount of rice, and some sugar. After long simmering, the soup is puréed and strained, and it's finished with a half pound [225 g] of tomato butter, made by working the butter with a stiff tomato purée.

Except for some salt and pepper, my favorite tomato soup contains one ingredient: tomatoes. I make it only from August to the beginning of October, when tomatoes are at their best and I can experiment with heirloom varieties grown by local farmers. Every variety of tomato has its own nuances of flavor. I look for yellow tomatoes (which have a soft texture and a lot of liquid) that look like they're ready to burst out of their skin. I usually serve this soup with a simple sauce of chopped fresh tarragon or basil stirred into lightly beaten heavy cream.

FOR THE SOUP:

12 very ripe medium-size tomatoes, preferably yellow (about 4 pounds/2.3 kg)

    salt

    pepper

FOR THE OPTIONAL FINISHING SAUCE:

3 tablespoons fresh tarragon leaves, or 1 handful fresh basil leaves

1 teaspoon olive oil

1 cup [250 ml] heavy cream

    salt

    pepper

TO PREPARE AND SERVE THE SOUP

PEEL the tomatoes by plunging them, 2 or 3 at a time, into a pot of boiling water for about 15 seconds and then immediately fishing them out and rinsing them with cold water. Cut out the little piece of stem at one end and pull away the peels with your fingers.

SET a fine-mesh strainer over a bowl. Slice the tomatoes in half, cutting crosswise through the equator, and squeeze the seeds and juice out from each half, over the strainer. Work the juice through the strainer with your fingers, leaving the seeds behind. Discard the seeds and reserve the juice.

CHOP the tomatoes fine, preferably by hand. (You can purée the tomatoes in a blender, but they turn pale and their flavor seems to lose some of its brightness.) Combine the chopped tomatoes with the reserved juice. Season to taste with salt and pepper. Serve chilled. If you're serving the sauce, pass it at the table or swirl a little on the top of each serving.

RUB the tarragon or basil leaves with the olive oil, to keep them from turning dark, and chop fine. Chill the heavy cream in a mixing bowl for 5 minutes in the freezer and beat, by hand or in an electric mixer, until the cream barely begins to thicken. Stir in the chopped herbs and season to taste with salt and pepper.

Variations: If the weather turns chilly, add 1 cup [250 ml] of cream to this soup and serve the soup hot, and you'll have the best cream of tomato soup imaginable. I sometimes swirl aïoli (see page 491), thinned with a little water, or pesto sauce (or the *pistou* sauce described on page 224) onto each serving of soup, or I pass the sauce at the table. I also like to garnish the soup with croutons that have been gently browned in olive oil or butter. Thin strips of bacon, stirred into the hot soup, are also a delicious touch.

USING BREAD TO THICKEN SOUPS

Thickening soups, sauces, and stews with bread is a technique that was used in medieval cooking before the discovery of roux and before potatoes were brought back from the New World. Older recipes for bisque call for thickening with bread crumbs (instead of the more modern rice, see Chapter 17), and Mediterranean paste-like sauces (Catalan *romesco* and *picada,* Provençal *rouille,* and some versions of pesto) are still thickened with bread (and/or ground nuts). Taillevent, in *Le Viandier,* written in the late fourteenth century, often calls for *pain hallé*—toasted bread—as a thickener for *potaiges lians,* which were more generous and stewlike than most modern soups. I like to use bread as a thickener in more subtly flavored soups, such as the artichoke soup below, because it isn't as full-flavored as potato or as starchy as flour. As a further precaution against starchiness, I (like a lot of people before me) cut the bread into quarter-slices or cubes and cook it gently in butter or olive oil before puréeing it with liquids, usually in a blender, to use as a thickener.

ARTICHOKE SOUP

PURÉE GEORGETTE

MAKES 6 FIRST-COURSE SERVINGS

One of the great things about this soup is that it captures all the flavor of artichokes but it's effortless to eat. And unlike a lot of French artichoke dishes that involve turning artichokes, thereby wasting the leaves, for this recipe you use almost the whole artichoke and strain out anything that's tough or fibrous. Most recipes have you rubbing the raw artichokes with lemon to prevent them from turning dark, but if you really want artichokes that are pale green with no gray patches, you need to marinate the cooked artichokes overnight with a little lemon juice to bleach them.

- 6 medium-size or 4 large artichokes (about 25 pounds [1.1 kg] total weight)
- 2 tablespoons olive oil
- 2 slices firm-textured white bread, such as Pepperidge Farm
- 4 tablespoons butter

  juice of 1 lemon
- 4 cups [1 l] cold chicken broth (page 209)
- ½ cup [125 ml] heavy cream

  salt

  pepper

CUT the top one-third off each artichoke and discard. Cut off the stems and reserve. Trim off and discard the outermost leaves by rotating each artichoke against a sharp paring knife or by just pulling away the leaves. Cut the artichokes vertically in quarters and peel the outermost fiber from the stems. Simmer the artichokes and stems in a non-aluminum pot with plenty of water to cover and 1 tablespoon of the olive oil. Put a plate on the artichokes to keep them from bobbing up.

CUT the crusts off the bread, cut the slices into quarters, and cook the quarters in the butter in a sauté pan, over medium heat, turning once, until the bread is golden brown on both sides.

WHEN the artichokes and stems are easily penetrated with a knife, after about 25 minutes, drain in a colander and toss with the lemon juice and the remaining olive oil.

PURÉE the artichokes and stems in a blender with the toasted bread and 3 cups of the cold chicken broth for about 1 minute. Start on slow speed and gradually increase the speed to high. Work the purée through a food mill, or work it through a coarse strainer with the back of a ladle. Strain a second time, ideally through a fine-mesh strainer. Combine the purée with the rest of the broth and the heavy cream. Bring to a simmer just before serving, and season to taste with salt and pepper.

Variation: Escoffier has a version of artichoke soup that includes hazelnut oil. I sometimes dribble a little hazelnut oil (made from toasted nuts) on each serving. (See page 37 for more about nut oils.)

USING EGG YOLKS TO FINISH CLASSIC SOUPS

Classic French recipes often call for egg yolks to finish sauces, stews (see *blanquette de veau*), and soups. Most of us are intimidated by egg yolks because they contain cholesterol and fats, but also because they are tricky to work with. If allowed to boil, they curdle; if not cooked hot enough, they taste eggy and they never take on the lovely velvety texture that is the whole reason for using them. Some writers claim that egg yolks used to finish sauces containing flour won't curdle, but I've found they always curdle unless the sauce contains an enormous amount of flour. So I always treat egg yolks in soups and sauces as though I were making *crème anglaise* (see page 641). There is one soup that makes hassling with egg yolks worth the trouble: *potage Germiny*, a rich, creamy soup made with sorrel.

CREAM OF SORREL SOUP

POTAGE GERMINY

MAKES 6 SERVINGS

Sipping this soup is like drinking satin. The soup is very rich, but the richness is delightfully contrasted with the tang of the sorrel. Sorrel is becoming easier to find in fancy grocery stores, especially in the summer. You can make the sorrel purée, described in the first paragraph of the recipe, earlier in the day or the day before. Traditionally, *potage Germiny* is decorated with chervil, but chervil can be hard to find and expensive, so I sometimes use fennel frond or little strips of sorrel leaves. Because the soup is so rich, the servings in this recipe are only about 6 ounces [175 ml] each. If it's a hot summer day, consider serving the soup cold.

½ pound [225 g] sorrel (about ½ cup tightly packed), washed

4 cups [1 l] White Chicken Broth (page 210; also see note below)

5 egg yolks

1 cup [250 ml] heavy cream

4 tablespoons butter

   salt

   pepper

6 tiny sprigs of chervil or fennel frond for decorating the bowls (optional)

REMOVE and discard the sorrel stems. Combine the sorrel in a pot with ½ cup [125 ml] of the chicken broth. Cover the pot and bring to a boil. Boil for about 1 minute, until all the sorrel turns gray and "melts." (Don't worry, sorrel is one vegetable that cannot be kept bright green.) Purée the contents of the pot in a blender and work the mixture through a food mill, or work it through a large strainer with the back of a ladle. To make the soup even silkier, work the sorrel mixture through a fine-mesh strainer with the ladle.

ABOUT 20 minutes before you're ready to serve, combine the sorrel purée with the rest of the broth and bring to a simmer. Remove from the heat. In a medium-size mixing bowl, whisk the egg yolks and cream until the mixture is smooth, and ladle about half the hot sorrel mixture into the cream mixture while stirring with a wooden spoon. Pour the cream mixture, again while stirring, into the pot with the rest of the hot sorrel mixture. Put the pot back on the stove, over medium heat, and keep stirring with a wooden spoon, reaching into the corners so no egg yolk collects there and curdles, until the soup thickens slightly and takes on a smooth, velvety consistency. Whatever you do, don't let it boil. Take the pan off the heat and stir for 1 minute more so the heat retained in the pan doesn't cause the yolks to curdle. Stir in the butter and season to taste with salt and pepper. Ladle into hot (but not scalding) bowls. Decorate the center of each serving with a chervil sprig or fennel frond.

Note: If you're serving this soup cold, use a light broth—or use half broth, half water—so the broth doesn't jell when it gets cold. For more about cooking liquids with egg yolks, see the recipe for crème anglaise on page 642.

FRENCH ONION SOUP

SOUPE À L'OIGNON

HOW TO	HOW TO	HOW TO	USING
MAKE FRENCH ONION SOUP WITHOUT MAKING BEEF BROTH	CARAMELIZE ONIONS	CONVERT SOUPS INTO CASSEROLES (GRATINS)	GARLIC SOUP AS A BASE FOR IMPROVISATIONS

THERE ARE TIMES WHEN THE DISTINCTIONS BETWEEN THE CAREFULLY laid-out categories of French cooking become murky. The traditional French onion soup, often described on the menus of restaurants in France as a *gratinée,* is a case in point. In some places it's more soup, on others, more gratin—what we might call a baked onion casserole. Onion soup is almost always gratinéed by slowly baking so that the layers of bread and cheese on top of the broth form a delicious savory crust, but every version is different, with some emphasizing bread and cheese more than onions and broth. When I lived in Paris, I was an habitué of what must have been the cheapest restaurant in town. For a couple of francs I could down an onion soup that was mostly bread, but eminently satisfying: a filling lunch for the price of a beer at a café on the Champs-Élysées. Years later I sipped a *soupe à l'oignon* at a chic little restaurant in Manhattan for four times the price of my Parisian lunches. What a delicate little thing it was: a bowl of clear broth, looking almost like consommé, with a few strands of onion and a tiny cheese-crusted crouton floating on top. It was conceptual onion soup, more idea than substance, not bad, but without the satisfying beauty of the old-fashioned and, to me at least, real thing.

I know of no one who doesn't adore onion soup, and there are those who'll put up with all sorts of travesties just to get a hit of that crunchy combination of toast, cheese, and onions. The typical onion soup in an everyday American restaurant is made with canned bouillon, indifferent cheese, and toasted white bread, but in the winter months it always manages to hit the spot, especially with a glass of wine to sip between mouthfuls.

When it comes to making onion soup at home, most of us give up when we see beef broth in the list of ingredients. If you're conscientious, you can make your own beef broth—make the pot-au-feu described on page 456 and withhold the broth when you serve it, so you have good meaty broth and don't waste the meat. Or you can use one of the products mentioned on page 4. But onion soup tastes so much like onions and cheese that you can get by using rather ordinary broth (but broth from a pot-au-feu, page 456, or oxtail soup, page 200, makes fantastic soup). I sometimes use Brown Chicken Broth (page 209), but my most practical and inexpensive solution is broth made with the leftover carcass from a roast turkey.

Another stumbling block is the cheese. I always use authentic Swiss Gruyère. Don't buy the kind of Swiss cheese with big holes, which is Emmentaler; it doesn't have enough taste and makes the soup stringy. Gruyère is never cheap, but if you shop around, it can often be had for the same price as ordinary American cheddar.

The least expensive ingredients are the onions. While any onion will do, I prefer big red onions, which seem to give the soup just the right amount of sweetness. But keep in mind one of the secrets to a great onion soup: a ton of onions. When you finish slicing the onions you'll be standing in front of a mountain. But don't lose faith, you're going to cook them down to about one-tenth of their volume before adding liquid. And now to the most important secret: The onions must be cooked very slowly, for almost an hour, until they've completely softened and have released all their natural juices. When the onions have softened and the juices they release evaporate, you must be very attentive, stirring almost constantly so that the juices caramelize and the onions take on color without burning. You then add a little broth, scrape up the caramelized juices clinging to the bottom of the pot, and let everything caramelize again. You add the rest of the broth and bring it to a simmer while scraping the bottom of the pot with a wooden spoon to dissolve the caramelized juices, and the liquid part of your soup is ready. The soup can be made up to 3 days ahead of time and kept covered in the refrigerator.

———————◯———————

CRYING

I've discovered only two things that sort of work and one thing that really works to solve the problem of crying when you cut onions. Contact lenses and, to a lesser extent, glasses will make you cry less. What really works is a pair of cheap plastic goggles from the hardware store.

FRENCH ONION
SOUP

SOUPE À L'OIGNON

MAKES 10 FIRST-COURSE SERVINGS

5	pounds [2.3 kg] onions, preferably red
4	tablespoons butter
10	cups [2.5 l] beef, turkey, or chicken broth
1	medium-size bouquet garni
	salt
	pepper
4	cups [120 g] ¾-inch [2 cm] cubes (about ½ pound [225 g]) cut from crusty slices of French bread, preferably sourdough
25	cups [280 g] finely grated Swiss Gruyère or other full-flavored firm cheese (about 5 pound)

PEEL and slice the onions as thin as you can. This is easiest with a plastic vegetable slicer, called a Benriner cutter (see page 13). Melt the butter over medium heat in a wide, heavy-bottomed pot large enough to hold the sliced onions. Add the onions and stir every few minutes over medium heat until they soften and release liquid, about 15 minutes. At this point, you can turn the heat to high to reduce the liquid, but keep a close watch and stir every minute or two so that the onions don't scorch. When most of the liquid has evaporated, after about 15 minutes, turn the heat back down to medium and keep stirring and scraping the bottom of the pot with a wooden spoon to keep the caramelized juices from burning. When all the liquid has evaporated and the bottom of the pot is coated with a shiny glaze, after 5 or 10 minutes, pour in 1 cup of broth and turn the heat to high. Stir the onions, again scraping off any caramelized juices that cling to the bottom and sides of the pot. When the broth completely evaporates and again forms a brown glaze on the bottom of the pot, add the rest of the broth and the bouquet garni.

GENTLY simmer the soup for 10 minutes. Be sure to scrape the bottom of the pot so that the caramelized juices dissolve in the soup. Season to taste with salt and pepper. Remove the bouquet garni.

WHILE the onions are cooking, spread the bread cubes on a sheet pan and bake them in a 400°F [200°C/gas mark 6] oven for about 20 minutes, turning them over every few minutes so that they brown evenly. Unless you're making the soup ahead of time, leave the oven on for baking the crocks of soup.

LADLE the hot soup into individual 10-to-12-ounce [300 ml to 375 ml] soup crocks or soufflé dishes. (You can also bake the soup in a large soufflé dish or soup tureen and ladle it into individual bowls at the table.) Sprinkle half the cheese over the soup and distribute the toasted bread cubes among the crocks. Sprinkle with the remaining cheese. Put the crocks on a sheet pan and bake them at 400°F [200°C/gas mark 6] until the cheese bubbles and turns light brown, about 10 minutes. Serve immediately. (You can also assemble the soups earlier in the day and refrigerate them until shortly before serving. When heating cold soups, bake them in a 375°F [190°C/gas mark 5] oven until they start to steam and bubble, about 25 minutes. By using the lower temperature you give the soup time to heat up without overbrowning the cheese.)

Variations: Most onion soup variations revolve around cheeses, including Brie, Cheddar, Comté, or almost any hard and flavorful cheese. (I once tried a version with Camembert—rind removed—that was gooey and delicious.) Fortified wines, such as semisweet Madeira or port, added when the onions are caramelized, give the soup a note of sweetness, and in the case of Madeira, a pleasing nutty complexity.

BREAD
AND ONION SOUP

SOUPE À L'OIGNON
EN PANADE

MAKES 10 SIDE-DISH SERVINGS

Onion soup can also be turned into a panade or a classic gratin. A panade is a soup with the bread already in it, but unlike most versions of soupe à l'oignon, which contain broth covered with a crunchy layer of bread and cheese, panades contain so much bread that all the liquid is absorbed. The panade is served in steaming, stringy, delicious mounds. Most panades are cooked gently in a pot, but if you spread the same mixture into a baking dish and sprinkle it with cheese, you can turn it into a gratin. This idea of turning soups into panades or gratins provides a great way to reuse soups the next day so that no one will recognize them as leftovers. Just layer the leftover soup in a pot with cubes of crusty sourdough bread, which retains its texture when soaked with liquid, and plenty of flavorful cheese and bake it. I sometimes serve panades as side dishes rather than first courses. They are great with stews or meat dishes with red-wine sauces.

The ingredients for this panade are the same as for the soupe à l'oignon on page 189, but the amounts of bread and cheese are doubled.

- 5 pounds [2.3 kg] onions, preferably red
- 4 tablespoons butter
- 10 cups [2.5 l] beef, turkey, or chicken broth
- 1 medium-size bouquet garni
- 8 cups [240 g] ¾-inch [2 cm] cubes (about 1 pound) cut from crusty slices of French bread, preferably sourdough
- 4 cups [450 g] finely grated Swiss Gruyère (about 1 pound)

PREPARE the onion soup as described on page 189 until you get to the point of assembling the individual soups in crocks. Preheat the oven to 400°F

[200°C/gas mark 6]. Spread the bread cubes on sheet pans and bake them, turning them over every few minutes, for about 20 minutes, until they are an even golden brown. Pour about 1 cup [250 ml] of onion soup into a relatively narrow pot that will hold 6 quarts [6 l], and over that sprinkle one-fourth of the bread cubes, one-fourth of the cheese, and 2 more cups [500 ml] of broth. Continue layering in this way, so that you end up with about 4 layers of bread and cheese, finishing with a layer of bread cubes, a ladle of broth, and the last of the cheese. Make sure, as you're ladling the broth layer by layer, that each layer gets its share of the onions. Turn the oven down to 375°F [190°C/gas mark 5] and bake for 50 minutes, uncovered. Bring the pot to the table and serve the panade with a big ladle onto hot plates.

Variations: Sometimes I sprinkle chopped thyme, marjoram, or sage over the layers. It might be interesting to try a different herb between each layer. I sometimes add cream, or cubes of cooked bacon or pancetta, or a sprinkling of chopped prosciutto end between the layers. Chopped leftover vegetables would also work. You can turn this panade into a gratin by making only 1 or 2 layers in a very large dish (or several) and baking until it is crusty on top, slightly less time than the 50 minutes required for the panade. A gratin differs from a panade only in that it has a larger surface area, so there's more crust.

SQUASH
AND BREAD SOUP

PANADE DE COURGE

MAKES 10 SIDE-DISH SERVINGS

One of the most dramatic dishes I know is a pumpkin panade made by hollowing out a pumpkin as though making a jack-o'-lantern, layering bread, broth, cream, and cheese inside, and then baking the pumpkin for a couple of hours and presenting it whole at the table. When serving, I scoop around the insides of the pumpkin so that the cooked pumpkin combines with the bread mixture. The dish never fails to get oohs and ahs. While it is, in fact, delicious (I give a recipe in my book *Splendid Soups*), pumpkin lacks the sweetness of the best winter squash. A panade made in a pot with winter squash won't be as dramatic, but it will be sweeter and more flavorful. I serve this dish as a side dish or as a first course.

3 pounds [1.5 kg] winter squash, such as acorn, buttercup, butternut, or turban

2 tablespoons melted butter, if you're seeding the squash before baking, plus 2 tablespoons butter for cooking the onion and garlic

8 cups [240 g] ¾-inch [2 cm] cubes (about 1 pound) cut from crusty slices of French bread, preferably sourdough

3 medium-size onions, chopped fine

2 cloves garlic, chopped fine

10 cups [2.5 l] beef, turkey, or chicken broth

1 small bouquet garni

   salt

   pepper

4 cups [450 g] finely grated Swiss Gruyère (about 1 pound), or 2 cups Gruyère and 2 cups Parmigiano-Reggiano or *grana padana*

CUT the squash in half and scoop out the seeds. If the squash is too hard to cut, it can be baked whole and seeded once it's cooked, but squash baked whole can be a little watery. If you've seeded the squash, brush the exposed flesh with melted butter, place the halves, flesh side up, on a sheet pan, and slide the pan into the oven. Baking the squash this way helps to evaporate its water and concentrate its flavor. Turn the oven to 375°F [190°C/gas mark 5]. If you're baking the squash whole, poke it in about eight places with a sharp knife so it doesn't burst open. Bake until the squash is completely soft and a knife slides easily in and out, from 45 minutes to 1½ hours—whole squash will take longer. If the exposed part of a seeded squash starts to get too brown, turn down the oven to 300°F [150°C/gas mark 2]. If you've baked the squash whole, cut it in half and scoop out the seeds.

SPREAD the bread cubes on sheet pans and bake them, turning them over every 10 minutes, for about 30 minutes, until they are an even golden brown. If there's room in the oven, you can do this while baking the squash.

WHILE the squash is baking, cook the onions and garlic in butter in a heavy-bottomed pot over medium heat, until the onions turn translucent, about 10 minutes. Keep stirring and turn down the heat if the onions start to brown. Add the broth and the bouquet garni and simmer gently for 20 minutes.

SCOOP the pulp out of the squash in large pieces. Be gentle—you don't want to turn the squash into purée.

POUR about 1 cup [250 ml] of broth into a 6-quart [6 l] or larger pot. Spoon one-fourth of the squash over the broth, sprinkle with salt and pepper, and add one-fourth of the bread cubes and one-fourth of the cheese. Pour over this 2 more cups [500 ml] of broth. Continue layering in this way, seasoning each layer of squash with salt and pepper, so you end up with 4 layers of bread, squash, and cheese, finishing with a layer of bread cubes, a ladle of broth, and the last of the cheese. Bake, uncovered, for 50 minutes at 375°F [190°C/gas mark 5]. Bring the pot to the table and serve the panade with a big ladle onto hot plates.

OTHER BAKED SOUPS

Leave it to the French to take a simple idea, like baking a crock of soup, to the height of refinement. Years ago I was lucky enough to taste such a soup at Paul Bocuse's elegant three-star restaurant just outside of Lyons. The soup was straightforward and yet incredibly extravagant. An individual high-sided soup crock, like those used to bake French onion soup, was filled with consommé, cubes of foie gras, and slices of black truffles. Instead of spreading cubes of bread and cheese on top, Monsieur Bocuse covered the top of the bowl with a round of puff pastry (*pâté feuilletée*) and then baked the soup so that the puff pastry rose into a golden dome, sealing in the aroma of the truffles and foie gras. It was up to me to break through the crust with my spoon and breathe in the fragrance.

A crock of soup covered with flaky puff pastry is so dramatic and satisfying that I've adapted it for more practical home cooking. Instead of using truffles, I flavor a good broth with dried cèpes (porcini) and morels and add foie gras only when I'm being extravagant. You can also make this soup with fresh wild mushrooms, but if you do, sauté them first to bring out their flavor. When shopping for dried cèpes, look for bags with large slices rather than little pieces. Feel through the bag if you can—good-quality dried cèpes should be leathery and slightly flexible, not completely dried out—and smell them. They should be so fragrant that you can smell them through the bag. (I find those from Italy to be the most fragrant.) You can make your own puff pastry, but it's tricky and takes time, so unless you're adept at it, you're better off buying ready-made frozen puff pastry. But beware: Some major brands of puff pastry are made with margarine or shortening and taste ghastly. Check the ingredients carefully to make sure the pastry is made with butter and contains nothing hydrogenated. (See Sources.) To make this soup you'll need soup crocks without rims. Large ramekins or 10-ounce or 12-ounce [300 ml to 375 ml] soufflé dishes will also work. The mushroom broth can be made up to three days ahead and baked just before serving.

BAKED DRIED CÈPES AND MOREL SOUP

SOUPE AUX CÈPES ET MORILLES SECHES

MAKES 12 FIRST-COURSE SERVINGS

This recipe is enough for 12 servings, rather a lot, but cutting the recipe down much smaller has you weighing out ridiculously small amounts of ingredients. If you want to serve less, you can make a whole batch of soup and freeze what you don't use.

1 ounce [30 g] dried cèpes (porcini), or ¾ pound [335 g] fresh

1 ounce [30 g] dried morels, or ¾ pound [340 g] fresh

½ cup [125 ml] semidry Madeira or good dry sherry (ideally, amontillado)

4 tablespoons butter or rendered duck or goose fat if you're using fresh mushrooms, or 2 tablespoons if you're using dried mushrooms

salt

pepper

1 medium-size onion, chopped fine

1 clove garlic, chopped fine

¼ pound [115 g] pancetta or prosciutto end, cut into ¼-inch [.5 cm] dice

½ teaspoon chopped fresh thyme or marjoram, or ¼ teaspoon dried thyme

8 cups [2 l] full-flavored broth such as Brown Chicken Broth (page 209) or beef broth (see page 219)

¼ pound [115 g] terrine of foie gras, preferably bloc or entier, cut into ¼-inch [.5 cm] cubes (optional; see page 96 for more about foie gras)

3 pounds [1.5 kg] puff pastry (pâte feuilletée) or 3 packages (14 ounces each [397 g]) store-bought frozen puff pastry made with butter (see note below)

1 egg

IF you're using dried mushrooms, rinse them in a colander under cold running water and toss them with the Madeira in a mixing bowl. Soak them for about 1 hour, moving them around in the Madeira periodically to make sure they soften evenly. Squeeze the Madeira out of the softened mushrooms and reserve it in a small bowl. If you're using fresh mushrooms, inspect them for dirt and sand. If they're dirty, quickly rinse them with cold water. You may need to cut clinging dirt or sand from the cèpes with a small knife.

IF you're using fresh mushrooms, slice the cèpes ¼ inch [.5 cm] thick, leave the morels whole, and sauté both together over high heat in 2 tablespoons of the butter for about 10 minutes, until they smell fragrant and any water they may have released boils down and is reabsorbed. Season with salt and pepper.

COOK the onion, garlic, and pancetta in the remaining butter in a 6-quart pot over medium heat. When the onions smell fragrant, after about 10 minutes, sprinkle in the thyme, cook for 1 minute more, and let cool. Pour the broth over the onion mixture, add the mushrooms and any Madeira from the dried mushrooms (leaving any grit behind in the bowl), and let cool. The soup must be cold or at least cool when you're putting on the puff pastry or the heat will melt the pastry.

DISTRIBUTE the cool soup, which may have jelled, and the optional foie gras into individual soup crocks and sprinkle salt and pepper over each one. Leave at least ½ inch of space between the top of the soup and the top of the crock. Refrigerate the crocks while you're preparing the pastry.

AT this point you can preheat the oven to 375°F [190°C/gas mark 5], but if your kitchen is not well ventilated, you may want to wait until you've rolled out the pastry. Look around the kitchen for a saucer or mixing bowl that's about 2 inches [5 cm] wider than the top of the crocks. Roll the pastry into sheets between ⅛ inch and ¼ inch thick [about .5 cm]. Using the saucer as a guide, make 12 round cutouts. Keep them in a cool place while you preheat the oven to 375°F [190°C/gas mark 5], if you haven't already done so. Use a fork to beat the egg with a big pinch of salt (for thinning the egg wash). Brush the egg wash over one side of each of the cutouts. One by one, place the cutouts, egg side down, on top of the soup crocks and press the pastry down along the sides of the crocks. Make sure that the pastry is well sealed to the crock. Brush the pastry tops with the egg wash. For a decorative touch, and to help prevent the pastry from cracking, use a sharp paring knife to make a series of arcs— like spokes of a bicycle, but curved instead of straight—from the center of the pastry to the edge, cutting no more than halfway through the pastry.

PUT the crocks on a sheet pan and bake until the pastry forms a shiny golden dome on each, about 45 minutes. Serve immediately.

Note: The exact amount of puff pastry you will need depends on the diameter of the crocks used for baking the soup. I use soufflé dishes that are almost 5 inches [12.5 cm] across at the top for making this soup. If you're using smaller dishes, you may be able to get by with less pastry. If you find yourself short of pastry, refrigerate the trimmings, left from cutting out the rounds, for about 1 hour and then roll them out into a new sheet. Pastry trimmings tend to be elastic. Don't force the pastry or you'll toughen it. As soon as you notice any elasticity, put the pastry into the refrigerator to rest for 30 minutes.

Variations: You can use this treatment for virtually any soup or stew, but since the purpose of the pastry covering is to seal in aromas that otherwise would be lost, it makes the most sense to use it for soups or stews that contain luxurious ingredients—like truffles, wild mushrooms, and foie gras—when you don't want to lose a single whiff of their precious perfume. It also makes sense for soups that contain herbs such as basil or tarragon, whose lovely fragrances dissipate during cooking. In addition, it is good for making pot pies, which otherwise can be disappointing because the bottom crust always ends up soggy. Making a pot pie in a pastry-covered soup crock circumvents this problem, and the crisp buttery crust makes a light and savory contrast to what's underneath. This method also allows you to keep the ingredients in the pie on the soupy side instead of thickening them with flour, which dulls their flavor and makes them pasty and heavy. One of my favorite methods is to stew some sliced leeks and some diced carrots in a little butter and combine them in the soup crocks with chunks of raw chicken breast and tarragon leaves or chopped basil before pouring a little broth and heavy cream over them. Needless to say, a few wild mushrooms aren't bad here either. I then seal on the covers and bake as above.

Garlic Soups
Soupes à l'Ail

GARLIC AND ONIONS ARE A NATURAL PAIR. Both are pungent and aromatic and profoundly comforting. They've provided sustenance, spiritual and physical, to the poor and hardworking for aeons. Many a simple dish is based on garlic or onions alone. Together or separately, they're indispensable for almost all savory dishes. It's hard to imagine life without them.

A number of French provinces have their own versions of *soupe à l'ail*, with slight variations, but in spirit virtually the same. Typically, a broken-up head of garlic is simmered in water until it softens, and the soup is strained and poured over a chunk of crusty bread. When the garlic is worked hard through the strainer, the garlic pulp adds a creamy body to the soup, but if the soup is just strained, it becomes a sort of tea, a tonic for the weary or sick. Some recipes call for flavoring the soup with bay leaves and thyme, others sage. I sometimes use fresh marjoram. In one version, a *soupe à l'ail* from the Auvergne, a slice of toast is rubbed with a garlic clove and dribbled with olive oil (like a Tuscan bruschetta), water is poured over it, and the serving is sprinkled with grated cheese. Some recipes call for chicken broth; others, more frugal, suggest using the cooking water from beans. In some regions, such as the Béarn, they add eggs or egg yolks and a dash of vinegar.

Garlic broth made by first roasting the garlic will have a subtle dimension that boiled garlic does not. Just wrap the unpeeled cloves in aluminum foil with a sprinkling of water and bake them in a 375°F [190°C/gas mark 5] oven for about 45 minutes. If you want to go all out, you can finish the garlic broth by whisking in some aïoli (about 3 tablespoons per cup of broth) and returning it to the heat, but don't let it boil or the egg yolk in the aïoli will curdle.

One word of warning: You and all who join you in eating this soup are going to reek for 24 hours. Avoid elevators and close contact with anyone except your fellow diners.

GARLIC SOUP
SOUPE À L'AIL
MAKES 4 SERVINGS (1 QUART)

- 4 small-to-medium heads of garlic, preferably the kind that's stained with purple, broken up into cloves and roasted (see garlic soups introduction at left)
- 5 cups (1.1 l) water, homemade chicken broth, cooking liquid from dried beans, or a mixture of all three
- 5 sprigs fresh thyme or marjoram and 3 sage leaves (or ½ teaspoon dried thyme and 1 bay leaf)
- salt
- pepper
- 1 tablespoon good wine vinegar, or more to taste
- 2 beaten eggs (optional)
- 2 tablespoons finely chopped parsley
- 4 slices crusty French bread, preferably a bit stale

DON'T bother to peel the roasted garlic cloves, just combine with the water and herbs in a small pot. Simmer, covered, for about 30 minutes, until the garlic is completely soft and you can easily crush one of the cloves against the inside of the pot.

WORK the soup through a food mill or purée it in a blender and then work it through a strainer with the back of a ladle to extract as much of the garlic pulp as possible. Season the soup to taste with salt, pepper, and vinegar.

IF you're using the beaten eggs, whisk some of the soup into them and return the mixture to the pot. Reheat the soup while stirring, but don't get it so hot that the egg curdles. Add the parsley, arrange a slice of bread in each heated soup plate, and ladle the soup over it.

Variations: I sometimes add cream, but only when I want to make the soup more substantial. I recently made a fabulous discovery: Garlic soup makes a delicious meatless broth to use as the basis for more elaborate soups and stewlike concoctions. One recent experiment involved gently sweating a little onion in duck fat, adding shredded duck confit (see page 383 for more about confit), pouring garlic broth over these, and garnishing the soup with little cubes of bread, also cooked in duck fat, to add crunch. Another evening, this evolved into a more substantial main course, involving slices of bread gently browned on both sides in duck fat, a heated confit duck leg placed on the bread, and, again, the garlic broth poured over and around. The bread can be replaced with cooked chard or spinach or a heap of cooked beans, and the shredded duck confit replaced with cubes of pancetta or prosciutto end. Garlic broth also makes an excellent base for tomato soup: Cut peeled, seeded, and chopped tomatoes into cubes and add them to the finished soup, or simmer the tomatoes with the garlic and strain everything at once. (For another tomato soup recipe, see page 183.)

Garlic broth—without the egg—also makes a great poaching or steaming liquid for seafood. Throw some mussels or clams into the strained soup and simmer until they open (some saffron and/or tomatoes could come into play here). Poach fish steaks in garlic broth, place the individual servings of fish on toasted bread slices or mounds of vegetables, and pour the garlic broth over and around.

You can also use garlic broth as the base for a vegetable soup: Just toss in fresh shell beans, peas, cubes of tomato, sections of string beans, shredded leafy greens (chard, spinach, sorrel), mushrooms (cultivated or wild), and fresh or dried chiles (chopped or, if dried, shredded and toasted in a skillet).

Try replacing the fava beans in the following recipe with baby peas (even frozen will do) or 1-inch [2.5 cm] lengths of thin string beans, which should be precooked in boiling salted water just until they loose their crunch, about 5 minutes.

GARLIC, DUCK CONFIT, FAVA BEAN, AND FRESH CHARD SOUP

SOUPE À L'AIL AUX CONFIT DE CANARD, AUX FÈVES FRAÎCHES, ET AUX BLETTES

MAKES 4 MAIN-COURSE SERVINGS

5 confit duck legs (see recipe, page 382, or Sources)

1 medium-size onion, chopped fine

2 tablespoons duck fat from confit

1 bunch green Swiss chard (1 pound) [450 g], white stems removed, leaves washed

1 quart (1 recipe) Garlic Soup (page 194), without the egg

   salt

   pepper

1 pound [450 g] fava beans, shucked and peeled (about ¾ cup; see page 65 for more about fava beans)

4 slices crusty French bread, preferably a bit stale, lightly toasted

PULL the meat off one of the confit legs. Combine the meat with the onion and duck fat in a heavy-bottomed pot and cook over medium heat while stirring, until the onion turns translucent, about 10 minutes.

ROLL up the chard leaves and slice them into ½-inch [1.5 cm] strips. Put the chard in a small pan large enough to hold the remaining 4 duck legs in a single layer. Arrange the duck legs on top of the chard and ladle 1 cup of the garlic broth over them. Cover the pan and place it over medium heat. When the liquid starts to boil, turn the heat down to low. Cook for about 10 minutes—long enough to heat through the legs.

POUR the remaining garlic broth into the onion mixture and simmer gently for 10 minutes. Season the broth to taste with salt and pepper, but leave it slightly undersalted because the confit is very salty. A couple of minutes before serving, toss the fava beans into the broth.

PLACE 1 slice of toast each in the bottom of 4 heated wide soup plates. Place a mound of chard on top of each slice, and a confit leg—handle them gently, they're fragile—on top of the chard. Pour the broth left in the pan used to heat the duck legs into the pot with the rest of the hot garlic broth. Ladle the broth into each plate, making sure everybody gets a share of fava beans.

SERVING CHICKEN WITH GARLIC BROTH: If you don't have confit duck legs and you don't want to toy with fava beans, you can make a similar dish using chicken. I recommend sweating a little prosciutto end, pancetta, or bacon with onions to round out the garlic broth's flavor and give it extra complexity, but these aren't essential. I like to use chicken breasts with the bone in and the skin attached; they have a lot more flavor. But if you're in a hurry, boneless chicken breasts are still great.

SAUTÉED CHICKEN BREASTS IN GARLIC BROTH WITH TOMATOES, SPINACH, SAFFRON, AND BASIL

POULET SAUTÉ À LA SOUPE À L'AIL, ET AUX TOMATES, SAFRAN, ET BASILIC

MAKES 4 MAIN-COURSE SERVINGS

2   double bone-in chicken breasts, or 4 individual bone-in half breasts

    salt

    pepper

2   to 4 tablespoons plus 1 teaspoon olive oil

1   medium-size onion, chopped fine

¼   pound [115 g] prosciutto end, pancetta, or bacon, cut into ¼-inch [.5 cm] cubes

1   pound [450 g] spinach, stemmed and washed, or two 10-ounce [280 g] bunches (optional)

1   quart (1 recipe) Garlic Soup (page 194), without the egg

    leaves from 1 bunch basil, about 40 leaves

3   medium-size tomatoes (about 1 pound total), peeled, seeded, and chopped

1   pinch saffron threads, soaked for 30 minutes or more in 1 tablespoon water (optional)

IF you're using double bone-in chicken breasts, turn them upside down and cut them in half by pressing a chef's knife straight down into the center of the underside of the breastbone and bringing the knife all the way through one side of the breast. Repeat, going in the other direction. Season the breasts with salt and pepper and sauté them skin-side down first, in a pan just large enough to hold them in a single layer, over medium heat in 2 tablespoons of olive oil.

WHEN the chicken breasts are well browned on both sides and bounce back to the touch (meaning they are cooked through), 8 to 10 minutes on each side, transfer them to a plate and keep them warm. Pour all but about 1 tablespoon of fat out of the sauté pan. (If the bottom of the pan has burned, wash the pan out and start over with 2 tablespoons of fresh oil.) Stir in the chopped onion and prosciutto cubes. Cook over medium heat, stirring every couple of minutes, until the onion turns translucent, about 10 minutes.

WHILE the onions are cooking, put the spinach in a pan with ½ cup [125 ml] of the garlic broth. Sprinkle the basil with 1 teaspoon of olive oil, chop coarse, and reserve.

WHEN the onions are done, put the pan with the spinach on high heat.

POUR the rest of the garlic broth, the tomatoes, and the saffron and its soaking liquid into the pan with the onions, or use a bigger pot if you need to, and bring the resulting soup to a simmer.

WHEN the spinach has "melted," after 1 or 2 minutes, spoon it into hot soup plates. Pour any broth left in the pan into the rest of the garlic broth. Place a chicken breast on top of the spinach. Stir the chopped basil into the soup and season to taste with salt and pepper. Ladle the soup over and around the chicken.

Variations: You can substitute any leafy vegetable you want—chard, sorrel, beet greens—for the spinach or just use a slice of toasted bread. If you want this dish to look really dramatic, "deconstruct" the various elements. Instead of the garlic broth, use a lightly creamed chicken broth; chop the basil very fine, almost like a pesto; heat the chopped tomatoes separately; and make a saffron aïoli (see page 491). Arrange the chicken breasts in the bowls, dribble the saffron aïoli over them; add the pesto; and dollop the tomatoes in little mounds here and there. The effect is a dramatic tangle of colors, and the flavors change with each bite.

OXTAIL SOUP

POTAGE DE QUEUE DE BOEUF

HOW TO	HOW TO	HOW TO	HOW TO
MAKE INEXPENSIVE, INTENSELY FLAVORFUL CLEAR BROTH	MAKE OXTAIL STEW	BREAD AND GRILL IN FRENCH STYLE	MAKE AN HERB VINAIGRETTE FOR MEATS

OXEN AND STEERS ARE, AS FAR AS I CAN TELL, THE SAME CREATURES—castrated bulls—except that oxen are made to work, whereas steers just hang around waiting to be eaten. To call a steer an ox does indeed imply a beast of a *certain age,* but in any case, "oxtail" certainly sounds better than "steertail" and whatever you end up buying will have come from some bovine animal, be it steer, cow, ox, or bull.

It is true that the oxtails I encounter in the United States are disappointingly small, perhaps because we slaughter beef younger than in France or because our breeds of cattle are smaller. This isn't really a problem unless you're setting out to stuff and braise a whole oxtail—a glorious thing—or want impressive big oxtail rounds for stew. My usual oxtail stew strategy is to serve one large and one small piece per person.

The French have long been fond of oxtails. They've been writing about them since the seventeenth century and no doubt eating them since long before that. Oxtail soup is derived from a kind of pot-au-feu called a *hochepot*, now encountered mostly in Flanders and Belgium. The word *hochepot* is the root of our "hodgepodge"—a fairly accurate description of the dish, since a *hochepot*, unlike most versions of pot-au-feu, often contains meats from different animals. It may or may not contain oxtail. Some cuts of meat— veal breasts, beef tongues, and of course oxtail—however, show up in seventeenth- and eighteenth-century cookbooks *en hochepot* by themselves, unaccompanied by other meats and simply simmered with aromatic vegetables, like a pot-au-feu except that the braising liquid (often enriched with a little extra veal broth) is reduced and the whole concoction served up in what sounds like a modern stew. The earliest recipe I can find of *hochepot* is in *Le Viandier*, where Taillevent describes a recipe for *hochepot de poullaille* made by cutting up what was presumably a chicken (the modern word is *poulet*); cooking it in lard; making a sauce out of toasted bread, the chicken livers, and beef broth; and then seasoning the whole thing with spices (unspecified) and *verjus* (a sour juice from underripe fruit).

Nowadays, except in places where you may encounter *le hochepot*, the only other dish with that name attached is *queue de boeuf en hochepot*. Oxtail served in this fashion is much like a *potée* (see page 464), except that oxtail is used instead of pork. But the usual vegetables—the carrots, turnips, onions, and wedges of cabbage—stay the same. Like so many traditional peasant *soupes, queue de boeuf en hochepot* has gone through various refinements on its way to becoming a *potage*. (For more about the difference between a *soupe* and a *potage*, see page 178.) In the middle of the nineteenth century, there were recipes for a *soupe de queue de boeuf* that was much like the *hochepot* version, except that the cabbage was gone. By the end of the century, the soup had reached its apotheosis and become *potage de queue de boeuf* (or, as named by Escoffier, *potage oxtail*, in deference to the English, who were big fans). It was a clear and luxurious double consommé.

My own version of oxtail soup is much like the classic late nineteenth-century versions, except that I leave out the tedious clarification involving extra meat and egg whites that's required to convert an already clear broth into something slightly more clear. Beware of recipes that have you add sherry or some other wine to an already clear broth. If the wine is added at the end, the acidity will cloud the broth by denaturing soluble proteins and making them insoluble. It's better, when flavoring a clear broth with wine, to add it at least an hour before the end of cooking. Ideally, you'd make a pot-au-feu and save the broth for cooking your oxtail. But you can use homemade Brown Chicken Broth (see page 209), or broth from a can or made from a concentrate. When I set out to make oxtail soup, I make a lot, since making a lot takes no longer than making a little.

OXTAIL SOUP

POTAGE DE QUEUE DE BOEUF

MAKES 10 FIRST-COURSE SERVINGS

FOR THE SOUP:

7 pounds [3.1 kg] oxtail, whole or cut into rounds about 1½ [4 cm] inches thick

4 quarts [4 l] full-flavored beef broth, preferably from a pot-au-feu or by dissolving 12 tablespoons demi-glace gold (see Sources) in 4 quarts [4 l] water, or more as needed to keep the oxtail covered

2 medium-size carrots, peeled, cut into 2-inch [5 cm] sections

2 medium-size onions, peeled, halved through the root end

1 clove, stuck into one of the onion halves

1 medium-size turnip, peeled and halved

1 small bouquet garni

1 cup [250 ml] dry sherry or semidry Madeira

salt

pepper

FOR THE OPTIONAL GARNITURE:

3 tablespoons finely chopped parsley (chopped at the last minute)

and/or

1 medium-size leek, cut into fine julienne

1 medium-size carrot, cut into fine julienne

1 medium-size turnip, cut into fine julienne

TO MAKE THE SOUP

IF you've bought whole oxtails, trim off any thick chunks of fat and divide the tails into 1½-to-2-inch [4- to 5-cm] rounds by cutting through each verte-bra with a chef's knife. Cut through what appears to be bone, not in between. Keep experimenting until the knife slides through the tail with firm, steady, even pressure.

IF you're buying oxtail already cut into rounds, just trim off any thick chunks of fat.

PUT the oxtails in a heavy-bottomed pot and pour enough cold water over them to cover. Bring to a boil over high heat, turn down to a simmer, and simmer for 1 minute. Drain the oxtails in a colander and rinse them thoroughly with cold water to eliminate scum and produce a clearer broth. Wash out the pot.

PUT the oxtails back in the pot and pour the beef broth over them. Bring to a gentle simmer, uncovered, over medium heat. Turn down the heat to keep the broth at a very gentle simmer—a bubble rising every 2 seconds—and skim off fat and scum, as they float to the surface, with a ladle held flat and quickly brushed along the surface of the broth. Simmer the oxtails for 4 hours or until the meat pulls away from the bone easily. After 2 hours of cooking, add the vegetables, the bouquet garni, and the sherry. If the broth evaporates so that the oxtails are no longer covered, add just enough water or more broth to keep them covered.

USE tongs to gently transfer the oxtails to a plate. Strain the broth. Gently press down on the vegeta-bles and bouquet garni, but don't push too hard or you'll cloud the broth. Strain the broth again through a fine-mesh strainer or a regular strainer lined with three layers of cheesecloth. Season the broth to taste with salt and pepper and set aside. Pull off and discard any fat clinging to the oxtails. Pull the meat away, cut it into ¼-inch [.5-cm] pieces, and combine it with the broth. Discard the bones. If you're not serving the soup within a cou-ple of hours, allow the broth to cool, uncovered, for about 1 hour, then cover and refrigerate until needed. The soup will keep for at least 3 days. Before reheating, spoon off any solidified fat from the top of the broth.

JUST before serving, bring the soup to a simmer and ladle into hot soup plates.

CLASSIC recipes from the beginning of the twentieth century, when *potage de queue de boeuf* was at the height of its popularity, suggest garnishing the soup with shaped, or "turned" (see page 21), carrots and turnips and diced celery. Other recipes insist that the vegetables be cut into *brunoise*, tiny cubes about ⅛ inch [3 mm] on each side. I sometimes leave out a garniture or simply swirl in a couple of tablespoons of finely chopped parsley just before ladling out the soup. If I'm trying to impress, I cut carrots, leeks, and turnips into fine julienne and simmer them for about 15 minutes in a little of the broth. I return the broth used for simmering the vegetables to the soup and distribute the vegetables among the bowls.

Variations: I love cold soups and especially cold brothy soups that set lightly, when chilled, into the texture of melting jelly. Unfortunately, a fair number of my guests are sent into a panic by the mere mention of anything resembling aspic. I've never understood this, especially in those who grew up eating Jell-O. My usual tactic is just to set the cold soup proudly in front of them, suggesting by my manner and excitement that they are very fortunate indeed to be tasting one of my favorite, and rather labor-intensive, dishes. No one dares make a peep. They're almost always converted and end up delighted.

Oxtail soup makes a perfect cold soup because it contains just the right amount of natural gelatin— enough so that it holds together, but not so much that it's rubbery. My usual system is to heat the soup, infuse it with herbs (usually parsley, chervil, and tarragon, alone or in combination), let it cool, and pour it into individual dariole molds or ramekins, making sure everyone will get a fair share of meat, and then chilling it. Sometimes I layer in extra little goodies such as cubes of diced cooked artichoke bottoms, reconstituted dried morels or cèpes (porcini), and, for favorite friends, truffles and cubes of foie gras. Just before serving the *hures*, I unmold them on plates. Sometimes I add a sauce, usually a tangy and creamy tomato sauce to contrast with the suave delicacy of the soup. With cold soup, I usually serve about half as much as I would when serving hot soup. So if you make one recipe of oxtail soup and serve three-quarters of it hot, you'll have enough left over to make the recipe that follows.

COLD OXTAIL SOUP WITH HERBS AND CREAMY TOMATO SAUCE

HURE DE QUEUE DE BOEUF AUX HERBES ET À LA SAUCE TOMATE CRÈMÉE

MAKES 6 FIRST-COURSE SERVINGS

I'm being somewhat fanciful calling this an hure, but I don't want to use the dreaded A-word, "aspic," or no one will ever give this dish a try. Nowadays, "aspic" has been largely replaced by the term en gelée. An hure was originally a kind of headcheese made by simmering a pig's (or boar's) head with aromatic vegetables and just letting the whole thing set. The result could then be sliced or cut into wedges. The term has evolved to mean a kind of terrine held together with cold, clear gelatinous broth instead of the more typical forcemeat of ground pork, sometimes veal, and pork fat. The problem with traditional hures is that the gelée must be stiff enough to hold the whole thing together. The rubbery result explains our aversion to aspic. When making individual hures, like those below, the gelée can be light, and melt instantly in your mouth. You can make the sauce by just simmering peeled and chopped tomatoes with cream. My approach, below, is a bit more fastidious.

FOR THE HURES:

3 cups [750 ml] Oxtail Soup (page 200)

2 tablespoons finely chopped parsley (chopped at the last minute)

1 tablespoon finely chopped chives (optional)

1 tablespoon finely chopped chervil (chopped at the last minute; optional)

salt

pepper

SLICING A LARGE ASPIC TERRINE "HURE"

One constant problem with making terrines that are held together with natural *gelée* is the necessity of making the *gelée* stiff enough to hold the terrine together without making it rubbery. One solution is to make individual servings in small molds that do not have to be sliced; in this way the trembling, melting texture of a well-made *gelée* can be left alone without adding extra gelatin. But there's nothing more dramatic than a well-made terrine e*n gelée*, served in glistening slices. To serve slices of delicate terrine *"en gelée,"* unmold the terrine, freeze it, and slice it with a serrated knife. Put frozen servings on the plates and let them thaw out before serving.

FOR THE OPTIONAL SAUCE:

2 medium-size tomatoes, peeled

½ cup [125 ml] heavy cream

1 tablespoon fresh tarragon leaves

   salt

   pepper

2 teaspoons sherry vinegar, or more to taste

TO MAKE THE HURES

BRING the broth to a simmer, remove from the heat, and stir in the herbs. Cover the pot and let cool to body temperature. Season with salt and pepper and ladle the soup into 4-ounce or 5-ounce [125- or 155-ml] dariole molds or ramekins, cover with plastic wrap, and chill for about 4 hours until the *gelée* has set completely.

TO MAKE THE OPTIONAL SAUCE

CUT the tomatoes into wedges, push the seeds out of each wedge with your forefinger, and discard the seeds. Cut the pulp out of the wedges and chop it coarsely. Cut the flat outside part of the wedges into tiny dice, between ⅛ and ¼ inch [about .5 cm] on each side. Combine the chopped inside pulp with the cream, simmer gently for about 3 minutes, and work through a strainer. Bring back to a simmer, stir in the tarragon leaves, tomato cubes, salt, pepper, and vinegar. Chill in the refrigerator.

TO UNMOLD AND SERVE THE HURES

JUST before serving, unmold each *hure* by running a knife along the inside of the mold, placing a chilled plate upside down on the mold, turning the whole thing over, and giving the mold a tap. If the *hure* won't come out, dip the bottom of the mold in a bowl of hot water for about 30 seconds. Check the consistency of the sauce—it may be too thick now that it's cold—and, if necessary, thin it with a little water. Spoon the sauce over the *hures.*

RED WINE OXTAIL STEW

MATELOTE DE QUEUE DE BOEUF

MAKES 8 MAIN-COURSE SERVINGS

Nowadays, a matelote is a stew made with fish (see chapter 18), but in the eighteenth century, a matelote could be any kind of stew, usually one made with red wine. I first encountered this dish in Paris, at Vivarois, where I did my first apprenticeship. At first it seemed like a prosaic sort of thing to be serving in such grand surroundings. We naturally made it ahead of time, since it takes almost 4 hours to cook, and then reheated it to order. Infinite care was taken in its preparation. The stewing liquid was enriched with *glace de viande* (see page 221) and the red wine was a mixture of good Burgundies and Bordeaux, from bottles left unfinished by the affluent clientele. As the oxtails neared completion, the chef would finish the sauce, adding old Armagnac and puréed foie gras trimmings left over from making foie gras terrines.

An oxtail stew is made just like any other stew. The tails, cut into rounds (see page 200), are browned, aromatic vegetables are browned in the same pan, and everything is simmered together slowly until the meat is falling off the bone. At this point, you have to be careful when taking the tails out of the pot because they can easily fall apart. I always find that a note of sweetness goes well with oxtails, so I include some Madeira in this recipe (also see variations).

7	pounds [3.1 kg] oxtail (at least 16 pieces), cut into rounds about 1½ inches [4 cm] thick
	salt
	pepper
4	tablespoons olive oil or vegetable oil
3	medium-size carrots, peeled and sliced
2	medium-size onions, peeled and sliced
4	cloves garlic, peeled and crushed
1	medium-size bouquet garni
1	cup [250 ml] semidry or semisweet Madeira, or port or cream sherry
1	bottle full-bodied red wine (see page 10)
1	cup [250 ml] beef broth, preferably concentrated (see page 219)
2	tablespoons finely chopped parsley (chopped at the last minute)

TRIM any thick chunks of fat off the oxtails. Season the oxtails liberally with salt and pepper. If there's time, let them sit in the refrigerator for several hours to give the seasoning time to penetrate the meat.

PAT the oxtails dry—the salt will have drawn moisture to the surface—and brown them over high heat, on both sides, in 2 tablespoons of the olive oil in a heavy-bottomed pot just large enough to hold them in a single layer. If your pot isn't large enough, brown them in two batches.

TAKE the oxtails out of the pot and discard the cooked oil. Put the remaining olive oil in the pot and cook the carrots, onions, and garlic over medium heat until they release their fragrance, about 10 minutes. Put the bouquet garni in the pot and put in the oxtails, ideally in a single layer. Pour in the Madeira, red wine, and broth. Bring to a simmer over medium heat, then turn the heat to low. If not all the oxtail pieces are submerged, cover the pot with a sheet of aluminum foil pushed down in the middle so the pieces will be basted from the inside. Cover the pot and cook very gently over very low heat on the stove or in a 325°F [165°F/gas mark 3] oven, adjusting the heat periodically so that a bubble rises to the surface of the stew every 2 or 3 seconds. If some of the oxtail pieces were protruding above the liquid, gently rearrange the pieces in the pot after 2 hours of cooking.

AFTER about 4 hours of cooking—the meat should be falling off the bone—gently transfer the oxtails to a platter or plate, using a skimmer or large slotted spoon. Cover them with aluminum foil, since braised meats dry out very quickly in the open air. If you're serving the oxtails right away, keep them in the oven, with the heat at the lowest setting. Strain the braising liquid into a clean saucepan. Press gently on the vegetables to extract as much liquid as possible. Discard the vegetables. (Some of the vegetables can also be puréed and used to thicken the stew—see Variations.)

BRING the braising liquid to a simmer. Place the pan to one side of the heat so the liquid bubbles up on one side, pushing the fat to the other. Skim off the fat and continue cooking down the braising liquid until only about 2 cups [500 ml] remain. (If you're serving the stew the next day, let the braising liquid cool, refrigerate it overnight, and then spoon off the congealed fat before reducing it.) Just before serving, stir in the parsley. Season the sauce to taste with salt and pepper.

PLACE the oxtails on hot soup plates—one large and one small piece per person—and spoon the broth-like sauce over them.

Variations: An oxtail stew can be treated like any other stew (see Rooster in Red Wine Sauce, Chapter 27, and Beef Stew with Pearl Onions, Mushrooms, and Bacon, Chapter 32, for ideas for different ways of finishing the sauce, garnitures, etc.), but I find that oxtails have an affinity for sauces that are slightly sweet, which is why I included the Madeira in the recipe above. I once worked in a place where we braised oxtails with bunches of whole muscat grapes. By the end of cooking, the grapes had liquified—we strained out the peels—and had given the sauce a delightful sweetness. Carrots also provide sweetness. You can purée the carrots used for braising and whisk them into the sauce as a thickener, or you can dice fresh carrots, sweat them gently in a little olive oil or butter, and spoon them as a garniture over each serving of oxtail. If you braise the oxtails with tomato purée and white wine, you'll end up with a southern French version, very similar to the Roman dish *coda alla vaccinara*.

BREADED AND GRILLED OXTAILS

QUEUES DE BOEUF À LA SAINTE-MÉNEHOULD

MAKES 4 MAIN-COURSE SERVINGS

Anything stewed is so good reheated that I always try to make more than I need so there are plenty of leftovers. Leftover stewed oxtails can be gently reheated and served just the way they were the night before. You can also pull the meat away from the bone, melt the braising liquid (reduce it a little if it didn't set firmly in the refrigerator), incorporate plenty of chopped herbs, and make a delicious terrine much like the one made out of leftover pot-au-feu on page 459. There is also another way: cooking à la Sainte-Ménehould. Sainte-Ménehould is a town in the Champagne region, famous for its pigs' feet à la Sainte-Ménehould, a dish supposedly enjoyed by Louis XVI before he was arrested at Varennes. The standard method involves long braising of the pigs' feet, coating with fresh bread crumbs, and grilling while basting with melted butter. I've never been a big fan of the dish, not because of the treatment, but because I'm not mad for pigs' feet. But in the eighteenth century, all sorts of things, including skate, pigeons, chicken wings, and of course oxtails, were grilled à la Sainte-Ménehould. If you don't feel like going outside and lighting a grill, especially in the middle of winter when you're most likely to have leftover braised things that take best to the Sainte-Ménehould treatment, you can use a hot oven or grill pan instead. Nowadays, breaded pigs' feet are served with nothing more than a little mustard, but two centuries ago, there were sauces for different eventualities. Skate à la Sainte-Ménehould was served with a cold *sauce ravigote*, a vinaigrette with herbs and capers (there's also a hot version, made by adding vinegar and shallots to a velouté). Oxtails à la Sainte-Ménehould were served with an herbaceous vinegar sauce called *sauce piquante*.

Because cooked oxtails are fragile, you'll need to wrap them in caul fat so that the meat doesn't fall off during the baking or grilling. You can wrap them in caul fat earlier the same day or the day before, but they should be breaded just before you're ready to cook them.

When I'm feeling up to it, I make an old version of a *sauce ravigote* (see page 205). If not, I pass the mustard.

4 large and 4 small (or 8 medium-size) braised oxtail rounds with their braising liquid from Red Wine Oxtail Stew (page 202)

6 slices firm-crumbed white bread, such as Pepperidge Farm, crusts cut off

8 squares caul fat, each large enough to wrap an oxtail round with a single layer (see page 88)

4 tablespoons melted butter

GENTLY pull the jelled braising liquid away from the oxtails and reserve in a small saucepan.

WORK the bread slices in a food processor until they're well broken up, about 1 minute, and work them through a large strainer, or drum sieve if you have one. This will be easier if the bread is slightly stale; you can also dry it out just slightly in a warm oven.

IF you're cooking the oxtails right away, preheat the oven to 375°F [190°C/gas mark 5] or light a grill. (If you're using a grill pan, wait until you're ready to start grilling.)

SPREAD the squares of caul fat, one at a time, on the work surface and wrap each piece of oxtail. The caul fat should not overlap too much on top.

WHEN you've wrapped all the oxtails, roll them in melted butter and then in the bread crumbs. Place them gently on a sheet pan and bake until the crust is golden brown, about 30 minutes, or grill gently on an outdoor grill or a grill pan over medium heat, turning several times so they're grilled on all sides, for a total of about 15 minutes.

SERVE with mustard or the old-fashioned Ravigote Sauce below.

OLD-FASHIONED RAVIGOTE SAUCE

This sauce has a peculiar history and, while it is always based on herbs, it has been made in several ways. Since the eighteenth century it has been served hot and made by adding various assorted herbs, chopped or crushed in a mortar, to a velouté sauce (basically broth thickened with flour). But throughout this time there have been cold versions, essentially vinaigrettes. These cold versions make delicious accompaniments to meaty foods, but their herbal freshness makes them especially delightful next to the richness of braised or poached dishes. Here's my favorite version:

MAKES 1¼ CUPS [300 ML] (ENOUGH FOR 4 GENEROUS SERVINGS)

3 tablespoons good-quality white-wine vinegar

2 teaspoons Dijon mustard

1 heaping tablespoon capers, drained, chopped fine

1 bunch parsley, large stems removed, chopped fine

1 medium-size bunch chives, chopped fine

1 medium-size bunch chervil, chopped fine (optional)

2 medium-size shallots, or 1 small onion, chopped fine

½ cup [125 ml] extra-virgin olive oil

salt

pepper

Whisk together the vinegar and mustard until smooth and then whisk in the capers, herbs, and shallots. Whisk in the olive oil in a thin stream and season to taste with salt and pepper.

CHICKEN CONSOMMÉ WITH SHREDDED CRÊPES

CONSOMMÉ CÉLESTINE

HOW TO	HOW TO	HOW TO
MAKE CLEAR, FAT-FREE BROTH	IMPROVISE YOUR OWN CONSOMMÉ VARIATIONS	MAKE BROTH FROM BONES

TO MANY OF US, CONSOMMÉ IS A DISTINCTLY UNPLEASANT GELATINOUS substance that comes out of a can, designed to torture us when we're not feeling well to begin with. This may explain why it has lost its popularity and rarely shows up on menus despite being one of the few delicious foods that don't have a speck of fat. This would seem to make it, in our calorie-obsessed age, a perfect candidate for rediscovery. As with so many foods first sampled in canned versions—creamed corn and tomato soup come to mind—our prejudice can be righted only by tasting the real thing in a good restaurant or by making it ourselves. Authentic consommé is simply a clear double bouillon (broth) made by using meat—usually beef—to make the second broth. More extravagant versions can be made by using the double broth to moisten more meat—the result being a triple broth. You can continue in this way, ad infinitum, until you give up or go broke.

"Consommé," from the French *consommé,* meaning perfect, was first mentioned in late eighteenth-century cookbooks, which describe it as a concentrated bouillon used to reinforce the flavor of sauces and as a base for *potages.* It wasn't until the nineteenth century that the word "consommé" was used to describe a perfectly clear and fat-free broth, which was called a *potage.* All through the nineteenth century, it was a soup only the rich could afford, because it required a shocking amount of meat.

By the end of the nineteenth century, there were scores of consommé variations, with Escoffier listing over 140, most of them essentially the same, a basic double beef bouillon, except for some variation in the garniture, which was often ridiculously elaborate. In Escoffier's list of consommé recipes you'll encounter *consommé Zola,* a basic consommé, really a clarified pot-au-feu broth, but with tiny gnocchi, flavored with white truffles, floating in each bowl. There's also *consommé Washington,* garnished with tiny squares of poached calf's head (cooked ahead with Madeira and the juices from a round of veal), finely julienned celery, and julienned truffles (also cooked separately in Madeira). There are miniature quenelles made from every conceivable creature; *royales,* miniature custards made with vegetables, or lobsters, or pureed peas and cut into different shapes; tiny profiteroles filled with elaborate stuffings; and so on.

Fortunately there are simpler and cheaper ways to go about it. Garnishes can be as simple as a little chopped parsley. You can make a *pot-au-feu* twice and use the broth from the first one to moisten the second. You can also make a chicken consommé much faster and for less money than a beef consommé.

Today, most consommé is made by clarifying broth by gently simmering the broth with a mixture of egg whites, eggshells, very lean ground meat, aromatic vegetables, and herbs. As the broth is heated with this clarification mixture, the egg whites slowly coagulate into long strands of protein that trap the minute specks of protein that make broth cloudy. The eggshells give the protein strands something to cling to and help them form into large clumps that make the consommé easy to strain. The meat, vegetables, and herbs are added to reinforce the consommé's flavor. But in the nineteenth century and before, very clear broths were made by gently simmering relatively large pieces of meat, instead of ground meat, in broth and then carefully straining the double broth, usually through muslin, without any clarification with egg whites. While a decent chunk of meat, such as a chuck roast suitable for pot roast, will cost more than ground meat, you can at least serve up the meat as you would a pot-au-feu, with mustard, coarse salt, and a few cornichons. Eating the ground meat used to make consommé is unpleasant at best.

Another money-saving trick is to make the first broth with bones (see page 219) and then use the bone broth to simmer the meat for the consommé. You can also make a very concentrated brown chicken broth, as in the recipe below, and either use it again to make a second broth or simply strain it through a cloth so that it's perfectly clear, achieving a broth that isn't technically a consommé because it isn't a double broth, but that is more concentrated than most double broths.

Before setting out to make consommé, you must first make a good clear broth. Broths are divided into two types: white and brown. A white broth is made with raw or lightly blanched meats and/or bones, while a brown broth is made by first browning the meat and/or bones and vegetables in the oven or on the stove. So-called white broth—or stock (see page 210)—is used for creamed soups and sauces in which it's important that the color remain very pale or green. Because brown broth has a more pronounced flavor and I like its golden color, I prefer it for making sauces, most soups, and certainly consommé (although traditional recipes use white broth). While brown broth requires an extra step, the browning, the actual cooking time is no greater because the cooking will have begun during the browning. When making a small amount of broth, it's easiest to brown the meat or bones on top of the stove; for larger amounts, use the oven. Brown broth has another advantage: If the browned meat or bones are moistened with cold water and simmered—not boiled—the broth will remain clear. White broth is trickier because raw bones and meat release proteins into the surrounding liquid, causing it to turn cloudy. To avoid this, the bones must first be blanched.

BROWN
CHICKEN BROTH

BOUILLON BRUN
DE VOLAILLE

MAKES 2½ QUARTS [2.5 L]

W hen I once made this broth for a friend who was in the hospital, his only complaint was that it was so concentrated that he had to dilute it with water. It is, in fact, so flavorful and meaty that you can strain it through a cloth (see page 213) and serve it as consommé. Or, if you want to go all out, use chicken broth instead of water in the recipe below to create an authentic double consommé.

To be sure of success, you must first cook the cut-up chickens or chicken parts in the oven—or, if you're making a very small amount, on the stove—until they're completely done, in fact overcooked, so that all the juices release into the pan, where they can mingle with those of the aromatic vegetables. Once released, the juices must then be cooked long enough that they evaporate completely and caramelize on the bottom of the pan, leaving the now easily discarded fat in a shiny layer above. The fat is spooned or poured out and the pan then deglazed with water or more broth.

This broth is best made with chicken drumsticks or wings, which have the most flavor and natural gelatin. But I sometimes cut up whole chickens, which are often less expensive than chicken parts, and use either the whole chickens or everything except the breasts, which I save. As a general rule, 3 pounds [1.5 kg] of whole chickens or chicken parts is enough for 1 quart [1 l] of brown chicken broth. (White chicken broth requires somewhat less; see page 210.) If I have them, I add some fennel stalks or fronds to the broth; they give it a lovely lightness without taking over. The size of the vegetables depends on how long the broth will be cooking; vegetables for beef broth, which cooks for hours, can be left almost whole while those for fish broth must be chopped very fine. For chicken broth, the size can be somewhere between the two—slices should be about ½ inch [1.5 cm] thick; onions can be quartered.

6 pounds [2.75 kg] whole chickens, chicken wings, chicken drumsticks, or chicken backs (each back broken up into at least 3 pieces with a cleaver)

1 large onion, root end cut off, quartered without peeling

3 medium-size carrots, greens removed, scrubbed but not peeled, halved lengthwise and sliced

1 stalk celery, sliced (optional)

1 handful fennel stalks (optional)

4 quarts [4 l] White Chicken Broth (page 210; optional)

1 small bouquet garni

IF you're using whole chickens, cut them up as described on page 17. Separate the drumsticks from the thighs, cut each of the whole breasts in two, and cut the backs into 3 pieces each.

SPREAD the chicken parts and the vegetables in a heavy-bottomed roasting pan just large enough to hold them in a single layer. If the pan is too large, the juices will burn; if it's too small, the chicken won't brown properly. Slide the pan into the oven and turn the oven to 400°F [175°C/gas mark 4]—there's no need for preheating—and bake for 1 to 1½ hours, stirring the vegetables and chicken a couple of times during the baking so that they brown evenly and thoroughly. From time to time, tilt the roasting pan and spoon out and discard excess fat. Don't, however, accidentally discard any still-liquid and uncaramelized juices that may be underneath the rendered fat, which is a perfectly clear liquid.

WHEN the chicken and vegetables are well browned and the bottom of the roasting pan is covered with a golden brown glaze, take the pan out of the oven and place it on top of the stove. If the chicken and vegetables have browned but there's cloudy liquid on the bottom of the pan, put the pan over high heat and stir the chicken pieces (but don't scrape the bottom of the pan) until any liquid—except fat—caramelizes into a glaze at the bottom of the pan. At this point you must be vigilant so that the juices don't burn. Tilt the pan and spoon out any more transparent liquid fat.

POUR 1 quart [1 l] of water (or 1 quart of the optional chicken broth) into the roasting pan, turn the stove on to high, and scrape the bottom of the pan with a wooden spoon until the water comes to a simmer and the glaze dissolves, about 5 minutes. Scrape everything out of the roasting pan into a heavy-bottomed pot. Ideally, the pot should be narrow and tall, so that it will be easier to skim. Add about 3 quarts [3 l] of cold water or broth—enough to cover the chicken by about 1 inch [2.5 cm]—and bring the broth to a simmer, but not a boil, over high heat. Turn down the heat to maintain at a murmur—a bubble rising every second or two—with the pot moved slightly to one side of the burner so the broth bubbles only on one side. This pushes the fat to one side and makes it easier to skim. Simmer for about 1½ hours, adding an additional 2 cups [500 ml] of broth or water to keep the chicken covered. Strain, let cool, and refrigerate. When the broth has jelled, spoon off and discard any congealed fat.

WHITE CHICKEN BROTH

BOUILLON BLANC

DE VOLAILLE

MAKES 3½ QUARTS [3.5 L]

Although I almost always prefer brown broth to white, I don't always want to make the effort a brown broth requires. Also, there are dishes, namely cream of vegetable soups, that brown broth will color a murky . . . well, brown.

In some ways, though, white broth can be trickier than brown broth, because uncooked bones and some meats can produce cloudy broth by releasing specks of insoluble protein that are so fine they're impossible to strain

out. Meat and bones from immature animals, such as calves and baby lambs, release so much of this protein that they must be blanched before they can be used to make broth. Raw chicken bones pose a similar problem; if you use them to make a white broth, the broth will be cloudy. But if you include some raw chicken meat—say a few legs or breasts—or if you use a stewing hen, the meat will clarify the broth by releasing different kinds of proteins, similar to those in egg white. In similar fashion, if you're planning to use white chicken broth to moisten browned chicken for a brown broth, the browned chicken will clarify the broth. If you're using white chicken broth to make a cream soup, it doesn't matter if the broth is cloudy.

2 chickens (3½ pounds [1.75 kg] each) or 1 stewing hen, cut up (page 17); or 6 pounds [2.75 kg] chicken legs, drumsticks, or wings; or carcasses from 3 roast chickens (4 pounds each); or a combination of the above

1 large onion, root end cut off, quartered without peeling

3 medium-size carrots, greens removed, scrubbed but not peeled, halved lengthwise and sliced

1 stalk celery, sliced (optional)

1 handful fennel stalks (optional)

1 small bouquet garni

4 to 5 quarts [4 to 5 l] chicken broth or water

IF you're using leftover chicken carcasses, break them up with a cleaver so that they take up less room in the pot—otherwise you'll need too much water to cover and your broth will be thin. Put the vegetables and bouquet garni in the pot first, so they don't float up and interfere with skimming. Then put in the chicken. Add just enough cold liquid (water or broth) to cover, usually 4 to 5 quarts [4 to 5 l], and place over medium heat. When the liquid comes to a simmer, move the pot slightly to one side of the burner and turn down the heat so it bubbles gently on one side. Simmer for 2 hours, skimming off fat and foam with a ladle every 20 minutes, and strain. Let cool for 1 hour at room temperature and refrigerate. When the broth has jelled, spoon off and discard any congealed fat.

TIPS FOR MAKING BROTH

START WITH COLD WATER OR BROTH. If you pour hot liquid over meat or bones, they quickly release minute specks of protein that are impossible to remove. When meats or bones are started in cold liquid, the proteins are released more slowly and form longer chains and clusters, which are easier to skim off or strain out.

DON'T EVER BOIL BROTH. As meats and bones simmer, they release fats and insoluble proteins that float to the top. If the broth is boiling, these get churned back into the broth, causing it to cloud and take on a muddy, greasy taste. Ideally, broth should just bubble gently on one side of the pot so that fat and froth move to the other side, where they can easily be skimmed off. This gentle bubbling is achieved by moving the pot to one side of the burner.

SKIM CONSTANTLY, ESPECIALLY AT THE BEGINNING. It is theoretically possible to make a perfectly clear broth without skimming at all, but if you don't skim, and the broth comes to a boil for even a few minutes, the froth and fat that floated to the top will get churned in. Professional cooks skim with a ladle, the bowl held almost parallel to the broth's surface, by quickly moving it along the inside wall of the pot, scooping up froth and fat while taking up very little broth. You can remove additional fat by chilling the broth overnight and scooping off the congealed fat.

DON'T ADD TOO MUCH LIQUID. Cooks often put too much liquid in the pot, producing a broth that is weak. Because meat and bones have a tendency to shrink and settle in the pot as they cook, you need to add only enough liquid to barely cover them. As a general rule, 2 to 3 pounds [900 g to 1.3 kg] of meat and/or bones are enough to make 1 quart of flavorful broth. For brown stocks, more meat and/or bones can be used, because they shrink during the preliminary browning.

CUT THE AROMATIC VEGETABLES (ONION, LEEKS, CARROTS, CELERY, FENNEL) INTO APPROPRIATE-SIZE PIECES. If you're making beef-bone broth that takes 7 hours to cook, you can practically use the vegetables whole, since they'll have plenty of time to release their flavor. You don't even need to peel them, just give them a good scrubbing. If, on the other hand, you're making the base for a fish broth, which cooks in 20 minutes, or a quick-cooking braised dish, the vegetables should be cut fine so they release their flavor almost immediately.

THE SIZE OF THE BOUQUET GARNI SHOULD CORRESPOND TO THE AMOUNT OF BROTH YOU'RE MAKING. A few cups of broth may require a bouquet garni only the thickness of your forefinger; a giant pot of beef broth will need much more (see page 219).

EITHER KEEP BROTH HOT OR COOL IT QUICKLY to prevent the growth of bacteria (see page 218).

CHIVE CRÊPES

MAKES ABOUT 8 SMALL CRÊPES

WISK together ½ cup [60 g] of all-purpose flour with 2 large eggs and just enough milk to make a smooth, thick mixture. Stir in 1 tablespoon of finely chopped fresh chives, ½ teaspoon of salt, and enough additional milk so that the batter has the consistency of heavy cream. Brush a crêpe or omelette pan with melted butter and make the crêpes by spreading the pan with a thin layer of the batter, cooking over medium heat until they're browned on one side, and turning them over carefully with your fingers.

CONSOMMÉ WITH SHREDDED CRÊPES

CONSOMMÉ CÉLESTINE

MAKES 10 SERVINGS

To follow a traditional recipe for consommé célestine, you must first make a rich beef broth with a couple of hens added; then clarify the broth with lean ground beef, chopped aromatic vegetables, and egg whites; and then carefully strain the soup and serve it with little strips of crêpes. To reproduce Escoffier's version, you must stuff the crêpes with a chicken forcemeat flavored with truffles—all of this to produce something that, frankly, isn't as good as a well-made concentrated broth. My own version is ridiculously simple, and it would have been heretically frugal to anyone living in the nineteenth century. But I think it is more satisfying. I make a brown chicken broth, carefully strain it through a cloth napkin, skim off any speck of fat, and then serve the soup with little strips of green herb crêpes. But even the bit about the crêpes is pushing it—I rarely make a batch of crêpes just to garnish a consommé. Instead I usually just use whatever I have around—fresh tarragon leaves, the tiniest sprigs of parsley, a julienned leek, a few cubes of tomato. But at this point I can no longer call it a consommé célestine, since to be called that the soup must contain crêpes.

If you really want to go wild, you can make the Brown Chicken Broth described on page 209 using White Chicken Broth, described on page 210, instead of water. But I think you'll find that brown broth made with water, and carefully strained and skimmed, is amazingly good. In the recipe below, I've made the crêpes optional. If you leave them out, serve the consommé plain or make up a garniture.

1 recipe (2½ quarts [2.5 l] Brown Chicken Broth (page 209)

8 Chive Crêpes (above; optional)

salt

2 tablespoons finely chopped fresh chives or parsley (optional)

SKIM every speck of fat off the broth. This is easy if the broth is chilled and jelled, but if it is still hot, keep skimming it with a small ladle.

IF the broth is relatively clear, strain it gently first through a fine mesh strainer. Then thoroughly rinse a large, clean cloth napkin, a piece of muslin sheet, or a kitchen towel to rid it of any traces of soap. (The fabric should be tightly woven so it strains out minute particles but not so thick that it absorbs a lot of broth.) Use the cloth to line the inside of a large strainer, and set the strainer over a pot. Ladle the hot broth into the strainer. As you're straining, you'll notice that the liquid will start to go through the cloth very slowly, because the minute openings in the cloth have become clogged. As this happens, gently pull the cloth to one side, repositioning it over the strainer, so the liquid is now sitting over a new patch of cloth. If the whole cloth becomes completely clogged, use a second cloth.

IF you're adding the Chive Crêpes, roll them up and slice them as thin as possible, into tiny shreds.

SEASON the consommé to taste with salt. Ladle the broth into heated bowls or cups and place a pinch of shredded crêpes into each serving. Garnish with chives or parsley.

CONSOMMÉ MADE CLEAR WITH EGG WHITES AND GROUND MEAT

MAKES 3 QUARTS OF CONSOMMÉ

Nowadays, consommé is usually clarified by combining a mixture of egg whites, aromatic vegetables, herbs, and lean ground meat with the cold broth and then gently heating the mixture until the egg white coagulates completely. If you make your broth following the tips on page 211, clarifying with egg whites and ground meat shouldn't be necessary. There are times, however, when the broth may have boiled, or the meat or bones used to make the broth were insufficiently blanched or roasted, and the broth doesn't come out perfectly clear, even after straining through cloth. If it's a real emergency, you can clarify it with egg whites and eggshells alone, but ideally you should add some very lean meat to the clarification mix-

ture to improve the consommé's flavor. If you're using chopped vegetables and/or meat, the eggshells are optional. They are, however, essential if you're just using egg whites, since the clarification works better when the coagulating proteins have something solid to attach to.

3½ quarts [3.5 l] full-flavored broth, or 1 recipe White Chicken Broth (page 210)

6 egg whites

eggshells from 6 eggs

3 pounds [1.3 kg] very lean meat such as top round of beef, rump steak, or boneless and skinless chicken breasts (optional)

1 medium-size bunch parsley or tarragon, including stems, chopped coarse (optional)

1 medium-size onion, chopped fine (optional)

½ stalk celery, chopped fine (optional)

IF the broth is cold, gently warm it so it melts, but don't let it get hot. If the broth is hot, let it cool. The broth should be warm, not hot, or the egg whites will coagulate prematurely and won't clarify it.

WASH your hands thoroughly so that there are no traces of fat on them to interfere with the action of the egg whites. If you're using the egg whites alone, beat them slightly to break them up and whisk them into the broth. Whisk hard for about 1 minute, to make sure the egg whites are well distributed in the broth. If you're using the optional meat, trim off any traces of fat, cut the meat into 1-inch [2.5-cm] chunks, and grind it to the consistency of hamburger meat in a food processor. (Unless you know and trust your butcher to grind some perfectly lean meat for you, meat that you buy already ground always contains a fair amount of fat, which will end up floating on your consommé and interfere with the clarification.) Work the egg whites, meat, and, if using, vegetables and herbs together with your fingers—the clarification works better if everything is coated with egg white. Then whisk this mixture thoroughly into the broth.

BRING the broth to a simmer over high heat in a heavy-bottomed pot with the pot moved to one side of the burner, so the broth comes to a boil on only one side and bubbles are coming up on one edge of the pot. Turn down the heat to maintain at a steady simmer—again, on one side only. Reposition the pot every 10 minutes so it's simmering up in a different place. The broth should be perfectly clear with just some particles floating in it. Don't stir the pot or you may break up the crust of coagulated protein—sometimes called a "raft"—on top of the pot, but after about 20 minutes gently slide a long wooden spoon against the inside bottom of the pot to dislodge any chunks of meat or other ingredients that may have become attached. Continue simmering the broth for 20 minutes more and check it by breaking through the crust on top with a spoon and looking at the broth underneath. It should be perfectly clear, with only a few flecks of coagulated protein. Continue the simmering and repositioning if it isn't completely clear.

GENTLY cut through the crust with a ladle, and ladle the broth into a fine-mesh strainer set over a pot. When you get near the bottom, just lift the pot of broth and gently pour everything into the strainer, in stages if necessary. Give the mixture about 15 minutes to drip through the strainer and discard what doesn't go through. Don't be tempted to push down on the mixture in the strainer. If your broth still contains specks, strain it again through a strainer lined with a well-rinsed cloth.

BEEF CONSOMMÉ

CONSOMMÉ ORDINAIRE

MAKES 12 SERVINGS

There's nothing ordinary about good beef consommé, but Escoffier called it ordinaire because with few exceptions it was the base for other consommés, which were made by simmering game, mutton, duck, stewing hens, or lobster shells in the beef broth to give it a particular flavor.

To make a classic beef consommé you have first to make a good beef broth and then use it to make a second broth, using more beef. The idea is to develop strategies for using all the cooked meat and keeping the cost under control. One of my favorite tricks is to make Oxtail Soup (page 200) and then, instead of pulling off the oxtail meat and putting it back in the broth, serve the oxtails with a little tomato cream sauce (see page 202) and save the broth. Later in the week—or, if I freeze the broth, maybe months later—I use the soup to make the pot-au-feu described on page 456 or the simplified version given below. You can of course reverse the order by making a pot-au-feu first and using the pot-au-feu broth for making the oxtail soup. You can do this any number of times, making the consommé more and more concentrated as you go. In classic versions of beef consommé, the meat isn't browned, but I like broths, soups, and sauces made with browned meats because they have a deeper flavor and color. Or you can use both methods, browning the meat for the first batch of broth and not the second. Some cooks like to make a broth with bones (see Bone Broth, page 219) and then clarify it with meat. This is a good strategy for saving money, but again you can get away with it only once, meaning that the second (or third and so on) batch of broth shouldn't contain bones (including oxtails) or the consommé will become too gelatinous and feel sticky in the mouth. A gelatinous broth is desirable in a stew, where it lends support to the meat for a satisfying meal, or in a sauce to which butter is added, mollifying the effect somewhat. But a consommé should be flavorful yet feel light in the mouth. Before converting a meat broth into consommé, taste it to see if any particular element seems too strong. For example, if the broth feels sticky in the mouth (or was rubbery when in the refrigerator), don't use bones or oxtails in the second broth; if it tastes too sweet, avoid additional onions or carrots, which contain large amounts of natural sugar; if a particular herb seems to dominate the broth, then leave it out of the bouquet garni on the next go-round. The recipe given below is a simplified version of how consommé was made in the nineteenth century. Whole meat is used, rather than ground, so you can serve it much as you would a pot-au-feu.

1 tied chuck roast suitable for pot roasting (4 to 5 pounds [1.8 to 2.3 kg]), visible fat trimmed off

4 quarts [4 l] broth from Oxtail Soup (page 200) or broth from a pot-au-feu (page 456) or bone broth (page 219)

1 medium-size bouquet garni

2 medium-size carrots, peeled, cut into 1-inch sections

1 medium-size onion, halved through the root end

½ stalk celery

1 medium-size bunch parsley, tarragon, or chervil

PUT the chuck roast in a heavy-bottomed pot just large enough to hold it. If the soup or broth has jelled, warm just enough to melt it, and then pour it over the roast. Add the bouquet garni and bring to a gentle simmer over medium heat. Turn the heat down to maintain at a gentle simmer, and simmer, partially covered, skimming off any fat or froth that floats to the surface. (If the pot is completely covered, the broth may cloud; if uncovered, too much will evaporate.) After simmering the meat for about 2 hours, add the optional carrots, onion, and celery—but don't add them, or don't use all three, if the broth already seems sweet. Simmer until a knife slides effortlessly in and out of the meat, about 1 hour more. Add water or more broth during the simmering, as needed, to keep the meat covered with liquid.

GENTLY take the meat and vegetables out of the broth with a skimmer. Serve the meat as you would a pot-au-feu, with a little mustard, coarse salt, and cornichons. Or use it in one of the recipes designed for using leftover simmered meats (beet salad, page 69; *hachis de boeuf* [beef hash] au gratin, page 446; or miroton, page 445).

COARSELY chop the herbs, toss them into the pot with the liquid, and cover the pot so the perfume of the herbs infuses in the broth. Let cool for 1 or 2 hours at room temperature, then strain through a fine-mesh strainer and, if necessary, through a cloth towel (see page 213). Refrigerate, covered, for up to 5 days. When serving, adjust the seasoning with salt. Don't use pepper because you'll see the flecks. Or if you insist on the flavor of pepper, cracked pepper can be wrapped in a little cloth and infused in the hot broth for 5 minutes before serving.

FLAVORED CONSOMMÉS

After wading through Escoffier's scores of more predictable consommé derivatives, we arrive at an interesting section devoted to consommés that are served in cups for late-night suppers. They are served either cold or hot, depending on the season, and because of this, they contain no garniture. To paraphrase Escoffier, "they must be perfect onto themselves." These understated recipes appeal to modern tastes because their emphasis is entirely on flavor. Here we encounter quail consommé, made by roasting quails, removing their breasts for another dish, and simmering the rest in the broth with other ingredients as part of the clarification process. Other variations include celery, tarragon, morel, pimento, and truffle, each made by infusing the ingredient in question in hot broth during the clarification process, and then straining. Various wines are used, usually sweet full-flavored wines such as Madeira, marsala, or muscat, but these wines must be added before the consommé is clarified because their acidity causes soluble proteins in the consommé to become insoluble and cloud the consommé.

So once you've made a basic consommé, you have some choices. You can serve it as it is, or flavor it and leave the flavoring ingredients in, or flavor it and strain them out. Flavoring possibilities are infinite, but you need to use ingredients according to how they behave. Because ingredients such as fresh herbs, wild mushrooms, and truffles have a fleeting aroma, add them to the finished consommé while it is still hot, cover the consommé, and let cool. I sometimes pour the hot consommé into a mason jar, add the aromatic ingredients, and immediately seal the lid. After about 1 hour, I put the jar in the refrigerator. If you're straining out the aromatic ingredients, just let the consommé cool to room temperature—any colder and it will set—before straining. If you're adding ingredients that you want to keep suspended in cold consommé, turn the mason jar upside down, then right side up, every few minutes as the consommé sets.

A crustacean-flavored consommé, such as lobster, crayfish, or shrimp consommé, should still be made with meat to give support and background to the flavors of the seafood and to provide natural gelatin. The best approach is to cook the seafood in a small amount of broth, take the flesh out of the shells, break up the shells with a rolling pin (as though making *lobster à l'américaine;* see page 333), and then combine the shells and the broth used for cooking the shellfish with egg whites, herbs, and aromatic vegetables and use this mixture to clarify the meat broth. The flesh from the crustaceans can be used for another dish, or be used as a garnish for the finished consommé. You can use a similar method for flavoring consommés with duck, or game birds such as pigeon or partridge. Cut off the breasts to use in another dish and brown the carcasses and legs with a little onion and carrot. Combine this mixture with the meat broth, before it is clarified, and simmer for about 30 minutes. Don't simmer for too long or the flavor of the birds will merge with the broth and the broth will lose its identity. Aromatic vegetables, such as celery, should be chopped, simmered in the clear broth for 15 minutes, and then strained out.

TOMATO CONSOMMÉ

CONSOMMÉ DE TOMATES

MAKES 6 FIRST-COURSE SERVINGS

A classic tomato consommé is made by simmering chopped tomatoes in beef consommé and then very gently straining the mixture through a piece of muslin, a clean kitchen towel, or a napkin. But in the last 10 years I've encountered delicious meatless consommés in restaurants in the United States and France. I don't know who first came up with the idea, but a tomato consommé made this way is surprisingly savory and takes relatively little time to prepare. Many of the flavorings and garnishes used for classic meat consommés can be used for this meatless tomato consommé. This version is a little bit spicy because it contains chiles. If you don't like their heat, leave them out. Or if you want flavors that are more authentically French, substitute 1 large bunch of fresh tarragon, coarsely chopped, for the chiles.

6 pounds [2.7 kg] medium-size, very ripe in-season tomatoes, cored and chopped coarse

1 medium onion, chopped fine

1 bunch parsley, stems and leaves chopped coarse

1 poblano chile, charred and peeled (see "Peeling and Seeding Bell Peppers," page 20), chopped coarse, or 1 large bunch fresh tarragon, including stems, chopped coarse

3 large eggs with shells

   salt

WORKING in batches, combine the tomatoes—seeds, peels, and all—in a blender with the onion, parsley, and chile or tarragon. Purée for about 1 minute. Separate the eggs, save the yolks for something else or discard them, and work the egg whites and the eggshells into the tomatoes by crushing everything together with your fingers in a medium-size, heavy-bottomed pot.

PUT the pot over medium heat, repositioning it every 5 minutes so the mixture heats through evenly. When the mixture comes to a simmer, turn the heat down to maintain a gentle simmer. Every 10 minutes, gently run a long wooden spoon along the inside bottom of the pot to detach any egg white that could scorch. Simmer for 30 minutes total.

USE a ladle to gently transfer the mixture to a fine-mesh strainer set over a clean pot. Unless you have a very large fine-mesh strainer, the straining will have to be done in batches. When liquid from one batch stops dripping out of the strainer, discard the contents of the strainer and fill it again. Don't be tempted to push down on the mixture or you'll cloud the consommé.

Variations: Serve tomato consommé hot or cold, and garnished however you like. I prefer very simple garnitures such as tarragon, chervil, or parsley leaves, tiny cubes of tomatoes, baby peas, cubes of thin-sliced string beans (haricots verts), fava beans, and small whole wild mushrooms such as morels or chanterelles. You can also serve the tomato consommé as a kind of sauce, with or without a garniture, around grilled fish fillets in wide soup plates.

COLD CONSOMMÉ

It's a pity that most of us are put off by cold consommé since the most delicate flavors, which would quickly evaporate if the consommé were served hot, are held in delicate suspension when it is served cold. A successful cold consommé must have just the right amount of gelatin so that it's neither too stiff nor too runny when you take it out of the refrigerator. It should slowly begin to liquify so that when you serve it, it barely holds together. If cold consommé contains too much gelatin it will be rubbery and unpleasant. If it doesn't contain enough gelatin, it will be completely liquid, which is a less serious problem. In fact, some people prefer it this way—but I enjoy the sensation of the trembling consommé dissolving in my mouth. To give your consommé the right consistency, use broth that's been made entirely with meat and clarify it with meat only. (You can also use Oxtail Soup, page 200.) Unlike bones, meat contains relatively little gelatin, so a broth made only with meat won't be too rubbery.

Cold consommé lends itself to sauces and luxurious ingredients that would cloud hot consommé. The Creamy Tomato Sauce for Cold Oxtail Soup, page 202, is one example, but you can get as sophisticated as you like and top the consommé with dollops of caviar, lobster cubes in a well-creamed *sauce à l'américaine* (see chapter 25), crayfish tails lightly bound in a cold cream sauce made from the shells, or a few paper-thin white truffles slices. I serve cold consommé in little bowls with high sides, in double espresso cups, or in tall wineglasses.

BEEF AND VEAL BONE BROTHS

Meat broths made with enormous amounts of meat, in the fashion of the nineteenth century and earlier, are so expensive that even the best restaurants use broth made from bones as the base for most of their brown sauces and some of their soups. Classic consommé must always be made with at least some meat, but the first broth—the one used to simmer the meat—can be made with bones.

Veal or beef bone broth is also used to make *glace de viande,* the base for most modern French brown sauces. Veal and beef bones, when simmered, release gelatin and a certain amount of meaty flavor, and they're inexpensive. Their main disadvantage is that they take 8 to 12 hours to release most of their flavor and gelatin. In a home kitchen on a hot day you'll probably want to do something other than stand around skimming broth. So save the project for cold winter weekends.

Traditionally, veal bones are used for white broth and beef bones for brown, but in fact there's very little difference between the two. Buy knucklebones, which can be recognized by the white and shiny joint; they will contribute gelatin to the broth. Don't buy marrowbones, which are cylindrical, with the marrow visible on the ends; they contain very little gelatin. The bones must be either blanched, for white broth, or browned in the oven, for brown broth. If you don't blanch or roast the bones before you use them to make broth, your broth will be gray and cloudy.

STORING BROTH

WHEN STORING BROTH, keep in mind that bacteria don't like hot or cold—they like warm things, like us. You can keep a pot of broth on the stove for years—the farmhouse pot-au-feu might be kept simmering for months at a time. But once the broth's temperature drops, you need to chill it fast. If you're making a few quarts of broth, chilling is rarely a problem. Just let the broth cool at room temperature for about an hour before putting it in the refrigerator. (Never put hot foods directly in the fridge or they'll warm everything else up and overwork the motor.) Once chilled, meat broth will keep for at least 5 days. If you want to refrigerate it longer, bring it back to a boil to kill any bacteria that may be thinking about taking up residence, let it cool as before, and you can keep it for another 5 days. You can do this indefinitely. Chilling large amounts of broth, which is something you may never have to do at home, requires a little more care because the broth takes longer to cool and spends more time being warm and hospitable to bacteria. If you've got a big pot of broth, let it cool for about an hour at room temperature and then set it in a bowl of ice to chill it quickly before sliding it into the refrigerator. If the pot is too big to fit in a bowl, fill a smaller pot with ice—make sure the outside of the pot is perfectly clean—and float it around inside the pot of broth. Do this until the broth is cool, then slide the pot of broth into the refrigerator.

BROTH CAN ALSO BE FROZEN FOR MONTHS OR EVEN LONGER. I rarely freeze broth because I don't have a stand-alone freezer and my small refrigerator freezer is filled with ice cubes for drinks and ice buckets. The standard advice for home cooks is to freeze broth in ice cube trays and then store the cubes in plastic storage bags, the idea being that you can use as little as you like without having to thaw a big container. This has never made any sense to me because most of us never need less than a quart or two [1 or 2 l] of broth at a time. (If you do have a large freezer, just freeze broth in 1-quart [1 l] plastic containers.) Freezing concentrated broth, however, makes a lot of sense since it takes up so little room.

WHEN I HAVE BROTH AROUND, I make soup later in the week. Or I simmer the broth down to a concentrated sauce base to make it much more compact and easy to refrigerate or freeze. I then use it as is to make sauces, or I add water to reconstitute it into broth for making soups. (For more information about concentrated sauce bases and *glace de viande,* see page 221.)

BONE BROTH

MAKES 5 QUARTS [5 L]

Since bone broth takes so long to cook, I recommend making a relatively large amount, using what you need in the next few days for soups, and then reducing the rest into *glace de viande* (see page 221), which takes up a lot less room and is great to have on hand for making sauces. I have a heavy-bottomed 40-quart [40 l] aluminum stockpot, which is the largest pot that will fit on my home-style kitchen stove without bumping into the exhaust hood. The recipe below requires a 20-quart [20 l] stockpot or larger, but adjust it according to what you have. Be careful of what you pay for the bones. If you can't find them really cheap, consider substituting oxtail, which is inexpensive, will provide meat you can eat, and is a lot more flavorful.

15   pounds [6.8 kg] veal or beef knucklebones, or oxtails

2   large onions, rinsed, root end removed, not peeled, halved through the root end

2   large carrots, greens removed, cut into 2-inch [5-cm] sections

1   head garlic, halved crosswise

1   stalk celery (optional; see page 220)

1   large bouquet garni

WHITE BONE BROTH: Put the bones in a stockpot with enough cold water to cover. (You may have to use two pots.) Bring to a boil over high heat and boil for 5 minutes. Drain in a large colander, rinse thoroughly with cold water, and thoroughly clean out the pot. Put the onions, carrots, garlic, and celery and the bouquet garni in the pot—they go in first so they don't float to the surface and interfere with skimming. Then put in the bones. Add enough cold water to cover by about 1 inch. Bring to a simmer over high heat. Turn down the heat to maintain the broth at a gentle simmer. Skim off fat and froth every 30 minutes or so. Simmer for 12 hours, adding cold water from time to time to keep the bones covered. Strain. Let cool, for 1 hour at room temperature and then in the refrigerator. Lift off any remaining fat with a spoon. Refrigerate or freeze until needed.

BROWN BONE BROTH: Put the vegetables in one or two heavy-bottomed roasting pans and put the bones on top to keep the vegetables from burning. Bake until the bones are well browned, about 1 hour at 500° [260°C/gas mark 10]. Ideally, the bones should be in a single layer. If your roasting pan isn't big enough, rotate the bones, moving those on the bottom to the top, so that all the bones brown. This may take 1 to 2 hours, depending on your oven. When the bones and vegetables are well browned, use tongs to transfer the vegetables to a heavy-bottomed stockpot. (You may have to use two pots.) Add the bouquet garni and then the bones. If there are caramelized meat juices in the roasting pan, put it on the stove over high heat with about 1 quart of water. Scrape up the caramelized juices with a wooden spoon for about 5 minutes and pour the liquid over the bones in the stockpot. Add enough cold water to cover the bones by about 1 inch. Bring to a simmer over high heat. Turn down the heat to maintain the broth at a gentle simmer. Skim off fat and froth every 30 minutes or so. Simmer until any cartilage that was adhering to the bones is falling away, about 12 hours, adding cold water from time to time to keep the bones covered. Strain and let cool for 1 hour at room temperature. Lift off any remaining fat. Refrigerate or freeze until needed.

USING CELERY

I'm always annoyed by recipes for broths, sauces, and stews that call for a stalk of celery. Who wants to go out and buy a whole bunch of celery, use a tiny bit, and then let the rest of the bunch go limp in the fridge drawer? First, celery is rarely essential in anything, except maybe celery soup, so it's no big deal if you leave it out. Second, you can freeze it. Celery that's been frozen will look limp and depressed—don't try to use it to make a crisp little salad—but its flavor will be intact, so you can use it for cooking. When you get the bunch, separate the stalks, wrap them tightly in a plastic bag, and freeze them. Take them out one at a time, as you need them.

REDUCING BROTH FOR SAUCES

Broth is used as a base for soups or sauces and to give body to stews or braised dishes such as pot roast. For soups, a simple broth usually has enough body and flavor to do the trick. For consommés, double broths are sometimes used to make the consommé more flavorful and nutritious. It's only in sauce making that we encounter broths that are cooked down into syrupy glazes and concentrates.

Until relatively recently, meat sauces were thickened with flour, which was usually cooked in butter to form a roux before broth was added. Typically, these sauces—called *veloutés* when made with white broth, *espagnole* when made with brown—were then carefully reduced to rid them of fat and any starchy taste from the flour, and to concentrate their flavor. This system worked fine when broths were made with large quantities of meat and were intensely flavorful to begin with. But meat has become too expensive, and our social system is no longer designed in such a way that the boiled meat can be given to the servants while the broth is used in the sauces. Nowadays the basic broths, or stocks, used for making the classic sauces are made almost entirely with bones. But a bone broth thickened with flour has very little to offer.

In France in the 1960s, chefs started eliminating flour from their sauces and began making meat sauces by reducing the basic broths into concentrated glazes. Classic sauces based on the flour-thickened *sauce espagnole* were replaced with *glace de viande* (meat glaze) made from beef and/or veal bones—finished with butter, and sauces based on *sauce velouté* were replaced with concentrated white stocks finished with cream. This system resulted in one of the most important changes of *la nouvelle cuisine:* Sauces became lighter textured and more intensely flavored.

For home cooks, an advantage to the new system is that these concentrated broths are easier to store and take up far less space than the equivalent amount of broth. When highly concentrated—reduced to a glaze—broth takes on a thick syrupy consistency and when refrigerated has the texture of hard rubber. This makes it convenient for making quick pan-deglazed sauces (see page 480), for which you need only about ½ tablespoon per serving, and for reinforcing the flavor of stews and braised dishes. You can also use it as a concentrate—about 4 tablespoons per cup to make instant broth.

Concentrating a large amount of broth into a small amount of *glace de viande* makes a lot more sense than filling your freezer with bags of broth cubes.

MEAT GLAZE

GLACE DE VIANDE

MAKES ABOUT 3 CUPS [750 ML]

In restaurants, meat glaze is usually made with brown beef or veal bone broth, but you can also make it with good chicken broth. Meat glaze is 10 to 15 times as concentrated as broth. Making meat glaze requires very little work, but it takes all day. I save the project for a cold, gray winter day.

1   recipe (5 quarts [5 l]) Brown Bone Broth (page 219) made from beef or veal bones

BRING the broth to a gentle simmer in a wide pot. (The wider the pot, the more quickly the broth will reduce.) Move the pot to one side of the flame so that the broth simmers on one side only and scum and fat are pushed to the other side. Skim off fat and scum about every 20 minutes with a small ladle or large flat kitchen spoon. When the broth has reduced to about one-third its original volume, after 4 to 6 hours, strain it through a fine-mesh strainer into a smaller pot. Continue simmering in the smaller pot until the broth, which will now be syrupy, cooks down again to about one-half its volume when you strained it into the smaller pot. Strain the meat glaze into small plastic containers or mason jars. (I use French-style jars with hinged clamp-on lids.)

MEAT glaze keeps in the refrigerator for at least a month and in the freezer for years. One convenient trick is to pour it into ice cube trays, let it set in the refrigerator, and then loosen the cubes by working around their sides with a knife. You can then freeze the cubes in batches in plastic bags or storage containers and use a cube at a time without having to thaw out the whole batch.

BUYING A BIG STOCKPOT

If you're not careful, you can end up paying a lot more than you should for a good stockpot. I bought my own stockpot, which is heavy nonanodized aluminum and was very inexpensive, at a restaurant supply store. Many people are nervous about cooking with aluminum because of reports, years ago, that aluminum may be a factor in Alzheimer's disease. I don't know about Alzheimer's, but aluminum does in fact turn certain foods, such as artichokes and egg yolks, dark, and interacts with relatively acidic foods such as tomatoes. However, it seems to be fine for simmering broth. Because of its price, aluminum is almost universal in professional kitchens. Good-quality stainless steel pots cost about 5 times the price of nonanodized aluminum ones. Dark anodized aluminum pots cost about as much as good stainless steel, and heavy copper stockpots, about 20 times as much (which might be worth it because they look so great). If you're making a small amount of broth, an enameled iron pot will also do the trick.

FRENCH COUNTRY VEGETABLE SOUP WITH BASIL AND GARLIC PASTE

SOUPE AU PISTOU

HOW TO	HOW TO
TURN A GOOD VEGETABLE SOUP INTO A FABULOUS ONE	IMPROVISE VEGETABLE SOUPS ACCORDING TO WHIM AND SEASON

PERHAPS IT'S HUMAN NATURE, BUT I HAVE FAR CRISPER MEMORIES OF cooking failures than I do of triumphs. The time my omelets for six all stuck to the pan, the raw roast beef, and the curdled hollandaise all come rushing to mind every time I get near a stove to try something adventurous. It's with a similar wave of angst and embarrassment that I remember my first vegetable soup, boiled up for a group of friends in my one-room Mont-Martre flat—the one with the radiator that never got hot and the horsehair blanket with "1939" embroidered on one corner. In my own defense, the soup's failure was partly due to poverty, but with a little of an old-fashioned French housewife's cunning frugality I might have been able to pull it off. Had I known how to make a *soupe au pistou,* one of the glories of Provençal cooking, my soup would surely have been a long-forgotten triumph.

In *soupe au pistou,* as in other mixed-vegetable soups, the vegetables are simmered until done in water or broth and are added in stages appropriate to their cooking times. What turns a vegetable soup into a *soupe au pistou* is *pistou*—a paste of garlic, Parmigiano-Reggiano cheese, and basil either swirled into the soup immediately before serving or passed at the table for guests to help themselves. The basil and garlic release their pungent perfumes and the cheese gives the soup a nutty richness right under the diner's nose.

To make a successful *soupe au pistou,* you must first make a vegetable soup, to which you then add some noodles, at least if you're concerned about authenticity. Most of us almost reflexively use broth when making soup, but a *soupe au pistou* is more often than not made without it, forcing us to derive its flavor and aroma from vegetables alone. This is one of the soup's advantages, since most of us find making broth a nuisance and canned broth rarely worth bothering with. But even if you're stuck with supermarket vegetables and the soup itself ends up a little insipid, the *pistou* will enliven it into something heady and satisfying.

The *pistou,* the Provençal relative of neighboring Liguria's pesto, is a cause of much bickering, mostly about whether the *pistou* can be made in a blender or food processor or must be made by hand with a mortar and pestle. True, it is better if you make it in a mortar, but how many of us have mortars large enough to make the process anything other than agonizing? The mortars and pestles sold at cooking supply stores work fine for crushing a pinch or two of herbs, but making a cup or two of *pistou* would take most of a day. So I must be honest and admit that I make *pistou* and pesto in a blender. It takes about a minute.

But now to the soup itself. The vegetables will vary according to the cooks you talk with, the cookbooks you read, and the time of year. Winter or summer squash are almost always available, as are fresh beans, either shell beans or string beans and sometimes both. Tomatoes are commonly but not universally used. They are often added to the *pistou,* but because they turn it a rather dull hue, I prefer to add them directly to the soup. Potatoes, zucchini, the root vegetables turnips, carrots, and celeriac, and onions or leeks are also commonly used. Some recipes call for sweating the root vegetables in olive oil before adding liquid, but usually the vegetables are combined all at once in a pot with water and simmered until done. More careful recipes use a bit more common sense and call for adding the vegetables in stages according to their cooking times. My own versions are almost entirely seasonal and depend more on what I stumble into at the farmers' market or supermarket than on any preconceived idea. My summer *soupe au pistou* invariably contains zucchini or summer squash, tomatoes, fresh cranberry or lima beans (if I can find them), and string beans. Winter versions contain winter squash (common in many traditional versions), potatoes, and turnips. Every version, regardless of season, contains leeks or onions and carrots. In traditional recipes, thick vermicelli noodles, called *méjanels,* are simmered in the soup just long enough to cook through. Most modern recipes call for vermicelli, but I use little macaroni instead.

I make *soupe au pistou* for a crowd because it's hard to make a small batch, since there's such a large variety of vegetables. Combined with bread, sprinkled with olive oil and cheese, and baked, leftover *soupe au pistou* becomes a gratin or panade (see page 190). Served at room temperature, it's similar to the Tuscan *ribollita.* I often serve *soupe au pistou* as a main course, especially in the summer, but it also makes a good first course. The *pistou* can be made earlier in the day or while the soup is cooking.

BASIL AND GARLIC PASTE
PISTOU

Though *pistou* is used mainly to convert vegetable soup into *soupe au pistou,* it's also delicious when dolloped, as a sauce, over grilled seafood, chicken, or vegetables.

MAKES ABOUT 3 CUPS

½ teaspoon salt (coarse if you're using a mortar and pestle, fine or coarse if you're using a blender)

4 cloves garlic, chopped

3 tightly packed cups fresh basil leaves (leaves from 2 large bunches)

¾ cup [175 ml] "pure" olive oil (or extra-virgin olive oil if you're using a mortar and pestle)

1 cup [250 ml] extra-virgin olive oil

3 cups [300 g] finely grated Parmigiano-Reggiano or *grana padana*

THE recipe calls for both "pure" olive oil and extra-virgin olive oil because, if you're using a blender to work the oil, garlic, and basil into a paste, extra-virgin olive oil may turn bitter. Because of this, the "pure" olive oil is puréed with the other ingredients in the blender, and the extra-virgin olive oil is added at the end by hand.

IF you have a large mortar and pestle, use all extra-virgin olive oil. Combine the coarse salt and the garlic and work it into a smooth paste. Add a handful of basil leaves at a time—enough to half-fill the mortar—and continue working until the mixture is smooth. Add a couple of tablespoons of olive oil. Continue in this way until you've used all the oil and basil. Work in the cheese.

IF you're using a blender, crush the chopped garlic with the side of a chef's knife to obtain a smooth paste. Combine the garlic and basil in the blender with the "pure" olive oil and purée until smooth. If the mixture is too stiff or won't turn around in the blender, push a wooden spoon handle down through the hole in the top, being careful not to touch the blade, to get the mixture to move around. When the mixture is smooth, work in the extra-virgin olive oil and the cheese by hand. Transfer the *pistou* to an attractive bowl you can pass at the table.

COOKING WITH WINTER SQUASH

When dishes, like *soupe au pistou,* call for sliced or diced raw squash, you're confronted with peeling and cutting up the squash. This isn't a problem if you're dealing with smaller squash with smooth skin, but larger squash are difficult to slice, and some squash, such as acorn squash, are impossible to peel because you can't get into the nooks and crannies with the peeler. One solution is to cut the squash in half and scoop out the seeds, or even leave it whole, and bake it until the flesh is soft—so that a knife slides easily in and out—and you can just spoon it out of the peel. You can also cook squash in the microwave—if you're cooking it whole, poke it in a few places with a knife so it doesn't explode. Turn the squash over and around in the microwave every few minutes so it cooks evenly. Cooked squash should be added to dishes near the end of cooking instead of at the beginning.

FRENCH COUNTRY VEGETABLE SOUP WITH BASIL AND GARLIC PASTE

SOUPE AU PISTOU

MAKES 8 MAIN-COURSE OR 12 FIRST-COURSE
SERVINGS (ABOUT 18 CUPS [4 L] OF SOUP)

1½ pounds [675 g] winter squash, such as acorn, buttercup, or butternut; or 1½ pounds [675 g] zucchini or summer squash

3 medium-size leeks with all but 2 inches [5 cm] of the greens cut off, or 1 large onion

3 tablespoons olive oil

4 cloves garlic, chopped

3 medium-size carrots, sliced into small triangles (en paysanne, see page 22)

1½ pounds [675 g] fresh cranberry beans, shucked (about 2½ cups [285 g] after shucking), or 3 cups [545 g] cooked dried beans (see page 468), or 1 pound [450 g] red or white waxy potatoes, peeled and cut into ½-inch [1.5-cm] cubes, kept under cold water until needed

3 pounds [1.3 kg] fresh tomatoes, peeled, seeded, and chopped, or 2 cans (28 ounces [793 g] each) whole tomatoes, drained, seeded, and chopped

1 pound [450 g] string beans, preferably haricots verts, ends removed, beans cut into ½-inch [.5-cm] lengths

1 cup [100 g] dry small macaroni

salt

pepper

1 recipe pistou (Basil and Garlic Paste, page 224)

IF you're using winter squash, peel and seed it, cut it into ½-inch [1.5 cm] dice (or cook it as described in "Cooking with Winter Squash," page 225, spoon out the seeds, and coarsely chop the flesh). If you're using summer squash, don't peel it, just cut it into ½-inch dice or slice it *en paysanne* (see page 22). If you're using leeks, wash and trim them and slice them thin. If you're using onion, chop it fine.

HEAT the olive oil in a 6-quart [6 l] or larger heavy-bottomed pot and stir in the leeks or onion, the garlic, the carrots, and the raw winter or summer squash. (If you've cooked the winter squash, don't add it yet.) Stir the mixture, over medium-to-high heat, until the leeks or onions turn translucent and any moisture released by the vegetables evaporates, about 15 minutes. Pour in 3 quarts [3 l] of water and bring to a simmer. Stir in the fresh cranberry beans or potatoes (don't add cooked beans yet) and the tomatoes and simmer the soup until the beans or potatoes soften, about 15 minutes. Stir in the string beans and the macaroni and simmer until they are both soft, about 10 minutes. If you're using cooked squash and/or cooked dried beans, add them and bring the soup to a simmer. Season to taste with salt. Ladle the soup into heated wide bowls, grind fresh pepper over each bowl, pass the *pistou* and plenty of bread at the table.

OTHER FRENCH MIXED VEGETABLE SOUPS

Some soups are designed to highlight a particular vegetable (see Chapter 13), while others contain assortments of vegetables and sometimes meats. Mixed vegetable soups can range in style from robust affairs containing at least as much meat as vegetable, typical of traditional farmhouse cooking, to delicate consommés (see Chapter 16) of sparkling clear broth with a few angel-hair strands of vegetable, served in china cups. Generous *soupes,* like *potées,* pot-au-feu, and *garbure,* are almost always served as main courses, while delicate *potages* are served at the beginning of a meal and set the tone, establishing a greater or lesser degree of formality, and alluding to things to come. Grimod de La

Reynière, in the early part of the nineteenth century, compared a *potage* to the overture of an opera, an entrance and a preview.

You can determine the formality of your soup and signal the formality of the upcoming meal by cutting the vegetables into more or less regular shapes. At a formal meal you'll want to cut the vegetables into perfectly even dice or julienne and make the pieces quite small. As the soup becomes less formal, the vegetables can be sliced instead of diced, and left in larger pieces. If you're using broth, its clarity will also reflect the soup's formality. A broth should always be clear, but a very clear broth, carefully skimmed of most if not all fat, will seem more formal than a broth with a few tiny droplets of fat left floating on it. Most formal of all is consommé, clarified with meat and egg whites (see page 213) and skimmed of every trace of fat. The vegetables you choose to include in your soup will also tell of your frugality (which is fine, frugal things are often best) or your extravagance: cabbage and turnips—frugality; truffles, wild mushrooms, foie gras—extravagance.

Regardless of your soup's style, there are almost universally applicable tricks for enhancing its flavor. Vegetable soups are almost always improved by good broth, but in a fresh summery soup, like *soupe au pistou,* broth can overpower and detract from the flavor and aroma of the vegetables. The simplest mixed vegetable soups are made by just simmering vegetables in liquid, the vegetables added at different times, depending on how long they take to cook. The flavor of root vegetables, especially onions and leeks, can be accentuated by a preliminary gentle cooking in fat—sweating—until they turn translucent and release their aroma. Depending on the soup, these vegetables, as well as garlic and other root vegetables such as carrots and turnips, can be cooked until they caramelize so they contribute a rich concentrated flavor and a deep color to the soup. (This is the principle behind French Onion Soup, page 189.)

Even though a vegetable soup should contain mostly vegetables, various meats may be used to lend support and to provide a savory backdrop. The most obvious way to use meat is to cook the vegetables in meat broth, which can be white or brown and more or less concentrated. Another simple way to use meat is to add a meaty bone to the soup at the beginning so that essentially you're making a broth at the same time you're cooking the soup. In Provence, a lamb bone is sometimes simmered in a *soupe au pistou*. One of the best and most convenient ways to extract the flavor of meat into a soup is to cut the meat into cubes and sweat it with root vegetables, allowing everything to caramelize lightly, before adding liquid. Almost any meat used in this way will enhance the flavor of the soup, but pork, in various forms—fresh, cured, or smoked—works best. Confit of duck or goose, shredded and cooked with the vegetables, adds a distinct and incomparable flavor.

If a soup is being served at the beginning of a rich meal, the proportion of liquid to solid ingredients should be higher, since you don't want to fill people up too soon. If, on the other hand, the soup *is* the meal, it should be made up mostly of solid ingredients, ideally ladled over a thick slice of stale or toasted (and maybe garlic-rubbed) bread. If you're setting out to make a soup that's going to suffice for dinner, you may want to add starchy ingredients—for example, rice, about 15 minutes before the soup is done, or dried pasta, about 10 minutes before. Croutons, cooked in a sauté pan with a little olive oil, butter, or duck fat and passed at the table, make a crunchy alternative to the slice of bread in the bowl.

Vegetable soups can also be enriched, to give them more body, make them more filling, or enhance their texture. Adding even a small amount of heavy cream shortly before serving helps unify a soup's flavors into a suave and sapid whole. Butter can also be whisked into the soup just before serving, or dolloped, at the discretion of the diner, into each bowl. To thicken a vegetable soup and give it a velvety texture without using extra fats, a certain amount of the soup can be puréed. The easiest way to do this is to stick an immersion blender in the soup and move it around until the soup has the consistency you like. You can also purée a portion of the soup in a regular blender and stir the purée back into the rest of the soup. If you prefer a perfectly smooth purée soup,

purée the entire soup with a food mill or blender and then strain it again through a fine-mesh strainer. Starchy ingredients such as cooked beans, potatoes, and rice can also be cooked separately, puréed, and whisked into the soup to give it body.

The great genius of a *soupe au pistou* is, as I said earlier, the *pistou* itself, stirred in at the table so none of its pungent aroma and flavor is cooked off, the burst of fresh garlic and basil giving the soup a vital freshness that would otherwise have been impossible. This principle—adding a fresh and flavorful ingredient just before serving—is useful to remember when making any vegetable soup. In some soups, especially summer soups with tomatoes, a couple of finely chopped and crushed garlic cloves stirred in 30 seconds before serving will work miracles. Fresh herbs, chopped fine so that they release their flavor quickly, will lend just the right note to an otherwise flat-tasting soup, tying the flavors together and giving the soup an identity. Tarragon is marvelous if you've used chicken broth, or included strips or cubes of chicken in the soup. Fresh marjoram is great with anything containing garlic, and is perfect if you've included a lamb bone in your soup or used a lamb broth. (I sometimes make a *pistou*-like paste with a tablespoon of fresh marjoram and a couple of cloves of garlic.) Fines herbes—chervil, chives, parsley, and tarragon, either all together or in different combinations—give a delicate finesse to vegetable soups, especially those containing a large proportion of green vegetables.

POSSIBLE INGREDIENTS FOR IMPROVISED VEGETABLE SOUPS

ROOT VEGETABLES (usually added first, either directly to liquid or first sweated in fat)

CARROTS, sliced in rounds, *en paysanne* (see page 22), diced, or julienned

GARLIC, crushed whole cloves, or chopped or sliced

LEEKS, usually sliced, occasionally julienned

ONIONS, chopped fine or sliced thin

TURNIPS, diced, chopped, or julienned

COOKING FATS (used at the beginning if root vegetables are being sweated)

OLIVE OIL

BUTTER

LARD

RENDERED BACON FAT

GOOSE OR DUCK FAT

MEATS (diced and caramelized with root vegetables at the beginning, simmered along with the soup, or added near the end)

PRESERVED PORK SUCH AS BACON, PANCETTA, OR PROSCIUTTO (see page 9), diced and sweated at the beginning or left in a chunk and simmered with the soup; HAM HOCKS, SMOKED OR UNSMOKED, simmered whole in the soup

MEATY BONES, SUCH AS LAMB, HAM, OR FRESH PORK BONES, simmered in the soup and removed before serving

CONFIT OF DUCK OR GOOSE, shredded and sweated along with the vegetables at the beginning or shredded and simmered in the soup shortly before serving

COOKED OR RAW TENDER MEATS SUCH AS CHICKEN, BEEF, OR LAMB, cut into cubes and simmered in the soup just before serving

LIQUIDS (used for simmering the vegetables)

WATER

BROTH, CHICKEN, BEEF, VEAL, OR LAMB; either white or brown (see pages 209 to 211)

MILK, used only if the soup is being completely or partially puréed (otherwise it will curdle)

STARCHY INGREDIENTS (added at various stages, depending on their cooking times)

BEANS, FRESH, added 10 to 20 minutes before soup is ready (fava beans cook faster, in about 2 minutes); or cooked dried, heated in soup just before serving

POTATOES, diced or sliced, simmered for about 20 minutes in the soup

RICE, rinsed and then simmered in the soup about 15 minutes (short-grain rice gives a creamy consistency to the soup, while long-grain does not)

PASTA, PENNE OR ORZO, simmered in the soup about 10 minutes (for dried pasta)

BREAD, TOASTED, PERHAPS RUBBED WITH GARLIC, placed in each bowl before ladling in the soup; or cut into cubes (croutons), lightly browned in olive oil or butter, and sprinkled over each serving or passed at the table.

GREEN VEGETABLES (usually added near the end)

ASPARAGUS, peeled, stalks diced, stalks and tips simmered in soup for 5 minutes

BROCCOLI, cut into small florets, simmered in soup about 5 minutes

CABBAGE, GREEN OR RED, shredded or cut into wedges, simmered for 20 minutes to 3 hours (you may want to cook it separately—as in the pot-au-feu recipe on page 456—so it doesn't take over the flavor of the soup)

STRING BEANS, ends broken off, beans diced or cut into sections of varying length, cooked 5 to 10 minutes, depending on size

KALE, trimmed, cut into pieces, simmered in soup 20 to 30 minutes

LEAFY VEGETABLES SUCH AS BEET GREENS, SORREL, SPINACH, SWISS CHARD, shredded, simmered in soup, 1 minute for sorrel, 2 minutes for spinach, 10 minutes for beet greens and Swiss chard

PEAS, FRESH, simmered in soup 2 to 4 minutes, depending on size; frozen, thawed, heated through in the soup just before serving

ARTICHOKES, not recommended since they are subtle; better in their own artichoke soup (see chapter 13)

WINTER SQUASH, precooked (see page 225), reheated in chunks just before serving; or raw, diced and simmered in the soup for 30 minutes

ZUCCHINI AND SUMMER SQUASH, sliced in rounds, en paysanne, or diced, simmered in the soup for 5 minutes; may be sautéed to accent the flavor before adding to soup

ENRICHENERS AND THICKENERS

HEAVY CREAM, added near end

BUTTER, PLAIN OR HERB, swirled in the soup immediately before serving or passed at the table

AROMATIC FINISHES

GARLIC, chopped fine or crushed to a paste

THYME, MARJORAM, SAVORY, LAVENDER, alone or in combination, chopped fine and combined with garlic paste

PISTOU (see page 224)

AÏOLI (traditional for the fish soup, bourride, but also works well in hearty vegetable soups; see page 491)

ROUILLE (the traditional accompaniment and finish to bouillabaisse, but may also be whisked into vegetable soups)

Clear Vegetable Soups

POTAGES

A SOUPE AU PISTOU IS A GENUINE SOUPE in the French sense of the word—abundant enough that it can be served as a whole meal instead of a prelude, and often served over a slice of stale or toasted bread, another characteristic that distinguishes *soupes,* the everyday staples of farmhouse cooking, from the more refined *potages.* Many of the same ingredients used to make *soupes* are used to make *potages.* But because *potages* have a different function, that of introducing a meal instead of constituting the meal itself, a *potage* will contain a higher proportion of liquid to solid ingredients, or if it's puréed, the purée will be thinner. (See chapter 13 for more information about puréed *soupes* and *potages.*) *Potages* are never poured over a slice of crusty bread in the soup bowl; if they contain any starchy ingredient at all, it will be more delicate and will likely consist of tiny croutons, thin shreds of crêpes, or a few strands of vermicelli.

By the early nineteenth century, the *potage* had essentially completed its evolution from the elaborate stews or *potée*-like dishes that centuries before were labeled *potages,* to a relatively refined and delicate soup. It was also the nineteenth century that saw the development of *la cuisine bourgeoise,* a hearty but refined style of cooking practiced in the homes of the well-to-do, but without the sometimes effete refinement of *la grande cuisine classique* that had developed in the courts of royalty, and later in restaurants. In *la grande cuisine,* most clear *potages* were made with consommé (clarified broth) while the *potages* of *la cuisine bourgeoise* were made with broth that was hearty and clear, but not clarified. Various consommés were also served in bourgeois homes, but vegetable *potages* made with broth were more common. In *la grande cuisine,* the distinction between a consommé and a vegetable *potage* (*potage de légumes*) was often little more than the amount and formality of the garniture.

Julienned Vegetable Soup

POTAGE JULIENNE

DURING MOST OF THE NINETEENTH CENtury and much of the twentieth, *potage julienne* was a cornerstone of solid bourgeois cooking. Lighter and more refined than a simple soup, but heartier and less cerebral than the fussy consommés served in the most elegant nineteenth-century restaurants and homes, *potage julienne* appears in cookbooks starting in the early nineteenth century.

The French have an almost fanatical love of nomenclature, and throughout the nineteenth century they came up with a multitude of vegetable *potages*, which were almost identical except for some minute variation in one of the ingredients or in the way the ingredients were shaped. A *potage julienne*, for example, contains julienned carrots, turnips, leeks, and celery, thin slices of onion, and shredded lettuce and sorrel. When the carrots, turnips, and celery are cut into *brunoise* (see page 22), and the *brunoise* are sweated in a little butter, the soup suddenly becomes *potage brunoise*. When the same ingredients are used, but instead of being gently cooked in butter before liquid is added are simmered directly in liquid, the soup becomes a *potage printanier*. When cabbage, peas, and string beans are added to the soup and the carrots and turnips are cut with less regularity, the soup becomes a *potage paysanne*, very close to a genuine peasant soup except that most writers are quite specific about leaving out bread. If bread is used, it must be sliced very thin, toasted, and passed at the table—the bourgeoisie must be careful not to get too down-to-earth. A *potage cultivateur* contains bacon and cabbage and the vegetables are cut into more-or-less regular cubes (unlike *brunoise*, which must be precise) or *en paysanne* (see page 22). If consommé, instead of simple clear broth, is used to make a *potage julienne*, it becomes a *consommé julienne*; similarly, a *potage brunoise* becomes a *consommé brunoise*.

Since few of us cook formal nineteenth-century *potages*, it makes much better sense to make a soup based on what's in season and let the vegetables retain at least some of their natural shape instead of laboriously forcing them into perfect *brunoise* or julienne. You can make a beautiful vegetable soup by simmering whole baby vegetables in a clear (but not clarified) broth, adding a few herbs, and maybe a couple of cubes of tomato. You can also combine approaches and use one or two baby vegetables; a root vegetable or two cut any way you like; a couple of leeks, sliced or julienned, or tiny rounds of scallions; a little shredded cabbage; a few mushrooms (whole morels look great); and a little shredded basil or a few tarragon leaves.

CLASSIC JULIENNED VEGETABLE SOUP

POTAGE JULIENNE CLASSIQUE

MAKES 8 FIRST-COURSE SERVINGS

This version is almost identical to the classic except that I simmer the carrots and turnips directly in the broth (like a *potage printanier*) instead of first sweating them in butter. See page 19 for a description of how to julienne carrots, turnips, and leeks.

1   stalk celery

2   medium-size carrots, peeled, cut into fine julienne

1   medium-size turnip, peeled, cut into fine julienne

1   medium-size leek, cut into fine julienne

1   small onion, sliced paper thin with a vegetable slicer

2   quarts [2 l] clear (but not clarified) White or Brown Chicken Broth (pages 210 and 209)

1   pale green butter lettuce leaf

1   handful sorrel leaves, stems removed (optional)

1   small bunch fresh chervil or curly parsley, chopped coarse

½   cup [75 g] fresh baby peas or thawed frozen baby peas

    salt

    pepper

¼   pound [115 g] unsalted butter or herb butter such as tarragon or basil butter, passed at the table for guests to dollop in their soup (optional)

PEEL the stringy outside of the celery with a vegetable peeler. Cut the stalk into 2-to-3-inch [5- to 7.5-cm] lengths and slice horizontally through each length, following the shape of the celery with the knife, to make it thinner. (Don't panic if it isn't perfect, celery doesn't like being julienned.) Cut the slices lengthwise into julienne.

COMBINE the julienned vegetables with the broth, bring to a simmer over medium heat, and turn the heat down to maintain at a very gentle simmer. Simmer until the vegetables have softened, about 20 minutes. While the vegetables are simmering, skim off any fat or froth that rises to the surface.

WHILE the vegetables are simmering, cut the crispy white stalk out of the middle of the lettuce leaf and discard it. Roll the leaf into a tight cylinder. Slice the cylinders as thin as you can with a chef's knife—the French call these little shreds *chiffonade*—and do the same thing with the sorrel leaves.

WHEN the julienned vegetables are done, toss in the lettuce, sorrel, chopped chervil, and baby peas and bring to a simmer. Season to taste with salt and spoon into hot bowls. Grind pepper over each serving or pass the pepper mill at the table. Pass the butter.

IMPROVISED SPRING VEGETABLE SOUP

POTAGE PRINTANIER FOU

MAKES 8 FIRST-COURSE SERVINGS

Even though this is called a spring vegetable soup (printanier means springlike), I enjoy it most in the summer, when more fresh vegetables show up at the farmers' market in Manhattan's Union Square. But you can make it, in one form or another, at any time of year. In the fall, I diverge from the classic and include bits of winter squash, wild mushrooms, artichoke bottoms, even chestnuts. At Christmas, I may even sneak in cubes of foie gras and sliced truffles. The idea is simply to simmer the best available vegetables in good broth. So here's a recipe, really just a snapshot of what came out of a particular day at the farmers' market, in which virtually everything, except onion or leek, can be replaced.

2   medium-size leeks, or 1 medium-size onion

2   medium-size carrots (about 12 ounces [340 g], not including the greens), peeled, or 8 baby carrots

1   medium-size turnip, peeled, or 8 baby turnips

2   quarts [2 l] full-flavored clear (but not clarified) chicken or beef broth (see pages 209 to 211)

½   pound [225 g] button mushrooms or fresh wild mushrooms, such as morels, washed and patted dry

½   pound [250 g] thin string beans, preferably haricots verts, ends broken off, cut into 1-inch lengths

8   asparagus tips

1   cup [145 g] fresh baby peas (1 pound [450 g] before shucking), or ¾ cup [115 g] fresh fava beans (1 pound [450 g] before shucking), shucked and individually peeled

1   tablespoon fresh tarragon, chervil, or flat-leaf parsley leaves

    salt

    pepper

¼   pound [115 g] unsalted butter or herb butter (optional)

IF you're using leeks, cut off all but 2 inches [5 cm] of the greens. Slice off the greens that surround the white part of the leek, removing the darkest and toughest outermost leaves. Cut the leeks in half lengthwise, wash them, and slice them fine or cut them into fine julienne.

IF you're using an onion, slice it as fine as you can, preferably with a vegetable slicer.

IF you're using medium-size carrots, slice them into thin rounds or cut them into julienne. If you're using baby carrots, scrape them with the back of a knife to take off the thin peel (don't use a peeler, it takes off too much) and leave about ½ inch [1.5 cm] of green attached. If you're not using them right away, wrap them in a wet towel so they don't turn brown.

IF you're using a medium-size turnip, peel and dice it—the size is up to you—or cut it into julienne. If you're using baby turnips, don't bother peeling them, just leave about ½ inch [1.5 cm] of green attached and cook them whole.

ABOUT 20 minutes before you're ready to serve the soup, bring the broth to a gentle simmer in a large pot. Skim off any froth or fat that rises to the top and add the leeks or onion, the carrots, and the turnip. Simmer the vegetables for 10 to 15 minutes, until they retain just a slight crunch or offer just a little resistance when poked with a knife—they should be soft but not mushy after the additional 7 minutes or so that it will take to cook the rest of the vegetables. You'll have to gauge the cooking times according to how you've cut the vegetables. Add the mushrooms and string beans, simmer until they both retain just the slightest crunch, about 5 minutes, and add the peas or fava beans. Simmer for 1 or 2 minutes more, add the tarragon or other herb, season to taste with salt, and ladle into heated bowls. If you've used baby vegetables or a small number or mushrooms, make sure they're distributed evenly in each bowl. Grind fresh pepper over the bowls or pass the pepper mill at the table. Pass the butter.

MEDITERRANEAN
FISH SOUP

BOUILLABAISSE

HOW TO	HOW TO	HOW TO	HOW TO	TRICKS FOR
TO IMPROVISE YOUR OWN FISH STEWS AND SOUPS	INTENSIFY FLAVOR WITH HERBS	THICKEN A SAUCE WITH BEURRE MANIÉ	WORK WITH EEL AND OCTOPUS	ORGANIZING YOURSELF AHEAD OF TIME

THE AUTHENTICITY OF A BOUILLABAISSE DEPENDS, MORE THAN ANY-thing, on one's point of view. There are those who insist that a bouillabaisse can be made only within sight of the Mediterranean—a condition that of course ensures the availability and freshness of the appropriate fish. Others, more liberal, admit to finding a decent version in Paris. And then there are those, usually owners of restaurants, who concoct their own versions in Arizona or Oklahoma, miles not just from the Mediterranean but from any water at all. But pontificating about the authenticity of any dish strikes me as dubious because good ingredients, lovingly prepared, will always result in something satisfying, with its own identity. Why should such a dish go unloved because it doesn't match exactly something we tasted halfway around the globe?

Whatever you call it, a bouillabaisse is a fish soup—or really a stew, since a soup has more liquid than solid—made by boiling up a bunch of different whole fish in a saffron-and-fennel-scented broth. The dish makes up a whole meal because the broth is served first, followed by the whole fish. Because this serving method is a problem for most of us Americans, who aren't terribly adept at avoiding a mouthful of bones by filleting our own whole cooked fish, I fillet the fish ahead of time and use the heads and bones to make the broth. Just before serving, I poach the fillets in the broth and serve broth and fillets together in a wide soup plate. This way, the soup is easier to eat, though it's true that the beauty of all those different whole fish is lost. Also, I'm assured of a flavorful broth because I have plenty of bones and heads.

Unfortunately, though, the usual bouillabaisse argument is based on the irrefutable fact that Mediterranean fish just have more flavor than most other fish. So unless you are cooking within fish-shopping distance of the Mediterranean, you'll need a trick or two to coax the flavor out of those fish you're able to find. The first requirement, besides freshness, is a reasonable variety of nonoily whole fish. Dogmatists insist on seven specific varieties, most of which are unavailable except from the Mediterranean—look for *rascasse, vive, girelle, saint-pierre, lotte, congre,* and *grondin* if you're there. But wherever you are, simply gather as many different kinds as you can. The more kinds you have, the more deeply flavored your soup will be. Don't, however, sacrifice freshness for variety, and don't be discouraged if you can only find two types— it's still worth the effort. If you can find very inexpensive fish, nab them to add extra flavor to your broth. Chinese and other ethnic markets are often good sources for very cheap little fish. I find baby sea bass on the East Coast and little rock fish on the West Coast. I also like to include mussels, ideally a few New Zealand mussels, whose shells contribute their bright green color. Both regular and New Zealand mussels add a briny sea-like flavor to the broth.

Most recipes for fish broth, the basis for your soup, suggest making the broth by simply combining fish heads and bones, an onion or two, some fennel, and a bouquet garni and simmering for 20 minutes before straining. A better strategy is to cook the fish heads with herbs and aromatic vegetables, including a lot of garlic, in olive oil until they form a brown coating on the bottom and sides of the pot before you add liquid. After this initial browning—the principle is the same as in making any brown broth—add garlic, a little wine, and a goodly amount of tomatoes so the broth, the soul of the soup, is good on its own.

Another trick is to whisk some of the rouille into the fish broth after you've poached the fish. The rouille, which gets its name from the French for "rust," is a thick pasty sauce made from ground dried chiles, some stale bread (softened with a little of the fish broth), garlic, and plenty of olive oil worked together in a mortar or a food processor. I sneak a little saffron into my version and sometimes use Spanish *pimentón*—a kind of smoked paprika—or roasted red bell pepper combined with cayenne instead of the *piment d'espagne* favored by the French. If the roughhewn look of rouille disturbs you, add an egg yolk to the mixture before working in the oil. But keep in mind that this method technically turns the rouille into a mayonnaise, which means that the sauce mustn't ever boil once added to the broth or the egg yolk will curdle.

Bouillabaisse is best made for a crowd, partly because it's a convivial kind of dish, and also because making a lot will allow you to buy a larger assortment of fish. The basic broth can be made earlier the same day, but the final poaching of the fish must be done at the last minute.

MEDITERRANEAN FISH SOUP

BOUILLABAISSE

MAKES 10 MAIN-COURSE SERVINGS

FOR THE FISH BROTH:

10 pounds [4.5 kg] assorted whole fish such as monkfish (not counting the head, which is rarely sold, but which you should include in the broth if you do find it), rockfish, John Dory, striped bass, Spanish mackerel (regular mackerel is too oily), red snapper, walleye, and kingfish. (Avoid salmon, sardines, and other oily, strongly flavored fish.)

4 pounds [1.8 kg] assorted inexpensive baby fish such as baby sea bass or rockfish for the broth, gutted and rinsed (these fish are optional)

3 leeks or 3 medium-size onions

½ cup [125 ml] extra-virgin olive oil

8 cloves garlic (don't bother peeling), chopped coarse

1 cup [250 ml] dry white wine

5 ripe tomatoes, chopped coarse

1 medium-size bouquet garni

¼ cup [60 ml] Pernod or Ricard

½ teaspoon saffron threads, soaked in 1 tablespoon water for 30 minutes

2 pounds [1 kg] mussels, preferably small cultivated

salt

pepper

FOR THE ROUILLE:

8 slices dense-crumb white bread (such as Pepperidge Farm), crusts removed

3 cloves garlic, peeled, chopped fine, crushed to a paste with the side of a chef's knife

2 red bell peppers, peeled and seeded (see page 20), puréed in a food processor for 2 minutes (not needed if you're using the pimentón)

1 heaping teaspoon cayenne pepper (not needed if you're using the pimentón)

1 tablespoons pimentón picante (see Sources; optional)

3 egg yolks (optional)

1 teaspoon saffron threads, soaked for 30 minutes in 1 tablespoon water (optional)

salt

2 cups [500 ml] extra-virgin olive oil

FOR FINISHING AND SERVING THE BOUILLABAISSE:

1 pound [450 g] New Zealand mussels (optional)

the reserved mussels

the reserved fish fillets

30 thin slices baguette, very lightly toasted in the oven, each rubbed with a peeled garlic clove

TO MAKE THE FISH BROTH, STEAM THE MUSSELS, AND PREPARE THE FISH FILLETS

HAVE the fishmonger fillet and skin the fish (see "Another Method for Cooking the Fish in a Bouillabaisse," page 238, for a do-ahead tip or a way to use fish skin). Make sure he gives you the bones and heads. If you're using the baby fish, you may have to gut them yourself; sometimes they're so cheap that the fishmonger isn't willing to do it. Cut the gills out of the heads of both the filleted large fish and the baby fish and discard the gills. Soak the bones and heads in a bowl of cold water for 2 to 3 hours, changing the water every half hour. This gets rid of the blood, which can discolor the broth. Drain the bones and reserve fillets and bones separately in the refrigerator.

IF you're using leeks, cut off and discard most of the greens, leaving about 4 inches [10 cm] of the green attached to the white. Slice the leeks in half down the middle and rinse out any sand or grit by holding them under running water and flipping through the leaves. Slice fine. If you're using onions, chop them coarse.

HEAT ¼ cup [60 ml] of the oil in a heavy-bottomed pot over medium heat and add the leeks or onions and the garlic. Stir these until they smell fragrant, about 5 minutes, and add the fish bones and heads and the whole baby fish. Turn the heat up to high, stirring every minute or two to make sure that nothing on the bottom of the pot is burning. After about 20 minutes the fish will have fallen apart completely—it'll all look like a ghastly mess—and you must keep stirring so nothing burns. Continue in this way until a brown caramelized layer forms on the bottom of the pot, about 10 minutes more, and pour in the white wine. Boil the white wine until it evaporates completely. Stir in the tomatoes and enough water to cover—about 1 quart [1 l]. Add the bouquet garni and pour in another ¼ cup [60 ml] of olive oil. (Bouillabaisse broth is one of the rare exceptions to the rule that broths must be gently simmered and carefully skimmed during cooking to prevent fats from becoming emulsified into the liquid. For this broth, the extra-virgin olive oil is in fact emulsified into the broth—the broth is cooked at a rolling boil—but instead of making it greasy, the oil provides body and flavor.) Boil the broth for 15 minutes and stir in the Pernod. Work the broth through a heavy-duty strainer (sometimes called a china cap; see page 16) with a wooden spoon or with the end of a European-style rolling pin (the kind with no handles), or work it through a food mill. You should end up with about 3 quarts [3 l] of broth. Strain the broth through a fine-mesh strainer. Add the saffron and its soaking liquid to the broth.

SCRUB and sort the regular mussels and pull off any large pieces of beard sticking out of the shells. Put the regular mussels, not the New Zealand ones, in a large pot with about 2 cups [500 ml] of the fish broth, cover the pot, and steam the mussels over high heat until they've all opened, about 5 minutes. Scoop the mussels out of the pot with a skimmer, take them out of the shells, discard the shells, and reserve the mussel meats. Reserve the liquid left in the pot.

CUT the fillets into manageable pieces but not so small that they loose their identity—each piece should still look like a fillet, not just a chunk, and be enough for at least 2 or 3 bites. Not all the pieces need to be the same size; if some of the fillets are small, they can be left whole. Keep in mind the number of guests you're having and cut the fish so that everyone gets the same amount of each one. Season carefully with salt and pepper (since mussels are salty).

TO MAKE THE ROUILLE

COMBINE the bread and the rest of the ingredients except the olive oil in the bowl of a food processor and purée until smooth. Transfer the mixture to a bowl and work in the olive oil with a wooden spoon until you end up with a thick paste. If the sauce is too thick, thin it with a little of the fish broth.

THE FINAL PREPARATION (IMMEDIATELY BEFORE SERVING)

PUT the New Zealand mussels in the pot with the liquid used to steam the regular mussels. Cover the pot and steam over high heat until all the mussels have opened, about 5 minutes. Scoop the mussels out, remove and discard their top shells (leave them in the bottom shells—they look pretty), put them in a large bowl, cover them with plastic wrap, and keep them warm. Carefully pour the cooking liquid into the fish broth, leaving any grit behind in the pot.

HEAT wide soup plates in a warm oven. Bring the fish broth to a gentle simmer in a pan large enough to hold the fillets in a single layer. (If you don't have a big enough pan, use two.) Slide the fillets into the simmering liquid, adjusting the timing according to the size of the fillets, with the thicker pieces added first. The fillets are usually done after about 9 minutes of simmering per inch of thickness, but a more reliable method is to press on the pieces with your finger—when they spring back to the touch, they are done. (If this seems too daunting, just cut into a piece. The flesh should look opaque, not translucent, but shouldn't flake.) Or see page 238 for another way of cooking the fillets.

WITH a skimmer or slotted spoon, arrange the fish fillets in the soup plates. Put the mussel meats and the New Zealand mussels in their bottom shells in the broth to reheat them. Spoon half the rouille into a bowl and whisk a couple of ladles of the hot fish broth into the rouille. Scoop the New Zealand mussels out of the broth and arrange them in the soup plates. Return the rouille mixture to the rest of the broth. (From this point on, especially if you've used the egg yolk, don't allow the broth to boil.) Ladle the hot broth and the mussel meats over the fish. Pass the toasted slices of baguette and the rest of the rouille so guests can spread rouille on both toasts and fish.

Other Fish Soups and Stews

EVERY REGION OF FRANCE HAS ITS OWN FISH soup or stew. The main differences, except for varieties of fish, are in the ingredients used to make the basic broth and the flavorful finishes sometimes added at the end. Again, the difference between a soup and a stew is simply a matter of the ratio of liquid to solid, less liquid being used to moisten a stew. To follow the continuum even further, a piece of fish with a concentrated sauce based on its head and bones is prepared in the same way as a fish soup or stew except that the liquid is highly reduced and perhaps finished, in the way of a sauce, with a little butter, cream, or beurre manié.

Southern French fish soups and stews, bouillabaisse being the star, are among the most interesting, primarily because Mediterranean fish taste so good and because of the natural affinity of fish for other Mediterranean ingredients such as garlic, fennel, saffron, wild thyme, oregano, and tomatoes. The bourride is probably the best known of bouillabaisse alternatives and is made in much the same way without aspiring to the same level of luxury, since it includes a smaller variety of fish. But the real genius behind the dish lies in the fact that the broth is whisked into an aïoli containing some extra egg yolks, and the broth is cooked gently on the stove—like the seafood equivalent of a *crème anglaise* (see page 642)—until the garlicky broth turns silky smooth. A *bourride sètoise* is a similar concoction except that the aïoli contains puréed monkfish liver.

Because monkfish are bottom feeders and toxins accumulate in the liver, this is a delicacy I avoid. A *soupe de poisson marseillaise* is a fish soup that has been puréed through a food mill so that all the flavor is extracted from the fish but enough of the finely divided flesh works through to give the soup some body. The soup contains no solid pieces of fish, unless of course as a refinement one were to poach pieces of fish in it or use it as the base for a bouillabaisse. An *oursinade* is a kind of bourride except that the broth is finished with egg yolks and sea urchin (*oursin*) roe whisked up into a kind of sabayon (a fluffy sauce similar to hollandaise; see page 257) and then served over or around the fish.

On the Atlantic coast, the Basques make a soup, *ttoro*, similar in concept to a bouillabaisse but with a completely different flavor. In addition to plenty of garlic and tomatoes, *ttoro* is spiced up with hot pepper and contains shrimp and mussels, and often clams. To the north, the Bretons and Normans have their own fish soups and stews (see page 242).

Inland areas offer an array of fish soups and stews made with freshwater fish and a variety of moistening liquids, almost always including wine, and often enricheners such as butter, cream, or egg yolks. Eel is a special favorite. It enters into the classic *matelote d'anguille*, a red wine stew, finished with the classic Burgundian garniture of mushrooms and bacon; but fortunately for those who aren't eager to literally wrestle with an eel (a live eel is essential), the same methods and ingredients are adaptable to almost any fish, freshwater or otherwise. The Burgundian *pauchouse* is much the same thing except that white wine replaces the red. In the Northeast of France, the *anguille au vert* is a classic. The poaching liquid is finished with finely chopped herbs and egg yolks, and again the eel can be replaced with just about any firm-fleshed fish. (I once made sand shark *au vert*.) You can convert any of these fish stews into a soup simply by using a higher proportion of liquid to fish and cutting the pieces of fish smaller. Conversely, the liquid can be reduced or thickened and used as a sauce, the principles for making stews, soups, and sauces being so similar.

ANOTHER METHOD FOR COOKING THE FISH IN A BOUILLABAISSE

Poaching fish fillets, especially at the last minute, can leave you scurrying around the kitchen while trying to look calm in front of your guests. Also, skin-on fillets curl when you poach them (because the skin contracts), and poached fish skin doesn't taste particularly good anyway. If I'm throwing a dinner party or lunch party, or if I just want to eat the fillets with the skin on, I season the fillets and sauté them skin-side down in olive oil in a nonstick pan over very high heat for about 30 seconds while pressing down on them with a spatula to keep them from curling. Before I begin to sauté, I cover a sheet pan with ice cubes and set another sheet pan on top. I rub the top sheet pan with olive oil. As soon as the fillets are sautéed I place them, skin-side down, on the cold sheet pan so they immediately stop cooking. When the fillets have chilled, I turn them over, so the skin is facing up, and refrigerate them. (If I have fillets of varying thicknesses, I arrange them on separate sheet pans.) Shortly before I'm ready to serve, I preheat the oven to 400°F [200°C/gas mark 6] and bake the fillets for 3 to 8 minutes, depending on their thickness. This way, I can be dealing with the broth while the fish is cooking and then just scoop the fillets off the sheet pan and arrange them in the soup plates. This method makes it easy to sort the various kinds of fillets ahead of time and leaves your fillets with the crispy, decorative skin still on.

PURÉED FISH SOUP

SOUPE DE POISSON À LA MARSEILLAISE

MAKES 4 FIRST-COURSE SERVINGS,
OR 6 FIRST-COURSE SERVINGS IF YOU'RE
USING PESTO OR AÏOLI

The beauty of this soup is that you don't have to worry about overcooking the fish. In fact, you want to overcook the fish so that it releases all its flavor into the surrounding liquid and falls apart into a smooth purée as you work it through a food mill. This soup is also great when you have fish with little bones that make it almost impossible to debone without tearing the fillets into shreds.

Traditional recipes tell you just to boil the whole gutted fish in a pot and then work everything through a food mill, but you end up with so many bones and pieces of head that the mixture becomes very difficult to work. A better method is to get the fish filleted, make a concentrated fish broth with the bones and heads (in the same way as the bouillabaisse on page 235), and then strain the fish broth. Once you have the fish broth, use it to simmer the skinless fillets (the skin can make the broth murky), and then work the mixture through the food mill. (I put a lot of tomatoes in the broth before working it through the food mill.) Once you get the basic soup, you can flavor it in the traditional way, with some saffron threads. I like to make an aïoli with some saffron in it and then whisk the broth into the aïoli as though making a bourride (see page 237). But you can use a simpler approach and just add some finely minced garlic and finely chopped herbs, such as marjoram or fresh oregano, or parsley. Or you can add basil, either chopped or crushed into a cheeseless pesto. I pass little toasts for people to drop into the soup or use for spreading with aïoli. You can also ladle the soup over a slice of stale bread in the bottom of each bowl.

3 pounds [1.3 kg] assorted whole fish such as rockfish, John Dory, striped bass, Spanish mackerel (regular mackerel is too oily), red snapper, walleye, and kingfish. (Avoid salmon, sardines, and other oily, strongly flavored fish, and don't use monkfish—unless you can get the delightfully hideous and gelatinous head—because it won't supply you with enough bones to make the basic broth.)

1 whole head garlic, plus 3 (optional) cloves garlic chopped fine, crushed to a paste with the side of a chef's knife

¼ cup [60 ml] extra-virgin olive oil

1 medium-size onion, chopped coarse

½ cup [125 ml] dry white wine

1 bouquet garni containing a 3-inch [7.5-cm] strip of orange zest and maybe a few sprigs of marjoram, savory, or oregano in addition to the usual bay leaf, parsley, and thyme

6 ripe tomatoes, chopped coarse

1 cup [225 ml] pesto without the cheese, or 1½ cups aïoli (see page 491) (use either of these if not using the crushed garlic cloves)

   salt

   pepper

30 thin slices baguette, very lightly toasted in the oven

FILLET the fish, or have them filleted. Skin the fillets, or have them skinned, and reserve in the refrigerator. Remove the gills from the heads and discard the gills. Soak the bones and heads in cold water for 2 to 3 hours, changing the water every 30 minutes.

CUT the head of garlic in half crosswise and break it up into cloves with your fingers. Heat the oil over medium heat in a heavy-bottomed pot and add the half-cloves of garlic and the onion. Stir over medium heat for about 15 minutes until the onion turns translucent, but don't let it brown. Add the fish heads and bones and the wine and turn the heat up to high. Stir the bones and heads until the wine and any liquid released by the bones has completely evaporated, about 8 minutes. Add the bouquet garni and 3 cups of water and bring to a gentle simmer. Simmer, covered, for 20 minutes. Strain into a clean pot, pushing down on the bones with the back of a wooden spoon to extract their juices.

PUT the fish fillets and the tomatoes in the strained broth and simmer for about 20 minutes, covered, until the fillets are falling apart and the tomatoes are mushy. Work the soup through a food mill with the finest mesh attachment. You should end up with about 4 cups [1 l], but you may end up with more or less depending on the ripeness of the tomatoes.

JUST before serving, whisk the crushed garlic or ½ cup of the pesto into the hot soup; or if you're using aïoli, put 1 cup of the aïoli into a mixing bowl, whisk in the soup, and pour the mixture back into the pot. Reheat the soup, while stirring, over medium heat— if you've used aïoli, don't let it boil—season to taste with salt and pepper, and ladle the soup into hot bowls. Pass the toasted slices of baguette and the extra aïoli or pesto at the table for guests to spoon into their soup or spread on the toasts.

TUNA BOURRIDE

THON EN BOURRIDE

MAKES 4 MAIN-COURSE SERVINGS

Many fish markets carry whole steaks from large fish such as tuna, swordfish, shark, or Chilean sea bass. While these firm-fleshed fish are perfect in fish soups and stews, you're left with the problem of not having heads or bones to make the broth. I sometimes make a broth with inexpensive whole fish, but since these aren't always easy to find, I often make a tomato broth—a kind of light tomato soup—to surround the fish in a wide soup plate. I then sauté or grill whole steaks of tuna and serve them sliced, surrounded by the tomato broth, which has been thickened and flavored with aïoli and saffron.

4   tuna, swordfish, shark, or other firm fish steaks (6 to 8 ounces [170 to 225 g] each), between ¾ inch and 1 inch [2 and 2.5 cm] thick, skin and dark meat (if you're using tuna) removed

1   tablespoon olive oil

1   small pinch saffron threads (optional)

3   ripe medium-size tomatoes, peeled

½   cup [125 ml] aïoli (page 491)

    salt

    pepper

RUB the steaks with olive oil and refrigerate them.

COMBINE the saffron threads with 1 tablespoon water and let sit for 30 minutes or longer.

CUT the tomatoes in half crosswise. Place a medium-size strainer over a small bowl and squeeze the seeds out of each tomato half over the strainer. Work the tomato juice through the strainer with your fingers and discard the seeds, which don't go through.

CHOP THE TOMATO HALVES fine and combine them with the tomato juice and ½ cup [125 ml] of water in a small saucepan. Cover the saucepan, bring to a simmer, and cook gently, covered, over low heat for 10 minutes.

WHISK the saffron threads and the tomato mixture into the aïoli. Pour the mixture into a saucepan, off the heat. Season to taste with salt and pepper.

SEASON the tuna steaks with salt and pepper and sauté them over high heat in olive oil or rub them with olive oil and grill them over a hot fire for 2 to 4 minutes on each side. Tuna is best left rare in the middle; other steaks should be cooked through, about 9 minutes per inch [2.5 cm] of thickness (see page 20 for more about cooking times for fish).

HEAT the aïoli/broth mixture over medium heat while whisking until hot but not boiling. (Boiling will cause the egg yolk to curdle.)

SLICE the tuna steaks into long strips and arrange them in rows in hot soup plates. (Other steaks can be left whole or be cut into large chunks.) Ladle the hot aïoli mixture around the tuna slices. Serve immediately.

Variations: By placing a slice of crusty bread or a mound of a cooked leafy vegetable such as spinach or Swiss chard in the center of each plate, you can keep the fish partially elevated above the broth so it doesn't overcook, and the presentation will look more dramatic. One of my favorite tricks is to lightly sauté French bread slices in a small amount of olive oil, rub each slice with a peeled garlic clove, and sprinkle it with fresh chopped marjoram.

EEL OR WHATEVER FISH WITH HERB SAUCE

ANGUILLE ON N'IMPORTE QUOI AU VERT

MAKES 4 MAIN-COURSE SERVINGS

In its original version, anguille au vert is a rough-and-tumble affair made by packing pieces of eel into a pot with shredded sorrel, lettuce, and chard, adding some white wine (or, in some places, beer), and simmering the whole thing until the eel is done. The cooking liquid is thickened by whisking in a little flour worked with some butter (beurre manié) and bringing the liquid to a simmer. The liquid is then whisked into egg yolks and the mixture gently heated, but not allowed to boil—a process that enriches it and gives it a silky texture. The idea of finishing a poaching liquid with egg yolks is well established in classic French cooking and the idea of incorporating an abundance of freshly chopped herbs into an egg yolk–thickened sauce has been adopted by some of France's most respected chefs.

In any case, you can apply the usual refinements, such as filleting the fish and making a fish broth with bones and heads for the sauce base. The secret to success, however, is to finish the sauce with lots of delicate herbs such as parsley, chervil, chives, tarragon (use less or it will obliterate the flavor of the other herbs), or sorrel. I make this recipe by simply adding the finely chopped herbs about 1 minute before the sauce is ready. I use an immersion blender to zap the sauce, to make it foamy and release the flavor and color of the herbs, but this final puréeing is optional. While the sauce can be thickened with egg yolks alone—either gently stirred like a crème anglaise (see page 642) or whisked enthusiastically like a sabayon (see page 11)—I add a little butter to cut the eggy taste. In another departure from classic recipes, I sweat the fish bones and heads (without allowing them to brown) so they fall apart in the pot and enable me to use a minimum of liquid and avoid reduction later, after straining.

4 pounds [1.8 kg] whole fish such as striped bass, Atlantic sea bass, Spanish mackerel, red snapper, walleye, kingfish, or any nonoily, firm-fleshed fish.

2 medium-size leeks

2 tablespoons butter (for cooking the leeks), plus 3 tablespoons butter (for finishing the sauce)

1 cup [250 ml] dry white wine

1 small bouquet garni

½ cup finely chopped herbs such as parsley, chervil, tarragon, basil (out of character for a Northern French dish but good anyway), sorrel (in chiffonade if you like), or chives, either alone or in combination. (Chop the herbs as close to the last minute as possible—with 2 teaspoons of olive oil if you're using tarragon and/or basil to prevent them from turning black.)

3 egg yolks

salt

pepper

FILLET the fish, or have it filleted. Skin the fillets and cut them into pieces that are manageable, but not so small that they loose their identity. (Remember this is a stew, not a soup.) I usually give each person about 3 pieces. Reserve in the refrigerator. Remove the gills from the heads and discard the gills. Soak the bones and heads in cold water for 2 to 3 hours, changing the water every 30 minutes.

CUT most of the greens off the leeks, leaving about 4 inches [10 cm] of green attached to the white. Cut the white in half lengthwise and rinse out any sand under running water. Slice fine.

MELT 2 tablespoons of butter in a heavy-bottomed pot and add the leeks. Cook over low to medium heat, stirring regularly, until the leeks smell fragrant, about 7 minutes. Don't let the leeks brown. Add the fish bones and heads, the wine, and the bouquet garni. Turn the heat up to high and stir regularly until the fish bones completely fall apart, about 15 minutes. Add 2 cups [500 ml] of water and simmer very gently, covered, for 15 minutes more. Strain and reserve the broth.

SHORTLY before you're ready to serve, poach the fish in the strained fish broth, and keep the fish warm. If you don't have enough broth to cover the fillets, use a large spoon to baste them while they are poaching. (Or bake the fish so you can make the sauce while the fish is cooking; see page 238.) Whisk the herbs into the egg yolks in a mixing bowl and whisk in the hot fish broth you used for poaching the fillets. (Keep the fish warm on a plate in the oven set to its lowest setting.) Pour the mixture back into the saucepan and cook over medium heat while stirring constantly with a wooden spoon. When the sauce takes on a satiny consistency, remove the sauce from the heat. Don't expect the sauce to be thick—it should have the consistency of cream soup. Stir in the butter and season to taste with salt and pepper. If you want a frothy sauce, whip it with an immersion blender for 30 seconds. Arrange the pieces of fish in warm soup plates and ladle the sauce, which will be almost like a rich soup, over and around them.

A SIMPLER METHOD: If you don't want to whisk your fish broth at the last minute with egg yolks—especially nerve-wracking if both your fish and your guests are waiting for you to finish the sauce and disastrous if the yolks curdle—skip the yolks and finish the sauce with a little cream and butter instead. Boil the fish broth down by one-third—to about 2 cups [500 ml]—add the herbs and ½ cup [125 ml] of heavy cream, and swirl in 4 tablespoons of butter. Whip the sauce, if you like, with the immersion blender, season, and serve.

More Fish Stews

MATELOTES

WHILE THE WORD MATELOTE IS USED ALL over France to mean fish stew, virtually every region has its own variations. *Matelote à la normande*, from Normandy, is made with saltwater fish and cider, but most matelotes are made with freshwater fish and red or white wine. A typical matelote is a rather slapdash affair made by heaping aromatic vegetables—the usual onions and carrots—in a pot with chunks of eel, perch, or carp; pouring in the wine; simmering or even boiling until the fish is cooked; and thickening the liquid with beurre manié. Many versions are garnished the same way as for a *boeuf bourguignonne*—with pearl onions, mushrooms, and little strips of bacon. Heart-shaped *croûtons,* their tips dipped in parsley, may surround the dish. The result is less than exciting. Neither wine nor vegetables have had time to cook by the time the fish is done. If red wine is used, the bones clarify and remove much of the color from the cooking liquid. The chunks of whole fish—bones and all—are hard to eat, surrounded as they are with the (usually overthickened) sauce. The *bourguignonne* garniture isn't bad, but there are so many other possibilities.

Yet the idea of munching on thick chunks of fish surrounded with a velvety sauce is too inviting to ignore. While white wine matelotes have their own advantages, it is a red wine sauce with fish—especially full-flavored fish like salmon—that makes a startling and unusual treat. The trick is to make a red wine fish broth with fish heads and bones and let it simmer long enough to cook the raw taste out of the wine. Here is an exception to the rule that only nonoily fish should be used to make fish broth; the full flavor of salmon and members of the mackerel family, such as king mackerel, Spanish mackerel, and wahoo, is balanced by the concentrated red wine. Caramelizing the fish bones in the pot, adding wine in several stages, and caramelizing after each addition except the last gives the sauce base a meaty complexity and a deep, almost black, color. This rich, dark liquid can be thickened with beurre manié and served around the fish in a soup plate, or it can be reduced, lightly thickened with less beurre manié or with plain butter, and served as a sauce. (The liquid is now too rich, too sparse, and too intensely flavored to qualify as a stewing liquid.) The garniture can be as simple as some chopped parsley added to the sauce at the end, but you can get as elaborate as you want and sauté wild mushrooms, blanch whole garlic cloves, glaze pearl onions, gently warm diced tomatoes, sweat little cubes of carrots, or boil fava beans or haricots verts and strew them over the finished stew on the plates.

IF YOU DO DECIDE TO USE EEL

Because the eels I find in the United States have a slightly muddy taste, I adapt most eel recipes so that they can be used with other fish. If you're lucky enough to get an eel or two that you know are good—perhaps you're cooking in Japan or Venice or you've caught your own—here's what to do: Grab the eel around the neck with a kitchen towel (to keep it from slipping out of your grip) and whack its head a couple of times, as hard as you can, on a hard surface. This will make you feel better, since it will be safe to assume that the eel has been knocked senseless, but it will do nothing to keep the body from wrapping around your arm and squeezing. Make a skin-deep cut around the base of the eel's head and start to peel the skin back toward the tail, working all around the cut. A small pair of pliers works well for this. Once you've starting peeling back the skin, grab it with a towel and pull it off the eel. It will come off like a glove. Clean the eel by making a cut into the anus, which is a few inches [about 2.5 cm] behind the head, and cutting up to the base of the head. Pull and rinse out any innards and discard them. Cut the eel into 2-inch sections. You'll need 3 or 4 sections per serving, depending on the thickness of the eel. Discard the head and use the sections for *anguille au vert*.

RED WINE SALMON MATELOTE

MATELOTE DE SAUMON

MAKES 6 MAIN-COURSE OR
12 FIRST-COURSE SERVINGS

3 pounds [1.3 kg] salmon fillet or mackerel-family fillet, skin removed unless you're sautéing (see variations below)

2 salmon heads, or 3 pounds [1.3 kg] fresh heads and bones from mackerel-family fish (ask your fishmonger—they should be free)

2 tablespoons butter (for cooking the salmon heads), plus 2 tablespoons (for the beurre manié) or 6 tablespoons (if you're not using beurre manié)

2 medium-size onions, chopped coarse

4 cloves garlic, crushed

1 medium-size carrot, peeled and sliced

1 fennel stalk (about 12 inches [30.5 cm]), sliced into 1-inch [2.5-cm] pieces (optional)

2 bottles full-bodied red wine (see page 10)

1 medium-size bouquet garni

2 tablespoons flour (if you're using beurre manié)

2 tablespoons finely chopped parsley

salt

pepper

FOR THE GARNITURE (OPTIONAL):

1 pound [450 g] wild mushrooms, such as morels, porcini, or lobster mushrooms, cut into bite-size pieces

2 tablespoons butter

PULL any pin bones out of the salmon with tweezers or needle-nose pliers and cut the salmon into 6 or 12 equal pieces. Refrigerate.

CUT the gills out of the salmon heads with heavy-duty scissors and discard the gills. Soak the heads for at least 20 minutes in cold water and drain.

HEAT 2 tablespoons of butter over high heat in a heavy-bottomed pan, and before the butter has a chance to burn add the onions, garlic, carrot, and fennel and the salmon heads. Stir every few minutes or so, to keep what is on the bottom of the pan from burning, until the head completely falls apart and a brown crust forms on the bottom and sides of the pan, after about 30 minutes. Pour in 1 cup [250 ml] of wine and boil it down while scraping the bottom and sides of the pan with a wooden spoon to dissolve the caramelized juices. When the wine has evaporated completely and the juices have caramelized—the bottom of the pan will be covered with hot, oily fat rendered from the salmon—add another cup of wine and repeat, scraping up the caramelized juices with a wooden spoon and caramelizing one more time. Pour in the rest of the wine, add the bouquet garni, and scrape the bottom of the pan for 1 minute with a wooden spoon. When the wine reaches a simmer, turn the heat down to low, and simmer gently for 30 minutes. Strain into a saucepan—press hard on the inside of the strainer to get the liquid out—and put the saucepan on medium heat, keeping the saucepan pushed to one side of the heat so the fat moves to the other side and is easier to skim off. Skim the fat off with a small ladle or spoon as it rises to the surface. If you're using the mushrooms, sauté them in 2 tablespoons of butter while you're reducing the red wine sauce, and season with salt and pepper.

AT this point you have a choice: You can reduce the liquid down to an almost syrupy consistency, as you would a meat sauce (*sauce genevoise* is the classic name for this rich red wine fish sauce), and swirl in some butter, or you can reduce the sauce less so you have more of it and then thicken it with beurre manié. (Sauce bases must already have a lightly syrupy consistency to be thickened successfully with butter alone.) I opt for the butter method if I'm serving only one kind of fish with a very simple garniture and the beurre manié method if I'm using more than one kind of fish or the garniture is more elaborate and I want to serve everything in a wide soup plate. If you're using the beurre manié, reduce the red wine fish broth down to 1½ cups [375 ml]. Work the 2 tablespoons of butter with the flour into a paste on a plate with the back of a fork and whisk the mixture into the simmering red wine mixture, simmer for about 30 seconds, and remove from the heat. If you're making a sauce using butter alone, reduce the red wine mixture down to about ½ cup [125 ml] and whisk in all 6 tablespoons of butter and remove from the heat.

SEASON the salmon pieces with salt and pepper and sauté or bake them (see page 238). Arrange the salmon on hot plates if you've made the rich butter sauce or in soup plates if you've made the lighter version with beurre manié. Spoon the sauce and the mushrooms over and around the salmon.

Variations: While salmon heads and bones make the best sauce, there's no need to limit the fish in this dish to salmon or to any single fish. If you want the dish to have more the character of a traditional matelote—with a variety of fish—just substitute smaller pieces of different fish for some of the salmon and include their bones and heads in the red wine fish broth. If this were a traditional matelote, the fish would be poached in the red wine broth, but this is inconvenient because you then have to keep the cooked fish warm while finishing the sauce. It's a lot easier just to bake the fish (see page 238) or sauté it lightly and then finish it, just before serving, in the oven. If you decide to sauté, you may want to leave the skin on the salmon. Sautéed salmon skin is crispy and juicy and makes a nice counterpoint to the melting texture of the flesh itself. (Poached fish skin, on the other hand, is sticky and rubbery.) Sauté the pieces, skin-side down first, in a nonstick pan over high heat. Press down on the fish pieces with a spatula during the first minute of sautéing. This prevents the pieces from curling and helps the skin crisp up evenly. If you're sautéing in advance and finishing in the oven, sauté the salmon on the skin side only and refrigerate immediately to stop the cooking (see page 238).

OCTOPUS DAUBE

POULPE EN DAUBE

MAKES 6 MAIN-COURSE SERVINGS

Until recently, unless you grew up in an Italian household or were fortunate enough to have traveled in Italy or Greece, eating octopus was not an option for an American. My own childhood exposure to octopus was limited to occasional forays with my mother to San Francisco's Chinatown, where we gaped in horror at the fish stalls. Later I watched reruns of It Came from Beneath the Sea, a movie about a giant octopus that pulled down the Golden Gate bridge and in which my father, playing the part of an admiral, ordered the firing of torpedoes.

It wasn't until years afterward, in the train station in Genoa and too hungry to be picky, that I discovered the delights of an octopus salad.

Although almost all fish or shellfish are ready to eat as soon as they are cooked through—rarely longer than a few minutes—squid, cuttlefish, and octopus are sturdy creatures whose flesh softens with long, gentle simmering, just like a chunk of meat. Pieces of octopus, treated in the same way as meat in a stew—slowly simmered in red wine with the usual aromatic vegetables and herbs—become meltingly tender and release their natural gelatin into the surrounding liquid, lending it a suave sapidity and depth of flavor. The result is meaty, rich, and delicious. There's no need to go through any of the elaborate processes (beating on rocks, dipping and redipping in simmering water) sometimes recommended to tenderize the octopus, because the octopus will be tender at the end of about an hour's cooking. I like to serve plenty of crusty bread and a bowl of aïoli for guests to dollop on the stew.

Most octopus comes frozen, which does it no harm, and already cleaned. But if you find a fresh creature, cut off the head just above the eyes and turn it inside out. Pull out any organs or viscera and rinse the head, which you can cut up and cook with the tentacles. Cut the eyes off the rest of the octopus and remove the small hard little beak by turning the octopus upside down and pressing against the opposite side of the "base" where all the tentacles meet. Push the beak through the opening in the middle. Give the octopus a thorough rinsing, kneading it with your hands in a sink full of cold water, and being sure to rinse out any mud that may be clinging to the inside of the suckers.

Any of the garnitures used for a meat stew can be used for an octopus daube. The classic burgundian garniture of mushrooms, pearl onions, and bacon is nice, but I like to add green vegetables such as string beans, peas, fava beans, or baby artichokes, pearl onions, or root vegetables such as baby carrots or turnips. (Mature root vegetables can be turned; see page 21.) Wedges of fennel, braised on the stove with a little white wine, are also nice, as are whole blanched garlic cloves and sautéed mushrooms, wild or cultivated.

2 octopuses (2 pounds [900 g] each) or the equivalent, cleaned

2 bottles full-bodied red wine

6 cloves garlic, chopped coarse

2 medium-size onions, chopped coarse

2 medium-size carrots, peeled and chopped coarse

1 medium-size bouquet garni

3 tablespoons finely chopped parsley

2 cups [500 ml] aïoli (optional; page 491)

BLANCH the octopuses by submerging them in a large pot of boiling water for 5 minutes. Drain, rinse with cold water, and cut the tentacles into 3-inch [7.5-cm] lengths and the center section into 2-inch [5-cm] chunks. In a nonaluminum bowl, combine all the ingredients except the parsley and the aïoli, and let marinate in the refrigerator for 4 to 12 hours. (Marinating is optional.)

POUR everything from the bowl into a heavy-bottomed pot, bring to a gentle simmer, and simmer, covered, very gently on the stove (or in a 325°F/165°C/gas mark 3 oven) until the octopus meat feels tender when you stick a fork into it, about 1½ hours.

STRAIN the stew into a clean saucepan. Over gentle heat, reduce the braising liquid to about 2 cups [500 ml], skimming off fat as it cooks, about 20 minutes. Pick through the solids, reserving the octopus and discarding the bouquet garni, onion, and carrot. When you're ready to serve, reheat the octopus in the reduced braising liquid, stir in the chopped parsley, simmer for 30 seconds, and serve. Pass the aïoli.

Caudières, Chaudrées, Cotriades, Chowders, and Pot-au-feu de Poisson

THE GREAT VARIETY OF FRENCH FISH SOUPS and stews has more to do with nomenclature than it does with differences in technique or with different kinds of seafood. Some of the best-known seafood soups and stews were invented by fishermen who threw whatever fish they figured they couldn't sell into a pot with perhaps a little wine, some onion, and some potatoes. Various traditions have evolved, and there are those who insist that certain soups be made only with this particular fish or that particular potato—much as we argue about New England versus Manhattan clam chowder. To me this is all nonsense and runs countercurrent to the common sense of good cooking, which dictates that we make the best use of what we have.

A *caudière* is a creamy fisherman's soup, popular around Dunkerque. Except for the use of cream, white wine, and a final egg yolk liaison (a refinement unlikely to be bothered with on a fishing boat), a *caudière* is virtually identical to an American fish chowder—fish trimmings or whole baby fish are simmered with water (originally, no doubt, sea water), onions, white wine, and bouquet garni herbs; the mixture is strained into a pot of sliced potatoes and simmered long enough to cook the potatoes; a few big handfuls of mussels are thrown in and simmered until they open; and the whole thing is finished off with heavy cream. A *chaudrée*, another fishermen's soup popular along the Atlantic coast north of Bordeaux, is similar to a *caudière* except that strips of cuttlefish are cooked in butter with onions and garlic before wine and water and a variety of fish are added. No potatoes or cream are used, but a goodly amount of butter is whisked in at the end. Exact recipes for *cotriade* are impossible to pin down, but the usual principles and ingredients apply: onions cooked in butter, potatoes added and simmered until done, pieces of fish added at the end. And while some recipes include sorrel, whose natural acidity goes well with fish, the *cotriade*'s special identity comes from wine vinegar, sprinkled on the fish just before it is served. In one recipe from Brittany, the fish broth is ladled into bowls over thick slices of bread and the fish, served after, is sprinkled with a little oil and vinegar and a few sprigs of *perce-pierre*, a salty, crunchy succulent that grows between rocks near the beach and has thin, pale green branches. Another, more picturesque version involves dipping the fish in vinegar heavily flavored with pepper, much like the *sauce mignonnette* served with raw oysters. A *marmite dieppoise* follows the same basic fish soup or stew formula—leeks, celery, and onions sweated in butter, fish broth and fish added, the soup finished with cream—except that curry powder and cayenne are added to the pot near the end.

A *pot-au-feu de poisson* is a nouvelle cuisine refinement designed as an analogue to the classic pot-au-feu made with meat. Essentially, a *pot-au-feu de poisson* is a fish soup consisting of a variety of fish served in a bowl surrounded with a rich fish broth, which in the fanciest versions has been clarified into a consommé, and miniature vegetables. Michel Guérard makes one in which each fish is cooked differently—sautéed, grilled, and poached. While the dish is stunning to look at, the flavors are rarely as satisfying as a well-made fish soup or stew, perhaps because the clarified broth contains no cream or butter or Mediterranean sauce such as aïoli—elements that, even in small amounts, are essential for unifying the flavors of the seafood into a satisfying whole.

INDIVIDUAL COLD OCTOPUS TERRINES
TERRINE DE POULPE EN GELÉE

If you have leftover Octopus Daube but you don't want to serve it again in the exact same way, melt the congealed red wine braising liquid, stir in a few tablespoons of finely chopped parsley or basil or a little tarragon, and season to taste with salt and pepper, keeping in mind that cold sauces taste less salty. Slice the leftover octopus into ¼-inch-thick [.5-cm] pieces and pour enough braising liquid into 5-ounce [155-ml] ramekins to come up about ¼ inch. Let set in the refrigerator. Fill the ramekins with octopus pieces and pour the rest of the cool—not cold, or it will set—braising liquid over them. Let set for 4 hours and unmold on chilled plates as a first course. If you use all the braising liquid and still find yourself with leftover octopus, you can toss it with a little chopped shallot, parsley, olive oil, and vinegar and serve it as a salad. If, when you unmold the terrines, the *gelée* seems tough or rubbery, let them sit at room temperature for about 15 minutes so the *gelée* will soften. Octopus daube can also be allowed to set in a terrine or loaf pan. It must be unmolded, frozen, and sliced with a bread knife while still frozen. The slices must then be allowed to thaw on the individual platters.

FRENCH-STYLE FISH AND SHELLFISH CHOWDER
CAUDIÈRE

MAKES 4 MAIN-COURSE OR 6 FIRST-COURSE SERVINGS

Even though I never balk at a steaming bowl of New England clam chowder, I'm always a little frustrated when it comes to making one at home. The traditional potatoes, onions, and bacon give the soup substance, but they also dilute the flavors of seafood. And whenever I've tried using milk, it ends up, partially curdled, clinging to the potatoes. I could solve this problem by adding flour, but then the soup would be too starchy. Instead I leave out the potatoes and bacon, replace the milk with a smaller amount of cream, and serve the seafood as an intensely flavored stew with none of the flavor of the ocean obscured. I don't rely on fish broth alone to provide liquid and flavor, but incorporate clams, mussels, or cockles to give an irresistible briny dimension to the stew. You can serve this "chowder" as a first course or a main course.

4 pounds [1.8 kg] whole firm-fleshed fish such as Atlantic sea bass, red snapper, Dover sole, pompano, or rockfish, filleted, bones and heads reserved, fillets skinned

2 leeks

2 tablespoons butter

1 small bouquet garni

1 cup [225 ml] dry white wine

2 dozen littleneck clams, or 2 pounds mussels or New Zealand cockles, well scrubbed

1 cup [225 ml] heavy cream

2 tablespoons finely chopped parsley

1 tablespoon finely chopped chives (optional)

pepper

REMOVE the gills from the fish heads and discard the gills. Soak the fish bones and heads in cold water for at least 2 hours, changing the water every 30 minutes. Cut the fish fillets into 4 or 6 pieces, as close to the same size as possible, and refrigerate.

CUT most of the greens off the leeks, leaving about 4 inches [10 cm] of green attached to the white. Cut the white in half lengthwise and rinse out any sand under running water. Chop fine. Cook the chopped leek gently in butter in a heavy-bottomed pot for about 5 minutes. Drain the fish bones, put them in the pot, add the bouquet garni, and stir every few minutes until the bones fall apart but don't brown, about 15 minutes. Pour in the white wine and 1 cup [225 ml] of water (don't worry if you don't have enough liquid to cover the bones completely), cover the pot, and simmer gently over low heat for 15 minutes. Strain into a clean pot large enough to hold the shellfish. You should have about 1½ cups [375 ml] of liquid.

PUT the shellfish in the pot with the fish broth, cover the pot, and cook the shellfish over medium to high heat until they've all opened, about 12 minutes for clams, 5 minutes for mussels or cockles. Scoop the shellfish out of the pot into a bowl and cover the bowl with aluminum foil to keep the shellfish warm and moist. (If you like, take one of the shells off of each of the shellfish so they take up less room on the plate.) If you see sand on the bottom of the pot used for steaming the shellfish, carefully pour the liquid into a clean pot, leaving the sand behind. At this point you should have about 3 cups of liquid. If you have less, add enough water to make 3 cups.

POACH the fish pieces in the steaming liquid—cover the pan if there is not enough liquid to cover—and scoop the pieces out onto hot soup plates. (Or bake the fish pieces; see page 238.) Surround the fish with the shellfish. Add the cream and herbs to the poaching liquid, season to taste with salt and pepper (be careful of the salt, the shellfish is very salty), bring back to a simmer, and spoon the liquid over the fish. Serve immediately.

Variations: The poaching liquid is easy to flavor with different herbs—try basil, marjoram, or tarragon. Spices, such as saffron and curry (curry cooked first in a little butter, traditional in a *mouclade*), are sublime with the briny shellfish. Cubes of in-season tomatoes (or tomatoes added to the fish broth) give the sauce a lovely sweetness and a pink hue. Spinach or sorrel, lightly creamed, can be placed in small mounds in the bottom of the soup plates and used for propping up the fish, making it look more dramatic and preventing it from overcooking in the sauce. New potatoes can be steamed and added to the stew at the end (so that they act as a gentle foil without absorbing the seafood flavors as they do when cooked in a chowder), as can pearl onions or baby turnips. Truffles (chopped or sliced) and morels (fresh or dried, left whole or halved; dried morels soaked, simmered in the liquid at the end) are marvelous. Subtle Mexican flavors can be incorporated by simmering a soaked, softened, and chopped dried chile (anchos or guajillos are easy to find, but my favorites are the hot and smoky *pasilla di Oaxaca* and the subtle-flavored black *chilhuacle negro*) in the finished poaching liquid. And of course all the garnitures you might use for a meat stew—little green vegetables, artichokes, glazed root vegetables—can be used here.

Improvising a Seafood Soup, Stew, or Sauce

FOR MEAT, STEWING USUALLY IMPLIES LONG cooking, but for seafood (with the exception of octopus, squid, and cuttlefish), cooking times are usually short. Seafood stews tend also to be rather formal and carefully controlled (fish poached at the last minute, arranged carefully in soup plates), whereas most soups are put together by just adding the ingredients at more or less the right time. Soups are then simply ladled out into bowls, instead of being arranged. But any soup, stew, or sauce is made following the same principles. Once you grasp the succession of techniques, you'll be able to make a soup or stew with just about anything that swims.

THE BASIC LIQUID

FISH BROTH: Simmer fish bones and heads (which may be browned first for a more assertive but less subtle flavor) with aromatic vegetables (maybe just a leek or onion, but often including carrots, celery, garlic, and fennel) and a bouquet garni. Moistening liquids are usually white wine and water, but red wine and hard cider can also be used.

SHELLFISH STEAMING LIQUID: The liquid released by shellfish such as clams, cockles, and mussels has an intense briny flavor of the sea that's never matched by fish broth. The only problem is that a relatively large number of shellfish are required to produce a small amount of liquid. This method is better for stews and sauces than it is for soups, because soups require too much liquid. Shellfish steaming liquid can also be used in combination with fish broth.

VEGETABLE BROTH (court bouillon): Some very delicate fish stews, and some versions of seafood pot-au-feu, are made with vegetable broth instead of fish broth. Vegetable broth (see page 283) can also be reduced to concentrate the natural sweetness of the vegetables.

THE FISH

Many of us can't find afford to be picky, because much of the time we can find only one or two varieties of fish that are truly fresh. Firm-fleshed fish are best because they won't fall apart while they sit in a hot broth or stewing liquid. If you can find only soft-fleshed fish like rockfish, you might want to make the *soupe de poisson à la marseillaise* described on page 238; since the fish is puréed into the soup, its texture is unimportant. One alternative is to buy firm-fleshed fish steaks, such as swordfish or shark steaks, and then buy small, soft-fleshed fish to make the broth. Unless you're making a red wine fish stew, avoid stronger-tasting fish such as salmon and mackerel.

FINISHES AND THICKENERS

Most seafood stews are slightly thickened or given a silky consistency with rich ingredients such as cream, butter, egg yolks, rouille (see page 236) or aïoli (see page 491), either alone or in combination. An American chowder is naturally somewhat thick because the potatoes release starch into the surrounding liquid; also, many of those who enjoy chowder stir in broken soda crackers, which act as a thickener. French seafood stews are sometimes thickened with flour, either by whisking fish broth into a roux to make a *velouté de poisson* or, more typical of red wine stews, by whisking beurre manié into the stew at the end. A *soupe de poisson à la marseillaise* is thickened with the puréed fish itself. Herb butters, lobster butter (see page 335), or sea urchin or scallop roe (puréed with an equal amount of butter) can also be whisked into a seafood stew or sauce as a final thickener and to provide nuance.

GARNITURES

Any garniture that is appropriate for a meat stew will work as well for a seafood stew. Little mounds of lightly creamed sorrel or spinach, or a combination, make a wonderful foil for creamy seafood stews. Baby green vegetables—haricots verts, fava beans, and peas—add color and a fresh crunch. Glazed root vegetables and mushrooms add flavor and give the stew body.

OYSTERS

HUÎTRES

HOW AND WHEN	HOW TO	HOW TO	HOW TO	HOW TO
TO SHOP FOR OYSTERS	SHUCK AN OYSTER	COOK AN OYSTER: GRILLING, BROILING, AND OYSTER STEW	MAKE HOLLANDAISE SAUCE	IMPROVISE YOUR OWN HOT OYSTER DISHES

SOME PEOPLE HATE OYSTERS AND OTHERS LOVE THEM. MY OWN observation has been that most of those who hate them have never tasted one. Some doggedly refuse to give them a try, having made the mistake of looking at one too closely, or even worse having glanced at an illustration in a cookbook, one with little arrows pointing out the oyster's various parts. Oysters are, in fact, not the most beautiful of creatures. Then there's the texture, which should at first be ignored, and the oyster swallowed whole. But once these initial anxieties are overcome, a fondness develops that borders on the religious, perhaps because nothing so completely captures the pure essence of the sea. There is also the question of raw versus cooked. As M.F.K. Fisher once explained, there are those who will only eat oysters raw, those who will only eat them cooked, and those who will eat them "hot, cold, thin, thick, dead, or alive." I belong to the latter group, but I also believe that once an oyster is cooked it descends from the realm of the divine into the reality of mere deliciousness.

There are those who quibble about which are the best oysters, and I too have my opinions, but part of an oyster's magic is its individuality—no oyster tastes exactly the same as another. Each has its own nuances. Almost all taste the way the ocean smells, but some have a distinctly metallic taste (which I especially love), others have a vague scent of sulphur (which is subtle and intriguing, not bad), and some have fragrances so particular to oysters that they're too difficult to describe. My own preference is for oysters from the coldest water, usually from the Pacific or the northern part of the Atlantic, because they often have the most intense flavor of ocean. Oyster bars these days offer an assortment from various places, making it easy to experiment and, if you're a beginner, discover your favorites.

Most oysters are named after the place they originally came from or come from now, but in fact there are only three major varieties that you're likely to encounter. The most common are what the French call *huîtres creuses*, "hollow oysters," because these oysters have deep bottom shells. They're elongated rather than round. If you're eating oysters in France, you'll notice that *huîtres creuses*, which until recently were called *portugaises*, and are now called *japonnaises*, come in various sizes and gradations. The gradations have to do with how long the oysters have spent in special brackish fattening beds, called *claires*, which are rich in plankton. You'll run into terms such as *améliorées en claires*, *fines de claires*, and *spéciales*, with *spéciales* being the fattest oysters. Most oysters you'll encounter in the United States are examples of "hollow oysters."

In addition to *huîtres creuses*, there are what the French call *huîtres plates*, "flat oysters," because the bottom shell is rather flat. Flat oysters are round rather than elongated. They were the original European oyster and until the twentieth century were the only oysters eaten in France. In the United States, flat oysters are cultivated in Maine and California and are usually sold under the name "belon," after a well-known variety from Brittany. In France, however, there are more than one kind of flat oyster, named after where they are harvested. So, in France at least, not all flat oysters are belons. There are also *marennes*, *gravettes*, and *bouzigues*—all flat oysters but with different nuances of flavor and color.

The third variety, native to America, is the Olympia oyster, which is hard to grow and rarely grows much larger than a quarter, but has a special intense flavor all its own.

Many of us who adore raw oysters have our own idiosyncrasies. There are those who insist on lemon wedges, others want hot sauce, francophiles require *sauce mignonnette* (see page 253), and others, like myself, require nothing, unless I'm in a French place, where I expect the traditional French accompaniments, brown bread and good butter—perfect foils for the briny oysters. Oysters should be served nestled in crushed ice on a platter or on individual plates. Because I don't have an ice crusher, I wrap ice cubes in a kitchen towel and smash them brutally on the sidewalk (my neighbors think I'm weird anyway). Whatever you do, if you set oysters out for any period of time—say, at a buffet—don't let the ice melt and get into the oyster. The water will leach out the flavor and turn the oyster into a nauseating slimy blob. You can also set oysters on a bed of seaweed—oyster sellers often have it on hand—but then you must eat the oysters right away before they warm up. Some people like to serve raw or cooked oysters on a plate of coarse salt, but this is messy and inevitably some of the salt gets on your lap and into the oyster, making something that is already salty, too salty.

It's hard to judge the condition of an oyster by just looking at one at the market, but there are two things to watch out for. Unlike perfectly healthy mussels, which sometimes open slightly when sitting around, oysters must be tightly closed. If they're not, they're probably old (or improperly trained—French oysters are actually taught to stay closed, by exposing them to the open air for short periods before they are harvested). But even when fresh and healthy, an opened oyster may dry out. Again, unlike mussels, which can be stored any which way as long as they're kept cold and have access to air, oysters should be stored flat so their brine doesn't seep out; even a tightly closed oyster will eventually dry out if kept on its side or stored haphazardly in a net bag. When you get your oysters home, stack them carefully, so they're all flat and top-side up, on a plate or platter and put them in the refrigerator. (The top is flat, and even on a flat oyster the bottom shell is slightly rounded.) There is also the question of seasons. Tradition has it that one should eat oysters only in months containing an *R*—good advice in the days before refrigeration, when oysters would quickly deteriorate in the heat of summer. Nowadays, in New York at least, I see people wolfing down oysters year-round. But I don't like most oysters during the summer because they're preparing to spawn and are filled with a milky substance—the French call such oysters *laiteuse*—that gives the oysters a slightly unpleasant texture and dulls their flavor.

Many fish stores will shuck oysters for you, sometimes for a small fee. But if you're not planning to eat the oysters within a few hours, or if the fish store hasn't shucked them and you have no way of keeping them flat on your way home, you're going to have to shuck them yourself. Until you've had a bit of practice, this can be tedious and somewhat risky business. First, you need a decent knife. An oyster knife, with a solid handle and a 5-inch [12.5-cm] blade that's pointed but not too sharp, is best. If you find yourself in a poorly equipped kitchen at a summer rental, you can make do with a regular dining-room knife. Don't use a kitchen knife, which is too sharp and can seriously hurt you if you slip, and don't use a clam knife—one with a short triangular blade—or you'll damage the oyster. Real pros hold the oyster in one hand and the knife in the other as they shuck, but I find it easier and safer to place the oyster on a double-folded towel on a steady work surface. I hold the oyster with the towel in my left hand (I'm right-handed) against the work surface and keep a fold of the towel partway up on top of the oyster so it's between my left hand and the knife. You then must scrutinize the oyster for a vulnerable point of entry. Elongated oysters are best approached at the hinge. Flat oysters—belons—are usually opened through the side. Usually it's easy to spot a space between the top shell and the bottom shell in which to stick the knife. Stick the knife firmly into this little gap and twist it. If all goes well, you'll feel the top give and see it separate slightly from the bottom shell. Slide the knife under the top shell, keeping the blade firmly against the underside of the top shell so that you neither damage the oyster, most of which sits nestled in the deeper bottom shell, nor waste any oyster by leaving some attached to the top shell. Remove the top. You can leave the oyster as it is or you can rinse it. I was shocked the first time I saw someone rinse out an oyster, but the oyster immediately refills with brine after the rinsing and any grit that may have fallen into the oyster while you were shucking is washed away. To rinse an oyster, hold it under a slow, steady stream of cold water from the tap for a second or two while running your finger around and under the oyster, letting the water get under and wash out grit. The next decision is whether or not to detach the oyster from the bottom shell. In France, oysters are always served attached and it's left to you, the diner, to cut the oyster away with a small oyster fork. But at home, I make life simpler for my guests and detach the oyster by running the oyster knife firmly against the bottom shell.

The French have loved oysters for centuries. As the weather starts to cool, usually in late September, wooden crates of oysters appear under the awnings of brasseries and fancier cafés. A half dozen oysters make a perfect first course at dinner or lunch, but you can also make a decent meal or luxurious afternoon snack out of a platter of oysters. Three dozen oysters—18 each—is usually about right for a couple of serious oyster eaters having an oyster meal or serious (and pricey) snack. I drink Chablis if I'm feeling flush, a good muscadet when I'm not.

SAUCE MIGNONNETTE

I'm such a purist about oysters that I rarely add anything to them. But the French insist on serving a mixture of cracked pepper, shallots, and wine vinegar called a *sauce mignonnette*. *Mignonnette* is also the word for cracked pepper. If you're having French friends over, you'll see them looking around for it, so here's the recipe:

MAKES 1 CUP [225 ML]

3 tablespoon black peppercorns

2 shallots, chopped very fine

¾ cup [175 ml] good-quality white wine vinegar or good-quality aged sherry vinegar

CRUSH the peppercorns by placing them on a cutting board and rocking over them with the corner of a heavy saucepan, leaning on them with all your weight. (You can also use already cracked pepper, but it's not as aromatic.) Combine with the shallots and vinegar and let sit, covered, for at least 1 hour but ideally overnight. Serve chilled.

HOW TO GET THE ROE OUT OF A SEA URCHIN

If you're buying whole sea urchins, cut off the top—the side with the hole in the middle—by cutting through the hole with a pair of heavy scissors all the way to the outer edge of the urchin. Cut around the sides of the urchin, remove the entire top, and scoop out the golden-orange roe with a small spoon.

Caviar is such a lovely addition to oysters that it's hard to imagine a more special treat. Caviar is often paired with crunchy things like toast or crackers, which make it harder to appreciate the caviar's delicate texture. Oysters, on the other hand, have a gentle texture that won't interfere with that of the caviar, and the flavors are an equal match, so neither one is lost. How much caviar to use per oyster is up to you, but if you can't afford to be relatively generous, you're better off leaving the oysters alone—the flavor and texture of too little caviar will go unnoticed. I recommend at least 1 teaspoon per oyster—1 ounce [30 g] of caviar per half dozen oysters.

Another of my favorite oyster tricks is to dollop a tiny bit of raw lobster roe and tomalley on each oyster, but unless your guests are Japanese, I'd be careful about going into too much detail. To get at the roe and tomalley you must cut up the lobsters while they're alive (see page 333), scoop out the roe and tomalley, and work them through a fine-mesh strainer. The roe is extremely perishable, so you have to perform this operation within an hour of the arrival of your guests and keep the roe-tomalley mixture in a bowl with a few drops of vinegar (to prevent clotting), set over another bowl filled with ice, in the refrigerator until just before serving. You can cook the lobster—now in pieces—and serve it later in the dinner or, cold, the next day.

Other sneaky little tricks involve adding literally 1 or 2 drops of various flavorful liquids to each oyster. (Use an eyedropper.) A drop of Pernod adds an exciting note, as does a drop or so of authentic balsamic vinegar (page 50) or truffled vinegar (see Sources) or truffle oil.

Because the delicate sea-like flavor of oysters is so easily compromised and is virtually impossible to improve, I limit additions to a few favorite delicacies. Sea urchin roe, which, if you can't get it at the fish store you should be able to buy at a Japanese restaurant, gives a slightly sweet yet still sea-like dimension to oysters. (The roe is expensive, but you won't need much.) Sea urchin roe is sold by itself, carefully arranged in little wooden boxes. In French restaurants it is served in the shell, often along with oysters on a raw seafood platter (*assiette de fruits de mer*). When the pieces of roe are relatively large—about 1 teaspoon— I cut them into smaller pieces, but I never chop the roe to the consistency of a purée, as this causes it to loose its texture and identity. Depending on the size of your oysters and your generosity, dollop slightly more or less than 1 teaspoon of roe on each oyster.

COOKED OYSTERS

One of the earliest cookbooks, Taillevent's *Le Viandier,* gives a recipe for oysters that, in typical medieval fashion, contains a collection of spices including saffron, ginger, cloves, cinnamon, and *graines de paradis* (a kind of pepper grown in Africa, used today in Moroccan and Tunisian cooking). The body of the sauce is provided by white wine held together with bread and puréed peas, a touch reminiscent of modern sauces held together with vegetable purées. Later recipes for cooked oysters, those that start to appear in cookbooks written in the seventeenth century, are more typical of modern French cooking. The spices are replaced with indigenous ingredients such as capers and herbs like thyme and chives. Bread continues to be the thickener of choice, usually in the form of bread crumbs (called *chapelure*), but lard, the favorite cooking fat of the Middle Ages, is supplanted by butter, and oyster stews (*ragoûts*) are used as accompaniments to or integral parts of an amazing variety of other seafood, meat, and poultry dishes.

Virtually every cookbook written in French since the fourteenth century contains some recipe for cooked oysters. A lot of these old recipes are impractical to prepare exactly as they were written, but with a little improvisation in the kitchen they can inspire dishes that are appealing to modern tastes and relatively light. One of the simplest recipes for cooked oysters is from Françoise Píerre La Varenne's *Le Cuisinier François,* first published in 1651. It suggests simply grilling the whole oysters in the shell. This is an easy way to cook oysters, because you don't have to shuck them. Just scrub them with a brush and put them whole on the barbecue or in the oven, so that as they cook, the oyster dies and lets go of its top shell, which you can then pull off. You can eat the oysters as they are or sprinkle them with sauce. Some people like Tabasco, which annihilates the taste of the oyster. I prefer to put a little chunk of butter in the oyster and leave it for a minute more on the grill until the butter melts.

You can serve oysters with more or less elaborate sauces and garnitures either in or out of the shell. Both methods require first shucking the oysters and gently poaching them in their own juices. (Never allow an oyster to boil or it will harden into a little flavorless ball.) If you're serving the oysters in the shell, you can put a garniture—such as duxelles (see page 96), creamed spinach or sorrel, diced or julienned vegetables or bacon gently sweated until soft—in the shell and place the oyster on top. You can then top the oyster with any number of sauces, which may or may not include the reduced oyster poaching liquid, and heat the oysters in the oven and slide them under the broiler. Here's one of my favorite ways of serving hot oysters in the shell, a recipe I learned at the Paris restaurant Vivarois.

GRATINÉED OYSTERS WITH CURRIED HOLLANDAISE SAUCE

HUÎTRES GRATINÉES AU CURRY

MAKES 4 GENEROUS FIRST-COURSE OR
8 LIGHT FIRST-COURSE SERVINGS

It was up to me, as the lowest-ranking member of the restaurant kitchen, to shuck the oysters for this dish (always to order, never ahead of time), whisk up the hollandaise, and get the plates of hot oysters into the hands of the snarling waiters as quickly as possible. Assuming your own work environment is a little less hectic, you can shuck the oysters and take them out of the shells earlier the same day, and blanch the spinach. However, you should make the hollandaise, which is very perishable, within an hour of serving the dish and cream the spinach and poach the oysters at the last minute. If you're serving these oysters as part of an elaborate dinner with lots of courses, give 3 per person (meaning this recipe will make enough for 8), but if you're following the oysters with a relatively light main course, give 6 per person.

- 2 bunches spinach (10 ounces [280 g] each)
  salt
- 24 medium-size oysters
- 1½ cups [375 ml] (one recipe) hollandaise (see page 257)
- 1 tablespoon good-quality curry powder
- 1 tablespoon butter
- 4 tablespoons heavy cream
  pepper
  mild Hungarian paprika

WASH the spinach, remove and discard the stems, and blanch the leaves for 30 seconds to 1 minute—until they "melt"—in 1 quart of boiling salted water. Drain the spinach in a colander and quickly rinse it under cold running water to cool it. Gently squeeze it in bunches to eliminate excess water. Chop it once or twice, just enough to break it up, and reserve it on a plate.

SHUCK the oysters into a bowl and discard the top shells. Scrub the bottom shells under running water and arrange them on a sheet pan covered with a sheet of crumpled aluminum foil, which will keep them flat on the sheet pan. Place the sheet pan in a 200°F [95°C] (or lowest setting possible) oven about 20 minutes before you're ready to serve the oysters, to dry out and heat the shells. Pick the oysters out of the bowl and arrange them on a clean kitchen towel. Pat them with a second towel and place them in a 2-quart sauce pan—all the grit and sand should be left adhering to the towels. Strain the oyster liquid left in the bowl through a fine-mesh strainer into the saucepan with the oysters. Refrigerate.

ABOUT 15 minutes before you're ready to serve, prepare the hollandaise. Combine the curry powder with the butter in a small saucepan and heat, while stirring, over low heat until you can smell the fragrance of the curry, about 1 minute. (This is to wake up the flavor of the spices contained in the curry.) Stir the curry mixture, a bit at a time, to taste, into the hollandaise.

BOIL the cream in a small, heavy-bottomed saucepan until it reduces by about half and gets very thick. Stir in the spinach. Continue stirring over medium heat until the spinach is hot, about 3 minutes. Season lightly with salt and pepper. Take the oyster shells out of the oven (unless you have a second oven or a separate broiler) and turn on the broiler.

PUT the saucepan containing the oysters over medium heat until the oysters just begin to curl around the edges, and take the pan off the heat. Put a spoonful of hot spinach on each oyster shell. Lift the oysters out of the saucepan with a spoon and arrange them in the shells over the spinach.

DOLLOP about 1½ tablespoons of curried hollandaise over each oyster. Quickly broil the oysters until the hollandaise bubbles up slightly, about 30 seconds. You'll need to reposition the sheet pan every few seconds so all the oysters brown evenly. Sprinkle with paprika and serve immediately.

Variations: Just about any hot in-the-shell oyster you encounter in a restaurant will be put together much like this one. Only the garniture in the shell and the sauce will differ. Most oyster sauces are based on the reduced oyster poaching liquid, which is often combined with white wine and sometimes with shallots before cream or butter is whisked in, as in making a beurre blanc (see page 281). One of the most common hot oyster dishes is oysters with champagne sauce, made by reducing Champagne with shallots and the oyster cooking liquid. Frankly, I'd rather drink the Champagne and use a wine with plenty of acidity, such as a muscadet. When the sauce is ready, it can be spooned over the oysters as is, or you can add other ingredients such as finely chopped herbs (chervil, parsley, chives, or tarragon), spices (curry mixtures, saffron), compound butters (especially Crustacean Butter, see page 335), chopped truffles, reduced mushroom cooking liquid (see page 8), reduced and strained tomato purée (coulis), or roe (lobster, sea urchin, sea scallop) to come up with your own versions.

Oysters Rockefeller is an American invention but is based on the same principle as its French cousins except that garniture—a combination of cooked spinach, bread crumbs, bacon, scallions, and a little hot sauce—goes on top of the oysters before they are broiled.

The garniture for underneath the oyster can be left out altogether, but it helps attenuate the richness of the sauce and the oyster itself and should be designed with this in mind. If, for example, you're using a tangy mock champagne sauce (made with white wine), you should avoid an acidic garniture such as tomates concassées or sorrel. On the other hand, if the sauce is less acidic and is finished with a rich ingredient such as sea urchin roe, you may want a tangy garniture (again, such as tomates concassées or lightly creamed sorrel) to contrast with the sauce and lighten the effect of the whole assembly. You can also use sauces from other dishes, such as the quick sauce américaine on page 340.

HOLLANDAISE SAUCE AND ITS COUSINS

A well-made hollandaise is an airy sauce made by combining egg yolks with a small amount of water and then whisking the mixture over medium heat until the egg yolks trap air and become frothy and eventually stiffen slightly into a sabayon. Butter—in cold cubes, melted, or clarified—is then gently whisked into the airy egg yolk mixture and the sauce is seasoned with salt and pepper and a little lemon.

When the egg yolks froth up and start to stiffen, immediately take the pan off the heat, whisk for a minute off the heat to cool the yolks, and whisk in the butter in a steady stream, or in chunks if you're using whole butter. Add lemon or other flavorings.

Hollandaise has a lot of relatives, all made basically the same way with flavorful ingredients replacing the water at the beginning or added at the end. A béarnaise sauce is flavored with a reduction of vinegar, black pepper, shallots, and tarragon; a *sauce Choron* is a béarnaise with tomato purée added; a *sauce paloise* is a béarnaise made with mint instead of tarragon; a *sauce maltaise* includes reduced blood-orange juice (or regular orange juice) added at the beginning and blanched orange zest whipped cream folded in at the end; and a *sauce vin blanc*, used for *sole Marguéry* (see page 310), is made by whisking

(continued)

the white-wine braising liquid from the fish with the egg yolks before adding the butter. A *sauce tyroli-enne* is made like hollandaise, but olive oil replaces the butter, resulting in a sort of hot mayonnaise. You can also invent your own variations (see page 257). To make 1½ cups [375 ml] of hollandaise or one of its derivatives, whisk together 2 egg yolks with cool water or a flavorful liquid such as fish broth.

French chefs argue about whether it is best to use whole butter, either cold or melted, or clari-fied butter for hollandaise sauces. It depends on the consistency you want. Clarified butter, because it contains no water, will produce a stiffer, more traditional sauce than whole butter. This is especially useful if you're combining a relatively large amount of liquid with the egg yolks at the beginning and you don't want to thin the sauce any more. Beurre noisette, butter that has been lightly caramelized (see page 7), has an intense buttery flavor that makes it useful in sauces in which you want to use just a little butter but you still want the sauce to taste buttery. Cold or melted whole butter will produce a thinner sauce because the butter contains water.

MAKES 1½ CUPS [375 ML]

2 sticks (½ pound [225 g]) butter

4 large egg yolks

4 tablespoons cold water

1 teaspoon lemon juice, or to taste

salt and white pepper

CLARIFY the butter by heating it in a heavy-bottomed saucepan over medium heat until the milk solids form golden-brown specks and the butter becomes clear and takes on a golden hue, about 10 minutes. Watch the butter carefully so you don't burn it. Strain the butter through a fine-mesh sieve or coffee filter and let it cool.

COMBINE the egg yolks with the cold water in a saucepan with sloping sides (a Windsor pan) or in a medium-size stainless steel mixing bowl. Whisk the mixture until it becomes light and frothy, about 30 seconds. Place the Windsor pan or mixing bowl on medium heat (if you're using a bowl, hold it on one side with a kitchen towel) and whisk rapidly until the mixture triples in volume and suddenly thickens—you will start to see the bottom of the saucepan or bowl while whisking. Immediately remove the egg mixture from the heat and continue to whisk for about 20 seconds so that it cools. Ladle the clarified butter into the egg mixture while gently stirring with the whisk. Add the lemon juice and season with salt and pepper.

GRATINÉED OYSTERS WITH BACON, TOMATOES, AND TARRAGON

HUÎTRES GRATINÉES AU LARD MAIGRE, AUX TOMATES ET À L'ESTRAGON

MAKES 4 GENEROUS FIRST-COURSE OR
8 LIGHT FIRST-COURSE SERVINGS

Oysters are often coupled with bacon—a tradition that seems to have been popular with the English. In most of the recipes I've tried, the flavor of the bacon is too strong and masks the taste of the oyster. In this dish, just a hint of bacon is used so that its smoky flavor balances the oyster's brininess. If you're serving these oysters as part of an elaborate dinner with lots of courses, give 3 per person (meaning this recipe will make enough for 8), but if you're following oysters with a relatively light main course, give 6 per person.

1	large carrot, peeled
1	large leek
2	slices bacon chilled, between ⅛ and ¼ inch [about .5 cm] thick
	salt
	pepper
3	medium-size tomatoes, peeled, seeded, and chopped fine
⅓	cup [75 ml] heavy cream
2	teaspoons fresh tarragon leaves
24	medium-size oysters
⅓	cup [35 g] finely grated Parmigiano-Reggiano or grana padana

CUT the carrot into tiny dice, between ⅛ inch and ¼ inch [about .5 cm] on each side. The easiest way to do this is to cut the carrot into 2-inch [5 cm] sections and then slice the sections along their sides with a plastic vegetable slicer, slice each of these flat slices into julienne with a chef's knife, and then slice the julienne into cubes. Cut the greens off the leeks and discard them or save for broth; cut the whites in half lengthwise and rinse out any sand. Peel the individual stalks off the leeks, 2 or 3 stalks at a time, and slice them lengthwise into a fine julienne. Slice across the julienne so you end up with tiny squares of leek. Cut the bacon into dice between ⅛ inch and ¼ inch [about .5 cm] thick. (This is easier if you first chill the bacon for 10 minutes in the freezer.)

HEAT the bacon cubes in a small sauté pan over low to medium heat until they just begin to render fat, about 3 minutes, and add the carrot cubes. Continue cooking the mixture, stirring every minute or so, for about 5 minutes, and add the leeks. Continue cooking the mixture until the vegetables have all softened, about 5 minutes more. Season the mixture with salt and pepper (it might not need salt because of the bacon) and reserve.

HEAT the tomatoes over medium heat in a small saucepan until they release their liquid and the liquid evaporates. Add the cream. Chop the tarragon leaves quite coarse and stir them into the tomato mixture. Simmer the mixture until it thickens slightly, about 3 minutes. Season to taste with salt and pepper and reserve.

SHUCK the oysters into a bowl and discard the top shells. Scrub the bottom shells under running water and arrange them on a sheet pan covered with a sheet of crumpled aluminum foil, which will keep them flat on the sheet pan. Place the sheet pan in a 250°F [120°C/gas mark ½] oven about 20 minutes before you're ready to serve the oysters, to dry out and heat the shells. Pick the oysters out of the bowl and arrange them on a clean kitchen towel. Pat them with a second towel and place them in a 2-quart [2 l] saucepan—all the grit and sand should be left adhering to the towels. Strain the oyster liquid in the bowl through a fine-mesh strainer into the saucepan with the oysters. If you're not serving the oysters right away, refrigerate them.

WHEN you're ready to serve, preheat the broiler and gently heat the bacon mixture and the sauce. Put the saucepan containing the oysters over medium heat until the oysters just begin to curl around the edges. Put 1 teaspoon of the bacon mixture in each oyster shell, put a hot oyster in each shell, and put 1 teaspoon of sauce over each oyster. Sprinkle each oyster with the cheese and slide the sheet pan under the broiler, moving it around so that the oysters are gratinéed evenly. Serve immediately.

OYSTER STEWS

An oyster stew can be more like a soup or more like a stew, depending on how much liquid you use and whether you thicken the liquid. Stews can be thickened with roux, vegetable purée (such as the puréed peas that are used to thicken Taillevent's *cretonnée de poys nouveaux,* with its spice-flavored broth), the bread crumbs (*chapelure*) called for in seventeenth- and eighteenth-century recipes, cooked puréed rice, a few puréed oysters, or the broken-up soda crackers served in American restaurants today.

In its simplest form, an oyster stew—sometimes misleadingly called "pan-fried" or "pan-roasted" oysters—is made by simmering freshly shucked oysters in heavy cream just long enough to heat the oysters through. Fresh pepper is ground over the top—salt is rarely needed—and the simple stew, surely one of the best of all things, is served forth. An oyster stew fits in any setting and is no more out of place on a greasy lunch counter than it is on a linen tablecloth in a chic French restaurant. Good oysters and good cream are all that is required.

Of course, there are those of us who like to take something perfectly good and try to make it better. A simple oyster is impossible to improve, but it can be varied almost limitlessly. When onions and/or potatoes are included, the stew is sometimes called a chowder (virtually the same as a New England clam chowder made with oysters). I like to turn an oyster

stew into something more substantial by garnishing the stew with vegetables such as pearl onions, baby peas, light creamed spinach or sorrel, fava or lima beans, tiny string beans, wild mushrooms, baby chard, or virtually any young, delicate, and colorful vegetable. Because oysters mustn't overcook for even a second, I prepare the vegetables separately and add them to the stew at the same time as, or sometimes even before, I add the oysters. The sauce itself I usually leave alone because I don't want anything to interfere with the pure essence of the oysters, but I have on occasion swirled in a little Crustacean Butter (see page 335) or added reduced mushroom cooking liquid (see page 8) or mussel cooking liquid. (Paradoxically, while most of us prefer oysters to mussels, the liquid released by mussels as they are steamed [see Chapter 20] is far tastier than that released by oysters.)

French oyster stews seem to have fallen from fashion. I rarely see them on menus in France, and even in those provinces where oysters are abundant, there are few recipes. In the classic French dishes described by Escoffier, the closest relatives to the oyster *ragoûts* written about in the eighteenth and early nineteenth centuries are sauces containing oysters used for fish dishes such as *sole à la normande.* You can, in fact, use any oyster stew as a sauce or garniture for a piece of poached or braised fish (with the fish braising liquid used as a base for the sauce) or poultry, but such dishes become frightfully complicated and too confusing to eat, much less cook. Here's one of my favorite oyster stews. While I've never encountered it in France, it is modeled after versions I've read in old cookbooks.

OYSTER STEW WITH SPINACH AND CHIVES

HUÎTRES EN RAGOÛT AUX EPINARDS ET À LA CIBOULETTE

MAKES 6 FIRST-COURSE SERVINGS OR 4 LIGHT
MAIN-COURSE SERVINGS

24	dozen medium-size oysters
2	bunches spinach (10 ounces [280 g], or 1½ pounds [675 g] total; look for the kind with large crinkled leaves, which take less time to stem)
	salt
2	medium-size shallots, chopped fine
1	tablespoon butter
¼	cup [60 ml] white wine
1	cup [225 ml] heavy cream
1	big handful sorrel leaves, stems removed (optional)
	pepper
1	tablespoon finely chopped fresh chives

SHUCK the oysters (see page 252 for more about shucking oysters) into a fine-mesh strainer set over a small bowl. Pick the oysters out of the strainer, roll them gently on a clean kitchen towel so that any grit clings to the towel, and put them in the bowl with their strained juices. Reserve in the refrigerator.

BRING about 6 quarts [6 l] of water to a rapid boil.

PULL the stems off the spinach leaves. (Peel the stems away from the backs of the leaves, don't just break them off where they join the leaf.) Wash the leaves thoroughly in a large bowl of water. Lift the leaves out of the water with your fingers. Repeat this process until there's no sand left in the bottom of the bowl. Toss a handful of salt into the boiling water and add the spinach. Stir the spinach in the hot water for 30 seconds to 1 minute, until the spinach "melts." Drain immediately in a colander and rinse with cold water. Squeeze the spinach gently to eliminate excess water.

COMBINE the shallots and butter in a small, heavy-bottomed saucepan and cook over medium heat until the shallots turn translucent, about 5 minutes. Pour in the wine and the juices from the bowl with the oysters—just hold the oysters back with your hand while pouring the juices out of the bowl. Simmer the mixture for about 5 minutes, until there are only a couple of tablespoons of liquid left. Pour in ¾ cup [175 ml] of the cream and simmer for about 5 minutes more, until the cream barely begins to thicken. Remove from the heat.

HEAT the remaining ¼ cup [60 ml] of cream in a small sauté pan over medium heat until the cream gets very thick, almost to the point where it's starting to break, and stir in the spinach and the sorrel, if you're using it. When the spinach is heated through and the sorrel turns gray-green, season the mixture to taste with salt and pepper and distribute it into 4 or 6 heated soup plates or small bowls.

ADD the oysters and chives to the wine sauce and heat gently just until the oysters shrink a little, but don't allow the sauce to boil. Adjust the seasoning and spoon the oysters and sauce into the plates with the spinach, giving 6 oysters per serving for a main course or 4 oysters per serving for a first course.

VARIATIONS ON OYSTER STEW

As with so many French dishes, it's easy to come up with variations by substituting ingredients at particular stages of the cooking process. Virtually every oyster stew is made in the same way—aromatic ingredients such as shallots or mirepoix are cooked in a small amount of fat or simmered directly in liquid (usually including the briny oyster liquid and white wine), the mixture is simmered and sometimes thickened, and the stew is finished with cream and/or butter and additional flavorings and garnitures.

FOR THE AROMATIC SAUCE BASE

DICED MIREPOIX (mixture of onions, carrots, and celery)

Onions alone

PROSCIUTTO, BACON, OR PANCETTA (cut into tiny cubes or little strips)

FATS FOR COOKING THE AROMATIC BASE

BUTTER (plain, flavored, or crustacean)

GOOSE OR DUCK FAT

FOIE GRAS FAT

OLIVE OIL

LIQUIDS FOR THE SAUCE

LIQUID RELEASED BY THE OYSTERS AS THEY ARE HEATED

FISH BROTH BRAISING LIQUID FROM FISH

CREAM

DRY WHITE WINE

OTHER WINES (semidry Madeira, sherry, port, Sauternes)

MILK (which has to be used in conjunction with a thickener, such as roux or vegetable purée, or it will curdle)

RED WINE OR RED WINE SAUCES (see page 483 for a recipe for bordelaise sauce)

MUSSEL COOKING LIQUID (see Chapter 20)

MUSHROOM COOKING LIQUID (see page 8)

PURÉED TOMATOES

THICKENERS FOR THE SAUCE

ROUX (flour can be added to mirepoix, shallots, or onions while they're being cooked in fat)

REDUCED CREAM (cream boiled until it thickens)

BUTTER (plain, herb, or crustacean, swirled in at the end)

VEGETABLE PURÉES (cooked baby peas, roast garlic, roast or sweated onions, reduced tomato purée, artichokes, mushrooms)

RICE (short-grain rice—the kind used for risotto—boiled until it's overcooked, puréed, whisked into the sauce)

OYSTERS (puréed and strained)

BROKEN-UP SODA CRACKERS

SAUCE FLAVORINGS

CURRY OR OTHER INDIAN SPICE MIXTURES (sweated at the beginning with aromatic vegetables or gently cooked in butter and whisked into the sauce at the end)

SAFFRON (soaked in a tiny bit of water, stirred at the end)

HERBS (finely chopped parsley, chervil, chives, tarragon, basil; stronger herbs such as thyme, sage, savory, cooked with aromatic vegetables at the beginning or simmered in sauce in a bouquet garni)

PERNOD

CRUSTACEAN ROE (worked through a strainer into a little Cognac)

CRUSTACEAN OIL OR BUTTER

SEA URCHIN ROE

GARNITURE

LEAFY VEGETABLES (spinach, sorrel, chard, all preblanched except the sorrel)

ROOT VEGETABLES (peeled and glazed pearl onions, baby carrots, turnips, celeriac)

MUSHROOMS (fresh or dried, wild or cultivated, sautéed or poached in the sauce)

ARTICHOKES (baby, or bottoms from large artichokes, chokes removed from large artichoke bottoms)

TOMATOES (peeled, seeded, diced)

FENNEL (diced or cut into wedges, braised in a small amount of water and butter)

NEW YORK STRIP STEAK WITH RED WINE AND OYSTERS

CONTRE-FILET À LA SAUCE VIN ROUGE ET AUX HUÎTRES

MAKES 4 MAIN-COURSE SERVINGS

Although seventeenth- and eighteenth-century recipes often combined oysters with poultry, the French have rarely combined oysters with red meats. The most popular oyster-meat combination is oysters served with hot sausages, a combination popular in the Bordelais. Here I've come up with this sauce, made with red wine, mushrooms, and fresh oysters, that makes a marvelous briny counterpoint to the rich, full flavor of red meat.

You can approach the sauce in one of two ways. You can sauté the steaks and use the method I give below by deglazing the pan with red wine and adding a little concentrated broth or *glace de viande*, if you have it, reducing the sauce until it's lightly syrupy, adding the oyster juices, reducing again, poaching the oysters in the sauce, and finishing with butter. Or, you can use the *sauce meurette* on page 115 and poach the oysters directly in the sauce just before serving. Spoon the sauce and oysters over the steaks on each plate.

16 medium-size oysters, preferably briny northern oysters such as belons

4 steaks such as New York strips (8 to 12 ounces [225 to 340 g] each), or 2 large steaks, such as porterhouse (about 1½ pounds [675 g] each), or 1 very large porterhouse (3 pounds [1.5 kg])

salt

pepper

2 tablespoons "pure" olive oil, clarified butter, or duck fat

2 medium-size shallots, chopped fine

1 cup [250 ml] full-bodied red wine (see page 10 for the best wines to use for cooking)

½ cup [125 ml] concentrated broth, or 3 tablespoons *glace de viande* (page 221)

finely chopped parsley

6 tablespoons butter

SHUCK the oysters into a fine-mesh strainer set over a small bowl. Pick the oysters out of the strainer, roll them gently in a clean kitchen towel so that any grit clings to the towel, and put them in the bowl with their strained juices. Reserve in the refrigerator.

SEASON the steaks with salt, preferably 1 or 2 hours before you're ready to sauté. If you're serving the steaks rare, let them sit at room temperature for about 2 hours before you cook them, so that they're not cold in the middle after browning. Pat the steaks dry with a paper towel and season with pepper.

HEAT the oil or fat over high heat in a sauté pan just large enough to hold the steaks until the fat just begins to smoke. Sauté the steaks to the doneness you like (see page 48). Pat the steaks on both sides with a paper towel to remove any burnt fat and transfer them to individual plates or a large platter. Keep them warm while making the sauce.

POUR the burnt fat out of the sauté pan, turn the heat down to medium, and stir in the shallots. Put the pan back over the heat and stir the shallots until you can smell them lightly toasting, about 30 seconds. Pour in the wine. Boil the wine down to about half over high heat and stir in the concentrated broth or *glace de viande*. Pour in the oyster liquid and continue boiling down the sauce until it's thicker than the consistency you like (the oysters will release liquid and thin the sauce). Whisk in the parsley and butter, add the oysters, and give them 30 seconds to heat through, but don't allow the sauce to boil. Season the sauce to taste with salt and pepper. Spoon the sauce over the steaks, making sure that each person gets 4 oysters. If you're serving porterhouse steaks, bring the sauce to the table and spoon it and the oysters over each serving as you carve.

STEAMED MUSSELS WITH WHITE WINE, SHALLOTS, AND PARSLEY

MOULES À LA MARINIÈRE

HOW TO	HOW TO	HOW TO	HOW TO
STEAM SHELLFISH	CONVERT SHELLFISH JUICES INTO SAUCES	MAKE SHELLFISH SOUPS AND STEWS	EAT AND COOK SEA URCHINS

LIKE OYSTERS, MUSSELS CAN BE EATEN BOTH RAW AND COOKED, SOMEthing I discovered at La Fête de l'Humanité, an annual Parisian fair sponsored by the French communist party, where I had been invited by a friend. Expecting tedious Marxist discourses, I was relieved that the fête seemed to be more about food than about politics and was crowded with happy French people, presumably communists, drinking wine and munching gourmet treats. Two adjoining booths offered raw shellfish—one, oysters; the other, mussels. The oysters were far more expensive than the mussels, and the booth offering raw mussels was more popular. I wondered if this would be true in a classless society.

Unlike oysters, which are celestial when eaten raw and are just plain good when cooked, mussels are best cooked, especially with white wine and something aromatic, such as shallots or garlic. Mussels are also fun to eat. I first witnessed the procedure in a French café as a chic, long-fingered woman deftly picked them out of their shells with a pair of still-hinged mussel shells.

Moules à la marinière is a simple dish. (Loosely translated, *marinière* means bargeman's wife.) It makes a perfect first course at an informal dinner or main course at a casual lunch. You steam the mussels until they open, in dry white wine that you've simmered with a little chopped shallot and parsley. You don't need a steamer, just a big pot, because the shells keep the mussels suspended above the boiling liquid. When the mussels have all opened, take them out of the pot and grind a little pepper into the steaming liquid, which now contains the marvelous briny juices released by the mussels, and if you like, whisk in some butter. You then serve the mussels in big bowls with plenty of the steaming liquid poured over them. I usually rush through the mussels, washing them down with crisp white wine, so I can get to the liquid and mop it up with French bread.

SELECTING, SORTING, AND CLEANING MUSSELS

Until recently, most of the mussels sold in the United States were wild and tended to be rather large. As much as I love mussels, there's something a bit creepy about having your mouth filled with a single giant. Also, wild mussels often contain a lot of sand. Despite having followed the recommendations of some chefs to soak the mussels in salt water to rid them of sand, I always managed to bite down on grit. Cultivated mussels are becoming more popular and easier to find; they're smaller, easier to clean, and virtually free of sand. Bright green New Zealand mussels are relatively free of sand and, while more expensive, they look beautiful on the plate. Their flavor, though, isn't dramatically different from that of regular cultivated mussels.

Many recipes insist you should use only mussels that are firmly closed. But in fact mussels tend to be lazy, and even when perfectly healthy they gape a little when left undisturbed. When you tap two together, they'll close, usually within a couple of seconds. If you have a mussel that won't close, give it a sniff—it should smell of the sea and nothing else—and push the shells away from each other sideways. If the mussel is dead, the shells will come apart in your hand.

When you get your mussels home, put them in a colander and rinse them off with cold water. If they're cultivated and look clean, just rub them together with your hands under cold running water to get rid of any grit clinging to the outside of the shells. If they're wild and large, you may need to wash them with a stiff brush (or do what the French do, scrape them with the back of a small knife) to rid them of mud and sand. Sort through them, pressing the upper and lower shells sideways in opposite directions so that any dead mussels come apart in your hand. Be especially suspicious of any that feel heavy, since these are probably dead and full of mud. Many recipes insist that you remove the "beard"—the little stiff black hairs that stick out of one side—before cooking the mussels. The beard is what the mussel uses to attach to rocks, and it is important to remove it if you're cooking large mussels with long, thick beards. But when cooking small cultivated mussels, I rarely bother. If you do decide to remove the beards, just grip them with a kitchen towel and give them a yank. Don't do this more than a couple of hours before cooking the mussels because the process will eventually kill the mussels.

If you've bought mussels a day or two before you plan to use them, store them in a colander in the refrigerator, covered with a wet kitchen towel and a handful of ice cubes. Set the colander over a bowl to catch water from the melting ice. Pour out the water that accumulates in the bowl so it doesn't reach up and soak the mussels. Whatever you do, don't store mussels in a bowl with ice—the ice will melt and the fresh water surrounding the mussels will kill them.

STEAMED MUSSELS WITH WHITE WINE, SHALLOTS, AND PARSLEY

MOULES À LA MARINIÈRE

MAKES 6 FIRST-COURSE SERVINGS OR
LIGHT MAIN-COURSE SERVINGS

6   pounds [2.7 kg] mussels, preferably small cultivated

4   large shallots, chopped or sliced thin

3   cups [750 ml] dry white wine such as muscadet or French sauvignon blanc

1   bunch parsley, chopped coarse just before you use it (about 4 tablespoons)

4   tablespoons butter (optional)

    pepper

    crusty French bread, preferably baguettes sliced into 1-inch-thick [2.5 cm] pieces (to accompany the dish)

WASH and sort the mussels as described on page 267.

COMBINE the shallots and wine in a pot about twice the size of your pile of mussels (to leave room for the mussels to open). Cover the pot, bring to a simmer, and simmer for about 5 minutes to infuse the shallots' flavor in the wine. Add the parsley and then the mussels. Cover the pot, turn the heat to high, and steam for about 4 minutes. Holding the lid firmly on the pot with a kitchen towel while also holding the pot handles, shake the pot, moving the back side up and toward you so the mussels that were on the bottom of the pot are redistributed to the top. Steam for about 2 minutes more, or until all the mussels have opened. Stand back when you remove the lid and don't put your hand in for a few seconds or the steam can burn you.

SCOOP the mussels—I use a skimmer or a frying spider—into large, hot bowls. If you notice some mussels that haven't opened, throw them out. Gently pour the hot liquid from the pot into a heat-proof bowl, leaving any grit or sand behind in the pot. Rinse out the pot and put the decanted liquid back in. Put the pot back on the stove and whisk in the butter. Season to taste with pepper. Ladle the hot liquid over the mussels in each bowl. Don't pour the liquid directly from the pot, because you want any sand or grit released by the mussels to stay behind in the pot. Serve with plenty of bread and wine.

Variations: The method of steaming used to make *moules à la marinière* is the starting point for virtually all hot mussel dishes. Variations can be as simple as adding different ingredients to the basic steaming liquid or submitting the steaming liquid, after the mussels have cooked, to additional processes. One of the best variations is *moules à la provençal*, essentially identical to *moules à la marinière* except that chopped garlic is used instead of, or in addition to, the shallots. Peeled, seeded, and chopped tomatoes are usually added and, occasionally, bay leaves. *Moules à la crème* are simply *moules à la marinière* with cream added and sometimes thickened with beurre manié (a paste of butter and flour). A *mouclade*, a famous regional dish made along much of France's Atlantic coast, is the same as *moules à la crème* except that curry powder or sometimes saffron is included as well as the cream. *Moules à la poulette* are similar to *moules à la crème* except that the braising liquid is thickened with egg yolks gently stirred until silky, and may or may not contain cream, butter, or beurre manié. Recipes from before the nineteenth century sometimes contained almonds (a typically medieval touch in which almond "milk" was used instead of cow's milk). In one recipe in Taillevent's *Le Viandier*, mint, along with spices including saffron, and butter, unusual in medieval cooking, were stirred into the cooking liquid in the same way as for *moules à la marinière*. I've experimented with the saffron and mint combination and found it delicious.

STEAMED MUSSELS WITH CREAM, SAFFRON, AND MINT

MOULES À LA CRÈME AU SAFRAN ET À LA MENTHE

MAKES 4 FIRST-COURSE SERVINGS

This dish is prepared in much the same way as moules à la marinière except that cream is added to the sauce and the sauce is flavored with saffron and mint instead of parsley. These mussels are also presented differently than moules à la marinière—the top shell is taken off of each mussel, because scooping mussels out of two shells can be messy when the sauce contains cream. The sauce is brothlike, almost like a soup.

50	to 60 small cultivated mussels (about 2 pounds [900 g])
1	cup [250 ml] dry white wine
2	medium-size shallots, chopped fine
1	small clove garlic, chopped fine, crushed to a paste with the side of a chef's knife
1	cup [250 ml] heavy cream
1	pinch saffron threads, soaked for 30 minutes in 1 tablespoon of water
25	fresh mint leaves
½	teaspoon olive oil
	pepper

WASH and sort the mussels as described on page 267.

COMBINE the wine, shallots, and garlic in a pot twice the size of your pile of mussels, cover the pot, and simmer gently for 5 minutes to infuse the flavors into the wine. Put the mussels in the pot, cover the pot, turn the heat to high, and steam for about 4 minutes. Holding the lid firmly on the pot with a kitchen towel while also holding the pot handles, shake the pot, moving the back side up and toward you so the mussels that were on the bottom of the pot are redistributed to the top. Steam for about 2 minutes more, or until all the mussels have opened. Stand back when you remove the lid and don't put your hand in for a few seconds or the steam can burn you.

SCOOP the mussels into a large bowl, leaving the steaming liquid behind in the big pot, and keep them warm while you're making the sauce.

GENTLY pour the mussel cooking liquid into a saucepan, leaving behind any grit or sand. Add the heavy cream and the saffron and its soaking liquid and bring to the simmer.

TAKE off and discard the top shell from each of the mussels and divide the mussels among 4 plates. Rub the mint leaves with the olive oil to keep the mint from turning black when you chop it, and chop it fine. Stir the mint into the sauce and season the sauce with pepper.

LADLE the sauce over the mussels in the soup plates, and serve immediately. If the mussels cooled off while they were waiting, rotate each plate of mussels (be sure the plates are ovenproof) under the broiler for 30 seconds or so.

Variations: This system—steaming open the mussels and converting their steaming liquid into a sauce—can be varied by adding other ingredients to the sauce base. Spices (curry makes the dish similar to a traditional *mouclade*), herbs (basil, tarragon, thyme), chives, reduced tomato purée, or other vegetable purées such as sorrel or garlic (see page 373) can be added to the sauce in various combinations. Vegetable purées not only contribute flavor but also help thicken the sauce, allowing you to use less cream. (The sauce can also be reduced to thicken it, but there's always the risk of making it too salty.) You can make the dish more substantial by taking the mussels out of their shells, placing a small mound of cooked vegetables, such as creamed spinach or sorrel, julienned or sliced leeks (softened in butter, creamed or not), duxelles (see page 96), or finely chopped onions or mirepoix (softened and lightly caramelized in butter), in the bottom shells, putting back the mussels, coating with a thickened sauce, and reheating the whole concoction in the oven. Instead of thickening and enriching the mussel steaming liquid with cream, you can whisk a few tablespoons of the mussel steaming liquid with egg yolks, and finish the sauce with butter as you would a hollandaise (see page 257). You can then replace the mussels in their bottom shells, spoon the sauce over them, and quickly brown the mussels under the broiler in much the same way as the gratinéed oysters on page 256.

BROILED MUSSELS WITH ONIONS AND MUSSEL-FLAVORED WHITE WINE SAUCE

MOULES GRATINÉES AUX OIGNONS ET À LA SAUCE VIN BLANC

MAKES 6 FIRST-COURSE SERVINGS

This dish is my own little invention, but each of its components is based on French classic cooking. The mussels are steamed open exactly as for moules à la marinière, a hollandaise-type sauce is made with steaming liquid from the mussels (a derivative of a classic sauce vin blanc, in which reduced fish broth is whisked with the egg yolks into a sabayon before the butter is added; described in the Sole Marguéry recipe on page 310), onions are sweated and caramelized and placed under the mussels in their shells, the mussels are coated with the sauce, and the whole thing is baked and then gratinéed.

1 large red onion (about 1 pound), chopped fine

2 tablespoons butter

plus ½ cup [125 ml] clarified butter (see page 7)

pepper

2 teaspoons red or white wine vinegar, or more to taste

½ teaspoon sugar (optional)

36 mussels, preferably small cultivated (about 1½ pounds [675 g] if the mussels are small)

2 medium-size shallots, chopped or sliced fine

½ cup [125 ml] dry white wine such as muscadet or French sauvignon blanc

2 egg yolks

pinch of paprika

COOK the onion in 2 tablespoons of butter in a heavy-bottomed pot or saucepan, starting on medium heat and stirring every few minutes until the onion releases liquid. Turn the heat up to high and continue cooking until all the liquid evaporates and the onion is completely soft and lightly caramelized, about 25 minutes. Season the onion with pepper, the vinegar, and, if you like, a little sugar. Don't add salt. Reserve.

SCRUB the mussels as described on page 267. Combine the shallots and white wine in a pot twice the size of the mussels, cover the pot, and simmer gently for 5 minutes to infuse the flavor of the shallots into the wine. Add the mussels, cover the pot, and steam over high heat until all the mussels have opened, about 5 minutes. (Because you're steaming so few mussels, you don't need to shake them around in the pot as for moules à la marinière.) Remove the mussels with a skimmer or large slotted spoon.

REMOVE the top shells from the mussels and discard. Take the mussels out of the bottom shells and reserve both shells and mussels. Crumple a large sheet of aluminum foil and spread it out on a sheet pan. Set the reserved mussel shells on the sheet pan, pressing them slightly down into the foil to keep them flat.

POUR the mussel steaming liquid through a fine-mesh strainer (or a strainer lined with cheesecloth) into a saucepan. Boil the liquid down to ¼ cup [60 ml] and set aside to cool for at least 5 minutes.

PREHEAT the oven to 250°F [120°C/gas mark ½].

WHISK the mussel cooking liquid with the egg yolks in a heavy-bottomed pan with sloping sides (a Windsor pan) or in a medium-size mixing bowl, off the heat, for about 1 minute, until the mixture becomes fluffy. Put the pan or bowl over medium heat while whisking until the egg yolks get even airier. (If you're using a mixing bowl, hold onto it on one side with a towel or oven mitt.) As soon as the egg yolks stiffen slightly, take the pan off the heat and whisk for a minute to cool the yolks. Whisk in the clarified butter, which should be no hotter than a hot bath or it will curdle the yolks. The sauce should be quite stiff. Season the sauce to taste with pepper—it won't need salt.

SPOON 1 teaspoon or so of the chopped onions into each shell. Place a mussel in each shell. Heat the mussels in the oven for 5 minutes and spoon the sauce over each one. Turn the oven up to 400°F [200°C/gas mark 6] and bake the mussels for about 5 minutes more to heat them through and make the sauce bubble up slightly. Sprinkle with paprika and arrange on 6 individual plates.

MINIATURE SERVINGS OF MUSSELS WITH SEA URCHIN SAUCE

CASSOLETTES DE MOULES À LA SAUCE D'OURSINS

MAKES 6 LIGHT FIRST-COURSE SERVINGS

People who aren't in the habit of going to sushi bars get spooked when I mention sea urchins, which they often confuse with sea anemones, those ghastly-looking tentacled creatures we've all seen at the aquarium. While it is true that sea urchins aren't particularly beautiful—they're black, round, spiked, with a hole in the middle—and are especially nasty if you step on one at the beach, they have their aficionados. In France, you'll find sea urchins served along with oysters and other raw seafood goodies on large platters called *assiettes de fruits de mer*. The top will have been cut off the sea urchins with a pair of heavy scissors and it will be left to you to spoon out the golden roe, one of life's ultimate delicacies, whose flavor magically combines the brininess of oysters with a subtle sweetness reminiscent of the best milk chocolate. You may be able to buy whole sea urchins at the fish market—you'll probably need to order them ahead—or you can do what I usually do and buy a couple of sashimi-size servings at the corner Japanese restaurant.

I've always been fascinated by using sea urchin roe to finish shellfish sauces and once, when I had my restaurant and sea urchins were cheap, I even made a soup out of it. In this dish, the roe is used in a sauce and as a garniture for a small dish of mussels. Since the combination is very rich, I like to serve this dish as a first course. In fancy restaurants in France, tiny servings of rich dishes are often served as starters—amuse-gueules or amuse-bouches—to an elaborate meal, usually in small elegant silver containers called *cassolettes*, which come in various shapes and sizes and often have lids. If you don't have such finery, you can bake rounds of puff pastry, cut them in half crosswise, place a mussel and sea urchin roe on the bottom half, and then place the little pastry lid on top.

1 sheet puff pastry (if you buy it, make sure it's made with butter), 10 by 6½ inches [25.5 by 16.5 cm] and between ⅛ and ¼ inch [about .5 cm] thick

1 large egg

1 teaspoon salt (for the egg wash), plus additional (for the sorrel)

6 sea urchins or 3 ounces sea [85 g] urchin roe (about 3 sashimi servings)

3 tablespoons butter, allowed to warm to room temperature

½ cup [125 ml] dry white wine

1 small shallot, chopped very fine

½ clove garlic, chopped fine, crushed to a paste with the side of a chef's knife

18 small cultivated mussels, scrubbed and sorted (see page 267)

2 tablespoons heavy cream (for the sorrel), plus ¼ cup [60 ml] (for the sauce)

1 large handful fresh sorrel or spinach leaves, stems peeled away from leaves, leaves washed

pepper

2 teaspoons finely chopped chives or parsley

PREHEAT the oven to 425°F [220°C/gas mark 6] and cut out 6 rounds from the puff pastry, 3 inches (7.5 cm) each in diameter. It's best to use a fluted cookie cutter, but if you don't have one, measure with something the right diameter and cut out the rounds with a knife. Sprinkle a small sheet pan with water to keep the bottom of the pastry from burning, and put the rounds of pastry on the sheet pan, upside down. Turning the pastry over before placing it on the pan Fkeeps the part that may have been slightly crimped as it was being cut, and so won't rise as well, on the bottom. Use a fork to beat the egg with 1 teaspoon of salt to thin it; beat until the egg

turns dark, about 1 minute. Brush the top of the pastry rounds with a thin layer of the egg mixture, being very careful not to let any of the mixture run down the sides of the pastry. (This can harden during baking and keep the pastry from rising.) With a paring knife, cut a series of decorative shallow arcs—like curved spokes of a wheel—from the center to the edge of each pastry round. Refrigerate for 10 minutes. Bake until the rounds are well puffed and golden brown on top, about 15 minutes. Allow to cool and cut each round laterally in half. Pull out any raw dough from inside the halves. Reserve the rounds.

IF you're using whole sea urchins, use a heavy pair of scissors or kitchen shears and cut each urchin, starting at the hole in the middle of the top and continuing to the outside edge of the shell. Cut completely around the sides and remove and discard the top. Scoop out the orange roe with a small spoon and reserve. Discard the rest of the urchin.

WORK half the roe (that you just scooped out or brought at the Japanese restaurant or fish store) through a strainer and work it with the softened butter, using a wooden spoon, in a small mixing bowl. Reserve the sea urchin butter and the reserved roe separately, covered, in the refrigerator.

SHORTLY before serving, set the oven to 200°F [95°C or lowest setting] and heat the puff pastry rounds and six small plates.

COMBINE the wine, shallot, and garlic in a saucepan twice as large as would be needed to hold the mussels, cover the pot, and bring to a gentle simmer to infuse the flavors in the wine. Simmer for 5 minutes, add the mussels, cover, and simmer for 5 minutes more, or until all the mussels have opened.

WHILE the mussels are cooking, bring 2 tablespoons of cream to a simmer in a heavy-bottomed saucepan. When the cream thickens, stir in the sorrel and cook until any excess cream evaporates, about 2 minutes. Season to taste with salt and pepper and reserve.

TAKE the mussels out of their shells, discard the shells, and reserve the mussels while you're making the sauce. If the mussels have released grit into the cooking liquid, carefully pour the liquid into a clean saucepan, leaving the grit behind. (You also leave behind the shallot and garlic but this is okay.) Add ¼ cup of cream to the mussel cooking liquid and boil the mixture down by about half—until it thickens slightly—and whisk in the chives and the sea urchin butter. Whisk over low heat to incorporate the butter, but don't allow the sauce to boil or the roe, like any other egg, will curdle. Season to taste with pepper. Stir the reserved mussels in the sauce to heat them through.

PLACE the bottom halves to the puff pastry rounds on heated plates and spoon a mound of sorrel on each one. Spoon the mussels over the sorrel and place the remaining sea urchin roe in the sauce to warm it. Spoon the sea urchin roe and sauce over the mussels. Place a puff pastry lid, slightly to one side, on top of each serving. Serve immediately.

MUSSEL SOUPS

Mussels make some of the most delicious seafood soups because the briny liquid they release is so flavorful. When I make mussel soup, I always seem to end up with a lot of mussels and a relatively small amount of the liquid needed as the base for the soup. There are several ways to get around this. You can serve the soup with tons of mussels, but then it becomes more stew than soup, and there's something cloying and monotonous about eating a big bowl of mussels already out of their shells with just a little bit of liquid. One classic method is to combine the mussel steaming liquid with fish broth, which is relatively bland, to stretch it. But this diminishes the briny mussel character of the soup. Some recipes suggest puréeing some of the mussels and adding them to the soup. This method thickens the soup and uses up the extra mussels, but it gives the soup a rough texture and colors it dull gray. My solution is a bit more circuitous and requires extra planning. Days, weeks, or even months before I make the soup, I make a pot of *moules à la marinière* (see page 268) and store the liquid in the refrigerator, where it will last for 2 or 3 days, or in the freezer, where it will last for several months. I then arrange the cooked mussels in their bottom shells, nestle them into some crumpled aluminum foil on a sheet pan, dollop them with parsley and garlic butter (the same butter used for snails) and sometimes a little chopped almond for texture, and broil them. I serve them as a first course (see page 274, Hot Broiled Mussels). No one misses the cooking liquid.

Once you have the mussel cooking liquid, making a soup is a snap, since the liquid is so flavorful. I always include heavy cream, which is essential for pulling together the oceanlike mussel flavors, which otherwise seem a bit austere, at least for my decadent tastes. For solid ingredients, there are of course the mussels; I like to leave them attached to the bottom shells and discard the top shells. But pieces of firm, white-fleshed fish, such as halibut or sea bass; shrimp; crabmeat; or cooked lobster will also give the soup substance. You can turn the soup into a chowder by adding cooked potatoes and gently stewed thin onion slices. I almost invariably add saffron, which gives the soup a great color, and tomatoes, if they're in season. You can also add a variety of vegetables—mushrooms (cultivated or wild), carrots, spinach, sorrel, baby turnips, carrots, artichokes—turning the soup into an elegant seafood stew. But if you're doing this, be sure to include some mussels or other seafood to make the stew's identity clear—otherwise guests might just wonder why the vegetables taste like fish.

Most of my favorite soups are relatively thin—I just like them that way. But if you want to thicken a mussel soup, or any soup, you have several options. You can whisk the soup into a roux, which will give it traditional New England clam chowder consistency, or whisk in a little mashed potato or other stewed and puréed vegetable such as garlic (surprisingly mild; see recipe below), reduced tomato purée, or purée of sorrel, fennel, or spinach. One Paris chef I know uses puréed creamed celery as the base for a glorious mussel soup.

MUSSEL SOUP WITH GARLIC PURÉE AND SAFFRON

SOUPE AUX MOULES À LA PURÉE D'AIL ET AU SAFRAN

MAKES 6 FIRST-COURSE SERVINGS

2 large heads garlic, cloves separated and peeled

30 cultivated mussels (slightly more than 1 pound), washed and sorted (see page 267)

½ cup [125 ml] dry white wine

4 cups [1 l] white wine–mussel cooking liquid, reserved from Steamed Mussels with White Wine, Shallots, and Parsley (page 268) or from 2 recipes of Hot Broiled Mussels with Garlic and Parsley Butter (recipe follows)

1 large pinch saffron threads, soaked for 30 minutes in 1 tablespoon of water

½ to 1 cup [125 to 250 ml] heavy cream

pepper

PUT the garlic cloves in a small pot with enough water to cover by 1 or 2 inches [2.5 to 5 cm]. Bring to a simmer and simmer gently until the cloves are soft, with the consistency of cooked boiled potatoes, about 20 minutes. Drain the cloves in a strainer, purée them in a miniature food processor or by working them through a strainer with a ladle or through a food mill, and reserve.

PUT the mussels in a pot with the wine and steam them open over medium to high heat, about 5 minutes. Take off the top shells and discard them. Reserve the mussels in their bottom shells and slowly pour their cooking liquid into a clean pot—large enough for all the soup—leaving any grit

behind. Add the additional white wine–mussel cooking liquid to the pot along with the saffron and its soaking liquid and the heavy cream. Whisk in the garlic purée and bring the soup to a simmer. Add the mussels, simmer for about 30 seconds to heat them through, and ladle the soup into heated bowls. Grind fresh pepper over each serving.

HOT BROILED MUSSELS WITH GARLIC AND PARSLEY BUTTER

MOULES GRATINÉES AU BEURRE D'ESCARGOTS

MAKES 8 FIRST-COURSE SERVINGS, OR HORS D'OEUVRES FOR 20

Most people I know who claim to love snails really love snail butter, the hot garlic butter the snails are baked in, because snails themselves don't have much flavor. This dish fills a dual purpose: It's delicious in itself and it will provide you with the cooking liquid from the mussels, which you can save to use in soups and sauces. The liquid keeps for months in the freezer, and it can be used instead of fish broth (although it's saltier and far more flavorful) or in any recipe that calls for bottled clam juice, which has an aggressive, fishy taste. Mussel cooking liquid was one of the staples of classic French cooking. Escoffier compares it to oyster cooking liquid, which he calls "insipid," and he uses mussel cooking liquid in sauce normande and other elaborate sauces. (See chapter 23 for more about fish sauces using mussel cooking liquid, and see the soup recipe on this page.)

- 1½ sticks (6 ounces [170 g]) butter, softened by being allowed to come to room temperature
- 2 cloves garlic, chopped fine, crushed to a paste with the side of a chef's knife
- 1 large bunch parsley, large stems removed
- ½ cup [70 g] blanched almonds, toasted for 10 to 15 minutes in a 350°F [175°C/gas mark 4] oven
- 2 slices dense-crumb white bread, crusts removed, or ½ cup [25 g] fresh bread crumbs
- 4 pounds [1.8 kg] mussels, preferably small cultivated or New Zealand green mussels
- 2 medium-size shallots, chopped or sliced fine
- 2 cups [500 ml] dry white wine such as muscadet or French sauvignon blanc

COMBINE the butter and garlic in a mixing bowl. (You can use an electric mixer with a paddle blade, but I just use a bowl and a big wooden spoon.) Chop the parsley very fine and work it into the butter. It's important that the parsley be chopped just before it's incorporated into the butter so that its flavor will be trapped. Chop the almonds by hand or pulse them in a food processor until they have the consistency of coarse sand, and work them into the butter. If you're using sliced bread, turn it into bread crumbs by grinding it in a food processor. Work the bread crumbs into the butter.

WASH and sort the mussels as described on page 267.

COMBINE the shallots and white wine in a pot about twice the size of your pile of mussels (to leave room for the mussels to open). Cover the pot, bring to a simmer, and simmer for about 5 minutes to infuse the flavor of the shallots in the wine. Add the mussels, cover the pot, turn the heat to high, and steam for about 3 minutes. Holding the lid firmly on the pot with a kitchen towel while also holding the pot handles, shake the pot, moving the back side up and toward you so the mussels that were on the bottom of the pot are redistributed to the top. Steam for

about 2 minutes more, or until all the mussels have opened. Stand back when you remove the lid and don't put your hand in for a few seconds or the steam can burn you.

SCOOP the mussels into a large bowl. Carefully pour the mussel steaming liquid through a strainer into a container, leaving any sand or grit behind. Store the liquid in the refrigerator or freeze it. There should be about 2½ cups [625 ml].

PREHEAT the oven to 450°F [230°C/gas mark 8].

TAKE off and discard the top shells from the mussels. Cut under the mussels to loosen them from the bottom shells (some will already have detached), but leave them in the shells. Cover 2 sheet pans with crumpled aluminum foil and press the mussels into the foil so they stay flat. Spoon a teaspoon of the garlic and parsley butter over each mussel and bake for about 5 minutes, until the butter is sizzling hot and the kitchen smells like garlic. Serve piping hot.

SNAILS

This method of cooking mussels with garlic and parsley butter is the same one used to cook snails. When I worked in Paris we bought live snails that came in big bushels. We'd keep them in the restaurant garden for a day or two before we could get to them, and it was my job to go out and catch those that had escaped and were making their way up the outer wall of the restaurant kitchen. The cleaning process was lengthy and rather unpleasant, but it's not something you'll have to worry about, since snails available in the United States come in a can already cleaned and precooked, and they taste none the worse for it. Nothing could be simpler than preparing them in the classic French bistro dish escargots à la bourguignonne (the best, fattest snails come from Burgundy). Just make the garlic and parsley butter described above (leave out the almonds), rinse off the snails, put them in snail shells (easy to find at a cooking supply store), force as much butter into the shell as you can, and bake them for 5 to 8 minutes in a 450°F [230°C/gas mark 8] oven, until the fragrance of garlic fills the room. The only problem you may run into is how to serve them. You can be extravagant and go out and buy individual escargot plates, which have indentations and special clamps. Or you can nestle the snails together in wide soup plates. You'll still need clamps (the shells must be piping hot) and oyster forks.

CLAMS AND COCKLES

French cooks use several kinds of clams that aren't available in the United States and one variety that is—the small hard-shell clams that we call little-necks (or, if larger, cherrystones) and they simply call *clams* (pronounced, of course, with a distinctly Gallic accent). The French also use cockles (*coques*), but a slightly different kind than the green-tinged New Zealand cockles we find in the United States. Clams or cockles can be used in any recipe that normally takes mussels; just the amounts and the price will be different. The liquid released by clams and cockles is even brinier and more delicious than the juices released by mussels, and I often make a simple sauce for a slice of fish by steaming open a few clams or a handful of cockles, adding cream and herbs to the steaming liquid, and serving the sauce and the clams or cockles around and over the fish. (For more about such sauces, see chapter 23.)

You will also notice that clams take longer to open than mussels, usually about 10 minutes instead of 5, and some, regardless of how long you steam them, will need to be opened with a knife. A mussel that doesn't open is probably dead or filled with mud and should be thrown out, but an unopened clam is usually perfectly fine. Just stick a knife between the two shells, give a little twist, and the clam should snap right open. Soft-shell clams, sometimes called steamers, have little spigots—actually siphons—sticking out at one end and never completely close because the poor clam can't draw the spigot in far enough to get it out of the way of the shell. Soft-shell clams (a misnomer, since the shells aren't really soft) often contain sand and, unlike mussels or hard-shell clams, benefit from an overnight bath in salted water kept in a cool place or in the refrigerator. (One cup of salt dissolved in 3 quarts [3 l] of water roughly approximates seawater.) Cockles, like mussels, are sold by the pound, so it is easy to substitute them in mussel recipes, but clams are usually sold by the dozen. Unless they're terribly small, I serve about 6 clams per person for a first course or in a fish sauce and 12 as a light main course.

SEA SCALLOPS POACHED IN VEGETABLE BROTH

COQUILLES SAINT-JACQUES

À LA NAGE

HOW TO	HOW TO	HOW TO	HOW TO	HOW TO
BUY, SHUCK, AND CLEAN SCALLOPS IN THE SHELL	PREPARE AND USE A VEGETABLE BROTH	POACH SEAFOOD	MAKE CLASSIC AND LIGHT VERSIONS OF BUTTER SAUCES	COOK À LA NAGE

UNTIL I MOVED TO FRANCE, THE ONLY SCALLOP SHELL I HAD EVER seen was at a gas station—the scallops occasionally found in California markets were sold already shucked. In Paris the scallops were sold alive in their shells. Like any pristine ingredient, perfect fresh scallops should be cooked following one of cooking's most important axioms: the better the ingredients, the simpler the cooking method. Such ingredients have to be cooked with a light touch (or not cooked at all) so that none of their delicate flavor and natural finesse is lost.

Scallops are now sold in the shell in fancy fish markets and sushi bars, mostly on the East Coast. This makes it easy to verify that they're still alive—the shell closes slightly when you squeeze it—and hence perfectly fresh. Most of these scallops, often called divers' scallops (meaning that they were harvested by divers instead of large dredges dragged along the ocean floor), are an American species with a relatively smooth shell and not the European variety with the classic ribbed shell. There's little difference in the two species, except that the European variety has a piece of roe shaped a little like a finger wrapping around the center muscle, the only part of the scallop that most of us eat. The American variety also has the roe, but it's often an unsightly gray and most cooks I know avoid it. European scallops are now being farmed on the West Coast of the United States and in Chile, so if you're able to buy them in the shell, don't ignore the roe, which is bright orange or sometimes white, depending on what sex the hermaphroditic scallop has taken up. Either cook the roe along with the rest of the scallop or use it in the sauce (see page 287).

If you don't have access to scallops in the shell, you'll have to buy them already shucked. The roe will have been discarded, and you'll have to look at and smell the scallops to judge their freshness and quality. If the scallops smell like anything other than a beautiful beach, don't buy them. You should also look for scallops that have never been soaked in tripolyphosphate solution, a mixture designed to keep dredge-harvested scallops "fresh" for days at sea and to prevent the scallops from releasing moisture and thus losing weight. (People in the industry speak of "drip loss.") Scallops that have been soaked are easy to spot because they all look perfectly white and are often covered with a milky and shiny froth as though they've been tossed with soap. Scallops that have not been soaked have slightly different nuances of color—some are pale orange, others white, others ivory—and appear dry, and while they have a smooth sheen, they're not what you'd call shiny.

If you've bought your scallops in the shell, you'll have to shuck them. Unlike oysters, scallops are easy to shuck because they gape slightly and it's easy to get a knife in between the shell and the adductor muscle, the part we eat. Just slide a dining-room or kitchen knife along the underside of the top shell, detaching the scallop and its coral, or roe, which tends to be orange, and its milt, or sperm, which tends to be gray or white, from the shell without leaving any of the muscle attached. Be careful not to cut yourself on the sharp shells. Pull off the top shell and slide the knife under the scallop and coral, detaching them from the bottom shell. Pull away and discard the mantle, which is the material surrounding the scallop and coral. There will be a small membrane surrounding the scallop that you'll have to cut through to remove the mantle. Rinse the scallops to eliminate any sand. Pull away the tiny muscle that runs up the side of the scallop, because it turns hard when you cook the scallops. (You will also need to do this with scallops already out of the shell.)

Scallops are a relatively recent discovery in mainstream French cooking, although it's hard to imagine that something so delicious hadn't long been eaten in coastal regions, such as Normandy and Brittany, where scallops are harvested. There's no mention of *coquilles Saint-Jacques* in any of my French cookbooks until the twentieth century, when they appear in Escoffier's *Le Guide Culinaire*. Escoffier's approach is phobic—the poor scallop is opened in a hot oven (hardly necessary, since they're easily opened raw), blanched for several minutes in a court bouillon, diced, put back in the shell (sometimes over a bed of duxelles), masked with a rich sauce, and then gratinéed under a salamander (what we nowadays, outside of restaurants, call a broiler). Needless to say, any delicacy or even flavor that once existed is completely destroyed.

On the other hand, the technique of cooking in vegetable broth with the vegetables still in it—*à la nage*—has existed in France for centuries, even if the use of the expression itself is relatively recent. My 1960s edition of *Larousse Gastronomique* mentions it, and a number of France's most famous chefs use it on their menus. The technique of simmering foods, especially shellfish, in court bouillon (vegetable broth) is written about in books from the seventeenth century, and it's hard to imagine that the technique wasn't used even earlier. In French classic cooking there are a number of versions of court bouillon. Some contain milk, which I never use, since the milk curdles and clings to the fish; others contain red wine—don't bother with these because the wine stains the fish; and others contain vinegar and are used for poaching fish, the most famous interpretation probably being *truite au bleu,* which is a whole trout poached in a vegetable broth containing a good amount of wine vinegar (see page 289). There's nothing difficult or mysterious about cooking *à la nage* (roughly translatable as "in the swim"), because all that's involved, with one important difference, is poaching in a vegetable broth called a court bouillon. The difference is that the vegetables used to make the court bouillon are left in for cooking *à la nage,* while for simple poaching they're strained out. When the vegetables are left in the broth, they must be cut in an attractive way instead of being quickly chopped up, as they can be when they're being strained out of the court bouillon and, having given their all, discarded. Cutting the vegetables in "an attractive way" may be as simple as keeping the slices the same thickness, but in classic cooking it might mean froufrou such as shaping carrot slices like cogwheels and cutting turnip slices into various other shapes. My own preference is to julienne the vegetables so they cook quickly and evenly and end up in a colorful and tasty and more spontaneous-looking tangle, over and around the poached scallops or whatever it is I've cooked *à la nage.*

HOW BUTTER WORKS IN BEURRE BLANC
AND OTHER SAUCES

Sometimes called *beurre nantais* (after the city of Nantes, where it supposedly originated), beurre blanc—a light, creamy sauce made almost entirely with butter—was once rarely known outside Brittany. In the 1960s, a restaurant was opened by a certain Mère Michel, who whipped it up as a sauce for poached fish. Before and during Madame Michel's restaurant reign, preparing a beurre blanc was considered beyond the abilities of mere mortals. The late Richard Olney, in his great book *Simple French Food,* describes the attitude of the times: "The utter simplicity of the thing, the paucity of elements, the absence of a binder . . . have engendered a wariness, distrust, or unbelief, than which there are no solider foundations on which to construct a myth. The story goes that only a very special kind of culinary genius with an inborn and mysterious twist of the wrist can produce a successful beurre blanc. . . ." After reading this passage, practically 30 years ago, I walked over to the stove and, following Olney's recipe and encouragement, whipped up my first beurre blanc—perhaps the easiest sauce I'd made until then or have made since.

To understand a beurre blanc, you need to know that it and most sauces are emulsions and the emulsions are mixtures of two liquids that normally won't combine. In other words, you can shake vinegar and oil together as long as you like, but you'll never end up with vinaigrette. To get the two to combine, you need an emulsifier, a substance—usually a protein—that attaches itself to micro-scopic globules of whatever it is you're trying to emulsify. In a mayonnaise, for example, molecules of a phospholipid found in egg yolks attach themselves to globules of oil in such a way that the globules can't coalesce into larger globules that then float to the top of the mixture, causing it to separate. Other emulsifiers are mustard, which emulsifies a vinaigrette; vegetable purées; and the proteins contained in butter. Flour and other starches also act as emulsifiers, although in a somewhat different way.

When butter is whisked with a small amount of liquid, the proteins—sometimes called milk solids—coat the minute particles of fat and keep the butter from turning oily. Emulsions also require a small amount of liquid—water, lemon juice, flavorful meat extracts such as *jus* or broth—to provide a medium for the emulsifier-coated globules of fat. If the proportion of liquid is too low, the fat globules are forced together and, despite being coated with an emulsifier, will coalesce and the mixture will separate. A beurre blanc or hollandaise sauce will also break if allowed to boil, because the integrity of the proteins that maintain the emulsion is compromised; the protein "denatures" and the sauce breaks or curdles.

So when making a beurre blanc, you need only to avoid letting it boil (although, unlike for a hollandaise sauce, boiling for a few seconds won't hurt it) and prevent the proportion of butter to liquid from getting too high. A successful buerre blanc should be only slightly thicker than cold heavy cream; if you try to make it thick, like a béchamel or reduced cream sauce, it will break. When cooks like myself discovered that making a bleurre blanc wasn't so hard after all, there arose a plethora of variations—e.g., ginger, grapefruit—most of which have, happily, fallen into desuetude. But the technique of whisking butter into a concentrated and flavorful reduction, a technique that has come to be called *monter au beurre*, changed French sauce-making so that many of the classic brown sauces, instead of being thickened with flour, are now finished with varying amounts of butter, which gives them a silky body and a luxurious flavor. See also chapter 35.

BEURRE BLANC

MAKES 1½ CUPS [375 ML]

4 medium-size shallots, chopped fine

¼ cup [60 ml] good-quality white wine vinegar, or more as needed

¼ cup [60 ml] dry white wine

2 tablespoons heavy cream (optional)

2 sticks (½ pound) (250 g) cold unsalted butter, each cut into 4 chunks, or more as needed

salt

white pepper

COMBINE the shallots, vinegar, and wine in a saucepan over medium heat. Be sure that the saucepan is at least as large as the heat source. If the heat source is larger, the insides of the saucepan will brown, causing the sauce to discolor when you whisk in the butter. (If you find that the inside walls of the saucepan have browned after you've simmered down the wine mixture, wipe them with a clean, damp towel.)

SIMMER the wine and vinegar until there's only 1 or 2 tablespoons of liquid left, barely enough to cover the shallots. Add the heavy cream (to traditionalists it's heresy, but I find that it stabilizes the sauce and no one knows it's there) and bring to a simmer over medium heat. Turn the heat to high,

(continued)

add the butter all at once, and continuously whisk the sauce until all the butter has melted, after 2 or 3 minutes. The butter needs to be kept in constant motion so the emulsion doesn't destabilize. Many recipes tell you to add the butter a chunk at a time, but this is unnecessary.

SEASON to taste with salt and pepper. If the sauce tastes flat, add another 1 to 2 teaspoons of vinegar; if it tastes too sharp, whisk in more butter. If at any point the sauce looks oily or waxy, add 1 or 2 tablespoons of liquid, such as heavy cream or water, to keep the sauce from breaking. As soon as all the butter is incorporated into the sauce, take the saucepan off the heat.

HOLDING AND REUSING BEURRE BLANC: Beurre blanc can be made a couple of hours before you need it, and kept warm in a covered pan on the back of the stove or in an oven turned to the lowest setting. (One friend of mine keeps hers in a thermos.) As a beurre blanc sits, you may find that it starts to thicken, in which case you should add a little cream or water as described above. If you have leftover beurre blanc, keep it in the refrigerator and reconstitute it by reducing ¼ cup [60 ml] of heavy cream over medium heat until it thickens slightly and then whisking in the now-congealed beurre blanc in chunks. This method, however, works only once. If you end up with leftover reconstituted beurre blanc, you can put the congealed beurre blanc on grilled meats or seafood, as you would other compound butters (see Chapter 35); you can whisk it into hollandaise-style sauces (egg yolks are more powerful emulsifiers than the milk solids in butter); or you can cook it until it separates and use it as clarified butter for sautéing meats or seafood, keeping in mind that it's going to have a distinct shallot taste—not a problem, just don't use it to make pastry.

COURT BOUILLON FOR COOKING À LA NAGE

COURT-BOUILLON POUR CUISSON À LA NAGE

MAKES 3 CUPS [750 ML] (ENOUGH FOR 4 MAIN-COURSE OR 6 FIRST-COURSE SERVINGS)

2 medium-size leeks

2 large or 3 medium-size carrots, preferably bought with greens attached, greens removed and discarded, cut into 3-inch [7.5 cm] sections

1 stalk celery

1 medium-size turnip

1 medium-size bouquet garni

1 cup [225 ml] dry white wine

CUT off and discard the greens and hairy roots from the leeks and cut the whites in half lengthwise. Rinse any sand out of the leeks by holding them, root-side down, under running water. Pull away the membranes, 2 at a time. Stack 2 of the membranes, fold them end to end, and slice them, lengthwise, as thin as you can.

USE a plastic vegetable slicer (see page 13) or thin knife to slice the carrot sections lengthwise in ⅛-inch [3 mm] slices. Stack 2 or 3 of the slices and slice them, lengthwise, as thin as you can.

PEEL away the stringy outside of the celery stalk with a vegetable peeler and cut the stalk in half lengthwise. Cut the halves into sections about 3 inches [7.5 cm] long and slice them, lengthwise, as thin as you can.

PEEL the turnip and slice it into ⅛-inch-thick [3 mm] slices with a vegetable slicer. Arrange the slices in a stack of 3 or 4 and slice the stacks as thin as you can.

COMBINE the julienned vegetables and the bouquet garni in a pot with 3 cups of water and bring to a gentle simmer. Simmer, partially covered, for 15 minutes, add the wine, and simmer for 10 minutes more. (The wine is added near the end because its acidity keeps the vegetables crisp and slows the release of their flavor.) Discard the bouquet garni.

IF you're making the court bouillon ahead of time, strain out the vegetables and reserve the vegetables and broth separately.

SIMPLE COURT BOUILLON

COURT-BOUILLON SIMPLE

A plain court bouillon—one in which the cooked vegetables are going to be strained out and discarded—is made in the same way as a court bouillon destined for cooking à la nage, except that the vegetables don't need to be cut into precise shapes. Use the same ingredients and procedure as given above, but just slice the cleaned leeks (you can even include the greens), carrots, celery, and turnips and simmer them together in the same way. When the vegetables have given their all, after about 30 minutes, strain them out and discard them, reserving the broth.

SEA SCALLOPS WITH VEGETABLE BROTH AND JULIENNED VEGETABLES

COQUILLES SAINT-JACQUES À LA NAGE

MAKES 4 MAIN-COURSE OR 6 FIRST-COURSE SERVINGS

12 large sea scallops, either in the shell or out (2 to 3 ounces [55 to 85 g] each, out of the shell)

3 cups [750 ml] (1 recipe) Court Bouillon for Cooking à la Nage (page 283)

salt

pepper

2 tablespoons coarsely chopped parsley or chervil, or 1 tablespoon whole tarragon leaves

IF the scallops are still in the shell, shuck them as described on page 278. Remove and discard the small muscle that runs up the side of each scallop. Cut the scallops in half laterally (crosswise). If the roe or milt is an attractive white or orange, leave it attached and cut it laterally in half with the rest of the scallop.

IF the vegetables are still in the court bouillon, strain it and keep the vegetables warm in a covered saucepan with about ¼ cup [60 ml] of the court bouillon on the lowest flame or in the oven. Bring the court bouillon itself to a gentle simmer, season it to taste with salt and pepper, and add whichever herb you're using.

ARRANGE the scallop halves in a pan, ideally one just large enough to hold them in a single layer, and ladle the simmering court bouillon over them.

Poach the scallop halves for 1 to 2 minutes—until their surface looks matte instead of shiny—and, using a slotted spoon, arrange them in heated soup plates, giving 6 halves per serving for a main course and 4 halves per serving for a first course. Use a pair of tongs to scatter the julienned vegetables over the scallops, doing your best to make the presentation look nonchalant but not sloppy. Ladle the court bouillon over the vegetables and scallops and serve immediately.

Variations: One of the advantages of cooking anything *à la nage* is that there's no added fat and nothing to distract from the lean delicacy of the food itself. But the French are never ones to leave things alone, and now that scallops are a well-respected (and expensive) delicacy served in the finest restaurants, you'll have no trouble finding variations on a simple poaching in court bouillon. When I worked in Paris in the 1970s, in fancy places most sauces were made almost entirely out of butter and/or cream. In one restaurant we steamed scallops *over* a boiling court bouillon and then served them surrounded with julienned vegetables. But instead of ladling the court bouillon over them, we radically reduced the court bouillon from the night before, whisked fistfuls of butter into the rather sweet reduction (the vegetables' natural sugars were concentrated during reducing), and flavored the whole thing with saffron. We then ladled this sauce, which had a brothlike consistency, around the scallops. The restaurant guests lapped it up by the spoonful, marveling at its flavor and apparently oblivious to the fact that they were drinking pure butter. I've since tried to duplicate the rich luxury of that dish without doing anyone in and have come up with a number of compromises, all based on variations of beurre blanc (see page 281 and the following recipe).

POACHED SEA SCALLOPS WITH VEGETABLE BROTH FINISHED WITH FLAVORED BUTTERS

COQUILLES SAINT-JACQUES À LA NAGE AU BEURRE COMPOSÉS

MAKES 4 MAIN-COURSE OR 6 FIRST-COURSE SERVINGS

When beurre blanc took over the world in the 1970s, it and its variations became so ubiquitous that even I, who would gladly get most of my calories from butter, got so sick of it that I gradually taught myself to make lighter sauces. But I have never given up entirely on cream and butter and am still convinced that no other ingredients are as useful in pulling together disparate flavors. So I've developed a couple of simple tricks. One is to dilute beurre blanc with the poaching liquid from scallops or other seafood, turning it into a creamy brothlike sauce. Another is to finish the beurre blanc with various butters flavored with herbs, wild mushrooms, crustacean shells, or even truffles. This allows me to come up with an infinity of flavors quickly and conveniently, since the compound butters can be made ahead of time and kept tightly wrapped in the fridge for weeks or in the freezer for months, and the beurre blanc derivatives can be whisked up in minutes. You can make the resulting sauce as rich or as lean as you like by combining different amounts of poaching liquid (the court bouillon) and the beurre blanc or beurre blanc variation.

In the variation given here, three flavored butters are whisked into a small amount of reduced court bouillon, which replaces the wine-vinegar-shallot mixture in a classic beurre blanc, and the scallops are poached in the court bouillon. When the poaching is completed, a larger amount of the court bouillon is whisked into the butter sauce. Remember, the choice of butters is up to you.

12 large scallops, either in the shell or out (2 to 3 ounces [55 to 85 g] each, out of the shell)

3 cups [750 ml] 1 (recipe) Court Bouillon for Cooking à la Nage (page 283) with its vegetables

¼ cup [60 ml] heavy cream

2 tablespoons parsley, chervil, or tarragon butter (see page 490) or plain unsalted butter

2 tablespoons morel, cèpe, or truffle butter (see pages 490-491) or plain unsalted butter

4 tablespoons Crustacean Butter (see page 335) or plain unsalted butter

1 teaspoon lemon juice, or more to taste

salt

pepper

IF you're using whole scallops in the shell, shuck them as described on page 278. Remove and discard the small muscle that runs up the side of each of the scallops. Cut the scallops in half laterally.

IF the julienned vegetables are still in the court bouillon, strain it and keep the vegetables warm with about ¼ cup [60 ml] of the court bouillon in a covered saucepan on the lowest flame or in the oven. Put 1 cup [225 ml] of the court bouillon into a 2-quart [2 l] saucepan and reduce it over medium to high heat to about ¼ cup [60 ml]. Add the heavy cream and reduce over high heat for about 1 minute. Whisk in the parsley and morel butters over medium to high heat as though making a beurre blanc. When these butters have emulsified into a sauce, whisk in the crustacean butter. (The crustacean butter is added last because it contains no milk solids; adding it to the already emulsified sauce is analogous to whisking oil or clarified butter into egg yolks to make mayonnaise or hollandaise sauce.) Reserve the sauce in a low oven or on the back of the stove. Bring the rest of the court bouillon to a gentle simmer.

ARRANGE the scallop halves in a pan, ideally one just large enough to hold them in a single layer, and ladle the simmering court bouillon over them. Poach the scallop halves for 1 to 2 minutes and, using a slotted spoon, arrange them in heated soup plates, giving 6 halves per serving for a main course and 4 halves per serving for a first course. Use a pair of tongs to scatter the julienned vegetables over the scallops. Whisk about 1 cup [250 ml] of the poaching liquid into the reserved butter sauce. Season the sauce to taste with lemon juice, salt, and pepper, and ladle it over the scallops.

SEA SCALLOPS À LA NAGE FINISHED WITH THE SCALLOPS' ROE

COQUILLES SAINT-JACQUES À LA NAGE ET AU BEURRE DE CORAIL

MAKES 4 MAIN-COURSE

OR 6 FIRST-COURSE SERVINGS

Only attempt this dish if you access scallops in the shell with bright orange or white coral or milt (see box page 287).

12 large scallops in the shell

4 tablespoons butter

3 cups [750 ml] (1 recipe) Court Bouillon for Cooking à la Nage (page 283)

¼ cup [60 ml] heavy cream

salt

pepper

SHUCK the scallops as described on page 278 and carefully cut away and reserve the tongue-shaped packet of roe that surrounds each one. Discard the small muscle that runs up the side of each scallop. Cut the scallops in half laterally. Purée the roe with the butter in a miniature food processor or by working the two together through a strainer with a sturdy wooden spoon. Refrigerate the roe butter.

IF the julienned vegetables are still in the court bouillon, strain it and keep the vegetables warm with about ¼ cup [60 ml] of the court bouillon in a covered saucepan on the lowest flame or in the oven. Put 1 cup [250 ml] of the court bouillon into a 2-quart [2 l] saucepan and reduce it over medium to high heat to about ¼ cup [60 ml]. Add the heavy cream and reduce over high heat for about 1 minute. Whisk in the roe butter over medium to high heat as though making a beurre blanc, but don't allow the sauce to boil or the roe will curdle. Reserve the sauce in a low oven or on the back of the stove. Bring the rest of the court bouillon to a gentle simmer.

ARRANGE the scallop halves in a pan, ideally one just large enough to hold them in a single layer, and ladle the simmering court bouillon over them. Poach the scallop halves for 1 to 2 minutes, until they just begin to lose their translucency, and, using a slotted spoon, arrange them in heated soup plates, giving 6 halves per serving for a main course and 4 halves per serving for a first course. Use a pair of tongs to scatter the julienned vegetables over the scallops. Whisk about 1 cup [250 ml] of the poaching liquid into the reserved butter sauce. Season the sauce to taste with salt and pepper and ladle it over the scallops.

Variations: While using scallop roe combined with butter as a flavorful finish to a scallop sauce makes good sense, seafood sauces finished with the roe from other shellfish can be at least equally delicious and more complex and intriguing. While such machinations aren't often practical in home kitchens, it doesn't hurt to give them a little thought. Roe from lobsters, extracted before the lobsters are cooked (see Chapter 25); or sea urchin roe, pulled out of fresh urchins or bought from the corner Japanese restaurant; or the roe from crabs adds a magnificent subtle complexity to seafood sauces.

BAY SCALLOPS (PÉTONCLES)

When I had a restaurant in New York in the early 1980s, we would occasionally get deliveries, from Long Island, of fresh bay scallops still in the shell. Now, most of the Long Island bay scallops have disappeared due to pollution and overharvesting. But because they are now aqua-farmed in China and are still harvested in parts of New England, bay scallops are easier than ever to find, both in and out of the shell.

Don't confuse authentic bay scallops, smaller cousins of sea scallops, with calico scallops, which are sometimes sold as bay scallops. Calico scallops, usually from Florida and almost always sold out of their shell, are much smaller than bay scallops and have a milky cast that's a result of their having been steamed open as part of an industrial shucking process. (They look a little like miniature marshmallows.) Authentic bay scallops are larger and have a clean white or slightly pink sheen. Bay scallops in the shell come in various colors and look like miniature European sea scallops (the ones with the classic striated shells).

Bay scallops in the shell make a marvelous starting point for hors d' oeuvres because, once the scallops are cleaned, the bottom shell makes a perfect holder for a flavorful base such as duxelles, creamed spinach or sorrel, or concentrated tomato sauce. The scallops can then be placed on the base, lightly sauced, and quickly broiled or baked. (I describe this in more detail in my book *Fish and Shellfish*.)

Bay scallops can be simmered *à la nage* in the same way as sea scallops, as long as you keep in mind that the cooking times should be shorter, no longer than 1 minute.

WHAT TO DO WITH THE SCALLOP ROE

If you track down whole scallops in the shell, the scallop will be partially surrounded with a tongue-shaped packet of roe (coral), which is orange, or with sperm (milt), which is white. (Gray or dull-looking roe or milt should be avoided—for appearance, if nothing else.) In France, the coral is eaten without hesitation, but in America there are those who warn against it because it absorbs toxins more readily than the adductor muscle (what we think of as the scallop itself). While cultivated scallops are grown in closely controlled conditions, wild scallops are not. Depending on where they've been harvested, they may contain toxins. Fortunately, most of the safety problems with scallops (and other bivalves) are well understood and the growing areas for shellfish are carefully monitored. When containers of shellfish arrive at the retail fish market or restaurant, they have a tag that describes their origin and date of harvest so that the buyer can avoid buying shellfish from contaminated water. Because retailers and restaurateurs are required to keep the tags for 90 days after the shellfish are sold, this method also allows health officials to track down the culprit if there is an outbreak of shellfish-borne illness. If you're concerned, you can ask the fishmonger to show you the shellfish tags, and you can check with state and local authorities to make sure the water is clean and safe.

Once you've established that the coral is safe to eat, you can just leave it attached and cook it along with the rest of the scallops, or you can purée it with an equal amount of butter and whisk the butter into the sauce as you would an herb butter or other flavored butter.

BAY SCALLOPS AND SHRIMP OR CRAYFISH À LA NAGE

PÉTONCLES ET CREVETTES OU ÉCREVISSES À LA NAGE

MAKES 4 LIGHT MAIN-COURSE
OR 6 FIRST-COURSE SERVINGS

This recipe is actually cheating a little, because instead of using a court bouillon, or vegetable stock—the classic poaching liquid for seafood à la nage—I call for crustacean broth made from shrimp or crayfish heads and shells finished with a little butter, and ideally, some crustacean butter. To learn more about crustacean sauces, see Chapter 25.

24 bay scallops, preferably in the shell

1 small onion, chopped

2 cloves garlic, chopped

3 sprigs fresh thyme, or ¼ teaspoon dried

1 tablespoon olive oil

12 large shrimp, preferably with the heads, or 24 live crayfish

3 ripe tomatoes, chopped coarse

1 cup [250 ml] chicken, fish, or vegetable stock or water

½ cup [125 ml] heavy cream

2 tablespoons Crustacean Butter (page 335; optional)

2 tablespoons finely chopped parsley

salt

pepper

SHUCK the bay scallops if they're still in the shell. The method is exactly the same as for sea scallops (see page 278) except there is no roe to worry about. Here, heads from the crustaceans are used, along with the shells to make a crustacean broth. They can also be reserved—they keep in the freezer for months—and saved up for making crustacean butter.

HEAT the onion, garlic, and thyme in the olive oil in a small pot over medium heat, stirring every couple of minutes until the onions turn translucent, about 10 minutes. Add the shrimp or crayfish, cover the pot, and cook for 4 minutes more. Take out the shrimp or crayfish with a slotted spoon and add the tomatoes and stock to the onion mixture. Simmer the mixture gently over low to medium heat.

TWIST the tails off the shrimp or crayfish, remove the shells from the tails, and devein the tails if necessary. Reserve the heads and tails. Put the shells and heads back into the mixture with the tomatoes and break up the shells and heads with the end of a French-style rolling pin or the front end of a cleaver held in the pot with the handle sticking straight up. Simmer gently, partially covered, for 20 minutes. Strain the shell/head mixture into a saucepan, pushing down firmly on the shells to extract as much liquid as possible. Discard anything that doesn't go through the strainer.

JUST before you're ready to serve, bring the crustacean broth to a gentle simmer and poach the reserved shrimp or crayfish tails and the bay scallops until the bay scallops lose their sheen, about 1 minute. Use a slotted spoon to transfer the bay scallops to heated soup plates. If you're serving the dish as a main course, give 6 bay scallops and 3 shrimp tails or 6 crayfish tails per serving. If you're serving it as a first course, serve everyone 4 bay scallops and 2 shrimp or 3 crayfish tails. Whisk the cream, crustacean butter, and parsley into the poaching liquid. Bring to a simmer and ladle it over the scallops. Season with salt and pepper.

BLUE TROUT

TRUITE AU BLEU

MAKES 4 MAIN-COURSE SERVINGS

Fish poached in a court bouillon containing vinegar is called *au bleu* because the acidic court bouillon causes the skin of some very fresh fish to turn blue. In the seventeenth and eighteenth centuries a number of fish were cooked *au bleu*, but the only remnant of the technique is *truite au bleu*, a delicate way to cook a very fresh trout.

If you're ever gone trout fishing or bought farmed trout straight out of the tank, you'll know that perfectly fresh trout are almost impossible to hold because they're so slippery. This slipperiness is caused by a coating that gradually erodes as the trout loses freshness. It is this coating that causes a trout to turn blue when it's plunged into a court bouillon acidulated with vinegar. Purists insist that the only way to make *truite au bleu* is with a live trout, but it is possible with a very fresh trout—one that is still slippery and very shiny. You must be careful not to rub off the slime layer. To protect this layer, wrap the trout in wax paper or in a plastic bag in your fishing creel or shopping bag. It's also essential that the trout be so fresh that it hasn't yet grown stiff from rigor mortis, because the hot court bouillon must cause the trout to suddenly contract and curl back in a characteristic spasm that allows *truite au bleu* aficionados to recognize the trout's perfect freshness. A perfectly fresh trout also turns blue, while a less than perfectly fresh trout, though perfectly edible, does not.

The most difficult part of *truite au bleu* is getting your hands on the trout. If you live in the right place, you can catch trout yourself, but more likely than not you'll end up ordering them at a local market that's supplied by a trout farm. Unfortunately, the quality of trout from trout farms varies so dramatically that some trout taste almost like they were just caught out of a rushing stream and others, to put it bluntly, taste like mud. Fortunately, I have an excellent source for trout (see Sources), which can be bought by mail order and shipped to other parts of the country; but while the trout will still be very fresh, they won't be fresh enough for *truite au bleu*. Your best bet is to try trout from different local sources.

If you have a live trout, kill it by gripping it in a towel (or, better, in a bunch of grass, which does less damage to the slime layer) and whacking its head on something hard to kill it instantly.

6 cups [1.5 l] (2 recipes) Simple Court Bouillon (page 283)

½ cup [125 ml] good-quality white wine vinegar

4 trout (12 ounces [340 g] each), ideally killed within 3 hours of cooking, gutted

1½ cups [375 ml] (1 recipe) Beurre Blanc (page 281; optional)

BRING the court bouillon to a simmer with the vinegar. Ladle about ¼ cup [60 ml] of the hot court bouillon into a heat-proof baking dish just large enough to hold the trout without overlapping. (The court bouillon will keep the trout from sticking to the baking dish.) Place the baking dish on the stove, using a flame tamer to help distribute the heat and, if the baking dish is glass, to keep it from breaking. Arrange the trout in the baking dish and ladle the rest of the simmering court bouillon over them. If there's not enough court bouillon to cover the trout completely, add some hot water. Simmer the trout gently for 10 to 12 minutes (about 10 minutes per inch [2.5 cm] of thickness at the thickest part) and check for doneness by gently lifting one of the trout out of the simmering liquid with a long spatula and then running a small paring knife along its back, to one side of the spine, and peering in to see if the flesh is still translucent and clinging to the bone. If it is, cook the trout a couple of minutes longer and check again. Serve the trout on individual plates. (If your trout is less than perfectly fresh and hasn't turned blue, remove the skin in the kitchen before serving. Otherwise leave it on so your guests will see that "blue trout" is indeed blue.) If your guests don't know how, show them how to pull off the skin by pinching it between a thumb and forefinger and just pulling it away or, if you're being fancy, hooking it onto the tines of a fork and rolling it up on the fork. Discard the skin. Pass the beurre blanc at the table or dilute it with a little of the poaching liquid—or just serve a little of the poaching liquid alone around the fish in large soup plates.

MEDALLIONS OF SALMON À LA NAGE

MÉDAILLONS DE SAUMON À LA NAGE

MAKES 4 MAIN-COURSE SERVINGS

Virtually any whole fish or piece of fish can be poached in a court bouillon and end up à la nage. Fish fillets are the most convenient because they contain so few bones, but fish steaks (what the French call *darnes* if they come from a round fish and *tronçons* if they come from a large flatfish like halibut) are also dramatic and work well. I like to poach thick salmon steaks that I first bone and then tie up into round medallions (see page 291).

You can poach salmon steaks as you would the sea scallops on page 284 (they take about 9 minutes per inch of thickness at the thickest part) and serve the poaching liquid and julienned vegetables around the cooked steaks in hot soup plates. You can also enrich the poaching liquid with various butters (see page 285) or just make a plain court bouillon, poach the salmon, and serve the steaks with a classic sauce such as a beurre blanc (see page 281), hollandaise (see page 257), or mousseline (see page 77).

4 salmon steaks (8 to 12 ounces [225 to 350 g] each), at least ¾ inch [2 cm] thick, boned and tied into medallions (see page 291)

3 cups [750 ml] (1 recipe) Court Bouillon for Cooking à la Nage (page 283) or Simple Court Bouillon (page 283)

optional sauces (beurre blanc, hollandaise, mousseline, etc.; see "Using Other Sauces to Finish Poaching Liquids," below)

ARRANGE the salmon steaks in a sauté pan (preferably one with straight sides) or heat-proof baking dish just large enough to hold them in a single layer. Bring the court bouillon to a simmer and pour it over the salmon. Place the salmon over medium heat—if you're using a glass baking dish, use a flame tamer—to maintain at a gentle simmer. Poach the salmon for about 9 minutes per inch of thickness. You may have to cut into a piece to judge when it's ready. Serve the salmon surrounded with the poaching liquid (and the julienned vegetables if you've used the Court Bouillon for Cooking à la Nage), or with one of the optional sauces.

USING OTHER SAUCES TO FINISH POACHING LIQUIDS

Throughout this book, classic sauces are combined with cooking liquids to enrich the liquids and to produce brothlike sauces that are less rich than their classic predecessors. Seafood braising liquid is used to make an egg yolk–butter sauce in Chapter 23; aïoli (garlic mayonnaise) is used to finish a bourride in Chapter 18; rouille is used to finish a bouillabaisse; and, in this chapter, various butters are emulsified in the style of a beurre blanc and combined with the poaching liquid to make creamy brothlike sauces.

BONING SALMON STEAKS AND TYING THEM
INTO ROUND MEDALLIONS

Buy salmon steaks that are at least ¾ inch [2 cm] thick—thinner steaks won't hold their shape. Unless your steaks come from near the salmon's tail, they'll have two stomach flaps hanging down on either side. Slide a paring knife along the inside of the two flaps and separate the bones from the flesh. Cut along the side of the bones that run up toward what was once the back of the salmon, following the bones all the way around the spinal column until you reach the top of the steak. Cut all the way to the top of the steak toward the skin, but don't cut through the skin. Repeat on the other side of the spinal column until you've removed all the spinal bones and ribs. Run your finger along both sides of the steaks to feel for any small pin bones that are left embedded in the flesh. Pull these out with tweezers or needle-nose pliers. Carefully cut away about 2 inches [5 cm] of the skin that wraps around one side of the stomach flaps so that raw skin isn't left on the inside of the medallion when this outer flap is wrapped inside the medallion. Fold the stomach flaps inside the medallion and tie it into a round shape with string.

SOLE WITH HOT BUTTER AND LEMON

SOLE MEUNIÈRE

WHAT	HOW TO	HOW TO	HOW TO	THE
"MEUNIÈRE" MEANS	FLOUR, BREAD, AND SAUTÉ WHOLE FLAT FISH AND FILETS	CLARIFY BUTTER	KNOW WHEN FISH IS DONE	DIFFERENCE BETWEEN SOLE AND FLOUNDER

IN LARGE AMERICAN CITIES THERE ARE CERTAIN OLD-FASHIONED French restaurants that are on the verge of extinction. Typically, such places have a maître d' who is likely to greet you with a discreet "bonsoir." In New York at least, such places have an overstuffed feel, with little tables and banquettes, low ceilings, and waiters in black jackets and bow ties pushing little carts to and fro, carving this and flambéing that. The menu is in French, usually without translation. It is filled with old standbys like lobster bisque, leeks with vinaigrette, rack of lamb, and sole meunière. There are no miso sauces or infused oils and none of the food looks like a skyscraper. I adore such places because they're cozy and comfortable and because they serve me the dishes I like most, unimproved by some "creative" chef.

My favorite of all the great classic French dishes is sole meunière, piping hot, tasting of the sea, butter, and a whisper of lemon. But it must be just right. And while I'm willing to settle for less at home, in an expensive restaurant the sole must be Dover sole, flown in from the eastern Atlantic. It must be cooked and presented whole, not in fillets. I prefer to carve it myself, on a small platter to the side of my plate, although in my fancy places a waiter will offer to do it for me.

Dover sole is the only flatfish we get in the United States that has a firm, almost meaty, texture and, at the same time, an indescribably delicate flavor. Like most fish, it is best cooked on the bone so the juices stay locked in. If you're serving it at home, you may have to show your guests how to carve it or, if you're serving for a small group, carve it yourself at the table. If carving in the dining room seems daunting, carve it in the kitchen, but cook it whole. If you can't find Dover sole or aren't willing to break the bank, use whole flounder, fluke, gray sole, lemon sole, rex sole, or petrale sole (all of which are technically flounder). Don't use "Dover sole" from the West Coast—again, this is a flounder, and one with rather soft and insipid flesh.

Cooking *à la meunière,* "like the miller's wife," is very simple. Dust the fish (or chicken breasts or slices of veal) with flour, pat off any excess, gently sauté the fish in butter (ideally, clarified), and sprinkle it with lemon juice and parsley. Throw out the cooked butter in the pan and heat fresh butter in the pan until it turns golden brown and spoon it over the fish. The butter froths up as soon as it hits the lemon, so it's important to serve the fish immediately, before the foam subsides.

I don't recommend serving sole meunière for more than four people because you'll need a large sauté pan—ideally nonstick and oval—for each 1 or 2 fish, depending on the size of the fish and the size of the pan. At fancy dinners, I sometimes serve sole meunière as a first course so I can give each person 2 fillets instead of 4 and so I can get by cooking fewer fish. It's hard to give only 1 fillet because the fillets on the bottom of the sole are smaller than those on top and someone's going to be cheated. If you're cooking more soles than you have pans, brown the fish quickly on both sides on high heat (for this, clarified butter is essential). When you've browned all the fish, transfer them to a baking sheet (or two) and slide them into a 350°F [175C°/gas mark 4] oven, for about 9 minutes per inch [2.5 cm] of thickness. (See "How to Know When Fish Is Done," page 20.) This is also a good way to do some of the work ahead of time—brown the fish just before the guests arrive, reserve in the refrigerator, and finish cooking in the oven at the last minute.

SOLE WITH HOT BUTTER AND LEMON

SOLE MEUNIÈRE

MAKES 4 FIRST-COURSE OR

LIGHT MAIN-COURSE SERVINGS OR 2 GENEROUS

MAIN-COURSE SERVINGS

2   whole Dover soles, flukes, or flounder (about 14 ounces [395 g] each)

    salt

    pepper

½   cup [60 g] all-purpose flour

3   tablespoons clarified butter (see page 296) or unsalted butter (for sautéing), plus 4 tablespoons unsalted butter (to finish fish)

1   tablespoon lemon juice

1   tablespoons finely chopped parsley

PREPARE the fish as described on page 297. Season the fish with salt and pepper, dredge them in the flour, pat off the excess, and spread them out on a sheet pan. Heat the clarified butter in a nonstick pan over medium to high heat. If you're using regular unsalted butter, don't get the pan too hot or the butter will burn.

SAUTÉ the fish for about 7 minutes on each side, until they feel firm to the touch on both sides or until the flesh no longer looks raw and translucent when you cut into it. (See page 20 for more about determining doneness.)

TRANSFER the fish to a platter or to individual plates. (If you're letting your guests carve their own, set a plate at everyone's place and put the fish on another set of plates or small oval platters to each person's left.) Sprinkle the fish with lemon and parsley.

DISCARD the butter used for cooking the fish and wipe out the pan with a paper towel. Put in the fresh butter and heat it over high heat until it froths. As soon as the froth begins to subside slightly, pour the butter over the fish. Serve immediately.

USING FILLETS

WHILE fillets of sole meunière never taste quite as good as a whole fish, they're easier to find and cook. When sautéing fillets, have the skin taken off, season the fillets and dust them with flour, and cook them in the same way as whole fish.

MEUNIÈRE VARIATIONS

The meunière technique is so adaptable that you're likely to encounter dishes that seemingly have no relationship to a simple sole meunière but that when analyzed reveal themselves as direct descendants. The most obvious are classic variations made by substituting vinegar for lemon juice or by adding ingredients such as capers (*à la grenobloise*) or almonds (*amandine*) to the hot butter sauce. Other classic variations include sole *dorée*, which is sole cooked *à la meunière* but without the frothy butter poured over it at the end, a good compromise for those watching their butter intake. Escoffier, in the 1902 edition of *Le Guide Culinaire*, describes variations such as sole meunière with eggplant, with porcini mushrooms, and with oranges, but these dishes are all essentially a classic sole meunière just decorated differently on the platter.

To make up dishes using the meunière technique as a starting point, it helps to understand what makes meunière different from dishes served with other kinds of sauces. Most sauces—beurre blanc, béchamel, hollandaise, mayonnaises—are emulsions in which microscopic globules of fat are suspended in the surrounding liquid, or, conversely, globules of liquid are surrounded in a medium of fat. Whole butter is already an emulsion that, when whisked into most sauces, stays emulsified and gives the sauce a special texture (see "How Butter Works in Beurre Blanc and Other Sauces," page 280). But when butter is cooked in a sauté pan before it is poured over foods, the heat destroys the emulsion and the milk solids lightly caramelize, creating a nutty-tasting and golden beurre noisette.

The meunière variations that we find in cookbooks or in restaurants are made by replacing one of the original components with something else. Olive oil or nut oils can replace the butter used for cooking the fish (or boneless chicken breasts or veal scallops) and for pouring over at the end. Vinegar is used in many classic variations as a substitute for the lemon juice, but with a little imagination different styles of vinegar can be used for different effects. Sherry vinegar, authentic balsamic vinegar, herb-infused vinegars, or even fruit-infused vinegars create subtle and not-so-subtle effects. (Please, no raspberry vinegar; try infusing lemon or orange zests in white wine vinegar instead.) Vinegar can also be infused with herbs or aromatic ingredients, such as shallots, and the infusion then sprinkled over the fish before the hot butter or oil is poured on top (see recipe, page 304). Alain Ducasse, perhaps France's most famous chef, infuses vinegar with shallots, pepper, and tarragon and sprinkles this mixture over the fish. He then heats butter until it's lightly browned and spoons this beurre noisette over the fish.

The flour coating can be left out or changed. Try using a classic coating of beaten eggs and bread crumbs (see recipe, page 304), or finely ground spices, finely chopped herbs, powdered dried cèpes (porcini), or finely chopped truffles. Traditional meunière garnitures may contain small or finely chopped ingredients such as lemon and capers (*à la grenobloise*), but you can improvise with other ingredients—minced shallots, olives, tomatoes, lemon zests, chiles, cornichons.

CARVING A COOKED WHOLE FLATFISH

One of the glories of a real Dover sole is that the fillets are firm enough that they don't fall apart when it comes time to carve. Other flatfish, such as flounder, require a bit more dexterity because of the fragility of the flesh.

If you're carving in front of your guests or family, put the fish on a heated oval platter and set a plate nearby for the bones. A long spatula, one that will slide under the whole length of the fish, is good for this; best of all is a long spatula with the flat part perpendicular to the handle that allows you to slide the spatula under the fish from the side. Spatulas should be perforated so that any fat in the pan is left behind.

The outside edge of flatfish is surrounded with a thin strip of flesh, called the frill, and a bunch of tiny bones. If you haven't removed these ahead of time (see page 297), push down on the edge of the fish, about ½ inch [1.5 cm] in from the side, with a small knife or spoon and push outward, pushing the frill and bones to the edge of the platter. Do this all the way around the fish, except up by the head.

Slide a flexible knife down the center of the fish, between the two fillets, separating them slightly from the bone. (If you're serving a Dover sole, you can use a spoon instead.) Starting from the center, near the head, slide the knife under each of the fillets, detaching them from the backbone. Gently slide the knife under the backbone, lifting it away from the bottom fillets. Detach the head and backbone and put them on the plate. Separate the two bottom fillets by cutting through the indentation that runs along the middle.

There are two methods for taking the milk solids out of butter to clarify it. If you're clarifying more than a couple of pounds, do what they do in restaurants: Melt the butter in a pot on the stove (ideally the pot should be tall and narrow to make skimming easier), let it sit, and skim off the froth with a ladle. Discard the froth and ladle out the pure, golden clarified butter. Don't reach too far down in the pot with the ladle or you'll bring up water and milk solids that have settled to the bottom. It's worth making more than you need, since clarified butter keeps for months in the fridge and forever in the freezer. If you're only clarifying a pound or two [450 to 900 g] of butter, cook the butter over medium heat in a heavy-bottomed saucepan. The butter will froth and bubble as the water in the butter boils away. (Butter is about 30 percent water.) After about 5 minutes, keep a close eye on the butter—tilt the pan and look at the bottom, where some of the milk solids will cling. When the milk solids coagulate, first into white specks, then lightly brown ones, remove the butter from the heat and set the bottom of the saucepan in a bowl of cold water for a few seconds to stop the cooking. Pour the butter into another container, leaving the golden brown milk solids clinging to the saucepan. Or if you're being fastidious, strain the butter through a fine-mesh strainer, a triple layer of cheesecloth, or a coffee filter. This second method produces a tastier version of clarified butter than the first, because the milk solids have caramelized, producing what French cooks call *beurre noisette* and Indians call *ghee*. Beurre noisette is used in the same way as clarified butter but can also be used in butter sauces (such as hollandaise) or in pastries to give a more pronounced butter flavor.

POMPANO

Unlike Europeans, who are blessed with Dover sole, turbot, and a tasty variety of Mediterranean fish, we Americans have to make do with flatfish that have mushy rather than firm flesh. Pompano, while not a flat fish, has a silvery skin and firm fillets very much like those from Dover sole. I like to cook pompano whole, either *à la meunière* or grilled, but you can also fillet it. I leave the skin on pompano fillets and sauté them in clarified butter, mostly on the skin side, while holding them down in the pan with a spatula to keep them from curling. If you want to dust the fillets with flour before sautéing, remove the skin.

GETTING FLATFISH READY FOR COOKING

Unless someone caught the fish for you, leave this to the guys at the fish market. If you have to do it yourself, cut the fins off the sides and around the edges of the fish with heavy scissors and cut the gills out of the base of the head. Discard the gills. Scale the bottom (white side) of the fish by scraping it with a fish scaler or the back of a knife. It's helpful to do this outside or by holding the fish in a clear, unscented garbage bag so the scales don't fly everywhere. Some cooks scale the top dark skin and leave it on, but European cooks always remove it. There are two ways to remove the dark skin. Dover sole, which has very firm flesh, is easiest to skin because the skin can be yanked off in one big piece. Make a shallow cut all around the fish about ¼ inch [5 cm] from the edge and ½ inch in from the end of the tail. Starting at the tail, slide the knife under the skin until you've loosened a small flap. Assuming you're right-handed, grip this flap with your right hand and hold down the fishtail with your left. (Use a kitchen towel if the skin is slippery.) Pull the skin toward the fish's head in one rapid movement until it comes away completely. This method doesn't work with flounder or American sole because the flesh is too soft and will tear. You'll need to cut the skin off in strips by sliding a long, thin, flexible knife under the skin.

Clean the fish by cutting away any frill, on the outside edge, revealed by removing the skin. Make a shallow slit along the stomach side of the fish, exposing the viscera. Don't cut too deeply or you'll damage the viscera and make the fish harder to clean. Pull out as much of the viscera as you can. Press any remaining viscera out of the fish by running the handle of a knife up along the side of the fish toward the opening. Rinse out the opening under cold running water.

PORTIONING FLATFISH FILLETS

Because flatfish fillets are not all the same size—the bottom ones are thinner—you may have to cut some of the fillets in half so everyone gets a fair share. If you are filleting a whole flatfish for two people, simply give each person one thick-top fillet and one thin-bottom fillet. If, however, you are serving the fish for four, you will need to halve the fillets—I like to cut them diagonally, so each person gets a half of a thick and a half of a thin fillet.

SKATE
WITH CAPERS
AND LEMON

RAIE À LA GRENOBLOISE

MAKES 4 MAIN-COURSE SERVINGS

Skate, which until recently could be found only in ethnic markets, has finally caught on in the United States. The French have been cooking it for years, and 20 years ago it was cooked in inexpensive restaurants and bistros with burnt butter, beurre noir. Beurre noir is now, happily, out of fashion, and chefs have taken to cooking in more imaginative ways, including meunière for which the butter is only caramelized into beurre noisette, not burnt. Dishes cooked à la grenobloise have been around for years, but the tangy and salty effect of the lemon and capers is delightful next to the rich, frothy butter and the melting texture of the skate.

In American markets, capers are usually sold in little jars, packed in brine, but in Europe they're often packed in salt, a method that I think better preserves their flavor. Whichever kind you use, try to find the relatively small capers labeled "non pareil."

Nowadays, skate is mostly sold already filleted, but in ethnic markets—mine are Chinese and Caribbean—you may encounter whole wings. To fillet the wings, use a long, flexible knife to cut down to just inside the thickest part of the wing. Press down on the knife so it bends, and slide it along the flat layer of cartilaginous bones. Keep sliding the knife outward toward the outer edge of the wing until the whole fillet comes loose. Turn the wing over and repeat on the other side. To skin a skate fillet, place it skin-side down on a cutting board and slide a long, flexible knife between the skin and the fillet. Press the knife so the blade is bending and pressing against the skin on the cutting board. Grip the skin, using a kitchen towel if it's slippery, and move it back and forth and pull while holding the knife. The skin usually comes completely off. If you're left with a few strips of skin adhering to the flesh, slide the knife under the skin and cut it off in strips.

4 skate fillets (6 to 8 ounces [170 to 225 g] each), or 2 bone-in skate wings (1½ to 2 pounds [675 g to 900 g] each)

   salt

   pepper

½ cup [60 g] all purpose flour

3 tablespoons clarified butter or unsalted butter (for sautéing), plus 8 tablespoons unsalted butter (for spooning over the skate)

2 tablespoons capers, drained if packed in brine, rinsed if in salt

1 lemon, cut into skinless wedges (see page 391), wedges cut into 30 pieces each

1 tablespoon finely chopped parsley

1 tablespoon lemon juice

IF you're using whole skate wings, fillet and skin them as described above. Just before you're ready to cook, season the fillets with salt and pepper and dredge them in the flour. Pat off the excess.

SAUTÉ the fillets in butter over medium to high heat, 3 to 5 minutes on each side, until they are golden brown on both sides and firm to the touch. Transfer them to hot plates or a platter. Discard the butter left in the sauté pan, wipe the pan out with a paper towel, and heat the new butter over medium heat until it's frothy. Take the pan off the heat, let cool for about 15 seconds, then toss in the capers and pieces of lemon. (The lemon and capers can cause butter that is too hot to burn.)

SPRINKLE the skate fillets with parsley and lemon juice and pour the hot butter, capers, and lemon pieces over them.

HOW TO PORTION FILLETS OF UNEVEN THICKNESS

When cutting up a fish fillet of uneven thickness, you need to analyze it so everyone gets the same amount. When I'm confronted with a salmon fillet, I cut it lengthwise down the middle, which leaves me with two halves, one thicker than the other. I cut crosswise through the two fillets and make the pieces I cut from the thinner side larger than those I cut from the thicker side. I cook the thin portions for a shorter time than the thick ones.

SALMON FILLETS WITH POWDERED CÈPES AND BALSAMIC VINEGAR

FILETS DE SAUMON À LA POUDRE DE CÈPES ET AU VINAIGRE BALSAMIQUE

MAKES 4 MAIN-COURSE SERVINGS

This elegant dish is made like sole meunière except that powdered cèpes (porcini) replace the flour coating and balsamic vinegar replaces the lemon. This dish is gorgeous with fresh wild mushrooms strewn over it just before serving. Thick slices of fresh cèpes would of course be ideal, but morels, chanterelles, hedgehogs, and other wild mushrooms will work, too. Don't not make the dish if you can't find wild mushrooms or don't want to spring for them—they're expensive. The balsamic vinegar can be any quality you like. Even inexpensive brands are rarely harsh, they're just not as interesting. But this is one time I break out and use my very best or my almost best. (See page 50 for more about balsamic vinegar.)

When buying the salmon, buy it in a single piece from the center of the fillet and cut it up yourself. If you leave it up to the fish store you're likely to get uneven pieces, but do go ahead and have them remove the skin. When you get the fillet home, pull out the pin bones and consider how best to cut it up. (See "How to Portion Fillets of Uneven Thickness," above.) I like square pieces of salmon about ½ inch [1.2 cm] thick and about 4 inches [10 cm] on each side, but this isn't always possible. This dish works with just about any fish fillet, as well as with boneless chicken breasts and slices of veal.

4 slices of salmon fillet (6 to 8 ounces [170 to 225 g] each)

salt

pepper

½ cup [125 g] (about ½ ounce) dried cèpes (porcini)

1 tablespoon butter (for sautéing the mushrooms), plus 2 tablespoons clarified butter or unsalted butter (for sautéing the salmon) and 4 tablespoons unsalted butter (for the sauce)

1 pound [450 g] fresh wild mushrooms such as cèpes, morels, or chanterelles (optional), hard parts trimmed off, brushed or rinsed clean

4 teaspoons balsamic vinegar

SPRINKLE the salmon fillets with salt and pepper, cover them with plastic wrap, and refrigerate them.

SPREAD the dried cèpes on a sheet pan and put them into a 200°F [95°C, or lowest setting] oven for 30 minutes to dry them out thoroughly. Let them cool, and grind them in a clean coffee grinder or blender for about 1 minute. Strain the dust through a fine-mesh strainer by rubbing it against the sides with your fingers. Repeat by grinding any pieces that don't go through the strainer and work this second batch through the strainer.

IF you're serving wild mushrooms, sauté them in 1 tablespoon of butter until they've softened and are fragrant. Season with salt and pepper.

WHILE the mushrooms are sautéing, dredge the salmon fillets in the cèpe dust so they're well coated on both sides. Sautè them in 2 tablespoons of butter in a nonstick pan over medium to high heat until they're browned on both sides and firm to the touch, about 4 minutes on each side for 1-inch [2.5 cm]-thick fillets. (If you're not using clarified butter, be careful not to let the butter burn.)

WITH a wide spatula, gently transfer the fillets to hot plates. Pour the butter out of the pan used for sautéing the fillets and wipe the pan clean with a paper towel. Put 4 tablespoons of butter in the pan and heat over medium heat until frothy. Spoon the butter over the fillets. Spoon 1 teaspoon of balsamic vinegar on top of each fillet. Spoon the mushrooms around and over the fillets and serve.

TROUT WITH PAPRIKA AND ALMONDS

TRUITE AMANDINE

AU PAPRIKA

MAKES 4 MAIN-COURSE SERVINGS

I've never been terribly fond of truite amandine, not because it's so old-fashioned that it's practically a cliché, but because restaurants that feature it are so stodgy that the cooking has lost any spark of ingenuity and enthusiasm. (You can tell a lot about a restaurant by how it smells, and these places smell dusty.) But I rediscovered it one evening when a friend who had just returned from Spain invited me over for dinner. As luck would have it, she's an expert smuggler and had waddled through customs with her favorite Spanish delicacies hidden under elaborate feminine garments. We had an assortment of cured fatty hams, chorizos, smoked Spanish paprika (pinmentón), and Spanish almonds. As she described a dish tasted in the Basque country, I remembered the trout that my mother used to cook in bacon fat when we'd camp by the side of a stream. And I remembered truite amandine. Trout amandine is a simple derivative of trout meunière—you just strew slivered almonds into the hot butter before spooning it over the fish. But when we cooked together that night, I substituted the Spanish paprika for the flour, the gently rendered fat from the ham for the butter, and plump and tasty Spanish almonds for the usual slivered ones.

The magnificent result was, of course, largely due to those illicit ingredients, but I've since come close, using whole almonds with the skin, good-quality mild Hungarian paprika or mild pimentón (pimentón dulce), fat rendered from Italian prosciutto, and, most important, good trout. To get the prosciutto fat, ask them at the market to slice a piece off the side of a prosciutto di Parma or other unsmoked cured ham, preferably without the rind. If this doesn't work, use pancetta, which is unsmoked bacon, usually sold rolled up.

2 tablespoons [35 g] whole almonds with skins

4 ounces [115 g] prosciutto fat (rind cut off) or pancetta,
   chopped fine by hand or in a food processor

4 trout (12 to 14 ounces [350 to 400 g] each), gutted

   salt

   pepper

4 tablespoons paprika, preferably Spanish pimentón dulce
   (see Sources)

4 tablespoons butter (optional)

1 tablespoon finely chopped parsley

TOAST the almonds in a 350°F [175°C/gas mark 4] oven until they smell fragrant, about 15 minutes.

HEAT the fat in a small, heavy-bottomed saucepan over low to medium heat until it releases its liquid fat, about 10 minutes. Don't let it burn. Strain the fat into a nonstick sauté pan large enough to hold the trout—if you don't have a large enough pan, use two—and reserve the little pieces of crackling that collect in the strainer.

SEASON the trout with salt and pepper and roll them in the paprika, coating them completely. Sauté them in the fat over medium heat until they're well browned, about 5 minutes on each side. They're done when they feel firm to the touch, but if you're unsure, make a little incision along the backbone and peek inside. If the fillets are still translucent and cling to the backbone, sauté the trout 1 or 2 minutes more and check again.

TRANSFER the trout to plates or a platter. Heat the little pieces of crackling and the almonds for about 1 minute in the fat left in the pan used for sautéing the trout and pour everything over the trout. (If the fat burned while you were sautéing the trout, pour it out and use the butter. Heat the butter until it is frothy and stir in the almonds, the crackling, and the parsley. Spoon the mixture over the trout.)

Variations: These trout and the salmon recipes on pages 299 to 300 are just two examples of how you can substitute different ingredients for the flour in a traditional meunière recipe. In American restaurants I often see fish coated with finely chopped nuts. In luxurious French restaurants, coating seafood, chicken, and sweetbreads with finely chopped truffles is a recent craze. Some chefs use truffles alone, while others combine them with finely chopped herbs, such as parsley.

SAUTÉED STRIPED BASS FILLETS WITH VEGETABLE "MARMALADE"

SAUTÉ DE FILETS DE BAR À LA MARMELADE DE LEGUMES

MAKES 4 MAIN-COURSE SERVINGS

I ran across a dish similar to this in a cookbook by Joël Robuchon, the now-retired chef of the restaurant Jamin in Paris. I once had lunch at Jamin, at the time considered by many to be the best restaurant in France, and was amazed not only by the perfection of the dishes but by the fact that the dishes were clearly derivatives of classic recipes. This is not to diminish Robuchon's cooking, for the execution was perfect and innovative juxtapositions, very much his own, lent the food its own special character. But this dish is a perfect example of how a classic dish can be used as a template for improvisation, with the basic techniques and identity of the dish left intact. When I tasted Robuchon's turbot with vegetable marmalade, I was immediately reminded of the capers in a sole à la grenobloise, and I realized that the ingredients that could be substituted for, or added to, the capers were limited only by our imagination. Here is my own version, very different than at Jamin, but much in the same spirit. The time-consuming part of this recipe, the "marmalade," can be prepared earlier the same day.

1 ½ to 2 pounds [675 g to 900 g] scaled skin-on fillet from a striped bass, red snapper, sea bass, or similar fish, or 2 or 4 smaller fillets (15 to 2 pounds [675 g to 900 g] total)

salt

pepper

1 ripe medium-size tomato, peeled

¼ cup [35 g] black olives (not canned), such as Gaeta, Kalamata, Nyons, or niçoise, pitted

1 tablespoon capers, preferably small nonpareil, rinsed and chopped fine

1 small pinch saffron threads, soaked for 30 minutes in 1 teaspoon of water

1 yellow or red bell pepper (or poblano chile, to give the marmalade a little bite)

1 lemon

1 small shallot, minced fine

10 fresh basil leaves, tossed with 1 teaspoon of olive oil to prevent blackening

⅓ cup [40 g] all-purpose flour

2 tablespoons "pure" olive oil or flavorless vegetable oil (for sautéing)

2 tablespoons extra-virgin olive oil (for the sauce)

USE a fish scaler or the back of a knife to scrape off any scales that are still attached to the fillet skin. If you have 1 or 2 fillets, cut them in quarters or halves so you have 4 equal-size pieces. Season on both sides with salt and pepper, cover with plastic wrap, and refrigerate.

CUT the tomato vertically into 6 wedges. Cut the pulp and seeds out of the wedges so you have only the bright red flesh. Cut the flesh into ⅛-inch [3 mm] dice and reserve in a small mixing bowl. Chop the olives until they are slightly smaller than the tomato dice and combine with the tomatoes. Stir the chopped capers and the saffron with its soaking liquid into the tomato mixture. Char and peel the bell pepper or chile (see page 20), cut out the stem, and then cut the pepper in half lengthwise. Scoop out and discard the seeds, cut out and discard any thick

strips of pale ribs, and cut the pepper into ⅛-inch [3 mm] dice. Add these to the tomato mixture. Cut a 3-inch-by-½-inch [7.5 by 1.5 cm] strip of zest from the lemon with a vegetable peeler or paring knife. Shave off any white pith still attached to the inside of the zest. Bring 1 cup [250 ml] of water to a boil, plunge in the strip of zest, and drain. Cut the zest into very thin strips and cut these crosswise into tiny dice. Combine with the tomato mixture. Squeeze the lemon and stir 1 tablespoon of the juice and the shallot into the tomato mixture. Refrigerate the mixture. Just before you're ready to cook the fish, chop the basil fine and stir it into the tomato marmalade.

DREDGE the fillets in the flour and pat off any excess. Heat the olive oil for sautéing in a nonstick pan over high heat and put the fillets in the pan, skin-side down. Press on the fillets with a spatula for the first couple of minutes to prevent them from curling. Sauté for 3 to 4 minutes on the skin side and 2 to 3 minutes on the flesh side, until the fillets are firm to the touch. The exact cooking time will depend on the thickness of the fillets. (See "How to Know When Fish Is Done," page 20.)

PUT the fillets, skin-side up, on hot plates. Wipe out the pan, pour in the tomato marmalade and the extra-virgin olive oil, and bring to a simmer over high heat. Season to taste with salt and pepper and spoon over and around the fish. Serve immediately so the skin doesn't get soggy from the marmalade.

Variations: The tomato marmalade is also delicious spooned over grilled fish or chicken. You can also make a less fastidious version by chopping the ingredients more or less randomly.

MORE WAYS TO SAUTÉ FISH FILLETS

Fillets are a quick and easy alternative when we don't have access to good whole fish or we don't feel like fiddling with bones. The first question when buying fillets is whether or not to leave the skin on. A rule of thumb is to leave the skin on when sautéing and to remove it when using moist cooking methods such as braising, poaching, or steaming. Sautéed fish skin turns delightfully crispy; poached fish skin can feel rubbery and unpleasant in the mouth.

When sautéing skin-on fillets, make sure the skin has been well scaled by running your fingers all along the surface to feel for rough patches. If you find scales, scrape them off with a scaler or the back of a kitchen knife. Keep in mind, also, that fish skin contracts as soon as it touches the hot sauté pan, causing the fillet to curl. To prevent this, put the fillets skin-side down in the hot pan and immediately press against the tops of the fillets with a spatula to keep them from curling and to keep the whole surface of the skin in contact with the heat so it browns evenly. You can also help prevent curling by making 3 or 4 shallow slashes in the skin in two directions. When the fillets cook, the skin contracts and reveals a crisscross pattern where the skin has pulled back from the little slashes.

BREADING: I never liked breaded foods until I had to teach them as part of a basic cooking class at a school in Manhattan. Teaching the class over and over again allowed me to refine the technique into something quite marvelous. Because most breaded foods are fried in oil, the breading absorbs the oil, coating the foods with a layer of grease. But when foods are coated with very fine fresh bread crumbs, the crust absorbs little fat. When the food is gently sautéed in clarified butter, the flavor is buttery but the breading isn't greasy. Regular unsalted butter works almost as well as clarified, but it leaves tiny brown specks of milk solids clinging to the breading.

The French, of course, have special terminology for different coatings. Foods coated only with flour are called *meunière* or *dorée;* when floured foods are in turn dipped in beaten egg, they're called *à la parisienne,* and when foods have been floured, dipped in beaten egg, and then dipped in bread crumbs, they are called *à l'anglaise.* When finely grated Parmigiano-Reggiano replaces the bread crumbs when breading *à l'anglaise,* the method is *à la milanaise.*

When the fillets are cooked *à l'anglaise* and surrounded by a classic garniture of cooked and strained egg yolks and egg whites, capers, and parsley, the dish is called *à la viennoise.*

When breading fish fillets for sautéing, it's best to use skinless fillets. This is because the skin is protected from the heat by the breading and will never get hot enough to turn crispy. Breaded foods are sautéed at lower temperatures than foods that have no coating or that have simply been floured, because the breading browns—and burns—at a lower temperature than skin or flesh. Because the coating absorbs a small amount of the fat used for sautéing, I like to use butter, which has the best flavor. If I'm being a perfectionist, I use clarified butter. You can use the same butter to sauté another round of fillets, but be sure to strain the butter through a fine-mesh strainer into a fresh pan so that flecks of breading that may have fallen off the first batch don't burn and leave specks.

Breaded fish fillets are delicious with just a squeeze of lemon, but frothy butter, cooked in the pan in the same way as when cooking *à la meunière,* is delicious, as are variations such as the caper sauce—*à la grenobloise*—on page 298. A little piece of herb butter, such as maître d' butter (page 490), can be dolloped on the fillets just as they are served, or the herb butter can be made to froth in the pan in the same way as whole butter in a classic sole meunière. The herb butter can also be passed at the table, either in disks or whipped. In classic French cooking, sauces containing water, wine, or other liquids aren't used for breaded foods because the breading absorbs the liquid and loses its delicate crispness. Beurre noisette, however, will not make the breading soggy because it contains no water. A favorite strategy of mine is to bread the fillets on one side only and spoon the sauce *around* the fillets, leaving the breading crisp and the whole dish less rich. Foods should be breaded immediately before they are cooked or the breading will get soggy. All of these methods for breading and cooking breaded fish will also work for boneless chicken breasts and thin slices of veal. (See page 2 for more about bread crumbs.)

FILLETS OF SOLE WITH A LIGHT BREAD-CRUMB COATING

FILLETS DE SOLE À L'ANGLAISE

MAKES 4 MAIN-COURSE SERVINGS

4 or 8 skinless fillets (or more, if you can find only small ones) of Dover sole or other firm-fleshed nonoily fish such as flounder, gray or lemon sole, Atlantic sea bass, or red snapper (1½ to 2 pounds [675 to 900 g] total)

7 slices dense-crumb white bread (such as Pepperidge Farm), crusts removed, or 1½ cups [65 g] fresh bread crumbs

2 large eggs

2 teaspoons salt

1 teaspoon ground pepper

1 cup [125 g] all-purpose flour

3 tablespoons clarified butter or unsalted butter, or more as needed (you'll need more if you sauté the fillets in batches)

 lemon wedges (optional)

¼ pound [115 g] herb butter, such as *beurre maître d'hôtel* (page 490), or unsalted butter (for making beurre noisette) (optional)

TRIM off and discard any frill left on the edges of the fillets. If the fillets are too long for your plates or sauté pan, cut them in half with a diagonal cut so the halves have the shape of whole fillets.

PROCESS the bread in a food processor for about 30 seconds and work the crumbs through a large strainer or drum sieve. If you don't have a food processor, just tear the bread into pieces before working it through the strainer. When you're ready for breading, spread the bread crumbs on a large plate or baking dish.

IN a small mixing bowl, lightly beat the eggs with the salt and pepper. The egg mixture contains a lot of salt and pepper because it is the fillets' only seasoning. The salt also loosens the egg so less adheres to the fish. When you're ready for breading, pour the egg mixture into a baking dish.

SPREAD the flour on a large plate or baking dish and dredge the fillets on both sides in the flour. Pat the fillets to get rid of excess flour so they are covered very lightly.

COVER a sheet pan with wax paper. Pinch the very end of each fillet and lower the fillet into the egg mixture. Wipe off the excess egg while holding the fillet over the egg mixture by running the fillet between the thumb and forefinger of your other hand. Lower the fillet into the bread crumbs and sprinkle more bread crumbs over it to coat both sides. Don't splash the egg mixture into the bread crumbs. Arrange the fillets on the sheet pan.

HEAT the clarified butter in a nonstick sauté pan over medium to high heat and gently put the fillets, more attractive side down, in the hot butter. Depending on the thickness of the fillets, sauté for 1 to 4 minutes on each side. When turning the fillets, use a long spatula that slides under the entire length of the fillets so you can turn the fillets without breaking them or cutting into the breading. The breading should end up golden brown. If it starts to darken too quickly, turn down the heat.

USING the long spatula, transfer the fillets to hot plates. Pass lemon wedges at the table; or put a dollop or disk of herb butter on top of each fillet; or discard the butter in the pan, wipe out the pan, heat unsalted butter until it is frothy, sprinkle the fillets with lemon juice, and spoon the frothy butter over each fillet.

IMPROVISING SOLE MEUNIÈRE VARIATIONS

THE COATING:

NATURAL (no coating at all; since this requires higher heat
for the fish to brown, clarified butter or oil must be used)

FLOUR (classic à la meunière)

FLOUR AND EGG (à la parisienne)

FLOUR, EGG, AND BREAD CRUMBS (à l'anglaise)

FLOUR, EGG, AND GRATED PARMIGIANO-REGGIANO CHEESE (à la milanaise)

POWDERED DRIED MUSHROOMS SUCH AS CÈPES (porcini), MORELS, OR SHITAKES

CHOPPED FRESH WILD MUSHROOMS OR TRUFFLES
(seafood or meat coated first with flour and egg)

HERBS SUCH AS PARSLEY, CHERVIL, OR TARRAGON, ALONE OR IN MIXTURES
(fish coated first with flour and egg)

CHOPPED NUTS

SPICES (curry powder, saffron, spice mixtures)

FAT FOR SAUTÉING
(most important when the coating, such as bread crumbs, is absorbent)

CLARIFIED BUTTER (CLASSIC)

WHOLE BUTTER

HERB BUTTERS (worked through a fine-mesh strainer so specks of herbs don't burn
during sautéing)

CRUSTACEAN BUTTERS (see page 335)

TRUFFLE BUTTER (see page 491)

OLIVE OIL

NUT OILS

RENDERED PORK FAT (from pancetta, prosciutto, bacon, etc.)

(continued)

FAT FOR SAUCE

WHOLE BUTTER (classic)

HERB BUTTERS

CRUSTACEAN BUTTERS

OLIVE OIL

NUT OILS (oils from toasted nuts are best, see page 37)

INFUSED OILS

ACIDIC INGREDIENTS (sprinkled on seafood or meat before pouring over sauce;
combined with the sauce, or swirled in the sauce on the plate)

LEMON (classic à la meunière)

WINE VINEGAR (classic for some meunière derivatives)

BALSAMIC VINEGAR

INFUSED VINEGARS

LIME JUICE

ORANGE JUICE

VERJUICE (the juice of underripe grapes)

GARNITURES (swirled into the sauce at the end)

CAPERS (à la grenobloise)

CHOPPED HERBS

DICED AROMATIC INGREDIENTS SUCH AS TOMATOES, OLIVES, ANCHOVIES, TRUFFLES, CHILES, CITRUS ZESTS

TINY CROUTONS (cooked in butter so they don't get soggy)

SOLE BRAISED WITH SHALLOTS AND WHITE WINE

SOLE BERCY

HOW TO	HOW TO	HOW TO	HOW TO
BRAISE WHOLE FISH AND FILLETS	MAKE FISH BROTH	CONVERT SEAFOOD COOKING LIQUIDS INTO SAUCES	GARNISH YOUR FISH WITH SHELLFISH AND SHELLFISH-BASED SAUCES

AS A BOY, I WOULD BE LURED INTO THE KITCHEN BY CERTAIN SMELLS. Buttery cookies and roasting meats were certain draws, as was anything cooked with wine, including my mother's fillets of sole, baked with a little butter and sherry. The juices from the sole mingled with the butter and sherry to make a simple and irresistible sauce. I didn't realize it at the time, but my mother's dish was, except for the sherry, virtually the same as *filets de sole Bercy,* one of the great classics of French cooking.

Sole Bercy is an example of what the French call cooking *en sauce,* a kind of braising, which is cooking in a small amount of liquid. For no reason I can imagine, other than a simple love of nomenclature, the term *en sauce* is used only for fish fillets, while the more general *braiser* is applied to whole fish. Just keep in mind that you can make a whole array of delicious fish dishes by baking fish—whole, fillets, or steaks—with a small amount of liquid, usually white wine and/or fish broth, and then serving the cooking liquid as the sauce. We could just leave it at that, but we'd miss out on the genius of French cooking—the ability to make dozens of variations using a single technique. In most classic French dishes, the cooking liquid is converted into a more or less elaborate sauce, often with cream or butter or egg yolks. Sometimes the sauce is used to glaze the fillets.

My mother's *sole Bercy* was perfectly delicious, but if you want to make the classic version, you'll need to make a fish broth. The most logical approach is to buy whole fish and have the fish store fillet them and give you the bones for the broth. My mother used sherry, which is fine, but the classic is made with dry white wine, which can be included in the fish broth used to cook the fish.

WHITE WINE FISH BROTH
(FUMET DE POISSON AU VIN BLANC)

MAKES 1 QUART [1 L]

2 pounds [900 g] bones and heads from nonoily fish, such as any flatfish,
sea bass, striped bass, or red snapper

1 medium-size onion, sliced thin

1 small bouquet garni

1 cup [250 ml] dry white wine

IF it hasn't already been done, cut the gills, which collect grit and discolor the broth, out of the base of the fish heads with heavy scissors and discard them. Pull out any viscera or clumps of blood from the body cavities; snap the backbones in couple of pieces, using your hands or a cleaver; and soak the bones for 2 hours in a bowl of cold water. Change the water every 30 minutes. In warm weather, put the bowl in the refrigerator with some ice in the water to keep it very cold.

PUT the onion and bouquet garni in a small pot and pack the bones tightly on top. Pour in the white wine and enough water—about 3 cups [750 ml]—to barely cover. Bring to a simmer on high heat, turn down the heat to maintain at a very gentle simmer, and simmer, uncovered, for 20 minutes. Don't overcook the bones or the broth will taste fishy. Strain and reserve. Fish broth will keep for several days in the refrigerator or for months in the freezer.

SOLE BRAISED WITH SHALLOTS AND WHITE WINE

SOLE BERCY

MAKES 2 MAIN-COURSE

OR 4 FIRST-COURSE SERVINGS

4   Dover soles, flukes or flounder (1 pound [450 g] each), or 2 flukes or flounder (2 pounds [900 g] each), filleted, bones reserved for the fish broth

    salt

    pepper

1   teaspoon butter (for the pan), plus 3 tablespoons unsalted butter (for the sauce)

2   shallots, chopped fine

½   cup [125 ml] White Wine Fish Broth (page 308)

SPRINKLE the fillets with salt and pepper, cover them with plastic wrap, and refrigerate them. If necessary, cut some of the fillets so everyone gets the same amount.

PREHEAT the oven to 350°F [175°C/gas mark 4]. Butter the bottom of one or two heat-proof baking dishes just large enough to hold the fillets in a single layer, and sprinkle the shallots over them. Arrange the fillets on top, with the more attractive side up, and add the fish broth, which should come about halfway up the sides of the fillets. Place the baking dishes on the stove over high heat, using a flame tamer if your dishes are glass or porcelain, and cook until the fish broth just begins to bubble, 1 or 2 minutes. Slide into the oven and bake for 3 to 8 minutes—2 minutes for thin fillets of sole, 8 minutes for almost-inch-thick filets of fluke. (See "How to Know When Fish Is Done," page 20.)

TURN off the oven. Transfer the fillets to hot plates with a long spatula—slide the spatula under the whole length of the fillets so they don't break. Place the plates in the turned-off oven—with the door open—to keep warm while you're making the sauce. Put the baking dishes back on the stove and boil down the braising liquid to reduce it by about one-third. If you've used more than one baking dish, combine the reduced braising liquid. Whisk the 3 tablespoons of unsalted butter into the hot braising liquid. Season the sauce to taste with salt and pepper, spoon it over the fish, and serve immediately.

FISH BROTH WITHOUT WINE (FUMET DE POISSON ORDINAIRE)

FOR recipes for braised fish that call for white wine, it isn't necessary to put wine in the fish broth. For these, make the fish broth above without the wine.

CLASSIC SOLE BERCY VARIATIONS

Classic recipes for fish cooked *en sauce* can be made with fillets, as in the recipe above, or they can be made with whole sole or other flatfish, such as flounder or fluke. When cooking whole flatfish, clean, scale, and prepare the fish as described on page 297, or have them do it at the fish store. Whole flatfish are best cooked in an oval pan just large enough to hold the fish, so less liquid is needed. If you don't have an oval pan, use a rectangular baking dish.

SOLE D'ANTIN: Prepare the fish in the same way as *sole bonne-femme*, below, but add 1 peeled, seeded, and finely chopped tomato to the pan with the shallots and mushrooms.

SOLE BONNE-FEMME: Sprinkle the bottom of the baking dish with 2 finely chopped shallots, 4 thinly sliced medium-size mushrooms, and 1 tablespoon of chopped parsley. Put the whole sole, the sole fillets, or other flatfish or flatfish fillets on top and pour ¼ cup of dry white wine and ¼ cup of fish broth over them. If you don't have fish broth, use ½ cup [125 ml] of wine. Bake in the same way as *sole Bercy*. Transfer the fish to a platter or hot plates, keep it warm, and pour ½ cup [125 ml] of heavy cream into the pan. Boil the sauce down over high heat until it has a lightly syrupy consistency. Whisk in 2 tablespoons of cold butter and season to taste. Spoon the sauce and mushrooms over the fish. If you like, follow the classic recipe and glaze the fish under a preheated broiler for a few seconds just before serving.

SOLE AU CHAMBERTIN: Classic recipes tell you to braise the sole in 1 cup [250 ml] of Chambertin. At $100 a bottle, drink the Chambertin and use an inexpensive full-bodied red wine for cooking the fish. If you follow the classic recipe, which is almost identical to a *sole Bercy* except that red wine replaces white wine, your sauce will be murky and acidic and specks of tannin will end up sticking to the fish. It's far better to prepare a red wine fish broth (see salmon recipe on page 243) using the sole or floun-der head and bones, reduce it to about 1 cup, and then use it instead of the wine and fish broth in the *sole Bercy* recipe.

SOLE À LA DIEPPOISE: Steam open about 30 mussels in white wine and use the mussel cooking liquid to braise the sole. Turn the braising liquid into a *sauce vin blanc* (see Fillets of Sole with White Wine, Butter, and Egg Yolk Sauce, below). Surround the fish with the mussels taken out of their shells and about ¼ pound of peeled bay shrimp. To be completely classic, you would coat the sole with the sauce, which is fine if you're using fillets but very messy if you're serving a whole fish. When serving whole fish, pass the sauce at the table.

SOLE DUGLÉRÉ: Make *sole Bercy* but replace half the white wine or fish broth with 2 peeled, seeded, and chopped tomatoes. After taking the fish out of the pan, add ½ cup [125 ml] of heavy cream, reduce until the sauce thickens slightly, and whisk in 2 tablespoons of butter. Season to taste.

SOLE À LA FLORENTINE: The combination of cheese and fish has never appealed to me, so I usually skip the cheese sauce that's served with this dish and just make a *sole Bercy* and serve it with spinach. But here's the classic: Cook fillets of sole in fish broth or white wine, set them on a bed of lightly creamed spinach, coat them with a mornay sauce (a béchamel sauce with cheese added), and glaze under the broiler.

FILETS DE SOLE MARGUÉRY: See below.

SOLE À LA NORMANDE: See page 313.

FILETS DE SOLE VÉRONIQUE: This eccentric dish is traditionally made only with fillets, not whole fish. For some mysterious reason, it caught on in French restaurants in the United States in the early part of the twentieth century. To make *sole véronique*, make *sole Bercy* without the shallots, boil down the braising liquid until it's lightly syrupy, and whisk in 4 tablespoons of butter. Spoon this sauce over the fillets. But here's what makes it *véronique*: spoon about 7 grapes—traditionally they should be peeled, seeded, and gently simmered muscat grapes—over each serving.

FILLETS OF SOLE WITH WHITE WINE, BUTTER, AND EGG YOLK SAUCE

FILETS DE SOLE MARGUÉRY

MAKES 2 MAIN-COURSE OR 4 FIRST-COURSE SERVINGS

Created at the Marguéry, a Parisian restau-rant that in the nineteenth century was world famous, the recipe for sole Marguéry was a closely guarded secret. It's rumored that

Diamond Jim Brady so insisted on eating the dish in New York that a well-known restaurateur took his son out of Harvard and sent him to work at the Marguéry to learn the recipe. As the story goes, after years of lowly work, the poor ex-student was finally admitted into the small circle of chefs and was given the secret recipe.

To understand the recipe, keep in mind that the myriad fish dishes cooked en sauce or braised are all prepared in the same way. It is only the braising liquid that is manipulated into a more or less elaborate sauce. In French classic cooking, whole fish and fish fillets are almost always braised in fish broth and/or wine, or occasionally the cooking liquid from mussels (see Chapter 20) or mushrooms (see page 8), and the braising liquid thickened with butter, cream, egg yolks, or a separate flour-thickened sauce such as fish velouté (fish broth thickened with roux) or béchamel (basically, milk thickened with roux). Minor additions to these basic variations might include tomatoes, meat glaze (glace de viande), various herbs, or red wine. Anyone familiar with French classic cooking at the time could have easily recognized the sauce on the sole Marguéry as a classic sauce vin blanc, essentially a hollandaise sauce made with the braising liquid from the fish. So much for our student.

2 Dover soles (14 ounces to 1 pound [395 to 450 g] each), or the same weight of another flatfish such as flounder, lemon sole, or fluke, cleaned, filleted, bones and heads reserved for the fish broth

   salt

   pepper

1 medium-size onion (for the fish broth)

1 small bouquet garni (for the fish broth)

1 cup [250 ml] dry white wine (for the fish broth)

1 tablespoon softened butter (for the baking dishes)

2 egg yolks

¼ pound [113 g] (1 stick) butter, clarified using the second method described on page 296

SEASON the fillets with salt and pepper, cover with plastic wrap, and keep in the refrigerator. Make a fish broth with the onion, bouquet garni, fish bones and heads, and wine, following the directions on page 308. Strain the broth and let it cool.

PREHEAT the oven to 350°F [175°C/gas mark 4]. Butter two heat-proof oval or rectangular baking dishes just large enough to hold the fillets in a single layer, and arrange the fillets, with the more attractive side up, in the dishes. Pour ⅓ cup [150 g] of the fish broth over and around the fillets. Place the dishes on the stove over high heat—if they're porcelain, use a flame tamer—until a bubble or two comes up, about 2 minutes. Slide the fillets into the oven and bake for 4 to 6 minutes, depending on their thickness, leaving them slightly underdone because they'll continue to cook while you're making the sauce.

USE a long spatula or two spatulas to support the weight of the fillets along their entire length as you transfer them to hot plates. Keep the plates in the turned-off oven with the door ajar while you're making the sauce. Put the baking dishes on the stove over high heat and boil the liquid for about 2 minutes. Strain the liquid through a fine-mesh strainer, measure out ⅓ cup [150 ml], and whisk this with the egg yolks in a heavy-bottomed pan with sloping sides or in a medium-size mixing bowl. Heat over medium to high heat while whisking until the egg yolks get fluffy, about 1 minute. As soon as the egg yolks stiffen slightly, take the pan off the heat and whisk for 1 minute to cool them. Whisk in the clarified butter, which should be no hotter than a hot bath or it will curdle the yolks. The sauce should be very stiff. Season to taste with salt and pepper. Pour off any liquid released by the fish while it's been waiting on the plates. Serve the sauce over the fish or at the table in a sauceboat.

Variations: Sole Marguéry is delicious, but the ingredients scare people because of all the butter and egg yolks. The genius behind the dish, and behind most braised fish dishes, is the use of the braising liquid, which contains the intrinsic flavor of the fish, for making a sauce. Michel Guérard, one of the first French chefs to adapt French cooking to the needs of a fat-conscious public, serves fish with feather-light sabayon sauces. These sauces are made in the same way as hollandaise sauce and its derivatives, such as the sauce for *sole Marguéry,* except that little or no butter is added to the airy emulsion. To make a sabayon sauce, whisk four egg yolks (two more than in the recipe above) with ½ cup of the braising liquid over medium heat. When the mixture is airy and stiffens slightly, serve it over the fish or pass it at the table. You can also prepare the classic sauce using half the butter or as much or as little butter as you like to the sabayon base.

Braised lean white-fleshed fish are delicious and elegant served with a crustacean sauce and garnished with pieces of cooked lobster, crayfish tails, shrimp, or crab. To prepare one of these dishes, braise the fish in a flavorful broth made from the crustacean shells, following the recipe for lobster *à l'americaine* on page 333. When the fish is cooked, convert the braising liquid into a light-textured sauce by combining it with cream and reducing it to the consistency you like and, if you have some on hand, whisking in a little Crustacean Butter (see page 335). You can also combine the reduced cooking liquid with egg yolks and make a sauce in the same way as for *sole Marguéry,* adding as little or as much butter as you like, and, again, finishing the sauce with 2 to 4 tablespoons of Crustacean Butter. Garnish the dish with pieces of the cooked crustaceans.

A more rustic dish, *merlan des mareyeurs,* from Brittany, made with whiting or fresh herring fillets, is prepared much like a *sole Bercy*—the fillets braised in dry acidic white wine infused with shallots and the sauce finished with parsley, mustard, and a good amount of butter. (The wine they use in Brittany is *gros plant,* an acidic poor cousin of muscadet that's perfect for cooking fish.) In Normandy fish are sometimes braised in hard cider. *Sole vallée d'Auge* is prepared with mushrooms and shallots, much like *sole bonne-femme,* except that cider is used as the braising liquid.

Vegetable purées can also be used to thicken and flavor seafood braising liquid (see Walleye with Sorrel, page 314). *Sole Rochebonne,* from Brittany, is again prepared much like *sole bonne-femme,* with mushrooms, except that the braising liquid is finished with artichoke purée. *Cabillaud à la bordelaise* is made by first browning the fish (cod, but you can substitute any lean white fish) and braising it with a purée of onions and tomatoes.

HALIBUT STEAKS WITH MUSSELS

FLÉTAN AUX MOULES

MAKES 4 MAIN-COURSE OR 8 FIRST-COURSE SERVINGS

One of France's great seafood classics is sole à la normande. Hardly anybody makes it anymore because it requires a sauce normande, a hopelessly elaborate concoction of fish broth, mussel cooking liquid, mushroom cooking liquid, fish velouté, and loads of butter, egg yolks, and cream. A garniture of shrimp, mussels, oysters, truffles, and puff pastry is then arranged on top of the whole cooked sole. But like so many classic dishes, sole à la normande can be simplified and lightened for modern tastes, and other fish, such as the halibut used here, can be substituted for the expensive Dover sole.

Perhaps the most brilliant component of sole à la normande is the use of mussel cooking liquid. Anyone who likes mussels steamed up with shallots (moules à la marinière; see page 268) knows that the best part of the dish is the flavorful liquid sitting in the bottom of the bowl. A great sauce trick, borrowed from sole à la normande, is to use this liquid as the basis for a sauce, and then use the cooked mussels, in the shell or out, as a garniture for the fish. The sauce is still best finished with cream and butter, but in far smaller amounts than in the classic.

Halibut, like sole, is a flatfish, but it is so large that it is usually cut crosswise into steaks instead of into fillets. When buying halibut steaks, notice that they're made up of four sections. You'll get four neat pieces of fish if you buy one thick steak and then separate the sections with a small knife. Depending on the size of the steaks, you can serve 1 section as a first course or 2 sections as a main course. If the halibut is being sold as fillets, just cut one piece into the number of sections you need.

I like to finish this dish with fines herbes, using fresh chervil, parsley, and chives but leaving out the tarragon because it tends to take over. If you don't have chervil or chives, just increase the chopped parsley to 1 tablespoon.

1   halibut steak (2 pounds [900 g]), 2 halibut steaks (1 pound [450 g] each), or 1½ to 2 pounds [675 to 900 g] halibut fillets or other lean white fish fillets

    salt

    pepper

2   pounds [900 g] mussels, preferably small cultivated

1   cup [250 ml] dry white wine

1   shallot, chopped fine

1   teaspoon softened butter (for the baking dish), plus 2 tablespoons butter (for the sauce)

½   cup [125 ml] heavy cream

1   teaspoon finely chopped chives

1   teaspoon finely chopped chervil

1   teaspoon finely chopped parsley

IF you're using halibut steaks, cut them into sections as described above. If you're using fillets of some other fish, cut them into 4 or 8 equal-size pieces. Season with salt and pepper, cover with plastic wrap, and refrigerate.

SCRUB the mussels under cold running water, throw out any that don't close when you tap them on the kitchen counter, and yank off any large beards sticking out of the sides of the shells. (See Chapter 20 for more about mussels.)

PREHEAT the oven to 350°F [175°C/gas mark 4].

PUT the wine and shallot in a pot large enough to hold the mussels and bring to a simmer over high heat. Put the mussels in the pot, cover, and steam over high heat until all the mussels open, about 5 minutes. Transfer the mussels to a large bowl, cover them loosely with aluminum foil to keep them warm, and gently decant their cooking liquid into a clean saucepan. (If you're being fastidious, strain it with a fine-mesh strainer.)

ARRANGE the halibut in a buttered baking dish just large enough to hold the pieces in a single layer. Bring the mussel cooking liquid back to a simmer and pour it over the halibut. Cover the dish loosely with aluminum foil and slide it into the oven.

TAKE the top shells off the mussels or remove the shells entirely. Reserve the mussels in a bowl, covered with a plate, in a warm place.

WHEN the halibut is no longer translucent when you cut into a piece, in 10 to 25 minutes, depending on its thickness, gently transfer the pieces to hot soup plates. Pour the braising liquid into a saucepan, bring it to a simmer, and pour in the heavy cream. Boil the sauce down for about 3 minutes to thicken it slightly. Stir in the herbs and whisk in the 2 tablespoons of butter.

ARRANGE the mussels over and around the halibut in each bowl and spoon the sauce over and around the seafood.

Variations: Clams or cockles make a delicious substitute for mussels. A pinch of saffron added to the sauce is glorious. The classic version of *sole à la normande* also contains mushroom cooking liquid (see page 8), which gives the sauce another dimension of complexity when you use it in conjunction with the mussel cooking liquid. This sauce is also enhanced with a tablespoon or two of crustacean butter whisked in at the end.

WALLEYE
WITH SORREL

SANDRE À L'OSEILLE

MAKES 6 MAIN-COURSE SERVINGS

The French love sorrel, especially with seafood. The most famous paring of sorrel with fish is *alose à l'oseille* (shad with sorrel). Lovers of the dish claim that the acidity of the sorrel dissolves the tiny shad bones, but because I've never had any success getting the bones to magically disappear, I don't recommend using whole shad. Use shad fillets or another fish altogether.

When I travel in the Midwest, teaching cooking classes, I'm often hard put to find fresh ocean fish. Fortunately, at least in the Great Lakes area, I'm almost always able to find walleye. Walleye is an underappreciated fish in this country, partly, no doubt, because it's abundant and cheap. But in France, walleye's close relative, *sandre*, is a delicacy you're likely to encounter only in the most expensive places. When shopping for walleye, don't look for clear, shiny eyes, because even an impeccably fresh specimen's eyes look like they've seen a lifetime of heavy drinking. Instead look for fish that have a healthy sheen and that, ideally, are stiff. Of course, you don't need to use walleye at all. Any lean, white, firm-fleshed fish will work perfectly well for this recipe.

Finding fresh sorrel can be a problem. But it's popping up more and more in green markets and it is worth tracking down because its tangy acidity makes it absolutely marvelous with fish. It's also available in jars and isn't half bad. It's also easy to grow.

6   walleyes (1 pound [450 g] each), filleted, skin removed, or 2½ to 3 pounds [1.1 to 1.3 kg] fillets or steaks from fish such as halibut, scrod, shad, or monkfish

     salt

     pepper

1   teaspoon butter (for the baking dish), plus 2 tablespoons (for the fish)

2   cups [500 ml] fish broth (see page 308), or 1 cup dry white wine

12   ounces [340 g] fresh sorrel, stemmed (4 tightly packed cups), or one 12-ounce jar

½   cup heavy cream

SEASON the fillets or steaks with salt and pepper, cover them with plastic wrap, and refrigerate them.

PREHEAT the oven to 350°F [175°C/gas mark 4]. Butter a baking dish just large enough to hold the pieces in a single layer, arrange the fillets or steaks in the dish, and pour the fish broth over them. (If you're using wine, dilute it with 1 cup of water.) Put pea-size dots of butter over the fish and loosely cover the dish with aluminum foil.

BAKE the fish for 12 to 20 minutes, depending on its thickness.

GENTLY transfer the fish to hot soup plates. Pour the braising liquid into a saucepan over high heat, bring it to a boil, and stir in the sorrel and the heavy cream. When the mixture comes back to a simmer—by which time the sorrel will have "melted"—simmer it for 2 minutes more. Purée the sorrel sauce with an immersion blender or in a regular blender. (If you're using a regular blender, be careful; see page 13.) Bring the sauce back to a simmer and season it to taste with salt and pepper. Spoon it over and around the fish.

Variations: Using sorrel in a fish sauce is an example of using a vegetable purée to give body to a sauce without using tasteless starches such as flour or large amounts of rich ingredients like egg yolks, cream, and butter. Other vegetable purées, such as garlic, onion, and mushroom, can be used (see page 374), but you'll need to use these purées already prepared because they take longer to cook.

Seafood

PROVENÇAL COOKS ARE FOREVER COOKING seafood *à la chartreuse*. Cooking *à la chartreuse* is hard to define except that the dish always contains a fair amount of finely sliced or chopped vegetables such as onions, garlic, and tomatoes, and almost always a shredded green vegetable such as Swiss chard, spinach, lettuce, or sorrel. Cooking *à la chartreuse* is *not* cooking with Chartreuse liqueur.

Technically, cooking *à la chartreuse* is cooking *en sauce,* the braising method used for cooking *sole Bercy* or *sole bonne-femme,* but the soul of seafood cooked *à la chartreuse* is rustic and distinctly southern French. The dish is typically flavored with savory, marjoram, or oregano, and plenty of olive oil. The fish themselves are likely to be fuller-flavored varieties such as sardines, tuna, mackerel, or red mullet (*rouget*). Usually there are no last-minute sauce-finishing machinations: the fish is just scooped out of the serving dish and served surrounded with vegetables and the cooking juices. At times the fish, once in the baking dish, is sprinkled with bread crumbs, giving the finished dish almost the effect of a gratin. Often, the whole fish are wrapped in blanched lettuce or cabbage leaves. Sometimes the fish are allowed to cool in their own juices and are served cool as a first course in much the same way as an *escabèche*. The fish in an *escabèche* are first sautéed and a hot vegetable, wine, or sometimes vinegar marinade is poured over. The fish cooks as it cools.

The best known *chartreuse* recipe is *thon à la chartreuse*, a dish that typically calls for larding thick pieces of tuna (*thon*) with anchovy fillets and then braising the tuna for close to an hour. The tuna is delicious but tends to be very dry, especially to those of us who are used to eating tuna raw in sushi bars or eating it grilled rare. I prefer cooking full-flavored fish such as mackerel, Spanish mackerel, or kingfish steaks. Mackerel has a bad reputation, which probably originated from eating it out of a can or when it wasn't perfectly fresh. Look for mackerel that is shiny, stiff, and blue or blue-green—it quickly loses its color when out of the water. Spanish mackerel should also be shiny and have distinct golden spots. Kingfish steaks are always a bit gray, but look for those with a clear sheen. Instead of braising, I prefer to prepare the vegetable mixture ahead of time. I then sauté the fillets and serve them immediately with the hot vegetable mixture, or I let them cool and serve them with the cold vegetable mixture.

MACKEREL À LA CHARTREUSE

MAQUEREAUX À LA CHARTREUSE

MAKES 4 MAIN-COURSE
OR 8 FIRST-COURSE SERVINGS

Traditional recipes call for cooking whole fish, but I fillet the fish ahead of time to make the dish easier to eat. When I'm serving this dish as a first course, I usually serve it cold; as a main course I serve it hot.

4 mackerel (14 ounces to 1 pound [395 to 450 g] each), or 2 Spanish mackerel (2 pounds [900 g] each), mackerel or Spanish mackerel filleted, skin left on, or 4 kingfish steaks (6 to 8 ounces [170 to 225 g] each)

salt

pepper

2 medium-size onions, sliced thin

1 medium-size carrot, peeled, sliced thin

6   garlic cloves, crushed

1   imported bay leaf

1   teaspoon finely chopped fresh marjoram, thyme, or
     savory

2   tablespoons olive oil (for cooking the vegetables), plus
     2 tablespoons (for sautéing the fillets)

3   medium-size tomatoes, peeled, seeded, and coarsely
     chopped

1   large handful sorrel or spinach leaves, stems removed,
     cut into chiffonade (see page 17)

½   cup [125 ml] dry white wine

¼   cup [60 ml] extra-virgin olive oil

1   tablespoon sherry wine vinegar

IF you're using mackerel or Spanish mackerel, run your fingers along the flesh side of the fillets to feel for the tiny pin bones. Take them out with tweezers or needle-nose pliers. Season the fish fillets with salt and pepper, cover with plastic wrap, and refrigerate.

COOK the onions, carrot, garlic, bay leaf, and marjoram in 2 tablespoons of olive oil in a heavy-bottomed pot over medium heat. Stir every few minutes until the onions and carrots are soft, about 20 minutes. Stir in the tomatoes, the sorrel, the wine, and the extra-virgin olive oil. Stir for 4 minutes over the heat—just long enough to cook the alcohol out of the wine over high heat. Stir in the vinegar and season to taste with salt and pepper. If you're serving the mackerel cold, let the vegetable mixture cool and then chill it in the refrigerator.

HEAT 2 tablespoons of olive oil in a large nonstick pan (or two pans) over high heat. Pat the fillets dry with paper towels and season them on both sides with salt and pepper. Place the fillets, skin-side down, in the hot pan. Press down on the fillets with the back of a spatula so the skin doesn't shrink and cause the fillets to curl. Cook the fillets about 5 minutes on the skin side and 1 minute on the flesh side—or more or less, depending on the thickness of the fillets—so the skin ends up very well cooked.

IF you're serving the mackerel hot, spread the hot vegetable mixture over heated plates and place 1 or 2 mackerel fillets (1 for first courses; 2 for mains) on top. If you're serving the mackerel cold, let the fillets cool and then put them in a dish with the cold vegetables and let them marinate in the refrigerator for 2 or 3 hours (or all day) before serving.

IMPROVISING FISH DISHES BRAISED
AND COOKED EN SAUCE

LIQUIDS FOR BRAISING THE FISH: Fish broth (see page 308); red wine fish broth (see page 243); court bouillon (see page 283); cooking liquid from mollusks such as mussels, clams, or cockles; cooking liquid from crustaceans (see Chapter 25); mushroom cooking liquid (see page 8); red or white wine or sherry; sweet wines such as port, Madeira, Malaga, Sauternes; hard cider; fruit juices (reduced or plain)

AROMATIC INGREDIENTS INFUSED IN THE BRAISING LIQUID BEFORE THE FISH IS ADDED: shallots, onions, mirepoix (onions, carrot, celery mixture), garlic, lemongrass, bouquet garni (classic or with other herbs, such as tarragon or marjoram); mushrooms; dried or fresh chiles; tomatoes

THICKENERS FOR BRAISING LIQUID: braising liquid left unthickened and served brothlike around fish fillets in soup plates; butter (dotted on the fish before baking, or whisked in at the end, or converted to a beurre blanc and combined with fish braising liquid before serving whole or clarified butter whisked into an egg yolk–braising liquid emulsion as for *sauce vin blanc*); cream (reduced with braising liquid; can be used in combination with other thickeners); egg yolks (used as the base for a *sauce vin blanc* as in *sole Marguéry* or combined with braising liquid and cooked like a crème anglaise, see page 642); crustacean or herb butters (whisked directly into braising liquid, beurre blanc, or egg yolk–braising liquid emulsion); vegetable purées (sorrel, garlic, etc., see page 373); flour (cooked in a roux, braising liquid whisked in or worked into a beurre manié, whisked into braising liquid); cornstarch (combined with water in a slurry, whisked into braising liquid)

FINAL FINISHES: Finely chopped herbs, herb butters, chopped truffles, chopped mushrooms (cultivated or wild, fresh or dried), spices (especially curry or saffron), squid or cuttlefish ink, sea urchin roe, sea scallop roe

MEDITERRANEAN SEA BASS GRILLED WITH FENNEL

LOUP DE MER GRILLÉ AU FENOUIL

ANYONE WHO HAS TRAVELED IN PROVENCE, THE REGION IN EASTERN France whose border on the Mediterranean forms the French Riviera (the Côte d'Azur), will have seen *loup de mer au fenouil* on restaurant menus. In flashy places, those catering especially to tourists, you'll encounter *loup de mer flambé au fenouil,* which involves the extra step of dousing the fish with pastis, a strong fennel-flavored drink, and igniting the now-etherized fish at the table. While I have nothing against pastis, it doesn't belong on a fish.

My first authentic grilled sea bass with fennel was in Provence, near Toulon, at the home of the late Richard Olney. Having read Mr. Olney's *Simple French Food,* I was determined to meet him. With the audacity of youth, I had the nerve to call on him, unannounced. A trucker helped me find him and drove me to the base of the hill where he lived. Since the truck couldn't make it up the hill, I walked up, admiring the countryside in the afternoon sun, knowing I was on the right track because I could hear the clickity-click of a type-writer. When I got to the top, Richard was sitting there under a grape arbor, tapping away on a 1930s Royal. Stark naked, he stood to greet me, and then with perfect aplomb he slipped on a tiny red bathing suit that had been hanging on the trellis and said, "Allow me to receive you." We started sipping wine almost immediately, but since my surprise appearance necessitated a quick trip to the village for provisions, we had to get in the car and drive down to buy fresh fruit and a fish. When we got home, Richard scaled and gutted the fish. He then lit an enormous fire in his hearth and grilled the fish, throwing some dried fennel stalks on the fire shortly before putting on the fish. The fennel was subtle but present, the fish juicy and redolent of the sea, and the only sauce was extra-virgin olive oil from a nearby mill.

Richard's dinner was a lesson in the beauty of simplicity and the marvel of fish cooked whole, an experience that many Americans have missed out on. We're afraid of whole fish because we don't know how to pick them out at the fish market and we don't know how to cook them. We're terrified of bones, and since we never get to practice filleting our own whole fish at the table, our phobia perpetuates itself. This is unfortunate, because the difference in flavor between a whole fish and a steak or fillet is similar to the difference between a poached boneless chicken breast (insipid) and a roast chicken (crisp, savory, and juicy). So I implore you to give whole fish a try.

First you must track down a good fish. Although authentic Mediterranean sea bass (*loup de mer*) is available in the United States, sometimes under its Italian name, *branzino,* the point is not so much what kind of fish you use but how fresh it is. Judging the freshness of a whole fish is always easier than determining the freshness of fillets or steaks, and you can be sure that fish stores that sell both whole and already-filleted fish are likely to fillet those whole fish that are starting to get a little stale. So when you buy a whole fish, you have an advantage. If you live in a city where there's more than one fish store, it pays to do a little comparison shopping. You can tell a lot about the fish by how the store smells (fresh, not fishy), by how the fish is arranged in the case (neatly on ice, paper between the ice and the fish to prevent "burning"), and sometimes by the customers. I often have the best luck shopping at fish stores that cater to Japanese customers, who are not only discerning but especially particular because they are likely to eat their fish raw. If you don't live near a fish store, you may be able to find good fish at the supermarket, but you may have to special-order whole fish. When you locate a fish that is the size you need, analyze it as best you can. Look at the eyes. Some fish have clear eyes that turn cloudy as the fish gets old. If you see several fish of the same variety, and some have cloudy eyes and some have clear, go for the clear. Since some fish have cloudy eyes even when perfectly fresh, a more reliable system is to notice how the eyes sit in the fish's head. Most fish eyes bulge slightly when fresh and sink back into the head as the fish ages. Notice also the general appearances of the fish. Fresh fish is shiny and may be covered with a clear, shiny slime. If the slime is cloudy, forget it. (Skate, however, has cloudy slime even when fresh.) Notice the tail. If it's dried out and curled up at the end, the fish may be fresh enough to eat but it won't be at its best. As you zero in on your catch, ask whoever's behind the counter to hold the fish up by the head, horizontally, with the tail sticking out. Ideally, the fish should be stiff—not limp and sagging—indicating that it's still in rigor mortis, a sure sign of freshness. Ask to see the gills. The fishmonger will have to pull back the flap of cartilage—the operculum—at the base of the head so that you can take a look at the gills, which should be bright red, not brown. Since gills are sometimes covered with mud, which makes it hard to see their color, ask to give them a sniff—any staleness or fishiness starts in the gills.

Because the only tricky part of grilling a whole fish is to keep it from sticking to the grill, cooks have developed a number of strategies for this. To avoid the problem altogether, just leave the scales on the fish and then peel the skin and scales off the fish before serving. This method is popular in restaurants in France, and it can be used either for the whole table, if it's a big fish, or for yourself, if it's a small fish. The layer of scales and skin seals in the fish's juices and flavor and the scales act as a nonstick surface for the fish. The only disadvantage to this method is that you can't eat the skin. If you want to eat the skin, which when grilled is crispy and delicious, you risk having the skin stick to the grill and tear when you turn over the fish or take it off the grill. While it seems impossible to avoid sticking every time, you can usually prevent it by making sure your grill is immaculate. I spray mine with heavy-duty oven cleaner, brush it with a steel brush, and rinse it thoroughly. I then get the grill burning-hot over the coals. After cutting off the fins with heavy scissors so I don't get poked, I brush or rub the fish with olive oil and sprinkle it with coarse salt immediately before setting it on the grill. Once you've set the fish on the grill, don't move it until you're ready to turn it over. When turning over the fish or taking it off the grill, don't just slide a spatula under it or you'll tear the skin. Instead, slide a long 2-pronged fork between the grill grids and gently lift up the fish, detaching it, before sliding a spatula underneath.

Another way to prevent sticking, at least when you turn the fish over, is to use a fish basket. There are two types. One is a fish-shaped metal cage with long handles and two pairs of feet. You place the oiled fish in the cage—there's something vaguely medieval about the whole method—and seal it up by bringing the two long handles together. You then place the cage over the coals, and when the fish is cooked on one side you turn the cage over. You don't need a grill. The other kind of fish basket, designed for small fish like sardines, consists of two square metal grills, which look somewhat like cake racks, held together at one end with a hinge, and with a handle at the end opposite the hinge. You put the little fish inside and turn them over by turning the whole basket over. But a fish basket isn't always the solution either, because the fish sometimes sticks to the basket itself, and when you pull apart the handles, the skin tears. Oiling and preheating the basket over the coals is helpful, but even this can fail. I sometimes pat the fish with coarse salt, which makes an interface between the basket and the fish; it's easily brushed off when the fish is cooked. This method also helps on a regular grill. Richard Olney told me that he sometimes wrapped the fish in grape leaves or fennel fronds and grilled it in a fish basket, and when he opened the basket the skin would adhere to the leaves or fronds, leaving a skinless fish. (Some fish, such as grouper or blackfish, should be served skinless anyway, since their skin has an unpleasant texture.)

You may also get home, fish in hand, only to find that your barbecue isn't big enough for the fish. Sometimes cutting off the head will get the fish to fit, but if you're really stuck, you'll have to improvise a grill. One of my favorite methods, devised one summer at a rented beach house, is to dig a pit about 8 inches [20.5 cm] deep, slightly longer and wider than the fish, and surround it with rocks or bricks to hold an improvised grill about 12 inches [30.5 cm] above the bottom of the pit. I build my fire in the pit, and when it dies down to coals, I take the two racks out of the oven, overlap them slightly, strap them together with wire, and place them—one long grill—on the rocks over the coals. If your idea of a summer barbecue doesn't involve digging up your garden and blackening your oven racks, you can always cut the fish in half, but its dignity and beauty will be lost.

Whenever you're grilling a fish without its scales—presumably so that you can eat the skin—adjust the distance of the fish from the heat source according to its size. To prevent sticking, the fish should be as close to the coals as possible and the grill burning-hot before you set the fish down. But if you do this with larger fish, the skin will burn before the heat reaches the center of the fish. When grilling fish, I build a very hot fire. If I'm grilling small fish such as sardines, I grill them about 4 inches from the coals; for medium fish, 1 to 1½ pounds [450 to 675 g] each, I grill them 6 to 8 inches [15 to 20.5 cm] from the coals. As the fish get larger, I grill them 10 to 12 inches [25.5 to 30.5 cm] from the coals.

Lastly, most recipes for grilled fish have you making slits in the side of the fish, presumably to let the heat penetrate, but they only encourage the juices to drain out. I don't recommend it.

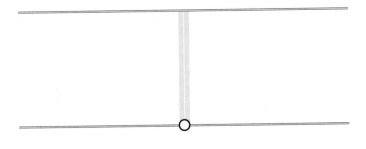

SCALING

This is a messy job best done at the fish market, but if you're stuck with it, cut off any sharp fins with a pair of heavy scissors, so the fins don't poke you, and hold the fish in a clear, unscented plastic garbage bag so you can see what you're doing but don't end up covered with scales. Scrape against the scales, working from head to tail, with a fish scaler or the back of a paring knife. Be thorough and especially conscious of the belly and underside of the fish, parts that are easy to miss. Rinse the fish thoroughly to get rid of loose scales—in grilling season I use the garden hose.

GRILLED WHOLE FISH

POISSON ENTIER GRILLÉ

MAKES 4 MAIN-COURSE SERVINGS

4, 2, or 1 whole fish such as Mediterranean sea bass (loup de mer, branzino), Mediterranean sea bream (daurade), Atlantic sea bass, red snapper, grouper, blackfish, striped bass, or rockfish, scaled (scaling optional; see "Grilling Whole Fish," page 320), gutted (about 5 pounds [2.3 kg] total weight)

1 large handful fennel stalks, dried by being left in a loose pile in a dry place for a couple of weeks or more (optional)

olive oil

coarse salt

lemon wedges (optional)

balsamic vinegar (optional)

freshly ground pepper

BUILD a hot charcoal fire in a barbecue or pit large enough to hold the fish.

IF you decide to grill the fish without its scales, have it scaled at the fish store. If you have to scale the fish yourself, see "Scaling," page 321. If you have to gut the fish yourself, do it after the fish has been scaled.

RUB the fish with olive oil and roll it in coarse salt.

WHEN the coals are ready, put the fennel on top and place the grill about 4 inches [10 cm] from the coals for small fish, or up to 12 inches [30.5] for larger fish. You may have to adjust the height of the grill, if yours is adjustable, or the height of the coals, depending on how hot your coals are and how the fish is doing. Let the grill get very hot. Brush the grill quickly and lightly with olive oil—too much will cause flare-up. Or rub it with a paper towel dipped in oil. Immediately set the fish on top. Grill the fish for about 10 minutes on each side for a fish that's 2 inches [5 cm] thick at the thickest point. (Increase or decrease the cooking time according to the thickness of the fish, figuring about 10 minutes total cooking time—5 minutes per side per inch [2.5 cm] of thickness.)

IF the fish skin is blackening too quickly, raise the grill or flatten the coals a couple of inches; if the fish isn't doing much (no sizzling), lower the grill or heap up the coals under the fish. Turn the fish by first detaching it from the grill with a two-pronged fork slid between the rungs of the grill and gently lifting up. Slide a wide spatula beneath the fish and turn it over.

TO tell when the fish is done, slide a thin paring or boning knife into the back of the fish alongside the backbone. Peek inside, between bone and flesh, and see if the flesh is still shiny and translucent, an indication that it's not yet cooked, or if it has turned opaque, meaning it's ready. There should be just the slightest trace of translucence left, because the fish will continue to cook as it rests.

WITH a dry brush, a kitchen towel, or a quick sweep of your hand, brush off any coarse salt clinging to the fish. Detach the fish from the grill by sliding a large two-pronged fork under it and then gently lifting. Slide a spatula under the fish and lift it off the grill. If the fish is big, have a guest help you and use two long spatulas slid under it at each end to lift it off the grill. For medium-size or small fish, you can also use a horizontal spatula—one in which the spatula part runs perpendicular rather than parallel to the handle. Set the fish on a heated platter.

IF you're serving each person his or her own fish, serve the fish on its own plate (ideally, an oval one) to the side of the dinner plate so your guests can leave the bones behind while serving themselves the fish. If you're doing the carving, see page 323.

PASS extra-virgin olive oil, salt, and if you like, lemon wedges or balsamic vinegar in small pitchers, and the pepper mill for guests to serve themselves. If, horror of horrors, you start to carve your fish and find that it's raw in the middle, don't panic. Just slide it in the oven and crank the temperature up to 400°F [200°C/gas mark 6]—or if the fish isn't too big, give it a quick zap in the microwave.

CARVING A WHOLE ROUND FISH

Approaching a whole cooked fish, knife in hand, for the first time can be a little unnerving. The fish stares at you, cynical and disapproving, while guests or family wait to judge your dexterity. But unless you've been foolhardy and baked a whole shad, which has a nightmarishly complicated bone structure, round fish are designed so that you can easily cut around and avoid most of the bones. (Round fish are shaped like trout; flatfish are shaped like flounder.)

Fish are easiest to dissect with a proper fish knife, one whose blade attaches to the handle at an angle, making it easier to slide the blade in sideways while comfortably holding the handle. But a regular chef's knife, a carving knife, or a pair of tablespoon-size spoons with oval bowls will do perfectly fine.

Arrange the fish on a platter with the tail facing you and the fish's back to your right.

If you've left the scales on the fish, you must first remove the skin, and the scales with it. Slide the knife under the base of the head, just above where the gills were. Once you've cut through the skin, continue until you run into the backbone. Slide the knife along the underside of the skin up against the flesh of the fish and lift away the skin covering the top of the fish all in one piece. Once you've removed the skin, you need to take the flesh off the backbone. The way you do this depends on the size of the fish. If it's a small or medium-size fish—large enough for one or two people—slide the knife under the base of the head (in the place where you started removing the skin) and then bring the knife (or a spoon) around along the back of the fish with the blade against the backbone and lift off the entire fillet. As you're removing the fillet, try to leave the ribs behind, still attached to the backbone. If the ribs come away with the fillet, turn the fillet skin-side down on the platter so the bones are on top and slide the spoon under the bones. Pinch the bones with a second spoon and pull them away from the fillet.

Once you've removed the top fillet, slide a spoon or knife under the backbone (between the bone and the flesh of the bottom fillet) and lift off the entire backbone and the head. If the ribs are still clinging to the bottom fillet, pull them away with two spoons. Separate the second fillet from the skin by sliding the knife or spoon under the flesh but above the skin. Pull the fillet away from the skin.

If you're serving a larger fish, removing the side of the fish in one piece is difficult. It's better to serve the fillets in two or more pieces. Notice the dark line running along the fillet, just above the backbone. Slide a knife or spoon along this line, going all the way down to the backbone, so that you're dividing the fillet into two lengthwise pieces. You can serve these two pieces or you can cut them in half crosswise before lifting them off the fish. Remove the backbone and continue carving the fish as above. If you haven't scaled the fish, leave the skin under the bottom fillet on the platter.

Use the same method to serve a whole scaled fish with the skin on.

In European restaurants that serve grilled fish, more often than not the fish isn't actually grilled, but is cooked under the broiler or baked in a very hot oven. The advantage to broiling or baking is that there's no grill to stick to. If you want to grill whole fish, or even fillets or steaks, you'll need to judge the heat of your broiler and experiment with arranging the fish at varying distances from the heat source, which is above, rather than below as it is when you're grilling. If your broiler is below the oven, you may have to actually lie down on the floor to check the fish's progress. The larger the fish, the farther it should be from the heat source so it won't brown before it has time to cook through. Unless you're cooking very small fish such as sardines, which should be started about 3 inches [7.5 cm] away from the heat source, start cooking whole fish as far from the heat source as you can. If after a few minutes nothing is happening—no sizzling, no bubbling up of the skin—raise the fish a notch or two. When broiling, place the fish on a sheet of well-oiled aluminum foil on a sheet pan. The sheet pan allows you to position the fish differently if it appears to be browning unevenly. When the fish is well browned on top, slide out the sheet pan, gently flip the fish on the aluminum foil, and cook it on the other side.

One disadvantage to broiling is that it leaves no attractive grill marks on the fish. If you want to cook inside and don't mind smelling up the house (or you have a good stove vent), and your fish isn't too large, you can use a grill pan. A grill pan is a heavy iron pan with riblike undulations that simulate the effect of grilling. Make sure the grill pan is very clean, and after getting it very hot on the stove, brush or rub it with oil as you would an outdoor grill. You can grill the fish completely on the grill pan, or you can leave it on the grill pan just long enough to give it the distinctive grill marks and then finish it under the broiler or in the oven.

Baked whole fish is one of the easiest dishes to manage, because all you need to do is slide the fish in the oven and take it out when it's ready. (To judge when a whole fish is done, see page 322.) I bake fish at fairly high heat and then adjust the temperature according to how the fish is cooking. Again, keep in mind that the larger the fish, the lower the temperature should be. In order to brown small fish without overcooking them, the oven temperature should be set very high—at about 500°F [260°C]—while large fish should be cooked at a lower temperature—about 350°F [175°/gas mark 4]—so they don't overbrown before cooking through. I cook most average-size fish, such as 1- to 2-pound [450 to 900 g] red snapper or sea bass, at about 400°F [200°C/ gas mark 6].

GRILLED SARDINES

SARDINES GRILLÉES

MAKES 6 FIRST-COURSE OR
4 MAIN-COURSE SERVINGS

Until recently, I never bothered with fresh sardines, since authentic sardines from the other side of the Atlantic were never sold in the United States. But since I now see them regularly in New York fish markets and in other parts of the country, I can no longer ignore them. They are among the juiciest and tastiest of foods you'll ever grill.

Sardines take perfectly to the grill because they are oily, and oily fish are best kept away from methods, such as sautéing or frying, that only serve to make them oilier. While you can also grill other small fish—I like grilled smelts and small Mediterranean red mullets (rouget)—sardines have the added advantage of rarely sticking to a very hot grill. If possible, grill sardines outside—they're in season in the summer anyway—or they'll "perfume" your house for days. I like to serve them as a first course, but they can also be served as a main course with a salad and followed with a bite of cheese.

24 plump sardines

olive oil

coarse salt

PREPARE a hot fire. Set up the barbecue so the grill will be between 2 and 3 inches [5 and 7.5 cm] away from the coals.

SCALE the sardines by rubbing them in your hands in both directions under cold running water. Clean the sardines by running your finger along the stomach cavity, starting at the base of the head. If you want to remove the heads, snap each one back first and then pull it away so that most of the viscera

come away with it. Run your finger along the stomach cavity to eliminate any viscera that didn't come away with the head. If you don't take off the heads, just pull the viscera out of the belly cavity with your fingers. Rinse the sardines under cold running water—again rub your finger along the inside of the belly cavity—and vigorously rub the outside of the sardines between your hands to eliminate any scales that may remain. Pat the sardines dry with paper towels.

TOSS the sardines in olive oil and rub away any excess to avoid flare-up. Sprinkle the sardines with salt. Get the grill very hot, place the sardines on the grill, and grill them for about 2 minutes on each side. Because they contain so much oil, sardines are forgiving if you overcook them slightly.

SERVE the sardines piping hot and encourage your guests to eat them with their fingers, nibbling on both sides and leaving the backbone behind, as though munching on an ear of corn.

Variations: In the spring, when wild dandelion greens are in season (I never use farm-raised dandelion greens since they're so bitter), I toss them in a salad with filleted grilled sardines. Just grill the sardines and pull the fillets away from the backbone by running a finger between the backbone and the fillets. Toss the salad with some good olive oil and vinegar or lemon juice.

In Provence, sardines are often boned, stuffed with spinach (flavored with garlic), rolled up starting at the head end, sprinkled with bread crumbs, and baked. I'm so fond of grilled sardines that I prefer to use the same treatment but instead of baking them, I grill them. I sometimes use Swiss chard in place of the spinach.

SARDINES STUFFED WITH SPINACH OR SWISS CHARD AND GRILLED

SARDINES GRILLÉES FARCIES AUX ÉPINARDS OU AUX BLETTES

MAKES 6 FIRST-COURSE
OR 4 MAIN-COURSE SERVINGS

These sardines have all the full flavor of plain grilled sardines, but they're flavored with garlic and made more substantial with cooked spinach or Swiss chard. Guests love them because most of the bones have been taken out, making them easy to eat with knife and fork or to pick up with fingers. If you have a square grill basket—the kind that looks like two cake racks with handles—use it for these sardines to make them easier to turn over. Heat the basket over the coals for about 30 seconds before putting in the sardines to help prevent sticking.

24 plump sardines

2 tablespoons extra-virgin olive oil

   salt

   pepper

2 cloves garlic, minced

1¼ pounds [565 g] spinach or Swiss chard, cleaned and destemmed (see page 22)

SCALE the sardines by rubbing them vigorously under cold running water. Snap off each head, backwards, and gently pull it away from the rest of the sardine, pulling out as much of the viscera as you can. Discard the heads and viscera. Run your finger along the inside of the stomach cavity, under cold running water, to rinse out any remaining viscera.

USE your fingers to pull the backbone away from the two fillets, leaving the fillets attached with the thin piece of skin that ran along the back of the fish. Pull away any bones clinging to the fillets but don't worry about tiny ones. Rub these double fillets on both sides with 1 tablespoon of olive oil and sprinkle the fillets on both sides with salt and pepper. Cover with plastic wrap and refrigerate.

HEAT the garlic in the remaining olive oil in a wide sauté pan over medium heat until it smells fragrant, about 1 minute. Turn the heat to high and add the spinach or chard leaves, a couple of handfuls at a time, stirring them with a wooden spoon. If you're using Swiss chard, add a couple of tablespoons of water to help it soften. As the leaves "melt" add more, until they are all in the pan. Cook the leaves, uncovered, stirring with a wooden spoon, over high heat until all the water they release evaporates, 3 to 5 minutes. Let cool and chop—not too fine—with a chef's knife or by pulsing in a food processor. Season to taste with salt and pepper.

PUT 1 spoonful of the spinach or Swiss chard mixture along the inside of each sardine and fold the two sides together around the stuffing so the sardine more or less regains its original shape. You can prepare the sardines earlier the same day you're serving them.

ABOUT 40 minutes before you're ready to serve, prepare a hot fire. Set up the barbecue or pile up the coals so the grill is about 4 inches away from the coals. Get the grill or grill pan very hot, place the sardines on it, and grill them for about 3 minutes on each side. Serve immediately.

Variation: Stuffed sardines are somewhat fragile, and they can come apart on the grill. If you prefer, bake them in a 400°F [200°C/gas mark 6] oven for about 12 minutes.

HOW TO STUFF A WHOLE FISH

Most French recipes for stuffed whole fish suggest putting the stuffing into the cavity after the viscera are removed. There are a couple of drawbacks to this method. One is that the flavor of the stuffing has a hard time penetrating the membrane between the cavity and the flesh, the other is that whole fish stuffed in this way is difficult to serve, since the stuffing is surrounded by ribs, which can easily come away when you reach in to remove the stuffing.

It's better to bone the fish and leave the head, tail, and fillets attached so that you still have a whole fish, but a boneless one that's easy to serve. There are two ways to bone a whole fish. The best method, boning through the back, requires a fish that hasn't yet been gutted. If the fish has already been gutted, then you can bone it through the stomach.

BONING A WHOLE FISH THROUGH THE BACK: Scale the fish as described on page 321. Remove the gills by turning the fish belly-side up and cutting through where the gills on both sides of the fish join at the base of the head. Cut along the underside of the gills—where they join the rest of the fish—and yank them away and discard them.

Set the fish on its side and slide a sharp, flexible knife along one side of the backbone, keeping the knife flush against the bone and following the contours of the ribs. Don't separate the fillets at the base of the head or along the top of the tail—remember, the fish should be kept whole. Keep cutting along the side of the backbone until you loosen the fillet on top. Be careful not to cut too deeply or you'll damage the viscera—making a mess—or worse, cut through the belly. Turn the fish over and repeat on the other side. When you've separated the two fillets from the backbone, use heavy scissors to cut the backbone where it joins the head and where it joins the tail. Gently pull out the bone—you can save it for fish broth or discard it—and then pull out the viscera. Inspect the inside of the fish carefully. If you've left the ribs attached to the fillets, slide the knife under the ribs and remove them. Rub a finger along the inside of the fillets, feeling for pin bones, and pull them out with tweezers or needle-nose pliers. Rinse out the fish.

BONING A WHOLE FISH THROUGH THE STOMACH: Use this method if the fish has already been gutted and the belly has been slit open. Set the fish on its side and slide a long, sharp, flexible knife lengthwise through the belly opening under the ribs with the blade facing outward toward the flaps on the outside. Keep sliding the knife under the ribs, separating them from the fillets until only the backbone is attached to the rest of the fish. Turn the fish over and around and repeat on the other side. Slide the knife carefully along the side of the backbone, as close to the skin as you can get, being careful not to poke through the back of the fish. Pull the backbone away and, with heavy scissors, cut it where it joins the head and tail and remove it. Rub a finger along the inside of the fillets, feeling for pin bones, and pull them out with tweezers or needle-nose pliers. Rinse out the fish.

WHOLE GRILLED OR BAKED BONELESS STRIPED BASS SCENTED WITH FRESH HERBS

BAR AMÉRICAIN DÉSOSSÉ, PARFUMÉ AUX HERBES FRAÎCHES

MAKES 8 MAIN-COURSE SERVINGS

Y ou can use this method with virtually any fish, large or small, and then serve the fish in crosswise slices instead of having to fillet it at the table. If you're using larger or smaller fish, calculate about 1 pound of whole fish (before boning and gutting) per person.

1, 2, or 4 wild striped bass (total weight 8 pounds [3.6 kg]), or other fish, such as Atlantic sea bass, red snapper, Mediterranean sea bass (loup de mer, branzino), or Mediterranean sea bream (daurade, orata), scaled but preferably not gutted

3 tablespoons freshly chopped herbs such as chervil, chives, parsley, basil, and tarragon, alone or in combination

3 tablespoons extra-virgin olive oil, plus additional (to pass at the table)

fine salt

pepper

coarse salt

balsamic vinegar or good wine vinegar (to pass at the table; optional)

lemon wedges (to pass at the table; optional)

IF the fish hasn't been gutted, bone it through the back; if it has been gutted, bone it through the stomach (see "How to Stuff a Whole Fish," page 327). Combine the chopped herbs with 1 tablespoon of the olive oil as soon as you chop them to make a coarse paste. Rub the inside of the fish with the herb paste and season it with fine salt and pepper.

IF you're grilling, set up the barbecue so the grill will be between 6 and 12 inches [15 to 30.5 cm] away from the coals (the larger the fish, the greater the distance). Get the grill very hot before putting on the fish. If your barbecue isn't big enough to hold the fish, you can cut the fish in half or remove the head, or you can dig a pit and use oven racks as described on page 321. Rub the grill with a paper towel dipped in 1 tablespoon of the olive oil and rub the outside of the fish with 1 more tablespoon of the olive oil. Sprinkle the fish liberally on both sides with coarse salt to help prevent sticking. Carefully place the fish on the grill or in a fish basket (which will help you turn it over, since boneless fish get very fragile as they cook). Cook the fish for a total of about 10 minutes per inch of thickness at the thickest part. If, for example, the boneless fish is 1½ inches [4 cm] thick, cook it for about 7 minutes on each side.

IF you haven't used a fish basket, carefully detach the fish from the grill with a two-pronged fork and use two long spatulas to transfer it to a long platter. Brush off any coarse salt clinging to the fish. At the table, slice the fish crosswise into 1½-to-2-inch [4 to 5 cm]-thick sections and serve it on heated plates. Pass olive oil and vinegar at the table in little pitchers, or serve lemon wedges instead of vinegar.

BAKING METHOD

IF you're baking your fish, preheat the oven to about 400°F [200°C/gas mark 6] (50°F/10°C more for very small fish; 50°F/10°C less for large fish). Cover a sheet pan with aluminum foil, rub the foil with oil, set the fish on it, and slide the pan into the oven. Bake for about 10 minutes per inch of thickness at the thickest part.

Variations: You can use virtually any mixture to stuff a fish, but I prefer to use small amounts of very flavorful ingredients (hence the herbs) instead of larger amounts of stuffing. If you use too much stuffing, not only can it fall out of the fish but you may have to overcook the fish to get the stuffing to heat through. Other than herbs, I sometimes use duxelles (chopped mushrooms cooked down until dry and flavorful; see page 96) or *tomates concassées* (peeled, seeded, and chopped tomatoes that have been cooked down to eliminate moisture). Chopped fennel fronds smeared over the inside of the fish with a little lemon and olive oil add a subtle note. You can also use the chopped spinach or chard mixture in the sardine recipe on page 326. Try adding sprigs of moistened dried fennel stalks, rosemary, or thyme to the fire a couple of minutes before the fish is ready. They will smoulder and impart a delicate scent to the fish. When serving grilled stuffed fish, a sauce is usually superfluous. In his marvelous book *Lulu's Provençal Table*, which describes the life of a Provençal family of winemakers and the recipes of its matriarch, Lulu, Richard Olney suggests serving grilled fish with tapenade (see Olive and Caper Spread, page 83) or a *tomates concassées* made by cooking chopped preserved anchovies in olive oil before adding the tomatoes.

GRILLED FISH
EN ESCABÈCHE

Some equivalent of the *escabèche* is made in virtually every country bordering the Mediterranean. Typically, an *escabèche* is made by sautéing or frying the fish and then smothering it with a marinade made with various herbs, usually cooked onions and garlic, and almost always vinegar. More exotic versions, from Venice, North Africa, or Sicily, may contain pine nuts, raisins, or pomegranate seeds. In Richard Olney's *Lulu's Provençal Table*, Lulu marinates raw fresh sardine fillets, which she calls *en escabèche*, but we might call the dish a ceviche, especially if lime juice replaced the vinegar. The principles behind a South American ceviche and Lulu's raw marinated sardine fillets are essentially the same. In addition to being a tasty way to serve fish or other seafood, the *escabèche* method—marinating *after* cooking—allows you to keep fish for a couple of days without it turning fishy.

It occurred to me one afternoon, after I'd grilled more sardines than I or my guests could eat, to turn the leftovers into a kind of *escabèche* made with grilled fish instead of fish that had been sautéed or deep-fried. The smoky flavors from the grill made a beautiful match for the vinegar, garlic, and onions. If you're grilling small fish, you can marinate them whole; if you're grilling larger fish, you can leave them whole, but they stay better in the marinade if you fillet them after you grill them. The *escabèche* method works especially well for oily fish, such as sardines, mackerel, and Spanish mackerel. You can also grill fish steaks or fillets of fish such as tuna and marinate the slices.

GRILLED FISH
EN ESCABÈCHE

POISSONS GRILLÉS
EN ESCABÈCHE

MAKES 6 FIRST-COURSE SERVINGS

FOR GRILLING:

18 small full-flavored fish, such as sardines, baby rougets, or smelts (about 2½ pounds [1.1 kg] total); or 6 medium-size fish such as small mackerel (6 to 8 ounces [170 to 225 g] each); or 3 larger fish, such as Spanish mackerel (about 12 ounces [340 g] each); or 1 thick tuna steak (about 1½ pounds [675 g])

2 tablespoons olive oil (for coating the fish and brushing the grill)

pepper

coarse salt

FOR THE MARINADE:

5 tablespoons olive oil

1 medium-size red onion, sliced very thin

1 small fennel bulb

1 clove garlic, chopped fine

¾ cup [175 ml] white wine

½ cup [125 ml] good-quality white wine vinegar

1 pinch saffron (optional)

salt

pepper

IF you're using whole fish, have them scaled and gutted. If you're using sardines, you may need to do this yourself, by running your finger along the inside of the stomach cavity, under cold running water, to remove the viscera and then rubbing the sardines, still under cold running water, to get rid of the scales.

AN hour before you're ready to serve, prepare a hot fire. Set up the barbecue so the grill is 4 to 6 inches away from the coals for sardines or 10 to 12 inches [25 to 30.5 cm] away for Spanish mackerel—the smaller the fish, the closer they should be to the coals. Get the grill very hot before putting on the fish.

RUB the fish with 1 tablespoon of olive oil and refrigerate until needed.

HEAT 1 tablespoon of the olive oil in a heavy-bottomed pot and stir in the onions. Cook the onion slices over medium heat, stirring every few minutes so they soften but don't brown, about 10 minutes. While the onions are cooking, cut the stalks and fronds off the fennel—you can save the stalks and let them dry for grilling—and coarsely chop the fronds. Pull off or cut away any dark patches on the fennel bulb. Peel away the outer stringy membrane with a vegetable peeler, as you would celery. Slice the fennel crosswise as close to paper-thin as you can, using a plastic vegetable slicer. Add the fennel slices to the pot with the onions and stir for another 10 minutes. The onions and fennel should be soft but with the slightest bit of crispiness. Stir in the garlic and cook for 2 minutes more. Pour in the wine and boil it for 1 minute to cook off its alcohol. Take the pot off the heat, add the vinegar and saffron and the rest of the olive oil for the marinade, and let cool.

RUB the grill with a paper towel dipped in 1 table-spoon of olive oil. Brush the fish on both sides with olive oil and sprinkle with coarse salt to help prevent sticking. Carefully place the fish on the grill. Cook small fish such as sardines for about 2 minutes on each side and larger fish a total of about 10 minutes per inch of thickness at the thickest part. If, for example, the boneless fish is 2 inches [5 cm] thick, cook it for about 10 minutes on each side. If you're grilling a tuna steak, cook it only for about 5 minutes per inch [2.5 cm] of thickness—2½ minutes on each side—so it stays rare in the middle and doesn't dry out. Transfer the fish to a work surface and let it cool for about 5 minutes. If you're serving small whole fish such as sardines, just leave them whole, but medium-size and large fish are better filleted once they've been grilled, and then allowed to cool a little (see page 323). If you're using tuna steak, slice it into strips about ¼ inch [.5 cm] thick.

ARRANGE the whole fish, or the strips of tuna steak, in alternating layers with the cool vegetable mixture in a decorative serving dish with sides, such as a large oval gratin dish, finishing with the vegetable mixture. Refrigerate for at least 1 hour before serving. Fish in *escabèche* can be kept, covered with plastic wrap, in the refrigerator for at least 2 days.

LOBSTER WITH TOMATO AND COGNAC SAUCE

HOMARD À L'AMÉRICAINE

HOW TO	HOW TO	AN	HOW TO	HOW TO
COOK LOBSTER	GET THE MOST FLAVOR FROM A LOBSTER	ASSORTMENT OF SAUCES FOR LOBSTER AND CRAYFISH	MAKE CRUSTACEAN BUTTER	MAKE A BISQUE

NO ONE KNOWS EXACTLY WHY THIS DISH IS NAMED AFTER AMERICA since there's nothing American about it except that Americans like lobster. After all, we boil our lobsters in a big pot instead of cutting them up and simmering them like a stew with Cognac. The more chauvinistic of French cooks insist that this is all a terrible misunderstanding and the original name was meant to be *homard à l'armoricaine,* named after the Armorique, a region that includes part of Brittany, which is of course famous for its lobster. But there's a problem: There aren't (or weren't) any tomatoes in Brittany.

Of course, none of this matters when it comes to cooking the dish, which is basically lobster, cut up while still alive (grisly, but quick and humane), cut into relatively small pieces, the pieces sautéed in olive oil (again, not Breton at all), a little chopped onion sweated in the still-hot oil, chopped tomatoes added along with the lobster, and the whole thing stewed for another 20 minutes. In fancy versions the sauce is finished with butter combined with the mashed coral (roe) and tomalley (liver). While I've always liked the idea of a lobster stew, *homard à l'américaine* has some serious problems. The lobster pieces curl up in the hot oil and then overcook and toughen in the sauce and are almost impossible to eat without covering yourself with tomato sauce. The coral and tomalley, while delicious, are next to impossible to work with butter, and when you stir the mixture into a boiling sauce it curdles anyway. A better system is to partially cook the lobster in larger pieces (so the meat is held in place by the shell and doesn't curl), take the flesh out of the shell, simmer the broken-up shells with the tomatoes, strain, and pour the sauce over and around the pieces of lobster, sliced and arranged in wide soup plates.

GETTING THE MEAT OUT OF A COOKED LOBSTER

To take the meat out of the tail, twist the tail away from the head (if the head and tail are still attached) and snap off the small flap at the end of the tail. Set the tail on its side and press gently with the heel of your hand until you hear a crunching sound. Don't press too hard or you'll crush the meat. Hold the tail in a kitchen towel with the underside facing you and pull the sides apart. The underside will split open. Push the tail meat out through one end with your finger. If you're using the head, cut it in half lengthwise and pull out and reserve any dark green coral or pale green tomalley (these can be puréed into the sauce). Pull out and discard the two halves of the grain sack near the front of the head—it's easy to recognize because it feels rough and pulls right out.

Remove the meat from the claws by gently wiggling the small pincer from side to side and then pulling back so that the small piece of cartilage embedded in the claw pulls out. Hold the claw on a cutting board with the thorny underside facing up. Hack into the shell about ¼ inch [.5 cm] with an old knife or cleaver and twist sideways. The shell should crack in two. Gently pull apart the shell, doing your best to leave the claw meat in one piece.

Remove the meat from the small joints connected to the claws by cutting them open with kitchen scissors. I usually don't bother taking the meat out of the little legs along the side of the lobster because I usually crush the legs and simmer them in liquid to make sauce. But if you want to extract their meat, roll a rolling pin along the length of the legs to push the meat out one end.

LOBSTER WITH TOMATO AND COGNAC SAUCE

HOMARD À L'AMÉRICAINE

MAKES 4 MAIN-COURSE OR 8 FIRST-COURSE SERVINGS

- 4 lobsters (1½ to 2 pounds [675 to 900 g] each)
- 3 tablespoons olive oil
- 1 medium-size onion, chopped fine
- 3 garlic cloves, chopped
- 4 medium-size tomatoes, seeded and chopped, or 1 can (28 ounces [800 g]) whole tomatoes, drained, seeds squeezed out, chopped
- ½ cup [125 ml] white wine
- 1 cup [250 ml] chicken or fish broth or water
- 1 medium-size bouquet garni
- ¼ cup [60 ml] Cognac
- 2 teaspoons coarsely chopped fresh tarragon (chopped at the last minute)
- ¼ cup [60 ml] heavy cream
- 4 tablespoons butter

  salt

  pepper

  chervil sprigs, fennel fronds, or chopped parsley (optional)

TO CUT UP THE LOBSTERS

RINSE the lobsters under cold running water, holding them by the back of the head. Place them, one at a time, on a cutting board—with the tail to your left if you're right-handed—and place a large chef's knife directly in the center of the head on top. Plunge the knife quickly straight down through the head all the way to the cutting board, and then bring the knife forward, splitting the front part of the head (actually called the thorax) and instantly killing the lobster. Hold the lobster over a bowl for a few seconds to catch the juices that run out. Snap off the claws where they join the thorax and twist off the tail. Take the rubber bands off the claws—be careful, the pieces of lobster will be twitching and the claws can pinch you—and rinse the claws again if there's grit under where the rubber band was. Finish cutting the thorax in half and pull the gritty little sac out of each side of the thorax and discard it.

TO COOK THE LOBSTERS

COOK the lobster pieces in 2 tablespoons of the oil over medium to high heat in a large, heavy-bottomed pot, turning every couple of minutes with tongs until the lobster pieces turn red, about 8 minutes. (See "Keeping Lobster Tails from Curling," below.) Remove the lobster pieces from the pan and let them cool. Put the onion and garlic in the pot with the remaining olive oil and cook over medium heat, stirring every few minutes, until they turn

KEEPING LOBSTER TAILS FROM CURLING

When lobsters cook, the tails curl tightly so that when you slice the meat you end up with uneven wedges instead of even slices. Some cooks tie them together with string, with the flipper sides facing each other to keep them straight, but in this way the initial cooking takes longer—about 12 minutes instead of 8. To avoid this, slide a small wooden skewer along the underside of the tail, between the thin translucent shell and the meat, to keep the tail straight.

translucent, about 8 minutes. Add the tomatoes, wine, chicken broth, and bouquet garni and simmer gently for 5 minutes. Remove the pot from the heat.

TAKE the lobster meat out of the tails and claws (see page 332), cut each of the tail meats into 4 slices, and reserve both tail and claw meat on a plate, covered with aluminum foil, while you're making the sauce.

TO MAKE THE SAUCE

PUT the shells in the pot with the tomatoes and break them up with the end of a French-style rolling pin (the kind without handles) or the front end of a cleaver, and simmer the mixture gently for about 20 minutes with the lid on. Strain the tomato mixture into a saucepan, pressing hard on the mixture with the back of a spoon to force out as much liquid as you can, and stir in the Cognac, tarragon, and cream. Simmer for about 5 minutes, or longer if you want a slightly thicker sauce. While the sauce is simmering, heat the lobster and the soup plates in an oven turned to the lowest setting. (The lobster mustn't get too hot or it will overcook.) Whisk the butter into the sauce and season to taste with salt, if necessary, and pepper.

ARRANGE the lobster pieces in the soup plates and spoon the sauce over and around them. Decorate each serving with chervil, fennel, or parsley.

THOUGHTS AND VARIATIONS ON LOBSTER STEW

Because I grew up in California, where no lobster swims (there is a local variety of what the French call *langouste,* but it's hard to find), I didn't taste one until my first visit to the East Coast, in my early twenties. Now, of course, live lobsters can be found just about anywhere, but in those days the only whole fresh crustacean available in California was Dungeness crab. When it was in season, we reveled in it, devouring it cold, in meaty chunks, with homemade mayonnaise. One afternoon a Filipino friend we had invited to lunch gasped in horror as he saw my mother scoop the crab's innards, his favorite part, into the trash. It wasn't until years later, while traveling and emulating the native eating habits of the French, Japanese, and Italians, that I discovered how right he was. The meat of shrimp, crab, and lobster is the creature's substance, but the flavor hides in the heads and shells and in the liver (the tomalley or, in crab parlance, the mustard) and roe (the eggs, or coral, found in the female).

Other than the obvious solution of sucking noisily on bits of lobster shell and on shrimp and crayfish heads, there are more elegant methods for getting the flavor out of every bit of a lobster or other crustacean. In making a crustacean sauce, stewing liquid, or soup, there are three sources of flavor: the juices released by the flesh as it cooks (juices that are lost when lobster is boiled in a big pot), the shells, and the tomalley and coral. Each of these flavor sources must be treated in a different way. The flesh is simple, in that it requires no special method to access its flavor, but it almost always gets overcooked. Crustaceans are best when cooked very gently, and they must never be cooked too long, just enough for the shell to turn red; however, if they are cooked less than that, the meat is very hard to separate from the shell. The shells require a different strategy because their flavor and color dissolve in fat, not in water, so that simmering a bunch of lobster shells in water as though making a fish broth will give you little of the flavor (and none of the color) contained in the shells. This is an inherent flaw in *homard à l'américaine*—the shells are simmered in tomato sauce with no fat in it. Sauciers who are aware of this either simmer the shells in cream (in addition, usually, to herbs, aromatic vegetables, and Cognac) or use the shells to make lobster butter, and some do both. Crustacean coral and tomalley require a different strategy altogether. They must be puréed and whisked into the sauce just before serving—but not worked with butter as suggested in most French cookbooks, or they will curdle in the same way as chicken eggs. I use my fingers to work the innards through a fine-mesh strainer into a bowl with a little Cognac, which prevents the juices from clotting.

CRUSTACEAN BUTTER

Almost any crustacean can be used to make an intensely flavored, bright orange crustacean butter, but crustaceans that turn bright red when cooked, such as lobster and crayfish (or shrimp, if you can find them with the heads), work the best. While lobster and crayfish produce the brightest butter, the kind of crustacean you use makes little difference in the flavor; crustacean butter has a generic crustacean flavor and little of the flavor of the particular variety. Crab shells are too hard.

Classic recipes suggest grinding crustacean shells with cold butter and then working the mixture through a drum sieve to eliminate pieces of shell, but it's better and easier to cook the butter with the broken-up shells to extract a maximum of flavor and color. I, who don't hesitate to take shells off guests' finished plates, save lobster or crayfish shells in a plastic bag in the freezer until I have a couple of pounds. I then work the shells in a heavy-duty mixer (such as KitchenAid or Hobart) with a slightly less than equal weight of butter. If I have fewer shells, or more tender ones, such as shrimp or crayfish shells, I use a food processor with an old blade I've saved and leave out the claw shells of crayfish and lobster because they are so hard that they'll jam up in the food processor.

MAKES ABOUT 1 POUND [450 G] NOT INCLUDING THE CLAW SHELLS

shells reserved from 4 medium-size cooked lobsters, or shells and heads from 4 pounds [1.8 kg] of cooked crayfish

1½ pound [675 g] cold butter, cut into about 8 chunks

COMBINE the shells with the butter in an electric mixer with a paddle blade or in a food processor. If you're using a mixer, hold a kitchen towel around the mixer and over the bowl for the first few minutes to keep the shells from working their way out before they've broken up and combined with the butter. Turn the mixer on low and work the shells with the butter for 20 minutes, until the butter turns a rich salmon color.

IF you're using a food processor, don't use the claw shells from lobster or crayfish because they are too hard and may damage the blade. (Discard lobster claw shells—they're simply too hard to release any flavor or color; crush crayfish claws with a mallet or the end of a French-style rolling pin and reserve.) Process the shells until they are broken into small fragments, about 3 minutes, scraping down the sides of the processor each time the butter clings to the sides, out of reach of the blade.

(continued)

HEAT the butter, ground-up shells and all, in a heavy-bottomed saucepan over low heat for about 30 minutes, stirring every few minutes. The butter is finished cooking when you see a layer of orange-colored oil instead of creamy melted butter at bottom of the pan. Don't overcook the butter and allow it to brown.

Pour enough hot water into the saucepan to completely cover the shells and set the pan in a bowl of ice water, or let cool and refrigerate overnight. The hot water keeps the butter molten long enough so that it floats on top of the water. When the butter has congealed into a solid orange layer on top of the saucepan, lift it off with a spoon (as though removing fat from cold broth) and transfer it to a clean saucepan. Discard the water and shells left in the saucepan. Melt the crustacean butter over low heat and strain it through a fine-mesh strainer into a clean saucepan. Heat over low heat to evaporate any traces of moisture left in the butter (which can cause it to turn rancid). Again, be careful not to burn it—once it starts bubbling and the butter is clear, it's done. Crustacean butter will keep for several months in a covered container in the refrigerator and even longer in the freezer.

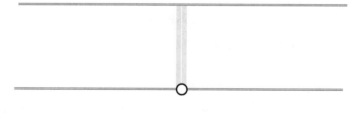

HOW TO TELL A LOBSTER'S SEX

Hold the lobster by the back of the thorax (better known as the head) and look at the bottom of the tail. Notice the little flippers along the length of the tail and look at the pair of flippers nearest the thorax. On a male lobster, these will be bone hard; on the female, they will be soft, thin, and flexible.

LOBSTER NEWBURG

HOMARD À LA NEWBURG

MAKES 4 MAIN-COURSE

OR 8 FIRST-COURSE SERVINGS

This is another of the great French classics that were once popular on American menus (in French restaurants, at least) but now are all but forgotten. This is a pity because, when well prepared, lobster Newburg captures the essence of lobster far better than lobster à l'américaine.

Lobster Newburg is made in the same way as lobster à l'américaine except that cream, marsala, and Cognac replace the tomatoes. I use semidry Madeira instead of marsala because I find most marsala too sweet. (See page 10 for more information about Madeira.) Traditional recipes also call for fish broth, but I prefer to use chicken broth or, in a perfect world, the cooking liquid from claims or mussels (see Chapter 20). Classic recipes are finished with the lobster coral and tomalley worked with butter, but I use lobster butter made from the shells (see page 335) and work the coral and tomalley through a strainer and combine it with the sauce. If you don't have lobster butter on hand or you don't want to deal with the coral, just leave these steps out—the lobster will still be delicious. If you plan to use the coral, be sure that at least 2 of your lobsters are females (see "How to Tell a Lobster's Sex," page 336).

4 lobsters (1½ to 2 pounds [675 to 900 g] each)

¼ cup [60 ml] plus 1 tablespoon Cognac

2 tablespoons olive oil

3 medium-size shallots, chopped fine

½ cup [125 ml] semidry Madeira or Spanish cream sherry

1 cup [250 ml] concentrated chicken or veal broth (see page 4)

1 cup [250 ml] heavy cream

4 tablespoons Crustacean Butter (page 335) or plain unsalted butter

1 tablespoon finely chopped parsley

salt

pepper

chervil sprigs (optional)

PREPARING THE TOMALLEY AND ROE

CUT up the live lobsters as described on page 333. Set a strainer, preferably one with a fine mesh, over a bowl containing 1 tablespoon of Cognac. Reach into the opening of each lobster tail—where it joined the thorax—with your finger and scoop any roe or tomalley into the strainer. Pull out and discard the grain sack from inside the split thorax. Pull out any tomalley and add it to the roe in the strainer. Work the roe and tomalley through the strainer with a wooden spoon. When you can't work through any more with the spoon, rub the mixture against the inside of the strainer with your fingers. Cover the strained mixture and refrigerate it.

COOKING THE LOBSTER AND MAKING THE SAUCE

IF you want the lobster tails to stay straight during cooking, slide a small wooden skewer through each one between the membrane that covers the underside of the tail and the meat itself (see page 333).

COOK the lobster pieces in the olive oil over medium to high heat in a large, covered, heavy-bottomed pot, turning every couple of minutes with tongs until the lobster pieces turn red, about 8 minutes. Remove the lobster pieces from the pan to let cool. Put the shallots in the pot and stir over medium heat until they turn translucent, about 5 minutes. Add the Madeira, the rest of the Cognac, the chicken broth, and the heavy cream. Bring to a simmer and remove the pot from the heat.

TAKE the lobster meat out of the shells (see page 332) and return the shells to the pot. Cut each of the shelled tails into 4 slices and reserve both tail meat and claw meat on a plate, covered with aluminum foil, while you're making the sauce.

BREAK up the lobster shells in the pot with the end of a French-style rolling pin or the front of a cleaver held on end and simmer gently for 20 minutes, uncovered. (Sauces containing cream should never be simmered covered or the cream will break.) Strain the sauce into a clean saucepan. (Sauces and soups containing hard shells should be strained first through a heavy-duty—or cheap—strainer because they can easily damage an expensive fine-mesh strainer. Strain the sauce a second time through a fine-mesh strainer.) Push down hard on the shells with the back of a wooden spoon to extract as much liquid as possible.

JUST before you're ready to serve, bring the sauce to a gentle simmer. Whisk every few minutes to keep the cream from separating. Whisk in the crustacean butter or unsalted butter. Pour the sauce into the bowl with the reserved coral and a tomalley while whisking. Return the sauce to the saucepan and heat very gently while whisking, until you see the sauce turn an intense orange. Don't let the sauce boil or the roe will curdle. Add the parsley to the sauce and season to taste with salt and pepper.

ARRANGE the lobster pieces on warmed (but not too hot) soup plates and spoon the sauce over and around them.

Variations: This lobster Newburg recipe includes all the methods for extracting the flavor from a lobster. The same or very similar methods also work for most other crustaceans. Admittedly, this is a complicated dish, but it's one that is easily simplified by leaving out the crustacean butter or by just leaving the tomalley and roe in the lobster instead of adding them to the sauce. You can use this recipe as a model for lobster stew, plugging in different ingredients at various stages during the cooking. Most of the great crustacean dishes in the fanciest French restaurants are made using these same techniques, substituting an ingredient here and there to give the dish its own identity. Here are some thoughts for variations.

THE AROMATIC VEGETABLES ADDED AT THE BEGINNING: Lobster à l'américaine calls for chopped onion and garlic; lobster Newburg, for shallots; but aromatic mixtures such as the classic mirepoix (chopped onion, celery, and carrot), mixtures of chopped fresh or dried chiles (for a Mexican note), mushroom stems or soaked dried mushrooms (later strained out), chopped fennel, or lemongrass (for a citrusy Thai aroma) can all be used.

THE LIQUIDS: Chopped tomatoes provide the liquid for lobster à l'américaine; cream and Madeira, for lobster Newburg. But you can use any liquid that could conceivably go well with lobster: Sauternes or other aromatic wines can replace the Madeira; clam or mussel cooking liquid (the clams or mussels added to the stew at the end) can replace the chicken broth; yellow tomatoes, tomatillos, red wine (reduced in advance with a little mirepoix and a bouquet garni), and various brandies or eaux-de-vies (such as kirsch or framboise) can replace or augment the Cognac. A few drops of Pernod or Ricard added at the end give the sauce a lovely hint of fennel.

FLAVORFUL FINISHES: Almost any herb can enhance a lobster stew. Parsley (used in the Newburg) is subtle and underrated; tarragon and basil have a natural affinity for crustaceans; stronger-flavored herbs such as thyme, marjoram, or savory can be finely chopped and added at the end or tied into a bouquet garni and simmered with the shells; spices (various curry mixtures or just plain curry powder, cooked first in a little butter; or saffron, soaked in a tablespoon of water) can be stirred into the sauce at the end. Herb butters can augment or replace the crustacean butter; they can be made in advance, whereas chopped herbs loose their aroma and may turn black (more about herb butters on page 490). Sea urchin roe (see page 272) or scallop roe (see page 287), worked with an equal amount of butter and strained, can replace or augment the lobster coral. Truffle butter, finely chopped black truffles, or white truffles shaved over the dish at the table aren't half bad either.

GARNITURES: Because a lobster stew is a rather intricate affair with lots of last-minute steps, I usually keep the garnitures to a minimum. But if you have someone to help you in the kitchen or you just can't resist making life complicated, adding vegetables or other seafood to the deeply flavored, bright orange lobster stew results in one of the most beautiful and complexly flavored dishes you may ever see or taste. I worked in one place where we added morels—dried, simmered in a little Madeira, the cooking liquid added to the sauce—and in another restaurant where we used tiny string beans, peas, and miniature carrots. Almost any green vegetable or baby root vegetable, lightly cooked in advance and kept warm while you're finishing the sauce, will enhance the stew.

THE EASY WAY: STEAMED LOBSTER WITH PARSLEY SAUCE

LE MOYEN FACILE:
HOMARD À LÀ VAPEUR,
SAUCE PERSILLÉE

MAKES 4 MAIN-COURSE
OR 8 FIRST-COURSE SERVINGS

Despite the fact that a lobster stew is one of the triumphs of French technique and tradition, it sometimes seems like too much hassle and we give up and just throw the lobsters into a pot of boiling water. But the boiling method bothers me because the lobster cooking juices are released into the water, never to be tasted again, and we have nothing on which to base a sauce. (Drawn butter is to me a bore, and it is fattier than any sauce.)

If you steam the lobsters in a small amount of water or wine (in the same way as mussels or clams), the liquids they release fall down into the steaming liquid, giving you a tasty liquid you can make a sauce out of. Once you've steamed the lobsters, just boil down the liquid left in the pot, add a little cream and some freshly chopped parsley (or other herb), and pass the sauce at the table. Steaming a lobster also makes it easier to cook it more slowly—essential for keeping the flesh from turning rubbery.

If you want to be elegant and make it easier for your guests to manage the lobster at the table, take the meat out of the claws, split the tails (with their shells) in half lengthwise, put 1 or 2 of the halves (depending on whether the lobster is a first or main course) in a wide soup plate for each guest, arrange the claw meat on top of the tails, and ladle the sauce over and around the lob-ster meat. Using a soup plate allows you to keep the sauce rather thin, so you don't have to use a lot of cream and butter to give it body. Give everyone a spoon in addition to a knife and fork.

4 lobsters (1½ to 2 pounds [565 to 900 g] each)

½ cup [125 ml] dry white wine

½ cup [125 ml] heavy cream

2 tablespoons finely chopped parsley (chopped at the last minute)

1 teaspoon Pernod (optional)

salt

pepper

RINSE the lobsters. Turn the lobsters over and cut the underside of the thorax (the head) in half with a heavy chef's knife, but don't cut all the way through the top of the shell. This is to kill the lobsters quickly and allow their juices to be released into the pot for the sauce. Cut off the rubber bands holding the claws together and if necessary rinse the claws again to get rid of any grit hiding under the rubber band. Put the lobsters in a heavy-bottomed pot and add the wine. Cover the pot and put it on low heat. With a pair of tongs, turn the lobsters around in the pot after about 10 minutes, redistributing them so that they cook evenly. Check the liquid in the pot every 5 minutes to make sure it doesn't evaporate completely. If it does, turn down the heat and add ½ cup [125 ml] water. (Cooking time will depend on the heat you use; the more slowly you cook the lobsters, the better.) When the lobsters have turned completely red, anywhere from 15 minutes to 1 hour, take them out of the pot with a towel or a pair of tongs, keep them warm, and add the cream to the liquid in the pot. Strain the liquid into a small saucepan, stir in the parsley and the optional Pernod, and bring to a simmer for 30 seconds to infuse the flavor of the parsley and to cook off the alcohol in the Pernod. Season to taste with salt and pepper.

YOU can serve the lobsters whole and let your guests grapple with them, or you can take the meat out of the lobsters, add the juices they release to the sauce, and serve the meat on warmed soup plates as described on page 334, with the sauce spread over and around it. The cooked tomalley and coral can be worked through a strainer, and added to the sauce.

Variations: It's easy to fool around with this simple and delicious sauce by using different herbs (basil and tarragon are naturals); adding fresh tomato purée (which lends a subtle sweetness and lovely color), Cognac (which gives the sauce a flavor reminiscent of an authentic *sauce américaine*), or chopped mushrooms or truffles; or whisking in crustacean or herb butters.

A QUICK SAUCE AMÉRICAINE

If you have Crustacean Butter on hand, here's a quick way to make a very satisfying little sauce with the character of a *sauce américaine* to serve over fish or shellfish.

MAKES ABOUT 1⅓ CUPS [325 ML] (ENOUGH FOR 6 SERVINGS)

¼ cup [60 ml] Cognac

1 ripe tomato, chopped

2 tablespoons concentrated veal or chicken broth (optional; see page 4)

¼ cup [60 ml] heavy cream

4 tablespoons Crustacean Butter (page 335)

4 tablespoons unsalted butter

½ teaspoon Pernod or Ricard (optional)

salt

pepper

COMBINE the Cognac, tomato, and concentrated broth in a small saucepan and simmer gently until the tomato softens, about 10 minutes. Add the cream, bring the mixture back to simmer, and strain, using the bottom of a small ladle to push it through the strainer into a clean saucepan. Simmer the sauce until it has the consistency you like—I like it just slightly thicker than cold heavy cream—and whisk in the crustacean butter, the unsalted butter, and the Pernod. If the sauce gets too thick, thin it with a little broth or water. Season to taste with salt and pepper. Serve on top of cooked shellfish or pieces of fish, with chicken (as in Chicken with Crayfish, page 341), or with the oysters on page 342.

CHICKEN WITH CRAYFISH

POULET AUX ÉCREVISSES

MAKES 4 MAIN-COURSE SERVINGS

I recently came across some old recipe ideas I had jotted down while studying cooking in Paris. Some of the ideas sounded good, although a bit extravagant (hot partridge mousse), but some combinations were just plain embarrassing (sliced raw beef with kiwis). At the time, I wasn't the only one who confused eccentricity with creativity. But seemingly unusual combinations in French cooking are nothing new. Medieval French cooks stewed meats with ginger, almonds, saffron, sugar, and galangal (still used in Southeast Asian cooking) and, at special feasts, covered their foods with gold leaf. During the seventeenth century, French cooks were far more daring than they were in the latter half of the nineteenth century and for most of the twentieth. Our own chefs are now catching up.

Particularly popular in the seventeenth century was the combining of poultry with seafood. Cookbooks from that time are sprinkled with recipes for chicken with oysters and pigeon or chicken with crayfish. Chicken with crayfish is still cooked in France and is considered one of the great dishes of French country cooking. But the genius behind these combinations lies in their economy. You can't serve a half dozen crayfish or oysters as a main course, but you can turn them into a sauce—or actually a little ragoût—and serve them atop a piece of chicken. You'll have a dish with all the finesse and flavor of expensive seafood, but with the substantial backdrop provided by the chicken.

During the nineteenth century the French considered crayfish far more luxurious than lobster, and by the early twentieth century most of France's streams and rivers had been fished out. Now, most of Western Europe's crayfish come from Eastern Europe. Although crayfish are plentiful in many parts of the United States, most of America's crayfish come from Louisiana or Oregon. Crayfish tails are also being imported from China, but if you want to use live crayfish—essential in French cooking not only as a means of ensuring freshness but because most of the flavor is in the shells and heads—you'll still need to get Louisiana or Oregon crayfish.

If you've never cooked crayfish before, the process can be a little nerve-wracking. The crayfish must all be alive, meaning that you have to sort through them and throw out any dead ones. I usually spread them out on a big sheet pan and push them, a few at a time, with a wooden spoon into a large colander, checking as I go, tossing out any dead ones and fighting off the most lively, which are by now clinging desperately to the spoon. Rinse the crayfish under cold running water. (Whatever you do, don't put them in a sink full of cold water or you'll give them a decided tactical advantage.) You can cook crayfish by plunging them in a pot of boiling water for a minute, but I always feel that valuable juices are released into the surrounding liquid, so I to sauté them in hot oil. (They do kick around a bit, so if this bothers you, use the water method.) Once they have turned red, after 30 seconds in the water or 5 minutes in the oil, I let them cool and take out the meat. (See page 343.)

2 tablespoons olive oil

24 live crayfish, rinsed

1 medium-size onion, chopped fine

1 medium-size carrot, peeled and chopped fine

5 tablespoons butter or Crustacean Butter (page 335) (for the sauce), plus 2 tablespoons butter (for cooking the chicken)

3 tomatoes, coarsely chopped

¼ cup [60 ml] Cognac

3 sprigs fresh thyme or marjoram

1 imported bay leaf

1½ cups [375 ml] chicken or fish broth or water

1 cup [250 ml] heavy cream

1 chicken (4 pounds [1.8 kg]), "quartered"; see page 17)

2 tablespoons finely chopped parsley, chives, or basil (or a combination), or 2 teaspoons chopped fresh tarragon

salt

pepper

½ pound [225 g] shelled cooked crayfish tails (bought already prepared; optional)

chervil sprigs (optional)

HEAT the olive oil over high heat in a heavy-bottomed pot large enough so that the crayfish come only one-fourth of the way up the sides. When the oil ripples—don't let it smoke—toss in the crayfish and stir them with a wooden spoon. When they've all turned bright red, after about 5 minutes, scoop them into a bowl and let them cool.

WHILE the crayfish are cooling, cook the onion and carrot in the oil in the pan with 1 tablespoon of butter or crustacean butter until the onion turns translucent, about 8 minutes.

TAKE out the crayfish meat (see page 343) and break up the heads and tail shells (leave out the claw shells) in a food processor for about 1 minute, scraping down the insides of the processor a few times during the process. The shells and heads should still be chunky. Don't overwork them or the sauce will have a dark, muddy color. Transfer the chopped shells and heads to the pot with the vegetables. If you don't have a food processor, put the heads and shells directly in the pot and break them up with the end of a French-style rolling pin or the front end, not the blade, of a cleaver. Crush the crayfish claws with the end of a rolling pin, a mallet, or a hammer with a towel wrapped around the end. Add the crushed claws, the tomatoes, Cognac, thyme or marjoram sprigs, bay leaf, chicken broth, and cream to the chopped shells and heads and simmer very gently for 30 minutes, stirring every few minutes with a wooden spoon. Strain the mixture through a coarse-mesh strainer or a china cap—a conical strainer made of smooth perforated stainless steel is perfect for this (see page 15)—pushing hard with a wooden spoon to extract the sauce from the shells. Discard the shells and strain the sauce a second time through a fine-mesh strainer into a saucepan.

COOK the chicken parts, skin-side down first, in 2 tablespoons of butter in a pan over medium to high heat for about 12 minutes on each side, until the chicken is very lightly browned and bounces back to

the touch (more about cooking chicken on page 26). Take the chicken out of the pan and arrange it on heated plates or, if you want to present the chicken in the pan, pour the fat out of the pan and put the chicken back in (I use a pretty copper pan that looks great on the table). Finish the sauce by whisking in the rest of the butter or crustacean butter and the chopped herbs. Season the sauce to taste with salt and pepper and heat the crayfish tails in it for a few seconds. Spoon the sauce and tails over the chicken on the individual plates or in the pan. Decorate each serving with the optional chervil sprigs.

Variations: The idea of turning a small seafood dish into a sauce or garniture for a less expensive (or at least more abundant) meat or seafood is so adaptable that you'll be able to think up dozens of original dishes. Here are few ideas for enhancing a simple sautéed piece of fish or chicken or veal. (Veal was often combined with seafood in the seventeenth and eighteenth centuries.)

OYSTERS: Poach oysters in their own juices combined with a little white wine and some chopped shallots. Just heat until the oysters curl slightly, but don't allow the liquid to boil; take the oysters out with a slotted spoon; roll them on a clean kitchen towel to rid them of any grit; reduce the poaching liquid with a little cream; if you like, whisk in flavored butter (crustacean, herb, roe, truffle, etc.) or plain butter; and sprinkle in herbs. Spoon the oysters and their sauce over the sautéed meat or seafood. The liquid released by clams and mussels can also be finished in the same way and used as a sauce. Oysters can also be gently poached in a finished crustacean sauce—don't let the sauce boil, especially if it contains coral—and the oysters served alone or over cooked chicken or seafood or over and around a small mound of cooked spinach.

SHRIMP: Even though shrimp are easy to find, they almost always come without the heads, leaving you very little with which to make a sauce. If you can't track down shrimp with the heads, you can collect shells in the freezer and use them to make the sauce, and use the shrimp tail meats in the same way as the crayfish in the main recipe. I recently made a delicious version of this dish (what now becomes *poulet aux crevettes*, or Chicken with Shrimp) with 1 pound of headless shrimp, using the shells to make the sauce and cooking the vegetables, shrimp, and chicken each in 1 tablespoon of crustacean butter (see page 335), and finished the sauce with 2 tablespoons more of crustacean butter to give it flavor and color.

LOBSTER: Even though lobster can be frightfully expensive, you can make a small amount of lobster *à l'américaine,* Newburg, or one of the variations on page 338 and use the lobster pieces and sauce as garniture and sauce for meat or fish. This method will provide a flavorful sauce for 4 servings with only one lobster.

CRAB: The relatively small blue crabs sold along the East Coast are delicious, but unless you're an expert at getting the meat out of the shells, they are frustrating to eat. To solve the problem, clean them (see page 346) and turn them into a sauce, using the same technique as you would for lobster or for Crab Bisque (page 344). Save any mustard or roe in the crabs, work it through a strainer with your fingers, and whisk it into the sauce at the end. Chunks of crabmeat, bought already shelled, can be used as a garniture.

TAKING THE MEAT OUT OF A CRAYFISH

When I was working as an apprentice, one of my jobs was to take the meat out of crayfish. The claw meat would take me an hour to get about half a cup [115 g]. Nowadays, I don't bother with the claw meat but instead just crush the claws with the end of a French-style rolling pin and simmer the claws, meat and all, in the sauce before it is strained. Most of the meat in a crayfish is in the tail, which you just twist off the thorax, the front part of the beast. To devein the tail, pinch the tiny flipper at the end and give it a gentle tug to pull out the vein. (If the vein doesn't come out, you'll have to take it out after removing the shell by gently pressing the back side of the tail to one side. This tears open the tail, and lets you get to the vein.) To take the meat out of the tail, pinch the tail between two fingers until you feel a little crack and then pull the shell away, using both hands and pinching each side of the tail shell between thumb and forefinger. Save the crushed claws, the tail and meat, and the heads and tail shells in separate piles.

Once you've cooked the crayfish and taken the tail meat out, make a sauce in the same way you would a sauce for a lobster stew—break up the heads and tail shells, cook them in butter with a little shallot or onion or mirepoix, add the crushed claws, simmer in cream and a little broth, and strain. You then sauté the chicken, simmer the chicken in the sauce, heat the reserved crayfish tails in the sauce for a few seconds, and serve. A half hour's work will give you plenty of shells and heads for making a delicious crayfish sauce but will give you very little meat. This is the advantage of serving a crayfish "ragout" as a sauce and garniture for chicken (or other meat or fish) rather than as a dish unto itself. If you want more crayfish tail meat, buy an extra ½ pound of shelled cooked tails and add them to the dish at the end.

Bisques

IT SEEMS THAT HARDLY ANYONE EATS BISQUE anymore. In fact, when I see them on the menu at an unfamiliar French restaurant, I go on alert, suspecting that this may be a stodgy establishment, lacking in flair and imagination. But I wait to pass judgment, because their presence may instead be a sign of understatement, modesty, and a hard-working classicist in the kitchen.

In some non-French restaurants, "bisque" is used synonymously with "soup," and many of us have had broccoli bisques, mushroom bisques, and heaven-knows-what bisques with no relationship whatever to an authentic bisque, which is essentially a crustacean broth thickened with rice or fresh bread crumbs and finished with crustacean butter, a little Cognac, and a purée of some of the crustacean flesh. Admittedly, bisques weren't always made with crustaceans. La Varenne, in *Le Cuisinier François*, described a bisque made with squabs that had nothing to do with shellfish. The only thing his recipe has in common with a "modern" bisque is that the liquid used for braising his pigeon was thickened with bread, in itself a holdover from medieval cooking when bread was used to thicken sauces. Gradually, "bisque" came to mean a dish with a crustacean sauce, like the Chicken with Crayfish on page 341, and by the era of Carême, near the beginning of the nineteenth century, it took on its current meaning.

Bisques may own a less-than-exalted status because they are very rich and contain a lot of butter. A big bowl of bisque is liable to fill you up and spoil your appetite for the main course. True, you can cut the amount of fat (I replace some of the butter with cream), but fats are essential for drawing the flavor out of crustacean heads and shells. My own solution is to serve the bisque in small consommé bowls or double espresso cups so it won't spoil anybody's appetite or waistline.

BLUE CRAB BISQUE

BISQUE DE CRABE

MAKES 10 SERVINGS

I make this crab bisque because blue crabs are relatively cheap in New York and I love their flavor but hate trying to pick out the meat. If you can't find blue crabs, the recipe will work with the shells from lobster, crayfish, or shrimp (ideally, with their heads, which contain most of the flavor). Don't try to make this soup with Dungeness crab—the shells are too hard.

1 medium-size onion, chopped

1 medium-size carrot, peeled and chopped

2 tablespoons olive oil

12 live blue crabs, cleaned and cut into 8 pieces each (see page 346)

1½ pounds [675 g] tomatoes, coarsely chopped, or 1 can (28 ounces [800 g]) whole tomatoes, seeds squeezed out

1 cup [250 ml] dry white wine

1 small bouquet garni

6 cups chicken broth (see page 209)

1 cup [250 ml] heavy cream

¾ cups [75 g] cooked rice (you'll need to boil ¼ cup/60 g of raw rice), or 3 slices white bread, crusts removed

½ pound [225 g] crabmeat, picked through for shells (optional)

4 tablespoons Crustacean Butter (page 335) or unsalted butter

⅓ cup [75 ml] Cognac

salt

pepper

PREHEAT the oven to 450°F [230°C/ gas mark 8].

SWEAT the onion and carrot in the olive oil over medium heat in a heavy-bottomed pot large enough to hold the crab pieces, until the onion turns translucent, about 8 minutes. Add the crab pieces in a single layer, and spread the tomatoes on top. Slide the pan into the oven for about 30 minutes until the crab pieces turn golden brown. Stir the crab pieces around every 10 minutes. Add the wine, bouquet garni, half the broth, and the cream and simmer gently for 30 minutes. Smash the crab shells up from time to time with a rolling pin, a big wooden spoon, or the end of a cleaver.

COMBINE the rice or the bread with the remaining broth in a blender and purée until smooth. Reserve in a bowl. If you're using the crabmeat, purée it with the crustacean butter or plain butter in a food processor (the classic method), or leave it whole and reserve.

STRAIN the crab mixture through a heavy-duty strainer, pushing hard on the shells with a wooden spoon to extract as much liquid out of the crabs as possible. Whisk the rice or bread broth mixture into the crab mixture. Stir in the Cognac, bring to a simmer, and simmer for about 2 minutes (to cook off the alcohol), and strain once more, this time through a fine-mesh strainer, using a small ladle to work the mixture through. Whisk the crustacean butter and butter/crab purée into the finished soup. Season to taste with salt and pepper.

PURÉED SOUPS

Until the end of the eighteenth century, bisques were defined by the fact that the meat, poultry, or seafood they contained was puréed. Nowadays we rarely if ever encounter a soup that contains purées other than vegetables or starches. One of the best-known soups in centuries past was *potage à la reine*. Early versions of the dish were often called blancmange, in reference to the fact that they contained almonds and puréed white meat, usually capon, not because they were sweetened as blancmange is today (see page 645 for more information about blancmange). In medieval versions of blancmange, the finished soup is sprinkled with pomegranate seeds. By the seventeenth century, La Varenne describes a blancmange that's set with the natural gelatin released by simmering a veal foot. It was at this time that soups flavored and thickened with almonds and puréed poultry evolved into *potage à la reine* and pure almond custards began to evolve into the modern sweet versions. La Varenne's recipe for *potage à la reine* is much like medieval versions of blancmange, except that bread is included as a thickener and the pomegranate seeds are augmented with slices of lemon. By the end of the nineteenth century, the almonds disappear entirely. Escoffier's version, which he calls a coulis, contains the same puréed poultry, rice used as a thickener, and plenty of cream and butter added at the end.

HOW TO CLEAN A BLUE CRAB

If the crabs are so ferocious that you can't get at them, pick them up with tongs and plunge them into a pot of boiling water for 30 seconds to kill them. Otherwise, kill them in what is said to be the most humane way, by turning them over and plunging a chef's knife into the shell, between the eyes and back from the eyes about ½ inch [1.5 cm]. Scrub them vigorously with a stiff brush while rinsing under cold running water. Be especially thorough on the underside of the crab between the legs, under the tail flap (called the apron), which you'll have to fold out, and the top shell, where mud tends to accumulate. Twist off the tail flap and discard it. Pull the top shell completely off by pulling it up on one side while holding the crab by the legs. Pull away and discard the rough gills clinging to the inside of the crab. Cut the top shell and the bottom part of the crab in quarters (so you end up with a total of 8 pieces) with a cleaver or heavy chef's knife.

ROAST CHICKEN

POULET RÔTI

HOW TO	HOW TO	HOW TO	HOW TO	HOW TO
ROAST CHICKEN AND TURKEY WITHOUT A THERMOMETER	TRUSS A CHICKEN WITHOUT A NEEDLE	MAKE FRENCH- AND AMERICAN-STYLE GRAVIES	STUFF CHICKEN UNDER THE SKIN	USE GARLIC AND FOIE GRAS TO FINISH SAUCES

WHEN I'M FEELING LAZY OR RUSHED AND DON'T WANT TO MAKE A BIG to-do in the kitchen, I roast a chicken, my equivalent to a TV dinner. I put the chicken in a 450°F [230°C/gas mark 8] oven for 50 minutes, until the skin's crispy and brown and the juices that accumulate in the cavity are no longer pink, and I serve and eat.

People make such a fuss over roast chicken—cookbooks abound with suggestions, more or less dogmatic, about the perfect temperature, the right roasting pan or oven rack, how the chicken has to be turned this way and that. It's no wonder most of us don't bother. True, you can overcook the chicken so the breast meat is dry (it'll still be delicious), or the juices can burn so you have no gravy (something I don't bother with on lazy nights any-way), or it may come out of the oven a little pale (use a higher temperature next time). But whatever you do to it, it's still going to be a lot better than a real TV dinner.

Now, if you're feeling more ambitious or have guests you want to impress, you can get into the nuances. The biggest mistake most of us make is overcooking the chicken and drying it out. This is easy to avoid. When the chicken has been roasting about 35 minutes, start checking the juices that accumulate in its cavity by putting the handle of a wooden spoon in the cavity and tilting the chicken so that some of the juices run out. (You can also reach in and scoop some of the juices out with a tablespoon.) At first, the juices will be pink and cloudy. When they turn oily, with streaks of dark red, the chicken is done. If you wait until the juices are completely clear, with no traces of red, the chicken will be over-cooked. You can also stick a metal skewer into the leg where the thigh joins the drumstick. The juices that ooze out should be clear, with no trace of pink. Or you can stick an instant-read thermometer into the skin between the breast and the leg—almost touching the joint where the thigh plugs into the rest of the chicken, but not touching any bone—and take the chicken out of the oven when the temperature reaches 140°F [60°C], keeping in mind that the temperature will increase by 5°F [2° to 3°C] when the chicken rests. (See "*Poulet Paranoia*," page 349.)

Another easy-to-avoid problem is the tendency of the chicken breasts to dry out by the time the legs are done. Tear off a small sheet of aluminum foil and fold it into a triangle just large enough to cover the breast meat on both sides of the chicken, but not the legs. (Traditional French cooks use a sheet of pork fat, called a *barde,* but the foil works just as well.) Butter one side of the foil and shape it, buttered-side down, over the whole chicken breast. Take the foil off after about 20 minutes of roasting, so the breast will have time to brown. Another nuance: Your chicken might look funny because the legs tend to hang off to one side, like a dog rolling on the floor to scratch its back. To deal with this, you can tie the ends of the two drumsticks together with a piece of string or one of those wire ties that come with garbage bags (don't use a plastic one). Or—don't panic—you can truss. When I taught French cooking, I had to teach three trussing methods, two of which required complicated knots. The only method I have ever needed takes only a few seconds (see "How to Truss a Chicken Without a Needle," page 349).

Partly because I like old-fashioned heavy-duty cooking things and partly because I lose things in the back of drawers, very few gadgets make it into my kitchen. Some gadgets, namely folding roasting racks, are useless. Half the time the rack (nonstick or otherwise) sticks to the bird or at least leaves strange markings. Worse, an oven rack keeps the meat above the roasting pan, causing the roasting pan to get too hot. As soon as the bird releases juices, they hit the hot pan and end up in smoke. Some recipes suggest putting a little water in the pan, but water produces steam and makes it harder to brown your bird. A better method is to use a small pan or heat-proof oval gratin dish that just fits the size of the bird. (An iron skillet works great.) Spread the giblets or a coarsely chopped onion in the pan and set the chicken on top. This prevents the chicken from sticking to the pan but keeps it close enough to the pan that the pan won't overheat and burn the juices. You can make an even better *jus* by buying a couple of chicken wings, chopping them up, and putting them in the roasting pan under the chicken.

HOW TO TRUSS A CHICKEN WITHOUT A NEEDLE

Cut a 2½-foot [76-cm] length of kitchen string. Place the chicken on a cutting board with the drumsticks facing you. Slide the middle of the string under the chicken, a couple of inches back. Grab the two ends of the string and move the left one to the right and the right one to the left, so the string is crossing over the ends of the drumsticks. Move the string from crossing on top of each drumstick end to underneath the drumstick, so the string forms an X. Pull the string to tighten it and bring the drumstick ends together. Bring the string back along the sides of the chicken and over the wings (be sure the wings are unfolded). Lift the chicken so the neck end is sticking straight up and continue turning it over until the chicken is breast-side down on the cutting board. Pull the string tight and tie the two ends together over the back. Fold the wing tips under the wings.

POULET PARANOIA: WHAT ABOUT SALMONELLA?

A properly roasted chicken is still a little pink (although not at all raw or translucent) on the inner part of the leg. Most of us overcook poultry out of fear of salmonella. This fear is well founded, since many of our chickens have been contaminated by careless handling, but our caution is often misplaced. Salmonella bacteria live on the surface and in the cavity of contaminated poultry, not within the meat. So as long as the surface of a chicken is well browned and the inside cavity has reached 145°F [62°C] (or even 140° [60°C]), there's little risk of infection. I have been criticized for cooking poultry to 140°F [60°C] between the leg and breast (the last part of any bird where the heat penetrates) and then letting the bird rest, which brings the temperature up to 145°F [62°C]. Salmonella is killed at 140°F [60°C], but the Food and Drug Administration says that poultry should be cooked to 170°F [76°C]. The choice is yours.

The biggest risk comes from mishandling the raw chicken and from stuffings. Once you get your chicken in the oven, wash your hands thoroughly and scrub any surfaces that the chicken touched, such as cutting boards, with hot water containing a splash of bleach. This prevents bacteria from being transferred to food, such as a salad, that you prepare while the chicken is roasting. I never put stuffing in the cavities of poultry because, in order to be safe, the inside of the stuffing must reach 145°F [62°C], by which time the bird itself is overcooked. If you do stuff the cavity, put the stuffing in the bird just before it goes into the oven, not ahead of time.

WHAT SIZE CHICKEN TO ROAST: I'm often tempted to roast one of those gigantic 6-pound [2.7 kg] roasting chickens if I'm cooking for a crowd or I want to have leftovers. But young chickens don't get that big naturally. The traditional method for making a giant chicken is to castrate the male and let it grow up into a 10-to-12-pound [4.5 to 5.4 kg] eunuch, a capon. Because this method is expensive, most modern capons and large roasting chickens, are given hormones to achieve a similar result. This all makes me very nervous, so I rely on "free-range" organic chickens, which I've never seen larger than 4½ pounds [2 kg]. If you get your hands on an authentic capon, roast it like a turkey (see page 358).

HOW MUCH TO SERVE: Americans who read cookbooks written in French get the impression that the French don't eat very much, because the portions seem so small. But we often forget that the French always serve a first course, which may be quite substantial and which they logically call the *entrée,* meaning, of course, entrance. French recipes say that a chicken will serve at least four, but many of the people I know (I'm not naming names) aren't satisfied with a single breast or leg and will eat one of each—unless I've served a first course such as a substantial salad or soup. The recipes I give here specify 4 servings per chicken, but if you're not serving something else first, a single chicken may be enough for only 2 servings.

MAKING A JUS OR GRAVY: A gravy and a *jus* are both made from a roast's natural drippings. The only difference is that a gravy is a *jus* that has been thickened with flour. Occasionally a *jus* is thickened with cornstarch or arrowroot and called a *jus lié,* a "bound" or thickened *jus.* A *jus* can also be thickened with cream, butter, vegetable purée (garlic, roasted in the pan with the chicken or meat, is marvelous), or foie gras (see recipe on page 355 for using garlic and foie gras together). When I roast a chicken, I rarely bother making a gravy but, instead, make a quick *jus.* There are two ways to do this. The first and most obvious is to simply pour off the juices that have accumulated in the bottom of the pan, skim off the fat, and serve. This is the best method for roast turkey, which releases a lot of flavorful liquid; but because roast chicken releases very little liquid, the roasting pan typically ends up covered with a layer of oily fat with a couple of tablespoons of juices floating under it—only enough *jus* for one or two people. If you've made a base—a *fonçage*—with vegetables or wings, much of the liquid will have been absorbed by the vegetables, so if you just strain it, you leave much of the flavor behind. Instead, deglaze the pan with a little broth or water to extract any flavor left in the *fonçage.*

Before you deglaze, there's another trick: Caramelizing the juices heightens their flavor and at the same time makes it very easy to get rid of the fat. To do this, take the chicken out of the pan and tilt it—I use the handle of a wooden spoon for this—so that any juices that have accumulated in the cavity drain into the roasting pan. Set the chicken aside and set the roasting pan on the stove on high heat. (If you've roasted in earthenware or porcelain, use a flame tamer.) Don't stir the contents of the pan at this point, but let the juices caramelize. The liquids will evaporate completely and leave a brown glaze on the vegetables and on the bottom of the pan. The fat will separate and will look like oil. Move the pan around as needed if the juices start to get too dark or if there are parts where the liquid hasn't yet caramelized and looks murky. When all the juices have caramelized—none of the liquid is murky, there's just oily fat over a brown glaze—spoon the fat out of the roasting pan or tilt the roasting pan over a strainer to let the fat run out. Put any vegetables or trimmings that may have fallen out into the strainer back into the pan. Deglaze the pan with about 1 cup of chicken broth or water. Put the pan back on the stove over high heat and scrape the bottom with a wooden spoon to dissolve the caramelized juices into the deglazing liquid. Continue boiling until all the liquid evaporates and caramelizes a second time. Deglaze again with another cup of chicken broth or water. Turn down the heat to medium and simmer the *jus* for about 3 minutes, stirring and scraping all the while to get the caramelized juices to dissolve in the broth. Strain and serve.

WHAT IS ROASTING?

Authentic roasting is done on a spit, in the open air, in front of a fire. It's different from grilling because grilling is done *over* the fire. A pan (*lèchefrite*) is placed under the spit to catch the juices released by the roast. These juices, called a *jus*, are quickly skimmed of some but not all of the fat, and then served with the roast birds or meats. Traditionally, the *jus* is passed at the table. Chicken roasted on a spit in front of an open fire is incomparable because it becomes lightly scented with wood smoke and delightfully crispy. But because for most of us spit roasting is impractical, we roast in the oven.

Oven roasting is closely related to an old-fashioned technique called *poêlage*, which involves wrapping the roast in parchment paper or caul fat containing a *matignon* and roasting it on a spit while basting with butter. A *matignon* is a mixture of chopped onions, celery, carrots, cured ham (such as prosciutto), a few sprigs of thyme, and a bay leaf that has been cooked gently in butter. When the roast is ready, the vegetables are simmered with Madeira or white wine and then stirred into the *jus* in the *lèchefrite* to add flavor. Modern *poêlage*, what we now call oven roasting, is simpler. The *matignon* is typically replaced with the same vegetables, but raw and without the meat (the meatless mixture is called a mirepoix) and spread on the roasting pan. At times, chopped-up bones or meat trimmings are added to the mixture to lend savor to the *jus* and to keep the roast from sticking to the pan. The French call this base mixture a *fonçage*. A typical French recipe, for example, might call for a *fonçage* of mirepoix and meat trimmings. To complicate matters even more, in recent times the term *poêlage* has taken on a different meaning and means simply to sauté in butter or simply to sauté.

ROAST CHICKEN

POULET RÔTI

MAKES 8 MAIN-COURSE SERVINGS

2 chickens (4 pounds [1.8 kg] each)

butter optional, for the aluminum foil

IF YOU'RE MAKING A JUS

1 pound [450 g] chicken wings (optional)

1 small carrot, chopped (optional)

1 small onion, chopped (optional)

½ stalk celery, chopped (optional)

2 cups brown chicken broth (see page 209) or water

PREHEAT the oven to 450°F [230°C/gas mark 8].

IF you wish, truss the chickens (see page 349) and make a small aluminum foil covering for the breast (see page 348). If you're making a *jus* and are using the optional ingredients to give it more flavor, chop up the wings with a cleaver or heavy chef's knife and spread the pieces, with the chicken necks and vegetables, in a heavy-bottomed roasting pan or skillet just large enough to hold the chickens. Put the chickens, breast-side up, on top of the wings and vegetables in the pan. Bake for 20 minutes, remove the aluminum foil, and bake for about 30 minutes more, until done. Transfer the chicken to a platter and let it rest for 15 minutes in a warm oven.

IF you want to make a *jus*, follow the directions on page 350.

CARVING: Roasting a chicken is easy enough, but carving can intimidate the most stalwart cook. It's worth learning, not just so you don't make a mess of the chicken, but so you can carve at the table—an elegant and satisfying ritual. I usually carve with an ordinary fork and small chef's knife and save the fancy carving set for more formal occasions. I have a favorite wooden cutting board, one with a moat

that catches the juices. In a pinch, set a regular cutting board in a sheet pan with rims—not very pretty, but it works.

If you're being really formal, put the chicken on a small heated platter to bring it out to the dining room and then, lifting with a fork held inside the cavity, move it onto the cutting board. On less exalted occasions, just bring it out on the cutting board. If you're right-handed, position the chicken with the drumsticks pointing to your left. Hold the chicken still by pressing down against the inside of the cavity with a fork. Cut through the skin separating the leg and breast and cut all the way down to the bone at the base of the thigh. Push the thigh down on the platter and away from the chicken so that the small round bone at the base of the thigh, where it joins the rest of the chicken, snaps out. Slide the knife along the side of the chicken where the thigh connects to the back, separating the leg completely from the chicken. Leave as little meat as possible attached to the back.

Cut sideways into the breast just above the wing and locate the joint where the wing connects to the body. The joint is set surprisingly deep in the chicken. Cut into the joint and detach the wing from the breast. Slide the carving knife along one side of the breastbone, as close to the bone as possible. Keep cutting, following along the side of the chicken and keeping the knife against the bone. Push the breast meat away from the bone with the back of the knife as you go. Detach the whole boneless breast. Turn the chicken around and repeat the whole process on the other side.

STUFFINGS: I never stuff chickens by filling the cavity with this mixture or that, because to get the stuffing hot you have to overcook the chicken. But I do put herbs, especially fresh tarragon, chervil, or parsley, just under the skin, between the skin and flesh. Begin by taking the stems off a small bunch of herbs and discarding the stems. With the drumsticks facing you, slide your finger underneath the chicken skin. Keep moving your finger in and about, snaking around under the skin of the leg, loosening the skin and separating it from the flesh. Don't try to separate the skin from the breastbone—where the two sides of the breast join—or the skin will tear. Push the herbs under the skin, again sliding your finger all around so both sides of the breast and the legs have herbs.

At holiday time, I use the same method to make a variation of the classic *poularde en demi-deuil* (chicken in half-mourning) by sliding slices of black truffle under the skin. The classic dish is made by poaching a specially fattened chicken called a *poularde*, but I use a regular chicken, and instead of poaching, I wrap the chicken in aluminum foil and bake it for about 1 hour. I then unwrap the chicken at the table—so everyone can smell the aroma—and serve in the same way as roast chicken, with the truffley juices that have accumulated in the foil.

ROAST CHICKEN STUFFED UNDER THE SKIN WITH SPINACH AND RICOTTA

POULET RÔTI, FARCI SOUS SA PEAU AVEC ÉPINARDS ET FROMAGE FRAIS

MAKES 4 MAIN-COURSE SERVINGS,
WITH 4 CHICKEN LEGS LEFT OVER

I first got the idea for this dish more than 20 years ago after reading Richard Olney's Simple French Food, in my opinion the best book ever written about French cooking. Olney's stuffing contains marjoram and zucchini, but this is one of those dishes where a couple of ideas and principles allow you to make up stuffings as you go along. Olney suggests splitting the chicken by cutting out the back and then splaying the chicken and sliding a surprisingly large amount of stuffing

under the skin of both breast and legs. Because this method works most dramatically on the chicken breasts (the stuffing protects the flesh from the heat while allowing the skin to get crispy) I leave the chicken as it is and put the stuffing under the breast skin only. When it comes time to serve, I carve the boneless breast with its stuffing and crispy skin. I save the legs as leftovers or for seconds. You can make the stuffing earlier the same day, but don't stuff the chicken until you're ready to roast. Because the stuffing protects the breast meat, I don't bother using the aluminum foil covering I describe in the basic recipe.

FOR THE STUFFING:

  1 small onion, chopped fine

  1 large clove garlic, chopped fine

  1 tablespoon butter or olive oil

  1 pound spinach, stemmed, leaves washed

  1 cup [245 g] ricotta

  2 teaspoons chopped fresh herbs, such as marjoram, sage, or thyme

  ¾ cup [75 g] freshly grated Parmigiano-Reggiano

  1 egg, beaten

  1 teaspoon salt

  1 teaspoon freshly ground pepper

THE CHICKENS:

  2 chickens (4 pounds [1.8 kg] each), giblets reserved

FOR THE JUS:

  1 pound [450 g] chicken wings, chopped coarse (optional)

  1 small carrot, chopped (optional)

  1 small onion, chopped (optional)

  ½ stalk celery, chopped (optional)

  2 cups [500 ml] brown chicken broth (see page 209) or water

TO MAKE THE STUFFING:

COOK the onion and garlic with the butter in a heavy-bottomed sauté pan over low to medium heat, stirring every few minutes, until the onion turns translucent, about 10 minutes.

PLUNGE the spinach in a pot of boiling water for 30 seconds, drain, rinse with cold water, and squeeze dry. Chop coarse.

COMBINE the cooked onion and garlic with the spinach, ricotta, herbs, Parmigiano-Reggiano, and egg. Season to taste with salt and pepper. (If you're worried about tasting the mixture with the raw egg in it, season before adding the egg.)

TO STUFF THE CHICKEN:

USE your forefinger to loosen (but not remove) the skin on each side of the breast, making space for the stuffing. Don't try to pull the skin away from the breastbone. Push the stuffing under the skin covering the breast, spreading it as best you can over the surface of the breast meat. If you truss the chicken (see page 349) it will look neater when it comes out of the oven, but trussing isn't essential.

TO ROAST THE CHICKEN AND PREPARE AN OPTIONAL JUS:

PREHEAT the oven to 450°F [230°C/gas mark 8].

SPREAD the chicken wings and vegetables—or just the giblets—in a heavy-bottomed roasting pan or an iron skillet just large enough to hold the chicken. Put the chicken, breast-side up, on top of the wings and vegetables or giblets. Bake for about 1 hour, until the juices in the cavity are clear and streaked with red or the temperature between the leg and the breast reaches 140°F [60°C] (see "*Poulet* Paranoia," page 349). Tilt the chicken to let any juices that have accumulated in the cavity drain into the roasting pan. Transfer the chicken to a serving platter or cutting board and keep it warm. Put the roasting pan on the stove and boil the juices until they caramelize—keep moving the pan to different positions over the heat so that the juices caramelize evenly. Tilt the roasting pan and spoon out the fat and discard it. Pour 1 cup [250 ml] of the broth or water for the *jus* into the pan and boil it over high heat to caramelize the juices a second time. Deglaze again with the rest of the broth or water and simmer gently, while stirring, for about 3 minutes. Strain the jus, pressing against the contents of the strainer to extract as much *jus* as possible.

TO SERVE:

CARVE off the legs and wings and gently remove the boneless breasts in one piece by sliding a long knife between the flesh and the breastbone, being careful not to tear the skin or dislodge the stuffing. Arrange the breasts, with their stuffing and crispy skin on top, on four hot plates and serve. Pass the *jus* at the table.

Varations: Chicken stuffings lend themselves to infinite variation. I typically start out cooking a little chopped onion and garlic in butter or olive oil. I add fresh chopped sage, marjoram, or thyme, then some vegetables (often leftovers), such as mushrooms (chopped, cooked until dry with the onion), zucchini (julienned, salted, wrung out, cooked until dry), spinach (blanched or steamed, coarsely chopped), squash purée (cooked on the stove until relatively dry and stiff, flavored with a little nutmeg and sage), Swiss chard or beet greens (blanched, chopped), sorrel (stewed until its liquid evaporates), and/or leeks (which replace the onion). After allowing the mixture to cool, I combine it with ricotta, an egg (to hold everything together), and freshly grated Parmigiano-Reggiano. If I have it, I also add ¼ cup [60 ml] or so of leftover roasting juices or stewing liquid or reduced broth such as *glace de viande*.

OTHER FINISHES FOR GRAVIES AND JUS: In the sixteenth, seventeenth, and eighteenth centuries, French cooks often added ingredients such as citrus juices and zests, vinegar, and *verjus* to roasting juices. But by the mid-nineteenth century the consensus was, as it is today, that a *jus* should contain the essence of the roast and that little if anything should be done to alter its flavor. In short, a *jus* is not a sauce in the way we usually think of one, made by building layers of flavor with aromatic ingredients, reduced broths, and thickeners, but ideally is the pure essence of roast meat or poultry. So any addition must be subtle. There are some ingredients that can enhance the intrinsic flavor of a *jus* without distorting it. Finely chopped subtly flavored herbs such as parsley, chives, chervil, and tarragon, either alone or in combination, can be simmered in the *jus* for about 30 seconds before serving. Aromatic ingredients such as wild mushrooms (whole or chopped, dried or fresh; morels or cèpes are best), or truffles (sliced, julienned, or chopped), will add their luxurious complexity without distortion.

Thickeners not only add body to the *jus* but often add a flavor of their own. Roux (flour cooked in fat, usually some of the fat from the roast) is the most popular thickener in American kitchens and converts a *jus* into a gravy. (See Roast Turkey with Giblet Gravy, page 358.) In traditional French kitchens, a *jus* is sometimes thickened with a small spoonful of cornstarch or arrowroot dissolved in a little water. While all of these starches are excellent thickeners, none contributes any flavor to the *jus*. One tasty way to give a *jus* flavor as well as body is to incorporate the bird's giblets—the liver, heart, gizzard, and occasionally the lungs (sometimes left in the cavity of squabs). American cooks typically cook the giblets and then incorporate the chopped cooked giblets and their cooking liquid into the gravy (as in the turkey gravy recipe on page 359), while French cooks are more likely to purée the giblets raw (sometimes with blood), combine the mixture with a little butter, and whisk it into the hot *jus* at the last minute without letting it boil. (For an example of this method, see Squab Salmis, page 377.) You can make a luxurious variation by whisking in foie gras, puréed with butter, and strained into the *jus* (as in Roast Chicken with Garlic and Foie Gras, at right). More recently, cooks have started using vegetable purées as thickeners for *jus* because the vegetables have a gentle flavor that won't mask the meat flavors and they add little fat and few calories. Roast garlic and caramelized onions are marvelous for this. Vegetable purées can be made ahead of time and whisked into the *jus* just before serving, or the vegetables can be used to surround the roast and be puréed at the last minute with the *jus*. The well-known *poulet rôti aux quarante gousses d'ail* (chicken with forty cloves of garlic) is an example of this method. The chicken is roasted surrounded with unpeeled garlic cloves. In informal versions, the garlic cloves are served whole, and guests squeeze out the purée-like pulp for themselves; but in formal versions, the roast garlic is puréed, strained, and whisked into the *jus*.

ROAST CHICKEN WITH GARLIC AND FOIE GRAS

POULET RÔTI À L'AIL ET AUX FOIE GRAS

MAKES 4 MAIN-COURSE SERVINGS

The first time I ate this dish, I embarrassed myself. A lady friend and I were in France at the three-star restaurant Georges Blanc, long famous for its fine chicken dishes made with the local *poulardes de Bresse*. When the chicken arrived, it was a study in understatement, just a plain roast chicken on a platter, surrounded with a pale brown sauce that looked a little like milk chocolate. When the waiter asked which piece of the chicken we would each prefer, I blurted out, "l'aile!"— the breast. Ignoring me, he turned to my friend with slow and deliberate (but again understated) disdain, and said, "Madame?" She got the breast. I was too intimidated to ask him to cut into the second side of the chicken.

But as I dug in I forgot my embarrassment. The sauce was creamy and deeply flavored, with the subtle flavor of roast garlic perfectly matching that of the foie gras without taking over. I've since experimented with this combination at home, and while it doesn't quite match Georges Blanc's (for one thing, I can't get *poulardes de Bresse*), it's one of the best chicken dishes I know. There are a couple of approaches you can take. The method used at Georges Blanc's, and the one given here, is to make a roast garlic purée and then to purée foie gras with an equal amount of butter. I use terrine of foie gras, store-bought or my own, instead of raw foie gras, because the terrine, having been cooked, contains less water and has a more concentrated flavor and silkier texture. The foie gras and garlic purées are then whisked into the jus just before serving. The exact amount of the purées depends on how much jus you have and the consistency you like. You can also make a variation of this dish by sliding thin slices of terrine of foie gras under the skin of the chicken so that the foie gras slowly bastes the chicken from the inside. (For more about stuffing under the skin, see page 352.) The only disadvantage to this method is that the flavorful fat from the foie gras ends up in the roasting pan, where it is skimmed off. Lastly, if you don't want to hunt down foie gras, purée a good-size chicken liver with the same amount of butter and use this mixture instead. Either chop the liver and butter together by hand until very fine or use a miniature food processor or a blender with a food processor attachment. Whichever method you do use, work the paste through a strainer with a wooden spoon or small ladle.

1 recipe Roast Chicken (page 352)

2 ounces [55 g] terrine of foie gras (or the chicken liver; see headnote)

2 ounces [55 g] unsalted butter

2 to 4 tablespoons Roast Garlic Purée (page 374)

salt

pepper

WHILE the chicken is roasting, purée the foie gras or chicken liver and butter by crushing them together with the side of a chef's knife. If you're using chicken livers, chop them very fine with the butter, or use a blender, and then work them through a strainer. Just before serving, whisk the foie gras or liver butter into the hot *jus*, then whisk in the garlic purée to taste. If the *jus* gets too thick, thin it with a little broth or, in a pinch, water. If the *jus* curdles, zap it with an immersion blender or quickly work it through a strainer. Season to taste with salt and pepper.

HOW TO MAKE JUS WITHOUT A ROAST

Usually a *jus* is made at the last minute, when the roast is done. This is fine if you're making roast chicken for four people, but it's a hassle if you're cooking for a crowd. In my restaurant, we used the *jus* from the roast chicken from the night before and saved the fresh *jus* for the next day, but this isn't practical at home. Cooks sometimes try to make *jus* by using a concentrated broth, but broth has a different character than a *jus* and, even when significantly reduced, a distinctly different flavor. Reduced broth has a gelatinous consistency that is disagreeable in a *jus*. It also has a kind of heaviness and lacks a certain vital freshness; next to a light and brightly flavored *jus,* it tastes flat.

If you want to make a batch of *jus* ahead of time or if you're roasting a piece of meat very rare (in which case there aren't enough drippings for a *jus*), the solution is to make a *jus* without a roast. There are two ways to do this. The first method is to make a basic brown broth from the bones and trimmings of whatever creature it is you're serving and then use this broth to deglaze a second batch of bones and trimmings that you brown in the oven with the usual aromatic vegetables.

The secret is to deglaze with only a small amount of broth—not even enough to cover—let the broth simmer with the trimmings for no more than 5 minutes while scraping the bottom of the pan with a wooden spoon, and immediately strain.

A second method is to caramelize broth repeatedly in a sauté pan with a few meat trimmings and aromatic vegetables, add more broth, and caramelize again. (Don't use canned broth for this, it's too salty.) You can repeat this process ad infinitum, your *jus* getting more syrupy and concentrated as you go.

MAKES ABOUT 2 CUPS [500 ML] CHICKEN JUS

2 pounds [900 g] chicken wings or drumsticks, hacked into small pieces with a cleaver

1 small onion, chopped coarse

1 small carrot, chopped coarse

5 cups [1.2 l] (or more if you want to caramelize more than once) homemade brown chicken broth (page 209)

SPREAD the chicken wings and vegetables in a single layer in a heavy-bottomed roasting pan or an iron skillet. Brown in a 375°F [190°C/gas mark 5] oven for about 45 minutes, or until the chicken is well browned and any liquid released caramelizes on the bottom of the pan. Put the pan on top of the stove over medium heat and pour in half the chicken broth and boil it down, changing the position of the pan on the stove every minute to avoid burning, until the broth has evaporated and formed a shiny golden glaze on the bottom of the pan. Tilt the pan and spoon out and discard any clear fat floating above the caramelized juices. Add the rest of the broth, and with the pan on the stove over medium heat scrape the bottom of the pan with a wooden spoon for about 5 minutes to dissolve the caramelized juices. (Or caramelize again, add more broth, and repeat the process to concentrate the *jus.*) Strain the *jus* into a saucepan or glass measuring pitcher and let it sit for 10 minutes. Spoon off and discard any fat that rises to the surface.

ROAST TURKEY WITH GIBLET GRAVY

DINDON RÔTI AVEC SON JUS AUX ABATS

MAKES 10 TO 15 SERVINGS, WITH LEFTOVERS

While you can still find delicious turkeys in France, turkeys are less popular now than they were during the eighteenth century, when they were all the rage—provided, of course, that they were stuffed with truffles. The turkey was one of the first foods from the New World to be embraced by the French, and during the sixteenth century it overtook the peacock as the largest bird to be served at feasts. The earliest suggestions included turkey garnished (not stuffed) with oysters and cardoons. By the seventeenth century, a number of recipes had been developed, including La Varenne's famous roast turkey stuffing with raspberries. By the eighteenth century, in addition to the opulent truffled turkey, there were recipes for turkey stews and pies.

When Thanksgiving rolls around, friends and former students call to ask me how to roast the turkey and how to make the gravy. You can roast a turkey exactly the same way as a chicken, keeping in mind the principle that the larger the roast, the lower the temperature should be. If, for example, you were to roast a large turkey in a 500°F [260°C/gas mark 10] oven, the skin would brown or even blacken before the heat penetrated all the way through and cooked the turkey meat. On the other hand, very small birds, such as quails, or birds with red meat, such as squabs and wild ducks, which need to be kept rare or medium rare, must be roasted at the highest temperature possible to get the skin to brown without overcooking the meat. In fact, because very few home ovens are hot enough to pull this off, it's best to brown these birds in a pan on top of the stove before sliding them into the oven.

Cooks often make the same mistake with turkey as they make with chicken—they overcook it. First, pull out that little pop-up thermometer that comes with most birds

these days. If you rely on it, you're guaranteed a dry turkey. Second, cover the breast meat for the first 45 minutes or so of roasting with a folded and buttered sheet of aluminum foil, as in roasting chicken (see page 348). Third, don't stuff the bird, because in order to cook the stuffing you have to overcook the turkey. Also, a stuffing will absorb the turkey juices, which is all very fine for the stuffing, but it leaves you little with which to make a gravy. If you really want a stuffing, bake it, covered with foil, in a dish next to the turkey for about 45 minutes and then moisten it with some of the turkey jus or a broth made from turkey parts. Most important, don't overcook the turkey. Most recommendations for cooking times and temperatures are frightful. I cook turkey (unstuffed) from 8 to 10 minutes per pound [450 g], to 145°F [62°C] (measured in the hollow area between the leg and breast), keeping in mind that the temperature will rise another 5°F [2° to 3°C] as the turkey rests.

When it comes to the sauce, I break from French tradition and make a giblet gravy instead of a simple unthickened jus. Because a turkey releases a relatively large amount of drippings, I don't bother to caramelize them on the stove as I do for smaller birds such as chickens. I just separate the fat by transferring all the juices to a glass measuring pitcher and then skim off the fat with a small ladle. (You can also use a degreasing cup; see page 18.) Most of the fat ends up in the trash, except for 2 or 3 tablespoons that I cook with flour to make the gravy. The giblets—the neck, gizzard, liver, and heart—get gently simmered for a couple of hours. Their cooking liquid is used, if needed, to stretch the gravy, and the chopped giblets themselves are stirred into the gravy just before serving. I buy 1½ pounds [675 g] of turkey per person (and a minimum of 15 pounds [6.8 kg]), a system that ensures there will be plenty of leftovers.

When shopping for my turkey, I always look for a free-range organic turkey that has never been frozen. Don't despair if you can't find a turkey that meets all these criteria. Do, however, avoid "butterball" turkeys, which are injected, not with butter, but with hydrogenated vegetable oil.

1   fresh turkey (15 to 20 pounds [6.8 to 9 kg], preferably free-range and organic

1   medium-size onion, peeled and sliced (for the roasting pan), plus 1 small onion, peeled and halved (for giblet broth)

1   small bouquet garni

3 cups [750 ml] brown chicken broth (see page 209) or turkey broth made in the same way using separately purchased turkey drumsticks (optional)

2 pounds [900 g] turkey or chicken parts, if you're not including giblets in your gravy

3 to 8 tablespoons flour (depending on how much gravy you want)

    salt

    pepper

TAKE the giblets and neck out of the turkey and reserve them. They may be hiding in the cavity or in the neck end, which is covered with a flap of skin. (If you don't like giblets in your gravy, spread them on the bottom of the roasting pan with the onion to contribute flavor to the *jus*.) Tie the ends of the drumsticks together with a piece of kitchen string to help the turkey hold its shape. Spread the sliced onion on the bottom of a heavy-bottomed roasting pan (to prevent the turkey from sticking) and set the turkey on top. Make sure the turkey isn't touching the sides of the pan, or the skin could tear when you take the turkey out of the pan. Cover the breast with a buttered triple-thick sheet of aluminum foil, buttered-side down, and slide the turkey into a 350°F [175°/gas mark 5] oven. Remove the aluminum foil after about 45 minutes to allow the breast skin to brown. Check the bottom of the pan from time to time to make sure the juices aren't burning. If they start looking too dark, pour in 1 cup of broth or water.

PUT the halved onion and the bouquet garni in a small pot with the giblets and neck or, if you've put the giblets under the turkey, 2 pounds [900 g] of turkey or chicken parts. Pour over enough water or broth to barely cover (not the broth called for in the recipe ingredients, which is for making the *jus*). Bring to a gentle simmer. Simmer for 2 hours, skimming off fat and froth that floats to the surface.

AFTER roasting the turkey for an amount of time based on 8 minutes per pound [450 g], insert an instant-read thermometer through the skin that stretches between the breast and leg, almost all the way down to the joint but not touching it. When the thermometer reads 145°F [62°C] (see "*Poulet* Paranoia," page 349), take the turkey out of the oven and transfer it to a platter. To do this, put a heavy wooden spoon or barbecue fork inside the cavity and lift the turkey straight up while using your other hand, covered with a kitchen towel, to hold and stabilize the turkey. If you can manage it, tilt the turkey over the roasting pan so that any juices that have accumulated in the cavity run out into the pan. Cover the turkey loosely with aluminum foil and keep it in a warm place for 30 minutes while you're making the gravy.

TO MAKE GIBLET OR PLAIN GRAVY:

SCRAPE the bottom of the roasting pan with a wooden spoon to loosen any coagulated drippings. Strain the juices from the pan into a glass measuring pitcher or a degreasing cup. If you're using a pitcher, skim the fat off the juices with a ladle and reserve the amount of fat you need for making the roux (see chart, page 360).

STRAIN the giblet or turkey broth and reserve the liquid. If you're using the giblets, peel as much meat as you can off the neck and discard the neck bone. With a chef's knife, chop the neck meat and giblets to the consistency of hamburger relish and reserve.

DECIDE how much gravy you need (make at least enough to use all the juices but not too much or you'll dilute its flavor) and put the appropriate amount of turkey fat and flour (see chart) back in the roasting pan. Put the roasting pan on the stove over medium heat and cook the flour-and-fat mixture—the roux—for about 2 minutes, until it forms a smooth paste and smells toasty. Pour in the degreased pan juices and, if necessary to make the amount of gravy you need, some or all of the giblet or turkey broth. Simmer the gravy for about 2 minutes in the pan while whisking to thicken it. If at this point the gravy has unsightly pieces of coagulated pan drippings, you may want to strain it. If you're making giblet gravy, stir in the giblets. Season to taste with salt and pepper.

TO BASTE OR NOT TO BASTE?

I rarely bother basting birds, because the fat contained in the skin bastes them automatically and I've found that basting makes only a slight difference—the skin of basted birds is softer and shinier, while the skin of unbasted birds is crispier. Basting also means that you have to keep opening the oven door, and this causes the temperature to drop and may interfere with browning, especially for smaller birds that require very high heat. Though some recipes suggest basting with liquids such as broth, wine, or the liquid (not the fat) in the roasting pan, basting with these causes the surface of a chicken or other bird to glaze rather than get crispy. Because authentic roasting requires the driest possible heat, whereas basting with liquid actually turns the roast into a kind of braise, purists insist that roasts be basted only with fat.

SERVINGS OF GRAVY PER PERSON AND AMOUNTS OF FAT, FLOUR, AND LIQUID NEEDED

Figure about ⅓ cup [75 ml] of gravy per person for a turkey dinner. (This is more than for other meals, because people tend to eat more at turkey dinners.) Decide how many servings you need and then use the amounts given here. Keep in mind that the less giblet liquid you need to add to stretch the juices, the tastier your gravy will be. I usually make only enough gravy for the first day, so there's none left over.

Servings	Fat	Flour	Liquid
6	2 tablespoons	3 tablespoons	2 cups [500 ml]
8	2½ tablespoons	4 tablespoons	2½ cups [625 ml]
10	3 tablespoons	5 tablespoons	3½ cups [875 ml]
12	4 tablespoons	6 tablespoons	4 cups [1 l]
14	4½ tablespoons	7 tablespoons	4¼ cups [1.1 l]
16	5 tablespoons	7½ tablespoons	5½ cups [1.3 l]

CASSEROLE ROAST CHICKEN

POULET EN COCOTTE

MAKES 4 MAIN-COURSE SERVINGS

In some parts of France, until the 1950s, many households didn't have ovens or even stoves and had to do all their cooking in the hearth. A chicken roasted on a spit in front of a blazing fire is a delicious thing, but it requires a blazing fire for at least an hour. This not only burns up a lot of wood, but in the summer months can make the house intolerably hot. The method of cooking food covered in a casserole made it possible to use the coals in the hearth —and nowadays the oven—to cook the bird and its garniture all at one time. The bird absorbs the aromas of the garniture and the garniture cooks in the chicken's juices.

Two recipes for *poulet en cocotte* are most common: *poulet en cocotte grand-mère*, made with cubes of unsmoked bacon (pancetta makes a good substitute), small or turned potatoes, and pearl onions; and *poulet en cocotte à la fermière*, made with carrots, onions, and celery, all gently cooked in butter, and string beans, added to the casserole along with the chicken. Typically, a little broth is added to the casserole to help steam the vegetables. I never follow either of these recipes exactly, but I use the cocotte method to make an easy and surprisingly elegant one-pot meal.

Your chicken will be easier to manage if you truss it (see page 349). Select a heat-proof lidded casserole just large enough to hold the chicken without the chicken touching the sides. An oval shape is best for birds. I use an enameled iron casserole, but earthenware, copper, or porcelain will also work.

¼ pound [115 g] pancetta, or 2 tablespoons butter

1 pound [450 g] wild mushrooms, such as cèpes (cut into ½-inch [1.5-cm]-thick slices) or morels (left whole if small; halved lengthwise if large), or cultivated mushrooms, preferably cremini (cut vertically in quarters, or left whole if small)

salt

pepper

1 chicken (4 pounds [1.8 kg])

4 new potatoes, scrubbed or peeled, or 2 medium-size waxy potatoes, peeled, cut into sections, and turned (see page 21) (about 1 pound [450 g] total)

4 baby carrots, peeled, or 1 large carrot, peeled, halved, cored, and cut into 1-inch [2.5-cm] sections (see page 21)

4 baby radishes, left whole, or 1 medium-size turnip, peeled and cut into 8 wedges

2 tablespoons chicken broth or water

PREHEAT the oven to 425°F [220°C/gas mark 7]. Cut the pancetta into ¼- to ½-inch [.5- to 1.5-cm] cubes and cook them gently in the casserole you'll be using to roast the chicken, until they render their fat and barely begin to crisp. (If the casserole is earthenware or porcelain, use a flame tamer.) Use a slotted spoon to transfer the pancetta to a small bowl, leaving the fat in the pan. Sauté the mushrooms in the rendered fat or the butter over high heat until they are well browned and any liquid they release evaporates. Season the mushrooms with salt and pepper and spread them evenly over the bottom of the casserole.

TRUSS the chicken, sprinkle it with salt and pepper, and place it on top of the mushrooms. Arrange the vegetables around the chicken and slide the dish, uncovered, into the oven. Roast the chicken for 40 minutes or until it is well browned. Spoon the broth or water over the chicken, put on the cover, and bake for 20 minutes more. Check for doneness by pricking a leg, near the joint between the thigh and the drumstick. When the juices run clear, the chicken is done. If the chicken is done but the vegetables aren't, take the chicken out of the casserole, cover, and bake until the vegetables are easily penetrated with a skewer. Remove the lid and put the chicken back in. Bring the whole casserole to the table and carve the chicken in the same way as roast chicken—transfer it to a cutting board by lifting it with a wooden spoon held inside the cavity. Surround each serving with vegetables and top with any juices left in the casserole.

ROOSTER IN RED WINE SAUCE

COQ AU VIN

THE DIFFERENCE	HOW TO	WHAT IS	HOW TO	HOW TO
BETWEEN LONG AND SHORT BRAISING	IMPROVISE YOUR OWN BRAISED CHICKEN DISHES	A FRICASSEE AND HOW DOES IT DIFFER FROM A SAUTÉ?	MAKE AND USE VEGETABLE PURÉES TO FINISH SAUCES	COOK A SQUAB

COQ AU VIN, ONCE A STANDBY DISH IN FRENCH RESTAURANTS IN THE United States, is making a comeback after years of neglect by chefs busy with nouvelle cuisine, California cuisine, fusion this and Mediterranean that. In truth, rarely are these dishes authentic *coq au vin,* made with a rooster, but are instead plates of chicken in red wine sauce, the more modest *poulet au vin rouge.* This isn't entirely a bad thing, but for a cook it's useful to understand the difference, because not only are these dishes made with different sorts of birds, they are made using different techniques.

Few of us are likely to encounter a rooster anymore—even in France they are seldom sold—and it's a rare cook who seeks one out in an effort to make the authentic dish. In fact, *coq au vin* was probably invented as a way of using an old bird that any other method would have made tough and stringy. Only long, slow stewing, for 2 or 3 hours, in something acidic such as red wine or vinegar, softens up an old rooster, and even this treatment leaves the breast meat dry. If you do somehow get your hands on a real rooster, you can solve the breast problem with thorough larding (see page 423) or by braising just the legs, which stay moist—in which case you'll need more than one rooster and you'll need to use the breasts for soup or broth.

A traditional *coq au vin* is finished with the rooster's blood, saved in a jar with a little Cognac and vinegar to keep the blood from clotting. The blood is added to the stewing liquid at the end to thicken it and give it the dark, muddy color that aficionados have learned to recognize and love.

Chicken with Red Wine Sauce (*poulet au vin rouge*) is a sensible alternative to a traditional *coq au vin* because you can use regular chickens, which need only be cooked long enough for the heat to penetrate all the way through. You can prepare the dish as a sauté (*poulet sauté au vin rouge*), by cooking the chicken in butter (or the traditional rendered fat from unsmoked bacon) in a pan until completely done, transferring the chicken to a serving dish to keep warm, pouring the fat out of the pan before deglazing the pan with red wine and broth, and finally thickening the sauce with beurre manié, plain butter, or a purée of roast garlic, onions, or foie gras. The finished sauce is poured over the chicken immediately before serving. You can also cook the bird in a kind of fricassée, by lightly browning it and then simmering it very gently in red wine.

I often throw together a delicious *poulet sauté au vin rouge* in about 45 minutes by skipping the marinade used for a classic *coq au vin,* by leaving the bacon and pearl onions out of the Burgundian garniture (*de rigueur* for an authentic version), and by deglazing the pan used to sauté the chicken (which I keep warm in a serving dish) with red wine and, if I have it, a chunk of store-bought demi-glace or *glace de viande* (see Sources). I simmer a couple of handfuls of button mushrooms in the sauce for 5 minutes, reduce the sauce until it has the consistency I like, and I'm done. If you don't have demi-glace or *glace de viande,* which give body to the sauce and thicken it, use a little broth and thicken the sauce at the end with some beurre manié, or reduce the sauce even more and whisk in whole butter (a technique called *monter au beurre;* see page 20).

While my simple *poulet sauté au vin rouge* has a very low work-to-deliciousness ratio, it has certain weaknesses. The chicken lacks the depth of flavor of an authentic *coq au vin,* and because the wine has had so little time to cook, the sauce may have a slightly aggressive raw-wine quality. To avoid this problem, the wine must be cooked and reduced before it is simmered with the chicken. You can just boil down a couple of bottles of wine by half (with a few aromatic vegetables and a bouquet garni) to add body to the sauce, but this will concentrate the wine's acids and tannins and give your sauce a rough, sharp flavor. The secret to a stunning sauce, rivaling any I've tasted, is to make a red wine brown chicken broth by browning chicken parts in the oven, deglazing with red wine, and then simmering for 2 hours. By the time this broth is used for cooking the chicken (or deglazing the pan), it already has a full, deep flavor. Another trick, and one often used in an authentic *coq au vin,* is to purée chicken livers with butter and whisk the mixture into the sauce just before serving. Other obvious refinements can be added to the dish at the end. They include wild mushrooms instead of cultivated ones (cèpes, sautéed separately, are fantastic) and assorted glazed root vegetables or blanched green vegetables (neither of these is traditional, but who cares—they look and taste marvelous).

HOW TO GET CHICKEN LEGS AND BREASTS
TO BE DONE AT THE SAME TIME AND HOW TO KNOW
WHEN SAUTÉED CHICKEN IS DONE

Depending on how you or your butcher cut up your chicken, the legs and breasts will cook differently. The legs usually take longer. To get them to cook in the same time as the breast, and to make them easier to eat, take the bone out of the thigh, leaving the bone in the drumstick. This is easy to do. Put the leg on a cutting board, flesh-side up (skin against the cutting board), and run a paring knife along the top and sides of the thigh bone. Continue cutting and scraping around and under the bone until you come to the joint where it connects to the drumstick bone. Twist the thigh bone around, cut through the joint, and remove the bone.

To judge when sautéed chicken is done, poke it with your finger. Raw chicken, which feels fleshy, like an unflexed muscle, will gradually firm up as it cooks. As soon as the fleshy feeling goes away completely, and the chicken feels firm to the touch, take the chicken off the heat. Most people overcook chicken, and as a result the chicken is dry. Don't be frightened if there is some red coloration on the inside of the thighs when you cut into them; this does not mean they are undercooked. If, however, they are pink *and* have a translucent sheen, put them back in the pan or zap them for a few seconds in the microwave.

CHICKEN WITH RED WINE SAUCE SIMPLEST METHOD

POULET AU VIN ROUGE

2 chickens (4 pounds [1.8 kg] each), quartered (see instructions on page 17)

   salt

   pepper

2 tablespoons butter (for sautéeing the chicken; see additional butter listed below)

2 large shallots or 1 medium-size onion, chopped fine

2 cups [500 ml] full-bodied dry red wine

2 tablespoons demi-glace or glace de viande, or 1 cup [250 ml] chicken broth (see page 363) (optional)

¾ pound [335 g] small cremini mushrooms or regular white cultivated mushrooms or larger mushrooms, or 1 package (10 ounces [280 g]) mushrooms, quartered from top to bottom

1 tablespoon finely chopped parsley

1 tablespoon flour worked to a paste with 1 tablespoon softened butter (beurre manié) (optional; not needed if you're using demi-glace) or 4 tablespoons unsalted butter (if you're not using the beurre manié; optional)

1 teaspoon red wine vinegar or more to taste

1 tablespoon Cognac (optional)

REMOVE the thigh bone from the chicken legs (see page 364) so the thigh cooks in the same time as the breast. Season the chicken parts with salt and pepper and cook them, skin-side down first, in 2 tablespoons of butter in a heavy skillet or sauté pan over medium to high heat until the skin turns crispy, about 12 minutes. As soon as you put the chicken in the pan, jerk the handle back and forth in a clockwise and then counterclockwise direction for about 1 minute to prevent the chicken from sticking. Turn the pieces over and cook them for about 10 minutes on the flesh side. (You'll need a 14-inch [35.5-cm] sauté pan to fit all the chicken pieces. If you don't have a pan this big, sauté in batches or use two pans. A nonstick pan will help to ensure that the chicken doesn't stick. If, despite all efforts, the skin sticks when you try to turn the pieces, let the skin brown a few minutes longer—it will often loosen itself.) When the chicken bounces back to the touch and no longer feels fleshy, transfer it to a plate and keep it warm. (If you can't judge doneness by touch, just cut into a piece somewhere discreet.) Pour the fat out of the pan and discard it.

STIR the shallots in the still-hot pan until they smell fragrant, about 1 minute. Add the red wine, the demi-glace or broth, and the mushrooms, and boil down over high heat until only about 1 cup [250 ml] of sauce is left. If the sauce has the consistency you like (I like the texture of hot real maple syrup), stir in the parsley, whisk in the optional butter, adjust the salt and pepper, vinegar and Cognac, and spoon the sauce and mushrooms over the chicken on plates or on a platter. If the sauce seems too thin (it will be thinner if you've used broth instead of demi-glace, which contains flour), you have two choices. You can whisk the beurre manié, a bit at a time, into the simmering sauce until the sauce has the right thickness, or you can reduce the sauce down even more—to about ½ cup—and then whisk in the plain butter. Add the parsley, vinegar, and Cognac; adjust the seasoning, and serve.

CHICKEN WITH RED WINE SAUCE BEST, ALBEIT MORE COMPLICATED METHOD

MAKES 8 MAIN-COURSE SERVINGS

Because the chicken in this dish is simmered only long enough to cook through (to an internal temperature of about 140°F [60°C]; see "Poulet Paranoia," page 349), a raw marinade will impart an unpleasant taste of alcohol to the flesh that short cooking won't eliminate. While it's not essential, it is best to cook the wine and aromatic vegetables long enough to cook the alcohol out of the wine before using the mixture to marinate the chicken.

THE CHICKENS:

- 2 chickens (4 pounds [1.8 kg] each), quartered, livers reserved

FOR THE MARINADE:

- 1 cup [250 ml] full-bodied red wine (see page 10 for information about cooking wines)
- 1 clove garlic, crushed
- 1 onion, sliced thin
- 1 carrot, peeled and sliced thin
- 1 bay leaf
- 3 sprigs thyme

LIVER MIXTURE (OPTIONAL) FOR FINISHING THE SAUCE:

- 2 reserved livers from the chickens
- 4 tablespoons unsalted butter
- 1 tablespoon Cognac (optional)
- 2 tablespoons finely chopped parsley

FOR COOKING:

- salt
- pepper
- 3 tablespoons butter
- 3 cups [750 ml] red wine chicken broth made by substituting red wine for the water in the brown chicken broth recipe on page 209

FOR THE GARNITURE:

- 1 pint [335 g] pearl onions, peeled
- ½ pound [225 g] small cremini mushrooms or regular white cultivated mushrooms or larger mushrooms, quartered
- 5 pound [225 g] bacon, preferably slab, cut into about 1-by-4-inch [2.5 by .5 cm] strips (lardons), gently cooked in a sauté pan until barely crisp, about 8 minutes, and drained on a paper towel
- 1 teaspoon red wine vinegar or more to taste

CUT the little stub off the end of the chicken legs with heavy kitchen shears or a cleaver. Pull out any bone that may splinter. Remove the thigh bone by cutting around it, starting from the flesh side of the thigh, and then cutting through the joint where it joins the drumstick bone. Don't remove the drumstick bone.

COMBINE the marinade ingredients in a small pot, bring to a simmer, simmer for 2 minutes, and let cool. Chill the mixture in the refrigerator or by setting the pan in a bowl of ice. It must be cool before you combine it with the chicken or it can cause the chicken to sour.

TOSS the chicken parts in a bowl with the marinade, cover with plastic wrap, and let marinate in the refrigerator for 4 to 6 hours or overnight. Turn the chicken around in the bowl a couple of times during the marinating. Don't be concerned that the marinade doesn't completely cover the chicken.

TAKE the chicken out of the marinade and wipe it dry with paper towels. Strain the marinade, reserving the wine and discarding the herbs and vegetables.

PREPARE the optional liver mixture by finely chopping the livers with the butter by hand or in a miniature food processor and then stirring in the Cognac and parsley. Work through a strainer with a wooden spoon and refrigerate.

SEASON the chicken with salt and pepper and lightly brown it, for about 5 minutes on each side, in 3 tablespoons of butter. While the chicken is cooking, cook the pearl onions for about 10 minutes (this won't cook them completely) in a small covered pot, with ½ cup [125 ml] of the red wine chicken broth. Transfer the chicken to a plate, discard the fat in the pan, and pour in the reserved wine from the marinade. Reduce the wine over high heat until it evaporates completely. Put the chicken back in the pan. Pour the mushrooms, the onions with their cooking liquid, and the red wine chicken broth over the chicken, and cover the pan. Cook on low heat until the chicken parts feel firm to the touch (see page 364), about 15 minutes.

ARRANGE the chicken pieces on plates or on a platter. If the sauce in the pan seems runny, reduce it slightly by simmering it until it takes on a lightly syrupy consistency. Whisk the liver mixture into the sauce in the pan—don't let the sauce boil at this point—and stir in the bacon strips to reheat them. Season the sauce to taste with vinegar, salt, and pepper, and spoon it, and the garniture, over the chicken.

AUTHENTIC COQ AU VIN

Now that you know how to simulate an authentic *coq au vin* using a chicken instead of a rooster, what if you do happen upon a big rooster? Unlike chicken, which we cook just long enough to heat it through—to about 140°F [60°C]—an old rooster takes long gentle simmering, about 3 hours, to tenderize it. Authentic long-braised dishes take prolonged cooking to higher temperatures—around 180°F [82°C] to soften the meats and release their flavor. This is a great way to cook if you're stewing meats that contain a certain amount of fat, which keeps the meat moist; but if you're braising something lean, such as a rooster, you have to insert strips of fat into the breasts and thighs to keep them moist and then submerge the rooster completely in red wine and simmer it very gently. When the braising is done, you have only to reduce the braising liquid until it has the consistency you like. (Keep the rooster covered and hot; you don't have to worry about overcooking as you would with a chicken.) Traditionalists thicken the braising liquid with beurre manié and the rooster's blood, saved in a jar with 1 teaspoon of Cognac to keep it from clotting. Just before serving, the reduced braising liquid is whisked into the blood—not the other way around—and never allowed to boil. Because I rarely get my hands on the blood, I resort to a little beurre manié or, in a richer interpretation, to butter alone after drastically reducing the braising liquid to about 1 cup for 6 servings.

IMPROVISING SAUTÉED CHICKEN DISHES

The method of sautéing a cut-up chicken and then immediately deglazing the pan to make a quick sauce is so versatile, and lends itself so well to improvisation, that it's worth understanding how to do it so you can make up your own dishes with different ingredients. First, cook the chicken completely in fat on medium to high heat so the skin turns crispy. You can use butter, oil, or a rendered fat such as lard, duck fat, or goose fat. Don't worry about the fat, it's not included in the dish and only helps flavor the chicken; in fact, it helps render the fat *out* of the chicken skin. Use a heavy-bottomed sauté pan that holds the chicken in a single layer with no leftover space. Chicken juices burn on empty spaces in the pan, which get too hot. If the pan has places that aren't covered, add pieces of the back or neck, parts that you might otherwise throw out or reserve for broth. For a single chicken, a 10-inch or 12-inch [25.5- or 30.5-cm] pan is usually the right size. I often use nonstick pans so that I don't risk tearing the skin, but otherwise I use pans that are silvery rather than black on the inside so that I can see the condition of the juices. If the caramelized juices burn in a black pan, you won't see them, and if you go ahead and deglaze, your sauce will be bitter.

When the chicken is completely cooked, transfer it to a plate and keep it warm in a low oven while making the sauce in the sauté pan. Pour out and discard the cooked fat. If you're cooking solid ingredients, such as chopped shallots, in the pan before deglazing with liquid, you may want to leave 1 or 2 teaspoons of the fat in the pan. If the fat, however, looks or smells burnt, pour it all out. Inspect the caramelized juices on the bottom of the pan. If they look black, rinse the pan with water and wipe it out with a paper towel before adding a little fresh fat and any other ingredients.

First add solid ingredients, such as shallots or finely chopped mirepoix, to the fat in the pan and stir them over medium heat for 5 to 10 minutes until they release their aroma. If you're using wine (you can use wine from the marinade), add it to the pan next and boil it for 1 minute to cook off its alcohol.

If you're using broth, reduced broth, demi-glace, or *glace de viande*, whisk it into the pan and adjust the consistency of the sauce by reducing (to thicken) or by adding liquid, such as water or a lighter broth (to thin). You can thicken the sauce with beurre manié, cornstarch dissolved in cold water (called a slurry), or heavy cream and then reduce it, or you can whisk butter or flavored butters (see page 489) into the sauce to give it a silky texture and a rich flavor. Final flavorings, such as chopped herbs, or spirits, such as marc or Cognac, should be added near the very end, with the sauce only brought to a quick boil to infuse the flavor of the herbs or cook the alcohol out of the spirits. Garnitures can be added at different stages, depending on whether they are raw or cooked. Mushrooms, for example, are either sautéed in a separate pan or sautéed directly in the pan used to sauté the chicken. Or they can be added raw, at the same time as the broth, so they are cooked right in the sauce. More complicated garnitures, such as assortments of glazed root vegetables, are best cooked separately and added to the sauce or spooned over the chicken at the end.

Cooking fat (for browning the chicken)

BUTTER

OLIVE OIL

RENDERED PORK FAT (from pancetta, prosciutto, or bacon)

RENDERED DUCK FAT

RENDERED GOOSE FAT

Solid Aromatic Ingredients for Deglazing the Pan

FINELY CHOPPED SHALLOTS, ONIONS, OR LEEKS

FINELY CHOPPED MIREPOIX (onions, carrots, and celery, and sometimes prosciutto)

FINELY CHOPPED GARLIC

Liquid or Semiliquid Aromatic Ingredients for Deglazing the Pan

DRY WHITE OR RED WINE

FORTIFIED WINES, SUCH AS PORT, MADEIRA, MALAGA, MARSALA, AND SHERRY

TOMATOES (peeled, seeded, and chopped if you want them chunky, just chopped and the sauce strained if the final sauce is to be smooth)

SHELLFISH COOKING LIQUIDS (see Chicken with Crayfish, page 341)

Broths and Reduced Broths for Giving Body to the Sauce

GLACE DE VIANDE (meat glaze; see page 221)

DEMI-GLACE (see page 3)

REDUCED BROTH (see page 4)

PLAIN WHITE OR BROWN BROTH (see page 209)

RED WINE BROTH (see page 363)

Thickeners and Enricheners

BEURRE MANIÉ (butter worked to a paste with flour; see page 436)

CORNSTARCH (dissolved into a slurry in an equal amount of cold water, see page 444)

HEAVY CREAM (reduced after adding, to increase thickness)

BUTTER (plain, herb, puréed with livers—see Squab Salmi, page 377—or puréed with the same amount of foie gras, see page 491)

CRUSTACEAN BUTTER; CRUSTACEAN ROE

VEGETABLE PURÉES, SUCH AS GARLIC, POTATO, SORREL, ONION, AND REDUCED TOMATO SAUCE (see pages 373 to 375)

Final Flavorings

HERBS (finely chopped parsley, chervil, and others)

SPIRITS (Cognac, marc, eaux de vie such as kirsch, whiskey)

WINE VINEGAR

Garnitures

LIMITLESS (see "Some Classic Chicken Sautés," page 370, for ideas)

○

"WHITE" CHICKEN SAUTÉS

Some classic chicken sauté recipes, designed to produce a very pale white sauce, insist that the chicken be thoroughly cooked without browning—that it be sautéed *à blanc*. To do this, cook the chicken in butter over lower heat just long enough to cook the outer surface lightly. Finish the chicken by covering the pan and baking in a 350°F [175°C/gas mark 4] oven.

Though many of the classic French chicken sautés were developed in the nineteenth century and are overly elaborate for today's tastes, they are good sources of inspiration and are easy to simplify. Here are a few examples, taken from Escoffier's *Guide Culinaire*.

POULET SAUTÉ ALGÉRIENNE: Sauté the chicken in butter, deglaze the pan with white wine, add finely chopped garlic and 1 or 2 peeled and seeded tomatoes, and reduce to the consistency you like. Traditionally served with chayote (*christophene*) and sweet potatoes that have been shaped like olives and cooked in butter.

POULET SAUTÉ ARCHIDUC: Gently sweat a sliced large onion in butter in the pan used first to sauté the chicken. Add Cognac and cream and reduce the sauce to the consistency you like. Finish with a little Madeira and lemon juice.

POULET SAUTÉ BERCY: Sauté the chicken in butter, pour out and discard all but 1 teaspoon of fat, sauté some chopped shallots, and deglaze the pan. Add white wine and reduce. Add concentrated veal broth (or demi-glace or *glace de viande*) and finish with sautéed mushrooms. Traditionally served with cooked sausages, but this seems a bit much.

POULET SAUTÉ À LA BRETONNE: Sauté the chicken *à blanc* (see page 369). Gently sweat chopped leeks in butter and sauté sliced mushrooms in butter while the chicken is cooking. Pour heavy cream over the combined cooked vegetables, reduce this mixture to the consistency you like, and pour it over the chicken.

POULET SAUTÉ AUX CÈPES: Sauté the chicken in butter or olive oil. Pour out and discard all but 1 teaspoon of fat. Sauté some chopped shallots and then deglaze the pan with white wine. Reduce the sauce to about half, and finish it with butter. Spoon

thickly sliced cèpes (porcini), sautéed with shallots, over and around the chicken.

POULET SAUTÉ CHASSEUR: Sauté the chicken in butter. Sauté mushrooms with chopped shallots in the pan used for sautéing the chicken. Add white wine and Cognac, reduce, add concentrated chicken or veal broth (or demi-glace or *glace de viande*), and reduce to the consistency you like. Finish with chopped tarragon and a little butter.

POULET AU CURRY: Cook curry powder in a small amount of fat in the pan used to sauté the chicken. Stir in unsweetened coconut milk and reduce. I like to add chopped cilantro at the end—more typical of Indian cooking than of French.

POULET SAUTÉ À L'ESTRAGON: Sauté the chicken in butter, deglaze the pan with white wine and reduced veal broth, and finish with chopped tarragon.

POULET SAUTÉ AUX FINES HERBES: Sauté the chicken in butter. Deglaze the pan with white wine and concentrated veal broth and reduce. Finish the sauce with chopped chervil, parsley, tarragon, and chives.

POULET SAUTÉ À LA HONGROISE: Sauté the chicken in butter. Brown chopped onion and a pinch of paprika in the pan used for sautéing the chicken. Add peeled, seeded, chopped tomatoes and cream. Reduce the sauce and pour it over the chicken.

POULET SAUTÉ MARENGO: Sauté the chicken in olive oil. Take out the chicken, keep it warm, discard the fat in the pan, and deglaze the pan with white wine, chopped tomatoes, cooked button mushrooms, and crushed garlic. Traditionally, *poulet marengo* is garnished with croutons, crayfish, and fried eggs.

POULET SAUTÉ À LA NORMANDE: Sauté the chicken in butter. Deglaze the pan with hard cider. Garnish with apple slices gently cooked in butter. Finish the sauce with cream and a little Calvados (apple brandy).

POULET SAUTÉ PARMENTIER: Sauté the chicken in butter. Deglaze the pan with white wine and veal broth. Garnish with potatoes "turned" into small egg shapes (or use little new potatoes) and cooked in butter.

POULET SAUTÉ SAINT-LAMBERT: Sauté the chicken in butter. Deglaze the pan with white wine and mushroom cooking liquid. Thicken the sauce with a cooked purée of carrots, turnips, onion, and mushrooms.

POULET SAUTÉ À LA VICHY: Sauté the chicken in butter. Deglaze the pan with veal broth. Garnish with glazed turned carrots.

Chicken Fricassees

FRICASSÉES DE POULET

THE FRENCH USE THREE BASIC METHODS for cooking cut-up chickens. They stew old hens and roosters for 2 or 3 hours in the same way as tough cuts of beef, lamb, or veal. An authentic *coq au vin* is an example of this method. They cook more tender chickens either as sautés or as fricassees. In a sauté, the chicken is completely cooked in a small amount of fat and comes into contact with liquid—the sauce—only at the very end. In a fricassee, the chicken parts are first lightly cooked in fat, usually butter, and in traditional recipes are sprinkled with flour while still in the pan. Then liquid, usually broth, is poured over the chicken parts and the parts are gently simmered until just cooked through, usually in 15 to 20 minutes. The method for making a fricassee is almost identical to that used for making a blanquette (See Chapter 30), except that the poaching liquid for a traditional blanquette is thickened *after* the meat is cooked—by being whisked into a roux—whereas the flour in a fricassee is sprinkled over or used to coat the chicken or meat at the beginning. The results of these techniques are similar but they produce subtle differences in flavor and texture.

The best known of all fricassees is *fricassee de poulet à l'ancienne,* made by lightly cooking chicken in butter, sprinkling the chicken with flour while it's still in the pan, adding broth, and gently simmering the chicken. When the chicken is done, the cooking liquid, now a chicken velouté, is gently heated, without boiling, with a mixture of heavy cream and, traditionally, egg yolks. The finished dish is garnished with pearl onions and little mushrooms. I leave out the egg yolks because they make the fricassee richer than necessary and they make it easy to curdle the sauce, especially when I'm rushing around before a dinner party.

As with so many basic French cooking methods, the beauty of a fricassee is its adaptability. You can really make it with any ingredients you wish, including the same ones you might use to make a chicken sauté (see chart, pages 368-369).

Since sautés and fricassees can be made with identical ingredients, why make one instead of the other? In fact, the results of cooking up a chicken as a fricassee and as a sauté are so similar that it doesn't matter too much which approach you use. I've gotten into the habit of making sauté because I like chicken skin brown and crispy and I think that the caramelized juices on the bottom of the sauté pan make a more savory sauce. But for subtly flavored dishes that call for delicate and expensive ingredients such as wild mushrooms or truffles, or for dishes that I want to have a perfectly white sauce, I prefer the paler and more subtly flavored fricassee. Because a fricassee allows the flavors of the sauce to work their way into the chicken in a way that a sauté does not, I fricassee a chicken if I have a particularly rich and delicious broth to use for the simmering.

CHICKEN FRICASSEE WITH DRIED CÈPES

FRICASSÉE DE POULET AUX CÈPES SECS

MAKES 4 MAIN-COURSE SERVINGS

If I have fresh cèpes, I prepare this dish as a sauté. I sauté the chicken and mushrooms separately (I sprinkle the mushrooms with a persillade of finely chopped parsley and crushed garlic). Then I spoon the mushrooms over the sautéed chicken just before serving. In this way, the mushrooms don't loose their meaty texture by being simmered in a sauce, as they would in a fricassee.

Unfortunately, fresh cèpes are a luxury most of us don't run into very often. It makes good sense to keep a bag of dried cèpes (usually sold as porcini) on hand for use as quick, easy, and luxurious flavoring for last-minute pasta sauces or improvised pan-deglazed sauces for chicken or veal. And while dried cèpes aren't cheap, I find that a tiny little handful gives the simplest dish such depth of savor and complexity of flavor that guests wonder what magical thing I did to the sauce.

Be careful when buying dried cèpes. Those of the best quality are thickly sliced and large, while those of lesser quality look like little broken-up pieces of wood. But most important is aroma. If the mushrooms are reasonably aromatic and fresh, you'll be able to smell them right through the bag. Buy as many as you can afford—they get cheaper when you buy them in amounts approaching a pound [450 g]—and keep them in the refrigerator or even in the freezer. The best cèpes I've encountered are from Italy. Cèpes from Chile are less flavorful but correspondingly less expensive.

1 ounce (about 1 cup loosely packed) [35 g], dried cèpes (porcini)

¼ cup [60 ml] semidry Madeira or semidry sherry such as oloroso (optional)

1 chicken (4 pounds [1.8 kg]), quartered

   salt

   pepper

2 tablespoons butter

2 tablespoons flour

2 cups [500 ml] white chicken or veal broth
(see pages 210 and 217)

½ cup [125 ml] heavy cream

1 tablespoon lemon juice, or more to taste

STIR the cèpes in a small bowl with the Madeira or with ¼ cup [60 ml] of water. Move them around in the bowl every 10 minutes to redistribute them in the liquid until they soften, in 30 minutes to 1 hour.

SEASON the chicken with salt and pepper and cook it uncovered in the butter, skin-side down first, in a sauté pan that has a lid, over medium heat for about 5 minutes on each side. Don't let the skin brown. Take the chicken out of the pan and stir in the flour with a small whisk. Whisk the flour into the butter and juices in the pan until smooth, and whisk in the broth. Bring to a gentle simmer, put the chicken back in the pan, and cover the pan. Cook over low heat, checking every few minutes, until the chicken is firm to the touch, about 15 minutes (see information on judging doneness, page 364). If you're still not sure whether the chicken is done, just cut into a piece.

WHILE the chicken is cooking, squeeze the liquid out of the cèpes into a small bowl and reserve it. Coarsely chop the cèpes.

TAKE the chicken out of the pan, set it on a plate, and keep it warm in the oven. Put the pan containing the stewing liquid on the stove over medium to high heat with the pan pushed to one side of the heat. Reduce the sauce, using a spoon to skim off fat that floats to the surface, until the sauce thickens slightly, about 5 minutes. Whisk in the cream and the cèpes. Carefully pour in the reserved mushroom soaking liquid so that you leave any grit behind in the bowl. Reduce the sauce for a minute or more to thicken it—it should have the consistency of a light syrup—or thin it with broth or water if it's gotten too thick. If any juices have run out of the chicken onto the plate, pour them into the sauce. Season the sauce to taste with salt,

pepper, and lemon juice and spoon it over the chicken in a serving dish or on individual plates.

Variations: Dried morels have a special smoky flavor that fresh morels lack, something that makes them wonderful in this dish. Just soak the same amount of dried morels as you would cèpes and use them in the same way, but don't chop them. You may also want to experiment with thickening fricassee sauces and other sauces with vegetable purées (see below) or foie gras worked with butter (see page 491).

USING VEGETABLE PURÉES TO FINISH SAUCES

Heavy cream is used in many traditional dishes, including a classic chicken fricassee, to give the sauce a silky texture. In some sauces, especially those that contain no flour, heavy cream, reduced with the sauce, is the only thickener. Most of us don't eat a lot of cream and aren't often going to cook a dish that blithely calls for a cup [250 ml] or more of heavy cream stirred in at the end. One solution is to finish sauces with a vegetable purée, almost as though making a cream soup. A vegetable purée gives the sauce texture, flavor, and sometimes color. You'll still need some cream, since a purée, no matter how smooth, doesn't duplicate the effects of the cream. But you'll be able to get by with much less, as little as 1 tablespoon per serving. Among my favorite purées are garlic, onion, tomato, and potato.

To thicken a sauce with a vegetable purée, cook the vegetable and purée it with the sauce in a blender just before serving. Vegetables, even quick-cooking green vegetables such as spinach and sorrel, must be cooked before you use them or they'll release liquid into the sauce and thin it instead of thicken it. An immersion blender—one that you put right into the saucepan—is the easiest for puréeing the vegetables with the sauce, but a regular blender will work, too. If you want a perfectly smooth sauce, or if you haven't peeled or seeded the vegetables, strain your sauce at the end. You can also prepare vegetable purées in advance and whisk them into the sauce just before serving. This method allows you to control more closely the exact thickness of the sauce and also lessens last-minute running around in the kitchen.

ROAST GARLIC PURÉE

MAKES 1 CUP [250 ML]

Roast garlic purée can be whisked into the cooking liquid from a fricassee, into a pan-deglazed sauce, or into the juices from a roasting pan to lightly thicken the mixture and give it a rich flavor. You can also spread garlic purée on toast (it makes the ultimate garlic bread) or thin it with broth or cream to turn it into a velvety sauce for grilled or sautéed meats and seafood. Garlic purée keeps for several weeks, in a small jar in the refrigerator, covered with a 6-inch layer of extra-virgin olive oil.

6 large heads garlic (about 1 pound [450 g])

BREAK up the heads of garlic into cloves (there's no need to peel them), sprinkle them with water to keep them from getting too brown, and wrap them in aluminum foil. Bake in a 400°F [200°C/gas mark 6] oven for about 45 minutes, or until the cloves feel very soft when you pinch them through the foil. Purée the cloves in a food processor for about 15 seconds and then work them through a strainer with the bottom of a ladle, through a drum sieve (see page 15), or through a food mill with the finest-mesh grid. If you're using a food mill, make a complete counterclockwise turn every once in a while to scrape up the garlic skins that are clogging the holes.

TOMATO PURÉE

MAKES 1 CUP [250 ML]

Tomato purée is the best-known vegetable (well, actually fruit) purée. It can be whisked into deglazed pans, especially those deglazed with wine, to give body to a sauce. A small amount of cream or butter whisked into the sauce at the end helps cut the tomatoes' acidity and gives the sauce a smooth consistency.

2 pounds [900 g] ripe tomatoes, halved crosswise, seeds squeezed out

CHOP the tomatoes coarse. Cook over medium heat in a heavy-bottomed pan, stirring and scraping against the bottom of the pan every few minutes

with a wooden spoon. When the mixture becomes thick and stiff, after about 30 minutes, work it through a strainer or food mill.

POTATO PURÉE

MAKES 2 CUPS [420 G]

Potato purée, essentially mashed potatoes without any liquid added, doesn't contribute much flavor to a purée-thickened sauce, but it makes a perfect thickener. You can simmer potatoes with other vegetables, as though you were making a soup, or you can make the potato purée given here and whisk it into sauces as needed for thickening.

1½ pounds [675 g] medium-starchy potatoes such as Yukon Golds or Yellow Finns, peeled and cut into chunks

PUT the potatoes in a pot with enough water to come halfway up their sides. Cover the pot and simmer until the potatoes are very easily penetrated with a knife, about 30 minutes. Drain. Work through a fine-mesh drum sieve (the best method) or through a strainer with the bottom or ladle, through a ricer, or through a food mill with the finest attachment.

POBLANO CHILE PURÉE

MAKES 1 CUP [250 ML]

Bell peppers are often used for making puree-based sauces, but poblano chiles have much more character and—be forewarned—a bit of heat.

4 poblano chiles (about 1 pound [250 ml])

1 tablespoon olive oil

GRILL or broil the chiles or roast them over an open gas flame until they are completely blackened but not white. Put them in a plastic bag or in a bowl covered with plastic wrap for 10 minutes and rub off the blackened peel. Cut out and discard the stems and cut the chiles in half lengthwise. Rinse out the seeds and chop the pulp. Cook the pulp in olive oil in a heavy-bottomed saucepan over medium heat for about 20 minutes. Purée the pulp in a food processor. If you want a perfectly smooth purée, work the purée through a strainer, food mill, or drum sieve.

ONION PURÉE

MAKES 2½ CUPS [590 ML]

Onion purée is the base for the classic sauce Soubise. But while sauce Soubise contains either rice or béchamel sauce to give it body, this simple onion purée is less rich and has a cleaner and sweeter flavor. Onion purée is perfect for finishing brown meat sauces.

2 large onions (1¼ pounds [565 g] total), preferably red onions, peeled and sliced

2 tablespoons butter

COOK the onions over low to medium heat in butter in a heavy-bottomed pot until they soften completely, about 30 minutes. Stir every few minutes to keep the onions from browning. Purée them in a blender or food processor. If you want a perfectly smooth purée, work the purée through a strainer or food mill.

DRIED CHILE PURÉE

MAKES 6 CUPS [175 ML]

Because some chile purées are hotter than others, whisk them into sauces a little bit at a time. They give flavor and heat and act as a thickener. Dried chile purées are great when used together with tomato purée and a little cream as a finish to chicken and seafood sauces.

2 ounces [60 g] dried pasillas, anchos, guajillos, New Mexico, or other dried chiles

WIPE the chiles with a damp towel to get rid of dust. Spread the chiles in an iron skillet and heat over medium heat for about 3 minutes until you smell their fragrance. Put the chiles in a bowl with enough hot tap water to cover. Soak for 30 minutes or until the chiles are soft and leathery. Drain, discarding the water. Cut off and discard the stems and cut the

chiles in half lengthwise. Rinse out the seeds. Purée the chiles in a food processor with 6 tablespoons of water (or more as needed to get the purée to move around) for 5 minutes, scraping down the sides of the food processor every minute with a rubber spatula. If you want a perfectly smooth purée, work the mixture through a strainer with the bottom of a ladle.

CHICKEN FRICASSEE WITH SPINACH AND SORREL

POULET FRICASSÉE À L'OSEILLE ET AUX ÉPINARDS

MAKES 4 MAIN-COURSE SERVINGS

This recipe is an example of how you can use green vegetables as a flavorful, light, and colorful last-minute thickener for a chicken fricassee. In this particular combination, the spinach provides color and body, while the sorrel gives the sauce a delicious acidic tang. If you can't find sorrel, make the dish with spinach alone. The method is also great with herbs such as parsley, chervil, or basil—just add a large handful of the leaves to the sauce and purée with a blender. The herbs release their flavor into the sauce and there's no chopping. If you can't get the blender to chop the herbs as fine as you like, strain the sauce after blending.

1   chicken (4 pounds [1.8 kg]), quartered (see page 17)

    salt

    pepper

2   tablespoons butter

2   tablespoons flour

2   cups [500 ml] white chicken or veal broth
    (see pages 210 and 217)

1   bunch spinach (10 ounces [280 g]), stemmed and
    rinsed

½   pound [250 g] fresh sorrel, stemmed and rinsed

½   cup [125 ml] heavy cream

2   tablespoons lemon juice, or more to taste

SEASON the chicken with salt and pepper and cook it uncovered in the butter, skin-side down first, in a sauté pan that has a lid, over medium heat for about 5 minutes on each side. Don't let the skin brown. Take the chicken out of the pan and stir in the flour with a small whisk. Whisk the flour with the butter and juices in the pan until smooth and whisk in broth. Bring to a gentle simmer, put the chicken back in the pan, and cover the pan. Set on low heat, checking every few minutes, until the chicken is firm to the touch, about 15 minutes (see information on judging doneness, page 364). If you're still not sure whether the chicken is done, just cut into a piece.

WHILE the chicken is simmering, bring ¼ cup [60 ml] water to a boil in a large skillet over high heat and stir in the spinach. Stir the spinach around for about 1 minute until it's completely limp. Press against the spinach with a spatula and pour off and discard the water in the pan. Add the sorrel to the pan with the spinach and stir it over the heat until it "melts," about 1 minute. Continue simmering and stirring until there's no liquid left in the pan, about 5 minutes. (The spinach water is discarded because it contributes little flavor, but the sorrel liquid is reduced to concentrate its acidity.)

WHEN the chicken is done, take it out of the pan, set it on a plate, and keep it warm in the oven. Put the pan containing the stewing liquid on the stove over medium to high heat with the pan pushed to one side of the heat. Reduce the sauce, skimming off fat and scum that float to the surface, until the sauce thickens slightly, about 5 minutes. Whisk in the cream and the spinach and sorrel, and purée the mixture with an immersion blender—in which case you may have to transfer the sauce to a smaller pan—or in a regular blender, starting at the lowest setting and pulsing in short bursts. Purée the sauce to the texture you like (I prefer a sauce flecked with chopped greens to one that's perfectly smooth). If the sauce is too thick, thin it with a little broth or water. If it's too thin, reduce it over medium heat for about 5 minutes. Season to taste with salt, pepper, and lemon juice. Spoon the sauce over the chicken on individual plates or in a serving dish.

Salmis

SALMIS

WE DON'T RUN INTO SALMIS MUCH ANY-more, probably because the method is best used for real wild game, not the farm-raised variety—the only kind that's legal to sell in the United States. A salmi is made using two basic techniques, roasting and braising, and is generally used for relatively small birds. The bird is partially roasted, the breasts and legs are carved off, and the carcass is chopped up and simmered in a concentrated broth. The partially cooked breasts and legs are then gently reheated (sometimes in a chafing dish) in the sauce. Depending on the variety of bird, the innards are worked into a paste and used to thicken the sauce, or they're spread on little pieces of bread and used to prop the pieces of bird up on the plate.

SQUAB SALMIS

PIGEONNEAU EN SALMIS

MAKES 4 MAIN-COURSE SERVINGS

To me, a salmis represents the height of French cooking, but some people simply don't like the livery flavor of game birds or of giblets. (Turkey giblet gravy, the closest most of us have come to a salmis, is a good gauge as to whether you'll like a salmis or not.) But having tasted a couple of salmis in France, I've always wanted to find a bird that would work here in the United States and a method that's practical without five assistants in the kitchen and a skilled carver in the dining room. In my search, squab is the hands-down winner. Squabs have a full, gamey flavor and thick breasts of tender red meat, and can usually be found with their livers and hearts, and sometimes their lungs. Instead of roasting, which requires working frantically to get the sauce ready while the partially cooked parts are drying out on a plate, I remove the breasts and legs before cooking the squabs, make a stock with the rest of the bones, and purée the innards (everything I find except intestines, which are rarely included anyway) with butter and work the mixture through a strainer. All of this can be done earlier in the day or even a day in advance. When I'm ready to serve, I sauté the breasts and legs, deglaze the pan with the broth, finish the sauce with the giblet butter, and pour the sauce over the breasts. A purist would simmer the breasts in the sauce, but I've found it does little except increase the risk of overcooking the squab and curdling the sauce. If your squabs come without innards, you can substitute chicken livers puréed with a little butter or a puréed small piece of foie gras, also worked with an equal weight of butter. If you don't like a livery taste in your sauce, just whisk 4 tablespoons of butter into the sauce at the end and leave out the innards. A few crushed and finely chopped juniper berries added to the marinade and/or to the giblet purée will magnify the squabs' gamey flavor. A teaspoon or so of Cognac, or better yet an earthy-flavored marc, added to a sauce about a minute before serving, also lends a characteristic gamey flavor.

4 squabs (about 1 pound [450 g] each), with as many of their innards as possible (see Sources)

salt

pepper

2 shallots, or 1 small onion, chopped fine

1 small carrot, peeled and chopped fine

1 clove garlic, chopped

2 tablespoons olive oil

3 cups [750 ml] rich chicken broth (see page 363) or veal broth (see page 217)

1 small bouquet garni

2 ounces [55 g] foie gras, or 2 chicken livers (either needed only if the squabs don't come with their innards)

4 tablespoon butter

1 tablespoon Cognac or marc

1 teaspoon red wine vinegar or more to taste

CUT the two outer wing sections off the squabs, leaving only the inner section of wing attached to the breast. Cut off the legs. Remove the breasts by sliding a knife along one side of the breastbone and, while keeping the knife flat against the bone, carving down toward the back and through the wing joint until the breast (with the wing section attached) comes away from the carcass. You should end up with 2 breast pieces (boneless except for the first wing section), 2 legs, the pieces of wing, the carcass, and the innards. Cut out the small bone in the thigh portion (not the drumstick) of each leg.

SEASON the breasts and legs with salt and pepper, put them on a plate, cover them with plastic wrap, and refrigerate. Take any innards out of each carcass; discard the intestines, if they were included, and reserve the rest. Chop the carcasses with a heavy knife or cleaver into about 10 pieces each, so that you don't need to use as much broth to cover. Brown the pieces of carcass and the reserved wing sections with the shallots, carrot, and garlic in 1 tablespoon of the olive oil in a small pot over medium to high heat for about 7 minutes. Add 1 cup [250 ml] of the broth and boil it down until it evaporates and caramelizes on the bottom of the pan. Be careful not to burn it. Add the bouquet garni and the rest of the broth and bring to a simmer. Simmer gently, occasionally skimming off fat and scum with a small ladle, for 1½ hours. Strain the broth into a small saucepan, pushing hard on the bones to extract as much liquid as possible. Discard the bones and reduce the broth until you have about ¾ cup [175 ml].

PURÉE the reserved innards, including the livers, hearts, gizzards, and lungs, with the remaining butter and the Cognac in a miniature food processor or a blender or by chopping very fine by hand. If your squabs came without innards, purée the butter with the foie gras or the chicken livers. Work either mixture through a strainer with a wooden spoon. If you're not serving the squabs right away, cover the liver or foie gras mixture with plastic wrap, which should touch the purée's surface so the purée doesn't darken, and refrigerate.

WHEN you're ready to serve, heat the remaining olive oil in a sauté pan just large enough to hold the breasts in a single layer, until it barely begins to smoke. Very high heat is essential for browning the breasts without overcooking them. Sauté the breasts and legs, skin-side down first, over high heat. Press down on the legs and breasts with a spatula to keep them flat. Sauté for about 2 minutes on the skin side and 1 minute more on the flesh side. It doesn't matter whether or not the legs cook all the way through, but the breast meat should be between rare and medium rare. Keep warm while making the sauce.

POUR the burnt fat out of the pan, wipe the pan out with a paper towel, and pour in the reduced broth. Bring the broth, which should have a lightly syrupy consistency, to a simmer and whisk in the butter mixture and the Cognac. Heat while whisking until the butter is completely integrated into the sauce, but don't allow the sauce to come to a hard boil. Don't panic if the sauce looks curdled; salmi sauces often have a rough, muddy look. If this bothers you, purée the sauce with an immersion blender. Season the sauce to taste with salt and pepper and a spot of vinegar. Arrange the breasts and legs on hot plates and pour the sauce over and around them.

DUCK À L'ORANGE

CANETON À L'ORANGE

HOW TO	HOW TO	HOW TO	HOW TO	WHAT
CUT UP A DUCK	SAUTÉ, GRILL, AND BRAISE DUCK	MAKE A GASTRIQUE AND USE IT IN SWEET AND SOUR SAUCES	MAKE CONFIT AND RILLETTES	PRESSED DUCK IS

MY FIRST ROAST DUCK ENDED IN DISASTER. THE SAN FRANCISCO WEATHER had turned suddenly hot, and my sweaty guests waited expectantly as I made the first tentative incision into the breast. My heart sank as the grease spurted out and everyone saw the sad fatty little slices. Fortunately, ducks have gotten meatier since then, and after years of fumbling around in the kitchen I've finally figured out how to cook one. Duck is often the perfect solution when we aren't in the mood for red meat like beef or lamb but don't quite feel like chicken or seafood. Duck is, in fact, easy to cook once you understand a few of its idiosyncracies, and duck *à l'orange,* clichéd or not, is one of the easiest and best duck dishes. But before we set out to cook duck *à l'orange,* let's examine a couple of methods for cooking ducks, *à l'orange* or otherwise.

American domesticated ducks, which are Pekin—not "Peking"—ducks, have very lean meat, but they're covered with a thick layer of fatty skin. If you roast such a duck as you would a chicken, the fat won't render by the time the meat is done. You'll end up with a fatty duck and a greasy sauce and you'll probably never try to cook duck again. The standby American restaurant solution to this problem has been to cook the duck for 2 or 3 hours until most of the fat renders and the skin finally turns crispy. When done carefully, with regular basting and eventual draining off of fat, you'll end up with something that's more like confit than like roast duck.

Because duck legs are considerably tougher than the breast, any attempt to roast an American duck without overcooking it is doomed to failure. In France, the standard *canard de Barbarie* has relatively thin skin containing less fat. (A *canard* is a duck and a *caneton* a duckling, but the two terms are often used interchangeably.) The problem is solved by roasting the whole duck, carving off the legs when the breast is ready and grilling the legs or finishing them off in a sauté pan. This method won't work with an American duck because there's just too much fat in the skin and the legs are still tough even after the extra cooking. The solution is to give up on roasting the duck and cook the breast and legs separately, using the technique that is best for each one.

If you live near sophisticated shopping, you may be able to buy boneless breasts from Long Island (Pekin) ducklings or, better yet, from mulard ducks. Mulard ducks are voracious hybrids of Muscovy ducks (which are becoming harder to find and can be tough) and mallards (lean ducks, rarely domesticated) that eat so much that their livers end up as unnaturally large foie gras and their breasts (marketed under the French word for duck breast, *magret*) weigh in at a pound [450 g] or more for each boneless single (that is, half) breast. Mulard breasts have a fuller and gamier flavor than the breasts from the easy-to-find Pekin duckling. While they're more expensive, they're tastier and also more convenient, since you don't have to cut up the duckling and figure out what to do with the legs. In most places, however, we must be content with the standard Pekin duckling, a creature we're likely to find frozen and wrapped in plastic. (Fortunately, ducks take well to freezing.) If you want to get straight to the point and make duck à l'orange, see the recipe on page 390.

―――――――――○―――――――――

CUTTING UP A DUCK

To cut up a Pekin (Long Island) duckling into 2 single breasts, 2 legs, and miscellaneous parts, begin by cutting off any loose chunks of fat or flaps of fatty skin (save the fat for making confit). Position the duck so that the legs are facing you. Pull one of the legs forward and, with a paring or boning knife, cut through the skin between the thigh and the breast with the knife closest to and pointing toward the inside of the thigh so you don't accidentally cut skin off the breast and expose the meat. Leave enough skin on the breast so that the meat is completely covered. Continue cutting through the skin where it meets the thigh and then fold open the leg, away from the body. Slide the knife along the back where it joins the inside of the thigh and through the joint that connects the thigh to the body. Pull the leg completely away and repeat on the other side. Cut off the wings where they join the rest of the duck. When you've removed both legs and the wings, slide a small knife along one side of the breastbone, keeping the knife against the bone so you don't cut into any meat. Slide the knife under the breast meat, folding the breast meat back as you go. Cut one side of the breast completely away from the duck and repeat on the other side. Trim off the fatty skin that surrounds the breasts and legs, but be sure to leave the layer of skin covering the meat. You can save the fat for rendering (see page 383) and the carcass for making broth.

SAUTÉED DUCK BREASTS

MAGRETS DE CANETON À LA POÊLE

When you sauté a duck breast you get rid of most of the fat in the skin and have perfect control over how much to cook the meat. French cooks roast whole ducks to a red-pink medium rare, and wild ducks even rarer. Don't think of duck as you would chicken or turkey, which is cooked completely through, to the equivalent of medium for red meat. When you cook duck breasts, you can peel off the fatty skin and sauté the breasts as you would a little steak, leaving the meat rare to medium rare and providing a piece of meat leaner than a boneless chicken breast and quite a bit tastier. But because much of the duck's flavor is in that layer of fat on the breast, you'll want to capture the best of both possible worlds—crispy flavorful skin with much of the excess fat cooked out and juicy rare-to-medium-rare meat. To do this, make a series of thin slashes diagonally across the skin of each breast, cutting as deep into the skin as you can without cutting all the way down to the meat, so you end up with about 20 slashes. Give the breast a 90-degree turn and make a new series of about 20 slashes that cross over the other ones. The slashes expose much of the fat contained in the skin so it will render quickly in the sauté pan. Season the breasts with salt and pepper and sauté them skin-side down over medium to high heat in a pan just large enough to fit them—there's no need to put oil in the pan—8 to 10 minutes for Long Island duckling breasts (12 to 14 minutes for mulard), or until the breasts just begin to feel firm to the touch and the skin looks brown and crispy. Turn the breasts over and cook them for 2 minutes (3 minutes for mulard breasts) over high heat, just long enough to brown the flesh side. If you're using Pekin duckling, serve everyone a whole single breast or slice the breasts into thin strips and fan them slightly over hot plates—a method that allows you to serve less than a whole breast per person. Strain the fat left in the pan and save it (see the information on page 383).

SALAD OF SAUTÉED OR GRILLED DUCK BREASTS

SALADE VERTE AUX MAGRETS DE CANARD

MAKES 4 FIRST-COURSE SERVINGS OR 2 MAIN-COURSE SERVINGS

Greens tossed just before serving with sliced sautéed or grilled duck make a great main-course or first-course salad.

- 4 handfuls of mixed salad greens, such as arugula, frisée, oak leaf lettuce, baby romaine, mâche, or basil

- 2 boneless single Long Island (Pekin) duckling breasts or 1 boneless single mulard breast (about 1 pound [450 g] total)

- 3 tablespoons extra-virgin olive oil

- 2 tablespoons sherry vinegar or good-quality red wine vinegar, or more to taste

  salt

  pepper

WASH and dry the greens and put them in a large bowl.

SAUTÉ the duck breasts as described above; slice them, crosswise, into thin strips; and distribute them over the salad greens. Pour out all but 1 tablespoon of the fat left in the sauté pan, or if the fat smells burnt, pour all of it out. Add the olive oil, vinegar, salt, and pepper. Pour this hot vinaigrette over the salad. Toss the salad and serve.

WHAT TO DO WITH THE LEGS

Whenever you see duck breasts on a restaurant menu, search around and you'll find out what clever dish the chef has invented for using the legs. Some places grill them, others turn them into confit; but the legs always show up somewhere. If you cook a lot of duck breasts, you, too, will be stuck with the legs. You can sauté them as you did the breasts, except that there's no need to score the skin, but they'll be tough. Cooking them until they're well done softens them somewhat, so that you can cut the meat off the bone in thin slices and toss it in a salad, but the meat is still a bit tough. I've found that legs are best either turned into confit or gently braised. Since neither of these methods is worthwhile for just a couple of legs, I braise or make confit only if I'm making duck for a crowd or I've saved up at least a dozen legs in the freezer.

DUCK CONFIT

CONFIT DE CUISSES

DE CANARD

MAKES 12 FIRST-COURSE SERVINGS, 6 MAIN-COURSE SERVINGS, OR 12 ACCOMPANIMENTS TO A DUCK BREAST MAIN COURSE

16   duck legs

2½   tablespoons freshly ground black pepper

¾   cup [180 g] coarse salt

7   cloves garlic, chopped, crushed to a paste with the side of a chef's knife

1½   tablespoons chopped fresh thyme

gizzards and hearts from 6 ducks

fat and skin from 8 Long Island ducklings (not including the fat attached to the legs and breasts), about 16 cups [3.75 l] before rendering, 12 cups [3 l] when rendered), or 12 cups [3 l] already rendered duck fat (see page 383)

LEAVE the skin attached to the legs but remove any excess that surrounds the meat. (You will probably have already done this in order to render the fat.)

COMBINE the pepper, salt, garlic, and thyme and rub the mixture into the duck legs, especially on the flesh side, and on the giblets (the hearts and gizzards). Place the duck legs and giblets in a bowl, cover with plastic wrap, and refrigerate 12 to 18 hours.

IF you haven't yet rendered the duck fat trimmings, chop them by hand or in a food processor. The more finely they are chopped, the more quickly they'll render their fat. Put the chopped fat in a 10-quart or 12-quart [10- to 12-l] heavy-bottomed pot over medium heat. Use a flame tamer to prevent the fat on the bottom of the pot from scorching.

WIPE excess salt off the duck legs and giblets with a moist towel and nestle the legs and giblets, skin-side down, into the pot with the warmed fat. Keep pressing the legs and giblets down. As the fat on the outside of the legs is rendered, it will cover the legs and giblets. Adjust the heat so that the surface of the confit is gently boiling, which tells you that the water contained in the duck is evaporating. Cook for 2 to 3 hours, until the fat is clear and a knife stuck into one of the legs slides in and out easily. Transfer the legs and giblets to jars, or into bowls if you're going to use them in the next few days. Strain the fat and ladle it, while hot, over the confit. If you're planning to store the confit for a week or more, make sure the meat is completely covered with fat, with no pieces of meat breaking the surface. Keep the jars in the refrigerator.

HOW TO USE CONFIT: You can serve whole confit duck legs as a main course—I like them with beans or lentils or atop a mound of creamed sorrel or spinach. Or you can serve them as an accompaniment to a main course of duck breast. Because duck confit is so flavorful, you can also use it as a flavoring. Try stirring blanched or steamed spinach or Swiss chard in a little hot duck fat with some of the shredded confit. Your guests will barely know the confit's there but they'll wonder why the spinach is so good. Or nestle the duck legs in a pot with some shredded cabbage and a little white wine and broth and bake for 1 hour. Or try the same thing with sauerkraut or beans (for more about beans, see Chapter 34). Duck confit also makes the most delicious possible rillettes (see page 384), a pâté-like spread. One of my favorite uses is the salad on page 284.

PREPARING AND USING DUCK FAT AND MAKING DUCK CONFIT

Rendered duck fat makes a delicious alternative to vegetable oil, and because it has a relatively high smoking point, it can be used for sautéing over higher heat than butter for browning meat, seafood, or vegetables. It also makes the best possible omelets. (Well, second best—goose fat makes *the* best.) To make rendered duck fat, chop up any chunks of fat and flaps of fatty skin you've saved that were attached to the duck carcasses and the skin surrounding (but not covering) the legs and breasts. (You may want to freeze the fat and skin until you've accumulated at least several cups.) Unless you want cracklings—the crispy pieces of skin left over after rendering—it's better to purée the skin and fat in a food processor before rendering, because when puréed, the skin and fat render more thoroughly and more quickly.

Cook the puréed or chopped fat in a heavy-bottomed saucepan or pot over low to medium heat until the fat turns clear and, if you've chopped the skin and fat by hand, the pieces of skin—which are now cracklings—barely begin to brown. Depending on how much fat you have, this can take anywhere from 20 minutes to 3 hours. Be very careful not to let the fat get too hot or it will burn and lose its delicate flavor. On the other hand, if the hot rendered fat is cloudy, there is likely to be liquid disbursed in the fat. Because this can cause the fat to turn rancid, boil the mixture at first and turn down the heat as soon as the fat starts to become clear. When it is perfectly clear, turn off the heat. Strain the fat, allow it to cool, and store it in a tightly covered container in the refrigerator, where it will keep for up to 6 months.

To save the fat that is rendered when you sauté duck breasts, cook the duck breasts in a pan just large enough to hold them in a single layer. If the pan is too large, it gets too hot in areas where it isn't covered with meat and the fat gets too hot. You can tell if the fat has burned by smelling it. It loses its delicate aroma and smells a little like burnt bacon. Usually, you'll be able to get about 16 cups [3.5 l] of skin and fat from 8 Long Island ducklings (while leaving the fat attached to the breasts and legs). When this fat is rendered, you should have 12 cups [3 l], just enough to make confit out of the 16 duck legs.

Make confit by gently cooking duck, or other foods such as pork or goose, completely immersed in rendered fat. This isn't as horrifying as it sounds because most of the fat is rendered out of the meat and isn't served with the confit—it's saved for sautéing other foods or for making rillettes (see page 384). Confit was originally limited to southwestern France, where it was used as a method of preserving duck and goose without refrigeration. In the 1970s it caught on in Paris and then in the United States. There are good reasons for confit's popularity. It's delicious and versatile, and if you serve a lot of duck breasts, it's perfect for using up the legs.

To make confit, save duck fat trimmings, any extra rendered fat you've saved from cooking the duck breasts, and the duck legs in the freezer until you've accumulated at least a dozen legs, enough to make the effort worthwhile. If you need extra fat or if you want to buy goose or duck confit instead of making it, gourmet stores sell rendered goose and duck fat and confit of duck and goose (see Sources).

WILD MUSHROOM AND DUCK CONFIT SALAD

SALADE VERTE AU CONFIT DE CANARD ET AUX CHAMPIGNONS SAUVAGES

MAKES 4 FIRST-COURSE SERVINGS

I used to serve this salad at my restaurant Le Petit Robert in Manhattan. I would hand-select the greens at a retail market (we were too small to order wholesale), and I would vary the salad according to what greens and mushrooms were in season. Since the combinations we came up with never failed to please, I suggest you do the same.

4 handfuls of mixed salad greens, such as arugula, frisée, oak leaf lettuce, baby romaine, mâche, or basil, and flowers, such as nasturtiums

1 pound [450 g] assorted wild mushrooms or cultivated mushrooms

2 confit duck legs

3 tablespoons duck fat from the confit

2 tablespoons extra-virgin olive oil

2 tablespoons sherry vinegar or good-quality red wine vinegar, or more to taste

salt

pepper

WASH and dry the salad greens. If the mushrooms are dirty, brush them clean or quickly rinse them in a colander. Depending on their size, leave the mushrooms whole or cut them in halves or quarters, following their natural shape. Don't cut them too small.

PULL the skin away from the duck legs and discard it. Pull the meat off the duck legs, leaving it in small chunks or shreds, and reserve.

JUST before you're ready to serve the salad, put the greens in a large bowl for tossing. Sauté the mushrooms in the duck fat in a heavy-bottomed pan until they're well browned and fragrant, about 5 minutes. Sprinkle the confit over them and sauté for 2 minutes more. Add the olive oil and vinegar. Season with salt and pepper (be careful with the salt—the confit is already salty) and pour the contents of the pan over the salad greens. Toss quickly. Taste a leaf—if it tastes bland, sprinkle a little more vinegar over the salad and toss again. Serve immediately.

DUCK RILLETTES

RILLETTES DE CANETON

MAKES A LITTLE MORE THAN 2 CUPS [450 G], ENOUGH FOR ABOUT 8 HORS D'OEUVRE SERVINGS

Whenever I get off the plane in France after a long absence, certain immediate cravings set in. A choucroute garnie (see Chapter 38) must be had within the first few days, as must a plate of oysters. But first and foremost—usually by the first lunch—there have got to be rillettes, preferably on the terrace of a café, served with crusty pain Poilane and a glass of good rouge. Here, you must be careful because, seeing an American, the waiter may ask if you want your rillettes en sandwich or comme ça. It's essential to have them comme ça, which in this context means that you get to spread them on the bread yourself, giving you control over the rillette-to-bread ratio of each bite and providing the right amount of distraction between sipping and people watching.

A description of rillettes scares a lot of people away: shredded very-cooked pork, duck, or goose worked with congealed fat and seasoned with spices rather than herbs. Goose and duck rillettes are best, but pork rillettes do perfectly fine on that first desperate day. I never bother making pork rillettes at home—American pork fat never tastes quite right to me—but when I'm feeling a bit ambitious and am getting tired of looking at those duck legs taking up space in the freezer, I set forth on a batch of rillettes de caneton.

4 duck confit legs (see Duck Confit, page 382)

¾ cup [175 ml] duck fat from the confit, skin pulled away
   and discarded

¾ teaspoon *quatre épices* (see Four Spice Mixture, page 386)

½ teaspoon salt

PULL the meat off the duck legs and shred it with your fingers. Stir it in a mixing bowl with the duck fat, the *quatre épices*, and the salt. Don't try to cut down on the fat or the rillettes will be dry, and don't be tempted to use the food processor, which will give you a pasty mixture with more the consistency of potted meat. Serve cool but not cold (take the rillettes out of the refrigerator 30 minutes before serving) with crusty French bread slices or small toasts. Let guests spread their own.

DUCK STEW

PETITE FRICASSÉE DE
CUISSES DE CANARD

MAKES 4 MAIN-COURSE SERVINGS
(2 LEGS PER SERVING), OR ADDITIONS TO
8 SERVINGS OF DUCK BREAST

Many older French recipes for duck, especially a duck that has passed its prime, call for braising rather than roasting. This makes no sense for whole American ducklings because the breast meat is tender and lean, perfect for cooking rare to medium rare but not for stewing, which would dry it out. Duck legs, on the other hand, are tough. Except for their relatively short braising time, you can cook duck legs in the same way you would any stew—brown them in fat, brown aromatic vegetables in the same fat (or new fat), moisten with wine and broth or water, nestle in a bouquet garni, cover, and gently simmer. (For moistening, a broth made from the duck carcass makes the most sense but

requires forethought.) Depending on the finished dish, the braising liquid is reduced and/or thickened with flour, cornstarch, or butter, or, as in this recipe, is used to glaze the legs. The braising liquid can also be used as a base for a sauce for the duck breasts (see "How to Make Brown Duck Broth," page 389).

Braised duck legs make a delicious main course in themselves (you'll need 2 per person), but they can also be served with sautéed duck breasts and the braising liquid used as a base for the sauce for both. By serving the legs, you'll get 3 or 4 servings out of a duck instead of 2 or 3 if you just serve the breasts.

8 duck legs

   salt

   pepper

2 to 4 tablespoons rendered duck fat (see page 383),
   butter, or oil

1 medium-size carrot, peeled and chopped fine

½ stalk celery, chopped fine

1 medium-size onion, chopped fine

4 cloves garlic, crushed, chopped coarse

1 cup [250 ml] red wine

2 cups [500 ml] duck or chicken broth (see pages 389
   and 209)

1 small bouquet garni

2 tablespoons chopped parsley

SEASON the legs with salt and pepper and brown them in 2 tablespoons of duck fat over medium to high heat in a heavy-bottomed pot large enough to hold them in a single layer. If your pot isn't large enough, brown them in batches or use a pan in addition to the pot. Brown the legs for about 8 minutes on each side and transfer them to a plate. If the fat in the pot smells burnt, pour it out and replace it with 2 tablespoons of new fat. Add the carrot, celery, onion, and garlic to the pot and stir them in the fat over medium heat until they barely begin to brown, about 10 minutes. Pour in the wine and boil it down until only about 2 tablespoons are left in the bottom of the pot, about 5 minutes. Put the duck legs, skin-side up, back in the pot along with any juices that have run out onto the plate. At this point, the legs don't need to be in a single layer, but nestle them in as tightly as you can. Pour in the broth, bring it to a boil over high heat, nestle in the bouquet garni, and turn down the heat to maintain at a gentle simmer. Cover the pot with a sheet of aluminum foil and press the foil down so that the legs not covered with broth are basted with condensing steam. Cover the pot and let it stew for 45 minutes over low heat, so that the braising liquid barely bubbles. Or slide the pot into a 325°F [165°C/gas mark 3] oven after first bringing it to a simmer. Check the duck legs after 10 minutes to make sure they're cooking at a low simmer—a bubble rising gently to the surface every couple of seconds—and adjust the oven accordingly.

USE a pair of tongs to transfer the legs to a dish and strain the braising liquid into a small saucepan. Press down on the aromatic vegetables and the bouquet garni in the strainer to extract as much of the liquid as you can. Discard the vegetables and the bouquet garni. Set the saucepan, a bit to one side,

over low to medium heat so that the liquid boils up on one side only. Use a small ladle or spoon to skim off fat and froth as they rise to the surface. Continue reducing and skimming for about 15 minutes, until the liquid has reduced by half and you've skimmed off most of the fat. You'll end up with about 1½ cups of reduced braising liquid.

AT this stage, you can use the degreased braising liquid as the base for a sauce for both the legs and the breasts or the breasts alone (see Sautéed or Grilled Duck Breasts with Classic Orange Sauce, page 390), or you can use it to glaze the legs. (If you use it for the breasts alone, since you'll have no sauce for the legs, you can toss the leg meat in a salad or reheat or grill the legs, sauceless, for tomorrow's dinner.) While the braising liquid is reducing, clean out the pan used for braising the legs and turn the oven up to 400°F [200°C/gas mark 6]. Place the legs, skin-side up, back in the pan and pour the reduced braising liquid over them. Baste the legs every 10 minutes until they are covered with a shiny glaze, 30 to 45 minutes. Transfer to a serving dish or plates, spoon any reduced liquid from the bottom of the pan over them, sprinkle them with parsley, and serve.

FOUR SPICE MIXTURE (QUATRE ÉPICES)

To make a small amount of the classic *quatre épices* mixture, which the French use for making pâtes and other dishes, combine 2½ teaspoons freshly ground white pepper, ¼ teaspoon ground cloves, ¾ teaspoon powdered ginger, and ¾ teaspoon ground nutmeg. I keep mine in a little jar in the freezer.

Cooking Duck with Oranges

EVEN THOUGH THE KINGS OF FRANCE planted oranges throughout the sixteenth century, —it had become *de rigueur* for royalty to have an orangerie—they didn't eat their own but instead imported oranges from Portugal. Oranges didn't really catch on in a big way in France until the seventeenth century. The earliest references to orange sauce in seventeenth-century cookbooks describe simply adding a little orange juice to the natural cooking juices—the *jus*—from a roast duck. This is still a great idea, except that we Americans seldom have access to ducks that are suitable for roasting. There is also the problem that when meat is roasted rare to medium rare it doesn't release much juice, so there's nothing to work with. By the eighteenth and nineteenth centuries, cookbook writers were describing orange sauce, or more accurately *sauce bigarade*, made with *blond de veau*, an especially extravagant predecessor to what was later to become demi-glace, used in most professional kitchens until the 1970s. (See page 3.)

Duck *à l'orange* is unusual in French cooking because it combines savory, sweet, and sour, a combination of tastes that the French have never been terribly fond of. Even during medieval times, when cooks in other places were combining the most unlikely foods with sugar, sometimes in prodigious amounts, French cooks used very little. During the sixteenth century, when sugar became more abundant, French cooks judiciously combined sweet and savory, but the trend pretty much died out by the end of the seventeenth century. Duck *à l'orange* is one of the few remaining examples of French sweet-and-sour dishes.

The classical name for duck *à l'orange* is actually duck or duckling (*caneton*) *à la bigarade*. A *bigarade* is a Seville orange, which has a bitter rind and sour juice that helps prevent the sauce from becoming cloyingly sweet. But a regular orange will work, provided you don't add too much sugar.

A classic orange sauce (*sauce bigarade*) is made by combining blanched orange zest, sugar, vinegar, orange juice, and rich veal broth. Because French cooks are wary of sugar, they caramelize it first and then add vinegar to create a sweet-and-sour mixture called a *gastrique*. The best way to use the *gastrique* is to add it bit by bit to the sauce, as you'd use a seasoning, until the sweetness is just right. If the sauce needs a tad more acidity, a few drops of good wine vinegar can be added at the last minute. (See page 390 for more about *gastrique*.)

Nowadays, chefs are more likely to infuse orange zests in orange juice and then round out the combination with *glace de viande* instead of the demi-glace. This leaves the home cook in a bit of a bind. We can of course make *glace de viande* (see page 221), a satisfying two-day project but one that most cooks are unwilling to undertake, or we can use a commercial brand of *glace de viande* or demi-glace. But to me, the most elegant solution is to braise the duck legs and then use the braising liquid as the base for the sauce for both the breasts and the legs. The beauty of this method is that it provides fantastic sauces—not just orange sauces—that can be varied almost infinitely. (See "Improvising Duck Dishes," page 392.)

ORANGE-GLAZED SAUTÉED DUCK BREASTS

MAGRETS DE CANARD GLACÉS À L'ORANGE

MAKES 4 MAIN-COURSE SERVINGS

This method will not provide the rich silky sauce of a classic duck à l'orange, but it will flavor the duck breasts with a sweet-and-sour orange glaze. Best of all, it doesn't require any broth.

4 boneless single Long Island duckling breasts or 2 mulard boneless single breasts (about 2 pounds [900 g] total)

salt

pepper

2 juicing oranges, preferably Seville, well scrubbed

4 teaspoons sugar

¼ cup [60 ml] good sherry vinegar, or more to taste

SCORE the duck breasts as described on page 381 and season with salt and pepper. Use a vegetable peeler to peel the zest off 1 of the oranges. Chop the zest coarse and squeeze the juice out of the orange. Stir the duck breasts in a bowl with the chopped zest, the orange juice, and 1 teaspoon of the sugar, and let marinate in the refrigerator for about 4 hours or overnight.

PEEL half the zest off the second orange and cut the zest into very fine julienne. (See page 19 for more about cutting in julienne.) Eliminate the bitterness in the zest strips by plunging them into 1 cup [250 ml] of boiling water for 30 seconds, draining them in a strainer, and rinsing them with cold water.

Squeeze the second orange, strain the seeds out of the juice, and combine the juice with the remaining sugar and the julienned zest in a small saucepan. Bring the mixture to a boil and remove it from the heat. Let the julienned zest steep in the hot juice for at least 5 minutes. Spoon or strain the zest out of the juice and reserve zest and juice separately.

ABOUT 20 minutes before you're ready to serve, take the breasts out of the marinade, pat them dry, wipe off any pieces of zest clinging to their surface, and sauté them, starting skin-side down, over medium to high heat for about 8 minutes (10 to 12 minutes for mulard breasts), until the breast barely begins to feel firm to the touch and the skin is well browned and crispy and has released a lot of fat. Turn the breasts over and cook them for 1 minute on the skin side. At this point, the breasts should be slightly underdone. Set the breasts aside on a plate while you're preparing the glaze. Pour the fat out of the pan and pour in the reserved boiled orange juice and the vinegar. Boil down the mixture over high heat until it starts to look syrupy, about 2 minutes, and put the breasts, skin-side down, back in the pan. Move the breasts around in the boiling orange juice mixture until they are well coated with the orange glaze, about 2 minutes. Turn the breasts over to glaze them on the meat side, and keep moving them around for about 1 minute. There should be a small amount of very thick glaze clinging to the breasts and to the pan. Be careful not to burn the glaze.

SLICE the breasts and arrange the slices on hot plates. If you're using Long Island duckling breasts, serve each diner a whole single breast. If you're using mulard breasts, give each diner half a single breast. Sprinkle the slices with the cooked julienned orange zests. If you like, decorate the plate with a few skinless orange wedges coupér à vif (see page 391).

Variation (Grilled Duck Breasts with Orange Glaze): Though the smokiness from a wood grill is the perfect accent to the mild, slightly gamey flavor of duck, the thick layer of fat on one side of the duck breasts makes them difficult to grill because the fat renders, drips down into the coals, and causes the fire to flare up and generate a lot of sooty smoke. The soot adheres to the breasts and gives them an unpleasant greasy flavor. The trick to grilling duck breasts is to cook the breasts, skin-side down, in a pan so they render most of their fat before you put them on the grill. Once sautéed, the duck breasts should be allowed to cool so they can be grilled without overcooking—a fact that means you can sauté the breasts beforehand and grill them at the last minute. If you want orange-flavored duck breasts, prepare the recipe above but sauté the Long Island duckling breasts for only 5 minutes on the skin side (8 minutes for mulard breasts) and 30 seconds on the meat side before glazing (glaze the breasts with the orange mixture as in the recipe above). Let the breasts cool for at least 20 minutes. (You can do this much earlier in the same day and refrigerate the breasts until you're ready to grill. To chill the breasts quickly, place them on a sheet pan set on another sheet pan covered with ice; see page 238.)

Wipe the grill with oil and grill the breasts, starting on the skin side. If the coals flare up, move the breasts to a part of the grill that is not directly over the flames. You may find yourself having to move the breasts almost constantly. If there starts to be a lot of fire over most of the surface of the coals, turn the breasts over and grill them on the flesh side. Grill Long Island duckling breasts for about 2 minutes on the skin side, turning them 90 degrees after 1 minute so you get a cross-hatch pattern on the skin side, and 5 minutes on the flesh side. (Grill mulard breasts 6 minutes on each side.) Serve on hot plates. Long Island duckling breasts can be served whole or sliced. Mulard breasts should be served sliced.

HOW TO MAKE BROWN DUCK BROTH

If you're feeling ambitious, you can make a broth out of the duck carcass. Coarsely chop the carcass, brown it in a pan with a little onion and carrot, add a bouquet garni and enough water or chicken broth to cover, and simmer for about 2 hours. You can then reduce this duck broth to use in sauces (see Sautéed or Grilled Duck Breasts with Classic Orange Sauce, page 390) or, the ultimate refinement, use it as the moistening liquid in the duck stew. Making quick little broths is an easy habit to get into. I sometimes even skip the vegetables and the bouquet garni, figuring I'll flavor the broth when I use it. If you cook a lot, you can use one broth to moisten another, so that by the end of the process you end up with very concentrated and delicious broth to use as a base for soups and sauces. Broth is, of course, easy to freeze.

SAUTÉED OR GRILLED DUCK BREASTS WITH CLASSIC ORANGE SAUCE

MAGRETS DE CANARD SATÉS OU GRILLÉS, SAUCE À L'ORANGE

INGREDIENTS FOR 8 MAIN-COURSE SERVINGS
(OR 4 MAIN-COURSE SERVINGS IF YOU DECIDE
NOT TO BRAISE THE LEGS AND SERVE
ONLY THE BREASTS)

This recipe calls for braising the duck legs as well as sautéing or grilling the breasts. The moistening liquid for the legs (see page 385) can be broth and/or red or white wine, or water.

The sauce can be finished with any combination of fines herbes (chives, chervil, tarragon, and parsley), basil, sautéed wild mushrooms, truffles, cream, green peppercorns, the puréed duck liver combined with an equal amount of butter, puréed foie gras, berries such as red or black currants or raspberries, chopped green olives, or crushed juniper berries. Because you're serving the legs and the breast, this method allows you to get 4 servings out of the one Long island duckling. If you don't want to bother with braising the legs, substitute a good concentrated duck, chicken, or veal broth for the duck-leg braising liquid.

- 2 Long Island (Pekin) ducklings, sectioned (see page 380)
- 4 cups [750 ml] full-flavored duck, chicken, or brown broth (see pages 389 and 209)
- 2 juicing oranges, preferably Seville, well scrubbed
- 3 tablespoons sugar
- ⅓ cup [150 ml] sherry vinegar, or more as needed
- 4 tablespoons unsalted butter
- salt
- pepper

FOR the tastiest sauce, braise the duck legs following the recipe for duck stew on page 385, using the broth called for in the recipe here, keeping in mind that you're making half the recipe because the 2 ducks will give you only 4 legs. Reserve the braised legs. Reduce and degrease the braising liquid as described in the recipe, but don't glaze the legs. Reserve the braising liquid. If you don't want to bother with this step, save the uncooked legs for another use. Bring the broth to a gentle simmer in a saucepan and reduce it by half.

PEEL half the zest off 1 of the oranges, being careful to avoid leaving any white pith attached. Cut the zest into fine julienne. Toss the zest into boiling water and boil for 30 seconds. Strain, rinse with cold water, and reserve. Squeeze the 2 oranges through a strainer into a small saucepan and boil the orange juice down to about 3 tablespoons.

PREPARE a *gastrique* by melting the sugar over medium heat in a small, heavy-bottomed saucepan while stirring with a wooden spoon. Use a pan with a shiny bottom so you can see the color of the caramel as it's cooking. When the sugar melts and turns the color of coffee, remove the saucepan from the heat and—while standing back—immediately pour in the vinegar. Swirl the *gastrique* gently over medium heat to dissolve all the caramel. Add a little more vinegar if necessary to get the caramel to dissolve. If the *gastrique* doesn't look syrupy, boil it down until it does. You'll end up with more *gastrique* than you need, but it's nearly impossible to control the sugar when making less. (*Gastrique* keeps for a couple of months in the refrigerator.)

COMBINE the reduced orange juice and the reduced duck-leg braising liquid or broth in a small saucepan and reduce slightly again until the mixture has the consistency of a light syrup. At this point, you should have about 1 cup [175 ml] of mixture. Stir in the julienned zest, simmer for 2 minutes more, and stir in the *gastrique* bit by bit until the sauce has the right sweetness. If the sauce starts to taste too sweet, add a few more drops of vinegar. Reserve this mixture.

SCORE the breasts as described on page 381 and season them with salt and pepper. Sauté them over medium to high heat, skin-side down in a pan just large enough to fit them—there's no need to put oil in the pan—for 8 to 10 minutes, or until the breasts begin to feel firm to the touch and the skin looks brown and crispy. Turn the breasts over and cook them for 2 minutes over high heat just long enough to brown the flesh side. If you braised the legs, gently heat them in a covered container in the oven or in the microwave. Give each guest a half breast (or a whole one if you're not using the legs), thinly sliced on an angle. Serve a few slices of braised duck leg with the breast. You can also decorate the plate with orange wedges (see "Cutting Orange Wedges without Membranes," below).

BRING the reserved orange juice mixture back to a simmer and whisk in the butter. Season to taste with salt and pepper and, if needed, extra vinegar or *gastrique*.

HOW TO CUT ORANGE WEDGES WITHOUT MEMBRANES (COUPER À VIF)

At times, the classic French aversion to texture runs against our contemporary appreciation of foods in a more natural state. Many people love mashed potatoes with the peels left on, none of us bothers peeling mushrooms anymore, and most of us would prefer a chunk of grilled tuna to a feather-light quenelle. But as far as I can tell, strips of membrane and pith left on an orange wedge thrill no one.

To cut an orange into membraneless and pithless wedges—the French call this *couper à vif*—slice both ends off the orange with a sharp paring knife, deep enough so you see the orange flesh. Set the orange on one end and carve off the peel, working from the top down. Follow the contours of the orange so you leave as little flesh attached to the peel as possible. When you've removed all the peel and, with it, the white pith, hold the orange in one hand over a bowl and slice along both sides of each of the thin membranes separating the wedges. Slice along the membranes only to the center of the orange, coaxing the wedges into the bowl as you go. When all the wedges—now called "supremes"—are in the bowl, squeeze the juice out of what's left of the orange, over the wedges.

Once you know the basic methods of cooking duck—sautéing and grilling of breasts, braising and confit of legs—almost any classic French duck dish is simply a variation on a theme. Many classic dishes—*caneton aux navets* (Duck with Turnips), *caneton aux olives* (Duck with Olives), *caneton aux petits pois* (Duck with Baby Peas), and *caneton aux cerises* (Duck with Cherries) are virtually the same except for the addition of a fruit or vegetable to the basic sauce (the sauce on page 390 without the orange) or to the garniture surrounding the duck.

When you serve a garniture such as turnips or baby peas, you should decide how much of an interchange of flavor you want between garniture and duck. If there's to be no interchange, the garniture, conceivably almost any vegetable, can be cooked independently of the duck. But most of the time, French cooks take advantage of the duck's savor for flavoring the garniture. When roasting a duck in the traditional way—either in the oven in a small roasting pan or in a pot (*en cocotte*)—the garniture is simply cooked along with the duck (in the case of turnips) or added as the duck approaches readiness (in the case of baby peas) so that the fat and juices released by the duck combine with the garniture. But because American ducks oblige us to use methods other than roasting, we need to find another way to get our vegetables or fruits to taste like duck. The simplest and most obvious method is to cook the vegetables in a small amount of rendered duck fat and perhaps with a few shreds of confit or braised duck legs. If we've braised the duck legs, the vegetables can be cooked in a small amount of the braising liquid. In the recipe given here for Duck with Turnips, the turnips are first lightly browned in duck fat and then glazed with the braising liquid. Some garnitures—currants or cherries, for instance—act as simple flavorings and are just simmered in the sauce for a few minutes before serving. Because these fruits release liquids as they cook, the sauces usually has to be reduced slightly before being served or before being finished with butter. Fruit sauces are usually flavored with *gastrique* (see page 387) in the same way as a classic orange sauce.

On some occasions, we may want to serve two vegetables, one that is integral to the cooking of the duck and has been cooked in duck fat and/or braising liquid, and a second that has been cooked independently and has no flavor of duck in it at all. Straw potatoes (deep-fried julienne potatoes) are the traditional French nonintegral garniture to roast duck (soufflé potatoes in really fancy places), but nowadays mashed potatoes seem to make more sense and are adaptable to all sorts of variations—flavoring with fennel, celeriac, mushrooms, and so forth. (See Chapter 41 for more about flavored mashed potatoes.)

DUCK WITH TURNIPS

CANETON AUX NAVETS

MAKES 4 MAIN-COURSE SERVINGS

3   medium-size turnips (about 1½ pounds [675 g] total)

2   tablespoons rendered duck fat or butter

    salt

    pepper

1   cup [250 ml] duck-leg braising liquid (see page 385) or concentrated veal or chicken or duck broth (see page 389)

4   boneless single Long Island duckling breasts, or 2 boneless single mulard breasts (about 2 pounds [900 g] total)

4   tablespoons unsalted butter

PEEL the turnips and cut them into wedges about ¾ inch [2 cm] thick at the thickest part. You should be able to get about 8 wedges out of a medium-size turnip. If you want, use a small paring knife to trim the edges off the wedges to give them a somewhat rounder shape.

SAUTÉ the turnips in the rendered duck fat or butter over medium heat until they turn golden brown but aren't cooked all the way through—they still offer a little resistance when you poke them with a knife—about 7 minutes, turning every couple of minutes. Spoon out any fat left in the pan, season the turnips with salt and pepper, and add 3 tablespoons of the braising liquid or concentrated broth to the pan. When you start cooking the duck breasts, partially cover the pan containing the turnips and place it over low to medium heat. Move the pan rapidly back and forth every few minutes to coat the turnips with glaze.

SCORE the breasts as described on page 381 and season them with salt and pepper. Sauté them over medium to high heat, skin-side down in a pan just large enough to fit them—there's no need to put oil in the pan—for 8 to 10 minutes (12 to 14 minutes for mulard breasts), or until the breasts just begin to feel firm to the touch and the skin looks brown and crispy. Turn the breasts over and cook them for 2 minutes (3 minutes for mulard breasts) over high heat, just long enough to brown the flesh side. If you're using mulard breasts, slice the breasts; if you're using Long Island duckling breasts, you can slice them or serve them whole. Take the lid off the turnips, which should be easily penetrated with a knife, and spoon them onto the plates. Pour the rest of the braising liquid or concentrated broth into the pan used to glaze the turnips, bring to a boil on high heat, and whisk in the butter. Season to taste with salt and pepper, and spoon the sauce over the duck.

OTHER VARIATIONS

DUCK WITH OLIVES (Caneton aux Olives): Squeeze or cut the pits out of ¾ cup [100 g] of green olives. Chop the olives very coarse. Sauté the duck breasts. While keeping the breasts warm, pour the fat out of the pan and deglaze the pan with 1 cup of concentrated broth or braising liquid. Reduce by about half, or until the liquid becomes lightly syrupy. Stir in the olives, whisk in 4 tablespoons of butter, and season to taste with salt and pepper. Spoon the sauce over the sliced or whole duck breasts.

DUCK WITH FRESH RED CURRANTS OR OTHER BERRIES (Caneton aux Groseilles ou aux Autres Baies): Set aside 1 cup of berries, such as red or black currants, blackberries, blueberries [all 150 g], or pitted sour cherries [250 g]. Prepare a *gastrique* as described on page 390. Sauté the breasts, pour out the rendered fat, deglaze the pan with concentrated broth or braising liquid, and reduce by about half, or until lightly syrupy. Stir the berries into the sauce and allow them to cook through, about 1 minute. If you notice that the sauce has gotten too thin because the berries have released liquid, remove the berries with a slotted spoon and reduce the sauce some more until it is, again, lightly syrupy. Add the *gastrique*, 1 teaspoon at a time, until the sauce has the right amount of sweetness and tartness. If it starts to get too sweet without being acidic enough, add a few drops of good wine vinegar; if it's too acidic, simmer it for 1 minute and, if it's still too acidic, add a pinch of sugar. Reduce again, if necessary, and whisk in 4 tablespoons butter and, if you like, a few drops of the appropriate eau de vie, such as kirsch (for cherries), framboise (for raspberries), and so on. Put the fruits back into the sauce, season to taste with salt and pepper, and serve over the duck breasts.

DUCK WITH BABY PEAS (Caneton aux Petits Pois): I hate to admit it, but baby peas are one of the few frozen vegetables that, most of the year, I prefer over fresh. Except for a week or two in late spring or early summer when fresh peas show up at farmers' markets, fresh peas are always too large and starchy. To get the most flavor and texture out of frozen baby peas, don't follow the directions on the box, which tell you to cook the peas in boiling water. This isn't necessary, since the peas have already been parboiled at the factory

Prepare the duck and the duck sauce in the same way as Duck with Olives. In a large sauté pan, heat 1½ cups boiled and drained fresh peas or a 10-ounce [285 g] package of thawed and drained frozen baby peas in a couple of tablespoons of duck fat. Stir in a few tablespoons of shredded confit, if you have any. Season well with salt and pepper.

PRESSED DUCK

It's tempting to make pressed duck as an excuse to buy one of those impressive-looking duck presses. Unfortunately, we Americans don't have access to the right kind of duck, and are unlikely ever to encounter pressed duck (*caneton à la presse* or *canard au sang;* "sang" means blood) on American shores or even in France. A few restaurants in France serve pressed duck, but the only restaurant I know that has it year-round is the Tour d'Argent, Paris's and probably the world's oldest restaurant. Of course, lunch here costs about the same as a duck press, but the views of Notre-Dame and the Seine are unforgettable, as is the preparation of the famous duck itself—listed on the menu as *caneton au sang*—conducted in a corner of the dining room. To see the process close up, tell the waiter you want to go over and watch.

Pressed duck does have one grim aspect. It is made from a Rouen duckling, which is killed by strangling instead of bleeding, so that the blood stays in the organs and tissues, giving the duckling its own particular flavor. The duck is then roasted so that the breast meat is rare and the legs are very rare. The legs are carved off in the dining room and rushed back to the kitchen, where they are quickly grilled. The breast meat is cut into strips—called *aiguillettes*—and placed in a small pan, while the carcass is pressed in the duck press to extract its intensely flavored juices. The juices are flavored with a little Cognac and a swirl of butter and are then used for gently reheating the strips of duck breast. (This is actually a salmis—the bird is roasted and lightly cooked in its own juices. See Squab Salmis, page 377.) At this point, quickly get back to your table so you make it there before the duck. The climax (or anticlimax) to the process is a rather unassuming plate of duck strips with a sauce that looks like mud. But such a dish needs no fanfare or elaborate decoration; all its eloquence is in its flavor. When you've been nibbling on your duck for 10 minutes, the grilled legs appear on little plates to the side. Near the end of the meal, you'll get a postcard with a painting of one of the former owners of the Tour d'Argent at the duck press. The card will have the number of the duck—the haute cuisine equivalent of "billions served."

I've tried pressing Long Island duckling carcasses in a friend's press and ended up with only ½ cup of grease. To simulate pressed duck, make a red wine sauce base by braising the duck legs in red wine and reducing and degreasing as on page 386; or brown the raw duck carcass with mirepoix, moisten with red wine instead of water, and reduce; or simply reduce concentrated brown veal or beef broth with an equal amount of red wine. When you get your red wine sauce base, purée the duck liver (or some foie gras) with an equal amount of butter, work the mixture through a strainer with a wooden spoon, and whisk the mixture into the red wine sauce base. Whisk in a little good Cognac. You can reheat the sliced duck breast in the sauce (again, turning the dish into a salmis) or just spoon the sauce over it. Don't let the sauce boil or it will look like curdled mud instead of just mud. (A curdled sauce can be quickly fixed by puréeing with an immersion blender.)

FRICASSEE OF YOUNG RABBIT WITH PEARL ONIONS, BACON, AND MUSHROOMS

LAPEREAU EN GIBELOTTE

HOW TO	HOW TO	HOW TO	HOW TO
DEAL WITH A RABBIT'S UNFAMILIAR ANATOMY	PARTIALLY BONE A RABBIT TO MAKE IT EASIER TO SERVE AND TO EAT	SAUTÉ, BRAISE, AND GRILL A RABBIT	COOK WILD RABBIT AND HARE

WE AMERICANS HAVE NEVER BEEN ESPECIALLY FOND OF RABBIT, because, it seems, rabbits make us think of Easter bunnies or childhood pets instead of a tasty dinner. But the needs of the epicure must override these associations. Rabbits make a very satisfying meal, with white flesh that's much like chicken, but more flavorful and with a firmer, meatier texture. Perhaps as a result of the bunny qualms, rabbit recipes are scarce. Rabbits also have a confusing anatomy that makes them tricky to eat.

Sometimes rabbits are roasted whole, but because they have no fatty skin to self-baste them, they must first be wrapped in a thin sheet of fatback—what the French call a *bard*—

to keep them from drying out, a process few of us want to bother with. More often, rabbits are cut up and sautéed in butter. Like chickens, rabbits can be cooked completely in a sauté pan in hot fat—the result is called a sauté—and a sauce made by deglazing the pan. Or they can be prepared in the style of a fricassee: cooked only partially in hot fat and then simmered in liquid. A *gibelotte* is a kind of fricassee made by simmering lightly sautéed rabbit pieces in white wine and broth, with the cooking liquid thickened into a sauce by flour that was sprinkled over the rabbit during the sautéing. The process, typical of home-style cooking, is called *singer*. Today, *gibelotte* always refers to a rabbit stew, but in the eighteenth century and earlier, the same treatment and name were used for stews made not only with rabbit, but with chicken and game birds. (See page 405 for information about wild rabbits and hares.)

HOW TO CUT UP A RABBIT

Because rabbits are sold whole and butchers can't be relied on to cut them up in the right way, you may have to cut yours up at home. This is easy, since a rabbit fits together into rather obvious pieces that are readily separated. If your rabbit comes with its head—valuable for adding flavor to the stew—just cut it off with a cleaver or heavy chef's knife. If the rabbit comes with its liver, save it and chop it to use as a stuffing for the saddle, or sauté it and sprinkle it, coarsely chopped, over rabbit stew. Cut through the thin layer of meat that attaches the forelegs to the body. There's no joint to cut through; the forelegs are attached with muscle alone. Cut the front section of the rabbit away from the hindquarters by turning the rabbit on its back. Count 3 ribs up from the hindquarters and slide a knife between the ribs to the rabbit's backbone until you hit the backbone and can't go any farther. Repeat on the other side. Use a heavy chef's knife to separate the front and back where the cuts that were made between the ribs join. Press down firmly, gently forcing the knife through the backbone. At this stage you should have the head, two forelegs, and the front section (these are cooked with the rest of the rabbit to reinforce the flavor of the braising liquid; they aren't served at formal meals), and the hindquarters (the saddle— two legs and the back).

Cut the legs away from the saddle by sliding a small paring knife into where the legs join at the backbone and cutting through the joint. Hack off the pointed end of the tailbone that's left when you remove the legs. Cut the saddle crosswise in half with a heavy knife. You may have to lean on the knife to cut through the bone. Season the underside of the flaps with salt and pepper and roll the flaps under each half of the saddle. Tie up each of these halves with two short lengths of string, to hold the flaps in place. If you're cooking 2-pound [900-g] rabbits, the size I recommend for *gibelottes* and other quick-cooking stews, you can get 3 servings per rabbit; a leg each for two diners and both saddle pieces for the third. But if you have hungry guests or want a more equitable division of rabbit parts, serve a leg and half a saddle per person, meaning of course that you'll only get 2 servings per rabbit. (Most people prefer the saddle, which is more tender and has more meat.) *Lapereau en gibelotte* is delicious served with buttered noodles.

FRICASSEE OF YOUNG RABBIT WITH PEARL ONIONS, BACON, AND MUSHROOMS

LAPEREAU EN GIBELOTTE

MAKES 4 GENEROUS MAIN-COURSE SERVINGS

- 1 pint [335 g] (12 ounces [about 280 g]) pearl onions, or 1 package (10 ounces [285 g]) frozen
- ½ pound [225 g] or 1 package (10 ounces [280 g]) small mushrooms, preferably cremini
- 2 rabbits (2 pounds [900 g] each, dressed) (if you're starting out with a rabbit with its fur, it should weigh 4 to 5 pounds)

  salt

  pepper

- 2 tablespoons butter
- 2 tablespoons flour
- ½ pound [225 g] thickly sliced lean bacon
- 2 cups [500 ml] dry white wine
- 1 cup [250 g] Brown Chicken Broth (see page 209)
- 1 small bouquet garni

PEEL the onions by first plunging them into a pot of boiling water, boiling for 1 minute, draining in a colander, rinsing with cold water, and then cutting the tiny root ends off with a sharp paring knife and pulling away the peel. Trim ⅛ inch (3 mm) off the bottom of the mushroom stems if they are dark, dirty, or dried out. If the mushroom caps are more than 1 inch in diameter, quarter the mushrooms vertically.

CUT up the rabbits as described on page 396. Chop the rib cage into 3 or 4 pieces with a cleaver and chop the head, if you have it, in half. Season the rab-

bit parts with salt and pepper and brown them in the butter, over medium heat, in one or two skillets just large enough to hold them in a single layer. When the parts are well browned, after about 8 minutes on each side, sprinkle them with the flour and cook them for about 2 minutes more on each side, to eliminate the flour's starchy taste.

WHILE the rabbit parts are browning, cut the bacon slices crosswise into ¼-inch [.5 cm] strips and cook the strips gently over medium heat in a small skillet until they barely begin to turn crispy. Remove them with a slotted spoon and reserve.

POUR the wine and the broth over the rabbit parts, nestle in the bouquet garni, and add the pearl onions and mushrooms. If you're using two skillets, use half the liquids, onions, and mushrooms in each one and nestle a small bouquet garni in each. Bring to a simmer over high heat, turn the heat down to low to maintain at a very gentle simmer, and cover. Simmer for about 15 minutes, until the rabbit feels firm to the touch.

TRANSFER the rabbit parts, onions, and mushrooms to a bowl and cover them loosely with aluminum foil. Pour the liquid in the pan into a small saucepan and gently simmer the sauce, while skimming off fat and scum, for about 10 minutes, until the sauce has a lightly syrupy consistency.

SORT through the rabbit parts with tongs, removing the head, the forelegs, and the cut-up front section. Cut the string off the pieces of saddle. Serve each guest a leg and half a saddle. Spoon the sauce, mushrooms, and pearl onions over each serving.

HOW TO BONE A RABBIT SADDLE

If your guests don't have experience eating rabbit, getting the meat off the saddle can be as frustrating for them as eating a small, bony crab. To cut the saddle into more elegant and easier-to-manage servings, you can bone it ahead of time and then slice it into boneless rounds, giving 1 or 2 rounds per guest to accompany the legs. Turn the saddle on its back and notice the two thin muscles that run along its length, next to the backbone. These are the tenderloins. Slide a knife under these muscles starting in the center, scraping them away from the underlying bone as you go. Slide the knife under the toothlike range of bones that were lying under the tenderloins and continue, following the bones' contours, until you detach the thicker—loin—muscles that run along the backbone closer to the back of the saddle. Continue in this way until you reach the small cartilaginous bones that protrude under the skin along the back. As you approach these bones, you may make a harmless tear or two, but try to keep the skin as intact as possible. Don't try to cut completely around the bones or you'll cut through the skin. When you've nearly detached the backbone—the skin should hang from the bone only along the very thin ridge of bones that practically protrude through the back—turn the saddle over, with the skin facing up. Gently pull the skin back and cut through the cartilaginous bones, one by one, while peeling back the skin. You'll have to leave a tiny bit of bone embedded in the skin; if you try to cut it out, you'll tear the skin. Continue in this way until you've cut through all the bones and the backbone comes away in one piece. Season the inside of the saddle and, if you wish, sprinkle it with chopped herbs. (I like to lay 2 sage leaves end to end between the loin muscles.) Roll up the flaps and tie the boneless saddle into what will look like a thick sausage. Brown it and simmer it in the same way you would a bone-in saddle, but don't slice it or cut it crosswise in half until you're ready to serve. When serving the rabbit, slide a knife along both sides of the tiny bones you left embedded along the saddle, making a tiny V and cutting out the bits of bone. Slice the saddle, depending on the number of guests, into slices from ½ to 2 inches [1.5 to 5 cm] thick, so that each person gets 1 or 2 slices.

VARIATIONS ON RABBIT SAUTÉ AND FRICASSEE

Any recipe for sautéed or fricasseed chicken (see Chapter 27) can be used for rabbit. The French have enjoyed rabbit for centuries and have developed dozens of recipes. In France, rabbit has never been considered an elegant or expensive dish, but it has always been available, especially in the country, where until recently virtually everyone had a rabbit hutch and fed the rabbits on kitchen scraps. Traditional recipes include blanquette, in which the cut-up rabbit is poached with aromatic vegetables and the poaching liquid is finished with roux, egg yolks, and cream and garnished like a *blanquette de veau*, with pearl onions and mushrooms (see Chapter 30). In *lapin aux pruneaux,* the rabbit is marinated with aromatic vegetables and vinegar and simmered in the marinade, and the marinade is finished with red currant jelly and prunes, to create a sweet-and-sour effect. Rabbit cooked *à la poulette* is much like a blanquette, except that potatoes replace the mushrooms, and the aromatic vegetables—carrots and turnips—are left in. Late eighteenth-century and early nineteenth-century recipes are more fanciful. Some sound modern and delicious: rabbit simmered in broth, the reduced broth worked into a lentil purée and served with the rabbit; rabbit with cucumbers; rabbit with mushrooms and artichokes; rabbit fillets tossed in a salad with capers, onions, and little strips of anchovies; rabbit smothered with peas and gently cooked. Others (rabbit with eels) border on the bizarre.

Now that rabbit is no longer banned from the menus of the best restaurants, chefs have come up with innovative, often luxurious, and sometimes frightfully complicated dishes to accommodate it. Many of these recipes use only the saddle, in French usually called the *râble* but on more affected menus called the *cul* (slightly vulgar, meaning roughly "rear end") or the *baron* (a word traditionally reserved for the two attached hind legs of larger creatures such as lambs). Michel Guérard simmers rabbit in chicken broth with baby turnips and their greens and serves the rabbit, quickly boned before serving, with a rich butter sauce made from the reduced stewing broth; he surrounds the rabbit fillets with the turnips, their greens, and lightly blanched spinach. Roger Vergé, at his Provençal restaurant Le Moulin de Mougins, cooks the rabbit saddle and legs in a covered pot with butter—this technique of cooking covered with little or no liquid is called *étuvage*—and makes a quick sauce in the pot with shallots, white wine, cream, parsley, and basil. Georges Blanc, a three-star chef in the Bresse region famous for its poultry, serves rabbit fillets with chayotes and a sauce made with crème fraîche and mustard. Claude Peyrot, chef-owner of Le Vivarois, serves thin strips of rabbit fillets in a salad with sautéed wild mushrooms.

The most complicated rabbit dish I've ever heard of is prepared by Alain Ducasse, France's only chef to hold six Michelin stars. While I'm not suggesting you run out and make it, I appreciate it because it makes use of virtually all the rabbit parts. Here's a synopsis: The legs are boned, wrapped in bacon, roasted, and served, sliced, in rounds. The forelegs and front section of the rabbit are braised with onions, rosemary, and garlic and the meat is shredded (almost like rillettes, see page 384) and stirred into the onion, rosemary, and garlic mixture. The rib cage is split down the middle of the backbone like a rack of lamb, and the miniature racks, as well as halves of the saddle, are served atop the onion mixture. The dish is garnished with black radishes (which the French call *navets noirs*, black turnips) and white turnips. Get right to work.

Despite these elegant interpretations, one of France's most popular, and conceivably best, rabbit dishes is rabbit with mustard sauce. Like almost all rabbit dishes, it is traditionally served with buttered fresh egg noodles.

RABBIT WITH MUSTARD

LAPIN À LA MOUTARDE

MAKES 4 MAIN-COURSE SERVINGS

While lapin à la moutarde is an old standby, there are several ways to go about cooking it. The most obvious method, and the one I'm most likely to use at home, is to sauté the rabbit and keep it warm while making a quick mustard sauce in the pan. After pouring off most of the fat, I typically stir a little chopped shallot or onion into the hot pan; add white wine and broth, if I have it; and pour in some heavy cream. At the end I add the mustard to taste, alone with whatever herb I happen to choose from what's growing in the garden or hanging to dry next to the stove. A common bistro method is to brush the rabbit pieces liberally with mustard before sautéing them in butter or oil and then making a white wine sauce in the pan, much like my usual home version, but without the mustard and often without the cream. When the cream is left out, a little flour is cooked with the chopped onions added to the sauté pan before the broth or wine is added, resulting in a velouté sauce that is less rich than my version yet still has a little body.

2   rabbits (2 to 2½ pounds [900 g to 1.1 kg] each, dressed)

    salt

    pepper

4   tablespoons butter

1   medium-size onion, or 4 shallots, chopped fine

1   cup [250 ml] dry white wine

1   cup [250 ml] Brown Chicken Broth (page 209) or rabbit broth made from the head and forequarters, including the forelegs

½   cup [125 ml] heavy cream

2   tablespoons Dijon or whole-grain (moutarde de Meaux), mustard, or more to taste

CUT up the rabbits as described on page 396. Save the head, forelegs, and rib cage for making broth. (If you're ambitious, make a rabbit broth by browning the coarsely chopped bones and simmering them with aromatic vegetables and a bouquet garni for 2 hours, reduce the broth, and add it to the sauce described here.) If you like, bone the saddle as described on page 398.

SEASON the rabbit pieces with salt and pepper and brown them in 2 tablespoons of the butter in a heavy-bottomed sauté pan over medium heat for about 10 minutes on each side, until done. (See "Knowing When Rabbit Is Done," page 401.)

TRANSFER Transfer the pieces to a platter and keep them warm while you're making the sauce.

POUR the cooked butter out of the sauté pan and replace it with the remaining 2 tablespoons fresh. Stir in the chopped onions or shallots. Cook over low to medium heat while stirring until the onions turn translucent, about 10 minutes. Pour in the wine and broth. Bring to a simmer over high heat and turn down the heat to maintain at a low simmer. Simmer for 5 minutes while using a spoon or small ladle to skim off froth and fat that float to the top. Pour any juices released by the rabbit into the sauce. Pour in the cream and boil the sauce for about 5 minutes, or until it has a lightly creamy consistency. Take the pan off the heat and whisk in the mustard. Season the sauce with salt and pepper. Spoon the sauce over the rabbit on the platter or over individual servings on heated plates.

KNOWING WHEN RABBIT IS DONE

Sections of young rabbit will feel firm to the touch when they're done. But because rabbit tends to be firm to begin with, the touch method is somewhat trickier than with chicken, which has a softer texture when raw and turns distinctly firm when cooked. You can stick a skewer into the rabbit and look at the color of the juices that come out. If they're pink, cook the rabbit some more, until the juices come out clear. You can also stick an instant-read thermometer through the thickest part of one of the rabbit sections—the rabbit is done when it has reached an internal temperature of 135°F [57°C]. When you are long-braising rabbit, as in the next recipe, temperature is irrelevant. Like stew meat, long-braised rabbit is cooked until a skewer slides in and out with no resistance.

COOKING OLDER RABBITS: RABBIT CIVETS

Nowadays most French recipes for rabbit call for one that's relatively young, no bigger than 3 pounds [1.3 kg] after dressing—a *lapereau* instead of a *lapin*. Like most modern cooks, French or not, I once assumed that younger animals are tastier or at least more tender than older ones. I discovered my error one day after a restaurant customer gave me two giant rabbits he thought too old to eat, from his farm. I knew the only solution was to braise them for hours as though making a stew, and because I feared the lean meat would dry out during the long cooking, I knew they needed to be well larded. I had been wanting to make an authentic *civet*, which is a stew finished with the animal's blood, like an authentic *coq au vin*. And now, since my farmer friend was killing the rabbits for me, I had my opportunity. I was thrilled with the results, but I knew that the real test would be the reaction of our largely French clientele. Several customers pronounced the rabbit a triumph, and one customer, from Alsace, who had grown up eating rabbit, pronounced it the best he had ever had.

If you want to prepare this dish yourself, don't panic about the blood, which needs to be saved in a jar with Cognac as soon as the rabbit is killed. It isn't essential. Whisking the blood into the braising liquid just before serving—the blood mustn't boil or it will curdle—thickens the sauce and makes it almost black, but doesn't do a whole lot for its flavor, which comes from the long braising. The large, delicious rabbit liver can be puréed with a little butter and the mixture worked through a strainer and whisked into the sauce to give it a deeper flavor, or you can sauté the liver, slice or chop it, and sprinkle it over the finished stew. If you want to pull out all the stops, work a couple of ounces of foie gras with an equal amount of butter with or without the rabbit's liver through a strainer and whisk the mixture into the sauce just before serving.

When buying your rabbit, ask for the biggest one. The butcher may try to talk you out of it and try to sell you a smaller creature, more suitable for a quick sauté or for grilling. He may have to special-order a big rabbit and it may come frozen, but because the rabbit is being braised, the freezing does it no harm. This recipe serves 4, but considering the time it takes, you may want to double it. Keep in mind, though, that a double recipe requires a very wide, shallow pot—what the French call a *rondeau*.

LONG·BRAISED RABBIT

LAPIN BRAISÉ À L'ANCIENNE

MAKES 4 MAIN-COURSE SERVINGS

1 rabbit (5 pounds [2.3 kg] or larger after dressing, or the largest you can find), liver reserved; blood also reserved, if possible, with 2 teaspoons Cognac added

1 pound [450 g] fatback, including the rind (see page 9)

1 large onion, sliced

1 large carrot, peeled and sliced

1 medium-size turnip, peeled and sliced

2 cloves garlic, crushed

1 medium-size bouquet garni

2 quarts [2 l] Brown Chicken Broth (page 209) or White Chicken Broth (page 210)

1 cup [250 ml] heavy cream (optional)

salt

pepper

CUT up the rabbit as described on page 396, except leave the saddle whole. Reserve the liver and blood, if you have them, in the refrigerator.

PLACE the fatback in the freezer for about 30 minutes to make it easier to slice. Cut the rind off the fatback by placing the fatback, rind-side down, on a cutting board and then sliding a long, thin knife between the fat and the rind. Cut the fat crosswise into strips ¼ inch [.5 cm] wide and about 5 inches [13 cm] long (the length will be the same as the width of the fatback). You'll need about 40 strips. Reserve the strips and the rind.

TO make carving easier, you can bone the saddle as described on page 398, but this isn't essential.

USE an interlarding needle, which looks a little like a trussing needle but with a hinged clamp on the end, to grip the strips of fatback and pull them through the rabbit legs on both sides and the outside of the saddle. Put about 20 strips of fatback in the legs—10 in each leg. Turn the saddle over and lard the outside with 10 strips each on the left and right sides. Cut off the strips of fatback, leaving about ¼ inch protruding from the rabbit; don't cut them all the way down, because they shrink during cooking. (See page 423 for more about larding.)

PREHEAT the oven to 450°F [230°C/gas mark 8] and spread the onion, carrot, turnip, and garlic in a shallow, heavy-bottomed pot (or straight-sided sauté pan) just large enough to hold the rabbit pieces (including the forelegs and forequarters) in a single layer. (The pot or pan should have a lid.) Place the fatback rind over the vegetables and arrange the rabbit pieces on top. Slide the pot, uncovered, into the oven and roast the rabbit until the top is well browned, about 45 minutes. Check underneath the rabbit after about 20 minutes to make sure the vegetables or rabbit juices aren't caramelizing and getting too dark. If they are, add ½ cup [125 ml] of water or broth. Turn the rabbit pieces over and brown them in the oven on the second side, about 30 minutes, again being careful not to allow the vegetables or juices to burn.

WHEN the rabbit is well browned on both sides, take the pot out of the oven and place it on the stove. Nestle the bouquet garni in among the pieces and pour in the broth. Bring to a gentle simmer on the stove and cover the pot, first with a sheet of aluminum foil pressed down in the middle (this causes moisture to condense and drip over the rabbit, basting it from the inside) and then with the lid. Keep the braising liquid at the barest simmer by placing the pan on the stove over the lowest flame or in the oven, turned down to 325°F [165°C/gas mark 3]. Check every 20 minutes or so to make sure the liquid is barely simmering (a bubble rising every 3 or 4 seconds). Simmer in this way until a skewer slides easily in and out of the rabbit, about 2½ hours.

GENTLY transfer the rabbit pieces to a bowl and strain the braising liquid into a saucepan. Press down on the vegetables and trimmings in the strainer with the bottom of a ladle to extract the juices. Discard the vegetables and trimmings (save the forelegs for nibblings). Gently simmer the braising liquid on the stove, keeping the saucepan to one side of the heat source and skimming off fat and froth, for about 10 minutes, until you're left with about 4 cups [1 l]. (The amount will depend on your pot, the exact oven temperature, and so on.) Wash out the pot used for braising the rabbit and arrange the cooked rabbit pieces in it. Pour in the reduced and degreased braising liquid and slide the pot, uncovered, back into the oven. Turn the oven up to 400°F [200°C/gas mark 6].

GLAZE the rabbit pieces by basting them, about every 10 minutes, until they are covered with a shiny glaze and the surrounding braising liquid is slightly syrupy, about 45 minutes. If you want to use the cream, which gives the sauce a little body and *suavité*, pour it over the rabbit, baste, and cook for 5 minutes more. (If you have the blood, whisk the sauce into it off the heat and reheat the sauce gently, while whisking, without allowing it to boil, until it thickens.)

ARRANGE the rabbit pieces on a platter (if you want to carve at the table) and season the sauce to taste with salt and pepper. At the table or in the kitchen, slice the saddle into 4 rounds if you've boned it or carve it off in strips if you haven't (see page 404). Slice the meat off the legs, placing a round or strip of saddle and a share of sliced leg on each of 4 heated plates. Spoon the sauce over each serving.

Variations: Any attempt to improve the flavor of this delicious dish might well incur the wrath of the gods. The melting rabbit flesh and the sauce should be as good as anything you've ever tasted. However, there's always room for excess. A handful of dried morels, softened in a little Madeira, simmered for a few seconds in the sauce (before adding any blood), and spooned over each serving, takes an already celestial dish to greater heights. Needless to say, truffles would do no harm.

Lightly creamed spinach or a mixture of spinach and sorrel placed under each serving cuts the richness and adds contrasting green to a study in browns, and the sorrel contributes a welcome acidic tang. Glazed carrots, pearl onions, or baby turnips add color, contrast, and flavor. Boiled string beans, baby peas, baby artichokes, or wedges of artichoke bottom can be mingled with the sauce and spooned over the servings. Red wine can replace the broth, giving the sauce a note of acidity and a coq au vin–like depth. Vinegar can be used in the braising or for finishing the sauce and its acidity balanced with fresh or dried fruits (prunes, softened in a little port, are marvelous) or red currant jelly (used in many classic game sauces). When the acidity and sweetness are both pronounced, the dish becomes sweet-and-sour (*lapin à l'aigre-doux*), the sauce providing a welcome contrast to the melting suaveness of the rabbit. Various well-buttered purées (especially chestnut and lentil, which again are classic with game) can be placed in small mounds under the servings or passed at the table. In addition to being a possible finish for the braising liquid, foie gras can be cut into thick strips and wrapped in the boned saddle.

GRILLED RABBIT

It doesn't occur to most of us to feature rabbit at an outdoor barbecue, but rabbits take well to grilling provided they are young and small, they aren't overcooked, and they are basted with olive oil or melted butter during the grilling. Unless you have guests who are used to eating rabbit and won't be confused by the rabbit saddle's unfamiliar anatomy, I suggest either boning the saddle before cooking (see page 398) or carving it at the table once it's done (see page 404).

HOW TO CARVE OR EAT A SADDLE OF RABBIT

No one has trouble eating rabbit legs, because they have almost the same structure as chicken legs; but I've seen the saddle bring dinner guests to the verge of tears. If you've ever seen a saddle of lamb, you'll soon realize that a rabbit saddle is put together in the same way and you'll know how to proceed. If, however, you're among the majority who have never seen a saddle of anything, you'll need a lesson.

The saddle is like the bottom half of your back. If you reach around and feel your spine, you'll notice that there are two muscles (actually groups of muscle) running vertically along each side. When you stare down at the rabbit saddle on your plate or cutting board, you'll notice similar muscles running lengthwise on both sides of the spine. Use a long, sharp knife to cut lengthwise down along one side of the bones that stick out from the vertebrae, which you can feel them by rubbing your hand or knife along the back of the saddle, until you hit a ridge of bone that runs along one side of the spinal column. Turn the knife outward, toward the side of the saddle, and while pressing the knife against the underlying bone, cut around the ridge and then outward until you detach the whole loin muscle. Turn the saddle around (not over) and repeat on the other side. You can serve the two long, tender loin muscles as they are, or slice them into rounds or strips. When you've sliced off both loins, turn the saddle over and repeat the process with the smaller tenderloin muscles that run along the spine on the underside of the saddle.

GRILLED YOUNG RABBIT

LAPERAU GRILLÉ

MAKES 4 GENEROUS MAIN-COURSE SERVINGS

2 rabbits (2 to 2½ pounds [900 g to 1.1 kg] each, dressed)

1 medium-size onion, sliced thin

½ cup [125 ml] dry white wine

4 tablespoons olive oil

1 tablespoon chopped fresh marjoram or thyme, or 4 fresh whole sage leaves

   salt

   pepper

4 tablespoons extra-virgin olive oil or melted butter

CUT up the rabbits as described on page 396. The forelegs can be grilled, but the rib cage and head should be saved for broth. Marinate the rabbit pieces with the onion, wine, and 2 tablespoons of the olive oil in a bowl, covered, for 2 to 12 hours, in the refrigerator. If you're not boning the saddles, include the marjoram, thyme, or sage in the marinade.

IF you want to make the saddles easier to eat, bone them (see page 398). Before marinating, sprinkle the inside with the salt, pepper, and chopped marjoram (or put in the sage leaves, end to end), and tie them up into large sausage shapes with string.

WHEN you're ready to grill, take the rabbit pieces out of the marinade and pat them dry with paper towels. Rub the rabbit pieces and the grill or grill pan with olive oil. Season the rabbit pieces with salt and pepper and grill, 6 to 8 inches [15 to 20.5 cm] from the bed of coals or in a grill pan over medium to high heat, for 15 to 20 minutes on each side, brushing them with extra-virgin olive oil or melted butter, at least twice on each side.

IF you've boned the saddles, slice them into 4 rounds each and serve everyone a leg and 2 rounds of the saddle. If you haven't boned them, you can carve them (see page 404) and serve everyone 1 or 2 slices and a leg each.

Variations: During the summer, I slice the meat off the grilled or sautéed legs and saddle and toss it in a salad of baby greens with olive oil and a little vinegar. When grilling a boned saddle of rabbit, I simply sprinkle a few chopped herbs or arrange a couple of sage leaves along the inside of the saddle before tying it up, but the sky's the limit on stuffings. The possibilities include wild mushrooms (or their stems), chopped and cooked on the stove until they release their moisture and turn into a duxelles; chopped truffles; the rabbit's liver (lightly sautéed, sliced, and arranged evenly within the saddle); strips of foie gras; or a brushing of mustard.

WILD RABBIT AND HARE

I am blessed to have a hunter friend who supplies me with various wild creatures he shoots in the forests of Pennsylvania. My freezer is filled with venison loins, wild turkey breasts, and wild rabbits. Wild rabbits, sold in France as *lapins de garenne,* are not sold in the United States, but if you are in Europe in the fall, you'll be able to recognize them in the markets by their slightly darker flesh. They have a delicious flavor, deeper than that of domestic rabbits, and they can be tough. Since predicting which ones will be tender and which tough can be tricky, I start cooking them like regular young domestic rabbits and if they feel tough when I stick a knife into a piece, I keep cooking them until they soften.

Although sometimes thought of as a big rabbit, a hare (*lièvre*) is a different animal altogether. It is one of the most delicious of all four-legged wild things. Unlike rabbits, wild or otherwise, hares have red meat and should be cooked according to their age—simply roasted when young, larded and braised when old. The saddle, however, even of older hares,

is almost always tender enough to roast; only the legs of older hares require braising. A hare is larger than a rabbit and has an elongated saddle that makes a generous and delicious roast for two.

If you get your hands on a hare (see Sources), you need to give some thought as to how to approach it. If you've never tasted hare, and want to appreciate it in its simplest unadulterated form, serve the saddle roasted rare to medium rare and carve the loin muscles lengthwise into gorgeous long red strips. Unlike a saddle of rabbit, typically cut away from the rib cage just 2 or 3 ribs up (see page 396), a saddle of hare includes most of the rib cage with the ends of the ribs trimmed off near the back loin muscles; the result is an elongated saddle with more meat. The trimmings of bone and the coarsely chopped forelegs are typically added to the roasting pan so they augment the juices released by the saddle and ultimately contribute to the flavor of the *jus* or sauce.

A *sauce poivrade* and a few of its derivatives are the most classic (and the most delicious) sauces for roast game. The first steps for making a poivrade are relatively predictable: The game's trimmings are gently browned with aromatic vegetables, and white wine (which has been used in the marinade) and full-bodied broth are added. But it is pepper and vinegar that give the sauce its special character. Derivatives soar to celestial heights. A *sauce grand veneur* is a poivrade finished with cream and a little red currant jelly; the sweetness of the jelly juxtaposed with the vinegar in the poivrade gives the sauce a marvelous sweet-and-sour quality. A *sauce Diane,* almost too decadent to imagine, is made by folding whipped cream and chopped truffles into the poivrade. A *sauce moscovite* is made by using Malaga in a *sauce poivrade* and infusing the sauce with crushed juniper berries, which are a natural with game. Other enhancements include puréeing the liver with a little butter (or with the hare's blood, saved with a teaspoon of Cognac to prevent clotting) and whisking the mixture into the sauce at the end.

If confronted with an older hare, you can lard it and braise it in the same way as a large rabbit (see page 402), replacing half the broth with a full-bodied red wine. If you have the blood and/or the liver, you can purée these (the liver puréed with butter or the blood) and whisk them into the sauce just before serving, turning the stewed hare into a *civet de lièvre*. You can also make a *lièvre à la royale*, of which there are many versions, all calling for cooking the hare for up to 7 hours, until the meat falls away from the bone. One of my favorite versions from my 1929 edition of *La Bonne Cuisine du Périgord* finishes the sauce with slices of fresh truffles and the hare's puréed blood and liver.

HARE WITH VINEGAR AND PEPPER SAUCE

LIÈVRE, SAUCE POIVRADE

MAKES 6 MAIN-COURSE SERVINGS

This dish has a natural economy because the lean and tender saddle of hare is cooked quickly in butter while the thighs, forelegs, and ribs are braised for 3 hours (the braising can be done in advance), and the braising liquid then converted into a sauce for both.

2   hares (4 pounds [1.8 kg] each, dressed), or 3 hares (2½ to 3 pounds [1.1 to 1.3 kg] each, dressed)

    salt

    freshly ground black pepper

2   tablespoons olive oil

1   medium-size carrot, peeled and sliced

1   medium-size onion, peeled and sliced

2   cloves garlic, crushed

1   cup [250 ml] white wine

½   cup [125 ml] excellent-quality white wine vinegar or sherry vinegar or balsamic vinegar, or more as needed to finish the sauce

4   cups [1 l] good-quality homemade or salt-free beef broth (see page 219) or Brown Chicken Broth (page 209)

1   medium-size bouquet garni

2   tablespoons butter

12   black peppercorns

CUT up each hare in the same way as a rabbit (see page 396), but cut the forequarters away from the saddle closer to the forelegs—leave more ribs attached to the saddle on both sides—so you don't waste any of the loin meat. Trim off the ends of the ribs and the flaps, using a knife and/or a pair of kitchen shears. Season this elongated saddle with salt and pepper, tie it up with a couple of loops of string, and refrigerate until needed. Save any trimmings.

USE a cleaver or heavy knife to chop each hare's rib cage into 2 pieces and split the heads in half. Season the hind legs and forelegs with salt and pepper and lard them, if you like (see page 402). Brown the legs in olive oil on both sides, in a heavy-bottomed pot with the rib cage, head, and other trimmings. Scoop out the hare parts and reserve. Put the carrot, onion, and garlic in the pot used to brown the legs and trimmings and cook over medium heat, stirring every minute or two, until the vegetables are lightly browned, about 15 minutes. Put the hare back in the pot with the vegetables. Pour in the wine, vinegar, and broth and nestle in the bouquet garni. Bring the liquid to a simmer, cover the pot, and simmer very gently for 3 hours on the stove or in a 325°F [165°C/gas mark 3] oven until a knife slides easily in and out of a leg.

GENTLY take out the hind legs and forelegs with tongs and reserve. Strain the braising liquid through a fine-mesh strainer into a saucepan, pressing gently on the vegetables and trimmings to extract as much of the flavorful liquid as possible. Reduce the braising liquid to about 2 cups [500 ml]—or until it takes on a lightly syrupy consistency—skimming off any fat or froth with a small ladle.

ABOUT 45 minutes before you're ready to serve, preheat the oven to 400°F [200°C/gas mark 6]. Melt the butter in a sauté pan and brown the saddle on both sides. Roast the saddles until an instant-read thermometer stuck into the middle of a saddle half reads 125°F [51°C], then take the saddle halves off the heat and cut them crosswise into sections so everyone gets 1 piece, or, if the saddle halves are thick, carve them in long, thin strips. (See "How to Carve or Eat a Saddle of Rabbit," page 404.) Heat the reserved hind legs in a little of the sauce.

CRUSH the peppercorns by leaning on them with a small pot, rocking the pot over the pepper. Simmer the pepper gently in the sauce for about 3 minutes and season to taste with salt and, if needed, more vinegar. Strain the sauce through a fine-mesh strainer.

ARRANGE the strips or chunks of saddle on 6 heated plates. Carve 2 chunks of meat off each of the hind legs and put a chunk on each plate. Pass the sauce at the table or pour it around—not over—the hare on each plate, so that everyone can see the color of the meat.

Variations: On those rare occasions when I get my hands on a hare, I may not want to bother making a poivrade sauce. In that case I make a simplified game sauce by infusing crushed peppercorns and 6 or 7 crushed juniper berries in concentrated beef broth (see page 4), whisking in some butter to smooth the sauce and give it body, and then straining out the pepper and juniper. I also like to add some marc (see page 10 for information about marc), which lends a gamey note to the sauce.

If you don't want to make a sauce at all, just grill the saddle and freeze the hindquarters and trimmings for more ambitious moments. If you want to stretch the saddle so you can get 4 servings out of it, bone it just like a rabbit saddle (see page 398), put thick strips of foie gras down the middle, tie it up, grill or roast it, and slice it into rounds. Needless to say, this drives guests wild, but you may have to think about a home equity loan.

VEAL STEW WITH CREAM AND MUSHROOMS

BLANQUETTE DE VEAU

WHEN I LIVED IN PARIS, I USED TO STROLL IN MONTMARTRE BECAUSE
it was pretty and convenient to my cramped little room. I'd head for the bustling summit—
la Butte—with its views of the rest of Paris and its square filled with painters dabbing paint
on faux-impressionist canvases to sell to the tourists. One night, two young Americans,
probably college students, were walking behind me. As I eavesdropped, I gathered that they
had been away from home for most of the summer. They talked longingly of what they
really missed about home. It was the food, but not just any food. It was the Big Mac.

When I meet foreigners I make it a habit to ask what foods they most miss from home.
Often I discover that their favorites are dishes I've never heard of—humble dishes that
were served by a loving mother or wife. A *blanquette de veau* is such a dish, or at least used
to be, in the days when more women stayed home and cooked.

A blanquette is essentially a stew made by poaching chunks of veal breast in broth or water, thickening the poaching liquid with roux (which turns the liquid into a *sauce velouté*), and finishing the thickened sauce with cream and egg yolks (which turns the *sauce velouté* into a *sauce suprême*). The pieces of cooked veal are then gently reheated in the sauce, which mustn't boil, and are served with rice or noodles. If you leave out the egg yolks, you don't have to worry about the sauce boiling; in fact, you can boil it down to just the consistency you like. Onions (one of which is stuck with a whole clove) and carrots are simmered with the veal to flavor the sauce. In the simplest blanquettes, these vegetables (which the French call *la garniture aromatique*) are served in the sauce along with the veal, but in the popular *blanquette de veau à l'ancienne,* they're picked out and discarded and replaced with cooked pearl onions and mushrooms.

French recipes for blanquette call for *tendron,* the part of the breast with the most cartilage (which turns into gelatin as it cooks and gives the sauce body). But because I've never been able to get a butcher to sell me just this part, I buy a whole or half veal breast (with the bones) or, in a pinch, cubes of veal stew meat. Veal stew meat is somewhat unpredictable because it's made up of trimmings from different parts of the calf; some cubes will cook perfectly, but others may be dry. Remember, also, that the breast is by far the cheapest cut of veal.

As with so many dishes, you can make blanquette the hard way or you can take shortcuts. When I'm making it the hard way, I trim a breast of veal and make a white veal broth, the day before or earlier the same day, with the bones. (A white broth is a broth in which the ingredients have not been browned before liquid is added.) Once I have the veal broth, I use it to poach the meat. If you don't want to go through all this, the blanquette will be plenty good if you just use water or, if you have any, homemade chicken broth. One tip: Veal meat and bones throw off an enormous amount of scum when they are first heated through. Both meat and bones must be parboiled starting in cold water. This eliminates most of the scum that would make the blanquette gray instead of white and would give it an unpleasant soapy flavor. While it may seem as though a lot of the meat's savor would be lost by parboiling, I've found that the meat doesn't start contributing flavor to the surrounding liquid until after about 20 minutes.

CREAMY VEAL STEW WITH MUSHROOMS AND BABY ONIONS

BLANQUETTE DE VEAU À L'ANCIENNE

MAKES 8 TO 10 SERVINGS

1 whole breast of veal (about 11 pounds [5 kg]), or 5 pounds [2.3 kg] veal stew meat

2 quarts [2 l] homemade white veal, chicken, or beef broth (see page 413) or water, or more as needed

3 medium-size carrots, peeled, cut into 1-inch [2.5 cm] sections

1 stalk celery

2 medium-size onions, peeled, halved through the root end

1 clove, stuck into one of the onions

1 medium-size bouquet garni

2 pints [670 g] pearl onions, or 1¼ pounds [565 g] walnut-size boiling onions, peeled

1 pound [450 g] small cultivated mushrooms, preferably creminis, left whole if small, quartered vertically if large

4 tablespoons all-purpose flour

4 tablespoons butter

4 egg yolks (optional)

2 cups [500 ml] heavy cream

juice of ½ lemon, or more as needed

salt

pepper, preferably white

1 tablespoon finely chopped parsley

IF you're using the breast of veal, cut off and discard any obvious chunks of fat. Cut off the meat in sections, sliding the knife along the bones. When you've taken off the meat, cut away and discard any large sections of sinew and the thin connective tissue that covers the meat. Don't get obsessive, though, because the fat and sinew run through the meat and are impossible to remove completely. What's more, they contribute to the flavor and texture of the meat.

IF you want to make a broth with the bones from the veal breast, cut through the cartilaginous rib ends with a chef's knife, separating them into the individual ribs. Put the bones in a pot, cover them with cold water, and bring to a simmer over high heat. Boil the bones for about 5 minutes, drain in a colander, and rinse with cold water. Rinse out the pot, put the bones back in, and again add just enough cold water or broth (which will produce a double broth) to barely cover the bones. Bring to a slow simmer, skim off any fat or froth that floats to the top, and simmer for 4 to 5 hours, replenishing the liquid as needed to keep the bones covered. Strain the broth and discard the bones.

CUT the breast meat into 1½-inch [4 cm] cubes and put them (or the veal stew meat) into a narrow, tall pot, which makes skimming easier and will enable you to use less liquid to cover the meat. Cover the meat with cold water. Bring to a boil on high heat, turn down the heat, and simmer for about 4 minutes. Drain the meat in a colander and rinse thoroughly with cold water. Wash out the pot and put in the carrots, celery, halved onions, bouquet garni, and meat. (Putting the meat on top holds down the vegetables and makes skimming easier.) Add enough broth or water to completely cover the meat. Bring to a simmer over medium to high heat and then turn down the heat to maintain at a gentle simmer. Partially cover the pot. (This allows the stewing liquid to evaporate and concentrate but keeps any meat protruding through the surface from turning dark.) Simmer for 1½ to 2 hours, until the meat is completely tender when you bite into a piece. Turn down the heat so the meat is kept hot but isn't simmering.

PUT the pearl onions and mushrooms in separate saucepans and ladle 1 cup of the veal cooking liquid over each. Cover the saucepans. Simmer the mushrooms for about 10 minutes and the onions for 10 to 15 minutes, until they're easily pierced with a skewer. Pour the liquid left in each saucepan back into the pot with the meat. (The mushroom cooking liquid may darken the veal liquid, but the flavor's worth it.) Reserve the mushrooms and onions.

DRAIN the meat in a colander set over a pot. Pick through the meat and throw out the vegetables and the bouquet garni. Bring the broth to a gentle simmer, skim off any fat or scum that floats to the top, and gently cook it down to about 2 quarts [2 l].

PREPARE a roux by combining the flour and butter in a heavy-bottomed pot large enough to hold the finished blanquette. Cook the butter and flour over medium heat while whisking until the mixture smells toasty and looks smooth, about 3 minutes. Whisk in the hot veal poaching liquid. Bring to a gentle simmer—set the pot on one side of the flame so the sauce bubbles only on one side. Skim off fat and scum as they float to the surface. Reduce the sauce until it cooks down to about 1 quart, about 20 minutes.

IF you're using the egg yolks, combine them with the cream and lemon juice in a mixing bowl. Whisk in about 2 cups [500 ml] of the veal cooking liquid and then whisk this mixture back into the rest of the veal cooking liquid (the velouté). If you're not using the egg yolks, just pour the cream into the velouté, boil down the sauce for a few minutes to thicken it slightly, and add lemon juice to taste. If you're using the egg yolks, stir the sauce over low heat until you see it take on a silky texture. This can be hard to recognize (see *crème anglaise*, page 642), so if you're in doubt, just take the sauce off the heat—it mustn't come to a boil or it will curdle. Season to taste with salt and pepper.

WHEN you've finished the sauce, stir the veal, onions, and mushrooms into the sauce. Put the sauce over low to medium heat while gently stirring to reheat the veal and the vegetables. Again, if you've used egg yolks, don't let the sauce come to a boil.

SPOON the blanquette into a serving dish or onto individual plates and sprinkle with parsley. Serve rice or egg noodles on the side.

Variations: Theoretically at least, any meat or poultry can be poached in the same way as veal, the poaching liquid finished with cream and egg yolks, and the meat or poultry served with a vegetable garniture, such as the classic *à l'ancienne* (mushroom and pearl onion) garniture. The latest trend in Parisian restaurants is the *blanquette d'agneau*, made with chunks of lamb shoulder (actually, the dish has been around for centuries). While it's easy to make a perfectly acceptable version of *blanquette d'agneau* using lamb shoulder (I just cut the meat out of lamb shoulder chops), it won't have the same flavor as the French version because our lamb is marketed older and has a stronger flavor. *Blanquette d'agneau* is, however, marvelous when made in the springtime with milk-fed baby lamb.

A blanquette lives up to its name (*blanc* means white) because, except for its sprinkling of parsley, it is entirely white or at least ivory colored. But one of the joys of blanquette, like so many old French dishes, is that it's almost infinitely adaptable and easily made colorful by replacing or augmenting the classic garniture with root vegetables such as turnips, carrots, or celeriac, glazed in a little broth or simmered in the velouté and stirred into the sauce at the end; or green vegetables such as baby string beans, asparagus tips, or spinach leaves, blanched, refreshed, and again, reheated in the sauce. The cultivated mushrooms can be replaced with wild mushrooms (dried or fresh morels are fantastic) and augmented with truffles, sliced or chopped and stirred into the sauce at the end; both wild mushrooms and truffles bring the homey blanquette into the realm of *haute cuisine*.

The *sauce velouté*—the thickened veal poaching liquid—is another rich source of ideas and variations. Until nouvelle cuisine took over much of French classic cooking in the 1970s, velouté was one of the cornerstones of serious restaurant cooking. Nowadays, restaurant sauces are flourless reductions enriched with cream, butter, or egg yolks or simple reductions left alone to pose as natural juices. Most cooks, even in fancy restaurants, don't bother making an authentic *sauce velouté* anymore, not only because the trend is away from flour-thickened sauce, but because veal broth is too expensive. But if you make a blanquette, you'll get a full-flavored velouté as part of the deal. If you want to use the velouté for something else, you have the problem of not having any sauce for your cooked veal. In restaurants this is handled by foisting off the cooked meat on the staff and using the velouté for other dishes. If you can pull this off with your family, you'll have an excellent velouté that you can use for refinements like the veal chops given below. I sometimes reheat the veal in a creamy little tomato sauce with tarragon, which isn't half bad.

You can thicken the veal poaching liquid with onion purée (see page 375) or a purée made from the aromatic garniture (the vegetables simmered with the meat). Just purée the cooked onions and carrots in a blender and whisk the purée into the reduced poaching liquid.

VEAL CHOPS WITH VEGETABLE BLANQUETTE

CÔTES DE VEAU AVEC LEUR BLANQUETTE DE LEGUMES

MAKES 8 SERVINGS

3 cups [750 ml] Velouté Sauce (page 413) or the roux-thickened cooking liquid (without the cream and egg yolks) from ½ recipe Creamy Veal Stew with Mushrooms and Baby Onions (page 410)

2 cups [500 ml] heavy cream

salt

1 pound [450 g] French string beans (haricots verts), ends broken off

2 bunches spinach (about 10 ounces [280 g] each), stems removed

6 medium-size carrots, peeled, cut into 1-inch [2.5 cm] sections, sections cored and turned (turning optional; see page 21)

4 medium-size turnips, peeled, cut into wedges, wedges lightly turned (see page 21)

2 ounces [55 g] dried morels or cèpes (porcini), soaked for 30 minutes in ½ cup [125 ml] warm water

8 veal loin or rib chops or boneless loin medallions, ¾ inch to 1 inch [2 to 2.5 cm] thick (6 to 8 ounces [170 to 225 g] each, or slightly heavier if you're using chops)

pepper, preferably white

1 truffle, cut into fine julienne (optional)

1 tablespoon finely chopped chives

1 tablespoon finely chopped parsley

1 tablespoon finely chopped chervil (optional)

juice of 5 lemon, strained

BRING the velouté to a simmer in a saucepan large enough to hold all the vegetables. Stir in the cream and reduce until the sauce—now a *sauce surprême*—has a creamy texture and will lightly coat the back of a spoon. Season to taste with salt, cover, and reserve.

BLANCH the string beans by plunging them into about 4 quarts [4 l] of rapidly boiling salted water and boiling them until they just lose their crunch, about 5 minutes. Take the string beans out with a skimmer and rinse them with cold water. Toss the spinach leaves in the same boiling water for 30 seconds. Drain the spinach in a colander, rinse with cold water, and press gently on the leaves to get rid of the water. Refrigerate the string beans and the spinach.

PUT the carrots and turnips in a pot with enough water to come one-third of the way up their sides. Partially cover the pot and simmer until all the water has evaporated and the vegetables offer only slight resistance when pierced with a fork.

SQUEEZE the excess water out of the mushrooms and carefully pour their soaking liquid into the velouté, leaving any grit behind in the bowl.

SEASON the veal with salt and pepper and sauté or grill it for about 7 minutes on each side (a bit less for boneless medallions), until the veal springs back to the touch—when it's cooked medium.

WHILE the veal is cooking, heat the vegetables, morels, truffle, herbs, and lemon juice in the *sauce suprême*. Season to taste with pepper.

ARRANGE the veal on plates—preferably, deep soup plates—and spoon the vegetable blanquette over and around it.

VELOUTÉ SAUCE

A *sauce velouté* is simply a white stock (one in which the bones and meat have not been browned) that's been thickened with roux. The most traditional velouté, a *velouté ordinaire,* is made with veal broth, essentially what you get when you make a blanquette. Nowadays, because of the price of veal, veal broth is rarely made with meat but instead is made with bones. Naturally, broth made with bones isn't going to taste as good as broth made with meat, but if you don't want to make a blanquette just to get the broth, make a white veal broth with veal knuckle bones.

To thicken 1 quart of veal stock (see recipe below) into a velouté, make a roux with 4 tablespoons of flour and 4 tablespoons of butter and whisk the broth into the roux. Simmer gently while skimming off fat and scum for at least 15 minutes. When the sauce is smooth and lightly creamy, you can finish it in the traditional ways (with cream and/or egg yolks) or with vegetable purée.

To make 6 quarts [6 l] of white veal stock, put 10 pounds [4.5 kg] of veal knuckle bones in a pot, cover them with cold water, and bring the water to a boil over high heat. Boil the bones for 10 minutes, drain them in a colander, and rinse them thoroughly under cold water. Wash the pot you used for blanching the bones and put in a large bouquet garni. (The onions, carrots, celery, and bouquet garni go into the pot first so they don't float up and interfere with skimming.) Put the bones back in the pot, cover with cold water, and bring to a gentle simmer. Simmer for 8 hours, skimming off froth and scum with a ladle and adding cold water as needed to cover the bones. Strain and discard the bones.

QUICK AND SIMPLE BLANQUETTE

MAKES 6 MAIN-COURSE SERVINGS

If you don't feel like boning a breast of veal or waiting a couple of hours while your veal simmers, you can make a simplified, or at least quicker-cooking, blanquette by preparing a velouté sauce ahead of time and then cooking cubes of veal taken from a tender cut instead of the relatively tough breast. This changes the technique from long braising, in which prolonged heat is used to break down sinew and muscle, to short braising, in which the meat is cooked only long enough for heat to penetrate to the inside. The only disadvantage to this method is that tender veal such as the top round I recommend here is relatively expensive. You also need to be careful not to overcook the veal—it'll dry out in a second.

If you have good chicken or veal broth, just thicken it with roux and reduce it for about ½ hour, as described in the velouté sauce instructions above, until it has about the consistency you want, remembering that you're going to add cream, which will thin it out. In the recipe given here, I'm assuming that your chicken broth is only so-so in flavor, hence the pieces of prosciutto to give it a little body. I have included the classic mushroom and onion garniture, but you can improvise with any vegetables you want (see Veal Chops with Vegetable Blanquette, page 412). A quick tip about the prosciutto: Try to buy prosciutto ends. They're too small to be sold in fine slices but are perfect for cooking and should be about one-fourth the price of prosciutto sold by the slice.

1   medium-size onion, chopped fine

1   medium-size carrot, peeled and chopped fine

½   stalk celery, chopped fine

1   clove garlic, chopped

¼   pound [115 g] end piece unsmoked prosciutto, such as prosciutto di Parma (or regular slices if ends are unavailable), chopped

5   tablespoons butter

3   tablespoons flour

1   quart [1 l] White Chicken Broth (page 210) or veal broth (see Velouté Sauce, page 413)

1   small bouquet garni

1   package (10 ounces [285 g]) small mushrooms

1   package (10 ounces [285 g]) pearl onions, peeled

2   cups [500 ml] heavy cream

1   top round of veal (about 3 pounds [1.3 kg])

    salt

    pepper

    juice of ½ lemon, strained

1   tablespoon finely chopped parsley

COOK the chopped vegetables and prosciutto in 3 tablespoons of the butter in a heavy-bottomed pot over medium heat. Stir with a wooden spoon for about 10 minutes, until the onion turns translucent and the vegetables and ham smell fragrant. Add the flour and continue stirring until it smells toasty, about 2 minutes. Whisk in the broth and continue to whisk for a few seconds to make sure the roux dissolves into the broth. Add the bouquet garni, bring to a simmer, and move the pot to one side of the flame so that it boils up on one side only. Simmer for about 40 minutes, skimming off fat and froth every 10 minutes or so, until the liquid has reduced by about half. Strain the sauce to eliminate the pieces of vegetables and prosciutto.

PUT the mushrooms and pearl onions in separate saucepans with about ½ cup [125 ml] of water in each one, and simmer gently, covered. The mushrooms will take about 10 minutes, the onions, 20. If, when the vegetables are done, there is any liquid left in their saucepans, pour this liquid into the velouté.

WHISK the cream into the velouté and continue reducing until the sauce lightly coats the back of a spoon or is the consistency you like.

CUT the veal into 1-inch [2.5 cm] cubes. Season the cubes with salt and pepper and gently sauté them, several at a time, in the remaining butter over medium to high heat for about 7 minutes, until they just begin to feel firm to the touch. This is a little tricky. Because veal contains a lot of water, if the heat isn't high enough the water will release into the pan and you'll end up with boiled veal. If the heat is too high, the butter may burn and the veal will brown—not bad in itself but inappropriate for a blanquette, which should be perfectly white. Be very careful not to overcook the veal. In fact, you should leave it a little undercooked because it will continue to cook in the sauce.

STIR the vegetables into the velouté and bring to a simmer. Stir in the veal and the lemon juice and season with salt and pepper. Bring back to a simmer over high heat and serve immediately. Serve the blanquette on hot plates or a platter and sprinkle it with parsley.

HOW TO KNOW WHEN A STEW IS DONE

An authentic blanquette is "long-braised" by simmering enough for tough proteins to soften, while this Quick and Simple Blanquette is "short-braised," simmered just long enough for the meat to heat through. When the meat is first browned, the French call these short-braised stews *sautés*. One familiar example is Beef Stroganoff (see page 453), made by simmering strips of tender beef in a velouté and then finishing the sauce with crème fraîche or sour cream.

DIFFERENT methods are used for determining when a long-braised stew and a short-braised stew are done. The meat in an old-fashioned long-braised stew is done when a skewer or fork stuck into one of the pieces slides easily in and out, or when a piece you bite into melts in your mouth, with little or no need to chew. Meat in a short-braised stew, however, is done as soon as the heat penetrates to the center of the meat. In the case of veal, pork, or chicken, the meat will have just lost its translucence when you cut into a piece, whereas beef, lamb, or duck may be left rare or medium rare, according to your own taste. Experienced cooks judge the meat's doneness by pinching a piece between thumb and forefinger. Meat that is cooked through will bounce back and no longer feel fleshy. Rare red meat will still feel fleshy, and medium-rare meat will just begin to spring back to the touch.

BRAISED SWEETBREADS IN THE STYLE OF A BLANQUETTE

BLANQUETTE DE RIS DE VEAU

MAKES 4 MAIN-COURSE SERVINGS

I understand why some people don't like liver and kidneys, because these organs have such an assertive flavor, and I understand why brains make some people nervous, because their fragility is a reminder of our own vulnerability. But I'm mystified as to why so many people don't like sweetbreads.

Sweetbreads have a delicate flavor that captures the essence of veal and a texture that is more reminiscent of tender muscle—the meat we usually eat—than of organ meat. Part of the problem may be that people don't know what a sweetbread is. Most of my students think it's a brain or a pancreas, and the information that a sweetbread is a thymus gland—part of the immune system—does little to relieve their anxiety. So I coax them along, hoping that the sweetbread's flavor will overcome their hesitation.

The sweetbread is made up of two sections, a relatively even, round part that the French call the noix and an irregular, elongated section they call the gorge. Often these two sections are still attached with a thin membrane, so you may have a hard time getting the butcher to give you the more presentable and easier-to-slice noix without the attendant gorge.

When you get your sweetbreads home, you can cook them right away, but if you have the time, it's a good idea to soak them overnight in heavily salted water. The salt draws out any traces of blood, which would turn gray when you cook the sweetbreads. This is also a good method if you need to keep the sweetbreads for 2 or 3 days without freezing them, because sweetbreads are very perishable and the salt helps preserve them.

Almost all recipes for sweetbreads insist that you first blanch them, starting in cold water, and then weight them for 4 to 6 hours with something flat and heavy like a cutting board. This is a good trick because it compresses the sweetbreads, makes them easier to trim and to slice evenly, and makes them look prettier on the plate. But if you're in a rush, or if you're executing the occasional recipe that has you remove most of the sweetbreads' membrane—a treatment that causes them to come apart in small pieces—skip the blanching and weighting.

Assuming, however, that you've blanched and weighted your sweetbreads, trim off any little loose pieces of fat or membrane. Don't remove too much membrane or the sweetbreads will fall apart. The sweetbreads are now ready for cooking.

Cook sweetbreads in one of two ways: Slice and bread them and sauté them in the same way as in the fillets of sole on page 304, or braise them. The technique for braising is much the same as the method used for making a blanquette, except that if we're being picky about nomenclature, the liquid in a blanquette completely covers the meat, so the meat is actually poached, while the braising liquid for sweetbreads is kept to a minimum, so the sweetbreads' flavor isn't overly diluted. The standard sweetbread-braising method consists of sweating onions, carrots, and celery (the aromatic garniture) in a little butter in a pan just large enough to hold the sweetbreads, and then adding and quickly reducing a little wine, adding a little broth and the sweetbreads, and covering the whole thing loosely with a sheet of parchment paper (or aluminum foil). The parchment paper traps steam so that any part of the sweetbread not covered with liquid cooks at the same rate as the part in the liquid. This would also happen if you just covered the pan. The loose covering of paper also allows the braising liquid to reduce and concentrate while the sweetbreads are cooking.

Once the sweetbreads are done, garnitures, such as the pearl onions and mushrooms called for here, or perhaps fava beans or string beans, can be cooked separately and served around the sweetbreads or in their sauce. The care to be taken cutting the vegetables for the aromatic garniture depends on whether or not you're straining the sauce.

2	pounds [900 g] veal sweetbreads
	coarse salt
1	medium-size carrot, peeled and chopped fine (or cut into ¼-inch [.5-cm] dice if you're not straining the sauce)
2	shallots, chopped fine
½	stalk celery, chopped fine (or cut into regular dice if you're not straining the sauce)
1	garlic clove, chopped fine
1	tablespoon butter
½	cup [125 ml] white wine
3	cups [750 ml] white veal broth (page 413) or White Chicken Broth (page 210)
1	small bouquet garni
20	pearl onions
½	pound [250 g] small cultivated mushrooms or wild mushrooms such as morels
½	cup [125 ml] heavy cream
1	teaspoon lemon juice, or to taste
	salt
	pepper
1	tablespoon finely chopped parsley

SOAK the sweetbreads overnight in a couple of quarts [liters] of water—enough to cover—with a handful of coarse salt thrown in. After soaking, drain and rinse the sweetbreads and put them in a pot with enough cold water to cover. Bring the water to a simmer over high heat, immediately drain the sweetbreads, and spread them on a sheet pan. Put a cutting board on the sweetbreads with a couple of small cans on top to weight it, and refrigerate for 4 to 6 hours or overnight.

PREHEAT the oven to 350°F [175°C/gas mark 4]. Gently sweat the chopped vegetables in the butter over low heat in an ovenproof pan just large enough to hold the sweetbreads in a single layer, until the vegetables turn translucent, about 10 minutes. With a paring knife, trim any loose pieces of fat or membrane off the sweetbreads. Pour the wine into the pan with the vegetables and boil it down over high heat until it evaporates completely, but do not let the vegetables brown. Pour in 1 cup [250 ml] of the broth and boil it down until it evaporates almost completely, but do not let it start to caramelize on the bottom of the pan. Pour in another cup of broth, add the bouquet garni, and spread the sweetbreads on top of the vegetables, with smaller portions in the center. Bring the broth to a simmer on top of the stove, cover the pan loosely with a sheet of parchment paper or aluminum foil, and slide the pan into the oven.

WHILE the sweetbreads are braising, cook the onions and mushrooms, covered, over medium heat, in separate small pots in ½ cup [125 ml] each of the remaining broth. When the onions are easily penetrated with a skewer, in about 10 minutes, and the mushrooms have released all their liquid, also in about 10 minutes, pour any liquid left in the pots with the vegetables into the pan with the sweetbreads. Set the vegetables aside.

WHEN the sweetbreads spring back to the touch, after about 25 minutes, transfer them to a plate and keep them warm. Tilt the pan and spoon off any fat that has floated to the top. If you are including the aromatic garniture in the sauce, stir the heavy cream into the braising liquid. (If you aren't including the aromatic garniture, strain the braising liquid into a saucepan before adding the cream.) Reduce slightly, until the sauce has the consistency you like, keeping in mind that it's better to err in the direction of too thin—in fact, this dish is best served in soup plates with a light sauce served around the sweetbreads. Stir the reserved onions and mushrooms into the sauce, add the lemon juice, season with salt and pepper, and sprinkle in the parsley. Slice the sweetbreads, on an angle, into ½-inch-thick [1.5 cm] slices and arrange them on a serving dish, such as an oval gratin dish, or on individual plates. If the sweetbreads have cooled while you were making the sauce, you can *very gently* reheat the slices in the sauce, but don't let the sauce boil for even a second or you'll toughen the slices. Spoon the sauce and vegetables over the sweetbreads and serve.

Variations: The braising liquid can be subtly altered with the addition of cream (as in a blanquette), vegetable purée (especially sorrel or tomato), butter, wild mushrooms (in chunks or chopped and cooked down into a duxelles), truffles, puréed or cubed foie gras, or chopped herbs. Variations can also occur earlier—the traditional mirepoix aromatic base can be replaced or augmented with mushrooms, fennel, shallots, prosciutto, or garlic, and the braising liquid can contain fortified wines, no wine at all, or even red wine (which must be precooked, as in the meurette sauce on page 115).

SWEETBREAD TERRINE

TERRINE DE RIS DE VEAU

MAKES 10 FIRST-COURSE SERVINGS

The French are masters at turning leftovers into savory dishes that are sometimes even better than the originals. In keeping with this idea, if I'm spending an hour or more making an elaborate dish for four or six people, I go ahead and make extra so I'll have leftovers. Much of the time a leftover main course, when refashioned the next day, makes a perfect first course. Remolding leftover cooked meats in a terrine or, more rustically, in a bowl, is a deviously elegant way to manage leftovers.

Terrines are made in several ways. A traditional country terrine (see Chapter 5) is usually held together with a good amount of pork and pork fat. Other terrines, sometimes called hures, are held together with aspic; in the best versions, the natural congealed braising or poaching liquid from a braised or poached dish is melted and layered with thin slices of the cooked meat in the terrine or bowl (see the beef terrine, page 427, and the jambon persillé, page 104). Here, however, the braising liquid for the sweetbreads has been finished with cream, which turns it into a chaudfroid. Chaudfroid (which means hot-cold) is an even more maligned concept than aspic. In its original seventeenth-century form, a chaudfroid was simply the congealed sauce from a fricassee, a dish similar to a blanquette in which the braising liquid has been finished with cream and egg yolks. In the nineteenth century the method devolved into a decadent covering for elaborate *pièces montées*—foods arranged to look more like architectural models than like something you'd want to eat. Because these baroque constructions, which can still be seen at culinary shows, sat for long hours at room temperature, it was essential that the chaudfroid be stiffened with so much gelatin that it became inedible (to say nothing of the long ripening at room temperature). Nowadays, chaudfroid is largely forgotten. But a natural chaudfroid—one whose texture is derived only from the natural gelatin contained in the braising liquid—is a subtle and infinitely adaptable cold sauce that lends itself to delicate flavorings such as finely chopped herbs, delicate fortified wines, foie gras, spices, and truffles. The terrine below, held together by the enriched sweetbread braising liquid flavored with finely chopped parsley and tarragon, can be made as elaborate as you like by inserting layers of foie gras, cooked artichoke hearts, blanched leeks, or juliennes of various vegetables. The chaudfroid itself can be colored and flavored with vegetable purées—spinach, sorrel (which admittedly turns a rather unappetizing gray but contributes a delicious tang), tomato, mushroom—or finely chopped chervil, tarragon, or other herbs.

To construct this terrine, prepare a recipe of Braised Sweetbreads in the Style of a Blanquette, or prepare a double recipe, serve half for dinner, and save the rest for the terrine. It's essential, when braising the sweetbreads, to use a homemade or very good quality natural broth that contains enough natural gelatin to help the terrine hold its shape.

1 recipe Braised Sweetbreads in the Style of a Blanquette (page 415), without the pearl onions and mushrooms

½ cup [125 ml] heavy cream (in addition to the cream called for in the blanquette recipe)

4 egg yolks

   salt

   pepper

   lemon juice

1 envelope (2½ teaspoons) unflavored gelatin, softened in 2 tablespoons water for 20 minutes

4 tablespoons finely chopped parsley, in addition to the parsley called for in the blanquette recipe

2 tablespoons coarsely chopped fresh tarragon (chopped at the last minute, leaves tossed with 1 teaspoon of olive oil before chopping to keep them from turning black)

½ teaspoon cayenne

PREPARE the braised sweetbreads and reserve them. Stir all the cream into a saucepan with the degreased sweetbread braising liquid, bring to a simmer, and reduce until you have a total of 2½ cups [625 ml] of the mixture. Beat the egg yolks in a mixing bowl and whisk in the hot cream mixture. Return the mixture to the saucepan and heat over medium heat while stirring constantly until the mixture takes on a satiny consistency—don't let it boil for even a second or it will curdle (see crème anglaise, page 642). Remove the saucepan from the heat and season the mixture to taste with salt, pepper, and lemon juice. (Keep in mind that foods taste less salty when chilled, so season generously.) Stir in the gelatin, parsley, tarragon, and cayenne. Set the saucepan in a bowl of ice water, stirring every few minutes until the mixture is cold but not set.

WET the inside of a 10-inch by 3½-inch by 3½-inch (6-cup [1.45 l]) terrine mold and line it with plastic wrap, leaving a little of the wrap hanging over the outside of the mold. Ladle about ½ cup [125 ml] of the cream mixture into the mold and set the mold in the refrigerator or, if you're in a hurry, a bowl of ice water, until the mixture has set. Cover the congealed layer with thin slices of sweetbreads, trimmed to fit in one tight layer. Spread another layer of the cream mixture over the sweetbread layer—heat the mixture just enough to melt it if it has congealed—chill, and spread over it another layer of sweetbread slices. Continue in this way until you've used up all the cream and the sweetbread slices. Chill the terrine for at least 3 hours in the refrigerator. Just before serving, put the serving plate or platter on top of the terrine and invert both plate and terrine. Give the whole thing a shake to dislodge the terrine. If the terrine won't come out of the mold, gently pull on the plastic wrap to dislodge it. Gently peel away the plastic wrap. Cut the terrine in slices with a long, sharp knife.

FRENCH·STYLE POT ROAST

BOEUF À LA MODE

HOW TO	HOW TO	HOW TO	TRICKS	HOW TO
BRAISE BEEF, VEAL, AND LAMB	USE FATBACK TO MAKE MEAT MOIST	WORK WITH AND APPRECIATE NATURAL MEAT JELLIES	WITH LEFTOVERS	COOK LAMB AND VEAL SHANKS

FOR THOSE OF US WHO THINK OF FRENCH FOOD AS DOMINATED BY rich, thick sauces, it comes as a revelation that a cornerstone of French cooking is made up of pot roast–like dishes—slow-cooked pieces of meat with wine, herbs, and aromatic vegetables whose disparate flavors merge miraculously into something robust yet subtle, deeply satisfying yet elegant. Nowadays, the "best," most tender cuts of meat are fashionable—we want a quickly grilled steak or a little roast we can cook up in an hour, not a dish that simmers for hours on end. This wasn't always the case. In the seventeenth and eighteenth centuries, the French were considered experts at braising (slow cooking with a small amount of liquid), while it was the English who were the esteemed masters of the roast. Slow-cooked dishes are still to be found in French country homes, where the traditions of good cooking remain more respected than in the cities. More recently, a craze for regional cooking has long-cooked dishes like pot-au-feu and *boeuf à la mode* showing up in chic restaurants.

The term "pot roast" is misleading, because authentic roasting requires cooking with dry heat—traditionally in the open air in front of a hearth—while "pot roasting" requires the presence of moisture. The only thing accurate about calling it "pot roasting" is that it's done in a pot. A widely held misconception is that cooking meat with liquid keeps the meat moist. Liquid has nothing to do with it. Tender cuts, best for roasting or steaks, stay moist if they're not overcooked, while tough and sinewy cuts, perfect for stews and braised dishes, are kept moist by the presence of fat and particular kinds of proteins that slowly break down into gelatin during long, moist cooking. Great care must be taken to make sure the braising liquid never boils, since that would cause the fat that is slowly released by the meat into the liquid to emulsify with the rest of the liquid, leaving the braising liquid murky and the meat stringy and dry.

The good news is that some of the cheapest cuts of beef make the best pot roasts, because certain proteins that make them tough when roasted make them melting and juicy when they're braised. Traditional French recipes call for rump. It may be that beef has changed over the years, but rump is far too lean and will end up dry. A chuck roast, with its marbling of fat and soluble sinew, is a much better bet. Look for a chuck roast that weighs between 3 and 5 pounds [1.3 and 2.3 kg]. The appropriate cuts have different names in different parts of the country. Ask your butcher to give you a chuck roast suitable for pot roasting.

Larding, now almost a lost art, was once considered essential to a successful pot roast. The idea is to insert strips of unsmoked fatty pork belly, called fatback, into the meat, parallel to the grain. Larding helps keep the meat moist (or helps it give the impression of moistness); the fatback strips are usually marinated, so they provide an extra little burst of flavor; and the little pieces of fatback embedded in each slice make a pretty checkered pattern. For most braises you can get by without larding, but larding will add another dimension of succulence to your pot roast.

The standard method for making a pot roast consists of marinating the meat in wine with aromatic vegetables, browning the meat, and browning the chopped carrots, onions, and celery used in the marinade. Wine is then added (including the wine used in the marinade), perhaps along with some broth or concentrated broth, and the pot is covered and gently simmered until the beef is tender throughout, at least 3 hours. In traditional recipes, strips of pork rind—the rind taken from a large strip of fatback—is simmered along with the meat to provide extra gelatin and add a natural unctuousness to the braising liquid. A calf's or pig's foot, split and blanched, is also sometimes added.

The moistening liquid chosen and the amount used also play an important part in the final flavor of the roast and its sauce. In a traditional American pot roast, a small amount (about 1 cup [250 ml]) of broth, water, or wine is used as the moistening liquid, making it more akin to what the French call an *étuvé,* a kind of braise cooked in a covered pot with very little or no liquid. A traditional *boeuf à la mode* is made with red wine and some beef broth (in old-fashioned farmhouse cooking, taken from the pot-au-feu). A *boeuf à la mode* gets called something different if the moistening liquid or the final vegetable garniture changes but the essentials stay the same. I make my own *boeuf à la mode* variations by substituting ends of wine bottles, white or red, and sometimes adding a splash of Madeira or port, some homemade vinegar, or even dark beer so that each pot roast has an identity all its own. There are other methods, some taken from *la cuisine ancienne,* that can be used to add depth of flavor to a traditional pot roast. One trick is to add pieces of meat, such as veal or beef trimmings, or pieces of prosciutto or pancetta, to the mirepoix, the aromatic garniture consisting of chopped onions, carrots, and celery, cooked at the beginning of the braising process.

Another method, called *pincer*, consists of getting the meat to release juices that are then caramelized with the aromatic garniture before liquid is added. One way to do this is to start the pot roast in the oven with the aromatic vegetables as though it were a regular roast. When the roast has released its juices and the juices have caramelized on the bottom of the roasting pan, after 1 to 1½ hours, you add the moistening liquid, bring to a gentle simmer on top of the stove, cover, and continue braising until the meat is easily penetrated with a skewer, in another 1 or 2 hours. This method, however, is tricky, because if the roasting pan is too large, the juices released by the meat can quickly burn, and if the pan is too small, the juices take too long to evaporate and the meat overcooks before you've even added wine or other liquid for the braising itself. This latter problem is more likely to occur if you've marinated the meat, because the absorbed marinade is released into the pot along with the meat's other juices. For these reasons, I only caramelize the meat juices in this way when braising meat that hasn't been marinated (see Veal Shoulder Pot Roast with Morels, page 428).

You can also improve the flavor of your pot roast by glazing it in the oven. When the pot roast is done, gently transfer it to a clean pot and, in a saucepan, lightly reduce and degrease the braising liquid by gently simmering it for 10 minutes and skimming off any fat or scum. Pour the degreased braising liquid back over the pot roast and slide the pot roast, uncovered, into a 375°F [190°C/gas mark 5] oven. Bake the pot roast for about ½ hour, basting every few minutes with the sauce, until the sauce has the consistency of a light syrup and the pot roast is covered with a shiny glaze. Reducing the braising liquid in this way—on the surface of the pot roast—gives the liquid an amazingly full flavor that you won't get if you just reduce it in a saucepan on top of the stove. Your pot roast will also be improved if you add concentrated broth or, better yet, demi-glace or *glace de viande*, to the braising liquid at the beginning of the braising.

Despite all these variations and seeming complexities, it's very hard to go wrong making a pot roast. Other than out-and-out burning, there is only one mistake that will turn your pot roast stringy and dry and make your sauce muddy and greasy: leaving the braising liquid at a rolling boil. Braised dishes must barely simmer. The French term for this hardly perceptible simmering is *mijoter*, which translates as cooking at a bare simmer with the occasional bubble coming to the surface every few seconds. It's also helpful to braise in a heavy-bottomed pot, for even heat and to prevent burning of the caramelized juices if you're roasting first, and in a pot that fits the size of the meat as closely as possible, so that less liquid will be needed to come halfway up the sides of the meat. Some recipes suggest basting the meat from time to time during the braising, but there are French cooks who insist that continually lifting the lid causes important aromas to be lost. (Old recipes called for sealing the lid with luting paste, a mixture of flour and water, in order to contain the perfume and protect the braise from ashes when it was nestled in the coals in the hearth.) To baste a pot roast without lifting the lid, place a sheet of aluminum foil over the top of the pot, before putting on the lid, and press it down in the middle, near the top of the roast. In this way, moisture condenses on the underside of the aluminum foil and drips down on the pot roast, basting it from the top. You will, however, need to check from time to time to make sure the surrounding liquid isn't boiling, but that an occasional bubble does rise to the surface. To completely avoid lifting the lid, bring a saucepan of water to a boil, cover it, and place it in the oven next to the pot roast. Check the water in the pot instead of the liquid surrounding the roast.

Recipes also differ as to how long to cook a pot roast. Nowadays, we usually cook a pot roast until a skewer slides easily in and out, but in centuries past, pot roasts were sometimes cooked *à la cuillière*—until the roast was tender enough that it could be served with a spoon. If you're willing to cook for 5 or 6 hours, this is still a magnificent way to cook a pot roast, but it requires that the roast be well larded so it doesn't dry out.

A classic *boeuf à la mode* is surrounded with carrots and little onions. In its simplest and most primitive form, what the French might call *à la ménagère* (meaning, roughly, housewives' style), the carrots and onions included in the marinade and used in the braising are the same carrots and onions served around the finished pot roast. A more refined style and nowadays the usual method (called *à la bourgeoise*), is to strain out the original vegetables and add new vegetables near the end of cooking or even to cook these vegetables separately (using a little of the braising liquid from the pot), on the stove, and reunite them with the pot roast just before serving.

BRAISING: WHITE, BROWN, LONG, AND SHORT

In the loosest sense, braising simply means cooking with a small amount of liquid. Poaching, on the other hand, is cooking with a lot of liquid, enough to completely cover what's being poached. Roasting is cooking with no liquid at all. Vegetables, seafood, and of course meats all lend themselves to braising, but braising in ways that are often subtly and sometimes radically different from the methods used for pot roast. Seafood (except octopus, cuttlefish, and sometimes squid), is braised only until it cooks through—a method I call short braising. Tender meats and poultry can also be cooked this way, and need only be cooked to the proper internal temperature. You determine their doneness in the same way you would a roast (see page 507). Long braising requires that the inside of the meat remain at a relatively high temperature—around 175°F [79°C]—for a prolonged period in order for sinew and tough muscle tissue to break down; measuring the temperature with a meat thermometer will not tell you if the pot roast is done or not. The doneness of long-braised dishes depends on texture, determined by sticking a skewer into the meat to see if it slides freely in and out.

Braises are also divided into brown and white, a distinction based on whether or not the meat or seafood was browned before liquid was added. The meat for most long braises is browned either in a sauté pan or by being roasted in the oven before liquid is added.

LARDING

If you decide to lard your pot roast, it will give a melting juiciness to the finished meat. I highly rec-ommend the technique not only for that reason but because it's delightfully anachronistic. (How marvelous in this age of ever more lean and tasteless meat to actually add fat!) There are two basic methods used for larding, and a different kind of larding needle is used for each. The method you'll use for the pot roast requires a larding needle—in French, a *lardoir*. A larding needle has a heavy handle and a hollow metal tube about 10 inches [25.5 cm] long. You insert a strip of fatback into the tube, slide the tube into the meat, parallel to the grain, and slide out the tube, leaving the stirp of fat embedded in the meat. Another method, more properly called interlarding, requires a smaller and thinner larding needle, one about 8 inches [20.5 cm] long, which looks like a small knitting needle with a toothed hinge at one end. This needle—in French, an *aiguille à piquer*—is used to lard smaller pieces of meat that a *lardoir* would mangle. To use an *aiguille à piquer*, you pinch one end of the fat-back strip in the little hinge, slide the needle through a section of the meat, and pull the needle through, leaving the fatback strip embedded in the meat. If you have trouble getting the needle through, grip the pointed end with a kitchen towel and pull it through.

To get the strips of fatback needed for larding, you'll need to buy a piece of fatback, which looks like a piece of slab bacon but is all fat with no lean. The butcher may try to sell you salt pork, but salt pork has a funny taste and won't work. The fatback may come frozen, and if you have the space in your freezer, it might be worth ordering more than you need to keep it on hand. When you're ready to use the fatback, thaw it out and cut off the rind with a long, sharp knife. Cut the fat into strips about ¼ inch [.5 cm] on each side. For most dishes, it's best to marinate the strips with some very finely chopped garlic and, if you like, a little Cognac, for 4 to 8 hours or overnight. Use the rind, left whole or cut into strips, to add gelatin and body to stews and braised dishes.

Traditional stews and braised dishes often call for a calf's or pig's foot to add gelatin to the braising liquid and give it more body. This gives the sauce a richer feel in the mouth and makes it easier to glaze large pieces of meat without having to reduce the liquid too much. Calves' and pigs' feet work equally well, but pigs' feet are smaller and usually easier to find. Pigs' feet should be split in half lengthwise; veal feet, since they are bigger, should be quartered by being split both lengthwise and crosswise (have the butcher do this for you). Before using pigs' or calves' feet, blanch them by putting them in a pot of cold water, bringing it to the boil, and boiling them for 15 minutes so that any scum they throw off won't end up in your stew or pot roast. After blanching, rinse them thoroughly with cold water.

You can also make a stock—a *fonds gelée*—ahead of time and use it for braising stews and pot roasts or for poaching ham, as in the *jambon persillé* recipe on page 104. Stock made from pigs' or calves' feet is also useful for cold dishes served *en gelée*, when you need a certain amount of natural gelatin to hold things together. To make 5 quarts [5 l] of stock, gently simmer 2 calves' feet split both lengthwise and crosswise (so they'll fit in the pot), or 5 split pigs' feet, with enough cold water to cover. Simmer gently, skimming off fat and froth, for 10 hours. You can keep *fonds gelée* for a week in the refrigerator or indefinitely in the freezer.

BASIC BOEUF
À LA MODE

1 chuck roast (3 to 5 pounds [1.3 to 2.3 kg]) for pot roasting

1 bottle full-bodied red wine (see page 10 for more about wines to cook with)

1 medium-size onion, peeled and quartered (for the meat marinade)

1 medium-size carrot, peeled and sliced (for the meat marinade), plus 4 medium-size carrots, peeled, cut into ⅛-inch-thick [3 mm] round slices (for cooking with the meat)

½ stalk celery, sliced (for the meat marinade)

3 cloves garlic, crushed (for the meat marinade), plus 3 cloves garlic, chopped fine and crushed to a paste (for the fatback marinade; optional)

1 medium-size bouquet garni

12 ounces [340 g] fatback with rind, rind removed and reserved (optional)

2 tablespoons Cognac (for the fatback marinade; optional)

salt

pepper

5 tablespoons olive oil

1 slice (2 ounces [5.5 g]) unsmoked cured raw ham such as jambon de Bayonne or prosciutto di Parma, cut into strips about 2 inches [5 cm] long and ⅛ inch [3 mm] wide

1 pig's foot, split lengthwise by the butcher, blanched (see page 424)

1 cup [250 ml] concentrated beef broth (optional; see page 4)

20 walnut-size onions, or 1 pint [335 g] (10- to 12-ounce [about 285 g] package) pearl onions, peeled

2 tablespoons finely chopped parsley

PUT the meat in a nonaluminum bowl with the wine, the vegetables for the meat marinade, and the bouquet garni, and let marinate in the refrigerator for 4 hours, or overnight.

PUT the optional fatback in the freezer for about 30 minutes to partially freeze it and make it easier to slice. Cut it into ¼-inch by 6-inch [.5 by 15 cm] strips and, in a small mixing bowl, toss the strips with the garlic for the fatback marinade and the Cognac. Cover with plastic wrap and let marinate in the refrigerator for 4 hours, or overnight.

PREHEAT the oven to 325°F [165°C/gas mark 3].

TAKE the meat out of its marinade, pat it dry, and, if you've chosen to lard it, insert the strips of fatback using a *lardoir* (see page 423). If your roast has an elongated shape (such as a chuck blade roast), lard it through the sides, but at an angle, so that as you serve the meat, you slice across the ends of the fatback strips and reveal a checkerboard pattern. Strain the marinade and reserve the liquid, the vegetables, and the bouquet garni. Pat the meat dry, season it with salt and pepper, and brown it on all sides in 3 tablespoons of the olive oil over high heat in a heavy-bottomed pot that closely fits its size. Take it out of the pot, pour out the cooked oil, and put the reserved vegetables, the remaining olive oil, and the ham in the pot. Stir over medium heat until the vegetables release their aroma, about 10 minutes. If you're using it, put the sheet of pork rind over the vegetables and set the meat on top. Nestle the blanched pig's foot next to the meat. Pour in the reserved marinade liquid and the broth. Push the reserved bouquet garni down into the liquid. Depending on the size of the pot and the size and shape of the meat, there should be enough liquid to come between halfway and all the way up the sides of the meat. If you need more liquid to reach halfway up the sides, add a little extra broth, wine, or water. Put the pot on top of the stove over high heat to bring the liquid to a simmer. Turn the heat down and simmer gently for 10 minutes, so the heat partially penetrates the meat. Unless the meat is completely covered with liquid, place a sheet of aluminum foil over the top of the pot and press down in the center so it almost touches the meat. Cover the pot and slide it into the oven. Every 30 minutes, check the liquid in the pot to make sure it stays at a gentle simmer, with a bubble rising to the surface every couple of seconds, and adjust the oven temperature accordingly. (Or use a little pot of water to check, as described above.)

COOK the pot roast until a skewer slides easily in and out, about 3 hours. Gently transfer the pot roast to a clean pot (or return it to the same pot, rinsed out), and keep it in a warm place. (Because the roast is very fragile, I lift it out with a long spatula that supports it along its entire length.) If you like, carefully lift the sheet of pork rind out of the pot with tongs and cut it into ½-inch-wide [1.5-cm] strips to serve with the meat. Or discard the rind if it's not to your taste. Strain the braising liquid into a small saucepan, pressing down on the vegetables in the strainer with the bottom of a ladle to extract as much liquid as you can. Discard the cooked vegetables and the bouquet garni. Put the braising liquid over low to medium heat with the pan moved to one side of the burner so the liquid boils up on one side only. Simmer for about 20 minutes, skimming off the fat with a small ladle (see page 18) every couple of minutes, until you're left with about 4 cups [1 l] of liquid. Put the small peeled onions and sliced carrots in the pot, around the sides of the roast. (If you're using pearl onions, don't add them yet.) Pour in the reduced braising liquid and bring to a simmer on top of the stove. Cover the pot and slide it back into the oven. Remove the lid, and baste the roast every 5 minutes for about 30 minutes, until it is coated with a shiny glaze and the carrots and onions are soft. If you're using pearl onions, add them 15 minutes into the basting. Put the strips of pork rind into the pot 5 minutes before you're done basting. When finished basting, transfer the pot roast to a hot deep platter or serving dish and surround it with the carrots and onions and the strip of rind, if you're using them. Whisk the parsley into the braising liquid, season to taste with salt and pepper, and ladle over the roast. Serve the roast in slices.

COLD FRENCH-STYLE POT ROAST

BOEUF À LA MODE FROID

I've always had a secret love of leftovers—the doggy bag from that fancy restaurant provides a more special treat the day after, when I can munch away, sitting in an old pair of shorts in my garden. French cooks have made an art out of les restes. They turn many a delicious hot dish into a transcendental cold one that has a magical depth and subtlety hot dishes often lack. But there's a problem. Many of the best cold dishes are surrounded by the congealed sauce or, as here, braising liquid, that sends many of us Americans screaming in horror. This isn't just lack of sophistication. We have our reasons for hating aspics— what the French call gelées—and anything that resembles them. We've been tortured by Jell-O salads, and by congealed canned consommé.

But it's not only we Americans who have sinned. Aspics, and their cream-enriched cousins chaudfroids (see page 417), were originally the natural braising liquids and sauces that set when cold. In the nineteenth century, chefs forgot what aspics and chaudfroids were originally about and used them to make elaborately constructed dishes in which cubes of golden aspic with the texture of rubber were used like bricks. But the braising liquid from a boeuf à la mode, a delicately trembling jelly when cold, is sublimely delicious and should melt in your mouth.

Traditional recipes for cold boeuf à la mode have you slice the leftover meat and layer it with the vegetables in a bowl or oval serving dish lined with the cold leftover braising liquid. Such an elaborate construction requires that the congealed braising liquid be very stiff. Instead, I recommend serving the sliced cold braised meat with a few spoonfuls of the gelée spread on top of each slice and the cold vegetables around it. I also like this terrine, which makes a delightful first course:

COLD BEEF TERRINE

TERRINE DE BOEUF EN GELÉE

MAKES 10 FIRST-COURSE SERVINGS

This elegant little terrine is a great way to use braised or boiled beef left over from a *boeuf à la mode* or a *pot-au-feu*. The only tricky part is getting the natural *gelée*—the cold braising liquid—to have the right consistency. If the *gelée* is too stiff, the terrine will be rubbery; if it's too loose, the terrine won't hold together. If the *gelée* is too stiff, unlikely unless you included the pig's foot in the braising of the *boeuf à la mode*, just thin the melted braising liquid with a little broth or water. If the *gelée* is too loose, you can reduce it to concentrate its natural gelatin (and its flavor) or, if you don't have enough, you can add packaged gelatin. When you've adjusted the *gelée* in one way or another, you'll need to chill a few tablespoons in a small bowl in the refrigerator to see how it sets and to judge its texture.

- 3 to 6 cups [750 ml] gelatinous braising liquid from *boeuf à la mode* or other braised meat or stew

- 1 packet (2½ teaspoons) unflavored gelatin, or more as needed (unnecessary if your *gelée* is already stiff)

  salt

  pepper

- 3 tablespoons chopped parsley or chervil, 1 tablespoon chopped tarragon, or a mixture of all three (chopped at the last minute)

- 1 pound [450 g] leftover *boeuf à la mode*, *pot-au-feu*, or other braised or poached beef, sliced thin (about 3 cups [590 ml] when pressed into a measuring cup)

CHILL the braising liquid in the refrigerator until it sets. Spoon off and discard any specks of fat on top. Check the texture of the braising liquid to see if it needs to be loosened or stiffened—it should have the consistency of Jell-O. Melt the braising liquid in a small saucepan, season to taste with salt and pepper, and strain it through a fine-mesh strainer or a clean kitchen towel. (Don't use a terry-cloth towel, it will absorb too much of your braising liquid.) Either of these may start to clog up and stop working, in which case you'll have to rinse out the strainer or reposition the kitchen towel. Adjust the texture of the braising liquid by thinning it with broth or water if it's too stiff, reducing it if it's too loose, or, again if it's too loose, by dissolving a packet of powdered gelatin—first softened in 2 tablespoons of water—in the heated *gelée*. You need 3 cups [750 ml] of *gelée* to make the terrine, so if you're reducing it to thicken it, start with 6 cups [1.5 l] of braising liquid and reduce to 3 [750 ml]. Chill, check the consistency, and, if necessary, add more gelatin or water. When you have the *gelée* ready, let it cool. Before it sets, stir in the parsley or other herb. You also have the option of freezing the terrine before slicing it (see page 202).

CHILL the braising liquid until it is cool but not cold, so it doesn't set before you put it into the terrine. Wet the inside of a 5-cup [1.25 l] rectangular terrine mold or loaf pan and line it with plastic wrap, leaving a little of the wrap hanging over the outside the mold. (The water helps the wrap cling to the terrine.) Pour ⅓ cup [75 ml] braising liquid into the mold and allow it to set in the refrigerator, about 20 minutes. (Make sure the mold is level so the liquid forms an even layer.) Cover the *gelée* layer with a sprinkling of herbs and 2 or 3 thin slices of meat in a single layer—you may need to trim the slices. Pour another ⅓ cup of the *gelée* over the meat and allow it to set again in the refrigerator. Continue in this way until you've used up the meat, herbs, and the *gelée*, or until you've filled the mold, finishing with a thin layer of meat slices. Refrigerate for at least another 2 hours before unmolding.

JUST before serving, put the serving plate on top of the mold and invert both plate and mold. Give the whole thing a quick up-and-down shake to dislodge the terrine. If the terrine won't come out of the mold, gently pull on the plastic wrap to dislodge it. Gently peel away the plastic wrap. When you're ready to serve, slice the terrine with a long, thin, and very sharp knife. You may need to gently press your hand against the end of the terrine as you slice, so that the slice comes away in your hand. Don't be dismayed if the slice breaks apart as it folds away from the terrine. Serve each slice with a couple of cornichons and, if you have any left over, a spoonful of the *gelée*. See also Ham and Parsley Terrine, page 104, for more ideas.

VEAL SHOULDER POT ROAST WITH MORELS

FRICANDEAU AUX MORILLES

MAKES ABOUT 10 MAIN-COURSE SERVINGS

I once worked in a restaurant where one of the owner's favorite dishes was a *vitello tonnato*, cold roast veal slices spread with a mayonnaise flavored with canned tuna and capers. Well, I like *vitello tonnato* but it's not a subtle dish, and it used to kill me to pour the jus from that wonderful roast into that fishy mayonnaise. To stave off boredom, I cooked the veal a little differently every day so that after months of experimentation I felt I had finally learned how to cook veal. Through much trial and error, I arrived at this dish, which as it turns out was one of the great classics of seventeenth- and eighteenth-century cooking.

RECIPES for *fricandeau* vary. Some recipes call for thick slices of veal loin, others for very lean round of veal, and some for my favorite, veal shoulder; all call for larding. When choosing a cut, it's essential to understand the difference between long and short braising (see page 422). A lean and tender cut of veal such as the rack, saddle, boneless loin, or round

will dry out if cooked a second beyond a barely perceptible, ever-so-slightly translucent pink, the equivalent of medium for beef; this translates to an internal temperature of about 137°F [58°C] (which means you have to cook the veal to 132°F [55°C] because the temperature will increase as it rests). Whether you roast these cuts completely without moisture—just a little basting with butter—or short-braise them with a little broth or wine, they have an exact point at which they are ready. Because eighteenth-century cooks, unlike people today, were fond of deeply flavored long-braised dishes, they adapted these lean cuts to long braising by thoroughly larding them. But there's no point in using an expensive cut that doesn't work as well as a naturally more gelatinous cheaper one, like the veal shoulder clod I call for here (your butcher should know what you're talking about).

THE shoulder clod is a boneless, meaty cut that seems to have muscles going every which way. If you're larding the meat to make it moister, don't have the butcher tie it. If the butcher offers you bones, snap them up and use them to enrich the braising liquid. You don't need to marinate veal, but the fatback strips will be tastier if you marinate them for a few hours or overnight with a little garlic and Cognac. The morels in this dish were almost an afterthought and are by no means essential. But the dish takes a lot of time and isn't cheap, so why not pull out all the stops and make it even more luxurious?

1 pound [450 g] fatback, rind removed and reserved, fat cut into strips about 6 inches long and 4 inches wide (see "Larding," page 423)

3 cloves garlic, chopped fine, crushed to a paste

1 veal chuck shoulder clod (about 5 pounds [2.3 kg])

salt

pepper

2 medium-size carrots, peeled, cut into 1-inch [2.5-cm] sections

2 medium-size onions, peeled and quartered

1 medium-size turnip, peeled and quartered

2 fennel stalks, cut into 1-inch [2.5-cm] lengths (optional)

1 quart [1 l] veal, beef, or chicken broth, or more as needed (optional)

1 medium-size bouquet garni

1 ounce dried morels, or ¾ pound fresh

2 tablespoons butter (if you're using fresh morels)

½ cup [125 ml] semidry Madeira or dry sherry (if you're using dried morels)

TOSS the strips of fatback with the garlic and let them marinate in the refrigerator for 4 hours, or overnight.

FOLD open the veal shoulder, skin-side down, and with a hinged interlarding needle (see page 423) sew strips of fatback into the various muscles. This seems monotonous at first, but it's strangely satisfying and you'll pick up speed. Try to distribute the fatback strips equally. Season the inside of the meat with salt and pepper and tie it with string into an elongated oval shape. To do this, turn the veal over, so the skin side is now on top, and bunch it up by pressing the edges under. Tie a loop of string loosely around the roast, going lengthwise. Then tie a series of loops around the roast, starting in the middle and subdividing until you have about 10 loops holding the shoulder together.

PLACE the veal in a heavy-bottomed pot and surround it the with the carrots, onions, turnip, and fennel and any bones the butcher may have given you. Slide it into a 400°F [200°C/gas mark 6] oven and roast for 1 to 1½ hours, until the veal releases its juices and the juices caramelize on the bottom of the pot. At this point, you don't have to worry about overcooking the veal—remember, it's a braise, not a roast, and the fatback will keep it moist. The purpose is to get the veal to release its juices so they caramelize with the vegetables on the bottom of the pot. (This preliminary caramelization, or *pincer*, was one of the cornerstones of eighteenth-century French cooking.) When the juices start to caramelize, check the bottom of the pot every 5 minutes until the juices form a thick brown syrup clinging to it. If

they don't brown enough, the braising liquid will be insipid; if, horror of horrors, they burn, your veal will be ruined. Turn the oven down to 350°F [175°C/gas mark 4], pour enough broth or water over the veal to come halfway up the sides, nestle in the bouquet garni, and put the pot on the stove over high heat. When the liquid comes to a simmer, cover the pot with a sheet of aluminum foil, press the foil down in the middle so it just touches the top of the veal, and put a lid on the pot and slide it into the oven. Braise for about 1 hour and turn the veal over so the half that was submerged is now protruding above the liquid. Braise for 1 to 1½ hours more, until a skewer slides easily in and out of the veal.

GENTLY transfer the veal to a clean pot, which can be slightly smaller, since the veal will have shrunk, and strain the braising liquid into a saucepan. Discard the vegetables and the bouquet garni, set the pan to one side of the burner so the liquid bubbles up on one side only, and gently reduce the braising liquid while skimming off fat with a small ladle or spoon for about 10 minutes, until you've removed most of the fat. If you're using dried morels, soak them in the Madeira or in ½ cup of water. Turn them around in the liquid every 5 minutes so they soften quickly.

POUR the degreased braising liquid over the veal and slide the pot, uncovered, into the oven. Baste the veal with the braising liquid every 5 minutes until the liquid turns lightly syrupy, after 20 to 30 minutes, and the veal is covered with a shiny glaze. If you're using fresh morels, sauté them in the butter, season them with salt and pepper, and reserve.

TRANSFER the veal to a platter. If you're using dried morels, squeeze out their liquid into the bowl and then pour the liquid, leaving any grit behind in the bowl, into the braising liquid. Stir the fresh or dried morels into the braising liquid. Bring the braising liquid to a quick simmer to cook off any raw Madeira. Slice the veal with a thin, sharp knife, place it on plates, and spoon the braising liquid and morels over it.

Variations: In eighteenth-century recipes, *fricandeau* is often served with lightly creamed sorrel, a sensible accompaniment since the acidity of the sorrel balances the suave richness of the meat. In the Anjou region of France, on the Loire River not far from where it runs into the Atlantic, the braising liquid is finished with cream and plenty of chopped fines herbes (parsley, chervil, tarragon, and chives). In Flanders, near Belgium, veal is braised with prunes, raisins, and cubes of dried apricot; in mountainous regions, braised or roast veal is often accompanied by chestnuts glazed with a little port. In the Bourbon, a region in central France, braised or roast veal is often accompanied by both black and green olives and mushrooms.

LEG OR SHOULDER OF LAMB BRAISED FOR SEVEN HOURS

GIGOT OU ÉPAULE D'AGNEAU À LA SEPT HEURES

MAKES 6 MAIN-COURSE SERVINGS

Supposedly gigot à la sept heures was invented by Alexandre Dumas, but it is a dish so in keeping with the traditions of old-fashioned French cooking that I hesitate to give him all the credit. In any case, this dish is just as it sounds, a leg of lamb cooked like a pot roast and braised for 7 hours, so long that it can be eaten with a spoon—à la cuillière. The first time I braised lamb this way, I cooked it just like the fricandeau on page 428, but I left it in the braising liquid for 5½ hours, so the total cooking time (including 1½ hours of preliminary roasting) met the requisite 7 hours. Perhaps because our lamb is leaner than that of Dumas, and despite my having obsessively larded it, the leg came out dry. And while a leg looks prettier and sounds better, you'll get much better results braising a lamb shoulder.

Unfortunately, most lamb shoulder these days is cut into shoulder chops, a cut that fails to make the best use of the shoulder and, when sautéed or grilled, leaves us hankering for the leaner and more tender loin or rib chops. If you have a good butcher, however, it shouldn't be a problem getting your hands on a lamb shoulder and having it boned. (Be aware that I'm talking about only one shoulder—primal [wholesale] cuts of lamb include both shoulders, and the whole thing is referred to as a shoulder—so you'll want only half the primal cut.)

Before tying up the shoulder, sprinkle the inside with any herbs you like—thyme, marjoram, savory, sage, or an herbes de Provence mixture—and then smear the inside with crushed garlic. Some cooks, when they see lamb, think reflexively of rosemary, which is very domineering; if you use it, chop it very fine and use it sparingly. Because lamb is popular in Provence, I tend to associate it with Mediterranean flavors and ingredients, meaning that I put plenty of herbs in the marinade, and maybe include a sprig of savory or a strip of orange zest in the bouquet garni, chopped tomatoes in the braising liquid, and plenty of garlic with the aromatic garniture. When the braising liquid has been strained and degreased and then reduced, either on the stove or, for a better taste, spooned over the lamb roast as part of the glazing process, I like to finish the sauce with typically Mediterranean flavorings and garnitures, such as coarsely chopped olives, chopped or shredded fresh basil, anchovies (crushed to a paste and whisked in the finished braising liquid), or whole peeled garlic cloves (blanched or cooked in the braising liquid during the last hour of braising). You may want to serve a vegetable accompaniment, such as a zucchini tian (see page 579) or artichokes à la barigoule (a Provençal dish in which baby artichokes are trimmed as described on page 68 and braised in olive oil and white wine with onions and garlic sweated in the oil before the artichokes are added). Or, for an especially stunning effect, you can cook baby onions, carrots, mushrooms, or baby artichokes in a little of the braising liquid and serve them atop the meat in wide soup plates. Sautéed wild mushrooms, finished with a garlic and parsley persillade and served over the sliced lamb, aren't bad either. The tying method I give here, called en ballon, is from a similar dish in Richard Olney's Simple French Food.

1   lamb shoulder (half a primal cut), boned, obvious fat
    trimmed off (about 9 pounds [4.1 kg] after boning)

2   cups [500 ml] dry white wine

2   cloves garlic, chopped

1   medium-size onion, quartered

1   medium-size carrot, peeled and sliced

2   teaspoons chopped dried thyme or marjoram or other
    herb, or a mixture, or 4 teaspoons fresh

2   large cloves garlic, chopped, crushed to a paste

    salt

    pepper

3   tablespoons olive oil

6   medium-size tomatoes, peeled, seeded, and coarsely
    chopped, or 1 can (35 ounces [990 g]) tomatoes,
    drained, seeded, and chopped

1   medium-size bouquet garni, which can contain a sprig
    of savory or marjoram or a strip of orange zest

20 large garlic cloves, peeled, simmered for 8 minutes,
    drained

WHEN you get your boned shoulder home, don't despair, it'll look like a mess. Just spread it out skin-side down on the cutting board and trim off any obvious chunks of fat. Marinate the shoulder with the wine, garlic, onion, and carrot and 1 teaspoon of the dried or fresh herbs in a nonaluminum bowl in the refrigerator for 4 hours, or overnight.

TAKE the shoulder out of the marinade, pat it dry, and spread it skin-side down on the cutting board. Smear it with the crushed garlic, sprinkle it with the remaining chopped herbs, and season it with salt and pepper. Strain the marinade, reserving both liquid and vegetables. Fold the outer edges of the shoulder toward the center, forming a more-or-less spherical packet. Tie it tightly with string with a series of ties—about eight 2-foot [61-cm] lengths—going under and around so that the string on top looks like spokes of a wheel.

PREHEAT the oven to 325°F [165°C/gas mark 3]. Sprinkle the meat with salt and pepper and brown it in the olive oil over medium to high heat in a heavy-bottomed pot, ideally one just large enough to hold it. Take the meat out of the pot and pour out the cooked fat. Put the meat—pretty side down—back in the pot and surround it with the vegetables and wine from the marinade and the tomatoes. Nestle in the bouquet garni. Bring to a simmer on top of the stove, cover the pot with a sheet of aluminum foil, press down on the center of the foil, put on the lid, and slide the pot into the oven. Braise for about 1½ hours and carefully turn the meat over, hooking it by the string with a long fork. Braise for about 1½ hours more, until a skewer slides easily in and out of the meat. Check every 20 minutes or so to make sure the braising liquid is barely bubbling. Take the meat out and turn the oven up to 450°F [230°C/gas mark 8].

GENTLY transfer the meat to a clean pot or a serving dish, such as a large oval gratin dish. Strain the braising liquid into a saucepan—you may have to press against the contents of the strainer with the bottom of a ladle to extract all the liquid from the vegetables and tomatoes. Place the saucepan over medium heat with the pan moved to one side of the burner so the liquid bubbles only on one side. Skim off the fat with a small ladle. When you've removed most of the fat, after about 10 minutes, ladle half the liquid, of which you should have about 3 cups [750 ml], over the meat, arrange the blanched garlic cloves around the meat, and slide the pot back into the oven. Bake the meat, uncovered, basting every 5 minutes, until it's covered with a shiny glaze, about 45 minutes. While the meat is baking, continue reducing the rest of the braising liquid on the stove until it's lightly syrupy. If the basting liquid you're using begins to run low, use some of the braising liquid that you're reducing on the stove. Shortly before you're ready to serve, pour the liquid from the stove over the meat and baste for 5 or 10 minutes more, until the meat is coated with a shiny reddish glaze.

SERVE the lamb, cut into rough wedges, in wide soup plates or pasta bowls with a few of the garlic cloves sprinkled around it and the braising liquid spooned over it.

Optional Garnitures and Finishes

5 BASIL LEAVES, shredded (cut into chiffonade; see page 17) and stirred into the braising liquid 1 minute before serving

2 TOMATOES, peeled, seeded, cut into dice, stirred into the sauce 1 minute before serving

8 ANCHOVIES, chopped finely, whisked into the braising liquid just before serving

40 PEARL ONIONS (about 1 pint [335 g]), OR 12 WALNUT-SIZE ONIONS; peeled; glazed with a small amount of water, broth, or braising liquid; or just cooked with the lamb the way the garlic is in the recipe above

12 BABY ARTICHOKES, leaves trimmed off, simmered in boiling water, drained

3 MEDIUM-SIZE CARROTS, sliced or sectioned; cored; turned (see page 21); glazed with water, broth, or braising liquid; or cooked with the lamb as the garlic is in the recipe above

1½ POUNDS [675 g] WILD MUSHROOMS, sautéed in olive oil, sprinkled with garlic and parsley mixture (persillade), spooned over each serving

---

BRAISED LAMB SHANKS WITH RED WINE

JARRETS D'AGNEAU AU VIN ROUGE

MAKES 4 MAIN-COURSE SERVINGS

A few years ago, braised lamb shanks, along with polenta and gnocchi, became one of the in foods at Manhattan restaurants. These are all delicious foods, but they are so inexpensive to make that it's irksome to be charged as though they were filet mignon. The obvious recourse is to make them at home.

Braising lamb shanks is a snap—they just take a while—and because they are naturally gelatinous, the meat always ends up meltingly soft and juicy. These shanks are delicious when served with a bowl of garlic mayonnaise, aïoli (see page 491), passed at the table for people to dollop on as they see fit.

4   lamb shanks (about 1 pound [450 g] each), trimmed of excess fat

salt

pepper

4   tablespoons olive oil

2   medium-size onions, chopped fine

3   cloves garlic, peeled

3   medium-size carrots, peeled, halved lengthwise, and sliced thin

4   cups [1 l] full-bodied red wine, plus 1 more cup if you're not using broth

1   cup [250 ml] concentrated beef, veal, or chicken broth (see page 4; optional)

1   medium-size bouquet garni

2   tablespoons chopped parsley

SEASON the lamb shanks with salt and pepper and brown them on both sides in a wide heavy-bottomed nonreactive pot (avoid cast iron and nonanodized aluminum) in 2 tablespoons of the olive oil. Set them aside. If the shanks are especially long or your pot is too small, you may have to brown them in stages. Pour out the cooked oil, replace it with the remaining oil, and add the onions, garlic, and carrots. Stir the vegetables over medium heat until the onions turn translucent and just begin to brown, about 10 minutes. Pour in 1 cup of the red wine and boil over high heat until just a thin film is left on the bottom of the pot. While the wine is reducing, scrape the bottom of the pot to dislodge and dissolve any caramelized juices.

PUT the shanks back in the pot, pour in 3 cups of wine, plus the broth or extra cup of wine, nestle in the bouquet garni, and bring to a gentle simmer. Cover the pot with a sheet of aluminum foil and press it down in the middle so moisture condensing on its underside will drip over the shanks. Put the lid on the pot and place the pot on a flame tamer set over a very low flame, so that the braising liquid barely bubbles, or slide the pot into a 325°F [165°C/gas mark 3] oven. Braise for 2 hours, or until a skewer stuck into one of the shanks slides easily in and out.

PUT the shanks on a plate and keep them warm. Strain the braising liquid into a saucepan—push down on the vegetables with the bottom of a ladle to extract as much liquid as possible—and gently reduce while skimming off fat until the braising liquid has reduced by half and is lightly syrupy. Discard the vegetables. Stir the parsley into the reduced braising liquid and spoon the liquid over the shanks on a platter or on individual plates.

Variations: This is a very simple recipe for lamb shanks because there's no garniture. If you like, garnish the shanks with vegetables such as whole peeled garlic cloves, whole peeled small shallots, or mushrooms cooked separately in a little of the braising liquid for about ½ hour just before the shanks are ready. I sometimes cut carrots into ¼-inch [.5 cm] dice, sweat them in a little butter, and spoon them over the shanks just before serving. (See also the list of optional garnitures for braised lamb shoulder, page 432.)

BRAISED VEAL SHANKS (OSSO BUCO) WITH VEGETABLE "CONFITURE"

JARRETS DE VEAU BRAISÉS AVEC LEUR CONFITURE DE LEGUMES

MAKES 6 MAIN-COURSE SERVINGS

A veal shank—osso buco—is a great cut of veal, provided you know how to cook it. Sautéed or grilled like a steak, it is tough and inedible. It must be braised.

The easiest of all methods, standard for most braises and stews, is to brown the shanks, sweat a few aromatic vegetables in the same pan, pour some wine, broth, or water over them, simmer very gently for 2 to 3 hours, and serve. The recipe given here, however, includes a small variation. Remember that traditional French pot roast can be prepared à la ménagère, which means that the aromatic garniture added at the beginning remains in the dish. When the dish is prepared à la bourgeoise, the aromatic vegetables are strained out and fresh vegetables, either cooked separately or finished in the braising liquid, are served with the final dish. The method used here is à la ménagère, but with a refinement: The aromatic vegetables are cut into julienne and are then served in a melting tangle on top of the shanks. The combination of flavors, with the slightly sweet vegetables redolent of the meaty juices from the veal, is unforgettable. A hint of orange is a final nuance.

6   rounds of veal shank (each 2 inches [5 cm] thick; the weight may vary from 10 to 18 ounces [280 to 505 g], but since larger pieces have more bone, there is a similar amount of meat), tied

salt

pepper

2 tablespoons olive oil

2 cups white wine

1 cup [250 ml] concentrated veal or beef broth (see page 4; optional) or water

1 medium-size bouquet garni containing 2 strips of orange zest (3 inches each) in addition to the regular herbs

2 large carrots, peeled

3 large leeks, washed

2 medium-size turnips, peeled

1 small celeriac (optional), peeled

1 bulb fennel, stalks removed

3 tablespoons finely chopped parsley

SEASON the shanks with salt and pepper. Over medium to high heat, brown them on both sides in the oil in a heavy-bottomed pot just large enough to hold them in a single layer, 8 to 10 minutes on each side. If the heat's too high, the shanks will burn; if it's too low, they will stew prematurely in their own juices. If you don't have a big enough pot, brown them in batches.

TAKE the shanks out of the pot, pour out the cooked oil, and stir in the wine and the broth or water. Scrape the bottom of the pot with a wooden spoon to dislodge any caramelized juices, and put the shanks back in the pot. Nestle the bouquet garni in between the shanks. Put the pot back on the stove until it returns to a simmer. Cover the pot with a sheet of aluminum foil pressed down in the middle, put on the lid, and simmer ever so gently on top of the stove or by sliding the pot into a 325°F [165°C/gas mark 3] oven. Check every 30 minutes to make sure the shanks are still at a low simmer, with a bubble rising to the surface about every 2 seconds. Turn the shanks to ensure even cooking.

JULIENNE the vegetables so they're about 3 inches [7.5 cm] long and ⅛ inch [3 mm] thick (see below)—you'll have an enormous pile. When the shanks have been braising for about 45 minutes, lift the foil, spread the vegetables on top of the shanks, put back the foil, and cover the pot. Continue braising for about 1 hour and 15 minutes more, until a skewer slides easily in and out of one of the shanks. Take out and discard the bouquet garni. Put each shank in a hot soup plate and spoon the braising liquid and the vegetables over it. Sprinkle each serving with parsley.

CARROTS: Peel the carrots and cut them into sections about 3 inches [7.5 cm] long. Slice the sections, with a knife or Benriner cutter (see page 13), between ⅛ and 1/16 inch [about 3 mm] thick on four sides until you reach the woody core. You should be able to get about 4 slices from each of the four sides of a large carrot. Discard the core. Stack 2 or 3 of the slices (or start with 1 if this makes you uncomfortable) and, using a chef's knife, slice them into julienne strips the same width as the slices are thick.

TURNIPS AND CELERIAC: Peel, cut into slices between 1/16 and ⅛ inch [about 3 mm] thick with a knife or Benriner cutter, and julienne by stacking the slices and then slicing the stack into strips having the same width as thickness.

LEEKS: A Benriner cutter is no help here. Cut off the leek greens, leaving little of the pale green attached, and cut the white in half lengthwise. Rinse the leek under cold running water with the green end facing down. Flip through the leaves while holding the leek under running water, rub off any clinging grit with your thumb, and shake out the water. Take 2 or 3 of the leaves a time, fold them over themselves end to end, and slice them into thin strips.

FENNEL: It's impossible to slice fennel into perfect julienne because it falls apart into pieces as soon as the individual layers are pulled away from the bulb. But you can come close by first peeling the stringy fiber off the outside of the bulb with a vegetable peeler and cutting around the core, detaching it, in a cone shape, from the individual layers. It's then easy to remove the layers, cut them into manageable sections, and spread them flat on the cutting board for slicing.

BEEF STEW WITH PEARL ONIONS, MUSHROOMS, AND BACON

BOEUF À LA BOURGUIGNONNE

HOW TO	HOW TO	GREAT TRICKS	HOW TO	HOW TO
MAKE BEEF STEW AND LAMB STEW AND INVENT YOUR OWN VARIATIONS	MAKE A STEW WITHOUT BROWNING THE MEAT	WITH LEFTOVERS	MAKE RAVIOLI	MAKE A MEAT "SAUTÉ" THAT LOOKS LIKE A STEW

I'M ALWAYS RELUCTANT TO GIVE A RECIPE FOR A STEW BECAUSE, IN my kitchen at least, the best stews come about almost by accident—a few unfinished bottles of wine, a little of my homemade vinegar, and a tomato or two might go into the pot, with results that are never entirely predictable. Perhaps because of the simple spontaneous delight of using what's around, these haphazard concoctions end up more satisfying than a perfectly executed recipe.

A stew is a dish in which the main ingredient has been cut into manageable pieces—usually into cubes 1 or 2 inches [2.5 to 5 cm] on each side—and then gently simmered in just enough liquid to cover. There are innumerable variations, each with its own, sometimes hazy, nomenclature. Stews, of course, are all braises, but they are rarely referred to as such, that word being reserved for relatively large cuts of meat such as pot roast, *fricandeau,* and their various relatives discussed in Chapter 31.

A blanquette is a stew that derives its identity from the veal strips' being poached directly in liquid, rather than browned in fat before liquid is added; from the poaching liquid's being thickened with roux, which turns the liquid into a velouté; and then from the dish's being finished with a classic mixture of cream and egg yolks. The same dish with the veal strips first cooked lightly in fat—not enough to brown the meat—before the addition of liquid becomes a fricassée. The fricassée approach has the slight advantage of not requiring a preliminary blanching of the meat, but other than that it is practically indistinguishable from a blanquette. Two other factors affect the character of a stew: whether and how it is thickened, and whether or not the meat is browned before liquid is added. Most red meat stews are browned before liquid is added, to enhance the color of the sauce and improve the flavor of the dish. Thickeners, usually flour, can be added at different stages and in different forms or be left out entirely. When no thickener is added, the body of the stewing liquid is provided by the natural gelatin that is slowly released by the meat into the surrounding liquid. Often, this natural gelatin is supplemented with pork rind from unsmoked bacon or with a calf's or pig's foot, cut in half lengthwise and blanched. Highly reduced broth, demi-glace, or *glace de viande* added to the stewing liquid will also contribute natural gelatin and additional savor.

One way to thicken a stew is to coat the pieces of meat with flour before browning or sprinkle flour over the meat as it browns, a method called *singer.* This browns the flour, eliminating its starchy taste, before you add liquid. But because flour is an emulsifier, it tends to keep the fat that's released by the meat in solution and make the fat harder to skim off during and after cooking. Stews can also be thickened at the end with *beurre manié,* a paste of flour and butter whisked into the simmering stewing liquid shortly before serving. This method allows you to degrease before thickening. However, if beurre manié is allowed to simmer for more than a minute or two, the sauce takes on a starchy taste. The trick is to get the flour to thicken before it releases too much starch. Four tablespoons of beurre manié (2 tablespoons each of butter and flour) is enough to thicken about 2 cups [500 ml] of liquid.

Cornstarch or some other soluble starch such as arrowroot or potato starch, worked into a thin paste with twice its volume of water, can also be whisked into a stew a few minutes before serving and the stewing liquid brought quickly to a boil for the thickening to take effect. Even though cornstarch is easy to use and perfectly effective, there's something decidedly un-French about the sheen it gives to the finished sauce. Vegetable purées, especially onion or garlic or the aromatic vegetables cooked along with the meat and puréed, can be whisked into the stew at the end to give the stew a natural body without tasteless starch. An elegant touch—although rich—is to reduce the stewing liquid to concentrate its flavor and enhance its natural body and then whisk in cold butter (*monter au beurre;* see page 20) as though making a modern brown sauce. Small amounts of foie gras can also be worked into a smooth paste with an equal amount of butter and then whisked into the reduced stewing liquid shortly before serving.

The French also call stews *sautés,* a habit that confuses things even more, since most of us think of sautés as simple dishes of meat, seafood, or vegetables that have been browned in a pan in hot fat. In addition to this obvious and usual usage, the word "sauté" can just refer to a meat, poultry, or seafood stew, or it can have a more specific meaning. A chicken sauté, for example, is a dish made by cooking the cut-up chicken entirely in a small amount of fat, usually butter, on top of the stove, setting the chicken aside, discarding the fat, and then making a sauce in the pan. The chicken is only reheated in the sauce just before serving (see pages 368 to 371). A sauté can also be a kind of mock stew in which tender cuts of meat (or pieces of leftover roasts or grilled meats) are browned (or not) and finished in a sauce and immediately served. Beef Stroganoff (page 453), finished with sour cream (or better, crème fraîche, which won't curdle), is the best known of these dishes, but virtually any meat or sauce combination can be used.

It is for good reason that wine is the liquid used most often in stews; its acidity and fruity complexity make the perfect foil for flavorful meat juices and merge almost miraculously with herbs and aromatic vegetables to create flavors and aromas far greater than the sum of the ingredients. But in regions where wine was expensive, stews evolved using the local alcoholic beverages, including beer (used in the northeast of France to make carbonnade), cider (used in Normandy to make *tripes à la mode de Caen*), tomatoes (which liquify when cooked; used in Provence and the Languedoc), vinegar (used in Alsace), and water (used in Irish stew, a dish that has been adopted enthusiastically by the French). Any of these liquids, alone or in combination, will give a stew its own special identity. Broth will give body and flavor to any stew but is usually used only to augment, rather than replace, other moistening liquids. Unless your broth is very concentrated, it can weaken the flavor of a stew rather than enhance it. In better French restaurants, a chunk of *glace de viande* is stirred into a stew to add body without diluting the flavors of moistening liquids such as wine.

With minor variations in method, such as the use of different herbs (either in the bouquet garni or sprinkled on the meat before moistening) or the use of different liquids or aromatic vegetables, most stews are made in much the same way. It is often the garnitures that are added near the end of cooking that give the stew its name and identity. A *boeuf à la bourguignonne* gets its name from the classic Burgundian garniture of pearl onions, mushrooms, and strips of bacon (also used with coq au vin), but once you permit yourself to improvise, the possible garnitures become almost endless. The simplest garniture is, of course, the aromatic vegetables, usually onions and carrots, that have cooked along with the meat; but in less homespun concoctions these vegetables are taken out and discarded, or occasionally puréed and used to thicken the stew. You can glaze onions and root vegetables such as carrots, turnips, parsnips, celeriac, and turnips on the stove in a little of the stew's liquid, or you can just cook them in the stew itself after you've removed the original aromatic vegetables. If you cook the vegetables on the stove, you can even spoon them over the individual servings so they aren't masked with sauce. Lots of cooks never think of it, but green vegetables—string beans, asparagus tips, green peas, fava beans, spinach, Swiss chard—can be quickly boiled or steamed and strewn over or stirred into the stew just before serving. Other vegetables, such as zucchini or wild mushrooms, can be quickly sautéed and added to the stew at the last minute.

Because American meat seems to be getting leaner, if I'm feeling particularly conscientious I lard each cube before browning.

BEEF STEW WITH PEARL ONIONS, MUSHROOMS, AND BACON

BOEUF À LA BOURGUIGNONNE

5 pounds [2.3 kg] beef chuck roast, preferably blade, cut into 1½-inch [4-cm] chunks

1 bottle full-bodied red wine

2 medium-size carrots, peeled, cut into ½-inch [1.5-cm] sections

2 medium-size onions, chopped coarse

2 cloves garlic, crushed, plus 2 cloves, chopped fine (for the fatback strips; optional)

1 medium-size bouquet garni

12 ounces [340 g] fatback (including rind), rind removed and reserved, fat cut into ¼-inch-by-6-inch [.5- by 15-cm] strips (optional)

4 tablespoons "pure" olive oil or vegetable oil (for sautéing the meat and vegetables), plus 2 tablespoons olive oil (for sautéing the mushrooms)

   salt

½ cup [375 ml] beef or veal broth (optional; see page 4)

1 pint [335 g] pearl onions, or 16 walnut-size onions, peeled (see "Peeling Pearl Onions," page 439)

1 pound small cultivated mushrooms, preferably cremini

   pepper

½ pound [225 g] thickly sliced bacon, cut into 1-inch [2.5-cm] strips

3 tablespoons all-purpose flour (for an optional beurre manié)

3 tablespoons butter (for an optional beurre manié)

STIR the beef chunks in a bowl with the red wine, carrots, chopped onions, garlic, and bouquet garni and let them marinate in the refrigerator for 6 to 12 hours. Stir the meat and vegetables once or twice during the marinating. If you're in a rush, skip the marinating.

IF you're larding the meat, toss the strips of fatback with the chopped garlic and let them marinate in the refrigerator while you're marinating the meat. Cut the reserved rind into strips about ½ inch [1.5 cm] wide and tie them in a bundle.

TAKE the meat out of the bowl and scoop out the vegetables, reserving both wine and vegetables. If you're larding the meat, insert a strip of fatback in each piece with a hinged interlarding needle (see page 423), cutting the strip of fatback off where it comes out of the meat, leaving a 1½-inch [1.5 cm] strip of fatback in each chunk.

OVER medium heat, heat 2 tablespoons of the oil in a heavy-bottomed pot large enough to hold the stew, or in a heavy-bottomed skillet. Brown the vegetables, stirring every few minutes until they have softened and lightly browned. Scoop out the vegetables and reserve. Pat the meat dry and season the chunks with salt. Over high heat, heat another 2 tablespoons of oil in the pot used to brown the vegetables, and brown the meat on all sides (see "Tricks for Sautéing Meats and Vegetables," page 440). If the oil is smoking and the bottom of the pot looks like it might be burning, turn down the heat to medium. When the meat is well browned, pour out the cooked oil and examine the bottom of the pot to see if it is black with burnt juices. If it is, rinse the pot and wipe out the burnt juices.

PUT the meat back in the pot and add the wine, the broth, if using, and the browned vegetables. Nestle the bouquet garni and the pork rind strips into the pot. Bring the stew to a gentle simmer on the stove, cover, and slide into a 325°F [165°C/gas mark 3] preheated oven. Cook for about 3 hours, checking every 30 minutes to make sure the stew isn't boiling, but that a bubble rises to the surface every second or so. Check if the meat is done by poking a piece with a paring knife—the meat is done when a chunk doesn't cling to the knife.

STRAIN the stew through a colander or large strainer into a clean pot. Pick out the meat with tongs and set it aside in a bowl covered with plastic wrap. (Never leave stewed meat uncovered or it will get dry and crusty.) Discard the bouquet garni, aromatic vegetables, and rind. Put the pot of braising liquid over low to medium heat, with the pan to one side of the burner so the liquid bubbles up on only one side. Skimming off the fat, simmer the cooking liquid down to 3 cups, about 20 minutes.

WHILE the cooking liquid is reducing, prepare the garniture. Put the pearl onions in a pan just large enough to hold them in a single layer, with ½ cup [125 ml] of the stewing liquid. Simmer, covered, until the onions are easily penetrated with the tip of a knife, 10 to 20 minutes. If the mushrooms are larger than 1 inch across, cut them in quarters vertically; otherwise leave them whole. Sauté them in 2 tablespoons of olive oil over high heat until they're well browned, and season them with salt and pepper. Pour any liquid left after cooking the mushrooms and onions back into the stew. Heat the bacon strips over medium heat for about 10 minutes until they release their fat and turn just slightly crispy. Scoop them out with a slotted spoon and drain them on paper towels.

JUST before serving, combine the meat with the stewing liquid and the garniture and gently reheat, keeping the meat at a very gentle simmer for about 5 minutes so that it heats through. Check to see if the liquid seems too thin. (It's a matter of taste—I like a brothlike stew and serve it in wide soup plates.) If you want to thicken the liquid, make a beurre manié (see page 436) by working the flour and butter into a paste with the back of a fork. Whisk half the paste into the simmering stew and judge the stewing liquid's consistency (dipping a spoon into the liquid makes it easier to see). If you still want it thicker, whisk in the rest of the beurre manié.

SERVE the stew on hot plates or in hot wide soup plates. Grind fresh pepper over each serving.

Variations: Every region of France has its own stew. In northern France, near Belgium, the *carbonnade* is a traditional dish. To prepare a carbonnade, replace the wine in the recipe above with dark beer, double the onions and leave them in the stew, and leave out the carrots and the Burgundian garniture. The traditional stew from Provence, the *daube Provençal,* is often made with beef, but it can also be made with lamb, rabbit or hare, or even octopus (see page 440). A traditional beef daube contains red wine, tomatoes, and a good amount of carrots and onions.

PEELING PEARL ONIONS

If you went out and bought one of those pint (10-ounce) [285-g] containers of pearl onions, you're liable to regret it once you start peeling. To make peeling easier, plunge the onions in a pot of boiling water for about 30 seconds, drain them in a colander, and rinse with cold water. The peels will come off much more easily.

Home cooks sometimes have problems sautéing because our stoves don't get hot enough to brown foods properly. Because all foods contain water that is released when the food is heated, sautéing requires high heat to evaporate this water as soon as it is released and to allow the outer surface of the food to develop a savory crust of caramelized natural sugars and other compounds. If your pan isn't hot enough, the water is released too quickly, the temperature of the pan is lowered even more, and your food boils or steams in its own juices and never browns. Other than going out and buying a professional stove that delivers intense heat, there are a couple of ways to prevent this. First, use the heaviest pan or pot you've got. Heavy pots and pans not only provide even heat, they *retain* heat so their temperature doesn't drop so quickly once you start adding food. Second, and perhaps most important, add foods to be sautéed only a little bit at a time, making sure that the foods start to brown before you add more. If you're sautéing meat, don't start turning it until the side touching the pan is completely browned, and when you do start turning, turn only a few of the pieces at a time. Last, if you have a choice, use a pan that's shiny rather than dark on the inside. This allows you to see if you're burning the juices. If you are, rinse out the pan while it's still hot, once you've browned all the meat.

PROVENÇAL LAMB STEW

MOUTON EN DAUBE À LA PROVENÇAL

MAKES 6 MAIN-COURSE SERVINGS

The French are fond of *daubes*, a type of dish whose name is derived from the Provençal word *daubière*, for a juglike earthenware stewing vessel with a narrow mouth. The term is now used to refer to a stew with Provençal idiosyncracies, such as including orange zest in the bouquet garni, adding tomatoes to the braising liquid, and using lots of garlic. Daubes differ from most stews because the meat isn't browned before liquid is added (making a daube especially easy to throw together). Nor is any thickener used except for pork rinds and/or a split calf's or pig's foot, which supply enough natural gelatin to give the stew body and a natural shiny sapidity. If you don't want to go out in search of pigs' feet and rinds, a daube is perfectly good without them; the stewing liquid will just be a little lighter. You can also add concentrated broth, which will contribute both flavor and natural gelatin. Or you can reduce the stewing liquid, so you'll have less liquid, but liquid with a more intense flavor.

Our lamb is older than French lamb and would be looked upon by a French cook as more mutton than lamb. But this is of little concern when making a daube, because in a daube, as in any stew, the meat is cooked long enough so that the meat, even of older animals, eventually tenderizes.

Shoulder meat or the meat from lamb shanks is best for stewing—the leg meat is expensive and dries out. If you have trouble finding lamb shoulder, buy shoulder chops and cut the bones out. Look for the thickest chops and buy almost twice the amount by weight as you would boneless lamb. If you have a good butcher, you may be able to get lamb shanks (see also page 509). Here again, figure almost half the weight will be bone. Whenever boning cuts of meat for stews or roasts, save the bones and simmer them in the stew or use them to surround the roast, to provide extra flavor.

5	pounds [2.3 kg] boneless lamb shoulder meat or lamb stew meat, or 9 pounds [4.1 kg] lamb shoulder chops or lamb shanks
1	bottle dry white wine
2	medium-size onions, chopped fine
5	cloves garlic, chopped fine
1	medium-size bouquet garni (including a 2-inch [5 cm] strip of orange zest)
1	pig's or calf's foot, cut in half lengthwise, calf's foot also cut crosswise by the butcher, boiled for 5 minutes, drained, and rinsed (optional)
	rind from fatback, about 6 by 12 inches [15 by 30.5 cm] or whatever you have (optional)
5	medium-size tomatoes, peeled, seeded, and chopped coarse, or 1 can (28 ounces) [795 g] drained, seeded, and chopped
	salt
	pepper

CUT the boneless shoulder meat into 1½-inch [4-cm] chunks. If you're using chops or shanks, take the meat off the bone and cut it into chunks or, if it's too thin, into strips about 2 inches [5 cm] long and ½ inch [1.5 cm] wide. Don't worry if you have some irregular pieces. Save the bones.

TOSS the lamb in a bowl with the wine, onions, garlic, and bouquet garni and let it marinate in the refrigerator for 4 to 12 hours.

PREHEAT the oven to 325°F [165°C/gas mark 3]. Place the split foot or the fatback rind in a heavy-bottomed pot. (Ideally, the pot should be narrow, emulating as closely as possible the traditional *daubière*, which has a squat shape and narrows near the top, making it easy to skim off fat.) If you're

using the rind, place it in the pot fat-side down, because the rind side can stick and burn. Put in the bouquet garni, any reserved bones, and the tomatoes and sprinkle with salt. Add the meat—sprinkle some more salt over it—along with the wine, 1 cup of water, and the vegetables from the marinade. If the meat is sticking out above the liquid, don't be tempted to add more liquid, which would dilute the sauce. Instead, cover the pot with a sheet of aluminum foil and press it down in the middle before covering the pot. This bastes the meat that's not covered with liquid. Bring the stew to a gentle simmer on top of the stove, cover the pot, and slide it into the oven. Check every 30 minutes to make sure the liquid isn't boiling but that a bubble floats to the surface about every second.

AFTER 2½ hours, when the meat should no longer cling to a paring knife stuck into one of the pieces, take the stew out of the oven. With a small ladle, skim off any fat that has floated to the surface, or let cool, refrigerate overnight, and remove the congealed fat the next day. Discard the bones or give them to the dog. Serve in soup plates.

Variations: Lamb stew can be varied like any other stew—the moistening liquid can be water, broth, wine, tomatoes, hard cider, or just about anything you can think of. While onions and garlic seem essential, they can be supplemented with turnips, fennel, dried mushrooms (porcini are marvelous), and, of course, carrots. A daube can be converted into the classic *navarin d'agneau* by browning the meat, sprinkling it with flour toward the end of browning (although I find that adding flour at this stage holds the lamb fat in suspension, making it more difficult to skim later), replacing the wine with broth or water, and then serving the lamb (aromatic garniture removed) with a garniture of pearl onions and baby potatoes, cooked separately or nestled into the stew during the last 30 minutes of cooking. *Agneau à la printanière* is much like the navarin, except that the garniture is more elaborate and contains baby carrots or turnips (or larger ones that have been turned) and occasionally string beans or asparagus tips or baby peas (blanched and drained and stirred into or sprinkled over the stew just before serving). Thawed frozen peas work amazingly well and can just be stirred into the stew (without boiling) 1 minute before serving. Shell beans are especially marvelous with lamb. Fresh boiled fava beans, added to the stew at the end, or fresh cranberry beans, simmered in the stew for about 20 minutes, make dramatic additions. Dried beans can also be added—either cooked separately with an onion and a bouquet garni and stirred in at the end (a pressure cooker will cut their precooking time to about 45 minutes), or added at the beginning so they cook along with the lamb and absorb the stewing liquid. (More about this in Chapter 34.) An Irish stew is perhaps the simplest variation, requiring no marinade or wine, and put together by layering the pieces of lamb with sliced onions and potatoes and baking until everything merges into a melting whole.

STEPS AND INGREDIENTS FOR MAKING A MEAT STEW

Meat Cuts

BEEF: CHUCK, SHANK, SHORT RIBS, CHEEKS

LAMB: SHOULDER, NECK, SHANKS

PORK: SHOULDER

VEAL: SHOULDER, SHANKS

VENISON OR BOAR: LEG, SHOULDER

Fat for Browning Meats

OLIVE OIL ("pure," not extra-virgin)

BUTTER (preferably clarified)

ANIMAL FAT, such as pork, duck, or goose, rendered

VEGETABLE OIL

Aromatic Garniture

VEGETABLES FROM THE MARINADE

DRIED MUSHROOMS, such as porcini (cèpes) or morels, or fresh mushrooms, frozen saved-up mushroom stems

CUBES OF PANCETTA (unsmoked bacon) OR PROSCIUTTO END (sweated along with aromatic garniture vegetables before adding liquid)

Moistening Liquids

WINE (usually taken from the marinade)

BROTH

CONCENTRATED BROTH OR JUS (glace de viande, demi-glace, drippings from a roast)

WATER

VINEGAR

BEER (preferably dark or amber Belgian style)

CIDER (soft cider will make the stew somewhat sweet; hard cider is more subtle)

Marinade Ingredients (optional)

ONIONS

CARROTS

CELERY

TURNIPS

FENNEL

ORANGE ZEST

HERBS (thyme and bay leaf are most common,
but marjoram, oregano, savory, sage, hyssop, lavender, or herbes de Provence mixture may also be used.
These herbs can be tied up into a bouquet garni or be left loose and strained out later.)

JUNIPER BERRIES, CRUSHED (for game)

WINE (red or white or a mixture)

VINEGAR

GARLIC AND PARSLEY, chopped (for marinating strips)

COGNAC (for marinating strips)

Larding Ingredients (optional)

FATBACK STRIPS

Herbs and Bouquets Garnis

ANY OF THE HERBS UNDER "MARINADE INGREDIENTS," above,
or a classic bouquet garni (bay leaves, thyme, parsley)

Thickeners

PORK RIND (from fatback): blanched, added whole or in pieces
to the stew at the beginning; provides natural gelatin

CALF'S OR PIG'S FOOT: split in half lengthwise, blanched,
cooked in stew from the beginning to provide natural gelatin

FLOUR: sprinkled over meat during browning; worked into a beurre manié and whisked at the end;
or cooked into a roux and the braising liquid added to the roux to make a velouté
(more typical when making a blanquette; see page 413)

(continued)

VEGETABLE PURÉES: the puréed aromatic garniture whisked into the braising liquid at the end;
OTHER VEGETABLE PURÉES SUCH AS ONION, GARLIC,
SORREL OR SPINACH (for a blanquette), MUSHROOM, ARTICHOKE, ROASTED AND PEELED BELL
PEPPERS OR POBLANO CHILES, SOAKED AND PURÉED DRIED CHILES (which will turn the stew into a mole)

CORNSTARCH/ARROWROOT/POTATO STARCH: whisked with an equal amount of cold water;
this slurry then whisked into simmering stew

BLOOD/LIVERS/VISCERA: sometimes used as thickeners for game stews (see Squab Salmis, page 377)

RUSSET POTATOES (for Irish stew)

Enrichers

BUTTER/HERB BUTTER: whisked into reduced and degreased stewing liquid at the end

FOIE GRAS: worked with an equal amount of butter; whisked into reduced and degreased stewing liquid at the end

HEAVY CREAM: reduced with degreased stewing liquid (more typical in "white" stews such as blanquette)

Final Flavorings

HERBS: finely chopped herbs whose flavor would be lost if simmered with the stew,
SUCH AS BASIL, PARSLEY, CHIVES, TARRAGON, CHERVIL

ANCHOVIES: crushed to a paste, whisked into the stewing liquid at the end

TRUFFLES: chopped, sliced, or cut into julienne

Final Garnitures

PEARL ONIONS: glazed in a small amount of stewing liquid

ROOT VEGETABLES: carrots, celeriac, turnips, rutabagas, etc., sectioned and shaped,
glazed in a small amount of stewing liquid and added to stew at the end

FENNEL: cut into wedges, braised

GREEN LEAFY VEGETABLES: SWISS CHARD, SPINACH, BEET GREENS, blanched or steamed, sautéed with garlic
CROUTONS: cubes of bread cooked in butter or olive oil or cut into classic heart shapes, dipped in parsley (see page 493)

BACON: cut into strips (lardons), rendered

SHELL BEANS (dry or fresh)

GREEN BEANS

PEAS

TOMATOES: peeled, seeded, cut into cubes

BABY ARTICHOKES: trimmed, boiled in water acidulated with lemon, sautéed in olive oil with garlic

CULTIVATED OR WILD MUSHROOMS: sautéed or braised in some of the stewing liquid,
stirred into the stew or sprinkled over it at the end

LEFTOVER STEWS: RAVIOLI AND THE MIROTON

What the French call *les restes,* a term little more enticing than our "leftovers," the Italians call the *incatenata*—the "chained up." The *incatenata* is a succession of dishes, each based on the one preceding it, that make up the weekly fare of a well-run but parsimonious kitchen. Anyone who cooks regularly and with a little imagination can create his or her own *incatenata.* In certain French kitchens, the use of leftovers has become almost formulaic—a leftover stew or braised dish reappears *en gelée* (see Cold French-style Pot Roast, page 426), and whatever's left of that may very well end up as a stuffing for ravioli, more likely in the south, or reheated in a kind of gratin called a *miroton,* more likely in the north.

Figuring out ways to use leftover stewed or poached meats is also very helpful when you're using the richly flavored braising liquid as the base for a brown sauce or for some elegant dish and don't know just what to do with the meat.

GRATIN OF LEFTOVER BEEF WITH ONIONS

BOEUF EN MIROTON

MAKES 4 MAIN-COURSE SERVINGS

This gratin is so delicious that I often like it at least as much as the original dish that provides the leftovers. A miroton is traditionally made with the meat from a pot-au-feu, but it also makes a great way to use leftover stew, braised chunks of meat, or leftover roast. You may have to gauge the amounts in this recipe to suit what you have left over.

1¼ pounds [565 g] waxy potatoes, peeled

2 pounds [900 g] onions (preferably red onions, which are mild and sweet), sliced thin

4 tablespoons butter

2 tablespoons flour

2 cups [500 ml] broth or water

salt

1 pound [450 g] (approximately) leftover meat from a pot-au-feu, meat broth, roast, or stew, cut in ¼-inch [.5 cm] slices

1 tablespoon good wine vinegar

4 tablespoons fresh bread crumbs (see page 2)

pepper

1 tablespoon finely chopped parsley

PUT the potatoes in a pot with just enough cold water to cover them. Bring to a gentle simmer and simmer until the potatoes can be penetrated with a knife but offer a slight resistance, 15 to 30 minutes, depending on the size of the potatoes. Drain and let cool.

COOK the onions over medium heat in a heavy-bottomed pot in 2 tablespoons of the butter. Keep stirring with a wooden spoon to prevent the onions from burning. When the onions have released their liquid and the liquid caramelizes on the bottom of the pot—this takes about 25 minutes—sprinkle the onions with flour, stir over the heat for about 2 minutes more, and pour in the broth or water. Bring to a simmer while scraping the bottom of the pot to dissolve the caramelized juices. Season to taste with salt and remove from the heat.

PREHEAT the oven to 400°F [200°C/gas mark 6]. Slice the potatoes into rounds about ¼ inch [.5 cm] thick and spread them in a gratin dish rubbed with 1 teaspoon of the butter. The dish should be just large enough to hold the potatoes in a single layer, with the potatoes overlapping slightly. (Mine is oval, 9 inches [23 cm] wide and 13 inches [33 cm] long.) Arrange the meat over the potatoes, spoon the onion mixture over it, dribble the vinegar over the mixture, and sprinkle with bread crumbs. Melt the remaining butter and dribble it over the gratin. Bake until the *miroton* is bubbling and the top has a crispy crust, 20 to 25 minutes. If the crust hasn't browned, slide the *miroton* under the broiler—watch it carefully—to brown it. Grind pepper over the *miroton*, sprinkle it with parsley, and serve.

Variations: The idea of turning meat leftovers into a gratin is so adaptable that you could make one with just about anything (well, not quite anything) that you find in your refrigerator. The sauce (made with onions and broth) and vegetables (the potatoes) in a traditional *miroton* can each be replaced. The cooked potatoes can be replaced with cooked turnips or rutabagas; cooked pasta; leftover cooked green vegetables, such as spinach or Swiss chard (cooked with garlic), or stewed and creamed sorrel; tomatoes (cooked down to a thick sauce); mushrooms (wild, to make your *miroton* suddenly luxurious); or combinations of these. The onion sauce can be replaced with a simple broth—toss some cubes of stale bread or layer slices in the gratin to absorb excess liquid during baking—or with milk or cream. Grated cheese (possibilities include Gruyère, Parmigiano-Reggiano, and aged Gouda) can be sprinkled on top and/or within.

BEEF HASH GRATIN

HACHIS DE BOEUF AU GRATIN

MAKES ABOUT 4 MAIN-COURSE SERVINGS

Hachis, no doubt a relative of our American hash, has a name that translates as "chopped," and it's a perfect dish for getting rid of leftover cooked meats that are already cut into small pieces, such as those from a stew or from a roast that has stopped yielding attractive slices. The version given here is ideal for using meats left over from roasts or from making broth. If you have leftover mashed potatoes, you're in real luck.

FOR THE OPTIONAL SAUCE:

1 medium onion, chopped fine

2 tablespoons butter

2 tablespoons flour

¾ cup [175 ml] white wine

¾ cup [175 ml] broth

2 tomatoes, peeled, seeded, and chopped, or 1 can (14 ounces) [395 g] whole plum tomatoes, drained, seeded, and chopped

½ cup [125 ml] heavy cream (optional)

salt

pepper

FOR THE POTATO COMPONENT:

3 cups [630 g] mashed potatoes

½ to 1 cup milk [125 to 250 ml] (to thin the mashed potatoes to the desired consistency)

or

1½ pounds [675 g] potatoes, preferably Yukon Golds, but russets will do

¾ cup [175 ml] milk, or more as needed to give potatoes the desired consistency

salt

pepper

FOR THE HASH GRATIN:

1 teaspoon butter

2 cups [900 g] (approximately) leftover stew meat with the stewing liquid, or meat left over from making broth, chopped coarse

1 tablespoon finely chopped fresh marjoram, or 2 tablespoons finely chopped parsley (chopped at the last minute)

salt

pepper

1 cup [115 g] grated Gruyère

IF you're using leftover stew that still has plenty of liquid, you don't need to make a sauce, but if you're just using pieces of meat, serve the dish with the simple tomato sauce given on page 580.

TO make the tomato sauce, cook the onion in the butter in a heavy-bottomed saucepan over medium heat, stirring regularly, until the onion softens and begins to brown very slightly, after 10 minutes. Sprinkle in the flour, stir for 2 minutes more, and pour in the white wine and broth. Whisk for about 2 minutes to eliminate lumps. Boil the sauce for about 5 minutes to cook off some of the flour taste and add the tomato and the cream. Turn down the heat and simmer gently for 10 minutes, or until the sauce has the consistency you like. Season to taste with salt and pepper, and set aside.

IF you're using leftover mashed potatoes, heat them on the stove or in the microwave and add just enough milk to give them the consistency you like. If you're making mashed potatoes, peel the potatoes and cut them into chunks about 1 inch [2.5 cm] square (so they cook faster) and put them in a pot with enough water to come halfway up their sides. Cover the pot

and simmer for about 25 minutes, until they offer no resistance when poked with a knife. Drain; work through a drum sieve, ricer, or food mill; and stir in the milk. Season to taste with salt and pepper.

RUB a gratin dish, ideally one just large enough to hold the meat in a single layer, with butter. Spread the chopped meat, along with any leftover stewing liquid, in the dish, in a layer ½ inch to 1 inch thick. Sprinkle the meat with the chopped marjoram or parsley and salt and pepper. If you're using the sauce or leftover liquid from the stew, pour it over the meat. Spread the mashed potatoes on top. Sprinkle with the cheese and bake in a 350°F [175°C/gas mark 4] oven for about 25 minutes, until the mixture is bubbling (in the center as well as the sides) and the cheese has formed a crust on top. If the cheese starts to get crusty too quickly, turn down the oven. If the mixture is bubbling but hasn't browned, brown it for a minute or so under the broiler.

BEEF MARROW

Because, as far as I know, no one has marketed beef marrow already out of the bone, you'll have to go to the butcher and ask for marrow bones. Make sure he doesn't give you knuckle bones, which don't contain much marrow, but instead gives you smooth, cylindrical bones, 2 to 3 inches [5 to 7.5 cm] long, taken from the leg. Some bones make it easy—you'll be able to extract the marrow by just pushing on it with your thumb at the narrower end of the bone. Other bones are more resistant. If you need to use marrow in presentable rounds (as in Steak with Red Wine Sauce, page 483), place each bone upright on a cutting board and give one side of it a whack with a cleaver. You may have to do this a couple of times to crack the bone so that you can pull it away from the marrow. If you're using marrow in a stuffing, you don't need to get it out of the bone in perfect rounds—just scoop it out with a demitasse spoon or with the end of a vegetable peeler.

Once the marrow is out of the bone, you can use it right away. But if you're worried about how it looks once cooked (irrelevant for the ravioli), soak it for 12 to 24 hours in well-salted water in the refrigerator. This not only preserves it but draws out any blood, which would turn an unsightly gray once cooked.

MEAT-FILLED RAVIOLI

RAVIOLI FARCIS
À LA VIANDE

MAKES 6 FIRST-COURSE OR 4 MAIN-COURSE
SERVINGS (ABOUT 50 MEDIUM-SIZE RAVIOLI)

While the Provençal habit of throwing together ravioli with various leftovers has always sounded to me like a clever way of disguising bits of meat and vegetables, the potential for brilliance didn't occur to me until I read the kolduny recipe in Richard Olney's Simple French Food. Apparently, koldunys, which are ravioli by a different name, originated somewhere in Eastern Europe, but the preparation and serving of koldunys involve two essential concepts first described in the early twentieth-century work Gastronomie Pratique, by Henri Babinsky, or Ali-Bab. The first idea is that the koldunys (or ravioli) must contain fat that melts when the koldunys are cooked and that bursts into the mouth at first bite. Ali-Bab uses beef suet (the brittle fat that surrounds the steer's kidneys), but Olney takes the refinement a step further and uses beef marrow. I've experimented with butter but find the effect most dramatic with marrow. The second idea is that the koldunys should be served surrounded with a bland sauce or broth so that the palate isn't desensitized to the filling. This highlights a mistake made by chefs who serve ravioli with a sauce that reflects the stuffing—the palate shouldn't be fatigued to the flavors of the filling by a closely related sauce surrounding the ravioli. All forks and knives must be kept out of reach of the guests—only spoons allowed—and the ravioli kept to a manageable size so each guest is obliged to eat them whole. The first bite releases the molten filling in a burst of flavor.

This all sounds rather daunting as a way to use up leftover stew, but the possibilities are endless. When I had my restaurant, I once served crayfish ravioli—crayfish heads and shells simmered in cream; the cream strained, reduced, and combined with the puréed tails, marrow,

and marjoram; and the laborious, unassuming little ravioli served surrounded with a purposely bland chicken broth. The waiters were directed to remove all unnecessary cutlery from the tables.

3 cups [755 g] leftover stew, including the stewing liquid

6 pieces beef marrow, each 2 inches [5 cm] long (see page 447), or ¼ pound [115 g] butter

1 tablespoon chopped fresh marjoram, or 2 teaspoons dried

salt

pepper

1 recipe pasta dough (see page 449)

2 cups [500 ml] hot chicken broth

BRING the stew to a gentle simmer and strain the melted stewing liquid—you should have about 1 cup—into a small saucepan. Reduce the stewing liquid to ½ cup [125 ml] over medium heat, skimming off fat and froth. Let cool, but not so much that the liquid sets. Chop the meat, which should be cool, and the marrow by hand or by pulsing in a food processor until the mixture has the consistency of hamburger meat. Combine with the marjoram and the reduced stewing liquid. Chill the mixture in the refrigerator until it's stiff enough to hold its shape. Sauté or poach a tiny patty so you don't have to taste the mixture raw, and season to taste with salt and pepper.

USE a pasta machine to roll out the pasta dough into thin 18-inch-long [45.5-cm] sheets. Place 1½-teaspoon portions of the filling, at intervals of about 1½ inches [4 cm], in two rows along the lengths of the pasta. Brush the pasta with cold water between the portions of filling and along the edges of the dough. Roll up a second sheet of dough, and unroll it over the first. Press between the mounds with your fingers, sealing the filling in the dough. Cut the dough into squares with a knife or fluted pastry cutter or with a square or round pasta cutter. Pinch the edges of each ravioli to make sure the filling is well sealed within. Reserve the ravioli, until you're ready to cook them, on a sheet pan covered liberally with semolina flour or cornmeal to prevent the ravioli from sticking to the pan.

SIMMER the ravioli in a large pot of water for about 5 minutes—don't cook them at a hard boil or they may burst. Drain and serve, surrounded with the chicken broth, in heated soup plates.

Variations: If I have leftover cooked meat-filled ravioli, I spread them on a buttered gratin or baking dish, sprinkle them with heavy cream and fine grated Parmigiano-Reggiano or *grana padana,* and bake them in a 375°F [190°C/gas mark 5] oven until the cream thickens and bubbles, about 25 minutes. The marrow–stew meat ravioli filling is also delicious rolled up in cannelloni and baked with a little liquid from a stew, or with broth or cream.

PASTA DOUGH

Combine 3 cups [375 g] of flour, 4 large eggs, 1 tablespoon of olive oil, and 1½ tablespoons cold water in a food processor. Pulse the mixture about 20 times, until it has the texture of coarse sand. If you don't have a food processor, just knead the ingredients together with the heel of your hand until the dough forms a ball. You may need to sprinkle it with up to 3 tablespoons of cold water, ½ tablespoon at a time, if it won't come together, or knead in a little flour if it feels sticky. Set up the pasta machine, divide the dough into manageable amounts, and feed the dough through the rollers, folding the flattened dough over itself between rollings until it's well kneaded and feels like suede. Sprinkle the dough with flour as you work to keep it from sticking to the machine. Set the rollers one notch closer together after each rolling. If the sheets of dough become long and unwieldy, cut them in half. Continue rolling until the pasta is very thin but not so thin that you can see through it, and finish with the last or next-to-last setting on the machine. If you're not using the pasta right away, spread it on well-floured sheet pans and cover it with plastic wrap.

This dough can also be made using an electric mixer with a paddle attachment for kneading. Combine ingredients in the bowl of the mixer, as above. While the mixer is set to medium speed, add up to 1 more tablespoon of olive oil and up to 1½ tablespoons of cold water, in ½-tablespoon increments. Stop the mixer and scrape up any flour from the bottom of the bowl; resume mixing at medium speed.

Let the mixer knead the dough for 8 minutes, or until completely smooth. If the dough does not bounce back when pushed slightly, allow the machine to knead it for another 2 minutes. Remove the dough from the mixer, form it into a cylinder, sprinkle with flour, and wrap it in plastic. Refrigerate for at least 2 hours. To roll out the dough, follow the directions above for using a pasta machine, ignoring the directions to fold the dough over itself between rollings.

Stewlike
Meat Sautés

WHILE A SAUTÉ CAN BE MADE TO LOOK LIKE a stew, stewing and sautéing are fundamentally different. Stews are cooked for at least 1 or 2 hours so that the relatively tough cuts of meat that enter into them have time to become tender. Sautéing is designed primarily to create a brown and savory crust on the outside of meats. While the meat used in many stews is sautéed before liquid is added, sautéing does little to tenderize the meat. For this reason, meats that are only being sautéed (without subsequent stewing) must be tender to begin with. In classic French cooking, sauté-type dishes are surrounded with a sauce, usually based on the contents of the deglazed pan. Most of these sauces may be based on finely chopped aromatic vegetables (often as simple as a little chopped shallot) added to the hot pan before liquids, such as wine, are added for the deglazing proper. In restaurant cooking, demiglace (*glace de viande*) is added to the pan to give the sauce body (in old-fashioned French home cooking a little broth from the pot-au-feu would fill this

role) and a garniture, such as sautéed mushrooms (*sauce chasseur*), olives, green or root vegetables, and so on, may be added to the sauce at the end. Enrichers, such as cream or butter, may also be added to give the sauce a velvety texture and a suave, more complex flavor.

Cubes of tender beef, lamb, or veal can form the basis of a sauté, such as the simple blanquette on page 413 or the Beef Stroganoff on page 453, and the whole thing may then be served up as though it were a classic stew made with a tougher and more flavorful cut of meat and simmered for hours. Although many of these sautés are delicious and their variety forms much of the backbone of French classic cooking, they rarely have the rich, savory complexity of an authentic stew. There is, however, a somewhat convoluted way around this: Make a stew, serve the meat in a simple sauce, and use the stewing liquid as the moistening liquid for your sauté. As extravagant as this may sound, there's little more spectacular than serving cubes of tender meat, still rare in the middle, enrobed in the succulent sauce of an authentic stew and presented as such. The first bite reveals the deception and amazes guests. (Be careful to enhance the drama by saying little more than that you're having stew for dinner.)

RED WINE BEEF BROTH

If you don't feel like spending the time or money to make a stew just to obtain the liquid for another dish, make a half recipe of the brown beef broth on page 219, substituting 3 bottles of red wine for the water. If 3 bottles isn't enough to cover the bones, add a little broth or water—just enough to barely cover the bones. When the broth is cooked, strain it and reduce it to 1 quart [1 l].

SAUTÉ OF BEEF OR LAMB EN SURPRISE

SAUTÉ DE BOEUF OU D'AGNEAU EN SURPRISE

MAKES 8 MAIN-COURSE SERVINGS

To pull this off you need to make a regular red meat stew using one of your favorite recipes or one of the recipes above, save the stewing liquid, and then serve the stewed meat in Quick Tomato Cream Sauce (page 451) or a simple onion sauce such as the one used for the *boeuf en miroton* on page 445. With the precious stewing liquid available (you can freeze it and use it whenever), you need only sauté the meat, prepare a garniture (see pages 442 and 444 for some ideas), and serve. The present example uses beef and a luxurious garniture of morels, but any garniture—including the classic Burgundian one of pearl onions, bacon, and mushrooms—will do. One thing to watch out for: Once you've put this dish together you'll have to work fast and serve it quickly or the meat will overcook—never a problem with a traditional stew.

The meat is best sautéed just before you assemble the "stew," but if that's too hard to organize, sauté it over very high heat, so that it browns without overcooking, and spread it out on a sheet pan to cool. (Don't heap it in a bowl or it will overcook.)

FOR THE SAUTÉ:

- 4 cups [1 l] red wine beef braising liquid from 8 servings of red wine beef stew, such as the *boeuf à la bourguignonne* on page 438, or from a simple daube made with red wine (see page 245); or Red Wine Beef Broth (page 450)
- 3 tablespoons butter (for a roux, if one is needed)
- 3 tablespoons flour (for a roux, if one is needed)
- 3 to 4 pounds [1.3 to 1.8 kg] fillet of beef, or, for lamb, leg or boneless loin, cut into 2-inch [5-cm] cubes (no smaller)

- salt
- pepper
- 2 tablespoons "pure" olive oil

FOR THE GARNITURE:

- 1 pound [450 g] fresh morels, or 1½ ounces [40 g] dried (the dried soaked in ½ cup [125 ml] of semidry Madeira or water for 30 minutes and the excess liquid squeezed out and reserved)
- 2 tablespoons butter
- salt
- pepper

SKIM off any fat that has floated to the top of the stewing liquid, or let the liquid set overnight in the refrigerator and then lift off the fat. Bring the liquid to a gentle simmer in a saucepan while you're sautéing the meat. If the stewing liquid seems thin, or if you're using the Red Wine Beef Broth, made from bones, prepare a roux by combining the butter and flour in a saucepan, cooking the mixture for about 5 minutes over medium heat while stirring, and then whisking in the broth. Simmer the stewing liquid for 15 minutes, skimming off any scum that floats to the surface, or until the broth has the consistency you like.

SEASON the meat cubes with salt and pepper and brown them in the olive oil over very high heat. (See page 440 for tips on sautéing.)

SAUTÉ the morels in butter over high heat, adding them to the pan before the butter has a chance to burn, and sprinkle them with salt and pepper. Sauté for about 10 minutes, until the morels smell fragrant and any liquid they may have released evaporates. (If you're using dried morels, cook them for 5 minutes, carefully pour their soaking liquid—leaving any grit behind—over them, and cook for about 1 minute more, until the liquid evaporates.)

IMMEDIATELY before serving, stir the sautéed beef cubes and the mushrooms into the hot stewing liquid. Season to taste with salt and pepper.

QUICK TOMATO CREAM SAUCE

When you've made a stew and stolen the braising liquid for fancier projects, reheat and serve the stew meat in this sauce.

MAKES ENOUGH FOR 8 MAIN-COURSE SERVINGS OF STEW

12 medium-size ripe tomatoes, or 2 cans (28 ounces [795 g] each)

1 onion, chopped

2 cloves garlic, chopped

2 tablespoons olive oil

1 cup [250 ml] heavy cream

2 tablespoons finely chopped fresh tarragon, or 1 tablespoon chopped fresh marjoram
(tarragon or marjoram chopped at the last minute), or 1 teaspoon dried thyme

salt

pepper

IF you're using fresh tomatoes, chop them coarse without bothering to seed or peel them. If you're using canned tomatoes, drain them, puncture the side of each one with your thumb, squeeze out and discard the seeds, and chop the tomatoes coarse.

GENTLY sweat the onion and garlic over medium heat, in olive oil, in a heavy-bottomed pot large enough to hold the tomatoes, about 8 minutes, until the onion turns translucent. Stir in the tomatoes and simmer, stirring about every 10 minutes so the tomatoes don't stick and scald, until the sauce thickens, about 40 minutes. Strain the sauce through a food mill or, with the bottom of a ladle, work it through a large coarse-mesh strainer into a clean saucepan.

STIR in the cream and the herb. Season to taste with salt and pepper.

BEEF STROGANOFF

MAKES 4 MAIN-COURSE SERVINGS

When I was growing up, beef stroganoff was one of those special-occasion dishes that had me in the kitchen pestering my mother in the hopes that we could eat dinner as soon as possible. It wasn't until years later that I realized it's an excellent way to use the leftover meat from tender roasts. (For that matter, the method works for lamb, chicken, or pork, as well as beef.)

Even though beef stroganoff is supposedly Russian in origin, the methods for making it are thoroughly French. Chunks or strips of tender beef are quickly browned (I leave this step out when using leftover beef), a little chopped onion is sweated in the pan, flour is added to make a quick roux, and then beef broth is added to make the basic sauce. I like to add a little wine. Traditional recipes suggest finishing the sauce with sour cream, but American sour cream, with its relatively low butterfat content, has a nasty tendency to curdle once it gets hot. Crème fraîche is better because it provides the necessary tang but won't curdle. Of course, crème fraîche is expensive, and while easy to make (see page 39), it takes a day's forethought. Heavy cream will work if you add a few drops of lemon juice to provide the necessary zing. Most of the work for beef stroganoff—browning the meat lightly and making the sauce—can be done ahead of time. You can serve beef stroganoff with rice, but I like it best with buttered fettuccine.

3 cups [680 g] leftover roast beef or steak, cut into strips about ½ inch by 1½ inches [.5 by 1.5 cm], the pieces cut roughly the same size

or

1½ pounds [675 g] of a tender cut of beef such as tenderloin (fillet), New York strip steak, or sirloin tip, cut into strips as above

salt

pepper

2 tablespoons butter, or more if needed

1 medium-size onion, chopped fine

1 tablespoon flour

¼ cup [60 ml] white wine or dry vermouth

1¼ cups [300 ml] beef broth

½ cup [125 ml] crème fraîche, heavy cream, or sour cream

lemon juice (if you're using heavy cream)

SEASON the meat with salt and pepper. If you're using raw meat, heat the butter in a heavy-bottomed sauté pan until it froths. Lightly brown the beef in the butter over high heat, about 2 minutes on each side. Don't overload the pan—cook the meat in a single layer. (You won't be able to get a crusty, deep brown coating to form on the meat because the butter would burn and you'd overcook the meat.) Remove the meat with a slotted spoon and spread it on a large plate. (Don't heap it in a bowl or it will overcook.) If you're using cooked meat, don't bother browning the meat, just melt the butter in the pan and go straight to the next step.

PUT the onion in the pan with the butter used for browning the meat—if the butter has burned, pour it out and replace it with fresh. Stir the onion over medium heat until it turns translucent, about 10 minutes. Add the flour and stir until the flour smells toasty, about 2 minutes. Whisk in the wine and the broth and bring the sauce to a gentle simmer. Simmer it gently for 10 minutes to reduce it slightly and to cook off the taste of the flour and the raw flavor of the wine. Whisk in the cream, and add lemon juice to taste if you're using heavy cream. Season the sauce with salt and pepper and stir in the meat and any juices it may have released. Simmer gently for about 30 seconds—just long enough to warm the meat—and serve immediately.

FARMHOUSE-STYLE POACHED BEEF AND VEGETABLES

POT·AU·FEU

A POT-AU-FEU, A POT OF SIMMERED BEEF AND VEGETABLES, IS TO THE French what apple pie is to Americans. Its mention evokes hearty, convivial meals and long weekend afternoons sitting at the family table. It's a grandmother's dish, not made much anymore in French households because it takes time to cook and eat, but it has a deep appeal in the French heart and brings up memories of home and hearth, and traditions lost. Now that old-fashioned French cooking has become stylish in Paris, it is more likely to be served in a restaurant so that we foreigners can sample it, but it's best eaten when there's a large group and a free afternoon. It's a copious dish and needs lots of red wine to keep everyone's appetite up.

Considering the importance of the pot-au-feu in the French psyche, it's peculiar that the dish is practically unknown to Americans and that it's hardly ever served in French restaurants in the United States. This is probably because French cooks, until recently, thought of it as a dish to be eaten at home, never in a restaurant. The fact that the name is hard to translate and pronounce doesn't help matters. *Pot-au-feu,* or "pot on the fire," is often loosely defined as "poached beef with vegetables"—more descriptive perhaps, but not terribly appetizing.

A pot-au-feu is made in the same way as a broth except that the emphasis is on the solids rather than the liquid. Traditionally, the broth from the pot-au-feu is served first, usually with a few little pieces of toast with cheese baked on them. The meat is served as the main course, accompanied by mustard, little sour pickles (cornichons), coarse salt, and occasionally tomato sauce or vinaigrette. A classic pot-au-feu is made from beef, usually the short ribs, the shanks, and the shoulder, with marrow bones added near the end. These are all inexpensive cuts that benefit from long and gentle simmering. When cooked, each cut has its own characteristics—the short ribs have a soft, melting texture, while the shoulder (chuck) and shanks are firmer and meatier. For a luxurious touch, I sometimes replace the beef shanks with veal shanks (osso buco), but these are more expensive. The marrow is scooped out of the shank bones, and any extra marrow bones, with a little spoon. If I'm making a smallish pot-au-feu, I leave out the shanks or even the chuck and just use short ribs.

I sometimes break with tradition and serve a light salad instead of the pot-au-feu broth as a first course, and then serve the broth, spooned over the sliced meat, in wide soup plates, all as one course. Guests seem to appreciate the greens before the onslaught of meat, and the broth functions as a light sauce, moistening the meat and vegetables, but without adding fat. If I'm serving the pot-au-feu at an informal dinner, I get stingy and save most of the broth for other dishes, for making sauces, or for *glace de viande.* If you're making beef broth, it's well worth making and serving a pot-au-feu so you're not left stuck with four days' worth of cold leftover beef.

While we set about making a pot-au-feu in the same way we do broth, we have to be careful not to over or under cook the meat and vegetables and to make sure they're still presentable when we take them out of the pot. The easiest approach is to cover the meat with cold water, add a bouquet garni, bring to a slow simmer, and skim carefully for 3 to 4 hours before adding the vegetables, either whole or cut into sections, and then simmering for 45 minutes more. If you want a richer broth and have the time, make a broth with beef bones and then use it, instead of water, for poaching the beef. In traditional recipes, about 1 quart [1 l] of water (or bone broth) is used per pound [450 g] of meat (not including the bones). If you plan to save the broth, and especially if you plan to reduce it for making sauces, you can get by using less liquid—just enough to cover—so your broth will be more concentrated.

The recipe below calls for three cuts of meat. Since it's hard to buy small quantities of certain cuts, such as chuck roast, it requires a 12- to 15-quart [liter] stockpot, not something we all have in our kitchens. You can start out using two pots—it doesn't matter what you put in which—and as the meats shrink during cooking, you can combine everything near the end. If you want to make a smaller amount, leave out one of the cuts, add fewer vegetables, and reduce the amount of liquid accordingly.

FARMHOUSE-STYLE
POACHED BEEF
AND VEGETABLES

P O T · A U · F E U

MAKES 12 SERVINGS

2   cloves

1   medium-size onion

1   large bouquet garni

4   rounds of beef or veal shank (each about 2 inches
    [5 cm] thick, about 3 pounds [1.3 kg] total), each tied
    in 2 directions

1   chuck roast appropriate for pot roasting (4 pounds
    [1.8 kg]), tied

3   pounds [1.3 kg] beef short ribs, preferably in a single
    piece, excess fat trimmed off, tied in 2 directions

8   quarts [8 l] beef bone broth (page 217) or water or a
    combination, or enough to cover

2½ pounds [1.1 kg] medium-size carrots, peeled

3   large turnips, peeled, each cut into 6 wedges

6   medium leeks, greens discarded, whites split
    lengthwise, rinsed, and tied in a bundle with string

12 marrow bones (each about 2 inches [5 cm] long;
    optional)

1   baguette (if you're serving the broth first)

½   cup [55 g] finely grated Gruyère (if you're serving the
    broth first)

    coarse salt (to accompany the dish)

    pepper (to accompany the dish)

    mustard (both a Dijon style and a whole grain, if you
    like, to accompany the dish)

    cornichons (to accompany the dish)

2½ cups (1 recipe) Sweet-and-Sour Tomato Sauce
    (page 460); toasted French bread (for serving)
    (optional)

INSERT the cloves into the onion and put the onion in a large pot with the bouquet garni. Arrange the meat on top and pour in enough beef broth or water to cover.

PUT the pot over medium to high heat. When it reaches a simmer, turn the heat down to maintain it at the barest simmer—the top of the meat should just barely vibrate. Simmer for 4 to 5 hours, until a knife slides easily in and out of the chuck roast. Use a ladle to skim off fat and scum that float to the top of the pot. You may need to add water to make up for evaporation. Add the carrots, turnips, and leeks and simmer for 45 minutes more—if you're using the marrow bones, tie them in bundles of 5 in cheesecloth and put them in the pot 15 minutes after you've added the vegetables.

IF you're serving the broth as a first course, slice the baguette into ⅛-inch-thick [3-mm] diagonal slices and toast the slices, on one side only, on a sheet pan in a 400°F [200°C/gas mark 6] oven. When the slices are dry on top, turn them over and sprinkle them with Gruyère. Bake for a few minutes more, until the Gruyère melts and gets slightly crusty.

IF you're serving the broth as a first course, season it with salt and bring it to the table in a soup tureen. Ladle it out at the table and pass the toasts for guests to put in their soup.

SLICE the chuck roast and arrange the slices on a large platter with the rest of the meats, the un-wrapped marrow bones, and the vegetables and march triumphantly into the dining room. If you haven't served the broth first and you're not diverting it for other projects, serve the meat in wide soup plates and pour a ladleful of broth over each serving. Pass the condiments at the table.

POT·AU·FEU VARIATIONS

Like so many of the great French dishes, the pot-au-feu has innumerable variations. In Central France—*le Massif Central*—a deluxe version called a *mourtayrol* or *mortier* is made by adding a small ham and a hen to a regular pot-au-feu of beef. A small mound of *panade,* a bread-crumb stuffing held together with an egg and in this case flavored with saffron, is put in each bowl before the broth is poured in. A Provençal version contains the usual cuts of beef, a large chunk of lamb shoulder, a little white wine (unusual in classic versions), a few seeded and chopped tomatoes, a dried melon rind, and juniper berries. In Gascony the pot-au-feu gets a chunk of lamb shoulder, a goose leg, and a hen stuffed with a spicy *panade.* Again in central France, in the Auvergne, cabbage leaves are blanched, made into little packets stuffed with a ground pork mixture, and braised in the oven. A packet of braised cabbage is then placed in each bowl before the broth is ladled in. (Don't ever cook cabbage directly in the pot-au-feu or it will flavor the whole thing.) The Burgundian version of pot-au-feu contains a small whole cabbage (sometimes cut into wedges through the root end) and a good amount of celery. If you're going to try the Burgundian version with the cabbage, cook the cabbage separately with some of the pot-au-feu broth.

The principle of poaching meats together in a flavorful broth isn't limited to pot-au-feu and isn't limited to France, as Italian *bollito misto,* Japanese sukiyaki, and Mongolian hot pot attest. The best-known pot-au-feu derivative is the *poule au pot,* made by poaching a hen in the broth and serving slices of hen along with everything else. A *hochepot,* from which our word "hodgepodge" descends, is a pot-au-feu sometimes made with a mixture of meats, often from different animals, the usual root vegetables, and potatoes. Recipes for *hochepot* vary from region to region—some versions are made only with oxtail, others with only short ribs, though all seem to contain a gelatinous pig part such as a foot or an ear. But what clearly distinguishes *hochepot* from other versions of pot-au-feu is that the meat is first browned in fat, as though making a stew. A *potée,* for which there are at least as many variations as there are regions, is a pot-au-feu made with different cuts of pork and, at times, sausages. Most *potées* contain cabbage; some versions contain dried or fresh beans, or potatoes. Unlike a pot-au-feu, which is served in courses, a *potée* is served all at once, broth and solids together, in big bowls. A *garbure,* from Gascony, contains plenty of beans and vegetables and, in addition to a large chunk of pork shoulder, confit of goose or duck. But because a *garbure* is so thick and is often gratinéed, I think of it as being more closely related to a cassoulet. (One way to think of a cassoulet is as a very thick *potée* that is baked.)

While regional pot-au-feu recipes undoubtedly evolved as a natural response to available natural products and much of the time to the necessity of making a filling and satisfying dish out of a limited number of ingredients, restaurant chefs have developed refinements with the opposite goal in mind: to make lighter interpretations with a wider range of ingredients, including some elegant and expensive ones. The petite marmite, popular in Parisian restaurants in the first half of the twentieth century, is a pot-au-feu—both broth and solids—served in individual little pots (*marmites*). Traditional recipes for petite marmite call for making the pot-au-feu with broth instead of water (so the final liquid is a kind of double consommé, but with a trace of fat left floating on top) and for cutting the meat and vegetables into smaller, more elegant, shapes. There is also the method of cooking *à la ficelle.* Meats to be cooked *à la ficelle* are held with a piece of string (*ficelle* means string) and submerged in the barely simmering pot-au-feu just long enough to cook rare, as though they were roasts. The best-known version, *boeuf à la ficelle,* is made by poaching a section of beef tenderloin in the pot-au-feu and then serving the rare sliced beef in addition to, or instead of, the long-simmered meats from the pot-au-feu, surrounded with the pot-au-feu vegetables and a ladleful of the broth. Any tender cut of meat or fowl can be poached and served this way, but the two versions I've seen most often are *gigot à la ficelle,* made with leg of lamb, and *canard à la ficelle,* made with duck breasts. While pot-au-feu is served with the broth that results from long poaching, the meat for dishes cooked *à la ficelle* and other derivatives isn't cooked long enough to make a tasty broth. In this situation, make a broth ahead of time and one that's appropriate to whatever is being poached. For example, I make a duck broth with the carcasses and duck thighs and use it for duck *à la ficelle*.

Finally there are the *pot-au-feu de luxe*. Michel Guérard, in his restaurant in Southwestern France, makes a *pot-au-feu du pot-au-feu* with plenty of duck confit. I've seen other versions, some with consommé, foie gras, and truffles, but none beats the *pot-au-feu Dodin Bouffant*. Dodin Bouffant is a fictional gourmet who lived in the French countryside in the early part of the nineteenth century. When Dodin is invited to dinner by a visiting prince and is served a pretentious dinner of heavy-handed dishes, he decides to teach the prince a lesson and invites him and his entourage to his home to dine. When the prince arrives and Dodin tells him they're having a *pot-au-feu*, the prince is insulted at the idea of such a peasant dish. But the pot-au-feu, an opulent assortment of meats, whole poached foie gras (poached in Chambertin, as I remember), and a whole truffled capon breast, is a work of genius.

POT-AU-FEU CONDIMENTS

In addition to the cornichons and coarse salt served with a pot-au-feu, strongly flavored condiments and sauces make a delicious counterpoint to the rich meatiness of the dish by balancing the flavors and making the whole thing seem lighter. Mustard is the easiest and most obvious, but some cooks, especially in the south of France, serve tomato sauce. Italian cooks make a sweet-and-sour tomato sauce, with sugar and vinegar, that is especially delicious (see page 460). I sometimes borrow another sauce from the Italians and serve a *mostarda di frutta di Cremona*, a syrupy mixture of whole candied fruit such as figs, plums, and apricots, lightly flavored with mustard oil, that has been used since the Renaissance. (According to Alan Davidson in his masterpiece *The Oxford Companion to Food*, a version from Emilia called *mostarda di Carpi* is restricted to pear, apple, and sometimes quince cooked in grape must.) I suppose it's possible to make at home, but I, like the Italians, buy it in jars in fancy food stores (see Sources). Italians also serve *salsa verde*, made by working chopped parsley, garlic, anchovies, capers, vinegar, bread crumbs, and extra-virgin olive oil into a loose paste. In restaurants, they often add an egg yolk, which turns this sauce into a mayonnaise—a kind of *gribiche* sauce (see page 549).

RED WINE POT-AU-FEU WITH SHORT RIBS

POT-AU-FEU DE PLAT DE CÔTES AU VIN ROUGE

MAKES 6 GENEROUS MAIN-COURSE SERVINGS

It occurred to me one afternoon, while setting out to make a pot-au-feu, to use red wine instead of water, as though I were making a stew. I also added a few tablespoons of store-bought demi-glace to give the broth a meaty richness. Of course, by doing all this I converted a modestly priced dish into a rather expensive one, but everyone at dinner that night agreed that the dish had the light brothiness of a pot-au-feu and the rich winy flavor of a beef stew. I also must admit that my favorite of all the beef cuts for pot-au-feu is short ribs, because they're so well marbled that they never dry out. They melt in your mouth.

12 beef short ribs (about 10 pounds [4.5 kg]), cut 5 to 6 inches [13 to 15 cm] long, tied

2 bottles full-bodied red wine (plus additional if not using broth; see below)

6 cups [1.5 l] beef broth or chicken broth, or an additional bottle of red wine and 3 cups [750 ml] water

1 large bouquet garni

1 large turnip, peeled, cut into 12 wedges

4 medium-size carrots, peeled, cut into 2-inch-long [5-cm] sections

2 parsnips, peeled, cut into 2-inch-long [5-cm] sections

6 medium-size leeks, or 3 large, greens removed, white split in half but left attached at the base (if you're using large leeks, don't leave the halves attached), rinsed, membranes rubbed to loosen sand, tied into a bundle with string

1 bulb fennel, cut through the base into 6 wedges

coarse salt (to accompany the dish)

cornichons (to accompany the dish)

mustard (to accompany the dish)

PUT the short ribs in a large, heavy-bottomed pot. Pour 3 cups of red wine and the beef broth (or the extra wine and the water) over the ribs and nestle in the bouquet garni. Bring to a simmer over high heat, immediately lower the heat when the wine reaches a simmer, and maintain at a gentle simmer, uncovered, for 2½ hours. Skim off fat and scum every 30 minutes or so—short ribs render a lot of fat.

ADD the vegetables—you may need to nestle them in among the short ribs to get them into the liquid. Simmer for 1 hour more. If at any point the pot doesn't contain enough liquid to cover the vegetables, add enough water or broth to cover. Serve the short ribs and vegetables in wide soup plates (transfer the vegetables gently with a slotted spoon). Discard the bouquet garni. Give the red wine broth a final skimming, season to taste with salt, and ladle it over the meat and vegetables. Serve the condiments at the table.

A TRICK WITH LEFTOVERS

If you have leftover pot-au-feu, slice the meat thinly and layer it in a terrine with gently warmed pot-au-feu broth, allowing each layer to set in the refrigerator before adding more. (If the broth doesn't set, add a little gelatin to it.) Freeze the terrine, unmold it, slice it with a serrated bread knife, and put the slices on the plates you're using for serving. Let them thaw in the refrigerator before serving.

SWEET-AND-SOUR TOMATO SAUCE
SAUCE DE TOMATES À L'AIGRE-DOUCE

MAKES 2½ CUPS [625 ML], ENOUGH FOR ONE RECIPE OF POT-AU-FEU

1 medium-size onion, chopped

3 cloves garlic, chopped

2 tablespoons olive oil

8 medium-size tomatoes (about 3 pounds [1.3 kg]), peeled, seeded, and chopped, or
2 cans (28 ounces [795 g] each; 4 cups [960 g] total) drained, seeded, and chopped

1 tablespoon sugar

1 to 2 tablespoons sherry vinegar or other good wine vinegar

salt

HEAT the onion and garlic in the olive oil in a heavy-bottomed, nonaluminum sauté pan over medium heat. Stir until the onion turns translucent, about 8 minutes. Stir in the tomatoes and simmer gently until the sauce thickens, about 45 minutes. While the sauce is cooking, scrape the bottom of the pot every 5 to 10 minutes with a wooden spoon to keep the sauce from sticking and scorching. Add the sugar, stir for 1 minute to dissolve it, and add vinegar and salt to taste.

CHICKEN POACHED IN BEEF BROTH

POULE AU POT

MAKES 4 MAIN-COURSE SERVINGS

This dish is supposed to be made with an old hen, but hens are hard to come by and their flesh, which is rather tough, is not to everyone's taste. I make it with a chicken instead. In old-fashioned farmhouse cooking, the hen is just pushed down into the pot-au-feu that is always simmering on the back of the stove, but I'd hate to limit making this dish to those rare times when I just happen to have a pot-au-feu handy. Good broth is the only essential ingredient that may require forethought, but it doesn't have to be pot-au-feu broth or even beef broth; a good chicken broth does fine.

A poule au pot made with a chicken (which becomes a poulet au pot) takes only about 45 minutes to cook. The vegetables you serve surrounding the slices of poached chicken are up to you, but they should include at least some of the classic pot-au-feu vegetables—leeks, carrots, and turnips. I sometimes add fennel wedges, sections of parsnip, tiny fingerling potatoes, or diced tomatoes. Baby carrots and turnips look beautiful in the soup bowls, but if you can't find these, cut the carrots into sections and the turnips into wedges. Leeks, if small, can be cut in half lengthwise and each guest given a half; otherwise, they can be cut into quarters. Sometimes, instead of sectioning the root vegetables, I slice them with a Benriner cutter (see page 13) and julienne them by hand. I like to slide tarragon leaves under the skin of the chicken. Poule au pot is served only with coarse salt, not the mustard or sauces sometimes used for pot-au-feu, which are too strong.

1   bunch fresh tarragon (optional)

1   large chicken (4 to 5 pounds [1.8 to 2.3 kg])

8   baby carrots, or 2 large carrots

8   baby turnips, or 2 medium-size turnips

4   small to medium-size leeks, all but a little of the greens discarded, whites split in half lengthwise and rinsed

1   medium-size bouquet garni (with 4 sprigs of fresh tarragon or the tarragon stems)

2   to 3 quarts [2 to 3 l] full-bodied Brown Chicken Broth (page 209), turkey broth (made the same way as Brown Chicken Broth using separately purchased turkey drumsticks), or beef broth (page 219), or more as needed to cover

    salt

    pepper

    coarse salt (to accompany the dish)

TAKE the leaves off the bunch of tarragon and slide them under the skin of the chicken, pushing the leaves under the breast skin and curling your finger around to get some of the leaves under the leg skin. Don't put leaves between the halves of the breast where they join or you may tear the skin. It's best to truss the chicken (see page 349), but not essential.

IF you're using baby carrots, scrub them with a nylon scrub pad or scrape them with the back of a knife to take off the very thin peel. Leave about ½ inch of the greens attached. If you're using large carrots, peel them with a peeler and cut them into 1-inch [2.5-cm] sections. Stand each section on end and cut it lengthwise into quarters, thirds, or halves, depending on the thickness of the section, so that each of the wedges is about the same size, and cut

out the core. Or you can julienne large carrots (see page 19). If you're using baby turnips, you don't need to peel them. Just wash them and cut off and discard all but ½ inch [1.5 cm] of the greens. If you're using medium-size turnips, peel them and cut each one into 8 wedges, or into julienne. Tie the leeks together with string or cut them into julienne.

PUT the chicken in a pot just large enough to hold it. (If the pot is too big, you'll need too much broth. Ideally, the pot should be narrow and tall.) Nestle in the bouquet garni and pour in enough broth to cover the chicken. Bring to a simmer over high heat, and as soon as the broth approaches a boil, turn down the heat to maintain only the very slightest shimmering on top of the liquid. Skim off fat and froth with a ladle. When the chicken has been simmering for 5 minutes, nestle the vegetables around it. Continue simmering about 30 minutes more, until the chicken is done—when you pierce the thickest part of the leg with a skewer and the liquid that runs out is clear—and the vegetables are almost completely soft. If the chicken is done before the vegetables, transfer it to a plate and keep it warm while the vegetables are finishing. Season the broth to taste with salt.

PULL off and discard the skin—use a kitchen towel to protect your fingers—and carve the chicken as you would roast chicken (see page 352). Spoon a ladleful of broth (about 6 ounces [185 ml]) into 4 hot soup plates and arrange some of the sliced chicken and the vegetables in each bowl. Season with pepper and serve immediately. Pass the coarse salt.

Variations: If carving a poached chicken into neat slices at the last minute seems like a headache, try poaching chicken breasts or a whole turkey breast in the broth with the same vegetables. The breasts will taste better if you poach them on the bone, but in a pinch, they can be poached boneless. Keep in mind that a turkey breast will be done in 25 to 35 minutes and boneless chicken breasts in about 5; time the poaching of the vegetables accordingly. Chicken breasts should be added to the already simmering broth, while a turkey breast can be started in cold broth and brought rapidly to a simmer. If started out in cold broth, boneless chicken breasts cook through before the broth reaches a simmer.

POACHED BEEF TENDERLOIN WITH POT-AU-FEU VEGETABLES

BOEUF À LA FICELLE

MAKES 6 MAIN-COURSE SERVINGS

Whenever I'm stumped for an elegant dish but want something that isn't too rich, I think of *boeuf à la ficelle*. True, beef tenderloin is rich, but in a *boeuf à la ficelle* there's no added fat, just slices of poached rare beef surrounded with vegetables and a golden broth. The only potentially time-consuming part is coming up with the broth. The traditional source of both broth and vegetables is a classic pot-au-feu. This is still the most logical method—you can even serve some of the pot-au-feu meats along with the tenderloin—but it takes time and planning. On the other hand, if you're making your own beef broth, you're essentially making a pot-au-feu anyway. But you can also make a simplified beef broth using store-bought demi-glace (see page 3). When shopping for the tenderloin, it's ideal to buy a chunk from the center, but I sometimes settle for a less expensive piece near the thick wedge end and just tie it. In France, beef tenderloin is served very rare. You can cook it to between rare and medium rare; I don't recommend cooking it more than that. Like *poule au pot*, *boeuf à la ficelle* is served with coarse salt, but not mustard.

2½ pounds [1.1 kg] beef tenderloin, in a single piece

    salt

    pepper

    vegetables and 1½ quarts [1.5 l] of broth from the pot-au-feu on page 456, or:

6 baby carrots, or 2 large carrots

6 baby turnips, or 2 medium turnips

3 medium-size leeks, all but a little of the greens discarded, whites split in half lengthwise and rinsed

1½ quarts [1.5 l] beef broth (see page 219)

½ medium-size bouquet garni

3 tablespoons coarsely chopped parsley

    coarse salt (to accompany the dish)

SEASON the tenderloin with salt and pepper several hours before you poach it so the seasonings penetrate it. Take it out of the refrigerator 1 or 2 hours before you're ready to poach it so it isn't too cold in the middle.

IF you have a pot-au-feu already simmering, just submerge the meat in the simmering broth. If you're using cold broth and vegetables from the pot-au-feu, or a broth made from store-bought demi-glace (see page 3), bring the broth to a simmer in a narrow 8-quart [8 l] pot and poach the meat in the simmering broth.

IF you're using raw vegetables, bring the broth to a simmer in a narrow pot large enough to hold the meat, add the vegetables and the bouquet garni, and simmer very gently, partially covered, until the vegetables begin to soften, about 20 minutes. Submerge the meat in the simmering broth—you can tie a string to it if you like, but I usually just fish it out with tongs—and poach it at a bare simmer.

WHICHEVER method you're using, start checking the meat's doneness after 20 minutes of poaching by sticking an instant-read thermometer into the thickest part. If the inside has reached 115°F [46°C], the tenderloin is very rare; at 120° [48°C], it's between rare and medium rare; at 125° [51°C], it's medium rare. If the meat isn't done, put it back in the broth and check it every 5 minutes.

WHEN the meat is ready, transfer it to a cutting board and let it rest, loosely covered with aluminum foil, for 5 minutes. If you've poached it in a pot-au-feu, just spoon vegetables into wide heated soup plates. If you're using previously cooked pot-au-feu vegetables, simmer them in the broth for 5 minutes to heat them through.

SIMMER the parsley in the broth for 30 seconds (skip this step if you're using an actual pot-au-feu). Season the broth to taste with salt. Remove the vegetables with a slotted spoon and arrange them in hot wide soup plates. Slice the meat into ¼-inch [.5-cm] slices (try to get 12 or 18 slices so each guest gets 2 or 3) and arrange the slices over the vegetables. Ladle the broth around the meat (not over it, since that would turn the meat gray). Pass the coarse salt.

Variations: If you want to make duck *à la ficelle,* poach whole duck breasts—1 single breast per person if you're using a Long Island ducking, ½ breast per person if you're using mulard—in the beef broth with the same vegetables, keeping in mind, of course, that a small duck breast will be done in about 5 minutes and a larger one in about 10. You can peel the skin off the breasts so the meat is perfectly lean, but because I like the flavor of the skin, I leave it on. However, because the fat in the breast won't render in the broth in the same way it does when you sauté duck breasts, I score and sauté the breasts as described on page 381 and then cook them in the broth for just a couple of minutes before serving. This gives the skin a better texture and flavor and makes it less fatty. Slice the breasts, which should be rare, and arrange them in soup bowls. Surround them with the vegetables and broth. Use beef broth the same way as in the recipe above, or make a duck broth with the duck carcass and legs and serve pieces of the simmered legs, along with the sliced rare breast meat and the vegetables.

Gigot d'agneau (leg of lamb) *à la ficelle* is done in the same way as beef, except that a leg of lamb takes about 50 minutes to cook through to medium rare, which is best for lamb. Buy the smallest leg of lamb you can find and have the butcher remove the hip bone. Trim off all the outer skin and fat and tie up the leg. Pour over it enough cold broth to cover, and bring to a gentle simmer. Simmer for about 10 minutes and skim off fat and scum that float to the top. Add the vegetables and a bouquet garni, and simmer until everything is done.

HOW TO KEEP RARE RED MEATS FROM TURNING GRAY

When rare red meat is surrounded with hot broth, the broth can easily slosh up onto the surface of the meat and turn it gray. The traditional way to prevent this is to arrange the meat on top of a slice of toasted country bread to keep it above the broth. Rubbing the toast with a little garlic is a nice touch. I sometimes place a mound of cooked spinach or Swiss chard in the center of each bowl and then arrange the meat on top of the mound.

PORK AND
CABBAGE SOUP

POTÉE

MAKES 10 MAIN-COURSE SERVINGS

A potée is essentially a pot-au-feu made with pork. In addition to the usual pot-au-feu vegetables, a potée contains cabbage (optional in a pot-au-feu) and usually some starchy ingredient, such as potatoes or beans. A potée is a substantial main course, something I imagine Gargantua enjoying, so packed with ingredients that there's at least as much solid as liquid. You can lighten it, or even turn it into a first-course soup, by adding more liquid, cutting the cooked meat into dice, and shredding the cabbage; or you can make it more dense by adding more potatoes or beans. You can even make it so thick that you can bake it in a dish and serve it as a gratin. (Adding beans turns a potée into a kind of pork cassoulet; adding potatoes, into a close relative of the Alsatian Bäckeofe; adding duck confit, into the southwestern French garbure—see variations, below). The recipe given here, because it contains beans, is typical of the Lorraine, a region in northeastern France near Alsace. Feel free to leave the beans out or to replace them with potatoes, sliced and added to the potée about 30 minutes before it's done. Pork shoulder comes either with the bone or without and, depending on how well it was trimmed, with varying amounts of fat. You should end up with 5 to 6 pounds of fairly well trimmed, boneless meat. If you can find only bone-in pork shoulder with a thick layer of fat and its rind attached, it may weigh as much as 9 pounds.

2 cups [400 g] dried white beans such as cannellini, borlotti, or Great Northern

5 to 6 pounds [2.3 to 2.7 kg] boneless trimmed pork shoulder (or up to 9 pounds [4.1 kg] before trimming if it includes fat and bone)

3 cloves garlic, crushed, peeled

1 medium-size bouquet garni

5 juniper berries, crushed with the side of a knife, tied up in cheesecloth (optional)

1 pound [450 g] slab bacon, preferably with rind, left whole

1 large cabbage (about 3 pounds [1.3 kg]), preferably Savoy

1 pound [450 g] sausage such as saucisson à l'ail (garlic sausage) or cervelas (see pages 530 and 532 for information about making your own sausages)

2 large carrots, peeled, quartered lengthwise, cut into 1-inch [1.5-cm] sections

1 medium-size turnip, peeled, cut into 8 wedges

1 medium-size onion, peeled

2 cloves (stuck into the onion)

   salt

10 thick slices from a country loaf of French bread, toasted

RINSE the beans and put them in a bowl with enough cold water over the beans to cover them by several inches so that they stay covered as they expand. Let sit for 4 to 12 hours, or overnight. Drain and reserve.

IF the shoulder still has a bone, carve around the bone and remove it. If the shoulder is covered with fat more than ¼ inch [.5 cm] thick, trim off the excess fat with a sharp knife. Tie the shoulder into an oval and put it in a large pot, ideally just wide enough to hold the shoulder, with the shoulder bone if there was one. Add the garlic, the bouquet garni, and the juniper berries. Pour in enough cold water to cover and bring to a gentle simmer. Cut the rind off the bacon and nestle both the rind and the bacon into the liquid with the shoulder. Simmer very gently, uncovered, using a ladle to skim off fat and froth that float to the top. Peel any wilted outer leaves off the cabbage and cut the cabbage, through the bottom core, into 10 wedges. Cut off the strip of core that runs along the inner edge of each wedge and discard. Slide a wooden skewer through the length of each of the wedges so they don't fall apart in the pot. When the shoulder has cooked for 1½ hours, add the beans. Simmer for 30 minutes more and nestle in the cabbage wedges, the sausage, and the rest of the vegetables. Simmer for 1 hour more. (The pork cooks for a total of 3 hours.) Strain the contents of the pot in a colander set over a bowl or a clean pot. Discard the bouquet garni and shoulder bone. Skim excess fat—you don't have to get it all—off the broth and season the broth to taste with salt. Slice the meats and discard the shoulder bone. Arrange the vegetables, beans, and broth in hot soup plates—each containing a slice of toast—or in a large soup tureen, and place the slices of shoulder, bacon, and sausage on top. Place a piece of toast in the bottom of each bowl before ladling over the soup.

Variations: If you want to serve the *potée* as a first-course soup, shred the cabbage by cutting it into 4 wedges and then slicing the wedges as thin as possible with a Benriner cutter (see page 13) or by hand. Cut the vegetables into cubes. When the meats are cooked, cut them into dice and stir them back into the soup. If you want to turn this *potée* into a *garbure,* the traditional dish from Gascony, use only half as much pork shoulder and add 8 confit duck legs (see page 383) 15 minutes before the *potée* is done.

FINISHING BROTH WITH HERBS

Long-simmered broths sometimes taste flat because the fresh aroma of vegetables and herbs has cooked off. One way to restore vitality to a broth is to add fresh herbs 1 or 2 minutes before serving. Whole or coarsely chopped parsley leaves are most often used for this, but other herbs, such as tarragon, basil, chervil, or chives, can also be chopped fine at the last minute and simmered briefly in the broth before serving. (Chop basil and tarragon with a little olive oil to keep them from turning black.) The herbs wake up the flavor of the broth and cover the meat and vegetables with colorful flecks.

BAKED BEAN AND DUCK CASSEROLE

CASSOULET

I'LL NEVER FORGET THE FIRST CASSOULET I TASTED IN FRANCE. I HAD driven from Paris to the Champagne region to have lunch with a friend's family. It was a crisp autumn day and my stomach was growling, anticipating great regional specialties and glass after glass of Champagne. When I arrived, we sat in my friend's family living room sipping an aperitif as I admired the elegantly set table in the dining room. When my friend's mother announced that we were having cassoulet, I thought it was a little peculiar because cassoulet comes from the Languedoc, almost at the opposite end of France. But I had no trouble envisioning the thick sausages, chunks of duck confit, and crusty beans. Finally, it arrived. I almost gasped—it was nothing more than a pot of canned beans spread out on a sheet pan with chunks of hot dogs strewn on top.

It wasn't until years later that I dispelled the vision of those pale hot dog chunks with the experience of an authentic cassoulet served in a restaurant in Carcassonne, in the Languedoc. But in cassoulet country one has to be very careful with the word "authentic," because cassoulet is one of those dishes that show the French at their dogmatic best. A few kilometers away it would have been unwise to mention that I had had an authentic cassoulet in Carcassonne. I'd have been told that such a thing wasn't possible, that the people of Carcassonne had used the wrong beans and the wrong meats, that they cooked everything all wrong, and that, in short, such a concoction would be almost *immangeable*—inedible.

While all of this can be intimidating, especially to someone setting out to make cassoulet for the first time, keep in mind that a cassoulet is essentially a bean casserole with meat in it. Unless you undercook the beans it's almost impossible to go wrong.

Cassoulet enthusiasts are divided into three camps, each originating in an ancient city of the French southwest—Castelnaudary, Toulouse, and Carcassonne. The Castelnaudary cassoulet (begrudgingly acknowledged even by rivals as the original) is based mainly on pork and occasionally goose; the Carcassonne version contains lamb; and the Toulouse version, a mixture of lamb, sausage, and goose or duck. Every version is made by gently simmering meat in water or broth and then simmering beans in the meat cooking liquid, sometimes while the meat is still cooking. In essence, a cassoulet is a lamb or pork stew in which beans have absorbed the liquid. Most cassoulets are also gratins, because after an initial cooking they are baked in a wide earthenware pot called a *cassole*—no doubt where the cassoulet got its name. Bread crumbs are sprinkled over the cassoulet so a crust forms on top, the crust is gently folded back into the beans, and more crumbs are sprinkled over so that a second crust forms. This process is repeated up to three times, so the crunchy bread crumbs are distributed throughout the cassoulet and contrast with the beans' melting texture. In many recipes, including the one given here, confit of duck or goose is layered with the beans along with the meat used for making the basic stew. Sausages are also added, but nearer the end of cooking so they aren't broken up during the folding. Pork rind, the sheet of skin running along one side of slab bacon or fatback, is used in cassoulets and all sorts of stews to provide gelatin, for a richer consistency without additional fat. It's best to use pork rind from fatback, which, unlike bacon, is unsmoked and won't take over the flavor of the stew. If you can't find pork rind, use a calf's or pig's foot, split in half lengthwise by the butcher. If you can't find any of these, just make the cassoulet without them.

Ideally, a cassoulet should be 4 or 5 inches [10 to 13 cm] thick when baked in an earthenware dish. Don't worry if you don't have just the right size baking dish—the thickness can range from 3 to 8 inches [7.5 to 20.5 cm]. In any case, you'll need a big dish. (You can use more than one, but it won't be as dramatic.) I use a large enameled iron pot—don't use cast iron, which can give the beans a metallic taste—or a large roasting pan.

TIPS FOR USING BEANS

SOAKING: If you're in a mad rush, soaking dried beans isn't essential, but if you have the time it will speed up cooking. Soak them in plenty of water—at least 3 times the depth of the beans—for 4 to 12 hours at room temperature. If the beans swell above the water, add more water to keep them covered. Dried beans will cook fastest after being soaked for 12 hours. Don't soak them longer than that or they may begin to sprout. Some people cook the beans in their soaking liquid. I use new water, although I've never noticed a difference in the results. Fresh beans never need soaking.

AMOUNTS: Two cups of dried beans, before soaking, weigh about 1 pound [450 g]. Each cup of dried beans will swell to between 2 and 3 cups [365 and 545 g] when cooked. Fresh beans don't expand significantly when cooked. A pound [450 g] of fresh cranberry or lima beans will give you between 1½ and 2 cups [290 and 400 g] of shucked beans. A pound [450 g] of fresh fava beans will give you about ¾ cup [110 g] of shucked beans. I count on ½ to ⅔ cup [90 to 120 g] of cooked beans per serving.

VARIETIES: French recipes for beans most often call for *haricots blancs* (large white beans, for which you can substitute Great Northerns, cannellini, or borlotti beans), *haricots rouges* (like our red kidney beans), flageolets (small, green, and smooth; sold dried in the United States), and fresh fava beans. In cassoulet country, *haricots blancs* are popular but purists insist on either *tarbais* or *lingots* (see Sources).

COOKING TIMES: Dried beans, depending on their age and how long they've been soaked, usually cook in 1 to 2 hours in simmering liquid, and in 30 to 45 minutes in a pressure cooker. For fresh beans, cooking time in simmering water ranges from 1 minute for baby fava beans to 20 minutes for full-grown lima or cranberry beans.

SEASONING: When simmering dried beans, it's best to add salt halfway through the cooking. Added at the beginning, it can toughen the beans; added at the end, it doesn't penetrate to the inside of the bean. When boiling fresh beans, you can add the salt at the beginning.

HOW MUCH LIQUID TO USE: Cook fresh beans in a large amount of boiling water, as you would a green vegetable. Dried beans will usually require three times their volume in liquid. If the liquid starts to run dry, add more. If when the beans are done they're swimming in liquid, drain them over a pot, boil down the liquid, and pour it back over the beans.

BAKED BEAN AND DUCK CASSEROLE

CASSOULET

4½ cups (2 pounds [900 g]) dried white beans such as tarbais or lingot (see Sources), cannellini or Great Northern

1 pork rind about 12 by 6 inches [30.5 by 15 cm], or
1 calf's or pig's foot, halved lengthwise, calf's foot also
halved crosswise

2 pounds [900 g] boneless pork shoulder (or butt), or,
if that is difficult to find, 4 pounds [1.8 kg] bone-in
shoulder pork chops

1 medium-size bouquet garni

2 medium-size onions, peeled

2 whole cloves, stuck into one of the onions

1 large carrot, peeled, cut in four sections

4 cloves garlic, crushed (for the pork stew), plus 1 clove,
peeled (for the baking dish)

1 tablespoon salt, or more to taste

12 confit duck legs (homemade, see page 383, or store-
bought, see Sources)

4 cups [180 g] coarse fresh bread crumbs made from
1 loaf dense-crumb white bread (see page 2)

2 pounds [900 g] thick sausages: pork (see page 532),
garlic (see page 534), or duck (see page 532)

RINSE the beans and put them in a bowl with
enough water to cover them by at least 8 inches [20
cm] so that they stay covered as they expand. Let
soak for 12 hours. Drain.

IF you're using pork rind, cut it crosswise into 1-by-
6-inch [2.5- by 15-cm] strips and tie the strips into
a loose bundle with string. If you're using a foot, put
the halves or quarters in a pot, cover them with cold
water, and bring to a simmer. Simmer for 5 minutes,
drain them in a colander, and rinse thoroughly.

IF you're using pork shoulder or butt, cut it into rectangular pieces about 2 inches [5 cm] long, 1 inch
[2.5 cm] thick, and 1 inch [2.5 cm] wide. If you're
using shoulder chops, cut the meat away from the
bone and cut the meat from each chop into 2 or 3
pieces. Put the meat pieces in a heavy-bottomed pot
with the rinds or feet, the bouquet garni, the stud-
ded onion with the cloves, the carrot, and the garlic.
Pour in enough cold water to cover by 3 inches
[7.5 cm] and bring to a gentle simmer. Simmer gently for about 15 minutes, skimming off froth and fat.
Cover the pot and turn the heat down to low. Cook
for 1 hour, then add the beans and enough water to
cover by 1 inch. Return to a simmer and cook for 45
minutes more. Add 1 tablespoon of salt and more
water, if needed, to keep the beans covered. Gently
stir the beans with a wooden spoon once or twice,
scraping against the bottom of the pot to make sure
they're not sticking. If necessary, add more water to
keep the beans moistened.

PICK out the foot halves or pork rinds, the onion,
carrot, and bouquet garni with tongs. Discard the
vegetables and the bouquet garni. Cut the pork rind
strips or any gelatinous meat from the foot into
½-inch dice and stir these into the beans. Taste the
beans—they'll be mealy, but don't worry—and add
more salt if necessary.

PREHEAT the oven to 350°F [175°C/gas mark 4].
Rub the inside of a large baking dish or roasting pan
or one or more gratin dishes with the garlic clove.

TRANSFER half the beans, meat, and any diced rind
or foot gelatin with a slotted spoon into the baking
dish, leaving the liquid behind in the pot. Wipe off
any excess fat clinging to the duck legs and arrange
the duck legs on top of the bean mixture. Add the
rest of the bean mixture, again leaving the liquid behind. Ladle in enough of the bean cooking liquid to
reach three-quarters of the depth of the beans in the
baking dish, reserving any liquid you haven't used.

SPREAD the top of the cassoulet with about one-
third of the bread crumbs and slide the dish into the

oven. When the cassoulet is bubbling and the bread crumbs have formed a crust, gently turn the crust into the beans with a large spoon. Sprinkle the top of the beans with half the remaining bread crumbs. If at any point the cassoulet seems dry and stiff, gently add 1 cup [250 ml] of the reserved bean cooking liquid (or water, if you run out of liquid). Bake for 1 hour more, until a second crust has formed. Turn down the crust as before. Nestle the sausages into the cassoulet, pushing the bean mixture aside and folding some of it over the sausages. Sprinkle with the rest of the bread crumbs. Bake until the last crust has formed, about 1 hour more, and serve.

FRESH BEAN "CASSOULETS"

I had never seen a fresh bean until I first went to Italy, where the markets were filled with garish heaps of scarlet-streaked cranberry beans. Years later, in New York, I could find fava beans in Italian markets where it seemed that, other than the occasional elderly Italian lady, I was the only one to buy them. Now, of course, fresh beans can be found in most farmers' markets. Beans in any form make a perfect foil for rich foods like duck, pork, and even foie gras, but fresh beans have a delicate texture all their own. They also have the advantage of cooking quickly and not needing to be soaked.

While fresh beans are not in season during the cold cassoulet months, and the long cooking would compromise their subtlety, I do like to cook fresh beans with little bits of rich, meaty things like duck confit, foie gras, pancetta, and bacon. When I'm trying to impress, I'll put the hot beans in a gratin dish, sprinkle them with bread crumbs, and slide them under the broiler to reinforce the cassoulet illusion, but the gratinéeing is mostly just for show.

FRESH FAVA BEAN "CASSOULET" WITH FOIE GRAS

"CASSOULET" AUX FÈVES ET AU FOIE GRAS

MAKES 4 SIDE-DISH SERVINGS

I once read in Jean-Anthelme Brillat-Savarin, who wrote in the early nineteenth century about food, that before inviting guests to an important dinner, it was essential to establish that they were worthy. He suggested that a dinner be served and, as was the custom in those days, the dishes be announced at the beginning of the meal. When the meal was well under way, you were to report, aghast, that one of the best dishes (he suggested a whole turbot) had been dropped in the kitchen and would not be served. At this critical point, you were to watch the reaction of the guests. Those who were not sufficiently upset were never to be invited again.

Even though I'd never pull such a cruel trick, there are certain dishes, especially those that have taken a lot of work or involve some luxurious ingredient, that I expect to evoke a reaction. These beans, which are rather ordinary looking, are among those dishes. Those in the know should recognize the fava beans and be highly impressed because fava beans take a lot of work—they have to be peeled twice. And those unfamiliar with fresh fava beans should stop in amazement when they take their first bite, for never will they have tasted beans like these. If they keep on gabbing with no pause, they're B-listed.

In any case, serve this dish when you're pulling out all the stops. I serve it as an accompaniment to sautéed duck breasts, roast pork, or the Squab Salmis, on page 377—either right on the plate or on the table as a gratin. But you can serve it with just about any roast or sautéed meat. When shopping for fava beans, buy the biggest pods you can find and feel them to make sure they're full of beans. You can also make this dish with fresh cranberry or lima beans.

3 pounds [1.3 kg] fresh fava beans in the pod, or
   1½ pounds [675 g] fresh lima or cranberry beans

1 slice (4 ounces [115 g]) Foie Gras Terrine (page 97), cut
   while cold into ¼-inch [.5-cm] cubes

1 tablespoon finely chopped parsley, chervil, or mint
   (chopped at the last minute), or 1 teaspoon finely
   chopped fresh savory

   salt

   pepper

½ cup [55 g] bread crumbs (if you want to serve the
   beans as a gratin)

SHELL the beans. If you're using fava beans, immerse the shelled beans in boiling water for 1 minute to loosen their peels. Drain in a colander and immediately rinse with cold water. Peel each bean by digging into the peel with your thumbnail and pinching the bean to slip it out of the peel.

BRING 2 quarts [2 l] of salted water to a boil and toss in the beans. Cook the beans until they're tender but not mushy—anywhere from 1 to 3 minutes for fava beans to about 12 minutes for lima beans. Drain in a colander. Unless you're using the beans right away, rinse them with cold water.

COMBINE the beans with the foie gras in a small, heavy-bottomed sauté pan. Toss or gently stir the beans over medium heat until the foie gras melts and the beans heat through, about 5 minutes. Sprinkle with the herb, season to taste with salt and pepper, and toss for 1 minute more. Unless you're serving the beans as a gratin, spoon them into a hot serving dish or onto the individual plates.

IF you want to present the beans as a gratin, spread the hot beans in a heated gratin dish large enough to hold them in a layer ½ inch to 1 inch [1.5 to 2.5 cm] thick. Sprinkle them with a layer of bread crumbs. Slide the gratin under the broiler—not too close, about 6 inches [15 cm] away is best—until the bread crumbs brown slightly. Watch very closely so you don't burn them. Present the whole dish at the table.

Variations: Made with foie gras, this is the ne plus ultra of bean dishes, but foie gras is expensive. Fava beans are also delicious with ¼ pound [115 g] of bacon, cut into ¼-inch [.5-cm] dice, cooked until barely crisp, and all but 2 tablespoons of the fat poured out of the pan, or with pancetta. Or you can use duck confit—the meat from 1 or 2 legs, pulled away from the bone, shredded with your fingers, 1 tablespoon of fat used for heating the beans, and then beans, fat, and meat stirred together. You can even use string beans in place of shell beans. For a dish called *haricots verts à la landaise*, after the Landes region in the French southwest, string beans are parboiled and cooked covered with a cured ham (such as prosciutto), goose fat, leeks, and garlic, and finished with some of the bean cooking liquid, an egg yolk, and a little vinegar. (I skip the egg yolk.) A similar treatment for fava beans, with butter replacing the goose fat and plenty of chopped parsley and chervil added at the end, is called *fèves à la tourangelle*, after Tours, a city in the Loire valley.

OTHER WAYS TO COOK DRIED BEANS

Beans are a wonderfully versatile starch that we often overlook, partly out of habit and partly, no doubt, because most bean recipes call for soaking (which isn't essential but does shorten cooking times) and long cooking. One solution is to use a pressure cooker; another is to buy dried beans from a store—maybe an Italian market—that has a large turnover, giving you a better chance to get beans from the last harvest, which will cook faster. Once the beans are cooked, you can heat them with a little bacon, pancetta, or confit, as described in the variations above; you can butter and season them and serve them with roast meats; you can toss them with extra-virgin olive oil and a little lemon juice and parsley and serve them cold as a salad; or you can purée them and add butter as though they were mashed potatoes.

Dried beans cooked with water in a pressure cooker have a delicate texture and flavor, but unlike beans that have slowly been simmered with pork or lamb, they won't have any flavor of meat. True, meat can be cooked in the pressure cooker along with the beans, but meat cooked in this way has a nasty habit of making the beans greasy. Lean, smoky meats such as ham hocks do, however, work all right in the pressure cooker—just put a ham hock in the pressure cooker at the same time as the beans and, when the beans are ready, peel the meat off the hock, chop it, and stir it back into the beans. You can also cook beans with water and, when they are done, stir them with reduced broth, or the reduced liquid from a stew and perhaps the meat from the stew; the result will be a simplified, nongratinéed cassoulet.

When cooking dried beans with meats such as pork or veal, you have to decide whether to cook the beans at the same time as the meat or to cook them separately. The easiest system is to just combine meat, liquid, and beans in a pot and simmer everything until both meat and beans are done. Sometimes, however, the meat or the beans will finish cooking before the other is done. You can cook the beans separately in broth or water and combine them with the meat at the end, but this method doesn't allow the meat's flavor to penetrate the beans. The surest method is first to cook the meat and then cook the beans in the meat cooking liquid, but this method means cooking in two stages and takes more time.

ROAST LEG OF LAMB WITH FLAGEOLET BEANS

GIGOT AUX FLAGEOLETS

MAKES 8 MAIN-COURSE SERVINGS

This classic of French bourgeois cooking might make up a solid Sunday lunch or a serious meal in a good bistro. Flageolet beans, even when dried, are pale green and smooth. (If they're wrinkled, they're old.) They can be soaked and then simmered in water for about 15 hours or cooked for 20 minutes in a pressure cooker. Classic recipes call for tossing the cooked beans with a sauce bretonne, a simple garlic and tomato sauce, but I prefer stirring the cooked beans around in the roasting pan, about 15 minutes before the roast is done, so they absorb the roast's juices.

2 cups flageolet, Great Northern [365 g], or cannellini beans [400 g], rinsed

1 whole leg of lamb (6 to 7 pounds [2.5 to 3 kg]), including any bones you remove or have removed

6 cloves garlic, peeled

1 medium-size onion, peeled

1 clove, stuck into the onion

1 small bouquet garni

1 cup [250 ml] chicken broth or water

salt (for the lamb), plus 1 teaspoon or more (for the beans)

pepper

SOAK the beans for 4 to 12 hours in enough water to cover by 8 inches [15 cm].

HAVE the butcher trim excess fat off the leg of lamb and cut out the hip bone and section of vertebrae. Be sure he gives you the bones. When you get the lamb home, trim any large clumps or strips of fat off the bones and discard the fat.

DRAIN the beans and combine them, in a heavy-bottomed nonaluminum pot, with the garlic and onion, the bouquet garni, the bones, and 6 cups [1.5 l] broth or water. Bring to a boil and simmer gently, uncovered, for 15 minutes, using a ladle to skim off fat and froth that float to the top. Cover the pot and adjust the heat to keep the beans at a very gentle simmer. When the beans have cooked for 30 minutes, sprinkle 1 teaspoon of salt over them. Continue simmering until the beans, when you bite into one, have lost their mealiness. Add more water, as needed, to keep the beans from drying out. If they're swimming in liquid when done, drain off the liquid, reduce it to about ¼ cup [60 ml], and pour it back over the beans. Take out and discard the onion, the bouquet garni, and the bones and season the beans to taste with pepper and more salt. Set aside.

WHILE the beans are cooking, preheat the oven to 375°F [190°C/gas mark 5]. Rub the roast with salt and pepper and, if the butcher didn't do it for you, tie a few loops of strings around it lengthwise so the flap of meat that once covered the hip bone is held snug against the roast. Put the roast in a heavy-bottomed roasting pan, as close to the size of the leg as possible. Roast for 1 hour to 1¼ hours, until the temperature at the thickest part reaches 125°F [51°C] (rare to medium rare) to 130° [54°C] (medium rare to medium). About 15 minutes before you expect the roast to be done, stir the beans into the juices in the roasting pan. When the roast is done, cover the pan loosely with aluminum foil and let it rest in a warm place for 20 to 30 minutes.

TRANSFER the roast to a cutting board with a moat to catch any juices. (Or set a regular cutting board over a sheet pan.) Carve the roast. Pour any juices from the cutting board into the beans, and stir. Serve the beans on hot plates next to the sliced lamb.

VEAL SHANKS (OSSO BUCO) WITH BEANS

JARRETS DE VEAU AUX HARICOTS

MAKES 6 MAIN-COURSE SERVINGS

Beans make a natural foil for slow-cooking, gelatinous cuts of meat. Pork is the meat most commonly cooked with them, and lamb is a close second, but veal has a subtle depth of flavor that makes it a perfect match for long-simmered beans. As with many bean dishes, you have a choice of cooking meat and beans together so that the beans absorb the juices from the meat, or, to gain more control, cooking the meat first and then using the meat braising liquid to cook the beans. Here, the beans are partially cooked in water and then finished in the braising liquid from the veal. In this way, the beans are flavored with veal juices, but because the beans are partially precooked, they don't absorb all the

juices. This leaves you with a delicious, somewhat soupy combination of veal, flavorful broth, and beans. The veal can be braised earlier the same day or even the day before.

1½	cups (10 ounces [280 g]) dried flageolet, cannellini, or Great Northern beans
6	rounds of veal shank (each 1½ to 2 inches [4 to 5 cm] thick)
	salt (for the meat), plus 1 teaspoon or more (for the beans)
	pepper
4	tablespoons olive oil, or more as needed
1	medium-size onion, chopped fine
1	medium-size carrot, peeled, diced
½	cup [125 ml] dry white wine
3	cloves garlic, peeled
6	medium-size tomatoes, peeled, seeded, and chopped, or 1 can (35 ounces [990 g]) Italian plum tomatoes, drained, seeded, and chopped
1	medium-size bouquet garni
3	cups [750 ml] veal broth (page 219), chicken broth (page 209), or water

SOAK the beans in enough water to cover by at least 8 inches [20 cm], for 4 to 12 hours.

SEASON the veal shanks with salt and pepper. Brown them on both sides over medium to high heat in 2 tablespoons of the oil in a heavy-bottomed pot just large enough to hold them in a single layer. If you can't fit all shanks in the pot, brown them in batches. Transfer the shanks to a plate. Pour the cooked oil out of the pan and add 2 tablespoons of fresh oil. Sweat the onion and carrot over medium heat until the onion turns translucent, about 8 minutes. Stir in the wine, garlic, and tomatoes, nestle in the shanks and the bouquet garni, and pour in the broth or water. Bring to a boil and turn down the heat to maintain at a bare simmer. Cover the top of the pan with a sheet of aluminum foil—press down on the foil so it just touches the top of the shanks—and cover the pan with a lid. Simmer the shanks for 2 hours, at which point they should just be slightly underdone—they'll offer a little resistance when you poke one with a paring knife.

WHILE the veal is braising, drain the beans and combine them with 3 cups [750 ml] water. Simmer gently, partially covered, for 20 minutes, stir in 1 teaspoon of salt, and simmer for 20 minutes more. If the liquid is absorbed before then, add another ½ cup of water and lower the heat.

WHEN the veal has cooked for 2 hours, remove and discard the bouquet garni and add the beans, including any of their cooking liquid that remains. Cover the pot and simmer gently, until the beans are soft and have lost their mealiness, usually in about 30 minutes more, and the veal offers no resistance when you poke it with a knife. Season the beans to taste with salt and pepper. (If the veal is done before the beans, gently take out the shanks with a slotted spoon and reserve them on a platter while the beans are cooking. Reheat the veal in a covered pot with the beans—and a little broth if everything seems too dry—before serving.)

USE a slotted spoon to transfer the veal shanks gently to hot soup plates. Spoon the beans over them, along with enough of the cooking liquid so there's about ½ inch of liquid in each bowl. Serve immediately.

Variation: This dish is also marvelous with lamb shanks. Just substitute 4 pounds [2 kg] of lamb shanks for the veal. Trim any excess fat off the shanks. For lamb, I use 6 cloves of garlic instead of 3.

SEAFOOD CASSOULET

The first time I saw a seafood cassoulet on a menu in France, I thought, here's another nouvelle cuisine monstrosity. But I've since discovered that *la morue aux haricots*—salt cod with beans—is a traditional dish from Gascony. A number of French chefs have experimented with the idea, including my old boss, Claude Peyrot at the Paris restaurant Vivarois, who makes a *cassoulet de lotte*—monkfish cassoulet—by simmering the beans with aromatic vegetables and bacon and then combining them with lightly sautéed monkfish slices in miniature soup crocks, sprinkling each serving with bread crumbs and quickly browning the individual "cassoulets" under the broiler. The dish is good but the juxtaposition of pork and seafood has never appealed to me. In the traditional salt cod version, the cod is soaked to remove the salt and then simmered with the beans so the beans take on some of its character. I once tried to get the beans to take on the character of seafood by making a broth out of the fish bones and heads and using this broth to cook the beans. The result was disastrous—the beans just tasted fishy. I then experimented with mussels, lobsters, and crabs and discovered that I could lightly precook the shellfish, make a crustacean broth with the shells (in the same way as for lobster *à la americaine*), steam the mussels in white wine, and cook the beans in the combined liquids. This way, the beans themselves taste intensely like seafood instead of pork, yet they don't taste fishy. Just before serving, I quickly combine the seafood with the beans, sprinkle with bread crumbs, and brown the "cassoulet" under the broiler before the shellfish has a chance to overcook. The finished dish is luxurious and a delight to look at.

LOBSTER AND MUSSEL CASSOULET

CASSOULET DE HOMARD ET DE MOULES

MAKES 4 MAIN-COURSE SERVINGS

Most of this dish—cooking the shellfish, making a shellfish broth, and cooking the beans in the broth—can be done the day before or earlier the same day.

- 2 cups (about 1 pound [450 g]) dried beans such as cannellini, Great Northern, or borlotti, rinsed

- 1 medium-size onion, peeled (for the beans), plus 1 (for the lobster), chopped fine

- 1 small bouquet garni

- 2 pounds small cultivated mussels, clams, or cockles, scrubbed and rinsed

- 1 cup [250 ml] dry white wine

- 2 lobsters (1¼ to 1½ pounds [565 to 675 g] each)

- 1 clove garlic, chopped fine

- 2 tablespoons olive oil

- ½ cup [125 ml] Cognac or good brandy

- 4 tomatoes, chopped, or 2 cups drained canned tomatoes (a 28-ounce [795-g] can)

- 2 cups [450 ml] chicken or fish broth or water, or more as needed

- 1 cup [45 g] fresh bread crumbs, or 4 slices fresh dense-crumb white bread turned into bread crumbs (see page 2)

- 3 tablespoons butter, melted

SOAK the beans in enough water to cover by 8 inches [20 cm] for 4 to 12 hours. (If you soak them for 12 hours, they triple in volume and cook faster.)

Drain the beans and put them in a heavy-bottomed pot with 3 cups [750 ml] of water, the peeled onion, and the bouquet garni. Simmer gently, uncovered, until the beans have absorbed almost all the water, 20 to 40 minutes. There should be about a ¼-inch [.5-cm] layer of liquid in the bottom of the pot, but the beans should remain undercooked (you can chew them but they're a bit mealy). If completely cooked at this point, they won't absorb the shellfish cooking liquid. Set aside.

PUT the mussels in a pot with the wine, cover, and bring to a boil over high heat. When the mussels have all opened, after about 5 minutes, remove the lid, let the mussels cool for a couple of minutes, scoop them out of the pot, and remove them from their shells. Discard the shells and slowly pour the cooking liquid into a bowl, leaving any sand or grit behind in the pot. Rinse out the pot and put the decanted liquid back in.

RINSE the lobsters and kill them by forcing a chef's knife quickly through the top of the thorax (the front part) and moving it quickly forward, cutting the front half of the thorax in two. (See page 333 for more grisly details.) To save the juices, immediately hold the lobster over the pot used for cooking the mussels. Twist off the claws and tails and tie the two tails together with string, undersides facing, so they won't curl as they cook. Finish cutting the thoraxes in half and remove and discard the gritty grain sack from each side. Put the lobster parts in the pot used for steaming the mussels, cover, and steam them in the mussel cooking liquid until the shells turn red, no longer, 8 to 10 minutes. Let cool and take the lobster meat out of the shells (see page 332). Reserve the meat, shells, and cooking liquid (you should have about 1½ cups [375 ml]).

IN a heavy-bottomed pot large enough to hold the lobster shells with plenty of room left over (so the shells don't fly around when you're breaking them up), cook the chopped onion, garlic, and lobster shells in olive oil over medium heat. Crush the shells with the end of a French-style rolling pin or the end of a cleaver. Stir the shells over medium heat until they smell fragrant, about 8 minutes. Pour the mussel and lobster steaming liquid into the pot. Add the Cognac, tomatoes, and broth and simmer, covered, over low heat for 20 minutes. Strain the shell mixture in a colander set over a large pot or bowl. Press down on the shells with the bottom of a ladle to extract as much liquid as possible—you should end up with about 4 cups. Discard the shells and vegetables and strain the liquid through a strainer.

POUR the strained liquid over the beans and simmer gently until the beans are soft but not mushy, and no longer mealy, 20 to 40 minutes. If the beans absorb all the liquid before they are cooked, add 1 cup of water. If the beans cook before they've absorbed all the liquid, drain off the liquid, reduce it to about 1 cup, and pour it back over the beans. The beans should be moist so they can be easily stirred without breaking apart, but they shouldn't be soupy.

CUT the lobster tails into 6 slices each and cut the 2 large claws (called the crusher claws) through the sides, dividing them into 2 attractive halves. Leave the 2 smaller claws (the pinchers) whole. At this point, the shellfish can be kept covered in the refrigerator, and the beans can be allowed to cool and then refrigerated. (For a more detailed explanation of how to get the meat out of a lobster, see page 332.)

WHEN you're ready to serve, preheat the broiler and, if the beans are cool, gently reheat them in a pot until they bubble up. The beans must be very hot because the dish will only be browned under the broiler, not reheated. Preheat an oval gratin dish or baking dish large enough to hold everything in a 2-inch-thick [5-cm] layer. (I use a 9-by-13-inch [23-by-33-cm] oval gratin dish.) Quickly layer the beans, mussels, and lobster in the dish, sprinkle the bread crumbs on top, drizzle the melted butter over the crumbs, and brown the "cassoulet" under the broiler. Watch it like a hawk so the bread crumbs don't burn. Bring the dish to the table and serve on hot plates.

Variations: You can use beans to absorb other seafood braising liquids. Cooking beans in some of the liquid from Octopus Daube (page 245) and serving chunks of octopus along with the beans is a natural. Squid or cuttlefish can be braised and simmered with the partially cooked beans in the same way. (If using cuttlefish, use the ink to finish the beans in a kind of bean risotto.) If you can find shrimp with the heads, cook the beans in a shrimp-heads-and-shells cooking liquid (just like the lobster above), and grill the tails and serve them on top of the beans, like a bean paella.

Bean salads, often containing bits of seafood or made with anchovies in the vinaigrette, are popular in Italy and somewhat less so in the south of France. You can improvise your own, using the same techniques as for the shellfish cassoulet—by cooking dried beans in the shellfish cooking liquid. But salads are better made with fresh beans, which benefit little from being cooked in a flavorful broth, since they don't absorb much liquid. In any case, a seafood and bean salad is best kept simple and fresh, the beans tossed with the cooked seafood, olive oil, parsley or basil, and a little lemon juice. The cooking liquid from the shellfish, especially from mussels or clams, can be reduced and added to the beans along with the olive oil and lemon.

STEAK WITH RED WINE SAUCE

ENTRECÔTE À LA BORDELAISE

WHERE DO	HOW TO	HOW TO	HOW TO	HOW TO
THE BEST STEAKS COME FROM?	SAUTÉ STEAKS	MAKE PAN-DEGLAZED RED WINE SAUCES AND OTHER BROWN SAUCES	MAKE BÉARNAISE, FLAVORED BUTTERS, AND MAYONNAISE	WORK WITH MARROW

VIRTUALLY EVERY RESTAURANT IN FRANCE HAS A STEAK ON THE MENU, sometimes because steaks happen to be the specialty of the house, but more often to accommodate diners who feel like having something simple and, as the French would say, *sans chichi.* The steak you'll get depends on the kind of place you're in. In an inexpensive corner restaurant, maybe one that specializes in *steak frites* (a steak served with French fries), you're likely to get a thin slice of *bifteck* taken from one of the many muscles that make up the steer's leg—a little on the tough side, but often a good value for a quick bite. Steaks served with a shallot and white wine sauce are almost ubiquitous on the menus of modest bistros. *Onglet aux échalotes* or *bavette aux échalotes* are the most common because both of these steaks are tasty and relatively inexpensive. The *onglet,* called hangar steak in English, is a long, irregular strip of meat that hangs inside the steer's rib cage. It's now catching on in the United States, so what used to be a bargain steak (albeit hard to find) is now getting pricey in the same way as the once inexpensive *bavette,* which we call flank steak. In more expensive (or pretentious) places, you're likely to encounter an *entrecôte,* served with any number of sauces and garnitures, which will vary according to where you are. In the fanciest restaurants in France, you may see *entrecôte du Charollais* or *entrecôte charollaise.* These are steaks taken from France's most famous steers, the Charollais, which are giant white steers that are allowed to live for six years instead of the usual five (or even four) so that they develop more flavor. Strictly speaking, an *entrecôte* is a boneless rib steak (versus a *côte de boeuf,* which is a giant rib steak, with the bone, usually served for 2); but nowadays, in good places at least, an *entrecôte* is often a *contre-filet* (what in New York is called a strip steak), and in cheap places, a *bifsteck* or *romsteck,* another inexpensive cut.

CHOOSING A GOOD STEAK CUT

Times of war and famine may have contributed to the French aversion to wasting food, but the end result has been a collection of techniques and recipes for virtually every part of a steer. Unlike cuts used for braising (see Chapter 31), stewing (see Chapter 32), or poaching (see Chapter 33), cuts used for steaks must be tender because they will not be exposed to prolonged heat, which tenderizes even the toughest cuts.

The best steak cuts run along the back of the steer. Boneless rib steaks are cut away from the ribs nearer the shoulder, usually from the seventh to the fifth rib (the rib numbers get larger as you move back along the steer), while club steaks are cut away from the eighth to the twelfth ribs, the ribs nearer the loin—the same ribs that are roasted for prime rib. Rib steaks have a chunk of fat in the middle, which is easy to eat around but which may be the reason rib steaks are often a good value, while club steaks don't have the fat and are usually more expensive. Nowadays, butchers and supermarkets sometimes don't make the distinction between rib steaks and club steaks, but sell the club steak section of the ribs as prime rib and the rest—the shoulder end of the ribs—as rib steaks.

Behind the steer's ribs is the loin section. Steers are sold to butchers already halved down the middle. When the butcher slices the whole loin section, starting from front to back, he comes up with a series of steaks: Delmonico steaks (which have only one main muscle and are very similar to club steaks), T-bone steaks (in which a piece of bone, shaped like a T, separates the main loin muscle and the thin end of the fillet), porterhouse steaks (almost the same as T-bones, but containing a larger section of the fillet), and then various sirloins. In Europe, whole T-bones and porterhouse steaks (in French, *aloyau*) are rarely served, because European steers are much larger than American steers (although this is beginning to change as American steers are being bred with their European cousins) and the T-bones and porterhouses are just too huge. (An exception is the famous *bistecca alla fiorentina,* a giant porterhouse taken from a Chianina steer, Italy's finest.)

In most parts of the United States, the two main muscles that make up the porterhouse—the tenderloin (also called the fillet) and the large loin muscle—are separated. The tenderloin is a long, tapering muscle that can be roasted whole or cut into various steaks (see page 492). The larger loin muscle, which before trimming can weigh from 17 to 30 pounds [7.7 to 13.6 kg], is also sliced into steaks, which in New York are called strip steaks if the bone has been removed or shell steaks if the bone is still attached. Outside of New York, both may be called New York cut. Shell or strip steaks (in French, *contre-filets* or *faux-filets*) are excellent in any recipe calling for *entrecôtes,* but they're usually more expensive than rib steaks or club steaks. Flank steaks, which are the flaps that hang down on either side of the porterhouse (they're cut off by the time you see them in the butcher's case), are easy to recognize because they have a long grain that runs the length of the steak. Hangar steaks are harder to find, but you should be able to order them from a good butcher. I sometimes use sirloin butt steaks when I want to sauté or grill a steak without breaking the bank.

STEAK QUALITY AND AGING

Once you've decided on your favorite cuts, the next problem is how to get the best quality and the best value. Most of us are at least vaguely familiar with "prime" and "choice"—the two top grades of meat—but there are also "good" and "commercial" and three grades even lower that aren't usually sold in retail stores. Most of the meat you'll encounter at the supermarket will be graded "choice," but unfortunately that is a very large category and can vary significantly in quality. Some retailers distinguish meat as "top choice"—the best quality within the choice grade. All grades above "commercial" must be from steers, which are castrated bulls (commercial grade beef can be taken from cows or bulls), and the meat from the better grades, "prime" and "top choice," must be well marbled with white fat. You'll rarely see prime beef, the best grade, at the supermarket; you'll have to go to a good butcher or a fancy restaurant.

There is also the question of aging. When large sections of beef—typically the whole hindquarter, loin, or rib section—are hung for 2 or 3 weeks or longer in a cold refrigerator, the meat loses moisture and certain enzymes tenderize the meat and improve its flavor. Good aged meat with its surrounding fat has a delicious nutty flavor and is usually more tender than meat that hasn't been aged. Unfortunately, aged meat is becoming almost impossible to find, especially outside of large cities. This is because, nowadays, meat is usually broken down and sealed in plastic—Cryovac—before being sold to butchers. The Cryovac helps the meat keep longer, but the meat, once broken down and sealed, can no longer be aged in the traditional way. Some restaurants advertise meat that has been aged, but aging in Cryovac has no positive effect. So if you see "aged" meat on a menu or on a meat label, ask if it is "dry aged" using the traditional method of hanging in a cold room. As with prime meat, the only places to buy dry-aged beef are at good butcher shops or in better restaurants. If given a choice, I prefer buying less expensive cuts (such as sirloin or flank steak) from a good butcher who specializes in prime aged meats to buying more expensive cuts (such as tenderloin) from the supermarket.

COOKING A STEAK

Steaks are sautéed (panfried), broiled, grilled, and occasionally fried (as for chicken-fried steak). I avoid broiling because my broiler doesn't get hot enough to brown the steak before overcooking it. This is less of a problem if you are broiling very thick steaks, which take longer to cook but no longer to brown, or if you like your steak cooked more than rare. Broiling also causes any juices released to drip down through the broiling pan so that they are lost or at least difficult to recover. Grilling, too, causes the juices to be lost—they drip down into the coals—but at least grilling contributes a lovely flavor of its own. In France, steaks are either grilled or sautéed—the broiler is used for quick browning and glazing, but I've never seen it used for cooking meats—and are then usually served with a simple dollop of flavored butter (for grilled steaks) or a sauce made by deglazing the pan (for sautéed steaks) or a sauce such as béarnaise, prepared in advance (for sautéed or grilled steaks).

SAUTÉING: Part of the reason the French are fond of sautéing meat is that it allows them to make a quick sauce by deglazing the sauté pan—stirring a little liquid into it after cooking the meat, dissolving the caramelized meat juices and forming the basis for a sauce. To sauté so that these juices form on the bottom of the pan and caramelize without burning, you need to use a heavy-bottomed pan just large enough to hold the steaks in a single layer. If the pan is too small, the steaks won't all come in contact with the heat and they'll steam instead of brown, leaving watery, insipid juices in the pan and the surface of the meat gray and dull with no caramelized brown crust. If, on the other hand, the pan is too large, the exposed parts of the pan that aren't covered with meat will become too hot and the juices released by the steak will burn, leaving you nothing with which to make a sauce. If you find yourself with a sauté pan that's just a little too large, fill the empty space with meat trimmings or bones, if you have them. The sauté pan should be thick and heavy or the heat from the stove won't be distributed evenly over its surface; there will be hot and cold spots, the steaks will cook unevenly, and, again, the juices will burn. Old-fashioned iron skillets make great sauté pans and they're cheap enough that it won't cost a fortune to have a collection in different sizes. They do, however, have one disadvantage. Because their inner surface is dark, it is difficult to judge the condition of the meat juices that have, one hopes, caramelized rather than burned on the pan's surface. The only way to know is to deglaze the pan and taste the juices.

DEGLAZING THE SAUTÉ PAN AND MAKING A SAUCE: The sauté pan used for cooking steaks is deglazed by first pouring out and discarding any fat that was used for browning the steak. Finely chopped aromatic vegetables such as shallots or garlic are sometimes stirred in the pan for a few seconds while it's still hot so they release their flavor before liquid is added. At times, liquid is added directly. The liquid can be water or broth, but very often it is wine—red or white wine or fortified wine such as port or Madeira— that is boiled for a few seconds to cook off its alcohol and stirred in the pan with a wooden spoon or whisk to dissolve the juices in the wine. If I'm cooking a steak for myself at home, I'll often leave it at that—I'll deglaze the pan with about ½ cup [125 ml] of red wine, boil the wine down to a couple of tablespoons, and spoon it over the steak. If I feel like having something fancier, I'll add some highly reduced broth that I've either made myself (see Chapter 16) or bought. If I have meat drippings from a leftover roast, I use those. I then boil down the sauce until it thickens to the consistency of a light syrup. (Broth contains gelatin that gets syrupy when concentrated, and some store-bought products contain flour, which also thickens the sauce.) At this point you can season the sauce and serve it as is, or go further and add chopped herbs (parsley, chervil, tarragon, or chives), mushrooms (wild or cultivated, sautéed with a little fresh thyme), green peppercorns, truffles, little cubes of foie gras, crushed juniper berries, slices of beef marrow (for bordelaise), and so on. As the coup de grace, I may swirl in a little butter to give the sauce a velvety consistency and to soften and help meld the flavors.

HOW TO DETERMINE WHEN A STEAK IS DONE

The easiest way to see if a steak is done is to cut into a piece and look inside, but people who cook a lot of meat learn to judge doneness by touch and by the look of the meat's surface. Meat is muscle, which contracts and becomes firm to the touch as it heats. As meat continues to heat through, it also releases juices, which form on its surface. Initially these juices are red, but as the meat approaches medium and medium well, the juices turn pink and then brown. To train yourself to judge by touch and appearance, cut into the meat but also poke it with a finger to test its firmness, and notice what the juices look like.

BLACK-AND-BLUE, OR VERY RARE (Bleu): Seldom ordered in American restaurants, this is meat that's literally raw—although not cold—in the middle, but well browned on the outside. To accomplish this, you need an extremely hot fire or sauté pan. Home stoves often aren't hot enough, unless the steak is very thick. Leave the steak out of the refrigerator for about 1 hour before cooking so it won't be cold in the middle. Black-and-blue steaks will feel fleshy and no juices will have formed on either side. When you cut into the steak, the meat will be bright red and, if the meat is well aged, slightly purple.

RARE (Saignant): Rare meat still feels fleshy to the touch, but you'll notice tiny red droplets forming on the surface before you turn it. When cut, the meat will be red in the middle and barely pink near the top and bottom.

MEDIUM RARE (À point): As soon as the steak starts to stiffen and lose its fleshiness, it's medium rare. You'll also notice red droplets forming on its surface, but there will be more of them than when the steak is rare. When you cut into the steak, the very center will be red surrounded by pink.

MEDIUM (À point): In French, there's no distinction between medium and medium rare and anything above *à point* is considered well done, seldom ordered except by foreigners. A steak has reached medium when all fleshiness is gone and the meat has the texture of a flexed muscle rather than a limp one. There will be a lot of pink juices on the surface of the meat. The meat is pink when you cut into it, with no trace of red translucency.

MEDIUM WELL AND WELL DONE (Bien cuit): The meat will feel very firm to the touch and the juices forming on its surface will be mostly brown for medium well and all brown for well done. The meat will be brown all the way through when you cut into it.

STEAK: BUYING, SEASONING, AND CARVING

The amount of steak you should buy depends largely on your guests. In France, an 8-ounce [225-kg] steak would be a generous portion, but when we Americans decide to splurge on a good steak, it's got to be a big one. When buying steaks, keep in mind that thin steaks are harder to brown without overcooking because by the time they brown, the meat is cooked through. Also be aware that some steaks—shell steaks, porterhouse, and rib-on rib steaks—are about 30 percent bone by weight. When buying boneless steaks, figure on 8 to 12 ounces [225 to 340 g] per person. For bone-in steaks, calculate 12 ounces to 1 pound [340 to 450 g] per person. If you're cooking for lighter eaters, calculate 6 ounces [170 g] (without the bone) per person, but to avoid the thin-steak problem, don't buy individual steaks, buy thicker steaks, large enough to serve 2 or more people, and slice them for your guests at the table. Starting with thicker steaks and then carving them is also a good idea when you're cooking for a crowd and you're short of pan or grill space.

When grilling or sautéing a steak, you want the steak to be as dry as possible so that it browns quickly—especially important if the steak is thin. Because salt draws moisture out of the meat and after a couple of minutes will make the surface of the steak wet, don't salt the steak and then wait 10 minutes before cooking it. The best method is to salt the steak liberally a couple of hours before grilling or sautéing and then pat it dry just before cooking. But if you're like me, you may forget about seasoning ahead of time. In that case, season with salt immediately before cooking. Season with pepper after cooking.

If you decide to serve a large porterhouse for more than one person, set the steak on a large wooden cutting board—the kind with a moat to catch juices. While holding the steak down with a fork, slice along the T-bone, separating the large oval loin muscle and the round tenderloin muscle from the bone. Slice both cuts, making sure everyone gets a fair share of each one.

STEAK WITH BORDELAISE SAUCE

ENTRECÔTE À LA BORDELAISE

MAKES 4 MAIN-COURSE SERVINGS

For the last 100 years or so, bordelaise sauce has been made with red wine and has contained little cubes of marrow. In the first half of the nineteenth century, it was made with white wine—Carême called for Sauternes, tarragon, lemon, cloves, bay leaf, and veal broth—but here I give the "modern" version. The marrow is a nuisance if you've decided to do this at the last minute, since marrow is best if soaked overnight in salt water. So unless you've got a butcher on the corner and are thinking ahead, forget the marrow. If you don't have broth or concentrated broth, just finish the reduced wine with the butter.

1 marrow bone, about 2 inches [5 cm] long (optional)

2 porterhouse steaks (about 1½ pounds [675 g] each, about 1 inch [2.5 cm] thick), or 1 porterhouse steak (about 3 pounds [1.3 kg], about 2 inches [5 cm] thick), or 4 strip or rib steaks (8 to 12 ounces [225 to 340 g] each), or 4 shell steaks (strip steaks with the bone; 12 ounces to 1 pound [340 to 450 g] each)

  salt

2 tablespoons olive oil

10 black peppercorns

1 shallot, chopped fine

½ imported bay leaf

1 cup [250 ml] full-bodied red wine (see page 10 for more information about cooking wines)

1 cup [250 ml] homemade beef broth or Brown Chicken Broth (page 209), or 4 tablespoons concentrated broth (see page 4), or 2 tablespoons concentrated demi-glace, softened in 2 tablespoons of water (see page 3)

4 tablespoons cold unsalted butter, cut in 4 pieces (optional)

IF you're using the marrow, try to push it out of the bone by pressing on the narrower end of the marrow with your thumb—often the marrow will just slide out in one clean cylinder. If it's being uncooperative, set the bone upright on an old cutting board and give the bone a whack with a cleaver. Try not to hack into the marrow, but just crack the outside bone. Crack the bone on two sides, pull it apart, and push out the marrow. If the marrow's warm, chill it before slicing. Slice the marrow into ⅛-inch-thick [3-mm] disks. If you have time, soak the marrow overnight in a bowl of very salty water in the refrigerator. The salt draws out the blood and keeps the marrow from turning gray when you cook it.

SEASON the steaks on both sides with salt and let them sit for a couple of hours before sautéing (see page 482). An hour before sautéing, take the steaks out of the refrigerator and let them come to room temperature.

HEAT the olive oil in a sauté pan over high heat until it starts to smoke. Pat the steaks dry and put them in the pan, holding each one away from you and then lowering it gently, so you don't get spattered with oil. Brown the steaks from 3 to 7 minutes on each side, depending on how thick they are and how you like them done. If you notice them getting too brown, as may happen if you're cooking a very thick steak to medium rare or beyond, turn down the heat.

CRUSH the peppercorns by putting them on a cutting board and rocking a heavy saucepan back and forth over them while leaning on it with all your weight.

WHEN the steaks are done, transfer them to a platter, plates, or a cutting board (if you're carving.) Ideally, the cutting board should have a moat to catch juices. Keep the steaks warm in the oven on the lowest setting. Pour the fat out of the sauté pan and add the shallots. Stir the shallots in the hot pan with a whisk or wooden spoon until you smell their fragrance, about 20 seconds. Add the bay leaf and pour in the wine. Boil the wine over high heat until you're left with about ¼ cup [60 ml]. Pour in the broth or concentrated broth. Boil the sauce down until it becomes lightly syrupy. Pick out the bay leaf and stir in the crushed peppercorns and the disks of marrow. Whisk in the butter. Season to taste with salt. Spoon the sauce over the hot steaks, making sure everyone gets his or her fair share of the marrow.

Variations: Once you get a sense of the sequence of events when making a pan-deglazed sauce—the initial deglazing (usually with wine), the addition of broth for body, and a final finishing with butter and/or delicate flavorings—it will become second nature to make up your own sauces or your own versions of the classics. My sauces are often based on the wine left in the bottle from last night's dinner or a little vinegar from my vinegar barrel. For more ideas, see "Ideas for Improvising Sautéed Chicken Dishes" (page 368); most of these ingredients (except the seafood cooking liquids) will work for steak sauces. See also New York Strip Steak with Red Wine and Oysters (page 264).

○

BROWN SAUCES

Once you've made a *sauce bordelaise,* you'll be able to prepare classic brown sauces and improvise your own variations. Though brown sauces are intimidating to beginning cooks, most of them are made in a somewhat formulaic way, so once you've mastered a few, you can make others (and improvise your own) by plugging in different ingredients. Often, a brown sauce is made by gently cooking aromatic ingredients such as mirepoix (onions, carrots, and celery), shallots, onions (alone), garlic, or prosciutto in a small amount of fat. A liquid is then added, often red or white wine or a fortified wine such as port or Madeira. In a classic poivrade sauce, vinegar is used at this stage. The sauce is then usually reduced and demi-glace (in traditional sauces) or *glace de viande* (in modern sauces) added for body and a meaty flavor. Some sauces are strained to take out the aromatic ingredients that have surrendered their flavor to the liquid. Cream is sometimes added and lightly reduced to thicken the sauce, unify its flavors, and give it body. Other, more delicate flavorings, such as finely chopped fines herbes (chervil, parsley, chives, and tarragon), alone or in combination; mustard (not so delicate, but it will separate if added earlier); chopped or sliced mushrooms; truffles; or delicate spirits like Cognac, are then often added. The sauce is finished with a swirl of butter to give it a satiny texture and, like cream, to unify the flavors. In more homespun red wine sauces, a paste of flour and butter (beurre manié) may be whisked in as a thickener. Traditional sauces, based on demi-glace, contain relatively little cream and butter compared to sauces made with *glace de viande,* because the flour in the demi-glace acts as a thickener. Here are some ideas for improvising your own brown sauces:

Aromatic Ingredients, Chopped Fine and Gently Sweated in a Small Amount of Fat before Liquid Is Added

MIREPOIX (onions, carrots, celery) (see Meurette Sauce, page 115)

ONIONS (alone)

SHALLOTS (see Bordelaise Sauce, page 483)

GARLIC (see Lamb Chops with Garlic and Marjoram, page 503)

MUSHROOMS (see Poulet Sauté Chasseur, page 370)

CUBES OF PROSCIUTTO, PANCETTA, OR MEAT TRIMMINGS (see Meurette Sauce, page 115)

Flavorful Liquids Added to the Aromatic Ingredients Already in the Pan and Cooked Down

WINES (red or white, Madeira, port, marsala, Sauternes)
(See Center-cut Tenderloin Steaks with Truffles and Foie Gras Tournedos Rossini, page 494)

VINEGAR (See Sauce Poivrade, page 406)

GASTRIQUE MIXTURE (made by adding vinegar to caramel; see page 390 for more about this method)

MUSHROOM COOKING LIQUID (see recipe, page 8)

CURRANT JELLY (see Sauce Poivrade, page 406)

FRUIT JUICES (such as orange juice for duck à l'orange)

Meat Base to Give Body to the Sauce

DEMI-GLACE (commercial or homemade)

GLACE DE VIANDE (homemade, see page 221; or commercial)

GOOD-QUALITY VEAL, BEEF, OR CHICKEN BROTH (the more concentrated the better, so you're not reducing at the last minute)

Enrichers/Thickeners

HEAVY CREAM

BUTTER

HERB BUTTER (see pages 490 to 491)

CRUSTACEAN BUTTER (page 335) AND SEE LOBSTER NEWBURG (page 337)

BUTTER FLAVORED WITH AROMATIC INGREDIENTS SUCH AS REDUCED TOMATO PURÉE, CHOPPED TRUFFLES, OR CÈPES
(porcini)

BEURRE MANIÉ (butter and flour paste; see pages 116 and 436)

FINAL AROMATIC INGREDIENTS AND FLAVORINGS

COGNAC OR OTHER SPIRITS, SUCH AS FRUIT BRANDIES (see page 10 for more about using spirits in cooking

DELICATE HERBS (tarragon, chervil, parsley, chives)

MUSHROOMS, chopped or sliced

TRUFFLES, chopped, julienned, or sliced

MUSTARD (see Veal Kidneys with Mushrooms, Mustard, and Port, page 543)

ROOT VEGETABLES (carrots, celeriac, onions) diced, caramelized

MEATS SUCH AS PROSCIUTTO, diced, caramelized (see Roast Top Round of Veal with Diced Aromatic Vegetables, page 521)

FRUITS

STEAK WITH GREEN PEPPERCORNS

ENTRECÔTE AU POIVRE VERT

MAKES 4 MAIN-COURSE SERVINGS

This dish is similar to the *entrecôte à la bordelaise* described on page 483, except that port is used instead of red wine, cream instead of butter is used to thicken the sauce, and the sauce is flavored with green peppercorns. Green peppercorns come from the same plant that produces white and black peppercorns. But instead of being picked when ripe or nearly ripe and then dried, green peppercorns are picked before they ripen and are packed in brine or sometimes freeze-dried, so their delicate, aromatic pine-like flavor stays intact. In the same way as black pepper, green peppercorns should be added to dishes and sauces shortly before serving so their aroma doesn't cook off.

2   porterhouse steaks (about 1½ pounds [675 g] each, about 1 inch [2.5 cm] thick) or 1 porterhouse steak (about 3 pounds [1.3 kg], about 2 inches [5 cm] thick), or 4 strip or rib steaks (8 to 12 ounces [225 to 340 g] each), or 4 shell steaks (strip steaks with the bone; 12 ounces to 1 pound [340 to 450 g] each)

salt

2   tablespoons olive oil

1   shallot, chopped fine

¾   cup [175 ml] ruby or tawny port

1   cup [250 ml] homemade beef broth or Brown Chicken Broth (page 209), or 2 tablespoons concentrated broth (see page 4), or 1 tablespoon concentrated demi-glace, softened in a tablespoon of water (see page 3)

½   cup [125 ml] heavy cream

1   tablespoon freeze-dried green peppercorns, crushed with the back of a fork or with a mixing bowl, or 1 tablespoon brine-cured green peppercorns, rinsed, chopped coarse

1   teaspoon white wine vinegar, or more to taste

SEASON the steaks on both sides with salt and let them sit for a couple of hours before sautéing (see "Steak: Bying, Seasoning, and Carving," page 482). An hour before sautéing, take the steaks out of the refrigerator so they come to room temperature.

HEAT the olive oil in a sauté pan over high heat until it starts to smoke. Pat the steaks dry and put them in the pan, holding each one away from you and then lowering it gently, so you don't get spattered with oil. Brown the steaks from 3 to 7 minutes on each side, depending on how thick they are and how you like them done. If you notice them getting too brown, as may happen if you're cooking a very thick steak beyond medium rare, turn down the heat.

WHEN the steaks are done, transfer them to a platter, plates, or a cutting board (if you're carving) and keep them warm. Pour the fat out of the sauté pan and add the shallots. Stir the shallots in the hot pan with a whisk or wooden spoon until you smell their fragrance, about 30 seconds. Pour in the port and boil it down over high heat until you're left with about ¼ cup [60 ml]. Pour in the broth or concentrated broth. Boil the sauce down until it becomes lightly syrupy. Pour in the heavy cream and reduce again until the sauce is very lightly syrupy. Don't over-reduce. If the sauce gets too thick, thin it with 1 or 2 tablespoons of water or broth. (Don't ever thin a sauce at the last minute with wine or you'll taste the raw alcohol and possibly the tannins in the wine.) Stir in the crushed peppercorns and the vinegar. Season to taste with salt and, if the sauce needs it, more vinegar. Spoon the sauce over the steaks.

HANGAR STEAK OR FLANK STEAK WITH SHALLOTS

ONGLET OU BAVETTE

AUX ÉCHALOTES

MAKES 4 MAIN-COURSE SERVINGS

You're likely to spot either of these steaks in a typical Parisian bistro, although lately it seems that hangar steak is beating out flank steak, probably because flank steak has gotten too expensive. A steer has only one hangar steak—which hangs down from the inside of the rib cage—usually just right for 2 servings. Hangar steaks are long and thin and look vaguely like big pieces of rope with knots tied in them. Running down the center of the steak is a strip of membrane that the butcher should take out for you. Or if your butcher isn't familiar with hangar steak, you can do it yourself by cutting lengthwise along both sides of the membrane, spreading the steak open as you go.

Unlike hangar steaks, which were virtually unknown in America until a couple of years ago, flank steaks have been around a long time. The flank steak is a flat and wide strip of meat that hangs down the sides of the steer behind the rib cage. If you put your hands on your hips, but a bit above your hip bone, you're clutching your flank steaks. Flank steaks used to be sold as London broil (London broil is now mostly chuck—flank steak is too pricey). They are easily to identify because they have a very distinct grain that runs the length of the steak. Because flank steak is tough (but delicious), slice the cooked steak in thin strips, across the grain. Lean the knife to about a 45-degree angle to make the strips wider.

This recipe is designed for 8-ounce [225-g] portions. If you've got hungry guests, up the amounts accordingly.

2 hangar steaks or flank steaks (about 1 pound [450 g] each), or 1 flank steak (2 pounds [900 g]), or 4 sirloin butt steaks (8 ounces [225 g] each)

salt

2 tablespoons olive oil

4 shallots, chopped fine

1 cup [250 ml] dry white wine

1 cup [250 ml] homemade beef broth or Brown Chicken Broth (page 209), or 2 tablespoons concentrated broth (see page 4), or 1 tablespoon concentrated demi-glace, softened in 1 tablespoon of water (see page 3)

4 tablespoons cold butter, cut in 4 pieces

pepper

SEASON the steaks on both sides with salt and let them sit for a couple of hours before sautéing (see "Steak: Bying, Seasoning, and Carving," page 482). An hour before sautéing, take the steaks out of the refrigerator so they come to room temperature.

HEAT the olive oil in a sauté pan over high heat until it starts to smoke. Pat the steaks dry and put them in the pan, holding each one away from you and then lowering it gently, so you don't get spattered with oil. Brown the steaks from 3 to 7 minutes on each side, depending on how thick they are and how you like them done. If you notice them getting too brown, as may happen if you're cooking a very thick steak beyond medium rare, turn down the heat.

WHEN the steaks are done, transfer them to a platter, plates, or a cutting board, preferably one with a moat (if you're carving), and keep them warm. Pour the fat out of the sauté pan and add the shallots. Stir the shallots in the hot pan with a whisk or wooden spoon until you smell their fragrance, about 30 seconds. Pour in the wine and boil it down over high heat until you're left with about ¼ cup [60 ml]. Pour in the broth or concentrated broth. Boil down the sauce until it becomes lightly syrupy—more boiling will be needed if you've used broth instead of concentrated broth. Whisk in the butter. Season to taste with salt and pepper.

IF you're serving flank steak, carve it crosswise in strips, put the strips on hot plates, and spoon the sauce over the strips. If you're serving hangar steaks, just cut them crosswise in half, put them on hot plates, and spoon the sauce over them.

BÉARNAISE SAUCE

Serve béarnaise in a sauceboat at the table, so guests can help themselves. (See page 257 for more about making hollandaise and its derivatives.)

MAKES ENOUGH FOR 4 MAIN-COURSE SERVINGS OF STEAK

2 shallots, minced

¼ cup [60 ml] dry white wine

¼ cup [60 ml] white wine vinegar or tarragon vinegar

10 black peppercorns

4 sprigs fresh tarragon, plus 2 tablespoons whole fresh tarragon leaves, leaves plunged in boiling water for 5 seconds, drained, rinsed with cold water (these leaves optional)

2 sticks (½ pound [225 g]) butter

3 egg yolks

salt

pepper

COMBINE the shallots, wine, and vinegar in a small saucepan. Crush the peppercorns by putting them on a cutting board and pressing down on them with the corner of a heavy saucepan and leaning on it with all your weight. Put them in a Windsor pan—a saucepan with sloping sides—with the above ingredients and the tarragon sprigs. Put the pan over low heat and simmer the mixture until only about 2 tablespoons of liquid are left. Let cool.

PUT the butter in a small saucepan over medium heat, simmer it for about 10 minutes until the foam subsides and you see brown specks form on the bottom of the pan (see page 296 for more about clarifying butter). Strain the butter through a fine-mesh strainer, a coffee filter, or a regular strainer lined with a thin kitchen towel. Let cool for about 10 minutes—the butter should be hot but not scalding when you add it to the sauce.

ADD the egg yolks and 2 tablespoons cold water to the shallot mixture. Whisk the mixture over medium heat until it thickens, and remove immediately from the heat. Whisk for about 30 seconds off the heat so the heat retained in the pan doesn't cause the yolks to curdle. Whisk in the clarified butter in a thin but steady stream. Work the mixture through a strainer into a clean saucepan and stir in the blanched tarragon leaves. Season to taste with salt and pepper. Thin if necessary with 1 or 2 teaspoons of water.

Unlike chicken or foods that take a long time to cook through, steaks require a very hot fire so they end up quickly coated with a very tasty brown and slightly crispy crust. If the fire isn't hot enough or the steaks are too far away from the heat source, by the time the crust has developed, the steak will be overdone. Ideally, grills should be adjustable so you can change the distance from the coals to the grill itself, and the grill should be made of heavy iron so it leaves distinct markings on the meat, although these markings are mainly for looks. To get the distinctive crosshatch pattern you see in restaurants, give the steaks a 90-degree turn after a few minutes of cooking on the first side, cook for a few minutes longer, and then turn them over. (There's no need for the 90-degree turn on the second side, since no one will see it.) A common mistake is to keep moving the steaks around on the grill; this makes them take longer to brown and interferes with the formation of the crosshatch pattern. In case of flare-up, however, you will have to move the steaks to keep them away from the flames. Foods should never be cooked over flames, because the flames produce soot that clings to them. To avoid flare-up when grilling steaks, trim off most of their fat—it's the fat that renders and drips into the coals and causes the flames.

SAUCES FOR GRILLED MEATS: The juices from grilled meats drip down into the grill, so you can't make a sauce by deglazing as you would for sautéed meats. The French deal with this problem by serving a sauce that isn't based on the juices released by the meat. In inexpensive restaurants, the only sauce will probably be a dollop of *beurre maître d'hôtel*, which is made by working or whipping butter with chopped parsley and lemon juice. The combination is surprisingly good. In more expensive (or experimental) restaurants, the same steak might be served with some other compound butter. Compound butters are simple mixtures of cold butter and flavorful ingredients. Escoffier lists almost 35 combinations (a few are described below), but you

can easily make up your own using non-French ingredients (tomatillos, reconstituted dried chiles, curry mixtures) or ingredients that weren't around in Escoffier's era (pink or green peppercorns). The other classic accompaniment to grilled steaks is béarnaise sauce and occasionally its cousin, *Choron,* which is a béarnaise with a little tomato purée in it. Either of these sauces is traditionally served in a sauceboat for guests to help themselves, never already on the steak.

My own béarnaise and compound butter alternatives include homemade flavored mayonnaises that I make much like the classic French versions except that I include more herbs and flavorful ingredients, such as capers or pickles, so the effect is somewhat like a salsa and there's less fat (and virtually no cholesterol) per serving. If I'm feeling conscientious, I'll make three or four differently flavored mayonnaises (from a single batch of basic mayo) and pass them around the table for guests to dollop on their steaks.

CLASSIC AND IMPROVISED FLAVORED BUTTERS: You can make these butters in one of two ways: whipped or worked. To make a "worked" compound butter, just work the softened butter with the rest of the ingredients in a bowl with a wooden spoon until everything is well combined. If you're making a big batch—you're using more than 1 or 2 sticks of butter—use an electric mixer with the flat paddle blade. You can serve the butter in a bowl at the table or put a dollop on each steak, or you can roll up the butter in a sheet of wax paper, twist the two ends in opposite directions so you end up with a kind of sausage, chill, remove the paper, and slice the butter into decorative disks. If you want whipped butter, you'll need an electric mixer. Start by working the butter with the paddle blade; when the butter has softened, switch to the whisk and beat the butter until it is fluffy, about 10 minutes. Serve the butter right away—especially important if it's a hot day—and don't refrigerate it or it will harden again and you'll have to rewhip it.

I could go on for pages giving recipes for flavored butters, but the principle is so simple and it's so easy to make up your own that it would be pointless. Virtually any ingredient can be worked with butter to produce the effect of a melting sauce and the ingredient's flavor made more suave by butter's magical ability to attenuate the aggressiveness of certain ingredients without diluting their flavor. Finely chopped herbs are an obvious choice. Ideally, they'll be chopped at the last minute, and some (basil, tarragon, marjoram) chopped together with a cube of butter so they don't turn black. Any herb that might taste good sprinkled on a grilled steak is probably going to taste even better in a butter. Finely chopped garlic, worked with butter and finely chopped parsley (again, chopped at the last minute, though not because of blackening but because its aroma is so fleeting), produces the classic escargot butter, which is the chief reason for the deliciousness of hot snails and is also great on a hot steak. Puréed tomatoes, cooked down to a stiff paste and allowed to cool, worked with butter and fresh tarragon and a few drops of vinegar, work wonders on a steak (and are even better on grilled fish and chicken). Peppers, not just bell peppers, but any chile, fresh (grilled and peeled) or dried (softened in a little water), chopped to a purée and worked with butter, is good on anything grilled. (If the chiles are hot, I sometimes work in some cilantro.) Savory little goodies like capers, cornichons, anchovies, and shallots can all be chopped fine and worked with butter, alone or in combination.

SOME FRENCH CLASSIC COMPOUND BUTTERS

BEURRE AUX CÈPES SÈCS (Dried Porcini Butter): Combine ½ cup [35 g] of dried porcini with ¼ cup [60 ml] of warm water in a mixing bowl and let sit for 30 minutes. Stir the mixture every few minutes so the mushrooms are all moistened and have softened. If the mushrooms still seem hard or dry, add 1 more tablespoon of water, but use as little water as possible. Squeeze the mushrooms firmly in your fist and discard the muddy liquid they release (or strain it and use it for sauces or soups). Chop the mushrooms and work them with ¼ pound [115 g] of butter.

BEURRE À L'ESTRAGON (Tarragon Butter): Chop about ¼ cup [20 g] of fresh tarragon leaves with 1 stick (¼ pound [115 g]) of unsalted butter. Tarragon is best *chopped* with the butter so the butter immediately coats it and keeps it from turning black.

BEURRE MAÎTRE D'HÔTEL (Maître d' Butter): Finely chop a small bunch of parsley (preferably the Italian flat-leaf kind, which is more aromatic). You should end up with about 2 tablespoons. Work or whip the parsley with 1 stick of butter and 2 teaspoons of lemon juice. Season to taste with salt and pepper. If you like, add a little mustard.

BEURRE MARCHAND DE VINS (Red Wine Shallot Butter): Combine 1 cup [250 ml] of full-bodied red wine with 1 finely chopped shallot and 2 tablespoons of concentrated beef or chicken broth. If you don't have any broth, skip it. Boil the mixture down to ¼ cup [60 ml]. Stir in 1 tablespoon of finely chopped parsley and 1 teaspoon of lemon juice and work or whip the mixture with 1 stick of butter. Season to taste with salt and pepper.

BEURRE MONTPELLIER (Herb Mayonnaise with Butter and Olive Oil): I have to warn you, making this butter is a bit of a pain. But if you're feeling up to the effort, the result is like a combination of the best herb butter and the best herb mayonnaise, because it contains not only butter but also olive oil (which gives it a creamier texture), and both raw and cooked egg yolks (which contribute to the mayonnaise effect). Plunge 1 medium-size bunch each of watercress, chervil, chives, tarragon, and parsley in a pot of boiling salted water for about 15 seconds, drain in a strainer, and immediately rinse with cold water. If you don't have all the herbs, just use more of those you do have. Wring out the herbs in your fists, press them dry in paper towels, and chop them coarsely by hand. Combine the greens with 1 finely chopped shallot, 3 cornichons, 2 tablespoons of drained capers, 1 finely chopped clove of garlic, 5 anchovy fillets, 2 raw egg yolks, 2 cooked egg yolks, ½ cup [125 ml] of extra-virgin olive oil, and 1½ [170 g] sticks of butter in a food processor. Purée the mixture, scraping it off the inside walls of the food processor every 30 seconds or so, until the mixture is smooth, about 5 minutes. Work the mixture through a drum sieve—working it with the back of a small metal mixing bowl is quickest—or through a strainer with the bottom of a ladle. Season with salt and pepper and a little vinegar.

BEURRE DE MOUTARDE (Mustard Butter): Just work or whip 1 tablespoon or more of your favorite mustard with the butter to taste. I often use whole-grain mustard.

BEURRE AUX TRUFFES (Truffle Butter): The obvious way to make this is to chop truffles and work them with the butter. But to get by without using any truffles, just store fresh truffles overnight in a sealed jar with a couple of unwrapped sticks of butter. The truffle aroma will scent the butter. (For more about truffles, see page 595.)

BEURRE AU FOIE GRAS (Foie Gras Butter): If given the choice, I'd rather just put a big slice of foie gras on top of my steak (see *Tournedos Rossini,* page 494) and let the heat of the steak soften it. But some inventions are inventions of economy instead of pure decadence, so if you want the flavor of foie gras on your steak, work *mousse de foie gras* with an equal amount of butter. You'll cut costs and the effect will be great. (See more about foie gras on page 96.)

FLAVORED HOMEMADE MAYONNAISE

It doesn't occur to most of us to put mayonnaise on a steak, and in fact most people find the idea peculiar at best until they taste the results. The secret is to make your own mayonnaise and flavor it with an abundance of full-flavored ingredients such as herbs, spices, capers, or aromatic vegetables, so that it functions almost like a salsa but is more saucelike.

As with so many classic sauces, there are lots of variations—Escoffier lists 14. Some of them are clearly outdated, but others are useful as jumping-off points for improvisation. I often make classic mayonnaises but double or triple the solid ingredi-

ents so the sauce is less rich and its flavor more assertive. You can use a lot of the same ingredients used to flavor the compound butters in the previous section. I sometimes take a Mexican route (unless I'm serving delicate wines) and flavor mayonnaise with cilantro and various chiles—either dried chiles that have been reconstituted, or fresh chiles, charred and peeled—including one of my favorites, chipotles, which are smoked jalapeños. Curry makes a great mayonnaise: Cook 2 tablespoons of curry powder for 30 seconds in oil and stir this mixture into a basic mayo to taste. But a word of warning: curry turns mayonnaise very stiff and may cause it to break, so thin the sauce with 1 or 2 tablespoons of water. Red or white wines, reduced with a little shallot, give mayonnaise a delightful tang (although red wine turns it a weird color).

SAUCE AÏOLI (Garlic Mayonnaise): This is the classic garlic mayonnaise from Provence, traditionally dolloped on cooked seafood or boiled vegetables and also used in bourride, the Mediterranean fish soup (see page 235). Most classic mayonnaise derivatives can be made by just adding ingredients to a basic mayonnaise made with vegetable oil, but aïoli is traditionally made with extra-virgin olive oil, so you have to start from scratch. To further complicate matters, extra-virgin olive oil has a tendency to turn bitter if beaten too hard—as in a blender, or even with a hand whisk. When it is worked in the traditional way, gently with a pestle, in a heavy mortar, bitterness isn't a problem. Since few of us own a good mortar and pestle, the best way to make aïoli is this: Finely chop 2 cloves of garlic and smash the chopped garlic into a paste by going back and forth over it with the side of a chef's knife, while leaning heavily on the knife. Combine this paste in a glass or porcelain bowl (avoid metal) with 2 egg yolks, 2 teaspoons of lemon juice, and a pinch of salt, and slowly work in about 1½ cups [375 ml] extra-virgin olive oil with a wooden spoon, until the mayonnaise gets stiff. If it starts to get too stiff, thin it with a little water. Aïoli is also magnificent flavored with a pinch of saffron threads, first soaked in 1 tablespoon of water, and the soaking liquid added too.

SAUCE ANDALOUSE (Tomato and Bell Pepper Mayonnaise): Peel, seed, and chop 6 tomatoes and cook them down to a stiff consistency. Let cool and combine with 1 recipe (1½ cups [375 ml]) Basic Mayonnaise (page 34). Use a wooden spoon to work ½ cup [125 ml] extra-virgin olive oil into the mayonnaise, 1 tablespoon at a time. If the mayonnaise gets too stiff, thin it with 1 or 2 teaspoons of water. Char and peel 3 bell peppers, ideally 3 different colors, and cut them first into strips and then into dice. Fold the dice into the mayonnaise. Season to taste with salt and pepper.

SAUCE RÉMOULADE (Herb, Caper, and Pickle Mayonnaise): This is a popular sauce for grilled fish, but I also like it on a grilled steak. Here, I've more than doubled the amounts of all the ingredients except the basic mayonnaise. To 1 recipe (1½ cups [375 ml]) Basic Mayonnaise (page 34), add 1 tablespoon Dijon mustard (in addition to the mustard in the basic mayo recipe); 8 cornichons, chopped to the consistency of relish; 3 tablespoons of capers (preferably the smaller nonpareil variety), drained and chopped; 1 tablespoon each of finely chopped parsley, chervil, and tarragon, chopped at the last minute with 1 teaspoon of oil to keep the tarragon from turning black; and 4 anchovy fillets, drained and minced (optional). If you don't have some of the herbs, just leave them out and use more of the others.

SAUCE SUÉDOISE (Swedish Applesauce and Horseradish Mayonnaise): This sweet and slightly dissonant sauce is also delicious on cold leftover meats. Combine ¾ cup [180 ml] of applesauce with 1 recipe (1½ cups [375 ml]) Basic Mayonnaise and 2 heaping tablespoons of finely grated horseradish. (I make my own applesauce by stewing 3 peeled and chopped apples until they soften and the mixture stiffens. I don't bother straining, but leave the apples chunky.) Season to taste with salt and pepper. If the sauce seems too sweet, add a little lemon juice.

BEEF TENDERLOIN

In the world of steak, beef tenderloin—often called by its French name, *filet*—holds a special place. It is the tenderest of all the beef cuts, and it makes beautiful steaks you can cut with a fork. It's easy to roast it whole and slice it and serve it in convenient, tender rounds. It's a status symbol because of its cost, and it makes it onto the menu of many an important banquet, not only because of its panache, but no doubt because it's easy to cook and serve.

Most of the time when buying tenderloin steaks you'll be buying steaks that have already been sliced or that you have the butcher slice for you. You may also want to buy a whole tenderloin—for roasting or because you want to cut your own steaks. In either case it helps to know a little about how whole tenderloins are butchered so you can recognize the best value. Whole tenderloins are often sold in supermarkets. They make great roasts, and are usually a better value than individual steaks. A tenderloin is a boneless, tapering strip of muscle, about 18 inches [45 cm] long. Tenderloins come covered with a thick layer of fat that can make up as much as 25 percent of the tenderloin's total weight. Usually, in supermarkets, this layer of fat has already been removed, but if you see suspiciously low prices for tenderloin, look to see if the tenderloin still has the fat. Tenderloins typically weigh from 5 to 7 pounds [2.5 to 3 kg] with the fat still on, and from 3 to 5 pounds [1.5 to 2 kg] with the fat removed. You should also be aware that a long, thin muscle, called the side muscle—*chainette* in French—runs along almost the entire length of the tenderloin. The side muscle is easy to recognize, because most of the steak will be a single round muscle, but will have a little side piece attached. Most supermarkets, butchers, and restaurants leave this muscle on—it is, in fact, perfectly delicious, it just makes the steaks look less perfect. But if you're being charged a premium price for either whole tenderloin or steaks, you should pay less per pound if the side muscle is left on. If you're buying a whole tenderloin, the choice is yours whether to leave the side muscle on; it pulls away so easily you almost don't need a knife. I usually leave it on unless I'm making something very fancy, like the *tournedos Rossini* on page 494. (If I do remove it, I cut it into chunks, sauté it, deglaze a few times with broth, and make a little sauce.) The tenderloin is also partially covered with a thin, shiny strip of connective tissue, called the silver skin. This is easy to remove, but if you're buying a whole tenderloin from a butcher, ask him to remove it.

What to do once you get your whole tenderloin home will depend on how thoroughly it was trimmed when you bought it. If the fat is still attached, just pull it off—it peels right off with just a little help from a sharp paring or boning knife. If you want to remove the side muscle, pull it away from the rest of the fillet with your fingers, using a knife only where it attaches on one end. Trim off the silver skin by sliding a paring knife or boning knife along the underside of the tissue, with the blade facing up so you don't cut into the meat, and cutting off the silver skin in strips.

Once you have a thoroughly trimmed tenderloin in hand, you can cut it into steaks or tie it up and roast it whole—or do both. Notice that the thick end, called the butt end, of the tenderloin divides in two. If you want to serve the tenderloin in steaks or roast it whole (see Chapter 37), you can tie the two parts of the butt end together with several loops of string (each steak will need its own loop to hold it in one piece), or you can cut the wedge off the butt end and tie it onto the thin end of the tenderloin, making the whole tenderloin roughly the same thickness. The advantage to this system is that you can slice the whole thing, or if you're roasting, it will cook evenly. The disadvantage, however, is that the steaks or slices on the two ends will actually be made of two pieces, which will separate on the plate. One solution is to cut off the butt end, tie it up, and serve it as a small roast—carving it lengthwise eliminates the problem of the slices being in two pieces. The center of the tenderloin is the most desirable piece of the whole cut, not because it tastes better, but because it is perfectly cylindrical and can be sliced into perfectly round, elegant steaks. The chateaubriand is a large piece—at least large enough for 2 servings—from the center of the tenderloin, which is grilled or sautéed and classically served with béarnaise sauce. Thin steaks (½ inch to 1 inch [1.5 to 2.5 cm] thick) taken from this same center-cut section of the tenderloin are called tournedos. Thicker steaks, taken from the thin part—but not the very end—of the tenderloin are the filets mignons.

CROÛTONS

The word "crouton" comes from the French *croûte*, which means crust. In French cooking, *croûton* has a broader meaning than "crouton" does in English. What we call croutons are little cubes of dried bread, all too often out of a box, that we sprinkle over salads or use to stuff turkeys. French cooks also use them in the same way. But in France, *croûtons* can also be slices of stale bread put in bowls before soup is ladled in; cubes of fresh bread cooked in butter or bacon or duck fat, for sprinkling in salads; or rounds of fresh bread cooked in butter or other fat and used as supports for poached eggs (see Poached Eggs in Red Wine Sauce, page 115), vegetables, and meats. The reason that the French so often cook *croûtons* in fat instead of just toasting the bread is not just for extra flavor, but because the fat gives the *croûton* crunch and at the same time waterproofs it so it resists the moist ingredients and sauces that would otherwise make it soggy. This makes good sense in salads and in dishes such as *tournedos Rossini,* when the crouton is going to be surrounded with sauce.

CENTER-CUT TENDERLOIN STEAKS WITH TRUFFLES AND FOIE GRAS

TOURNEDOS ROSSINI

MAKES 6 MAIN-COURSE SERVINGS

I serve this dish once every few years, only to very good friends and during the holidays, when I can better justify its wanton excess. It's a dish that nouvelle cuisine chefs used to make fun of for being old-fashioned, pretentious, and excessive. Well, give me a little pretense and excess anytime, because tournedos Rossini is a marvelous thing and makes a glorious main course for a luxurious dinner. Because it's so very rich, you can get by serving relatively small portions. Still, be prepared to spend a lot of money.

Traditionally, the tournedos are set on round slices of bread cooked in butter, topped with a slice of foie gras, and served with truffles and a Madeira sauce. I sometimes leave out the rounds of bread, which the French call croûtons (see page 493). If you decide to use the croutons, they can be made earlier the same day.

- 1 section (2 pounds [900 g]) center-cut tenderloin (trimmed of all fat, silver skin and side muscle removed; see headnote)

  salt

  pepper

- 6 thin slices dense-crumb white bread such as Pepperidge Farm (only if you're making the croûtons)

- 1 stick (¼ pound [115 g]) butter, clarified (see page 296) (only if you're making the croûtons)

- 1 chunk (12 ounces [340 g]) foie gras terrine (bloc or entier) (see page 96 for more information about foie gras)

- 1 black winter truffle (1 ounce [30 g], or as large as you can afford; see page 594)

- 3 tablespoons clarified butter, duck or goose fat, or olive oil (for sautéing the steaks)

- ½ cup [125 ml] semidry or semisweet Madeira

- ½ cup [125 ml] concentrated beef broth (see page 4)

- 3 tablespoons butter (for the sauce)

CUT the tenderloin into 6 steaks. Rub the steaks liberally with salt and pepper, cover them with plastic wrap, and refrigerate them until 1 hour before you're ready to serve.

CUT the bread slices into rounds that match the size of the steaks as closely as possible. Use a round cookie cutter or, if you don't have one, hold the bottom of a glass on each bread slice and cut around it with a paring knife. Cook the bread rounds on both sides in clarified butter in a wide sauté pan over medium heat until they are golden brown on each side. Reserve.

AN hour before you're ready to serve, take the steaks out of the refrigerator. Thirty minutes before you're ready to serve, preheat the oven to 200°F [90°C]. If you've made the *croûtons* ahead of time, put them on a sheet pan in the oven to warm. Cut the foie gras into 6 slices, ideally just large enough to cover each steak. Put the slices on a plate, cover with plastic wrap, and allow them to come to room temperature.

PEEL the truffle with a small paring knife, chop the peelings fine, and cut the truffle into thin slices with a small knife, vegetable slicer, or truffle slicer.

JUST before you're ready to start sautéing, pat the steaks dry with paper towels.

PUT the clarified butter or other fat in a sauté pan just large enough to hold the steaks in a single layer. Heat the pan over high heat until the butter ripples and barely begins to smoke. Sauté the steaks just long enough to brown them, 2 to 3 minutes on each side, so they stay very rare—they'll continue to cook in the oven while you're making the sauce.

Quickly transfer the steaks to a plate, put a foie gras slice on each one, and keep them in the warm oven. Pour the cooked fat out of the pan.

DEGLAZE the sauté pan with the Madeira, boil the Madeira down over high heat to about half, and add the concentrated broth. Boil the sauce down until it has a lightly syrupy consistency. If it gets too thick, thin it with a little water. Whisk in the 3 tablespoons of butter and the chopped truffle peels and truffle slices. Simmer gently while stirring with a whisk, about 1 minute. Season to taste with salt and pepper.

PLACE each *croûton* in the center of a hot plate and place a foie gras–covered steak on top of it. Spoon the sauce over the steaks.

PORK NOISETTES WITH PRUNES

NOISETTES DE PORC AUX PRUNEAUX

WHAT IS	HOW TO	WHAT ARE	HOW TO
THE MOST TENDER CUT OF PORK AND HOW TO COOK IT	COOK ACCORDING TO THE CUT OF MEAT: SAUTÉING VERSUS BRAISING	CHOPS, MEDALLIONS, AND NOISETTES	COOK VEAL CHOPS AND LAMB CHOPS

PORK WITH PRUNES IS A POPULAR DISH IN THE TOURAINE, THAT PART of the Loire valley famous for its chateaux and for Vouvray wine. The combination is an intriguing one and can be adapted to several methods, including sautéing and long and short braising. When I taught cooking regularly, pork with prunes was part of the repertoire of the school's most basic cooking class. After teaching the dish every week for years, I kept my sanity by changing it in subtle ways until I came up with different methods, each with its own nuances.

The quickest and most obvious approach, and the one I was supposed to teach, consisted of first pitting the prunes and soaking them in Vouvray. This makes good sense because Vouvray is from the same region as the dish and the wine in bottles marked "*demi-sec*" or "*moelleux*" has a sweetness that enhances that of the prunes but enough acidity to offset the richness of the pork. In the basic recipe, the chops were sautéed, the pan was deglazed with the prune soaking liquid, cream was added to give the sauce body, and the prunes, simmered in the sauce, were spooned over the chops. Because modern center-cut pork chops can be tough, instead of chops I sometimes ordered pork tenderloins, which are small: ½ to 1 pound [225 to 450 g], about 8 inches [20.5 cm] long and 1 or 2 inches [2.5 or 5 cm] in diameter at the thick end and tapering to a very thin tip. We trimmed the tenderloins and cut them into inch-thick [2.5-cm] noisettes, thick little rounds with a diameter scarcely more than that of a quarter. (The French word *noisette* means hazelnut.) Three noisettes made a generous serving of perfectly tender little morsels. But sometimes we'd be stuck with shoulder chops, which are tough and fatty. They aren't good sautéed because the meat and fat don't have time to soften. Instead, pork shoulder chops should be gently braised for a couple of hours until the meat softens and the fat renders. To do this, soak the prunes in Vouvray or other slightly sweet wine, sauté the chops, sweat finely chopped mirepoix (onions, carrots, and celery) in the pan, put the chops back in, nestle in a bouquet garni, pour the wine used for soaking the prunes over the chops, and gently braise the chops for 2½ to 3 hours. When the chops are done—a knife slides easily in and out— degrease and reduce the braising liquid, add cream, simmer the prunes in the sauce, and spoon the prunes and the sauce over the chops. The result is one of the best pork dishes there is, and from the lowliest and least expensive cut.

The lesson is that dishes with identical flavorings and garnitures can be cooked in different ways, appropriate to the particular cut of meat. Lean, tender cuts should be sautéed (or if they're large, roasted), while tough cuts should be braised or stewed. Lean and tough cuts are best larded before they are braised (see page 423). But our shoulder chops had enough fat of their own to keep them moist, and after the long, gentle cooking the fat gave the chops a smooth, melting texture. An additional advantage to braising pork chops is that much of the fat liquifies, so it can be skimmed off the braising liquid before you make the sauce.

Here are recipes for both approaches:

SAUTÉED PORK NOISETTES WITH PRUNES

NOISETTES DE PORC SAUTÉES AUX PRUNEAUX

MAKES 4 MAIN-COURSE SERVINGS

20 pitted prunes

1 cup [250 ml] Vouvray demi-sec or moelleux, or ½ cup [125 ml] authentic Portuguese white port combined with ½ cup [125 ml] dry white wine

1½ to 2 pounds [675 to 900 g] pork tenderloins (2 or 3 whole tenderloins)

salt

pepper

2 tablespoons clarified butter or unsalted butter

½ cup [125 ml] concentrated brown veal or beef broth (see page 4) or Brown Chicken Broth (page 209) (optional)

½ cup [125 ml] heavy cream

2 teaspoons good-quality white wine vinegar or sherry vinegar, or more to taste

COMBINE the prunes with the wine in a small mixing bowl and let them soak for 1 to 2 hours. If the thin shiny skin—the silver skin—is still attached to the tenderloins, slide a small paring knife under it and trim it off in strips. Cut the tenderloins into noisettes by slicing the thick end between ¾ inch and 1 inch [2 and 2.5 cm] thick and then cutting the slices progressively thicker as the tenderloin tapers, so that each noisette has the same amount of meat. Plan to end up with 12 noisettes. Take the slices from the thinner end of the tenderloin, place them end-down on the cutting board, and press on them with the heel of your hand, flattening them so that all the noisettes end up being about the same thickness. Season the noisettes with salt and pepper.

DRAIN the prunes, reserving them and the wine separately. Heat the butter in a sauté pan just large enough to hold the noisettes. Heat clarified butter until it ripples; heat whole unsalted butter until it foams and the foam begins to subside. Put in the noisettes. Sauté from 4 to 5 minutes on each side, until one of the noisettes springs back when you press on it with your finger. (If you're unsure, cut into one.)

TRANSFER the noisettes to a heated plate and pour the cooked fat out of the sauté pan. Pour in the wine and reduce over high heat, while scraping the bottom of the pan with a wooden spoon, to about ¼ cup [60 ml]. Add the broth, if using, and boil down again until the mixture is lightly syrupy. Pour in the cream, stir in the reserved prunes, and simmer while whisking until the sauce has the consistency you like. Be careful not to make it too thick. Stir in the vinegar and any juices released by the noisettes, and simmer for a few seconds more. Season to taste with salt, pepper, and, if you like, more vinegar. Arrange the noisettes on heated plates—3 on each plate—and spoon the sauce and 5 prunes over each serving.

BRAISED PORK SHOULDER CHOPS WITH PRUNES

CÔTES DE PORC BRAISÉES AUX PRUNEAUX

MAKES 6 MAIN-COURSE SERVINGS

While French butchers separate meats into large boneless cuts suitable for braising or stewing, American butchers cut meat to get the maximum number of steaks or chops, because these are more familiar and take less time to cook. Francophile that I am, I prefer the French system because it's designed to get the best that each cut has to offer. I've never seen pork shoulder chops in France; the French prefer to braise or roast the shoulder or cure it and turn it into *jamboneau*, the French equivalent or our "picnic ham."

If you sauté or grill pork shoulder chops, you'll be disappointed because they're fatty and gristly, and quick cooking won't render the fat or tenderize the meat. But when they are braised, the meat softens, the fat dissolves, and the juices released by the meat create the base for a savory sauce. I make this dish for at least 6 because it takes 3 hours to cook. It also makes great leftovers.

Don't be surprised by the amount of meat called for here. Much of it is bone, and the meat shrinks during braising.

30 pitted prunes

2 cups [500 ml] Vouvray *demi-sec* or *moelleux*, or 1 cup [250 ml] authentic white port from Portugal combined with 1 cup [250 ml] dry white wine

6 double pork shoulder chops or large center-cut pork chops taken from the relatively fatty shoulder end of the whole loin (5 to 7 pounds [2.3 to 3.1 kg] total)

salt

pepper

3 tablespoons clarified butter, "pure" olive oil, or vegetable oil

1 tablespoon butter

1 medium-size onion, chopped fine

1 medium-size carrot, peeled, chopped fine

1 stalk celery, chopped fine (optional)

1 medium-size bouquet garni

3 cups [750 ml] brown veal or beef broth (see page 219) or Brown Chicken Broth (page 209)

1 cup [250 ml] heavy cream

2 tablespoons finely chopped parsley (chopped at the last minute)

1 tablespoons good-quality white wine vinegar or sherry vinegar, or more to taste

COMBINE the prunes with the wine in a small mixing bowl and let them soak for 1 to 2 hours.

CUT the bones off the chops and reserve the bones. If you like, tie the chops with a few rounds of string each to hold them together in attractive medallions.

SEASON the medallions with salt and pepper and brown them on both sides in 3 tablespoons of clarified butter in the widest sauté pan or pot with a lid that you own, ideally one just large enough to hold them in a single layer. If you don't have a big enough pan, sauté them in stages. The medallions take about 8 minutes on each side to brown. Set them on a large plate and pour the butter out of the pan. Put 1 tablespoon of fresh butter in the pan used for browning the pork and gently sweat the chopped vegetables over medium heat, stirring the vegetables every few minutes until they soften and the onion turns translucent, about 10 minutes.

DRAIN the prunes, reserving them and the wine separately.

ARRANGE the meat on top of the vegetables—if your pot isn't big enough, you'll have to stack the medallions—and nestle in the bouquet garni. Put the reserved bones on top of the medallions. Pour the reserved wine and the broth over the bones and medallions. Bring to a gentle simmer on top of the stove and place a sheet of aluminum foil over the pot, pressing down on the middle so moisture will condense on the foil and drip down on the chops from the inside. Cover the pot with its lid and simmer very gently, so that a bubble rises to the serve every 1 or 2 seconds, on top of the stove or in a 325°F [165°C/gas mark 3] oven. If you've stacked the chops, rearrange them after 1 hour of simmering so those that were on the top are now on the bottom and surrounded with liquid. Continue simmering in the same way for 1½ to 2 hours more, until a knife or skewer slides easily in and out of the boneless chops.

GENTLY transfer the chops to a plate. Remove the string, if you've used it, cover the chops with aluminum foil, and keep them in warm place, such as a low oven. Strain the braising liquid into a saucepan, using a small ladle to push firmly against the vegetables to extract as much liquid as possible. Discard the vegetables and the bouquet garni. Bring the braising liquid to a medium simmer and move the pan to one side of the heat so it simmers on one side only, to make skimming easier. Reduce the sauce to about 2 cups [500 ml], skimming off the fat with a small ladle. (You can also pour the braising liquid into a degreasing cup and then pour the fat-free liquid into the saucepan to reduce it. You'll still have to skim it, but just a little. See page 18.)

POUR in the heavy cream and continue to reduce the sauce until it has a lightly syrupy consistency. Stir in the prunes, any liquid released by the chops as they sat on the plate, the parsley, and vinegar and season to taste with salt and pepper. If you like, add more vinegar to balance the sweetness of the wine and prunes. Spoon the sauce and prunes over the chops on hot plates.

Variations: Once you've mastered sautéing and braising you'll be able to handle any chop, medallion, or noisette that comes your way. (See below for the differences between these cuts.) Because the delicate sweetness of fruit pairs so well with pork, it's worth experimenting with apples, apricots, pitted cherries, and underripe peaches. I peel apples and peaches, cut them into wedges, and simmer them separately in a little broth instead of in the sauce because, unlike prunes, which are done as soon as they're heated through, apples and other fresh fruits need to cook for several minutes to soften. By cooking the fruits separately, you can control their cooking time and add them and the little bit of braising liquid to the sauce at the end. The flavor of the fruits can be reinforced by braising them in hard cider instead of wine (for apples) and finishing with an appropriate eau-de-vie (such as Calvados for apples, kirsch for cherries). Red wine is sometimes used in a traditional recipe from the Touraine in which lean center-cut pork chops, not shoulder chops, are simply sautéed and a red wine sauce, sweetened with a little port, is made separately and thickened at the end with a little beurre manié (butter worked with flour), producing a sauce almost identical to the meurette sauce on page 115. The advantage to such a sauce is that it requires no broth—although a little concentrated broth added along with the wine would do no harm. The prunes are simmered in the sauce as in the two recipes above. If you're braising shoulder chops and want to use red wine, just substitute one-half port and one-half red wine (soak the prunes in the port for the white wines).

The French don't limit their treatment of pork chops to fruits. In fact, they are more likely to pair pork with savory ingredients like mustard (*côtes de porc à la moutarde*), or mustard and finely sliced cornichons (*côtes de porc à la charcutière*). Home cooks make these dishes by sautéing the chops in lard (which makes sense, but I use butter), sweating a little chopped onion in the pan after removing the chops, cooking flour with the onions for a couple of minutes to make a roux, deglazing with white wine, and finishing the sauce with just mustard or a combination of mustard and cornichons. Restaurant versions omit the flour, add broth or concentrated broth, and finish the sauce with cream or butter before adding the mustard and, for *côtes de porc à la charcutière*, cornichons. I like home-style butterless or creamless versions more—although I usually skip the roux—because the lean acidic sauce cuts the richness of the pork. (Roux is typical in homespun dishes made with white wine; beurre manié is the thickener of choice when red wine is used.)

You can also braise a whole boneless pork shoulder as you would a veal pot roast (see page 428), except that there's no need to lard it because pork shoulder has enough natural fat of its own. (Ask for a boneless picnic shoulder or boneless skinned shoulder butt.) A braised pork shoulder is also a lot cheaper than a veal pot roast. Garnitures—fruits, wild or cultivated mushrooms, or vegetables such as carrots, small onions, and turnips—can be added to the braising liquid during the final glazing.

OTHER CHOPS, MEDALLIONS, AND NOISETTES

A chop is (or at least should be) a lean, tender cut of meat with the bone attached, suitable for sautéing or grilling. A medallion is a larger chop with the bone removed or a round piece of steak such as tenderloin; the meat is sometimes pounded slightly to flatten it. A noisette is a small, round, boneless piece of meat such as a lamb chop with no bone. You can also make medallions and noisettes by slicing a boneless (veal or pork) loin into medallions and a tenderloin into noisettes as described on page 498.

The technique for sautéing chops, medallions, and noisettes is virtually identical for all. Red meats such as lamb or venison should be cooked less—between rare and medium rare—while pork and veal should be cooked to medium, until no translucency remains when you cut into one, 137°F [58°C]. At home it's easiest to make a pan-deglazed sauce, constructing it by adding flavorful ingredients to the pan in stages. (See page 480 for more about pan deglazed sauces.) Roasts are cooked to a lower temperature than sautéed meats because the inside of a roast rises by about 5°F [2 to 3°C] as the roast rests.

VEAL: As with pork chops, there are three kinds of veal chops: shoulder chops, center-cut rib chops, and loin chops. The shoulder chops are the least expensive of the three; they are slightly tougher and have an irregular muscle structure that makes them less pretty. If you have a sudden hankering for veal and aren't splurging for a fancy dinner, shoulder veal chops are perfectly fine and, unlike pork shoulder chops, are relatively tender and lean. Center-cut rib chops include the eight ribs closest to the rear of the animal except for one or two ribs that are some-

times left attached to the saddle. The center-cut chops have the ribs attached and contain a neat and compact rib-eye muscle. Loin chops are cut farther down toward the calf's back; they contain, instead of a rib, a section of backbone and both the rib-eye muscle and the tenderloin, and look like miniature T-bone steaks. Loin chops and center-cut rib chops are both very expensive, and the two are equally good. Some people prefer loin chops because they include a piece of the very tender fillet (tenderloin), while others, like myself, prefer rib chops because we can trim the end of the rib (french it) so it looks very dramatic on the plate. Some butchers bone the rib-eye muscle completely and will sell you slices—medallions—of boneless veal loin. Whole veal tenderloins are almost impossible to find, because when calves are broken down into the wholesale primal cuts, part of the tenderloin is left attached to the leg and another part attached to the saddle.

FARM-RAISED VEAL

Veal is generally sold in one of two forms. So-called conventional veal is taken from older calves—usually about 6 months old—that have been milk fed for the first 24 hours after their birth but are then fed grass or hay. The diet of grass or hay causes their flesh to turn deep pink, almost red, but not as red as beef. Purists insist that "conventional" veal shouldn't be called veal, but is more accurately described as baby beef. The very pale pink, almost white, meat that most of us associate with veal is called nature veal, which is something of a misnomer because there's nothing natural about how "nature veal" is raised. Instead of being fed hay or being allowed to graze, calves destined for making nature veal are fed milk formula for about four months so their flesh doesn't turn red and retains the delicate milky flavor of veal. There are people who argue that this is inhumane because the calves aren't allowed to graze and exercise and are kept isolated in small pens. Others insist that the treatment is humane, that the pens provide ample room and are kept spotlessly clean. I've never visited a veal farm, so I can't form my own opinion, but it is possible to order veal from small farms that raise their calves in a traditional way, letting them drink their mother's milk, and not isolating them or so tightly restricting their diet (see Sources).

VEAL CHOPS OR MEDALLIONS WITH BASIL SAUCE

CÔTES OU MEDAILLONS DE VEAU AU BASILIC

MAKES 4 MAIN-COURSE SERVINGS

This is the first recipe for veal chops listed in Escoffier's 1903 Le Guide Culinaire. His version is made by deglazing the sauté pan with white wine, giving the sauce body with glace de viande, and finishing the sauce with basil butter. This is exactly the way pan-deglazed sauces are made in French restaurants today. You may wonder why the sauce is finished with basil butter instead of just a swirl of plain butter and a little chopped basil. The reason is that if you chop basil by itself, it turns black almost immediately, but if you chop it with butter, the butter protects it from air so it retains both its color and its flavor.

4 center-cut veal rib chops, loin chops, or shoulder chops (each 10 ounces [280 g] or larger), 4 medallions (slices) boneless veal loin (each 6 to 8 ounces [170 to 225 g])

salt

pepper

5 tablespoons butter

leaves from 1 small bunch basil (about 15 leaves, or ¼ cup [15 g] tightly packed)

½ cup [125 ml] white wine

2 tablespoons glace de viande or commercial concentrated demi-glace, or ¾ cup [185 ml] concentrated Brown Chicken Broth (page 209) or veal broth (page 219) (optional)

SEASON the chops or medallions with salt and pepper. Ideally, this should be done 2 hours before and the moisture drawn out by the salt patted off immediately before sautéing.

HEAT 2 tablespoons of the butter over medium to high heat, until it foams, in a sauté pan just large enough to hold the chops or medallions. Sauté the chops for 5 to 7 minutes—less if you're sautéing medallions—on each side, until both sides are golden brown and the veal bounces back when you poke it with your finger. If you're not sure it's done, cut into a piece. (If you're sautéing a chop, cut along the bone, where it will be least done and where the cut will be least conspicuous.) When done, the inside of the veal should be pink but not shiny.

WHILE the veal is sautéing, chop the basil with the rest of the butter.

TAKE the veal out of the pan and reserve it in a warm place on a heated platter. Pour the cooked butter out of the pan and pour in the wine. (Escoffier says to leave the butter in the sauce, but I find the sauce rich enough and the butter is often too cooked.) Reduce the wine by about half and whisk in the glace de viande, demi-glace, or broth. If you're using glace or demi-glace, to get it to dissolve you may need to thin the sauce with a little broth or water. If you're using broth, boil the sauce down until it becomes lightly syrupy.

WHEN the sauce has the consistency you like, whisk in any liquid released by the veal. Whisk in the basil butter. Season the sauce with salt and pepper and spoon it over the veal on individual heated plates, or pass it, in a sauceboat, at the table.

Variations: In classic French cooking, veal chops are subjected to fanciful tricks, such as stuffing (a deep slit is made in the side of the chop and duxelles or other ingredients are sneaked in), breading (à l'anglaise, see page 304), coating with thick sauces and then breading, and cooking en papillotte (baking in a parchment-paper envelope). In eighteenth-century recipes, veal chops are larded not only with fatback but with truffles, ham, even anchovies. Today, the diner is more likely to encounter a veal chop simply sautéed and served with a more or less simple sauce.

Veal chops, because they are expensive, and are leaner and more delicately flavored than pork or lamb chops, call for less aggressive treatment. I wouldn't make a mustard sauce for them, as I would for pork, or a garlicky sauce, as I might for lamb. Since I'm spending a lot of money anyway, I'm likely to go for luxurious ingredients such as wild mushrooms and truffles. One of my favorite sauces is constructed like the basil sauce given above, but Madeira replaces the white wine, cream or plain butter replaces the basil butter, and morels (sautéed first if fresh; soaked in the Madeira, and the soaking liquid incorporated into the sauce, if dried) are simmered in the sauce at the last minute, just long enough to heat them through. I sometimes add quickly blanched fresh green beans or fresh fava beans to a morel sauce for contrasting color and texture.

LAMB: Other than whole roasting cuts such as racks, legs, and saddles (see Chapters 31 and 37), most lamb is sold in chops. Shoulder chops, which have an irregular muscle structure and a lot of connective tissue, are better suited for stewing than they are for sautéing or grilling. I often buy shoulder chops when I'm at the supermarket and can't find lamb stew meat. I just cut the meat off the bones and simmer it, along with the bones (which contribute flavor and which I remove before serving), in a stew. Rib chops are made by cutting between the ribs of a rack; because they are lean and tender, they should be sautéed or grilled. If the chops are taken from a very small rack of lamb, such as New Zealand lamb or small farm-raised lamb, they are usually cut into double chops or even quadruple chops, each with two or four ribs; otherwise they are simply too small. Loin chops are prepared by cutting the half saddle crosswise; like other loin chops, they look like miniature T-bone steaks. Loin chops may come in almost any thickness because there are no ribs to dictate where the butcher cuts them. Occasionally (more likely in Great Britain), you'll see double loin chops, which are made by cutting the whole saddle crosswise. A double loin chop has two pieces of loin muscle and two pieces of tenderloin. Some butchers sell lamb loin—the completely boned ribeye and loin muscles—which you can cut into noisettes. These boneless cuts are, needless to say, very expensive because they are all meat.

LAMB CHOPS WITH GARLIC AND MARJORAM

CÔTELETTES D'AGNEAU À L'AIL ET À LA MARJOLAINE

MAKES 4 MAIN-COURSE SERVINGS

Since half the year I have marjoram growing in my garden and there's always plenty of garlic around, this is the dish that often comes about when I decide to sauté lamb chops. Garlic is a natural with lamb, but you can always substitute shallots or a little onion. Marjoram is one of my favorite herbs. Don't confuse it with oregano, whose flavor is more aggressive and is better on grilled foods. If you don't grow marjoram and can't find it at the greengrocer, substitute thyme or a little fresh sage. A lot of cooks associate rosemary with lamb, but I find rosemary so aggressive that I prefer to sprinkle it, chopped fine, on grilled foods or wet it and put it right on the fire so it smoulders and contributes its flavor more subtly.

I deglaze the pan used for sautéing the lamb with white wine, chopped garlic, and marjoram, and then add concentrated broth (ideally made from lamb trimmings), if I have it. I finish the sauce with a little swirl of butter, season it with salt and pepper, and serve it at the table in a sauceboat. I don't use too much butter, because lamb is rich and the sauce, rather than being thick, should have the consistency of a jus. If you end up with very little sauce—because you didn't use broth—spoon ½ tablespoon over each chop before serving. Both clarified butter and olive oil are ideal for sautéing lamb chops because they can be heated to a very high temperature before you put in the meat. If you have very thick chops, you can use whole butter because the chops can be cooked at a lower temperature—they'll have more time to brown before they overcook.

8 rib or loin lamb chops if cut from large American lamb, or 8 double rib chops or inch-thick loin chops if cut from baby lamb such as New Zealand lamb (about 2 pounds total)

   salt

   pepper

1 teaspoon fresh marjoram leaves

1 teaspoon olive oil (for chopping the marjoram)

2 tablespoons clarified butter, whole butter, or olive oil (for sautéing)

½ cup [125 ml] dry white wine

1 large clove garlic, chopped fine, crushed to a paste with the side of a chef's knife

½ cup [125 ml] brown lamb broth, brown beef broth (page 219), or Brown Chicken Broth (page 209)

4 tablespoons butter (for finishing the sauce)

SEASON the lamb chops with salt and pepper—ideally 1 or 2 hours before sautéing—and pat them dry just before you put them in the pan. (Seasoning ahead of time causes the salt and pepper to penetrate the meat and allows you to pat off the moisture drawn out by the salt, which would inhibit browning.)

STIR the marjoram leaves with the olive oil, chop them fine, and reserve.

HEAT the butter or oil in a sauté pan just large enough to hold the chops. If you're using clarified butter or oil, heat it until it ripples before putting in the chops. If you're using whole butter, wait until it foams and the foam begins to subside. Arrange the chops in the pan and brown them from 2 to 5 minutes on each side, depending on their thickness. I calculate 2 to 2½ minutes on each side per ½ inch [1.5 cm] of thickness. When the chops are browned on both sides and bounce back to the touch, or are a juicy pink when you cut into one, transfer them to hot plates and pour the cooked fat out of the pan.

POUR the wine into the still-hot pan and immediately stir in the garlic and marjoram. Boil the wine

down by half. If you're using broth, pour it in and reduce the sauce again by half. (The exact amount of reduction will depend on the concentration of your broth. Keep the sauce light and don't let it get syrupy.) Whisk in the 4 tablespoons of butter and season to taste with salt and pepper. Spoon the sauce over the chops or serve it at the table in a sauceboat.

Variations: You can fool around with the usual sauce variations (see page 484) by adding different aromatic vegetables, substituting slightly sweet or fortified wines for the dry white wine, and finishing the sauce with different herbs or herb butters. Lamb chops are also delicious when grilled and served simply. Use a good hot fire. (See "Grilling," page 489.)

Classic lamb chop recipes in Escoffier may be what gave French classic cooks the reputation of not ever leaving a good thing alone. The poor chops are flattened, breaded, stuffed, and cooked and cooked again until they're hopelessly rich and their innocence is lost. Breading was the favorite habit, but instead of being simply breaded *à l'anglaise* (see page 304)—with flour, eggs, and bread crumbs—the chops were often coated with thick sauces (usually *sauce parisienne*, a velouté thickened with egg yolks) before being wrapped in caul fat and coated again with bread crumbs and plenty of butter. Even grilled chops didn't escape the breading treatment and were breaded by being first dipped in butter and then in the bread crumbs, a method called *paner au beurre* or *paner à la française*. To me, none of these treatments improves a simple grilled or sautéed chop.

Lamb loins can be cut into noisettes in the same way as pork tenderloins—they're usually about the same size, except that lamb loins don't taper. They can then be quickly grilled or sautéed in the same way as chops.

BUYING LAMB

There are four distinct categories of lamb, although recently the distinctions among the four have broken down somewhat. Baby milk-fed lambs that have pure white flesh—even paler than veal—are sold whole for a few weeks around Easter and are roughly the size of suckling pigs. Their tender meat is very delicate and they're best roasted. You can also buy sections of the baby lamb such as the baron, the whole rear end of the animal that comprises part of the saddle and the two hind legs. Second, there is "spring lamb," which used to be available from March through October, and is now available year-round, making the term meaningless.

"Regular" lambs are grown larger than in the past and, at least to my palate, often have a strong, unpleasant gamey taste, more like mutton. When buying any cut of lamb, look for lower weights, which indicate that the lamb was slaughtered at a younger age, and ideally that it was from a small farm (see Sources). Don't confuse regular lamb, which has red flesh, with milk-fed lamb that is very small and has white flesh like veal. You can also buy New Zealand lamb, which is true lamb because it is small and young. The only drawback to New Zealand lamb is that it has been frozen. Third, there are yearlings, which are larger and have an even stronger flavor. Last is mutton, which is meat from a two-year-old castrated male—the ovine equivalent to a steer. I've never seen authentic mutton in the United States and rarely ever see it in France. It is most popular in England.

ROAST RACK OF LAMB WITH PARSLEY AND GARLIC CRUST

CARRÉ D'AGNEAU PERSILLÉ

HOW TO	HOW TO	HOW TO	WHAT ARE	HOW TO
ROAST RED MEATS AND KNOW WHEN THEY'RE DONE	PREPARE AND ROAST RACKS AND SADDLES OF LAMBS	USE BRINE TO ENHANCE PORT ROASTS	CROWN ROASTS AND WHY SHOULD THEY BE AVOIDED?	USE MEAT TRIMMINGS TO ENHANCE THE FLAVOR OF A "JUS"

MOST OF US EAT RACK OF LAMB IN RESTAURANTS, WHERE IT'S OFTEN the most expensive item on the menu, instead of at home. Home-cooked lamb is more likely to be a roast leg (see page 430), a lamb stew (see page 440), or maybe lamb chops (see page 503). The rack of lamb intimidates, in part, no doubt, because of its price, and in part because it comes trimmed differently and to different degrees, depending on the skill and generosity of your butcher. But rack of lamb, like other roasts, makes far more sense to have at home, where you can carve it at the table—it's one of the easiest of all roasts to carve. In a restaurant, for the most part, it arrives already sliced into chops, the dramatic presentation of the whole rack and the ritualistic carving lost.

As with any roast, the only trick to cooking a rack of lamb is to cook it just the right amount, which for lamb is rare (but not too rare) to medium rare. To me, rack of lamb should be roasted to a higher internal temperature than rare beef, but it should never be cooked beyond the point where it loses most of its color—not medium, and never medium well. If you like your lamb cooked more than medium rare, instead of a rack roast a leg of lamb, which takes better to more cooking. It's easy enough to tell when the rack is done—in a surprisingly short amount of time, about 25 minutes—by sticking an instant-read thermometer into the center. The thermometer should read 125°F [51°C] for rare or 130°F [54°C] for medium rare. These temperatures will rise slightly when you let the rack rest. If you don't have a thermometer, you can judge the doneness of the rack by pressing on it at both ends with the middle finger of each hand. It's done as soon as it springs back to the touch instead of feeling fleshy.

You'll find dozens of recipes for rack of lamb in French cookbooks, but the basic method for roasting the rack is virtually the same in all of them. The differences involve either the garniture, vegetables that are cooked separately or in the pan with the rack; the *jus* or gravy, to which various ingredients such as wine, herbs, tomato purée, or thickeners such as cornstarch are sometimes added; and occasionally, as for *carré d'agneau persillé*, the application of a crust, which usually contains bread crumbs (or occasionally ground nuts), often garlic, and usually herbs such as parsley.

———○———

JUS AND GRAVY FOR RED MEAT ROASTS

In Chapter 26 I discussed how to make a *jus* or gravy (a thickened *jus*) from the pan drippings from a roast chicken or turkey, but making a *jus* from red meat roasts requires a slightly different approach. This is because red meats such as lamb, beef, and venison are cooked to a lower internal temperature so that they stay red or pink in the middle. And meats cooked to a lower temperature release few juices, if any. In classic French cooking, the amount and flavor of roast meat juices is enhanced by roasting the meat over a bed of meat trimmings and sometimes bones and vegetables—called a *fonçage*—so that the trimmings provide the necessary juices. This method works as well for red meats as it does for white meats, but there's a problem. The relatively short cooking time for red meat roasts doesn't give the trimmings enough time to brown, caramelize, and release their flavorful juices before the roast is done. Because of this, the *fonçage* ingredients should be browned—either in the oven or on top of the stove—in the roasting pan before the cooking of the roast begins or after, while the roast is resting. It's also possible to make a "fake" *jus* (see pages 4 and 356) with appropriate meat trimmings and just forget about making a *jus* or gravy at the last minute.

WHAT A RACK OF LAMB IS AND HOW TO BUY ONE

Lambs are cut across into four wholesale pieces called primal (not to be confused with prime) cuts: the shoulder, the rack, the saddle, and the baron, which is the loin with the two legs left attached. A double rack of lamb, the cut sold to your butcher, is essentially the middle of the lamb's rib cage; it contains 16 chops, eight ribs on each side. One or two ribs are often left attached on each side of the saddle—nearer the rear of the animal—and four or five are left attached to each side of the shoulder. Most of us, unless we've worked in restaurants, never see a double rack of lamb; we only see the racks of lamb that are made by sawing the double rack in half. These "single" racks are then sold whole or are sliced into rib chops.

If you buy your rack of lamb at the supermarket, you're likely to be sold the single rack, untrimmed. This can be a problem because half the spinal bones—the chine bones—that unite the ribs are left attached to the rack, making it impossible to carve the rack by slicing between the ribs. Sometimes the butcher will have made cuts through the chine bones, so you can get the knife through when carving. This way he can charge you for the bone, which is better cut off entirely. If you're buying your rack at the butcher's, ask him if the chine bone has been sawed off. If it hasn't, ask the butcher to saw it off and give it to you for the roasting pan.

Once you've settled the chine problem, look at the rack and notice the length of the ribs. The tip of the ribs should be no farther than 4 inches [10 cm] from the round of meat in the center of the rack, the rib eye. Look at the rack on both the loin end (the back end that was once connected to the saddle) and the shoulder end. (You'll notice that the loin end is much neater, while the shoulder end has a variety of different muscles, separated by fat.) For the rack to be called "oven ready," 1 inch [2.5 cm] of fat and rib should have been cut off so the distance from the ends of the ribs to the rib-eye muscle is 3 inches [7.5 cm] instead of 4 [10 cm]. It's perfectly fine to cook the rack this way. Just have the butcher trim off the outer membrane and any thick layers of fat—but have him leave a thin layer of fat covering the rib eye and remove the shoulder blade. If you bought your rack at the supermarket, you can do this trimming at home (see page 509).

FRENCHING A RACK OF LAMB: If you want to achieve the ultimate dramatic effect, a rack of lamb must be frenched. This simply means that the ribs must be sawed or hacked off with a cleaver about 3 inches [7.5 cm] from the rib eye (the solid round muscle that runs the length of the rack) and that fat and meat covering the last 2 inches [5 cm] of the ribs must then be removed, leaving the clean ribs exposed and only an inch-wide strip of fat and/or meat covering the ribs (1 inch out from the rib eye). Unless you go to a very fancy or cooperative butcher, you may have to do this yourself. There's nothing terribly tricky about it, but until you get the knack it can be tedious. Turn the rack so that what was the animal's back is facing up. Make a slit in the fat and meat, 1 inch from the rib-eye muscle, first on the loin side (which looks neater and more compact), where you should cut all the way down to the rib, and then on the shoulder side, where the knife will run into the cartilaginous shoulder blade. Join these two marks by cutting through the fat and meat all the way down to the ribs. As you cut across each rib, push the knife down between the ribs so it comes out on the inside (the concave side) of the rack. When you get to the shoulder blade, cut away the fat that covers it and then slice under the shoulder blade and remove it. (I throw it out since it contributes little to the roasting juices.) Cut down to the ribs, again connecting the two slits at each end with a straight line, and again poking the knife so it sticks out through the ribs on the other side.

There are two ways to trim the ribs, which must be left with no meat or membrane attached or they will burn during roasting and make the rack unattractive. The more straightforward, but more time-consuming, method is to simply cut off the layer of fat and meat that covers the ribs from where you made the line connecting the two slits and then scrape the ribs free of fat and membrane.

The second method allows you to peel the layer of meat and fat away from the ribs so that the ribs are left completely clean. To do this, turn the rack over so you're looking at the inner side of the ribs. You'll see a row of tiny slits that you made when you poked the knife through when cutting through the fat on the other side. With a sharp paring or boning knife, make a line, as you did on the other side, cutting through the thin membrane that covers the bones. Cut down so that you're also cutting through the membrane that covers the sides of the ribs. Scrape the knife against the bone, to help cut through the membrane and expose the bone. Next, cut through the membrane along the center of each of the ribs—moving parallel with the ribs—starting at the horizontal cut you made through the membrane and continuing all the way out to the end of the ribs. Use the knife to push and scrape, not cut, the membrane off the ribs, pushing it to the side of each of the ribs. When you've moved the membrane completely to the side of each of the ribs, use the back of the knife to push the membrane down and away from the eye. It's important at this point not to cut through the membrane.

Now, use a kitchen towel to grip the layer of meat and fat that covers the ribs. Grip it tightly, right up against the first rib on the loin end, and peel it back from the ribs, one at a time, so that it comes off in a single strip and leaves the ribs perfectly white. If there are pieces of meat or membrane left attached to the ribs, scrape them off with a knife.

At this point, you need to cut off the outermost 2 inches [5 cm] of the ribs so only 1 inch [2.5 cm] of a rib is left attached to the rack. To do this, place the rack with the outer, rounded side facing down on a cutting board. Cut the ribs, one at a time, using a sharp, quick whack with a cleaver.

TRIMMING THE RIB EYE: *Regardless of whether or not you're frenching a rack of lamb,* the thin membrane, the fat, and meat that cover the rib eye, especially on the shoulder end, need to be trimmed. Some butchers remove all the fat and most of the meat that covers the shoulder end, but this wastes much of the tasty meat covering the shoulder. My favorite method, and the one usually used in France, is to cut through the layer of fat crosswise down the middle of the rack to between ⅛ inch and ¼ inch [about .5 cm] away from the rib-eye muscle, being very careful not to cut all the way down (much less into) the rib-eye muscle itself. I peel this whole thick layer of meat and fat away from the shoulder end and then just lightly trim the membrane and fat off the loin end, again leaving a layer between ⅛ inch and ¼ inch thick [about .5 cm]. This method leaves some of the meat attached to the shoulder end but ensures that the rack will cook evenly.

BREAKING DOWN A WHOLE DOUBLE RACK AT HOME

Start by feeling the bones running along the back of the double rack with your fingers. Carefully slide a boning knife along one side of the bones until it hits bone and won't go any farther. Continue, cutting the rib-eye muscle away from the center bones by following the bone contours until you separate the meat from the small ridge that runs along one side of the center bones and close to where the ribs join at the middle. Don't cut beyond this point or you'll completely separate the rib-eye muscle from the ribs.

Turn the rack around and repeat on the other side of the center bones. Stand the double rack on end and press the two sides of the rib cage together so you create a space between the rib-eye muscles and the center bones. With a cleaver, using quick, abrupt motions, cut through the ribs where they join the center bones at the spine. Slant the cleaver slightly toward the center so you don't accidentally cut into any of the rib-eye muscle. Continue in this way until you've cut through and separated six of the ribs from the center bones. Repeat on the other side of the center bones, this time continuing all the way down to the cutting board and completely separating the second rack from the center bones. Go back to the first rack and use the cleaver to chop away the center bones. Chop up the bones and save them for the roasting pan. (These and most of the other butchering and carving techniques called for in this book are illustrated in my book *Essentials of Cooking.*)

RACK OF LAMB WITH PARSLEY AND GARLIC CRUST

CARRÉ D'AGNEAU PERSILLÉ

MAKES 8 MAIN-COURSE SERVINGS

Traditionally, a rack of lamb consists of eight ribs, so that each person gets 2 rib chops; but some racks of lamb, such as the baby lamb racks from New Zealand, are so small that 2 rib chops aren't enough and you're better off serving 4 chops—half a rack—per person.

2 racks of lamb, trimmed and frenched (about 1½ to 2 pounds [675 to 900 g] each after trimming and frenching), trimmings reserved if you're preparing a jus (frenching optional; see page 509), or 4 trimmed and frenched New Zealand racks (12 ounces [340 g] each)

1 pound [450 g] lamb stew meat or lamb shoulder (if you're making a jus and don't have any trimmings)

1 medium-size onion, chopped coarse (if you're making a jus)

1 medium-size carrot, chopped coarse (if you're making a jus)

salt

pepper

3 tablespoons butter, at room temperature

4 slices dense-crumb white bread such Pepperidge Farm, crusts removed, ground for 1 minute in a food processor, or 1 cup [45 g] fresh bread crumbs

1 bunch parsley, chopped fine just before using

4 cloves garlic, chopped fine, crushed to a paste with the side of a chef's knife

2 cups [500 ml] Brown Chicken Broth (page 209) or beef broth (see page 219) (if you're making a jus)

½ cup [125 ml] dry white wine

PREHEAT the oven to 450°F [230°C/gas mark 8].

IF you're making a jus using lamb trimmings, trim the meat away from the fat on the trimmings and discard the fat. Cut the meat into thin strips, about ½ inch [1.5 cm] on each side. If you're using lamb shoulder meat, cut it into thin strips. If you're using stew meat, cut it into cubes or strips about ½ inch [1.5 cm] on each side. Spread the meat trimmings, onion, and carrot in a roasting pan or an ovenproof oval gratin dish just large enough to hold the racks. Slide the pan into the oven and roast until the trimmings and vegetables start to brown and release their juices, about 25 minutes.

SEASON the racks with salt and pepper. Put them, fat-side up, in the roasting pan on top of the trimmings—or if you're not making a jus or are making a "fake" jus (see pages 4 and 356), just put them in a roasting pan large enough to hold them. Slide the pan into the oven.

WHILE the lamb is roasting, work together the butter, bread crumbs, parsley, garlic, salt, and pepper in a mixing bowl with a wooden spoon. When the lamb has been roasting about 10 minutes, take it out of the oven and evenly spread the outside (the fat side) of each rack with the parsley mixture. Keep the rack facing down in the pan so the bread-crumb mixture doesn't fall off. Return the lamb to the oven and roast for 15 to 20 minutes more for an American rack or 5 to 10 minutes more for a New Zealand rack, or until an instant-read thermometer stuck into the middle of the rib eye reads from 125°F to 130°F [51° to 53°C] (keeping in mind that the temperature will increase as the racks rest), or until the meat just begins to spring back when you press on it at both ends. Transfer the racks to a heated plate, cover them loosely with aluminum foil, and keep them in a warm place—such as the back of the stove or the turned-off oven with the door open—for 15 minutes.

IF you're making a jus, pour 1 cup of the broth and the wine into the roasting pan with the trimmings or stew meat and place the pan on the stove over high heat. Stir the trimmings as the broth is boiling and continue for about 5 minutes, until all the broth has evaporated and caramelized on the surface of the pan, leaving only a layer of clear liquid fat. Tilt the roasting pan and spoon out and discard the hot fat. Stir in the rest of the broth and set the roasting pan back on the stove over low to medium heat, so it's gently simmering, and stir for about 5 minutes to dissolve the caramelized juices. Pour any juices released by the racks on the plate into the juices. Strain the *jus* and serve it in a heated sauceboat. Arrange the racks on a heated platter. If you're serving 2 racks, face them toward each other, with the ribs of each one interlaced with the ribs of the other.

CARVING: Set a small cutting board at the head of the table—or directly in front of where whoever is carving will sit—and place the platter behind the cutting board. With the carving fork and knife, transfer the racks to the cutting board. Slice between individual ribs and place 2 ribs per person on heated plates. (If you're serving New Zealand racks, cut between every *other* rib and serve each person 2 double rib chops.) Traditionally, rack of lamb is carved alternating between the shoulder end and the loin end so no one person gets stuck with only shoulder chops while someone else gets the loin chops. Pass the *jus* for guests to serve themselves.

Variations: Most of the classic presentations of rack of lamb differ only in the accompaniments. Potatoes, in one form or another, are deservedly part of many classic recipes. *Carré d'agneau à la beauharnais* is served with *pommes noisettes* (potatoes scooped into hazelnut shapes with a tiny melon baller–like device made specially for this), browned in butter, and artichoke bottoms filled with béarnaise sauce. *Carré d'agneau à la bonne femme* is made by roasting the rack at a lower temperature than usual (so the surrounding vegetables have time to cook through) in a Dutch oven (*cocotte*) surrounded with small onions, strips of bacon (*lardons*), and again melon-ball potatoes, but slightly larger ones than *pommes noisettes* (and fitting with the French addiction to nomenclature, given another name, *pommes parisiennes*). *Carré d'agneau parmentier* is made by cooking the rack of lamb with diced potatoes. While some garnitures get progressively more rococo and impractical, others are relatively straightforward and just plain delicious. *Carré d'agneau à la bordelaise* contains potatoes shaped to look like olives

(you can use little new potatoes, with their peels, instead) and thickly sliced cèpes (porcini) cooked together with the rack. My own garnitures are dictated by what I spot at the market and how hard I'm trying to impress. If I really want to show off, I make the vegetable stew on page 584 and spoon it around the rack on the platter; but usually I serve potatoes (like the *gratin dauphinois* on page 571 or the sautéed potatoes on page 601), or spinach (blanched, lightly creamed), and often sautéed cultivated or wild mushrooms. I also like to serve tomatoes *à la provençal* (see page 565); they look pretty on the platter and their garlicky flavor goes well with lamb.

If I'm making a *jus* (see page 507), I add a little dry white wine to give it a bit of vinous acidity. Chopped herbs such as chives or fresh marjoram wake up the *jus* and make it look prettier on the plate.

The bread-crumb crust is certainly not essential. Coating roasts with bread crumbs is a holdover from the seventeenth- and eighteenth-century habit of coating roasts with various mixtures, such as chopped aromatic vegetables, and securing the mixtures against the roast with buttered parchment paper or caul fat. This was a method that augmented the flavors of the *jus* when roasts were cooked in front of a fire on a spit, in the same way a *fonçage* (the base of aromatic vegetables, meat trimmings, and/or bones; see page 507) contributes flavor to roasts cooked in the oven. But essential or not, a flavorful crust contributes texture and flavor that both contrast with and support those of the meat. Chopped nuts can replace some or all of the bread crumbs; herbs such as marjoram (my favorite), thyme, rosemary, sage, or lavender can replace the parsley; but nothing really can replace the garlic. The crust can also be replaced with a "rub." Rubs, as their name implies, are mixtures that are rubbed on roasts to contribute flavor. They can be pastes of herbs and garlic ground with a mortar and pestle; mixtures of dried spices, moistened or not; or finely ground dried mushrooms such as cèpes or morels.

For some unfathomable reason, cooks setting out to serve a luxurious roast think first of a crown roast. A crown roast is simply two or more racks of lamb, veal, or pork in which incisions are made between the ribs on the inside so that the roast can be wrapped into a circular shape with the ribs sticking out all along the top, forming the distinctive crown. The problem is that the inside of the rib eye, the juiciest part of the roast, is exposed by the incisions, allowing the juices to escape. At the same time, the meat exposed by these cuts never really browns properly, so a crown roast can never be as juicy, as perfectly cooked, or—to my mind—as attractive as a simple rack. To be blunt, a crown roast is just a pretentious way of serving a rack.

ROAST SADDLE OF LAMB WITH BASIL-SCENTED JUS

SELLE D'AGNEAU RÔTIE AU BASILIC

MAKES 6 MAIN-COURSE SERVINGS

When you ask for a whole saddle of lamb, be prepared for a certain amount of confusion. The butcher's likely never to have sold one, even though the saddle is the most tender and delicious cut of lamb, outdoing even the rack because it contains no fatty shoulder-end chops. In case you're wondering what happens to all those saddles of lamb, they're turned into lamb loin chops—which look like miniature T-bone steaks—by using the bandsaw to first cut the saddle in half lengthwise and then to cut it crosswise into chops. Since there are no ribs dictating the thickness of the chops, loin chops can vary from ½ inch to 2 inches [1.5 to 5 cm] thick.

If you want to get a sense of where the saddle is on the lamb's body, feel the back of your torso and locate the base of your rib cage, which is the bottom of your very own rack—the loin end—and the top part of your saddle, which extends all the way down to the small of your back. Actually, with a saddle of lamb, one or two ribs are usually left attached, so don't be surprised when you see them. You or the butcher will be removing them.

Chances are, when you get your whole saddle, your butcher is going to ask all sorts of confusing questions about what you plan to do with it. Or if he's a grouch, he'll just hand it over and let you figure it out. Don't panic, a saddle is easy to trim—much easier than a rack. The saddle is well named because that's just what it looks like. There will be a thick center loin section with rather long flaps hanging down on both sides—these are what you feel if you put your hands on your hips, and on a steer they are called flank steaks. If you look at the saddle from one end, you'll notice two large muscles on top that run its length. These are the loin muscles, which are an extension of what was the rib eye on the rack. You'll also notice two smaller muscles on the underside. These are the tenderloins, sometimes called fillets. Occasionally you may run into a saddle with the kidneys and surrounding fat still attached. Here's what to do or have the butcher do: Pull out the kidneys and fat. Let the butcher keep the fat—he'll be delighted, since butchers sell lamb fat for turning into cosmetics—and unless you like grilled lamb's kidneys (see Chapter 39), tell him he can keep the kidneys.

Now have him cut off the flaps about ½ inch [1.5 cm] away from where they join the center loin, being careful not to leave any of the loin meat attached to the flaps. This may also require removing the one or two ribs often left attached to each side of the saddle by sliding a small boning knife or paring knife under the ribs where they join the loin muscle and then just twisting them off. Be sure the butcher gives you the flaps and the ribs so you can use them in the roasting pan for your fonçage. Next, have him trim off the outer membrane and most of the fat that covers the outer loin muscles, but be sure he leaves a thin layer of white fat—between ⅛ and ¼ inch [about .5 cm] thick—covering the outer part of the loin. The saddle is now ready for roasting. Now, unless he's very cooperative indeed, you'll need to trim the flaps yourself. They're mostly fat, but they contain a nice flat sheet of meat that will add a lot of flavor to your jus. (Some butchers trim the flaps while leaving them attached to the rest of the saddle, roll them under, and tie the whole saddle up with string. This method will give you more meat, since you'll be able to serve the flaps along with everything else. But it makes it difficult to cook the saddle evenly, because the heat has to get through the flaps to the tenderloins, by which time you may overcook the loin muscles.)

To trim the flaps, place them one at a time flat on a cutting board and slide a thin, flexible knife under the flat piece of meat that runs along the inner side of the flap. Keep the flap taut and peel back the flap of meat as it comes away from the fat. When you've separated the meat from the fat, discard the fat and cut the flap meat into strips about ¼ inch [.5 cm] on each side, to use in the roasting pan. When preparing the aromatic ingredients— the meat strips and vegetables—that go under the saddle in the roasting pan, keep in mind that they should be browned for about 45 minutes in a 425°F [220°C/gas mark 7] oven before the roast is added, or they won't have time to release their juices (see page 507).

If your butcher doesn't have a saddle with the flaps attached, buy 1 or 2 shoulder lamb chops so you'll have some meat for your fonçage.

1 saddle of lamb (6 to 8 pounds [2.7 to 3.6 kg], including flaps, kidneys, fat, etc., before trimming; or 3 to 4 pounds [1.3 to 1.8 kg] after trimming and removal of the flaps)

1 small onion, peeled, quartered

1 medium-size carrot, sliced

2 cloves garlic, crushed

2 pounds lamb stew meat, or 2½ pounds [1.1 kg] lamb shoulder chops, bones removed and saved (if your saddle comes without flaps)

salt

pepper

2½ cups [625 ml] Brown Chicken Broth (page 209) or beef broth (page 219)

½ cup [125 ml] dry white wine

10 basil leaves

1 teaspoon olive oil

PREHEAT the oven to 425°F [220°C/gas mark 7].

TRIM the saddle as described in the headnote and spread the strips of meat from the flaps, the onion, carrot, and garlic in a roasting pan just large enough to hold the saddle. If your saddle comes without flaps, put the lamb stew meat, cut into 1-inch [2.5 cm] cubes, in the bottom of the pan with the vegetables instead. Slide the pan—without the saddle— into the oven and roast the meat trimmings and vegetables until they brown and have released their juices, about 45 minutes. (If you start roasting the meat trimmings and vegetables with the saddle, they won't have enough time to brown and release juices.)

SEASON the saddle on both sides with salt and pepper. Place it, back-side up, in the roasting pan and roast for about 25 minutes, until an instant-read thermometer stuck into the center of one of the loin muscles reads 115°F [46°C]. Turn the saddle over, so the tenderloins are on top, and roast for about 10 minutes more, until the thermometer stuck into the center of the tenderloins reads 125°F [50°C] (for rare to medium rare).

TRANSFER the saddle to a heated plate while you prepare the *jus*. Pour 1 cup [250 ml] of the broth and the wine into the roasting pan and place the pan on the stove over high heat. Stir the trimmings as the broth is boiling and continue stirring for about 5 minutes, until all the broth has evaporated and caramelized on the surface of the pan, the meat trimmings, and the vegetables, leaving only a layer of clear fat. Tilt the roasting pan and spoon out and discard the hot fat. Stir in the rest of the broth, set the roasting pan back on the stove over low to medium heat—so it's gently simmering—and stir for about 5 minutes to dissolve the caramelized juices.

RUB the basil leaves with the olive oil and chop them, not too fine. Pour any juices released by the saddle on the plate into the juices in the pan. Strain the juices, stir in the basil, and serve the basil-scented *jus* in a heated sauceboat. Serve the saddle on a heated platter.

CARVING: There are two ways to carve a saddle of lamb. The first, and most elegant, is to hold the saddle in place with a fork and use a long, thin carving knife to cut lengthwise just to the right of the long series of bones (the tips of the vertebrae) that run down the center of the saddle. Cut down until you run into bone. Then slice the loin muscle lengthwise into long strips, slicing inward from the side. The first cut you make will be the layer of fat and membrane that covers the top of the meat and shouldn't be served. Continue slicing lengthwise into long strips until all the meat has been removed and you only see bone. (If the strips seem too long for your plates, cut the long muscle in half crosswise before slicing.) Turn the saddle completely around and repeat with the second loin.

TURN the saddle upside down and slide the knife along the right side of the center bones, as you did before, and then slide it, moving in from the side, against the bone underlying the tenderloins and completely separate the first tenderloin. Cut the tenderloin into strips or small rounds and serve it with the long strips. It's useful to have a small cutting board at the table to do this.

THE second carving method will provide your guests with the dainty little rounds of lamb that the French call *noisettes*. It requires that you have a cutting board in place next to the platter. Slice lengthwise along the top of the loins to remove the layer of fat and membrane. Cut along the right side of the center bones that run along the top of the saddle, keeping the knife pressed against the bones so you don't leave any meat attached to the bones, and cutting all the way down until you run into a ridge of bones. Follow the ridge, gently moving the knife along the ridge toward the side of the saddle until you've cut around it and run into another set of bones. Next, slide the knife inward from the right side, keeping the knife pressed against the bones that extend from the center bones. When you reach the center bones, the whole loin should come away from the bones. Transfer it to a cutting board and slice it into noisettes—slices between ½ inch and 1 inch [1.5 and 2.5 cm] thick. Turn the saddle around and repeat with the other loin. Turn it upside down and repeat with the tenderloins.

Variations: When I owned a restaurant in Manhattan in the early 1980s we were always strapped for funds, and while our clientele liked the food, the place lacked amenities. The dining room was always too cold in the winter, and the growling air conditioner was no match for New York's hot, humid summers. But these seasonal temperature fluctuations had the advantage of forcing us to serve food that was appropriate for the time of year. (In New York, the reverse is usually true—buildings are sweltering in winter and freezing in summer.) So the hot roasts we'd serve during the winter would metamorphose into cold variations in the summer. One of the most popular of these summer dishes was cold saddle of lamb with its cold barely-set *jus*, infused with strips of basil, spread over the top of the meat. The effect was striking because no one had ever seen lamb in such perfect strips and the cool *gelée* was refreshing to the eye and to the palate. To pull this off at home, just roast the saddle of lamb and make the *jus* in the usual way. Let the saddle cool and then refrigerate it, wrapped in plastic wrap, for a few hours or overnight. Add little strips of basil (or other herbs) to the hot *jus* and then let the *jus* set in the refrigerator. (If you're in a hurry, set the container in a bowl of ice.) Gently lift off any fat that will have floated to the top of the *jus* and congealed. Slice the saddle into strips as described above, arrange it on a chilled platter or plates, and spread the lightly congealed *jus* over the slices.

BONING AND ROASTING A WHOLE SADDLE OF LAMB

If last-minute carving in front of guests sounds like too much, bone the saddle of lamb before roasting so that all four muscles, the two loins and the two tenderloins, are tied together in a neat sausagelike package that's easy to carve—it's just sliced—at the table. Older recipes call for stuffing a boneless saddle of lamb with elaborate mousses and forcemeats, but I limit the "stuffing" to a sprinkling of herbs, salt, and pepper.

To bone a saddle of lamb, turn it upside down so the fillets are facing you. Slide a long, flexible knife under the fillets, starting from the middle and, keeping the knife pressed against the bones, working toward the outside until the tenderloin is barely hanging from the edge of the bones. If it becomes completely detached, don't worry about it. Rotate the saddle and repeat on the other side. With the tenderloin side facing you, slide the knife under the bones that were hidden by the tenderloins, between the bones and the loin muscles again, keeping the knife pressed upward against the bones so you don't lose any meat. Continue around, keeping the knife against the bone, until you come to the center of the saddle, where the ridge of bones protrudes slightly along the center of the back. Rotate the saddle again, and repeat with the other side. At this point, you will have detached the tenderloins and the loins from the bones except where the backbones attach to the membrane that connects the two sides. Cut carefully along the backbones so you don't cut through the membrane and end up cutting the saddle in half, until you've removed the bones completely. With a cleaver, chop the bones to use in the roasting pan for your *fonçage*. Season the inside of the saddle with salt and pepper and, if you like, a sprinkling of herbs (marjoram is great), and tie up the roast with string. Season the outside with salt and pepper, brown the roast in a pan on the stove, and roast it at 450°F [230°C/gas mark 8] for about 35 minutes, to between rare and medium rare (between 125°F and 130°F [50° and 54°C] when you stick an instant-read thermometer into the center of one of the loin muscles).

PORK ROASTS

French classic cooks have long been snooty about pork. In *Le Guide Culinaire*, Escoffier states that pork is better suited to home cooking than to *"la grande cuisine"*—an ungrateful attitude, considering that, at least in the kitchen, pork is by far the most versatile of animals and may very well be the tastiest. It's also the least expensive.

Like lamb, veal, and beef, pork is broken down into several primal cuts that, traditionally at least, are then made into smaller retail cuts by the butcher or restaurant. Unlike lamb and veal, which are cut crosswise into hindquarters, saddle, rack, and shoulder, pork is split lengthwise before being broken down further. In other words, unless you make special arrangements, you'll never see a saddle or double rack of pork, because the pig was already halved before it even got to the butcher.

The best cut for roasting is the loin. A whole pork loin is at least a couple of feet long, and it contains all the ribs—as many as 13—and also the back part of the loin, which is the lower saddle end (corresponding to the small of your back). The lower part of the whole loin is sawed into loin chops—those little T-bones again—and the 8 ribs closest to the loin are cut into center-cut rib chops. The ribs closest to the shoulder are cut into shoulder chops.

When most cooks set out to roast pork, they roast a boneless section of the loin, which cooks quickly and is easy to carve. But like most boneless roasts, this cut lacks flavor, especially when taken from a modern pig, which has less fat and flavor than its forebears. There's a tastier and more dramatic way to go about it. Tell your butcher you want a center-cut rack of pork and ask him to cut off the chine bone, which is the part of the spinal column left attached to the ribs. If it's left on, the roast will be impossible to carve. Ask him to trim off excess fat—but not all the way down to the meat—so the roast is covered with a layer ⅛ inch to ¼ inch [about .5 cm] thick. Be sure he gives you any bones and meat trimming so you can put them in the roasting pan. You can make a decent roast with as few as 4 chops (count 1 chop per serving unless you've got teenagers), or you can go all-out and get an 8-rib roast, which will look fabulously dramatic and, if you don't serve it all, will give you great leftovers.

You can roast the rack as is or you can french it in the same way as Rack of Lamb (see page 511) to make it far more dramatic. Notice the small oval muscle next to the main loin muscle. Cut the meat off the ends of the ribs as you would when frenching a rack of lamb (see page 509), but leave this muscle attached to the roast. This will usually leave you about 1 inch of ribs protruding from the roast.

As with all roasts, the recipes differ only in the garniture. *Carré de porc* (rack of pork) *à l'alsacienne* just means that you serve the pork surrounded with sauerkraut. When making rack of pork *à la bonne femme,* surround it with peeled baby new potatoes—browned first on the stove—and baby onions. My own favorite recipe, which also happens to be cheap and easy, is *carré de porc aux choux rouges*—rack of pork with red cabbage.

Unlike red meats such as lamb and beef, which are cooked to varying degrees of doneness, white meats such as veal and pork should always be cooked to the exact point where they're slightly pink in the center but with no hint of translucent rawness. Conveniently enough, this is always 137°F [58°C], and it is also the point when the roast springs back to the touch on all its surfaces, with no trace of fleshiness. (You can practice judging doneness by using a thermometer and then poking the roast to see what a particular temperature feels like. Soon you'll be able to do without the thermometer.) Remember, however, that for the roast to end up at 137°F [58°C], you'll have to take it out of the oven at about 133°F [55°C] and let it rest, loosely covered with aluminum foil, for 20 minutes.

ROAST RACK OF PORK WITH RED CABBAGE

CARRÉ DE PORC AUX CHOUX ROUGES

MAKES 8 MAIN-COURSE SERVINGS

1 center-cut rack of pork (8 ribs; about 6 pounds [2.7 kg]), chine bone removed (frenching optional)

salt

pepper

½ pound [225 g] ¼-inch [.5 cm] thick lean bacon slices

1 small red cabbage

½ cup [125 ml] good-quality red wine vinegar or sherry vinegar, or more to taste

PREHEAT the oven to 400°F [200°C/gas mark 6]. Rub the roast with salt and pepper and set it in an oval roasting pan or heat-proof gratin dish with a little extra room left around the roast for the cabbage. If you don't have the right size roasting pan, use a heavy-bottomed pot or Dutch oven. Slide the pan into the oven and roast until the meat feels firm to the touch when you press on it in the middle, or until a meat thermometer measures about 132°F [55°C], about 50 minutes or longer if the meat came straight out of the refrigerator.

CUT the bacon slices crosswise into little strips (lardons) ¼-inch [.5-cm] on each side. Cook the bacon in a heavy-bottom pot large enough to hold the shredded cabbage, over low to medium heat, until the strips just begin to turn crispy, about 10 minutes.

PULL off and discard any wilted outer leaves from the cabbage. Cut the cabbage in quarters, cutting through the white core at the bottom. Cut the section of core out of each quarter and discard it. Slice across the quarters, shredding the cabbage as thin as you can. (I like to use a Benriner cutter, but you can also use a knife.)

SPOON out all but about 4 tablespoons of bacon fat from the pot used to render the bacon. Discard the excess fat or save it for other uses. Put the cabbage in the pot with the bacon, stir, and cook it, partially covered, for about 15 minutes, stirring every few minutes to keep it from sticking. Stir in the vinegar. Season the cabbage to taste with salt and pepper and, if it needs it, more vinegar.

WHEN the roast has been in the oven about 30 minutes, surround it with the cabbage and bacon. It doesn't matter if you heap the cabbage up around the roast. Continue roasting until the meat is done. If during roasting you notice the cabbage drying out or browning, stir it around in the roasting pan.

PRESENT the roast at the table and carve it by just slicing between the ribs. Carving is so simple, I usually carve it on a platter and don't bother with a cutting board.

Variations: In Alsace, plums simmered in sugar syrup are served around a pork roast along with the cabbage. The sweet plums make a perfect counterpoint to the acidic cabbage. You can turn this dish into a complete meal by nestling some new potatoes into the cabbage about 10 minutes before you transfer it to the roasting pan—giving the potatoes about 25 minutes to cook through. Or try cooking cubes of apples along with the cabbage.

A CARVING TIP FOR BIG DINNER PARTIES

When serving a big roast, especially one like a turkey that requires a platter *and* a cutting board, there's often not enough room at one end of the table for the roast, the cutting board, a stack of heated plates, bottles of wine, and so on. It will make your life easier to set a small serving table next to your place and to carve there instead of at the main table. In that way, your guests get to see the carving but you have more room to work.

VEAL ROASTS

I know I'm being extravagant when the guy at the wine store asks me if he should gift wrap the half bottle I'm buying for lunch and when the butcher tells me the roast I want is a "specialty item." When you're buying your veal roast, bring a lot of cash, because with the exception of shoulder roasts, the top cuts of veal—those best for roasting—are expensive. Whole veal is cut in cross sections and is butchered in much the same way as lamb. Unlike legs of lamb, veal legs are too large to roast, but you can roast a whole top round of veal—a perfectly lean, dome-shaped piece weighing 3 to 5 pounds [1.3 to 2.3 kg]—a whole saddle, or a rack. Of the three choices, the round is the most manageable; it can be found smaller and it requires no trimming. It is also perfectly tender. Veal saddles and racks are prepared in the same way as lamb saddles and racks, except that the cooking times are longer, not just because the cuts are bigger, but because like all white meats they are cooked to 137°F [58°C]. (The meat thermometer should read 133°F [56°C] because the temperature will increase as the meat rests.)

Older recipes for round of veal—called the *noix de veau*—insist on careful larding and long braising, but veal round is so lean that even when well larded it ends up dry. The shoulder clod is less expensive and takes better to braising (see page 428). French chefs today either roast whole veal round or pot roast it with a very small amount of concentrated veal broth (a method called *à l'étuvée*), but just until it cooks through in the same way as a roast, to 132°F [55°C] (137°F [58°C] after resting). Roasting a round of veal is tricky because if overcooked even slightly it will dry out. If the oven temperature is too high, the surface of the meat will toughen or even burn, although frequent basting with butter helps avoid this problem. If the oven temperature is too low, the roast will release liquid and end up braising in its own (uncaramelized) juices, leaving the meat dry and the *jus* insipid. The trick is to brown the veal round thoroughly in clarified butter before roasting and then keep a close eye on it and adjust the oven temperature or cover or uncover the pot as needed. If the roast is browning very quickly or sizzles in the butter in the pot, turn down the oven heat or put the lid on the pot (you can also add a little broth, in which case you end up using the pot roast method whether you planned to or not). However you approach it, the idea is to get the roast to release its juices at the same rate that they caramelize. If they caramelize too quickly and threaten to burn, deglaze the pan with the broth (or water). If the roast is releasing juices and they're accumulating on the bottom of the roasting pan without caramelizing, turn up the oven heat, remove the pot lid if it was on, or, if there are a lot of juices, put the roasting pan on the stove over high heat and boil down the juices—with the roast still in the pan—until they caramelize.

You can serve roast round of veal with almost any vegetable. With most roasts, aromatic vegetables such as onions, turnips, and carrots are cooked in the pan at the same time as the roast. They can be left whole or cut into relatively large pieces to function as the garniture, or they can be cut more finely and added to the *fonçage* to add aromatic support to the *jus*. Because, when roasting a round of veal, I may be adjusting the heat in ways that could cause the vegetables to burn or not to caramelize properly, I cook the vegetables separately so I can control their cooking. I then combine them with the *jus* at the end and serve them diced, as an integral part of the *jus*, over the slices of veal. A *matignon* is almost identical to a mirepoix (a mixture of onions, carrots, and celery), except that it may sometimes contain cubes of cured ham and is always served as a garniture, whereas a mirepoix may be used just for flavoring and then be strained out. Traditionally, the vegetables and ham for the *matignon* are cut into perfect cubes, an undertaking that I think is worth the effort because you're serving the *matignon* with an elegant roast and the little cubes look great atop the slices of veal. But if you're not feeling up to elegance, just chop them roughly into pieces that are slightly smaller than ¼ inch [.5 cm] on each side. When ordering your round of veal, tell the butcher you want the "cap" (a layer of muscle that covers part of the round) removed.

BRINING

In recent years, pork has become so lean that if you're not careful and you overcook it, it will quickly dry out and toughen. Soaking a pork roast overnight in a brine made with salt and sugar and your own favorite herbs will moisten it, make it more savory, and give it a subtle sweetness. To brine a rack of pork, combine 6 quarts [6 l] of water with 6 cups [1.6 kg] of salt (preferably sea salt) and 3 cups [600 g] of granulated sugar. If you like, make a bouquet garni with 2 bay leaves, a few sprigs of fresh thyme, and a bunch of parsley. If I have them, I add a handful of fennel stalks and fronds and about 10 crushed juniper berries. Bring everything to a simmer in a big enameled iron or stainless steel pot—not tinned copper or aluminum, which would react with the brine. Simmer until the salt and sugar dissolve. Let cool. Immerse the roast in the brine and refrigerate it most of the day and overnight—a 5-pound or 6-pound [2.3- or 2.7-kg] roast with bones should stay in the brine about 24 hours. A boneless loin of pork should be brined for only 12 hours. For a more thorough curing, make the *demi-sel* on page 528.

LETTING ROASTS REST

When you take your roast out of the oven, don't carve it right away. Cover it loosely with aluminum foil (not tightly, or it will steam) and leave it in a warm place, such as the turned-off oven with the door open, for 15 to 20 minutes, depending on the size of the roast. There are several reasons for doing this. The first is to allow the heat to penetrate to the inside of the roast. When you take a roast out of the oven, it's hotter on the outside than it is in the center. If you roast the meat until the inside is at the temperature you want, the outside is going to be overcooked. But if you let the roast rest, there will be time for the heat to be distributed evenly so the inside of the roast cooks through without the outside overcooking. Second, the roast contracts as it cooks, putting the juices under pressure and toughening the meat. If you cut into a roast as soon as it comes out of the oven, you'll notice large amounts of juice spurting out onto the platter. As a roast rests, the muscle relaxes and reabsorbs the juices so they stay in the meat.

ROAST TOP ROUND OF VEAL WITH DICED AROMATIC VEGETABLES

NOIX DE VEAU RÔTIE AU MATIGNON DE LÉGUMES

MAKES 6 TO 10 MAIN-COURSE SERVINGS

1 top round of veal (3 to 5 pounds [1.3 to 2.3 kg]), without the cap

salt

pepper

10 tablespoons clarified butter (see page 296)

3 medium-size leeks, greens removed and discarded, whites halved and rinsed

1 slice prosciutto (⅛ inch [3 mm] thick; about 2 ounces [55 g]; optional)

2 medium-size turnips, peeled, cut into dice slightly smaller than ¼ inch [.5 cm] on each side

2 large or 4 medium-size carrots, peeled, cut lengthwise into 6 strips, strips sliced slightly less than ¼ inch [.5 cm] thick

2 cups [500 ml] concentrated veal or beef broth (see page 4)

2 tablespoons finely chopped parsley (chopped at the last minute)

PREHEAT the oven to 400°F [200°C/gas mark 6].

SEASON the veal on all sides with salt and pepper. Brown it on all sides over high heat in 6 tablespoons of the clarified butter in a heavy-bottomed pot that is just large enough to hold it with 1 or 2 inches [2.5 to 5 cm] left around the sides and that will fit in your oven. Be sure the pan is very hot—but not so hot that the butter smokes—before you add the veal, because veal contains a lot of water, which is released as soon as the veal is heated. At the same time, be careful not to let it burn anywhere—turn down the heat if it browns too quickly—and don't let the juices burn on the bottom of the pot. Brown the veal completely on the top, rounded side and then on the flat side; don't keep turning it over in the pan. The browning should take about 10 minutes. Slide the pot with the roast into the oven. Baste it every 5 minutes with the butter that settles to the bottom of the pot. (If you don't have a baster, tilt the pot and pull up the butter with a long spoon.) If the juices completely caramelize on the bottom of the pot, cover the pot. Keep checking the roast every 10 minutes or so, covering or uncovering as necessary to keep the juices just on the edge of caramelizing. The roast is usually done after about 45 minutes for a 3-pound [1.3 kg] roast to 1½ hours for a 5-pound [2.3 kg] roast. It's done when the internal temperature reaches 133°F [56°C], the roast springs back to the touch, and you see spots of white juices forming on the roast's surface. (The white shows that the proteins in the juices are hot enough to coagulate.)

WHILE the roast is cooking, cut the leeks into coarse julienne (see page 77 for more about leeks) and then slice the julienne so you have little squares slightly smaller than ¼ inch [.5 cm] on each side. Cut the prosciutto in ⅛-inch [3-mm] dice.

COOK the leeks, prosciutto, turnips, and carrots in the remaining clarified butter in a heavy-bottomed pot or straight-sided sauté pan over medium heat. Stir them every few minutes and regulate the heat so they soften and caramelize slowly and evenly, about 20 minutes. Pour in ½ cup of the broth, turn the heat to high, and boil down the broth while stirring until it caramelizes on the bottom of the pan. Stir enough to keep the vegetables from sticking but not so much that you break them up. Pour the rest of the broth into the vegetables and simmer for 1 minute while stirring with a wooden spoon to dissolve the caramelized juices on the bottom of the pot. Remove from the heat and reserve the mixture.

WHEN the roast is ready, transfer it to a platter and let it rest, covered loosely with aluminum foil, for about 15 minutes, during which time the internal temperature will rise to 137°F [58°C]. Stir the reserved vegetable mixture into the roasting pan so that any juices in the pot end up in the *jus*. (This is one situation in which I don't degrease the *jus*, because the fat is pure butter; but if you're watching fats or the butter smells burnt, skim off the butter with a spoon or small ladle.) Bring the *jus* to a simmer in the roasting pan and scrape against the sides and bottom of the pan with a wooden spoon to loosen any caramelized juices. Add the parsley and season to taste with salt and pepper. Carve the roast, slicing it at an angle into scallopini-like slices. Spoon the *matignon* and *jus* over each slice.

Variations: I like to add 1 pound of cremini mushrooms or 1 ounce of dried morels (morels soaked in a little Madeira or water) to the finished *jus*, cover the pot, and simmer for 10 minutes so they cook and release their own flavorful juices into the veal *jus*. I also sometimes replace the ½ cup [125 ml] of broth that's added to the vegetables with port or Madeira to give the sauce a pleasant sweetness.

ROAST BEEF

While the traditional American roast beef is the prime rib—the beef analogue to a rack—I have never encountered a beef rib roast in France. This may be because French steers are larger, which makes a rib roast ungainly to cook and serve, or because roasting is less embedded in cooking tradition in France than it is in England or America. Whatever the reason, roast beef is better suited to home cooking, or to restaurants that specialize in roast beef, where the drama of carving is an important part of the dining ritual. The French are more likely to use the rib section of the steer to make steaks with the bone removed (*entrecôtes de boeuf*) or, for a more dramatic effect, giant chops with the bone attached (see chapter 35 for more about steak cuts).

In addition to rib roasts, the steer offers several other delicious roasts that are every bit as tasty if not as exciting to look at. The tenderloin (or fillet), as its name implies, is the tenderest of the bunch and often the most expensive. Tenderloins cook quickly and evenly and come in a manageable size, usually right for about 10 people. Another luxurious cut is the shell or strip, which is analogous to the loin muscles on a saddle of lamb or veal—again, analogous to the muscles that run up and down your back on each side of your spine. Usually this muscle (actually a collection of muscles) is sliced into New York strip steaks (see Chapter 35 for more about steaks), but sections of the shell or strip make fantastic roasts, especially if the meat has been dry aged. If you're ordering a section of strip or shell for roasting, ask for the end nearest the ribs, which has a neater, more regular musculature than the rear end. You can also roast a boneless prime rib—called the rib eye—which is tender but contains more fat than the strip and lacks the drama of the big rib bones.

In France, where beef is usually served very rare, the tradition in classic cooking is to serve beef roasts with more or less elaborate sauces rather than with a simple *jus* made from the roast's drippings. This may be because a very rare roast releases hardly any juices, so you either have to make a "fake" *jus* with bones and trimmings (see page 356) or serve the roast with a sauce such as béarnaise (see page 488) or a sauce based on concentrated broth (see page 4).

ROAST WHOLE BEEF TENDERLOIN

FILET DE BOEUF RÔTI

MAKES 6 TO 10 SERVINGS

The weight of a whole tenderloin will vary depending not only on the size of the steer but on how thoroughly the tenderloin has been trimmed. (For information about trimming tenderloin yourself, see page 492.) If you buy your tenderloin from a wholesaler or from a supermarket that's trying to make it seem inexpensive, it may have a thick covering of fat. At most butcher shops and supermarkets,

this fat will have been removed and a tenderloin with the same amount of meat will weigh considerably less. At fancy shops, the little muscle running down the side of the tenderloin will also have been removed, making the tenderloin even lighter. I like to buy tenderloin with the little side muscle attached so I have the choice of leaving it on or using it make a "fake" jus as described on page 356. Count on serving 6 to 8 ounces [185 to 250 ml] of completely trimmed fillet per person.

1 whole tenderloin (6 to 7 pounds [2.7 to 3.1 kg] if the fat is left attached, 4 to 5 pounds [1.8 to 2.3 kg] if the fat has been removed, and 3½ to 4½ pounds [1.5 to 2 kg] if the side muscle has been removed)

salt

pepper

2 tablespoons clarified butter or "pure" olive oil

OPTIONAL SAUCES (3 TABLESPOONS OF SAUCE PER SERVING):

"Fake" jus, made with the side muscle (see page 356)

Béarnaise (see page 488)

Truffle sauce (see page 596)

Bordelaise sauce (see page 483)

Additional brown sauces (see page 484)

IF the roast is still coated with a thin membrane, called the silver skin, slide a paring knife under one end of the silver skin and cut, with the blade facing upward, toward the end of the silver skin, detaching it from the meat. While holding the flap of silver skin that you detached, cut along the silver skin—again with the blade facing up—in the opposite direction. Keep trimming off the silver skin in strips until you've taken it all off. Tie the roast by cutting off the thin tail where it's about 1 inch thick—usually 4 to 5 inches [10 to 12.5 cm] from the thin tip—and use several loops of string to tie it onto the thin end of the tenderloin. This method will still leave the thinner part of the roast more cooked than the thicker butt end. Most of the time this is fine, because you can serve your guests meat that's cooked either rare or medium rare. If you want your roast to cook completely evenly, cut a section off the side of the wedge end of the tenderloin and tie it to the thin end such that the roast has the same thickness its entire length.

PREHEAT the oven to 500°F [260°C/gas mark 10]. Season the tenderloin with salt and pepper and brown it in clarified butter or in oil in a large sauté pan over high heat. You'll probably need to move it around in the pan to get it to fit. (If it doesn't fit, you can cut it half—a pity if you want to present it and carve it in front of your guests. Or you can skip the initial sautéing and roast it on a sheet pan with the oven set to the highest heat.) When the roast is completely browned, slide it into the oven—you can roast it right in the sauté pan or in a roasting pan—and roast it until a ready-read thermometer stuck into the thickest part reads 120°F (for very rare) to 125°F [48° to 50°C] (for between rare and medium rare). Cover the roast loosely with aluminum foil and let it rest for 15 minutes in a warm place, such as the turned-off oven with the door cracked open. (But not the oven that was just at 500°F [260°C].)

CUT and remove the string and bring the roast out into the dining room on a heated platter. Because tenderloin is so tender, you can carve it into thick slices directly on the platter. Pass one of the sauces in a sauceboat at the table or spoon the sauce over each serving. (Traditionally, egg-yolk sauces such as béarnaise are passed and never served already on top of the meat.)

OTHER BONELESS ROASTS

Meat always ends up more flavorful when it's roasted on the bone, but boneless roasts are easier to prepare and trim (so butchers like to sell them), they cook faster, and they're easier to carve. For these reasons, you're more likely to see tenderloins and boneless pork loins at the supermarket or at the butcher's than you are a rack of pork. At fancy shops, you may also see lamb loin—the boned rib-eye or loin muscle from a rack or saddle—or veal loin, veal tenderloin, or venison loin, and of course you'll see boneless beef roasts from the rib or loin sections. Needless to say, these cuts cost a lot per pound since there's no bone or fat.

Most boneless roasts—except large beef roasts—cook surprisingly quickly, so you have to be careful not to overcook them. This is especially true with lamb and venison, which are, of course, red meats and need to be cooked less than veal or pork. I, in fact, often sauté whole lamb or venison loin or pork tenderloins (which are very small) instead of roasting them, since by the time I've thoroughly browned them on the stove, they've cooked enough. I then present them as though they were roasts and carve them at the table. (Pork tenderloins, however, are too small to present this way). Before cooking, you may instead decide to cut these roasts into noisettes (which are pieces of meat ¾ inch to 1 inch [2 to 2.5 cm] thick and 1 or 2 inches in diameter) or medallions (¼ inch to ½ [.5 and 1.5 cm] and about 3 inches across) and sauté them (see Chapter 36).

A NOTE ON SIZES OF ROASTS

Most American lamb and veal is much larger than what you would find in Europe, so the cooking times in recipes translated from French cookbooks tend to be much shorter because the roasts are smaller. If you're lucky enough to find organic lamb or veal from a small farm, the roasts will also be smaller than you'll see at a typical butcher shop. This is also true of New Zealand and Australian lamb, sold in already trimmed and frenched racks that look miniature compared to an American rack.

SAUERKRAUT WITH SAUSAGES, BACON, AND PORK SHOULDER

CHOUCROUTE GARNIE À L'ALSACIENNE

HOW TO	HOW TO	HOW TO	HOW TO	HOW TO
MAKE YOUR OWN SAUSAGE	BRAISE A SHOULDER OF PORK	MAKE YOUR OWN SAUERKRAUT	MAKE QUENELLES	COOK RED CABBAGE

MY FIRST EXPOSURE TO SAUERKRAUT WAS BY WAY OF A JAR THAT MY father kept in the back of the refrigerator along with his Limburger and Liederkranz—smelly things that the rest of the family wouldn't touch. As my tastes matured and I realized that some foods taste a lot better than they smell, sauerkraut became an essential accompaniment to beach-picnic hot dogs, its tart crunchiness being the perfect foil for rich porky things. The French, of course, have taken the ballpark frank to their own heights and serve sauerkraut on groaning platters heaped (*garnie*) with various pork sausages and pork chops and, in elegant places, with such delicacies as duck or goose confit or even foie gras.

Choucroute garnie (*choucroute* means sauerkraut; *garnie* is whatever you serve with it) comes from Alsace, which at times has been part of Germany, and at other times part of France. Because of this history, Alsace shares the Germanic taste for a wide variety of pork products, and over the years it has brought these tastes into the mainstream of French cooking, as Alsatians have moved to Paris and opened brasseries. The French word *brasserie* means brewery, and since Alsatians, like Germans, love beer, it's not hard to imagine the day when beer was brewed in the same place that food was served, as in some of today's micro-breweries.

A modern brasserie is hard to define because some are casual, inexpensive little corner places while others are chic and dressy. But certain characteristics prevail. Beer is served, and it's often on tap. In the cooler months oysters are shucked, usually outside in front. And one can always find a choucroute garnie. In short, a good brasserie provides life's essentials and what may be the world's most perfect leisurely meal: a platter of oysters, plenty of crisp Alsatian wine, and a choucroute.

Now, if you want to duplicate these conditions at home, I suggest inviting over a bunch of friends for a big Sunday lunch. It's important that no one has any dinner plans and that all dietetic considerations be put on hold. Buy lots of wine, preferably an Alsatian Riesling, Sylvaner (a crisp but humble cousin of the noble Riesling), or pinot blanc, or, for that matter, a selection of different wines. The oysters aren't essential but they're a light way to start, and nowadays most places will shuck them for you so you can dedicate your energy to the choucroute, which requires little in the way of last-minute preparation anyway.

Your choucroute can be simple or complex: You can buy the sauerkraut in bags or jars, and buy some different sausages, some slab bacon, and some pork chops. Or you can get crazy and make your own sausages, cure your own pork, and ferment your own cabbage. You can use virtually any pork products you like, but at least one (usually the bacon) should be smoked. Pork chops (smoked or plain) are sometimes sautéed and added to the sauerkraut at the end, but I like to braise a pork shoulder, which will stay more moist and will soften during braising so it melts in your mouth. (In Alsace, they use smoked pork shoulder called *Schifela*.)

If you're buying pork shoulder, you may have to buy a whole one, including the bones, rind, and a fair amount of fat, and bone and trim it yourself. A 9-pound [4.1 kg] bone-in untrimmed pork shoulder will leave you with about 5 pounds [2.3 kg] when you bone it and trim off the rind and fat. If you encounter whole shoulders that are larger than 9 pounds, ask for a 5-pound boneless Boston butt, which is the part of the shoulder best for braising.

SAUERKRAUT WITH SAUSAGES, BACON, AND PORK SHOULDER

CHOUCROUTE GARNIE À L'ALSACIENNE

MAKES 10 SERVINGS

1 boneless trimmed pork shoulder (5 pounds [2.3 kg]) or Boston butt (raw or cured into demi-sel; see page 528)

3 medium-size onions, chopped

3 cloves garlic, chopped

2 tablespoons duck fat, goose fat, or bacon fat

1 medium-size bouquet garni

1 bottle dry white wine

5 pounds [2.3 kg] sauerkraut, preferably homemade (see page 529) or sold in bags, rinsed under cold running water, excess water squeezed out

15 juniper berries

1 teaspoon caraway seeds (optional)

1¾ pound [790 g] slab bacon (without the rind; 2 pounds [900 g] with), preferably double-smoked, as lean as possible

2½ pounds [1.1 kg] garlic sausage (1 recipe Simple Garlic Sausages, page 534), pork sausages (1 recipe Pork Sausages, page 532) or boudins blancs (1 recipe Chicken Mousse Sausages, page 535), or store-bought garlic, sausage, or kielbasa

20 small new potatoes, peeled

TIE the pork shoulder with several loops of string. This not only helps it hold its shape, but makes it easier to get out of the pot.

COOK the onions and garlic over medium heat in the fat in a pot just large enough to hold the pork shoulder. When the onions turn translucent, after about 10 minutes, put in the pork shoulder and the bouquet garni and pour the wine over them. The wine should come at least halfway up the sides of the pork shoulder; if it doesn't, add a little water. Bring to a simmer on the stove, add the sauerkraut if you like it soft (see below if you like it crunchy), and bring back to a simmer. Cover the pot with a sheet of aluminum foil (shiny-side down—the shiny side is less reactive) so that moisture will drip down and baste the pork. Cook the pork shoulder on the stove over very low heat—just enough so a bubble rises up about every second—for 45 minutes. Gently turn the pork shoulder over, so the part that was above the liquid is now below. Replace the foil and simmer gently for 45 minutes more.

CRUSH the juniper berries by rocking a saucepan over them while leaning on it with all your weight. Sprinkle the juniper berries into the liquid around the shoulder. Chop the caraway seeds, wrap them in cheesecloth, and nestle the bundle next to the meat. Add the bacon in 1 or 2 pieces, and add the sauerkraut (if you like it crunchy). Cover the pot with the foil and lid and simmer gently for 30 minutes more. Nestle the sausages around the pork shoulder. (If you've bought large sausages and they're too big for the pot, cut them into 2 pieces each. Don't worry, though, if the sausages aren't completely submerged.) Add the potatoes, cover the pot as before, and simmer gently for 30 minutes, until the potatoes are easily penetrated with a knife.

GENTLY reach into the pot with a skimmer or large slotted spoon and take out the sauerkraut and potatoes. Pull out the pork shoulder and remove the string. Discard the bouquet garni and the bundle of caraway seeds. Arrange the meats, potatoes, and sauerkraut on a heated platter. Set a cutting board next to the platter so you can slice the shoulder, sausages (if they're large), and bacon. Serve a large mound of sauerkraut on each plate and top it with the various meats. Put two potatoes on each plate.

Variations: Alsatian and French cookbooks abound with choucroute garnie variations, including recipes for sauerkraut made with turnips instead of cabbage and versions containing multitudes of sausages, and smoked meats. I like to include sautéed duck breasts instead of or in addition to the pork. (Mulards are especially marvelous; for more about duck see chapter 28.) I also make a simple version in which I just cook the sauerkraut in wine and broth for about 1 hour and then serve it in a mound with sautéed or grilled pork chops, smoked or cured pork loin, or the sautéed duck breasts. If you're using pork loin, which doesn't need to be braised in the same way as shoulder, since it is more tender and needs only to be heated through, skip the initial 1-hour braising. Instead, nestle the pork loin, which should still have its bones attached, into the sauerkraut and cook it, along with the sauerkraut, for a total of only 1 hour. This is especially good when done with cured bone-in pork loin or smoked pork loin.

DEMI-SEL

Parisian charcutiers sell a variety of pork products, called *demi-sel* ("half-salt"), that have been cured in salt or brine. As is true for so many preserved things, the curing process intensifies flavors, adds complexity, and tenderizes. Since it's hard to find *demi-sel* in the United States, I make my own by rubbing pork loin, pork shoulder, pork butt (which is a part of the shoulder), or the sirloin end of a fresh ham with salt and turning it in the salt several times a day for 3 to 6 days depending on its size—3 days for a 5-pound [2.3-kg] piece and 6 days for 10-pound [4.5-kg] piece. Traditional French recipes call for *sel rose* ("pink salt"), which contains a small amount of saltpeter. The saltpeter, which is potassium nitrate, contains traces of potassium nitrite, which helps the meat retain its natural pink color instead of turning a sullen gray. Paradoxically, once the meat is cured, it has to be soaked before it is cooked to eliminate excess salt.

To cure a 5-pound [2.3-kg] boneless trimmed pork shoulder (rind and large layers of fat removed) or a 4-pound [1.8 kg] section of pork loin (ribs attached), combine 1½ cups [360 g] coarse salt with ½ cup [100 g] sugar; ½ teaspoon of saltpeter; 2 cloves of garlic, chopped fine and crushed to a paste; and 10 crushed juniper berries. (The saltpeter is optional. You can buy it at a drugstore or kitchen supply store, or see Sources.) Rub this mixture over the meat and put the meat and the mixture in a food-grade plastic tub or a stainless steel, glass, or earthenware bowl. Cover the bowl with plastic wrap and keep it in the refrigerator for 3 days. Twice a day, turn the meat in the salt mixture, which by now will contain some liquid, rubbing the wet salt paste all over the meat and rind each time. When the 3 days are up, rinse the meat with cold water, pat it dry, and wrap it in plastic wrap. It will keep, refrigerated, for at least 1 week. You can also cure the meat for up to 2 weeks to give it more flavor. If you do use this longer cure, soak the meat for 3 days in cold water, changing the water every day, before you cook it, to get rid of some of the salt. (You can also double the ingredients and the curing time, and cure a 10-pound [4.5 kg] section of ham—the sirloin end, not the shank.) When using saltpeter, immediately wash any utensils that have come in contact with it so you don't accidentally get it on any other meat. Meats that have saltpeter on them will look raw no matter how long you cook them.

SIMPLEST SHOULDERLESS CHOUCROUTE GARNIE

MAKES 4 MAIN-COURSE SERVINGS

If you're intrigued by the idea of a choucroute garnie but don't want to braise a pork shoulder, try this version, which requires only sausages and bacon.

2	tablespoons butter, duck fat or goose fat
2	medium onions, chopped
2	cloves of garlic, chopped
½	bottle of dry white wine
1	cup chicken stock
2½	pounds [1.1 kg] homemade sauerkraut
1	bouquet garni
½	teaspoon caraway seeds wrapped in cheesecloth
8	juniper berries, crushed
½	pound [225 g] thick sliced smoked bacon
1½	pounds [675 g] garlic sausage

HEAT butter or fat in a large saucepan until the fat melts. Add onions and garlic, and cook over medium heat until the onions are translucent, about 10 minutes. Add the wine and stock and bring to a boil. Lower heat to a simmer, and add sauerkraut, bouquet garni, caraway seeds, and juniper berries; cover and simmer 15 minutes. Add the bacon and simmer another 15 minutes. Nestle the sausage into the sauerkraut and simmer 30 minutes. Remove cheesecloth and serve.

HOMEMADE SAUERKRAUT

CHOUCROUTE MAISON

MAKES ENOUGH FOR ABOUT 20 SERVINGS OF CHOUCROUTE GARNIE

Unless you live near an ethnic market where you can buy "homemade" sauerkraut, your sauerkraut will be crunchier and more flavorful if you make it yourself. To make sauerkraut at home you need two things: a large nonmetal or stainless steel crock to hold the cabbage while it ferments and a cool place to store the crock of cabbage for 3 to 4 weeks. I have a big glazed terra-cotta crock, but finding it at a garage sale was just luck. A more practical solution is to use two 4-gallon [16 l] food-safe plastic buckets, which are easy to find at cooking supply stores. (Don't be tempted to use just any bucket—if you're using plastic, it must be food grade.)

You can slice the cabbage by hand with a knife or a vegetable slicer.

6	tablespoons coarse salt (for the brine), plus 12 tablespoons (for tossing the shredded cabbage)
15	pounds [6.8 kg] green cabbage

COMBINE the 6 tablespoons of coarse salt with 4 quarts [4 l] of water, bring to a boil, and boil until the salt dissolves. Let cool.

PULL off and discard any wilted outer leaves from the cabbages. Wash your hands thoroughly. Cut the cabbages vertically in half and then cut each half, through the core, in half again. Cut the core out of each quarter and discard it. Slice the cabbage quarters into thin shreds, ⅛ inch to 1/16 inch [about 3 mm] thick, with a chef's knife or plastic vegetable slicer. Put the cabbage in a colander, rinse it thoroughly under running water, squeeze out the excess water, and toss the cabbage with the 12 tablespoons of coarse salt in a large mixing bowl (you may have to work in batches). Pack the cabbage into one or two immaculately clean nonmetal food-grade containers large enough so that the containers are not more than three-quarters full. Pour in enough brine to barely cover the cabbage.

FILL two or more (depending on the number and size of your containers) large Ziplock bags with brine and place two of these on top of each container of cabbage to weight it down. (The bags are filled with brine instead of water in case one leaks.) Make sure the top of the container is completely covered with the brine-filled bags to prevent the growth of yeasts and mold. Cover the top of the container with a clean kitchen towel.

STORE the cabbage for 3 to 4 weeks in a cool place, but not in the refrigerator. Every day, skim off any mold or scum that floats to the top of the container above the bags. When the cabbage is fermented to the degree you like it—smell it and bite into a piece to decide when it's ready (it gets stronger and smellier)—use it as needed. If you're not using it right away, store it, covered, in the refrigerator. This will almost completely stop the fermentation.

HOMEMADE SAUSAGES

If you live in a cosmopolitan city or in any place with an ethnic population, you'll have little problem finding an assortment of interesting sausages. But you can also make sausages yourself. The process is amazingly easy and limitlessly versatile. Most people are intimidated by making sausages because you have to order the casings from the butcher in advance, mail-order them (see Sources), or get them from a pork store—and not every town in America has a pork store.

Every region in France has its own sausages, but basically there are only two kinds: sausages made by stuffing chopped or puréed meat or seafood into a pig's, lamb's, or beef's intestines, and patty sausages, what the French call *crépinettes*, from *crépine*, the word for caul fat (see page 8). *Crépinettes* are what you make if you don't have a sausage stuffer—you just shape the sausage meat into patties. You can then wrap the patties in caul fat so they hold their shape, but if you put a little egg in the filling, you don't have to bother.

The principles behind making your own sausages are almost identical to those involved in making pâtés (see Chapter 5), and in fact any pâté filling can be stuffed into a casing or shaped into a *crépinette* and used as a sausage. When you make sausage fillings by hand, you may want to include any of the same decorative and flavorful garnitures you'd use in a pâté—pistachio nuts, cubes of fat, pieces of wild mushrooms, cubes of black truffles. Flavorings for sausage are also similar to those used in a pâté, and like pâtés, sausages are almost always improved with a little garlic. Chopped onions or shallots, first sweated in a little butter, lard, or bacon fat, also give sausages extra flavor.

Sausages can also be made with a mousseline mixture prepared by puréeing meats (see page 535) into a smooth paste and then working in cold heavy cream. More traditional recipes for these sausages—called *boudins blancs* because they are white and presumably because they have the same shape as *boudins noirs*, which are black blood sausages—are made by combining the puréed meat (usually pork, veal, or chicken) with fatback (fatty, unsmoked bacon, not salt pork), sweated onions, *quatre épices* (a mixture of ground ginger, cloves, nutmeg, and white pepper; see page 386), bread crumbs soaked in milk, and a little egg to hold the mixture together. When raw beef suet (the brittle fat that surrounds a steer's kidneys) replaces the fatback, the mixture is called *godiveau*. When cream is added to the *godiveau* mixture, you end up with *godiveau à la crème*. Truffled *boudins blancs*, recognizable because they look like they have round black bruises, show up in French charcuteries around Christmastime.

BUYING AND STUFFING SAUSAGE CASINGS

Cleaned and salted intestines (called casings) come in various sizes and can usually be bought in 1-pound tubs, enough for a lot of sausages. Lambs' intestines are used for small link sausages; hogs' intestines for medium-size sausages, such as those given here; and beef intestines for very large sausages, such as mortadella. Unless you live near a pork store, you may have to get your butcher to order them for you or you may have to mail-order them (see Sources). Because the salt preserves the sausage casings (they can be kept in the refrigerator for up to a year) and they're inexpensive, it's worth tracking them down and stocking a small supply. Some sausage casings are sold with the salt already rinsed out. If you have extra casings that came with the salt rinsed out, or that you rinsed out yourself, toss them with enough salt to coat them well and store them in the refrigerator.

If you're stuffing sausage casings and the casings haven't already been soaked and are encrusted with salt, soak those that you need in cold water for about 10 minutes. Fit the end of one on the kitchen tap and gently run cold water through it for about 30 seconds. Start running the water slowly, so if the casing has a crimp, you have time to straighten it before the casing bursts. Stuff the rinsed casings with a hand sausage-stuffer (which looks like a giant syringe) or with the sausage-stuffing attachment on an electric mixer. If you're using the electric mixer, don't use the grinding blades (some mixers grind and stuff at the same time); if your machine obliges you to use blades, use the coarsest ones, since you will have already ground or pureéd the meat in a food processor. Use the largest tube attachment and rub it with shortening to lubricate the casings and make them easier to work with. Roll the 7-foot [2 m] length (or smaller pieces) of casing up on the stuffing tube and begin feeding in the sausage mixture with the mixer set on low speed. When you have a sausage the right length—in Homemade Pork Sausages, between 4 and 5 inches [10 and 12.5 cm]—turn off the machine and pull the sausage 1 or 2 inches [2.5 to 5 cm] away from the stuffing tube so you have some empty casing with which to make a knot. Push the sausage mixture into the casing so that the sausage is firm and there are no air pockets. Cut the sausage casing where it joints the tube and tie a knot at both ends of the sausage. Repeat until you've used all the stuffing.

HOMEMADE
PORK SAUSAGES

SAUCISSES MAISON

MAKES 10 LINK SAUSAGES ABOUT 1½ INCHES [4 CM]
THICK AND 4 TO 5 INCHES [10 TO 12.5 CM] LONG,
OR 20 SAUSAGE PATTIES (5 MAIN-COURSE SERVINGS
IF YOU'RE SERVING THE SAUSAGES WITHOUT OTHER
MEATS; 10 SERVINGS IF YOU'RE SERVING THEM
AS PART OF A CHOUCROUTE GARNIE)

1 recipe pâté filling for Country-style Pork Pâté (page 87)

7 feet [2 m] hog sausage casings for sausages about 1½
   inch [4 cm] in diameter, preferably in a single piece (see
   page 531), or 1½ pounds [675 g] caul fat (see page 8)

   shortening (unless you're making patty sausages)

1 additional egg, if needed

IF you're using sausage casings, follow the directions on page 531.

IF you're using caul fat, cut it into squares about 6 inches [15 cm] on each side. If you're using neither sausage casings nor caul fat, work the extra egg into the pâté mixture. Form the sausage mixture into about 20 patties. Wrap each patty in caul fat, if you're using it. Sausages made with caul fat should be gently sautéed before being incorporated into dishes such as cassoulet or choucroute garnie.

SAUSAGES can be refrigerated for up to 2 days before they are cooked (see below).

Variations: You can make duck sausages by using the duck pâté mixture on page 88; this will give you twice as much as the recipe above.

OTHER WAYS TO SERVE SAUSAGE

The French eat sausages far more often then they eat *choucroute,* and since you're likely to find these sausages very tasty, you may want to serve them in various guises. A French favorite is *saucissons, pommes à l'huile,* which means sausages served with potato salad. Just poach the sausages for 20 minutes, slice them, and serve them on the same plate with the potato salad on page 43.

FRENCH REGIONAL SAUSAGES

It seems that every region of France has its own sausages, with picturesque names whose origin has long since been lost, but the character and identity of the sausages still intact. French sausages can be divided into several main categories: *saucisses, saucissons secs, andouilles* and *andouillettes,* and boudins. *Saucisses,* what we call sausages, are filled with raw meat and flavorings and are meant to be cooked within a few days of being stuffed. *Saucissons secs* are the equivalent to our salami, essentially sausages that have been hung to dry and age so the meat hardens and continues to develop flavor. The meat is never actually cooked, but is cured in the same way as prosciutto or salami, and can be eaten raw. Andouilles and andouillettes differ from one another primarily in size—andouilles are made with the hog's large intestines, andouillettes from the small. For the most part they are stuffed with tripe and sold already cooked and often smoked so they can be eaten cold, like salami; or they can be braised, broiled, or grilled and be served with potatoes or purées of beans, onions, or other vegetables. Andouilles and andouillettes are made all over France. Troyes, Nancy, and even Lourdes (where they make an andouillette shaped like a rosary) claim to make the best. French gourmets indulge in vehement debates about the merits of each and have even created a club, the AAAAA (Association Amicale d'Amateurs d'Authentiques Andouillettes). Boudins, except for *boudins blancs* (see page 535), are blood sausages made from the blood of a just-killed pig combined with cubes of fat. Like andouilles, boudins are poached as soon as they are made to preserve them and so they can be eaten cold (we ate them at dawn with our coffee where I picked grapes), but are more typically served grilled or sautéed, often with apples.

Variations on all the above seem to be infinite. *Larousse Gastronomique* lists 16 sausages from Alsace alone, including various boudins, one of which includes tongue; two varieties of Strasbourg sausages, one of which is *Knackwurst,* the others a *saucisse de Strasbourg* (a smoked sausage that contains beef); *Leberwurst; Burelewerwursht;* and *Waedele* (all made with liver); a ham sausage; a sausage made of rolled veal (one version has truffles); and a giant sausage with big cubes of fat called a *Bierwurst.* Lyon is also famous for its sausages, including the *rosette de Lyon* (a large sausage flavored with marc) and the *cervelas de Lyon,* which once contained brains (hence its name; *cervelle* means brains) but now is made with pork and no brains. The Lyonnais are also fond of garlic sausages (see recipe, page 534), which they sometimes jazz up with pistachios and truffles and serve with steamed potatoes (or hot potatoes with oil and vinegar) or wrap in brioche and serve in thick slices. In short, virtually anything you can cut up and stuff into a hog (or beef or lamb) intestine or wrap up in caul fat can be made into a sausage.

SIMPLE GARLIC SAUSAGES

SAUCISSONS À L'AIL

MAKES 10 LINK SAUSAGES ABOUT 1½ INCHES
[4 CM] THICK AND 4 TO 5 INCHES [10 TO 12.5 CM]
LONG, OR 20 PATTY SAUSAGES (5 MAIN-COURSE
SERVINGS IF YOU'RE SERVING THE SAUSAGES
WITHOUT OTHER MEATS; 10 SERVINGS IF
YOU'RE SERVING THEM AS PART OF A
CHOUCROUTE GARNIE)

The best sausages are made by chopping the ingredients by hand or by pulsing them in a food processor in the same way as the pâté mixtures on pages 87 and 88. These handmade mixtures, however, take longer to make than mixtures made by simply grinding meats and fat together in a meat grinder. Some meat grinders have a sausage attachment that allows you to grind and stuff at the same time, but I try to avoid these since I like to cook a sample of the ground sausage mixture before I use it to stuff casings or wrap it in caul fat. Garlic sausages are popular in France and are great as part of a choucroute garnie.

- 1 pound [450 g] pork shoulder or pork butt (or 1½ pounds [675 g] pork shoulder chops with the bones and sinew cut away so you end up with 1 pound [450 g] of meat), cut into ½-inch [1.5-cm] cubes

- ¾ pound [340 g] fatback (weight without rind), rind removed, cut into ½-inch [1.5-cm] cubes

- ½ pound [225 g] chicken livers, cut in half

- 2 large eggs, beaten

- 4 slices dense-crumb white bread such as Pepperidge Farm, crusts removed

- 1 cup [250 ml] milk

- 4 cloves garlic, chopped fine, crushed to a paste with the side of a chef's knife

- 1 tablespoon fresh thyme leaves, chopped fine, or 2 teaspoons dried thyme, chopped fine

- 2 teaspoons fine salt

- 2 teaspoons freshly ground black pepper

- ½ teaspoon ground cloves

- ½ teaspoon ground ginger

- ¼ teaspoon ground nutmeg

- 1 tablespoon oil (for sautéing mixture for testing)

- 1 length of hog casing (7 feet [2 m]) or the equivalent in smaller pieces (see page 531), or 1½ pounds [675 g] caul fat (see page 8)

  shortening

CHOP the meat in batches in the food processor, pulsing the mixture until it has the consistency of coarse hamburger meat. (You can also have the butcher grind it for you or grind it yourself if you have a meat grinder or a meat-grinding attachment for your electric mixer.)

COMBINE the ground pork, fatback, chicken livers, and eggs in a large mixing bowl.

SOAK the bread in the milk and squeeze out and discard any excess milk. Combine the bread with the pork mixture and the garlic, thyme, salt and spices. Work the mixture with your hands until the ingredients are evenly distributed. Sauté a small patty of the sausage mixture, taste it, and adjust the salt and pepper. Refrigerate the mixture until needed, up to 2 days.

IF you're using sausage casings, follow the directions on page 531.

IF you're using caul fat, cut it into 20 squares about 6 inches on each side. If you're using neither sausage casings nor caul fat, form the sausage mixture into about 20 patties. Wrap each patty in caul fat, if you're using it.

CHICKEN MOUSSE SAUSAGES

BOUDINS BLANCS

MAKES 12 SAUSAGES ABOUT

1 INCH THICK AND 6 INCHES LONG

(6 MAIN-COURSE SERVINGS IF YOU'RE SERVING

THE SAUSAGES WITHOUT OTHER MEATS;

UP TO 20 SERVINGS IF YOU'RE SERVING THEM

AS PART OF A CHOUCROUTE GARNIE)

Nothing could be less like a traditional boudin noir—blood sausage—than these creamy, rich, ivory-colored sausages. To prepare boudins blancs you first make a mousseline mixture by puréeing boneless chicken breasts (or veal or seafood) in a food processor. Then, over a period of several hours, you work in heavy cream in increments, allowing the mixture to rest in the refrigerator between the additions. The best mousselines should melt in your mouth and have a creamy, almost souffle-like texture that barely holds together. To achieve this, you must balance the amount of protein (the meat and egg whites) with just the right amount of cream. When you're making boudins blancs, the mixture must also be stiff enough when cold so that it stays in the casings, whereas if you're baking a mousseline in a mold, the raw mixture can be as runny as you like, because the mold contains the mixture as it cooks. When making a mousseline mixture for boudins blancs, you want to work as much cream into the mixture as you can without making it too runny. You then need to poach a dollop of the mixture in simmering water to make sure that it holds together once it's cooked. If it doesn't, you need to add more egg white. If, when you add more egg white, the mixture becomes too runny to stuff into casings, you have to purée more chicken and work the runny mixture into the puree—so it's best to add the minimum amount of cream and start testing the mixture before adding too much liquid. You can then stuff the sausage into the casings with the sausage attachment to an electric mixer or a pastry bag with a ½-inch [1.5 cm] tip.

2¾ pounds [565 g] boneless and skinless chicken breasts or top round of veal

3 egg whites, or more as needed

1¾ tablespoon salt, or more as needed

1¾ teaspoon freshly ground white pepper, or more as needed

⅓ teaspoon nutmeg

3 to 3½ cups [625 to 750 ml] heavy cream (or more, as needed), well chilled

8 feet [2 m] hog casings for medium-size sausages (see page 531)

TRIM any fat and sinew off the chicken breasts, including the small tendon that runs along the tenderloin, which is the small strip of meat that runs along one side of the breast. Just pull the tendon and place one end of it on a cutting board. Hold the end against the cutting board with your fingernail and slide a thin, flexible knife along the top of the tendon, pulling on the tendon until you cut it off. Cut the chicken into 1-inch [2.5 cm] cubes. If using veal, trim off any pieces of gristle or silverskin.

COMBINE the chicken or veal with the egg whites, salt, pepper, and nutmeg in a food processor. Work the mixture into a smooth paste, about 2 minutes. Scrape down the sides of the processor at least once with a rubber spatula so nothing escapes the blade. Transfer the mixture to a nonreactive mixing bowl large enough to hold the mixture with plenty of room left over. Cover the mixture with plastic wrap, pressing the plastic against the top of the mixture to prevent a crust from forming, and refrigerate for at least 2 hours, or overnight.

USE a wooden spoon to work 1 cup [250 ml] of the heavy cream, about one-quarter at a time, into the mixture. Clean the sides of the bowl with a spatula, and incorporate into the mixture. Cover the mixture again with plastic wrap, and refrigerate for 2 hours. Again work 1 cup of cream into the mixture, one-quarter at a time. Cover with plastic wrap, chill the mixture, and work in another cup [125 ml] of cream.

BRING about 1 quart of water to a simmer with 1 teaspoon of salt. Dollop a mounded teaspoon of the mousseline mixture into the simmering water and simmer gently for about 5 minutes. Adjust the texture of the mousseline (see headnote) and season to taste with salt and pepper. If necessary, repeat the test. If the mixture is cold, and holding together well, stuff the casings at this point. If not, cover the mixture with plastic wrap and refrigerate it for at least 2 hours, or as long as overnight.

CUT the sausage casing into twelve 8-inch lengths and soak the casings in cold water for about 10 minutes. Fit the end of one of the casings on the kitchen tap and gently run cold water through the casing for about 30 seconds. Start running the water slowly, so if the casing has a crimp, the water won't cause it to burst. Repeat with the other casings. Fill a pastry bag with a ½-inch [1.5 cm] tip three-quarters full with the mousseline mixture and lay the filled bag on a level surface. Fit ¾ of each sausage casing over the end of the pastry bag and, while holding the casing onto the end of the bag, pipe in the mixture until you have about 6 inches of mousseline per sausage, leaving an inch free at both ends of the casing. (You can also use a hand sausage stuffer or an electric sausage stuffer, but I find the mixture easier to stuff using a pastry bag.) As you're stuffing the sausages, tie the ends either by making a little knot with the extra casing or by tying the casing with string. You can refrigerate the sausages for up to 1 day before you cook them (see page 532).

Variations: Because the *boudins blancs* mixture is less dense than that of other sausages, you don't need to prick the casings before cooking. Because *boudins blancs* are so delicately flavored, you can add luxurious ingredients to the basic mousseline mixture without losing the flavor or texture of these ingredients. Try stirring 6 ounces of terrine of foie gras (*bloc;* see page 96), cut into ¼-inch [.5-cm] dice, into the mousseline mixture just before stuffing the casings. Diced or chopped black truffles—as many as you can afford—take the boudins into transcendental realms. You can also add a little truffle juice or truffle oil to the mousseline so you don't actually need whole truffles. Dried morels (about 1 ounce for the recipe above) are a less expensive but still magnificent alternative to truffles. You stir them with a little Madeira until they're softened; squeeze out the liquid and incorporate it into the mousseline mixture, being careful to leave any grit or sand behind in the soaking dish; chop the morels coarse; and cook them in a sauté pan for 1 or 2 minutes to cook off the alcohol in the Madeira. Cubes of meat—the same meat used as the base for the mousseline or something more flavorful and distinctive, such as duck or squab—can be folded into the mixture, as can coarsely chopped pistachios, which add color and a little crunch. The mousseline itself can be made with more flavorful meats, such as squab, duck, hare, or rabbit, and the trimmings used to make a flavorful broth, which you can reduce to a glaze and incorporate into the mousseline. Trimmings of mousse of foie gras (which is less expensive than *bloc;* see page 96) can be puréed with the chicken, veal, or other meat.

Seafood *boudins blancs,* served alone or as part of the garniture in the seafood version (*choucroute garnie aux poissons et aux fruits de mer*) on page 538, can be made by substituting scallops, lean white fish such as cod, or salmon for the meat in the mousseline base. Cubes of cooked lobster or other crustaceans, such as shrimp or crayfish, can also be stirred into the mousseline. Puréed lobster roe can be incorporated into the mousseline base, turning it an ugly green when raw but a bright orange when cooked—a trick that must be done within a few hours of cooking the boudins since lobster roe is so perishable. Smoked salmon or other smoked fish can also be puréed into the mousseline mixture or cubed and folded in before stuffing the sausages.

Don't limit your enjoyment of *boudins blancs* by eating them only with sauerkraut. You can grill them or sauté them in a little butter for about 5 minutes on each side.

OTHER TRICKS WITH CABBAGE

The tanginess of sauerkraut makes a perfect foil to rich meats, especially pork, and seafood, especially salmon. But unless we're fanatics, it's unlikely that we're going to have a crock of homemade sauerkraut at the ready, and we may not feel like using something out of a bag or jar. You can simulate the tanginess of sauerkraut, if not the exact flavor, by cooking cabbage with bacon and vinegar. I like to use red cabbage, which seems to hold its texture better and looks pretty, and I add apples to balance the acidity of the vinegar. I thought I had invented this dish, but later discovered that it's the same thing as *chou à l'ardennaise* described in Anne Willan's wonderful book *French Regional Cooking* and similar to the *chou rouge braisé à l'alsacienne* described in Austin de Croze's classic *Les Plats Régionaux de France.*

PORK CHOPS WITH RED CABBAGE FLAVORED WITH VINEGAR, APPLES, AND BACON

CÔTES DE PORC AU CHOU ROUGE À L'ARDENNAISE

MAKES 6 MAIN-COURSE SERVINGS

In this recipe, the red cabbage with apples and bacon is served as an accompaniment to pork chops, but as with the variations for choucroute garnie, you can also serve the cabbage with various sausages, smoked meats, sautéed or grilled duck breasts, or confit (see page 382).

¼ pound [115 g] bacon, sliced ¼ inch [.5 cm] thick

1 medium-size red cabbage (about 1½ pounds [675 g])

1 cup [250 ml] white wine

12 juniper berries, crushed with the side of a knife or under a small pot

2 teaspoons caraway seeds, chopped coarse (optional)

3 medium-size tart apples such as Granny Smiths, peeled, cored, diced into ¼-inch [.5-cm] cubes

6 center-cut pork chops, about 1 [2.5 cm] inch thick

salt

pepper

2 tablespoons sherry vinegar, or more as needed

CUT the bacon slices crosswise into strips (*lardons*) about 1 inch [2.5 cm] long and ¼ inch [.5 cm] on each side. Put the strips in a heavy-bottomed pot large enough to hold the shredded cabbage and cook over low heat. Stir them every couple of minutes so they cook evenly. Be careful not to burn the fat. As soon as the bacon strips begin to turn crispy, turn off the heat, take them out of the pot with a slotted spoon, pour the fat into a small bowl, and reserve bacon and fat separately.

PULL off and discard any wilted outer leaves from the cabbage. Quarter the cabbage by cutting through the core at the bottom. Cut the core out of each of the quarters and discard it. Shred the cabbage by slicing the quarters about ⅛ inch [3 mm] thick with a knife or vegetable slicer.

PUT the cabbage in the pot and pour the wine over it. Add the juniper berries, caraway seeds, reserved bacon, and apples and toss everything together until the ingredients are evenly distributed. (If you don't like biting into juniper berries and caraway seeds, you can wrap them in cheesecloth.) Put the pot on high heat until the wine comes to a boil and then turn the heat down to low. Cover the pot and simmer gently for 45 minutes. Keep an eye on the pot, stirring every few minutes, so you don't allow all the liquid to evaporate and the cabbage to burn. If after 45 minutes the cabbage is floating in lots of liquid, remove the lid and turn the heat up to high to evaporate the liquid, again being careful not to burn the cabbage.

SEASON the pork chops with salt and pepper. Sauté them in the reserved bacon fat, over high heat, in a sauté pan or skillet just large enough to hold them in a single layer—or use two pans—until they are firm to the touch, or pink but not translucent when you cut into one, 3 to 8 minutes on each side, depending on their thickness.

ADD the vinegar to the cabbage and season to taste with salt, pepper, and more vinegar if it needs it. Serve the pork chops with a mound of the cabbage on heated plates.

Variations: Cabbage is delicious when simmered with cured pork loin, shoulder, or butt that has been soaked to eliminate salt (see *"Demi-sel,"* page 528). If you want to serve a seafood version of pork chops with red cabbage, just sauté pieces of salmon or other fish and use cubes of smoked salmon instead of bacon in the cabbage.

SEAFOOD WITH SAUERKRAUT

CHOUCROUTE GARNIE AUX POISSONS ET AUX FRUITS DE MER

MAKES 10 SERVINGS

The first time I heard of this, in the 1970s, I was skeptical because I had already encountered so many nouvelle cuisine monsters, obvious but ill-conceived derivatives of traditional dishes. But years later I read a recipe for salmon with sauerkraut in an 1842 edition of an Alsatian cookbook, one of the first cookbooks ever written about a regional cuisine. So I decided that combining sauerkraut with seafood was worth a try.

Coupling salmon with sauerkraut has a certain logic, since salmon is a rich fish in the same way pork is (or was) a rich and relatively fatty meat. But I've also had fun (and rave reviews from friends) making more abundant and luxurious versions of seafood choucroute by including seafood boudins blancs (see page 536), chunks of lobster, and a variety of poached firm fish, especially monkfish. Unlike pork, for which exact cooking times aren't critical when you cook it nestled in with the sauerkraut, seafood requires more precision and should be cooked separately and coupled with the sauerkraut just before serving.

3   medium-size onions, chopped

3   cloves garlic, chopped

3   tablespoons duck fat, goose fat, or olive oil

5   pounds [2.3 kg] sauerkraut, preferably homemade (see page 529) or sold in bags, rinsed under cold running water, excess water wrung out

1   medium-size bouquet garni

15   juniper berries, crushed

1   bottle dry white wine

⅓ (about 6 ounces [150 g]) smoked salmon, cut in ¼-inch [.5-cm] dice (optional)

20 small new potatoes, peeled

1 recipe Chicken Mousse Sausages (page 535) using salmon, scallops, or other lean white fish instead of the chicken (or 10 individual boudins blancs, 4 or 5 inches [10 to 12.5 cm] long—if they're larger use half as many and cut them in half)

3 pounds [1.3 kg] salmon fillet, with skin (pin bones removed), or 3 pounds other firm fish fillets

salt

pepper

10 medium-to-large sea scallops (optional)

COOK the onions and garlic over medium heat in 1 tablespoon of the fat in a pot large enough to hold the sauerkraut and boudins. When the onions turn translucent, after about 10 minutes, put in the sauerkraut, the bouquet garni, and the juniper berries. Pour in the wine, bring to a simmer on the stove, and cover the pot. Simmer very gently over very low heat—just enough so a bubble rises up about every second—for 1 hour. Stir in the diced smoked salmon and nestle in the new potatoes. After 10 minutes, nestle the *boudins blancs* into the sauerkraut. Cook for 20 minutes more, or until the potatoes are easily penetrated with a knife or skewer.

SEASON the salmon fillet or other fish fillets on both sides with salt and pepper. If the fillets vary in thickness, cut them into two or more pieces so that each piece is of the same thickness. Over medium to high heat, sauté the fillet or fillets skin-side down, in 1 tablespoon of the fat, for 4 to 6 minutes depending on their thickness, holding them down with a spatula to prevent the skin from contracting. Turn and sauté on the flesh side until the fillets are firm to the touch (or are cooked through when you cut into one), 2 to 3 minutes (a total of about 10 minutes per inch of thickness). Sauté the scallops over high heat in the last of the fat, 1 to 2 minutes on each side depending on their thickness. Cut the fish into 10 equal portions.

DISCARD the bouquet garni and spoon the sauerkraut onto heated plates. Arrange a boudin, a piece of fish, a scallop, and 2 new potatoes next to and over the mound of sauerkraut on each plate.

Variations: You can make a seafood choucroute as simple or as complicated as you like. I rarely go to the trouble of making seafood boudins and assorted seafood to go with sauerkraut unless I'm serving a special meal. Usually I just cook a salmon or other fish fillet or fish steak and serve it with a mound of sauerkraut (or the braised red cabbage on page 537) next to it on the plate. Going in the direction of complexity, you can add lobsters, crayfish, and shrimp, all cooked at the last minute, and serve them with the sauerkraut for an especially luxurious version.

QUENELLES

Egg- or sausage-shaped purées of chicken, veal, game, or seafood, poached or baked, quenelles have long been famous in and around Lyonnais. The quenelle was once synonymous with French cooking at its finest (or at least at its most elaborate). My first quenelle was a disaster, sampled in the dining room of a cheap hotel on Lake Nantua—after which the famous *quenelles Nantua* (quenelles with crayfish sauce) were named—and little different from a pasty hot dog with canned tomato sauce on top.

I'm guessing that much of the quenelle's prestige has to do with how difficult it once was to make. Meat or seafood had to be worked into a purée in a large mortar and the mixture then worked through a drum sieve. Nowadays the food processor does this work, so anyone can make quenelles fairly easily at home. Quenelle mixtures come in various forms. Older recipes call for *panades* of flour and eggs and veal kidney fat, while more contemporary versions use a mousseline mixture, based on cream and identical to the mixture used for making *boudins blancs* on page 535.

If you want to make quenelles, make the *boudin blanc* mixture using chicken, veal, or a lean white fish as the base, and then shape the mixture into egg shapes with two spoons dipped in cold water to prevent sticking. Or use a pastry bag with a ¾-inch [2-cm] tip to pipe the mixture into small sausage shapes. Preheat the oven to 350°F [175°C/gas mark 4], put the quenelles in a buttered baking dish— if you're using a pastry bag, pipe them directly into the dish—and pour in enough boiling water to get the quenelles to float. Cover the dish loosely with aluminum foil and bake for 10 minutes or so until the quenelles are cooked through. Cut one in half to make sure it isn't raw in the middle. Drain the quenelles and serve them with a tomato sauce, or a lobster or crayfish sauce (see Chapter 25). Or cover them with béchamel and cheese and gratinée them. Serve quenelles as a first course.

VEAL KIDNEYS WITH MUSHROOMS, MUSTARD, AND PORT

ROGNONS DE VEAU AUX CHAMPIGNONS, À LA MOUTARDE ET AU PORTO

WHETHER	HOW TO	HOW TO	HOW TO	SAFETY TIPS
OFFAL IS REALLY AWFUL	COOK KIDNEYS, BRAINS, TONGUE, AND LIVER	MAKE A MEDIEVAL DIPPING SAUCE	WORK WITH COATINGS AND BATTERS FOR FRYING	FOR FRYING AND SAUTÉING

UNLIKE AMERICANS, WHO TEND TO AVOID ORGAN MEATS, THE FRENCH consider many of what we euphemistically call variety meats and the British call offal to be among the best that a particular animal—usually a lamb or a calf—has to offer. True, there's a hierarchy of animal parts, with veal or lamb sweetbreads reigning as the most expensive and luxurious, closely followed by kidneys, livers, and brains. Tripe (stomach tissue), tongues, and lungs form a second category, while odder things, such as eyes, testicles, and teats, popular in the eighteenth century, form a third category and are rarely eaten anymore even by the adventurous French.

I confess to never having developed a taste for tripe, although I've tried dozens of versions, and fortunately I haven't ever had to try eyes. Other animal organs, for the most part, I find delightful. When I land in France after a too-long absence, I soon order a dish of kidneys, often the most expensive item on the menu because the French love them and each animal, of course, only has two. Because kidneys do have a lot of flavor (those who don't like them describe them as strong), they go well with robust sauces and are often paired with mustard.

Some people prefer lamb kidneys to veal kidneys, but even in France you'll rarely encounter them. Because the lamb kidneys I've found in the United States have a strong, gamey taste, I always opt for veal kidneys. Veal kidneys are often sliced and sautéed, a treatment that can easily turn them tough and rubbery. I prefer to roast them in a small pot or Windsor pan, discard their juices (whose flavor has the potential to be aggressive), make a sauce in the pot or pan, and very gently reheat the sliced roast kidneys in the sauce, not allowing the sauce to reach a boil, which would cause the slices to curl and toughen.

During roasting, kidneys should ideally be coated with a thin layer of fat to prevent them from drying out. In France, kidneys are sold with a layer of their own white, brittle fat—*graisse de rognon*—which when rendered makes the best possible fat for French fries, but in the United States kidneys are usually sold without the fat. If you can find caul fat (see page 8), use it to wrap the kidneys, but if it's unavailable, don't worry about it.

VEAL KIDNEYS WITH MUSHROOMS, MUSTARD, AND PORT

ROGNONS DE VEAU AUX
CHAMPIGNONS, À LA
MOUTARDE ET AU PORTO

MAKES 4 MAIN-COURSE SERVINGS

2   veal kidneys (about 1 pound [450 g] each)

    salt

    pepper

2   small sheets caul fat (large enough to wrap the kidneys with a single layer) (optional)

1   pound [450 g] cultivated or wild mushrooms

2   tablespoons butter (for sautéing the mushrooms), plus 4 tablespoons (for finishing the sauce)

2   medium-size shallots, chopped fine

½   cup [125 ml] port, preferably tawny

2   tablespoons *glace de viande* or demi-glace (see page 3); ¼ cup [60 ml] concentrated beef, veal, or chicken broth (see page 4); or 1 cup [250 ml] Brown Chicken Broth (page 209)

½   cup [125 ml] heavy cream

2   tablespoons Dijon mustard

2   tablespoons finely chopped parsley (chopped at the last minute)

PREHEAT the oven to 425°F [220°C/gas mark 7].

IF the kidneys come with a layer of fat, trim most of it off so that the kidneys are coated with only a thin layer, about ¼ inch [.5 cm]. Rinse them, pat them dry, and season them with salt and pepper. If the kidneys aren't coated with fat, rinse, dry, and season them, and wrap them in a single layer of caul fat, if you have it.

TRIM any dark or gritty sections off the mushrooms. If you're using small mushrooms, leave them whole. If you're using large cultivated mushrooms, quarter them vertically. If you're using large wild mushrooms, cut them into smaller pieces, following their natural contours.

BROWN the kidneys over high heat in an ovenproof sauté pan or small pot just large enough to hold them, or in a saucepan with sloping sides (a Windsor pan), again just large enough to hold them. When the kidneys are well browned on all sides, slide the pan into the oven and roast them for about 20 minutes, just until they bounce back when you press on them with a finger, or until an instant-read thermometer, stuck into the middle of one of the kidneys, reads 133°F [56°C].

WHILE the kidneys are roasting, sauté the mushrooms in 2 tablespoons of butter over medium to high heat until they brown and any liquid they release evaporates. Season the mushrooms with salt and pepper. Set the pan aside.

TAKE the kidneys out of the oven, cover the pan loosely with aluminum foil, and let the kidneys rest for 20 minutes.

TRANSFER the kidneys to a plate and pour out and discard any juices that have accumulated in the bottom of the sauté pan. Put the shallots into the pan (don't worry if there's no fat) and cook them over medium heat, stirring with a whisk, until you smell their fragrance, about 1 minute. Pour in the port and boil it down to about half. If you're using *glace de viande*, demi-glace, or concentrated broth, add it and stir with the port over medium heat until it dissolves. If you're using chicken broth, add it and boil it down for about 5 minutes, until you have slightly more liquid than there was port left in the pan before you added the broth. Pour in the cream and simmer the sauce until it thickens slightly, about 5 minutes. Whisk in the remaining butter, the mustard, and the parsley and season the sauce to taste.

WHILE the liquids from your sauce are reducing, cut into the underside of each kidney and cut away the small clump of fat and any large veins. Cut the kidneys crosswise into slices slightly thinner than ¼ inch [.5 cm]. Discard any juices the kidneys released on the plate. Put the slices in the sauce and gently reheat over low to medium heat, stirring gently, for about 2 minutes, just long enough to heat the slices through. Don't allow the sauce to boil. Put the mushrooms back on the stove over medium heat for about 2 minutes to reheat them. Spoon the kidneys onto individual heated plates or into a serving dish and spoon the mushrooms over them.

Variations: Of the 15 recipes Escoffier lists for veal kidneys, most are similar to the recipe given here, except that Madeira, white wine, or, in a Breton version, cider may replace the port, and wild mushrooms—specifically cèpes, whose meaty texture matches that of the kidneys—replace the cultivated mushrooms. Pieces of bacon, either cubes or *lardons*, lightly blanched to reduce their smokiness, are included in some recipes; they closely match the texture of the kidneys and their full flavor doesn't dominate the dish as it would so many others.

Kidneys are also good grilled. Split them in half lengthwise and cut out any chunks of fat and large veins. Run two large metal skewers sideways through both halves and grill them over a hot fire for about 10 minutes on each side, brushing them every few minutes with a little melted butter. Escoffier suggests serving grilled kidneys with *maître d'hotel* butter (made by working butter with chopped parsley and lemon juice) or *beurre Bercy* (made by working butter with a reduction of white wine and shallots). I like to serve grilled kidneys with a runny pesto sauce—made with enough olive oil so that the sauce stays more liquid than solid—which contrasts with and lightens the effect of the kidneys' rich, full flavor. Some contemporary chefs cut kidneys into thick slices and bread them with flour, beaten egg, and bread crumbs (breading *à l'anglaise*, see page 304) for a delicately crunchy addition to the already toothsome texture of the kidneys. Some also include crushed juniper berries in the sauce to give it a slightly gamey flavor.

BRAINS

Of all organ meats, brains have the most delicate flavor and texture, yet they cause as much anxiety the others. But brains have become one of my favorite organ meats, and they are always a special treat, not because they're expensive, but because the butcher doesn't carry them on a regular basis and I rarely have the foresight to order them ahead of time. Since they are very perishable, it isn't a good idea to buy them more than a day ahead of time.

Like sweetbreads (see page 415 for more about sweetbreads), brains can be cooked exactly the way they come, but they'll look better if you remove the thin outer membrane and then soak them overnight in salty water to draw out any traces of blood that would turn a sullen gray in cooking. Because brains are fragile, they can be difficult to work with when they're raw. I blanch them quickly, starting in cold water to stiffen them and make them easier to slice.

Brains are quite versatile—they're delicious fried, sautéed, or served poached in a vinaigery court bouillon. However, they shouldn't be served with strong sauces, which completely overwhelm them.

SAUTÉED CALVES' BRAINS WITH "HAZELNUT" BUTTER

CERVELLES DE VEAU AU BEURRE NOISETTE

MAKES 6 MAIN-COURSE SERVINGS

This used to be a common bistro dish, but instead of being served with beurre noisette, which is butter that's cooked only until its milk solids caramelize, the brains were served with beurre noir, which is butter that's cooked until it's actually slightly burnt. The French, who are surprisingly health conscious, although in ways different than we are in the United States, actually outlawed beurre noir because burnt milk solids are known to be carcinogenic and, as the French have long known, burnt butter is *indigeste* (indigestible) anyway. To the French, a beurre blanc, as rich as any sauce could be, is digestible and perfectly fine, while beurre noir is not. In any case, we could also call this dish *cervelles de veau à la meunière* (see page 294 for more about this technique), since the brains are lightly floured, sautéed, sprinkled with lemon, and sauced with the beurre noisette.

- 4 calves' brains (slightly more than ½ pound [225 g] each)
- salt
- pepper
- ½ cup [60 g] all-purpose flour
- 4 tablespoons clarified butter (see page 296)
- 1 tablespoon lemon juice
- 6 tablespoons whole butter
- 1 tablespoon finely chopped parsley

SOAK brains in cold water for 2 hours to loosen the outer membrane. Starting at the side, pinch the mem-

brane and gently peel it off. It should come off quite easily unless the brains were frozen. (If you can't get it off, just leave it on.) Discard the membrane. Put the brains in a bowl of fresh water—enough to cover abundantly—with a small handful of salt and refrigerate them overnight. Give them a quick rinse and put them in a pot with enough cold water to cover. Bring to a simmer over high heat. As soon as the water reaches a simmer, drain the brains in a colander and rinse them with cold water. Handle them gently, they're fragile.

TRIM off and discard any loose membrane, veins, and the white brain stem.

CUT the brains crosswise into slices about ⅓ inch [about 1 cm] thick and season the slices with salt and pepper. Dredge the slices in flour and pat each slice between your hands to eliminate excess flour. (Don't flour the slices in advance, or the coating will get gummy.)

HEAT the clarified butter over medium heat in a sauté pan large enough to hold the slices in a single layer—or use two pans—and cook the slices for about 4 to 5 minutes on each side, until they are pale golden brown. Immediately transfer the slices to a heated serving dish or individual heated plates and sprinkle them with the lemon juice.

POUR the cooked butter out of the sauté pan and add the whole butter. Cook the whole butter over medium heat until it foams and the milk solids turn golden brown. Add the parsley to the butter and spoon the hot beurre noisette and parsley over the brains. Serve immediately.

Variations: I sometimes add capers to the hot butter, along with the parsley, to give a briny tang that contrasts nicely with the richness and gentle flavor of the brains. (This is essentially the same treatment as the *raie à la grenobloise* on page 298.) Brains also take well to frying because the crispy outer coating of the breading contrasts beautifully with the melting brains inside. Brains, poached in a lightly acidic court bouillon and cut into thin slices, are often combined with French-style scrambled eggs (*les oeufs brouillés*; see page 127). The juxtaposition of the two similar textures is intriguing and satisfying.

CALVES' BRAINS FRITTERS

CERVELLES DE VEAU
EN BEIGNETS

MAKES 4 FIRST-COURSE SERVINGS

In France, beignets are usually made by dipping sliced fruits into a batter, deep-frying them, and sprinkling them with powdered sugar. The same kind of frying batter can be used to fry savory things. It works particularly well with brains because the crispy outer coating provides contrasting crunch.

2 calves' brains (about ¾ pound [340 g] each)

salt (for soaking)

FOR THE MARINADE:

¼ cup [60 ml] dry white wine

1 small shallot, chopped fine

1 teaspoon chopped fresh marjoram, or ½ teaspoon chopped dried marjoram (or try thyme or tarragon)

FOR THE BATTER (START PREPARING AT LEAST 2 HOURS BEFORE YOU'RE READY TO SERVE):

1 cup all-purpose flour

1 teaspoon salt, plus additional salt (for sprinkling over the beignets)

2 egg whites

tiny pinch cream of tartar (unless you're using a copper bowl)

FOR FRYING:

2 quarts [2 l] "pure" olive oil

OPTIONAL SAUCES:

Sauce Cameline (page 547)

Sauce Gribiche (page 549)

Sauce Rémoulade (page 492)

Tartar Sauce (page 549)

SOAK the brains in cold water for 2 hours to loosen the membrane. Starting at the side, pinch the membrane and gently peel it off. It should come off quite easily unless the brains have been frozen. (If you can't get it off, just leave it on.) Discard the membrane. Put the brains in a bowl of fresh water—enough to cover abundantly—with a small handful of salt and refrigerate them overnight. Give them a quick rinse and put them in a pot with enough cold water to cover. Bring to a simmer over high heat. As soon as the water comes to a simmer, drain the brains in a colander. Treat them gently, they're fragile. Rinse for 1 or 2 minutes with cold water to cool the brains, and refrigerate them for 1 hour.

REMOVE any loose membrane, veins, and the white brain stem. Cut the brains crosswise into ⅓-inch-thick [about 1 cm] slices. Gently toss the brain slices with the marinade ingredients, cover, and refrigerate for 1 to 6 hours.

TO make the batter, use a small whisk to work water—usually, a bit more than a cup—into the flour and ½ teaspoon of salt in a mixing bowl, to form a smooth paste. Work in just enough water to make a thick batter that you can smooth out by stirring with the whisk. Once the batter is smooth, add the rest of the water. Cover the bowl with plastic wrap and leave it undisturbed for 2 hours.

COMBINE the remaining ½ teaspoon of salt with the egg whites, add the cream of tartar if you're not using a copper bowl, and beat the whites until they form stiff peaks. Whisk half the beaten egg whites into the batter and then fold in the rest with a rubber spatula.

HEAT the oil in a heavy-bottomed pot to 360°F [182°C]. (See Safety Tips for Frying," page 550.) Pat the brain slices dry with a clean kitchen towel—don't use paper towels, which will stick and tear. Dip the slices in the batter. Lower them into the hot oil with your fingers (go slowly to keep the oil from splashing up on your hand) and fry for 2 to 3 minutes on each side, turning them over with a slotted spoon, until they are pale golden brown. Place them on a paper towel–lined sheet pan for a few seconds to get rid of excess oil, sprinkle with salt, and serve immediately. Pass one of the optional sauces at the table or serve in a bowl for dipping.

OPTIONAL SAUCES: Most French recipes for fried brains don't include a sauce, and those that do suggest sauces such as mayonnaises (tartar sauce, *gribiche*) or cream sauces. To me these seem too rich for most fried foods and especially for brains, which already have a texture that's creamy and saucelike. I prefer the Asian habit of serving fried foods with sweet-and-sour, strongly flavored dipping sauces. But the kind of sauce I'm looking for, something sweet-and-sour, lean and acidic, is rare in French cooking, until one goes back to the Middle Ages, when sauces were often made without fat and seem to have contained a large proportion of acidic ingredients such as vinegar or verjuice (*verjus*), the acidic juice of under-ripe grapes, crab apples, or currants.

Many medieval sauces were thickened with bread—a good technique for producing thick, condiment-like sauces such as rouille (see page 236) or *pistou* (see page 224), designed to dollop on foods or stir into soups. But medieval sauces were often unthickened infusions of spices such as ginger, saffron, nutmeg, garlic, cinnamon, perhaps *graines de paradis* (a kind of African pepper), and galingale (a gingerlike rhizome) in vinegar or verjuice. These sauces sound similar to certain Asian dipping sauces, except that most of the flavorings are different; most importantly, breadless medieval sauces contain no sugar to counteract the acidity of the vinegar. Sugar, long a luxury, was rarely used in early medieval cooking, although sweet fruits and honey were often included in vinegary sauces that were probably very much like modern Indian fruit chutneys. Here's my own version of a *sauce cameline* taken from Taillevent's *Le Viandier*. I'm guessing on the spice quantities (there's no way to know), and I have left out the bread and added sugar to balance the acidity of the vinegar.

MEDIEVAL SPICE DIPPING SAUCE
SAUCE CAMELINE

MAKES ½ CUP [125 ML]

½ cup [125 ml] good-quality white wine vinegar

2 teaspoons grated fresh ginger

½ teaspoon ground cinnamon

⅛ teaspoon ground cloves

¼ teaspoon powdered nutmeg

½ teaspoon saffron threads

2 tablespoons sugar

COMBINE all the ingredients in a heavy-bottomed saucepan and bring to a gentle simmer over medium heat. Stir until the sugar completely dissolves and remove from the heat. Cover the saucepan—to trap the aroma of the spices—and let the sauce cool. Serve slightly cool or at room temperature.

COATINGS AND BATTERS FOR FRYING

Frying may be the most abused of all cooking techniques and when done poorly produces truly revolting food. But it must also be said that frying seals in the flavors and aromas of certain foods in ways that other techniques do not and that the contrast of steaming hot crust and often molten interior is hard to resist.

Properly fried foods must be hot—like a good bowl of soup, almost too hot to touch—and coated with a fragile, crispy crust. The oil must be of high quality. I use "pure" olive oil, which has a clean flavor and doesn't cost as much as extra-virgin olive oil, but rendered beef suet, duck fat, and goose fat are also excellent. I don't use vegetable oils, which to me have a fishy taste, but most people don't seem to notice or mind this. The oil must be free of burnt food particles. It must be reasonably fresh, which is to say that there's no hint of rancidity, and that it hasn't been used more than once or twice and never got so hot it smoked. If the oil is being used for frying fish, then it must be used for fish and fish alone.

But the most contentious arguments are about which coating is best for which food. Some foods, such as potatoes, form their own crispy crust and need no additional coating. Other foods, such as chicken, whose skin becomes the crust when the chicken is fried, benefit from a simple dredging in flour. Vegetables do well with a simple mixture of water and flour or flour and club soda—the carbon dioxide in the club soda provides an additional subtle crunch. Some French recipes say to combine beer or even white wine with flour, insisting that yeast in the beer or wine will leaven the batter and make it lighter. This has never made sense to me since there is little, if any, active yeast left in most bottles of beer or wine. I do sometimes use beer or wine for the flavor it imparts, and I sometimes add yeast to a simple flour and water batter to provide leavening. But I never use yeast and wine together in a batter, because the alcohol in the wine retards the action of the yeast. Classic French beignet batter includes beaten egg whites folded with a mixture of flour and water and a little oil or clarified butter to coat the particles of flour and prevent the activation of the gluten, which can make the batter tough. Tempura batter is made by barely combining flour with egg yolks so there are still lumps of flour in the batter. The result is surprisingly good because the uncombined flour lumps provide extra crunch. Some recipes recommend coating foods to be fried with flour, beaten egg, and bread crumbs (a method called *paner à l'anglaise*), a method I think is better suited to gentle sautéing in clarified butter since the bread crumbs absorb a fair amount of the surrounding fat. (See page 641 for more about this method.)

HOMEMADE MAYONNAISE WITH CAPERS, CORNICHONS, AND HERBS
SAUCE GRIBICHE

MAKES 2 CUPS [500 ML]

This tangy mayonnaise is delicious with fried or grilled foods, especially seafood. I put a lot more capers and cornichons in mine than classic recipes call for, and I also add a little extra-virgin olive oil. This lightens the effect of the mayonnaise and gives the sauce a brighter, tangier, and more direct flavor.

1 tablespoon Dijon mustard (in addition to the mustard in the Basic Mayonnaise)

¼ cup [60 ml] extra-virgin olive oil

1 recipe (1½ cups [375 ml]) Basic Mayonnaise (page 34)

2 heaping tablespoons coarsely chopped capers

6 cornichons, chopped coarse

2 tablespoons finely chopped parsley

1 tablespoon finely chopped chives

1 tablespoon finely chopped fresh tarragon

salt and pepper

STIR the mustard and olive oil into the mayonnaise with a wooden spoon until the oil is completely incorporated. Stir in the rest of the ingredients.

Tartar Sauce: For what reason I don't know, some recipes for tartar sauce call for making the basic mayonnaise with cooked egg yolks instead of raw egg yolks. Because it's hard to get mayonnaise made with hard-boiled egg yolks to emulsify and hold together, most modern recipes use raw egg yolks. To make the simplest version of tartar sauce, stir 3 heaping tablespoons of finely minced shallots, 1 tablespoon of mustard (in addition to that contained in the mayonnaise), and 2 heaping tablespoons of finely chopped chives into 1 recipe (1½ cups [375 ml]) Basic Mayonnaise (see page 34). If you're concerned about using raw egg yolks in your mayonnaise, make a sabayon as though making a hollandaise and finish it with oil instead of clarified butter, see page 257.

When frying, it's best to use enough oil or fat to cover the food by at least 1 or 2 inches [2.5 to 5 cm]. If you use too little oil, the temperature of the oil will drop as soon as you add the food and the food will fry too slowly and absorb too much oil. Because you'll be dealing with a pot or frying pan containing a fair amount of hot oil that if accidentally spilled or allowed to spatter can cause nasty burns, use a heavy pot, skillet, deep-fryer, or electric frying pan and set it on the back of the stove or counter so you don't accidentally bump into it. Never fill whatever container you're using more than halfway up with oil, because the oil will bubble up a lot when you start adding food and if you're using too much oil, the oil may boil over. Make sure the deep-fryer, electric frying pan, or deep-frying pot is completely dry before you put in the oil. Any traces of liquid will cause the oil to spatter. Add food to the oil with a spoon, tongs, or a "spider" (which looks like a metal spider web with a long handle). If you must use your fingers—some batter-coated foods are hard to manage with a spider—hold the food within 1 inch of the hot oil before dropping it in; held any higher, it may splash you. Add food a few pieces at a time, especially at the beginning, until you can judge how much the oil is going to boil up. Have a box of baking soda or salt handy in case the oil spills over and starts a grease fire. If a fire starts, pour a lot of baking soda or salt on it. Don't skimp. You'll make a mess, but at least you won't burn the house down.

Most of us have tasted tongue in a sandwich. (I like mine on pumpernickel with plenty of mustard.) But hot tongue, slowly and lovingly braised, rarely appears on restaurant menus and no one I know ever cooks it at home. In any case, tongue cooked in a number of ways can be found in any French cookbook written before the Second World War. Oddly, it has disappeared from both cookbooks and restaurant menus, but no doubt it will become popular again and reappear in French bistros in the same way as other old-fashioned, slow-cooking foods such as short ribs and beef cheeks. It's simply too good to ignore.

Tongue can be simmered in a pot-au-feu—not a bad idea as long as you blanch it for 15 minutes (see the recipe that follows) to get rid of scum. But tongue really comes into its own when it's braised like a pot roast, in much the same way as the *boeuf à la mode* described in Chapter 31. The basic braising techniques, garnitures, and variations that work for pot roast also work for tongue. You can braise it in red or white wine (I prefer red), Madeira (combined with broth), cider, or even beer, and then reduce the braising liquid to concentrate its flavor and natural body. Or instead of reducing the liquid, you can follow the advice of French cookbooks designed for home cooks, and thicken the braising liquid with arrowroot that's been combined with an equal amount of cold water and is used in the same way as cornstarch. (Arrowroot is preferable to cornstarch, not because it has more thickening power, but because it's more stable. Liquids thickened with cornstarch, when cooked for more than 10 or 15 minutes, start to thin.) Like most braised meats, tongue is better if it's larded, and because of its shape, it is easy to lard; but this isn't essential. Again, as with any braised meat, the sauce benefits if you add something to the pot to provide extra gelatin, which will give natural body to your sauce so that you won't have to reduce or thicken it as much. The most common addition is the rind from fatback, which you should have on hand anyway if you're larding; but a calf's foot, split lengthwise, split again in half crosswise (so it fits into the pot), and blanched, will also provide extra gelatin. In place of the calf's foot, I often use 2 pig's feet, which are easier to find. I have the butcher split them

in half lengthwise only, because they're smaller, and blanch them in the same way. Tongue loses a lot of weight and volume when it's trimmed and braised, so a 4-pound [1.8 kg] tongue makes just 4 main courses. Since braising a whole tongue is a long process, you may want to braise 2 tongues, using the same amounts of the other ingredients as given below except, if you're larding, for the fatback, which should be doubled.

BRAISED BEEF TONGUE

LANGUE DE BOEUF BRAISÉE

MAKES 4 MAIN-COURSE SERVINGS

1   beef tongue (4 pounds [1.8 kg])

¾   pound [340 g] fatback, rind removed, fat cut into strips about 6 inches [15 cm] long and ¼ inch [.5 cm] thick (optional)

2   tablespoons "pure" olive oil or vegetable oil, or 1 sheet of fatback rind, about 6 by 8 inches [15 by 20.5 cm]

1   large onion, peeled, sliced thin

3   medium-size carrots, peeled, sliced thin

1   calf's foot, split in half lengthwise and again crosswise, or 2 pig's feet, split in half lengthwise (optional)

2   cups [500 ml] full-bodied red wine

1   medium-size bouquet garni

3   cups [750 ml] brown beef broth (page 219) or Brown Chicken Broth (see page 209), or more as needed

    salt

    pepper

WHEN you get the tongue home, trim off and discard the rough top surface, silverskin, and loose pieces of arteries and fat near the back of the tongue. If you're not using the tongue right away, you can store it for up to 24 hours, submerged in water, in a bowl in the refrigerator.

IF you're larding the tongue, push the strips of fat-back diagonally through the sides of the tongue with a larding rod (not a larding needle; see page 423 for an explanation of the difference). By larding diagonally you end up with cross-sections of fat-back strips when you slice the tongue.

PREHEAT the oven to 400°F [165°C/gas mark 3].

IF you're using oil, pour it into a heavy-bottomed pot just large enough to hold the tongue. (An oval pot would be ideal.) If you're using the fatback rind, place it fat-side down on the bottom of the pot. Put the tongue in the pot, surround it with the sliced onion and carrots, and place in the oven, uncovered, for 1 hour, until the meat is browned and the vegetables are starting to color. Transfer to the stovetop and cook over high heat until all pan juices evaporate. Deglaze with the wine, scraping up brown bits. Reduce until evaporated.

NESTLE the bouquet garni, feet, and fatback rind (if using), into the pot next to the tongue and pour in the broth. There should be enough broth to come about two-thirds of the way up the sides of the tongue. Add more if it's needed and bring the broth to a simmer over medium heat. Cover the pot with a sheet of aluminum foil with the less reactive shiny side down; press down slightly on the foil so that moisture condenses during braising and drips down over the tongue. Let the tongue braise on the stovetop for 3 more hours. After 1 hour of braising, turn the tongue over in the liquid. After another hour, turn it over again so it braises evenly. Check the pot at the same time to make sure the braising liquid is barely simmering, with a bubble rising to its surface every 1 or 2 seconds, and adjust the oven accordingly.

THE tongue is done when a skewer slides in and out with no resistance. Transfer the tongue to a clean pot and strain the braising liquid into a saucepan, pressing down on the vegetables to extract as much liquid as possible. Bring the liquid to a simmer and skim off any fat. Pour the braising liquid back over the tongue and slide the pot into the oven. Turn the oven down to 375°F [190°C/gas mark 5] and baste the tongue with the braising liquid every 5 minutes for about 30 minutes, until the liquid is reduced by about half and the tongue is lightly glazed. Season the liquid with salt and pepper.

SERVE the tongue in thick slices surrounded with its braising liquid in wide soup plates.

Variations: After straining out the onion and carrots and degreasing the braising liquid, I sometimes surround the tongue with pearl onions, carrot sections, fennel wedges, or turnips (left whole if small, peeled and cut into wedges if large), gently simmered in the tongue's braising liquid. The easiest way to do this is to add the vegetables to the broth surrounding the tongue during the final glazing. A more elaborate way is to steal a few ladles of the braising liquid about ½ hour before serving, simmer the vegetables in covered pans on top of the stove, and put the vegetables and the liquid back in the pot with the tongue at the end of the glazing.

Another trick, spectacular if you have leftovers (or even worth braising a tongue for), is to layer thin slices of the cold tongue in a terrine with the braising liquid, let the whole thing set, and serve it in slices, with mustard and cornichons, as a first course. If you didn't use a foot of some kind when you braised the tongue, the braising liquid may need more gelatin. Experiment with stirring ½ packet of unflavored gelatin into the melted *gelée*, and add more as needed. If you don't have enough leftover braising liquid, you may have to augment it with some concentrated beef or chicken broth. You can sprinkle the layers of tongue with freshly chopped herbs, such as parsley or chervil. You can also get very fancy and layer in thinly sliced or finely chopped truffles, slices of cooked artichoke bottoms, slices of foie gras, simmered leeks, or paper-thin slices of prosciutto. Make sure the braising liquid is concentrated enough so that it sets firmly when cold or the terrine will fall apart when you try to slice it. Or if it's fragile, consider slicing it frozen (see page 202).

LIVER

Those who don't like liver have trouble convincing me that their dislike doesn't come from having tasted beef liver or what's sometimes called, euphemistically, "baby beef" liver, both of which have an aggressive flavor, instead of authentic calves' liver. To make matters worse, most of us have tasted liver cooked in rather thin slices, which are difficult to brown properly without overcooking, and have never tasted liver cooked in the relatively thick slices recommended in many French recipes, to say nothing of slices of whole roasted liver—a popular dish before the Second World War and a different experience entirely. If you want to try it, buy a 2- to 3-pound [900 g to 1.3 kg] liver or liver section and have the butcher remove the thin transparent tissue that covers it. Brown the liver in clarified butter and then roast it at 400°F [200°C/ gas mark 6] to an internal temperature of 135°F [57°C], which will increase to 140° [59°C] as the roast liver rests.

When buying liver, look for pale pink calves' liver and avoid the liver you're likely to see in most supermarkets, labeled "beef liver" or "baby beef liver," which is dark red or purple. Getting authentic calves' liver may be harder than you think; you may have to order it ahead from a butcher or better supermarket. If you're buying the liver already sliced, make sure the slices are of even thickness (so they cook evenly) and are at least ½ inch [1.5 cm] thick. If they're too thin, you'll have a hard time getting them to brown without overcooking them. If you're buying the liver from a butcher, make sure he or she removes the thin outer membrane before slicing the liver. If this almost invisible membrane is left on, it will contract when you're cooking the liver slices and cause them to curl and to cook unevenly. If you've bought your liver already sliced and see the shiny membrane around the slices, don't try to peel it off—that's next to impossible—but make little cuts through it in several places around the slice to allow the membrane to contract without causing the slice to curl.

Always season and coat liver slices with flour just before sautéing or grilling so that a savory crust forms quickly and prevents the release of juices. It's also essential to cook sliced liver over very high heat, so the slices brown quickly. If you're grilling the slices, grill them 4 to 6 inches above a bed of hot coals; if you're sautéing, use a cooking fat. I usually use clarified butter, but olive oil or duck, goose, or bacon fat will also work. Don't use whole butter, which will burn. Make sure your pan is very hot before putting in the liver. On a home stove, this may mean using two or more skillets and leaving them on the highest heat for a few minutes—until the fat ripples but doesn't smoke—before adding the liver. (Nonstick or seasoned cast-iron skillets work best.) If you try adding too many slices to one large pan, a single burner may not be hot enough. Unlike steaks, which are cooked to different degrees of doneness depending on preferences, liver should only be cooked until it feels firm to the touch and when pink pearls of juices form on its surface after you've turned it. The inside should be pink but with none of the translucent sheen of raw liver.

SAUTÉED SLICED CALVES' LIVER WITH MADEIRA SAUCE

ESCALOPES DE FOIE DE VEAU SAUTÉE, SAUCE MADÈRE

MAKES 4 MAIN-COURSE SERVINGS

Most of my favorite French cookbooks are noncommital about which sauce to serve with liver. A typical recipe will give detailed directions on how to select and sauté, but conclude with "then finish with your favorite sauce," assuming the reader is familiar with a variety of sauces or will have little trouble making one up. I use Madeira because its nutty sweetness, balanced with a hint of vinegar, seems the perfect match for liver, but of course it's easy enough to make up your own sauces by deglazing the sauté pan with different aromatic ingredients both solid (shallots, garlic, mirepoix, thyme) and liquid (white wine, red wine, port, Sauternes), giving the sauce extra body with broth or *glace de viande* (see page 221) if you have either one, finishing with delicate herbs (parsley, chervil) or more assertive aromatic ingredients (mustard, capers, chopped cornichons, diced mushrooms, slivers of prosciutto, truffles), and swirling in a little chunk of butter for a satiny texture and to tie the flavors together.

- 4   slices calves' liver (about ½ inch [1.5 cm] thick and 6 to 8 ounces [170 to 225 g] each)

    salt

    pepper

- ½   cup [60 g] all-purpose flour

- 4   tablespoons clarified butter (see page 296); duck, goose, or bacon fat; or "pure" olive oil

- 2   medium-size shallots, or 1 small onion, chopped fine

- ½   cup [125 ml] semidry or semisweet Madeira, port, marsala, or cream sherry

- ½   cup [125 ml] concentrated brown beef or chicken broth (see page 4), or 2 tablespoons *glace de viande* or demi-glace dissolved in ½ cup [125 ml] water (see page 3)

- 2   teaspoons good-quality red or white wine vinegar or sherry vinegar, or more to taste

- 1   tablespoon Cognac or Armagnac (optional)

- 1   tablespoon finely chopped parsley

- 3   tablespoons butter

JUST before cooking, pat the liver slices dry, season them with salt and pepper, and dredge them in flour. Pat off any excess flour.

HEAT the clarified butter or other fat, over high heat, in one or two heavy-bottomed nonstick or iron skillets just large enough to hold the liver slices in a single layer. When the fat just begins to smoke, put in the slices (see "Safety Tips for Sautéing," page 555). Brown the slices 2 to 3 minutes on each side, until a crust has formed, the slices feel firm to the touch, and you see little pearls of pink juices forming on the second side, the side that's already been browned.

IMMEDIATELY place the slices on a sheet pan and pat them on both sides with paper towels to eliminate burnt fat. Unless the juices in the bottom of the pan have burned, pour the cooked fat out of the pan and stir the chopped shallots in the pan (or just one of the pans if you've used two) for about 30 seconds, until you smell the aroma of toasted shallots. (If the juices have burned, make the sauce in a clean pan or saucepan.) Pour in the Madeira and boil it down, by about half, over high heat. If you're using broth, add it to the pan and boil it down until the sauce has a lightly syrupy consistency. If you're using *glace de viande* or demi-glace, whisk it into the Madeira until it dissolves. (If this causes the sauce to become too thick, thin it with a little water or broth.) Add the vinegar and the Cognac, if you're using it. If you are using the Cognac, simmer the sauce for 30 seconds to cook off the alcohol. Whisk in the parsley and the whole butter. Adjust the thickness of the sauce by thinning it with a little water or broth or thickening it by boiling it for a few seconds. (In general, sauces finished with butter shouldn't be boiled, but a few seconds won't matter.) Adjust the seasoning with salt and pepper and, if you want a little more tang, more vinegar.

ARRANGE the liver slices on a heated platter or plates and spoon the sauce over them.

Variations: Sauce variations are again limited only by your imagination, but the sautéing treatment itself also offers possibilities. I sometimes like to buy one or two 1½-inch-thick [4-cm] slices of liver, sauté them in the same way as in the main recipe, but turn down the heat to medium after the initial browning, and cook until the liver bounces back to the touch, after a total of about 15 minutes; I then serve the slices sliced again into strips and coated with sauce. You can also bread sliced liver, which eliminates the need for extremely high heat, but you shouldn't serve breaded foods covered with a sauce, which would make the breading soggy. Traditional recipes use compound butters or beurre noisette instead. Serve the sauce in a sauceboat at the table or bread only one side of the liver slices and serve the sauce around, not over, the slices on individual plates.

I've never had any success broiling thin slices of liver because the broiler doesn't get hot enough and it's hard to control, but if you're cooking slices that are 1 inch thick or more, you can finish each slice with a bread-crumb and mustard coating by first browning it on both sides in a sauté pan, then brushing one side with mustard, dipping the mustard-coated side in bread crumbs, and broiling the slice, breaded-side up, just long enough for the bread crumbs to form a crust. The sauce should be assertive enough to match the mustard.

Liver with onions seems to be the only way that liver is served in the United States. In France it appears as *foie de veau à la lyonnaise* (*à la lyonnaise* is a designation that almost always ensures lots of onions and vinegar) or in combination with tomatoes in the Provençal *foie de veau moissonnière*, and in Italy as *fegato alla veneziana*. Whenever using onions in large amounts (versus a sprinkling to deglaze a pan), remember to slowly sweat them in some kind of fat so they soften and the liquid they release caramelizes on the bottom of the pan, a process that can take close to an hour, before incorporating them and their deglazed juices into a sauce.

Liver is great grilled. Flour it as you would if sautéing, cook it over very high heat, and brush it during the grilling with melted butter. The French like to serve it with compound butters such as *beurre maître d'hôtel* (parsley and lemon butter; see page 490) or *beurre Bercy*, butter worked with a reduction of shallots and white wine.

Sautéed mushrooms (cultivated or wild; ideally, thickly sliced cèpes) *à la bordelaise*, sprinkled with finely chopped shallots and parsley during the last 2 minutes of sautéing, spooned over the liver slices at the table, are among my favorite accompaniments.

SAFETY TIPS FOR SAUTÉING

When adding slices of meat, seafood, or vegetables to a pan of smoking hot fat, always lay the slices gently in the fat, setting them down so that the part you're holding ends up toward the back of the stove. In this way, if you're working quickly or the slice slips out of your fingers, the fat will splash away from you instead of toward you. You may also want to use tongs.

GLAZED SLICED CARROTS

CAROTTES À LA VICHY

HOW	HOW TO	HOW TO	HOW TO
ROOT VEGETABLES ARE COOKED DIFFERENTLY THAN GREEN VEGETABLES	GLAZE VEGETABLES AND CONCENTRATE THEIR FLAVOR	ROAST VEGETABLES	STUFF VEGETABLES AND MAKE UP YOUR OWN STUFFINGS

IN FRENCH COOKING, THE CARROT IS NEARLY AS IMPORTANT AS THE onion. It enters into almost every stew, broth, and braised dish, adding its sweet and subtle counterpoint to the richness of meat and some seafood. It's one of the three aromatic vegetables, along with onions and celery, in the classic combination mirepoix. Often its physical presence is hidden or altogether eliminated when the stewing liquid or broth is strained and the aromatic garniture—the mirepoix—discarded, having given its essence to the surrounding liquid.

So when I mention to assembled guests that we're having carrots as a vegetable, there are no oohs and ahs as there might be for, say, asparagus. This isn't the carrot's fault—the blame rests with the innumerable restaurants and cooks who have served up carrots boiled and drained, and, if the diner is lucky, dolloped with a pat of butter. This sorry state of affairs is the result of a fundamental misunderstanding of how to cook vegetables. Other than a few oddities like artichokes and salsify, most vegetables are cooked using one of two basic approaches: They're cooked with a small amount of fat or other liquid to concentrate their flavor, as with carrots and onions, or they're cooked with a lot of boiling water, as with most green vegetables (the method the French call cooking *à l'anglaise;* see page 587). If you mix up these approaches, you're in trouble. Slowly cooking green vegetables in a small amount of liquid (cooking them *à la française;* again see page 587), while once popular, will turn them gray, and cooking root vegetables in a lot of boiling water will leach out all their natural sugars and flavors and leave them tasting not much different from the water they were cooked in. Carrots and other root vegetables must be cooked in a small amount of water or broth, partially covered or covered with a sheet of parchment paper or aluminum foil, so the liquid evaporates as the carrots cook, leaving them coated with a sweet and flavorful glaze. The idea is to add just the right amount of liquid and to cook the carrots at the right temperature so the evaporation of the surrounding water to a syrupy glaze coincides with the carrots' being cooked through. This isn't as intimidating as it sounds, since you can start out with a small amount of liquid and monitor the carrots as they cook, adding more water if you need to, and adjusting the temperature of the oven or stove.

Carottes à la Vichy should not be difficult or time-consuming. The carrots are simply peeled and sliced, cooked in a little water (traditionally, mineral water from Vichy), finished with butter, and sprinkled with parsley. Classic recipes call for adding the butter before the carrots are cooked, but I find that the butter turns oily and I prefer to toss it gently with the cooked carrots just before serving.

GLAZED SLICED CARROTS

CAROTTES À LA VICHY

MAKES 6 SIDE-DISH SERVINGS

12 medium-size carrots with greens (to ensure their freshness)

1 cup [250 ml] Vichy water or regular water, or more as needed

salt

pepper

4 tablespoons butter

1 tablespoon finely chopped parsley

CUT the greens off the carrots, peel the carrots, and slice them into ⅛-inch-thick [3-mm] rounds. Spread the carrots in a 12-inch or 14-inch [30.5- or 35.5-cm] sauté pan or baking dish just large enough to hold them in a layer 1 inch deep. If you don't have a pan exactly the right size, don't worry, it's not critical.

POUR the water over the carrots and sprinkle them with salt. Cover the carrots with a sheet of parchment paper or aluminum foil, bring the water to a boil over high heat, and then turn the heat down to low to maintain the liquid at a gentle simmer. If you prefer, slide the pan into a 400 F° [200°C/gas mark 6] oven.

AFTER about 20 minutes, poke at the carrots with a fork and notice the amount of water left in the pan. If the carrots are still hard and there's very little water left, add another ½ cup; if the carrots have softened and there's a lot of liquid left in the pan, take off the parchment paper and turn the heat up to high (or the oven up to 500° F [260°C/gas mark 10]) to evaporate the liquid quickly so the carrots don't overcook.

WHEN the carrots are done—all their crunch should be gone—after about 30 minutes, gently pour them into a heated bowl (ideally, the one you're going to serve them in), season them with pepper, and add the butter and parsley. Toss the carrots in the bowl by giving the bowl a quick upward jerk, slightly toward you so the carrots turn over by themselves. (If this makes you nervous, use a spoon, but be very gentle so you don't break up the carrots.) Pass the bowl at the table or serve the carrots on heated plates.

GLAZED BABY CARROTS

CAROTTES NOUVELLES GLACÉES

MAKES 6 SIDE-DISH SERVINGS

(OR ENOUGH FOR A GARNITURE FOR 6 SERVINGS

OF STEW OR POT ROAST)

Glazed sliced carrots—carottes à la Vichy—make a simple and excellent side dish for just about any main course, but if you want a more elegant effect or if you want to integrate the carrots into a stew such as a blanquette de veau (see Chapter 30) or a braise such as a red wine pot roast—boeuf à la mode (see Chapter 31)—you may want to glaze whole baby carrots, cored and shaped sections of larger carrots (see instructions on page 21), or the peeled little carrots sold in bags. The cooking method for all of these is virtually the same as for carottes à la Vichy except that the carrots should be arranged in a single layer in a pan or baking dish rather than spread in a layer 1 inch deep.

30 baby carrots with greens (5 per person) or more or fewer depending on their size, or 6 medium-size carrots with greens, or 1 bag (1 pound [450 g]) peeled baby carrots

1 cup [250 ml] water

salt

pepper

2 tablespoons butter

1 tablespoons finely chopped parsley or chervil (optional)

IF you're using baby carrots, cut off most of the greens but leave about ¼ inch [.5 cm] attached—it adds color and shows off their freshness—and peel them. If you're using medium-size carrots, remove the greens completely, peel the carrots, and cut them into equal sections between 1 inch and 1½ inches [2.5 and 4 cm] long, depending on the size of your carrots. If you're feeling conscientious, cut the cores out of the sections and shape them (see page 21).

SPREAD the carrots in a sauté pan—or two—ideally just large enough to hold them in a single layer. Pour in the water and bring to a gentle simmer over medium heat. You can loosely cover the carrots with a round of parchment paper or aluminum foil as for *carottes à la Vichy*, but I just cook the carrots partially covered with the pan lid and shake the pan every few minutes so they cook evenly. Simmer the carrots gently until they're easily penetrated with a knife but, unlike *carottes a la Vichy*, retain a little of their texture, usually about 20 minutes. If, at any point during the cooking, the pan threatens to run dry, add ¼ cup of water. If the carrots seem close to done and there's still a fair amount of liquid in the pan, remove the covering and turn the heat up to high to quickly evaporate the liquid until it forms a syrupy glaze.

SEASON the carrots with salt and pepper and add the butter. Toss over low heat—you can also use a spoon, but be gentle—until the carrots are coated with a shiny glaze. Sprinkle them with the parsley and serve.

GLAZED OR CREAMED ONIONS

OIGNONS GLACÉS OU À LA CRÈME

MAKES 6 SIDE-DISH SERVINGS

Onions are glazed in the same way as carrots, by cooking them in a small amount of water or broth and butter in a partially covered pan or in a pan with the onions covered by a sheet of parchment paper or aluminum foil. Depending on how conscientious you are, you can glaze the tiny pearl onions that come in pint boxes—it's the peeling that takes the time—or you can use walnut-size white onions, sometimes called boiling onions. When they're in season, you can use small green onions (not to be confused with scallions), which, like boiling onions, have bulbs the size of walnuts, and leave a little of their greens attached. Glazed onions are a delicious accompaniment to roasted or braised meats and stews. If you're serving them with a pot roast (such as the *boeuf à la mode* on page 425) or stew, you can glaze them with some of the braising liquid—or just add them to the pot after you've strained out the aromatic vegetables—and use them to surround the meat just before serving so they become an integral part of the dish. When serving them with a roast, either pass them at the table or put them on the individual plates next to the slices of meat. If you're serving glazed onions with a roast, you can also finish them with cream, turning them into the creamed onions described at the end of this recipe.

2 packages (1 pint, or 10 ounces [280 g], each) pearl onions, or 30 walnut-size "boiling" onions, or 30 green onions (round onions with the greens attached, not scallions)

2 tablespoons butter

salt

pepper

BRING about 3 quarts of water to a rapid boil and put in the onions all at once. Boil the onions for 1 minute, drain them in a colander, and rinse them under cold running water. If you're using pearl onions or boiling onions, cut off the tiny root ends and pull away the peel, pinching it between your thumb and the side of a paring knife. If you're using green onions, the peels may be so thin that you don't need to peel them. If the outermost peel seems dry, however, peel them by cutting off the root ends and peeling away the thinnest amount of peel you can. Leave about ½ inch [1.5 cm] of the green stalk attached.

ARRANGE the peeled onions in a pan—or two—just large enough to hold them in a single layer. Avoid piling the onions on top of one another, since this will cause them to steam instead of glaze. Pour enough water into the pan to come about one-third of the way up the sides of the onions. (You can also use broth.) Add the butter, cover with parchment paper or aluminum foil, or partially with the pan lid, and bring to a gentle simmer over medium heat. Adjust the heat so the evaporation of the water down to a syrupy glaze coincides with the doneness of the onions. When the onions are cooked—from 10 to 25 minutes, depending on their size—there should be only a small amount of syrupy liquid coating them. Season with salt and pepper and serve.

IF you want to make brown-glazed onions (see page 561), continue cooking the onions until a brown glaze forms on the bottom of the pan. Add 2 tablespoons of water to the pan and swirl the onions around in the pan so they are coated with the caramelized glaze. If you want to make creamed onions, pour in ¼ cup [60 ml] of heavy cream and cook over high heat for about 2 minutes until it coats the onions.

GLAZED TURNIPS, CELERIAC, OR PARSNIPS

NAVETS, CÉLERI-RAVE, PANAIS, OU RADIS GLACÉS

MAKES 6 SIDE-DISH SERVINGS

If you have baby vegetables, glaze them exactly as you would the glazed baby carrots on page 558. If you have larger vegetables, shape them as described on page 21. Like small onions, other glazed root vegetables can be served as a side dish for roast meats or can be incorporated directly into the braising liquid from a pot roast or stew.

30 baby turnips, baby celeriac no larger than small walnuts, or baby parsnips no more than 3 inches [7.5 cm] long; or 7 small to medium-size turnips, celeriac, radishes, or parsnips; or 6 medium-size turnips, celeriac, parsnips, or radishes (25 pounds [1 kg] total weight)

1 tablespoon butter

salt

1 teaspoon sugar

pepper

IF you're using baby turnips, don't bother to peel them. Do, however, peel baby celeriac or parsnips. If you're using medium-size vegetables, shape them as described on page 21.

ARRANGE the vegetables in a pan just large enough to hold them in a single layer. If the pan's too small, the vegetables will be heaped on top of one another and will steam rather than glaze; if the pan's too big, any glaze on the unoccupied areas may burn. Pour enough water or broth into the pan to come about one-third of the way up the sides of the vegetables. Add the butter, sprinkle with salt and sugar, cover with a round of parchment paper or aluminum foil, or partially with the pan lid, and bring to a gentle simmer over medium heat. Adjust the heat so the reduction of the water to a syrupy glaze coincides with the doneness of the vegetables. When the vegetables are cooked—from 15 to 25 minutes, depending on their size—they should be coated with a small amount of glaze. Season with pepper and serve.

CONFIT OF TURNIPS WITH FOIE GRAS AND PORT WINE

CONFIT DE NAVETS AU FOIE GRAS ET AU PORTO

MAKES 6 FIRST-COURSE SERVINGS

I first tasted this dish at Alain Chapel's three-star restaurant in Mionnay, a small town outside Lyon. Mionnay is somewhat confusing to find, so instead of hitchhiking, my friend and I decided to take a country bus that stopped at every village along the way. When we got to the ticket window and asked for the tickets, the eyes of the grumpy woman behind the counter grew wide with excitement: "Vous savez il y a un très grand restaurant là bas!" (You know, there's a great restaurant there.) With equal enthusiasm I answered, "Oui, nous y allons." (Yes, that's where we're going.) Knowing nothing about any restaurant, her younger associate at the adjoining window asked her about it. As the older woman handed us our tickets, she glared at the young one with a disdain so complete—that

totally withering look fully mastered only by French waiters and bureaucrats—that it was as though the poor young woman had never heard of the pyramids.

When we reached the restaurant we ordered the menu dégustation. Among the first in a long line of dishes came these turnips with foie gras—not a single slice of turnip with a stingy sliver of foie gras, but a beautiful silver dish artfully layered with overlapping port-glazed turnip slices and a piece of sautéed foie gras the size of a main-course serving of calves' liver. Undaunted, we dug in and discovered a magical juxtaposition of sweetness from the port, gentle bitterness from the turnips, and the unctuous melting richness of the hot foie gras.

Alain Chapel had clearly used a slice of whole raw foie gras that he quickly sautéed at the last minute. I've experimented with sautéing slices of American foie gras from the Hudson valley and have found that they release water and fat so quickly in the hot pan that there's barely anything left to serve. There are two ways around this problem. Use whole French duck foie gras, which holds up better in the pan, or use terrine of foie gras (bloc or entier; see page 96), which has already been at least partially cooked so that it contains less water.

6   slices (¼ inch [.5 cm] thick; about 2 ounces [55 g] each) terrine of foie gras bloc or entier or raw French duck foie gras; 6 slices (½ inch [1.5 cm] thick; about 3 ounces each) raw whole duck foie gras liver

    salt

    pepper

3   medium-size turnips, peeled, sliced into ¼-inch-thick [.5 cm] rounds

½   cup [250 ml] tawny port

PREHEAT the oven to 200°F [95°C].

SEASON the slices of foie gras on both sides with salt and pepper. Heat a nonstick sauté pan over high heat for about 2 minutes and quickly sauté the foie gras slices about 30 seconds on each side, until they brown. Immediately take the pan off the heat, so as not to burn the fat. Transfer the browned foie gras to a plate and slide it into the warm oven.

PUT the turnip slices in the pan used to sauté the foie gras. Leave the fat in the pan unless it burned, in which case replace it with 2 tablespoons of butter or duck fat. Gently cook the slices over medium heat until they are lightly browned and easily penetrated with a knife, about 5 minutes on each side. Gently turn the turnip slices with a spatula or tongs and season them to taste with salt and pepper. Pour the port and any liquid released by the foie gras in the oven over the turnips. (Ideally, your pan should be large enough to cook the turnip slices in a single layer; if it isn't, work in batches, using half or one-third of the foie gras fat or other fat and the port for each batch. Or use two or three pans at once.) As you're cooking the turnips, boil the port down until it caramelizes and adheres to the slices.

ARRANGE the glazed turnip slices on hot plates. Arrange the slices of foie gras over the turnips on each plate and spoon any syrupy liquid left in the sauté pan over them.

ROAST VEGETABLES

Virtually any root vegetable can be cooked with a small amount of liquid, the liquid becoming a glaze that combines the flavors of the cooking liquid and the flavors released by the vegetable itself. (The liquid is usually water, but it can also be broth or cream.) This is the system used for glazed carrots, onions, and turnips. Unlike glazed vegetables, roast vegetables, in the strictest sense, are cooked in the oven with no liquid except for a small amount of oil or melted butter to keep them from drying out. Sometimes vegetables for roasting are peeled and at other times vegetables (beets, winter squash) are roasted unpeeled. Vegetables intended for roasting can be left whole or can be shaped (see page 21) in the same way as glazed vegetables, but the size is important only for appearance and, if a combination of vegetables is being roasted, to ensure that the vegetables take the same time to cook. Green vegetables are rarely roasted, because they need boiling water or steam to soften them; roasting only turns them gray and hard.

While the distinction between glazing—actually a form of braising—and roasting is easy to understand, in the real world, and especially in French cooking, the distinction becomes hazy. A favorite French method for roasting vegetables is to use the vegetables to surround a roast of meat, so while in fact both meat and vegetables are roasting, the juices and fats from the meat mingle with the juices of the vegetables in such a way that the vegetables start out roasting but end up glazing. When I roast vegetables, I often simulate the effect of their having been cooked with meat by first tossing them with a little melted butter and roasting them until they soften and their flavor has become concentrated, in large part through evaporation of the water they contain. Then, shortly before serving, I pour in a small amount of concentrated broth and let it evaporate and coat the vegetables with a savory sheen.

MIXED ROAST ROOT VEGETABLES

PANACHÉ DE LÉGUMES RÔTIS

MAKES 6 SIDE-DISH SERVINGS

2   medium-size carrots, or 6 baby carrots

2   medium-size parsnips, or 6 baby parsnips

2   medium-size turnips, or 6 baby turnips

1   medium-size fennel bulb

6   walnut-size boiling onions, or 1 pint [335 g] pearl onions, peeled

3   tablespoons melted butter or extra-virgin olive oil

    salt

    pepper

½   cup [125 ml] concentrated broth or jus (optional)

Because it's no harder to make an assortment of roast vegetables than it is to roast only one kind—and the effect is far more interesting—I scour the market for as many root vegetables as I can find. In the spring there's an abundance of baby turnips, onions, and carrots at the local farmers' market and in the early fall I find the same vegetables in adult form. In the winter I rely on the supermarket. Baby vegetables require little if any preparation, but larger vegetables may need to be cut into wedges or sections and, if you're conscientious, cored or shaped. Ideally, the vegetables should be the same size. If they're not, estimate their cooking times and add them to the roasting pan at different times, so they finish at the same time. Don't worry if some of the vegetables are undercooked while others are not; just cook all the vegetables a little longer.

If you're roasting vegetables around a chunk of meat, perhaps a leg of lamb, you'll need to time the cooking so meat and vegetables are ready together. Remember, also, not to confuse roast vegetables that you intend to serve with the meat with what's called the fonçage (see Chapter 37), a mixture of more or less coarsely chopped vegetables, cooked under the roast along with meat trimmings and bones and used to provide aromatic support to the jus. If you want to serve roast vegetables and flavor them with the drippings from the roast, but at the same time you want to use a fonçage for your jus, you're better off roasting the vegetables separately and glazing them at the last minute with the drippings, both fat and liquid, from the roast, some concentrated broth, or the finished jus. If you can't find all the vegetables listed below, just use more of the others. For that matter, this same system can be used for a single vegetable.

IF you're using medium-size carrots, cut off and discard their greens, peel the carrots, and cut them into pieces 1 inch long. If you like, core and shape the carrots as described on page 21. If you're using baby carrots, lightly peel them and leave about ¼ inch [.5 cm] of their greens attached.

PREPARE the parsnips in the same way as the carrots.

IF you're using medium-size turnips, peel them and cut them into 6 wedges each. If you like, round off the sharp edges to make the wedges more attractive. If you're using baby turnips, just cut off all but about ¼ inch [.5 cm] of the greens; don't bother peeling them.

CUT the stalks off the fennel bulb and peel off the stringy outer fiber from the bulb with a vegetable peeler. Cut the fennel through the center core at the base into 6 wedges. Be sure to leave a small section of the center core attached to each wedge so the wedges hold together.

TOSS the vegetables with the butter or oil and salt and pepper and spread them in a roasting pan or gratin dish, ideally in a single layer. (Or use them to surround a meat roast.) Roast at 400° F [200°C/gas mark 6], until all the vegetables are easily penetrated with a knife, from 30 minutes for baby vegetables to 1 hour for larger vegetables. If you're roasting meat at a different temperature in the same oven, just put the vegetables in earlier or later.

WHEN the vegetables are done, you can serve them as they are or give them a final glazing by pouring broth or *jus* into the hot roasting pan and shaking the pan every few minutes to coat the vegetables, until the broth has evaporated and formed a shiny glaze. If everything else is ready and you're in a hurry, put the roasting pan on the stove on high heat and shake it back and forth to evaporate the broth and glaze the vegetables quickly.

BAKED STUFFED VEGETABLES

For practical purposes, roasting and baking are the same thing, although strictly speaking roasting means cooking on a spit in front of an open fire, something we're unlikely to do with vegetables. But roasting also implies an intense heat designed to seal in flavor quickly and perhaps even to cause the outside of the vegetable to caramelize. Baking implies cooking at a lower temperature so that the moisture in the vegetables slowly evaporates and the vegetable's flavor is slowly concentrated.

French cooks are geniuses at making something delicious out of a few leftovers and raw ingredients. In the south of France, where there's an abundance of vegetables, cooks often improvise stuffings for vegetables to give them savor and to turn them into bright hors d'oeuvres or side dishes or, if there's enough variety, even a main course. The stuffing is usually based on the pulp carved out of vegetables such zucchini, eggplants, and tomatoes, and is usually cooked with garlic and onions, sometimes pieces of leftover meat or ham, often bread crumbs or rice, and herbs. If an assortment of stuffed vegetables is being served, the herbs and other flavorings should be varied as much as possible so that each vegetable has its own special identity and all the vegetables taste different. Don't worry about following these recipes too closely. You can exchange the stuffing flavorings with those for different vegetables.

You can make a dramatic platter of several stuffed vegetables if you can find an assortment of baby vegetables or, if the vegetables are larger, you can stuff one or two and serve them as a first course or a side dish for meat or fish.

STUFFED ZUCCHINI

COURGETTES FARCIES

MAKES 4 FIRST-COURSE OR SIDE-DISH SERVINGS

4   medium-size zucchini, (each about 6 inches [15 cm] long, 1½ inches [3.5 cm] across)

1   tablespoon extra-virgin olive oil (for baking the zucchini), plus 1 tablespoon (if you're using pancetta) or 2 tablespoons (if you're using prosciutto)

1   small onion, chopped fine

1   large clove garlic, chopped fine

1   slice (2 ounces [55 g]) pancetta or prosciutto end, chopped fine

2   teaspoons chopped fresh marjoram, or 1 teaspoon fresh thyme leaves or ¼ teaspoon dried thyme leaves

1   slice dense-crumb white bread, crusts removed

¼   cup [60 ml] milk

½   cup [50 g] finely grated Parmigiano-Reggiano, *grana padana*, or other flavorful hard cheese

    salt

    pepper

PREHEAT the oven to 400° F [200°C/gas mark 6]. Wash the zucchini thoroughly, trim off the stems, and cut the zucchini in half lengthwise. Rub the zucchini with olive oil and arrange them flat-side down on a sheet pan. Bake for 25 to 35 minutes, or until the zucchini feel soft when you pinch them gently. Take them out of the oven but leave the oven on.

WHILE the zucchini are baking, cook the onion, garlic, and pancetta in olive oil in a sauté pan over low to medium heat until the onion turns translucent, about 10 minutes. Sprinkle with the marjoram and cook for 1 minute more.

SOAK the bread in the milk.

SCOOP the pulp out of the zucchini with a spoon or melon baller, being careful not to break through the skin—it's okay to leave some pulp attached to the skin. Combine the pulp with the onion mixture and continue to cook it on the stove to evaporate the moisture in the zucchini pulp. Stir in the bread and cheese and season to taste with salt and pepper. Carefully put the stuffing back into the zucchini— the stuffing will form a mound—and return the zucchini to the oven. If the zucchini won't stay level on the sheet pan, spread crumpled aluminum foil on the sheet pan and press the zucchini gently into the foil. Bake in a 400°F [200°C/gas mark 6] oven until golden brown on top, about 20 to 25 minutes, and serve.

STUFFED TOMATOES

TOMATES À LA PROVENÇAL

MAKES 6 FIRST-COURSE OR SIDE-DISH SERVINGS

With typical French thrift, Roger Vergé, one of Provence's most renowned chefs, stuffs tomatoes by using leftover meat from a stew or a pot-au-feu. If you don't happen to have any pot-au-feu hanging around, you can use leftover meat from roast beef, lamb, chicken, or turkey. You just scoop out the inside of the tomato and cook the pulp with herbs, onion, and garlic. Some cooks add sausage meat,

but I've never cared much for it unless I've made it myself, so I substitute my standby favorites, pancetta or prosciutto end or even bacon (whose smokiness catches everyone delightfully off-guard). Stuffed tomatoes are best served as a first course or side dish.

6   medium-size tomatoes

    salt

1   medium-size onion, chopped fine

2   cloves garlic, chopped fine

1   tablespoon extra-virgin olive oil (if you're using pancetta), or 2 tablespoons (if you're using prosciutto or leftover meat), plus 1 tablespoon (for the sheet pan)

1   slice (4 ounces [115 g]) pancetta or prosciutto end, chopped fine, or 1 cup [450 g] meat from a stew, pot roast, or pot-au-feu, roast bird, or roast beef or lamb, chopped coarse (to about the size of large peas)

5   fresh sage leaves (don't use dried sage), or 1 tablespoon finely chopped fresh marjoram leaves (chopped at the last minute with a few drops of olive oil), or ½ teaspoon dried thyme leaves

2   cups [380 g] cooked long-grain rice (you'll need to boil about ⅔ cup [125 g] raw rice to get this amount)

1   cup [100 g] finely grated Parmigiano-Reggiano or other full-flavored hard cheese

    pepper

CUT the stem end out of each of the tomatoes and then cut a slice off the top, about ½ inch [1.5 cm] down, so the slice forms a lid. Reserve the lids. Hold the tomatoes upside down and gently squeeze them to force out the seeds. Reach into the little crevices with your finger to pull out any remaining seeds. Discard the seeds and the liquid that comes out of the tomatoes and cut around the inside of each tomato with a melon baller or sharp paring knife, cutting out as much of the interior pulp as you can without cutting into the pulpy outer body of the tomato. Reserve the pulp. Sprinkle the insides of the hollowed-out tomatoes with salt and turn the tomatoes upside-down on a paper towel to drain. Chop the reserved pulp.

WHILE the tomatoes are draining, cook the onion and garlic in olive oil in a sauté pan over low to medium heat until the onion turns translucent, about 10 minutes. If you're using pancetta or prosciutto, cook it along with the onion and garlic. If you're using leftover meat, add it to the pan after the onion has cooked. Sprinkle in the sage, add the chopped tomato pulp, and cook for about 3 minutes more. Combine the mixture with the rice and cheese and season to taste with salt and pepper.

PREHEAT the oven to 350° F [175°C/gas mark 4]. Set the tomatoes upright and gently stuff them—the stuffing should mound slightly on top. Place a tomato lid on each one. Brush a sheet pan with olive oil and arrange the tomatoes on it. Slide the pan into the oven and bake for 45 minutes to 1 hour.

STUFFED
MUSHROOMS

CHAMPIGNONS FARCIS

MAKES 25 INDIVIDUAL HORS D'OEUVRES,

OR 6 FIRST-COURSE OR SIDE-DISH SERVINGS

The great thing about stuffing mushrooms is that they provide the base for their own stuffing mixture—the stems. The usual approach is to chop the stems, cook them down until they release their water, and then add ingredients such as cream or bread crumbs for texture and to help hold them together, and herbs such as parsley, chervil, or tarragon—that is, make duxelles. More fanciful versions can be made with fresh cèpes (porcini) or portobellos; luxurious stuffings such as foie gras or snails (dolloped with garlic-parsley butter) can replace or augment the usual duxelles. Duxelles cooked in foie gras fat—the yellow fat that forms on top of a terrine (see page 96) or the gently rendered fat from a chunk of foie gras—is divine.

35 medium-size mushrooms (about 1½ inches [4 cm] across the top), such as cremini, portobellos, cèpes, or regular cultivated mushrooms

1 tablespoon butter, foie gras fat, or duck fat (for cooking the duxelles), plus 1 teaspoon butter (for the sheet pan)

1 small clove garlic, chopped fine

1 shallot, chopped fine

½ cup [125 ml] heavy cream

3 tablespoons finely chopped parsley (chopped at the last minute)

salt

pepper

PUT the mushrooms in a colander and rinse them under cold running water while tossing them quickly but gently. Cut away any dark or dirt-encrusted parts from the bottom of the stems. Snap the stems away from the caps and chop the stems and 5 whole mushrooms fine, by hand or in a food processor. (If you're using a food processor, cut the 5 mushrooms into several pieces each and pulse the stems and pieces until they have the consistency of hamburger relish—not purée.)

PREHEAT the oven to 375° F [190°C/gas mark 5].

HEAT the fat in a sauté pan and gently sweat the garlic and shallot for about 3 minutes until they smell fragrant. Add the chopped mushroom stems, turn the heat to high, and cook the mixture, stirring every 1 or 2 minutes, until the shopped stems release their liquid and the liquid evaporates, leaving the mixture dry. Add the heavy cream and boil it down until the mixture has thickened, about 5 minutes. Stir 2 tablespoons of the parsley into the duxelles and season to taste with salt and pepper. Fill the caps with the duxelles, forming mounds on the inverted caps. Arrange the mushrooms on a buttered sheet pan and bake for 20 minutes. Sprinkle with the remaining parsley and serve piping hot.

STUFFED
EGGPLANTS

AUBERGINES FARCIS

MAKES 4 FIRST-COURSE OR SIDE-DISH SERVINGS

This is another one of those dishes for which you take out the vegetable's inside pulp, flavor it with herbs, onion, garlic, and cheese, put it back in, and bake it. My own little trick is to stew the stuffing with tomatoes and douse it with a good amount of freshly chopped basil and garlic. If you have the same aversion to eggplant seeds as I do, you'll like this stuffing, since the seeds are strained out. This recipe is designed for long, thin Japanese eggplants or, better yet, the paler purple Chinese ones, which have a gentler flavor. Long Italian-style eggplants will do in a pinch and the fat, bulbous eggplants usually sold in the supermarket can be used as a last resort.

2 Chinese, Japanese, or Italian eggplants (about 8 inches [20.5 cm] long and ¼ pound [115 g] each)

3 tablespoons extra-virgin olive oil

1 medium-size onion, chopped fine

2 cloves garlic, chopped fine

3 tomatoes, peeled, seeded, chopped

   salt

   pepper

20 fresh basil leaves

12 anchovy fillets, soaked for 5 minutes in cold water and patted dry, or 24 olive halves (optional)

PREHEAT the oven to 400° F [200°C/gas mark 6]. Cut the eggplants in half lengthwise and trim off the stem ends. Coat the eggplants with 1 tablespoon of the olive oil. Place them flat-side down on a sheet pan and bake them for about 20 minutes, until a skewer goes through one of them with no resistance. Take the eggplants out of the oven and let them cool.

WHILE the eggplants are baking, cook the onion and garlic in a saucepan in 1 tablespoon of the olive oil over medium heat for about 5 minutes, until they smell fragrant, and add the tomatoes. Cook the mixture over medium heat until it stiffens, 10 to 15 minutes. Take the saucepan off the heat and set a fine-mesh strainer or a food mill (with the finest plate) over it. Scoop the pulp out of the cooled eggplants into the strainer or food mill. Leave a little of the pulp adhering to the skins so the eggplants don't fall apart. Work the pulp through the strainer with a ladle, or through the food mill, into the tomato mixture. Stir the mixture and check its consistency. If the mixture is runny, cook it over medium heat until it stiffens. Season to taste with salt and pepper.

TOSS the basil leaves with the remaining tablespoon of olive oil (to keep the leaves from turning dark) and chop them fine. Spread the mixture evenly along the bottom of the hollowed-out eggplant halves and spoon in the tomato mixture, forming a mound running along the length of each half. Bake the stuffed eggplants on a sheet pan for 10 minutes, to heat them through. Decorate each one with anchovies or olive halves and heat in the oven for 1 minute more.

PETITS OIGNONS FARCIS

MAKES 18 HORS D'OEUVRES,

OR 6 FIRST-COURSE OR SIDE-DISH SERVINGS

This is another recipe inspired by Roger Vergé, who roasts whole onions, scoops out the insides, and fills each onion with a mixture of cheese and the chopped insides. In this version, I include thyme, Gruyère cheese, and cream. The size of the onions is up to you, but this recipe is designed to make 18 individual hors d'oeuvres or, if you give each person 3 onions, a first course. If you want to use medium-size onions, use 6 onions and double the amounts of the other ingredients to make 6 first courses or side dishes.

18 boiling onions (each slightly larger than a walnut, if possible)

½   teaspoon fresh thyme leaves or ¼ teaspoon dried thyme

1   tablespoon butter

1   slice dense-crumb white bread, crust removed

½   cup [125 ml] heavy cream

⅔   cup [75 g] finely grated Gruyère

    salt

    pepper

PREHEAT the oven to 400°F [200°C/gas mark 6] and bake the onions for about 25 minutes, until a skewer slides in and out of one with no resistance. Leave the oven on and let the onions cool enough so you can handle them. Cut off the root end, being careful not to cut too far into the onion, and gently pull away the peel. Reach in through the top of the onion (the side away from the root end) by sliding a small teaspoon between the layers and pull out most of the inside of the onion, but leave enough of the outside intact to hold the stuffing.

CHOP the insides you've taken out of the onions and cook them with the thyme, in butter, in a small sauté pan for about 5 minutes. Transfer the mixture to a mixing bowl and add the bread and cream. Work the mixture with your hands to break up the bread, but don't overwork it or you'll make it heavy. Stir in the cheese and season the mixture to taste with salt and pepper.

CAREFULLY spoon the mixture into the onions and gently arrange the onions in a baking dish, ideally just large enough to hold the onions upright. (If you have trouble keeping the onions upright, nestle them in a sheet of crumpled aluminum foil. When served they will be softer and should stay upright on the plate.) Bake the onions for 15 to 20 minutes and serve.

BAKED CREAMED
POTATO GRATIN

GRATIN DAUPHINOIS

WHAT ARE	HOW TO	TRICKS	HOW TO	HOW TO
GRATINS AND HOW TO MAKE THEM	MAKE BÉCHAMEL SAUCE	WITH POTATOES	MAKE A "TIAN," A PROVENÇAL GRATIN WITH FRESH TOMATO SAUCE	IMPROVISE YOUR OWN GRATINS

I SO LOVE HEAVY CREAM THAT A FRIEND ONCE REMARKED THAT ALL my recipes could be pared down to very simple directions: Pour heavy cream over it and bake. In my own defense, this is true only for potatoes and certain other gratins. With little variations here and there, a *gratin dauphinois* is essentially a baking dish filled with sliced potatoes stacked in layers, with heavy cream poured over each layer, and baked. While strictly traditional recipes for *gratin dauphinois* don't contain cheese, I sprinkle the layers of potato with Gruyère simply because I like the flavor and the strings of cheese that pull away from the gratin as everyone takes a bite. Other nuances include rubbing the gratin dish with garlic—this is a solid tradition and shows up in most recipes—and sprinkling the layers with a little nutmeg—essential to some, heretical to others. My own approach is to use a tiny bit.

Except for heat-wave summer days when I live on tomatoes and salads, I could eat *gratin dauphinois* every day. Some recipes try, mostly in vain, to lighten a *gratin dauphinois* by replacing the heavy cream with milk. In fact, replacing some of the heavy cream with milk is a good idea because the gratin is lightened without taking away from the effect of richness, but if you try replacing more than half the cream with milk, the milk will separate and leave the potatoes specked with little pieces of milk solids instead of a creamy and gooey coating. There are three other issues that are often debated: what kind of potatoes to use, how thick to slice them, and whether to wash the slices. Frankly, you can make a *gratin dauphinois* out of any potato you want; the effect will just differ accordingly. Russet potatoes have a slightly mealy texture, but they hold together nicely; yellow-fleshed potatoes like Yukon Golds and Yellow Finns have a delicious flavor and a melting texture, but I find them to be a bit too fragile. I use white waxy potatoes because they hold together well and have a fine creamy texture (although not as creamy as a Yukon Gold's) when baked. I buy the largest ones I can find so there aren't as many to peel. Most recipes insist that the potatoes for a *gratin dauphinois* not be washed after slicing, the idea being that the starch left attached to the potato helps bind the sauce. I haven't been able to tell much difference between gratins made with washed and unwashed potatoes. I wash the potatoes when I've peeled and sliced them ahead of time so they don't turn dark, but I skip the washing when I'm constructing the gratin as I go along, which is most of the time. The thickness is, again, up to you. Thick-sliced and thin-sliced potatoes work equally well; you'll just end up with different effects. A gratin made with thin-sliced potatoes will hold together in a kind of cake, while a gratin made with thick potatoes will almost look like a gooey and creamy potato stew when you serve it.

How thick you make the gratin will depend on what kind of baking dish you use. You can make it any thickness you like, but I like to make it rather thin so that there's a large proportion of browned crust. This isn't always possible if I'm cooking for a crowd and don't want the gratin to take up all the space in the oven. My own favorite for a gratin large enough to serve 8 people is a tin-lined oval copper dish measuring 9 inches [23 cm] wide by 13 inches [33 cm] long.

One tip: Don't skimp on the cheese. Use authentic Swiss Gruyère and not Emmentaler (the kind with the big holes), because Emmentaler doesn't have as full a flavor and it will be too stringy. If you want to substitute a different cheese entirely, just use one with a lot of flavor—aged cheddar (I prefer the farmhouse English or American kind that hasn't been dyed orange), Comté, Parmigiano-Reggiano, aged Gouda, or a good blue cheese (Roquefort, Gorgonzola, or Stilton—not Danish blue, which is too strong)—but, for blue cheese, use half the amount that's in the recipe below, broken up into little pieces since it's too soft to grate.

BAKED CREAMED POTATO GRATIN

GRATIN DAUPHINOIS

MAKES 8 SIDE-DISH SERVINGS

2½ pounds [1 kg] red or white waxy potatoes (about 3 very large or 6 medium-size)

1 small garlic clove, crushed with the side of a chef's knife

1 tablespoon softened butter

2 cups [500 ml] heavy cream, or 1 cup [250 ml] milk and 1 cup [250 ml] cream (mixed together), or 2 cups [500 ml] half-and-half

salt

pepper

nutmeg (tiny pinch)

¾ pound [340 g] Gruyère, grated fine (about 4 cups when grated)

PEEL the potatoes and put them in a bowl of cold water to keep them from turning dark.

PREHEAT the oven to 350°F [175°C/gas mark 4].

THOROUGHLY rub the inside of a large gratin dish or baking dish with the garlic clove. Smear the inside of the dish with the butter to make the dish easier to wash. Bring the cream to a simmer in a saucepan and pour enough into the dish to form a thin layer. Sprinkle salt and pepper and a tiny bit of nutmeg into the cream. Slice the potatoes about ⅛ inch [3 mm] thick (the thickness of 2 quarters) and spread them over the layer of cream, overlapping them slightly. Sprinkle the potatoes with cheese, pour more cream over them, and season again with salt, pepper, and nutmeg. Repeat until you've used everything up, finishing with a layer of cheese.

IF you've used a flame-proof dish, place the dish on top of the stove and move it gently back and forth, positioning it in different spots, over medium heat, until the cream comes to a simmer, about 5 minutes. Bake for 1 hour (or slightly more if you didn't heat it on the stove), until the top of the gratin is golden brown nd a knife slides easily in and out of the potatoes.

Variations: It's hard to imagine that until the beginning of the nineteenth century, the French didn't eat potatoes. It was Antoine Augustine Parmentier, a French economist, who recognized that the potato, easy to grow in difficult soil and climates, could be helpful when other crop yields were low. Parmentier spent the latter part of his life getting the French to eat potatoes, and a number of classic potato dishes have his name attached to them. By the end of the nineteenth century, there were more than 100 potato recipes in the classic repertoire, with potatoes (*pommes de terre*) cooked in every conceivable way—fried, puréed, glazed, roasted, baked into gratins. Potato gratin variations are easy to imagine. Baked with cooked onions and broth, the dish becomes *pommes de terre à la boulangère*; cooked covered with lots of butter and unmolded into a cake, it becomes *pommes Anna* (see page 572). I often make a simple gratin of my own by just layering the potatoes in a dish while seasoning and spooning melted butter over each layer. It's also easy to include other vegetables in a potato gratin that if made into their own gratin would have too strong a taste, or would be too dense, or not starchy enough. Turnips are an example. If baked into their own gratin, they're a bit strong and the gratin doesn't hold together very well because there's relatively little starch. But if turnips are used to replace *half* of the potatoes in a *gratin dauphinois*, the results are magnificent. The same is true of celeriac.

Some vegetables can be interspersed between the layers of a *gratin dauphinois* as flavoring. Lyonnaise versions often contain onions (leeks are even better), sweated first in a little butter. Old classic versions (or modern ones in very expensive restaurants) often contain truffles between the layers. Potato gratins can also be made by combining mashed potatoes with cheese or herbs or other flavorings, sprinkling the top with more grated cheese, and quickly heating in the oven. Sometimes a little cooked bacon and bacon fat are added to the mashed potatoes or sprinkled over sliced potatoes in a gratin to give them a smoky flavor, but almost any flavorful ingredient—including onions, garlic, cubes of cooked artichoke bottoms, cubes of leftover meat or poultry—can be folded into mashed potatoes or layered in a potato gratin. One of the classics of French home cooking is the *boeuf en miroton* (see page 445), a gratin made by layering cooked rounds of potato with slices of leftover meat and a sauce made by sweating onions in butter, stirring in a little flour to make a roux, and finishing with some broth. A *rapée morvandelle* (*rapée* means grated and *morvandelle* refers to the Morvan) is much like a *gratin dauphinois*, except that the potatoes are grated before they are mixed with cream, eggs, and cheese and baked.

POTATO CAKE

POMMES ANNA

MAKES 1 "CAKE," ENOUGH FOR ABOUT
8 SIDE-DISH SERVINGS

In the winter when air fares are low and the tourists are gone, I often take a quick jaunt to Paris. I keep costs down by staying in a hotel that's a little worn around the edges, but budgetary concerns end whenever my nose and stomach are involved. I always treat myself to a copper pot or two in one of the cooking supply shops near the edge of what was once Les Halles. For anyone who likes to cook, these shops, glistening with beautiful thick hammered copper, are hard to resist. One especially pretty object is a copper pommes Anna pan, a low, straight-sided pot with a lid that fits down along the sides of the pot about an inch. Since pommes Anna—essentially slices of potato cooked into a cake—contains a lot of butter, the pan is designed to let you to turn the cake over before serving without the butter running out or the cake falling apart. You can make pommes Anna without such an elegant device, but it's a fine excuse to buy something that will look good in the kitchen. (See Sources for some kitchenware shops in Paris.)

8 large red or white waxy potatoes (about 4 pounds [1.8 kg] total)

½ pound [225 g] (2 sticks) butter, softened

salt

pepper

PEEL the potatoes up to a day ahead and leave them in a bowl of cold water until you're ready to slice them.

PREHEAT the oven to 400°F [200°C/gas mark 6].

RUB the inside (including the sides) of a 10-inch [25.5-cm] pommes Anna pan or a straight-sided 10-inch [25.5-cm] nonstick ovenproof sauté pan with a thick layer of softened butter, about ½ stick. Place a round of parchment paper in the pan—

make sure it fits exactly—and rub it with 3 tablespoons more of the butter. Slice the potatoes into 2-inch [5-cm] rounds about the thickness of quarters with a mandoline (see page 13) or chef's knife. (For added drama, rotate one of the potatoes against the blade of a knife, doing your best to shape it into a perfect cylinder. Slice this potato, which will yield perfect rounds, and layer the rounds in the pan first.) Don't rinse the potato slices or you'll rinse off the starch that holds them together in the cake. Arrange the slices in a rosette pattern in the pan. When you've arranged one layer of potatoes, season the layer with salt and pepper and dot it with pieces of butter about the size of hazelnuts. Put another layer of potatoes over the first. (You don't have to be as careful about arranging the potatoes perfectly, since no one will see this layer.) Continue in this way, layering, seasoning, and dolloping with butter until you've used up all the potatoes. If you don't have a pommes Anna pan, reserve 2 tablespoons of the butter.

IF you're using a pommes Anna pan, put the lid on. If you're using a straight-sided sauté pan, press a round of parchment paper or aluminum foil, spread thickly with the reserved butter, on top of the potatoes to keep those on top from becoming too brown. Slide the pan into the oven and bake for 1 hour. At this point, if you're using a pommes Anna pan, take off the lid—or if you're using a regular pan, take off the parchment paper—to allow the moisture in the potatoes to evaporate. Bake for 60 to 90 minutes more, until the pommes Anna is about half as thick as the potatoes were when you put them in the pan and the top—the eventual bottom—is golden brown.

IF you're using a regular sauté pan, tilt it sideways and pour off as much excess butter as you can while holding the potatoes in place by pressing on top of them with the back of a spatula. Quickly move the pommes Anna pan or sauté pan handle back and forth clockwise and counterclockwise to loosen the potatoes. Place a round serving dish on top of the pan and quickly turn the whole thing over and lift away the pan. Peel the parchment paper away from the potatoes. Serve in wedges.

IF you're making this a day ahead, cool the pan overnight in the refrigerator. To unmold, warm the pan over low heat until the *pommes Anna* has loosened slightly. Place a plate on top of the pan and invert.

Variation: Other ingredients, such as sautéed wild mushrooms, thinly sliced zucchini, truffle slices, or slices of full-flavored cheese, can be put between the layers of potatoes. Because *pommes Anna* with truffles is such an extravagance and much of the flavor of the truffle is lost during the long cooking, I make it only when I have an abundance of black summer truffles, which are far less expensive.

IMPROVISING GRATINS

The method of covering foods with liquid and baking until the flavors concentrate and the food becomes coated with a savory crust is infinitely versatile. A bubbling-hot gratin taken right out of the oven and served at the table makes an impressive sight, provoking oohs and ahs that are all the more satisfying be-cause most gratins require very little energy to make.

Most of the best-known gratins are made by pouring heavy cream or a sauce such as béchamel or tomato sauce over vegetables or pasta, sprinkling with cheese, and then baking until the foods cook through and a savory crust forms on top. Much of the time, foods to be gratinéed should be cooked first so that they need less time in the oven and, in the case of vegetables, so that the moisture they contain is released during the precooking instead of remaining in the gratin, where it would dilute the surrounding sauce.

USING HEAVY CREAM: Many foods, including potatoes, turnips, and celeriac, can simply be layered in a gratin dish, the layers doused with heavy cream, grated cheese sprinkled on top, and the whole thing baked. For many dishes, though, heavy cream is just too rich. But two of my favorite gratins, both of them delicious and made with plenty of cream, are stand-bys in my kitchen: pasta gratin and leek gratin.

JUDGING WHEN A GRATIN IS DONE

It's impossible to give exact recipes for gratins because there are so many variables, such as the thickness of the mixture in the dish (itself dependent on the size dish you use) and the exact temperature of your oven. It's important to recognize, especially when making gratins with cream, that if the cream is cooked too long, it will break and turn into butter. The trick is, obviously, to cook it less. But what if your gratin isn't browning properly? There are a couple of things you can do. You can cook the gratin at a higher temperature for less time so the crust forms while the cream has less time to evaporate. Check the gratin from time to time to see if the cream is thickening and a crust is forming. If neither is happening, turn up the heat. If the cream is thickening but the top isn't browning, either turn up the heat to high to quickly brown the top without overcooking the cream, or, if it looks as if the cream is about to break, slide the gratin under the broiler to brown it on top. Gratins made with béchamel sauce are more forgiving than those made with cream, but they can still break if over-cooked. Again, judge the oven temperature by seeing if the béchamel is thickening and a brown crust is forming, and adjust the oven temperature accordingly.

PASTA GRATIN

GRATIN DE MACARONI

MAKES 6 SIDE-DISH SERVINGS

Pasta gratins have long been popular in southern France and in Italy (where they are usually called *pasticcii*). They make the perfect accompaniment to stews and braised meat dishes, especially those containing red wine. I'll serve a pasta gratin with just about anything because it's a snap to make and my guests always go nuts when they take their first bite.

My own version of pasta gratin is really nothing more than macaroni and cheese, except that I don't limit myself to elbow macaroni but sometimes use fettuccine, linguine, or ziti for slightly different effects. My choice of pasta is often dictated by what's left over from the night before or what happens to be in the cupboard. My own version is also made with heavy cream—I know it's shocking, but I can't help it—and Parmigiano-Reggiano, sometimes combined with grated Gruyère. I spread the pasta in a buttered gratin or baking dish (buttered to make the dish easier to clean). My favorite dish is a 9-by-13-inch [23 by 33 cm] oval, and the pasta ends up no more than 1 inch [2.5 cm] thick, so there's plenty of crust. I let the crust form twice, as with a cassoulet, turning the first crust under and into the pasta, sprinkling with more cheese, and allowing a second crust to form. The result is half custard, half crunch, and it's magnificent. Don't hesitate to make a lot. Your guests will probably eat twice as much as you thought possible, and should you have any left over, pasta gratin is great reheated.

1   pound [450 g] dried pasta such as elbow macaroni, linguine, ziti, or fettuccine, or 1½ pounds [675 g] fresh

1   tablespoon butter, softened

    salt

    pepper

2½ cups [625 ml] heavy cream, or as needed

2½ cups [600 ml] (½ pound) finely grated Parmigiano-Reggiano or grana Padano, or other dry, hard cheese, such as Gruyère or aged Gouda

PREHEAT the oven to 375°F [190°C/gas mark 5].

COOK the pasta until it's about done—it doesn't matter if it's a little underdone or overdone—and drain it in a colander.

RUB the butter on the inside of a gratin dish or baking dish big enough to hold the pasta in a layer about 1 inch [2.5 cm] thick.

SPREAD the pasta in an even layer in the dish. Sprinkle liberally with salt and pepper. (Lots of pepper is good, but go easy on the salt, since the cheese is salty.) Pour the cream over the pasta, but don't use enough to drown it, only enough so that the cream covers it when you push down on the pasta with the back of a fork. Sprinkle half the grated cheese over the pasta.

BAKE until a crust forms, about ½ hour, and gently fold the crusty pasta on top down into the cream so there's no crust left on top. Sprinkle with the rest of the cheese, press down on the pasta with the back of a fork as before, and bake until a second crust forms and all the cream thickens and coats the pasta, about ½ hour more. Serve at the table. If the cream starts to break and look oily (the cream turns into butter when all its water is baked out), the gratin is starting to overcook, so take it out of the oven and serve it immediately.

Variations: There isn't much you can do to make this gratin any better than it is, but there is one thing—add saffron. Soak a pinch of saffron threads in the cream for about 1 hour before assembling the gratin or, as an ultimate refinement, make saffron pasta by soaking a healthy pinch of saffron in a tablespoon of water for 30 minutes and then working the saffron and the soaking liquid into the pasta dough. If you want a lighter gratin, replace the cream with half-and-half or, lighter yet, milk or flavorful broth.

Most fresh pasta you'll encounter in France is made in the same way as fresh pasta is made in Italy. Flour is combined with eggs and a little olive oil and rolled out by hand or with a machine. The French, however, have noodles of their own. Probably the best known are *spaëtzle*, from Alsace, made by working a runny pasta dough through the holes of a colander set over a pot of simmering water. They are drained and sautéed in butter.

Richard Olney, in *Simple French Food,* describes a wonderfully light noodle—*nouille à la poche*—made by piping a cakelike batter into a pan of simmering water. He recommends improvising a cone with a piece of parchment paper and cutting off the tip; I use a pastry bag.

LEEK GRATIN

GRATIN DE POIREAUX

MAKES 6 SERVINGS

I like to demonstrate this gratin at cooking classes. As I pour the cream over the dish, my students have that horrified I'll-never-make-that look, but when I serve the leeks, usually at the same time as other things, I hear, "Ah, the leeks . . ."

In classic French cooking, tradition dictates that you blanch the leeks and then cover them with a Mornay or béchamel sauce (see Cauliflower Gratin, page 578) and bake or broil them until a crust forms on top. That's all very fine, and is actually the method I prefer for most vegetables, but leeks have a natural silkiness that makes blanching unnecessary and the cream so perfect.

6   medium-size leeks or 3 large

1   teaspoon butter, softened

1   to 1½ cups [250 to 375 ml] heavy cream

     salt

     pepper

PREHEAT the oven to 350°F [175°C/gas mark 4].

CUT the roots off the ends of the leeks and cut off the greens, leaving about 2 inches [5 cm] of the palest green attached to the whites. Discard the greens (or use them in broths). Cut the whites in half lengthwise and rinse them under cold running water with the root end facing up. Flip through the stalks, rubbing each one between your thumb and forefinger to release sand.

BUTTER a gratin dish or baking dish just large enough to hold the leeks in a single layer, and arrange the leeks, flat-side down, in a single layer in the dish. Pour the heavy cream over them and season liberally with salt and pepper. Bake for about 40 minutes, pressing the leeks down into the cream with the back of a fork after 15 minutes. After 10 minutes more, press the leeks down again, or even turn them over, to prevent those parts of the leeks that protrude above the cream from drying out. If this happens anyway, pull off and discard the dried outermost membranes just before serving.

Variations: Try gently cooking little cubes of bacon, pancetta, or prosciutto and combining them, along with a little of their rendered fat, with the cream you use for the leeks. If the richness of all of this is too horrifying, replace the cream with broth and about 1 tablespoon of butter, or replace the cream with béchamel and sprinkle the gratin with grated Gruyère or another tasty cheese before baking. The same recipe can be used for ramps, although you'll need less sauce because ramps are smaller and the gratin won't be as thick; I strongly recommend the bacon variation to balance the ramps' strong, wild flavor.

Tomatoes are also delicious baked in cream, although I wait until near the end of the season when there's a little nip in the air (even I am daunted by a rich, creamy gratin in the middle of the summer). Keep in mind that tomatoes contain a lot of water. To make a tomato gratin and deal with the water, peel the tomatoes (see salad recipe on page 42 for how to do this) and cut them into wedges. Seed each wedge by pushing out the seeds with your finger and arrange the wedges, overlapping them slightly, in a single layer in a gratin dish. Bake for about 20 minutes in a 375°F [190°C/gas mark 5] oven. At this point, you'll notice the gratin is full of liquid. Gently pour or spoon the liquid out of the gratin into a small saucepan, put the gratin back in the oven, and pour cream into the liquid in the saucepan and boil it down until the mixture barely begins to thicken. (If you like, put cooked bacon cubes into the cream mixture. A little tarragon is also delicious.) Pour the cream mixture back over the tomatoes, sprinkle with Parmigiano-Reggiano, and bake until a crust forms. Don't overcook the gratin or the cream will separate.

Winter squash is also great baked with cream, but I prebake the squash to make it easier to get out of the skin. You can also bake spaghetti squash, scoop out the "spaghetti," and use it as though it were the pasta in the pasta gratin on page 574. Or you can cook other kinds of squash, scoop the pulp out in big pieces—unless you want it to turn into a purée—and bake with cream and cheese.

USING BÉCHAMEL SAUCE

Béchamel sauce and its descendant Mornay sauce (béchamel with cheese) are the most traditional sauces for making gratins. Béchamel has the advantage of being lighter than heavy cream. It also can be made quite thick—thicker than heavy cream, which breaks if overreduced. I avoid béchamel in gratins made with ingredients that are already starchy, such as pasta and potatoes, but prefer it to cream for gratins made with most other vegetables because it's less rich.

If you follow most recipes for béchamel you'll end up with something very bland (not necessarily a bad thing, but a situation that is easily improved). Modern béchamel is made by adding milk to a simple roux, and at most flavoring it with a little nutmeg and cayenne. This wasn't always the case. Escoffier's recipe, now about 100 years old, contains onion, along with cubes of veal and a sprig of thyme, sweated in butter before the flour and milk are added. Some 70 years before Escoffier, Carême gives a recipe for béchamel made by adding a ham-enriched concentrated veal broth to a roux—producing what's now called a *sauce velouté*—and then converting the velouté into béchamel by adding heavy cream. The resulting sauce is actually closer to what was later called a *sauce suprême*. About 80 years before Carême, Menon, in his *Les Soupers de la Cour* (1755), gives a recipe in which slices of raw ham, mushrooms, shallots, garlic, cloves, bay leaves, and basil are gently cooked in butter until colored (before the nineteenth century, béchamel sauce wasn't a white sauce as it is today), flour is sprinkled over all, and the mixture moistened with cream. I'm not suggesting you go out and buy 10 pounds [4.5 kg] of veal to improve your béchamel sauce, but a few veal trimmings or bits of prosciutto end will work wonders. Here's my own béchamel. If you don't have some of the ingredients, leave them out—your sauce will still be a lot better than the standard version. If you're in a mad rush, just make a roux with the butter and flour, skip the vegetables and prosciutto, and simmer, skim, and season as described on the following page.

BÉCHAMEL SAUCE

MAKES 3 CUPS [750 ML]

2 tablespoons butter

1 small onion, or 2 large shallots, chopped fine

1 piece celery (4 inches [10 cm] long), chopped fine

1 small carrot, chopped fine

1 clove garlic, crushed

1 slice (4 ounces [115 g]) prosciutto end, pancetta, or veal or pork trimmings, chopped fine

1 bay leaf

3 sprigs fresh thyme or ½ teaspoon dried thyme leaves

5 tablespoons all-purpose flour

1 quart [1 l] milk or half-and-half

nutmeg

salt

pepper

MELT the butter in a heavy-bottomed 4-quart [1 l] saucepan over medium heat. Add the chopped vegetables and prosciutto end while stirring with a wooden spoon. Continue cooking until the vegetables have softened and the mixture smells fragrant, about 10 minutes. Don't let the ingredients or the inside bottom of the pan brown, unless you don't mind having a sauce that isn't perfectly white. (An off-white sauce never bothers me, and it often tastes better.) Add the bay leaf and thyme, sprinkle with the flour, and cook for about 2 minutes more. Pour in 2 cups [500 ml] of milk, turn the heat to high, and whisk the sauce until it thickens. Pour in the rest of the milk and bring the sauce to a simmer while whisking. Turn down the heat and move the saucepan to one side of the heat so it simmers only on one side. Simmer the sauce for about 20 minutes, skimming off scum and froth with a ladle. Strain and season to taste with nutmeg (be careful, it's very strong), salt, and pepper.

Mornay Sauce: Stir ½ cup [50 g] finely grated Parmigiano-Reggiano and ½ cup [50 g] of finely grated Swiss Gruyère into 3 cups [750 ml] of Béchamel Sauce. Stir over low heat until the cheese melts into the sauce, but don't let the sauce boil or the cheese may separate or turn stringy.

CAULIFLOWER
GRATIN

GRATIN AU CHOUFLEUR

I confess. I'm not mad about cauliflower and I do what Americans have long accused the French of doing—cover up a questionable ingredient with rich sauce. But apparently I'm not alone. I've published a similar recipe in my book *Vegetables*, and have had grateful readers tell me they've finally found a way to fix cauliflower that they really like.

- 2 tablespoons salt
- 1 head cauliflower (about 2 pounds)
- 1 teaspoon butter, softened
- 3 cups (750 ml) (1 recipe) Béchamel Sauce (page 577)
- 2 cups [225 g] grated cheese such as Gruyère (about ⅓ pound)

PREHEAT the oven to 375°F [190°C/gas mark 5].

BRING about 4 quarts [4 l] of water to a rolling boil with the salt. Break off and discard the green leaves around the cauliflower. Cut the cauliflower into florets by cutting around the core from the bottom. Cut the florets into smaller florets by cutting through them at the base—the flower end of each floret should be about 1 inch across.

BUTTER a gratin dish or baking dish just large enough to hold the florets in a single layer. (I use an 11-by-7-inch [28 by 18 cm] oval dish.)

BOIL the florets for about 5 minutes over high heat, drain them in a colander, and let them sit for 5 minutes so they steam dry. Spread the florets in a single layer in the gratin dish. Pour the béchamel sauce over them and sprinkle with the cheese. If there seems to be too much cheese, work some of it into the béchamel with a fork.

BAKE the gratin until a golden crust forms on top, about 25 minutes. If a crust hasn't formed, slide the dish under a hot broiler, watching carefully so you don't burn the gratin, for 30 seconds to 1 minute.

Variations: I use this method for broccoli gratin and as a way of reheating leftover cooked vegetables, such as asparagus, string beans, leeks, and spinach, that have lost some of their sheen. Unlike cauliflower, which doesn't suffer from slow, gentle cooking, green vegetables will turn gray—especially if they're left over to begin with—when baked for more than a few minutes. In these situations, I turn on the broiler, put the gratin dish in the oven while the broiler is on to get it hot, heat the vegetables in a little butter on top of the stove, spread them out in the hot dish, pour the hot béchamel over them, sprinkle them with the cheese, and then brown the gratin under the broiler for 1 or 2 minutes and serve immediately.

USING TOMATO SAUCE: Gratins based on cream or béchamel sauce are typical in northern France, especially Lyons, but in the south of France, vegetable gratins—called *tians*—are simple affairs, often made with no more sauce than a drizzling of olive oil and a sprinkling of Parmigiano-Reggiano. There are innumerable versions, some of which involve puréeing the vegetables. *Tians* also may include rice. One of my favorite methods for making a *tian* is to use a simple tomato sauce—a *coulis* or a *concassée* (see "Simple Tomato Sauces," page 580). This method keeps the vegetables moist and gives the *tian* a sweet tang that relieves the richness of cheese and olive oil.

HOW TO MAKE CRÊPE GRATIN WITH LEFTOVER TURKEY OR CHICKEN

To turn leftover pieces of chicken or turkey into a presentable meal, add about ½ cup [125 ml] of sherry or Madeira to 3 cups [750 ml] (1 recipe) of Béchamel Sauce (page 577) and simmer the sauce for about 5 minutes to cook off the alcohol. Combine the pieces of chicken or turkey with half the sauce, season to taste with salt and pepper, and spoon the poultry mixture into crêpes (see Basic Crêpes, page 648), allowing 2 crêpes per serving. Arrange the crêpes in a buttered gratin dish or baking dish, cover them with the remaining sauce, sprinkle with cheese, and bake for about 25 minutes in a 350°F [175°C/gas mark 4] oven until the sauce is bubbling and a brown crust has formed on top.

ZUCCHINI GRATIN

TIAN DE COURGETTES

MAKES 6 SIDE-DISH SERVINGS

Because zucchini contain a lot of water, the best way to enhance their flavor is to use a technique that causes the water to evaporate—grilling, baking, sautéing, roasting—and not a method like boiling or steaming that will cause them to absorb water. To make this *tian*, sauté the zucchini first (grilling is even better), with plenty of herbs and garlic, to evaporate most of the water and intensify the flavor, before spreading the zucchini out in the gratin dish. The finely chopped basil is spooned over the tian just before serving—instead of before baking—so its aroma isn't lost during cooking.

3 medium-size zucchini (about 1½ pounds [675 g] total), scrubbed, ends sliced off

2 tablespoons extra-virgin olive oil

2 cloves garlic, chopped very fine

1 tablespoons chopped fresh marjoram, or 1 teaspoon chopped fresh thyme, or ½ teaspoon dried thyme leaves

salt

pepper

3 cups (750 ml) Tomato Coulis (page 581)

1 cup [100 g] finely grated Parmigiano-Reggiano or grana padana

12 basil leaves

SLICE the zucchini into ⅛-inch-thick [3-mm] rounds with a vegetable slicer or chef's knife. Sauté the zucchini in 2 tablespoons of the olive oil in a wide sauté pan over high heat until the slices are completely limp and lightly browned, about 10 minutes. Sprinkle with the garlic, marjoram, salt, and pepper and sauté for about 2 minutes more.

PREHEAT the oven to 350°F [175°C/gas mark 4].

SPREAD half the tomato coulis on the bottom of a gratin dish or baking dish large enough to hold the zucchini, overlapping, in a single layer. (Again, I use a 9-by-13-inch [23 by 33 cm] oval gratin dish.) If you're using a smaller gratin dish—so that you'll need to make two layers of zucchini—spread the dish with only one-third of the coulis. Spread the zucchini rounds in a single layer, overlapping each round about halfway over the next. If you're making two layers, spread the zucchini with half of the remaining tomato sauce and lay a second zucchini layer on top. Spread the rest of the coulis on top of the zucchini, sprinkle with the cheese, slide into the oven, and bake until the edges are lightly browned and a crust has formed on top, about 30 minutes.

WHILE the *tian* is baking, finely chop the basil. When the *tian* comes out of the oven, garnish with fresh basil on top. Serve immediately.

Variations: You don't have to limit yourself to zucchini when making a *tian*. Many *tians* contain artichokes—use baby artichokes, precooked and halved vertically—and/or eggplant. I sometimes also add mushrooms (first sautéed in a little olive oil), and I like sliding thin layers of cheese (smoked mozzarella, Camembert) between the layers of vegetables. If I have anchovy fillets, I make a crisscross pattern over the *tian* about 15 minutes before it comes out of the oven. I also use strips of grilled and peeled bell peppers and olives. If you're improvising a *tian*, think of it as you would a pizza—almost anything that goes well on a pizza will work.

SIMPLE TOMATO SAUCES: COULIS AND CONCASSÉE

Traditional French tomato sauces are long-cooked affairs made by gently sweating mirepoix (a mixture of onions, carrots, and celery) with unsmoked bacon and adding flour to make a roux, before pouring in tomato purée. The mixture is then simmered for several hours until it thickens.

There's nothing wrong with long-cooked tomato sauces; some of world's best sauces are tomato sauces from Bologna or Naples that are simmered for many hours. But the trend in French restaurants is toward sauces that are cooked quickly so that the freshness of the tomato is left intact. There are basically two types of these new sauces: *coulis*, which is a sauce that has been strained so that it doesn't contain any lumps, and *concassée*, which is a tomato sauce left chunky. Both *coulis* and *concassée* can be either raw or cooked. Apart from the task of straining, which is easy to do with an inexpensive food mill, *coulis* is quicker to make than *concassée* because there's no need to peel and seed the tomatoes, since the peels and seeds will be strained out. Raw *coulis* and *concassée* contain a fair amount of water from the tomatoes. We need to get rid of much of the water so that the tomatoes will hold together in a sauce. In a long-cooked sauce, the sauce is cooked until the water evaporates and the sauce thickens, but in a sauce where the freshness of the tomatoes is important and long cooking isn't a solution, we have to eliminate water in other ways. When making a tomato *concassée* or *coulis*, my favorite method is to peel (for a *concassée*), seed, and chop the tomatoes; cook them in a saucepan just long enough to get them to release their liquid; drain them in a strainer; and then boil down the liquid that goes through the strainer. When the liquid boils down to a syrup, I recombine it with the tomato pulp. At this point, if I'm making a *concassée*, I'm done. If I'm making a *coulis*, I work the mixture through a food mill, which also eliminates peels and seeds.

TOMATO COULIS
COULIS DE TOMATES

MAKES 3 CUPS [750 ML]

12 medium-size tomatoes (about 4½ pounds [2 kg] total)

CUT the tomatoes in half crosswise and squeeze out the seeds. Chop to a chunky consistency, so that each piece is roughly ½ inch across. Put the tomatoes in a nonaluminum saucepan and bring to a simmer on high heat, stirring almost constantly with a wooden spoon so the tomatoes don't stick. When the tomatoes are at a full boil, turn down the heat and simmer them for 10 minutes. Take the pan off the heat and let sit for 5 minutes.

POUR the tomatoes into a strainer set over a large bowl and let them drain for about 15 minutes. Put the liquid released by the tomatoes back into the saucepan and boil it down until you have about ¼ cup [60 ml] of lightly syrupy liquid. Work the tomato pulp through a food mill or strainer and combine it with the syrup.

PROVENÇAL VEGETABLE STEW

RATATOUILLE

FORTUNATELY, RATATOUILLE IS EASIER TO MAKE THAN TO PRONOUNCE, but then again it's not that easy to make well. In its usual form, ratatouille is a vegetable stew made by gently cooking together onions, tomatoes, eggplant, and zucchini in olive oil. Most restaurant versions I've encountered are too oily, and they prickle my mouth from the eggplant and taste too strongly of bell peppers. More carefully prepared versions are made by sautéing each of the ingredients separately, so that each better keeps its identity, and combining them at the last; but of course such a concoction isn't really a stew, but a sauté made to look like a stew. Some recipes specify that each ingredient be cut into tiny dice, for a thick paste that can be dolloped on toasts, while others say it's essential that the vegetables be cut into relatively large slices or chunks so that you can taste and see them individually.

Some versions contain garlic, basil, olives, parsley, thyme, or capers, but the only unalterable ingredients are eggplant, tomatoes, peppers, zucchini, onions, and olive oil.

I cook all the vegetables together, but instead of stewing them in a big pot, I roast them in the oven, so I can get by with using less oil and the ratatouille never seems too oily. I cut everything into relatively large pieces, which shrink during cooking, but if you want a kind of salsa that you can dollop on grilled meats or fish or serve over toasts as a first course, you can dice the ingredients finer. I solve the eggplant-prickle problem by using the lavender Chinese eggplants they sell in Asian markets. If I can't find those, I use Japanese eggplants or the elongated (rather than bulbous) dark Italian eggplants. I toss the cubed eggplant in a little olive oil and then spread the cubes on a sheet pan and bake them. I often add chopped olives and capers for a little zing, but if it means an extra trip to the store, I leave them out. I love to include marjoram. In the summer, which is the only time I make ratatouille anyway, I stir in lots of finely chopped basil and garlic just before serving, so the flavors of both stay fresh and bright. Most versions of ratatouille are taken over by the flavor of the peppers, but I roast the peppers on top of the stove instead of stewing them in oil. This way, the ratatouille is less oily, and because the peppers haven't flavored the oil, they're less domineering. Finally, I use more tomato than most.

PROVENÇAL VEGETABLE STEW

RATATOUILLE

MAKES 6 SIDE-DISH SERVINGS

1 medium-sized onion, chopped coarse

1 cup [250 ml] extra-virgin olive oil

10 medium-size tomatoes, peeled, seeds squeezed out, cut into ½-inch [2.5 cm] cubes

1½ pounds [675 g] eggplant, preferably Chinese, or the same weight of Japanese or Italian eggplants, peeled, cut into 1-inch [2.5-cm] cubes

3 medium-size zucchini (about 1½ pounds [675 g] total), scrubbed, cut into 1-inch [2.5-cm] pieces

1 tablespoon chopped fresh marjoram, or 1 teaspoon chopped fresh thyme, or ½ teaspoon dried thyme leaves

1½ cup [200 g] black olives, pitted, chopped coarse (optional)

4 tablespoons capers, preferably the small nonpareil type (optional)

2 bell peppers, preferably 1 red and 1 yellow, charred, peeled, seeded, cut into fine dice (see page 20 for information on peeling peppers)

leaves from 1 large bunch basil (1 cup [60 g], tightly packed)

2 cloves garlic, minced, crushed to a paste with the side of a chef's knife

salt

pepper

TOSS the onions, half the olive oil, the tomatoes, eggplant, zucchini, and marjoram and spread them on a sheet pan. Slide the pan into the oven and bake at 400°F [200°C/gas mark 6] for about 90 minutes, until any liquid released by the tomatoes has evaporated. Fold the mixture over on itself once every 30 minutes so it cooks evenly. Remove from the oven, let cool, and transfer to a large mixing bowl. Stir in the olives, capers, and peppers.

JUST before serving, combine the basil, garlic, and remaining olive oil in a blender or food processor and purée to a smooth paste, pushing the mixture down with a wooden spoon as needed to get it to turn around. (Be careful not to touch the blade.) You can also chop the basil very fine with a chef's knife or work it to a paste with the garlic in a mortar. Stir the basil mixture into the cooled ratatouille. Season to taste with salt and pepper. Serve the ratatouille at room temperature as a side dish. Or if you cut the vegetables into smaller dice, as suggested in the headnote, serve the mixture as a sauce to dollop on grilled meats or seafood, or spread it in mounds on little toasts and serve it as an hors d'oeuvre.

Variations: This can be served with crackers as an hors d'oeuvre or with toast as bruschetta.

OTHER VEGETABLE STEWS

Most of us prepare a single vegetable at a time, usually as an accompaniment to a main course of meat or seafood. In French classic cooking, there are long lists of "garnitures" made with combinations of vegetables, cooked in various ways, and then served, either combined or arranged in separate mounds, on a platter with roast meat or fish. Some vegetable "stews" aren't really stews at all, but elaborate affairs in which the vegetables, each cooked separately, are combined just before serving. Other versions, more rough-hewn but equally satisfying, are made by adding vegetables to a pot containing a little water or broth and gently stewing the vegetables so their juices intermingle into a light natural sauce. When using this method, I usually swirl a small amount of butter or cream into the sauce at the end of cooking to pull the flavors together and get the sauce to coat the vegetables lightly. I often add herbs, maybe just a little parsley chopped at the last minute, or tomato coulis, or sometimes a flavorful purée of watercress or roast garlic to give the sauce its own identity and color.

Combinations of vegetables, subtly seasoned with herbs or sauces, can be stunning, whether they're based on inexpensive vegetables like carrots and turnips or include more extravagant things like artichokes, wild mushrooms, or even truffles. I often serve more complicated vegetable stews as first courses so that everyone pays attention to the vegetables instead of being distracted by the meat. At other times, I serve a vegetable stew as a side dish. But one of my favorite ways to use a luxurious mixture of vegetables is to spoon it over grilled or sautéed pieces of meat, poultry, or seafood, so the vegetables lend their delicacy and bright colors and become integral to the dish.

Almost any vegetable can be added to a pot with a little liquid and cooked, covered, until done; the only trick is judging how long each vegetable will take. If, for example, you want to make a little stew of pearl onions, string beans, fava beans, and fresh peas, you need to figure out the cooking time for each vegetable and then add it to the pot accordingly. If you're being meticulous, you may want to use a different technique for each one and then combine them at the last minute. This method is also useful when you want to precook certain vegetables and then just reheat them together shortly before serving. Cooking the vegetables separately is especially helpful if you're using a strongly flavored vegetable such as cabbage that if cooked with the other vegetables would take over the flavor of the stew. You may also feel that some vegetables—wild mushrooms, for instance—have a better flavor when sautéed over high heat than when simply steamed in a covered pot with other vegetables.

Herbs, of course, can be used in an infinity of combinations. When I'm cooking a vegetable stew with olive oil and summer vegetables such as zucchini, eggplant, and tomatoes, I use so-called herbes de Provence (thyme, marjoram, oregano, savory, and lavender flowers, alone or in combination), but instead of the dried mixtures sold in jars, I use fresh herbs. Savory is classic with fava beans; mint goes well with cucumbers. Parsley and other fines herbes (chervil, chives, tarragon) work best with delicate green vegetables such as asparagus and string beans. Tarragon is wonderful with regular cultivated mushrooms. Garlic can be used in several ways. Whole peeled cloves can be boiled until soft and added whole to the stew at the end

or puréed and added to the sauce; minced garlic can be sprinkled over zucchini or wild mushrooms while they're sautéing.

Small amounts of flavorful meats add savor and complexity to a vegetable stew. Tiny cubes or thin shreds of prosciutto can be simmered in cream and used in the sauce, or they can just be tossed into the stew at the end. *Le cousinat à la bayonnaise* is a vegetable stew flavored with the local Bayonne ham. Bacon or pancetta can be gently rendered and used in the sauce, along with a little of the rendered fat; or the cubes, without any fat, can be tossed with the vegetables at the end. Little cubes of foie gras work wonders (they're celestial with wild mushrooms). They can be tossed in at the end or puréed into the sauce. The yellow foie gras fat that forms at the top of foie gras terrines is also marvelous, just tossed with the vegetables and allowed to melt. If the vegetable stew is functioning as a garniture for seafood, you might even add little cubes or slivers of smoked salmon or little slices or cubes of lobster.

White or black truffles, julienned, cubed, chopped, or thinly sliced, stirred into the stew a few minutes before it is done—or in the case of white truffles, shaved over each serving—add high drama; they're best when the sauce contains cream or butter. A little truffle oil or truffle juice will add flavor, but there will be none of the dramatic black (or gray) of actual truffle pieces.

Savory ingredients including olives, anchovies, cubes or strips of charred and peeled bell peppers (see page 20), and capers are good in any vegetable stew with a Mediterranean feel, like ratatouille. Curry powder (1 or 2 teaspoons cooked in butter for 30 seconds and stirred into the sauce) is great with fennel and other green vegetables. Saffron (threads soaked, liquid and threads added to the sauce) is also good with fennel and tomatoes.

STEW OF SPRING VEGETABLES

RAGOÛT PRINTANIER

MAKES 6 FIRST-COURSE OR
SIDE-DISH SERVINGS OR GARNITURES

In classic cooking, this little stew of carrots, turnips, pearl onions, string beans, and peas is made by cooking all the vegetables separately. The carrots and turnips are glazed using two methods, and the peas and string beans are cooked separately with lots of boiling salted water, a method the French call cooking "à l'anglaise" (see page 587). The mushrooms are steamed, and the liquid they release provides the base for a small amount of sauce that coats the vegetables. Typically, the little stew is then strewn over a meat stew, or, in more formal presentations, each vegetable is arranged around the meat in its own separate mound. I also like to serve the vegetables, all tossed together, as a side dish.

Ideally, the vegetables should be combined and served as soon as they are done, but this isn't always practical. You can get this stew started earlier in the day by glazing the root vegetables and allowing them to cool, and by cooking the string beans and peas (if you're using fresh), leaving them a tad undercooked and draining and rinsing them under cold running water or plunging them in ice water. You can also steam the mushrooms and reserve them and the liquid they release.

12 baby carrots, scraped (see page 587), or 3 medium-size carrots, peeled

12 baby turnips, unpeeled; or 2 medium-size turnips or 1 medium-size celeriac (about ¾ pound [340 g], peeled)

1 pint (10 ounces [280 g]) pearl onions, or 12 walnut-size boiling onions

1 tablespoon butter (for the carrots and turnips), plus 3 tablespoons (for the sauce)

1 teaspoon sugar

10 ounces [280 g] small-to-medium cremini or regular cultivated mushrooms

½ cup [125 ml] heavy cream

½ pound [225 g] baby string beans (ideally, haricots verts), ends broken off, the string beans cut into 2-inch [5-cm] lengths

salt

1 pound [450 g] fresh baby peas, shucked (about 1 cup), or 1 package (10 ounces [280 g]) frozen baby peas, thawed

pepper

2 tablespoons freshly chopped parsley, chervil, or chives, or a combination

IF you're using medium-size carrots, peel them and cut them into about 4 sections each. Cut the thickest sections in half lengthwise and cut out their cores (see also page 21). If you're using medium-size turnips or celeriac, cut them into wedges—you should get about 6 out of each turnip and 12 out of a celeriac.

GLAZE the carrots and turnips or celeriac à blanc (see page 561), using about ½ tablespoon of butter and a pinch of sugar for each vegetable. Ideally, the carrots and turnips should be glazed separately, but if you don't have enough pans, glaze them together. If you're using pearl onions, peel them by plunging them in boiling water for a minute, draining in a colander, and rinsing under cold water.

GLAZE the pearl onions or walnut-size onions à brun, again using about ½ tablespoon of butter and a pinch of sugar (see page 561).

RINSE the mushrooms and put them in a pot with ½ cup [125 ml] of water. Cover the pot and bring to a boil. Turn down the heat to maintain the water at a bare simmer and simmer for 15 minutes. Scoop the mushrooms out with a skimmer and reserve. Add the cream to the liquid left in the pot and simmer until it reduces about one-third and begins to thicken slightly.

PLUNGE the string beans into about 3 quarts of boiling, heavily salted water and cook them until they've lost their crunch, usually 5 to 7 minutes, and drain. (Most people these days undercook string beans.) If you're using fresh peas, give them the same treatment—you can use the same water if you fish the string beans out with a skimmer—but cook them for only 1 or 2 minutes. If you're using frozen peas, don't boil them.

COMBINE the cooked vegetables in a pot. If they've cooled off, or if you've cooked them ahead of time, put 1 tablespoon of water in the pot, cover the pot, and heat over medium heat for about 4 minutes.

BRING the mushroom sauce to a simmer and whisk in the remaining butter and the parsley. Season the sauce to taste with salt and pepper and add it to the cooked vegetables. Toss or gently stir. Serve immediately.

CARROTS: SCRAPE OR PEEL?

Large carrots and other vegetables such as turnips are best peeled with a regular vegetable peeler, but if you're peeling baby vegetables, the peel is so thin that if you use a regular peeler, you'll waste a good part of the vegetable. If you have baby carrots, just scrape them a little with the back of a knife shortly before you use them. Baby turnips can also be scraped, but since the skin is so thin, I usually leave it on.

COOKING GREEN VEGETABLES À L'ANGLAISE OR À LA FRANÇAISE

In French classic cooking, there are two ways to cook green vegetables: slowly and covered—*à la française*—and quickly and uncovered—*à l'anglaise*. Cooking *à l'anglaise*, which we Americans sometimes call blanching or parboiling, is the method most of us are familiar with and the most popular method in an era when we like our vegetables bright green, lightly cooked, with a little resistance to the bite. The first time I saw something (sweet peas) cooked *à la française*, in a fancy Paris restaurant, I was shocked. The peas, after cooking for about half an hour, had a pleasant sweetness but looked and tasted like they came out of a can. I've since found that some vegetables benefit from long, slow cooking in a covered pot. Broccoli and broccoli rabe, cooked with olive oil and lots of garlic, develop a depth of flavor that they don't have when cooked *à l'anglaise*.

MOREL,
FAVA BEAN,
AND ASPARAGUS
FRICASSEE

FRICASSÉE DE MORILLES,
FÈVES, ET ASPERGES

MAKES 4 FIRST-COURSE OR

SIDE-DISH SERVINGS OR GARNITURES

One of the joys of living in France was the constant appearance and disappearance of vegetables, fruits, seafood, and game. I had no choice but to cook according to what was in season, and I could often tell what to buy by spying on older neighborhood women as they poked, made faces, and haggled. The best way to come up with a vegetable stew in which the vegetables have a natural harmony is to pay attention to what's in season. This is getting harder to do, since almost everything seems to be in season year-round. But if you go to a local farmers' market, grow your own vegetables, or just notice what things cost, you'll regain a sense of seasonality.

Morels, fava beans, and asparagus are all in season in the spring, and they make a gorgeous and delicious combination that can be served as a first course or a side dish, or can be spooned over a slice of pork roast or veal, fish, or sautéed chicken. Strictly speaking, to qualify as a stew, the vegetables should be steamed together in a covered pot in their own juices (the French call this cooking à l'étuvée, a term that is related to the word for "to smother," étouffer) or with a small amount of some other liquid, such as broth or cream. Fricassée has a similar meaning, but it implies that the foods are sautéed before being simmered in liquid. (The word is most often applied to chicken dishes; see Chapter 27.) Because many wild mushrooms, and particularly morels, release their best flavor when sautéed, I sauté them before combining them with the other ingredients. And because fava beans and asparagus keep their color when quickly boiled, I give them a quick blanching before combining them with the morels.

If you can't find morels, other mushrooms will do. If you can't find fava beans or don't want to deal with the double peeling, substitute peas, another fresh bean, or 1-inch [2.5-cm] lengths of string beans, preferably haricots verts.

1   pound [450 g] fresh morels, or 1 ounce dried

20   thick asparagus

    salt

3   tablespoons butter

1   shallot, chopped fine

½   cup [125 ml] heavy cream (optional)

2   pounds [900 g] fresh fava beans, shucked and peeled, or 1½ cups [215 g] shucked peas or other fresh beans

1   tablespoon freshly chopped chervil or parsley

    pepper

IF you're using fresh morels, check them carefully—look in the hollow interiors—for dirt and bugs. If the morels are very large, cut them in half lengthwise. If they seem dirty, rinse them quickly in a colander and pat them dry with paper towels. If you're using dried morels, put them in a bowl with ½ cup [125 ml] water for 30 minutes, moving them around with your fingers after 15 minutes so they absorb the water evenly. (The idea is to use a minimum of water to reconstitute the mushrooms so their flavor doesn't go into the water.) Remove the morels from the water and reserve both.

CUT the tips off the asparagus just below the flower. The tips should be about 3 inches [7.5 cm] long. Save the stalks for making soup. (They freeze well, tightly wrapped in plastic.)

ABOUT 20 minutes before serving time, bring 3 quarts [3 l] of water to a rapid boil and add a small handful of salt.

SAUTÉ the morels in the butter over medium to high heat until they soften and smell fragrant, about 10 minutes. Dried morels may take slightly longer. Sprinkle with shallots and sauté for 1 minute more. If you're using dried morels, add the soaking liquid, leaving grit behind. Reduce until liquid disappears. Pour the optional cream over the morels and simmer until the cream thickens very slightly and coats them.

SLIDE the asparagus tips into the boiling water and boil for 2 to 5 minutes, depending on their thickness, until they retain only the slightest crunch. Scoop them out with a skimmer or slotted spoon and put them in the pan with the morels. Put the fava beans in the boiling water, boil for 1 minute, and drain in a colander. Add them to the pan. Sprinkle with the chervil and stir or toss gently to combine the ingredients while seasoning to taste with salt and pepper. Serve immediately.

BABY ARTICHOKES, FENNEL, LEEKS, GARLIC, AND PEAS WITH WATERCRESS SAUCE

PETITE FRICASSÉE D'ARTICHAUTS, FENOUIL, POIREAUX, AIL, ET PETITS POIS AU CRESSON

MAKES 6 FIRST-COURSE
OR SIDE-DISH SERVINGS OR GARNITURES

Most vegetable stews end up lightly coated with the natural moisture the vegetables release as they cook, this moisture often given body with a little cream or butter. Leafy vegetables such as spinach, sorrel, or watercress can be added to stews as whole leaves, or they can be chopped or shredded into chiffonade. Another method is to blanch and purée green vegetables, leafy or otherwise, combine them with a little cream and the cooking liquid from the vegetable, and stir them into the stew just before serving so the puréed vegetables don't lose their color but give the stew a bright color and a subtle freshness and function as a sauce. Garlic purée (see page 374), tomato coulis (see page 581), sorrel (melted in a little cream and puréed), and watercress (blanched and puréed) are some of my favorite natural sauce thickeners, and all are perfect for a vegetable stew. As is true with meats and seafood, the difference between a stew and a soup is simply that a stew has more solid to liquid than a soup. So, if you want, you can convert this stew into a soup by making more of the watercress sauce (by thinning it with broth) and cutting the vegetables into smaller pieces.

The vegetables can all be prepared in advance, but the stew should be cooked just before it is served.

FOR THE VEGETABLE STEW:

1 large bulb fennel

6 small to medium-size leeks, or 3 large

18 baby artichokes, leaves trimmed off (see page 68), or 4 large artichokes, turned but chokes left in (see page 69), either tossed with lemon juice

3 tablespoons dry white wine

18 garlic cloves, peeled, boiled in 1 quart of water until soft (about 15 minutes), drained

1 pound [450 g] fresh baby peas, or 1 package (10 ounces [280 g]) frozen peas

1 tablespoon coarsely chopped fennel fronds or finely chopped parsley (if you're not making the watercress sauce)

3 tablespoons butter (if you're not making the watercress sauce)

salt

pepper

FOR THE OPTIONAL WATERCRESS SAUCE:

salt

1 cup [250 ml] heavy cream

1 bunch watercress

CUT the stalks and fronds off the fennel, saving a small handful of the leafy fronds, and pull away and discard any dark or cracked sections. With a vegetable peeler, remove the stringy outer membrane from the bulbs. Cut the fennel bulb through the bottom core into 6 wedges—or 12 if the bulb is really enormous. (It's important that each wedge includes part of the core to hold it together.) Put the wedges in an 8-quart [8 l] or larger nonaluminum pot.

CUT the greens off the leeks, leaving only a couple of inches [about 5 cm] of the palest green attached to the whites. Discard the greens (or use them in broths). Cut the roots away, being careful not to cut too far up the stalk, which would cause the leek to fall apart. Cut the leeks in half, hold them under running cold water with the root end facing up to rinse out any sand, and put them in the pot with the fennel.

PUT the artichokes in the pot with the fennel and leeks. (The choke is left in the large artichokes because it is much easier to remove when the artichokes have been cooked.)

POUR ½ cup [125 ml] water into the pot and bring it quickly to a simmer over high heat. Turn the heat down to low and cover the pot. After about 10 minutes, pour in the wine, cover the pot, and continue cooking. Check periodically to make sure the liquid doesn't run dry. After a total of 25 minutes, test the vegetables with a paring knife, which should slide easily through each vegetable, with only the artichokes offering a little resistance. Usually the vegetables cook at the same time, but if you notice that one is done before the others, gently take it out of the pot and put it on a plate.

WHILE the fennel, leeks, and artichokes are cooking, make the watercress sauce, if you're using it. Bring about 1 quart [1 l] of water to a boil and toss in about 1 tablespoon of salt. Bring the cream to a simmer in a small saucepan and simmer gently—down to ¾ cup [175 ml]—until it thickens slightly, about 5 minutes. Don't overreduce it or it will turn to broken butter. Cut the stems off the watercress—don't

worry about the little stem attached to each leaf, just cut the bottom half of the bunch off with a knife. Wash the leaves and drop them into the boiling water. Boil for 1 minute to remove the cress's bitterness, and drain in a colander. Rinse with cold water and then take the leaves in your fist and squeeze out the water. Just before you're ready to serve the stew, combine the watercress and the hot cream in a blender and purée at high speed for about 1 minute. (See page 13 for information about blender safety.)

WHEN the fennel, leeks, and artichokes are ready, if you've used large artichoke bottoms, take them out of the pot, scoop out their chokes with a spoon, cut each bottom into 6 wedges, and put the wedges back in the pot, along with any vegetables you may have taken out earlier. Put the garlic cloves and the peas in the pot, cover, and simmer for about 1 minute. At this point there should be only 2 or 3 tablespoons of liquid left in the pot. If there's more than that, remove the lid and boil the liquid down over high heat. Swirl in the butter, or toss the vegetables with the sauce. Sprinkle with the fennel fronds or parsley and season to taste with salt and pepper.

Variations: Most of the time, the best sauces for vegetable stews are made by swirling a little butter or cream into the liquid released by the vegetables while they are cooking. More elaborate sauces, like the watercress sauce, are best based on vegetable purées (see pages 373 to 374). You can also try whisking the cooking liquid from the stew into a little hollandaise, beurre blanc, or aïoli and gently tossing the sauce with the vegetables or spooning the sauce around or over each portion.

IMPROVISING VEGETABLE STEWS

You can make a vegetable stew with just about any vegetable, if you rely on common sense and intuition about what goes with what. You need to decide when to add the vegetable (on the basis of how long each one takes to cook), as well as what cooking liquid to use (water, wine, or broth); whether to finish the stew with cream, butter, or some kind of sauce; whether to steam the vegetables together in one big pot or to use different techniques (glazing, sautéing, roasting, grilling) to get the most flavor out of each vegetable; and what flavorings (herbs, spices, strips of prosciutto, cubes of bacon or foie gras), if any, to use. The vegetables listed below are grouped according to when they should be added to the pot.

Root vegetables and other long-cooking vegetables (root vegetables can be gently stewed in the pot or glazed separately and combined at the end)

ARTICHOKES (turned; simmered in a nonaluminum pot; chokes left in baby artichokes; chokes removed from big artichoke bottoms after cooking, bottoms cut into wedges after cooking)

BEETS (roasted or boiled separately; peeled; sliced or cut into bâttonets; carefully arranged on the plates with the other vegetables when serving—if cooked or tossed with the other vegetables, they discolor the whole stew)

CARROTS (if baby, left whole, scraped, with tiny bit of green left attached; if larger, peeled, sections, cored (see page 21), turned (turning optional)

CELERIAC (always peeled; same treatment as turnips)

CHESTNUTS (roasted, peeled, and glazed; combined with other vegetables at the end)

CUCUMBERS (peeled; halved lengthwise; seeds spooned out; sectioned)

FENNEL (stalks removed; fronds reserved and chopped, bulb peeled and cut through the core into wedges)

LEEKS (halved lengthwise if large)

ONIONS (walnut-size boiling onions and large green onions [not scallions], peeled, left whole; pearl onions glazed separately or added about 20 minutes before the stew is done)

PARSNIPS (same treatment as carrots)

TURNIPS (if baby, left whole with tiny bit of green left attached, unpeeled; if larger, peeled, cut into wedges or battonêts, turned (turning optional)

Vegetables that are best sautéed before being added to stew at the end

EGGPLANT (sautéed in olive oil or butter or brushed with oil or butter and baked; sliced or cubed)

WILD MUSHROOMS (sautéed in butter or olive oil or duck fat; sprinkled with herbs and/or garlic and shallots)

ZUCCHINI AND SUMMER SQUASH (sliced, cubed, or sectioned; sautéed in olive oil; sprinkled with herbs [marjoram is great] and minced garlic)

Quick-cooking vegetables best added near the end of stewing or blanched and added at the very end

ASPARAGUS (tips only; or tips and peeled stalks cut into 1-inch [2.5-cm] sections)

CAULIFLOWER (cut into small florets)

CORN (kernels cut off ear with a knife; always cooked directly in the stew—not blanched)

BROCCOLI (cut into small florets)

FAVA BEANS (shucked, peeled)

GARLIC (whole cloves, peeled; boiled for 15 minutes until soft; drained)

HERBS

SHELL BEANS (shucked, blanched until no longer mealy)

SNAP PEAS (ends broken off, string pulled away from side, blanched about 5 minutes)

SNOW PEAS (same as snap peas)

SORREL (leaves rolled up and sliced into shreds—chiffonade—or chopped)

SPINACH (small leaves left whole; larger leaves rolled up and sliced into shreds—chiffonade)

STRING BEANS (preferably haricots verts, ends broken off, cut into 1-inch [2.5-cm] sections, blanched about 7 minutes)

SWISS CHARD (same as spinach)

TRUFFLES (grated, sliced, chopped, or julienned)

Sauces

VEGETABLE PURÉES (such as watercress, sorrel, or garlic, combined with heavy cream)

STEWING LIQUID (finished with herbs and/or cream or butter)

STEWING LIQUID (combined with a classic sauce such as hollandaise (see page 257), flavored mayonnaise and compound butters (see pages 490 to 492)

HOW TO TURN A VEGETABLE STEW INTO A VEGETABLE TERRINE

It was sometime in the late 1960s or early 1970s that vegetable terrines started appearing on the menu of virtually every "fancy" French restaurant in Paris and New York. While it sounded like a good idea, most of them were dismal. The standard approach was to embed precooked vegetables into some kind of mousseline, usually veal or pork puréed and worked with heavy cream (see page 535 for more about mousselines) and then slowly bake the whole concoction, let it cool, and serve it sliced like a regular pâté. The problem was that the vegetables ended up getting cooked twice (and the second cooking, in the oven, was long and slow) and the surrounding mousseline was so heavy and rich that you couldn't taste the vegetables. But I've long been fascinated by the idea of a vegetable terrine because the slices, especially if the vegetables aren't overcooked, are so pretty. Instead of making a mousseline, which has to be cooked, I make a sauce, like the watercress sauce on page 589, and while the sauce is still warm, I add gelatin, chill the mixture slightly (but not enough so that it sets), and fold it with cream whipped to medium peaks, turning the sauce into a vegetable Bavarian cream. I then spread a layer of the Bavarian mixture in a terrine mold, get it to set quickly by placing the mold in a bowl of ice water, arrange a layer of cooked vegetables over the mixture, spread another layer of the Bavarian mixture over that, chill, and continue until I've filled the mold. (The vegetables can't be too hard or large, or the terrine will be impossible to slice.) I put the terrine in the fridge for a couple of hours or overnight, and then I unmold it onto a platter and slice it at the table. If it's too hard to slice, I freeze it, and slice it with a bread knife and let the slices thaw on the individual plates.

43

BAKED WHOLE TRUFFLES

TRUFFES SOUS LA CENDRE

EVERY YEAR A COUPLE OF CLOSE FRIENDS AND I GET TOGETHER FOR the December holidays and cook truffles. When I describe our festivities to students and normal people who are more likely to spend any extra cash on a vacation or a new car, I encounter a shocked incredulity that at times borders on disgust. Because any attempt at putting such extravagance into perspective (a pound [450 g] of truffles costs the same as a fancy restaurant dinner for four—at least in New York—and such meals are memorable for life) only worsens matters, I've learned to keep my mouth shut except around dedicated foodies, whose only reaction is envy.

When it comes to truffles, don't skimp. The flavor of truffles measured out in paper-thin slices is lost. So if you're going to splurge on a truffle, use it up all at once and don't be stingy. If you've never cooked truffles, your first mission is to track them down. While there are dozens of varieties from all over the world, you'll likely run into only three kinds—and rarely at the same time. The most famous truffles, at least in French cooking, are black winter truffles (*Tuber melanosporum*), which are found in several regions in France, but most notably in the Périgord, a region toward the southwest of the hexagon that is France. This same species is found in Provence and in Umbria and here and there in other parts of Europe. Black winter truffles start to show up in markets in November but are better in December and January, after the first frost. While thoroughly black on the outside—they look a little like black golf balls—authentic black winter truffles have a fine white filigree pattern when sliced, a characteristic that distinguishes them from other, less aromatic (and less expensive) varieties. At least equal in fame are white truffles (*Tuber magnatum*), less appreciated in France than in Italy, where they are shaved raw over fresh pasta, veal, seafood, and just about anything you can think of. In much the same way that the best-known black truffles come from the Périgord, the most famous white truffles come from the Piedmont in northern Italy and to a far lesser extent from other parts of northern Italy, and they are even more expensive than black winter truffles. Last are black summer truffles (*Tuber aestivum*), which are found in Tuscany and other parts of Italy. Summer truffles are less aromatic than their winter cousins but can still be a good value if you buy them fresh, and you're paying about one-fourth of what you'd pay for black winter truffles. Slices of summer truffles don't have the white filigree pattern you'll see in winter truffles. Summer truffles are rougher-looking on the outside than winter truffles. They're not as delightfully smelly as black winter truffles, but they should still have a pronounced aroma.

When buying fresh truffles you have to be sure they're fresh. If you have a fancy grocer whom you trust, just ask what day the fresh truffles come in, make your plans accordingly, and use the truffles within a day or two. If you don't know your grocer, you'll have to use your judgment when picking out your truffles. This can be challenging if you've never before tasted or smelled one. I sometimes play food spy and check the store every day, memorizing the shape of each truffle in the display case (the truffles are always behind glass like a necklace at Harry Winston), and then make my pick when some new ones show up. But if you're not up to this kind of subterfuge, ask to smell the truffles. Black winter truffles should have an intense aroma that's different from anything you've smelled before, yet somehow familiar. (I have a friend who describes the smell as "prenatal.") To me a good black truffle smells like a combination of mildew, mushrooms, and the ether they put me out with when as a child I broke my arm. The perfume should be intriguing and complex, like a good wine, and leave you at a loss for words, as I am, to describe exactly what it is you're smelling. It should *not* smell like ammonia—which means the truffle is rotting—and there should be no soft or wet spots. If the smell is right, ask to handle the truffle so you can inspect it. Black summer truffles smell similar to black winter truffles, but the aroma isn't as pronounced. The aroma of white truffles has the same elusive quality as that of black truffles, but it is distinctly different, something like a combination of garlic, a gas leak, and a seedy barroom, yet strangely mouthwatering.

If the prospect of shopping for truffles is just too daunting (or no one near you sells them), you're better off mail-ordering them from one of the suppliers listed in the Sources section of this book; they deal with truffles in larger quantities than retail stores and move them through more quickly. Year-round, you can also buy frozen truffles that are often more aromatic than fresh ones because they've been frozen almost as soon as they come out of the ground. The only difference in a thawed frozen truffle is the texture, which is less firm that that of a fresh truffle, making it difficult to slice the truffle thin or chop it fine.

A BIT OF TRUFFLE HISTORY

Strangely, truffles were never called for in French cookbooks written before the seventeenth century, but they were described in Platina's *De Honesta Voluptate et Valentudine* (On Right Pleasure and Good Health) published (in Latin) in Italy in the fifteenth century. The Italian humanist extols the virtues of North African truffles, which he considers the best, but describes those found in Greece and Syria to be sweeter and those from Olympus the most noble. He makes no mention of French truffles, but says, "The skill of a Norcian sow is wonderful, for she easily finds out where they grow, and . . . she sets them down unharmed when her ear is touched by the farmer." Norcia is still an important Umbrian truffle center, such that black winter truffles from Umbria are often called Norcia truffles. Apicius, a Roman epicure who wrote in the first century A.D, gives a number of recipes for truffles, including several that call for grilling them on skewers and finishing them in various sauces made from sweet wines, honey, pepper, olive oil, and cilantro. In the seventeenth century, French cookbook authors start using fewer of the spices so prevalent in medieval cooking and depend more on herbs and other indigenous ingredients, such as mushrooms and truffles. While truffles were never considered cheap, seventeenth- and eighteenth-century cookbooks call for them with a nonchalance more suggestive of onions than of something rare or expensive. In the beginning of the twentieth century, Escoffier suggests serving truffles as a vegetable—an extravagance that raises even my eyebrows.

BAKED WHOLE TRUFFLES

TRUFFES SOUS LA CENDRE

MAKES 4 FIRST-COURSE SERVINGS

If you want to taste truffles in a pure, unadorned state, baking them whole (or, if you have a fireplace, cooking them under the coals) is the surest way to appreciate them. While this is a classic preparation—it's Platina's first suggestion—it is shamelessly extravagant. The cost, however, may be somewhat offset by the fact that whenever the subject of truffles comes up you will have tasted them as have few others.

Until French families started using stoves, foods were cooked in or in front of the hearth. Thus, recipes for *truffes sous la cendre* (literally, "truffles under the ash") had you wrapping the seasoned truffle in a thin sheet of fatback and then wrapping the whole concoction in three thicknesses of greased parchment paper. Why the paper didn't just burn up, I don't know, but nowadays that risk can be avoided with aluminum foil. If you're committing yourself to this folly, serve everyone a whole truffle as a first course and let them unwrap it themselves so they can inhale its aroma.

4 black winter truffles, as big as you can afford

4 tablespoons duck fat, goose fat, clarified butter, or extra-virgin olive oil, or more to taste

salt, preferably *fleur de sel* (see page 598)

pepper

IF you're cooking the truffles the old-fashioned way, build a fire in the fireplace and let it die down to coals.

IF the truffles are dirty, brush them with a soft toothbrush, rinse them under cold running water, and pat them dry in a dish towel. Rub them generously with the fat or oil—each truffle should be accompanied by 1 tablespoon of fat—and sprinkle them with salt and pepper. Wrap each truffle in a double layer of aluminum foil. Make sure the foil clings to the truffles tightly and that they are well sealed.

IF you're not using the fireplace, preheat the oven to 400°F [200°C/gas mark 6].

PUSH the truffles under the hot coals—use something blunt-ended like a sharpening steel so you don't poke through the foil—or put them in the oven. Leave them under the coals for 15 to 20 minutes or in the oven for 20 to 25 minutes, depending on their size. Put each one, still wrapped in foil, on an individual plate. Let your guests unwrap their own. Pass a pepper mill, some good salt such as *fleur de sel,* some good butter (since you've dug into your savings you might want to buy French butter), and some crusty French bread so your guests can smear the bread with butter and mop up the truffle juices.

COOKING WITH TRUFFLES

There are very few ingredients that aren't enhanced by the flavor of truffles. Often, especially when used in lesser amounts, truffles have an almost magical ability to make foods taste more like themselves—eggs taste more like eggs, chicken more like chicken, and oysters more like oysters. But there are a few tricks for getting the most flavor and aroma out of a truffle. The scent and flavor of truffles are best trapped in emulsified fats such as egg yolks, butter, cream, and oils (emulsified into vinaigrettes or mayonnaises). When flavoring a dish or a sauce with truffles, you should cook the truffles for only a short time so their aroma, which is volatile and fleeting, doesn't cook off (white truffles are usually left raw). If you're using truffles in a long-cooked dish, make sure the dish is well covered or sealed in some way so the truffle perfume doesn't escape.

One way to get the most flavor out of your truffles is to leave the truffles in contact with whatever it is you're cooking before you actually begin cooking. If, for example, I'm baking a truffled chicken, I slide the truffles under the chicken's skin, wrap the chicken in aluminum foil, and leave it for several hours or overnight in the refrigerator before baking it. When making a truffled hollandaise, I store the eggs and butter with the truffles overnight (see below), add the chopped truffles to the finished hollandaise, and then let the hollandaise sit, covered, for 30 minutes before serving. (Don't let hollandaise sit for longer. Because it is warm and not hot, it's a perfect medium for bacteria.) If you're making a sauce flavored with truffles, make sure that the sauce contains some fat, such as butter or cream. When finishing a sauce with butter, chop the truffles into the butter or just use the butter stored with the truffles overnight in a jar. If you're finishing a truffle sauce with cream, reduce the cream ahead of time (most cream sauces require boiling down the cream to thicken it), add the chopped or sliced truffles to the reduced warm cream, and let them infuse, covered, for 15 minutes to 1 hour before finishing the sauce with the cream. You can also use truffle oil and truffle juice as flavorings for cooking (see page 62).

TRUFFLES WITH EGGS (TRUFFLE FLAN): Eggs and truffles go so well together that you can use truffles in virtually any dish made with eggs— *oeufs en cocotte* (eggs baked in ramekins; see Chapter 7), *oeufs brouillés* (French-style scrambled eggs; see Chapter 8), hollandaise sauce (see page 257), and omelets (see Chapter 8). Because the smell of truffles often reminds me of garlic, it occurred to me to combine the two in a flan. Remember, a flan is the same thing as a custard—a liquid held together with whole eggs, egg yolks, egg whites, or combinations of yolks or whites and whole eggs.

STORING TRUFFLES

Ideally, you should use truffles as soon as you get them so they don't lose any aroma. A favorite way to keep them is to bury them in a bowl of rice, which keeps them from rotting because the rice doesn't trap their moisture as would plastic wrap or aluminum foil. Theoretically at least, the rice becomes scented with the truffles, but since rice takes so long to cook, any perfume imparted by the truffles cooks off. If I'm using truffles within a few days, I store them in a large jar with a tight-fitting lid and put eggs, in their shells, and butter, taken out of its wrapper, in the jar. I seal the lid and keep the whole thing in the refrigerator. I use the eggs (now redolent of truffles) to make scrambled eggs or an omelet (see pages 127 and 123) and the butter (which can be frozen) to finish sauces, add to mashed potatoes, or to stir into a risotto.

If you have more truffles than you can use within a few days, you should first count your blessings and then wrap each truffle tightly in plastic wrap and then twice in aluminum foil, put the truffles in a jar, and freeze them. They won't have the same texture once they thaw, but their flavor will be intact, and for most dishes the texture of the truffles isn't important anyway.

FLEUR DE SEL

Every decade has its trendy ingredients. In the 1960s it was green peppercorns, in the 1970s there were kiwis and raspberry vinegar, in the 1980s it was pink peppercorns, and in the 1990s, *fleur de sel*. It used to be that salt was salt. Sophisticated kitchens may have had coarse salt or kosher salt, but that was about it. I discovered *fleur de sel* a couple of decades ago while riding my moped across the Ile de Ré, a small island off the coast of Brittany. Until recently, whenever friends went to France and asked me if there was anything they could bring back, I asked for *fleur de sel*, available at Fauchon in the Place de la Madeleine. I felt like a Roman soldier, accepting favors in salt. Because *fleur de sel* is now available in the United States (at exorbitant prices), I'll have to think of something else.

But why all the fuss? Well, first of all, *fleur de sel* looks different. It has flat crystals that sparkle in a particular way and look rather dramatic when sprinkled on foods just before serving or when passed at the table. On special occasions I serve it in my grandmother's saltcellars with salt spoons—it won't come through the holes in a shaker because it's slightly moist, as is any salt that doesn't include some kind of desiccating agent. Until the early part of the twentieth century, all salt was a bit damp, because salt absorbs moisture from the air. Additives are now added to most salt to keep it dry.

Does *fleur de sel* taste different? It may be the power of suggestion, but *fleur de sel* and other natural sea salts taste milder and seem more delicate than regular processed salt. *Fleur* means flower, and *fleur de sel* got its name from the distinctive flowerlike pattern that forms on the surface of the salt beds as the sea water is allowed to dry in the sun. This salt—the *fleur*—is raked off. The salt that sinks to the bottom is then sold as regular sea salt.

Sel de Guérande is a less expensive yet still excellent sea salt, but instead of the flat crystals characteristic of *fleur de sel*, it has a dull gray appearance and medium-size crystals, between the size of coarse salt and fine salt. In my own kitchen I use a number of salts: regular coarse or fine salt for boiling vegetables (in which case the salt is thrown out with the water), *sel de Guérande* for day-to-day seasoning and cooking, and *fleur de sel* for special occasions.

WHITE TRUFFLES

Whether out of chauvinism or ignorance, French chefs have, except for a few nineteenth-century eccentricities, neglected white truffles. In Italy, white truffles are almost always served raw, but when I first started serving them in my Manhattan restaurant Le Petit Robert, not knowing any better, I cooked them. The results were marvelous. I served a *poulet en demi-deuil,* the classic French dish made by sliding slices of black truffles under the skin of a chicken and then poaching it, or, in Lucien Tendret's late nineteenth-century version, steaming it; but I used white truffles instead of black, and instead of poaching or steaming, I simply wrapped the whole chicken in aluminum foil and baked it. When the waiters unwrapped it in the dining room before a table of truffle enthusiasts, customers at other tables turned around in bewilderment wondering what on earth that weird smell was.

I was recently reading a book called *L'Atelier d'Alain Ducasse,* and it appears the French, led by the renowned Monsieur Ducasse, are catching on. He makes a dish similar to my aluminum foil–wrapped concoction, but uses a pig's bladder. (Don't be shocked, this has been going on for years—anything cooked in a bladder is called *en vessie.*) In addition to the chicken with the truffle slices slid under its skin, he loads the bladder with foie gras, Cognac, port, and other goodies and constructs a *sauce Albufera,* a classic sauce finished with puréed foie gras, out of the juices released by the chicken. The recipe goes on for a while, but you get the idea. His book includes other recipes using raw white truffles—thinly sliced over gnocchi (Italian enough, but Frenchified with a little heavy cream and veal broth), over caramelized winter vegetables, over poached eggs and sweetbreads, and over a little stew made with celeriac and sea scallops.

ROAST GARLIC AND BLACK TRUFFLE FLANS

FLANS À L'AIL RÔTI ET AUX TRUFFES NOIRES

You can serve these individual flans as first courses or as side dishes for red meat, poultry, or game dishes.

1	black winter truffle, as big as you can afford
½	cup [250 ml] milk
1½	cup [250 ml] heavy cream
4	large egg yolks
½	teaspoon salt
¼	teaspoon freshly ground pepper
2	large heads garlic, broken up into cloves, cloves unpeeled
1	tablespoon extra-virgin olive oil
2	teaspoons softened butter

IF the truffle is dirty, brush it with a soft toothbrush, rinse it under cold running water, and pat it dry in a dish towel. Grate the truffle using the finest teeth on a hand grater. If your grater doesn't have fine teeth, but has only little punch-outs that will turn the truffle into mush, slice the truffle with a plastic vegetable slicer, a knife, or a truffle slicer and then chop the slices fine.

COMBINE the grated or chopped truffle with the milk and cream. Beat the egg yolks with the salt and pepper and strain them into the truffle mixture. Cover the mixture with plastic wrap and refrigerate it for 2 to 12 hours to let the flavor of the truffle infuse.

TOSS the garlic cloves with the olive oil, wrap them all together in foil, and sprinkle them with 1 tablespoon of water to keep them from burning. Wrap them up into a packet and bake them in a 350°F [175°C/gas mark 4] oven (there's no need to pre-heat it) for about 30 minutes, until when you squeeze one of the cloves through the foil, it's completely soft. Turn the oven down to 275°F [165°C/gas mark 3] for baking the custards.

LET the garlic cool for 10 minutes and then squeeze the pulp out of each of the cloves. Work the pulp through a strainer with the bottom of a ladle and whisk the pulp into the truffle mixture.

BRUSH the inside of six 4- or 5-ounce [120- or 150-ml] ramekins or Pyrex custard dishes with butter and ladle in the truffle mixture. After each ladling, stir the mixture remaining in the mixing bowl so that each custard gets an equal amount of chopped truffles. Arrange the ramekins in a baking dish with sides at least 2 inches high (to act as a bain-marie; see page 634). Fill the baking dish with enough hot tap water to come halfway up the sides of the ramekins and slide it into the oven. Bake for 45 minutes, or until no ripples form when you jiggle the ramekins back and forth. To be sure that all the flans are done, jiggle them individually—ovens are often uneven. Run a knife around the inside of each mold and unmold the flans on heated plates.

Variations: If these flans are intended as a first course, you might want to serve them with a sauce, such as a bordelaise sauce (see page 483), with or without the beef marrow, and perhaps some more chopped truffles. Sautéed wild mushrooms spooned over each of the flans make them pretty to look at, provide a contrasting texture, and a magnificent flavor. You can also deglaze the pan with a little Madeira and dribble it over the flans. In one experiment, I tried lining the ramekins with thinly sliced truffles (simmered for 2 minutes in 2 tablespoons of Madeira, the Madeira added to the flan mixture), but they floated up into the mixture during baking. A better solution is to cook the truffle slices in the Madeira, arrange them on top of each flan once you've unmolded the flans onto the plates, and dribble the truffle-infused Madeira over each flan. You can also use the truffle and morel fricassée described on page 604 as a topping for these flans.

TRUFFLES WITH POTATOES: First it should be said that any potato dish made with truffles can also be made without, but needless to say truffles add a dramatic *je ne sais quoi*. Since potatoes and most vegetables contain very little fat of their own, they're hard to infuse with the aroma of truffles unless they are cooked in some fat, such as butter or cream. Virtually any cooked vegetable can be enrobed in a cream, butter, or egg yolk sauce flavored with truffles, but two vegetables—potatoes and wild mushrooms—are most dramatic with truffles, probably because potatoes make a perfect medium for fats (such as butter or duck fat) and wild mushrooms have earthy notes that are enhanced by the truffles. (Things that grow in the same place often go well together.)

The classic French repertoire is filled with potato dishes calling for truffles. Escoffier mentions *pommes Anna aux truffes* (see page 572 for a plain *pommes Anna*); puréed potatoes with truffles (see page 602); and *pommes de terre Berny,* for which a potato croquette mixture is loaded with chopped truffles, and the mixture is formed into apricot shapes, breaded, and deep-fried. *Pommes de terre Mirette* are potatoes cut into small dice, cooked gently in butter, and finished with julienned truffles, meat glaze, and Parmigiano-Reggiano; they are then browned under the broiler. To make *pommes de terre Ninon,* you must bake the potatoes, scoop out the pulp and work it with chopped truffles and foie gras, and then bake it in tartlet shells. After unmolding, the tartlets are coated with a chateaubriand sauce, made with white wine, herbs, and butter. The list goes on in similar baroque fashion. In places where truffles are found, cooks are more likely to combine them with potatoes in more straightforward and traditional ways than those of classic chefs, usually with more satisfying results. *Pommes de terre sarladaise,* from the French southwest, are simply sautéed potatoes with chopped truffles added at the end. Named after the town of Sarlat in the Dordogne valley, they are derived from a classic and deceptively simple dish of sautéed potatoes, *pommes de terre sautées à cru,* which simply means sautéed raw potatoes. The tricky part is getting the potatoes to brown evenly. They must be served immediately or they'll turn soft.

SAUTÉED POTATOES SPRINKLED WITH CHOPPED TRUFFLES

POMMES SAUTÉS DE TERRE SARLADAISE

MAKES 4 SIDE-DISH SERVINGS

5   medium-to-large white or red waxy potatoes (about 2½ pounds [1.1 kg] total), peeled, kept submerged in water until you're ready to cook

½   cup [125 ml] duck or goose fat (see page 383), or ¼ pound butter

1   black winter truffle as big as you can afford

salt

pepper

SLICE the potatoes to about the thickness of 2 quarters with a mandoline (see page 13) or chefs' knife and pat them dry in kitchen towels. (Don't use paper towels, which stick and tear.) Heat the fat or butter in two 10- to 14-inch [25.5- to 35.5-cm] nonstick pans or well-seasoned iron pans until you smell the fat or the butter froths. (You need two pans so you don't have to stack the potatoes too thickly, causing them to steam instead of sauté.) Don't get the fat too hot—it shouldn't ripple, much less smoke, or you'll destroy its aroma. Add the potatoes, separating any that cling together, evenly in the pans. Cook the potatoes for about 12 minutes over medium to high heat. Shake the pans continuously for the first 1 or 2 minutes to keep the potatoes from sticking together, and then every couple of minutes until they are well browned on the bottom—gently lift one up and peek at its color. Don't try to turn the potatoes until they are brown. When they are well browned, turn the slices over one by one with a spatula, being very gentle so you don't break through the crispy outer surface, causing them to release starch and to stick. Continue turning the potatoes over as needed until they are all evenly browned. You'll need another 12 to 15 minutes.

WHILE the potatoes are sautéing, chop or grate the truffle.

WHEN the potatoes are browned, sprinkle them with salt and pepper. (Don't add salt before this or it will draw the moisture out of the potatoes, making it more difficult to brown them.) Add the chopped truffle. Toss or gently turn for 1 minute more. Serve immediately.

Variations: *Pommes sautées à cru* are plenty good served plain, but you can also finish them with ingredients less rarefied than truffles. One of the best mixtures for finishing most sautéed foods is a persillade made by combining fresh parsley, chopped at the last minute, with garlic that has been chopped and crushed to a paste with the side of a chefs' knife. Sprinkle the persillade over the potatoes about 1 minute before serving so the garlic releases its perfume but doesn't have a chance to burn. French cooks use other mixtures ending in *-ade* (pronounced "add"), such as *anchoïade*, made by crushing anchovies in a mortar with garlic, bread crumbs, and olive oil. The *anchoïade* is then spread on toasts as an hors d'oeuvre. An *oursinade* is a Provençal mayonnaise made with sea urchin roe and used to finish fish soups. A *truffade* is a paste made with truffles and olive oil and spread on toasts. (Don't confuse this with the Lyonnaise cake called *la truffade*, made with potatoes, bacon, and cheese.) It's easy to make your own variation on the theme by chopping various herbs with crushed garlic and sprinkling the mixture over sautéed vegetables or seafood such as shrimp or scallops. I once made a *"lavandade"* with garlic and lavender flowers I sprinkled over sautéed wild mushrooms. (The garlic balanced the flavor of the lavender so that no one was reminded of soap.) Thyme, herbes de Provençe mixture, marjoram, oregano, and sage are obvious possibilities.

PURÉED POTATOES WITH TRUFFLES

PURÉE DE POMMES DE TERRE AUX TRUFFES

MAKES 8 SIDE-DISH SERVINGS

American restaurants, from the corner diner to the most elegant and expensive establishments, have been going through a phase that involves serving lumpy mashed potatoes or, worse, mashed potatoes with the skin left on. How this deviant behavior came about I don't know, but its justification may have had something to do with the peels being healthy and the lumps somehow being homey. But the real reason, I suspect, has been laziness.

While I try to be flexible in the kitchen, my tolerance ends here. "Mashed" potatoes should not be mashed (using a masher invariably leaves lumps) but should be puréed until perfectly smooth and silky. And while I enjoy eating the peel of a baked potato, the peels for puréed potatoes should go into the trash or compost heap.

You can purée potatoes in one of several ways. Some cooks use a food mill, but certain potato varieties are overworked by a food mill and turn glutinous and gluey. A ricer is also a handy gadget and makes quick work of things, but the best device of all is a drum sieve (see page 15).

Another important factor when making mashed potatoes is the kind of potato you use. I prefer medium-starchy potatoes such as Yukon Golds, Yellow Finns, or *rattes* (little finger-shaped potatoes), but in a pinch I use russets, which are perfectly fine, just a tad mealy. I usually peel my potatoes before cooking them, but if you're using small potatoes such as *rattes*, it's easier to cook them with the peels on and then pull away the peels before the potatoes have time to cool. If, however, you're being an absolute perfectionist, you should know that peeling after cooking may very slightly discolor your purée because of the coloration left on the potato by the peel.

Cooks often assume, wrongly, that the only suitable liquids for mashed potatoes are butter (which of course is liquid when hot), heavy cream, and whole milk. When I make truffled mashed potatoes, I do use heavy cream and butter, because these ingredients help trap the flavor of the truffles. But much of the time, when making plain mashed potatoes, I thin the purée with some of the cooking liquid and finish it with relatively small amounts of butter and cream, or just butter. The amount of butter or cream you use is up to you. I've seen recipes that contain as much as a stick of butter per pound of potatoes and then thin the potatoes to the desired consistency with heavy cream. The result is delicious, but when I make them this way I keep my mouth shut in front of the guests.

You can incorporate the truffle into the mashed potatoes in various ways. The least expensive is to store your butter overnight in a jar with the truffle, add the butter to the potatoes, and use the truffle for something else. You can also just chop the truffle and incorporate it into the potatoes about 10 minutes before serving to give its aroma time to permeate. Another good trick is to bring 1 cup of heavy cream to a simmer, turn off the heat, put the chopped truffle in the cream, cover the pan, and let the truffle steep for about 15 minutes. You then stir the cream into the potatoes just before serving. Perhaps the most elegant approach is to pass a grater or truffle slicer with the truffle and let your guests help themselves.

3 pounds [1.3 kg] potatoes, such as Yukon Golds, Yellow Fins, rattes, or russets, peeled, kept submerged in cold water to prevent darkening

1 cup [250 ml] heavy cream or milk, or more as needed

1 black winter truffle, as big as you can afford

6 tablespoons butter or truffle butter (or less or more if you so choose)

salt

pepper

IF the potatoes are large, cut them in halves or quarters. Put the potatoes in a pot with enough cold water to come two-thirds of the way up the sides of the potatoes. (Potatoes should be started in cold water so that the heat penetrates them more slowly, causing them to cook more evenly.) Bring to a boil over high heat and then turn the heat down to maintain at a gentle simmer. When the potatoes are easily penetrated by a knife, after about 15 to 30 minutes, depending on their size, drain them in a colander, reserving the cooking liquid in case you need it to thin the mixture. Pull the peel away in strips with a paring knife while holding each potato in a towel.

WHILE the potatoes are cooking, bring the cream or milk to a simmer in a small saucepan and remove from the heat. Chop the truffle, add it to the cream, cover the pan, and let steep for 15 minutes.

WORK the potatoes through a drum sieve or ricer and transfer them to a clean pot. Put the pot over low heat and stir in the truffle cream and the butter. If you want the potatoes runnier, stir in some of the reserved cooking liquid or more cream or butter. Season to taste with salt and pepper and serve immediately.

Variations: To reheat mashed potatoes the next day, thin them with some milk and stir them gently on the stove, or heat them in the microwave for 30 seconds at a time, stirring between each reheating so they heat through evenly. Unless your mashed potatoes contain a large amount of butter or cream, you can turn them into a tasty *galette*—a pancake—by working them with beaten eggs (about 1 egg for every ¾ cup [160 g] of purée) and cooking them in butter in a nonstick sauté pan in a layer about ½ inch [1.5 cm] thick. If you like, add chopped chives or scallions or a little minced garlic for extra flavor.

Fortunately, plain mashed potatoes are marvelous without any special flavoring, and if you make them using one of the medium-starchy varieties (Yukon Golds, Yellow Finns, or *rattes*) and use a drum sieve, they're likely to be better than anything you or your guests have tasted anywhere. But the gentle flavor of mashed potatoes makes them a perfect medium for a variety of ingredients, including fennel, garlic, celeriac, dried cèpes (porcini) or morels, and saffron. If you're using fennel, garlic, or celeriac, just cook the chopped fennel bulb (about 1 bulb per 6 large potatoes), or the whole unpeeled garlic cloves (1 head per 6 large potatoes) or a peeled and chopped celeriac (about 1 medium-size root per 6 large potatoes) with the potatoes and work all the ingredients through the drum sieve or ricer together. If you're using dried mushrooms, soak them in a little Madeira or water—just enough to moisten them—chop them, and stir them into the potatoes after puréeing (½ ounce per 6 large potatoes is enough, but more won't hurt). A good pinch of saffron should be soaked in 1 tablespoon of water for 30 minutes before being stirred into the potatoes just before serving.

TRUFFLES WITH WILD MUSHROOMS: If you're lucky enough to have both of these on hand at the same time, get ready to enter celestial realms. If you have fresh chanterelles, morels, black chanterelles, hedgehog mushrooms, or cèpes, just sauté them in butter or duck or goose fat and sprinkle them with salt and pepper and chopped or grated black truffles about 2 minutes before you're ready to take them out of the sauté pan. Serve them as a first course or a side dish, or spoon them over slices of roast veal, sautéed veal chops, sautéed chicken, or fillets of full-flavored seafood such as salmon, or over the truffle and garlic flans described on page 600.

Truffles go especially well with dried morels, and the two together, simmered with a little port, cream, and meat glaze, make a sublime sauce for beef or veal. I also like to combine them with artichokes.

TRUFFLES, MORELS, AND ARTICHOKES FRICASSEE

TRUFFES, MORILLES, ET ARTICHAUTS EN FRICASSÉE

MAKES 4 LUXURIOUS FIRST-COURSE SERVINGS

To make this modest little vegetable stew you'll need fresh morels that aren't too small. They should be large enough—at least ¾ inch [2 cm] across at the widest part, just above the stem—so that you can stuff them with foie gras. If you decide not to use the foie gras, the size of the morels isn't important.

- 4 large artichokes
- juice of 1 lemon
- 2 tablespoons olive oil
- 1 pound [450 g] fresh assorted wild mushrooms, one-third of which need to be fresh large morels
- 3 ounces [85 g] foie gras bloc or entier (optional; see page 96 for more about foie gras)
- 4 tablespoons duck or goose fat or melted butter
- salt
- pepper
- ¼ cup [60 ml] tawny or ruby port
- 1 tablespoon meat glaze (optional; see page 3)
- ½ cup [125 ml] heavy cream
- 1 large black truffle, sliced thin

TURN the artichokes as described on page 21 and cook them in enough water to abundantly cover, with half the lemon juice and half the olive oil, in a nonaluminum pot until they are easily penetrated with a knife but still offer a little resistance, about 20 minutes. Drain in a colander and let cool for 10 minutes. Scoop the choke out of each artichoke with a spoon and discard the choke. Cut the artichoke bottoms into 4 or 6 wedges each, depending on the size of the artichoke, and toss the wedges with the remaining olive oil and lemon juice. (If you do this the day before, the lemon juice will bleach the artichokes to a delightful pale green.)

IF the mushrooms are dirty—look inside the morels through their stems—quickly stir them in a bowl of cold water, drain in a colander, and pat dry with towels. Cut the foie gras into strips about ¼ inch [.5 cm] on each side. Use the top of a pencil or chopstick to push the strips into the morels, and continue until you've used all the foie gras. Reserve the morels and other mushrooms.

HEAT the fat or butter in a sauté pan and sauté the mushrooms and artichoke wedges over high heat for about 5 minutes. Stop sautéing if the foie gras starts to leak out of the morels. Season with salt and pepper. Pour the port into the sauté pan and boil it for about 30 seconds over high heat to cook off its alcohol. Add the meat glaze and the heavy cream and boil for 1 or 2 minutes, until the sauce barely begins to thicken. Add the truffles and simmer for 1 minute more. Season to taste with salt and pepper. Serve on small plates or in little bowls or *cassolettes* (see page 271 for more about *cassolettes*). Or use as a topping for the truffle and garlic flans on page 600, in which case this recipe will make enough for 6 first-course servings.

Variations: When I worked at Vivarois in Paris, the most striking dishes were often the simplest. One was a large artichoke bottom served with a thick slice of foie gras on top—a classic Lyonnaise dish. A somewhat more complicated concoction was called a *belle humeur*. A 3-inch [7.5-cm] round of flaky puff pastry (*pâte feuilletée*) was stacked with alternating layers of truffles and foie gras. The edge of the pastry was brushed with beaten egg and a larger round was placed on top and pinched onto the bottom layer. The whole assembly was kept in the refrigerator until some lucky customer ordered it. When ordered, it was deep-fried for 2 minutes, patted free of oil, and served with a sauce similar to a *sauce périgourdine*—reduced port wine, meat glaze, truffles, and a little butter.

TRUFFLE SANDWICHES

Apparently someone in Paris is now famous for a truffle grilled cheese sandwich, which I must say sounds pretty good. I did make a truffle and ham sandwich once when my friend Sally Schneider, author of *A New Way to Cook*, returned from Spain with some celestial Serrano ham. We made miniature toasts, smeared them with a thick layer of French butter, spread a layer of black truffle slices over that, and then put thin slices of the ham on top. The result was one of the best things I've ever eaten.

APPLE TART

TARTE AUX POMMES

DURING THE YEARS I WAS STUDYING COOKING, I WAS DRAWN TO THE front door of every restaurant I happened upon so I could analyze its menu and even peer through its window to watch what people were eating. I had turned into a food voyeur.

The pastry cart is an invention well suited to food voyeurism because it gives you a chance to make a quick visual study and, with a little experience, to judge the skills of a restaurant's pastry chef before the maître d' even gets you to your table. On every pastry cart in France, in both modest and elegant places, you'll spot an apple tart in one guise or another. You may get a quick glance at a simple classic apple tart, made by baking apple wedges in a pastry shell coated with a layer of applesauce made from the ends of the apples; a *tarte Tatin*, which is an upside-down apple tart; a *tarte alsacienne*, in which the apples are surrounded with custard; or a thin and crispy *feuilletée* tart. The only version you won't see is an apple pie. Pies, which the French call *tourtes*, have a sheet of dough on top, covering what's inside. French cooks usually reserve this treatment for savory dishes such as hot pâtés.

Most cooks setting out to make an apple tart for the first time are stumped by three things: making the dough, knowing what kind of apples to use, and arranging the apples in the tart shell so they look pretty. The most classic and simple apple tart is made with the basic tart dough, what the French call *pâte brisée*, described on pages 155 to 157, the same dough used for making quiche. The pastry shell for a basic apple tart doesn't need to be prebaked because apples, unlike most fruits, release hardly any liquid as they cook, so the shell won't become soggy but instead will bake and turn crispy at the same time the apples are cooking. The kind of apple you use will depend on the season and where you live (see "Apples for Baking," below); if you don't have access to any special or unusual varieties, Golden Delicious apples (unlike Granny Smiths) retain their texture during baking and have a decent flavor.

PEELING AND SLICING APPLES: It's best to peel apples just before you're ready to use them and immediately rub them with a lemon half, but some apples begin browning after just a couple of minutes, lemon or no lemon. Cut the stem out of each apple by rotating the tip of a vegetable peeler or paring knife around the base of the stem, at the same time removing the bit of peel in the indentation. Peel the apples and cut each one vertically in half. Cut the core out of each half with a paring knife or melon baller. Cut the apple halves crosswise into slices between ¹⁄₁₆ inch and ⅛ inch [about 3 mm] thick. Don't toss the slices with lemon juice, but instead gently fan them out between both hands and then sprinkle them with lemon juice. They'll be much easier to arrange in the tart shell if they stay together in the order in which you sliced them. Do not soak the apples in lemon water or acidulated water, which leaches out the apples' natural sugars and flavor.

———○———

APPLES FOR BAKING

The availability of baking apples will vary according to where you live and the time of year. You should be able to find Golden Delicious and Rome apples in the supermarket at any time of the year. While these are good standby apples, be on the lookout for more flavorful apples, such as Baldwins, Cortlands, Empires, Galas, Macouns, Northern Spys, Reinettes du Canada, and Rhode Island Greenings. I always prefer to buy one of these "heirloom" varieties when I can find them, usually in the fall.

Professional pastry chefs glaze finish tarts by brushing them with a diluted apricot jam called *abricotage* (for apples or pears) or red currant jelly (for red fruits such as raspberries). While brushing with a glaze will give a tart an appealing sheen, don't overdo it or the tart will be sticky and it will end up tasting more like the glaze than like the fruit. To make enough light glaze for one 10-inch [25.5-cm] tart, combine 2 tablespoons of apricot jam or red currant jelly with 2 tablespoons of water in a small saucepan or nonmetal bowl or cup. Put the pan over medium heat or the bowl in the microwave for 30 seconds. Press down on the jam with a pastry brush or the back of a fork to get it to dissolve completely. When there are no specks of undissolved jam, remove the glaze from the heat, strain it (unless it's perfectly smooth), and lightly brush it over the cool tart.

CLASSIC HOME-STYLE APPLE TART

TARTE AUX POMMES
À LA MÉNAGÈRE

MAKES 6 DESSERT SERVINGS

(ONE 10-INCH [25.5-CM] TART)

1 recipe Basic Pie and Tart Dough (pâte brisée) (page 155)

6 Golden Delicious apples, or enough of another variety to make 2 pounds [1 kg]

2 tablespoons lemon juice

1 tablespoon granulated sugar, or to taste (for the applesauce)

1 tablespoon butter

1 tablespoon granulated sugar (for sprinkling over the tart before baking)

2 tablespoons apricot jam (for the glaze; optional; see above)

2 tablespoons confectioners' sugar (if you're not using the apricot glaze)

1 recipe Crème Chantilly (page 609) (for serving)

LINE a 10-inch [25.5-cm] tart pan with the dough, as described on page 157. Don't prebake the shell, just refrigerate it while you're preparing the apples. Peel and slice the apples as described on page 607. Take 2 or 3 of the small slices from each end of the apple halves—you should end up with about 2 cups of trimmings—and place them in a saucepan with 2 teaspoons of the lemon juice, ¼ cup [60 ml] of water, 1 tablespoon of granulated sugar, and 1 tablespoon of butter. Cover the pan and simmer gently over low to medium heat, stirring every few minutes with a wooden spoon and scraping the bottom of the pan so the apples don't stick, until the apples have softened and are easy to crush against the side of the pan, about 20 minutes. If the apples start to scorch at any point before they soften, add 2 more tablespoons of water. If there's liquid left in the pan once the apples have softened, take off the lid and simmer the applesauce, while stirring, until it's stiff. Usually the applesauce will end up smooth just from stirring. A few lumps don't matter, but if it contains firm chunks, work it through a strainer with a small ladle. Chill the applesauce for 20 minutes in the refrigerator and spread it evenly over the tart shell.

PREHEAT the oven to 400°F [200°C/gas mark 6]. Fan out the apple slices—don't toss them, or it will be more work fanning them out in the tart—and rub them with the remaining lemon juice. Set aside. After you've spread the applesauce in the tart shell, arrange the apple slices along the inside perimeter of the shell, with one end—what would be the bottom of the fan—facing the center of the tart. Overlap the slices so that each one covers about half the slice under it. Do this by fanning the apples out between both hands and placing the wider part of the fan against the inner rim of the tart. Make a second round inside the first, using the smaller slices from the ends of the apple halves. Arrange small slices—you may need to trim them to make them fit—at the center of the tart in a rosette pattern. Sprinkle the tart with granulated sugar.

PLACE the tart on a sheet pan and bake it for about 40 to 50 minutes, until the rim is pale brown and you can easily pierce the apples with a paring knife. If you're not using the apricot glaze, sprinkle the hot tart with half the confectioners' sugar by work-ing the sugar through a fine-mesh strainer with your fingers while holding the strainer over the tart. Let cool. If you're using the glaze, prepare it as described on page 608 and brush it over the apples (try not to get it on the rim). If you're not using the glaze, sprinkle the cool tart with the rest of the confectioners' sugar just before serving. Serve the tart in wedges. Pass the *crème Chantilly* at the table.

Variations: In Alsace, apple tarts—*tartes alsaciennes*—are often made with a rich custard surrounding the apples. To make one, prepare the tart above without the applesauce, dotting it with 1 tablespoon of butter and sprinkling 1 tablespoon of sugar over it. Take it out of the oven and let it cool for 10 minutes so it doesn't curdle the custard. Turn the oven down to 325°F [165°C/gas mark 3]. While the tart is cooling, make a custard batter by combining 1 cup [250 ml] of milk (or half-and-half or heavy cream) with 2 beaten eggs, 4 tablespoons of granulated sugar, and 1 teaspoon of vanilla extract. When the sugar has dissolved, pour the mixture over the tart (don't spill any on the rim). Put the tart on a sheet pan in case it leaks, and gently put the tart back in the oven and bake it for about 30 minutes, or until the custard has set—it doesn't move when you jiggle the tart back and forth.

CRÈME CHANTILLY

While it's true that there isn't a great deal of difference, *crème Chantilly* is not to be confused with whipped cream. Whipped cream is simply cream that has been whipped until it stiffens. *Crème Chantilly*, or Chantilly cream, contains a little vanilla (usually vanilla extract) and some sugar. To make enough for 4 to 6 servings, combine 1 cup [250 ml] of heavy cream with ½ teaspoon of vanilla extract and 1 tablespoon of confectioners' or superfine sugar in a mixing bowl. (Some people like their cream sweeter, so adjust the sugar to your own taste.) Put the mixing bowl and whisk (or whisk attachment for the electric mixer) in the freezer for 5 minutes before you use them. The colder the cream, the more quickly it will beat up. If it's a hot day, you may even want to beat the cream over a bowl of ice. If the cream isn't well chilled, it won't whip.

UPSIDE-DOWN APPLE TART

TARTE TATIN

MAKE 8 DESSERT SERVINGS

(ONE 10-INCH [25.5-CM] TART)

Before the days of nonstick pans, making a tarte Tatin was risky business because the apples could easily stick to the pan and burn. Now, with a little care and attention, a tarte Tatin is as easy to make as an ordinary tart and will guarantee oohs and ahs at the table. Acting nonchalant when serving will make your handiwork all the more impressive.

8   large Golden Delicious apples (Rome apples for firmer texture), or enough of another variety (see "Apples for Baking," page 607) to make 4 pounds [1.7 kg]

2   tablespoons lemon juice

6   tablespoons granulated sugar

6   tablespoons butter

1   recipe Basic Pie and Tart Dough (pâte brisée) (page 155)

1   recipe Crème Chantilly (or 2, if you're feeling piggy) (page 609) or 2 cups [500 g] Classic Vanilla Crème Anglaise (page 642) (for serving)

PEEL the apples and cut them in half vertically and then cut the halves in half so you end up with 4 wedges per apple. Cut the core off the side of each wedge with a paring knife. Toss the wedges with lemon juice and 2 tablespoons of the sugar. Toss again 10 minutes later, until the sugar dissolves and you don't feel it under your fingers.

USE a wooden spoon to stir the butter and the remaining sugar over medium heat in a 10-inch [25.5-cm] nonstick pan with sloping sides, preferably (but not essentially) one that has no rivet or nodule on the inside where the handle attaches. (Make sure the pan fits in the oven and doesn't have

a handle that will melt.) Continue stirring until the sugar dissolves and the butter foams, about 5 minutes. Remove from the heat.

PLACE the apple wedges in the pan. As you keep adding apples, they'll start to stand on end from bottom to stem. Add as many apples as you can until the pan is full and the apple wedges are all standing on end. Cram as many wedges into the pan as you can—they shrink as the tart cooks.

PREHEAT the oven to 400°F [200°C/gas mark 6]

PLACE the pan with the apples on the stove over medium heat. Use a flame tamer to help distribute the heat (it's easy to scorch the apples, especially if your pan is thin). Move the pan about every 5 minutes so the heat is under a different part and the apples brown evenly. As the apples cook, they'll release liquid, sometimes enough so that the liquid comes halfway up the sides of the wedges. The apples also shrink, allowing you to force in more wedges. It's important that the pan be completely full or the mass of apples won't hold its shape. Continue cooking the apples until most of the liquid boils away and you're left with a thickened caramel that comes halfway up the sides of the wedges, 45 minutes to 1 hour. At this point, the apples can easily burn. To check how they're doing, gently slide a knife down the side of the pan and lift up one of the wedges to see if it's golden brown on the bottom. Carefully replace the wedge. Do this in a couple of places around the pan.

WHEN the apples are well browned, make sure they're not sticking by quickly moving the handle of the pan clockwise and then quickly reversing to counterclockwise. Do this until you see the apples form a cohesive mass—they no longer move with the pan. If they're stuck, gently slide a knife or thin spatula down and under the apples, loosening the mass here and there without breaking up the apples. Take the tart off the heat and let it cool for 30 minutes at room temperature and for 30 minutes more in the fridge. The apples must be cool or they'll melt the dough when you unroll it over them.

ROLL the dough slightly less than ¼ inch [.5 cm] thick and cut out a round 2 inches [5 cm] larger in diameter than the outside rim of the sauté pan. (The extra inches [5 cm] are needed because the dough shrinks during baking.) Roll the round up on a rolling pin and unroll it over the apples. Tuck the dough around the inside of the pan, enclosing the apples. Place the tart on a sheet pan and slide it into the oven. Bake until the dough is golden brown, about 40 minutes. Remove the tart from the oven and again give the handle of the pan a quick back-and-forth turn to make sure none of the apples are sticking.

LET the tart cool for 2 hours at room temperature and for 2 hours more in the refrigerator, until it is thoroughly chilled. (You can also set the pan in a bowl over ice if you're in a rush.) Place the tart over high heat and, with your hand spread over the dough, gently rotate the tart a full 360 degrees within the pan. This ensures that the tart won't stick to the sides of the pan. Place a flat serving plate upside-down over the tart, and while holding the plate firmly against the tart with one hand, and firmly gripping the handle of pan with the other (use a kitchen towel or oven mitt), turn the tart over. Gently lift away the pan. Serve the tart in wedges. Pass the *crème Chantilly* at the table.

PASTRYLESS APPLE TART

TARTE AUX POMMES SANS CROÛTE

MAKES 8 DESSERT SERVINGS

(ONE 9-INCH/23 CM TART)

In all my travels I've never encountered this version of an apple tart. Instead, I learned it from my friend Fanny Brennan, who spent many years in France and worked on a marvelous newsletter called *Parties People Remember*. Fanny insists that red-skinned apples such as Rome Beauties be used and the peels be spread over the tart during baking so they impart a lovely pink color. This tart is similar to a *tarte Tatin* except that there's no pastry, so the final tart is less rich and makes a perfect finish to a long dinner. Also, there's no pastry to fuss with. Since the apple slices shrink from the long baking time, the height of the tart depends upon the pans in your kitchen. Using a 9-inch [22.5-cm] springform pan with sides 3¾ inches [8.5 cm] high creates a tart 2 inches [5 cm] tall that is easy to unmold.

15 tablespoons butter, softened

1 cup [200 g] granulated sugar

8 large red-skinned apples such as Rome Beauties or Cortlands or other red-skinned variety, but not Macintosh (5 pounds total)

1 recipe Crème Chantilly (page 609), or 2 cups Classic Vanilla Crème Anglaise (page 642) (for serving)

PREHEAT the oven to 375°F [190°C/gas mark 5].

RUB or brush softened butter on the inside of a 9-inch [23-cm] springform with 3¾-inch [8.5-cm] or higher sides. Cut a round of parchment paper one inch larger than the diameter of the pan and place it in the bottom, smoothing extra paper onto the sides of the pan. Rub or brush it liberally with butter and sprinkle ½ tablespoon of the sugar over it. Line the outside of the springform pan with aluminum foil.

PEEL the apples and reserve the peels. Cut the apples vertically in half and cut out the cores. Thinly slice the apple halves crosswise. Arrange the apple slices in a decorative overlapping rosette pattern on the bottom of the baking dish, and then layer in the rest of the slices, sprinkling each layer with sugar. (Only the bottom layer, which will end up on top, needs to be arranged decoratively.) Spread the reserved peels on top and slide the tart into the oven. Place a sheet pan underneath the tart to catch any juices that drip out of the bottom of the springform pan. These juices can be spooned over the top of the tart.

BAKE for 30 minutes, lower the heat to 300°F [150°C/gas mark 2], and bake 3½ hours longer. Press down on the tart every hour with a spatula. If at the end of this time you see a lot of juice still in the mold, siphon it off with a bulb baster, reduce it to a syrup on the stove, and pour it back over the tart. Remove the peels, which by now will have turned black. Set the tart on a rack and let it cool to room temperature. Refrigerate it overnight.

WHEN you're ready to unmold the tart, place it on the stove over medium heat. Move the pan to different spots over the heat source for 2 to 3 seconds at a time to loosen the tart. Flip the tart over and onto a plate, release the hinge, and remove the sides of the pan, metal bottom, and parchment round. Serve the tart in wedges with the crème anglaise or *crème Chantilly*.

PUFF PASTRY TARTS AND TARTLETS

The French have a variety of tarts made by sealing a filling between two rounds of puff pastry before baking. The best known of these, *le pithiviers*, is made by sandwiching a filling of ground almonds and butter, held together with egg, between the two rounds of pastry. A small hole is made in the center of the tart so that steam can escape without bursting open the tart, and a spiral design is made on top of the tart for decoration and to allow the pastry to expand without cracking. In the southwest of France they make a *feuilleté béarnaise* by sandwiching apples with a little goose fat between rounds of puff pastry. In Normandy they make an apple tart with a stiff applesauce baked in a tart pan lined with puff pastry and covered with a puff pastry lattice. In northern France, they seal pastry cream between two rectangles of puff pastry to make a tart called a *dartois*.

The same techniques are used throughout France to make savory tarts. In Burgundy, dollops of cheese mixture are placed in the middle of small rounds of puff pastry and the puff pastry is folded up around the cheese and pinched together. The individual pastries—*corniottes*—are then brushed with egg wash, baked, and served hot. In the Auvergne they make a potato *tourte* by baking sliced potatoes between two rounds of puff pastry, with a hole in the middle just like for a *pithiviers*, but they then pour crème fraîche into the hole about 5 minutes before taking the *tourte* out of the oven and serving.

THIN APPLE TART MADE WITH PUFF PASTRY

TARTE AUX POMMES FEUILLETÉE

MAKES 6 DESSERT SERVINGS

(ONE 12-INCH [30.5-CM] TART)

This delicate apple tart is thin, crispy, and buttery without being greasy. The acidity of the apples contrasts beautifully with the rich puff pastry. Crème chantilly is an almost essential accompaniment.

- 1 package (14 ounces or 1 pound [400 to 450 g]) puff pastry made with butter (see Sources)
- 3 Golden Delicious apples, or more if your apples are smaller (1½ pounds [675 g] total)
- ½ cup [100 g] granulated sugar
- 1 stick (¼ pound [115 g]) butter
- 1 recipe Crème Chantilly (page 609) (for serving)

ROLL the dough out—between ⅟₁₆ inch and ⅛ inch [about 3 mm] thick. If the dough becomes hard to roll or springs back after each roll, let it rest in the refrigerator for 30 minutes and roll some more. Don't force the dough, or it will contract during cooking. Sprinkle a sheet pan with 1 tablespoon of cold water to keep the bottom of the tart from burning. Roll the dough out onto the sheet pan and cut around it so you end up with a 12-inch [30.5-cm] circle, pulling away the trimmings from the outside. (I use a pan lid as a guide and cut with a sharp knife.) The pastry is cut after being placed on the sheet pan because otherwise it would lose its perfectly round shape when transferred from the work surface to the sheet pan. Poke the dough in about 20 places with a fork to help prevent it from puffing. Refrigerate for 30 minutes.

PREHEAT the oven to 425°F [220°C/gas mark 7].

PEEL the apples, cut them in half vertically, cut out the cores with a paring knife or melon baller, and slice the halves crosswise, as thin as you can. Pull away and reserve about 3 of the smallest slices from each side of the halves. Fan out the large slices and arrange them, overlapping them slightly, in a circle around the outside of the dough, leaving a ¼-inch [.5-cm] border. By having one end of your imaginary fan point toward the center of the tart, you'll be able to lay the slices evenly.

USE the reserved smaller slices—but not the little end pieces—to make a second circle within the outer circle, this time going in the opposite direction. Make sure the smaller slices are touching the larger slices, because the apples shrink as they cook and would otherwise leave too large a space. Fill the exposed center of the tart with the remaining slices, overlapping them in a rosette pattern.

SPRINKLE the tart with sugar. Slice the stick of butter as thin as you can—I usually get about 15 slices —and distribute the butter slices over the tart.

SLIDE the sheet pan into the oven and bake until the border of the tart is a deep golden brown, about 45 minutes. Because the pastry tends to puff, forming large blisters that would disrupt your careful arrangement of the apples, check the tart every 10 minutes and use a thin-pronged fork or skewer to pop the blisters as they form and to nudge any apples back into their original position.

WHEN the tart is done, let it cool for 10 minutes. Slide a long metal spatula under it to detach it from the sheet pan. (Unless you use a nonstick sheet pan, the tart always sticks.) Transfer the tart to a work surface and, while gently lifting it, one side at a time, with the spatula, inspect the bottom. If there are any burnt patches, scrape them off with a sharp knife. Serve the tart in wedges, preferably while it is still warm. (You can reheat it, but it's best served within hours of first coming out of the oven.) Pass the *crème Chantilly* at the table.

APPLE CHARLOTTE

CHARLOTTE AUX POMMES

MAKES 6 DESSERT SERVINGS

There are two basic kinds of charlotte: apple charlotte and the gooey kind of charlotte made by filling a ladyfinger-lined charlotte mold with chocolate mousse or some kind of fruit Bavarian mixture—a mixture of fruit purée, crème anglaise, and whipped cream held together with gelatin. (A charlotte mold looks like a little metal fez with heart-shaped handles.) These ladyfinger concoctions always strike me as too sweet, and the elaborateness of the construction contributes only to the visual effect, accomplishing little in the realms of flavor and texture.

Apple charlotte is something else entirely and is surely one of the best things that can be done with apples. It is made by lining a mold with buttered bread, filling the mold with cooked apples, and then baking until the bread turns golden brown. The charlotte is unmolded and a crème anglaise is served around it.

Many traditional recipes call for making one large charlotte, but a large charlotte requires a very stiff filling (bread crumbs assist in this role) to hold it together. Because this makes the filling starchy, I prefer to make individual charlottes, which are more dramatic anyway. Instead of using charlotte molds, which are expensive, I use versatile 5-ounce ramekins (mine are 3¼ inches [8.5 cm] in diameter and 1¼ inches [3 cm] high).

When buying the apples, look for a variety that won't turn into applesauce when you cook it and ideally one with an acidic tang and plenty of flavor. (See "Apples for Baking," page 607.)

- 8 Golden Delicious apples, or enough of another variety to make 4 pounds
- 12 tablespoons butter
- 12 to 15 slices white bread, preferably thin-sliced dense-crumbed bread, crusts removed
- 2 cups [500 ml] Classic Vanilla Crème Anglaise (page 642)

PEEL the apples, halve them vertically, and cut out the cores. Cut each half into 4 to 6 wedges (4 if the apples are small) and cut each of the wedges crosswise into 3 pieces. Heat 4 tablespoons of the butter in a heavy-bottomed pot. Stir in the apples. Cook gently, stirring every 5 minutes to prevent sticking, until the apples are soft but not mushy and there's no liquid in the pan, about 30 minutes. Don't stir any more than necessary to prevent sticking or the apples may break apart.

WHILE the apples are cooking, use a cookie cutter (or one of the ramekins and a paring knife) to cut 6 rounds of bread the same size as the outside diameter of the ramekins. (The rounds are made slightly large because they shrink during baking.) Melt the remaining butter and liberally brush both sides of the bread rounds. Push the rounds into the ramekins—they should fit snugly. Next, cut the 6 remaining slices of bread into 3 equal strips each, and butter both sides of the strips. Using 2 to 3 strips on their sides lengthwise, line the ramekins. Fit them snugly, since they will shrink during baking.

PREHEAT the oven to 350°F [175°C/gas mark 4].

SPOON the apples into the bread-lined ramekins, heaping them so they form a mound in each. (The apples shrink and settle as they bake.)

PUT the ramekins on a sheet pan and slide them into the oven. Bake until the bread is golden brown on the outside—slide a knife along the outside of the bread and press the bread back gently so you can see it—and the apples have shrunk and browned on top, about 1 hour and 10 minutes.

TAKE the ramekins out of the oven and let cool for about 15 minutes. (The charlottes should be served warm.) Use a bread knife to cut off any excess bread sticking over the top. Turn the charlottes out onto plates. Serve the crème anglaise around—not over—each charlotte. (If you make the charlottes ahead of time, don't reheat them in the microwave or the crust will turn soggy. Use the oven.)

A MORE DRAMATIC CHARLOTTE CRUST

The charlottes look more dramatic if the walls are made with thin strips of bread arranged vertically instead of on their sides. To do this, brush the inside of the ramekins with melted butter so the bread strips will cling, making the charlottes easier to construct. Prepare the bread rounds and insert them into the ramekins in the same way as described in the recipe. Instead of lining the sides with long strips of bread, cut the bread into 3 strips per slice, as in the recipe, but then cut each of these strips crosswise in half. Brush the rectangles (they're almost squares) with butter and arrange them vertically along the sides of the ramekins, overlapping them so about one-third of the strip underneath is covered. You'll need about 6 rectangles per ramekin. Each of the rectangles should touch the bread round on the bottom and reach about ¼ inch [.5 cm] over the top of the ramekin. Fill with the apple mixture, bake, and serve in the same way described in the recipe.

OTHER FRUIT TARTS

Every region of France has its traditional fruit tarts and professional pastry chefs are always inventing variations of their own. It's all a lot simpler than you might think, because the differences in fruit tarts are easy to understand. First of all, some tarts contain raw fruit, others cooked. Berries, such as strawberries and raspberries, which turn soft and release a lot of liquid when cooked, are usually arranged in a precooked tart shell, the fruit itself remaining raw. This is different from American berry pies in which the fruit is usually combined with cornstarch to thicken the liquid released by the fruit and to try (often unsuccessfully) to prevent the liquid from making the bottom piecrust soggy.

When raw berries or other fruits are to be arranged in a prebaked tart shell, the basic tart dough is often sweetened with sugar to contrast with the acidity of the fruit. When a relatively small amount of sugar is used, the sweetened tart dough is called *pâte brisée sucrée*, which simply means sweetened tart dough. For some tarts, an even sweeter dough called *pâte sablée* ("sandy dough") is used. Because of its fine, crumbly texture and because it contains extra butter, *pâte sablée* is almost identical to shortbread dough. Occasionally, almond flour is used to replace some of the flour in a *pâte sablée*, producing an even more fragile and crumbly crust called *pâte à linzer*, the dough used for making a linzertorte. Though most French recipes are very specific about which dough goes with which fruit or filling, you can use your own common sense. Very sweet fillings such as cream fillings or fruits cooked in sugar are best in an unsweetened tart shell of *pâte brisée*, while sour mixtures such as lemon curd are best contrasted with sweetened dough such as *pâte brisée sucrée* or *pâte sablée*.

Fruits that release relatively small amounts of liquids, such as apples, can be sliced or halved and left raw before being arranged in an uncooked tart shell, and the tart then baked—the shell and fruit cooking at the same time—in the same way as the basic apple tart on page 608.

Fruits that release larger amounts of liquid present different problems. Provided they are ripe, such fruits, including peaches and pears, can be arranged raw in a precooked tart in the same way as berries (although pears served in this way have a nasty habit of turning dark). The fruit can also be cooked separately with a little sugar and butter in the oven or in a sauté pan and arranged in a precooked tart shell shortly before serving (to keep the crust from getting soggy). Or the fruit can be cooked directly in an uncooked tart shell and be surrounded with a filling that absorbs any liquid the pear releases. Two examples of this kind of tart are the cherry clafoutis on page 651 (except that it has no pastry shell) and the pear tart on page 617. Other than the crêpe batter used for a clafoutis, fillings for such tarts are almost invariably mixtures of eggs, milk, and sugar, and they often include almond flour. Frangipane, a mixture containing almond flour (see recipe for Almond Pear Tart, page 617), is one such filling. Another popular filling is pastry cream (*crème patissière*), which is similar to the crêpe batter used in a clafoutis, except that pastry cream is cooked before it is added to the tart, and so it ends up being cooked twice.

When raw fruit is arranged in a precooked shell, a filling is usually spread over or baked in the shell before the fruit is added. Pastry cream can be left as is, since it's already been cooked, and the fruit arranged on top, or it can be cooked (a second time) in the shell and allowed to cool before the fruit is added. One of my favorite fillings is lemon curd, a sour lemon custard that contrasts well with a sweet tart shell made with *pâte sablée*. Uncooked lemon curd can be baked in the shell as though one were baking a lemon tart, or it can be cooked on the stove and spread over the shell before the fruit is arranged on top. Some fruits, especially berries, can also be completely submerged in the tart filling before baking, again like the cherry clafoutis.

FRESH RED BERRY TART

TARTE AUX BAIES ROUGES

MAKES 6 DESSERT SERVINGS

(ONE 10-INCH [25.5-CM] TART)

Make this tart with whatever berries are ripe and in season. In this recipe, I tell you to spread the bottom of the tart with a sour lemon curd before arranging the berries on top, but if your berries are moist and sweet, go ahead and skip this step.

1 recipe Shortbread Dough (pâte sablée) (page 620)

3 lemons, or more as needed to provide you with 6 tablespoons juice

3 eggs

6 tablespoons granulated sugar

2 tablespoons butter

2 to 3 pints [595 to 895 g] ripe strawberries, or 1 pint [245 g] raspberries, blackberries, blueberries, or currants

1 tablespoon red currant jelly (optional)

LINE a 10-inch [25.5-cm] tart mold with the shortbread dough and bake the shell *à blanc* (see page 157).

TO prepare the lemon curd, begin by grating the zest of one of the lemons and squeezing the lemons. Combine 6 tablespoons of the lemon juice with the eggs, zest, and sugar in a medium-size stainless steel mixing bowl. Set the bowl over a saucepan of boiling water. Make sure the saucepan is smaller than the bowl so the bowl sits on top out of the water and you can take it off quickly. (Don't use a double boiler with an insert that fits all the way into the pan underneath because it's hard to remove the insert quickly and the steam can shoot out and burn you.) Whisk the mixture with a stainless steel whisk (older, tin-coated whisks may give the lemon curd a metallic taste) until it thickens to the consistency of mayonnaise. Take the bowl off the saucepan and stir in the butter while the lemon curd is still hot. Let cool.

SPREAD the lemon curd over the tart shell and arrange the fruit on top. If you're being meticulous, arrange the berries in neat rows, starting from the outside rim of the tart and working around the tart. If you're being lazy, just scatter them in. If you're using strawberries, you'll get a more dramatic effect if you cut a small flat wedge out of the side of each of the berries so that you can nestle the berries more closely together.

IF you like, make a glaze for the tart by combining the jelly with 2 tablespoons of water in a small saucepan and gently boiling the mixture until the jelly dissolves. Brush the berries lightly with the glaze. Serve the tart lightly chilled.

ALMOND

PEAR TART

TARTE BOURDALOUE

MAKES 6 DESSERT SERVINGS

(ONE 10-INCH [25.5-CM] TART)

This is an example of a tart in which raw fruit is cooked in the tart. Because most raw fruits release liquid as they cook, such tarts are cooked with a filling so the filling absorbs the liquid and of course adds its own flavor and rich consistency. Frangipane, a creamy mixture made with almond flour (which you can make yourself by grinding almonds in a food processor), was invented by the chef to the Comte Frangipani, who in turn gave the recipe to Marie de Medici, who became the queen of France in 1600. The mixture has been popular in France ever since.

This recipe calls for underripe pears (see "Pears," page 618), which are first baked in the oven with butter and sugar until the pears soften and the butter and sugar caramelize into a kind of pear-butterscotch sauce. This sauce is then combined with the frangipane mixture before the tart is baked. If your pears are ripe, don't bother baking them, just combine the frangipane with the melted butter and sugar called for in the recipe.

1 recipe Sweetened Tart Dough (pâte sucrée) (page 619)

4 large underripe pears

1 tablespoon lemon juice

1 stick (¼ pound [115 g]) butter

½ cup [100 g] sugar

FOR THE FRANGIPANE:

½ cup [100 g] blanched almonds

1 egg plus 1 egg yolk

¾ cup [150 g] granulated sugar

½ cup [100 g] all-purpose flour

1 cup [250 ml] boiling milk

3 tablespoons butter (from the roasted pears)

¼ teaspoon almond extract

2 teaspoons vanilla extract

LINE a 10-inch [25.5-cm] tart mold that has a removable bottom with the tart dough and bake it *à blanc*, as described on page 157.

PREHEAT the oven to 400°F [200°C/gas mark 6].

PEEL the pears, cut them in half lengthwise, and cut out the cores with a melon baller or paring knife. Use a paring knife to cut out the strip of stem that runs from the center core to the top of each pear half. Toss the pear halves with a lemon juice and put them in a heavy-bottomed stainless steel or enamel-coated pot just large enough to hold them in a single layer. (Don't use a pot made of aluminum or cast iron, which will discolor the pears.) Put the stick of butter in the pot and sprinkle the sugar over the pears. Bake the pears until they release their liquid and soften, from 30 minutes to 1 hour, depending on how underripe they are. Turn them over gently after 20 minutes of baking so they don't discolor or dry out. Baste them with the melted butter in the pot every 10 minutes. Watch carefully so the pears, butter, and sugar don't burn. With a slotted spoon, transfer the pears to a plate. Reserve the hot butter mixture in the pot.

TO prepare the frangipane, toast the almonds in a 350°F [175°C/gas mark 4] oven for 15 minutes, or until they are pale brown and smell fragrant. Beat the egg and egg yolk with the sugar until they are pale yellow and able to hold a ribbon shape for a few seconds. Combine the flour in a food processor with the almonds and work the mixture for about 2 minutes. Stir the almond/flour mixture into the egg mixture, and add the hot milk in a steady stream. Transfer to a pan and cook over low heat for 5 minutes to cook the flour. Beat in the buttery juices from the pears and vanilla and almond extracts.

PREHEAT or turn down the oven to 350°F [175°C/gas mark 4].

SLICE the cooked pear halves lengthwise, leaving the slices attached at the narrow end. Fan out 6 of the pear halves by pressing down on them gently with your hand. Arrange these pear halves evenly around the tart shell with the narrow end pointing toward the center. Place one or both of the remaining pear halves (depending on the size of the pears) in the center of the tart. Spoon the frangipane over the pears, place the tart on a sheet pan, and bake until the frangipane puffs slightly and turns golden brown, about 30 minutes. Let cool for about 15 minutes. Serve the tart warm in wedges, cutting it so that each serving has an entire pear half.

Variations: Frangipane is a useful mixture for baking any number of fruits. The Alsatians make a *tarte aux quetsches* (little red plums) by spreading a prebaked tart shell with frangipane, nestling in the plums, and then baking. This works with plums or apricots (halved or just pitted, depending on their size), berries, less-than-perfect peaches (which can be prebaked like the pears in the recipe above), and tropical fruits.

PEARS

We'd all eat more pears if we could find them ripe, but fortunately pears ripen *off* the tree. In fact, unlike peaches or tomatoes, which ripen best when left on the tree or plant, pears must be picked before they are fully ripe and then be allowed to spend a few days at room temperature to soften. So, you can give up searching for a ripe pear. If your pears must be ripe, allow at least 3 days—sometimes you'll need as long as a week—for them to ripen.

SWEETENED
TART DOUGH

PÂTE BRISÉE SUCRÉE

MAKES ENOUGH FOR ONE 10-INCH [25.5-CM] TART

This dough is identical to the Basic Pie and Tart Dough on page 155, except that sugar has been added to sweeten the dough.

1   stick (¼ pound [115 g]) plus 1 tablespoon butter

1¾ cups [220 g] all-purpose bleached flour

4   tablespoons granulated sugar

1   large egg plus 1 egg yolk, right out of the refrigerator, beaten with a fork with ¼ teaspoon salt for 1 minute

1–2 tablespoons cold water, added ½ tablespoon at a time

PUT the butter and flour in the freezer for about 20 minutes so they're very cold but not frozen. Use a chef's knife to cut the stick of butter in half lengthwise, turn the stick of butter on its next side, and again cut it in half lengthwise so you end up with 4 sticks the length of the stick of butter. Keeping the sticks together, slice them crosswise into eighths so you end up with 32 perfect little cubes. Combine the butter, flour, and sugar in a mixing bowl, stir the mixture to distribute the sugar, and put the bowl in the freezer for 20 minutes.

IF you're working by hand, dump the chilled flour and butter onto the work surface and chop them together with a pastry scraper on the side of a spatula until the butter is in pieces the size of baby peas. Finish working the dough by quickly lifting it, a bit at a time, with the tips of your fingers and quickly crushing the butter into the flour. When you're done—don't do this for more than 1 minute—the dough should look like gravel, with little if any loose flour. Make a mound with the flour mixture and use your fingertips to make a well in the middle.

Pour the egg mixture into the well and put all the fingertips of one hand into the liquid. Move your fingers in a circular motion, gradually eroding and bringing in the inside walls of the flour. Continue in this way until the egg mixture is incorporated into the flour and you end up with a rough heap. Starting at the back of the pile, crush about one-sixth of the dough with the heel of your hand and smear it backwards, away from the rest of the pile. Continue in this way until you've crushed all the dough. If the dough is still crumbly, add ½ tablespoon of water at a time. It's sometimes necessary to *fraise* (the French word for the quick working together of butter and flour) three times to get the dough to come together. (Most recipes warn against this repetition, but as long as the butter doesn't start to melt—in which case, put the dough in a bowl and back in the freezer—it isn't a problem.) Press the dough into a disk about ½ inch [1.5 cm] thick, to let it chill more quickly and make it easier to roll out into the shape of the tart pan. Wrap the dough in plastic wrap and refrigerate it for 2 hours, or overnight.

WHEN using a food processor, most of the work is done for you. Once you have added the amount of water to make the dough come together in a ball around the blade, stop immediately or you will make a highly elastic dough that will shrink when baked. Pulse the flour mixture, 2 to 3 seconds per pulse, about eight times, until the mixture has the consistency of fine gravel and there is no loose flour in the bottom of the bowl. Add the egg mixture and pulse two to three times more. Add the water a half tablespoon at a time, pulsing to combine after each addition. When the dough comes together into a ball, transfer it to a floured work surface. Press the dough into a disk about ½ inch thick. Wrap the dough in plastic wrap and refrigerate it for 2 hours, or overnight.

SHORTBREAD DOUGH

PÂTE SABLÉE

This dough is so sweet and crumbly you can shape it into a cylinder, slice the cylinder into rounds, and bake the rounds as shortbread butter cookies. (The French call these *sablées*.)

When you use this pastry to line a tart, you've lined the tart with a sweet, buttery, and fragile cookie dough. Pâte sablée is made in the same way as sweetened pie dough (*pâte brisée sucrée*), except that more butter and sugar are used.

1½   sticks (⅜ pound) plus 1 tablespoon butter (15 tablespoons total)

1¾   cups [220 g] all-purpose bleached flour

2   large eggs, right out of the refrigerator, beaten with a fork with ¼ teaspoon salt for 1 minute

¼   cup [50 g] plus 2 tablespoons granulated sugar

1–2   tablespoons cold water, added ½ tablespoon at a time

PREPARE the dough exactly as described in the Sweetened Tart Dough recipe on page 619. Because of the extra butter, this pastry gets very hard when you refrigerate it. Pounding it with a rolling pin or letting it warm slightly makes it easier to roll out. When you're rolling it out, it may crack, again because of the extra butter. If it gets too warm it may melt, turn sticky, and become difficult to work with. The good news is that the sugar and the extra butter make it much harder to activate the gluten and toughen the dough. So if it cracks when you roll it out, knead it a little with the heel of your hand until it comes together. If it starts to melt or get sticky, flatten it into a disk (so it will cool more quickly) and refrigerate it for 15 minutes.

KEEPING TART SHELLS FROM GETTING TOO BROWN

Sometimes when you bake a tart shell, especially if baking it twice, the outer rim may get too brown before the tart has finished baking. If this starts to happen, cover the outer rim of the tart with a strip of aluminum foil to protect it from the heat of the oven.

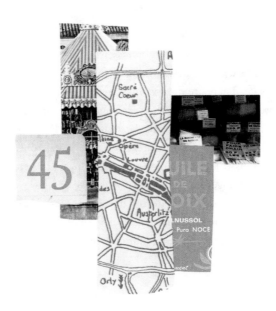

CHOCOLATE MOUSSE

MOUSSE AU CHOCOLAT

MY FIRST ENCOUNTER WITH CHOCOLATE MOUSSE HAPPENED THE DAY after my parents had returned from a dinner party. The hostess had been kind enough to send them home with leftovers, including a little plastic tub of chocolate mousse. I had tasted chocolate pudding, but this dense, rich mound of chocolate revealed a new universe of childhood ecstasy.

Not that I have anything against chocolate pudding, but chocolate mousse and chocolate pudding are different creatures entirely. A chocolate pudding is essentially a chocolate crème anglaise thickened with cornstarch and allowed to set. But a mousse is frothy—in

French, *mousse* means foam—and chocolate mousse requires that something airy, invariably whipped cream or whipped egg whites, or both, be folded together with a flavorful base containing the chocolate. There are dozens of recipes and it's impossible to say which is best because each produces a mousse with a somewhat different texture and flavor. The only certainty is the importance of using the best chocolate, but beyond that you may want to experiment until you find your favorite approach.

When making a mousse, first prepare the chocolate base. To make the simplest base, and one of the best, whisk together sugar, water (or coffee), and egg yolks. Warm the mixture gently with some chunks of chocolate and flavor the mixture with a little vanilla extract, brandy, or liqueur. When the base mixture is smooth, fold it with whipped cream or beaten egg whites. If you want a denser, more unctuous mousse, include some butter in the base mixture.

WHAT TO DO ABOUT LUMPS IN CHOCOLATE

If you're not careful, bittersweet chocolate—the best kind for a mousse—has a nasty tendency to form lumps. This sometimes happens when a small amount of liquid is added to melted chocolate. Even melting chocolate in a mixing bowl that isn't perfectly dry can cause the chocolate to clump up into a thick and grainy paste. If this happens, just stir 1 or 2 tablespoons of water, coffee, heavy cream, or other liquid into the chocolate to smooth it out. But don't add so much liquid that the chocolate mixture gets too thin, or the mousse won't hold together.

Other times, lumps are caused by overheating the chocolate mixture, in which case the chocolate coagulates and the egg yolks, if you've included them, curdle.

Whatever precautions you take, there are going to be times when you don't discover the lumps until it's too late and you've already folded the egg whites or whipped cream with the base mixture. If this happens and you don't want to start over, fold some toasted and chopped walnuts into the mousse. With the crunchy nuts in it, no one will notice that there are also little lumps of chocolate.

SIMPLEST CHOCOLATE MOUSSE

MOUSSE AU CHOCOLAT LA PLUS SIMPLE

MAKES 6 DESSERT SERVINGS

This mousse used to be made with raw egg yolks, which made it even simpler, but nowadays our anxieties about uncooked eggs compel us to cook the yolks.

- 6 large eggs, allowed to come to room temperature
- 2 tablespoons water or strong coffee
- 1 tablespoon Cognac, Grand Marnier, marc, kirsch, or any favorite brandy or liqueur (if you don't want to include this, add 1 more tablespoon of water or coffee to the 2 tablespoons given above)
- 1 teaspoon vanilla extract (optional if you're using a brandy or liqueur)
- 4 tablespoons sugar
- 6 ounces [170 g] of the best bittersweet chocolate you can find (see page 669), chopped coarse
- 4 tablespoons unsalted butter
- ¼ teaspoon cream of tartar (unless you're beating the egg whites in a copper bowl)

SEPARATE the eggs, reserve the whites, and combine 4 of the egg yolks in a medium-size heat-proof mixing bowl (stainless steel is ideal) with the water, Cognac, vanilla extract, and 2 tablespoons of the sugar. (Save the extra 2 egg yolks for something else or throw them out.) Set the bowl on top of a small saucepan of simmering water, but don't let the bowl touch the water. Whisk the egg mixture until you begin to see the bottom of the bowl. Be sure you keep the whisk moving over the whole surface of the bowl or the eggs will overheat in those spots not touched by the whisk, and they'll curdle. Take the bowl off the saucepan, immediately add the chocolate and butter and whisk until the mixture is smooth. If necessary, return the bowl to the saucepan of hot water to fully incorporate the ingredients.

COMBINE the egg whites with the cream of tartar in a mixing bowl (if you're using a copper bowl, skip the cream of tartar). Beat the whites with a whisk (or the whisk attachment on an electric mixer) until the whites are fluffy and have formed soft peaks, 4 to 7 minutes. Add the remaining 2 tablespoons of sugar and continue beating until the whites are smooth and stiff, 2 to 3 minutes more, depending on whether you're beating by hand or with the electric mixer. To make sure you've beaten them enough, hold the whisk above the bowl. The whites should form a point that sticks straight out and doesn't sag.

WHISK about one-fourth of the beaten egg whites into the chocolate mixture until the mixture is smooth and you see no traces of white. (This is to lighten the mixture so it will fold more evenly into the chocolate mixture.) Pour this chocolate mixture over the beaten whites and fold together by cutting into the mixture with a plastic spatula, sliding the spatula along the bottom of the bowl (where the chocolate settles), and folding the chocolate over the whites. When the mousse is well combined, with no streaks of egg white, scoop it out into a large, pretty serving bowl or into individual bowls or ramekins. Cover with plastic wrap, pushing the wrap down so that it touches the surface of the mousse (otherwise a dark film will form). Chill the mousse in the refrigerator for 2 to 12 hours. Mousse will keep in the fridge for at least 3 days.

Variations: Some chocolate mousses are made by folding cold chocolate *crème anglaise* (see page 641) with whipped cream, beaten egg whites, or both. The advantage to this method is that the egg yolks are thoroughly cooked and the crème anglaise ensures that the finished mousse will have a velvety texture. The density and flavor of the mousse can be controlled by adding extra chocolate, which makes the mousse stiffer, or by whisking butter into the hot crème anglaise, which also makes the mousse stiffer and gives it a melting, unctuous texture.

Because most recipe writers seem more concerned about raw egg yolks than raw egg whites, modern mousse recipes either use no yolks at all (the chocolate base mixture contains only water, sugar, bittersweet chocolate, and flavoring), or the egg yolks are cooked in a double boiler with the chocolate; or, as in the recipe above, the egg yolks are cooked into a kind of sabayon sauce (see page 256) with the flavorings, and the chocolate is then stirred into the mixture (sometimes with butter) until it melts. Professional pastry chefs often use somewhat more complicated methods for making chocolate mousse than do home cooks. One favorite method for making both regular and frozen chocolate mousse is to whisk hot sugar syrup (cooked to the "soft ball" stage) into the egg yolks, cooking them and at the same time giving them a thick, velvety texture. The chocolate is stirred into this still-hot mixture and melted. The same hot sugar syrup is also whisked into egg whites as they are beaten, cooking them and turning them into Italian meringue, the soft, fluffy white meringue sometimes used in America as a frosting for chocolate cake. The Italian meringue, the cooked egg yolks, the flavorings, and sometimes whipped cream are then all folded together and allowed to set in the refrigerator, or are frozen. Sometimes the mixture is frozen in soufflé dishes with paper collars, so it is held above the rim of the soufflé dish—the top of each frozen "soufflé" is sprinkled with powdered sugar and the paper removed just before serving.

Some cooks make chocolate mousse more dense by incorporating butter along with the chocolate and by using a smaller proportion of the airy egg whites or whipped cream, and serve it as a chocolate "terrine" or, in a more old-fashioned way, as the filling for a charlotte. Any charlotte, except the apple charlotte discussed in Chapter 44, is made by allowing some kind of mousse mixture, and sometimes Bavarian cream, to set in a ladyfinger-lined charlotte mold. Michel Guérard has invented his own fantasy, half charlotte, half terrine, by lining a terrine with ladyfingers and then filling the terrine with a dense mousse mixture. The terrine is chilled and then sliced as though it were a pâté, with each slice surrounded with ladyfingers. Here is a simpler version, without the ladyfingers.

DENSE CHOCOLATE TERRINE

TERRINE DE CHOCOLAT

MAKES 12 SERVINGS

This buttery-textured terrine is dense and rich enough that it is served in slices rather than in molds. With its deep bittersweet flavor and melting texture, it combines the best qualities of butter and chocolate.

- 1 tablespoon softened butter (for the terrine mold), plus 2½ sticks (10 ounces [280 g]) unsalted butter, cut into ¼-inch-thick slices and allowed to come to room temperature (for the filling)

- 7 egg yolks

- ¾ cup [150 g] granulated sugar

- 6 ounces [170 g] bittersweet chocolate (see page 669 for information about different kinds), chopped fine, by hand or in a food processor

- ¾ cup [65 g] unsweetened Dutch-process cocoa powder

- 2 cups [500 ml] heavy cream

- 1 teaspoon vanilla extract

BRUSH the inside of a 6-cup [1.5 l] terrine mold or loaf pan with softened butter. Cut 5 pieces of waxed paper the same sizes as the inside walls and bottom of the mold. Press the waxed paper against the sides and bottom of the mold—the butter keeps the waxed paper clinging to the mold. Refrigerate the mold while making the filling.

COMBINE the egg yolks and sugar in a large mixing bowl or electric mixer bowl and whisk for about 2 minutes, until the egg yolks lighten in color and the sugar completely dissolves. Add the chocolate to the yolk mixture and set the mixing bowl over a saucepan of gently simmering water, but don't let the bowl touch the water. Whisk the mixture constantly until the chocolate melts—this is hard work, so you may want to use a hand mixer—and whisk in the butter. Keep whisking until the butter melts and is incorporated into the mixture. Remove from the heat, sift the cocoa powder into the mixture, and whisk until the mixture is smooth and just slightly warm. (If the mixture is too hot it will deflate the whipped cream.)

COMBINE the heavy cream and vanilla in a mixing bowl or in an electric mixer bowl and chill the cream, the bowl, and the whisk in the freezer for 5 minutes. Beat the cream until soft peaks form. Whisk about one-fourth of the whipped cream into the chocolate mixture to lighten the mixture before folding in the rest of the cream. Spoon the rest of the whipped cream over the mixture and fold the mixture with a rubber spatula until it is perfectly smooth. Pour the mixture into the chilled mold and tap the terrine on a cutting board to settle the mixture. Cover the top of the terrine with plastic wrap—to keep a skin from forming, press on the wrap so it touches the surface of the mousse. Chill the terrine for at least 6 hours. (This terrine can be made 1 or 2 days ahead of time.)

JUST before serving, run a paring knife around the inside of the terrine mold, between the waxed paper and the walls, and place a serving platter upside down over the mold. Hold the mold against the platter and turn them over together. While holding the mold against the platter, give them a quick up-and-down shake to get the terrine out of the mold. Peel off the waxed paper. Slice the terrine, dipping the knife in water and wiping it clean after each slice for a neater result. Serve the slices on chilled plates.

Variations: This terrine is perfectly satisfying as it is, but if you're going all out you might want to serve it with a sauce. A *crème anglaise* is one of the most classic accompaniments, and it's easy to flavor in interesting ways so it complements the flavor of the chocolate. Pistachio and hazelnut pralines (see Sources) are especially elegant and tasty, as are marc, whiskey, and espresso (see page 642). You can pass the sauce at the table or decorate the *crème anglaise* on the plate with swirls of chocolate or colorful fruit coulis (a fruit purée with the seeds strained out). Fruit coulis can replace a classic crème anglaise and fresh berries can be spooned on top of the terrine slices; the cool texture and acidity of the fruit help keep the chocolate from seeming overwhelm-

ingly rich. The terrine mixture can also be used to fill a ladyfinger-lined charlotte mold and lightened, using the classic technique of folding it with pieces of cake or ladyfingers sprinkled with spirits. You can also use the terrine mixture between the layers of a cake.

FRUIT MOUSSES, OTHER FLAVORED MOUSSES, AND BAVARIAN CREAMS

Chocolate lends itself perfectly to making mousse because it hardens as it cools and helps the mousse keep its shape. Other ingredients, such as fruits and coffee, unless used in a frozen mousse, require different treatment because there's nothing in them to help hold the mousse together. The usual solution to this problem is gelatin, which sets when cool. But gelatin can be tricky to work with. If you use too much, the mousse will be rubbery; if you don't use enough, the mousse will stay liquid. A mousse made with gelatin—a Bavarian cream—is prepared by adding fruit purée or other flavorings and gelatin to a crème anglaise, letting the mixture cool (but not too much, or it will set), and folding it with whipped cream and occasionally beaten egg whites. The Bavarian cream is then poured into a mold (traditionally, a charlotte mold lined with ladyfingers—but I skip the ladyfingers) and allowed to set in the refrigerator. More modern versions dispense with the crème anglaise, incorporate the gelatin into the fruit purée, and fold the mixture with whipped cream before allowing it to set. In most Bavarian creams, raw fruit is used, but tropical fruit purées such as pineapple or passion fruit must be quickly brought to a boil or the protease enzymes they contain will break down the gelatin in the Bavarian cream and it will never set.

Frozen mousses are easier to deal with because they don't need any gelatin to help hold their shape. The simplest fruit versions are mixtures of fruit purée combined with whipped cream and/or Italian meringue (see variations to Simplest Chocolate Mousse, page 623) that are then frozen, often in soufflé molds. A more sophisticated version is a *parfait*, which in the American version is a sort of ice cream sundae, with layers of ice cream and sauces in a tall glass, but in France is an ice cream–like mixture made by whisking hot sugar syrup into egg yolks, flavoring the mixture, and then folding it with Italian meringue and whipped cream before freezing.

FROZEN RASPBERRY SOUFFLÉS

SOUFFLÉS GLACÉS AUX FRAMBOISES

MAKES 8 SERVINGS

To make these soufflés, or more accurately frozen mousse presented like soufflés, I use frozen raspberries because they're inexpensive and usually have a better flavor than fresh raspberries, especially out of season. Once thawed, frozen raspberries have a mushy texture, but for purées this doesn't matter.

FOR THE RASPBERRY PURÉE:

2 packages (10 or 12 ounces [280 or 340 g] each) frozen raspberries (the kind sold loose in bags, not frozen in syrup; the best choice is IQF, Individually Quick Frozen), thawed

FOR THE WHIPPED CREAM:

2 cups [500 ml] heavy cream

FOR THE ITALIAN MERINGUE:

6 egg whites

¼ teaspoon cream of tartar (unless you have a copper bowl for your electric mixer)

1¼ cups [250 g] granulated sugar

FOR TOPPING THE SOUFFLÉS:

confectioners' sugar

TO MAKE THE RASPBERRY PURÉE

HEAT the thawed frozen raspberries and any juice they've released in a heavy-bottomed saucepan over medium heat. Stir every few minutes until the raspberries soften completely and the mixture stiffens slightly, about 20 minutes. This is to get rid of excess water and to concentrate the flavor of the berries. Purée the berries by working them through a strainer with the bottom of a small ladle. If you want to eliminate the tiny seeds, strain the purée through a fine-mesh strainer.

TO PREPARE THE MOLDS

FOLD 8 sections of wax paper into triple-thick strips long enough to wrap around the outside of eight 4-ounce or 5-ounce [125- or 155-ml] soufflé molds or ramekins and 2 inches [5 cm] wider than the molds are high. Fold the strips so they stick up above the edge of the molds by about 1 inch. Secure the end of the wax paper to the ramekin with tape. Wrap the strips around the molds and attach them to the other end of the wax paper and across the base with tape. Place a rubber band around the ramekin to hold the collar on. Refrigerate the molds.

TO WHIP THE CREAM

PUT the heavy cream and a whisk in a mixing bowl (if you need the mixing bowl you used for the meringue, combine the purée with the meringue as described below) and put the bowl in the freezer for 5 minutes. Beat the cream by hand or in an electric mixer until it stiffens and forms soft mounds—don't beat it until it's completely stiff, or the mousse will seem dry.

TO MAKE THE ITALIAN MERINGUE

PUT the egg whites and cream of tartar in the bowl of an electric mixer (if you're using a copper bowl attachment, skip the cream of tartar). Put on the whisk attachment, but don't start beating until you're cooking the sugar syrup.

COMBINE the sugar with ½ cup [125 ml] of water in a heavy-bottomed saucepan and bring to a simmer over medium to high heat. When the sugar dissolves and the mixture begins to look syrupy, start testing it by dipping a spoon handle into the hot syrup and then immediately into a glass of cold water (not ice water). When the syrup starts to adhere to the back of the spoon, turn the mixer on medium-to-high. Continue simmering and testing the syrup. When the syrup forms a ball on the end of the spoon with the texture of chewing gum that's been chewed—I wish I had a more elegant comparison—or measures 240°F [120°C] on a candy thermometer, and the egg whites are fluffy and stiff, pour the hot syrup in a steady stream over the egg whites with the mixer on medium speed. As best you can, pour the syrup between the side of the bowl and the whisk—if syrup lands on either of these it will congeal and form hard little balls. When you've added all the syrup, leave the mixer on and continue beating the meringue to cool it slightly, about 3 minutes.

TO ASSEMBLE THE SOUFFLÉS

WHISK one-fourth of the Italian meringue into the raspberry purée until smooth, to lighten the purée. With a rubber spatula, fold the purée with the Italian meringue until you don't see any streaks of white in the mixture. Gently fold the whipped cream with this mixture. Spoon the mixture into the molds—there should be enough to come 1 inch [2.5 cm] or 1½ inches [4 cm] above the rim. Put the soufflés in the freezer. After about 2 hours, quickly wrap each of the soufflés with plastic wrap to help prevent them from absorbing freezer odors, and return them to the freezer. (The long freezing time is so that you can make the soufflés in advance. Don't make them more than 1 week ahead or they'll take on a stale freezer taste.) Just before serving, sprinkle the tops of the soufflés with confectioners' sugar and take off the wax paper.

HOT DESSERT SOUFFLÉS

Soufflés are little more than mousses that get baked. Soufflés usually contain less flour than cakes—and sometimes none at all—because they're served right out of the oven and don't have to stay risen when cool in the same way as cakes. (Flour stabilizes airy mixtures.)

In classic French cooking, a dessert soufflé is based on pastry cream (*crème patissière*), a thick, rather starchy filling that most of us have tasted as the filling in éclairs. The pastry cream is made by cooking flour and sometimes cornstarch with eggs and milk. It is flavored and, just before baking, folded with beaten egg whites. (A little sugar is often added to the egg whites to stabilize them.) Most "modern" soufflés are made without pastry cream or even entirely without flour. The effect is lighter, but since there's no flour to stabilize the soufflé, a flourless soufflé will fall more quickly than one made with flour. The usual way to make a flourless soufflé is to make a sabayon sauce by beating egg yolks, sugar, and flavoring together over gentle heat until the mixture turns light and airy. This sabayon is then folded with beaten egg whites and immediately baked.

Sometimes there's little difference between a soufflé and a cake, except that cakes are usually served at room temperature and contain more flour than soufflés. The recipe for chocolate soufflé cakes given below is much like a chocolate mousse with sifted flour folded in. There is, however, one essential difference. A mousse is lightened with whipped cream or beaten egg whites, while this soufflé mixture is lightened with whole eggs that have been beaten with sugar until they triple in volume. This is the method used for making the classic French sponge cake, *génoise*, except that more flour is folded into a *génoise* mixture after the beating and very little flavoring is added. (Too much flavoring—especially chocolate—will make the cake dense and cause it to fall.) Freeze these soufflés before baking so that they end up molten in the middle and cake-like on the outside.

SUGAR SYRUP

If you boil sugar in water, you'll make sugar syrup. As you cook the syrup it goes through various stages, from a relatively light syrup of equal parts sugar and water (called simple syrup), used for moistening cakes; to "soft ball," used for making Italian meringue; to "soft crack" and "hard crack," used for making certain candies; and eventually, when all the water has evaporated and the sugar begins to brown, to caramel (see page 639 for more about making caramel).

You can use a candy thermometer to determine when a sugar syrup has reached the stage you want, but professional pastry cooks usually judge when their syrups are ready by dipping their fingers in the syrup and then immediately into a bowl of cold water. Since the mere thought of this is terrifying, I dip the handle end of a spoon into the syrup and then immediately into a bowl of cold water (but not ice water). I then pinch the more-or-less congealed syrup between thumb and forefinger and judge by its texture. Here are a few stages.

Threads

TEMPERATURE: 230°F [110°C]

CONSISTENCY: forms threads when pinched between thumb and forefinger and the thumb and forefinger are pulled apart

USES: Butter creams, candied fruits, jellies

Soft Ball

TEMPERATURE: 240°F [115°C]

CONSISTENCY: like chewed-on chewing gum

USES: Butter creams, meringues, glazes

Hard Ball

TEMPERATURE: 260°F [126°C]

CONSISTENCY: very firm but still pliable

USES: Candies

Soft Crack

TEMPERATURE: 280°F [137°C]

CONSISTENCY: hard to the touch but gives slightly when squeezed firmly

USES: Candies

Hard Crack

TEMPERATURE: 300°F [148°C]

CONSISTENCY: hard to the touch, doesn't give when squeezed

USES: Candies, worked sugar decorations

HOT CHOCOLATE SOUFFLÉS

SOUFFLÉS CHAUDS
AU CHOCOLAT

MAKES 6 SERVINGS

1 tablespoon softened butter (for the ramekins), plus ¾ stick (6 tablespoons) unsalted butter (for the flavoring mixture)

1½ teaspoons unsweetened Dutch-process cocoa powder, sifted through a strainer, or more as needed

6 ounces [170 g] bittersweet chocolate, chopped coarse

½ teaspoon vanilla extract

3 large eggs, allowed to warm to room temperature

¼ cup [50 g] sugar

2 tablespoons all-purpose flour

confectioners' sugar (optional)

Crème Chantilly (page 609; optional)

Classic Vanilla Crème Anglaise (page 642; optional)

vanilla ice cream (optional)

BRUSH the inside of six 5-ounce [185 ml] oven-proof ramekins or Pyrex custard cups with the softened butter. Put the cocoa powder in a ramekin and rotate the ramekin so the cocoa completely coats the inside walls. Pour the cocoa powder from one ramekin to another until they're all coated. Tap firmly on the bottom of each ramekin after coating it with cocoa so there aren't large clumps of cocoa left clinging to the inside. Put the ramekins on a sheet pan and slide them into the refrigerator.

COMBINE the 6 tablespoons of unsalted butter, the chocolate, and the vanilla extract in a small heat-proof mixing bowl. Place the bowl over a saucepan of simmering water (but don't let the bowl touch the water) and stir with a whisk until smooth. Or, using a nonmetal bowl, heat in the microwave for 30 seconds.

COMBINE the eggs and sugar in the bowl of an electric mixer. They take a lot of beating, so try to avoid beating them by hand. Whip on high speed for 2 to 4 minutes with the whisk attachment until the eggs triple in volume—eggs at room temperature froth up more quickly than cold ones. When you lift the whisk about 6 inches [15 cm] out of the bowl, the mixture should slowly fall in a steady stream—bakers call this a ribbon—about 1 inch [2.5 cm] thick.

SCOOP the egg mixture over the chocolate mixture. Put the flour in a strainer and sift a small amount over the egg-chocolate mixture by gently shaking the strainer. Fold everything together with a rubber spatula, sifting the flour over the mixture about four times during the folding. Pour the mixture into the ramekins, filling them about three-fourths full. Put the soufflés in the freezer for at least 1 hour but no longer than 1 week. (If you're freezing the soufflés for more than 1 day, cover each of them with plastic wrap so they don't absorb odors.)

THIRTY minutes before serving, preheat the oven to 425°F [220°C/gas mark 7]. Slide the sheet pan with the ramekins into the oven and bake for 17 minutes, until the mixture has risen about ¼ inch above the edges. The soufflés should be cakelike on the outside and still runny in the middle.

YOU can serve the soufflés in their molds—just sprinkle them with a little confectioners' sugar like a soufflé—or you can quickly run a knife around the inside of the ramekins and unmold the cakes on hot plates. Serve immediately with one of the optional accompaniments.

GRAND MARNIER
SOUFFLÉS

SOUFFLÉS AU GRAND
MARNIER

MAKES 6 SERVINGS

When living in France, I read as much French literature as I could, so even if I couldn't pronounce anything, I'd at least learn the vocabulary. Colette was a favorite, partly because of her ability to describe the pleasures of food and drink. I remember one scene in her short and lovely novel *Chéri*. Chéri is a young and spoiled man-about-town, but endearing, partly because of his unabashed decadence. One night he dines out and for dessert is served a vanilla soufflé with a bright red ball of red currant sorbet hidden in the middle. Collette's description of the acidic little sorbet next to the frothy and exotic perfume of the vanilla is something I've never forgotten.

The vanilla–red currant combination is hard to manage. Red currants have a short season and I've never found them frozen, the sorbet requires an ice cream machine, and it's tricky getting the soufflé to cook without melting the little red frozen ball. A Grand Marnier soufflé is a lot easier to pull off and, in its own way, at least as satisfying. In this version, no flour is used. The egg yolks are simply whisked with sugar and then folded with beaten egg whites, and the whole thing is immediately baked. One tip: grand Marnier is expensive, but don't try to substitute another orange liqueur. Grand Marnier has a pure orange flavor.

1 tablespoon softened unsalted butter (for the soufflé dishes)

2 tablespoons superfine sugar (for soufflé dishes), plus ¼ cup [50 g] plus 2 tablespoons (for the soufflé mixture) (see "Superfine Sugar," page 631)

6 eggs, separated

¼ cup [125 ml] Grand Marnier liqueur

¼ teaspoon cream of tartar (unless you're beating the egg whites in a copper bowl)

BRUSH the inside of six 6-ounce [185-ml] soufflé dishes with softened butter. Roll 4 tablespoons of the superfine sugar around in one of the dishes to coat the interior, pour what doesn't stick into another mold, and continue in this way until you've coated all the molds. Refrigerate the molds.

PREHEAT the oven to 375°F [190°C/gas mark 5].

WHISK the egg yolks with the ¼ cup [50 g] of superfine sugar and the Grand Marnier in a small mixing bowl and reserve. (Do this just before beating the egg whites, or the yolks will become crusty.)

COMBINE the cream of tartar with the egg whites (unless you're using a copper bowl) and beat the whites to soft peaks in an electric mixer or by hand. The whites should be fluffy but sag slightly when you pull out the whisk and hold it sideways. Sprinkle the 2 tablespoons of sugar over the whites and beat until the whites are very stiff—they stick straight out when the whisk is held sideways—but not dry, 1 or 2 minutes more.

WHISK one-fourth of the egg whites into the egg yolk mixture until smooth and pour this mixture down the side of the bowl with the whites. Fold the mixture, turning it over with a rubber spatula while scraping against the sides and bottom of the bowl so the none of the mixture escapes the folding. When there are no traces of uncombined egg white left in the mixture, pour it into the molds.

RUN your thumb around the inside rim of each mold so there's a tiny moat, about ½ inch [1.5 cm] deep, along the edge. Put the soufflés on a sheet pan and slide them into the oven. Bake until the soufflés rise about 1 inch above the edge of the molds, about 15 minutes. Serve immediately.

HOW TO KNOW WHEN A SOUFFLÉ IS DONE

Soufflés are really very easy to make, but knowing when they're done can be tricky. A soufflé should be lightly crisp on the outside, fluffy near the edges, and creamy in the center. French writers often mention that the inside of the soufflé should form the sauce for the outer part. If a soufflé is underdone, you're left with a lot of raw eggs. If a soufflé is overdone, it will be dry inside and will fall almost the instant it comes out of the oven. The question, of course, is when to take the soufflé out of the oven. If you make soufflés regularly, in the same mold and the same oven, you'll learn to judge the cooking time just from experience. Otherwise, the best way to determine when a soufflé is done is to give it a little back-and-forth jiggle. When it's underdone, you'll be able to sense the center sort of sloshing around, meaning that it's still liquid, by the way the top of the soufflé moves. If it's overdone, the whole thing will stay stiff. Ideally, the inside does slosh around, but just slightly. If all of this is too daunting, don't be afraid to just dig into one with a spoon. (You can even bake an extra soufflé on which to perform your tests.) Undercooked soufflés are more stable than most of us think and will keep their height for several minutes, so if you get to the table and discover the soufflés are underdone, just gather them up and put them back in the oven.

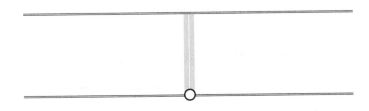

SUPERFINE SUGAR

Regular granulated sugar will sometimes not dissolve quickly enough in dessert mixtures. When it's used to coat buttered soufflé dishes and it doesn't dissolve, your soufflé ends up with an unpleasant grittiness. If you don't want to go out and buy superfine sugar, you can make it yourself by working granulated sugar in a food processor for about 3 minutes.

CARAMEL-GLAZED CREAM CUSTARD

CRÈME BRÛLÉE

HOW TO	HOW TO	HOW TO	HOW TO	HOW TO
MAKE SWEET CUSTARDS	MAKE CARAMEL AND BUTTERSCOTCH	WORK WITH WHOLE VANILLA BEANS	MAKE LIQUID CUSTARD CRÈME ANGLAISE	MAKE ICE CREAM AND THE WORLD'S BEST HOLIDAY EGGNOG

IT'S IRONIC IN THIS LOW-FAT AGE THAT CRÈME BRÛLÉE, A RICH CUS-
tard of cream and egg yolks covered with a sheet of caramelized sugar, is one of the most
popular desserts served in French (and non-French) restaurants. Of course there's nothing
terribly surprising about its popularity. After all, its richness and creaminess are not only
irresistible, they're irresistibly taboo. Best of all, the fat-starved dieter gets to give a determined whack to the glasslike layer of hardened melted sugar to break through to the
creamy delight underneath.

The traditional *crème brûlée*, or "burnt cream," has an obscure history. I once saw a similar dish mentioned in an eighteenth-century French cookbook, Menon's *Cuisinière*

Bourgeoise. Menon refers to it as a *crème gratinée* and calls for thickening the mixture with flour and flavoring it with lemon rind. But then the dish disappears for two centuries. Despite its popularity in American French restaurants, until very recently I never saw it on a menu in France. Now it seems to have made a kind of backward migration (although there are those who claim that it's English rather than French in origin).

Though its history may be obscure, there's nothing very mysterious or even that original about crème brûlée. European cooks have been toying with cream, eggs, and sugar in various combinations for centuries, and crème brulée, a simple custard, is one of the most obvious and least contrived dishes among the various *talmousses* (*tartelettes*), *poupelains* (giant cream puffs), and darioles (small molds lined with puff pastry and filled with frangipane) that represented the best French desserts of the seventeenth and eighteenth centuries.

A custard is a combination of eggs and milk or cream that is gently baked until it sets. Sweet custards, like crème brulée, contain sugar, but savory custards, including various quiche fillings, contain salt and often cheese. You can control the richness and texture of a custard by using whole eggs, egg yolks, or egg whites, and by using varying proportions of cream or milk. The lightest custards are made with milk—even skim milk—and egg whites, while richer custards, such as *pots de crème*, are made with egg yolks. Crème brûlée, the richest custard of all, is made with egg yolks and heavy cream. A custard made with cream and egg yolks has a melting, clotted cream–like consistency, while a custard made with egg whites or whole eggs and milk has a lighter, trembling texture more typical of what we associate with custard. Crème caramel is one example.

Neither sweet nor savory custards require much effort, and once you've made one you'll be able to make them all. A couple of things to remember: 1 egg (or 3 yolks or 2 whites) will set ⅔ to ¾ cup [175 ml] of liquid, which is all you need to know about the proportions, since you can just stir sugar in to taste. Keep in mind also that a custard mustn't get too hot or it will have little pits on its surface or, if things have really gotten out of hand, it will puff up and curdle, and you'll end up with scrambled eggs. To keep this from happening, bake custards in a pan of hot water—a bain-marie (see "How to Use a Bain-marie," page 634)—so they cook evenly and are protected from the direct heat of the oven. I usually bake custards at 325°F [165°C/gas mark 3].

Crème brûlée is usually baked in low round or oval dishes with little wing handles on each side, or in individual fluted quiche dishes. I sometimes use small oval gratin dishes, or I make one giant crème brûlée in a large gratin dish and then spoon it out at the table. In a pinch, you can use individual ramekins or Pyrex custard cups. Whichever dish you use, it should have a large surface area so you end up with a higher proportion of the crunchy glaze. The best thing about the glaze, apart from its being an outlet for aggression, is that it provides a textural contrast to the soft custard. But don't get hung up if you don't have the "right" containers.

HOW TO USE A BAIN-MARIE

Sometimes called a water bath, a bain-marie is just a pan of hot, sometimes barely simmering water. Custards, soufflés, flans, and other heat-sensitive mixtures are often baked in a bain-marie to prevent the temperature surrounding the molds from exceeding 212°F [100°C], the boiling point of water. A bain-marie also helps distribute heat evenly so that separate portions of food cook at the same time, even in an oven that isn't the same temperature throughout. While theoretically one could bake custards in a 212°F [100°C] oven, oven temperature settings are notoriously unreliable, home ovens cook unevenly, and cooking custards in such a low oven would take hours because air is a less efficient conductor of heat than water is.

In professional kitchens, a bain-marie is also sometimes set on top of the stove, over a low flame, to keep foods warm.

To make a bain-marie for baking custards or other mixtures, choose a baking dish with high sides—the hot water will need to come at least halfway up the sides of the molds—and, ideally, one that's just large enough to hold the molds without a lot of space left over. Place the filled molds in the dish and place the dish in the oven. Using a teakettle, if you have one, carefully pour hot tap water into the baking dish on one side, until the water comes halfway up the sides of the molds.

VANILLA BEANS:
THE PASTRY CHEF'S TRUFFLE

I once read the results of a taste test, done by a well-known cooking magazine, in which people were asked to taste cookies and determine whether real vanilla extract or artificial vanilla had been used to make them. The tasting wasn't just a man-on-the-street kind of thing; the tasters were cooking professionals, and to my utter amazement they couldn't tell the difference. True, if you've never paid any attention to such things, you might not know what to look for, but if you bake a lot it won't take you long to distinguish the two. Artificial vanilla smells like vanilla— almost too much so—but it's one-dimensional, and because of this it quickly becomes cloying. It's tempting at first but is soon tiresome. Real vanilla extract is more subtle and complex, and if you pay attention you'll notice that it has nuances of aroma and flavor that artificial vanilla does not.

But we're still in the anteroom to the sanctum sanctorum, because the subtlety of vanilla cannot be captured in a bottle; it is found only in the bean. The first time I put my nose to one, I was struck by an aroma that was so primal and exotic that I was immediately hooked. We don't use vanilla beans often because they're expensive, two beans costing about the same as a small bottle of extract, and their flavor is difficult to infuse into dry or cold mixtures such as cake batters. But in dishes such as custard or ice cream, for which the beans are infused in simmering liquid, they're heavenly.

Vanilla beans are very dark brown, almost black, and about the length of a ballpoint pen but not as thick. They should be flexible and vaguely rubbery—when they dry out they turn brittle—and should be deeply but not aggressively fragrant. To use them, cut them in half lengthwise, exposing the almost microscopic fragrant seeds, and simmer them in liquids such as milk or cream. When they've softened after a few minutes of simmering, fish out the halves, scrape out the goopy seeds with a paring knife, and put the seeds back in the liquid, along with the pod, so every part, especially the seeds, can release its flavor.

CRÈME BRÛLÉE

CRÈME BRÛLÉE

MAKES 6 DESSERT SERVINGS

3   cups [750 ml] heavy cream

1   vanilla bean, split in half lengthwise, or 2 teaspoons vanilla extract

8   egg yolks (from large eggs)

¾   cup [150 g] granulated sugar (for the custard), plus ⅔ cup (for glazing), or as needed (the exact amount will depend on the shape and size of the molds)

PREHEAT the oven to 325°F [165°C/gas mark 3].

BRING the cream to a simmer in a heavy-bottomed nonaluminum pot with the vanilla bean halves (if you're using extract, don't add it yet). Let the cream sit, covered, for 15 minutes to infuse the flavor of the vanilla. Spoon the vanilla bean halves out of the hot cream. Scrape out the tiny seeds with a paring knife. Put the seeds and the pod back into the cream.

LIGHTLY whisk the egg yolks with the ¾ cup [150 g] sugar in a mixing bowl. If you're using vanilla extract instead of the bean, whisk it into the egg yolk mixture.

STRAIN the hot cream, a bit at a time, into the egg mixture. Don't use too fine a strainer or you'll strain out the specks of vanilla, which look great in the crème brûlée. Discard the pod. Stir the egg mixture with the whisk for a few seconds after each addition of cream so the hot cream doesn't curdle the yolks. Don't whisk the egg mixture or you'll make it frothy and it won't be smooth on top when you bake it. Just stir it gently, making sure you're incorporating the egg yolks into the cream.

LADLE the cream mixture into one medium-size gratin dish or baking dish large enough that the mixture forms a layer between ½ and 1 inch [1.5 and 2.5 cm] thick, or six 5-ounce or 6-ounce [155- to 185-ml] individual round or oval gratin dishes, ramekins, or custard cups. Arrange the dish or dishes of custard in a baking dish with high sides and place it on one of the oven racks. Use a teakettle or ladle to pour in enough hot tap water to come halfway up the sides of the molds. Cover the bain-marie with a sheet of aluminum foil to prevent the custards from forming a crust on top.

START checking the custards after about 45 minutes—if they're deep they'll take longer—by peeling back the foil and wiggling them very slightly back and forth. If they're not done, the surface will ripple. As they continue to cook, the ripples will appear only in a smaller area near the center of the custard. When there's no rippling at all on the custards you've checked, take the foil off all the custards and wiggle the whole bunch so that, if your oven doesn't cook evenly, you'll catch any that are underdone. When all the custards are done, take the bain-marie out of the oven, and then take the custards out of the bain-marie. Let them cool for about 30 minutes. Refrigerate them for at least 1 hour, but preferably overnight. At this stage you can leave them, covered with plastic wrap, in the fridge for several days.

WHEN you're ready to glaze the custards, which should be cold, glaze them within a couple of hours of serving. Use a spoon to sprinkle them with a thin layer of granulated sugar just thick enough so you can't see the top of the custard. If your custard molds are deep (and so, less wide), you'll need less sugar than the recipe calls for.

IT'S easiest to glaze the crème brûlées by waving the flame of a small propane torch (sold at kitchen supply stores) or larger torch (sold at hardware stores) over their surface, until the sugar melts into a shiny caramel glaze. If you don't have a torch, light the broiler about 5 minutes before you're ready to glaze the custards. Put the custards on a sheet pan so it will be easier to move them around under the broiler. (Unless you're used to this, and know your broiler, it's probably best to glaze them one by one.) Slide the sheet pan into the oven, with the tops of the custards 1 or 2 inches away from the flames or coils. Watch them like a hawk, rotating them or moving them around so the layer of sugar bubbles up and browns evenly without burning. Allow them to cool for 5 minutes before serving.

Variations: Despite being a big fan of crème brulée, I find it overwhelmingly rich, especially when it follows one of my "company" dinners, which aren't light to begin with. It's also a dessert that people eat a lot in restaurants, and I don't like being upstaged. So I make a few changes here and there to the basic recipe to give it an element of surprise. One is to flavor the basic custard mixture with something like coffee, chocolate, or a fruit purée (more about this under "*Pots de crème*," below). I make a mango version that's not half bad, but frankly none of these variations is a big improvement on basic vanilla, especially when a whole vanilla bean is used and not vanilla extract. But one marvelous trick is to make a single large crème brulée, cover it just before serving with fresh raspberries or other berries—I use 1 pint of berries with the amounts in the recipe above—and then spoon it out onto plates at the table. The thick cream and thin sheets of crunchy sugar become a luxurious sauce for the berries.

POTS DE CRÈME: A *pot de crème*, or "little pot of cream," is a custard baked in an individual characteristic plump little dish with a lid. If you make *pots de crème* a lot it might be worth buying a set of *pot de crème* molds, but they come from France and if you need a set of 6 they can be a bit expensive. Mine have long since lost their lids, so I just cover them with aluminum foil, as in making crème brulée. You can use small ramekins instead. I can hardly say that *pots de crème* are low-cal, but they are lighter than crème brulée because, in my version at least, they're made with half cream and half milk instead of all cream. Of course, as with any custard, you can make them as light or as rich as you want by varying the proportions of cream and milk. Traditionally, *pots de crème* are made, like crème brulée, with egg yolks, not whole eggs.

Pots de crème can be flavored in the same way as any custard, but whereas my favorite flavor for crème brulée is vanilla, *pots de crème* lack the contrasting texture and subtle bitterness of that lovely sheet of caramelized sugar, and so call out for more assertive flavors such as chocolate or coffee, fruit purée, or, as in the recipe below, ginger.

GINGER POTS DE CRÈME
POTS DE CRÈME
AU GINGEMBRE

MAKES 6 SERVINGS

My first job in a Parisian restaurant was in a little place in Montmartre called Le Petit Robert, named after its diminutive owner. I got my foot in the door because a friend of mine, who had a job there washing dishes, went back to America for a month, and they needed a fill-in. I'd quickly scrub the dishes in a little sink in the back and then rush into the kitchen to watch the chef, ask questions, and in general make a pest of myself. When August rolled around and the kitchen staff went south for the month, Robert kept me on as substitute chef. One of the dishes he taught me was this, his version of pots de crème. And while I'm not wild about ginger in other things, its gentle, spicy heat makes it the perfect balance to the creamy richness of these custards.

1½ cups [375 ml] milk

1½ cups [375 ml] heavy cream

2 ounces [55 g] fresh ginger (about a 4-inch [7.5-cm] piece), peeled, sliced thin

9 egg yolks (from large eggs)

¾ cup [150 g] granulated sugar

6 pieces candied ginger (available in the spice rack at the supermarket)

COMBINE the milk, cream, and ginger slices in a heavy-bottomed saucepan and bring to a simmer. Remove from the stove, cover the pot, and let sit for 30 minutes to infuse the flavor of the ginger.

PREHEAT the oven to 275°F [165°C/gas mark 3].

WHISK the egg yolks with the sugar in a mixing bowl until smooth and slowly stir in the milk mixture. Stir the egg mixture as you add the milk mixture so the yolks don't curdle. Slowly whisk the egg mixture into the cream. Don't be overzealous, or you'll make it frothy and it won't be smooth on top when you bake it. Strain the mixture into a mixing bowl and skim off any froth with a ladle.

PUT a piece of candied ginger in the bottom of each of six 5-ounce [155-ml] *pot de crème* molds, 5-ounce or 6-ounce [155- to 185-ml] ramekins, or Pyrex custard cups. Pour the egg yolk mixture into the molds—a pitcher is easier to use than a ladle. If you're using *pot de crème* molds, put on their lids. Arrange the custards in a high-sided baking dish and place the baking dish on one of the oven racks. Using a teakettle or ladle, pour enough hot tap water down the side of the baking dish, to come halfway up the sides of the molds. Place the little lid on each mold. If you're using ramekins instead of *pot de crème* molds, cover the baking dish with a sheet of aluminum foil.

AFTER 30 minutes, rotate the pan to ensure even cooking. Start checking the custards after 10 minutes more by lifting a lid or peeling back the aluminum foil and wiggling them back and forth very slightly. They usually take 45 to 50 minutes more. If they're not done, the entire surface will ripple. As they continue to cook, the ripples will appear only in a smaller area near the center of the custard. When there's only a slight rippling left in the center—it's okay if *pots de crème* are a tiny bit underdone—take the custards out of the oven, then out of the bain-marie, and let them cool for about 30 minutes. Refrigerate for at least 1 hour before serving. If you serve them at this point, they'll still be a tad warm (a nice effect), but you can leave them in the fridge for several days.

Variations: To flavor a *pot de crème*, it's helpful to consider when in the whole process to add the flavoring. Some flavorings, including cocoa, strong coffee (espresso or, in a pinch, instant coffee), and ground spices such as cinnamon, powdered saffron, or cardamon, should be whisked with the egg yolks and sugar before the hot milk is added. Whole vanilla beans (split down the middle), chunks of cinnamon sticks or other whole spices, and ground coffee—best for making coffee *pot de crème*—should be infused in the hot milk and then strained out before the milk is combined with the egg yolks. Fruit purées, fruit brandies (eaux-de-vie), and extracts such as vanilla, almond, or lemon should be added to the *pot de crème* mixture just before it is poured into the molds so these ingredients, which are volatile and fleeting, are cooked as little as possible. (See Crème Anglaise, page 641, for more flavoring ideas.)

CRÈME CARAMEL: In Spanish or Latin restaurants, crème caramel is sometimes called flan. But if you ask for flan in a French pastry shop, you'll get something totally different—a kind of starchy and pie-shaped sweet custard, sold in wedges. In fancy restaurants a flan can be any kind of custard, sweet or savory. And you won't find crème caramel on a French menu (at least in France), because in France it's called *crème renversée*, which means "inverted" or "turned over," which is what you do to get it out of the molds.

A classic crème caramel is less rich than crème brûlée or *pot de crème* because it's made with whole eggs and milk instead of yolks and cream. Other than a little vanilla, its only flavoring is a trace of delightful bitterness from the caramel-lined mold. Below is a delicious variation on the classic, flavored with orange.

CARAMEL, CARAMEL SAUCE, CARAMEL SYRUP, AND BUTTERSCOTCH

All of these terms cause confusion because they mean different things to different people. In French cooking, caramel is the hard, dark, and brittle result of cooking sugar, without liquid, in a heavy-bottomed pot. To make caramel, just heat granulated sugar in a heavy-bottomed nonaluminum saucepan over medium heat while stirring with a wooden spoon. (French pastry chefs have a special untinned copper pot just for making caramel.) The sugar will gradually melt, look lumpy and disastrous (no need to worry), and turn pale golden and then deep red. As soon as it is smooth, it must be used right away—as for lining molds for crème caramel—or liquid has to be added immediately to keep the sugar from burning. If you add 1 cup of water to 1 cup of still-hot caramel, the mixture will boil up furiously—stand back—and you'll have caramel syrup, which you can boil down to the consistency you like, not a bad sauce for ice cream. If you add 1 cup of heavy cream instead of the water, you'll end up with a rich and creamy caramel sauce.

If you want to make 1 cup of butterscotch, which is composed of both caramelized sugar and caramelized butter, make a caramel with ½ cup [100 g] of granulated sugar, and when it's deep red-brown, pour in ½ cup [125 ml] cold water—stand back, it spatters. Boil the syrup for 1 or 2 minutes to dissolve the caramel and stir in 4 tablespoons of unsalted butter. Cook this mixture for about 5 minutes while stirring, to the "soft ball" stage. To know when you've reached the soft ball stage, dip the handle end of a spoon into the sauce and then quickly dip it in a glass of cool tap water. Pinch the end of the spoon. When the sauce feels like a clump of chewed-on chewing gum, it's ready. (You can also use a candy thermometer, which should read 240°F [115°C].) Immediately add ½ cup [125 ml] of heavy cream to the mixture and simmer gently, while stirring, until the sauce is smooth, about 1 minute.

ORANGE-FLAVORED CRÈME CARAMEL

CRÈME RENVERSÉE
À L'ORANGE

MAKES 6 DESSERT SERVINGS

I got this idea from Michel Guérard's book *Cuisine Minceur*, first published in France in the mid-1970s. Michel Guérard was the first French chef to explore ways of reducing the fat and calories in French classic cooking. His book is marvelously innovative, but sometimes a bit extreme. This custard, for example, he makes with artificial sweetener. Even though I've put the sugar back in, this is a reasonably light dessert, and the orange gives it a refreshing nuance. The custards can be made up to 2 days in advance.

To make a classic crème caramel, infuse a vanilla bean, split down the middle, in the hot milk instead of using the orange zests.

FOR THE CARAMEL:

1 cup [200 g] granulated sugar

FOR THE CUSTARD:

2 large navel oranges

3 cups [750 ml] milk

5 large eggs

⅔ cup [135 g] granulated sugar

HEAT the sugar for the caramel in a heavy-bottomed nonaluminum saucepan over medium heat while stirring with a wooden spoon. When the sugar melts, any lumps disappear, and it turns deep red, pour it immediately into six 6-ounce [185-ml] ramekins. Work quickly so the caramel doesn't overcook or harden. Pour just enough caramel into the molds to coat the bottoms. You shouldn't end up using all the caramel—you just made a cupful because it's diffi-

cult to cook a smaller amount. Try not to spatter any caramel on the inside of the ramekins. (When you're done with the saucepan, put about 1 cup of water in it and boil it for a few minutes to dissolve the caramel and make it easier to wash the saucepan.)

PREHEAT the oven to 325°F [165°C/gas mark 3].

PEEL the zest off the oranges in strips with a sharp paring knife or vegetable peeler. Try to avoid leaving the white pith attached to the zest, but don't worry if you leave a little. Blanch the strips of zest, to eliminate any bitterness, by boiling them for 30 seconds in 1 cup [250 ml] of water and immediately draining in a strainer.

COMBINE the drained zests with the milk in a heavy-bottomed saucepan and bring to a simmer over medium heat. Remove from the heat, cover the pan, and set aside for 30 minutes to let the zests' flavor infuse in the milk.

BEAT the eggs with the sugar until the mixture is smooth. Bring the milk back to a simmer, strain it into a clean saucepan or mixing bowl, and then gradually ladle it into the eggs while stirring with a wooden spoon. Continue stirring, scraping the spoon along the bottom and sides of the bowl to make sure all the egg mixture gets dissolved in the milk. (Don't leave the spoon sitting in the hot milk or the spoon may impart a stale wood flavor.) Ladle off any foam.

STRAIN through a fine-mesh strainer into a clear bowl or small pitcher to remove zests and any coagulated egg.

LADLE the custard mixture into the ramekins or use a small pitcher to pour it. Arrange the ramekins in a baking dish and slide the dish onto one of the oven racks. Pour enough hot tap water into the dish to come halfway up the sides of the ramekins. Cover the baking dish loosely with a sheet of aluminum foil. Bake the custards until they're set—no ripples form on the top of the custards when you give the dish a tiny back-and-forth shake—1¼ to 1½ hours.

TAKE the custards out of the bain-marie and let them cool at room temperature for 1 hour, uncovered. (If you cover them, moisture will condense on the covering and drip down on the custards.) Refrigerate, still uncovered, for 2 hours. If you're saving them longer than that, cover them with plastic wrap until you're ready to serve.

JUST before serving, run a paring knife along the inside of the ramekins to loosen the custards. Place an individual serving plate on top of one of the custards, hold the two together, and quickly flip plate and custard over so the custard is upside-down on the plate. While holding the plate with your fingers and the ramekin with your two thumbs, give a gentle up-and-down shake to dislodge the custard. Gently lift off the ramekin—a light caramel sauce will surround the custard. Repeat with the other custards.

Variations: I sometimes buy an extra orange and cut it and the orange used to provide the zest into skinless wedges (see page 391). I then use the wedges to decorate the servings of custard. In the summer I surround and top the custards with fresh berries. Crème caramels, like *pots de crème*, can be flavored in any number of ways (see page 637 for some ideas). In some regions of France, including the Languedoc, pieces of peeled chestnuts are folded into the custard mixture before baking. I imagine this would be magnificent with *marrons glacés*.

Custard Cream

CRÈME ANGLAISE

THE FRENCH HAVE A PECULIAR HABIT OF naming their own dishes after other places. There are all manner of things *à la grecque*, like nothing ever seen in Greece but popular in Parisian bistros; various dishes *à la milanaise* never to be encountered in Milan; dishes named something-or-other *maltaise*, implying the presence of orange, and any number of dishes *à l'americaine*. The list goes on, but the English are the clear winners, their identity tagged onto an array of dishes and techniques. Knowing the French disdain for English cooking, the first time I saw something *à l'anglaise* I suspected a disclaimer. I anticipated something designed to satisfy English tourists during the days of the grand tour, something never to be enjoyed by the French themselves and for which they assumed no responsibility. But in fact things cooked *à l'anglaise* are pretty good. Green vegetables *à l'anglaise* keep their color and crunch while the same vegetables cooked *à la française* turn mushy and gray. Veal scallops breaded *à l'anglaise*, with eggs and bread crumbs, are a triumph of fine cooking. Crème anglaise is fundamental to the art of French dessert making, it's hard to imagine the French giving others the credit.

Crème anglaise is custard kept liquid by being stirred on the stove instead of being allowed to set in molds in the oven. It can be flavored with anything that tastes good with sweets, including a number of ingredients (saffron, truffles, cardamom) that you'd never suspect. It's used as a sauce for fruit, tarts, and cakes, but it also gets turned into other things. Stick it in an ice cream machine and you've got French ice cream. Work it with butter to make butter cream, put in some gelatin and let it set and you've got *panna cotta*, or add whipped cream before allowing it to set and you've got a Bavarian cream. Layer it with pieces of stale cake and you've got trifle. Cook it with some cornstarch and allow it to set in bowls and you have American-style pudding. Lace it with brandy, whisky, or rum and fold in whipped cream and you've got the best eggnog on the planet, with no anxiety about raw egg yolks. It's useful stuff to know how to make.

CLASSIC VANILLA CRÈME ANGLAISE

CRÈME ANGLAISE À LA VANILLE

MAKES 1 QUART

Crème anglaise can be more or less rich, depending on how many egg yolks you use. Classic recipes call for 2 to 5 yolks per cup [250 ml] of milk. I compromise and settle on 3 egg yolks (from large eggs) per cup of milk. This recipe calls for somewhat less sugar than classic recipes do.

3 cups [750 ml] milk

1 vanilla bean, split in half lengthwise, or 1 teaspoon vanilla extract (see page 635 for more about vanilla)

9 egg yolks (from large eggs)

¾ cup [150 g] sugar

BRING the milk to a simmer in a heavy-bottomed nonaluminum pot with the vanilla bean halves (if you're using extract, don't add it yet).

WHILE the milk is coming to a simmer, whisk the egg yolks with the sugar in a mixing bowl until the egg yolks turn pale yellow, about 2 minutes. If you're using vanilla extract instead of the bean, whisk it into the egg mixture.

TAKE the vanilla bean halves out of the hot milk with a spoon or skimmer and scrape out the tiny seeds with a paring knife. Put the seeds and the pod back into the milk.

POUR half the hot milk, a bit at a time, while stirring, into the egg mixture. Stir the egg mixture with a wooden spoon or spatula for a few seconds after each addition of hot milk so the hot milk doesn't curdle the yolks. Pour the milk-egg mixture into the saucepan with the rest of the milk and put the saucepan on the stove over medium heat. Stir constantly with the spoon or spatula, reaching into the corners of the saucepan so no egg yolk accumulates and curdles. Continue stirring until the mixture thickens. (See "How to Know When Crème Anglaise Is Done," page 643.) Don't expect too dramatic a thickening, just a subtle shift from wateriness to silkiness. Take the pan off the heat and keep stirring for a couple of minutes so the heat retained in the pan doesn't overcook the crème anglaise. Strain the crème anglaise into a bowl (use a regular strainer, not a fine-mesh one, or you'll strain out the specks of vanilla). Discard the pod. Cover the bowl with plastic wrap, allow to cool for 30 minutes at room temperature, and then chill in the refrigerator.

Variations: Crème anglaise can be flavored with just about anything we might associate with a dessert. Spirits are great—between ¼ cup and ½ cup [60 and 125 ml] added to 1 quart [1 l] of crème anglaise will work wonders. My favorites are eaux-de-vie—dry, clear, fruit brandies, including kirsch (made from cherries), Poire William (made from pears), and framboise (made from raspberries). Good pot-stilled dark rum (the best comes from Martinique), bourbon (it should say "straight bourbon" on the bottle, not "blended bourbon"), marc or grappa (usually clear brandies made from grape skins and pits), and Cognac are wonderful flavorings for crème anglaise destined as a sauce for a chocolate or fruit dessert. Crème anglaise with any of these flavorings can also be turned into ice cream—you can make glorious flavors that you'd never be able to find at the supermarket. (Keep in mind that ice cream with spirits will stay softer, since alcohol lowers its freezing point.) One tip: Don't add spirits to a crème anglaise until after it has cooled, or their aroma will evaporate.

You can flavor a crème anglaise by stirring in a fruit purée. Frozen strawberries and raspberries, stirred in after the crème anglaise is cooked, are an inexpensive year-round source. Or you can give the crème anglaise a citrus flavor by simmering strips of the zest from 1 orange or 2 lemons or limes in the milk in the same way as the vanilla bean is used in the basic recipe above.

Chocolate is an obvious flavoring choice. You can use it in one of two ways. You can whisk ½ cup of cocoa powder into the egg yolks–sugar mixture in the basic recipe and just enough milk—about ½ cup [125 ml]—to make the mixture smooth before adding the rest of the milk. Or you can chop ½ pound [225 g] of bittersweet bar chocolate (or 4 ounces [115 g] of bitter baking chocolate) and stir this into the still-hot crème anglaise after it has thickened but before you strain it.

Coffee crème anglaise is easy to make by stirring about ½ cup (4 fluid ounces [125 ml], not half an espresso cup) of strong espresso into 1 quart of vanilla—or unflavored—crème anglaise. (In a pinch, you can make the espresso with instant coffee.) But you'll end up with a far more delicious and subtly flavored sauce by combining ¼ pound [115 g] of finely ground dark-roast coffee with the 3 cups of milk as it comes to a simmer, finishing the crème anglaise in the usual way, and then straining it through a fine-mesh strainer to get the coffee grounds out.

If you want mocha crème anglaise, use both coffee and chocolate.

You can also flavor crème anglaise with nuts—almonds and hazelnuts are best. To do this, roast 1 cup of nuts for about 15 minutes in a 350°F [175°C/gas mark 4] oven and grind the nuts in a food processor for 5 minutes, scraping down the sides. Grind until the nuts have the consistency of peanut butter. Stir the hot crème anglaise, a small amount at a time, into the nut paste until the mixture is smooth, and then strain. Don't whisk the nut paste directly into the crème anglaise, or it will take too long to dissolve. Store-bought nut pastes (hazelnut, almond, pistachios) can be whisked into the hot crème anglaise to taste. I usually cut the amount of sugar in the crème anglaise by ¼ cup when using these pastes, which tend to be very sweet.

HOW TO KNOW WHEN CRÈME ANGLAISE IS DONE

Crème anglaise is easy to make except for one thing: If it gets too hot it will curdle. On the other hand, if you don't cook it enough you'll end up with eggy-tasting milk. The first few times you make it, you might want to use an instant-read thermometer and as soon as the mixture reaches 180°F [82°C] take it off the heat, but if your thermometer is off by even a few degrees, this won't work. Most cookbooks tell you to judge the doneness of a crème anglaise by stirring it with a wooden spatula, holding the spatula level and drawing your finger through the liquid that clings to it, and seeing if the line stays there. I've never found this easy, and if you're not careful the crème anglaise will overcook and curdle—even if you take it off the heat—while you're staring at the spatula. Instead, I look at the ripples that form on the surface of the liquid while I'm stirring. Initially, the ripples are very small, almost frothy, and there are lots of them. Then, suddenly, the little ripples disappear and form smooth, rounder waves. As soon as this happens, the crème anglaise is done.

THE BEST HOLIDAY EGGNOG

MAKES 8 SERVINGS (1 CUP EACH)

Stir 1 to 2 cups [250 to 500 ml] of bourbon, brandy, or rum into 1 recipe of Classic Vanilla Crème Anglaise, chilled. I like straight bourbon, not blended, because it has more flavor. For the brandy I use an inexpensive but genuine Cognac. For the rum, Martinique is best, but good Jamaican dark rum is fine, too; Puerto Rican doesn't have enough flavor. Cover the mixture and refrigerate it for at least 2 hours. Beat 1 cup of heavy cream to medium peaks and fold it into the crème anglaise mixture. Serve in chilled cups or glasses. Grate a little nutmeg over each serving.

RICE CAKES AND PUDDINGS

The best-known French rice pudding is *riz à l'impératrice*, a frightfully elaborate dome- or fez-shaped structure of custard, candied fruit, and, of course, rice. But all rice puddings or cakes are really flans—milk held together with eggs—and are made in essentially the same way. In *riz à l'impératrice*, long-grain, neutral-tasting Carolina rice is simmered in milk and the milk is then turned into a crème anglaise. (This is one dish in which American white rice works best.) The starch from the rice dissolves in the milk and helps thicken it, but gelatin is added for additional body. Whipped cream is folded in, as for a Bavarian cream, and the whole thing—the cooked rice and the rice-starch-thickened Bavarian cream mixture—is allowed to set in a large charlotte mold lined with cut-outs of candied fruit. Simpler versions, such as the Norman *terrinée* (sometimes called *bourgoule*) and the rice pudding my mother used to make, are simple flans made by simmering the rice with milk and sugar (and sometimes spices, vanilla, or citrus zests), letting the mixture cool slightly, combining it with beaten eggs, and then baking it as you would any flan, in a bain-marie in a medium oven until it sets.

SWEET ALMOND CUSTARD:
BLANCMANGE

I first read about blancmange in Richard Olney's *The French Menu Cookbook*, in which he suggests serving it as a perfect accompaniment to a glass of good Sauternes. Sometimes called *blancmanger*, it is one of France's oldest dishes (it's first described in the fourteenth century) but is almost never served in French restaurants. I encountered it once, served as a tiny hors d'oeuvre at Joël Robuchon's three-star restaurant Jamin, where it was served in tiny glasses and topped with finely chopped tomatoes—a combination impossible to imagine but one that worked.

Modern versions of blancmange are made by setting sweetened almond milk (almonds puréed in a blender with water and strained through muslin) with gelatin, much like a *panna cotta*. Sometimes whipped cream is folded into the mixture, turning it into an almond Bavarian cream. French recipes call for 4 or 5 bitter almonds to every 100 sweet almonds, but since bitter almonds are illegal in the United States (they contain traces of a cyanide-related compound), I use a few drops of almond extract to replace the bitter almonds.

HOT CRÊPES WITH ORANGE BUTTER SAUCE

CRÊPES SUZETTE

AS A CHILD I WAS FASCINATED BY ADULT THINGS. WHEN THE ITEM IN question was also luxurious or, better yet, taboo, my curiosity grew boundless and I'd pester parents and teachers with questions until the mystery was solved. At some early age I found out that crêpes suzette, along with caviar, French Champagne, and pâté de foie gras, inhabited a celestial realm in which even teachers and parents were vague and inexperienced. Best of all, crêpes suzette involved fire.

One morning, during my annual summer stay at her place, my doting aunt Jane announced that we could make any dessert I wanted. Well, no chocolate cake or hot fudge sundae for me—it had to be baked Alaska, cherries jubilee, or crêpes suzette. After some discussion, crêpes suzette (French, more sophisticated) won. Out came *Larousse Gastronomique,* the chafing dish, a pound of butter, and a fortune in expensive, flammable, and taboo liquor. I spent the afternoon rubbing sugar cubes on the outsides of oranges, working butter in a bowl with a wooden spoon, and measuring out the booze while Jane labored over the crêpes. That night I got to light the hot brandy and spoon it over the crêpes, which were carefully folded and arranged in the chafing dish. Jane served the buttery brandy-laden crêpes on my grandmother's Limoges and all was good in the world.

Crêpes suzette, which now seem anachronistic and overly showy (as does anything flambéed), have all but disappeared from the menus of French restaurants, but they're still my all-time favorite dessert. Having outgrown my pyromania, I don't own a chafing dish, and I save a fortune by making my own orange infusion and by using a relatively inexpensive Cognac instead of the classic Grand Marnier. The crêpes themselves are easy to make and can be made a few days (or, if frozen, even months) ahead of time. The orange butter sauce takes about 20 minutes.

BASIC CRÊPES

MAKES EIGHTEEN TO TWENTY 5-INCH [12.5-CM]

CRÊPES (6 SERVINGS OF 3 EACH)

Some recipes for crêpes suzette call for flavoring the crêpes themselves with orange. This is a silly and needless complication, since no one will notice the delicacy of an orange-flavored crêpe under an intensely flavored orange sauce. I use the same crêpe recipe for both sweet and savory crêpe dishes and most of the time don't even measure the ingredients. I just break eggs into a bowl—1 egg per 2 servings—add enough flour to make a stiff but smooth paste, and then thin the mixture with enough milk until it has the consistency of heavy cream. I strain the mixture, stir in 1 tablespoon of melted butter per serving, sprinkle in a little salt, and I'm done. Crêpe batter is supposed to rest for a few hours so the gluten in the flour relaxes and the crêpe ends up a bit more tender, but many an evening or morning I've gotten a sudden inspiration and thrown together a batch of crêpes and been perfectly happy. Older recipes insist on well-seasoned iron crêpe pans, but these are expensive and useful for nothing else. I prefer nonstick pans, which never stick, something even well-seasoned iron pans can do. Since I like to keep four pans going at once and I don't have four matching crêpe pans, I end up using what I have around: a single nonstick crêpe pan, an omelet pan, and two nonstick sauté pans. I don't even worry if my crêpes aren't all the exact same size—when they're folded or rolled up, minor differences go unnoticed. I seldom bother making just a few crêpes. I make a big batch and eat, in various guises, those I don't use right away. Or I freeze them—they keep for months.

1 cup [125 g] all-purpose flour

5 large eggs

1¼ cup [310 ml] milk

½ teaspoon salt

6 tablespoons butter, melted (for the batter), plus about 1 tablespoon, softened (for the pans)

COMBINE the flour and eggs in a mixing bowl and add just enough of the milk to allow you to work the mixture gently into a smooth paste with a whisk. Don't overwork the mixture—which would activate the gluten—and don't worry about a few lumps, which will be strained out anyway. Gently whisk in the rest of the milk. Strain the batter and then stir in the salt and melted butter. (If the butter is added before straining, it congeals in the cold batter and gets strained out.) If you have time, cover the batter and let it rest in a cool place or in the refrigerator for at least 2 hours, or up to 24 hours.

COOKING crêpes is one of those things that take a little practice, so if you're new at it, count on ruining a few until you get the hang of it. First, the pan has to be at the right temperature. If it's too hot, the batter will seize up in the pan where you first ladle it in and form a thick area in the crêpe. Also, because you won't have time to spread the batter over the entire surface of the pan before it sets, the crêpe will be too thick overall. If the pan isn't hot enough, the crêpe may stick (unless you're using a nonstick pan), and of course it will take longer to cook. If you're making crêpes for the first time, start with a single pan. Use a paper towel to rub the inside of the pan with a very thin layer of softened butter (or use a brush). Put the pan over medium heat. When the butter foams and the foam begins to subside ever so slightly, as in making an omelet, ladle in enough batter to just cover the surface of the pan with a thin layer. If you add too much, pour the excess out of the pan. After a couple of crêpes, you'll be able to judge how much to fill the ladle so you can add the right amount each time. If, when you pour the excess out, none of the batter sticks to the pan, the pan isn't hot enough. If the batter sizzles as soon as it hits the pan, the pan is too hot.

AS soon as you add the batter, quickly lift the pan and gently rotate it and tilt it at different angles at the same time to coat it with the batter as quickly as possible. Put the pan on the stove for about 1 minute, until the batter loses its sheen. Pinch each side of the crêpe between thumb and forefinger of both hands or use a small, wide metal spatula, and lift the crêpe entirely off the pan, turn it over onto the pan, and cook it for about 45 seconds more. Don't try to flip crêpes—it's impossible, since they cling to the pan. If the crêpe starts to tear as you're trying to turn it, you probably need to cook it a little longer. If cooking the first crêpe longer doesn't work, beat another egg and stir it into the batter. If the next crêpe tears, you've probably made the batter too thin. Work 2 tablespoons of flour with milk until smooth and whisk this into the batter. If your crêpes come out too thick, thin the batter with milk.

NORMALLY, you won't need to butter the pan before every crêpe, but if the crêpes stick, rub the surface of the pan with more butter. If you're using an iron pan and the crêpes stick, don't try to scrape the batter off the pan or you'll just make matters worse. Instead, keep the pan on the heat until the clinging batter gets dark brown, then gently coax it off with a knife. Once you've removed all the batter, rub the pan vigorously with butter and try again.

AS you get better at making crêpes, try making more than one at a time, so that while one is cooking, you're ladling in the batter for another. As you take the crêpes out of the pan, arrange them on a platter in overlapping rows—don't just stack them, because they cling together and you'll have a hard time separating them. Once you've filled the platter with a single layer of crêpes, cover the first layer with a sheet of wax paper before adding another layer. Cover the plate with plastic wrap and refrigerate it until you're ready to use the crêpes, up to 5 days. If you're freezing the crêpes, stack them with small sheets of wax paper between them and tightly wrap the whole bundle in plastic wrap.

SIMPLIFIED ORANGE BUTTER CRÊPES

CRÊPES AU BEURRE D'ORANGE

MAKES 6 DESSERT SERVINGS

I'm not calling these crêpes suzette because I've replaced some of the traditional steps used to make crêpes suzette with simpler methods and used less expensive ingredients. Most modern recipes call for Grand Marnier, a marvelous orange-flavored liqueur, but frightfully expensive. Many cooks, when they run out to the liquor store to buy a bottle, panic at the price and substitute Triple Sec or orange curaçao. Unfortunately, the sauce ends up tasting like hair tonic. My own solution is to make an orange-flavored sugar syrup, flavor it with Cognac and butter, and pour it over the hot crêpes. Be sure to buy authentic Cognac. (See page 10 for more information about choosing spirits for cooking.)

1 recipe Basic Crêpes (page 648) (eighteen 5-inch [12.5 cm] crêpes)

1 tablespoon softened unsalted butter (for the serving dish), plus 1 stick (¼ pound [115 g]) cold unsalted butter, cut into 6 pieces (for the sauce)

4 navel oranges

⅓ cup [70 g] granulated sugar

⅔ cup [150 ml] Cognac

FOLD the crêpes in half with the more attractive side on the outside, and fold again to form little wedges. (You can also roll the crêpes up into cigar shapes.) Rub the softened butter on a heat-proof serving dish, such as an oval gratin dish, large enough to hold the folded crêpes in a single layer, with the crêpes partially overlapping.

RINSE off the oranges. With a vegetable peeler or sharp paring knife, remove all the zest in strips from 2 of the oranges. Toss zests into boiling water for 30 seconds, drain, rinse under cold water, and reserve. Squeeze the 4 oranges—you should end up with about 1½ cups [375 ml] of juice. Combine the strained juice, zest strips, and sugar in a small saucepan. Bring to a gentle simmer over low heat and simmer gently until you're left with about ⅔ cup [150 ml] of orange-flavored sauce. Strain the syrup into a clean saucepan. If you like, you can make the syrup up to 1 week in advance and keep it in the refrigerator.

TWENTY minutes before you're ready to serve, preheat the oven to 325°F [165°C/gas mark 3]. Cover the dish of crêpes with a sheet of aluminum foil, and 10 minutes before you're ready to serve, slide it into the oven. Bring the orange syrup to a simmer and whisk in the Cognac and the 6 pieces of butter. When all the butter has melted into the syrup, taste the sauce. If it tastes too strongly of Cognac, boil it for about 30 seconds. Spoon the hot sauce over the hot crêpes in the serving dish, or arrange the crêpes on hot plates and spoon some sauce over each serving.

Variations: Anyone who has strolled in Paris for more than 20 minutes will have encountered one of the ubiquitous street corner *crêperies* with their mouth-watering assortment of crêpes flavored with various sweet, and occasionally savory, fillings. One of my own favorite breakfasts or afternoon snacks is a hot crêpe that's been sprinkled with sugar, smeared with butter, and rolled up. Brushing a hot crêpe with butter and sprinkling it with a mixture of 1 part unsweetened cocoa powder to 3 parts sugar, while it's still in the pan, before rolling it up converts it instantly into a chocolate crêpe; a light sprinkling of Grand Marnier, into an orange-flavored one; and a smearing of Nutella—the sweet Italian equivalent to peanut butter, made with hazelnuts and chocolate—into a delicious *crêpe Nutella*.

Savory crêpes are popular in Brittany, where they're made with buckwheat flour and called *galettes*, and where they're likely to be served with cold hard cider. One of the easiest and tastiest *galettes* is made with ham and cheese—just sprinkle grated cheese and chopped ham in a crêpe, fold it in wedges, and cook it gently in a sauté pan in a little butter until the cheese melts (see Chapter 11).

Crêpes also provide a quick way of making leftovers more elegant. I sometimes heat bits of leftover chicken and turkey in a cream sauce—one recipe béchamel (see page 577) sauce with a half cup or more of cream added—roll the mixture up in crêpes, arrange the crêpes in a baking dish, top them with more sauce, and bake. This method also works with leftover vegetables—spinach and mushrooms are especially good. Stew the vegetables for 1 or 2 minutes in a little cream, arrange them in a crêpe with grated cheese, and bake. If you start out making crêpes to use with savory fillings, try flavoring the crêpe batter itself with an herb such as tarragon or marjoram (but not the two together) or with a spice such as saffron (great with seafood).

Clafoutis

CLAFOUTIS

A CLAFOUTIS IS A KIND OF TART OR VERY thick crêpe from the Limousin, a region near the center of France whose most famous city is Limoges. The traditional clafoutis par excellence is the *clafoutis aux cerises*, made from cherries. In its simplest and most rustic form, the unpitted cherries are spread out in a distinctive metal clafoutis pan, which looks vaguely like a paella pan, and enough sweetened crêpe batter just to cover the cherries is poured over them. The whole thing is baked until the batter sets and lightly browns. Just before serving, the clafoutis is sprinkled with powdered sugar. Cookbooks abound with variations based mainly on substituting other fruits, such as strawberries or plums, and, most important, pitting the cherries so you're not sitting there spitting out pits as you eat your wedge of clafoutis. More sophisticated versions may replace the crêpe batter with pastry cream, which is very similar except that it's been cooked on the stove and thickened before it is used. Some recipes add powdered almonds, turning the batter into a kind of frangipane and the clafoutis into a tart called a *tarte bourdaloue* (see page 617) or *tarte alsacienne*. All of these mixtures can be used to make excellent fruit tarts, but to my mind a clafoutis is a simple and rustic dessert that if toyed with too much stops being a clafoutis. I do make one important addition: melted butter. Butter not only flavors the clafoutis but, because it coats the particles of flour, makes the batter lighter and less starchy. I use whatever fruit is in season, but you should keep in mind that some fruits (red berries, peaches, nectarines) contain a large amount of water that's released as they bake so that each piece of fruit is surrounded by a little puddle of liquid when the clafoutis comes out of the oven. As the clafoutis cools, this liquid is reabsorbed into the surrounding, now rather cakelike, batter. If you're fussy, you can cook the fruit ahead of time and incorporate the liquid it releases into the batter before baking (although it may turn the batter a somewhat sickly pink).

CHERRY CLAFOUTIS

CLAFOUTIS AUX CERISES

MAKES 8 DESSERT SERVINGS

Traditional versions call for black cherries or sometimes sour cherries, but I use regular Bing cherries, which are plump, sweet, and easy to find. This recipe contains a higher proportion of cherries than most versions so that the clafoutis seems to be almost entirely fruit barely held together with batter, for a lighter overall effect. If you want a more traditional version, use 1 pound of cherries instead 1½ pounds.

- 1 teaspoon butter (for baking dish), plus 4 tablespoons butter, melted (for the batter)
- ⅔ cup [135 g] sugar
- 3 eggs
- ¾ cup [95 g] flour
- 1 cup [250 ml] milk

pinch of salt

- 2 teaspoons vanilla extract or kirsch
- 1½ pounds [675 g] Bing cherries, pitted (if you don't have a cherry pitter, push out the pits with a chopstick)

confectioners' sugar (optional)

BUTTER a 10-inch [25.5-cm] round baking dish or porcelain quiche dish and refrigerate until it's needed. (Don't use a tart pan with a removable bottom or the batter will just leak out.)

WHISK the sugar and eggs in a mixing bowl. Add the flour and just enough milk so that you can gently work the mixture, with a whisk, until it is smooth. Gently stir in the rest of the milk, the salt, the vanilla, and the melted butter. Let the mixture rest at room temperature for about 1 hour. (Skip the resting if you're in a rush; it just makes the dough a little more tender.)

PREHEAT the oven to 325°F [165°C/gas mark 3]. Spread the cherries in the baking dish and pour the batter over them. Put the dish with the clafoutis on a sheet pan, in case it overflows, and bake for 1 hour. Let cool slightly before serving—clafoutis is best just slightly warm. If you like, glaze the top of the clafoutis by sprinkling it with confectioners' sugar and sliding it under the broiler—watch it carefully—or by moving the flame of a propane torch quickly back and forth over its surface.

PEAR CLAFOUTIS

CLAFOUTIS AUX POIRES

MAKES 8 DESSERT SERVINGS

This is the tastiest version of clafoutis that I know. And unlike the traditional cherry clafoutis or clafoutis made from other berries, it can be made year round. It is also a perfect dessert for using underripe pears. In fact, the pears must be underripe, since ripe pears will fall apart. The pears are roasted with butter and sugar and the caramelized sugar-butter mixture is incorporated into the crêpe batter. The pear halves are then arranged in a baking dish, the batter is poured over them, and the clafoutis is baked. Like all clafoutis, pear clafoutis is best served warm.

- 4 large underripe pears (any variety is okay, but Bosc is best)
- ⅔ cup [135 g] granulated sugar
- 1½ sticks (6 ounces) [170 g] unsalted butter, cut into chunks (for the batter), plus 1 tablespoon softened butter (for the baking dish)
- 3 large eggs
- ¾ cup [95 g] all-purpose flour
- 1 cup [250 ml] milk
- pinch of salt
- 2 teaspoons vanilla extract
- 1 tablespoon confectioners' sugar (optional)

PEEL the pears, cut them in half lengthwise, and core the halves with a melon baller or paring knife. Cut the stem out of each half. Arrange the pear halves, cut-side down, in a stainless steel or enameled iron pan or pot just large enough to hold them in a single layer. (Aluminum or iron will turn the pears dark.) Pour the sugar over the pears and arrange the chunks of butter on top. Slide the pan

into the oven and turn the oven to 400°F [200°C/gas mark 6]—there's no need to preheat the oven unless you're in a rush. Bake the pears, basting them every 10 minutes, until they have softened—a paring knife slides easily in and out—and are lightly browned, 30 minutes to 1 hour, depending on their ripeness. When the pears are done, take them out of the oven and turn the oven down to 325°F [165°C/gas mark 3].

WHILE the pears are cooking, gently work the eggs into the flour with a whisk and add just enough milk so that you can bring the mixture to a smooth paste. Stir in the rest of the milk and the salt and vanilla extract. Allow the batter to rest at room temperature while the pears are cooking.

BUTTER a round baking dish or quiche pan just large enough to hold the 8 pear halves in a rosette pattern. (I use a 10-inch [25.5-cm] ceramic quiche pan.) Arrange the pear halves, flat-side down, in a circle, with the thinner ends pointing toward the center. Stir any liquid left in the pan used to roast the pears into the crêpe batter. If there's caramel adhering to the pan, deglaze the pan with ½ cup [125 ml] of water and add this to the batter. Pour the batter over the pears—it should almost, but not quite, cover them. Bake until the batter has set and lightly browned, about 40 minutes. Let the tart rest for 10 minutes before serving. (You can also make the clafoutis a day ahead of time, keep it wrapped in the refrigerator, and reheat it in a 250°F [120°C/gas mark ½] oven for 30 minutes.)

IF you like, immediately before serving, sprinkle with confectioners' sugar by putting the sugar in a strainer, holding the strainer over the clafoutis, and rubbing the sugar through the strainer with your fingers. Serve warm.

Adding Yeast to Crêpe Batter:

BLINI, SAVARINS, AND BABAS AU RHUM

A CRÊPE IS THE FRENCH EQUIVALENT TO THE American pancake and differs only in that American pancakes are usually leavened with baking powder and the batter is made thicker. Baking powder contains sodium bicarbonate (baking soda) and tartaric acid or some other source of acidity. When the mixture is moistened, the baking soda reacts with the acid and forms carbon dioxide, which becomes trapped in the gluten structures of the flour and causes the batter to rise. Blini, pancakes originally made with a mixture of buckwheat and regular flour, are instead leavened with beaten egg whites and yeast. Yeast ferments sugars and starch contained in the flour and, like baking powder, produces carbon dioxide, which causes the batter to rise. When you add yeast to a thick crêpe batter and let the mixture rise for a couple of hours in a warm place or overnight in the refrigerator, you can ladle the batter onto a hot buttered griddle or nonstick pan and make yeast-leavened pancakes, which are very similar to blini. You can bake yeast-leavened crêpe batter in a savarin mold (a ring mold) and you'll end up with a kind of cake, called a savarin, suitable for dipping in syrup flavored with rum or other liquor. If you fold yellow raisins into the batter and bake it in individual dariole molds, you'll get babas. Dip the babas in a rum syrup, and you'll have *babas au rhum.*

YEAST-LEAVENED PANCAKES

BLINI

Blini have a wonderful yeasty flavor that makes them much tastier than regular pancakes. You can serve them with butter and maple syrup or jam, although traditionally they are served with caviar and surrounded with a generous amount of melted butter. They are in fact the perfect accompaniment to caviar because their gentle texture, unlike the distracting crunch of a cracker or couton, doesn't override the texture of the caviar. But if most of us ate blini only when we ate caviar, it wouldn't be very often. A somewhat more modest alternative is smoked salmon or other smoked fish instead of the caviar, and crème fraîche instead of, or in addition to, the melted butter. This simplified recipe contains no beaten egg white, and the buckwheat flour is optional.

2 cups [500 ml] milk

1 teaspoon active dry yeast

pinch of sugar

1¾ cups [220 g] all-purpose flour, or 1 cup [125 g] all-purpose flour combined with ¾ cup [95 g] buckwheat flour

4 large eggs

¼ teaspoon salt

2 tablespoons softened butter, or more as needed (for the pan)

WARM the milk in a saucepan until it feels tepid. (If it's too hot it will kill the yeast, and if it's cold, the batter will take much longer to rise.) Combine one-fourth of the warm milk with the yeast and sugar to activate the yeast. Combine the flour and eggs in a mixing bowl. (The batter's going to double in size, so use a bowl that allows you plenty of room.) Gently work the mixture to a smooth, thick paste with a whisk. If the mixture is too stiff, work in some of the milk. When the mixture is smooth, stir in the yeast mixture and whisk in the rest of the milk, until the batter has the consistency of heavy cream. Whisk in the salt. Cover the mixture with plastic wrap and let it rise until doubled in volume, about 2 hours in a warm place, or overnight in the refrigerator.

TO make the blini, brush a nonstick or seasoned cast iron frying pan or omelet pan with the softened butter. Give the batter a quick whisking—it tends to separate during rising—and heat the pan over medium heat. Ladle the batter into the pan, making the blini any size you like, but keeping in mind that you have enough batter for thirty-two 4-inch [10-cm] blini. After about 2 minutes, bubbles will form on the surface of the blini. When the bubbles begin to break, after another minute, turn the blini over and cook for 1 or 2 minutes on the other side. If the blini brown too much before the bubbles break, turn down the heat. Place the blini on a parchment paper–covered sheet pan as you make them. If you end with more than one layer, cover the first layer with another sheet of parchment paper to keep them from sticking. You can make blini up to a day in advance and reheat them in a 250°F [120°/gas mark ½] oven for 10 minutes.

KIRSCH-FLAVORED SAVARIN CAKE

SAVARIN AU KIRSCH

MAKES 8 SERVINGS
(ONE 12-INCH [30.5-CM] SAVARIN)

A savarin is a doughnut-shaped cake that's dipped in, or brushed with, a liquor-flavored sugar syrup shortly before it is served. The great thing about a savarin is that you can make it days ahead of time. It doesn't matter if it gets stale, because it will be saturated with flavored syrup when you serve it. In addition to being easy to make and convenient, it's also a particularly delicious cake that is always moist.

A savarin batter is almost identical to a crêpe batter except that, like blini batter, it contains yeast and more flour. The difference, of course, is that a cake is not a pancake. For a savarin, you let the batter rise in the mold and then bake it, and you finish by unmolding the savarin and coating it with syrup. A savarin is really a bread, but one that's soaked in flavorful syrup.

To make a savarin, you'll need a special mold, a ring 10 or 12 inches [25.5 or 30.5 cm] in diameter. If you're going out to buy a new one, which shouldn't be expensive, you might as well get a nonstick one to make unmolding easier.

FOR THE CAKE:

1 teaspoon active dry yeast

1 cup [250 ml] milk, warmed until just slightly warm to the touch

4 eggs

pinch of salt

1 tablespoon granulated sugar

1½ cups [190 g] all-purpose white flour

2 tablespoons unsalted butter, softened

FOR THE SYRUP:

1 cup [200 g] granulated sugar

½ cup [125 ml] kirsch

COMBINE the yeast with 2 tablespoons of the milk and let sit in a warm place for about 10 minutes. Whisk the eggs, salt, and sugar in a large mixing bowl. Stir in the flour and add just enough of the milk so that you can work the mixture to a smooth paste. When the mixture is smooth, stir in the rest of the milk and the yeast mixture.

COVER the bowl with plastic wrap and leave in a warm place for about 1 hour, or in the refrigerator for about 4 hours, until the batter increases in volume by about 50 percent. (Don't let the batter rise too much or the savarin will become crumbly when you wet it with the syrup.)

SMEAR the softened butter on the inside of the mold—don't miss any spots—and refrigerate the mold for 15 minutes. Smear the mold with butter again and gently pour in the batter. Cover the mold with plastic wrap and leave it at room temperature for 30 minutes. Preheat the oven to 350°F [175°C/ gas mark 4].

PUT the mold on a sheet pan and bake for 25 to 30 minutes, until a paring knife slid into the savarin comes out with no batter clinging to it. Turn the savarin out of the mold as soon as it comes from the oven—if allowed to cool in the mold, it may stick. If you can't get it out of the mold, wrap the mold in aluminum foil for 10 minutes and try again. The trapped steam should loosen the savarin. Let the savarin cool, unwrapped, for 45 minutes. If you're not using it the same day, wrap it in plastic wrap and refrigerator it for up to 3 days. To freeze it instead, wrap it again in aluminum foil; it will keep for up to 3 months.

A few hours before you plan on serving the savarin, prepare a sugar syrup by combining the 1 cup [200 g] of sugar with 2 cups [500 ml] of water in a small saucepan, bringing the mixture to a boil just long enough to dissolve the sugar, and letting it cool to room temperature. Don't be tempted to reduce the amount of sugar in the syrup. If there's not enough sugar, the water weakens the savarin's structure and makes it crumbly. Stir the kirsch into the cooled syrup. (Flavorful spirits such as eaux-de-vie should never be added to hot mixtures, which would cause their flavor to evaporate.)

POKE the savarin with a skewer in about 8 places to help the syrup penetrate the crust. Set the savarin on a small cake pan and place the pan on a large baking dish or sheet pan with a rim to catch any syrup that flows off the savarin. Ladle the syrup over the savarin. When you've used all the syrup, scoop up the syrup that has run off the savarin and spoon it over again. Keep this up for about 5 minutes, until the savarin is completely soaked and there's hardly any syrup left. (Another method is to put the savarin back in the mold and spoon the syrup into the mold in increments, unmolding the savarin onto a platter when it won't absorb any more syrup.) Gently transfer the savarin to a serving dish, cover it with plastic wrap, and refrigerate for about 1 hour before serving. (Ideally, the savarin should be served cool but not cold.) Serve it in wedges at the table. Savarin is delicious with red berries and whipped cream, but these aren't essential.

Variations: If you want to make individual babas instead of a savarin, you'll need some 2-ounce or 3-ounce [60 to 90 ml] metal dariole molds. Make the savarin batter, but just before pouring it into the molds fold in ½ cup [70 g] of raisins that have been soaked for 30 minutes, or overnight, in barely enough kirsch, rum, or water to cover. Bake in a 350°F [175°C/ gas mark 4] oven for 20 to 25 minutes. To unmold, use a paring knife.

Pancakes, Waffles, and Madeleines

IF YOU MAKE A THICK CRÊPE BATTER WITH flour into which you've sifted a small amount of baking powder, you'll have pancake or waffle batter. But if you separate the eggs called for in a crêpe batter, add the yolks to the batter, and beat the egg whites and fold them into the batter, you'll end up with light and luxurious waffles and pancakes with none of the soda taste that sometimes sneaks through in recipes that include baking powder. If you take the same ingredients in crêpe batter, increase the amount of butter, add sugar and a tad of baking powder, and work the ingredients in a somewhat different order, you'll have madeleine batter. Madeleines are the little cakelike lemon cookies shaped like scallop shells that Proust made famous. They're worth learning how to make because they're easy and delicious and they cost about a dollar each in fancy pastry shops. The only downside is that madeleines require a special flat mold with scallop-shaped indentations, but this is a one-time purchase. It used to be that the only tricky part to making madeleines was getting them not to stick to the mold, but now you can buy nonstick molds that solve this problem. The molds, even nonstick versions, need to be brushed with softened butter to prevent sticking.

CLASSIC MADELEINES

MADELEINES CLASSIQUES

MAKES 24 MADELEINS

2 tablespoons softened butter (for brushing the molds), plus 1 stick (¼ pound [115 g]) unsalted butter, melted (for the batter)

1 lemon

2 cups [250 g] all-purpose flour

1½ teaspoons baking powder

3 large eggs

¾ cup [150 g] granulated sugar

⅔ cup [150 ml] milk

BRUSH 2 madeleine molds (assuming your molds make 12 madeleines each) with softened butter and slide the molds into the refrigerator. After about 15 minutes, brush them again, making sure you brush the butter around the indentations on top—otherwise, as the madeleines expand, they may stick to the top of the mold. Refrigerate again for at least 15 minutes.

GRATE the zest off half the lemon with the finest grater you have, and reserve the zest. Squeeze the lemon and reserve the juice.

WHISK the flour and baking powder in a mixing bowl to make sure the baking powder is well distributed in the flour.

MELT the butter and set it aside.

WHISK the eggs with the sugar, lemon zest, and lemon juice, by hand or in an electric mixer, for about 30 seconds. (There's so little beating involved in this recipe that I usually do it by hand.) Don't overwork the mixture.

THIN the mixture with ½ cup [125 ml] of the milk. Add the flour all at once—do this part by hand even if you started out using a mixer—and use a whisk to work the mixture just long enough to eliminate any lumps. Again, don't overwork the mixture or you'll work out the carbon dioxide produced by the baking powder and make the madeleines heavy. Gently stir in the rest of the milk and the melted butter. Refrigerate the batter for 20 minutes so that it stiffens slightly and becomes easier to work with. Stir once, quickly.

PREHEAT the oven to 425°F [220°C/gas mark 7].

PIPE the batter into the molds with a pastry bag, or use a spoon. Fill the molds to the top but no higher. Slide the molds into the oven and bake for 15 to 20 minutes, until the madeleines turn golden brown on top and rise above the top of the molds. (Turn the molds around halfway through the cooking so the madeleines all cook at the same time.) Immediately unmold the madeleines by turning them out onto a cake rack. Don't let them cool in the molds or they'll be too moist. Madeleines can be frozen, tightly wrapped, or kept in a tightly sealed tin or plastic bag for 3 days.

Turning Crêpe Batter into a Cake

ALL FRENCH PASTRIES ARE MADE BY MANIPU-lating four basic ingredients—butter, sugar, flour, and eggs—and sometimes milk or nuts, and occasionally yeast or baking powder, in different ways. Most of these methods are designed to incorporate air or, when yeast or baking powder is used, carbon dioxide, into the batter or dough so that once baked, the mixture rises instead of hardening into a leaden chunk. Two of France's lightest cakes are made by beating sugar and whole eggs (to make a sponge cake called *génoise*) or separated eggs (to make *biscuit*—a cake—or ladyfingers) and then folding the airy mixture with flour and sometimes melted butter.

If you change the amounts in crêpe batter and work the ingredients in a different way, you can make some of the most delicious cakes, called cream cakes, by first "creaming" butter with sugar, beating in eggs one by one, and sifting in flour. At times, baking powder is included to give the cake a little extra push and to make it lighter.

Frosted cakes are often too rich, and layers of very sweet and very rich frosting obscure the delicacy of the cake itself. My favorite of all cakes is pound cake, because it has real texture, so it doesn't need icing, and most of all because it tastes like butter. It's also easy to remember the recipe, because the name came from the amounts used—a pound of butter, a pound of flour, a pound of eggs, and a pound of sugar—although I usually cut the sugar a bit. (In French, pound cake is *quatre-quarts*, which means four quarters.) Pound cake is delicious just flavored with vanilla, but I like to add lemon zest. Most recipes for pound cake call for baking powder, which does make the cake lighter. Since I can always taste the baking powder and I like pound cake dense and rich, I leave it out. Making a pound cake light with no leavening, however, can be tricky and requires superfine sugar, ingredients at room temperature, and a large loaf pan to allow the heat to penetrate. If you don't want to go out and buy superfine sugar, which dissolves quickly, you can make it by working regular granulated sugar in a food processor for 3 minutes.

LEMON AND VANILLA POUND CAKE

QUATRE-QUARTS AU CITRON ET À LA VANILLE

MAKES 10 TO 12 SERVINGS (ONE 2-QUART [2 L] LOAF)

I like to serve this cake with a dollop of whipped cream and, if they're in season, fresh berries. It's even better, sliced and lightly toasted, for breakfast or with an afternoon coffee.

- 1 tablespoon softened butter (for the loaf pan), plus 2½ sticks (10 ounces [280 g]) unsalted butter at room temperature

  finely grated zest from 1 lemon

- 1 cup [200 g] superfine sugar, either store-bought or homemade (see headnote)

- 5 large eggs, allowed to come to room temperature

- 1 teaspoon vanilla extract

- ¼ cup milk

- ¼ teaspoon salt

- 2 cups [250 g] all purpose flour

BRUSH or rub the inside of a 2-quart [2-l] loaf pan with softened butter. (I get the best results using a pan 10 inches [25.5 cm] long, 5¼ inches [13 cm] wide, and 3 inches [7.5 cm] high.) Line the bottom and sides of the loaf pan with rectangles of parchment paper and brush or rub the rectangles with more butter. Put the lined loaf pan in the refrigerator while you're making the batter.

PREHEAT the oven to 350°F [175°C/gas mark 4].

ADD the lemon zest to the butter, and cream the butter by beating it in an electric mixer with the paddle blade until it becomes creamy and light, about 5 minutes. You can also cream it by hand, with a wooden spoon, but be warned, this is laborious and takes 12 to 15 minutes. Work the sugar into the creamed butter, one-fourth at a time, and beat for 5 minutes more in the electric mixer or 10 minutes more by hand to incorporate air.

WITH the electric mixer or by hand, work the eggs into the butter mixture one by one, waiting until each one is incorporated before adding another. Don't worry if the egg-butter mixture separates. Beat in the vanilla extract and milk.

ADD the salt and the flour all at once and work the mixture quickly in the mixer or by hand. You want to work it as little as possible, so you don't activate the gluten and make the cake heavy. As soon as the flour is incorporated, stop beating.

POUR the batter into the lined loaf pan and rap the pan on the kitchen counter a couple of times to get rid of any bubbles. Run a knife lengthwise down the middle of the cake, about 1 inch into the batter, so that an even opening forms along the length of the cake as it bakes. (Otherwise the cake may crack in an unsightly way.) Slide the pan into the oven. Bake until a paring knife, slid through the top into the middle of the cake, comes out clean and the cake pulls away from the sides of the loaf pan, 60 to 70 minutes.

LET cool for about 5 minutes and turn the cake out of the pan. Pound cake can be wrapped tightly in plastic wrap and kept at room temperature for up to 1 week (refrigerating dries it out). Or it can be wrapped again in aluminum foil and frozen for up to 3 months. The whole pound cake, or individual slices, can be reheated gently in the oven.

REGIONAL BUTTER CAKES

Most people who visit Paris for the first time gain several pounds because they can't resist the displays of pastry in patisserie windows. Because many of the elaborate *gateaux, tartes,* and creamy fantasies of classic French pastry-making require years of training to make, most French people buy such desserts at the corner patisserie. Simple cakes and tarts, which I find more satisfying than their sweeter and more elaborate classic cousins, are sometimes made at home. Many regions in France have their own dessert specialties, the most popular of which are simple cakes made with flour, sugar, eggs, plenty of butter, and sometimes yeast and sometimes nuts. Brittany has several such cakes, including the *far breton,* which has become popular in Paris patisseries. The Parisian version is dome-shaped and black on top, as though it spent too much time in the oven, but in Brittany a *far* is a kind of sweet porridge, containing raisins or prunes and plenty of eggs, that is baked into what looks like something between a cake and a flan. Breton cooks also make a yeast butter cake, *kuoing aman,* which is made in much the same way as croissant dough and puff pastry, by rolling out a yeast-leavened dough with butter folded up into it and then continually folding the pastry over itself and rolling so that the number of layers, multiplied by three during each rolling, reaches into the hundreds. A *gâteau breton* is almost identical to pound cake, except that it's even richer (egg yolks replace the whole eggs), it's baked in a tart mold, and it has a lattice design on top. In nearby Normandy, a yeast-leavened cake called a *fallue,* or sometimes a *gâche,* is made much like brioche except that the dough is folded over itself a couple of times (like puff pastry or croissant dough) and baked into flattened ovals.

In the southwest, you'll run into a *pignola* (from *pignon,* meaning pine nut), which is a butter cake containing almonds and pine nuts baked in a sweet tart shell. In the Basque country, and nowadays in plenty of other places, you'll encounter *gâteau basque,* made by sandwiching rum-flavored pastry cream (the stiff custard-like cream used as a filling for éclairs) between two rounds of pastry dough and baking. (Sometimes the pastry cream is replaced with the more regional *milhassou,* a pastry cream made with corn flour.) In the Béarn region, in the Pyrenees mountains, they make *le feuilleté béarnais,* a cake made by baking an almond pastry cream between two rounds of puff pastry, which is first folded over itself in the usual way but is finished by being rolled out into thin sheets and layered over the filling. Older recipes call also for goose fat. The better known *pithivier,* from the region of Orléans, is made by sandwiching almond paste between two rounds of puff pastry. A more rustic cousin, from nearby, is the *tartouillat,* made much like a *gâteau béarnais,* but filled with apples and squash (!) instead of pastry cream.

(continued)

Alsace has its own cakes, the most famous of which is no doubt the *kugelhopf*, made in a distinctive fluted mold with a hole in the middle, in English called a tube pan. Much like a brioche, a *kugelhopf* is made with yeast but is less rich because it contains less butter. It also contains raisins and almonds. *Berawecka* is a kind of fruitcake made with dried fruits, nuts, spices, and plenty of eau-de-vie, usually kirsch or quetsch, which is made from little red plums.

A *galette pérougienne*, made in several regions in France, is one of my favorites of all sweet things. To make it, roll out a large round of brioche and bake the pastry in a hot oven. When the brioche is golden brown on top, sprinkle it liberally with sugar and dollop it generously with créme fraîche (some recipes use butter instead). Cook it for about 10 minutes more, until the cream is absorbed into the *galette*.

FLOATING ISLANDS

ÎLES FLOTTANTES

HOW TO	HOW TO	HOW TO	HOW TO
MAKE CARAMEL THREADS	MAKE MERINGUE AND USE IT IN DIFFERENT WAYS	MAKE TWO KINDS OF CHOCOLATE FROSTING	MAKE MACARONS AND LADYFINGERS

FOR SOME REASON, FLOATING ISLANDS SEEM TO HAVE GONE OUT OF fashion. I rarely see them on menus anymore, perhaps because they're simple and we've come to expect elaborate desserts in restaurants. Or perhaps it's because they contain no chocolate, or because the flavor of their principal ingredient, the egg, is left virtually undisguised, as it might be in a piece of cake. For me, a floating island holds the same bittersweet nostalgia as an Edith Piaf song. It evokes something profoundly French, something lost. I eat it with a kind of contented sadness.

Another reason for floating islands' lack of popularity may be that almost everyone confuses them with *oeufs à la neige*, a dish that nowadays is far more likely to appear on the menu of an inexpensive corner restaurant in France. The difference is simple. Both are made with barely cooked meringue—egg whites beaten with sugar—but the meringue for floating islands is combined with hazelnuts and baked in a mold, while *oeufs à la neige* (the name can be loosely translated as "snow eggs") are made by poaching dollops of the meringue in sweetened milk or water. *Îles flottantes* are unmolded and served surrounded with crème anglaise—hence the impression of an island—while *oeufs à la neige* are left to float on the crème anglaise, like puffy clouds. Often, thin threads of caramel are pulled over the top of the clouds for decoration (see page 665).

Both of these dishes have a natural economy, since the egg whites are used to make the meringue and the yolks used to make the sauce, the crème anglaise. *Îles flottantes* require a few crushed hazelnuts. In France, pralines, which are sugar-coated hazelnuts, are used, but I haven't been able to find them in the United States and the sugar coating to my mind is superfluous. I toast whole hazelnuts to bring out their flavor and help remove their skins and then crush them in a towel by leaning on them with the bottom edge of a pot. My favorite molds for *îles flottantes* are small charlotte molds—fez-shaped metal molds with heart-shaped handles—but since these are expensive, you can substitute 5-ounce [155 ml] ramekins. The molds are best brushed on the inside with hazelnut oil (see page 36 for more about nut oils), but a flavorless vegetable oil will also work. Floating islands can be made earlier the same day, and in fact this is better because it gives you time to chill the crème anglaise. They should be unmolded as soon as they come out of the oven and kept, covered with plastic wrap, in the refrigerator or in a cool place.

FLOATING ISLANDS

ÎLES FLOTTANTES

FOR THE FLOATING ISLANDS:

⅔ cup [90 g] hazelnuts

2 teaspoons hazelnut oil or flavorless vegetable oil (for rubbing the inside of the molds)

6 egg whites (from large eggs; yolks reserved for the crème anglaise)

   tiny pinch of cream of tartar (unless you're using a copper bowl for beating the egg whites)

¾ cup [150 g] superfine sugar

FOR THE CRÈME ANGLAISE:

2 cups [500 ml] milk

1 vanilla bean, split in half lengthwise, or 1 teaspoon vanilla extract

6 egg yolks (from large eggs)

½ cup [100 g] granulated sugar

PREHEAT the oven to 350°F [175°C/gas mark 4]. Bake the hazelnuts on a sheet pan until they smell toasty, about 15 minutes, and immediately pour them out onto a clean kitchen towel and sprinkle them with cold water. Turn the oven down to 325°F [165°C/gas mark 3]. Fold over the towel and roll the hazelnuts with your hands over the towel on the counter to scrape off as much of the thin, dark skin as you can. Pick the nuts out of the towel—don't worry if some of the skin stays stuck to the nuts—and place them on the counter. Place a small pot or saucepan on top of the nuts and rock it back and forth to crush them. Don't overdo it—the nuts should just be broken into a few pieces, not turned into flour.

BRING about 3 quarts [3 l] of water to a boil for a bain-marie (water bath; page 634). There should be enough water to come halfway up the sides of the molds for the floating islands.

RUB the inside of the molds with the oil.

BEAT the egg whites with the cream of tartar (don't use the cream of tartar if you're using a copper bowl) in an electric mixer on high speed until they are stiff, about 1½ minutes. Add the sugar and beat for about 45 seconds more, until the whites get very stiff and shiny. Taste a dollop of the meringue to make sure the sugar has dissolved and there's no hint of crunch. (If you're beating the egg whites by hand, count on 4 to 5 minutes of vigorous beating before adding the sugar and then 2 to 3 minutes more beating after adding the sugar.) Fold the hazelnuts into the beaten egg whites with a rubber spatula, sliding the spatula down the side of the bowl and gently lifting up from the bottom, until the hazelnuts are distributed evenly throughout the meringue.

USE the spatula to transfer the meringue to the molds. If you're using 5-ounce [155 ml] ramekins, fill them to the top and smooth off the top with the spatula. Put the molds in a baking dish or straight-sided pan with sides that are at least the height of the molds. Pour the boiling water into the dish so that it comes halfway up the sides of the molds. Place the baking dish on the stove over high heat for about 2 minutes, until you hear the water barely begin to bubble up under the molds. Bake for about 25 minutes, until the meringue rises about 1 inch.

WHILE the floating islands are baking, prepare the crème anglaise with the reserved egg yolks and the rest of the ingredients listed above, following the directions on page 642. Refrigerate the crème anglaise, covered with plastic wrap (to prevent a skin from forming on its surface). Or, if you're in a hurry, put it in a bowl over another bowl of ice water and stir it until it's cool.

WHEN the floating islands are ready, let them cool for 5 minutes. Gently invert the molds. If they stick, run a knife around the inside of the molds. Unmold the floating islands onto individual plates with deep rims and spoon the crème anglaise around them.

MERINGUE SNOW EGGS

OEUFS À LA NEIGE

MAKES 6 DESSERT SERVINGS

These are even easier to make than îles flottantes because you don't need molds and you don't need hazelnuts. If you want to make an easy and inexpensive (and very French) dessert when all you have in the house are eggs, milk, and sugar, oeufs à la neige are the answer.

Most recipes for oeufs à la neige have you poach amorphous cloudlike dollops of the meringue in sweetened milk. The milk is then combined with the reserved egg yolks and cooked into a crème anglaise. I prefer to use sweetened water for poaching the meringue and make the crème anglaise separately, because milk tends to separate and leave tiny curds on the meringue.

FOR THE CRÈME ANGLAISE:

6　large eggs

2　cups [500 ml] milk

1　vanilla bean, split in half lengthwise, or 1 teaspoon vanilla extract

½　cup [100 g] granulated sugar

FOR THE SNOW EGGS:

½　cup [100 g] granulated sugar

6　egg whites (from large eggs—you will have used the yolks for the crème anglaise)

　tiny pinch of cream of tartar (unless you're using a copper bowl to beat the egg whites)

¼　cup [50 g] superfine sugar

FOR THE OPTIONAL CARAMEL:

1　cup [200 g] granulated sugar (see page 639)

SEPARATE the eggs. Reserve the whites at room temperature in a bowl covered with plastic wrap.

Prepare the crème anglaise with the egg yolks and the rest of the ingredients listed above, following the directions on page 642. Chill the crème anglaise in the refrigerator, covered with plastic wrap, or by stirring it in a bowl set in another bowl of ice water.

COMBINE the granulated sugar with 2 quarts [2 l] of water in a wide sauté pan or baking dish with high sides. Place the pan on the stove and bring the water to a boil. Turn the heat down to keep the water at a bare simmer.

BEAT the reserved egg whites with the cream of tartar (don't use the cream of tartar if you're using a copper bowl) in an electric mixer on high speed until they are stiff, about 1½ minutes. Add the superfine sugar and beat for about 45 seconds more until the whites get stiff and shiny. Taste a dollop of the meringue to make sure the sugar has dissolved and there's no hint of crunch. (If you're beating the egg whites by hand, count on 4 to 5 minutes of vigorous beating before adding the sugar and then 2 to 3 minutes more beating after adding the sugar.)

TAKE the meringue out of the bowl with a large spoon and place a large dollop—one-sixth of the mixture—on the simmering sweetened water. Add 5 more dollops, being careful not to let them touch one another. You'll probably have to work in batches. Poach the meringues—they won't really poach, because they float on top of the liquid—for about 10 minutes. Flip them over with a spatula or slotted spoon and poach them on the second side for 10 minutes more. Use a slotted spoon—or two if the snow eggs are being unwieldy—to transfer them to a sheet pan covered with a sheet of wax paper. Let them drain for at least 15 minutes so that any water they release doesn't end up in the crème anglaise.

POUR the crème anglaise into a dish or platter large enough to hold it and all the meringues. Gently place the snow eggs on top of the crème anglaise with a slotted spoon. If you like, decorate them with caramel threads. (See "Caramel Threads," page 665.)

CARAMEL THREADS

If you make caramel (see page 639), you can pull it into threads and then swirl the threads over *oeufs à la neige*. The effect is mainly decorative, and the technique, while easy to master, looks terribly impressive. To try this, dip a fork into the hot caramel, which you should first cool slightly by immersing the bottom of the pan in a bowl of cold water for about 3 seconds. Pull the caramel away from the tines of the fork with your fingers. Initially the caramel will be too thin (and too hot to touch), but as it cools on the fork, you'll be able to pull it away in long threads. I work directly over the snow eggs so the threads just fall on top. As the caramel cools on the fork, it will harden and become difficult to work. When this happens, just dip the fork again into the pan of caramel. If the caramel in the pan starts to harden, heat it over low heat, while stirring with the fork, until it thins again.

If you're feeling ambitious and need lots of threads, make them the professional way. Use a pair of wire cutters to cut the tops off the wires of a large balloon whisk just where they begin to curve. You'll end up with a bizarre-looking gadget that looks like it was electrocuted—the wires will stick straight out. To make the threads, stand at the end of a table (ideally marble or metal) that you've rubbed lightly with vegetable oil and dip your new instrument about 1 inch [2.5 cm] into the caramel. Swing the whisk forward and quickly snap it back as though fly-fishing. This will take practice because the temperature (and thus the consistency) of the caramel has to be just right, but once you get the knack, the threads of caramel will fly off the ends of the whisk and before you know it, you'll have a big pile.

You can also use threads of caramel to make dome-shaped cages that you can place over individual servings of dessert. To do this, select a stainless steel bowl that's the size you want for the cage and rub it on the inside with vegetable oil. Make the caramel threads a bit on the thick side, using the fork method, and line the inside of the bowl with a random crisscross pattern. Let the caramel set for a couple of minutes and then carefully place your hand against the inside of the bowl and rotate the bowl and release the cage. Don't try making these cages more than a few hours before you need them or they'll begin to sag. If the day is hot and humid, you can still use threads—make them shortly before serving—but put off the cages for another time.

During the seventeenth and eighteenth centuries, when pastry cooks started separating eggs and working the whites and yolks in different ways, they invented many of the basic dessert mixtures still used today. We've already seen what happens when the best-known meringue, sometimes called French meringue, is cooked in a mold in a bain-marie (*îles flottantes*) or directly in simmering liquid (*oeufs à la neige*). It ends up having a soft and delightfully spongy texture. When a very similar meringue (still French meringue, but made with some powdered sugar to keep it dry) is baked, we end up with the crunchy white and sweet meringue that's served with whipped cream or ice cream. In France, a cake called a *vacherin* is made by layering various ice creams or sorbets between rounds of baked meringue.

Swiss meringue, which has almost exactly the same proportions of sugar and egg white, is made by heating the egg whites while they are beaten and beating them longer than for French meringue. The result is a firmer mixture that is used for making cookies or the small decorative mushrooms on a *bûche de noël,* or is piped through a pastry bag to make meringue cups for holding ice cream, sorbet, or mousse. While Swiss meringue holds up better than French meringue, it lacks the delicate, crunchy (yet melt-in-the-mouth) texture of French meringue.

Italian meringue is made by pouring hot sugar syrup, cooked to the soft-ball stage (see page 628), into egg whites while they're being beaten. The result is the fluffy white mixture that, in America at least, is most often used as an icing for cakes. In France, Italian meringue is combined with fruit purée as a base for frozen soufflés and for various mousses. It is also used to make the French equivalent of baked Alaska, *omelette norvégienne* (Norwegian omelet), a cube of ice cream covered on all sides with a square of layer cake, finished with Italian meringue, and flambéed.

One of the earliest cakes, a kind of sponge cake called *biscuit* (pronounced bees-KWEE), is made by combining sweetened beaten egg whites with egg yolks and flour and then baking it like a cake or piping it out into short strips with a pastry bag to make ladyfingers. When French meringue is combined with powdered hazelnuts (or a mixture of powdered hazelnuts and almonds) and flour and then baked in rounds, it becomes a *succès.* A similar mixture is used to make rounds for a cake called a *dacquoise.* Powdered nuts, combined with raw meringue and piped out into little disks, are baked into little cookies. A bit of jam is placed on the bottom of the cookies and the bottoms are pressed together, two at a time, to make *macarons* (not to be confused with macaroons, which are made with coconut).

BAKED MERINGUE CUPS WITH CHANTILLY CREAM

MERINGUES À LA CHANTILLY

MAKE 6 DESSERT SERVINGS

Once you bake these meringues, you can fill them with whipped cream, ice cream, or chocolate mousse. I like whipped cream more than ice cream because it can be made far less sweet, although you can make mousse or your own ice cream by putting crème anglaise (see page 641) in an ice cream machine and, if you like, use less sugar. Classic Chantilly cream is different from whipped cream because it contains sugar and vanilla. When I use it to fill meringue cups, I use very little sugar. When baking meringue, remember that you're actually drying it out rather than cooking it, and this requires long cooking at a low temperature. If the oven gets too hot, it will turn the meringues brown when, in fact, they should be perfectly white. Meringues can be made up to 3 days in advance and kept tightly sealed in plastic bags.

FOR THE MERINGUES:

6   egg whites (from large eggs)

    tiny pinch of cream of tartar (unless you're using a
    copper bowl to beat the egg whites)

¾   cup [150 g] superfine sugar

1   cup [120 g] confectioners' sugar

FOR THE CHANTILLY CREAM:

2   cups [500 ml] heavy cream

1   teaspoon vanilla extract

1   tablespoon confectioners' sugar

PREHEAT the oven to 200°F [95°C].

BEAT the egg whites with the cream of tartar in an electric mixer on high speed until they are stiff, about 1½ minutes. (Don't use the cream of tartar if you're using a copper bowl.) Add the superfine sugar and beat for about 45 seconds more, until the whites get very stiff and shiny. Taste a dollop of the meringue to make sure the sugar has dissolved and there's no hint of crunch. (If you're beating the egg whites by hand, count on 4 to 5 minutes of vigorous beating before adding the sugar and then 2 to 3 minutes more beating after adding the sugar.) Whether using a mixer or working by hand, work the confectioners' sugar through a strainer over the egg whites and fold the sugar by hand into the whites until the mixture is smooth.

USE a ramekin or small plate and a pencil to draw six 4-inch [10-cm] diameter rounds on a sheet of parchment paper. Fit a pastry bag with a number 6 tip (½ inch [1.5 cm] in diameter) and load the pastry bag with the meringue. Put a tiny dollop of the meringue on 4 corners of a sheet pan to hold the parchment in place, and place the sheet of parchment paper, circles down—you'll be able to see them through the paper—pushing down in the corners. Pipe the meringue, starting in the center of each circle and working toward the outside, until you have six 4-inch-diameter [10 cm] rounds. Pipe walls around the edges of the circles so the

meringue is about 3 rings high, making a holder for the cream. Make a total of 6 meringue holders. If you don't have a pastry bag, use a large spoon to arrange the meringue within the circles into 6 individual mounds, each about 4 inches [10 cm] in diameter. Be sure they don't touch each other on the sheet pan. Press down in the middle of each of the mounds with the back of a spoon you've dipped in cold water, making an indentation to hold the whipped cream. Slide the sheet pan into the oven and bake the meringues for 3 to 5 hours. Test for doneness by touching one of the meringues. There should be no hint of stickiness. If they feel dry, pull one away from the parchment and feel its heft—when the meringues are done they should feel very light. If they're not done, bake for 30 minutes more and test again.

WHEN the meringues are done, prepare the Chantilly cream by combining the cream, vanilla, and sugar in a mixing bowl or the bowl of an electric mixer. Put the bowl in the freezer for 5 minutes and then beat quickly (or on high speed) until the cream is stiff. Mound the cream in the center of each meringue and serve.

Variations: The *montblanc*, a dessert you're likely to encounter in a Parisian café, is made by spreading a layer of sweetened chestnut purée (*crème de marrons*), which you can make yourself but is perfectly acceptable out of a can, in a meringue shell, dolloping Chantilly cream over it, and then grating bittersweet chocolate on top. The best brand of chestnut purée is from Clément Faugier, which makes both a sweetened version (which is what you need) and an unsweetened one. The unsweetened version, with some butter added, is good with game or red meat.

Fresh whole berries, puréed berries, or sorbet can provide a delightfully tart contrast to the sweetness of the meringue. Ice cream isn't bad either.

INDIVIDUAL CHOCOLATE MERINGUE CAKES

GÂTEAUX MERINGUÉS

MAKES 8 DESSERT SERVINGS

I first sampled one of these cakes in a restaurant in the east of France, Chez la Mère Blanc, and thought it was the most delicious thing I had ever tasted. I assumed that making anything so good required years of training, so it came as a pleasant surprise when I realized that it involved only two basic mixtures: meringue, which is actually the "cake," and ganache, a simple mixture of cream and chocolate. The only possibly scary thing is that you'll need a pastry bag with a ¼-inch [.5-cm] tip to make the rings and a ½-inch [1.5 cm] tip for the chocolate; but this recipe is straightforward and in fact is a good way to get used to a pastry bag. The filling is made by whipping ganache—essentially chocolate that's been melted in hot heavy cream—and the outside is coated with ganache that hasn't been whipped. You can control the consistency of a ganache by adjusting the amount of chocolate to heavy cream. A ganache that's perfect for chocolate sauce on ice cream is made with equal parts chocolate and cream—8 ounces [225 g] of bittersweet chocolate to 1 cup of heavy cream—but to ice a cake you need a slightly thicker mixture, about 10 ounces [280 g] of chocolate to 1 cup of cream. You can control the sweetness of ganache by using varying amounts of bittersweet, bitter, or sweet chocolate. In this recipe I make the chocolate quite bitter to balance the sweetness of the meringue.

The meringue disks can be made up to 1 week in advance if they're kept tightly sealed in plastic bags, and the cakes can be assembled up to 24 hours in advance.

FOR THE MERINGUE DISKS:

4 egg whites (from large eggs)

tiny pinch cream of tartar (unless you're using a copper bowl to beat the egg whites)

¾ cup [150 g] superfine sugar

1 cup [120 g] confectioners' sugar

FOR THE GANACHE:

2½ cups [525 ml] heavy cream

1½ pounds [675 g] bittersweet chocolate (see "Chocolate," page 669)

2 teaspoons vanilla extract

TO PREPARE THE MERINGUE DISKS

PREHEAT the oven to 200°F [95°C].

BEAT the egg whites with the cream of tartar with an electric mixer on high speed until they are stiff, about 1½ minutes. (Don't use the cream of tartar if you're using a copper bowl.) Add the superfine sugar and beat for about 45 seconds more, until the whites get very stiff and shiny. Taste a dollop of the meringue to make sure the sugar has dissolved and there's no hint of crunch. (If you're beating the egg whites by hand, count on 4 to 5 minutes of vigorous beating before adding the sugar and then 2 to 3 minutes more beating after adding the sugar.) Work the confectioners' sugar through a strainer over the egg whites and fold the sugar, by hand, into the whites until smooth.

WITH a pencil, draw eight 3½-inch [9-cm] circles on each of two sheets of parchment paper just large enough to fit into 12-by-18-inch [30.5-by-45.5-cm] sheet pans. (I draw around a 5-ounce [155-ml] ramekin.) Put the parchment paper, drawing side down, into the two sheet pans.

FIT the pastry bag with a number 1 (¼ inch [.5 cm]) tip and load it with the meringue mixture. Pipe a tiny dollop of meringue under each corner of the parchment paper to hold it down. Pipe out the meringue, starting in the center of a pencilled ring (which will be visible through the paper) and forming a spiral until you get to the outside line. Hold the tip of the pastry bag about ¾ inch [2 cm] above the paper. If you hold it too low, you'll flatten the meringue; if you hold it too high, it will be hard to control. Continue until you've made all 16 disks.

SLIDE the meringue disks into the oven and bake for 3 hours. Test for doneness by touching one of the disks—there should be no hint of stickiness. If the meringue starts to brown, turn the oven down to warm. Remove from the oven, let cool, and gently pull the disks off the parchment paper and reserve. (If the meringues refuse to cook, take them out of the oven for 10 minutes and touch them again—they sometimes don't feel crunchy until they cool.)

TO PREPARE THE WHIPPED AND REGULAR GANACHE AND ASSEMBLE THE MERINGUE CAKES

BRING 1 cup [250 ml] of cream to simmer in a saucepan (or in a cup in the microwave) and pour it into the mixing bowl of an electric mixer. While the cream is coming to a simmer, use a knife to break half the chocolate into pieces about the size of hazelnuts. Put the chocolate into the hot cream and let it sit, off the heat, for 5 minutes. Add the vanilla and gently stir the mixture—the ganache—with a whisk until it's perfectly smooth. (I use the whisk attachment to the mixer.) Put the bowl with the mixture in the refrigerator for about an hour, until the bottom of the bowl

feels cold to the touch. Beat the mixture on high speed until it looks whipped and gets paler, about 3 minutes. Put it back in the refrigerator for 5 minutes to stiffen it.

FIT a pastry bag with a number 6 (½ inch [1.5 cm]) plain tip. Put the whipped ganache into the bag and pipe it in a spiral pattern along the top of 8 of the meringue disks. Place another disk on top of each ganache-topped disk—top turned down side against the chocolate—and gently press. If you have any ganache left over, pipe it around the outside of each meringue cake and even it off with a spatula. Refrigerate the meringue cakes while you prepare the regular ganache.

BRING the rest of the cream to a simmer in a saucepan (or in a cup in the microwave) and take it off the heat. While the cream is coming to the simmer, use a knife to break the rest of the chocolate into pieces about the size of hazelnuts. Put the chocolate into the hot cream and let sit, off the heat, for 5 minutes. Add the vanilla and gently stir the ganache with a whisk until it's perfectly smooth. Put the ganache in the refrigerator until it stiffens slightly and it's just slightly warm to the touch, about 20 minutes.

CHOCOLATE

Many cooks are stumped when they try to replicate a chocolate dessert tasted in a restaurant and are left wondering why their own version doesn't taste as good. Most of the time it has to do with the quality of the chocolate. In Europe, chocolate is required by law to have the percentage of cocoa—the flavorful aromatic component in chocolate—printed on the package. In general, the higher the cocoa content, the more flavorful the chocolate. For bittersweet chocolate, the cocoa content ranges from around 50 percent all the way up to around 70 percent. Other factors, such as the origin of the cocoa beans (those from Central America are considered the best) and the way the chocolate is processed also influence the quality. My favorite brands are Scharffen Berger, made in Berkeley, California, and Valrhona, from France (see Sources).

PUT the sheet pan holding the meringue cakes on a level surface and ladle 2 tablespoons [30 ml] of the ganache over the center of each one so that the tops of the meringues are completely covered. (A 1-fluid-ounce ladle comes in handy here.) Refrigerate the meringue cakes and the ganache, or leave them in a cool place, so the ganache gets stiff enough to spread and the ganache on top of the meringue cakes sets, about 30 minutes. Use a small knife or spatula to spread the stiffened ganache along the sides of the meringue cakes. Serve within 48 hours.

ALMOND MERINGUE COOKIES WITH FRUIT JAM

MACARONS

MAKES ABOUT 30 COOKIES

Macarons, not to be confused with macaroons, are made using a mixture similar to a basic meringue except that the beaten egg whites used to make the *macaron* mixture are combined not only with sugar, as they are when making meringue, but also with powdered almonds. The mixture is piped out into small rounds on a sheet pan and the little cookies, once baked, are stuck together with a dollop of fruit jam. You can use any jam you like. For that matter, you don't have to use jam at all. You can use chocolate (for a ganache filling, see the recipe for Individual Chocolate Meringue Cakes, page 668). Or you can even use peanut butter or Nutella (Italian hazelnut butter).

- 1 cup [145 g] blanched almonds, toasted for 10 to 15 minutes in a 350°F [175°C/gas mark 4] oven, until pale brown and fragrant
- 1 cup [120 g] confectioners' sugar
- 5 egg whites (from large eggs)

  pinch of cream of tartar (unless you're beating the egg whites in a copper bowl)
- ¼ cup [50 g] superfine sugar
- ½ cup [160 g] flavorful good-quality fruit jam such as strawberry or raspberry, or an assortment

WHEN the toasted almonds have cooled, combine them with the confectioners' sugar in a food processor and purée the mixture. After 2 minutes, use a rubber spatula to scrape down the inside of the food processor to make sure the almonds are being ground evenly. Beat for a total of 4 minutes. Transfer the mixture to a bowl and break any remaining lumps with your fingers.

PREHEAT the oven to 300°F [150°C/gas mark 2].

BEAT the egg whites with the cream of tartar in an electric mixer on high speed until they are stiff, about 1½ minutes. (Don't use the cream of tartar if you're using a copper bowl.) Add the superfine sugar and beat for about 45 seconds more, until the whites get very stiff and shiny. Taste a dollop of the meringue to make sure the sugar has dissolved and there's no hint of crunch. (If you're beating the egg whites by hand, count on 4 to 5 minutes of vigorous beating before adding the sugar and then 2 to 3 minutes more beating after adding the sugar.)

FOLD the almond mixture into the egg whites by folding the whites with a rubber spatula—be sure to scrape the sides and bottom of the bowl—while sprinkling them with the almond mixture. Try to do this in less than a minute so you don't overwork the whites.

PUT a dollop of the *macaron* mixture in the corners of 2 sheet pans and cover each pan with a sheet of parchment paper.

FIT a pastry bag with a ⅓-inch [1-cm] tip and pipe rounds of the mixture, about 1 inch [2.5 cm] across, onto the sheet pans. To do this easily, hold the tip of the pastry bag about ½ inch [1.5 cm] above the sheet pan and squeeze out the mixture. When the mixture spreads into an inch-wide round, quickly jerk up the pastry bag tip. Smooth out any points with a finger dipped in cold water. Make 60 rounds (it takes 2 rounds to make each *macaron*). Slide the sheet pans into the oven and bake for about 15 to 20 minutes, until the *macarons* are pale blond. Halfway through the baking, turn the sheet pans around and switch them so the *macarons* bake evenly. Take the *macarons* out of the oven, let cool completely on the sheet pan, and pull them off the paper. Spread about ½ teaspoon of jam on the bottom of one *macaron* and press the bottom of another macaron onto it. Continue until you've made 30 cookies.

LADYFINGERS
BISCUITS À LA CUILLER

MAKES ABOUT 35 LADYFINGERS

Most of us who've tasted ladyfingers out of a box have been unimpressed. They taste stale and sugary. If we ever used them it was likely to be in a dessert such as tiramisù or trifle, or to line a charlotte mold. But homemade ladyfingers, made the same day, are an entirely different experience. Their texture is ever so slightly crunchy on the outside yet cakelike on the inside. Ladyfingers are great when served as you would any cookie—with a cup of tea or coffee or as an accent to a dessert such as ice cream.

Ladyfingers are made with the same mixture used to make the French sponge cake, called biscuit, in which egg whites and egg yolks are beaten separately, both with sugar, and the two folded together while being sprinkled with flour. When used for a cake, this mixture is just put in cake pans and baked; when used to make ladyfingers, it is piped out in strips with a pastry bag.

Ladyfingers are best straight out of the oven, but if tightly sealed in plastic bags they will keep for up to 2 weeks at room temperature. You don't need perfectly fresh ladyfingers when they are incorporated into other desserts in which their subtlety is lost.

  5 large eggs

  ¾ cup [95 g] superfine sugar

     pinch of cream of tartar (unless you're using a copper bowl for beating the whites)

  ¾ cup [95 g] flour, sifted onto a sheet of wax paper

  1 tablespoon softened butter

  2 tablespoons flour (for coating the sheet pans)

  ¾ cup [90 g] plus 1 tablespoon confectioners' sugar

PREHEAT the oven to 375°F [190°C/gas mark 5].

SEPARATE the eggs, putting the whites directly in the bowl you plan to use for beating them—one that's large enough for folding the finished mixture.

COMBINE ¼ cup [30 g] of the superfine sugar with the egg yolks and stir the mixture with a small whisk until the sugar dissolves and the yolks turn paler. A ribbon made in the yolks should hold its shape for 4 seconds. Gently stir in ¼ cup [30 g] of the flour. Stir just until the mixture is smooth. Don't overwork the flour or the mixture will be heavy.

COMBINE the egg whites with the cream of tartar (unless you're using a copper bowl) and beat the whites to stiff peaks with an electric mixer on high speed until they are stiff, about 1½ minutes. Add the remaining superfine sugar and beat for about 45 seconds more, until the whites get very stiff and shiny. Taste a dollop of the meringue to make sure the sugar has dissolved and there's no hint of crunch. (If you're beating the egg whites by hand, count on 4 to 5 minutes of vigorous beating before adding the sugar and then 2 to 3 minutes more beating after adding the sugar.)

POUR the egg yolk mixture over the beaten egg whites—use a rubber spatula to get all the yolk mixture out of the bowl. Add half the remaining sifted flour to the mixture, and fold the two mixtures and the flour together, sliding the rubber spatula along the sides of the bowl all the way down to the bottom and then lifting and folding the bottom over the top. Add the rest of the sifted flour to the mixture. Fold only until all the ingredients are evenly incorporated. Don't overwork the mixture.

PUT a small dollop of the mixture in the corners of 2 sheet pans and cover each pan with a sheet of parchment paper, pressing the paper down on the dollops to hold it in place. Brush the paper with the softened butter and put the 2 tablespoons of flour in one of the sheet pans. Working over a sink or large work surface, shake the pan until the paper is completely coated with flour and then dump the flour that doesn't cling into the second pan. Shake it in the same way. Hit the back of the sheet pans to get rid of excess flour.

FIT a pastry bag with a ½-inch [1.5-cm] tip (see page 14), load it with the mixture, and pipe out the mixture in 4-inch [10 cm] strips, about 20 per sheet pan. While piping, hold the tip of the pastry bag about 1 inch [2.5 cm] above the surface of the sheet pan. Hold a strainer over the ladyfingers, fill it with half the confectioners' sugar, and shake the sugar over the ladyfingers.

IMMEDIATELY slide the sheet pans into the oven. Check the ladyfingers after 8 minutes—they should be turning pale blond—and if necessary turn the sheet pans around or switch them so the ladyfingers bake evenly. If the ladyfingers haven't turned pale blond, bake them for up to 2 minutes more. They should be pale blond and slightly crisp on top. Remove from oven. Cool for 5 minutes and sprinkle them with the remaining confectioners' sugar. When the ladyfingers have cooled completely, peel away the parchment paper.

STRAWBERRY PRESERVES

CONFITURE DE FRAISES

FOR MOST OF US, IT'S HARD TO ENVISION A WORLD WITHOUT REFRIGERators and freezers. Since Roman times, and no doubt earlier, humans have done their best to keep foods from rotting by drying them; packing them in salt, honey, vinegar, or spices; or smoking them in the hearth. Until relatively recently, fruits and other sweet foods were impossible to preserve without seriously altering their flavor or texture. Early recipes call for drying fruits in the sun or preserving them in salt or in vinegar. (Cherries in vinegar are still served in parts of France as an accompaniment to pâtés.) While storing fruits in honey altered their flavor and texture less than using vinegar or drying them, honey is hygroscopic—it absorbs moisture from the air—and therefore it's useless for making the candied and preserved fruits that we know today.

It wasn't until the sixteenth century, when methods for making high-quality, relatively inexpensive sugar were perfected, that cooking fruits in sugar syrup became practical. Although the Italians were the first to learn how to work with sugar, techniques for preserving fruits were first written about in French—by Michel de Nostredame, or Nostradamus, more famous for his astrological predictions and his subsequent falling-out with the pope than for his writings about food.

Sugar has certain surprising characteristics. When a small amount is combined with water, it can be fermented by yeasts, whether they are introduced on purpose to produce alcohol, or by accidental contamination. But when sugar is concentrated into a syrup, it resists bacteria and *prevents* fermentation. Concentrated sugar solutions—syrups—are susceptible to molds, but molds are much slower to attack foods than are bacteria and if the sugar solution is kept sealed they are rarely a problem. Cooking fruits in sugar syrups of different concentrations creates different effects. Poaching fruit in a light syrup will soften the fruit and sweeten it, making poaching a good method for dealing with underripe or inferior fruit, but it won't preserve the fruit, because the sugar isn't concentrated enough to prevent fermentation. Poaching fruit in a more concentrated sugar syrup and then sealing it results in the familiar fruit preserves that we like to spread on toast. Dipping fruits repeatedly in hot concentrated syrup and allowing them to dry between dippings produces candied fruit.

Another discovery, which predated the widespread use of sugar, was distillation. Distillation is the technique by which liquid mixtures are gently heated in a still so that the more volatile components turn to vapor. The vapor is then cooled, and thereby liquefied, so it can be trapped. Described by Aristotle as a method of getting the salt out of seawater, distillation was later used by Arabs to produce alcohol, most likely used for medicinal purposes rather than in the kitchen or for drinking. In the fourteenth and fifteenth centuries, alcohol was distilled by French alchemists and later *limonadiers*, street vendors who sold both nonalcoholic citrus drinks, such as lemonade, and liqueurs. Like sugar, alcohol is a preservative and, especially when unsweetened fruit brandies are combined with sugar, a very tasty one at that. Preserving fruits in distilled spirits makes it possible to use less sugar and to cook the fruit less so that its texture stays more intact.

Preserving Fruits With Sugar

MOST FRUIT PRESERVE RECIPES TELL YOU to combine the fruits with a sugar syrup and cook the mixture down to a certain thickness or until it registers a certain temperature on a candy thermometer—a method that leaves the fruits without form or texture, more like jam than individual tasty berries or pieces of larger fruits. I prefer to prepare the syrup and dip the washed whole, sliced, or diced fruit in the syrup in batches only long enough to cook the fruit and get it to release its flavorful juices into the surrounding liquid, usually 5 to 15 minutes, depending on the size and ripeness of the fruit or fruit pieces. I remove the fruit and boil down the syrup (which the liquid released by the fruit will have thinned) to its original volume. I then add another batch of fruit and continue until all the fruit has been cooked, reducing the syrup after each addition. Finally, I put the fruit back in, bring everything back to a quick simmer to sterilize it, and pack it in sterilized jars (see page 676).

Make the following recipe when strawberries are at their tastiest and least expensive. On the East Coast this means June, on the West Coast earlier in the spring.

I make two versions of preserved fruit. One, what the French call *fruits en conserve*, are fruits preserved in a relatively light syrup; they are best as a topping for cakes, shortcake, or yogurt. The other, what we call fruit preserves and the French call *confiture*, contains almost twice as much sugar and is more suitable for spreading on toast in the same way as jam.

STRAWBERRIES IN SYRUP

FRAISES EN CONSERVE

MAKES 6 OR 7 PINTS [4 OR 4.5 KG]

10 pounds [4.5 kg] ripe strawberries
2¼ cups [450 g] granulated sugar

PUT the strawberries in a bowl of cold water, swirl them around for a second, and drain them in a colander. Don't let them soak, or the water will leach out their sweetness. Hull them by rotating the tip of a small paring knife around the stem. Don't just cut off the stem end, or you'll waste strawberry.

BRING the sugar to a simmer with 2 cups [500 ml] of water in the widest nonaluminum pot you have. If you're lucky enough to have one of those old-fashioned wide copper *bassins à confiture,* now's the time to use it. Use a skimmer or large spoon to skim off any froth that floats to the top. Older recipes constantly remind the reader to skim, probably because sugar was less pure than it is now. Note the level of the liquid, and gently pour in just enough strawberries—1 or 2 pounds—so that none are pushed up above the syrup, but don't worry if a few float. Keep the heat on medium, wait for the strawberries to come back to a simmer, simmer for 3 to 5 minutes, and then use a skimmer or slotted spoon to gently transfer the strawberries to a colander set in a mixing bowl. (You'll need two colanders to hold all the strawberries.) Boil down the syrup slightly to evaporate the liquid released by the strawberries, and add another batch. Repeat, reducing the syrup each time, until you've used all the strawberries. When you're done, pour any liquid that's accumulated under the strawberries in the mixing bowl and pour it back into the syrup. Boil the syrup down—again, until it reaches more or less its original volume—and put all the strawberries in the colander back into the syrup. Bring to a very gentle simmer and simmer for 8 minutes. Gently spoon the strawberries into sterilized mason jars (see below) and ladle in enough hot syrup to cover the fruit. These preserves will keep at least several months in the refrigerator.

Variations: While this is an especially dramatic (and delicious) technique for making preserves out of berries, it works for any fruit I've ever used it for. Fruits such as pears, apples, peaches, and apricots should of course be peeled and pitted or cored and then cut into pieces. I like to keep the pieces relatively large (pears and apples quartered, whole apricots halved, peaches halved or quartered) to emphasize that these are whole fruit preserves and not just jam.

If you want to make strawberry preserves (*confiture*), prepare the strawberries as described above, but dissolve 4 cups of sugar [800 g] in 3 cups [750 ml] of water instead of 2¼ cups [450 g] of sugar.

MAKING PRESERVES, JAMS, AND JELLIES

If you're blessed with an abundance of fresh fruit or are making jam for gifts, a few precautions will prevent—or delay—the growth of mold. The easiest-to-use jars for storing preserves are the French-style mason jars that have a clamp-on lid with a rubber gasket instead of the screw-on top on American mason jars. Jars destined for storing preserves should be sterilized before they are used. I put the jars and their lids in a large pot with enough water to come about 1 inch up the sides of the jars. I bring the water to a rapid boil. Then I cover the pot, steam and boil the jars for 10 minutes, and, with a pair of tongs, turn the jars and lids top-down on a clean kitchen towel.

If you want to reuse American mason jars, you'll need to replace the lids, because the integrity of the small rubber ring that runs around the perimeter of the lid itself (not the screw-on ring that holds it down) is easily compromised, and may not provide a perfect seal when reused. On French jars, the rubber gasket that fits around the clamp-on lid is heavy and reusable. If, however, the gaskets on your jars have started to dry out or crack, you'll need to replace them. French jars and gaskets can be sterilized in the same way as American jars and lids. Put preserves in the jars while the preserves are still boiling hot and wipe the rims of the jars with a damp paper towel before screwing or clamping on the lid. Any particles on the rim can interfere with the seal. As the preserves cool, they will form a vacuum inside the jar such that you should hear a little hiss when you first open one.

FIG JAM WITH WALNUTS

CONFITURE DE FIGUES AUX NOIX

I've never tasted this jam in France because it seems to be one of those foods, once made every year in homes, that no one has time for anymore. I first read about a fig and walnut jam in Robert Courtine's Cent Merveilles de la Cuisine Française. Courtine describes pieces of watermelon rind, almonds, and walnuts "held as prisoners in a black and sugary juice." Seduced by that description, I've fooled around with a simpler version, using only walnuts. I've left out the almonds because they are too hard in the mouth and the watermelon rind because it's difficult to find at the same time as figs, in the fall.

4 pounds [1.8 kg] ripe figs

½ cup [100 g] granulated sugar

2 cups (½ pound [225 g]) walnut halves, chopped coarse

CUT the stems off the figs and rinse the figs thoroughly under cold running water.

COMBINE the sugar with ½ cup [125 ml] of water in a heavy-bottomed nonaluminum pot large enough to hold the figs. Bring the mixture to a boil, and boil just long enough to dissolve the sugar. Add the figs. Bring the mixture back to a simmer, cover the pot, and turn down the heat to maintain at a gentle simmer. Cook for 15 minutes to soften the figs and get them to release liquid. Take off the lid and stir the mixture with a wooden spoon or spatula, crushing the figs against the inside of the pot. Cook over low to medium heat, stirring continuously to prevent burning, until the mixture has the consistency of stiff jam, about 45 minutes. Stir in the walnuts and pack immediately into sterilized jars (see page 676). If you want to eliminate the peels, work the jam through a coarse drum sieve, food mill, or strainer before adding the walnuts.

JAMS AND JELLIES

Sometimes the distinctions between jams, jellies, and preserves are hazy, but I usually think of fruit preserves as containing pieces of whole fruit, and of jam as more like a purée. Jelly is the juice of fruit that is made to jell with pectin, either entirely from the fruit itself or augmented with the pectin from apples (an apple jelly is made as the base) or store-bought pectin. Pectin is a carbohydrate found in the cell walls of fruit; when dissolved in water, it unravels into long chains of sugar molecules. These chains become entangled and cause liquid mixtures to jell. The action of pectin in cool solutions is similar to that of starch, such as flour (also made of long chains of sugar molecules), in hot solutions, and analogous to that of gelatin (made of soluble proteins, themselves chains of amino acid molecules) in cold mixtures.

QUINCE PASTE

PÂTE DE COINGS

MAKES ONE 1-QUART [1-L] LOAF

The Spanish have a marvelous custom of serving quince paste and pastes made from other fruits with Manchego and other firm cheeses. Now, even when I serve a platter of French cheeses, I include a slice or two of quince paste, which admittedly I usually buy. But after poking around in my library, I've discovered that the French were once quite fond of quince paste. La Varenne, in *Le Confiturier François*, gives recipes for two versions, both of which he calls *cotignac*. According to Barbara Wheaton in her excellent book about the history of French cooking, *Savoring the Past*, Nostradamus gave a recipe for quince paste and described it as already old-hat, since it had been popular as early as the fourteenth century. *Marmelo*, Portuguese for "quince," is probably the origin of our word "marmalade." This seems especially likely since La Varenne gives "marmelade" recipes for quinces and apples, but not for citrus fruits. *Pâtes de fruits* (literally, fruit pastes) are usually very sweet and are thought of as candies (see pages 694 to 698). This version, while still sweet, is less so than candy. Since quinces have such a short season, I also make this recipe with apples.

4   pounds [3.6 kg] quinces or tart apples, peeled

2   cups [400 g] granulated sugar

      zest and juice of 1 lemon

CUT the quinces (or apples) vertically into 6 wedges and put them into a heavy-bottomed pot with 2 quarts [2 l] of water. Bring the liquid to a boil, partially. Cover the pot and simmer until the quinces are completely tender, about 30 to 40 minutes. Work the quinces through a food mill to eliminate the skins and seeds and produce a purée. Combine the purée (about 2 quarts [2 l]) with the sugar and the strained cooking liquid in a wide, heavy-bottomed pot or frying pan. Cook it over high heat while stir-

ring with a wooden spoon until the mixture is a deep pink color and pulls away from the sides of the pot in a goopy mass. Stir in the lemon juice and zest and continue stirring, scraping the spoon against the bottom of the pot, until the quinces begin to leave a brown stain on the bottom of the pot, indicating that they're scorching (about 90 minutes).

SCOOP the mixture into a 1-quart [1 l] heat-proof nonstick loaf pan. If you don't have a nonstick loaf pan, line a regular loaf pan or cake pan with plastic wrap before putting the quince paste into it. Smooth the top of the paste with a rubber spatula dipped in cold water. Refrigerate until firm. Take the quince paste out of the mold and serve it in slices or wedges.

Variations: I've also seen some versions of fruit paste made with figs and some made with plums, but I've never attempted them. Presumably the process should work with most fruits.

GRAPE "BUTTER" WITH PEARS AND QUINCES

RAISINÉ

MAKES 4 CUPS [1.25 KG]

Even though sugar became widely available in France in the sixteenth century, it wasn't until the nineteenth century, when an industrial process for extracting it from sugar beets came into use, that it became a staple most everyone could afford. Fruits are, of course, a natural source of sugar, and grapes, common in France, were crushed when ripe and boiled down to a concentrated juice that would set into a stiff pastelike jelly that could be eaten with bread or be used as a sweetener in other dishes. A similar process is used today in making so-called natural sweet drinks or other sweetened products on whose label the manufacturer doesn't want to put the word "sugar" but can put "concentrated grape juice" or "concentrated apple juice" instead.

Raisiné is an old-fashioned jamlike paste, rarely made anymore. In his book *La Cuisinière Provençal*, written near the end of the nineteenth century, J.-B. Reboul already states that *raisiné* has fallen out of favor in country homes because of the cheapness of sugar and the "*maladies de la vigne*," referring no doubt to the phylloxera that struck French vineyards in the second half of that century. Burgundian recipes almost always include pieces of pears and quince in the jelly. Theoretically, you could make a sort of *raisiné* by cooking down grape juice into a very thick syrup, but it probably wouldn't set because commercial grape juice doesn't have enough pectin, which is contained in the skins of the grapes.

10 pounds [4.5 kg] sweet white or red grapes such as muscat or Concord or other sweet varieties, stemmed and rinsed

4 medium-size pears and 2 quinces, or 4 pears and 3 tart apples

½ lemon

2 cups [400 g] granulated sugar, or more to taste

PUT the grapes into a heavy-bottomed nonaluminum pot over medium heat. Crush them with a potato masher while they're in the pot. When the grapes come to a boil in their own juices, turn down the heat to maintain them at a gentle simmer. Simmer for 2 hours, uncovered, stirring and crushing now and then with the potato masher. Work the grapes through a food mill set over another pot or a bowl. Discard the skins and seeds. Rinse out the pot you used for simmering the grapes, and strain the grape juice back into it through a fine-mesh strainer. Simmer the juice for about 3 hours, skimming off froth with a ladle, until you're left with about 4 cups [1 l] of juice, which will now have a pasty consistency.

PEEL the pears and apples and immediately rub the peeled fruit with the lemon half. Cut the pears in half—again, rub the exposed parts with the lemon—and remove their cores and stems with a melon baller or a paring knife. Core the apples in

the same way. Cut the fruit into ½-inch [1.5 cm] dice and put the dice into the pot with the grape paste. Simmer the mixture gently until the dice have softened but aren't mush, about 20 minutes. Bring the mixture back to a simmer and stir in the sugar. Simmer long enough to dissolve the sugar and then remove from the heat.

SPOON the hot *raisiné* into sterilized jars and seal the jars (see page 676).

Poached Fruits

I'M NOT THE ONLY ONE TO LAMENT THE tasteless fruit that shows up in even the fanciest grocery stores and at the height of the season. While in the summer I can usually track down decent fruit at a farmers' market, grocery-store fruit is hopeless. When I'm hankering for fruit but am stuck with something tasteless or underripe, I make poached fruit. In the winter, when my friends and I are fruit starved, I make an assortment of poached fruits and pass them around the table for guests to spoon over vanilla ice cream.

Fruits are poached in virtually the same way as they are when making preserves—simply simmered in a sugar syrup and allowed to cool before they're served. But while the principle is the same, the amount of sugar needed for poaching fruits is far less than for preserves because the cooked fruit is served within a day or two. I make a very light sugar syrup—far lighter than most recipes call for—so that once I've used it to poach the fruit I can boil down and concentrate the juices released by the fruit without overconcentrating the sugar and making the syrup too sweet. After reducing the poaching liquid, I let it cool, reinforce its flavor with unsweetened fruit brandy or other spirits (although spirits aren't essential), and put the fruit back in. In France, dry fruit brandies are available for seemingly every fruit that grows. In the United States, we're limited to three or four, even in big cities. (See page 683 for more about fruit brandies.)

POACHED STRAWBERRIES

FRAISES POCHÉES

Makes 6 dessert servings when served with ice cream, and proportionately more if other poached fruits are being served at the same time.

2 pints [595 g] strawberries (about 2 pounds)

1 recipe Basic Poaching Liquid for Fruits (page 682)

¼ to ½ cup [60 to 125 ml] eau-de-vie de fraises (dry strawberry brandy, available only in France), or framboise (raspberry brandy), or kirsch (cherry brandy) (optional)

PUT the strawberries in a bowl of cold water, swirl them around for a second, and drain them in a colander. Don't let them soak, or the water will leach out their sweetness. Hull them by rotating the tip of a small paring knife around the stem. In a heavy-bottomed pot, bring the poaching liquid to a simmer. Put in the strawberries and simmer them gently until they soften and are easily penetrated with a knife but still retain some texture, 3 to 8 minutes, depending on the ripeness, size, and variety of strawberry. With a skimmer or slotted spoon, transfer the strawberries to a colander set over a mixing bowl. Boil down the poaching liquid—adding any liquid that has accumulated in the mixing bowl—to about half its original volume. Keep the pot to one side of the heat source so it boils only on one side and any froth accumulates on the other side. Skim off and discard any froth or scum.

TAKE the syrup off the heat and put the strawberries back in. Let cool, uncovered, at room temperature, and then chill in the refrigerator. Stir in the brandy to taste.

POACHED RASPBERRIES

FRAMBOISES POCHÉES

Makes 6 dessert servings when served with ice cream, and proportionately more if other poached fruits are being served at the same time.

4 cartons raspberries (½ pint [125 g] each)

1 recipe Basic Poaching Liquid for Fruits (page 682)

¼ to ½ cup [60 to 125 ml] framboise (raspberry brandy), or kirsch (cherry brandy) (optional)

BECAUSE raspberries are fragile, I poach them for only a few seconds. Bring the poaching liquid to a simmer and turn off the heat. Put the raspberries, in batches, in a skimmer, dunk them in the hot liquid for about 5 seconds, and transfer them to a bowl. When you've done this with all the raspberries, boil the liquid down to half its original volume and let it cool before adding the eau-de-vie, the raspberries, and any liquid the raspberries have released into the bowl.

OTHER POACHED BERRIES: Blueberries, red currants, black currants, and blackberries can all be prepared in the same way as the strawberries. Poached blueberries should be served warm, as soon as they are poached, because they contain so much pectin that they will otherwise jell. Red currants, because they are so sour, may require that the syrup be reduced a little more to concentrate its sweetness.

POACHED PINEAPPLE

ANANAS POCHÉS

Makes 8 dessert servings when served with ice cream, and proportionately more if other poached fruits are being served at the same time.

1 pineapple

1 recipe Basic Poaching Liquid for Fruits (page 682)

¼ to ½ cup [60 to 125 ml] kirsch (cherry brandy) (optional)

MOST pineapples are best served raw—*ananas aux kirsch* (raw pineapple with kirsch) is an old-fashioned bistro favorite—if you're stuck with one that's tough and sour, twist off the top, and cut off the bottom and top just deep enough to expose the flesh. To peel the pineapple quickly and easily, set it on end and cut the peel off with a chef's knife, deep enough so that the little brown pits are left attached to the skin. This method, however, wastes a lot of pineapple, so if you have the patience, cut the little pits out individually, or cut the pits out by following them, on a diagonal, down and around the pineapple, leaving the pineapple surrounded with spiral-shaped grooves. When you've peeled the pineapple, cut it lengthwise in half through the core and then cut each half lengthwise in half or in thirds, depending on the size of the pineapple. Cut off and discard the hard core that runs the length of each section. Slice the sections into wedges about ⅓ inch [1 cm] thick. Poach the wedges in the simmering poaching liquid for about 5 minutes, transfer them to a colander set over a mixing bowl, and boil the poaching liquid—adding any liquid that has accumulated in the mixing bowl—down to half its original volume. Put the pineapple wedges back in, let cool at room temperature, and then chill them in the refrigerator. Flavor to taste with kirsch.

POACHED BANANAS

BANANES POCHÉES

Makes 6 dessert servings when served with ice cream, and proportionately more if other poached fruits are being served at the same time.

I admit that the idea of poached bananas never really grabbed me until I discovered the secret ingredient: good dark rum. This is also the way to go if you're in a hurry to use underripe bananas.

3 large bananas

1 recipe Basic Poaching Liquid for Fruits (page 682)

¼ to ½ cup [60 to 125 ml] dark rum, preferably from Martinque or Jamaica (optional)

PEEL the bananas, cut them in half crosswise, and then cut each piece in half lengthwise. Poach the pieces in the simmering poaching liquid for 4 minutes and transfer them to a colander set over a mixing bowl. Boil the poaching liquid down to half

its original volume. Put the banana pieces back in, let them cool at room temperature, and then chill them in the refrigerator. Flavor to taste with rum.

POACHED PEARS

POIRES POCHÉES

Makes 6 dessert servings when served with ice cream, and proportionately more if other poached fruits are being served at the same time.

I, frankly, have never been fond of pears poached in red wine, especially when domineering spices like cinnamon and cloves have been added. A simple poaching in a plain sugar solution and ideally a final reinforcement of the pear flavor with unsweetened pear brandy (usually sold as Poire William) makes a dessert that is far more delicious and tastes of pears, nothing else. In this recipe, the pears are quartered, but for a more dramatic effect, peel the pears, leave them whole, and core them from the bottom. Poached whole pears require slightly more poaching liquid to cover, so add more as needed. (You can also cook them covered and baste them from time to time with the poaching liquid.) I serve poached whole pears standing up in chilled soup plates and surrounded with the poaching liquid, and I pass Crème Chantilly (page 609) or, better yet, lightly sweetened whipped crème fraîche (its acidic tang is a delightful accent next to the pears).

1½ recipes Basic Poaching Liquid for Fruits (page 682), or more as needed if you're poaching the pears whole

1 vanilla bean, split in half lengthwise (optional)

6 pears

¼ to ½ cup [60 to 125 ml] Poire William (unsweetened pear brandy) (optional)

BRING the poaching liquid to a gentle simmer with the vanilla bean before you peel the pears so the pears don't have time to darken. Peel the pears. If you're leaving them whole, core them through the base with an apple corer. Otherwise, cut them in half lengthwise and use a melon baller or paring knife to cut the core and stem out of each half. Halve each half lengthwise again so each pear yields 4 lengthwise wedges. Poach the wedges until they're easily penetrated with a knife but still offer a little resistance. Depending on the ripeness of the pears, this can take from 8 to 20 minutes. When the pears are done, take out the vanilla bean and transfer the pears to a mixing bowl. Boil down the poaching liquid to half its original volume. Scrape the tiny seeds out of the vanilla bean halves and put them into the still-hot poaching liquid. Put the pears back in, let cool, and chill. Flavor to taste with Poire William.

POACHED APPLES

POMMES POCHÉES

Makes 6 dessert servings when served with ice cream, and proportionately more if other poached fruits are being served at the same time.

1 recipe Basic Poaching Liquid for Fruits (below), or

more as needed

6 apples

¼ to ½ cup [60 to 125 ml] Calvados (apple brandy) (optional)

BRING the poaching liquid to a gentle simmer and peel the apples. Cut them in half, cut out the cores with a melon baller or paring knife, and cut each half into 3 or 4 wedges, depending on the size of the apples. Poach the wedges until they soften slightly but can be penetrated with a small knife, about 7 minutes, depending on the apples. (If the poaching liquid doesn't completely cover the wedges, poach them with the lid on the pot.) Transfer the wedges to a colander set over a mixing bowl. Boil down the poaching liquid—adding any liquid that's accumulated in the mixing bowl—to half its original volume. Put the wedges back in the mixing bowl, let cool at room temperature, and then chill them in the refrigerator. Flavor to taste with Calvados.

BASIC POACHING LIQUID FOR FRUITS

To make enough liquid to poach about 2 pounds [900 g] of fruit, combine ½ cup [100 g] of granulated sugar with 3 cups [750 ml] of water. Bring the mixture to a simmer and use it immediately to poach the fruits, or let it cool. If you're not using it right away, keep it refrigerated, but for no longer than several days. Because the liquid has a relatively low concentration of sugar, it's susceptible to alcoholic fermentation. To poach more than 2 pounds [900 g] of fruit, change the ingredient amounts accordingly. If you find that you don't have enough liquid to cover a batch of fruit, cover the pot during poaching so that fruit that isn't submerged is steamed. Gently turn the fruit over itself after a couple of minutes so that it cooks evenly.

Liqueurs, Ratafia, Fruits in Eau-de-vie

ALCOHOL HAS BEEN USED IN FRANCE SINCE at least the sixteenth century as a base for liqueurs, ratafia, and in sweetened and alcohol-preserved fruits, *fruits à l'eau-de-vie. Ratafia* is a creole word for a fruit liqueur made by steeping the fruits in alcohol or fruit brandy and then sweetening. A liqueur is made much like a ratafia, except that the alcohol is flavored with herbs, nuts, or spices instead of fruits, and is sweetened with sugar. Recipes for liqueur and ratafia were almost always included in cookbooks written in the seventeenth and eighteenth centuries and the early part of the nineteenth century, but later works, including Antonin Carême's *L'Art de la Cuisine Française au Dix-neuvième Siècle,* leave them out.

Most recipes for ratafia suggest combining fruits with eau-de-vie and sugar syrup, macerating the mixture for anywhere from a few days to a few months, and then working it through a strainer. The result is a fruit liqueur with the flavor of the fruit marvelously intact because the fruit is never cooked. You can make your own ratafia by infusing fruits for a week or more in a combination of sugar syrup and 100-proof vodka, which is 50 percent alcohol and has a neutral flavor that won't interfere with that of the fruit, and then straining. (In some states you can buy pure grain alcohol—actually 95 percent alcohol, the equivalent of 190 proof—which allows you to use a higher proportion of fruit without making the ratafia too weak.) You can also experiment with flavorful distilled spirits such as grape brandies (Cognac or Armagnac) or, ideally, clear brandy (eau-de-vie) made from whatever it is you're infusing—for example, framboise (clear raspberry brandy) for raspberries. (See page 10 for more about eaux-de-vie and other spirits.) The only disadvantage to this second method is that eaux-de-vie are more expensive than 100-proof vodka and have a lower alcohol content.

RASPBERRY CORDIAL

RATAFIA DE FRAMBOISES

MAKES 6 CUPS

1 cup [200 g] sugar

1 pint [245 g] raspberries

1 liter good-quality 100-proof vodka or framboise

COMBINE the sugar with ⅔ cup [150 ml] of water in a small saucepan and simmer just long enough to dissolve the sugar. Allow to cool.

CRUSH the raspberries with the back of a fork or large spoon and combine them with the sugar syrup and vodka in a tightly covered glass bowl or wide-mouthed jar. Let sit, at room temperature, for 2 weeks, giving the bottle a shake every few days.

WORK the mixture through a large strainer, pushing on the raspberries with a heavy wooden spoon to extract as much of their juice as possible. Discard what doesn't go through and strain the ratafia through a fine-mesh strainer. If you want the ratafia to be perfectly clear, strain it through a coffee filter or a strainer lined with a clean piece of muslin.

KEEP the ratafia in a tightly corked bottle and serve it as an after-dinner drink, as a flavoring for fruits (it's great tossed with fresh berries), or as a topping for ice cream.

Variations: Even though I know testing the recipes would be a lot of fun, I haven't made ratafia with a wide variety of fruits. But I don't see why the above method wouldn't work for just about anything. In reading my old recipes, the only difference I've seen is that relatively firm fruits such as apples, quinces, apricots, or peaches should be puréed before being combined with the alcohol and sugar. Old books say to grate them, but you can use a food processor instead. Keep in mind, though, that fruits contain varying amounts of sugar, so you might have to adjust the quantity of sugar syrup accordingly. If the fruit is very sweet, start with less sugar than I call for above. You can always add sugar syrup to taste at the end.

One problem with most homemade ratafia is that it has too little alcohol. Because alcohol is essential to balance the sweetness of the fruit and sugar, a liqueur with too little alcohol tastes cloyingly sweet. My own taste is for a liqueur of about 90 proof (45 percent alcohol). There are two solutions to this alcohol problem. If you can buy pure grain alcohol, use it in the recipe above, but double the sugar and raspberries. When the ratafia is finished, just dilute it with good bottled water to taste. If you can't find pure alcohol—in most states it's illegal— you can cook the fruit down to concentrate its flavor and cook off much of its water, which dilutes the vodka; but then your ratafia will lose much of the natural freshness of raw fruit.

CHERRIES
IN KIRSCH

CERISES À L'EAU-DE-VIE

MAKES 25 AFTER-DINNER OR LATE-NIGHT SNACK
(OR NIGHTCAP) SERVINGS

This delightful little concoction is both a dish and a drink. I first tasted it at the Lapin-Agile, an old-fashioned Montmartre cabaret where I went, when I could afford it, to listen to comedians and story tellers. Everyone sat on benches at long tables eating and sipping *cerises à l'eau-de-vie*, and even a few blocks from the tourist-packed "Butte" there were few foreigners, since everything was in French. I pretended, no doubt unsuccessfully, to be French.

Along with the various syrups, preserves, and liqueurs found in old cookbooks, there are also cherries and other fruits preserved in eau-de-vie. The recipes are similar for various fruits and the basic technique, identical. The fruits are first dipped in simmering sugar syrup, then allowed to drain and dry slightly. The syrup is reduced, the fruits are dipped again, and the process is

repeated from one to several times, depending on the fruit. The process is similar to making candied fruits (see page 686), except that the candying process isn't completed and the partially candied fruits and the cooled syrup are combined with eau-de-vie. The mixture is macerated for several days to several months, depending on the fruit and how much it was cooked before being combined with the alcohol. The fruits are then served, surrounded with the sweet eau-de-vie soaking liquid.

- 4 pounds [1.8 kg] cherries
- 2 cups [400 g] granulated sugar
- 2 cups [500 ml] good-quality kirsch (see page 142)

RINSE and drain the cherries. Don't worry about the stems and pits.

PUT the cherries in a heatproof jar or nonreactive bowl (such as heatproof glass or stainless steel). Combine the sugar with 6 cups [1.5 l] of water, bring to a simmer, stir to dissolve the sugar, and pour the hot syrup over the cherries. Cover the cherries and let sit for 24 hours. Gently drain the cherries in a colander set over a pot and put the cherries back into the bowl. Bring the syrup in the pot to a gentle simmer. Using a ladle to skim off any froth that floats to the surface, simmer the syrup for about 10 minutes to concentrate it and evaporate the liquid released by the cherries. Pour the hot syrup over the cherries, cover, and let sit again for 24 hours. Repeat this process for 3 more days and gently transfer the lightly candied cherries to clean jars with clamp-on lids or decorative wide-mouthed bottles. Gently simmer the sugar syrup on the stove, again skimming off froth, until it is thick and syrupy, leaving you with about 2 cups [500 ml]. Let cool for an hour and stir in the kirsch (don't add the kirsch while the syrup is hot or it will cook off the kirsch's aroma). Pour the kirsch syrup mixture over the cherries, cover the jars, and let macerate for 1 week. Serve chilled, in small bowls or glasses. *Cerises à l'eau-de-vie* will keep for 1 year.

Variations: In France, this same treatment is applied to the little golden plums called *mirabelles,* and *eau-de-vie de mirabelle* is substituted for the kirsch. I've never seen the plums in this country, and while *eau-de-vie de mirabelle,* known here simply as mirabelle, can be found, it isn't easy. A more accessible and delicious version is made with white grapes. I use muscat grapes if I can find them, but I pour the sugar syrup over the grapes only three times after blanching instead of five times. I replace the kirsch with a good French marc. *Grappa di moscato* in place of the marc would no doubt be delicious, but frightfully expensive. My favorite of all fruits in eau-de-vie are clementines, partially candied in the same way as the cherries, and finished with good vodka and the reduced cooking syrup.

CLEMENTINES OR MANDARIN ORANGES IN SWEETENED VODKA

CLEMENTINES OU MANDARINES À L'EAU·DE·VIE

MAKES 20 SERVINGS (1 CLEMENTINE PER PERSON AS AN AFTER-DESSERT TREAT)

When I owned a restaurant in Manhattan in the early 1980s, I would pull out all the stops for my annual New Year's Eve dinner. I charged our guests a hefty sum to spend the evening and the wee hours of the morning at my restaurant, but I was so extravagant I always lost money on the whole affair. The last in a long line of special dishes, each accompanied by a Champagne, were these alcohol-laced clementines, eaten whole, skin and all, which I served to accompany a good marc. As stuffed as they were, guests could never resist one last bite. If you want these for the December holidays, make them with the first clementines you see in November. You can also use mandarins (although they have seeds), but don't try tangerines—their skin is too thick.

24 small clementines or mandarin oranges (the 4 extra are for sampling)

7 cups [1.8 kg] granulated sugar

2 cups [500 ml] good-quality vodka, or more as needed

THOROUGHLY rinse the clementines and remove any stems and leaves. Bring about 6 quarts [6 l] of water to a boil over high heat and add the clementines. When the water returns to a simmer, turn down the heat. Gently simmer the clementines for 15 minutes, drain in a colander, and discard the blanching water. Let cool and prick each clementine about 15 times with a pin to allow the syrup and vodka to penetrate.

COMBINE 3 cups [600 g] of the sugar with 2 quarts [2 l] of water in a heavy-bottomed nonaluminum pot large enough to hold the clementines. Bring to a simmer, stir to dissolve the sugar, and add the clementines. Simmer for 10 minutes, turn off the heat, and transfer both syrup and clementines to a heat-proof bowl. (If you've used a stainless steel pot, just leave them in the pot.) Cover and leave at room temperature overnight. The next day, bring the clementines and their syrup to a simmer, simmer for 5 minutes, transfer again to the heatproof bowl (or leave in the pot), cover, and let sit overnight. Repeat this process one more time and drain them in a colander—handle them gently. Discard the syrup.

COMBINE the remaining sugar with 3 quarts [3 l] of water, bring to a simmer, and stir to dissolve the sugar. Put the clementines in the hot syrup, gently set a heat-proof plate on them to keep them from bobbing up, and let sit overnight. The next day, simmer the clementines for 10 minutes, uncovered, in the syrup and let cool. Repeat this process for 2 to 5 more days, sampling a clementine after 2 days. Bite into the clementine to make sure that the syrup has penetrated it, that the skin is soft and sweet but not mushy, and that the syrup has made it all the way to the center of the fruit. You may use up a couple of clementines—hence the extras—until you get it right. The number of days of cooking and soaking will depend on the size of the clementines and the thickness of their skins.

WHEN the clementines are sweet all the way through, use a slotted spoon to transfer them gently to wide-mouth jars, preferably with clamp or cork tops. Boil down the syrup, skimming off any froth, to 4½ cups [1.1 l], by which time it should have the consistency of maple syrup. Let cool. Combine 1⅓ cups [500 ml] of the reduced syrup with the vodka, and pour the mixture over the clementines. If there's not enough liquid to cover, add more syrup-vodka mixture. Soak for 2 to 3 weeks, gently twirling the jar every couple of days to redistribute the clementines. Serve in small chilled glasses or bowls. Beware: Eating one of these is roughly the equivalent of having an after-dinner drink. Leftover clementine-vodka juice is a welcome addition to vanilla ice cream.

CANDIED FRUITS

Most people nowadays would rather eat their fruit fresh instead of candied and would be happier just to find a good peach than to bite into an expensive, arduous-to-make candied fruit. But before chocolate was brought back from the New World, and candies of various sorts became commonplace, candied fruit bordered on the miraculous.

Candied fruits are made by repeatedly dipping fruits in hot sugar syrup and allowing the fruits to dry for 24 hours between dippings. As the dippings, which go on for from 5 days to 3 months, progress, a slightly more concentrated sugar syrup is used and a small amount of glucose (a different kind of sugar) is added to the syrup to keep it from crystallizing.

The sudden crystallization of a concentrated sugar syrup for no apparent reason is the result of supersaturation. Solutions are said to be supersaturated when more of a particular solid is dissolved in a liquid than the liquid can, under normal conditions, contain. To make a supersaturated sugar syrup, dissolve as much sugar as you can in a given amount of boiling water and then let the syrup cool. Because hot liquids will dissolve more solids than cold liquids, the syrup becomes supersaturated as it cools. If a stray sugar crystal—one that's formed on the side of the pan, perhaps—falls into the syrup, it initiates crystallization and the whole thing turns into a mass of wet crystals. Adding glucose helps prevent recrystallization because pure solutions (solutions of one kind of sugar), which form identical crystals, are much more likely to join together in matching crystals than impure ones. Some recipes call for adding a little cream of tartar or lemon juice, instead of glucose, to concentrated sugar solutions. Acids such as these cause sucrose—table sugar—to break down into invert sugar (a mixture of glucose and fructose), which also helps to keep the syrup from crystallizing.

COOKIES
AND CANDIES

PETITS·FOURS SECS

HOW TO	HOW TO	HOW TO
MAKE SHORTBREAD COOKIES	MAKE OLD-FASHIONED FRENCH REGIONAL COOKIES	MAKE CHOCOLATE TRUFFLES, CANDIED CITRUS RINDS, AND FRUIT JELLIES

YEARS AGO A CLOSE FRIEND AND I TOOK A THREE-WEEK TRIP TO THE French countryside, where we indulged in a variety of gustatory excesses. As we'd approach a new town or city, I'd run my finger down the page in the Michelin guide and call from a pay phone at a gas station to book a table. To avoid financial ruin, our one compromise was to skip desserts—hardly a sacrifice since we'd be ready to burst anyway. But while I'm not a big dessert eater, a good meal always leaves me hankering for a cup of strong espresso and just a little something sweet. In fancy restaurants, petits fours—tiny little cakes, candies, and cookies—are served as a prelude to dessert. For us they *were* dessert—the perfect end to an evening spent eating.

French pastry chefs divide petits fours into two kinds: *petits-fours secs,* which include various cookies and candies, and *petits-fours frais,* which are miniature cakes—including the familiar little square ones—or pastries that contain creamy mixtures. When I worked in restaurants in France, petits fours were made in the morning and those that weren't eaten at lunch were served to the staff. Fresh petits fours were made for dinner and any leftovers were eaten with our morning coffee. For a recipe for French *macarons* (meringue cookies), see page 670. For ladyfingers, see page 671.

Cookies

MOST COOKIES ARE COMBINATIONS OF BUT-
ter, flour, sugar, and eggs. Nuts are sometimes added
for flavor and texture, and flavorings such as chocolate, coffee, and vanilla are worked into the batter.
Some cookies are made much like cakes, by beating
egg whites and folding them with flavorful mixtures
of ground nuts, sugar, and/or flour.

SHORTBREAD COOKIES

SABLÉS

MAKES 48 COOKIES

Shortbread cookie dough is almost identical
to the shortbread dough used for lining sweet
tarts, except that even less liquid is used and
the finished cookie is even more fragile. *Sablé*
means "sand," and that is exactly the effect a shortbread
cookie should produce when you bite into one—not grit,
of course, but the feeling of the cookie instantly crumbling. The large proportion of butter to liquid keeps the
gluten in the flour from being activated, and the mixture,
once the flour is added, is worked as little as possible.

13 tablespoons (1½ sticks [170 g] plus 1 tablespoon)
   butter

½ cup [100 g] granulated sugar

½ teaspoon salt

1 teaspoon vanilla extract

1¾ cups [220 g] all-purpose flour

1 egg white (from a large egg), lightly beaten with a fork
   with ¼ teaspoon salt

½ cup [100 g] crystallized sugar, sanding sugar,
   granulated sugar, or "sugar in the raw"

WORK the butter, granulated sugar, salt, and vanilla
together in a mixing bowl with a heavy wooden
spoon or in an electric mixer with the paddle blade,
until the mixture is smooth and creamy, about 2
minutes. Scrape down the sides of the bowl every 30
seconds with a rubber spatula. If you're working the
flour in by hand, add it all at once and work it just
long enough to incorporate it until it has the consistency of gravel. If you're using the electric mixer,
turn off the mixer and pour the flour on top of the
butter mixture. Hold a kitchen towel over the mixer
bowl—be careful not to let it get caught in the
blade—and turn the mixer on low. Work the mixture for about 15 seconds on low and then 30
seconds on high, until it has the consistency of
gravel but doesn't come together into a mass. Pour
the dough out onto the work surface and crush it
several times with the heel of your hand until it
comes together into a single mass.

DIVIDE the dough into 3 parts and refrigerate, covered with plastic wrap, for 30 minutes, just long
enough for it to firm up slightly, but not to harden.
Use your hands and then a spatula to roll the dough
into 3 cylinders about 1½ inches [4 cm] thick. Press
on both ends of each cylinder to flatten them. Wrap
each cylinder in plastic wrap. Chill for 3 hours, or
overnight.

PREHEAT the oven to 375°F [190°C/gas mark 5].

COVER 2 sheet pans with parchment paper.

BRUSH one of the dough cylinders on all sides
(except the ends) with the egg white. Spread the
crystallized sugar on a sheet pan or work surface
and roll the dough in it to coat it. Slice the dough
into cookies about ⅓ inch [1 cm] thick. Arrange
them on sheet pans, leaving at least ½ inch between
cookies. Repeat with the remaining cylinders. Bake
the cookies until they are pale blond, not brown,
about 15 minutes. (If the oven heat isn't perfectly
even, you may have to rotate the pans so the cookies cook at the same time.) Transfer the cookies to
cake racks and let cool.

Variations: Basic shortbread dough can be flavored in any way you like. Many regional specialties, including the Norman cookies called *sablés de bourg-dun*, which are flavored with grated orange or lemon zest, are one example. Other regional cookies are made by adding chopped anise seeds, ginger (you end up with a rich ginger snap), spices such as cinnamon or cloves, or orange flower water.

LINZER DOUGH: It's hard to imagine, but there is a dough that's even shorter (more crumbly) than *sablé* dough: linzer dough. Linzer dough is used to make linzertorte, but it can also be used to make cookies just like the *sablés* above. To make a batch of linzer dough, replace ½ cup [65 g] of the flour in the *sablé* dough on page 689, with ground almonds. Toast ½ cup [75 g] blanched almonds in a 350°F [175°C/gas mark 4] oven for 15 minutes, allow them to cool, and then grind them in a food processor for 3 minutes. You can then turn the dough into cookies as you would the *sablés*, or you can make raspberry linzer cookies (see next recipe).

RASPBERRY LINZER COOKIES

LINZER PETITS-FOURS AUX PÉPINS DE FRAMBOISES

MAKES 32 FILLED COOKIES

Whenever you make raspberry coulis (a purée with the seeds strained out), as for the *fromage blanc* tart described on page 152 or the raspberry soufflés on page 626, freeze the tiny seeds that won't go through the strainer and use them to fill your cookies, much like a Fig Newton. (You can also strain a thawed 14-ounce [395 g] package of frozen raspberries just for this recipe and freeze the coulis.) If you don't want to deal with the seeds, use good-quality store-bought preserves or make your own (see page 676). You can also make these little cookies with leftover shortbread dough (*pâte sablée*) instead of linzer dough.

1 recipe linzer dough (see variations to Shortbread Cookies recipe, at left)

¾ cup [125 g] raspberry or strawberry seeds left over from straining purées, or ¾ cup [160 g] good-quality fruit preserves

2 tablespoons granulated sugar, or more to taste (if you are using berry seeds)

PREPARE, roll, and chill the linzer dough in the same way as the shortbread dough on page 689.

COMBINE the raspberry seeds with the sugar in a small saucepan and cook, while stirring, over low to medium heat, until the sugar dissolves and the mixture gets very stiff, about 10 minutes. Let the mixture cool and then chill it in the refrigerator. Fruit preserves can be used as they are.

PREHEAT the oven to 375°F [190°C/gas mark 5].

SLICE the cylinders of linzer dough into rounds between ⅛ and ¼ inch [about .5 cm] thick and put them on sheet pans covered with parchment paper. Bake the pastry rounds until they are pale blond, 8 to 10 minutes, and let cool. Spread half the rounds with a thin layer of the raspberry seed mixture and gently press the remaining rounds on top.

BUTTER ALMOND COOKIES

FINANCIERS

MAKES ABOUT 30 COOKIES

While life in Paris had its hardships, getting up every morning had a touch of luxury because my roommate and I lived near an excellent patisserie. Except for very well-known shops like Fauchon or Lenôtre, whose excellence goes unquestioned, the best pastry shops have a sign in the window that reads PUR BEURRE, meaning that no speck of margarine or shortening is ever used. If only we could be so reassured in this country. But we lived near such a place, Chez Pierre, and took turns going out to get pastries to eat with our morning coffee. Croissants were of course de rigeur, but whenever I went, I picked up a few financiers, buttery and nutty cookies. The ingredients for financiers are similar to those for linzer dough—almonds and plenty of butter (the butter is cooked into beurre noisette to accentuate its flavor)—but the effect is more cakelike because egg whites are used instead of whole eggs. The mixture is then baked in individual rectangular or elongated oval financier molds (see Sources), which if you become a financier addict may be worth the investment. Otherwise you'll have to use tartlet molds (again, see Sources), which aren't cheap either but are more versatile, or you can use a madeleine mold, which is cheaper still. This recipe makes about 30 financiers, but if you don't want to go out and buy 30 molds, just bake the cookies in batches.

12 tablespoons (1½ sticks) butter (for the batter), plus 2 tablespoons softened butter (for the molds)

2 cups [400 g] confectioners' sugar

¾ cup [150 g] plus 2 tablespoons blanched almonds, toasted for 10 to 15 minutes in a 350°F [175°C/gas mark 4] oven, allowed to cool

⅓ cup [40 g] plus 1 tablespoon flour

5 egg whites (from large eggs)

PREHEAT the oven to 450°F [230°C/gas mark 8]

MELT the butter for the batter in a heavy-bottomed saucepan over medium heat. It will boil for about 10 minutes while the water cooks out of it and then it will start to froth. At this point you must watch it carefully so you caramelize the milk solids without burning them. Tilt the pan so you can see the milk solids clinging to the bottom. As soon as they turn brown, plunge the bottom of the pan in a bowl of cold water for a few seconds to stop the cooking.

COMBINE the sugar and almonds in a food processor and grind by pulsing until they have a sandy consistency. Use a wooden spoon to combine the almond mixture with the flour and egg whites in a mixing bowl until smooth. Work in the hot beurre noisette. Refrigerate the batter overnight.

BRUSH the financier molds or 1-inch [2.5-cm] tartlet molds with softened butter. Chill the molds for 10 minutes and brush again. They must be very thickly coated with butter or the cookies will stick. Spoon the batter into the molds (or use a pastry bag), filling the molds about three-quarters full because the mixture expands. Put the molds on a sheet pan and slide them into the oven. Bake for 5 minutes, turn the oven down to 400°F [200°C/gas mark 6], and bake for 6 to 7 minutes more, until the cookies are brown on top. Let the cookies cool for 1 minute before turning them out onto a rack.

Variation: The *mirlitons* popular in Paris and Normandy are made much like *financiers* except that the *financier* batter is baked in small tartlet shells made with *pâte sucrée*.

PALM TREE COOKIES

PALMIERS

MAKES ABOUT 30 COOKIES

Assuming you buy puff pastry instead of making it yourself, these crispy little cookies are a snap to make. Just make sure that the puff pastry you buy (see Sources) is made with butter and not margarine or shortening—the only ingredients should be flour, butter, and salt.

1 package (14 ounces [395 g]) frozen puff pastry
    confectioner's sugar, as needed for rolling and coating

ALLOW the pastry to thaw and roll it out into a rectangle between ⅛ and ¼ inch thick (³⁄₁₆ inch [about .5 cm]), 6 inches [15 cm] wide, and 14 inches [35.5 cm] long. (This can be cut in half to make it more manageable, so that you have two pieces each 7 inches long.) If your pastry weighs slightly more or less than the weight listed above, just roll it out longer or shorter, keeping the thickness and width the same. Instead of using flour to coat the surface you're rolling on and the top of the pastry, use confectioner's sugar.

FOLD the sides (not the ends) of the rectangle so they meet in the center, leaving you with a rectangle the same length, twice as thick, but only 3 inches wide. Sprinkle the rectangle with confectioners' sugar and roll it gently with the rolling pin—just enough to press the layers together, not enough to make the rectangle larger. Fold the sides in again so they leave you with a strip between 1½ and 2 inches [4 and 5 cm] wide and 4 sheets of pastry thick. Press on the strip with your hands, again not to roll it out

but just to press it together so it doesn't unfold when baking. Freeze the pastry for 20 minutes. Preheat the oven to 400°F [200°C/gas mark 6].

CUT the partially frozen strip of pastry into ¼-inch-wide [.5-cm] slices and place them on a sheet pan, sprinkled with water, at least 1 inch away from one another. Don't butter the pan—a slight sticking helps prevent the *palmiers* from unfolding during baking. Chill the cookies for 20 minutes and bake them for 15 to 20 minutes until they are deep golden brown on the bottom. Gently turn the cookies over with a spatula and bake for about 5 minutes more, until the bottoms are, again, deep brown. Let cool for 15 minutes before taking the *palmiers* off the sheet pan with a spatula.

FRENCH REGIONAL COOKIES

Most of the cookies you'll encounter in French restaurants and pastry shops are prepared using elaborate methods that have evolved over the centuries in European kitchens. And while most of these concoctions are delicious, and some are brilliant in their conception, the simple understatement of regional specialities is often more appealing.

Most French regional cookies and other pastries predate their classic descendants and are more likely to reflect the cooking of centuries past because no one has updated them. In some regions, these pastries contain spices such as ginger, allspice, or anise seeds that are remnants of medieval cooking, or citrus flavorings, often in the form of orange flower water, that were popular in the sixteenth century. Nowadays, sweet pastries are almost always made with butter, but in parts of France, regional specialties are sometimes still made with fats—such as olive oil in Provence, nut oils in the Périgord, and goose or duck fat in Gascony—that until recently were the only ones available or affordable. Other ingredients, such as pine nuts, almonds, or hazelnuts, indigenous to particular regions, are also common in regional desserts.

Alsatian *bretzels* are sweet butter cookies shaped into figure eights like soft pretzels. Flemish almond cookies, *pains aux amandes,* are made out of sweetened bread dough flavored with spices. The dough is baked into a loaf and the loaf sliced thin and baked again in the same way as biscotti. (The words *biscotti* and *biscuit* both mean "twice cooked.") Cookies made in this way—the dough baked in a loaf, then sliced and baked again—are called *pains biscuit,* sometimes translated as "rusk" or "biscuit cake."

PROVENÇAL CANDLEMAS COOKIES

NAVETTES DE LA CHANDELEUR

MAKES 60 COOKIES

These are cookies are traditionally baked on Candlemas, February 2, when the church candles are blessed. They are really nothing more than simple butter cookies, except that they are shaped like little boats. (A *navette* is an incense holder or incense boat.) The pecans are my own addition. They add flavor and crunch. If you don't want to bother shaping your cookies like boats, use the dough to make plain round cookies, and top them with pecan halves.

¾ cup [150 g] granulated sugar

8 tablespoons (1 stick [115 g]) butter

½ teaspoon salt

2 large eggs

2 cups [250 g] all-purpose flour

60 pecan halves

CREAM together the sugar, butter, and salt with a heavy wooden spoon in a mixing bowl or in an electric mixer with a paddle blade. Work in the eggs, 1 at a time, and add the flour all at once. Work the mixture just long enough to work in the flour. Refrigerate the dough for 2 hours. Scoop out heaping teaspoonfuls of dough and quickly (so they don't warm) roll them into balls between your palms. Gently pinch the ends, so the cookies take on an oval shape, and make a slit with the back of a paring knife about one-third of the way into each cookie along its length, but not quite reaching the ends.

ARRANGE the cookies on two sheet pans covered with parchment paper, leaving about 1 inch between cookies. (If you don't have two sheet pans, work in batches.) Put the pans in the refrigerator for 1 hour. Press a pecan half into the top of each cookie. Preheat the oven to 350°F [175°C/gas mark 4] and bake the cookies until they are pale golden brown, about 30 minutes. If the cookies are browning unevenly, rotate the pans.

Candies

MOST CANDY IS SO INTENSELY SWEET THAT I have little taste for it, except for a piece or two after dinner. Because your guests presumably will want only a little bit, there's no limit to how rich, sweet, or chocolatey you make any candy.

CHOCOLATE TRUFFLES

TRUFFES AU CHOCOLAT

MAKES ABOUT 40 TRUFFLES

Chocolate truffles are such a well-known treat that many people think truffles are made of chocolate; they've never heard of the kind you dig up out of the ground. As with many other popular foods, there are dozens of recipes for chocolate truffles, but all of them are based on a few basic ingredients and principles. Generally, they are simple combinations of bittersweet chocolate, butter, and sometimes cream, and they can be flavored with just about anything. Vanilla, espresso, eaux-de-vie (kirsch, framboise, and others), Cognac, Armagnac, marc, and bourbon are a few possibilities. Traditionally, portions of this mixture are rolled around in unsweetened cocoa that—while it's stretching a point—looks vaguely like the dirt clinging to a real truffle. More elaborate recipes call for dipping the truffles in melted tempered chocolate.

While truffles are easy to make, the secret to success is to use the best chocolate you can find. My favorites are Sharffen Berger, made in California, and Valrhona, made in France (see Sources). The truffle can be made more firm by using a larger proportion of butter and made creamier by incorporating heavy cream. For a very light, creamy filling, a mixture of melted chocolate and heavy cream called ganache (see page 668) is beaten, but this

mixture is so sticky and melts so quickly that it's best used for truffles that are coated with melted tempered chocolate instead of cocoa powder.

12 ounces [340 g] bittersweet chocolate

1 cup [250 ml] heavy cream

1 teaspoon vanilla extract

8 tablespoons (1 stick [115 g]) butter, cut into 8 pieces, allowed to warm to room temperature

½ cup [45 g] unsweetened Dutch-process cocoa powder

BREAK up the chocolate into about 30 pieces by leaning on it with a chef's knife.

BRING the cream to a simmer in a saucepan, take the saucepan off the heat, and add the chocolate and the vanilla extract. Let sit for 10 minutes to allow the hot cream to melt the chocolate. Whisk or stir the mixture until it's smooth. If you're using an electric mixer to add the butter, use a rubber spatula to transfer the mixture to a mixing bowl or electric mixer bowl. Work the butter into the mixture, a piece at a time, with the paddle blade attachment to the mixer. If you're adding the butter by hand, leave it in the original bowl and add butter pieces, one at a time, stirring with a wooden spoon until completely combined. Leave the mixture in the bowl and chill it in the refrigerator for 4 hours, or overnight.

SIFT the cocoa powder onto a tray or small sheet pan. Use a teaspoon or a small (1-inch [2.5-cm]) ice cream scoop (or wing it with a regular teaspoon) to scoop out a heaping teaspoonful of the truffle mixture and roll it quickly between your palms until you get a ball about 1 inch [2.5 cm] in diameter. If the mixture is too hard, work it in an electric mixer or warm it slightly and work it with a heavy wooden spoon. Set the ball on the sheet pan with the cocoa powder and repeat with the rest of the mixture. If the truffle mixture gets too soft and starts to stick to your hands, put the bowl over a bowl of ice while you're working, or refrigerate the mixture for 20 minutes. If the mixture keeps sticking—which may mean that your hands are too warm—dip your hands in a bowl of ice water for as long as you can stand it and quickly pat them dry with a towel before continuing.

WHEN you've formed all the truffles, put the sheet pan into the refrigerator. After 20 minutes, take the pan out of the refrigerator and roll the truffles around on it, moving the pan back and forth until they are well coated with cocoa powder. Keep the truffles refrigerated until you're ready to serve them.

Variations: As I mentioned earlier, truffles can be flavored in any number of ways. As a start, just replace the vanilla extract with some other flavorful liquid. Or make delicious hazelnut truffles by working ½ cup [115 g] of praline paste into the truffle mixture at the same time you work in the butter. Praline paste, the hazelnut equivalent to sweetened peanut butter, is available in gourmet stores or by mail order (see Sources). To make your own, make a caramel (see page 639) with 1 cup [200 g] of sugar. When the caramel is ready, immediately pour in 1 cup [135 g] of hazelnuts that have had at least part of their dark inner skin removed (buy them this way or toast them for 10 minutes in a 350°F [175°C/gas mark 4] oven and rub them in a towel). Stir the hazelnuts in the caramel for about 30 seconds to cook them and bring out their flavor, then scoop the mixture out onto a sheet pan or marble surface that has been rubbed with vegetable (or, if you're really being a purist, hazelnut) oil and let it cool. You now have what the French call *nougatine,* a dark, glasslike mixture that professional pastry chefs pound into shape for decorating cakes and other elaborate desserts. Purée the *nougatine* in a food processor, scraping down the sides every minute for 5 minutes, until the praline has the consistency of peanut butter.

CANDIED GRAPEFRUIT OR ORANGE RINDS

ÉCORCES DE PAMPLEMOUSSE OU D'ORANGE CONFITES AU SUCRE

MAKES ABOUT 60 TINY CANDIES

These delightful little strips of candied citrus rind are easy to make and are sweet, bitter, and sour all at the same time.

2 grapefruits, or 4 navel oranges
2 cups [400 g] granulated sugar

CUT the ends off the fruit just far enough in so you can see the flesh on each side. Set the fruit on one end and cut the rind and pith away with a knife, following the contours of the fruit so that very little flesh is left attached to the rind and very little rind is left attached to the fruit. (You can cut the fruit into wedges to use in a fruit salad or, with a little raspberry purée, and maybe some whipped cream, as a dessert; see the directions on page 391.)

PUT the sections of rind in a pot with 2 quarts [2 l] of water and bring to a rapid boil. Boil for 10 minutes and drain. Bring another 2 quarts [2 l] of water to a boil. While it is heating, square off any irregularities on the sides and ends of the rinds and cut the rinds into strips about 1½ inches [4 cm] long by ⅓ inch [1 cm] wide. Plunge the strips into the boiling water and boil for 10 minutes. Drain.

COMBINE 1 cup [200 g] of the sugar with 2 cups [500 ml] of water in a heavy-bottomed pot and bring to a gentle simmer. Stir in the rinds and simmer gently, uncovered, for approximately 40 minutes, stirring every 10 minutes, until the sugar mixture gets very syrupy. Take the rinds out of the syrup with a slotted spoon and spread them on cake racks set over sheet pans. Let them cool and drain for 1 hour. Keep them in a dry place for 24 hours to allow them to dry.

SPREAD the remaining sugar evenly over a sheet pan and spread the candied rinds on top. Gently move the rinds around in the sugar until they're coated on all sides. Store on a sheet pan covered with wax paper until you're ready to serve them.

FRUIT JELLY CANDIES
PÂTES DE FRUITS

When I reminisce about my childhood taste for junk foods, including those little cellophane packets of sugar-coated jellies, I wonder why I'm still alive. I still see those jellies near the counters in discount drugstores, and I suspect there's not a drop of real fruit in them.

It wasn't until I got a job translating a book on French desserts that I realized that fruit jellies were once made with real fruit, and in some special places still are. Homemade jellies don't look as pretty as the electric green and red ones packaged in cellophane, but they have a bright, clean, authentic flavor. Fruit jellies are made by cooking fruit pulp with sugar until the mixture becomes so concentrated that it sets when cold. Pectin is added to help the candies set and to give them their characteristic melting consistency. Lemon juice is usually added to the fruit to give the mixture some acidity, to balance its sweetness, and to help activate the pectin. Professional chefs also add glucose, which helps prevent the sugar in the mixture from crystallizing. Instead of glucose, I use corn syrup—a mixture of glucose and fructose—because I can find it at the supermarket.

To make fruit jellies, you must first make a smooth fruit purée, sometimes called a coulis. If the fruit is already soft, you can purée it in a food processor and, depending on its consistency, work it through a fine-mesh strainer or a drum sieve to eliminate any seeds and make a perfectly smooth purée. If you're using hard fruits such as apples, quinces, or underripe pears, you'll have to peel, seed, and simmer the fruits in water with sugar to soften them before you purée them. Once you have the purée, you need to reduce it and combine it with hot sugar syrup containing corn syrup, lemon juice, and pectin. After a few minutes' additional cooking, you pour the mixture into a baking dish lined with parchment paper and lightly dusted with cornstarch to prevent sticking, and you allow the mixture to set. Last, the jellies are cut out, dried, and rolled in sugar.

RASPBERRY JELLY CANDIES

PÂTES DE FRAMBOISES

MAKES 64 CANDIES

3   packages (12 or 14 ounces [340 or 395 g] each) frozen raspberries (whole unsweetened raspberries, not the kind packed in syrup), thawed

1   cup [200 g] granulated sugar (for the sugar syrup), plus 1 cup [200 g] (for coating the candies)

3   tablespoons lemon juice

3   tablespoons powdered pectin

TO make the raspberries easier to work through a strainer, you can first purée them in a food processor, but this isn't essential. Work the raspberries through a food mill, and then through a fine-mesh strainer with a small ladle, or through a drum sieve with a large wooden spoon or rubber spatula (see page 15 for more about drum sieves). Freeze the seeds that don't go through the strainer for the linzer cookies described on page 690. Put the purée into a heavy-bottomed saucepan over medium heat and stir it with a wooden spoon, carefully reaching into corners of the saucepan to prevent burning, until the mixture has reduced to 1½ cups [375 ml], about 30 minutes.

STIR 1 cup [200 g] of sugar into the raspberry purée and simmer the mixture for 5 minutes to dissolve the sugar. Stir in the lemon juice and pectin and cook, stirring constantly, for about 10 minutes, until the mixture is shiny, translucent, and thickened and registers 218°F [103°C] on a candy thermometer.

BRUSH an 8-by-8-inch [20.5 by 20.5 cm] baking dish with a thin coat of vegetable oil and cover it with a sheet of parchment paper just large enough to cover the bottom of the dish.

POUR the raspberry mixture into the baking dish, let cool, and refrigerate for 2 hours. Run a knife around the edge of the mixture and lift up a corner to get the raspberry mixture to start to detach from the pan. Turn the mixture out onto a cake rack, peel away the parchment paper, and let it dry for 24 hours.

CUT the candies by making eight 1-inch-wide [2.5 cm] rows in two directions so you end up with 64 square candies about 1 inch on each side. Roll the candies in granulated sugar.

NORMALLY, fruit jellies can be stored for 2 to 3 weeks if well covered and kept in a cool place. If, however, you notice after a day or two that the jellies are starting to get wet, arrange them on a sheet pan covered with parchment paper and leave them in a 225°F [107°C] oven for 45 minutes to dry them out. Roll them again in sugar before storing them. If you stack them, put parchment paper between the layers to prevent sticking.

Variations: Other fresh or frozen berries, such as strawberries, blueberries, or currants, can be substituted for the raspberries. Use about 3 pounds [1.3 kg] of fresh berries, 2½ pounds [1.1 kg] of frozen ones. If using blueberries, leave out the pectin; they have enough. High-quality frozen fruit purées, available in some gourmet stores or by mail (see Sources), allow you to make these candies with virtually any fruit, regardless of season. Because some fruits are sweeter or more sour than others, you may have to adjust the sugar accordingly. Don't leave out the lemon juice, since it activates the pectin.

If you want to make fruit candies with citrus fruits, you'll need to use another fruit as well to give the candies body and contribute pectin. French pastry cooks often use apricot purée for this, but except for a short period during the summer, this requires a mail order. I use apples. Since apples contain a lot of pectin, I leave out the packaged pectin (see recipe that follows).

ORANGE
JELLY CANDIES

PÂTES D'ORANGE

MAKES 64 CANDIES

3 large navel oranges

3 pounds [1.3 kg] tart apples such as Granny Smith, stem removed, quartered (not peeled or cored)

3 tablespoons lemon juice

1 cup [200 g] granulated sugar (for the sugar syrup), plus 1 cup [200 g] (for coating the candies)

3 teaspoons pure orange extract, or 2 teaspoons pure orange oil, or more to taste (see citrus oils under Sources)

2 teaspoons vegetable oil (for brushing the mold)

SLICE zests off the oranges, leaving as little pith attached to the zests as possible. Squeeze the oranges and reserve the juice.

SLICE the applies and combine them, in a nonaluminum pot that has a lid, with the lemon juice, orange juice, and orange zests. Cover the pot and bring to a simmer over medium heat. Simmer, covered, for 15 minutes, remove the lid, and continue simmering, stirring every 1 or 2 minutes, until the apples turn into applesauce. Continue simmering until the mixture gets very thick and shiny, about 15 minutes. At this point you'll have to stir almost continuously to prevent burning. Work the mixture through a strainer or drum sieve to eliminate the orange zests, apple peels, and any lumps. Put the mixture into a medium-size heavy-bottomed saucepan and stir it over medium heat. While you're heating the apple mixture, prepare the sugar syrup by combining 1 cup of sugar with ⅓ cup [75 ml] of water and cooking to the "soft crack" stage (280°F [137°C]; see page 628 for more about sugar syrups). Stir the syrup into the apple mixture and continue cooking the mixture until it registers 225°F [107°C] on a candy thermometer, again about 15 minutes. At

this point the mixture should be goopy, and no longer completely liquid. If it is still very liquidy, cook it until it thickens, for about 10 more minutes. Take the saucepan off the heat and stir in the orange extract or oil. Taste the mixture—be careful, it's hot—and add more extract or oil if it's needed.

BRUSH an 8-by-8-inch [20.5-by-20.5-cm] baking dish with vegetable oil and cover it with a sheet of parchment paper just large enough to cover the bottom of the dish. Pour in the apple mixture and smooth its surface with the back of spoon or, ideally, a small metal offset spatula (available at cooking supply stores; see Sources). Let the mixture set in the refrigerator for 2 hours.

TURN the square of orange candy out onto a clean work surface and peel away the parchment paper. Put the candy on a cake rack and let it dry in a clean, warm part of the kitchen for 24 hours. Cut the candies by cutting eight rows in two directions so you end up with 64 square candies about 1 inch on each side. Roll the candies in granulated sugar.

NORMALLY, fruit jellies can be stored for 2 to 3 weeks if well covered and kept in a cool place. If, however, you notice after a day or two that the jellies are starting to get wet, arrange them on a sheet pan covered with parchment paper and leave them in a 250°F [120°C/gas mark ½] oven for 45 minutes to dry them out. Roll them again in sugar before storing them. If you stack them, put wax paper between the layers to prevent sticking.

SOURCES

INGREDIENTS AND SPECIALTY COOKWARE

The numbers appearing in parentheses that follow each list entry refer the reader to the list of suppliers that begins on page 701.

Anchovies, packed in salt (24, 27, 33)

Balsamic vinegar, aged authentic (24, 34)

Beans and other legumes, dried:
    Borlotti (7, 10)
    Canellini (7, 10)
    Green flageoles (7, 10)
    Le Puy green lentils (7, 10)
    Lingot (7)
    Tarbais (7)

Cheesemaking supplies:
    Butter muslin (cheesecloth for draining
      soft cheeses) (17)
    Rennet, animal and vegetable (17)
    Starter cultures (17)

Chocolate:
    Scharffen Berger (13, 26)
    Valrhona (7, 13, 18)

Citrus oils:
    Boyajian orange oil (7, 13, 18)

Cooking equipment:
    Benriner cutters (3, 12)
    Cassolettes (2, 12)
    Coeur à la crème molds (2, 12)
    Charlotte molds (2, 12)
    Chinoise strainers (2, 12, 22)
    Conical strainers (2, 12, 22, 29)
    Crème brûlée dishes (2, 12, 29, 32)
    Dariole molds (2, 12)
    Drum sieves (2, 12)
    Financier molds (2, 12, 18)
    Flame tamers (13, 32)
    Gratin pans and dishes (2, 12, 22, 29)
    Knives (2, 12, 22)
    Madeleine pans (molds) (2, 7, 12, 18)
    Mandolines (2, 12, 22, 29, 33)

Pâté molds, porcelain (2, 12, 22, 33)

Quiche dishes (porcelain) (2, 12)

Raclette makers (32)

Rolling pins, European style (2, 7, 12, 22, 29)

Rondeaux pans (2, 12, 22)

Savarian and baba molds (2, 12)

Scoops (ice cream, about 1 inch [25 mm]) (2, 7, 12, 13)

Soufflé dishes and ramekins (2, 3, 12, 29, 33)

Stockpots (3, 22, 33)

Tart pans (with removable bottom) and tartlet molds (2, 18, 29, 33)

Terrine molds, enameled cast iron, and porcelain (Le Creuset) (2, 3, 12, 22, 32, 33)

Truffle slicers (2, 7, 12)

Windsor pans (2, 7, 12)

Cornichons (7, 33, 34)

Dairy products:

Crème fraîche (31)

Fromage blanc (31)

Demi-glace (4, 16)

Herbs, spices, and other seasonings:

Fleur de sel (4, 7)

Ginger, candied Australian (21)

Herbes de Provence (7, 21, 32)

Pimentón (27)

Saffron (27)

Flours and starters:

Almond flour (13)

Buckwheat flour (13)

Chickpea flour (in Indian stores also called besan) (13)

Sourdough starter (13)

Fruit purées and coulis (23)

Meat and poultry products:

Bacon, double-smoked (7)

Duck confit and magrets (6)

Duck, farm-raised Pekin (14)

Duck fat (6, 16)

Foie gras (bloc, mousse, and raw) (6)

Garlic sausages (6, 7)

Goose fat (6, 7)

Ham, cured unsmoked (7)

Hare (20)

Lamb, farm-raised (11)

Pancetta (7)

Pork, farm-raised (9, 19)

Quail (6)

Sausage-making supplies (25)

Squab (20)

Veal, farm-raised (20)

Mushrooms:

Dried wild (15, 24, 30)

Fresh in season (15, 30)

Nut oils

Le Blanc (roasted hazelnut, pistachio, walnut) (7, 24)

Nut pastis (see Praline paste)

Olive oil

Premium Ligurian olive oil, called Schiapa, from Aldo Armato (24)

Assorted artisanal oils (34)

Praline paste (13, 18)

Puff pastry (8)

Salt cod (27)

Saltpeter (5)

Sugar (sanding and crystallized) (13, 18)

Trout, farm-raised (28)

Truffles and truffle products (7, 15, 30)

Vinegar-making supplies (1)

1. BEER & WINEMAKING SUPPLIES, INC.
   413-586-0150

2. BRIDGE KITCHENWARE
   800-274-3435; 212-688-4220
   www.bridgekitchenware.com

3. BROADWAY PANHANDLER
   212-966-3434
   www.broadwaypanhandler.com

4. THE CMC COMPANY
   800-262-2780
   www.thecmccompany.com

5. C. O. BIGELOW CHEMISTS
   800-793-5433
   www.bigelowchemists.com

6. D'ARTAGNAN
   800-327-8246
   www.dartagnan.com

7. DEAN & DELUCA
   877-826-9246
   www.deandeluca.com

8. DUFOUR PASTRY KITCHENS
   212-929-2800

9. EGG & I PORK FARM
   860-354-0820
   www.eggandiporkfarm.com

10. INDIAN HARVEST
    800-346-7032
    www.indianharvest.com

11. JAMISON FARM
    800-237-5262
    www.jamisonfarm.com

12. J. B. PRINCE
    800-473-0577   212-683-3553
    www.jbprince.com

13. KING ARTHUR FLOUR
    800-827-6836
    www.kingarthurflour.com

14. LIBERTY DUCKS
    800-95-DUCKS
    www.libertyducks.com

15. MARCHÉ AUX DELICES
    888-547-5471
    www.auxdelices.com

16. MORE THAN GOURMET
    800-860-9385
    E-mail: info@morethangourmet.com
    www.morethangourmet.com

17. NEW ENGLAND CHEESEMAKING
    Supply Company
    413-628-3808
    www.cheesemaking.com

18. NEW YORK CAKE AND BAKING DISTRIBUTOR
    800-942-2539

19. NIMAN RANCH
    510-808-0340
    www.nimanranch.com

20. OTTOMANELLI'S MEAT MARKET
    212-675-4217

21. PENZEYS SPICES
    800-741-7787
    www.penzeys.com

22. PROFESSIONAL CUTLERY DIRECT
    800-859-6994
    www.cutlery.com

23. QZINA SPECIALTY FOODS INC.
    800-661-2462
    www.qzina.com

24. ROSENTHAL WINE MERCHANT
    800-910-1990
    www.madrose.com

25. THE SAUSAGE MAKER
    716-876-5521

26. SCHARFFEN BERGER CHOCOLATE MAKER
    800-884-5884
    www.scharffenberger.com

27. THE SPANISH TABLE
    206-682-2827
    www.tablespan.com

28. STAR PRAIRIE TROUT FARM
715-248-3633
www.starprairietrout.com

29. SUR LA TABLE
800-243-0852
www.surlatable.com

30. URBANI TRUFFLES & CAVIAR
800-281-2330
www.urbani.com

31. VERMONT BUTTER & CHEESE COMPANY
800-884-6287
www.vtbutterandcheeseco.com

32. WILLIAMS-SONOMA
800-699-2297; 877-812-6235
www.williams-sonoma.com

33. ZABAR'S
800-697-6301
www.zabars.com

34. ZINGERMAN'S DELICATESSEN
888-636-8162
www.zingermans.com

PARIS KITCHENWARE SHOPS

E. DEHILLERIN
18-20, Rue Coquillière
Paris 1
Metro stop: Les Halles
Telephone: 01.42.36.53.13
www.e-dehillerin.fr

BOUTIQUE LAGUIOLE
1, Place Saint-Opportune
Paris 1
Metro stop: Chatelet–Les Halles
Telephone: 01.40.28.09.42

M.O.R.A.
13, Rue Montmartre
Paris 1
Metro stop: Les Halles
Telephone: 01.45.08.19.24

B.H.V. (BAZAAR DE L'HÔTEL DE VILLE)
52, Rue de Rivoli
Paris 4
Metro stop: Hôtel de Ville
Telephone: 01.42.74.90.00

INDEX

B

G

M

S

T